**FOR REFERENCE**

Do Not Take From This Room

# HANDBOOK OF PSYCHOLOGY

# HANDBOOK OF PSYCHOLOGY

## VOLUME 10:   ASSESSMENT PSYCHOLOGY

Second Edition

*Volume Editors*

## JOHN R. GRAHAM AND JACK A. NAGLIERI

*Editor-in-Chief*

## IRVING B. WEINER

**WILEY**

John Wiley & Sons, Inc.

*Library of Congress Cataloging-in-Publication Data:*

Handbook of psychology / Irving B. Weiner, editor-in-chief. — 2nd ed.
  v. cm.
 Includes bibliographical references and index.
 ISBN 978-0-470-61904-9 (set) — ISBN 978-0-470-89127-8 (cloth: Volume 10); ISBN 978-1-118-28676-0 (ebk);
 ISBN 978-1-118-28204-5 (ebk); ISBN 978-1-118-28381-3 (ebk)
1. Psychology. I. Weiner, Irving B.
 BF121.H213 2013
 150—dc23

                2012005833

Printed in the United States of America
10 9 8 7 6 5 4 3 2 1

*Parents are powerful forces in the development of their sons and daughters.*
*In recognition of that positive influence,*
*we dedicate our efforts on this book to the loving memory of*
*Craig Parris (1920–2001)*
*and*
*Sam Naglieri (1926–2001).*

# Editorial Board

**Volume 1**
**HISTORY OF PSYCHOLOGY**

*Donald K. Freedheim, PhD*
Case Western Reserve University
Cleveland, Ohio

**Volume 2**
**RESEARCH METHODS IN PSYCHOLOGY**

*John A. Schinka, PhD*
University of South Florida
Tampa, Florida

*Wayne F. Velicer, PhD*
University of Rhode Island
Kingston, Rhode Island

**Volume 3**
**BEHAVIORAL NEUROSCIENCE**

*Randy J. Nelson, PhD*
Ohio State University
Columbus, Ohio

*Sheri J. Y. Mizumori, PhD*
University of Washington
Seattle, Washington

**Volume 4**
**EXPERIMENTAL PSYCHOLOGY**

*Alice F. Healy, PhD*
University of Colorado
Boulder, Colorado

*Robert W. Proctor, PhD*
Purdue University
West Lafayette, Indiana

**Volume 5**
**PERSONALITY AND SOCIAL PSYCHOLOGY**

*Howard Tennen, PhD*
University of Connecticut Health Center
Farmington, Connecticut

*Jerry Suls, PhD*
University of Iowa
Iowa City, Iowa

**Volume 6**
**DEVELOPMENTAL PSYCHOLOGY**

*Richard M. Lerner, PhD*
*M. Ann Easterbrooks, PhD*
*Jayanthi Mistry, PhD*
Tufts University
Medford, Massachusetts

**Volume 7**
**EDUCATIONAL PSYCHOLOGY**

*William M. Reynolds, PhD*
Humboldt State University
Arcata, California

*Gloria E. Miller, PhD*
University of Denver
Denver, Colorado

**Volume 8**
**CLINICAL PSYCHOLOGY**

*George Stricker, PhD*
Argosy University DC
Arlington, Virginia

*Thomas A. Widiger, PhD*
University of Kentucky
Lexington, Kentucky

# Contents

# *Handbook of Psychology* Preface

The first edition of the 12-volume *Handbook of Psychology* was published in 2003 to provide a comprehensive overview of the current status and anticipated future directions of basic and applied psychology and to serve as a reference source and textbook for the ensuing decade. With 10 years having elapsed, and psychological knowledge and applications continuing to expand, the time has come for this second edition to appear. In addition to well-referenced updating of the first edition content, this second edition of the *Handbook* reflects the fresh perspectives of some new volume editors, chapter authors, and subject areas. However, the conceptualization and organization of the *Handbook*, as stated next, remain the same.

Psychologists commonly regard their discipline as the science of behavior, and the pursuits of behavioral scientists range from the natural sciences to the social sciences and embrace a wide variety of objects of investigation. Some psychologists have more in common with biologists than with most other psychologists, and some have more in common with sociologists than with most of their psychological colleagues. Some psychologists are interested primarily in the behavior of animals, some in the behavior of people, and others in the behavior of organizations. These and other dimensions of difference among psychological scientists are matched by equal if not greater heterogeneity among psychological practitioners, who apply a vast array of methods in many different settings to achieve highly varied purposes. This 12-volume *Handbook of Psychology* captures the breadth and diversity of psychology and encompasses interests and concerns shared by psychologists in all branches of the field. To this end, leading national and international scholars and practitioners have collaborated to produce 301 authoritative and detailed chapters covering all fundamental facets of the discipline.

Two unifying threads run through the science of behavior. The first is a common history rooted in conceptual and empirical approaches to understanding the nature of behavior. The specific histories of all specialty areas in psychology trace their origins to the formulations of the classical philosophers and the early experimentalists, and appreciation for the historical evolution of psychology in all of its variations transcends identifying oneself as a particular kind of psychologist. Accordingly, Volume 1 in the *Handbook*, again edited by Donald Freedheim, is devoted to the *History of Psychology* as it emerged in many areas of scientific study and applied technology.

A second unifying thread in psychology is a commitment to the development and utilization of research methods suitable for collecting and analyzing behavioral data. With attention both to specific procedures and to their application in particular settings, Volume 2, again edited by John Schinka and Wayne Velicer, addresses *Research Methods in Psychology*.

Volumes 3 through 7 of the *Handbook* present the substantive content of psychological knowledge in five areas of study. Volume 3, which addressed *Biological Psychology* in the first edition, has in light of developments in the field been retitled in the second edition to cover *Behavioral Neuroscience*. Randy Nelson continues as editor of this volume and is joined by Sheri Mizumori as a new co-editor. Volume 4 concerns *Experimental Psychology* and is again edited by Alice Healy and Robert Proctor. Volume 5 on *Personality and Social Psychology* has been reorganized by two new co-editors, Howard Tennen and Jerry Suls. Volume 6 on *Developmental Psychology* is again edited by Richard Lerner, Ann Easterbrooks, and Jayanthi Mistry. William Reynolds and Gloria Miller continue as co-editors of Volume 7 on *Educational Psychology*.

Volumes 8 through 12 address the application of psychological knowledge in five broad areas of professional practice. Thomas Widiger and George Stricker continue as co-editors of Volume 8 on *Clinical Psychology*. Volume 9 on *Health Psychology* is again co-edited by Arthur Nezu, Christine Nezu, and Pamela Geller. Continuing to co-edit Volume 10 on *Assessment Psychology* are John Graham and Jack Naglieri. Randy Otto joins the Editorial Board as the new editor of Volume 11 on *Forensic Psychology*. Also joining the Editorial Board are two new co-editors, Neal Schmitt and Scott Highhouse, who have reorganized Volume 12 on *Industrial and Organizational Psychology*.

The *Handbook of Psychology* was prepared to educate and inform readers about the present state of psychological knowledge and about anticipated advances in behavioral science research and practice. To this end, the *Handbook* volumes address the needs and interests of three groups. First, for graduate students in behavioral science, the volumes provide advanced instruction in the basic concepts and methods that define the fields they cover, together with a review of current knowledge, core literature, and likely future directions. Second, in addition to serving as graduate textbooks, the volumes offer professional psychologists an opportunity to read and contemplate the views of distinguished colleagues concerning the central thrusts of research and the leading edges of practice

in their respective fields. Third, for psychologists seeking to become conversant with fields outside their own specialty and for persons outside of psychology seeking information about psychological matters, the *Handbook* volumes serve as a reference source for expanding their knowledge and directing them to additional sources in the literature.

The preparation of this *Handbook* was made possible by the diligence and scholarly sophistication of 24 volume editors and co-editors who constituted the Editorial Board. As Editor-in-Chief, I want to thank each of these colleagues for the pleasure of their collaboration in this project. I compliment them for having recruited an outstanding cast of contributors to their volumes and then working closely with these authors to achieve chapters that will stand each in their own right as valuable contributions to the literature. Finally, I would like to thank Brittany White for her exemplary work as my administrator for our manuscript management system, and the editorial staff of John Wiley & Sons for encouraging and helping bring to fruition this second edition of the *Handbook*, particularly Patricia Rossi, Executive Editor, and Kara Borbely, Editorial Program Coordinator.

Irving B. Weiner
Tampa, Florida

# Volume Preface

The title of this volume, *Assessment Psychology*, was deliberately chosen to make the point that the assessment activities of psychologists constitute a legitimate and important subdiscipline within psychology. The methods and techniques developed by assessment pioneers were central in establishing a professional role for psychologists in schools, hospitals, and other settings. Although interest in psychological assessment has waxed and waned over the years and various assessment procedures and instruments have come under attack, the premise of this volume is that assessment psychology is alive and well and continues to be of paramount importance in the professional functioning of most psychologists. In addition, assessment psychology contributes greatly to the well-being of the thousands of individuals who are assessed every year.

A primary goal of this volume is to address important issues in assessment psychology. Some of these issues have been around a long time (e.g., psychometric characteristics of assessment procedures), whereas others have come on the scene more recently (e.g., computer-based psychological assessment). This volume also has chapters devoted to the unique features of assessment in different settings (adult and child mental health, schools, medical centers, business and industry, forensic and correctional, and geriatric). Other chapters address assessment in various domains (e.g., cognitive and intellectual, interests, personality and psychopathology). Still other chapters address various approaches used in the assessment process (e.g., interviews, behavioral methods, performance approaches, and self-report inventories). The final chapter summarizes the major conclusions reached by other authors in the volume and speculates about the future of assessment psychology.

We should also state clearly what this volume does not include. Although many specific tests and procedures are described (some in more detail than others), the volume is not intended as a practical guide for the administration and interpretation of tests and other procedures. There are other excellent interpretive handbooks already available, and many of these are referenced in the various chapters of the volume.

It is our hope that the detailed and insightful consideration of issues and problems will provide a strong foundation for all who are part of the discipline of assessment psychology, regardless of the techniques or instruments that they employ. We will view this volume as having been successful if it raises the sensitivity of assessment psychologists to the important issues inherent in the use of assessment procedures in a wide variety of settings and to the strengths and weaknesses of the various approaches and instruments.

This volume is intended for several audiences. Graduate students in psychology, education, and related disciplines should find the chapters informative and thought provoking as they master the assessment process. Psychologists who engage in psychological assessment, either routinely or on a more limited basis, should find the various chapters to be enlightening. Finally, those who use the results of psychological assessment (e.g., medical and social work professionals, teachers, parents, clients) should become more informed consumers after reading the chapters in this volume.

We want to thank those who contributed to the completion of this volume. Of course, the most important contributors are those who wrote the individual chapters. Their efforts resulted in informative and thought-provoking chapters. The editor-in-chief of the series of which this volume is a part, Irving Weiner, deserves considerable credit for his organizational skills in making the project happen as planned and for his specific contributions to chapters in this volume.

John R. Graham
Jack A. Naglieri

# Contributors

**R. Michael Bagby, PhD**
Departments of Psychology and Psychiatry
University of Toronto
Toronto, Ontario

**Yossef S. Ben-Porath, PhD**
Department of Psychology
Kent State University
Kent, Ohio

**Bruce A. Bracken, PhD**
School of Education
The College of William and Mary
Williamsburg, Virginia

**Jeffery P. Braden, PhD**
Department of Psychology
North Carolina State University
Raleigh, North Carolina

**Leslie M. Guidotti Breting, PhD**
Department of Psychiatry and Behavioral Sciences
NorthShore University HealthSystem
Evanston, Illinois

**James N. Butcher, PhD**
Department of Psychology
University of Minnesota
Minneapolis, Minnesota

**Andrew D. Carson, PhD**
Kaplan University
Winfield, Illinois

**Robert J. Craig PhD, ABPP**
Department of Psychology
Roosevelt University
Chicago, Illinois

**Philip DeFina, PhD**
International Brain Research Foundation
New Jersey Institute for Neuroscience
Secaucus, New Jersey

**Kevin S. Douglas, LL.B., PhD**
Department of Psychology
Simon Fraser University
Burnaby, BC, Canada

**Barry A. Edelstein, PhD**
Department of Psychology
West Virginia University
Morgantown, West Virginia

**Kurt F. Geisinger, PhD**
Buros Center for Testing
    and Department of Educational
    Psychology
The University of Nebraska–Lincoln
Lincoln, Nebraska

**Lindsay A. Gerolimatos, M.S.**
Department of Psychology
West Virginia University
Morgantown, West Virginia

**Elkhonon Goldberg, PhD**
Department of Neurology
New York University School of Medicine
New York, New York

**John R. Graham, PhD**
Department of Psychology
Kent State University
Kent, Ohio

**Leonard Handler, PhD**
Psychology Department
University of Tennessee
Knoxville, Tennessee

**Richard J. Klimoski, PhD**
School of Management
George Mason University
Fairfax, Virginia

**Gerald P. Koocher, PhD, ABPP**
Associate Provost and Professor of Psychology
Simmons College
Boston, Massachusetts

**David Lachar, PhD**
Department of Psychiatry and Behavioral Sciences
The University of Texas—Houston
Houston, Texas

**Rodney L. Lowman, PhD**
Organizational Psychology Programs
CSPP/Alliant International University
San Diego, California

**Brandee E. Marion, MA**
Department of Psychology
University of Alabama
Tuscaloosa, Alabama

**Ronald R. Martin, PhD, RD Psych.**
Faculty of Education
University of Regina
Regina, Saskatchewan, Canada

**Mark E. Maruish, PhD**
Southcross Consulting
Burnsville, Minnesota

**Carina McCormick, MA**
Department of Educational Psychology
University of Nebraska—Lincoln
Lincoln, Nebraska

**Edwin I. Megargee, PhD**
Department of Psychology
Florida State University
Tallahassee, Florida

**Jack A. Naglieri, PhD**
Devereux Center for Resilient Children
University of Virginia
Charlottesville, Virginia

**William H. O'Brien, PhD**
Department of Psychology
Bowling Green State University
Bowling Green, Ohio

**James R. P. Ogloff, JD, PhD**
School of Psychology, Psychiatry,
    and Psychological Medicine
Monash University and Institute of
    Forensic Mental Health
Victoria, Australia

**Tulio M. Otero, PhD**
Clinical Psy.D. and School
    Neuropsychology Programs
The Chicago School of
    Professional Psychology
Chicago, Illinois

**Kenneth Podell, PhD**
Department of Neuropsychology
Henry Ford Health System
Detroit, Michigan

**Celiane Rey-Casserly, PhD, ABPP-CN**
Neuropsychology Program
Children's Hospital
Boston, Massachusetts

**Cecil R. Reynolds, PhD**
Department of Educational Psychology
Texas A& M University
College Station, Texas

**Bridget Rivera, PsyD**
Psychology Department
Loyola University
Baltimore, Maryland

**Martin Sellbom, PhD**
Department of Psychology
University of Alabama
Tuscaloosa, Alabama

**Justin D. Smith, PhD**
Child and Family Center
University of Oregon
Eugene, Oregon

**Paul M. Spengler, PhD**
Department of Counseling Psychology
Ball State University
Muncie, Indiana

**Yana Suchy, PhD**
Department of Psychology
University of Utah
Salt Lake City, Utah

**Lisa A. Suzuki, PhD**
Department of Applied Psychology
New York University
New York, New York

**Jerry J. Sweet, PhD, ABPP**
Department of Psychiatry & Behavioral Sciences
NorthShore University HealthSystem
Evanston, Illinois

**Steven M. Tovian, PhD, ABPP**
Independent Practice and Department
    of Psychiatry & Behavioral Sciences
Feinberg School of Medicine Northwestern University
Chicago, Illinois

**Donald J. Viglione, PhD**
California School of Professional
    Psychology
Alliant University
San Diego, California

**John D. Wasserman, PhD**
American Institute of Psychology
Burke, Virginia

**Irving B. Weiner, PhD, ABPP**
Department of Psychiatry and
    Neurosciences
University of South Florida
Tampa, Florida

**Torrey R. Wilkinson**
Booz, Allen Hamilton
Herndon, Virginia

**Nancy Howards Wrobel, PhD**
Behavioral Sciences Department
University of Michigan—Dearborn
Dearborn, Michigan

**Kathleen M. Young, PhD, MPH**
Department of Family Medicine
University of Mississippi Medical Center
Jackson, Mississippi

PART I

# Assessment Issues

# CHAPTER 1

# The Assessment Process

IRVING B. WEINER

Assessment psychology is the field of behavioral science concerned with methods of identifying similarities and differences among people in their psychological characteristics and capacities. As such, psychological assessment comprises a variety of procedures that are employed in diverse ways to achieve numerous purposes. Assessment has sometimes been equated with testing, but there is more to the assessment process than giving tests. Psychological assessment involves integrating information gleaned not only from test protocols but also from interviews, behavioral observations, collateral reports, and historical documents. In this regard, the *Standards for Educational and Psychological Testing* (American Educational Research Association [AERA], American Psychological Association, & National Council on Measurement in Education, 1999) specify that

> the use of tests provides one method of collecting information within the larger framework of a psychological assessment of an individual.... A psychological assessment is a comprehensive examination undertaken to answer specific questions about a client's psychological functioning during a particular time interval or to predict a client's psychological functioning in the future. (p. 119)

The diverse ways in which assessment procedures are employed include many alternative approaches to obtaining and combining information from different sources, and the numerous purposes that assessment serves arise in response to a broad range of referral questions raised in clinical, educational, health care, forensic, and organizational settings. Chapters in this volume elaborate the diversity of assessment procedures, the nature of the

assessment questions that arise in various settings, and the types of assessment methods commonly employed to address these questions.

This introductory chapter sets the stage for what is to follow by conceptualizing assessment as a three-stage process of information input, information evaluation, and information output. Information input involves collecting assessment data of appropriate kinds and in sufficient amounts to address referral questions in meaningful and useful ways. Information evaluation consists of interpreting assessment data in a manner that provides accurate descriptions of respondents' psychological characteristics and behavioral tendencies. Information output calls for using descriptions of respondents to formulate conclusions and recommendations that help to answer referral questions. Each of these phases of the assessment process requires assessors to accomplish some distinctive tasks, and each involves choices and decisions that touch on critical issues in conducting psychological assessments.

## COLLECTING ASSESSMENT INFORMATION

The process of collecting assessment information begins with a formulation of the purposes that the assessment is intended to serve. Knowing why an assessment is being conducted helps examiners identify tests and other sources of information that are likely to provide a basis for relevant conclusions and useful recommendations. Also helpful in planning the data collection process is attention to examiner, respondent, and data management characteristics that influence the nature and utility of whatever findings are obtained.

## Formulating Goals

Psychological assessments are instigated by referrals that pose questions about aspects of a person's psychological functioning or likely future behavior. Clearly stated and psychologically relevant referral questions help psychologists determine what kinds of assessment data to collect, what considerations to address in examining these data, and what implications of their findings to emphasize in their reports. Referral questions that lack clarity or psychological relevance require some reformulation to give direction to the assessment process. For example, a referral in a clinical setting that asks vaguely for personality evaluation or differential diagnosis needs to be made more specific in consultation between the psychologist and the referring person to identify why a personality evaluation is being sought or what diagnostic possibilities are at issue. Assessment in the absence of a specific referral question can be a sterile exercise in which neither the data collection process nor the psychologist's inferences can be focused in a meaningful way.

Even when referral questions are adequately specified, they may not be psychological in nature. Assessors doing forensic work are often asked to evaluate whether a criminal defendant was insane at the time of an alleged offense; however, *sanity* is a legal term, not a psychological term. No assessment methods are designed to identify "insanity," nor are there any research studies in which "being insane" has been used as an independent variable. To help assessors plan their procedures and frame their reports in such instances, the referral must be translated into psychological terms, as in defining *insanity* as the inability to distinguish reality from fantasy.

As a further challenge in formulating assessment goals, referral questions that are specific and framed in psychological terms may still be unclear if they concern complex and multidetermined patterns of behavior. In employment evaluations, for example, a referring person may want to know which of three individuals is likely to perform best in a position of leadership or executive responsibility. To address this type of question adequately, assessors must first be able to identify psychological characteristics that are likely to make a difference in the particular circumstances, as by proceeding, in this example, with the presumption that being energetic, decisive, assertive, self-confident, and relatively unflappable is likely to contribute to effective leadership. The data collection process can then be planned to measure these characteristics, and the psychologist's eventual report can specify their presence or absence as the basis for whatever hiring decision is recommended.

## Selecting Tests

The multiple sources of assessment information mentioned include:

- the results of formal psychological testing with standardized instruments;
- responses to questions asked in structured and unstructured interviews;
- observations of behavior in various types of contrived situations and natural settings;
- reports from relatives, friends, employers, and other collateral persons concerning an individual's previous life history and current characteristics and behavioral tendencies; and
- documents such as medical records, school records, and written reports of earlier assessments.

Individual assessments vary considerably in the availability and utility of these diverse sources of information. Assessments may at times be based solely on record reviews and collateral reports, because the person being assessed is unwilling to be seen by an examiner or is for some reason prevented from doing so. Some people being assessed are quite forthcoming when interviewed but are reluctant to be tested; others find it difficult to talk about themselves but are quite responsive to testing procedures; and in still other cases, in which both interview and test data are ample, there may be a dearth of collateral input or documented information on which to draw.

There is little way to know before the fact which sources of information will prove most critical or valuable in an assessment process. What collateral informants say about a person may sometimes be more revealing and reliable than what the person says about him- or herself, and in some instances historical documents may prove more informative and dependable than either first-person or collateral reports. Behavioral observations and interview data may on occasion contribute more to an assessment than standardized tests or may even render testing superfluous, whereas in other instances formal psychological testing may reveal vital diagnostic information that would otherwise not have been uncovered.

The fact that psychological assessment can proceed effectively without psychological testing helps to distinguish between these two activities. As previously noted, the terms *psychological assessment* and *psychological testing* are sometimes used synonymously, but psychological testing is only one of several sources of information typically utilized in the assessment process. (See Matarazzo, 1990; Meyer et al., 2001.) Testing, however, is the most complex and specialized of the data collection procedures used in psychological assessment, starting with the selection of an appropriate test battery from among an extensive array of available measuring instruments. (See Geisinger, Spies, Carlson, & Plake, 2007; see also Ben-Porath; Lowman and Carson; O'Brien and Young; Otero, Podell, DeFina and Goldberg; Viglione and Rivera; and Wasserman, this volume). The chief considerations that should determine the composition of a test battery are:

- the psychometric adequacy of the measures being considered;
- the relevance of these measures to the referral questions being addressed;
- the likelihood that these measures will contribute incremental validity to the decision-making process; and
- the additive, confirmatory, and complementary functions that individual measures are likely to serve when used jointly.

### Psychometric Adequacy

As elaborated in the *Standards for Educational and Psychological Testing* (AERA et al., 1999) and in Wasserman and Bracken, this volume, the psychometric adequacy of an assessment instrument consists of the extent to which it

- involves standardized test materials and administration procedures;
- can be coded with reasonably good interscorer agreement;
- demonstrates acceptable reliability;
- has generated relevant normative data; and
- shows valid corollaries that serve the purposes for which it is intended.

Assessment psychologists may at times choose to use tests with uncertain psychometric properties, perhaps for exploratory purposes or for comparison with a previous examination in which these tests have been used. Generally speaking, however, formal testing as part of a psychological assessment should be limited to standardized, reliable, and valid instruments for which there are adequate normative data.

### Relevance

The tests selected for inclusion in an assessment battery should provide information relevant to answering the questions that have been raised about the person being examined. Questions that relate to personality functions (e.g., "What kind of approach in psychotherapy is likely to be helpful to this person?") call for personality tests. Questions that relate to educational issues (e.g., "Does this student have a learning disability?") call for measures of intellectual abilities and academic aptitude and achievement. Questions that relate to neuropsychological functions (e.g., "Are there indications of memory loss?") call for measures of cognitive functioning, with special emphasis on measures of capacities for learning and recall.

These examples of relevance may seem too obvious to have warranted mention. However, they reflect an important and sometimes overlooked guiding principle in psychological assessment, namely, that test selection should be justifiable for each measure included in an assessment battery. Insufficient attention to justifying the use of particular measures in specific instances can result in two ill-advised assessment practices: (1) conducting examinations with a fixed and unvarying battery of measures regardless of what questions are being asked in the individual case, and (2) using favorite instruments at every opportunity even when they are unlikely to serve any central or unique purpose in a particular assessment.

The administration of minimally useful tests that have little relevance to the referral question is a wasteful procedure that can evoke deserved criticism of assessment psychologists and the assessment process. Likewise, the propriety of charging fees for unnecessary procedures can rightfully be challenged by persons receiving or paying for these services, and the competence of assessors who give tests that make little contribution to answering the questions at issue can be challenged in such public forums as the courtroom. (See Weiner, 2009.)

### Incremental Validity

*Incremental validity* in psychological assessment refers to the extent to which additional information increases the accuracy of a classification or prediction above and beyond the accuracy achieved by information already available. Assessors pay adequate attention to incremental validity by collecting the amount and kinds of information they need to answer a referral question, but no more than that. In theory, then, familiarity with the incremental validity of various measures when used for certain purposes, combined with test selection based on this information, minimizes redundancy in psychological assessment and satisfies both professional and scientific requirements for justifiable test selection.

In practice, however, strict adherence to incremental validity guidelines often proves difficult and even disadvantageous to implement. As already noted, it is difficult to anticipate which sources of information will prove to be most useful in an assessment. Similarly, with respect to which instruments to include in a test battery, there is little way to know whether the tests administered have yielded enough data and which tests have contributed most to understanding the person being examined, until after the data have been collected and analyzed.

In most practice settings, it is reasonable to conduct an interview and review previous records as a basis for deciding whether formal testing would be likely to help answer a referral question—that is, whether it will show enough incremental validity to warrant its cost in time and money. Likewise, reviewing a set of test data can provide a basis for determining what kind of additional testing might be worthwhile. However, it is rarely appropriate to administer only one test at a time, to choose each subsequent test on the basis of the preceding one, and to schedule a further testing session for each additional test administration. For this reason, responsible psychological assessment usually consists of one or two testing sessions comprising a battery of tests selected to serve specific additive, confirmatory, and complementary functions.

### Additive, Confirmatory, and Complementary Functions of Tests

Some referral questions require selection of multiple tests to identify relatively distinct and independent aspects of a person's psychological functioning. For example, students receiving low grades may be referred for an evaluation to help determine whether their poor academic performance is due primarily to limited intelligence or to personality characteristics that are fostering negative attitudes toward achieving in school. A proper test battery in such a case would include some measure of intelligence and some measure of personality functioning. These two measures would then be used in an additive fashion to provide separate pieces of information, both of which would contribute to answering the referral question. As this example illustrates, the additive use of tests serves generally to broaden understanding of the person being examined.

Other assessment situations may create a need for confirmatory evidence supporting conclusions based on test findings, in which case two or more measures of the same psychological function may have a place in the test battery. Assessors conducting a neuropsychological examination to address possible onset of Alzheimer's disease, for example, ordinarily administer several memory tests. Should each of these tests identify memory impairment consistent with Alzheimer's, from a technical standpoint, only one of them would have been necessary, and the others have shown no incremental validity. Practically speaking,

however, the multiple memory measures taken together provide confirmatory evidence of memory loss. Such confirmatory use of tests strengthens understanding and helps assessors present conclusions with confidence. The confirmatory function of a multitest battery is especially useful when tests of the same psychological function measure it in different ways. The advantages of multimethod assessment of variables have long been recognized in psychology, beginning with the work of Campbell and Fiske (1959) and continuing with the reports of the American Psychological Association's (APA's) Psychological Assessment Work Group, which stress the improved validity that results when phenomena are measured from a variety of perspectives (Kubiszyn et al., 2000; Meyer et al., 2001):

> The optimal methodology to enhance the construct validity of nomothetic research consists of combining data from multiple methods and multiple operational definitions.... Just as effective nomothetic research recognizes how validity is maximized when variables are measured by multiple methods, particularly when the methods produce meaningful discrepancies... the quality of idiographic assessment can be enhanced by clinicians who integrate the data from multiple methods of assessment. (Meyer et al., 2001, p. 150)

Such confirmatory testing is exemplified in applications of the Minnesota Multiphasic Personality Inventory (MMPI, MMPI-2) and the Rorschach Inkblot Method (RIM), the two most widely researched and frequently used personality assessment instruments (Butcher & Rouse, 1996; Hogan, 2005). As discussed later in this chapter and in Viglione and Rivera and in Ben-Porath, this volume, the MMPI-2 is a relatively structured self-report inventory, whereas the RIM is a relatively unstructured measure of perceptual-cognitive and associational processes. (See also Exner, 2003; Graham, 2006; Greene, 2011; Weiner, 2003.) Because of differences in their format, the MMPI-2 and the RIM measure normal and abnormal characteristics in different ways and at different levels of a person's ability and willingness to recognize and report them directly. Should a person display some type of disordered functioning on both the MMPI-2 and the RIM, this confirmatory finding becomes more powerful and convincing than having such information from one of these instruments but not the other, even though technically in this instance no incremental validity derives from the second instrument. (See Weiner, 2005.)

Confirmatory evidence of this kind often proves helpful in professional practice, especially in forensic work. As described by Heilbrun (2001; see also Heilbrun, Grisso, & Goldstein, 2009), multiple sources of information pointing in the same direction bolster courtroom testimony, whereas conclusions based on only one measure of some characteristic can result in assessors being criticized for failing to conduct a thorough examination.

Should multiple measures of the same psychological characteristics yield different instead of confirmatory results, these results usually can serve valuable complementary functions in the interpretive process. At times, apparent lack of agreement between two purported measures of the same characteristic has been taken to indicate that one of the measures lacks convergent validity. This negative view of divergent test findings fails to take adequate account of the complexity of the information provided by multimethod assessment, and it can result in misleading conclusions. To continue with the example of conjoint MMPI-2 and RIM testing, suppose that a person's responses show elevation on indices of depression on one of these measures but not the other. Inasmuch as indices on both measures have demonstrated some validity in detecting features of depression, the key question to ask is not which measure is wrong in this instance but rather why the measures have diverged.

Perhaps, as one possible explanation, the respondent has some underlying depressive concerns that he or she does not recognize or prefers not to admit to others, in which case depressive features might be less likely to emerge in response to the self-report MMPI-2 methodology than on the more indirect Rorschach task. Or perhaps the respondent is not particularly depressed but wants very much to give the impression of being in distress and needing help, in which case the MMPI-2 might be more likely to show depression than the RIM. Or perhaps the person generally feels more relaxed and inclined to be forthcoming in relatively structured than relatively unstructured situations; then the MMPI-2 is more likely than the RIM to reveal whether the person is depressed.

As these examples show, multiple measures of the same psychological characteristic can complement each other when they diverge, with one measure sometimes identifying the presence of a characteristic (a true positive) that is missed by the other (a false negative). Possible reasons for the false negative can contribute valuable information about the respondent's test-taking attitudes and likelihood of behaving differently in situations that differ in the amount of structure they provide. The translation of such divergence between MMPI-2 and RIM findings into clinically useful diagnostic inferences and individual treatment planning has been elaborated by Finn (1996) and Ganellen (1996). Whatever measures may be involved, the complementary use of divergent test findings frequently enriches the interpretive yield of an assessment process.

## Examiner Characteristics

Two characteristics of the examiners who conduct psychological assessments are likely to influence the amount and kind of data they collect. One of these characteristics consists of their qualifications and competence in using assessment procedures, and the other concerns ways in which their personal qualities may affect how different kinds of people respond to them.

### Qualifications and Competence

There is general consensus that persons who conduct psychological assessments should be qualified by education and training to do so. The Ethical Principles and Code of Conduct promulgated by the APA (2002) offers the following guideline in this regard: "Psychologists provide services, teach, and conduct research with populations and in areas only within the boundaries of their competence, based on their education, training, supervised experience, consultation, study, or professional experience" (Ethical Code 2.04[a]). Particular kinds of knowledge and skill that are necessary for test users to conduct adequate assessments are specified further by Krishnamurthy and Yalof (2010) and in the test user qualifications endorsed by the APA (Turner, DeMers, Fox, & Reed, 2008). Of further note is the identification in the *Standards* for Educational and Psychological Testing (AERA et al., 1999) of who is responsible for the proper use of tests in psychological assessments: "The ultimate responsibility for appropriate test use and interpretation lies predominantly with the test user. In assuming this responsibility, the user must become knowledgeable about a test's appropriate uses and the populations for which it is suitable" (p. 112).

Despite the clarity of these statements and the detailed guidelines they contain, two persistent issues in contemporary assessment practice remain unresolved. The first issue is that, typically, adequate qualifications are assumed for psychologists who are licensed and present themselves as competent to provide psychological testing services. However, until such time as the criteria proposed in the test user qualifications become incorporated into licensing procedures, being licensed to use psychological tests does not ensure being competent in using them.

Being competent in psychological testing requires familiarity with the latest revision of whatever instruments an assessor is using, with current research and the most recent normative data concerning these instruments, and with the manifold interpretive complexities they are likely to involve. Assessment competence also requires appreciation for a variety of psychometric, interpersonal, sociocultural, and contextual issues that affect not only the collection of assessment information but also its interpretation and utilization. The chapters that follow in this volume bear witness to the broad range of these issues and to the steady output of research findings, practice guidelines, and new or revised measures that make assessment psychology a dynamic and rapidly evolving field with a large and burgeoning literature. Only by keeping reasonably current with these developments can psychological assessors remain competent, and only by remaining competent can they meet their ethical responsibilities (Kitchener, 2000; Koocher & Keith-Spiegel, 2008; Weiner, 1989).

The second persistent issue concerns assessment by persons who are not psychologists and are therefore not bound by this profession's ethical principles or guidelines for practice. Nonpsychologist assessors who can obtain psychological tests are free to use them however they wish. When easily administered measures yield test scores that seem transparently interpretable, as in the case of an elevated Borderline scale on the Millon Multiaxial Clinical Inventory–III (MCMI–III; Millon, 2006) or an elevated Paranoia scale on the Personality Assessment Inventory (PAI; Morey, 2007), unqualified examiners can draw superficial conclusions that fail to consider the complexity of these instruments, the interactions among their scales, and the limits of their applicability. It accordingly behooves assessment psychologists not only to maintain their own competence but also to call attention, when necessary, to assessment practices that fall short of reasonable standards of competence.

### Personal Influence

Assessors can influence the information they collect by virtue of their personal qualities and by the manner in which they conduct a psychological examination. In the case of self-administered measures such as interest surveys or personality questionnaires, examiner influence may be minimal. Interviews and interactive testing procedures, however, create ample opportunity for an examiner's age, gender, ethnicity, or other characteristics to make respondents feel more or less comfortable and more or less inclined to be forthcoming. Examiners accordingly need to be alert to instances in which such personal qualities may be influencing the nature and amount of the data they are collecting.

The most important personal influence that examiners cannot modify or conceal is their language facility. Psychological assessment procedures are extensively language-based, both in their content and in the instructions that introduce nonverbal tasks, and accurate communication is essential for obtaining reliable assessment information. It is widely agreed that both examiners and whomever they are interviewing or testing should be communicating either in their native language or in a second language in which they are highly proficient (AERA et al., 1999). The use of interpreters to circumvent language barriers in the assessment process rarely provides a satisfactory solution to this problem. Unless an interpreter is fully conversant with idiomatic expressions and cultural referents in both languages, is familiar with standard procedures in psychological assessment, and is a stranger to the examinee (as opposed to a friend, relative, or member of the same closely knit subcultural community), the obtained results may be of questionable validity.

Likewise, in the case of self-administered measures, instructions and test items must be written in a language that the respondent can be expected to understand fully. Translations of pencil-and-paper measures require close attention to the idiomatic vagaries of each new language and to culture-specific contents of individual test items, in order to ensure equivalence of measures in the cross-cultural applications of tests (Allen & Walsh, 2000).

Unlike their fixed qualities, examiners' manner in conducting the assessment process is within their control, and untoward examiner influence can be minimized by appropriate efforts to promote a full and open response to the assessment procedures. To achieve this end, an assessment typically begins with a review of its purposes, a description of the procedures that will be followed, and efforts to establish a rapport that will help the person being evaluated feel comfortable and willing to cooperate with the assessment process. Variations in examiner behavior while introducing and conducting psychological evaluations can substantially influence how respondents perceive the assessment situation—for example, whether they see it as an authoritarian investigative process intended to ferret out defects and weaknesses or as a mutually respectful and supportive interaction intended to provide understanding and help. Even while following closely the guidelines for a structured interview and adhering faithfully to standardized procedures for administering various tests, examiners need to recognize that their manner, tone of voice, and apparent attitude are likely to affect the perceptions and comfort level of the person being assessed and, consequently, the amount and kind of information that person provides. (See Masling, 1966, 1998.)

## Respondent Issues

Examiner influence in the assessment process inevitably interacts with the attitudes and inclinations of the person being examined. Some respondents may feel more comfortable being examined by an older person than a younger one, for example, or by a male than a female examiner, whereas other respondents may prefer a younger and female examiner. Among members of a minority group, some may prefer to be examined by a person with a cultural or ethnic background similar to theirs, whereas others are less concerned with the examiner's background than with his or her competence. Similarly with respect to examiner style, a passive, timid, and dependent person might feel comforted by a warm, friendly, and supportive examiner approach that would make an aloof, distant, and mistrustful person feel uneasy; conversely, an interpersonally cautious and detached respondent might feel safe and secure when being examined in an impersonal and businesslike manner that would be unsettling and anxiety provoking to an interpersonally needy and dependent respondent. With such possibilities in mind, skilled examiners usually vary their behavioral style with an eye to conducting assessments in ways that will be likely to maximize each individual respondent's level of comfort and cooperation.

Two other respondent issues that influence the data collection process concern a person's right to give informed consent to being evaluated and his or her specific attitudes toward being examined. With respect to informed consent, the introductory phase of conducting an assessment ordinarily must include not only the explanation of purposes and procedures mentioned previously, which informs the respondent, but also an explicit agreement by the respondent (or persons legally responsible for the respondent) to undergo the evaluation. As elaborated in the Standards for Educational and Psychological Testing (AERA et al., 1999), informed consent can be waived only when an assessment has been mandated by law, as in the case of a court-ordered evaluation, or when it is implicit, as when a person applies for a position for which being assessed is a requirement (i.e., a job for which all applicants are being screened psychologically; see also Kitchener, 2000, and the chapters by Geisinger & McCormick and by Rey-Casserly & Koocher, this volume).

Having given their consent to be evaluated, moreover, respondents are entitled to revoke it at any time during the assessment process. Hence, the prospects for obtaining adequate assessment data depend not only on whether respondents can be helped to feel comfortable and be forthcoming but even more basically on whether they consent in the first place to being evaluated and remain willing during the course of the evaluation.

Issues involving a respondent's specific attitudes toward being examined typically arise in relation to whether the assessment is being conducted for clinical or for administrative purposes. When assessments are being conducted for clinical purposes, the examiner is responsible to the person being examined, the person being examined is seeking some type of assistance, and the examination is intended to be helpful to this person and responsive to his or her needs. As common examples in clinical assessments, people concerned about their psychological well-being may seek an evaluation to learn whether they need professional mental health care, and people uncertain about their educational or vocational plans may look for help in determining what their abilities and interests suit them to do.

In administrative assessments, by contrast, examiners are responsible not to the person being examined but to some third party who has requested the evaluation to assist in arriving at some judgment about the person. Examiners in an administrative assessment are ethically responsible for treating the respondent fairly and with respect, but the evaluation is being conducted for the benefit of the party requesting it, and the results may or may not meet the respondent's needs or serve his or her best interests. Assessment for administrative purposes occurs commonly in forensic, educational, and organizational settings when evaluations are requested to help decide such matters as whether a prison inmate should be paroled, a student should be admitted to a special program, or a job applicant should be hired. (See Heilbrun, 2001; Monahan, 1980.)

As for their attitudes, respondents being evaluated for clinical purposes are relatively likely to be motivated to reveal themselves honestly, whereas those being examined for administrative purposes are relatively likely to be intent on making a certain kind of impression. Respondents attempting to manage the impression they give tend to show themselves not as they are but as they think the person requesting the evaluation would view favorably. Typically such efforts at impression management take the form of denying one's limitations, minimizing one's shortcomings, attempting to put one's very best foot forward, and concealing whatever might be seen in a negative light.

Exceptions to this general trend are not uncommon, however. Whereas most persons being evaluated for administrative purposes want to make the best possible impression, some may be motivated in just the opposite direction. For example, a plaintiff claiming brain damage in a personal injury lawsuit may see benefit in making the worst possible impression on a neuropsychological examination.

Some persons being seen for clinical evaluations, despite having come of their own accord and recognizing that the assessment is being conducted for their benefit, may nevertheless be too anxious or embarrassed to reveal their difficulties fully. Whatever kind of impression respondents may want to make, the attitudes toward being examined that they bring with them to the assessment situation can be expected to influence the amount and kind of data they produce. These attitudes also have a bearing on the interpretation of assessment data. The further implications of impression management for malingering and defensiveness are discussed later in the chapter.

## Data Management Issues

A final set of considerations in collecting assessment information concerns appropriate ways of managing the data that are obtained. Examiners must be aware in particular of issues concerning (a) the use of computers in data collection; (b) the responsibility they have for safeguarding the security of their measures; and (c) their obligation, within limits, to maintain the confidentiality of what respondents report or reveal to them.

### Computerized Data Collection

Software programs are available to facilitate the data collection process for most widely used assessment methods. Programs designed for use with self-report questionnaires typically provide for computerized administration of test items, automated coding of item responses to produce scale scores, and quantitative manipulation of these scale scores to yield summary scores and indices. For instruments that require examiner administration and coding (e.g., a Wechsler intelligence test), software programs accept test scores entered by the examiner and translate them into the test's quantitative indices (e.g., the Wechsler IQ and Index scores). Many of these programs store the test results in files that can later be accessed or exported, and some even provide computational packages that can generate descriptive statistics for sets of test records held in storage.

These features of computerized data management bring several benefits to the process of collecting assessment information. Computerized administration and coding of responses help respondents avoid mechanical errors in filling out test forms manually, and they eliminate errors that examiners sometimes make in scoring these responses. (See Allard & Faust, 2000.) For measures that require examiner coding and data entry, the utility of the results depends on accurate coding and entry, but, once these raw data are entered, software programs eliminate examiner error

in calculating summary scores and indices from them. The data storage features of many software programs facilitate assessment research, particularly for investigators seeking to combine databases from different sources, and they can also help examiners meet requirements in most states and many agencies for keeping assessment information on file for some period of time. Presumably for these reasons, many assessment psychologists have indicated in surveys that they use software for test scoring and feel comfortable doing so (McMinn, Ellens, & Soref, 1999).

Computerized collection of assessment information has some potential disadvantages as well, however. When assessment measures are administered by computer, first of all, there is a possibility that the reliability of the data collected could be compromised by a lack of equivalence between the automated procedure and the noncomputerized version of it. As elaborated by Butcher, Perry, and Dean (2009) and by Butcher, this volume, however, available data suggest fairly good equivalence for computerized administrations based on pencil-and-paper questionnaires, especially those used in personality assessment. (See also Butcher, Perry, & Hahn, 2004.) Specifically with respect to the MMPI, for example, a meta-analysis by Finger and Ones (1999) of research comparing computerized with booklet forms of the inventory showed them to be psychometrically equivalent. Good congruence with the original measures has yet to be demonstrated for computerized versions of structured clinical interviews, however, and Garb (2007) has reported only "poor to fair" concordance between diagnoses based on clinician interviews and diagnoses based on computer interviews.

A second potential disadvantage of computerized data collection derives from the ease with which it can be employed. Although frequently helpful to knowledgeable assessment professionals, automated procedures also simplify psychological testing for untrained and unqualified persons who lack assessment skills and would not be able to collect test data without the aid of a computer. The availability of software programs thus creates possibilities for assessment methods to be misused and respondents to be poorly served. Such outcomes are not an inescapable by-product of computerized assessment procedures, however. They constitute instead an abuse of technology by uninformed and irresponsible practitioners.

### Test Security

Test security refers to restricting public access to test materials and answers to test items. Such restrictions address two important considerations in psychological assessment. First, publicly circulated information about tests can undermine their validity, particularly if they comprise items with right and wrong or more or less preferable answers. Prior exposure to tests of this kind and information about correct or preferred answers can affect how persons respond to them and prevent an examiner from being able to collect a valid protocol. The validity of test findings is especially questionable when a respondent's prior exposure has included specific coaching in how to answer certain questions.

As for relatively unstructured assessment procedures that have no right or wrong answers, even on these measures various kinds of responses carry particular kinds of interpretive significance. Hence, the possibility also exists on relatively unstructured measures that a person can be helped to make a certain kind of impression by pretest instructions concerning what various types of responses are taken to signify. However, the extent to which public dissemination of information about the inferred meaning of responses does in fact compromise the validity of relatively unstructured measures has not been examined empirically and is a subject for further research.

Second, along with helping to preserve the validity of obtained results, keeping assessment measures secure protects test publishers against infringement of their rights by pirated or plagiarized copies of their products. Ethical assessors respect copyright law by not making or distributing copies of published tests, and they take appropriate steps to prevent test forms, test manuals, and assessment software from falling into the hands of persons who are not qualified to use them properly or who feel under no obligation to keep them secure. Both the Ethical Principles and Code of Conduct (APA, 2002, section 9.11) and the Standards for Educational and Psychological Testing (AERA et al., 1999, p. 117) address this professional responsibility in clear terms.

These considerations in safeguarding test security become particularly relevant in forensic cases should an attorney request to have a psychological examination observed by a third party. Such intrusions on traditional examination procedures pose a threat to the validity of the obtained data in two respects. First, there is no way to judge or measure the impact of an observer on how the test taker chooses to respond. Second, the normative standards that guide test interpretation are derived from data obtained in two-person examinations, and there are no comparison data available for examinations conducted in the presence of an observer. Validity aside, exposing test items to an observer can compromise test security in the same way as distributing test forms or manuals to persons who are under no obligation to keep them confidential.

## *Confidentiality*

A third and related aspect of appropriate data management pertains to maintaining the confidentiality of a respondent's assessment information. Like certain aspects of safeguarding test security, confidentiality is an ethical matter in assessment psychology, not a substantive one. The key considerations in maintaining the confidentiality of assessment information, as specified in the Ethical Principles and Code of Conduct (APA, 2002, Section 4) and elaborated by Kitchener (2000), involve:

- clarifying the nature and limits of confidentiality with clients and patients prior to undertaking an evaluation;
- communicating information about persons being evaluated only for appropriate scientific or professional purposes and only to an extent relevant to the purposes for which the evaluation was conducted;
- disclosing information only to persons designated by respondents or to other duly authorized persons or entities, except when otherwise permitted or required by law; and
- storing and preserving respondents' records in a secure fashion.

Like the matter of informed consent discussed previously, confidentiality is elaborated as an ethical issue in Rey-Casserly and Koocher, this volume.

## INTERPRETING ASSESSMENT INFORMATION

Following the collection of sufficient relevant data, the process of psychological assessment continues with a phase of evaluation in which these data are interpreted. The interpretation of assessment data consists of drawing inferences and forming impressions concerning what the findings reveal about a respondent's psychological characteristics. Accurate and adequately focused interpretations result in summary descriptions of psychological functioning that can then be utilized in the final phase of the assessment process as a foundation for formulating conclusions and recommendations that answer referral questions. Reaching this output phase requires consideration during the evaluation phase of the basis on which inferences are drawn and impressions are formed, the possible effects on the findings of malingering or defensiveness, and effective ways of integrating data from diverse sources.

## Basis of Inferences and Impressions

The interpretation of assessment data involves four sets of alternatives with respect to how assessors go about drawing inferences and forming impressions about what these data indicate. Interpretations can be based on either empirical or conceptual approaches to decision making; they can be guided either by statistically based decision rules or by clinical judgment; they can emphasize either nomothetic or idiographic characteristics of respondents; and they can include more or less reliance on computer-generated interpretive statements. Effective assessment usually involves informed selection among these alternatives and some tailoring of the emphasis given each of them to fit the particular context of the individual assessment situation.

### *Empirical and Conceptual Guidelines*

The interpretation of assessment information can be approached in several ways. In what may be called an *intuitive* approach, assessment decisions stem from impressions that have no identifiable basis in the data. Instead, interpretations are justified by statements like "It's just a feeling I have about her" or "I can't say where I get it from, but I just know he's that way." In what may be called an *authoritative* approach, interpretations are based on the pronouncements of well-known or respected assessment psychologists, as in saying "These data mean what they mean because that's what Dr. Authority says they mean." The intuition of unusually empathic assessors and reliance on authority by well-read practitioners who choose their experts advisedly may on occasion yield accurate and useful impressions, but both approaches have serious shortcomings.

Unless intuitive assessors can identify specific features of the data that help them reach their conclusions, their diagnostic sensitivity cannot be taught to other professionals or translated into scientifically verifiable procedures. Unless authoritative assessors can explain in their own words the basis on which experts have reached the conclusions being cited, they are unlikely to impress others as being professionally knowledgeable themselves or as knowing what to think without being told what to think by someone else. Moreover, neither intuitive nor authoritative approaches to interpreting assessment information are likely to be as consistently reliable as approaches based on empirical and conceptual guidelines.

Empirical guidelines to decision making derive from the replicated results of methodologically sound research. When a specific assessment finding has repeatedly been found to correlate highly with the presence of a particular psychological characteristic, it is empirically sound to infer the presence of that characteristic in a respondent who displays that assessment finding. Conceptual guidelines to decision making consist of psychological constructs that provide a logical bridge between assessment findings and the inferences drawn from them. For example, if subjectively felt distress contributes to a person's remaining in and benefiting from psychotherapy (for which there is evidence; see Clarkin & Levy, 2004), then it is reasonable to expect that moderate but not excessive elevations on test indices of subjectively felt distress will increase the likelihood of a favorable outcome in psychotherapy (which they do; see Butcher & Perry, 2008; Weiner, 2004).

Both empirical and conceptual guidelines to interpretation bring distinct benefits to the assessment process. Empirical perspectives are valuable because they provide a foundation for achieving certainty in decision making. The adequacy of psychological assessment is enhanced by quantitative data concerning the normative distribution and other psychometric properties of measurements that reflect dimensions of psychological functioning. Lack of such data limits the confidence with which assessors can draw conclusions about the implications of their findings. Without being able to compare an individual's test responses with normative expectations, for example, or without a basis for estimating false positive and false negative possibilities in the measures they have used, assessors can be only speculative in attaching interpretive significance to their findings. Similarly, the absence of externally validated cutting scores detracts considerably from the certainty with which assessors can translate test scores into qualitative distinctions, such as whether a person is mildly, moderately, or severely depressed.

Conceptual perspectives are valuable in the assessment process because they provide some explanation of why certain findings are likely to identify certain kinds of psychological characteristics or predict certain kinds of behavior. Having such explanations in hand offers assessors the pleasure of understanding not only how their measures work but also why they work as they do; these explanations help assessors focus their attention on aspects of their data that are relevant to the referral question to which they are responding; and they facilitate the communication of results in terms that address characteristics of the person being examined and not merely characteristics of the data obtained. As a further benefit of conceptual formulations of assessment findings, they foster hypotheses concerning previously unknown or unexplored linkages between assessment findings and dimensions of psychological functioning, and by so doing they help to extend the frontiers of knowledge.

Empirical guidelines are thus necessary to the scientific foundations of assessment psychology, as a basis for certainty in decision making, but they are not sufficient to bring assessment to its full potential. Conceptual guidelines do not by themselves provide a reliable basis for drawing conclusions with certainty. However, by enriching the assessment process with explanatory hypotheses, they point the way to increased understanding of why people are as they are and behave as they do.

For the purposes they serve, then, both empirical and conceptual guidelines should figure prominently in the interpretation of assessment information. At times, concerns about preserving the scientific respectability of assessment have led to assertions that only empirical guidelines constitute an acceptable basis for decision making and that unvalidated conceptual guidelines have no place in scientific psychology. McFall and Treat (1999), for example, maintain that "the aim of clinical assessment is to gather data that allow us to reduce uncertainty concerning the probability of events" (p. 215). From their perspective, the information value of assessment data resides in scaled numerical values and conditional probabilities. By contrast, Hunsley and Mash (2010), in a more balanced perspective on evidence-based assessment, offer this observation: "Psychological assessment is, however, much more than just the data collected from psychometrically strong measures. At its heart, assessment is inherently a decision-making task in which the psychologist must iteratively formulate and test hypotheses" (p. 8).

Let it further be observed in this regard that the river of scientific discovery can flow through inferential reasoning that suggests truths long before they are confirmed by replicated research findings. Newton grasped the reason that apples fall from trees well in advance of experiments demonstrating the laws of gravity, Einstein conceived his theory of relativity with full confidence that empirical findings eventually would prove him correct, and neither man has been challenged with respect to his credentials as a scientist. Even though empirical guidelines are on average more likely to produce reliable conclusions than conceptual formulations, logical reasoning concerning the implications of clearly formulated concepts can also generate conclusions that serve useful purposes and stand the test of time. The process of arriving at conclusions in individual case assessment is accordingly likely to involve creative as well as confirmatory aspects of scientific thinking, and the utilization of assessment to generate hypotheses and fuel speculation may in the course of scientific endeavor increase rather than decrease uncertainty by virtue of identifying new alternative possibilities to consider.

### Statistical Rules and Clinical Judgment

Empirical guidelines for decision making have customarily been operationalized by using statistical rules to arrive at conclusions concerning what assessment data signify. Statistical rules for interpreting assessment data comprise empirically derived formulas, or algorithms, that provide an objective, actuarial basis for deciding what these data indicate. When statistical rules are applied to the results of a psychological evaluation, the formula makes the decision concerning whether certain psychological characteristics are present (as in deciding whether a respondent has a particular trait or disorder) or whether certain kinds of actions are likely to ensue (as in predicting the likelihood of a respondent's becoming suicidal or performing well in some occupation). Statistical rules have the advantage of ensuring that examiners applying a formula correctly to the same set of data will always arrive at the same conclusion concerning what these data mean. As a disadvantage, however, the breadth of the conclusions that can be based on statistical rules and their relevance to referral questions are limited by the composition of the database from which they have been derived.

For example, statistical rules may prove helpful in determining whether a student has a learning disability but provide little information about the nature of this student's disability; they may predict the likelihood of a criminal defendant's behaving violently but offer few clues to the kinds of situations most likely to trigger this person's becoming violent; and they may help identify an individual's suitability for one type of position in an organization but be mute with respect to his or her suitability for other types of positions in the organization. In each of these instances, moreover, a statistical rule derived from a group of people possessing certain demographic characteristics (e.g., age, gender, ethnicity, socioeconomic status) and having been evaluated in a particular setting may not generalize to persons with different demographic characteristics evaluated in other kinds of settings. Garb (2000) has noted in this regard that "statistical-prediction rules are of limited value because they have typically been based on limited information that has not been demonstrated to be optimal, and they have almost never been shown to be powerful" (p. 31).

In other words, the scope of statistical rules is restricted to findings pertaining to the particular kinds of persons, psychological characteristics, and circumstances that were anticipated in building these rules. For many of the varied types of people seen in actual assessment practice, and for many of the complex and specifically focused referral questions raised about these people, statistical rules that can by themselves provide fully adequate answers may be in short supply.

As a further limitation of statistical rules, they share with all quantified assessment scales some unavoidable artificiality that accompanies translation of numerical scores into qualitative descriptive categories. On the Beck Depression Inventory (BDI; Beck, Steer, & Brown, 1996), for example, a score of 14 to 19 is taken to indicate "mild depression" and a score of 20 to 28 indicates "moderate depression." Hence two people who have almost identical BDI scores, one with a 19 and the other with a 20, will be described differently by the statistical rule, one as mildly depressed and the other as moderately depressed.

Similarly, in measuring intelligence with the Wechsler Adult Intelligence Scale–IV (WAIS–IV; Wechsler, 2008), a Full Scale IQ score of 109 calls for describing a person's intelligence as "average," whereas a person with almost exactly the same level of intelligence and a Full Scale IQ of 110 falls in the "high average" range. According to the WAIS–IV formulas, a person with a Full Scale IQ of 91, like someone with a 109 IQ, would be labeled as having "average" intelligence; a person with a Full Scale IQ of 119, like someone with a 110 IQ, would be labeled as having "high average" intelligence. Assessors can minimize this problem by adding some further specificity to the WAIS-IV categories, as in labeling a 109 IQ as the high end of the average range and a 110 IQ as the low end of the high-average range. Although additional categorical descriptions for more narrowly defined score ranges can reduce the artificiality in the use of statistical rules, there are limits to how many quantitative data points on a scale can be assigned a distinctive qualitative designation.

Conceptual guidelines for decision making have been operationalized in terms of clinical judgment, which consists of the cumulative wisdom that practitioners acquire from their experience. Clinical guidelines may come to represent the shared beliefs of large numbers of practitioners, but they emerge initially as impressions formed by individual practitioners. In contrast to the objective and quantitative features of statistical rules, clinical judgments constitute a subjective and qualitative basis for arriving at conclusions. When clinical judgment is applied to assessment data, decisions are made by the practitioner, not by a formula. Clinical judgments concerning the interpretive significance of a set of assessment data are consequently less uniform than actuarial decisions and less

likely to be based on established fact. The applicability of clinical judgments, however, is infinite. Their breadth and relevance are limited not by any database but by the practitioner's capacity to reason logically about possible relationships between psychological characteristics identified by the assessment data and psychological characteristics relevant to addressing referral questions, whatever their complexity and specificity.

The relative merit of statistical rules and clinical judgment in the assessment process has been the subject of considerable debate since this distinction was first formulated by Meehl (1954) in a classic book, *Clinical versus Statistical Prediction*. Contemporary publications of note concerning this important issue include contributions by Ægisdóttir et al. (2006), Garb (1998, 2005), Grove and Meehl (1996), Grove, Zald, Lebow, Snitz, and Nelson (2000), and Westen and Weinberger (2005). Much of the literature on this topic has consisted of assertions and rebuttals concerning whether statistical methods generally produce more accurate assessment results than clinical methods. In light of the strengths and weaknesses inherent in both statistical prediction and clinical judgment, as elaborated by Spengler in this volume, such debate serves little purpose and is regrettable when it leads to disparagement of either approach to interpreting assessment data.

As testimony to the utility of both approaches, it is important to note that the creation of good statistical rules for making assessment decisions typically begins with clinically informed selection of both (a) test items, structured interview questions, and other measure components to be used as predictor variables and (b) psychological conditions, behavioral tendencies, and other criterion variables to which the predictor variables are expected to relate. Empirical methods of scale construction and cross-validation are then employed to shape these selected predictor variables into valid actuarial measures of the relevant criterion variables.

Hence good statistical rules should almost always produce more accurate results than clinical judgment, because they encompass clinical wisdom plus the sharpening of this wisdom by replicated research findings. Clinical methods of assessment at their best depend on the impressions and judgment of individual practitioners, whereas statistical methods at their best constitute established fact that has been built on clinical wisdom. Relying only on clinical judgment in decision-making situations for which adequate actuarial guidelines are available disregards fundamental principles of evidence-based practice. Even the best judgment of the wisest practitioner can at times be clouded by inadvertent bias, insufficient consideration of base rates, and other sources of influence discussed in the final section of this chapter and in Reynolds and Suzuki, this volume. When there is a reasonable choice, assessment decisions are more advisedly based on established fact than on clinical impressions.

The previously noted diversity of people and of the circumstances that lead to their being referred for an evaluation mean that assessment questions regularly arise for which there are no available statistical rules, and patterns of assessment data often resemble but do not quite match the parameters for which replicated research has demonstrated certain correlates. When statistical rules cannot fully answer questions being asked, what are assessors to do in the absence of fully validated data? Decisions could be deferred, on the grounds that sufficient factual basis for a decision is lacking, and recommendations could be delayed, pending greater certainty about what recommendations should be made. Alternatively, assessors in a situation of uncertainty can supplement whatever empirical guidelines they have at their disposal with logical reasoning and clinical wisdom to arrive at conclusions and recommendations that are more responsive, more timely, and at least a little more likely to be helpful than saying nothing at all.

As these observations indicate, statistical rules and clinical judgment can properly be regarded as complementary components of effective decision making rather than as competing and mutually exclusive alternatives. Each brings value to assessment psychology, and each has a respectable place in it. Geisinger and Carlson (2009) comment in this regard that "it is time to move beyond both purely judgmental, speculative interpretation of test results as well as extrapolations from the general population to specific cases that do not much resemble the remainder of the population" (p. 109).

Assessment practice should accordingly be subjected to and influenced by research studies, lest it lead down blind alleys and detract from the pursuit of knowledge and the delivery of responsible professional service. Concurrently, however, lack of unequivocal documentation should not deter assessment psychologists from employing procedures and reaching conclusions that in their judgment will assist in meeting the needs of those who seek their help. Meehl (1957) himself allowed that, in the absence of research findings to provide guidance, clinicians may have to "use our heads instead of the formula"; as for when we should use our heads instead of the formula, he said, "'Always' and 'Never' are equally unacceptable" (p. 268). Zeldow (2009) has more recently echoed Meehl by observing that "clinicians will always have to deal with

uncertainty, values, and uniqueness; they will always have to use their heads for certain purposes and to rely on clinical expertise, not only because the appropriate research has not yet been conducted, but also because that is the nature of clinical work" (p. 1).

### Nomothetic and Idiographic Emphasis

Empirical guidelines and statistical rules constitute a basically nomothetic approach to interpreting assessment information, whereas conceptual guidelines and clinical judgment underlie a basically idiographic approach. Nomothetic interpretations address ways in which people resemble other kinds of people and share various psychological characteristics with many of them. Hence these interpretations involve comparisons between the assessment findings for the person being examined and assessment findings typically obtained from groups of people with certain known characteristics, as in concluding that "this person's responses show a pattern often seen in people who feel uncomfortable in social situations and are inclined to withdraw from them." The manner in which nomothetic interpretations are derived and expressed is thus primarily quantitative in nature and may even include specifying the precise frequency with which an assessment finding occurs in particular groups of people.

Idiographic interpretations, by contrast, address ways in which people differ from most other people and show psychological characteristics that are fairly unique to them and their particular circumstances. These interpretations typically comprise statements that attribute person-specific meaning to assessment information on the basis of general notions of psychological processes, as in saying that "this person gives many indications of being a passive and dependent individual who is more comfortable being a follower than a leader and consequently may not function effectively in an executive position." Deriving and expressing idiographic interpretations is thus a largely qualitative procedure in which examiners are guided by informed impressions rather than by quantitative empirical comparisons.

In the area of personality assessment, both nomothetic and idiographic approaches to interpretation have a long and distinguished tradition. Nomothetic perspectives in personality assessment derive from the work of Cattell (1946), for whom the essence of personality resided in traits or dimensions of functioning that all people share to some degree and on which they can be compared with each other. Idiographic perspectives in personality theory were first clearly articulated by Allport (1937), who conceived the essence of personality as residing in the uniqueness and individuality of each person, independently of comparisons to other people.

Over the years, assessment psychologists have at times expressed different convictions concerning which of these two traditions should be emphasized in formulating interpretations. Practitioners typically concur with Groth-Marnat (2010) that data-oriented descriptions of people rarely address the unique problems they may be having and that the essence of psychological assessment is an attempt "to evaluate an individual in a problem situation so that the information derived from the assessment can somehow help with the problem" (p. 3). Writing from a research perspective, however, McFall and Townsend (1998) grant that practitioners must of necessity provide idiographic solutions to people's problems but maintain that "nomothetic knowledge is a prerequisite to valid idiographic solutions" (p. 325) and that the clinical science of assessment should accordingly focus on nomothetic variables.

In light of what has already been said about statistical and clinical prediction, these nomothetic/idiographic differences of opinion can be tempered by recognizing that idiography can readily be managed in a scientific fashion (see Westen & Weinberger, 2004), and clinicians seeking solutions to idiographic problems can freely draw on whatever nomothetic guidelines will help them frame accurate and useful interpretations. In this vein, Stricker's (1997, 2007) concept of the "local clinical scientist" incorporates a frame of reference and a set of values that can characterize both office practitioners and laboratory researchers: "The local clinical scientist brings the attitudes and knowledge base of the scientist to bear on the problems that must be addressed by the clinician in the consulting room" (Stricker & Trierweiler, 2006, p. 37).

Issues of definition aside, then, there seems little to be gained by debating whether people can be described better in terms of how they differ from other people or how they resemble them. In practice, an optimally informative and useful description of an individual's psychological characteristics and functioning will address both the person's resemblance to and differences from other people in similar circumstances about whom similar referral questions have been posed. Nomothetic and idiographic perspectives thus complement each other, and balanced attention to both promotes the fullest possible understanding of a person who is being evaluated.

### Computer-Generated Interpretive Statements

For most published tests, there are software programs that not only assist in the collection of assessment data, as already discussed, but also generate interpretive statements that describe the test findings and present inferences based on them. Like computerized data collection, computer-based test interpretation (CBTI) brings some distinct advantages to the assessment process. By virtue of its automation, CBTI guarantees a thorough scan of the test data and thereby eliminates human error due to overlooking items of information in a test protocol. CBTI also ensures that a pattern of test data will always generate the same interpretive statement, uniformly and reliably, thus eliminating examiner variability and bias as potential sources of error. Additionally CBTI can facilitate the teaching and learning of assessment methods, by using computer-generated narratives as an exercise requiring the learner to identify the test variables that have given rise to particular interpretive statements.

The potential benefits of computerizing test interpretations, as well as some drawbacks of doing so, are elaborated in Butcher, this volume. (See also Butcher, Perry, & Dean, 2009.) Four limitations of CBTI have a particular bearing on the extent to which examiners should rely on computer-generated statements in formulating and expressing their impressions. First, although test software generates interpretive statements by means of quantitative algorithmic formulas, these computer programs are not entirely empirically based. Instead, they typically combine empirically validated correlates of test scores with clinical judgments about what various patterns of scores are likely to signify, and many algorithms involve beliefs as well as established fact concerning what these patterns mean. Different test programs, and even different programs for the same test, vary in the extent to which their interpretive statements are research based. Although CBTI generally increases the validity and utility of test interpretations, considerable research remains to be done to place computerized interpretation on a solid empirical basis. (See Garb, 2000.) In the meantime, computer-generated interpretations will embody at least some of the strengths and weaknesses of both statistical and clinical methods of decision making, and, as noted by Garb (2007), "it is recommended that computer assessment be combined with clinical judgment" (p. 207).

Second, the previously noted limitation of statistical rules with respect to designating quantitative score ranges with qualitative descriptors carries over into CBTI algorithms. Cutting points must be established, below which one kind or degree of descriptive statement is keyed and above which a different kind or degree of description will be generated. Consequently, as illustrated earlier for the BDI and WAIS, two people who score similarly on some test index or scale may be described by a computer narrative in quite different terms with respect to psychological characteristics measured by this index or scale.

Third, despite often referring specifically to the person who was examined (i.e., using the terms *he, she,* or *this person*) and thus giving the appearance of being idiographic, computer-generated interpretations do not describe the individual who took the test. Instead, these interpretations describe test protocols; that is, they indicate what research findings or clinical wisdom say about people who show the same or similar test scores and patterns as those in the protocol being scanned by the computer. Hence computer narratives are basically nomothetic, and most of them phrase at least some of their interpretive statements in terms of normative comparisons or even the specific frequencies with which the respondent's test patterns occur in certain groups of people. However, because no two people are exactly alike, and no individual matches any comparison group perfectly, some computer-generated interpretive statements may not describe a test taker accurately.

For this reason, well-developed test software narratives include a caveat indicating that (a) the interpretive statements in the report describe groups of people, not necessarily the person who took the test; (b) misleading and erroneous statements may occur as a reflection of psychological characteristics or environmental circumstances unique to the person being examined and not widely shared within any normative group; and (c) other sources of information and the assessor's judgment are necessary to determine which of the statements in an interpretive narrative apply to the respondent and which do not.

Fourth, the availability of computer-generated interpretive statements raises questions concerning their proper utilization in the preparation of an assessment report. Ideally, assessors should draw on computer narratives for some assistance, as for example in being sure that they have taken account of all of the relevant data, in checking for discrepancies between their own impressions and the conclusions reached by the machine, and perhaps in getting some guidance on how best to organize and what to emphasize in their report. Less ideal is using CBTI not merely for supportive purposes but as a replacement for assessors being able and willing to generate their own interpretations of the data they have obtained. Most of the assessment psychologists responding to the previously mentioned McMinn et al. (1999) survey reported that they never use CBTI as their primary resource for case formulation and would question the ethicality of doing so.

Even among ethical assessors, however, CBTI can present some temptations, because many computerized narratives present carefully crafted sentences and paragraphs that communicate clearly and lend themselves to being copied verbatim into a psychological report. Professional integrity would suggest that assessors relying on computer-generated conclusions should either express them in their own words or, if they are copying verbatim, should identify the copied material as a quotation and indicate its source. Regrettably, the previously mentioned software accessibility that allows untrained persons to collect and score test protocols by machine also makes it possible for them to print out narrative interpretations and reproduce them fully or in part as their report, without indicating their source. Aside from its questionable ethicality, the verbatim inclusion of computer-generated interpretations in assessment reports is likely to be a source of confusion and error because of the previously mentioned fact that these printouts are nomothetically rather than idiographically based and hence often include statements that are not applicable to the person being examined.

## Malingering and Defensiveness

Malingering and defensiveness consist of conscious and deliberate attempts by persons being examined to falsify the information they are giving and thereby mislead the examiner. *Malingering* involves intent to present oneself as being worse off psychologically than is actually the case and is commonly referred to as *faking bad*. *Defensiveness* involves seeking to convey an impression of being better off than one actually is and is commonly called *faking good*. Both faking bad and faking good can range in degree from slight exaggeration of problems and concerns, or of assets and capabilities, to total fabrication of difficulties never experienced or accomplishments never achieved. These two types of efforts to mislead examiners arise from different kinds of motivation, but usually both types can be detected from patterns of inconsistency that appear in the assessment data, unless respondents have been coached to avoid them.

### Identifying Motivations to Mislead

People who fake bad during psychological assessments are usually motivated by some specific reason for wanting to appear less capable or more disturbed than they really are. In clinical settings, for example, patients who are concerned about not getting as much help or attention as they would like to receive may exaggerate or fabricate symptoms in order to convince a mental health professional that they should be taken into psychotherapy, that they should be seen more frequently in outpatient treatment than is currently the case, or that they should be admitted to an inpatient facility or kept in one if they are already there. In forensic settings, plaintiffs seeking damages in personal injury cases may malinger the extent of their neuropsychological or psychosocial impairments in hopes of increasing the amount of the settlement they receive, and defendants in criminal actions may malinger psychological disturbance in hopes of being able to minimize the penalties that are be imposed on them. In employment settings, claimants may malinger inability to function in order to begin or continue receiving disability payments or unemployment insurance.

People who fake good during psychological assessments, in an effort to appear more capable or better adjusted than they really are, also show a variety of motivations related to the setting in which they are being evaluated. Defensive patients in clinical settings may try to conceal the extent of their difficulties when they hope to be discharged from a hospital to which they were involuntarily committed or when they would like to be told or have others told that they do not have any significant psychological problems for which they need treatment. In forensic settings, making the best possible impression can be a powerful inducement to faking good among divorced parents seeking custody of their children and among prison inmates requesting parole. In personnel settings, applicants for positions, candidates for promotion, and persons asking for reinstatement after having been found impaired have good reasons for putting their best foot forward during a psychological evaluation, even to the extent of overstating their assets and minimizing their limitations.

### Detecting Malingering and Defensiveness

Attempts to mislead psychological assessors usually produce patterns of inconsistency that provide dependable clues to malingering and defensiveness. In the case of efforts to fake bad, these inconsistencies are likely to appear in three different forms. First, malingerers often produce inconsistent data within individual assessment measures. Usually referred to as *intratest scatter*, this form of inconsistency involves failing relatively easy items on intelligence or ability tests while succeeding on more difficult items of the same kind or responding within the normal range on some portions of a personality test but in an extremely deviant manner on other portions of the same test.

A second form of inconsistency frequently found in the assessment data of malingerers occurs between test results and the examiner's behavioral observations. In some instances, for example, people who appear calm and relaxed during an interview, talk clearly and sensibly about a variety of matters, and conduct themselves in a socially appropriate fashion produce test protocols similar to those seen in people who are extremely anxious or emotionally upset, incapable of thinking logically and coherently, out of touch with reality, and unable to participate comfortably in interpersonal relationships. Such discrepancies between test and interview data strongly suggest deceptive tactics intended to create a false impression of disturbance.

The third form of inconsistency that proves helpful in detecting malingering consists of a sharp discrepancy between the interview and test data collected by the examiner and the respondent's actual circumstances and past history as reported by collateral sources or recorded in formal documents. In these instances, the person being evaluated may talk and act strangely during an interview and give test responses strongly suggestive of serious psychological disturbance but never previously have seen a mental health professional, received counseling or psychotherapy, been prescribed psychotropic medication, or been considered by friends, relatives, teachers, or employers to have any emotional problems. Such contrasts between serious impairments or limitations suggested by the results of an examination and a life history containing little or no evidence of these impairments or limitations provide good reason to suspect malingering.

Defensiveness in an effort to look good is similarly likely to result in inconsistencies in the assessment data that help to detect it. Most common in this regard are guarded test protocols and minimally informative interview responses that fall far short of reflecting a documented history of psychological disorder or problem behavior. Although being guarded and tight-lipped may successfully conceal difficulties, it also alerts examiners that a respondent is not being forthcoming and that the data being obtained probably do not paint a full picture of his or her psychological problems and limitations. As another possibility, fake-good respondents may, instead of being guarded and closemouthed, become quite talkative and expansive in an effort to impress the examiner with their admirable qualities and many capabilities, in which case the assessment information becomes noteworthy for claims of knowledge, skills, virtues, and accomplishments that far exceed reasonable likelihood. These and other guidelines for the clinical detection of efforts to mislead assessors by faking either good or bad are elaborated by Rogers (2008a) and by Berry, Sollman, Schipper, Clark, and Shandera (2009).

Most self-report inventories include validity scales that are based on inconsistent and difficult-to-believe responses that often can help to identify malingering and defensiveness. (See Greene, 2008.) A variety of specific interview, self-report, and ability measures have also been developed along these lines to assist in identifying malingering, including the Structured Interview of Reported Symptoms (SIRS; Rogers, Gillis, Dickens, & Bagby, 1991; Rogers, Jackson, Sewell, & Salekin, 2005) and the Test of Memory Malingering (TOMM; Teichner & Wagner, 2004; Tombaugh, 1997). (See also Berry & Schipper, 2008; Rogers, 2008b; Smith, 2008.)

Commonly used performance-based assessment instruments do not include formal validity scales but nevertheless are sensitive to inconsistencies in performance that suggest malingering or defensiveness. (See Ganellen, 2008; Sewell, 2008.) Moreover, because relatively unstructured measures convey less meaning to respondents than self-report questionnaires concerning what their responses might signify, there is reason to believe that they may be less susceptible to impression management or even that the fakability of an assessment instrument is directly related to its face validity (Bornstein, Rossner, Hill, & Stepanian, 1994; Weiner, 2005). This does not mean that unstructured measures like the Rorschach Inkblot Method and Thematic Apperception Test are impervious to malingering and defensiveness, which they are not, but only that efforts to mislead may be more obvious on these measures than on relatively structured measures and may be less likely to convey a desired impression.

### Coaching

A companion issue to the ease or difficulty of faking assessment measures is the extent to which respondents can be taught to deceive examiners with a good-looking or bad-looking performance. Research findings indicate that even psychologically naive participants who are given some information about the nature of people who have certain disorders or characteristics can shape their test behaviors to make themselves resemble a target group more closely than they could have done without such instruction. Misleading results are even more likely to occur when respondents are coached specifically in how to answer certain kinds of questions and avoid elevating validity scales (Gorny & Merten, 2007; Storm & Graham, 2000; Victor & Abeles, 2004). The group findings in these research studies have not yet indicated whether a generally instructed or specifically coached respondent can totally mislead an experienced examiner in actual practice, without generating any suspicion that the obtained results may not be valid, and this remains a subject for further investigation.

With further respect to individual assessments in actual practice, however, there are reports in the literature of instances in which attorneys have coached their clients in how to answer questions on self-report inventories (e.g., Lees-Haley, 1997; Wetter & Corrigan, 1995; Youngjohn, 1995), and a website on the Internet claims to provide a list of supposed good and bad responses for each of the 10 Rorschach inkblots. As previously mentioned in discussing test security, prior knowledge of test questions and answers can detract from the practical utility of psychological assessment methods that feature right and wrong answers. The confounding effect of pretest information on unstructured measures, for which correct or preferable answers are difficult to specify out of context, may be minimal, but the susceptibility of these measures to successful deception by well-coached respondents is another topic for future research. Less uncertain are the questionable ethics of persons who coach test takers in dishonesty and thereby thwart the legitimate purposes for which these respondents are being evaluated.

### Integrating Data Sources

As noted at the beginning of this chapter, psychological assessment information can be derived from administering tests, conducting interviews, observing behavior, speaking with collateral persons, and reviewing historical documents. Effective integration of data obtained from such multiple sources calls for procedures based on the previously described additive, confirmatory, and complementary functions served by a multimethod test battery. In some instances, for example, a respondent may during an interview report a problem for which there is no valid test index (e.g., having been sexually abused) and may demonstrate on testing a problem that is ordinarily not measured by interview data (e.g., poor perceptual-motor coordination). These two data sources can then be used additively to suggest that the person may have both a chronic traumatic stress disorder and a neuropsychological impairment. In another instance, a person who describes him- or herself during an interview as being a bright, well-educated individual with good leadership skills and a strong work ethic, and who then produces reliable documents attesting these same characteristics, offers assessors an opportunity for confirmatory use of these different data sources to lend certainty to a positive personnel report.

A third and somewhat more complicated set of circumstances may involve a respondent who behaves pleasantly and deferentially toward the assessor, reports being a kindly and even-tempered person, and produces limited and mostly conventional test responses that fall in the normal range. At the same time, however, the respondent is described by friends and relatives as an angry and abusive person, and police reports show an arrest record for assault and domestic violence. Familiar to forensic psychologists consulting in the criminal justice system, this pattern of discrepant data usually can be explained by using them in a complementary fashion to infer defensiveness and a successful fake-good approach to the interviewing and testing situations. As a further example in educational settings, if a student whose poor grades suggest limited intelligence but whose test performance indicates an above-average IQ and no specific learning disability, assessors can draw in a complementary fashion on these divergent data to infer the possibility of psychologically determined underachievement.

Because of the increased understanding of people that can accrue from integrating multiple sources of information, thorough psychological evaluation utilizes all of the available data during the interpretation phase of the assessment process. This consideration in conducting psychological assessments touches on the question of how much data should be collected for the purposes of an evaluation. Theoretically, there can never be too much information in an assessment situation. There may be redundant information that provides more confirmatory evidence than is needed, and there may be irrelevant information that serves no additive function in answering the referral question, but examiners can choose to discard the former and ignore the latter. Moreover, all of the test, interview, and observational data that are collected reflect some psychological characteristics of people being evaluated and may therefore signify something important to know about them.

Practically speaking, however, there are limits to how much assessment information should be collected to guide the formulation of interpretations. Psychological assessors are responsible for conducting evaluations in a cost-effective manner that provides adequate responses to referral questions with the least possible expense of time and money. As noted previously, practitioners who provide and charge for services that they know will have little import are exploiting the recipients of their services and jeopardizing their own professional respectability. Assessment psychologists may differ in the amount and kind of data they regard as sufficient for a fully adequate evaluation, but they are ethically obligated to refrain from collecting information beyond what they genuinely believe could be helpful.

With respect to providing answers to referral questions, two additional guidelines can help assessment psychologists draw wisely and constructively on the assessment data at their disposal. First, by taking account of indications of both psychological strengths and weaknesses in people they examine, assessors can present a balanced description of their assets and liabilities. Psychological assessment has tended over the years to address mainly what is wrong with people while giving insufficient attention to their adaptive capacities and admirable qualities. In keeping with a currently increasing focus in psychology on wellness, happiness, optimism, and other positive elements of the human condition, assessment serves its purposes best when the interpretive process gives full measure to coping strengths as well as functioning limitations. (See Duckworth, Steen, & Seligman, 2005; Linley, Harrington, & Garcea, 2010; Seligman & Csikszentmihalyi, 2000.)

Second, by recognizing that the strength of the evidence supporting the inferences and impressions they derive from assessment data is likely to vary, examiners can couch their interpretive statements in language that conveys their level of confidence in what they have to say. Most respondents provide clear and convincing evidence of at least some psychological characteristics, which examiners can then appropriately report in what may be called the *language of certainty*. The language of certainty states in direct terms what people are like and how they are likely to conduct themselves, as in saying "This student has a moderately severe reading disability," or "Mr. A appears to be an impulsive person with limited self-control," or "Ms. B is an outgoing and gregarious person who seeks out and enjoys interpersonal relationships." For other characteristics of a person being evaluated, the evidence may be fragmentary or suggestive rather than compelling and conclusive, in which case impressions are properly reported in what may be called the *language of conjecture*. Conjectural language suggests or speculates about possible features of a person's nature or behavioral tendencies, as in saying "There is some evidence to suggest that this child may have an auditory processing deficit," or "She appears prone on occasion to jump to conclusions and exercise poor judgment, which might limit her ability to make good decisions," or "The data provide some basis for speculating that his lack of effort represents a passive-aggressive way of dealing with underlying anger and resentment he feels toward people who have made a lot of demands on him."

## USING ASSESSMENT INFORMATION

The assessment process culminates in using descriptions of psychological characteristics and behavioral tendencies to formulate conclusions and recommendations.

Interpretations of assessment information are now translated into their implications for various decisions, and the overall purpose and eventual goal of assessment can be conceived as a way of facilitating decision making about classification, selection, placement, diagnosis, and treatment of people being evaluated. In this output phase, however, account must be taken of the fact that assessment data and the descriptions they generate may have different implications for different kinds of people living in different circumstances. Most important in this regard are possible sources of bias, applicable base rates, value judgments that call for cutting-score adjustments, and the cultural background and social context of the person being evaluated. Good assessment decisions depend on recognizing these considerations and preventing them from exerting undue influence on conclusions and recommendations.

## Bias and Base Rates

As elaborated in Reynolds and Suzuki, this volume, bias occurs in the utilization of assessment information when examiners allow preconceived notions and previously held beliefs to influence how they view the implications of their data. Assessment bias may arise either inadvertently, from attitudes of which examiners are unaware, or consciously, as purposeful intent on their part. Whether inadvertent or intentional, assessment bias takes the form of expectations that derive from demographic beliefs, environmental impressions, or epidemiological notions and that affect the meaning assigned to a set of findings.

As an example of demographic beliefs, an assessor who thinks that older people and males are generally likely to perform better as managers than younger people and females may advise hiring a 45-year-old man and not hiring a 30-year-old woman for a managerial position, even if their psychological assessment information would be seen by most examiners as comparable or even favoring the female candidate. Similarly, assessors who harbor a conviction that blue-collar African Americans are generally less likely to respond to psychotherapy than white-collar Caucasians may discourage psychotherapy for the former and recommend it for the latter, even when they are looking at assessment information showing equivalent treatment accessibility.

Environmental impressions as a source of biased expectations relate to the setting in which assessors are conducting an evaluation. Psychologists working in an inpatient facility in which a large percentage of patients are psychotically disturbed come to expect most of the people they examine to be psychotic, at least on admission, and accordingly they may be inclined to infer psychosis from a set of assessment data that would not have led them to this conclusion had they obtained it in an outpatient clinic in which psychotic disturbance is rarely seen. Similarly, psychologists assessing prison inmates, among whom antisocial personality disorder is commonly found, may be more likely to expect and diagnose this disorder than they would if they were working with similar data in a university counseling center.

As for epidemiological notions, examiners may be consciously or inadvertently influenced in the conclusions they draw by how they view the nature and incidence of various conditions. Those who believe that borderline personality disorder is widespread are likely to diagnose this condition more frequently than those who think this diagnostic category lacks precision and is too frequently used. Those who believe that attention-deficit/hyperactivity disorder (ADHD) occurs mainly in boys and adolescent anorexia mainly in girls are relatively unlikely to diagnose ADHD in girls and anorexia in boys.

In all such instances of possible untoward influence stemming from demographic, environmental, and epidemiological expectations, the challenge for assessment psychologists is to recognize their personal biases and prevent them as much as possible from affecting the conclusions they derive from their assessment data and the recommendations they base on these conclusions. As indicated by the examples just given, however, epidemiological and environmental expectations may have some basis in fact. There *are* more psychotic patients in hospital than in clinic populations, there *are* more antisocial individuals in prison than on college campuses, and there *are* gender differences in the incidence of ADHD and anorexia. From a strictly actuarial point of view, then, being hospitalized does increase the probability of being psychotic, being incarcerated does increase the probability of being antisocial, and being male or female does increase the probability of being attention disordered or anorexic, respectively. To take adequate account of such actual setting and group differences while preventing them from resulting in biased conclusions, examiners need to be alert to whatever base-rate information may be applicable in the individual case.

*Base-rate information* consists of the expected frequency of a characteristic or behavior in a particular set of persons or circumstances. Attention to applicable base rates provides a way of estimating the utility of assessment procedures, particularly with respect to their efficiency in assessing rare events. As first identified by Meehl and Rosen (1955), base rates can become problematic for measuring instruments when the expected frequency of an event falls very far below 50%. For example, in a clinical setting in which 10% of the patients are suicidal, a valid test of suicidality that has a hit rate of 60% (i.e., is correct 60% of the time in identifying people in general as suicidal or nonsuicidal) is technically less efficient than simply calling all of the patients nonsuicidal, which would be correct 90% of the time.

Although technically correct from a psychometric perspective, this type of base-rate emphasis on efficiency does not always satisfy priorities in actual assessment practice. Assessment methods that are inefficient in assessing suicidality, given its low base rate even in most patient populations, may nevertheless correctly identify a subgroup of patients in whom suicidal behavior is relatively likely to occur. An examiner can then use this information to recommend suicide precautions for this apparently suicidal subgroup, which is preferable to overlooking the self-destructive potential of the high-risk group by exercising the technically more efficient option of calling all of the patients nonsuicidal.

The base-rate problem can also be minimized by focusing assessment efforts on restricted populations in which the expected frequency of the characteristic being evaluated is less rare than in the general population. Kamphuis and Finn (2002) note in this regard that the more closely a base rate approximates 50%, the better prospects a valid measure has of improving on the efficiency of concluding that either everyone or no one has a certain characteristic or behavioral tendency. As an example of increasing the base rate by restricting the population, efficient prediction of violent behavior among people in general is difficult to achieve, because most people are nonviolent. In a population of criminal offenders, however, many of whom have a history of violence, a valid measure of violence potential may prove quite efficient in identifying those at highest risk for violent behavior in the future.

## Value Judgments and Cutting Scores

Value judgments in the present context relate to the purposes for which a respondent is being evaluated and the frequency of false-positive and false-negative outcomes that an assessment variable is likely to produce. False-positive outcomes result in concluding that people have certain conditions and tendencies that they in fact do not have; false-negative outcomes result in concluding that people lack certain conditions and tendencies that in fact do characterize them. When assessments are being conducted to assist in making decisions about psychological

characteristics and behavioral tendencies that most people would consider as undesirable, such as being suicidal or homicidal, false positives may be of less concern than false negatives. A false-positive decision concerning dangerousness might result in a person's being unnecessarily supervised or even restrained, which is a regrettable but not a fatal outcome. A false-negative decision, however, by failing to identify existing dangerousness to oneself or others, can result in loss of life.

Conversely, false-positive outcomes may be more problematic than false-negative outcomes when referral questions concern desirable characteristics and probable outcomes, such as whether a person should be given a scholarship, a job, a promotion, or a parole. False negatives in this kind of assessment situation may result in denying people opportunities for which they are qualified and deserving, which is disadvantageous and perhaps unfair to them as individuals. However, when false positives lead to promoting personnel to positions of responsibility that exceed their capacities or paroling felons whose criminal tendencies have not abated, many people other than the individual are likely to suffer regrettable consequences.

In relation to such value judgments, then, a set of assessment data may have different implications in different assessment circumstances and thereby call for assessors to select carefully the cutting scores they use in formulating their conclusions and recommendations. For quantifiable dimensions of assessment that correlate positively with the presence of a characteristic or behavioral tendency, moving up the numerical scale produces a progressively decreasing percentage of false positives and moving down the scale produces a progressively decreasing percentage of false negatives; just the opposite is the case for assessment dimensions that are inversely correlated with what they measure. As a way of deciding the implications of assessment findings in a particular circumstance, cutting scores can thus be selected to minimize the likelihood of false-positive outcomes in examinations concerned with desirable consequences and to minimize false-negative outcomes in the estimation of undesirable consequences.

## Culture and Context

Just as assessment information may have different implications for people examined in different settings and for different purposes, it may also vary in its significance for respondents coming from different cultures or living in different social contexts. Hence the utilization phase of the assessment process must always take account of how characteristics of individuals identified in the interpretive phase are likely to affect their psychological functioning in their particular circumstances. Attention to cross-cultural influences has a long history in assessment psychology (see, e.g., Hallowell, 1951; Lindzey, 1961) and has seen a recent resurgence of interest, as described in Geisinger and McCormick, this volume, and in contributions by Dana (2000, 2005), Hambleton, Merenda, and Spielberger (2005), and Suzuki and Ponterotto (2008).

The distinction drawn in this overview of the assessment process between interpreting and using assessment information provides guidelines for a two-step process in taking account of background and situational differences among respondents. The interpretive phase of assessment provides the first step, which consists of arriving at descriptive statements that identify a respondent's psychological characteristics as they exist independently of his or her cultural context and circumstances. Having superior intelligence, being orderly and compulsive, experiencing memory loss, being emotionally reserved, having an assertive and competitive bent, and being prone to acute anxiety in unfamiliar surroundings are examples of characteristics that define the nature of the individual. Any such characteristics identified by the assessment data obtained from people will be present in these individuals regardless of where they live, from whence they come, and in what they are involved.

The utilization phase of the assessment process provides the second step, which consists of being sufficiently sensitive to respondents' cultural and experiential contexts to estimate accurately the implications of their psychological characteristics in their particular life circumstances. Especially important to consider in this regard are whether the psychological characteristics people show are likely to prove adaptive or maladaptive in their everyday world and what kinds of successful or unsuccessful adaptations might result from these characteristics.

Research findings document that cultural differences can lead to cross-cultural variation in modal psychological characteristics and that the demands and expectations people face often determine the implications and consequences of certain characteristics, especially with respect to how adaptive these characteristics are. (See Kitayama & Cohen, 2007; Stevens & Gielen, 2007.) For example, a generally passive, dependent, agreeable, and acquiescent person may experience adjustment difficulties in a cultural context that values autonomy, self-reliance, assertiveness, and competitiveness. Conversely, a fiercely independent and highly competitive person might feel comfortable and flourish psychologically in a subculture that values individuality and assertiveness but feel alienated and adapt poorly in a society that subordinates individual needs and preferences to the wishes and welfare of the group and in which a passive and acquiescent person could get along very well.

These contextual influences on the implications of psychological characteristics extend to specific circumstances in persons' lives as well as their broader sociocultural contexts. A modest level of intelligence can be a source of comfort and success to young people whose personal and family expectations are that they graduate from high school but a source of failure and dismay to those for whom graduation from a prestigious college is a minimum expectation. Similarly, a person with good coping skills and abundant adaptive capacities who is carrying a heavy burden of responsibilities and confronting numerous obstacles to meeting them may be susceptible to anxiety, irritability, and other consequences of a stress overload, whereas a person with limited coping skills and few adaptive capacities who is leading a narrowly restricted life and facing very few demands may be able to maintain a comfortable psychological equilibrium and experience little in the way of subjectively felt distress. A contemplative person who values being painstakingly careful in completing tasks and reaching conclusions may perform well in a job situation that calls for accuracy and thoroughness and involves little time pressure; this same person may perform poorly in a position that imposes strict deadlines or requires rapid decisions on the basis of sketchy information and in which a more decisive and action-oriented person would function effectively.

As illustrated by this final example and those that have preceded it in this chapter, psychological assessment is a complex process. Diverse perspectives and attention to interacting variables are necessary in assessment psychology as elsewhere in behavioral science to expand knowledge and guide its practical application, and there is little to be gained from doctrinaire pronouncements or unidimensional approaches. Collecting, interpreting, and using assessment data effectively call for giving just due to each of the issues identified in this introduction to the assessment process, and the 24 chapters that follow are designed for this purpose.

## REFERENCES

Ægisdóttir, S., White, M. J., Spengler, P. M., Maugherman, A. S., Anderson, L. A., Cook, R. S., . . . Rush, J. D. (2006). The meta-analysis of clinical judgment project: Fifty-six years of accumulated research on clinical versus statistical judgment. *Counseling Psychologist, 34*, 341–382.

Allard, G., & Faust, D. (2000). Errors in scoring objective personality tests. *Assessment, 7*, 119–129.

Allen, J., & Walsh, J. A. (2000). A construct-based approach to equivalence: Methodologies for cross-cultural/multicultural personality assessment research. In R. H. Dana (Ed.), *Handbook of cross-cultural and multicultural personality assessment* (pp. 63–86). Mahwah, NJ: Erlbaum.

Allport, G. W. (1937). *Personality: A psychological interpretation*. New York, NY: Holt.

American Educational Research Association, American Psychological Association, and National Council on Measurement in Education. (1999). *Standards for educational and psychological testing*. Washington, DC: American Educational Research Association.

American Psychological Association. (2002). Ethical principles of psychologists and code of conduct. *American Psychologist*, *57*, 1060–1073.

Beck, A. T., Steer, R. A., & Brown, T. K. (1996). *Beck depression inventory manual* (2nd ed.). San Antonio, TX: Psychological Corporation.

Berry, D. T. R., & Schipper, L. J. (2008). Assessment of feigned cognitive impairment using standard neuropsychological tests. In R. Rogers (Ed.), *Clinical assessment of malingering and deception* (3rd ed., pp. 232–252). New York, NY: Guilford Press.

Berry, D. T. R., Sollman, S. J., Schipper, L. J., Clark, J. A., & Shandera, A. L. (2009). Assessment of feigned psychological symptoms. In J. N. Butcher (Ed.), *Oxford handbook of personality assessment* (pp. 613–642). New York, NY: Oxford University Press.

Bornstein, R. F., Rossner, S. C., Hill, E. L., & Stepanian, M. L. (1994). Face validity and fakability of objective and projective measures of dependency. *Journal of Personality Assessment*, *63*, 363–386.

Butcher, J. N., & Perry, J. N. (2008). *Personality assessment in treatment planning: Use of the MMPI-2 and BTPI*. New York, NY: Oxford University Press.

Butcher, J. N., Perry, J. N. & Dean, B. E. (2009). Computer-based assessment. In J. N. Butcher (Ed.), *Oxford handbook of personality assessment* (pp. 163–182). New York, NY: Oxford University Press.

Butcher, J. N., Perry, J. N., & Hahn, J. (2004). Computers in clinical assessment: Historical developments, present status, and future challenges. *Journal of Clinical Psychology*, *60*, 331–345.

Butcher, J. N., & Rouse, S. V. (1996). Personality: Individual differences and clinical assessment. *Annual Review of Psychology*, *47*, 87–111.

Campbell, D. T., & Fiske, D. W. (1959). Convergent and discriminant validation by the multitrait-multimethod matrix. *Psychological Bulletin*, *56*, 81–105.

Clarkin, J. F., & Levy, K. N. (2004). The influence of client variables on psychotherapy. In M. J. Lambert (Ed.), *Bergin and Garfield's handbook of psychotherapy and behavior change* (5th ed., pp. 194–226). Hoboken, NJ: Wiley.

Cattell, R. B. (1946). *Description and measurement of personality*. New York, NY: World Book.

Dana, R. H. (2005). *Multicultural assessment: Principle, applications, and examples*. Mahwah, NJ: Erlbaum.

Dana, R. H. (Ed.). (2000). *Handbook of cross-cultural and multicultural personality assessment*. Mahwah, NJ: Erlbaum.

Duckworth, A. L., Steen, T. A., & Seligman, M. E. P. (2005). Positive psychology in clinical practice. *Annual Review of Clinical Psychology*, *1*, 629–651.

Exner, J. E., Jr. (2003). *The Rorschach: A comprehensive system. Vol.1. Foundations* (4th ed.). Hoboken, NJ: Wiley.

Finger, M. S., & Ones, D. S. (1999). Psychometric equivalence of the computer and booklet forms of the MMPI: A meta-analysis. *Psychological Assessment*, *11*, 58–66.

Finn, S. E. (1996). Assessment feedback integrating MMPI-2 and Rorschach findings. *Journal of Personality Assessment*, *67*, 543–557.

Ganellen, R. J. (1996). *Integrating the Rorschach and the MMPI in personality assessment*. Mahwah, NJ: Erlbaum.

Ganellen, R. J. (2008). Rorschach assessment of malingering and defense response sets. In C. B. Gacono & F. B. Evans (Eds.), *Handbook of forensic Rorschach assessment* (pp. 89–120). New York, NY: Routledge.

Garb, H. N. (1998). *Studying the clinician*. Washington, DC: American Psychological Association.

Garb, H. N. (2000). Computers will become increasingly important for psychological assessment: Not that there's anything wrong with that! *Psychological Assessment*, *12*, 31–39.

Garb, H. N. (2005). Clinical judgment and decision making. *Annual Review of Clinical Psychology*, *1*, 67–89.

Garb, H. N. (2007). Computer-administered interviews and rating scales. *Psychological Assessment*, *19*, 4–12.

Geisinger, K. F., & Carlson, J. F. (2009). Standards and standardization. In J. N. Butcher (Ed.), *Oxford handbook of personality assessment* (pp. 99–111). New York, NY: Oxford University Press.

Geisinger, K. F., Spies, R. A., Carlson, J. F., & Plake, B. S. (Eds.) (2007). *The seventeenth Mental Measurements Yearbook*. Lincoln: University of Nebraska Press.

Gorny, I., & Merten, T. (2007). Symptom information—warning—coaching: How do they affect successful feigning in neuropsychological assessment? *Journal of Forensic Neuropsychology*, *4*, 71–97.

Graham, J. R. (2006). *MMPI-2: Assessing personality and psychopathology* (4th ed.). New York, NY: Oxford University Press.

Greene, R. L. (2008). Malingering and defensiveness on the MMPI. In R. Rogers (Ed.), *Clinical assessment of malingering and deception* (3rd ed., pp. 159–181). New York, NY: Guilford Press.

Greene, R. L. (2011). *The MMPI-2/MMPI-2-RF: An interpretive manual* (3rd ed.). Boston: Allyn & Bacon.

Groth-Marnat, G. (2010). *Handbook of psychological assessment* (5th ed.). Hoboken, NJ: Wiley.

Grove, W. M., & Meehl, P. E. (1996). Comparative efficiency of informal (subjective, impressionistic) and formal (mechanical, algorithmic) prediction procedures: The clinical-statistical controversy. *Psychology, Public Policy, and Law*, *2*, 293–323.

Grove, W. M., Zald, D. H., Lebow, B. S., Snitz, B. E., & Nelson, C. (2000). Clinical versus mechanical prediction: A meta-analysis. *Psychological Assessment*, *12*, 19–30.

Hallowell, A. I. (1951). The use of projective techniques in the study of the socio-psychological aspects of acculturation. *Journal of Projective Techniques*, *15*, 27–44.

Hambleton, R. K., Merenda, P., & Spielberger, C. D. (Eds.). (2005). *Adapting educational and psychological tests for cross-cultural assessment*. Mahwah, NJ: Erlbaum.

Heilbrun, K. (2001). *Principles of forensic mental health assessment*. New York, NY: Kluwer Academic/Plenum.

Heilbrun, K., Grisso, T., & Goldstein, A. M. (2009). *Foundations of forensic mental health assessment*. New York, NY: Oxford University Press.

Hogan, T. P. (2005). 50 widely used psychological tests. In G. P. Koocher, J. C. Norcross, & S. S. Hill III. *Psychologists' desk reference* (2nd ed., pp. 101–104). New York, NY: Oxford University Press.

Hunsley, J., & Mash, E. J. (2010). The role of assessment in evidence-based practice. In M. M. Antony & D. H. Barlow (Eds.), *Handbook of assessment and treatment planning for psychological disorders* (2nd ed., pp. 3–22) New York, NY: Guilford Press.

Kamphuis, J. H., & Finn, S. E. (2002). Incorporating base rate information in daily clinical decision making. In J. N. Butcher (Ed.), *Clinical personality assessment* (2nd ed., pp. 257–268). New York, NY: Oxford University Press.

Kitayama, S., & Cohen, D. (Eds.). (2007). *Handbook of cultural psychology*. New York, NY: Guilford Press.

Kitchener, K. S. (2000). *Foundations of ethical practice, research, and teaching in psychology*. Mahwah, NJ: Erlbaum.

Koocher, G. P., & Keith-Spiegel, P. (2008). *Ethics in psychology and the mental health professions: Standards and cases* (3rd ed.). New York, NY: Oxford University Press.

Krishnamurthy, R., & Yalof, J. A. (2010). The assessment competency. In M. B. Kenkel & R. L. Peterson (Eds.), *Competency-based education for professional psychology* (pp. 87–104). Washington, DC: American Psychological Association.

Kubiszyn, T. W., Meyer, G. J., Finn, S. E., Eyde, L. D., Kay, G. G., Moreland, K. L.,. . . Eisman, E. J. (2000). Empirical support for psychological assessment in clinical health care settings. *Professional Psychology*, *31*, 119–130.

Lees-Haley, P. R. (1997). Attorneys influence expert evidence in forensic psychological and neuropsychological cases. *Assessment*, *4*, 321–324.

Lindzey, G. (1961). *Projective techniques and cross-cultural research*. New York, NY: Appleton-Century-Crofts.

Linley, P. A., Harrington, S., & Garcea, N. (Eds.) (2010). *Oxford handbook of positive psychology*. New York, NY: Oxford University Press.

Masling, J. M. (1966). Role-related behavior of the subject and psychologist and its effect upon psychological data. In D. Levine (Ed.), *Nebraska symposium on motivation* (pp. 67–104). Lincoln: University of Nebraska Press.

Masling, J. M. (1998). Interpersonal and actuarial dimensions of projective testing. In J. Handler & M. J. Hilsenroth (Eds.), *Teaching and learning personality assessment* (pp. 119–135). Mahwah, NJ: Erlbaum.

Matarazzo, J. D. (1990). Psychological assessment versus psychological testing. *American Psychologist*, *45*, 999–1017.

McFall, R. M., & Townsend, J. T. (1998). Foundations of psychological assessment: Implications for cognitive assessment in clinical science. *Psychological Assessment*, *10*, 316–330.

McFall, R. M., & Treat, T. A. (1999). Quantifying the information value of clinical assessments with signal detection theory. *Annual Review of Psychology*, *50*, 215–241.

McMinn, M. F., Ellens, B. M., & Soref, E. (1999). Ethical perspectives and practice behaviors involving computer-based test interpretations. *Assessment*, *6*, 71–77.

Meehl, P. E. (1954). *Clinical versus statistical prediction*. Minneapolis: University of Minnesota Press.

Meehl, P. E. (1957). When shall we use our heads instead of the formula. *Journal of Counseling Psychology*, *4*, 268–273.

Meehl, P. E., & Rosen, A. (1955). Antecedent probability and the efficiency of psychometric signs, patterns, or cutting scores. *Psychological Bulletin*, *52*, 194–216.

Meyer, G. J., Finn, S. E., Eyde, L. D., Kay, G. G., Moreland, K. L., Dies, R. R., et al. (2001). Psychological testing and psychological assessment: A review of evidence and issues. *American Psychologist*, *56*, 128–165.

Millon, T. (2006). *Millon Clinical Multiaxial Inventory—III (MCMI–III) manual* (3rd ed.). Minneapolis, MN: Pearson Assessments.

Monahan, J. (Ed.). (1980). *Who is the client?* Washington, DC: American Psychological Association.

Morey, L. C. (2007). *Personality Assessment Inventory professional manual* (2nd ed.). Lutz, FL: Psychological Assessment Resources.

Rogers, R. (2008a). Detection strategies for malingering and defensiveness. In R. Rogers (Ed.), *Clinical assessment of malingering and deception* (3rd ed., pp. 14–35). New York, NY: Guilford Press.

Rogers, R. (2008b). Structured interviews and dissimulation. In R. Rogers (Ed.), *Clinical assessment of malingering and deception* (3rd ed., pp. 301–322). New York, NY: Guilford Press.

Rogers, R., Gillis, J. R., Dickens, S. E., & Bagby, R. M. (1991). Standardized assessment of malingering: Validation of the Structure Inventory of Reported Symptoms. *Psychological Assessment*, *3*, 89–96.

Rogers, R., Jackson, R. L., Sewell, K. W., & Salekin, K. L. (2005). Detection strategies for malingering: A confirmatory factor analysis of the SIRS. *Criminal Justice and Behavior*, *32*, 511–525.

Seligman, M. E. P., & Csikszentmihalyi, M. (2000). Positive psychology: An introduction. *American Psychologist*, *55*, 5–14.

Sewell, K. W. (2008). Dissimulation on projective measures. In R. Rogers (Ed.), *Clinical assessment of malingering and deception* (3rd ed., pp. 207–217). New York, NY: Guilford Press.

Smith, G. P. (2008). Brief screening measures for the detection of feigned psychopathology. In R. Rogers (Ed.), *Clinical assessment of malingering and deception* (3rd ed., pp. 323–339). New York, NY: Guilford Press.

Stevens, M. J., & Gielen, U. P. (Eds.) (2007). *Toward a global psychology: Theory, research, intervention, and pedagogy*. Mahwah, NJ: Erlbaum.

Storm, J., & Graham, J. R. (2000). Detection of coached malingering on the MMPI-2. *Psychological Assessment*, *12*, 158–165.

Stricker, G. (1997). Are science and practice commensurable? *American Psychologist*, *52*, 442–448.

Stricker, G. (2007). The local clinical scientist. In S. G. Hofmann & J. Weinberger (Eds.), *The art and science of psychotherapy* (pp. 85–99). New York, NY: Routledge.

Stricker, G., & Trierweiler, S. J. (2006). The local clinical scientist: A bridge between science and practice. *Training and Education in Professional Psychology*, *S*, 37–46.

Suzuki, L. A., & Ponterotto, J. G. (Eds.) (2008). *Handbook of multicultural assessment*. San Francisco, CA: Jossey-Bass.

Teichner, G., & Wagner, M. T. (2004). The Test of Memory Malingering (TOMM): Normative data from cognitively intact, cognitively impaired, and elderly patients with dementia. *Archives of Clinical Neuropsychology*, *19*, 455–465.

Tombaugh, T. N. (1997). The Test of Memory Malingering (TOMM): Normative data from cognitively intact and cognitively impaired individuals. *Psychological Assessment*, *9*, 260–268.

Turner, S. W., DeMers, S. T., Fox, H. R., & Reed, G. M. (2008). APA's guidelines for test user qualifications: An executive summary. In D. N. Bersoff (Ed.), *Ethical conflicts in psychology* (4th ed, pp. 279–282). Washington, DC: American Psychological Association.

Victor, T. L., & Abeles, N. (2004). Coaching clients to take psychological and neuropsychological tests: A clash of clinical obligations. *Professional Psychology: Research and Practice*, *35*, 373–379.

Wechsler, D. (2008). *Wechsler Adult Intelligence Scale* (4th ed.). Minneapolis, MN: Pearson.

Weiner, I. B. (1989). On competence and ethicality in psychodiagnostic assessment. *Journal of Personality Assessment*, *53*, 827–831.

Weiner, I. B. (2003). *Principles of Rorschach interpretation* (2nd ed.). Mahwah, NJ: Erlbaum.

Weiner, I. B. (2004). Rorschach Inkblot Method. In M. E. Maruish (Ed.), *The use of psychological testing for treatment planning and outcome evaluation* (Vol. 3, pp. 553–588). Mahwah, NJ: Erlbaum.

Weiner, I. B. (2005). Integrative personality assessment with self-report and performance-based measures. In S. Strack (Ed.), *Handbook of personology and psychopathology* (pp. 317–331). Hoboken, NJ: Wiley.

Weiner, I. B. (2009). Anticipating ethical and legal challenges in personality assessments. In J. N. Butcher (Ed.), *Oxford handbook of personality assessment* (pp. 599–612). New York, NY: Oxford University Press.

Westen, D., & Weinberger, J. (2004). When clinical description becomes statistical prediction. *American Psychologist*, *59*, 595–613.

Westen, D., & Weinberger, J. (2005). In praise of clinical judgment: Meehl's forgotten legacy. *Journal of Clinical Psychology*, *61*, 1257–1276.

Wetter, M. W., & Corrigan, S. K. (1995). Providing information to clients about psychological tests: A survey of attorneys' and law students' attitudes. *Professional Psychology*, *26*, 474–477.

Youngjohn, J. R. (1995). Confirmed attorney coaching prior to neuropsychological evaluation. *Assessment*, *2*, 279–284.

Zeldow, P. B. (2009). In defense of clinical judgment, credentialed clinicians, and reflective practice. *Psychotherapy: Theory, Research, Practice, Training*, *46*, 1–10.

# CHAPTER 2

# Clinical Versus Mechanical Prediction

PAUL M. SPENGLER

The debate over clinical versus mechanical prediction dates back to Meehl's (1954) seminal book, *Clinical vs. Statistical Prediction: A Theoretical Analysis and a Review of the Evidence*. Meehl (1986) later referred to this as his "disturbing little book" because of the extensive misunderstanding about his reflection on the benefits of both statistical prediction *and* clinical prediction. Meehl (1954, 1986, 1996) never argued against there being a place and utility for clinical prediction; instead, he discussed applications where clinical prediction cannot be functionally replaced by mechanical methods. What he did argue is that mechanical methods of prediction, when available, are likely to improve prediction accuracy and should be used by the practitioner. Meehl (1996) did make some claims that later were found to be partially inaccurate; these claims generally concerned his espousing the *robust* superiority of statistical prediction methods.

Nearly 50 years later, this "debate" has been resolved by two independently conducted meta-analyses. Both Grove, Zald, Lebow, Snitz, and Nelson (2000) and Ægisdóttir et al. (2006) found the same overall *d* effect size of .12 in favor of mechanical prediction over clinical prediction. Grove et al. (2000) reflected superiority of mechanical prediction by a positive effect, whereas Ægisdóttir et al. (2006) reported negative effect sizes in favor of mechanical prediction. To simplify discussion in this chapter, when referring to Ægisdóttir et al., the direction of the effect is reversed such that a positive effect also reflects the superiority of mechanical prediction. The effect found is considered to be a "real" effect in the sense that it is greater than zero, the 95% confidence interval is above zero, and the variance is homogeneous when outlier effects are removed (Ægisdóttir et al., 2006). Contrary to the

general conclusion by scholars of the robust superiority of mechanical prediction (Dawes, 1994; Dawes, Faust, & Meehl, 1989, 1993, 2002; Garb, 1994; Goldberg, Faust, Kleinmuntz, & Dawes, 1991; Grove & Meehl, 1996; Grove et al., 2000; Kleinmuntz, 1990; Marchese, 1992; Meehl, 1986; J. S. Wiggins, 1981), this is a small effect by any standard. According to Cohen's (1988) convention for the behavioral sciences, a *d* of .20 is considered a small effect, a *d* of .50 is considered a medium effect, and a *d* of .80 is considered a large effect. Nonetheless, these two independent meta-analyses provide a foundation of scientific support for the relative superiority of mechanical prediction, with several caveats explored in this chapter.

The development of and debate over clinical versus mechanical prediction techniques has followed several paths. To date there have been over 150 published and unpublished studies comparing clinical versus mechanical prediction for mental health judgments. Innumerable studies looking solely at clinical prediction and solely at statistical prediction exist (e.g., see Garb, 1998). The purpose of this chapter is to review these findings, provide an update on central issues since Garb's (2003) chapter in the previous *Handbook of Psychology,* and suggest directions for future research, graduate training, and the practice of psychological assessment with regard to the relative utility of clinical versus mechanical prediction.

## CLINICAL VERSUS MECHANICAL PREDICTION

There are basically two "bridges"—clinical and mechanical—that can be used to integrate client-related input data to predict personality traits, diagnoses, behavior, and other criteria. J. S. Wiggins's (1980) description of a basic research design for comparisons of clinical and statistical prediction is useful for also providing practitioners with a fundamental understanding about how client data can be combined. On the input side, there are a multitude of sources of data that might be used in either prediction method, including demographics, behavioral observations, clinical interview, psychological inventories and test scores, and population base rates based on group membership (e.g., gender, age, and race). In the field of psychology, relevant output criteria might include diagnostic or descriptive, causal or etiological, evaluative, and predictive statements. There are three possible outcomes in any clinical versus statistical prediction comparison: one where statistical prediction is superior, one where clinical prediction is superior, and one where the two techniques are equivalent in either their concurrent or predictive validity.

Before proceeding further it might be helpful to define clinical and mechanical approaches to prediction. Statistical approaches have been more broadly referred to as mechanical prediction to inclusively embody both traditional statistical methods, such as regression equations, and include mechanical or automated methods for prediction, such as clinician-generated algorithms for test interpretations (e.g., Minnesota Clinical Report; Butcher, 2005) and models of the clinical judge's decision-making process (e.g., Goldberg, 1965). Grove et al. (2000) defined mechanical prediction as "including statistical prediction (using explicit equations), actuarial prediction (as with insurance companies' actuarial tables), and what we may call algorithmic prediction (e.g., a computer program emulating expert judges)" (p. 19). Some studies have examined models of clinical judgment (mechanization of clinicians' judgment processes), which are also considered mechanical forms of prediction (Ægisdóttir et al., 2006). The utility of mechanical approaches optimally rests on the foundation of empirical relations (when statistically determined), and all forms of mechanical prediction (including models of the clinical judge) have the distinct advantage over unassisted clinical methods because the conclusions reached are 100% reliable or "reproducible" (Garb, 2003, p. 29). That is, the formula never tires, does not have a bad day, and does not vary in other ways characteristic of humans.

Clinical prediction techniques have been referred to in various manners but generally converge on some reference to the clinician using "intuition" to combine the input data. The data still might include empirically driven input, such as test scores, research findings, and the like, but the key point is that the clinician uses his or her cognitive powers to integrate these various data to form a prediction or judgment about present or future behavior, personality traits, and other psychological phenomena. Clinical judgments and judgmental processes are not 100% reliable, a fact that, by the very nature of the relation between reliability and validity, is thought to lower their potential validity (see Schmidt & Hunter, 1996). Whereas mechanical methods are 100% reproducible, clinical judgment is thought to be both negatively and positively affected by an array of judgment heuristics and biases and other impediments to human decision making (e.g., see Bell & Mellor, 2009; Cline, 1985; Dana & Thomas, 2006; Dawes, 1994; Dumont, 1993; Faust, 1986, 1994; Gambrill, 2005; Garb, 1989, 1992, 1997, 1998, 2005; Lopez, 1989; Rabinowitz, 1993; Ruscio, 2007; Schalock & Luckasson, 2005; Turk & Salovey, 1985; Wedding & Faust, 1989; Widiger & Spitzer, 1991).

## Narrative Research Summary

Paul Meehl's (1954) book marks a distinctive point in the history of the debate on clinical versus mechanical prediction and marks a distinctive moment in the history of the study of human judgment (W. M. Goldstein & Hogarth, 1997). Meehl's (1954) frequently cited treatise and review was the first synthesis of extant research. Prior to and since that time there have been clear camps in favor of clinical prediction and those in favor of statistical prediction. The issues that have been debated range from the unique benefits of clinical judgment (e.g., Holt, 1958, 1970; Zeldow, 2009) to ethical concerns if clinicians do not use a formula (e.g., Dawes, 2002, Grove et al., 2000; Meehl, 1997). Not much has changed in the perspectives of many scholars since Meehl's book (1954) except, one could argue, that there are now more sophisticated methods of prediction (e.g., discriminant function analyses, Bayesian strategies, computer automated programs). One aspect of this debate that apparently has not changed much is the difficulty encountered in encouraging graduate students and professionals to use mechanical methods of prediction (Vrieze & Grove, 2009). Greater clarity should also be put forth by proponents of mechanical prediction for when clinical judgment is optimal, as opposed to admonishments to use mechanical methods of prediction (e.g., Grove & Meehl, 1996).

In Meehl's (1954) original narrative review of 16 to 20 studies, he reported only one instance where clinical judgment was superior (Hovey & Stauffacher, 1953). He qualified this finding by stating that "this study must be interpreted with extreme caution... it indicates at most the superiority of a skilled MMPI [Minnesota Multiphasic Personality Inventory] reader to an undoubtedly nonoptimal linear function" (p. 112). He humorously added, "Out of the kindness of my heart, and to prevent the scoreboard from absolute asymmetry, I shall score this study for the clinician" (p. 112). Grove and Meehl (1996) later noted that due to inflated chi-squares, Hovey and Stauffacher should have been scored as equal. Approximately half of the comparisons Meehl considered to be "ties" or close to ties (Blenkner, 1954; Bobbitt & Newman, 1944; Dunlap & Wantman, 1944; Hamlin, 1934; Schiedt, 1936; Schneider, Lagrone, Glueck, & Glueck, 1944). In the remaining studies, Meehl interpreted statistical prediction to be superior (Barron, 1953; Bloom & Brundage, 1947; Borden, 1928; Burgess, 1928; Conrad & Satter, 1954; Dunham & Meltzer, 1946; Kelly & Fiske, 1950; Sarbin, 1942; Wittman, 1941; Wittman & Steinberg, 1944). The types of predictions made in these studies had to do with success in academic or military training, recidivism, parole violation, prognosis, and psychosis remission. It is interesting to note that in reviewing some of these studies, Meehl took great pains to decipher their results (e.g., Kelly & Fiske, 1950). At times he expressed difficulty deciphering the findings due to unfair comparisons usually in favor of the clinician, methodological confounds, and the sheer absence of reported statistical analyses (e.g., Schiedt, 1936; Schneider et al., 1944). Meehl (1954) stated: "In spite of the defects and ambiguities present, let me emphasize the brute fact that we have here, depending upon one's standard for admission as relevant, from 16 to 20 studies involving a comparison of clinical and actuarial methods" (p. 119). Despite others' clear categorization of the studies reviewed by Meehl (e.g, see J. S. Wiggins's "box score," 1980, p. 184), it is difficult to determine how Meehl classified every study in his narrative review.

In subsequent reviews, either using narrative or box score methods (i.e., a table with a count of study characteristics), the same conclusions were reached about the relative superiority of mechanical prediction techniques (Meehl, 1957, 1965; Sawyer, 1966; J. S. Wiggins, 1980, 1981). For example, Meehl (1965) reviewed 51 studies and found only one instance where clinical prediction was superior; 17 were ties; and 33 studies supported the superiority of mechanical methods of prediction. Generally speaking, other reviewers reached the same conclusion (Dawes et al., 1989; Garb, 1994; Grove & Meehl, 1996; Kleinmuntz, 1990; Russell, 1995; Sawyer, 1966; J. S.

Wiggins, 1980, 1981). These reviews almost always supported Meehl's report of the relative superiority or, at minimum, equivalence of mechanical prediction (for a rare exception, see Russell, 1995).

Over the years, debate has at times been contentious. The positions of reviewers often come through more clearly than the data. Returning to Meehl's (1954) book, what is often misunderstood is he did not dismiss the utility of either method of prediction (Dana & Thomas, 2006). To the contrary, he concluded: "There is no convincing reason to assume that explicitly formalized mathematical rules and the clinician's creativity are equally suited for any given task, or that their comparative effectiveness is the same for different tasks" (Meehl, 1996, p. vi). While several shifts in psychology have occurred toward a greater emphasis on scientifically based practice (e.g., evidence-based treatments, Norcross, Beutler, & Levant, 2006; outcome measurement, Shimokawa, Lambert, & Smart, 2010), there continues to be a lack of emphasis in training programs on decision making (Harding, 2007), judgment research (Spengler & Strohmer, 2001), and the use of mechanical prediction techniques (Vrieze & Grove, 2009). Several efforts have been made to influence this resistance, or perhaps this misunderstanding, perceived by some proponents of mechanical prediction (e.g., Grove & Meehl, 1996) to be maintained by practitioners and possibly by some academics. A recent survey suggests that the strongest predictor of clinicians' use of mechanical prediction techniques is whether they were *discussed* (not necessarily taught) in graduate school (Vrieze & Grove, 2009). The underlying arguments in favor of mechanical prediction have been its general superiority to clinical methods of prediction, its 100% reliability, and its foundation in empiricism, which is thought to counter the inherently biased nature of clinicians' judgments.

Recently two independent research laboratories (Ægisdóttir et al., 2006; Grove, Zald, Lebow, Snitz, & Nelson, 2000) invested countless hours to provide the first meta-analyses on clinical versus mechanical prediction. Both sets of researchers arrived at the same exact conclusion: There is a *slight* edge in favor of mechanical prediction over clinical prediction. These two comprehensive empirical reviews warrant discussion as they serve as a foundation for future research and thinking about clinical versus mechanical prediction in psychological assessment. When Garb (2003) wrote the first chapter on clinical versus mechanical prediction for the *Handbook of Psychology,* only the Grove et al. (2000) meta-analysis had been published. Garb referred to this as "the most comprehensive and sophisticated review of studies on clinical versus mechanical prediction" (p. 28). Independently conducted research by Ægisdóttir et al. (2006) replicated, strengthened, and extended Grove et al.'s findings.

## Meta-Analyses on Clinical Versus Mechanical Prediction

Meta-analysis involves collecting effect sizes from various studies, usually one per study, and analyzing these analyses; thus the term *meta-analysis*. Meta-analyses can be contrasted with narrative reviews of mechanical versus clinical prediction that have historically dominated the literature to this point (Hunt, 1997). As noted, there are also a few examples of box score reviews (e.g., J. S. Wiggins, 1980) in which existing studies are placed in a table with characteristics of the studies summarized and the statistical significance of the findings tabulated. The inherent problem with narrative or box score reviews is neither approach helps research consumers to see the forest for the trees. Hunt (1997) concluded that narrative reviews are "the classic and inadequate—solution" (p. 6) for the scientific scrutiny of a body of literature because of the inevitable subjectivity of reviewer's impressions. That is, given the cognitive challenges and complexities inherent in making sense of vast amounts of research, it is likely that reviewers and researchers alike will have a difficult time making sense of the data and not imposing their own biases on the findings.

While meta-analysis is not a panacea and has its unique methodological challenges and limitations (for discussion, see Cooper & Hedges, 1994), the two independently conducted analyses (Ægisdóttir et al., 2006; Grove et al., 2000) for the first time provided a view of the research forest rather than of the trees. Instead of attempting to make sense of findings based on a study-by-study review, the meta-analyses provided an empirical method for obtaining a more reliable and valid population estimate of the relative utility of clinical versus mechanical prediction. The "debate" over clinical versus mechanical prediction is partially resolved by these reviews which clarify population estimates from extant research. Garb (2003) called the Grove et al. (2000) meta-analysis a "landmark study" (p. 29). With the addition of a second independently conducted meta-analysis (Ægisdóttir et al. 2006), the possibility exists for research on clinical versus mechanical prediction to evolve past the most basic question about relative superiority that has dominated research. The mechanical versus clinical prediction debate remains in its infancy and has not paid the dividends expected. The results of these meta-analyses may spur researchers to investigate additional questions and invest in more sophisticated programmatic research.

Before reporting on the findings of the meta-analyses, it may be helpful to briefly compare and contrast research developments in another area of psychology—psychotherapy efficacy and effectiveness—and the role meta-analysis has played in shaping the debate about the benefits of psychotherapy. Ironically, around the same time that Meehl (1954) wrote his book, Eysenck (1952) wrote a similarly controversial review on psychotherapy outcomes. Eysenck concluded that psychotherapy is not effective and may even be harmful, causing an increase in symptoms for some patients (for further discussion, see Lambert & Ogles, 2004). What is relevant to the current discussion is that Eysenck's publication stimulated a flurry of psychotherapy outcome research and, ultimately, inspired the first ever meta-analysis in the social sciences. Most notably, Smith and Glass (1977) conducted a meta-analysis on the efficacy of psychotherapy. They found an overall effect of .68, indicating that psychotherapy patients on average were better off than 75% of patients in waitlist or control groups (for more extensive discussion, see Smith, Glass & Miller, 1980).

Smith and Glass's (1977) meta-analysis led to a number of subsequent psychotherapy meta-analyses, including reanalyses and critique of their findings. More psychotherapy research ensued, and a number of psychotherapy meta-analyses were conducted over the years on new developments and questions (e.g., common treatment factors, Norcross, 2002, 2011; empirically validated treatments, Nathan & Gorman, 2002; and dose-effect curves, Lambert, Hansen & Finch, 2001; Shimokawa et al., 2010). Reflecting on the status of psychotherapy research, Kazdin (2008) commented, "[T]housands of well-controlled outcome studies (randomized controlled trials or RCTs) have been completed, reviewed, and meta-analyzed. Indeed, reviews of the reviews are needed just to keep track of the advances" (p. 146). The study of psychotherapy has flourished, with new and productive questions being researched that go far beyond the initial question of whether psychotherapy works or not. Methodological pluralism has since characterized psychotherapy research resulting in intense study of in-session change processes (e.g., Elliott, 2010) and investigations of the effectiveness of psychotherapy in naturalistic settings (e.g., Seligman, 1995). For the first time in the history of psychology practitioners are reporting that they benefit from psychotherapy research findings and are using them to some degree in their practice.

The impact of meta-analyses with research on clinical versus mechanical prediction has been quite different. The development of research on clinical versus mechanical prediction has been weighed down by the most basic question: Which technique is superior? The meta-analyses to be discussed provide the initial answer to this question—with limitations based on the quality of existing research that was input into these analyses. A modest difference was found in favor of mechanical prediction techniques. It is hoped that researchers will turn their focus to developing better mechanical prediction models (e.g., prediction of violence; Hilton, Harris, & Rice, 2006), better clinical judgment models (e.g., mental health case simulations; Falvey, Bray, & Hebert, 2005), and better ways to train graduate students and clinicians in decision making (e.g., scientist-practitioner model for assessment; Spengler, Strohmer, Dixon, & Shivy, 1995).

## Grove, Zald, Lebow, Snitz, and Nelson (2000)

Grove et al. (2000) conducted the first-ever meta-analysis in any area of clinical judgment research except for an earlier and smaller meta-analysis on diagnostic overshadowing (White, Nichols, Cook, Spengler, Walker, & Look, 1995). What distinguishes Grove et al. (2000) is they were broad and inclusive in their study selection; they included clinical versus mechanical prediction studies from the areas of mental health, academia, medicine, finance/business, corrections/legal, advertising/marketing, and personnel selection/training. This is the case despite their claim that they included "[o]nly studies within the realm of psychology and medicine" (p. 20), and common reference by others to the same (e.g., Garb, 2003; Grove & Meehl, 1996). Grove et al. (2000) did not provide a focused review on psychological assessment but their contribution was significant for the broad debate on the relative utility of clinical judgment versus mechanical prediction in various and unrelated fields.

Despite their broad coverage, the overall effect size reported by Grove et al. (2000) was $d = .12$, which is the exact same effect reported by Ægisdóttir et al. (2006)—who analyzed just studies that focused on predictions of psychological constructs made by mental health professionals (e.g., psychologists, social workers, counselors, graduate students) and a mechanical method of prediction. Again, this $d$ is a small effect and might even be considered inconsequential in other areas of psychology (e.g., psychotherapy research; Norcross, 2011). If we place these findings into a binomial effect size display (Rosenthal & Rubin, 1982), there is a slight advantage

of 13% in favor of mechanical prediction over clinical judgment (Ægisdóttir et al. 2006). This means that in 100 comparisons of mechanical and clinical prediction, mechanical would be more accurate 53% of the time and clinical would be more accurate 47% of the time. To further place this effect into perspective, for an effect size of $d = .10$, it would take roughly 20 comparisons to identify 1 instance where mechanical prediction is superior to clinical judgment (see "number needed to treat," Norcross & Wampold, 2011, p. 130). This is not to say that the effect size favoring mechanical prediction is inconsequential. By way of comparison, the number needed to treat is 129 for aspirin as a preventive measure for heart attacks, an acceptable medical practice that was found to be so significant that a clinical trial was stopped to offer this treatment to controls (see Rosenthal, 1991).

Grove et al. (2000) found few moderators of this overall effect. Whereas Ægisdóttir et al. (2006) found no variance in the most rigorous comparison of studies, Grove et al. (2000) did perhaps because they included studies from so many different domains. There was a trend ($p = .07$) showing differences between these various domains, with the largest effects found in medical ($d = .82$) and forensic settings ($d = .89$). Issues of statistical power likely obscured detecting differences between these domains, given the apparently much larger effects in medical and forensic settings. The mechanical method was found to be superior to clinical judgment when interview data and medical data served as the predictors. There were no other significant moderators. Training and experience did not improve clinical judgment accuracy compared with mechanical techniques. Likewise, there was no advantage when human judges had access to more data than a formula or when a statistical formula was cross-validated or not. (Shrinkage often occurs with cross-validation.) Grove et al. (2000) concluded that these results, while modest, establish the superiority of mechanical methods of prediction.

## Ægisdóttir, White, Spengler et al. (2006)

Ægisdóttir et al.'s (2006) meta-analysis is part of a larger federally funded project called the Meta-Analysis of Clinical Judgment (MACJ) project (Spengler et al., 2000). For studies to be included in the MACJ database, they had to focus on mental health predictions or judgments, and the human judges had to be mental health practitioners or graduate students. (For a full description of the methodology, see Spengler et al., 2009.) Studies not included in Grove et al. (2000) were included, by nature of the different search strategies, the different time frames, and the different focus on only mental health applications. The types of criteria investigated included brain impairment, personality, length of hospital stay or treatment, diagnosis, adjustment or prognosis, violence or offense, IQ, academic performance, if an MMPI profile was real or fictional, suicide attempt, and "diagnosis" of homosexuality. Because the focus of Ægisdóttir et al. (2006) was strictly in the realm of mental health and psychology-related judgments, this meta-analysis more directly addresses issues about the relative utility of clinical judgment versus mechanical prediction for psychologists and other mental health professionals.

As noted, Ægisdóttir et al. (2006) found the same overall effect of $d = .12$ reflecting modest superiority of mechanical prediction over clinical judgment. The effect was slightly larger ($d = .16$) when Oskamp (1962) and Goldberg (1965) were included and when outlier effects were included ($d = .14$). Oskamp and Goldberg produced so many effects that they were treated as separate cases. Oskamp reported hit rates for 16 different cross-validated formulas and compared each of these with the predictive accuracy of the average clinical judge. Likewise, Goldberg reported the predictive accuracy of 65 different formulas compared with the average clinical judge. As with Grove et al. (2000), the preferred comparison with clinical judgment was with a cross-validated formula, resulting in the effect size of $d = .12$; otherwise the formula would have an artificial advantage due to chance associations or spurious findings (Dawes et al., 1989; Meehl, 1954).

Effect sizes ranged from $-.57$ in favor of clinical prediction to .73 in favor of mechanical prediction. A slightly broader range was found when outlier effects were included, ranging from $-.63$ to .81. Using Grove et al.'s (2000) scheme for categorizing the results, 52% of the studies had effects greater than .10 and were considered to favor mechanical prediction (Alexakos, 1966; Barron, 1953; Bolton, Butler, & Wright, 1968; Carlin & Hewitt, 1990; Conrad & Satter, 1954; Cooke, 1967b; Danet, 1965; Devries & Shneidman, 1967; Dunham & Meltzer, 1946; Evenson, Altman, Sletten, & Cho, 1975; Fero, 1975; Gardner, Lidz, Mulvay, & Shaw, 1996; Goldberg, 1970; Gustafson, Greist, Stauss, Erdman, & Laughren, 1977; Halbower, 1955; Hall, 1988; Kaplan, 1962; Klehr, 1949; Leli & Filskov, 1981, 1984; Meehl, 1959; Melton, 1952; Moxley, 1973; Oxman, Rosenberg, Schnurr, & Tucker, 1988; Perez, 1976; Shagoury & Satz, 1969; Stricker, 1967; Szuko & Kleinmuntz, 1981; Taulbee & Sisson, 1957; Thompson, 1952; Walters, White, Greene, 1988; Watley, 1966; Watley & Vance, 1964; Webb, Hultgen, &

Craddick, 1977; Wedding, 1983; Weinberg, 1957; Werner, Rose, Yesavage, & Seeman, 1984; N. Wiggins & Kohen, 1971; Wirt, 1956; Wittman & Steinberg, 1944); 38% had effects between $-.10$ to .10 and were considered ties (Adams, 1974; Astrup, 1975; Cooke, 1967a; Dickerson, 1958; Gaudette, 1992; Goldberg, 1965, 1970; Grebstein, 1963; Holland, Holt, Levi, & Beckett, 1983; Johnston & McNeal, 1967; Kaplan, 1962; Kelly & Fiske, 1950; Kleinmuntz, 1967; Lefkowitz, 1973; Lemerond, 1977; Lewis & MacKinney, 1961; Lindsey, 1965; Lyle & Quast, 1976; K. Meyer, 1973; Moxley, 1973; Oxman et al., 1988; Popovics, 1983; Sarbin, 1942; Shaffer, Perlin, Schmidt, & Stephens, 1974; Taulbee & Sisson, 1957; Weinberg, 1957); and only 10% were more negative than $-.10$ favoring clinical prediction (Blumetti, 1972; S. G. Goldstein, Deysach, & Kleinknecht, 1973; Heaton, Grant, Anthony, & Lehman, 1981; Holt, 1958; Hovey & Stauffacher, 1953; Klinger & Roth, 1965; McHugh & Apostolakos, 1959; Miller, Kunce, & Getsinger, 1972; Oskamp, 1962; Shaffer et al., 1974).

Based on arguments in the literature over the years, several moderators were tested. (Moderators are essentially interaction effects that address when a variable is most strongly associated with an outcome variable; see Frazier, Tix, & Barron, 2004.) One of the most interesting moderator findings was that *only statistically derived formulas were superior to clinical prediction*. Logically constructed rules (e.g., algorithms) were no better than clinician prediction. There were too few studies to test a third type of mechanical prediction, where the clinician's judgments are modeled (e.g., using think-aloud technique; Ericsson & Simon, 1994), to reach conclusions about modeling the clinical judge. Contrary to the assumption put forth by Holt (1970) that the clinician would do better with more information, the opposite was found to be true: More information led to a decline in clinical judgment accuracy compared with the formula. This finding also contradicts Grove and Meehl's (1996) assertion that the clinician fared well in any of these studies because of "the informational advantage in being provided with more data than the formula" (p. 298). Others have suggested that there are limits to human information processing that relate to this finding (see Dawes et al., 1989; Faust, 1986, 2003; Grove et al., 2000, Spengler et al., 1995). Overall, there was no specific type of judgment (e.g., prognostic or diagnostic) in which clinical judgment prevailed over mechanical prediction.

A few moderators suggest important directions for future research. One in particular was a trend suggesting that when clinicians were informed of base rates for the criterion they were predicting, their accuracy improved to the level of the formula. This finding contradicts the common theoretical assumption that humans tend to ignore base rates when making judgments under ambiguous conditions (Kahneman, Slovic, & Tversky, 1982; Nisbett & Ross, 1980). Providing clinicians with the statistical formula, however, did not improve their judgment accuracy (cf. Dawes et al., 1989; Sines, 1970), a finding that raises questions about how to make mechanical prediction more user-friendly, acceptable, and understood in graduate training. A common argument is that it is unfair to compare the average judge with the best formula (Holt, 1970) (for exceptions, see Goldberg, 1965; Oskamp, 1962) and that fair comparisons should be made between a cross-validated formula and expert judges. Only seven studies could be located where clinicians were considered to be experts in the judgment task. These studies yielded an effect size of .05 and the confidence interval included zero, indicating no true difference. A larger effect of $d = .12$ was found in the 41 studies with judges not considered experts. Therefore, contrary to majority opinion by most scholars (Brehmer, 1980; Brodsky, 1999, 2005; Dawes, 1994; Faust, 1986, 1994; Faust et al., 1988; Faust & Ziskin, 1988; Garb, 1989; Garb & Boyle, 2003; Garb & Grove, 2005; Lichtenberg, 1997, 2009; Wedding, 1991; J. S. Wiggins, 1980; Ziskin, 1995), expert judges do as well as the formula. Nonexpert mental health professionals were consistently outperformed.

Based on the relative consistency of these findings, Ægisdóttir et al. (2006) concluded like most other reviewers that statistical formulas, when available, ought to be used. They commented with this qualification:

> Although the statistical method is almost always the equal of the clinical method and is often better, *the improvement is not overwhelming*. Much more research is needed—in particular, programmatic lines of research on statistical prediction—that translates into practical applications for practicing psychologists (e.g., Quinsey et al., 1998). Likewise, supporters of clinical decision making must show how their approach can be improved. (p. 367, emphasis added)

## CRITIQUE OF MECHANICAL PREDICTION

The impact of Grove et al.'s (2000) meta-analysis on the debate regarding clinical versus mechanical prediction has been huge. At the time of the writing of this chapter, their article had been cited 347 times in the PsychInfo electronic database. Most of these scholars cited the significant advantage of mechanical prediction over clinical judgment (e.g., Myers, 2008; Peterson, Skeem & Manchak, 2011; Scurich & John, 2012; Vrieze & Grove, 2009), with some noting the presumed (but not yet tested) additional benefit of lowered costs of mechanical prediction (e.g., Grove & Meehl, 1996; Vrieze & Grove, 2009). A few noted that a meta-analysis does not establish solid evidence in favor of mechanical prediction or the necessity to replace clinical judgment with statistical formulas (Zeldow, 2009). Garb (2003) wrote: "[I]n light of these findings, comments made by statistical prediction advocates seem too extreme" (p. 28). Grove et al. (2000) also commented, "Our results qualify overbroad statements in the literature opining that such superiority (of mechanical prediction) is completely uniform" (p. 25). This statement contrasts with Grove and Meehl's (1996) arguments of the robust difference in favor of mechanical prediction.

It has become commonplace for adherents of mechanical prediction methods to refer to a frequency count of the number of studies that "score" in favor of mechanical prediction techniques relative to the number of ties and the even smaller number in favor of clinical prediction while ignoring the small size of this effect. For example, Myers (2008), citing results from Grove et al. (2000), wrote, "Clinical intuition surpassed 'mechanical' (statistical) prediction in only eight studies. In sixty-three studies, statistical prediction fared better. The rest (out of 134) were a tie" (p. 159). Vrieze and Grove (2009) noted, "With few exceptions, study after study have supported the conclusion that in making behavioral and medical predictions, mechanical (formal, statistical, algorithmic, actuarial) data combination performs as well as or better than clinical (informal, judgmental) combination" (p. 525). Westen and Weinberger (2005) stated, "Those who believe they can 'beat the odds' of a well-developed, well-validated formula would do well to keep their wagers small" (p. 1258). These comments are not much different from those made by Meehl (Grove & Meehl, 1996; Meehl, 1954, 1996). What they ignore is the small *empirical* difference between mechanical and clinical prediction methods.

Yes, mechanical prediction is superior, and yes, it should be used particularly in high-stakes judgments (e.g., prediction of violence; Hilton et al., 2006), but its relative utility compared to clinical prediction for mental health judgments has, in a sense, only begun to be investigated. There is a near absence of systematic programs of research allowing for clear conclusions about the relative utility of the two approaches for a variety of prediction tasks across different settings. As was recognized by the American Psychological Association task force on the use of psychological assessment (J. J. Meyer et al., 1998), mechanical prediction techniques are scarce for the majority of judgment tasks. Systematic empirical comparisons between clinicians and the formula are even scarcer (see Grove et al., 2000; Ægisdóttir et al., 2006). Problems with generalizability of logically constructed rules across settings and populations exist. For example, despite being extensively cross-validated, Goldberg's (1965) rules for classifying patients as psychotic or neurotic from the MMPI did not generalize well to psychiatric and nonpsychiatric populations (Zalewski & Gottesman, 1991). Training programs (Vrieze & Grove, 2009) and practitioner-friendly approaches to mechanical prediction are needed (cf. "frugal heuristics," Katsikopoulos, Pachur, Machery, & Wallin, 2008). As Grove and Meehl (1996) speculated, "Poor education is probably the biggest single factor responsible for resistance to actuarial prediction" (p. 318). In short, several important questions remain to be studied to advance this potentially fruitful area of psychological assessment research.

Clinicians do not have to use purely statistical prediction techniques, as many have argued for a hybrid model (e.g., Gonzach, Kluger, & Klayman, 2000; Holt, 1970; Kleinmuntz, 1990; Litwack, 2001; Mumma, 2001; Webster & Cox, 1997). Others have argued that mechanical prediction is so clearly superior that using some combination of the two is a violation of the beneficence principle (e.g., Grove et al., 2000). While research to date suggests that, whenever possible, statistical methods should be used, there remains much room for the development of mechanical prediction models. Likewise, proponents of mechanical prediction models must show that graduate students can be effectively trained in their use and in their development and cross-validation in local settings (cf. local clinical scientist; Stricker & Trieweiler, 1995). It would behoove proponents of mechanical prediction to design and test approaches for training graduate students in the development, adaptation and use of mechanical prediction techniques. One conclusion that can be supported from the existing research is that mechanical prediction techniques are probably most useful for diagnostic and prognostic types of judgments (which have empirical support); they may not apply to all aspects of psychological assessment.

## Utility of Mechanical Prediction

Spengler et al. (1995) defined psychological assessment as occurring along a continuum of decision making, ranging from micro to macro levels of judgments. In a therapy session, clinicians' micro decisions abound and include their immediate impressions of a client (e.g., Sandifer, Hordern, & Green, 1970), decisions about which verbal response to use (e.g., reflection or interpretation), and timing decisions about use of techniques. The hundreds of micro decisions made in the therapy hour are probably not amenable to mechanical prediction techniques, at least at this point in time and history. Increasingly sophisticated psychotherapy research, however, provides guidance for the scientifically informed clinician at key junctures, such as when to use interpretation (e.g., Crits-Christoph, Cooper, & Luborsky, 1988) and whether to use empathic listening or a Gestalt two-chair technique in response to a client split (e.g., Greenberg & Dompierre, 1981). However, because no known research program has striven to use mechanical formulas to inform these types of micro decisions, the closest a scientifically minded clinician can get is to strive to consume and incorporate psychotherapy research findings to inform many, but certainly not the vast majority, of these moments in a therapy hour.

Meehl (1954) never intended to convey that the formula would replace the clinician in these and many other similar activities (see Dana & Thomas, 2006; Grove & Meehl, 1996; Meehl, 1986; Wooten & Weinberger, 2005; Zeldow, 2009). In relation to clinical formulations, Meehl (1954) did argue that clinicians might be trained to access "statistical frequencies" related to specifics in therapy. He noted, "[W]e still would have to create (in the therapist) a readiness to invent particular hypotheses that exemplify the general principle in a specific instance" (p. 50). More than likely, however, the delivery of psychotherapy will remain in the purview of the clinician (cf. Zeldow, 2009) and the utility for mechanical methods will apply mostly to what Spengler et al. (1995) called "macro" levels of decisions.

Spengler et al. (1995) defined macro decisions as the more static criteria that are the focus of mechanical versus clinical prediction research. These are the judgments noted earlier in this chapter that largely include diagnostic and prognostic predictions. In Ægisdóttir et al.'s (2006) review, 51% (48/95) of the comparisons examined *diagnostic judgments* (e.g., brain impairment, Wedding, 1983; psychiatric diagnoses, Goldberg, 1965, 1970; malingering, Walters et al., 1988; lie detection, Szuko & Kleinmuntz, 1981; and personality characteristics, Weinberg, 1957); 46% (44/95) examined *prognostic judgments* (e.g., occupational choice, Webb et al., 1977; academic performance, Kelly & Fiske, 1950; marital adjustment, Lefkowitz, 1973; career satisfaction, Lewis & MacKinney, 1961; length of hospitalization, Evenson et al., 1975; length of psychotherapy, Blumetti, 1972; suicide attempt,

Gustafson et al., 1977; violence, Gardner, Lidz, Mulvay, & Shaw, 1996; and homicidality, Perez, 1976); and 3% (3/95) examined other judgments (e.g., real versus random MMPI, Carlin & Hewitt, 1990). It seems reasonable to assume, at this stage in technology development, that optimal use of mechanical prediction applies principally to macro-level judgments. This conclusion is not much different from Meehl's (1954) position on the matter almost 60 years ago.

## Challenges to Mechanical Prediction

The true advantage of mechanical prediction is that once the model is developed, it can be used on its own. Input into the model may still include clinical interview data or clinical observations, coded in a standardized manner, but the model would not vary. This inherent 100% reliability is directly related to the validity of statistical prediction, as the reliability coefficient places a cap on the possible size of a validity coefficient. Many of the challenges inherent to mechanical prediction are not unique and also apply to clinical prediction, although arguably the intuitive nature of clinical prediction makes it vulnerable to more threats to validity, as discussed later (e.g., judgmental heuristics; Nisbett & Ross, 1980). A mechanical formula is only as good as the input into the formula, which ideally is based on good research and adequate study of the empirical relations between identified predictors and the criterion. Theory and clinician-generated hypotheses enter into the selection of both predictor and criteria variables.

## Predictor-Criterion Contamination

One of the greatest challenges to mechanical prediction is *criterion contamination*—that is, the criteria used in some formulas are contaminated because of their similarity with the predictors. This would occur, for example, if clinician input was based on history and interview and the criterion was generated from the same type of clinician-generated data. In a series of studies on the use of the MMPI to predict whether a client was psychotic or neurotic, the criterion was in some cases also determined by patients' MMPI profiles (e.g., Goldberg, 1965, 1969, 1972; Goodson & King, 1976). Giannetti, Johnson, Klingler, and Williams (1978) suggested that conflicting results from these various studies may have been a result of criterion contamination. In fact, in the most contaminated samples, Goldberg (1965) found validity coefficients of .42 and .40 for the Meehl-Dahlstrom rules and the Taulbee-Sisson signs for differentiating psychotic from neurotic MMPI

profiles. These coefficients shrank to .29 and .27 for the least contaminated sample. To avoid criterion contamination, different input is needed for both the predictors and the criterion.

## Criterion Validity and Fuzzy Constructs

The predictive validity of a mechanical formula is directly related to the reliability and validity of the criterion. If the criterion has poor reliability and validity, a ceiling is placed on the potential accuracy of the formula (for further discussion, see Schmidt & Hunter, 1996). In some of the mechanical prediction studies, questionable criterion validity exists (see Ægisdóttir et al., 2006). For example, Kelly and Fiske (1950) used peer or supervisor ratings of academic performance with no demonstration of reliability or validity. Others have gone to great lengths to ensure the validity of their criterion (e.g., malingering, Walters et al., 1988; brain impairment, Leli & Filskov, 1981, 1984; Wedding, 1983). For example, Wedding (1983) verified presence and localization of brain impairment by autopsy and other highly reliable medical data. Several constructs of interest in psychology might be considered fuzzy and difficult to predict regardless of the method (cf. Kazdin, 2008).

## Predicting Personality Traits Versus (Observable) Behavior

Some have argued that mechanical methods of prediction are best for prediction of observable behavior and less good for personality traits and diagnoses. Behavioral observations occur at a lower level of inference, and should have higher reliability, than assessment of higher-order constructs, such as personality traits and diagnoses (cf. Pepinsky & Pepinsky, 1954). Behavioral observation is not without its challenges, however. For example, Werner et al. (1984) studied predictions of inpatient violence verified by nurses' entries in the patients' charts. Thus, the criterion was based on the behavior having been both observed and judged by the nurses as meeting the policy requirement for recording it in the chart, revealing several potential points of breakdown in the reliability of the criterion. Similarly, statistical assessments of future violence at parole board meetings may best predict who gets caught as opposed to the intended criterion of measuring future aggression (cf. Litwack, 2001). Often researchers equate other criteria with the intended behavioral criterion of aggression after release (e.g., recidivism, Kozol, Boucher, & Garafolo, 1972;

violence in the hospital, Mullen & Reinehr, 1982; short-term assessment of violence, Sepejak, Menzies, Webster, & Jensen, 1983).

## Low Base Rate Problems

Problems that occur infrequently are understandably difficult to predict using a formula or clinical judgment. A key example of a low base rate problem for psychological assessment is the prediction of suicide. In 2007, the national base rate for suicide in the general population was 11.3/100,000 (Centers for Disease Control and Prevention, 2010). The base rate increases for certain subpopulations, for example, the rate goes up to 36.1/100,000 for males over the age of 75. Suicide attempts occur 25 times more than completions, making suicide *risk* easier to predict (cf. Gustafson et al., 1977; Lemerond, 1977; Shaffer et al., 1974). Despite several efforts, mechanical prediction methods have not been successful at accurately predicting this important mental health problem (e.g., R. B. Goldstein, Black, Nasrallah, & Winokur, 1991; Pokorny, 1983, 1993). For example, R. B. Goldstein et al.'s (1991) mechanical prediction model resulted in 45 false negatives out of 46 completed suicides and only 1 accurate prediction of suicide out of 5 in a group of 1,906 patients followed over several years.

## Costs and Complexities of Longitudinal Research

In their response to common arguments against incorporating mechanical methods of prediction, Grove and Meehl (1996) stated: "A notion seems to exist that developing actuarial prediction methods involves a huge amount of extra work of a sort the one would not ordinarily be doing in daily clinical decision-making and that it then requires some fancy mathematics to analyze the data; neither of these things is true" (p. 303). This position might be true especially for concurrent validity studies, but the costs of predictive validity studies are well known. After all, if longitudinal research were not so much more time consuming and costly, the field of psychological assessment would have a preponderance of predictive rather than concurrent validity research.

## Limited Data Assessed for the Formula

A general criticism of mechanical prediction rules is that often little effort is put into identifying the very best predictors. Garb (1998) noted that "[s]tatistical-prediction rules would probably be more powerful if there was a

concerted effort to identify and use the best available input information" (p. 217). Proponents of mechanical prediction cite research examples when a minimal number of predictors in a formula still outperform clinical predictions (e.g., Grove & Meehl, 1996). This is not really the point that the statistical model can be parsimonious. Given the modest increase in accuracy using a formula, it seems that a concerted effort would be placed on identifying the very best predictors in sustained research programs (e.g., violence predictions; see Hilton et al., 2006). In short, there are considerable challenges and difficulties in constructing effective prediction formulas for the social sciences that have not yet been addressed or resolved by proponents of mechanical prediction methods.

## CRITIQUE OF CLINICAL PREDICTION

Clinical judgment research abounds both in comparative studies with mechanical prediction and in far greater numbers related to a variety of other clinical judgment questions. Mental health clinical judgment researchers study what are called *clinical judgmental biases* related to people characteristics (e.g., age, race, ethnicity, gender, intelligence, socioeconomic status; see Garb, 1998; MACJ project, Spengler et al., 2009). Research on clinical judgmental biases focuses on clinical information processing strategies related to inaccurate or biased clinical judgment. For example, in an impressive naturalistic study, Potts, Burnam, and Wells (1991) demonstrated the presence of gender bias in diagnoses of depression made by 523 mental health and medical professionals of 23,101 patients. Comparing their informal judgments with a standardized interview, medical professionals were found to *under*diagnose men whereas mental health professionals *over*diagnosed women with depression. A third important area of clinical judgment research has to do with the study of *clinician characteristics* (e.g., experience, confidence, cognitive complexity, scientific training, and theoretical orientation; see Garb, 1998; MACJ project, Spengler et al., 2009) as moderators of clinical judgment accuracy and judgmental biases. Overconfidence, for example, is thought to relate to decreases in judgment accuracy (e.g., Desmarais, Nicholls, Read, & Brink, 2010; Smith & Dumont, 2002). This may be because increased confidence is associated with testing fewer hypotheses and processing a narrower range of client data.

Clinical judgment researchers investigate decision-making processes (e.g., amount and quality of information; Berven, 1985; Berven & Scofield, 1980; Falvey &

Hebert, 1992; Gambrill, 2005; Shanteau, 1988) and the use of judgmental heuristics or cognitive shortcuts by clinicians (e.g., anchoring, availability, representativeness, confirmatory hypothesis testing, primacy/recency effects, and illusory correlation). Judgmental heuristics are cognitive shortcuts that professionals in all fields (e.g., medicine, law, and psychology) and laypeople alike have been found to use. The general conclusion is that clinicians are vulnerable to the same cognitive errors that affect all other decision makers (see Nisbett & Ross, 1980). The seriousness of the subject matter, however, warrants that clinicians learn about these shortcuts and learn how to prevent potentially associated judgment errors (see Zeldow, 2009). A series of studies, for example, suggest that clinicians have a tendency to confirm or seek client data to support their hypotheses (e.g., Haverkamp, 1993; Pfeiffer, Whelan, & Martin, 2000; Strohmer & Shivy, 1994; Strohmer, Shivy, & Chiodo, 1990). Such a strategy differs from a scientist-practitioner approach to assessment where disconfirmatory and alternate hypotheses are also tested (see Spengler et al., 1995). Martindale (2005) suggested that some clinicians may consciously engage in a related phenomenon he called confirmatory distortion.

While clinical judgment is a rich area of psychological assessment research and has been reviewed many times (e.g., Bell & Mellor, 2009; Cline, 1985; Dana & Thomas, 2006; Dawes, 1994; Dumont, 1993; Faust, 1986, 1994; Gambrill, 2005; Garb, 1989, 1992, 1997, 1998, 2005; Lopez, 1989; Rabinowitz, 1993; Ruscio, 2007; Schalock & Luckasson, 2005; Turk & Salovey, 1985; Wedding & Faust, 1989; Widiger & Spitzer, 1991), few firm conclusions can be reached about the strengths and pitfalls of decision making by mental health professionals. A primary reason is that, for the most part, this abundant area of research has not yet been synthesized by methods other than by narrative reviews. The same arguments made earlier in relation to clinical versus mechanical prediction hold: Without empirical synthesis, scholars and practitioners alike have difficulty seeing the forest for the trees. Some exceptions exist, such as two recent meta-analyses on the role of experience in clinical judgment (Pilipis, 2010; Spengler et al., 2009) to be described. Other problems and limitations characterize the study of clinical judgment. As with research on mechanical prediction techniques, there are few systematic research programs, which, consequently, has resulted in few useful guidelines for practitioners. There are also few examples of research efforts designed to *improve* clinical judgment through training on decision making (cf. Harding, 2007; Meier,

1999; Nurcombe & Fitzhenry-Coor, 1987; Kurpius, Benjamin, & Morran, 1985; Smith & Agate, 2002; Spengler & Strohmer, 2001; Vrieze & Grove, 2009). The study of mental health clinical decision making lags behind developments in medical decision making, where, for example, students and interns are routinely trained and tested using high-fidelity patient simulators (for review, see Cook & Triola, 2009). In this type of training, physicians' decision-making strategies can be evaluated; immediate feedback is provided to help students and interns learn optimal medical decision making. The few examples of computer simulations designed to train mental health clinicians are logically constructed, or they model the judgment processes of presumed experts (e.g., Falvey, 2001; Falvey et al., 2005; Falvey & Hebert, 1992). There is no assurance that the "expert" standard to which clinicians are taught to aspire provides the best model for clinical judgment.

This section highlights some of the issues thought to affect the reliability and validity of clinical judgment, especially in relation to its relative utility compared with mechanical methods of prediction. A caveat seems in order related to the clinical judgment literature: The vast majority of this research has relied on analogue methodology. Analogue clinical judgment research attains high internal validity (experimental control) at the expense of external validity (generalization) by, for example, studying clinicians' judgments of artificially constructed clinical vignettes (versus studying real-life judgments). Bias toward such a singular method retards growth in any area of research and limits its generalizability from the laboratory to practice settings. In their comprehensive clinical judgment experience meta-analysis, Spengler et al. (2009) found that 84% (62/74) of the studies used analogue methodology whereas a mere 5% (4/74) of studies used in vivo judgments. (The remaining 11% of the studies were archival.) A prototypical clinical judgment study provides clinicians with materials to review, usually in written form, but it could also include visual and other forms of media. A variable is manipulated, such as the gender or race of the client, the order of the information, or the availability of a statistical formula, and clinicians are asked to form their impressions in response to the materials provided by the experimenters. Often little emphasis is placed on establishing the validity of the stimulus materials, and in over 50% of the clinical judgment studies, it is impossible to determine what constitutes an accurate judgment (see MACJ project; Spengler et al., 2009). These limitations to clinical judgment research have slowed developments in this field despite over 50 years of accumulated research.

## Experience and Judgment Accuracy

The greatest challenge thought to limit the accuracy of clinicians' judgments is the lack of benefit from experience. This is the most common explanation offered for why clinical judgment is thought to not fare as well as mechanical prediction (Garb, 2003; Meehl, 1997). Several writers have asserted that judgment accuracy will not improve with experience; some have even speculated it may worsen due to repeated use of cognitive errors (Brehmer, 1980; Brodsky, 2005; Dawes, 1994; Faust, 1986, 1994; Faust et al., 1988; Faust & Ziskin, 1988; Garb, 1989; Garb & Boyle, 2003; Garb & Grove, 2005; Lichtenberg, 1997, 2009; Wedding, 1991; J. S. Wiggins, 1980; Ziskin, 1995). Others have argued that clinical experience has a role in clinical decision making, and judgment processes used by more experienced clinicians may even serve as the standard for measuring cognitive growth in novice clinicians (Berven, 1985; Berven & Scofield, 1980; Falvey & Hebert, 1992; Falvey et al., 2005; Gambrill, 2005; Shanteau, 1988; Zeldow, 2009). Embedded in this argument is usually a discussion of the many potential pitfalls that exist in clinical decision making. On one hand, Westen and Weinberger (2004) argued that accuracy should improve from clinical experience because of the immediate feedback obtained. On the other hand, Garb (2003) noted problems with client feedback due to its subjectivity. In fact, Hatfield, McCullough, Frantz, and Krieger (2010) found that therapists were unable to accurately detect client deterioration from client self-report. Errors related to judgments with this level of importance should concern practitioners and motivate them to optimize their decision making.

A key reason clinicians are thought to not learn well from their experience is that they apparently fail to routinely collect feedback on the accuracy of their psychological assessments and other types of judgments. As Garb (2003) noted, "In most cases, for mental health professionals to determine the accuracy of a judgment or decision, longitudinal or outcome data would have to be collected . . . but most clinicians find this [sic] data to be too expensive and time consuming to collect in clinical practice" (p. 37). A near absence of research on feedback exists in clinical judgment research. In the Spengler et al. (2009) meta-analysis, only 2 out of 74 studies assessed the impact of feedback on the experience-accuracy effect. In a subsequent experience meta-analysis, Pilipis (2010) found only 3 out of 36 studies assessed the benefits of feedback. Meehl (1954) noted years ago that if clinicians do not receive feedback, they cannot expect to improve their

decision making (cf. Dawes et al., 1989; Garb & Boyle, 2003; Lichtenberg, 1997). Garb and Boyle (2003) noted problems with the ambiguity of client feedback in practice (e.g., Barnum effects) and the unlikely benefits of feedback under these conditions. Some recent developments have been promising; for example, Lambert et al. (2001) found that giving simple feedback on patient response to treatment leads clinicians on their own to optimally change the course of psychotherapy treatment (see *patient progress feedback*; Shimokawa et al., 2010). Functioning like a scientist-practitioner in assessments warrants using a systematic method of data collection (Ridley & Shaw-Ridley, 2009; Spengler et al., 1995); the regular use of feedback data may be one of the keys to improving clinical decision making. Consider, for example, how often psychologists collect follow-up data to assess the accuracy of their conclusions in their psychological assessments.

Clinicians are thought to not fare as well as mechanical prediction because of the inability or impaired ability to learn from experience. These impediments to learning come from a variety of sources, including the tendency to rely on cognitive shortcuts called judgmental heuristics (Kahneman et al., 1982; Nisbett & Ross, 1980). The representativeness heuristic occurs when clinicians readily access a stereotype without consideration of base rates. When clinicians readily invoke a client explanation that is easily accessed from memory, they are using the availability heuristic. Clinicians invoke the anchoring heuristic when they place undue weight on clinical information that is processed first. Recent research suggests that some judgments may actually be enhanced with the use of some heuristics (see Gigerenzer & Brighton, 2009). The best-selling book *Blink: The Power of Thinking Without Thinking* (Gladwell, 2005) described these findings for the general public. Nisbett and Ross (1980) likewise noted that if judgment heuristics were always inaccurate, we as a species would not survive. The increased risk for inaccurate judgments by clinicians exists, however, when cognitive shortcuts are invoked outside of their awareness.

On the more positive side, there are several accounts of clinicians' judgment *processes* (not necessarily their judgment accuracy) improving with clinical experience. Experts compared with novice clinicians may differ on a number of cognitive dimensions, including (a) broader knowledge structures, (b) greater number of ideas generated, (c) more efficient use of their time spent on client conceptualizations, (d) better quality schemata about client case material, and (e) better short- and long-term memory for domain-specific information (Cummings, Hallberg, Martin, Slemon, & Hiebert, 1990;

Falvey, 2001; Falvey & Hebert, 1992; Falvey et al., 2005; Holloway & Wolleat, 1980; Kivlighan & Quigley, 1991; Martin, Slemon, Hiebert, Hallberg, & Cummings, 1989; Mayfield, Kardash, & Kivlighan, 1999; O'Byrne & Goodyear, 1997). The problem with this area of research is that these judgment processes have not been related to judgment accuracy or other outcomes that show their benefit. Findings from other areas of psychology suggest that experts can better use statistical heuristics and thereby avoid common decision-making errors. This occurs, however, only if it is apparent that statistical reasoning is appropriate for the judgment (Nisbett, Krantz, Jepson, & Kunda, 1983). Others have argued that much of clinical judgment occurs under conditions of uncertainty (Tversky & Kahneman, 1974) and in domains sufficiently unstructured to lessen the perceived utility of statistical heuristics (Kleinmuntz, 1990). Of greatest concern, debriefing clinician research participants suggests that much of their biased judgment processes occurs outside of their awareness (DiNardo, 1975). This lack of awareness is thought to be a key reason clinicians do not learn well from their clinical experience (Einhorn, 1986).

If clinicians do not learn from clinical experience, perhaps they do from their training and education. Regarding educational experience, Garb and Grove (2005) stated, "[T]he value of training has been consistently demonstrated" (p. 658), whereas Faust (1986) argued there is no support for benefits from general education experience. Developmental training and supervision models suggest that judgment accuracy should actually improve with experience (e.g., see Loganbill, Hardy, & Delworth, 1982; Stoltenberg, McNeill, & Delworth, 1998). Whereas clinical experience may allow clinicians the opportunity to repeat the same errors over and over again, increased educational experience may improve the quality of decision making, especially if decision-making strategies are taught (Swets, Dawes, & Monahan, 2000). Scholars have emphasized the importance of learning competent clinical decision-making skills (Elman, Illfelder-Kaye, & Robiner, 2005; Faust, 1986; Garb, 1998; Garb & Boyle, 2003; Garb & Grove, 2005; Harding, 2004; Kleinmuntz, 1990; Lilienfeld, Lynn, & Lohr, 2003; Meehl, 1973; Mumma, 2001; Tracey & Rounds, 1999; Westen & Weinberger, 2005). Unfortunately, fewer than 50% of clinical psychology graduate programs train their students in decision making, and none offers a stand-alone decision-making course (Harding, 2007) despite recommendations from an APA Division 12 (Society of Clinical Psychology) Task Force that ranked training in decision theory and clinical judgment second only in importance to ethics training (Grove, 2001, cited by Harding, 2007).

The conclusion that clinicians fail to learn from experience has been repeated so many times that singling out any one quote seems arbitrary and potentially capricious. Recent findings from the Meta-Analysis of Clinical Judgment project (Spengler et al., 2009), replicated in an updated meta-analysis (Pilipis, 2010), found a small but reliable effect reflecting improved judgmental accuracy with clinical and educational experience. Meehl's (1997) reflection on the limitations of clinical experience still has merit:

> Since clinical experience consists of anecdotal impressions by practitioners, it is unavoidably a mixture of truths, half-truths, and falsehoods. The scientific method is the only known way to distinguish these, and it is both unscholarly and unethical for psychologists who deal with other persons' health, careers, money, freedom, and even life itself to pretend that clinical experience suffices and that quantitative research on diagnostic and therapeutic procedures is not needed. (p. 91)

In Garb's (2003) earlier version of this chapter, he concluded, "[A] large body of research contradicts the popular belief that the more experience clinicians have, the more likely it is that they will be able to make accurate judgments" (p. 32). Contrary to years of conclusions along this line, two recent meta-analyses found that educational and clinical experience is associated with a modest but reliable increase in mental health judgment accuracy ($d = .12$, Spengler et al., 2009; $d = .16$, Pilipis, 2010). As with the clinical versus mechanical prediction effect, the experience-accuracy effect is equally small. It is understandable why authors of narrative reviews do not detect it. Clinical judgment studies investigating experience, unless they have large sample sizes, will tend to have low statistical power, and most will report statistically nonsignificant findings between experience and accuracy. Spengler et al. (2009) noted that studies with $n = 200$ per group (200 expert clinicians and 200 novice clinicians) and an alpha of .05 will have power of only .22 to detect an effect of this size. In other words, roughly only 1 in 4 studies with sample sizes this large would detect a statistically significant relation between experience and judgment accuracy. Spengler et al. concluded, "In light of the historical overemphasis on statistical significance, it is not difficult to understand why scholars have concluded that experience does not count" (p. 381). Besides informing the field, the results of these meta-analyses demonstrate the need to synthesize other areas of clinical judgment research and to further assess common assumptions about clinical judgment, to advance its practice and study.

## Meta-Analyses on Experience and Clinical Judgment

Too few studies in the area of clinical versus mechanical prediction have investigated the role of experience or expertness to support claims commonly made for the lack of impact from experience. Ægisdóttir et al. (2006) found only seven studies where experience or expertness was assessed and the *experts actually performed as well as the formula*. These studies yielded an effect size of $d = .05$ in favor of mechanical methods, although with the confidence interval crossing zero. This is not considered a true effect. In the remaining 41 studies, where the judges were considered to be nonexperts, the effect size was $d = .12$ in favor of mechanical methods. Ægisdóttir et al. concluded that "when judgments are made by expert clinicians, the difference between clinical and statistical methods seems to disappear" (p. 366). It holds to reason that if the experience-accuracy effect is $d = .12$ (Spengler et al., 2009), and it is a real effect and the same size as the clinical versus mechanical prediction effect of $d = .12$ (see Ægisdóttir et al.; Grove et al., 2000), this bump in accuracy for experienced clinicians would lead to equivalence between experienced clinicians and the formula. Based on extant research, it is premature to make claims of the robust superiority of mechanical prediction techniques, promising as they are, and to simultaneously claim that experienced clinicians are unable to compete with the formula.

Spengler et al. (2009) and Pilipis (2010) both produced meta-analyses on the relation between experience (clinical and educational) and clinical judgment accuracy. Spengler et al.'s study is part of the MACJ project where an archival data set was exhaustively constructed for the years 1970 to 1996. Their search process is a distinct advantage of the MACJ project, in this case resulting in 75 clinical judgment studies, where the accuracy judgments of 4,607 clinicians were assessed in relation to their clinical or educational experience. Pilipis updated the Spengler et al. experience meta-analysis following an adapted version of their search process to locate experience studies for the years 1997 to 2010. Both meta-analyses included studies of mental health judgments, by mental health practitioners or graduate students, where some form of experience was measured and the accuracy of the judgment could be determined. Pilipis identified 37 studies that assessed the relation between mental health experience and the judgments

made by 6,685 clinicians. Together these two studies cover nearly 40 years (1970–2010) of research examining the association between experience and accuracy.

## Spengler, White, Ægisdóttir et al. (2009)

Spengler et al. (2009) found an overall effect of $d = .13$ that was heterogeneous. One study (Garcia, 1993) produced a very large effect size of 3.08, indicating a large positive difference for experience. After this outlier was removed, the overall effect dropped to $d = .12$, the variance was homogeneous, and the confidence interval did not cross zero, indicating that this is a true effect. Overall, 67% of the studies had positive effects. If the format used by Grove et al. (2000) to "score" the studies is used, 43% (32/74) had effects greater than .10 and are considered to favor more experienced clinicians; 42% (31/74) had effects between −.10 to .10 and are considered ties; and only 15% (11/74) were more negative than −.10 favoring less experienced clinicians (recalculated from Grove et al., 2000, Table 2, p. 372). Following the logic put forth by proponents of mechanical prediction techniques, this indicates that experienced clinicians form clinical judgments as well and often better than less experienced clinicians.

Few moderators were significant, which is to be expected when the overall effect is homogeneous. This means that experienced clinicians are simply more accurate than less experienced clinicians across a range of tasks and settings. They were more accurate at diagnosing ($d = .15$) and at implementing practice guidelines ($d = .24$) (cf. APA Presidential Task Force on Evidence-Based Practice, 2006; Westen & Weinberger, 2004). A publication bias was evident by larger effects for studies published in APA journals ($d = .27$) compared with those in non-APA outlets ($d = .04$). A trend suggested that more experienced clinicians are better at diagnosing criteria with low validity ($d = .22$) compared with high validity ($d = .04$). Spengler et al. (2009) commented: "This finding may reflect that experience improves accuracy the greatest where more refined and nuanced understanding is required (e.g., when the criteria is [*sic*] "fuzzy") or under conditions of greater uncertainty" (p. 384). There was no difference between clinical and educational experience or when clinicians had specific versus general experience with the judgment task.

Several important questions could not be answered by this meta-analysis because of limitations with clinical judgment research. For example, Spengler et al. (2009) noted an intractable problem with quantifying the range of clinical and educational experience because of the various units of measurement used in these studies. They observed that "the modal study focused on restricted ranges of experience" (p. 388) and speculated that this may have produced a more conservative estimate of the effect size than if broader ranges of experience could be assessed. Research is needed that investigates longitudinal changes in judgment accuracy, akin to the Collaborative Research Network of the Society of Psychotherapy Research (Orlinsky & Rønnestad, 2005). This group has used cross-sectional and longitudinal methods to study changes in therapist expertise. There were too few studies to assess important questions for clinical judgment practice, such as the impact of specialized training or feedback on judgment accuracy.

While the overall effect is small, Spengler et al. (2009) argued that it is not trivial when considering the years of debate about the perceived lack of benefit of experience and conclusions by some that experience may actually lead to a worsening of judgment accuracy (e.g., Berven, 1985; Berven & Scofield, 1980; Brehmer, 1980; Brodsky, 2005; Dawes, 1994; Falvey & Hebert, 1992; Faust, 1986, 1994; Faust et al., 1988; Faust & Ziskin, 1988; Gambrill, 2005; Garb, 1989, 1998; Holt, 1970; Lichtenberg, 1997; Shanteau, 1988; Wedding, 1991; J. S. Wiggins, 1980; Ziskin, 1995). Spengler et al. stated: "Where decisions have a higher degree of importance, consumers of mental health services (e.g., clients, judges, hospital administrators, and custody litigants) may correctly assume that there is a practical gain achieved by having more experienced clinicians making these judgments" (p. 380).

### Pilipis (2010)

Pilipis (2010) extended Spengler et al.'s (2009) work by reviewing studies from the years 1997 to 2010. The overall effect size found was $d = .16$ after removal of one outlier ($d = 1.86$; Rerick, 1999), indicating a high degree of consistency in these two meta-analyses. Pilipis tested the same moderators as Spengler et al. with the addition of profession type (psychology, psychiatry, social work, counseling, psychiatric nursing) and, in an attempt to capture the no experience level, comparisons with non–mental health professionals. In discussing their results Spengler et al. hypothesized that the greatest gain in judgment accuracy may be from the level of no to some experience (cf. Lambert & Ogles, 2004; Lambert & Wertheimer, 1988; Skovholt, Rønnestad, & Jennings, 1997). Pilipis also found that more experienced clinicians were better at forming accurate diagnoses ($d = .29$) and better at assessing constructs with low criterion validity ($d = .20$). The comparison between no experience

with some experience was not a significant moderator. There also were no differences within profession type, but there were too few studies for each profession to draw conclusions. As with Spengler et al., there was a publication bias with the largest effects found in APA journals ($d = .54$). Once again there were too few studies to assess the effects of feedback, which has been speculated as essential to enhancing learning from experience (see Ericsson & Lehmann, 1996; Faust, 1991; Garb, 1998; Lichtenberg, 1997). Spengler (1998) stated, "To ensure judgment accuracy as a local clinical scientist, some form of feedback mechanism is needed" (p. 932). This is an area of research that should be more fully developed.

The results from Pilipis (2010) were remarkably similar to those from Spengler et al. (2009). They replicated and strengthened the conclusions reached that experience leads to a modest improvement in judgment accuracy. In light of the continued skepticism and critical stance toward the validity of clinical judgments (e.g., Lichtenberg, 2009; Lilienfeld et al., 2003) as well as the ongoing debate over the benefits of statistical methods in comparison to unaided clinical judgment, mental health clinicians may welcome this as a positive finding. Yet when considering the almost 40-year time span between the two meta-analyses (1970–2010), the small, stable experience-accuracy effect may be disappointing and surprising for some clinicians. Ridley and Shaw-Ridley (2009) referred to these findings as "sobering and instructive" (p. 402).

### Utility of Clinical Judgment

As Westen and Weinberger (2004) observed, "Meehl's arguments against informal aggregation stand 50 years later, but they have no bearing on whether, or under what circumstances, clinicians can make reliable and valid observations and inferences" (p. 596). Consistent with the previous discussion on the utility of mechanical prediction, it seems that there are many instances when clinical judgment will prevail or provide the organizing umbrella under which mechanical prediction techniques are used. Far too many types of decisions are being made for which there are no formulas available (e.g., guilty by reason of insanity—a legal definition measured retrospectively) or where it is impossible to construct formulas (e.g., micro decisions, Spengler et al., 1995). Grove and Meehl (1996) admonished clinicians to construct mechanical prediction formulas for almost every conceivable type of judgment. At an extreme point, their penchant for mechanical prediction was evident when they said, "A computerized rapid moment-to-moment analysis of the patient's discourse as a signaler to the therapist is something that, to our knowledge, has not been tried; however, given the speed of the modern computer, it would be foolish to reject such a science fiction idea out of hand" (pp. 304–305).

In response to strong advocates of mechanical prediction, much has been written about the continued role of clinical judgment in decision making (e.g., see Kazdin, 2008; Westen & Weinberger, 2005; Zeldow, 2009). The meta-analyses that have emerged since Garb (2003) wrote the previous version of this chapter point to only a small benefit from *both* mechanical prediction and experienced clinical judgment. Either method should be used with recognition of its inherent strengths and limitations; ultimately such use involves clinical judgment of how to combine the data. An example of a clinical judgment activity conducted in this manner may be a helpful illustration. The greatest challenge to a custody evaluator is no set criterion represents the legal standard of "best interest" of the child; therefore, a formula cannot be constructed to predict "best interest." Instead, what occurs in a complex assessment of this nature is the intelligent consideration (i.e., clinical judgment) of observations, test findings, theory, and scientific findings. Embedded in this assessment could conceivably be the use of mechanical prediction techniques for constructs subsumed under "best interest" (e.g., parenting competencies, parent–child attachment, risk of child abuse, risk of substance abuse). Ultimately, the greatest confidence should be placed in findings where multiple forms of data converge (observations, test scores, formulas, scientific findings; Spengler et al., 1995). This intelligent consideration of the data for a complex construct like best interest by necessity involves clinical judgment.

Even the use of mechanical prediction techniques involves clinical judgment. Grove and Meehl (1996) made it sound otherwise, as if it is a matter of setting up the formula and entering the data with no further considerations. Take, for example, the use of cutoff scores from the Minnesota Multiphasic Personality Inventory-2 (MMPI-2; Butcher, Dahlstrom, Graham, Tellegen, & Kaemmer, 1989) substance abuse scales (i.e., Addiction Potential Scale, Addiction Admission Scale, MacAndrew Alcoholism Scale—Revised) used to form a judgment about the probability a parent in the above custody evaluation has a substance abuse disorder. Examination of these scales is not a simple process that can arguably be handled by a formula alone. For example, the selection of a cutoff score involves several decisions related to forming an optimal balance between false positives and false negatives or examining the fit of the parent with the sample used to establish the cutoff scores. Predictive formulas from one MMPI-2 study of these scales (e.g., Stein, Graham, Ben-Porath, & McNulty, 1999) do not necessarily agree with those from another (e.g., Rouse, Butcher, & Miller, 1999). There is no one cutoff score determined for use by the formulas—it requires a decision by the clinician that is, one hopes, based on his or her knowledge of test construction, statistical prediction issues, and the scientific bases of the MMPI-2.

Proponents of mechanical prediction offer little with regard to these types of judgment issues that occur within a complex assessment process like a custody evaluation. On this matter, Grove et al. (2000) commented:

> Clinical and mechanical predictions sometimes disagree (Meehl, 1986). One cannot both admit and not admit a college applicant, or parole and imprison a convict. To fail to grapple with the question—Which prediction should one follow?—is to ignore the obligation of *beneficence*. Hence, the comparison of clinical judgment and mechanical prediction takes on great importance. (p. 19, emphasis added)

What would Grove do if there was more than one formula and the formulas did not agree, as in the earlier example of the need to resolve findings that differ between research studies? If a formula exists for predicting a criterion that is well defined (e.g., a good criterion for assessing college performance), arguably it should be used. Even here questions exist: Should it be the grade point average? Or should it be the number of years to degree completion? Or some form of a multivariate outcome measure?

It should be apparent from this brief discussion that several moments of "clinical judgment" must occur even when a clinician seeks to use methods of statistical prediction. Use of mechanical prediction techniques cannot conceivably involve a simple process of identifying one formula and using it without intelligent consideration of these types of issues, which constitutes what could be called *scientific judgment*. The formula does not resolve these issues; thus enters the clinician who must form a judgment about the use and application of a mechanical formula. These issues are not as simple as the prevailing question in the literature of which is superior, clinical or mechanical prediction? This brief discussion is not intended to deny that there are challenges to clinical decision making and that clinicians should function as much as possible in a scientific manner, including efforts to improve their decision making by keeping records of their accuracy. More research is needed on how to improve clinical decision making.

When using clinical judgment, several debiasing techniques have been recommended that may improve judgment accuracy (cf. Spengler et al., 1995). Improving clinical judgment likely involves using many of the tools available, including recommendations to use mechanical prediction formulas, especially for prognostic and predictive judgment tasks. Recent statements about evidence-based practice standards have come to recognize the importance of clinical experience as another source of evidence when making optimal treatment judgments for clients (e.g., see American Psychological Association Presidential Task Force, 2006). To some extent, this recommendation seems to be supported by the experience meta-analyses by Spengler et al. (2009) and Pilipis (2010). Zeldow (2009) provided a useful discussion on the role of clinical experience and decision making, in the context of empirically validated treatments, that takes into consideration nuances and times when it is necessary to adjust scientific findings to fit the cultural or individual nature of a client's needs.

## CONCLUDING REMARKS

What Garb (2003) wrote in the previous version of this chapter may still hold true today: "Although there are reasons to believe that statistical prediction rules will transform psychological assessment, it is important to realize that present-day rules are of limited value" (p. 30). Comparative research studying clinical judgment and mechanical prediction has not advanced such that there are clear directions for when and how to use either prediction technique. One intent of this updated chapter was to contrast developments in the study of psychotherapy to encourage a shift in research on clinical versus mechanical prediction. Both areas of research involve efforts to establish what works best, but the study of psychotherapy has a richness and maturity not found in the clinical versus mechanical prediction research. One reason put forth for this difference is that the forest has not been seen for the trees because of a predominance of piecemeal research and thought pieces. The clinical judgment meta-analyses conducted since Garb's last chapter in the *Handbook of Psychology* shed some new light on the basic question of which technique is superior and on a few other age-old controversies.

From these meta-analyses, it appears that there is a small (not robust) increase in accuracy for mechanical prediction compared with clinical judgment. Likewise, contrary to opposite impressions, experience is actually associated with a small but reliable improvement in judgment accuracy. These meta-analyses have limitations—they are only as good as the research that was input—and several important questions remain. Until additional research proves otherwise, it appears that *only* statistical formulas (i.e., not all forms of mechanical prediction) outperform the clinician, at least for mental health–related judgments (Ægisdóttir et al., 2006). It also may be that the expert is as good as the formula, clinicians do better with less information, and providing base rate information improves the clinician to the level of the formula, again for mental health–related judgments (Ægisdóttir et al., 2006).

Based on these findings, it still seems reasonable to recommend the use of mechanical prediction techniques when feasible, but with several caveats. It is time for both areas of study to grow beyond the dominance of analogue research. Programmatic lines of research are needed that advance conclusions about specific areas of application. There are few to no examples of research over the years of systematic comparison of clinical versus mechanical methods of prediction. Several judgment outcomes are looked at only in a cursory manner, such as prediction of career satisfaction, but they have been studied extensively outside of comparative studies (e.g., see *Handbook of Vocational Psychology,* Walsh & Savickas, 2005). Research is needed to develop user-friendly approaches to statistical prediction, and graduate-level training programs should be instituted, empirically tested, and implemented to improve clinical decision making. Conclusions cannot be reached on many potentially important topics of interest because they have not been sufficiently studied; one of these is the presumed benefits of feedback to improve clinical judgment.

One programmatic area of study warrants discussion related to a simple use of statistical feedback to aid clinical judgment. Lambert (2010) and Lambert et al. (2001) reported on a beneficial use of feedback for signal detection cases or the minority of patients found to deteriorate in psychotherapy. Using the Outcome Questionnaire-45 (Lambert et al., 1996), Lambert and colleagues formed dose-response curves for over 10,000 patients at varying levels of disturbance. Clinicians provided treatment as they chose to and received feedback each session in the simple format of a colored dot on the client's folder: white (patient is improved to normal levels, stop treatment), green (change is typical, no change in treatment recommended), yellow (change is deviating from expected recovery curve, modify treatment), and red (prediction of treatment failure, change course of treatment). This simple form of statistically derived feedback resulted in significant reduction in signal cases. Compared with a no-feedback group (23% deterioration rate), the statistical feedback group had only a 6% deterioration rate. (For a meta-analysis of these findings, see Shimokawa et al., 2010.) This line of research demonstrates the benefits of a simple, creative form of statistical feedback that is user friendly and improves the clinician's otherwise unassisted performance.

A great deal has been written about why clinicians do not use mechanical prediction formulas (see Vrieze & Grove's [2009] survey; see Harding [2007] on decision-making training; see Grove & Meehl, 1996; Kleinmuntz, 1990). Statistical prediction abounds in various fields. For example, it has been shown repeatedly that investing according to an index of the stock market beats investment portfolios that are actively managed. In sports, there is constant reference to probabilities, and commentators discuss on the correctness of coaching decisions based on these probabilities. If some form of statistical prediction is widely used in something as relatively unimportant (in the scheme of life) as sports, why is it not widely used by mental health practitioners who can be engaged in life-and-death decisions (e.g., judgments of suicide, homicide, or child abuse)? Rather than admonish clinicians to use mechanical prediction methods, proponents should develop more consumer-friendly approaches and training programs designed to overcome apparent resistance, misunderstandings, and lack of knowledge. Likewise, much remains to be done to improve clinical judgment research, practice, and training, including the very real need for the development of effective, empirically supported training programs.

# REFERENCES

Adams, K. M. (1974). *Automated clinical interpretation of the neuropsychological battery: An ability-based approach*. (Unpublished doctoral dissertation). Wayne State University, Detroit, Michigan.

Ægisdóttir, S., White, M. J., Spengler, P. M., Maugherman, A., Anderson, L. A., Cook, R. S., ... Rush, J. D. (2006). The Meta-Analysis of Clinical Judgment project: Fifty-six years of accumulated research on clinical versus statistical prediction. *The Counseling Psychologist, 34*, 341–382.

Alexakos, C. E. (1966). Predictive efficiency of two multivariate statistical techniques in comparison with clinical predictions. *Journal of Educational Psychology, 57*, 297–306.

American Psychological Association Presidential Task Force on Evidence-Based Practice (2006). Evidence based practice in psychology. *American Psychologist, 61*, 271–285.

Astrup, C. A. (1975). Predicted and observed outcome in followed-up functional psychosis. *Biological Psychiatry, 10*, 323–328.

Barron, F. (1953). Some test correlates of response to psychotherapy. *Journal of Consulting Psychology, 17*, 235–241.

Bell, I., & Mellor, D. (2009). Clinical judgements: Research and practice. *Australian Psychologist, 44*, 112–121.

Berven, N. L. (1985). Reliability and validity of standardized case management simulations. *Journal of Counseling Psychology, 32*, 397–409.

Berven, N. L., & Scofield, M. E. (1980). Evaluation of clinical problem-solving skills through standardized case-management simulations. *Journal of Counseling Psychology, 27*, 199–208.

Blenkner, M. (1954). Predictive factors in the initial interview in family casework. *Social Service Review, 28*, 65–73.

Blumetti, A. E. (1972). *A test of clinical versus actuarial prediction: A consideration of accuracy and cognitive functioning*. (Unpublished doctoral dissertation.) University of Florida, Gainesville.

Bloom, R. F., & Brundage, E. G. (1947). Prediction of success in elementary schools for enlisted personnel. In D. B. Stuit (Ed.), *Personnel research and test development in the Bureau of Naval Personnel* (pp. 263–261). Princeton, NJ: Princeton University Press.

Bobbitt, J. M., & Newman, S. H. (1944). Psychological activities at the United States Coast Guard Academy. *Psychological Bulletin, 41*, 568–579.

Bolton, B. F., Butler, A. J., & Wright, G. N. (1968). Clinical versus statistical prediction of client feasibility [Monograph VII]. *Wisconsin Studies in Vocational Rehabilitation*. University of Wisconsin Regional Rehabilitation Research Institute, Madison, WI.

Borden, H. G. (1928). Factors for predicting parole success. *Journal of American Institutes of Criminal Law and Criminology, 19*, 328–336.

Brehmer, B. (1980). In one word: Not from experience. *Acta Psychologica, 45*, 223–241.

Brodsky, S. L. (1999). *The expert expert witness: More maxims and guidelines for testifying in court*. Washington, DC: American Psychological Association.

Brodsky, S. L. (2005). Forensic evaluation and testimony. In G. P. Koocher, J. C. Norcross, & S. S. Hill (Eds.), *Psychologists' desk reference* (pp. 591–593). New York, NY: Oxford University Press.

Burgess, E. W. (1928). Factors determining success or failure on parole. In A. A. Bruce (Ed.), *The workings of the indeterminate sentence law and the parole system in Illinois* (pp. 221–234). Springfield, IL: Illinois Division of Pardons and Paroles.

Butcher, J. N. (2005). *User's guide for the Minnesota Clinical Report—4th edition*. Minneapolis, MN: Pearson Assessments.

Butcher, J. N., Dahlstrom, W. G., Graham, J. R., Tellegen, A., & Kaemmer, B. (1989). *Minnesota Multiphasic Personality Inventory–2 (MMPI-2): Manual for administration and scoring*. Minneapolis: University of Minnesota Press.

Carlin, A. S., & Hewitt, P. L. (1990). The discrimination of patient-generated and randomly generated MMPIs. *Journal of Personality Assessment, 54*, 24–29.

Centers for Disease Control and Prevention. (2010). *Web-based Injury Statistics Query and Reporting System*. Atlanta, GA: National Center for Injury Prevention and Control. Retrieved from www.cdc.gov/injury/wisqars/index.html

Cline, T. (1985). Clinical judgment in context: A review of situational factors in person perception during clinical interviews. *Journal of Child Psychology and Review, 26*, 369–380.

Cohen, J. (1988). *Statistical power analysis for the behavior sciences* (2nd ed.). Hillsdale, NJ: Erlbaum.

Conrad, H. S., & Satter, G. A. (1954). *The use of test scores and quality-classification ratings in predicting success in electrician's mates school. Project N-106: Research and development of the Navy's aptitude testing program*. Princeton, NJ: Research and Statistical Laboratory College Entrance Examination Board.

Cook, D. A., & Triola, M. M. (2009). Virtual patients: A critical literature review and proposed next steps. *Medical Education, 43*, 303–11.

Cooke, J. K. (1967a). Clinicians' decisions as a basis for deriving actuarial formulae. *Journal of Clinical Psychology, 23*, 232–233.

Cooke, J. K. (1967b). MMPI in actuarial diagnosis of psychological disturbance among college males. *Journal of Counseling Psychology, 14,* 474–477.

Cooper, H., & Hedges, L. V. (Eds.) (1994). *The handbook of research synthesis.* New York, NY: Russell Sage Foundation.

Crits-Christoph, P., Cooper, A., & Luborsky, L. (1988). The accuracy of therapist's interpretations and the outcome of dynamic psychotherapy. *Journal of Consulting and Clinical Psychology, 56,* 490–495.

Cummings, A. L., Hallberg, E. T., Martin, J., Slemon, A., & Hiebert, B. (1990). Implications of counselor conceptualizations for counselor education. *Counselor Education and Supervision, 30,* 120–134.

Dana, J., & Thomas, R. (2006). In defense of clinical judgment . . . and mechanical prediction. *Journal of Behavioral Decision Making, 19,* 413–428.

Danet, B. N. (1965). Prediction of mental illness in college students on the basis of "nonpsychiatric" MMPI profiles. *Journal of Counseling Psychology, 29,* 577–580.

Dawes, R. M. (1994). *House of cards: Psychology and psychotherapy built on myth.* New York, NY: Free Press.

Dawes, R. M. (2002). The ethics of using or not using statistical prediction rules in psychological practice and related consulting activities. *Philosophy of Science, 69,* S178–S184.

Dawes, R. M., Faust, D., & Meehl, P. E. (1989). Clinical versus actuarial judgment. *Science, 243,* 1668–1674.

Dawes, R. M., Faust, D., & Meehl, P. E. (1993). Statistical prediction versus clinical prediction: Improving what works. In G. Keren & G. Lewis (Eds.), *A handbook for data analysis in the behavioral sciences: Methodological issues* (pp. 351–367). Hillsdale, NJ: Erlbaum.

Dawes, R. M., Faust, D., & Meehl, P. E. (2002). Clinical versus actuarial prediction. In T. Gilovich, D. Griffin, & D. Kahneman (Eds.), *Heuristics and biases: The psychology of intuitive judgment* (pp. 716–729). New York, NY: Cambridge University Press.

Desmarais, S. L., Nicholls, T. L., Read, J. D., & Brink, J. (2010). Confidence and accuracy in assessments of short-term risks presented by forensic psychiatric patients. *Journal of Forensic Psychiatry & Psychology, 21,* 1–22.

Devries, A. G., & Shneidman, E. S. (1967). Multiple MMPI profiles of suicidal persons. *Psychological Reports, 21,* 401–405.

Dickerson, J. H. (1958). *The Biographical Inventory compared with clinical prediction of post counseling behavior of V.A. hospital counselors.* Unpublished doctoral dissertation. University of Minnesota, Minneapolis.

DiNardo, P. A. (1975). Social class and diagnostic suggestion as variables in clinical judgment. *Journal of Consulting and Clinical Psychology, 43,* 363–368.

Dumont, F. (1993). Inferential heuristics in clinical problem formulation: Selective review of their strengths and weaknesses. *Professional Psychology: Research and Practice, 24,* 196–205.

Dunlap, J. W., & Wantman, M. J. (1944). *An investigation of the interview as a technique for selecting aircraft pilots.* Washington, DC: Civil Aeronautics Administration, Report No. 33.

Dunham, H. W., & Meltzer, B. N. (1946). Predicting length of hospitalization of mental patients. *American Journal of Sociology, 52,* 123–131.

Einhorn, H. J. (1986). Accepting error to make less error. *Journal of Personality Assessment, 40,* 531–538.

Elliott, R. (2010). Psychotherapy change process research: Realizing the promise. *Psychotherapy Research, 20,* 123–135.

Elman, N. S., Illfelder-Kaye, J., & Robiner, W. N. (2005). Professional development: Training for professionalism as a foundation for competent practice in psychology. *Professional Psychology: Research and Practice, 36,* 367–375.

Ericsson, K. A., & Lehmann, A. C. (1996). Expert and exceptional performance: Evidence of maximal adaptation to task constraints. *Annual Review of Psychology, 47,* 273–305.

Ericsson, K. A., & Simon, H. A. (1994). *Protocol analysis: Verbal reports as data* (2nd ed.). Cambridge, MA: MIT Press.

Evenson, R. C., Altman, H., Sletten, I. W., & Cho, D. W. (1975). Accuracy of actuarial and clinical predictions for length of stay and unauthorized absence. *Diseases of the Nervous System, 36,* 250–252.

Eysenck, H. J. (1952). The effects of psychotherapy: An evaluation. *Journal of Consulting Psychology, 16,* 319–324.

Falvey, J. E. (2001). Clinical judgment in case conceptualization and treatment planning across mental health disciplines. *Journal of Counseling and Development, 79,* 292–303.

Falvey, J. E., Bray, T. E., & Hebert, D. J. (2005). Case conceptualization and treatment planning: Investigation of problem-solving and clinical judgment. *Journal of Mental Health Counseling, 27,* 348–372.

Falvey, J. E., & Hebert, D. J. (1992). Psychometric study of clinical treatment planning simulation (CTPS) for assessing clinical judgment. *Journal of Mental Health Counseling, 14,* 490–507.

Faust, D. (1986). Research on human judgment and its application to clinical practice. *Professional Psychology, Research, and Practice, 17,* 420–430.

Faust, D. (1991). What if we had really listened? Present reflections on altered pasts. In D. Cicchetti & W. M. Grove (Eds.), *Thinking clearly about psychology. Volume I: Matters of public interest* (pp. 185–217). Minneapolis: University of Minnesota Press.

Faust, D. (1994). Are there sufficient foundations for mental health experts to testify in court? No. In S. A. Kirk & S. D. Einbinder (Eds.), *Controversial issues in mental health* (pp. 196–201). Boston, MA: Allyn & Bacon.

Faust, D. (2003). Holistic thinking is not the whole story: Alternative or adjunct approaches for increasing the accuracy of legal evaluations. *Assessment, 10,* 428–411.

Faust, D., Guilmette, T. J., Hart, K., Arkes, H. R., Fishburne, F. J., & Davey, L. (1988). Neuropsychologists' training, experience, and judgment accuracy. *Archives of Clinical Neuropsychology, 3,* 145–163.

Faust, D., & Ziskin, J. (1988). The expert witness in psychology and psychiatry. *Science, 241,* 31–35.

Fero, D. D. (1975). *A lens model analysis of the effects of amount of information and mechanical decision making aid on clinical judgment and confidence.* (Unpublished doctoral dissertation). Bowling Green State University, Bowling Green, OH.

Frazier, P. A., Tix, A. P., & Barron, K. E. (2004). Testing moderator and mediator effects in counseling psychology research. *Journal of Counseling Psychology, 51,* 115–134.

Gambrill, E. (2005). *Critical thinking in clinical practice: Improving the accuracy of judgments and decisions about clients* (2nd ed.). Hoboken, NJ: Wiley.

Garb, H. N. (1989). Clinical judgment, clinical training, and professional experience. *Psychological Bulletin, 105,* 387–396.

Garb, H. N. (1992). The trained psychologist as expert witness. *Clinical Psychology Review, 12,* 451–467.

Garb, H. N. (1994). Toward a second generation of statistical prediction rules in psychodiagnosis and personality assessment. *Computers in Human Behavior, 10,* 377–394.

Garb, H. N. (1997). Race bias, social class bias, and gender bias in clinical judgment. *Clinical Psychology: Science and Practice, 4,* 99–120.

Garb, H. N. (1998). *Studying the clinician: Judgment research and psychological assessment.* Washington, DC: American Psychological Association.

Garb, H. N. (2003). Clinical judgment and mechanical prediction. In J. R. Graham & J. A. Naglieri (Eds.), *Handbook of psychology: Assessment psychology* (Vol. 10, pp. 27–42). Hoboken, NJ: Wiley.

Garb, H. N. (2005). Clinical judgment and decision-making. *Annual Review of Clinical Psychology, 1,* 67–89.

Garb, H. N., & Boyle, P. A. (2003). Understanding why some clinicians use pseudoscientific methods: Findings from research on clinical judgment. In S. O. Lilienfeld, S. J. Lynn, & J. M. Lohr (Eds.), *Science and pseudoscience in clinical psychology* (pp. 17–38). New York, NY: Guilford Press.

Garb, H. N., & Grove, W. M. (2005). On the merits of clinical judgment. *American Psychologist, 60,* 658–659.

Garcia, S. K. (1993). *Development of a methodology to differentiate between the physiological and psychological basis of panic attacks.* (Unpublished doctoral dissertation). St. Mary's University, San Antonio, TX.

Gardner, W., Lidz, C. W., Mulvay, E. P., & Shaw, E. C. (1996). Clinical versus actuarial predictions of violence in patients with mental illnesses. *Journal of Consulting and Clinical Psychology, 64,* 602–609.

Gaudette, M. D. (1992). *Clinical decision-making in neuropsychology: Bootstrapping the neuropsychologist utilizing Brunswik's lens model.* (Unpublished doctoral dissertation). Indiana University of Pennsylvania, Indiana, PA.

Giannetti, R. A., Johnson, J. H., Klinger, D. E., & Williams, T. A. (1978). Comparison of linear and configural MMPI diagnostic methods with an uncontaminated criterion. *Journal of Consulting and Clinical Psychology, 46,* 1046–1052.

Gigerenzer, G., & Brighton, H. (2009). Homo heuristics: Why biased minds make better inferences. *Topics in Cognitive Science, 1,* 107–143.

Gladwell, M. (2005). *Blink: The power of thinking without thinking.* New York, NY: Little, Brown.

Goldberg, L. R. (1965). Diagnosticians vs. diagnostic signs: The diagnosis of psychosis vs. neurosis from the MMPI. *Psychological Monographs: General and Applied, 79*(9), 1–27.

Goldberg, L. R. (1969). The search for configural relationships in personality assessment: The diagnosis of psychosis vs. neurosis from the MMPI. *Multivariate Behavioral Research, 4,* 523–536.

Goldberg, L. R. (1970). Man versus model of man: A rationale, plus some evidence, for a method of improving clinical inferences. *Psychological Bulletin, 73,* 422–432.

Goldberg, L. R. (1972). Man versus mean: The exploitation of group profiles for the construction of diagnostic classification systems. *Journal of Abnormal Psychology, 79,* 121–131.

Goldberg, L. R., Faust, D., Kleinmuntz, B., & Dawes, R. M. (1991). Clinical versus statistical prediction. In D. Cicchetti & W. Grove (Eds.), *Thinking clearly about psychology: Essay in honor of Paul E. Meehl, Vol. 1: Matters of public interest* (pp. 173–264). Minneapolis: University of Minnesota Press.

Goldstein, R. B., Black, D. W., Nasrallah, M. A., & Winokur, G. (1991). The prediction of suicide. *Archives of General Psychiatry, 48,* 418–422.

Goldstein, S. G., Deysach, R. E., & Kleinknecht, R. A. (1973). Effect of experience and amount of information on identification of cerebral impairment. *Journal of Consulting and Clinical Psychology, 41,* 30–34.

Goldstein, W. M., & Hogarth, R. M. (1997). Judgment and decision research: Some historical context. In W. M. Goldstein & R. M. Hogarth (Eds.), *Research on judgment and decision making* (pp. 3–65). Cambridge, UK: Cambridge University Press.

Gonzach, Y., Kluger, A. N., & Klayman, N. (2000). Making decisions from an interview: Expert measurement and mechanical combination. *Personnel Psychology, 53,* 1–20.

Goodson, J. H., & King, G. D. (1976). A clinical and actuarial study on the validity of the Goldberg index for the MMPI. *Journal of Clinical Psychology, 32,* 328–335.

Grebstein, L. C. (1963). Relative accuracy of actuarial prediction, experienced clinicians, and graduate students in a clinical judgment task. *Journal of Consulting Psychology, 27,* 127–132.

Greenberg, L. S., & Dompierre, L. M. (1981). Specific effects of Gestalt two-chair dialogue on intrapsychic conflict in counseling. *Journal of Counseling Psychology, 28,* 288–294.

Grove, W. M. (2001, Fall). Recommendations of the Division 12 Task Force: "Assessment for the century: A model curriculum." *Clinical Science, 8.*

Grove, W. M., & Meehl, P. E. (1996). Comparative efficiency of informal (subjective, impressionistic) and formal (mechanical, algorithmic) prediction procedures: The clinical-statistical controversy. *Psychology, Public Policy, and Law, 2,* 293–323.

Grove, W. M., Zald, D. H., Lebow, B. S., Snitz, B. E., & Nelson, C. (2000). Clinical vs. mechanical prediction: A meta-analysis. *Psychological Assessment, 12,* 19–30.

Gustafson, D. H., Greist, J. H., Stauss, F. F., Erdman, H., & Laughren, T. (1977). A probabilistic system for identifying suicide attempters. *Computers and Biomedical Research, 10,* 83–89.

Halbower, C. C. (1955). *A comparison of actuarial versus clinical prediction to classes discriminated by the Minnesota Multiphasic Personality Inventory.* (Unpublished doctoral dissertation). University of Minnesota, Minneapolis.

Hall, G. C. N. (1988). Criminal behavior as a function of clinical and actuarial variables in a sexual offender population. *Journal of Consulting and Clinical Psychology, 56,* 773–775.

Hamlin, R. (1934). Predictability of institutional adjustment of reformatory inmates. *Journal of Juvenile Research, 18,* 179–184.

Harding, T. P. (2004). Psychiatric disability and clinical decision-making: The impact of judgment error and bias. *Clinical Psychology Review, 24,* 707–729.

Harding, T. P. (2007). Clinical decision-making: How prepared are we? *Training and Education in Professional Psychology, 1,* 95–104.

Haverkamp, B. E. (1993). Confirmatory bias in hypothesis testing for client-identified and counselor-generated hypotheses. *Journal of Counseling Psychology, 40,* 303–315.

Hatfield, D., McCullough, L., Frantz, S. H. B., & Krieger, K. (2010). Do we know when our clients get worse? An investigation of therapists' ability to detect negative client change. *Clinical Psychology and Psychotherapy, 17,* 25–32.

Heaton, R. K., Grant, I., Anthony, W. Z., & Lehman, R. A. (1981). A comparison of clinical and automated interpretation of the Halstead-Reitan battery. *Journal of Clinical Neuropsychology, 3,* 121–141.

Hilton, N. Z., Harris, G. T., & Rice, M. E. (2006). Sixty-six years of research on the clinical versus actuarial prediction of violence. *The Counseling Psychologist, 34,* 400–409.

Holland, T. R., Holt, N., Levi, M., & Beckett, G. E. (1983). Comparison and combination of clinical and statistical predictions of recidivism among adult offenders. *Journal of Applied Psychology, 68,* 203–211.

Holloway, E. L., & Wolleat, P. L. (1980). Relationship of counselor conceptual level to clinical hypothesis formation. *Journal of Counseling Psychology, 27,* 539–545.

Holt, R. R. (1958). Clinical and statistical prediction: A reformulation and some new data. *Journal of Abnormal and Social Psychology, 56,* 1–12.

Holt, R. R. (1970). Yet another look at clinical and statistical prediction: Or, is clinical psychology worthwhile? *American Psychologist, 25,* 337–349.

Hovey, H. B., & Stauffacher, J. C. (1953). Intuitive versus objective prediction from a test. *Journal of Clinical Psychology, 9,* 341–351.

Hunt, M. (1997). *How science takes stock: The story of meta-analysis.* New York, NY: Russell Sage Foundation.

Johnston, R., & McNeal, B. F. (1967). Statistical versus clinical prediction: Length of neuropsychiatric hospital stay. *Journal of Abnormal Psychology, 72,* 335–340.

Kahneman, D., Slovic, P., & Tversky, A. (1982). *Judgment under uncertainty: Heuristics and biases.* London, UK: Cambridge Press.

Kaplan, R. L. (1962). *A comparison of actuarial and clinical predictions of improvement in psychotherapy.* (Unpublished doctoral dissertation). University of California, Los Angeles.

Katsikopoulos, K. V., Pachur, T., Machery, E., & Wallin, A. (2008). From Meehl to fast and frugal heuristics (and back): New insights into how to bridge the clinical-actuarial divide. *Theory and Psychology, 18,* 443–464.

Kazdin, A. E. (2008). Evidence-based treatment and practice: New opportunities to bridge clinical research and practice, enhance the knowledge base, and improve patient care. *American Psychologist, 63,* 146–159.

Kelly, E. L., & Fiske, D. W. (1950). The prediction of success in the VA training program in clinical psychology. *American Psychologist, 5,* 395–406.

Klehr, R. (1949). Clinical intuition and test scores as a basis for diagnosis. *Journal of Consulting Psychology, 13,* 34–38.

Kleinmuntz, B. (1967). Sign and seer: Another example. *Journal of Abnormal Psychology, 72,* 163–165.

Kleinmuntz, B. (1990). Why we still use our heads instead of formulas: Toward an integrative approach. *Psychological Bulletin, 107,* 296–310.

Klinger, E., & Roth, I. (1965). Diagnosis of schizophrenia by Rorschach patterns. *Journal of Projective Techniques and Personality Assessment, 29,* 323–335.

Kozol, H. L., Boucher, R. J., & Garafolo, R. F. (1972). The diagnosis and treatment of dangerousness. *Crime and Delinquency, 12,* 371–392.

Kurpius, D. J., Benjamin, D., & Morran, D. K. (1985). Effect of teaching a cognitive strategy on counselor trainee internal dialogue and clinical hypothesis formulation. *Journal of Counseling Psychology, 32,* 262–271.

Kivlighan, D. M. Jr., & Quigley, S. T. (1991). Dimensions used by experienced and novice group therapists to conceptualize group processes. *Journal of Counseling Psychology, 38,* 415–423.

Lambert, M. J. (2010). *Prevention of treatment failure: The use of measuring, monitoring, and feedback in clinical practice.* Washington, DC: American Psychological Association.

Lambert, M. J., Hansen, N. B., & Finch, A. E. (2001). Patient-focused research: Using patient outcome data to enhance treatment effects. *Journal of Consulting and Clinical Psychology, 69,* 159–172.

Lambert, M. J., Hansen, N. B., Umphress, V., Lunnen, K., Okiishi, J., Burlingame, G., . . . Reisinger, C. (1996). *Administration and scoring manual for the Outcome Questionnaire (OQ 45.2).* Wilmington, DE: American Professional Credentialing Services.

Lambert, M. J., & Ogles, B. M. (2004). The efficacy and effectiveness of psychotherapy. In M. J. Lambert (Ed.), *Bergin and Garfield's handbook of psychotherapy and behavior change* (5th ed., pp. 139–153). Hoboken, NJ: Wiley.

Lambert, L., & Wertheimer, M. (1988). Is diagnostic ability related to relevant training and experience? *Professional Psychology: Research and Practice, 19,* 50–52.

Lefkowitz, M. B. (1973). *Statistical and clinical approaches to the identification of couples at risk in marriage.* (Unpublished doctoral dissertation). University of Florida, Gainesville.

Leli, D. A., & Filskov, S. B. (1981). Clinical-actuarial detection and description of brain impairment with the W-B Form 1. *Journal of Clinical Psychology, 37,* 623–629.

Leli, D. A., & Filskov, S. B. (1984). Clinical detection of intellectual deterioration associated with brain damage. *Journal of Clinical Psychology, 40,* 1435–1441.

Lemerond, J. N. (1977). *Suicide prediction for psychiatric patients: A comparison of the MMPI and clinical judgments.* (Unpublished doctoral dissertation). Marquette University, Madison, WI.

Lewis, E. C., & MacKinney, A. C. (1961). Counselor vs. statistical prediction of job satisfaction in engineering. *Journal of Counseling Psychology, 8,* 224–230.

Lichtenberg, J. W. (1997). Expertise in counseling psychology: A concept in search of support. *Educational Psychology Review, 9,* 221–238.

Lichtenberg, J. W. (2009). Effects of experience on judgment accuracy. *The Counseling Psychologist, 37,* 410–415.

Lilienfeld, S. O., Lynn, S. J., & Lohr, J. M. (Eds.). (2003). *Science and pseudoscience in clinical psychology* (pp. 461–465). New York, NY: Guilford Press.

Lindsey, G. R. (1965). Seer versus sign. *Journal of Experimental Research in Personality, 1,* 17–26.

Litwack, T. R. (2001). Actuarial versus clinical assessments of dangerousness. *Psychology, Public Policy, and Law, 7,* 409–443.

Loganbill, C., Hardy, E., & Delworth, U. (1982). Supervision: A conceptual model. *The Counseling Psychologist, 10*(11), 3–42.

Lopez, S. R. (1989). Patient variable biases in clinical judgment: Conceptual overview and methodological considerations. *Psychological Bulletin, 106,* 184–203.

Lyle, O., & Quast, W. (1976). The Bender Gestalt: Use of clinical judgment versus recall scores in prediction of Huntington's disease. *Journal of Consulting and Clinical Psychology, 44,* 229–232.

Marchese, M. C. (1992). Clinical versus actuarial prediction: A review of the literature. *Perceptual and Motor Skills, 75,* 583–594.

Martin, J., Slemon, A. G., Hiebert, B., Hallberg, E. T., & Cummings, A. L. (1989). Conceptualizations of novice and experienced counselors. *Journal of Counseling Psychology, 36,* 395–400.

Martindale, D. A. (2005). Confirmatory bias and confirmatory distortion. *Journal of Child Custody: Research, Issues, and Practices, 2,* 31–48.

Mayfield, W. A., Kardash, C. M., & Kivlighan, D. M. (1999). Differences in experienced and novice counselors' knowledge structures about clients: Implications for case conceptualization. *Journal of Counseling Psychology, 46,* 504–514.

McHugh, R. B., & Apostolakos, P. C. (1959). Methodology for the comparison of clinical with actuarial predictions. *Psychological Bulletin, 56,* 301–309.

Meehl, P. E. (1954). *Clinical vs. statistical prediction: A theoretical analysis and a review of the evidence.* Minneapolis: University of Minnesota Press.

Meehl, P. E. (1957). When shall we use our heads instead of the formula? *Journal of Counseling Psychology, 4,* 268–273.

Meehl, P. E. (1959). A comparison of clinicians with five statistical methods of identifying psychotic MMPI profiles. *Journal of Counseling Psychology, 6,* 102–109.

Meehl, P. E. (1965). Seer over sign: The first good example. *Journal of Experimental Research in Personality, 1,* 27–32.

Meehl, P. E. (1973). When shall we use our heads instead of the formula? In P. E. Meehl, *Psychodiagnostics: Selected papers* (pp. 81–89). Minneapolis: University of Minnesota Press.

Meehl, P. E. (1986). Causes and effects of my disturbing little book. *Journal of Personality Assessment, 50,* 370–375.

Meehl, P. E. (1996). Preface to the 1996 printing. In P. E. Meehl, *Clinical versus statistical prediction: A theoretical analysis and a review of the evidence* (pp. v–xii). Minneapolis: University of Minnesota Press.

Meehl, P. E. (1997). Credentialed persons, credentialed knowledge. *Clinical Psychology: Science and Practice, 4,* 91–98.

Meier, S. T. (1999). Training the practitioner-scientist: Bridging case conceptualization, assessment, and intervention. *The Counseling Psychologist, 27*(6), 846–869.

Melton, R. S. (1952). *A comparison of clinical and actuarial methods of prediction with an assessment of the relative accuracy of different clinicians.* (Unpublished doctoral dissertation). University of Minnesota, Minneapolis.

Meyer, J. J., Finn, S. E., Eyde, L. D., Kay, G. G., Kubiszyn, T. W., Moreland, K. L., . . . Dies, R. R. (1998). *Benefits and costs of psychological assessment in healthcare delivery: Report of the Board of Professional Affairs Psychological Assessment Work Group* (Part I). Washington, DC: American Psychological Association.

Meyer, K. (1973). *The effect of training in the accuracy and appropriateness of clinical judgment.* (Unpublished doctoral dissertation). Adelphi University, Garden City, NY.

Mullen, J. M., & Reinehr, R. C. (1982). Predicting dangerousness of maximum security forensic mental patients. *Journal of Psychiatry and Law, 10,* 223–231.

Mumma, G. H. (2001). Increasing accuracy in clinical decision-making: Toward an integration of nomothetic-aggregate and intraindividual-idiographic approaches. *The Behavior Therapist, 24,* 7–85.

Myers, D. (2008). Clinical intuition. In S. O. Lilienfeld, J. Ruscio, & S. J. Lynn (Eds.), *Navigating the mindfield: A user's guide to distinguishing science from pseudoscience in mental health* (pp. 159–174). Amherst, NY: Prometheus Books

Miller, D. E., Kunce, J. T., & Getsinger, S. H. (1972). Prediction of job success for clients with hearing loss. *Rehabilitation Counseling Bulletin, 16,* 21–29.

Moxley, A. W. (1973). Clinical judgment. The effects of statistical information. *Journal of Personality Assessment, 37,* 86–91.

Nathan, P. E., & Gorman, J. M. (Eds.). (2002). *A guide to treatments that work* (2nd ed.). New York, NY: Oxford University Press.

Nisbett, R. E., Krantz, D. H., Jepson, C., & Kunda, Z. (1983). The use of statistical heuristics in everyday inductive reasoning. *Psychological Review, 90,* 339–363.

Nisbett, R. E., & Ross, L. (1980). *Human inference: Strategies and shortcomings of social judgment.* Englewood Cliffs, NJ: Prentice Hall.

Norcross, J. C. (Ed.). (2002). *Psychotherapy relationships that work: Therapist contributions and responsiveness to patient needs.* New York, NY: Oxford University Press.

Norcross, J. C. (Ed.) (2011). *Psychotherapy relationships that work* (2nd ed.). New York, NY: Oxford University Press.

Norcross, J. C., Beutler, L. E., & Levant, R. F. (2006). *Evidence-based practices in mental health: Debate and dialogue on the fundamental questions.* Washington, DC: American Psychological Association.

Norcross, J. C., & Wampold, B. E. (2011). What works for whom: Tailoring psychotherapy to the person. *Journal of Clinical Psychology: In Session, 67,* 127–132.

Nurcombe, B., & Fitzhenry-Coor, I. (1987). Diagnostic reasoning and treatment planning: I. Diagnosis. *Australian and New Zealand Journal of Psychiatry, 21,* 477–499.

O'Byrne, K. R., & Goodyear, R. K. (1997). Client assessment by novice and expert psychologists: A comparison of strategies. *Educational Psychology Review, 9,* 267–278.

Orlinsky, D. E., & Rønnestad, M. H. (2005). *How psychotherapists develop: A study of therapeutic work and professional growth.* Washington, DC: American Psychological Association.

Oskamp, S. (1962). The relationship of clinical experience and training methods to several criteria of clinical prediction. *Psychological Monographs: General and Applied, 76,* 1–27.

Oxman, T. E., Rosenberg, S. D., Schnurr, P. P., & Tucker, G. J. (1988). Diagnostic classification through content analysis of patients' speech. *American Journal of Psychiatry, 145,* 464–468.

Pepinsky, H. B., & Pepinsky, N. (1954). *Counseling theory and practice.* New York, NY: Ronald Press.

Perez, F. I. (1976). Behavioral analysis of clinical judgment. *Perceptual and Motor Skills, 43,* 711–718.

Peterson, J., Skeem, J., & Manchak, S. (2011). If you want to know, consider asking: How likely is it that patients will hurt themselves in the future? *Psychological Assessment, 23,* 626–634.

Pfeiffer, A. M., Whelan, J. P., & Martin, J. M. (2000). Decision-making bias in psychotherapy: Effects of hypothesis source and accountability. *Journal of Counseling Psychology, 47,* 429–436.

Pilipis, L. A. (2010). *Meta-analysis of the relation between mental health professionals' experience and judgment accuracy: Review of clinical judgment research from 1997 to 2010.* (Unpublished doctoral dissertation). Ball State University, Muncie, IN.

Pokorny, A. D. (1983). Prediction of suicide in psychiatric patients: Report of a prospective study. *Archives of General Psychiatry, 40,* 249–257.

Pokorny, A. D. (1993). Suicide prediction revisited. *Suicide and Life-Threatening Behavior, 23,* 1–10.

Popovics, A. J. (1983). Predictive validities of clinical and actuarial scores of the Gesell Incomplete Man Test. *Perceptual and Motor Skills, 56,* 864–866.

Potts, M. K., Burnam, M. A., & Wells, K. B. (1991). Gender differences in depression detection: A comparison of clinician diagnosis and standardized assessment. *Psychological Assessment, 3,* 609–615.

Quinsey, V. L., Harris, G. T., Rice, M. E., & Cormier, C. A. (1998). *Violent offenders: Appraising and managing risk.* Washington, DC: American Psychological Association.

Rabinowitz, J. (1993). Diagnostic reasoning and reliability: A review of the literature and a model of decision making. *Journal of Mind and Behavior, 14,* 297–316.

Rerick, K. E. (1999). *Improving counselors' attitudes and clinical judgement towards dual diagnosis.* (Unpublished doctoral dissertation). University of South Dakota, Vermillion.

Ridley, C. R., & Shaw-Ridley, M. (2009). Clinical judgment accuracy: From meta-analysis to metatheory. *The Counseling Psychologist, 37,* 400–409.

Rosenthal, R. (1991). *Meta-analytic procedures for social research* (rev. ed). Newbury Park, CA: Sage.

Rosenthal, R., & Rubin, D. (1982). A simple general purpose display of magnitude of experimental effects. *Journal of Educational Psychology, 74,* 166–169.

Rouse, S. V., Butcher, J. N., & Miller, K. B. (1999). Assessment of substance abuse in psychotherapy clients: The effectiveness of the MMPI-2 substance abuse scales. *Psychological Assessment, 11,* 101–107.

Ruscio, J. (2007). The clinician as subject: Practitioners are prone to the same judgment errors as everyone else. In S. O. Lilienfeld & W. T. O'Donohue (Eds.), *The great ideas of clinical science: 17 principles that every mental health professional should understand* (pp. 29–47). New York, NY: Routledge/Taylor & Francis Group.

Russell, E. W. (1995). The accuracy of automated and clinical detection of brain damage and lateralization on neuropsychology. *Neuropsychology Review, 5,* 1–68.

Sandifer, M. G., Hordern, A., & Green, L. M. (1970). The psychiatric interview: The impact of the first three minutes. *American Journal of Psychiatry, 127,* 968–973.

Sarbin, T. L. (1942). A contribution to the study of actuarial and individual methods of prediction. *American Journal of Sociology, 48,* 593–602.

Sawyer, J. (1966). Measurement and prediction, clinical and statistical. *Psychological Bulletin, 66,* 178–200.

Schalock, R., & Luckasson, R. (2005). *Clinical judgment.* Washington, DC: American Association on Mental Retardation.

Schiedt, R. (1936). *Ein beitrag zum problem der rückfallsprognose.* (Unpublished doctoral dissertation). Münchner-Zeitungs-Verlag, Munich.

Schmidt, F. L., & Hunter, J. E. (1996). Measurement error in psychological research: Lessons from 26 research scenarios. *Psychological Methods, 1,* 199–223.

Schneider, A. J. N., Lagrone, C. W., Glueck, E. T., & Glueck, S. (1944). Prediction of behavior of civilian delinquents in the armed forces. *Mental Hygiene, 28,* 456–475.

Scurich, N., & John, R. S. (2012). Prescriptive approaches to communicating the risk of violence in actuarial assessment. *Psychology, Public Policy, and Law, 18,* 50–78.

Seligman, M. E. P. (1995). The effectiveness of psychotherapy: The Consumer Reports study. *American Psychologist, 50,* 965–974.

Sepejak, D., Menzies, R. J., Webster, C. D., & Jensen, F. A. S. (1983). Clinical predictions of dangerousness: Two-year follow-up of 406 pre-trial forensic cases. *Bulletin of the American Academy of Psychiatry and the Law, 11,* 171–181.

Shaffer, J. W., Perlin, S., Schmidt, C. W., & Stephens, J. H. (1974). The prediction of suicide in schizophrenia. *Journal of Nervous and Mental Disease, 150,* 349–355.

Shagoury, P., & Satz, P. (1969). The effect of statistical information on clinical prediction. *Proceedings of the 77th Annual Convention of the American Psychological Association, 4,* 517–518.

Shanteau, J. (1988). Psychological characteristics and strategies of expert decision makers. *Acta Psychologica, 68,* 203–215.

Shimokawa, K., Lambert, M. J., & Smart, D. W. (2010). Enhancing treatment outcome of patients at risk of treatment failure: Meta-analytic and mega-analytic review of psychotherapy quality assurance system. *Journal of Consulting and Clinical Psychology, 78,* 298–311.

Sines, J. O. (1970). Actuarial versus clinical prediction in psychopathology. *British Journal of Psychiatry, 116,* 129–144.

Skovholt, T. M., Rønnestad, M. H., & Jennings, L. (1997). Searching for expertise in counseling, psychotherapy, and professional psychology. *Educational Psychology Review, 9,* 361–369.

Smith, J. D., & Agate, J. (2002). Solutions for overconfidence: Evaluation of an instructional module for counselor trainees. *Counselor Education & Supervision, 44,* 31–43.

Smith, J. D., & Dumont, F. (2002). Confidence in psychodiagnosis: What makes us so sure? *Clinical Psychology and Psychotherapy, 9,* 292–298.

Smith, M. L., & Glass, G. V. (1977). Meta-analysis of psychotherapy outcome studies. *American Psychologist, 32,* 752–760.

Smith, M. L., Glass, G. V., & Miller, T. L. (1980). *Benefits of psychotherapy.* Baltimore, MD: Johns Hopkins University Press.

Spengler, P. M. (1998). Multicultural assessment and a scientist-practitioner model of psychological assessment. *The Counseling Psychologist, 26,* 930–938.

Spengler, P. M., & Strohmer, D. C. (2001, August). *Empirical analyses of a scientist-practitioner model of assessment.* Paper presented at the annual meeting of the American Psychological Association, San Francisco, CA.

Spengler, P. M., Strohmer, D. M., Dixon, D. N., & Shivy, V. A. (1995). A scientist-practitioner model of psychological assessment: Implications for training, practice, and research. *The Counseling Psychologist, 23,* 506–534.

Spengler, P. M., White, M. J., Ægisdóttir, S., Maugherman, A., Anderson, L. A., Cook, R. S., . . . Rush, J. D. (2009). The Meta-Analysis of Clinical Judgment project: Effects of experience on judgment accuracy. *The Counseling Psychologist, 37*(3), 350–399.

Spengler, P. M., White, M. J., Maugherman, A., Ægisdóttir, S., Anderson, L., Rush, J., & Lampropoulos, G. K. (2000, August). *Mental health clinical judgment meta-analytic project: Summary 1970–1996.* Paper presented at the meeting of the American Psychological Association, Washington, DC.

Stein, L. A. R., Graham, J. R., Ben-Porath, Y. S., & McNulty, J. L. (1999). Using the MMPI-2 to detect substance abuse in an outpatient mental health setting. *Psychological Assessment, 11,* 94–100.

Stoltenberg, C. D., McNeill, B. W., & Delworth, U. (1998). *IDM supervision: An integrated developmental model for supervising counselors and therapists.* San Francisco: Jossey-Bass.

Stricker, G. (1967). Actuarial, naïve clinical, and sophisticated clinical prediction of pathology from figure drawings. *Journal of Consulting Psychology, 31,* 492–494.

Stricker, G., & Trieweiler, S. J. (1995). The local clinical scientist: A bridge between science and practice. *American Psychologist, 50,* 995–1002.

Strohmer, D. C., & Shivy, V. A. (1994). Bias in counselor hypothesis testing: Testing the robustness of counselor confirmatory bias. *Journal of Counseling and Development, 73,* 191–197.

Strohmer, D. C., Shivy, V. A., & Chiodo, A. L. (1990). Information processing strategies in counselor hypothesis testing: The role of selective memory and expectancy. *Journal of Counseling Psychology, 37,* 465–472.

Swets, J. A., Dawes, R. M., & Monahan, J. (2000). Psychological science can improve diagnostic decisions. *Psychological Sciences in the Public Interest* (Suppl. to *Psychological Science*), *1*(1).

Szuko, J. J., & Kleinmuntz, B. (1981). Statistical versus clinical lie detection. *American Psychologist, 36,* 488–496.

Taulbee, E. S., & Sisson, B. D. (1957). Configurational analysis of MMPI profiles of psychiatric groups. *Journal of Consulting Psychology, 21,* 413–417.

Thompson, R. E. (1952). A validation of the Glueck Social Prediction Scale for proneness to delinquency. *Journal of Criminal Law, Criminology, and Police Science, 43,* 451–470.

Tracey, T. J., & Rounds, J. (1999). Inference and attribution errors in test interpretation. In J. W. Lightenberg & R. K. Goodyear (Eds.), *Scientist practitioner perspectives on test interpretation* (pp. 113–131). Needham Heights, MA: Allyn & Bacon.

Turk, C. T., & Salovey, P. (1985). Cognitive structures, cognitive processes, and cognitivebehavior modification: II. Judgments and inferences of the clinician. *Cognitive Therapy and Research, 9,* 19–33.

Tversky, A., & Kahneman, D. (1974). Judgment under uncertainty: Heuristics and biases. *Science, 185,* 1124–1131.

Vrieze, S. I., & Grove, W. M. (2009). Survey on the use of clinical and mechanical prediction models in clinical psychology. *Professional Psychology: Research and Practice, 40,* 525–531.

Walsh, W. B., & Savickas, M. L. (Eds.) (2005). *Handbook of vocational psychology: Theory, research, and practice* (3rd ed.). Mahwah, NJ: Erlbaum.

Walters, G. D., White, T. W., & Greene, R. L. (1988). The use of MMPI to identify malingering and exaggeration of psychiatric symptomatology in male prison inmates. *Journal of Consulting and Clinical Psychology, 1,* 111–117.

Watley, D. J. (1966). Counselor variability in making accurate predictions. *Journal of Counseling Psychology, 13,* 53–62.

Watley, D. J., & Vance, F. L. (1964). *Clinical versus actuarial prediction of college achievement and leadership activity.* (Unpublished doctoral dissertation). University of Minnesota, Minneapolis.

Webb, S. C., Hultgen, D. D., & Craddick, R. A. (1977). Predicting occupational choice by clinical and statistical methods. *Journal of Counseling Psychology, 24,* 98–110.

Webster, C. D., & Cox, D. (1997). Integration of nomothetic and ideographic positions in risk assessment: Implications for practice and the education of psychologists and other mental health professionals. *American Psychologist, 52,* 1245–1246.

Wedding, D. (1983). Clinical and statistical prediction in neuropsychology. *Clinical Neuropsychology, 5,* 49–55.

Wedding, D. (1991). Clinical judgment in forensic neuropsychology: A comment on the risks of claiming more than can be delivered. *Neuropsychology Review, 2,* 233–239.

Wedding, D., & Faust, D. (1989). Clinical judgment and decision making in neuropsychology. *Archives of Clinical Neuropsychology, 4,* 233–265.

Weinberg, G. H. (1957). *Clinical versus statistical prediction with a method of evaluating a clinical tool*. (Unpublished doctoral dissertation). Columbia University, New York.

Werner, P. D., Rose, T. L., Yesavage, J. A., & Seeman, K. (1984). Psychiatrists' judgment of dangerousness in patients on an acute care unit. *American Journal of Psychiatry, 141,* 263–266.

Westen, D., & Weinberger, J. (2004). When clinical description becomes statistical prediction. *American Psychologist, 59,* 595–613.

Westen, D., & Weinberger, J. (2005). In praise of clinical judgment: Meehl's forgotten legacy. *Journal of Clinical Psychology, 61,* 1257–1276.

White, M. J., Nichols, C. N., Cook, R. S., Spengler, P. M., Walker, B. S., & Look, K. K. (1995). Diagnostic overshadowing and mental retardation: A meta-analysis. *American Journal on Mental Retardation, 100,* 293–298.

Widiger, T. A., & Spitzer, R. L. (1991). Sex bias in the diagnosis of personality disorders: Conceptual and methodological issues. *Clinical Psychology Review, 11,* 1–22.

Wiggins, J. S. (1980). *Personality and prediction: Principles of personality assessment*. Reading, MA: Addison-Wesley.

Wiggins, J. S. (1981). Clinical and statistical prediction: Where are we and where do we go from here? *Clinical Psychology Review, 1,* 3–18.

Wiggins, N., & Kohen, E. S. (1971). Man versus model of man revisited: The forecasting of graduate school success. *Journal of Personality and Social Psychology, 19,* 100–106.

Wirt, R. D. (1956). Actuarial prediction. *Journal of Consulting Psychology, 20,* 123–124.

Wittman, M. P. (1941). A scale for measuring prognosis in schizophrenic patients. *The Elgin Papers, 4,* 20–33.

Wittman, M. P., & Steinberg, L. (1944). Follow-up of an objective evaluation of prognosis in dementia praecox and manic-depressive psychosis. *The Elgin Papers, 5,* 216–227.

Zalewski, C. E., & Gottesman, I. I. (1991). (Hu)man versus mean revisited: MMPI group data and psychiatric diagnosis. *Journal of Abnormal Psychology, 100,* 562–568.

Zeldow, P. (2009). In defense of clinical judgment, credentialed clinicians, and reflective practice. *Psychotherapy Theory, Research, Practice, Training, 46,* 1–10.

Ziskin, J. (1995). *Coping with psychiatric and psychological testimony* (5th ed., Vols. 1 3). Los Angeles, CA: Law and Psychology Press.

# CHAPTER 3

# Fundamental Psychometric Considerations in Assessment

JOHN D. WASSERMAN AND BRUCE A. BRACKEN

"Whenever you can, count!" advised Sir Francis Galton, according to his biographer Karl Pearson (1924, p. 340), who reported that Galton seldom went for a walk or attended a lecture without counting something. The father of contemporary psychometrics, Galton is credited with applying the normal probability distribution to the study of individual differences and initiating the first large-scale efforts to measure physical, sensory, motor, and higher-order mental characteristics in his London Anthropometric Laboratories. Moreover, Galton is recognized for his discovery of the phenomena of regression, his conceptualization of the covariance between variables as a basis for understanding bivariate relations (with the product-moment correlation coefficient introduced by Pearson), and his execution of the first multivariate analyses (e.g., Stigler, 1999, 2010). Galton quantified everything from fingerprint characteristics, to variations in weather conditions, to the number of brush strokes taken by artists while he sat for portraits. At scientific meetings, he was known to count the number of times per minute that members of the audience fidgeted, computing an average and deducing that the frequency of fidgeting was inversely associated with level of audience interest in the presentation.

Of course, the challenge in contemporary assessment is to know what to measure, how to measure it, and when the measurements are meaningful. In a definition that still remains appropriate, Galton (1879) defined *psychometry* as "the art of imposing measurement and number upon operations of the mind" (p. 149). Derived from

the Greek *psyche* (ψυχή, meaning "soul") and *metro* (μετρώ, meaning "measure"), psychometry may be best considered an evolving set of scientific rules for the development and application of psychological tests.

Construction of psychological tests is guided by psychometric theories in the midst of a paradigm shift. Classical test theory (CTT), epitomized by Gulliksen's (1950) *Theory of Mental Tests,* dominated psychological test development through the latter two-thirds of the 20th century. Item response theory (IRT), beginning with the work of Rasch (1960) and Lord and Novick's (1968) *Statistical Theories of Mental Test Scores,* is growing in influence and use, with calls by its advocates for a "velvet revolution" in psychological measurement (Borsboom, 2006b, p. 467). Embretson (2004) summarized the current status of the paradigm shift from CTT to IRT: "[A]t the end of the 20th century, the impact of IRT on ability testing was still limited. Only a few large-scale tests had applied IRT by the late 1990s. The majority of psychological tests still were based on classical test theory that was developed early in the 20th century" (p. 8).

This chapter describes the most salient psychometric characteristics of psychological tests, incorporating elements from both CTT and IRT. It provides guidelines for the evaluation of test technical adequacy. Although psychometricians frequently warn that such guidelines are oversimplified, we consider them to be rules of thumb that have practical value for test consumers using an applied handbook. The guidelines may be applied to a wide array of tests, including those in the domains of academic achievement, adaptive behavior, cognitive-intellectual abilities, neuropsychological functions, personality and psychopathology, and personnel selection. The guidelines are based in part on conceptual extensions of the *Standards for Educational and Psychological Testing* (1999; currently undergoing revision) and recommendations from such authorities as Anastasi and Urbina (1997; see also Urbina, 2004); Bracken (1987); Cattell (1986); Cohen (1992); Neuendorf (2002); Nunnally & Bernstein (1994); Salvia, Ysseldyke, & Bolt (2010); and Streiner (2003).

## PSYCHOMETRIC THEORIES

The psychometric characteristics of mental tests are generally derived from one or both of the two leading theoretical approaches to test construction: CTT and IRT. Although it is common for psychometricians to contrast these two approaches and advocate for more contemporary techniques (e.g., Embretson, 1995; Embretson & Hershberger, 1999), most contemporary test developers in practicality use elements from both approaches in a complementary manner (e.g., Nunnally & Bernstein, 1994). For many challenges in test development, CTT and IRT findings may be largely interchangeable; Fan (1998) reported empirical findings indicating that person and item statistics derived from both theories are functionally comparable.

## CLASSICAL TEST THEORY

CTT traces its origins to the procedures pioneered by Galton, Pearson, C. E. Spearman, and E. L. Thorndike, and is usually defined by Gulliksen's (1950) classic book. CTT has shaped contemporary investigations of test score reliability, validity, and fairness as well as the widespread use of statistical techniques such as factor analysis.

At its heart, CTT is based on the assumption that an obtained test score reflects both true score and error score. Test scores may be expressed in the familiar equation:

$$\text{Observed Score} = \text{True Score} + \text{Error}$$

In this framework, the *observed score* is the test score that was actually obtained. The *true score* is the hypothetical amount of the designated trait specific to the examinee, a quantity that would be expected if the entire universe of relevant content were assessed or if the examinee were tested an infinite number of times without any confounding effects of such things as practice or fatigue. *Measurement error* is defined as the difference between true score and observed score. Error is uncorrelated with the true score and with other variables, and it is distributed normally and uniformly about the true score. Because its influence is random, the average measurement error across many testing occasions is expected to be zero.

Many of the key elements from contemporary psychometrics may be derived from this core assumption. For example, internal consistency reliability is a psychometric function of random measurement error, equal to the ratio of the true score variance to the observed score variance. By comparison, validity depends on the extent of nonrandom measurement error. Systematic sources of measurement error negatively influence validity, because error prevents measures from validly representing what they purport to assess. Issues of test fairness and bias are sometimes considered to constitute a special case of validity in which systematic sources of error across racial and ethnic groups constitute threats to validity generalization.

CTT places more emphasis on test score properties than on item parameters. According to Gulliksen (1950), the essential item statistics are the proportion of persons answering each item correctly (item difficulties, or *p*-values), the point-biserial correlation between item and total score multiplied by the item standard deviation (reliability index), and the point-biserial correlation between item and criterion score multiplied by the item standard deviation (validity index).

As a critic, Borsboom (2006a, 2006b; Borsboom, Mellenbergh, & Van Heerden, 2004) has argued that CTT has grave limitations in theory and model building through its misplaced emphasis on observed scores and true scores rather than the latent trait itself. Moreover, he has argued that it thereby creates a never-ending black hole need for continued accumulation of construct validity evidence (Borsboom 2006a, p. 431). At a more specific level, Hambleton, Swaminathan, and Rogers (1991) identified four limitations of CTT: (1) it has limited utility for constructing tests for dissimilar examinee populations (*sample dependence*); (2) it is not amenable for making comparisons of examinee performance on different tests purporting to measure the trait of interest (*test dependence*); (3) it operates under the assumption that equal measurement error exists for all examinees (*invariant reliability*); and (4) it provides no basis for predicting the likelihood of a given response of an examinee to a given test item, based on responses to other items. In general, with CTT, it is difficult to separate examinee characteristics from test characteristics. IRT addresses many of these limitations.

## Item Response Theory

IRT may be traced to two separate lines of development. Its origins may be traced to the work of Danish mathematician Georg Rasch (1960), who developed a family of IRT models that separated person and item parameters. Rasch influenced the thinking of leading European and American psychometricians such as Gerhard Fischer and Benjamin Wright. A second line of development stemmed from research at the Educational Testing Service that culminated in Frederick Lord and Melvin Novick's (1968) classic textbook, including four chapters on IRT written by Allan Birnbaum. This book provided a unified statistical treatment of test theory and moved beyond Gulliksen's earlier CTT work.

IRT addresses the issue of how individual test items and observations map in a linear manner onto a targeted construct (termed the *latent trait,* with the amount of the trait denoted by $\theta$). The frequency distribution of a total score, factor score, or other trait estimates is calculated on a standardized scale with a mean $\theta$ of 0 and a standard deviation (*SD*) of 1. An item response function (IRF; also known as an item characteristic curve, ICC) can then be created by plotting the proportion of people who have a score at each level of $\theta$, so that the probability of a person's passing an item depends solely on the ability of that person and the properties of the item. The IRF curve yields several parameters, including item difficulty and item discrimination. Item *difficulty* is the location on the latent trait continuum corresponding to chance responding or, alternatively, the probability of responding accurately (or not) given a specified ability level. Item *discrimination* is the rate or slope at which the probability of success changes with trait level (i.e., the ability of the item to differentiate those with more of the trait from those with less). A third parameter denotes the probability of answering correctly by *guessing in low-ability respondents* (as with multiple-choice tests). A fourth parameter describes the probability of *carelessness in high-ability respondents* (i.e., those may answer an easy item incorrectly). IRT based on the one-parameter model (i.e., item difficulty) assumes equal discrimination for all items and negligible probability of guessing, and is generally referred to as the Rasch model. Two-parameter models (those that estimate both

item difficulty and discrimination) and three-parameter models (those that estimate item difficulty, discrimination, and probability of guessing) may also be used. Only now are four-parameter models being considered of potential value, especially for their relevance in psychopathology (e.g., Loken & Rulison, 2010).

IRT posits several assumptions: (1) *unidimensionality and stability* of the latent trait, which is usually estimated from an aggregation of individual items; (2) *local independence* of items, meaning that the only influence on item responses is the latent trait and not adjacent (or any other) items; and (3) *item parameter invariance*—that is, item properties are a function of the item itself rather than the sample, test form, or interaction between item and respondent. Knowles and Condon (2000) argued that these assumptions may not always be made safely. While IRT offers technology that makes test development more efficient than CTT, its potential to lead to future advances in psychometrics is questionable. As Wainer (2010) asked rhetorically, "What more do we need to know about IRT to be able to use it well?" (p. 18).

## SAMPLING AND NORMING

Under ideal circumstances, individual test results would be referenced to the performance of the entire collection of individuals (*target population*) for whom the test is intended. Statewide educational tests given to all students at specified grade levels have this potential, although they are often used only as criterion-referenced benchmarks of academic progress. Without government mandates, it is rarely feasible to measure performance of every member in a population. Accordingly, standardized tests are developed with the use of *sampling* procedures designed to provide an unbiased estimation of the score distribution and characteristics of a target population within a subset of individuals randomly selected from that population. Test results may then be interpreted with reference to sample characteristics, which are presumed to accurately estimate stable population parameters.

### Appropriate Samples for Test Applications

When a test is intended to yield information about examinees' standing relative to peers of some kind, the chief objective of sampling should be to provide a reference group that is representative of the greater population for whom the test is intended. *Norm-referenced* test scores provide information about an examinee's standing relative to the distribution of test scores found in an appropriate peer comparison group. As a point of comparison, *criterion-referenced* tests yield scores that are interpreted relative to predetermined standards of performance, such as proficiency at a specific academic skill or activity of daily life.

If the test is intended to compare the performance of an individual to that of the general population, the sample may need to be stratified on demographic variables, typically those that account for substantial variation in test performance. Stratification divides the target population into smaller subpopulations, which can then be randomly sampled, provided that the population proportions in the strata are known (Kalton, 1983). Variables unrelated to the trait being assessed need not be included in the sampling plan. For example, a developmentally sensitive test needs to be stratified by age level, but a test that shows little variation in performance as a function of maturation may cover broad age ranges and not require age stratifications. The advantages of stratified sampling include greater ease of sampling and estimation, improved likelihood of representing important subpopulations in the normative sample, the option to conduct additional analyses on samples within strata (if independent from each other), and enhancement of sampling precision (e.g., Lehtonen & Pahkinen, 2004).

Variables frequently used for sample stratification include:

- Sex (female, male)
- Race (White, African American, Asian/Pacific Islander, Native American, Other)
- Ethnicity (Hispanic origin, non-Hispanic origin)
- Geographic region (Midwest, Northeast, South, West)
- Community setting (urban/suburban, rural)
- Parent educational attainment (less than high school degree, high school graduate or equivalent, some college or technical school, 4 or more years of college)

The most challenging of stratification variables is socioeconomic status (SES), particularly because it tends to be associated with cognitive test performance and is difficult to define operationally (e.g., Oakes & Rossi, 2003). Parent educational attainment is often used as an estimate of SES because it is readily available and objective and because parent education correlates moderately with family income. For children's measures, parent occupation and income are also sometimes combined as estimates of SES, although income information is generally difficult to obtain. Community estimates of SES add an additional level of sampling rigor, because the community in which an individual lives may be a greater factor in the child's everyday life experience than his or her parents' educational attainment. Similarly, the number of people residing in the home or whether one or two parents head the family are all factors that can influence a family's SES. For example, a family of three that has an annual income of $40,000 may have more economic viability than a family of six that earns the same income. Also, a college-educated single parent may earn less income than two lesser-educated cohabiting parents. The influences of SES on construct development clearly represent an area of further study, even as the relation of SES to cognitive and behavioral outcome proves complex (e.g., Turkheimer, Haley, Waldron, D'Onofrio, & Gottesman, 2003).

A classic example of an inappropriate normative reference sample is found with the original Minnesota Multiphasic Personality Inventory (MMPI; Hathaway & McKinley, 1943), which was normed on 724 Minnesota White adults who were, for the most part, relatives or visitors of patients in the University of Minnesota Hospitals. The original MMPI normative reference group was primarily composed of Minnesota farmers.

When test users intend to rank individuals relative to the special populations to which they belong, it may also be desirable to ensure that proportionate representation of those special populations are included in the normative sample (e.g., individuals who are intellectually disabled, conduct disordered, or learning disabled). Alternatively, it is not unusual to collect norms on special reference groups, such as individuals with a known diagnosis (e.g., autism spectrum disorders), when level of test performance is important in understanding the nature and severity of any impairments (e.g., specification of high-functioning autism versus lower-functioning autism). Millon, Davis, and Millon (1997) noted that tests normed on special populations may require the use of base rate scores rather than traditional standard scores, because assumptions of a normal distribution of scores often cannot be met within clinical populations.

## Appropriate Sampling Methodology

One of the principal objectives of sampling is to ensure that each individual in the target population has an equal and independent chance of being selected. Sampling methodologies include both probability and nonprobability approaches, which have different strengths and weaknesses in terms of accuracy, cost, and feasibility (Levy & Lemeshow, 1999).

Probability sampling is a randomized approach that permits the use of statistical theory to estimate the properties of sample estimators. Probability sampling is generally too expensive for norming educational and psychological tests, but it offers the advantage of permitting the determination of the degree of sampling error, such as is frequently reported with the results of most public opinion polls. *Sampling error* may be defined as the difference between a sample statistic and its corresponding population parameter. When sampling error in psychological test norms is not reported, an important source of true score error that transcends measurement error alone will be neglected.

A probability sampling approach sometimes employed in psychological test norming is known as *multistage stratified random cluster sampling*; this approach uses a sampling strategy in which a large or dispersed population is divided into a large number of groups, with participants in the groups selected via random sampling. In two-stage cluster sampling, each group undergoes a second round of simple random sampling based on the expectation that each cluster closely resembles every other cluster. For example, a set of schools may constitute the first stage of sampling, with students randomly drawn from the schools in the second stage. Cluster sampling is more economical than random sampling, but incremental amounts of error may be introduced at each stage of sample selection. Moreover, cluster sampling commonly results in high standard errors when cases from a cluster are homogeneous (Levy & Lemeshow, 1999). Sampling error can be estimated with the cluster sampling approach, so long as the selection process at the various stages involves random sampling.

In general, sampling error tends to be largest when nonprobability-sampling approaches, such as convenience sampling or quota sampling, are employed *Convenience samples* involve the use of a self-selected sample that is easily accessible (e.g., volunteers, college subject pool participants, or examinees personally known to the examiner). *Quota samples* involve the selection by a coordinator of a predetermined number of cases with specific characteristics. The probability of acquiring an unrepresentative sample is high when using nonprobability procedures. The weakness of all nonprobability-sampling methods is that norms may not be applicable to the population being served, statistical theory cannot be used to estimate sampling precision, the likelihood of sampling bias is elevated, and accordingly sampling accuracy can be evaluated only subjectively (e.g., Kalton, 1983).

An example of best practice in sampling may be found in the approach used with the Achenbach System of Empirically Based Assessment (ASEBA; Achenbach & Rescorla, 2001), a family of scales that includes the Child Behavior Checklist (CBCL/6–18), a leading behavior rating scale for children and adolescents with behavior problems. A multistage national probability sample was collected in the process of updating the norms for these scales:

- One hundred primary sampling units were selected by an institute of survey research to be collectively representative of the U.S. population.
- Trained interviewers were assigned to households across the various sampling units to visit homes to determine the age and gender of residents eligible for participation (i.e., children and adolescents with no major physical or intellectual disability, with one English-speaking parent).
- Eligible residents were identified, and candidate participants were selected by stratified randomized procedures to match an overall target demographic specification, with no more than one candidate included from each household.
- Interviews with parents or youths were conducted to complete the rating scales.
- After receipt of completed scales, ASEBA staff telephoned respondents to verify that interviews actually had been conducted.

A completion rate of 93.0% was reported for eligible CBCL/6–18 participants, suggesting a low likelihood for sampling selection bias. Of the 2,029 children whose parents completed the CBCL/6–18, 276 (13.6%) were excluded after data collection based on parent reports of mental health, substance abuse, and special education services, yielding a final nonreferred normative sample of $N = 1,753$. The systematic and random sampling techniques used to norm the ASEBA behavior rating scales may be contrasted with the less randomized sampling techniques found with many other psychological tests and behavior rating scales.

## Adequately Sized Normative Samples

How large should a normative sample be? If population parameters are to be estimated, effect sizes are to be calculated, or specific hypotheses are to be tested with null hypothesis significance testing, minimal sample sizes may be specified. The number of participants sampled at any given stratification level needs to be sufficiently large to provide acceptable sampling error with stable parameter estimations for the target populations. Depending on how the data are to be used, the *alpha level, effect size,* and *power* need to be specified in advance and can drive determination of minimal sample sizes necessary.

The minimum number of cases to be collected (or clusters to be sampled) also depends in part on the sampling procedure used; Levy and Lemeshow (1999) provided formulas for a variety of sampling procedures. Up to a point, the larger the sample the greater the reliability of sampling accuracy and the more precise the parameter estimate. Estimates that are biased will generally become less biased as sample size increases (e.g., Kelley & Rausch, 2006). Cattell (1986) noted that eventually diminishing returns can be expected when sample sizes are increased beyond a reasonable level. Julious (2005) recommended the use of a cost benefit analyses, where the point at which increased sample size yields diminished effect in estimating relevant population parameters.

The smallest acceptable number of cases in a sampling plan may also be driven by the particular statistical analyses to be conducted. Hertzog (2008) recommended samples of $n = 25$ to 40 for pilot studies during instrument development, $n = 20$ to 25 for intervention efficacy pilot studies (capable of detecting large effect sizes), and $n = 30$ to 40 per group for pilot studies comparing groups. In contrast, Zieky (1993) recommended that a minimum of 500 examinees be distributed across the two groups compared in differential item function studies for group administered tests. For individually administered tests, differential item function analyses require substantial oversampling of minorities. With regard to exploratory factor analyses, Riese, Waller, and Comrey (2000) have reviewed the psychometric literature and concluded that most rules of thumb pertaining to minimum sample size are not useful. They suggested that when communalities are high and factors are well defined, sample sizes of 100 are often adequate, but when communalities are low, the number of factors is large, and the number of indicators per factor is small, even a sample size of 500 may be inadequate. As with statistical analyses in general, minimal acceptable sample sizes should be based on practical considerations, including such considerations as desired effect size, power, and alpha level.

As rules of thumb, group-administered tests undergoing standardization generally sample over 10,000 participants per age or grade level, whereas individually administered tests typically sample 100 to 200 participants per level (e.g., Robertson, 1992). In IRT, the minimum sample size is related to the choice of calibration model used. In an integrative review, Suen (1990) recommended that a minimum of 200 participants be examined for the one-parameter Rasch model, at least 500 examinees be examined for the two-parameter model, and at least 1,000 examinees be examined for the three-parameter model. Using the WISC-IV normative data set, Zhu and Chen (2011) reported that representative sample sizes as small as $N = 50$ per age cohort were capable of yielding comparable (or even improved) norms relative to a substantially larger sample, based on results with an inferential norming method (Wilkins & Rolfhus, 2004).

Confidence in the use of smaller normative samples may soon be enabled by advances in data resampling procedures (with replacement), such as the bootstrap, the jackknife, and permutation methods, that have been shown to provide stable estimates of statistical parameters without requiring assumptions as to normality or homogeneity of variance. In particular, the bootstrap technique has been utilized in two recent normative updates for the Cognitive Abilities Test (CogAT, Form 6; see Lohman & Lakin, 2009) and the Woodcock-Johnson III (WJ III; see McGrew, Dailey, & Schrank, 2007). Efron and Tibshirani (1993) described how the bootstrap might be used to construct a 95% confidence interval (CI) for the latent trait statistical parameter $\theta$:

1. Draw 1,000 bootstrap samples with replacement from the original sample, each time calculating an estimate of $\theta$.
2. Use the results to generate a (simulated) distribution of $\theta$, sorting these estimates in ascending order.
3. Calculate the 2.5th percentile (i.e., the average of the 25th and 26th observations) and the 97.5th percentile (i.e., the average of the 975th and 976th observations) from the 1,000 simulated values.
4. The resulting values form the lower confidence limit and the upper confidence limit.

Mooney and Duval (1993) considered bootstrapped approximations of parameter estimates and CIs to be relatively high quality "when $n$ reaches the range of 30–50, and when the sampling procedure is truly random" (p. 21).

## Sampling Precision

As we have discussed, sampling error and bias is difficult to ascertain when probability sampling approaches are not used, and most educational and psychological tests do not employ true probability sampling. Given this limitation, there are few objective standards for the sampling precision of test norms. Angoff (1984) recommended as a rule of thumb that the maximum tolerable sampling error should be no more than 14% of the standard error of measurement. He declined, however, to provide further guidance in this area: "Beyond the general consideration that norms should be as precise as their intended use demands and the cost permits, there is very little else that can be said regarding minimum standards for norms reliability" (p. 79). For large-scale assessments normed through two-stage cluster sampling, a conventional recommendation has been that the magnitude of the 95% CI around a mean score should be less than 10% of the score's SD (e.g., Foy & Joncas, 2004; Wu, 2010). CIs that are greater than 10% of the SD may indicate problematic deviations from random sampling, inadequate sample size, and insufficient power. Wu (2010) noted that large sampling error can easily account for spuriously large differences in group mean scores, such as those that might be expected between regions or over time as a product of instruction.

In the absence of formal estimates of sampling error, the accuracy of sampling strata may be most easily determined by comparing stratification breakdowns against those available for the target population. As the sample more closely matches population characteristics, the more representative is a test's normative sample. As best practice, we recommend that test developers provide tables showing the composition of the standardization sample within and across all stratification criteria (e.g., Percentages of the Normative Sample according to combined variables, such as Age, by Race, or by Parent Education). This level of stringency and detail ensures that important demographic variables are distributed proportionately across other stratifying variables according to population proportions. The practice of reporting sampling accuracy for single-stratification variables "on the margins" (i.e., by one stratification variable at a time) tends to conceal lapses in sampling accuracy. For example, if sample proportions of low SES are concentrated in minority groups (instead of being proportionately distributed across majority and minority groups), then the precision of the sample has been compromised through the neglect of minority groups with high SES and majority groups with low SES. The more the sample deviates from population proportions on multiple stratifications, the greater the effect of sampling error.

Manipulation of the sample composition to generate norms is often accomplished through sample weighting (i.e., application of participant weights to obtain a distribution of scores that is exactly proportioned to the target population representations). Weighting is used more frequently with group-administered educational tests, because educational tests typically involve the collection of thousands of cases. Weighting is used less frequently with psychological tests, and its use with these smaller samples may significantly affect systematic sampling error because fewer cases are collected and therefore weighting may differentially affect proportions across different stratification criteria, improving one at the cost of another. Weighting is most likely to contribute to sampling error when a group has been inadequately represented with too few cases collected.

An illustration of problematic reporting of sample weighting may be found in the Wechsler Memory Scale (WMS-III; Wechsler, 1997). While this test's technical manual reports a standardization sample of 1,250 examinees (Tulsky, Zhu, & Ledbetter, 1997), subsequent independent reports indicated that this was a "weighted" $N$ and that 217 or 218 participants were exact duplicates of participants in the "unweighted" $N$ of 1,032 (see Tulsky, Chiaravallotti, Palmer, & Chelune, 2003; also Frisby & Kim, 2008). This approach to weighting a normative sample is not clearly disclosed in test technical materials (see, e.g., *Standards for Educational and Psychological Testing,* 1999) and does not meet accepted weighting procedures (e.g., Rust & Johnson, 1992).

## Recency of Sampling

How old can norms be and still remain accurate? Evidence from the last two decades suggests that norms from measures of cognitive ability are susceptible to becoming "soft" or "stale" (i.e., test consumers should use older norms with caution). Use of outdated normative samples introduces systematic error into the diagnostic process and may negatively influence decision making, such as denying services (for mentally handicapping conditions) to sizable numbers of children and adolescents who otherwise would have been identified as eligible to receive services (e.g., Reschly, Myers, & Hartel, 2002). Sample recency is an ethical concern for all psychologists who test or conduct assessments. The American Psychological Association's (2002) Ethical Principles and Code of Conduct directs psychologists to avoid basing decisions or recommendations on results that stem from obsolete or outdated tests.

The problem of normative obsolescence has been most robustly demonstrated with intelligence tests. The term *Flynn effect* (Herrnstein & Murray, 1994) is used to describe a consistent pattern of population intelligence test score gains over time and across nations (Flynn, 1984, 1987, 1994, 1999). For intelligence tests, the rate of gain is about one-third of an IQ point per year (3 points per decade), which has been a roughly uniform finding over time and for all ages (Flynn, 1999). The Flynn effect appears to occur as early as infancy (Bayley, 1993; Campbell, Siegel, Parr, & Ramey, 1986) and continues through the full range of adulthood (Tulsky & Ledbetter, 2000). The effect implies that older test norms may yield inflated scores relative to current normative expectations. For example, the Wechsler Intelligence Scale for Children—III (WISC-III; Wechsler, 1991) currently yields higher Full Scale IQs than the fourth edition of the WISC (Wechsler, 2003) by about 2.5 IQ points.

How often should tests be revised? There is no empirical basis for making a global recommendation, but it seems reasonable to conduct normative updates, restandardizations, or revisions at time intervals corresponding to the time expected to produce 1 standard error of measurement (SEM) of change. For example, given the Flynn effect and an overall average WISC-IV Full Scale IQ SEM of 2.68, one could expect about 10 years to elapse before the test's norms would "soften" to the magnitude of 1 SEM. We note, however, that some evidence has suggested that the Flynn effect may have diminished or even reversed in recent years (e.g., Teasdale & Owen, 2005).

## CALIBRATION AND DERIVATION OF REFERENCE NORMS

This section describes several psychometric characteristics of test construction as they relate to building individual scales and developing appropriate norm-referenced scores. *Calibration* refers to the analysis of properties of gradation in a measure, defined in part by properties of test items. *Norming* is the process of using scores obtained by an appropriate sample to build quantitative references that can be used effectively in the comparison and evaluation of individual performances relative to "typical" peer expectations.

### Calibration

The process of item and scale calibration dates back to the earliest attempts to measure temperature. Early in the 17th century, there was no method to quantify heat and cold except through subjective judgment. Galileo and others experimented with devices that expanded air in glass as heat increased; use of liquid in glass to measure

temperature was developed in the 1630s. Some two dozen temperature scales were available for use in Europe in the 17th century, and each scientist had his own scales with varying gradations and reference points. It was not until the early 18th century that more uniform scales were developed by Fahrenheit, Celsius, and de Réaumur.

The process of calibration has similarly evolved in psychological testing. In CTT, item difficulty is judged by the *p*-value, or the proportion of people in the sample that passes an item. During ability test development, items are typically ranked by *p*-value or the amount of the trait being measured. The use of regular, incremental increases in item difficulties provides a methodology for building scale gradations. Item difficulty properties in CTT are dependent on the population sampled, so that a sample with higher levels of the latent trait (e.g., older children on a set of vocabulary items) would show different item properties (e.g., higher *p*-values) than a sample with lower levels of the latent trait (e.g., younger children on the same set of vocabulary items).

In contrast, IRT includes both item properties and levels of the latent trait in analyses, permitting item calibration to be sample independent. The same item difficulty and discrimination values will be estimated regardless of trait distribution. This process permits item calibration to be sample free, according to Wright (1999), so that the scale transcends the group measured. Embretson (1999) has described one of the new rules of measurement: "Unbiased estimates of item properties may be obtained from unrepresentative samples" (p. 13).

IRT permits several item parameters to be estimated in the process of item calibration. Among the indices calculated in widely used Rasch model computer programs (e.g., Linacre & Wright, 1999) are item fit-to-model expectations, item difficulty calibrations, item-total correlations, and item standard error. The conformity of any item to expectations from the Rasch model may be determined by examining item fit. Items are said to have good fits with typical item characteristic curves when they show expected patterns near to and far from the latent trait level for which they are the best estimates. Measures of item difficulty adjusted for the influence of sample ability are typically expressed in logits, permitting approximation of equal difficulty intervals.

### Item and Scale Gradients

The *item gradient of a test* refers to how steeply or gradually items are arranged by trait level and the resulting gaps that may ensue in standard scores. In order for a test to have adequate sensitivity to differing degrees of ability or any trait being measured, it must have adequate item density across the distribution of the latent trait. The larger the resulting standard score differences in relation to a change in a single raw score point, the less sensitive, discriminating, and effective a test is.

For example, on the Memory subtest of the Battelle Developmental Inventory (Newborg, Stock, Wnek, Guidubaldi, & Svinicki, 1984), a child who is 1 year 11 months old who earned a raw score of 7 would have performance ranked at the first percentile for age, while a raw score of 8 leaps to a percentile rank of 74. The steepness of this gradient in the distribution of scores suggests that this subtest is insensitive to even large gradations in ability at this age.

A similar problem is evident on the Motor Quality index of the Bayley Scales of Infant Development Behavior Rating Scale (BSID-II; Bayley, 1993). A 36-month-old child with a raw score rating of 39 obtains a percentile rank of 66. The same child obtaining a raw score of 40 is ranked at the 99th percentile.

As a recommended guideline, tests may be said to have adequate item gradients and item density when there are approximately three items per Rasch logit, or when passage of a single item results in a standard score change of less than one third $SD$ (0.33 $SD$) (Bracken, 1987). Items that are not evenly distributed in terms of the latent trait may yield steeper change gradients that will decrease the sensitivity of the instrument to finer gradations in ability.

## Floor and Ceiling Effects

Do tests have adequate breadth, bottom and top? Many tests yield their most valuable clinical inferences when scores are extreme (i.e., for scores that are very low or very high). Accordingly, tests used for clinical purposes need sufficient discriminating power in the extreme ends of the distributions.

The floor of a test represents the extent to which an individual can earn appropriately low standard scores. A floor is usually considered the lowest, nonzero raw score that may be earned for any instrument; zero raw scores have ambiguous meaning, because a wide array of construct-irrelevant explanations can account for zero scores. An intelligence test intended for use in the identification of individuals diagnosed with intellectual disabilities must, by definition, extend at least 2 SDs below normative expectations (IQ < 70). In order to serve individuals with severe to profound intellectual disability, test scores must extend even further to more than 4 SDs below

the normative mean (IQ < 40). Tests without a sufficiently low floor may not be useful for decision making for more severe forms of cognitive impairment.

A similar situation arises for test ceiling effects. An intelligence test with a ceiling greater than 2 SDs above the mean (IQ > 130) can identify most candidates for intellectually gifted programs. To identify individuals as exceptionally gifted (i.e., IQ > 160), a test ceiling must extend more than 4 SDs above normative expectations. There are several unique psychometric challenges to extending norms to these heights, but recently the publisher of the leading school-age intelligence test, the WISC-IV, increased its highest global scores beyond 150–160 to extended standard scores as high as 210 (Zhu, Cayton, Weiss, & Gabel, 2008). The Stanford-Binet, Fifth Edition also offered an Extended IQ Score (EXIQ) that extends up to 225 (Roid, 2003). These advances may enable the identification of exceptionally gifted students at levels not previously possible.

As a rule of thumb, tests used for clinical decision making should have floors and ceilings that differentiate the extreme lowest and highest 2% of the population from the middlemost 96% (Bracken, 1987, 1988). Tests with inadequate floors or ceilings are inappropriate for assessing children with known or suspected intellectual disability, intellectual giftedness, severe psychopathology, or exceptional social and educational competencies.

## Derivation of Norm-Referenced Scores

IRT yields several different kinds of interpretable scores (e.g., Woodcock, 1999), only some of which are norm-referenced standard scores. Because most test users are most familiar with the use of standard scores, we focus on the process of arriving at this type of score. Transformation of raw scores to standard scores involves a number of decisions based on psychometric science and more than a little art.

The first decision involves the nature of raw score transformations, based on theoretical considerations (*Is the trait being measured thought to be normally distributed?*) and examination of the cumulative frequency distributions of raw scores within and across age groups (e.g., Daniel, 2007). The objective of this transformation is to preserve the shape of the raw score frequency distribution, including mean, variance, kurtosis, and skewness. *Linear transformations* of raw scores are based solely on the mean and distribution of raw scores and are commonly used when distributions are not normal; linear transformation assumes that the distances between scale points reflect true differences in the degree of the measured trait present. *Area transformations* of raw score distributions convert the shape of the frequency distribution into a specified type of distribution. When the raw scores are normally distributed, they may be transformed to fit a normal curve, with corresponding percentile ranks assigned in a way so that the mean corresponds to the 50th percentile, $-1$ *SD* and $+1$ *SD* correspond to the 16th and 84th percentiles respectively, and so forth. When the frequency distribution is not normal, it is possible to select from varying types of nonnormal frequency curves (e.g., Johnson, 1949) as a basis for transformation of raw scores or to use polynomial curve-fitting equations.

Following raw score transformations is the process of smoothing the curves. Data smoothing typically occurs within and across groups to correct for minor irregularities, presumably those irregularities that result from sampling fluctuations and error. Quality checking also occurs to eliminate vertical reversals (such as those within an age group, from one raw score to the next) and horizontal reversals (such as those within a raw score series, from one age to the next). Smoothing and elimination of reversals serve to ensure that raw score to standard score transformations progress according to growth and maturation expectations for the trait being measured.

Beyond computing norms one age group at a time, *continuous norming* (Gorsuch, 1983b; Gorsuch & Zachary, 1985) began as a way of using test scores across a large number of overlapping age groups to generate polynomial regression equations that could accurately capture the developmental progression of test scores. Continuous norming enabled improved estimation of raw to standard score transformations and age-based percentile ranks while minimizing the effects of sampling and artifactual irregularities. This approach has evolved into *continuous parameter estimation methods* (Gorsuch, 2010; Roid, 2010) that permit computerized estimation of statistical parameters such as mean, SD, and skewness for different samples as a function of salient population characteristics (e.g., gender, education, ethnicity, and age), thereby providing a context for transforming test raw scores to standard scores. Continuous parameter estimation methods may also be used to compute and model reliabilities, standard errors of measurement, and various forms of validity as a function of other variables (Gorsuch, 2010; Roid, 2010).

## TEST SCORE VALIDITY

Validity traditionally has been concerned with the *meaning* of test scores, or whether a test measures what it purports to measure (e.g., Cronbach & Meehl, 1955; Kelley, 1927). In an influential definition that sought to unify all forms of test score validity under the umbrella of *construct validity* and extend its reach to encompass the applied use of test results and their interpretations, Messick (1989a) defined *validity* as "an integrated evaluative judgment of the degree to which empirical evidence and theoretical rationales support the *adequacy* and *appropriateness* of *inferences* and *actions* based on test scores or other modes of assessment" (p. 13; emphasis in original). From this mainstream perspective, validity involves the inferences made from test scores and is not inherent to the test itself (e.g., Cronbach, 1971; Sireci, 2009; *Standards for educational and psychological testing,* 1999).

Yet Borsboom and his colleagues (Borsboom, Cramer, Kievit, Scholten, & Franić, 2009; Borsboom et al., 2004) argued that the traditional concept of validity was always indefensible, if just because it focused on test scores and their interpretations, whether they made sense in terms of psychological theories, and even on the justifiability of social actions based on test scores, rather than the measurement tools per se. Stripping excess requirements but covering less ground, they proposed a narrower formulation: that "validity is a property of measurement instruments [that] codes whether these instruments are sensitive to variation in a targeted attribute" (Borsboom et al., 2009, p. 135).

Lissitz (2009) provided an accessible compilation of controversies in contemporary perspectives on test score validity, from mainstream concepts of validity, to calls for radical change, and to *applications-oriented* forms of validity. In recent years, mainstream notions of test score validity have increasingly relied on the ambiguous concept of *construct validity*, which has come to represent something of a bottomless pit in terms of the ongoing accumulation of evidence for the validity of a test. Consumers of psychological test results expect the tests to have broad and diverse foundations and to be applied interpretatively in a manner supported by research. In a test-centered society, the narrow and more radical definition of validity espoused by Borsboom and his colleagues has a purist quality that appears inadequate, given the expectations of test consumers. The applications-oriented perspective takes the very functional approach that the optimal array of evidence necessary to support test validity varies according to the nature and applications of the test.

From a mainstream perspective, evidence of test score validity may take different forms, many of which are detailed in this chapter, but ultimately they are all concerned with construct validity (Guion, 1977; Messick,

1995a, 1995b). Construct validity involves appraisal of a body of evidence determining the degree to which test score inferences are accurate, adequate, and appropriate indicators of the examinee's standing on the trait or characteristic measured by the test. Excessive narrowness or broadness in the definition and measurement of the targeted construct can threaten construct validity. The problem of excessive narrowness, or *construct underrepresentation,* refers to the extent to which test scores fail to tap important facets of the construct being measured. The problem of excessive broadness, or *construct irrelevance,* refers to the extent to which test scores that are influenced by unintended factors, including irrelevant constructs and test procedural biases.

Construct validity can be supported with two broad classes of evidence: *internal* and *external* validation, which parallel the classes of threats to validity of research designs (Campbell & Stanley, 1963; Cook & Campbell, 1979). Internal evidence for validity includes information intrinsic to the measure itself, including content, examinee response processes, and substantive and structural validation. External evidence for test score validity may be drawn from research involving independent, criterion-related data. External evidence includes convergent, discriminant, criterion-related, and consequential validation. This internal–external dichotomy with its constituent elements represents a distillation of concepts described by Anastasi and Urbina (1997); Jackson (1971); Loevinger (1957); Messick (1995a, 1995b); Millon et al. (1997); and Slaney and Maraun (2008), among many others.

## Internal Evidence of Validity

Internal sources of validity include the intrinsic characteristics of a test, especially its content, assessment methods, structure, and theoretical underpinnings. In this section, several sources of evidence internal to tests are described—including content validity, substantive validity, and structural validity.

### Content Validity

*Content validity* is the degree to which elements of a test, ranging from items to instructions, are relevant to and representative of varying facets of the targeted construct (Haynes, Richard, & Kubany, 1995). Content validity is typically established through the use of expert judges who review test content, but other procedures may also be employed (Haynes et al., 1995; Vogt, King & King, 2004). Hopkins and Antes (1978) recommended that tests include a table of content specifications, in which the

facets and dimensions of the construct are listed alongside the number and identity of items assessing each facet. More recently, Mislevy and his colleagues (e.g., Mislevy & Haertel, 2006) have proposed *evidence-centered design* (ECD), in which test developers use model-based reasoning and data-based warrants to formulate evidentiary arguments logically connecting test substance to meaningful claims about examinee performance and proficiency. Through this approach, for example, educational test items are written with the sole intent of eliciting explicitly defined forms of evidence to support inferences of interest, such as student mastery of a specific academic curriculum. According to Brennan (2010a), the validity claims of ECD, including the implied assertion that ECD-developed tests have validity built into the test a priori, need to be more rigorously substantiated.

Content differences across tests purporting to measure the same construct can explain why similar tests sometimes yield dissimilar results for the same examinee (Bracken, 1988). For example, the universe of mathematical skills includes varying types of numbers (e.g., whole numbers, decimals, fractions), number concepts (e.g., half, dozen, twice, more than), and basic operations (addition, subtraction, multiplication, division). The extent to which tests differentially sample content can account for differences between tests that purport to measure the same construct.

Tests should ideally include enough diverse content to adequately sample the breadth of construct-relevant domains, but content sampling should not be so diverse that scale coherence and uniformity is lost. Construct underrepresentation, stemming from use of narrow and homogeneous content sampling, tends to yield higher reliabilities than tests with heterogeneous item content, at the potential cost of generalizability and external validity. In contrast, tests with more heterogeneous content may show higher validity with the concomitant cost of scale reliability. Clinical inferences made from tests with excessively narrow breadth of content may be suspect, even when other indices of validity are satisfactory (Haynes et al., 1995).

Content validity is particularly valued for educational achievement testing, vocational testing, and some self-report measures of personality and psychopathology, because the congruence of test content with test interpretation is quite linear. For state educational assessments, for example, Crocker (2003) observed that the match between test content and curricular requirements buttresses the legal defensibility of standardized tests: "When scores are used for educational accountability, the 'load-bearing wall' of that [validity] argument is surely content representativeness" (p. 7).

In the field of personality assessment, the development of the Minnesota Multiphasic Personality Inventory, Second Edition (MMPI-2) Restructured Clinical Scales and the subsequent publication of the MMPI-2 Restructured Form (MMPI-2-RF; Ben-Porath & Tellegen, 2008; Tellegen & Ben-Porath, 2008) has marked a shift toward improved content validity in this most widely used personality test, because empirically keyed "subtle" items and items saturated with a primary "demoralization" factor have been removed from the clinical scales, eliminating some 40% of MMPI-2 items to generate a new form, the MMPI-2-RF, in which item content is easily mapped onto the clinical dimension being measured. This was not always true for previous editions of the MMPI, which included items with unclear content relevance for personality and psychopathology.

- I used to like drop-the-handkerchief.
- I liked *Alice's Adventures in Wonderland* by Lewis Carroll.

In a special journal issue dedicated to a possible paradigm shift away from MMPI and MMPI-2 empirically derived item traditions, Weed (2006) outlined the strengths, limitations, and controversies associated with the new MMPI-2-RF.

## Examinee Response Processes

An examination of *how* individuals solve problems or answer questions is potentially important in establishing that a test measures what it purports to measure. The Standards for Educational and Psychological Testing (1999) stated that evidence based on response processes concerns "the fit between the construct and the detailed nature of performance or response actually engaged in by examinees" (p. 12). For example, a test measuring mathematical proficiency should not be difficult because its vocabulary is not understood; alternatively, a pictorial measure should not appear difficult merely because the picture is confusing. While item-level statistical analyses will normally identify test items that do not perform adequately from a psychometric perspective, new qualitative methods are being developed to identify the mental processes by which examinees understand and respond to test items.

The most compelling of these methods are Ericsson and Simon's (1980) "thinking aloud" procedures, which involve focusing on a challenging task while concurrently giving verbal expression to thoughts entering attention. A meta-analysis has shown that the think-aloud method shows no evidence of reactivity (or other influence on the accuracy of performance) (Fox, Ericsson, & Best, 2011). A representative think-aloud procedure consists of this directive given to a test taker:

> I would like you to start reading the questions aloud and tell me what you are thinking as you read the questions. After you have read the question, interpret the question in your own words. Think aloud and tell me what you are doing. What is the question asking you to do? What did you have to do to answer the question? How did you come up with your solution? Tell me everything you are thinking while you are doing the question. (Ercikan et al., 2011, p. 27)

For educational achievement testing, the think-aloud responses are recorded and scored according to four themes: understanding of the item, difficulty of the item, aspects of the item that are helpful in arriving at a solution, and aspects of the item that are confusing and difficult to understand (Ercikan, Arim, Law, Domene, Gagnon, & Lacroix, 2011).

Other methods to study examinee response processes include interviews of examinees, observation of test session behaviors, examination of item reaction times, eye movement tracking, and even simultaneous functional brain mapping methodologies. For our narrow goal of improving test score validity, think aloud protocols represent an economical way to ensure that test items are eliciting responses that tap the targeted construct and not construct-irrelevant responses.

## Substantive Validity

The formulation of test items and procedures based on and consistent with a theory has been termed *substantive validity* (Loevinger, 1957). The presence of an underlying theory enhances a test's construct validity by providing scaffolding between content and constructs, which logically explains relations between elements, predicts undetermined parameters, and explains findings that would be anomalous within another theory (e.g., Kuhn, 1970). As Crocker and Algina (1986) suggested, "[P]sychological measurement, even though it is based on observable responses, would have little meaning or usefulness unless it could be interpreted in light of the underlying theoretical construct" (p. 7).

Many major psychological tests remain psychometrically rigorous but impoverished in terms of theoretical underpinnings. For example, conspicuously little theory is associated with most widely used measures of intelligence (e.g., the Wechsler scales), behavior problems (e.g., the Child Behavior Checklist), neuropsychological functioning (e.g., the Halstead-Reitan Neuropsychology Battery), and personality and psychopathology (the MMPI-2). It may well be that there are post hoc benefits to tests developed without theories; as observed by Nunnally and Bernstein (1994), "Virtually every measure that became popular led to new unanticipated theories" (p. 107). Moreover, tests with well-articulated theories may be easier to discredit than tests without accompanying theory—because falsifying the theory will undermine the substantive validity of the test.

Personality assessment has taken a leading role in theory-based test development, while only now, with the rise of the Cattell-Horn-Carroll framework for understanding human abilities, is cognitive-intellectual assessment increasingly relying of theory. Describing best practices for the measurement of personality some three decades ago, Loevinger (1972) commented, "Theory has always been the mark of a mature science. The time is overdue for psychology, in general, and personality measurement, in particular, to come of age" (p. 56).

### Structural Validity

Structural validity relies mainly on factor-analytic techniques to identify a test's underlying dimensions and the variance associated with each dimension. Also called *factorial validity* (Guilford, 1950), this form of validity may utilize other methodologies, such as multidimensional scaling, to help researchers understand a test's structure. Structural validity evidence is generally internal to the test, based on the analysis of constituent subtests or scoring indices. Structural validation approaches may also combine two or more instruments in cross-battery factor analyses to explore evidence of convergent validity.

The two leading factor analytic methodologies used to establish structural validity are exploratory and confirmatory factor analyses. Exploratory factor analyses (EFAs) allow for empirical derivation of the structure of an instrument, often without a priori expectations, and are best interpreted according to the "psychological meaningfulness" of the dimensions or factors that emerge (e.g., Gorsuch, 1983a). Confirmatory factor analyses (CFAs) help researchers evaluate the congruence of the test data with a specified model and measure the relative fit of competing models. Confirmatory analyses explore the extent to which the proposed factor structure of a test explains its underlying dimensions as compared to alternative theoretical explanations. Thompson (2004) asserted, "Both EFA and CFA remain useful today, and our selection between the two classes of factor analysis generally depends on whether we have specific theory regarding data structure" (p. 6).

As a recommended guideline, the underlying factor structure of a test should be congruent with its composite indices (e.g., Floyd & Widaman, 1995), and the interpretive structure of a test should be the best-fitting structural model available. For example, the transformation of the Wechsler intelligence scales from a historically dichotomous interpretive structure (i.e., verbal and performance IQ, subordinate to the Full Scale IQ) to a four-factor interpretive structure (i.e., the verbal comprehension index, perceptual organization index, working memory index, and processing speed index, each contributing to the superordinate Full Scale IQ) reflects the relative importance of factor-analytic studies in driving test design and structure (Wechsler, 2003, 2008).

In the areas of personality and psychopathology assessment, leading instruments have long been plagued by inadequate structural validity. The MMPI and its restandardization, the MMPI-2, have received highly critical reviews as being "suboptimal from the perspective of modern psychometric standards" (Helmes & Reddon, 1993, p. 453), particularly for the mismatch between their psychometric and interpretive structure (e.g., Horn, Wanberg, & Appel, 1973). Some improvement is reported in the factorial support for the MMPI-2-RF Restructured Clinical scales, which extracted items tapping demoralization content (that saturated the clinical scales) to an independent scale, thereby leaving the restructured clinical scales more unidimensional with higher reliability (Hoelzle & Meyer, 2008; Tellegen, Ben-Porath, McNulty, Arbisi, Graham, & Kaemmer, 2003).

A different problem with structural validity has been observed with the widely recognized "Big Five" five-factor model of normal range personality, which has been repeatedly supported with exploratory factor analyses and disconfirmed with confirmatory factor analyses (e.g., Gignac, Bates, & Jang, 2007; Vassend & Skrondal, 2011). The five-factor model represents personality trait structure in terms of five orthogonal factors—neuroticism, extraversion, openness to experience, agreeableness, and conscientiousness—and is most commonly assessed with the NEO Personality Inventory (NEO-PI-3; Costa & McCrae, 2010). In response to consistent findings of poor model fit via CFA, McCrae, Zonderman, Costa, Bond, and Paunonen (1996) have asserted that confirmatory factor analysis is systematically flawed, capable of showing poor fits for reliable structures, and they warn of "the dangers in an uncritical adoption and simplistic application of CFA techniques" (p. 563).

The cases of the MMPI-2 and the NEO-PI-3 suggest that a reasonable balance needs to be struck between theoretical underpinnings and structural validation; that is, if factor-analytic techniques do not consistently support a test's underpinnings, further research is needed to determine whether that is due to limitations of the theory, the factor-analytic methods, the nature of the test, or a combination of these factors. Carroll (1983), whose factor-analytic work has been influential in contemporary cognitive assessment, cautioned against overreliance on factor analysis as principal evidence of validity, encouraging use of additional sources of validity evidence that move "beyond factor analysis" (p. 26).

## External Evidence of Validity

Evidence of test score validity also includes the extent to which the test results predict meaningful and generalizable behaviors independent of actual test performance. Test results need to be validated for any intended application or decision-making process in which they play a part. This section describes external classes of evidence for test construct validity, including convergent, discriminant, criterion-related, and consequential validity, as well as specialized forms of validity within these categories.

### Convergent and Discriminant Validity

In a classic 1959 article, Campbell and Fiske described a multitrait-multimethod methodology for investigating construct validity. In brief, they suggested that a measure is jointly defined by its methods of gathering data (e.g., self-report or parent report) and its trait-related content (e.g., anxiety or depression). They noted that test scores should be related to (i.e., strongly correlated with) other measures of the same psychological construct (*convergent* evidence of validity) and comparatively unrelated to (i.e., weakly correlated with) measures of different psychological constructs (*discriminant* evidence of validity). The multitrait-multimethod matrix allows for the comparison of the relative strength of association between two measures of the same trait using different methods (monotrait-heteromethod correlations), two measures with a common method but tapping different traits (heterotrait-monomethod correlations), and two measures tapping different traits using different methods (heterotrait-heteromethod correlations), all of which are expected to yield lower values than internal consistency reliability statistics using the same method to tap the same trait.

The multitrait-multimethod matrix offers several advantages, such as the identification of problematic method variance. *Method variance* is a measurement artifact that threatens validity by producing spuriously high correlations between similar assessment methods of different traits. For example, high correlations between digit span, letter span, phoneme span, and word span procedures might be interpreted as stemming from the immediate memory span recall method common to all the procedures rather than any specific abilities being assessed. Method effects may be assessed by comparing the correlations of different traits measured with the same method (i.e., monomethod correlations) and the correlations among different traits across methods (i.e., heteromethod correlations). Method variance is said to be present if the heterotrait-monomethod correlations greatly exceed the heterotrait-heteromethod correlations in magnitude, assuming that convergent validity has been demonstrated.

Fiske and Campbell (1992) subsequently recognized shortcomings in their methodology: "We have yet to see a really good matrix: one that is based on fairly similar concepts and plausibly independent methods and shows high convergent and discriminant validation by all standards" (p. 394). At the same time, the methodology has provided a useful framework for establishing evidence of validity.

### Criterion-Related Validity

How well do test scores predict performance on independent criterion measures and differentiate criterion groups? The relationship of test scores to relevant external criteria constitutes evidence of *criterion-related validity,* which may take several different forms. Evidence of validity may include criterion scores that are obtained at about the same time (*concurrent* evidence of validity) or criterion scores that are obtained at some future date (*predictive* evidence of validity). External criteria may also include functional, real-life variables (*ecological* validity), diagnostic or placement indices (*diagnostic* validity), and intervention-related approaches (*instructional* and *treatment* validity).

The emphasis on understanding the functional implications of test findings describes *ecological validity* (Neisser, 1978). Banaji and Crowder (1989) suggested, "If research is scientifically sound it is better to use ecologically lifelike rather than contrived methods" (p. 1188). In essence, ecological validation efforts relate test performance to various aspects of person–environment functioning in everyday life, including identification of both competencies and deficits in social and educational adjustment. Test developers should show the ecological relevance of the constructs a test purports to measure as well as the utility of the test for predicting everyday functional limitations for remediation. In contrast, tests based on laboratory-like procedures with little or no discernible relevance to real life may be said to have little ecological validity.

The capacity of a measure to produce relevant applied group differences has been termed *diagnostic validity* (e.g., Ittenbach, Esters, & Wainer, 1997). When tests are intended for diagnostic or placement decisions, diagnostic validity refers to their utility in differentiating the groups of concern. The process of arriving at diagnostic validity may be informed by decision theory, which involves calculations of decision-making accuracy in comparison to the base rate occurrence of an event or diagnosis in a given population. Decision theory has been applied to psychological tests (Cronbach & Gleser, 1965) and other high-stakes diagnostic tests (Swets, 1992) and is useful for identifying the extent to which tests improve clinical or educational decision making.

Contrasted groups is a common methodology to demonstrate diagnostic validity. In this methodology, test performance of two samples that are known to be different on the criterion of interest is compared. For example, a test intended to tap behavioral correlates of anxiety should show differences between groups of "normal" individuals and individuals diagnosed with anxiety disorders. A test intended for differential diagnostic utility should be effective in differentiating individuals with anxiety disorders from diagnoses that appear behaviorally similar. Decision-making classification accuracy may be determined by developing cutoff scores or rules to differentiate the groups, so long as the rules show adequate sensitivity, specificity, positive predictive power, and negative predictive power, as defined next.

- *Sensitivity*: The proportion of cases in which a clinical condition is detected when it is in fact present (true positive)
- *Specificity*: The proportion of cases for which a diagnosis is rejected when rejection is in fact warranted (true negative)
- *Positive predictive power*: The probability of having the diagnosis given that the score exceeds the cutoff score
- *Negative predictive power*: The probability of not having the diagnosis given that the score does not exceed the cutoff score

All of these indices of diagnostic accuracy are dependent on the prevalence of the disorder and the prevalence of the score on either side of the cut point.

Findings pertaining to decision making should be interpreted conservatively and cross-validated on independent samples because (a) classification decisions should in practice be based on the results of multiple sources of information rather than test results from a single measure, and (b) the consequences of a classification decision should be considered in evaluating the impact of classification accuracy. A false negative classification, meaning a child is incorrectly classified as not needing special education services, could mean the denial of needed services to a student. Alternatively, a false positive classification, in which a typical child is recommended for special services, could result in a child being labeled unfairly.

Bayesian methods to calculate evidential probabilities hold considerable promise in enhancing applied decision making, by permitting prior probabilities to be specified and then updated with relevant data such as test results. For example, the Bayesian *nomogram* represents a simple and practical strategy that is empirically derived, flexible, and easy to use as an aid to clinical decision making; it enables base rate information and test findings to be integrated to arrive at the probability for any likely outcome (e.g., Bianchi, Alexander, & Cash, 2009; Jenkins, Youngstrom, Washburn, & Youngstrom, 2011).

*Treatment validity* refers to the value of an assessment in selecting and implementing interventions and treatments that will benefit the examinee. "Assessment data are said to be *treatment valid,*" commented Barrios (1988), "if they expedite the orderly course of treatment or enhance the outcome of treatment" (p. 34). Other terms used to describe treatment validity are *treatment utility* (Hayes, Nelson, & Jarrett, 1987) and *rehabilitation-referenced assessment* (Heinrichs, 1990).

Whether the stated purpose of clinical assessment is description, diagnosis, intervention, prediction, tracking, or simply understanding, its ultimate raison d'être is to select and implement services in the best interests of the examinee, that is to guide treatment. In 1957, Cronbach described a rationale for linking assessment to treatment: "For any potential problem, there is some best group of treatments to use and best allocation of persons to treatments" (p. 680).

The origins of treatment validity may be traced to the concept of aptitude by treatment interactions (ATIs) originally proposed by Cronbach (1957), who initiated decades of research seeking to specify relationships between the traits measured by tests and the intervention methodology used to produce change. In clinical practice, promising efforts to match client characteristics and clinical dimensions to preferred therapist characteristics and treatment approaches have been made (e.g., Beutler & Clarkin, 1990; Beutler & Harwood, 2000; Lazarus, 1973; Maruish, 1994), but progress has been constrained in part by difficulty in arriving at consensus for empirically supported treatments (e.g., Beutler, 1998). In psychoeducational settings, tests results have been shown to have limited utility in predicting differential responses to varied forms of instruction (e.g., Reschly, 1997).

Turning the model that test results can predict effective treatment upside-down, recent federal mandates in the reauthorized Individuals with Disabilities Education Act (IDEA) have led to the practice of identifying learning disorders by Response to Intervention (RTI). RTI addresses the educational needs of at-risk students by delivering a series of instructional interventions accompanied by frequent progress measurements; students who do not benefit are considered in need of special education and are referred for further assessment and intervention. More than anything else, in RTI, it is the inadequate response to the initial treatment (i.e., evidence based forms of instruction) that becomes diagnostic of a learning problem and potentially qualifies a student for special education (e.g., Vaughn & Fuchs, 2003).

### Consequential Validity

The most recently proposed source of evidence for test score validity is concerned with both the intended and the unintended effects of test usage on individuals and groups. Messick (1989a, 1989b, 1995b) argued that test developers must understand the social values intrinsic to the purposes and application of psychological tests, especially those that may act as a trigger for social and educational actions. In this context, *consequential validity* refers to the appraisal of value implications and the social and legal impact of score interpretation as a basis for action and labeling as well as the actual and potential consequences of test use (Messick, 1989a, 1989b; Reckase, 1998).

Legal rulings and legislative actions have played a substantial role in establishing consequential validity, which was addressed in the landmark legal case of *Larry P. v. Riles* (343 F. Supp. 306, 1972; 495 F. Supp. 926, 1979), in which the court wrote that the consequences of test usage must be aligned with valid interpretation about what the test purports to measure. More recently, the text of the federal No Child Left Behind Act of 2001 (NCLB, 2002) legislation included a validity clause stating that

assessments must "be used for purposes for which such assessments are valid and reliable, and be consistent with relevant, nationally recognized professional and technical standards" [20 U.S.C. § 6311(b)(3)(C)(iii)(2002)]. For large-scale, high-stakes educational testing, this clause has been interpreted as taking on meanings associated with social and racial equity:

> Couched in this statutory framework, the exact meaning of the validity clause becomes extremely important. One possible definition of the validity clause would ensure only that NCLB tests have certain statistical relationships with behaviors that students exhibit in a non-test environment. Other possible definitions of the validity clause would control the quality of testing practices to a much greater extent. For example, some meanings of the validity clause would mandate consideration of whether NCLB testing practices disproportionately affect students on the basis of race. Other notions of the validity clause would go even further by considering how well NCLB accountability measures achieve their statutory goal of boosting academic achievement. (Superfine, 2004, p. 482)

The immediate effect of the validity clause appears to have been to codify requirements for proportionate classification of racial and ethnical minorities in special education, with applications to grade retention and promotion policies and a wide array of other educational practices. Linn (1998) suggested that when governmental bodies establish policies that drive test development and implementation, the responsibility for the consequences of test usage must also be borne by the policy makers—and this form of validity extends far beyond the ken of test developers.

Consequential validity represents an expansion of traditional conceptualizations of test score validity. Lees-Haley (1996) urged caution about consequential validity, noting its potential for encouraging the encroachment of politics into science. The *Standards for Educational and Psychological Testing* (1999) recognized but carefully circumscribed consequential validity:

> Evidence about consequences may be directly relevant to validity when it can be traced to a source of invalidity such as construct underrepresentation or construct-irrelevant components. Evidence about consequences that cannot be so traced—that in fact reflects valid differences in performance—is crucial in informing policy decisions but falls outside the technical purview of validity. (p. 16)

Evidence of consequential validity may be collected by test developers during a period starting early in test development and extending through the life of the test

(Reckase, 1998). For educational tests, surveys and focus groups have been described as two methodologies to examine consequential aspects of validity (Chudowsky & Behuniak, 1998; Pomplun, 1997). The extent to which test results yield statistical evidence of disparate or discriminatory results on protected groups may also constitute compelling evidence of test score consequential (in)validity with legal implications (e.g., Superfine, 2004). As the social consequences of test use and interpretation are ascertained, the development and determinants of the consequences need to be explored. A measure with unintended negative side effects calls for examination of alternative measures and assessment counterproposals. Consequential validity is especially relevant to issues of bias, fairness, and distributive justice.

After a comprehensive survey of validity research published or presented in the past decade, Cizek, Bowen, and Church (2010) reported that consequential validity research was "essentially nonexistent in the professional literature" (p. 732), leading them to call it "a flaw in modern validity theory" (p. 739). They hypothesized that it is not possible to include consequences of test usage as a logical part of validation, in part because of the difficulty of synthesizing and integrating consequential value judgments with more traditional psychometric data per se. Moreover, they recommended differentiating the validation of score inferences from justifications for test use.

### Validity Generalization

The accumulation of external evidence of test validity becomes most important when test results are generalized across contexts, situations, and populations and when the consequences of testing reach beyond the test's original intent. According to Messick (1995b), "The issue of generalizability of score inferences across tasks and contexts goes to the very heart of score meaning. Indeed, setting the boundaries of score meaning is precisely what generalizability evidence is meant to address" (p. 745).

Hunter and Schmidt (1990; Hunter, Schmidt, & Jackson, 1982; Schmidt & Hunter, 1977) developed a methodology of *validity generalization,* a form of meta-analysis, that analyzes the extent to which variation in test validity across studies is due to sampling error or other sources of error such as imperfect reliability, imperfect construct validity, range restriction, or artificial dichotomization. Once incongruent or conflictual findings across studies can be explained in terms of sources of error, meta-analysis enables theory to be tested, generalized, and quantitatively extended.

## TEST SCORE RELIABILITY

If measurement is to be trusted, then it must be *reliable*. It must be consistent, accurate, and uniform across testing occasions, across time, across observers, and across samples—at least to the extent that the trait or construct being measured is stable. In psychometric terms, *reliability* refers to the extent to which measurement results are precise and accurate, reproducible, and free from random and unexplained error. Reliability has been described as "fundamental to all of psychology" (Li, Rosenthal, & Rubin, 1996, p. 98), and its study dates back nearly a century (Brown, 1910; Spearman, 1910). Reliability is the ratio of true score variance to observed score variance or, alternatively, the squared correlation between true and observed scores (e.g., Lord & Novick, 1968). Although traditional statistics such as Cronbach's coefficient alpha remain preeminent in published reliability research (Hogan, Benjamin, & Brezinski, 2000), somewhat newer important concepts in reliability include generalizability theory (albeit several decades "new"; Cronbach, Gleser, Nanda, & Rajaratnam, 1972) and reliability generalization (Vacha-Haase, 1998), both of which have important implications for how reliability is reported (e.g., Fan & Thompson, 2001). In this section, reliability is described according to CTT and IRT. Guidelines are provided for the objective evaluation of reliability.

The idea that reliability is a fixed property of a test or scale has been described as the primary myth about reliability still ubiquitous in test manuals (e.g., Streiner, 2003). As articulated by Wilkinson and the APA Task Force on Statistical Inference (1999), "Reliability is a property of the scores on a test for a particular population of examinees" (p. 596). More specifically, reliability is dependent on total score variance, so factors such as sample composition and test score variability will affect score reliability. For a fixed error variance, reliability will generally be large for a heterogeneous sample with large true score variance but small for a more homogeneous sample with small true score variance (e.g., Meyer, 2010).

Because any selected research sample may have test score reliabilities that differ significantly from the score reliabilities reported for normative standardization samples in test manuals, psychometric authorities have recommended that reliability indexes be calculated anew and reported as new samples are collected for research (Vacha-Haase, Kogan, & Thompson, 2000). Moreover, it is helpful for normative samples to report not only score reliabilities for each age cohort and score but also for any sample subgroups that may exhibit different levels of heterogeneity.

## Generalizability Theory

While CTT decomposes observed score variance into true score variance and undifferentiated random error variance, an extension of CTT termed *generalizability theory* (Cronbach et al., 1972) includes a family of statistical procedures that estimates and partitions multiple sources of measurement error variance (facets) and their interactions. Generalizability theory posits that a response score is defined by the specific conditions under which it is produced, such as scorers, methods, settings, and times, and employs analysis of variance (ANOVA) methods to untangle the error associated with each of these conditions (e.g., Brennan, 2010b; Cone, 1978). Generalizability theory provides two reliability indexes: a *generalizability coefficient* (analogous to a reliability coefficient in CTT, estimating relative reliability for a wide range of scores), and a *dependability coefficient* (an estimate of absolute reliability in making criterion-referenced decisions, such as the reliability of passing and failing an academic proficiency exam with a cut score). Thompson (2003) noted that generalizability theory has the advantages of simultaneously enabling quantification of (a) multiple sources of measurement error variance, (b) interactions that create additional sources of measurement error variance, and (c) reliability for different types of decisions (i.e., relative or absolute). In spite of the powerful techniques found in generalizability theory, its use appears conspicuously absent from mental measures created in recent years (Hogan et al., 2000).

### Internal Consistency

Determination of a test's internal consistency addresses the degree of uniformity and coherence among its constituent parts. Tests that are more uniform and unidimensional tend to be more reliable. As a measure of internal consistency, the reliability coefficient is the square of the correlation between obtained test scores and true scores; it will be high if there is relatively little error but low with a large amount of error. In CTT, reliability is based on the assumption that measurement error is distributed normally and equally for all score levels. By contrast, IRT posits that reliability differs between persons with different response patterns and levels of ability but generalizes across populations (Embretson & Hershberger, 1999).

Several statistics typically are used to calculate internal consistency. The split-half method of estimating reliability effectively splits test items in half (e.g., odd items and even items) and correlates the score from each half of the test with the score from the other half. This technique reduces the number of items in the test, thereby reducing the magnitude of the reliability. Use of the Spearman-Brown prophecy formula permits extrapolation from the obtained reliability coefficient to original length of the test, typically raising the reliability of the test. By far the most common statistical index of internal consistency is Cronbach's alpha, which provides a lower-bound estimate of test score reliability equivalent to the average split-half consistency coefficient for all possible divisions of the test into halves (Hogan et al., 2000).

Several recent studies serve to elucidate the limitations of Cronbach's alpha, specifically that it is strongly affected by scale length, that a high score does not ensure scale unidimensionality, and that excessively high scores (> .90) on subtests or scales are potentially risky. The effects of scale length on alpha have been long known, but Cortina (1993) demonstrated that when item incorrelations are held constant, increasing the length of a scale will substantially (and spuriously) raise its coefficient alpha—even when scales consist of two or three uncorrelated subscales. Cortina concluded: "If a scale has more than 14 items, then it will have an α of .70 or better even if it consists of two orthogonal dimensions with modest (i.e., .30) item intercorrelations. If the dimensions are correlated with each other, as they usually are, then α is even greater" (p. 102).

Accordingly, alpha has limited value as a measure of scale unidimensionality or homogeneity (Cortina, 1993; Streiner, 2003). As alpha rises above .90, it becomes possible that its capacity to estimate high internal consistency may instead signal item redundancy (essentially the same content expressed with different verbiage), leading Streiner to caution against use of single scales and tests with an alpha great than .90. Clark and Watson (1995) concurred in principle, observing: "Maximizing internal consistency almost invariably produces a scale that is quite narrow in content; if the scale is narrower than the target construct, its validity is compromised" (pp. 316–317). Nunnally and Bernstein (1994, p. 265) stated more directly: "Never switch to a less valid measure simply because it is more reliable." Conversely, highly homogeneous item sets may evidence high reliability as a function of limited content or construct sampling. Table 3.1 provides practical guidelines for evaluating test reliability coefficients, with higher coefficients needed when high-stakes individual student decisions are to be made.

**TABLE 3.1  Guidelines for Acceptable Internal Consistency Reliability Coefficients**

| Test Methodology | Purpose of Assessment | Median Reliability Coefficient |
|---|---|---|
| Group Assessment | Programmatic decision making | .60 or greater |
| Individual Assessment | Screening | .80 or greater |
| | Diagnosis, intervention, placement, or selection | .90 or greater |

## Local Reliability and Conditional Standard Error

Internal consistency indexes of reliability provide a single average estimate of measurement precision across the full range of test scores. This approach assumes that measurement error variance is similar for all scores, an assumption that is generally false (e.g., Dimitrov, 2002). In contrast, *local reliability* refers to measurement precision at specified trait levels or ranges of scores. *Conditional error* refers to the measurement variance at a particular level of the latent trait, and its square root is a conditional standard error. Whereas CTT posits that the standard error of measurement is constant and applies to all scores in a particular population, IRT posits that the standard error of measurement varies according to the test scores obtained by the examinee but generalizes across populations (Embretson & Hershberger, 1999). In Rasch scaling, Wright (2001) observed, "once the test items are calibrated, the standard error corresponding to every possible raw score can be estimated without further data collection" (p. 786). Accordingly, reliability may be determined locally for any location in the score distribution (and level of latent trait) through IRT.

As an illustration of the use of CTT in the determination of local reliability, the Universal Nonverbal Intelligence Test (UNIT; Bracken & McCallum, 1998) presents local reliabilities from a CTT orientation. Based on the rationale that a common cut score for classification of individuals as mentally retarded is an FSIQ equal to 70, the reliability of test scores surrounding that decision point was calculated. Specifically, coefficient alpha reliabilities were calculated for FSIQs from −1.33 and −2.66 *SD*s below the normative mean. Reliabilities were corrected for restriction in range, and results showed that composite IQ reliabilities exceeded the .90 suggested criterion. That is, the UNIT is sufficiently precise at this ability range to reliably identify individual performance near to a common cut point for classification as intellectually disabled.

Two recent investigations have provided evidence supporting the importance of conditional error variance.

Hopwood and Richards (2005) reported an increased frequency of scoring errors for high-ability samples on the Wechsler Adult Intelligence Scale (WAIS-III; Wechsler, 1997). In a follow-up investigation, Erdodi, Richard, and Hopwood (2009) reported evidence of significantly greater scoring errors in high- and low-ability samples on the Wechsler Intelligence Scale for Children (WISC-IV; Wechsler, 2003). These findings suggest that local reliabilities may be more appropriate within specified ability ranges than the single reliability estimates more conventionally used.

IRT permits the determination of conditional standard error at every level of performance on a test. Several measures, such as the Differential Ability Scales (Elliott, 1990) and the Scales of Independent Behavior (SIB-R; Bruininks, Woodcock, Weatherman, & Hill, 1996), report local standard errors or local reliabilities for every test score. This methodology not only determines whether a test is more accurate for some members of a group (e.g., high-functioning individuals) than for others (Daniel, 1999) but also promises that many other indexes derived from reliability indexes (e.g., index discrepancy scores) may eventually be tailored to an examinee's actual performance. Several IRT-based methodologies are available for estimating local scale reliabilities using conditional *SEM*s (Andrich, 1988; Daniel, 1999; Kolen, Zeng, & Hanson, 1996; Samejima, 1994), but none has yet become a test industry standard.

## Temporal Stability

Are test scores consistent over time? Test scores must be reasonably consistent to have practical utility for making clinical and educational decisions and to be predictive of future performance. The stability coefficient, or test-retest score reliability coefficient, is an index of temporal stability that can be calculated by correlating test performance for a large number of examinees at two points in time. Two weeks is considered a preferred test-retest time interval (Nunnally & Bernstein, 1994; Salvia, Ysseldyke, & Bolt, 2010), because longer intervals increase the amount of error (due to maturation and learning) and tend to lower the estimated reliability. Because test-retest reliability and internal consistency forms of reliability are affected by different sources of error, it is possible for one to be high while the other is not (e.g., Nunnally & Bernstein, 1994).

Bracken (1987) recommended that a total test stability coefficient should be greater than or equal to .90 for high-stakes tests over relatively short test-retest intervals, whereas a stability coefficient of .80 is reasonable for low-stakes testing. Stability coefficients may be spuriously high, even with tests with low internal consistency, but tests with low stability coefficients tend to have low internal consistency unless they are tapping highly variable state-based constructs such as state anxiety (Nunnally & Bernstein, 1994). As a general rule of thumb, measures of internal consistency are preferred to stability coefficients as indexes of reliability.

### Interrater Consistency and Consensus

Whenever tests require observers to render judgments, ratings, or scores for a specific behavior or performance, the consistency among observers constitutes an important source of measurement precision. Two separate methodological approaches have been utilized to study consistency and consensus among observers: interrater reliability (using correlational indexes to reference consistency among observers) and interrater agreement (addressing percent agreement among observers; e.g., Tinsley & Weiss, 1975). These distinctive approaches are necessary because it is possible to have high interrater reliability with low manifest agreement among raters if ratings are different but proportional. Similarly, it is possible to have low interrater reliability with high manifest agreement among raters if consistency indexes lack power because of restriction in range.

*Interrater reliability* refers to the proportional consistency of variance among raters and tends to be correlational. The simplest index involves correlation of total scores generated by separate raters. The *intraclass correlation* is another index of reliability commonly used to estimate the reliability of ratings. Its value ranges from 0 to 1.00, and it can be used to estimate the expected reliability of either the individual ratings provided by a single rater or the mean rating provided by a group of raters (Shrout & Fleiss, 1979). Another index of reliability, Kendall's *coefficient of concordance,* establishes how much reliability exists among ranked data. This procedure is appropriate when raters are asked to rank order the persons or behaviors along a specified dimension.

*Interrater agreement* refers to the interchangeability of judgments among raters, addressing the extent to which raters make the same ratings. Indexes of interrater agreement typically estimate percentage of agreement on categorical and rating decisions among observers, differing in the extent to which they are sensitive to degrees of agreement correct for chance agreement. Neuendorf (2002) reviewed rules of thumb proposed by a variety of researchers and concluded that "coefficients of .90 or greater would be acceptable to all, .80 or greater would be acceptable in most situations, and below that, there

exists great disagreement" (p. 145). The criterion of .70 is often used for exploratory research. More liberal criteria are usually used for the indices known to be more conservative. An example is Cohen's kappa, a widely used statistic of interobserver agreement intended for situations in which raters classify the items being rated into discrete, nominal categories. Kappa ranges from −1.00 to +1.00; kappa values of .75 or higher are generally taken to indicate excellent agreement beyond chance; values between .60 and .74 are considered good agreement; those between .40 and .59 are considered fair; and those below .40 are considered poor (Fleiss, 1981).

Interrater reliability and agreement may vary logically depending on the degree of consistency expected from specific sets of raters. For example, it might be anticipated that people who rate a child's behavior in different contexts (e.g., school versus home) would produce lower correlations than two raters who rate the child within the same context (e.g., two parents within the home or two teachers at school). In a review of 13 preschool social-emotional instruments, the vast majority of reported coefficients of interrater congruence were below .80 (range 12–89) Walker and Bracken (1996) investigated the congruence of biological parents who rated their children on four preschool behavior rating scales. Interparent congruence ranged from a low of .03 (Temperamental Assessment Battery for Children [TABC], Ease of Management through Distractibility) to a high of .79 (TABC, Approach/Withdrawal). In addition to concern about low congruence coefficients, the authors voiced concern that 44% of the parent pairs had a mean discrepancy across scales of 10 to 13 standard score points; differences ranged from 0 to 79 standard score points.

Interrater reliability studies are preferentially conducted under field conditions to enhance generalizability of testing by clinicians "performing under the time constraints and conditions of their work" (Wood, Nezworski, & Stejskal, 1996, p. 4). Cone (1988) described interscorer studies as fundamental to measurement because without scoring consistency and agreement, many other reliability and validity issues cannot be addressed.

Lombard, Snyder-Duch, and Bracken (2002) recommended that interrater reliability be reported with this information at minimum:

- Size of the reliability sample
- Method for selection of the sample
- Description of the relationship of the reliability sample to the full sample
- Number of and identity of the reliability raters

- Approximate training time required to reach adequate reliability
- Amount of coding completed by each rater
- How rating disagreements were resolved
- Indices selected to calculate reliability with a justification
- Interrater reliability for each variable selected
- Where and how consumers can obtain detailed information about the coding instrument, procedures, and instructions

### Congruence Between Alternate Forms

When two parallel forms of a test are available, correlating scores on each form provides another way to assess reliability. In CTT, strict parallelism between forms requires equality of means, variances, and covariances (Gulliksen, 1950). A hierarchy of methods for pinpointing sources of measurement error with alternative forms has been proposed (Nunnally & Bernstein, 1994; Salvia et al., 2010): (1) assess alternate-form reliability with a 2-week interval between forms; (2) administer both forms on the same day; and, if necessary, (3) arrange for different raters to score the forms administered with a 2-week retest interval and on the same day. If the score correlation over the 2-week interval between the alternative forms is lower than coefficient alpha by .20 or more, considerable measurement error is present due to internal consistency, scoring subjectivity, or trait instability over time. If the score correlation is substantially higher for forms administered on the same day, the error may stem from trait variation over time. If the correlations remain low for forms administered on the same day, the two forms may differ in content with one form being more internally consistent than the other. If trait variation and content differences have been ruled out, comparison of subjective ratings from different sources may permit the major source of error to be attributed to the subjectivity of scoring.

In IRT, test forms may be compared by examining the forms at the item level. Forms with items of comparable item difficulties, response ogives, and standard errors by trait level will tend to have adequate levels of alternate form reliability (e.g., McGrew & Woodcock, 2001). For example, when item difficulties for one form are plotted against those for the second form, a clear linear trend is expected. When raw scores are plotted against trait levels for the two forms on the same graph, the ogive plots should be identical.

At the same time, scores from different tests tapping the same construct need not be parallel if both involve sets of items that are close to the examinee's ability level.

As reported by Embretson (1999), "Comparing test scores across multiple forms is optimal when test difficulty levels vary across persons" (p. 12). The capacity of IRT to estimate trait level across differing tests does not require assumptions of parallel forms or test equating.

### Reliability Generalization

In recognition that reliability is not inherent to a test itself and is influenced by test score hetereogeneity within a given sample, Vacha-Haase (1998) proposed *reliability generalization* as a meta-analytic methodology that investigates the reliability of scores across samples, studies, and administrative conditions. An extension of validity generalization (Hunter & Schmidt, 1990; Schmidt & Hunter, 1977), reliability generalization investigates the stability and variability of reliability coefficients across samples and studies and has now been reported for a number of measurements (see, e.g., Thompson, 2003). In order to demonstrate measurement precision for the populations for which a test is intended, a test should show comparable levels of reliability across various demographic subsets of the population (e.g., gender, race, ethnic groups) as well as salient clinical and exceptional populations. It is now considered best practice to report score reliabilities with CIs in recognition of the variability that may be found in test precision across samples (e.g., Fan & Thompson, 2001; Meyer, 2010).

### TEST SCORE FAIRNESS

From the inception of psychological testing, concerns about fairness and potential bias have been apparent. As early as 1911, Alfred Binet (Binet & Simon, 1911/1916) was aware that a failure to represent diverse classes of SES would affect normative performance on intelligence tests. He intentionally deleted classes of items that related more to quality of education than to mental faculties. Early editions of the Stanford-Binet and the Wechsler intelligence scales were standardized on entirely white, native-born samples (Terman, 1916; Terman & Merrill, 1937; Wechsler, 1939, 1946, 1949). In addition to sample limitations, early tests also contained items that reflected positively on whites. Early editions of the Stanford-Binet included an Aesthetic Comparisons item in which examinees were shown a white, well-coiffed, blond woman and a disheveled woman with African features; the examinee was asked "Which one is prettier?" The original MMPI (Hathaway & McKinley, 1943) was normed on a convenience sample of White adult Minnesotans and contained items referring to culture-specific games ("drop-the-handkerchief"), literature (*Alice's Adventures in Wonderland*), and religious beliefs (the "second coming of Christ"). Most contemporary test developers now routinely avoid such problems with normative samples without minority representation as well as racially and ethnically insensitive items.

In spite of these advances, the fairness of educational and psychological tests represents one of the most contentious and psychometrically challenging aspects of test development. The examination of test psychometric properties across various groups, including majority and minority groups, may be considered a special form of test score validity. Numerous methodologies have been proposed to assess item and test properties for different groups of test takers, and the definitive text in this area is Jensen's (1980) thoughtful *Bias in Mental Testing*. Most of the controversy regarding test fairness relates to the legal, political, and social perceptions that group differences in test scores, or differences in selection rates, constitute evidence of bias in and of itself. For example, Jencks and Phillips (1998) stressed that the test score gap is the single most important obstacle to achieving racial balance and social equity.

In landmark litigation, Judge Robert Peckham in *Larry P. v. Riles* (343 F. Supp. 306, 1972; 495 F. Supp. 926, 1979) banned the use of individual IQ tests in placing black children into educable mentally retarded classes in California, concluding that the cultural bias of the IQ test was hardly disputed in this litigation. He asserted, "Defendants do not seem to dispute the evidence amassed by plaintiffs to demonstrate that the IQ tests in fact are culturally biased" (Peckham, 1972, p. 1313) and later concluded, "An unbiased test that measures ability or potential should yield the same pattern of scores when administered to different groups of people" (pp. 954–955).

The belief that any group test score difference constitutes bias has been termed the *egalitarian fallacy* by Jensen (1980):

This concept of test bias is based on the gratuitous assumption that all human populations are essentially identical or equal in whatever trait or ability the test purports to measure. Therefore, any difference between populations in the distribution of test scores (such as a difference in means, or standard deviations, or any other parameters of the distribution) is taken as evidence that the test is biased. The search for a less biased test, then, is guided by the criterion of minimizing or eliminating the statistical differences between groups. The perfectly nonbiased test, according to this definition, would

reveal reliable individual differences but not reliable (i.e., statistically significant) group differences. (p. 370)

However this controversy is viewed, the perception of test bias stemming from group mean score differences remains a deeply ingrained belief among many psychologists and educators. McArdle (1998) suggested that large group mean score differences are "a necessary but not sufficient condition for test bias" (p. 158). McAllister (1993) has observed that "[i]n the testing community, differences in correct answer rates, total scores, and so on do not mean bias. In the political realm, the exact opposite perception is found; differences mean bias" (p. 394).

The newest models of test fairness describe a systemic approach utilizing both internal and external sources of evidence of fairness that extend from test conception and design through test score interpretation and application (Camilli & Shepard, 1994; McArdle, 1998; Willingham, 1999). These models are important because they acknowledge the importance of the consequences of test use in a holistic assessment of fairness and a multifaceted methodological approach to accumulate evidence of test fairness. This section describes a systemic model of test fairness adapted from the work of several leading authorities.

## Terms and Definitions

Three key terms appear in the literature associated with test score fairness: *bias, fairness,* and *equity*. These concepts overlap but are not identical; for example, a test that shows no evidence of test score bias may be used unfairly. To some extent these terms have historically been defined by families of relevant psychometric analyses—for example, bias is usually associated with differential item functioning, and fairness is associated with differential prediction to an external criterion. In this section, the terms are defined at a conceptual level.

*Test score bias* tends to be defined in a narrow manner, as a special case of test score invalidity. According to the most recent *Standards for Educational and Psychological Testing* (1999), bias in testing refers to "construct under-representation or construct-irrelevant components of test scores that differentially affect the performance of different groups of test takers" (p. 172). This definition implies that bias stems from nonrandom measurement error, provided that the typical magnitude of random error is comparable for all groups of interest. Accordingly, test score bias refers to the systematic and invalid introduction of measurement error for a particular group of interest. The statistical underpinnings of this definition have been underscored by Jensen (1980), who asserted, "The assessment of bias is a purely objective, empirical, statistical and quantitative matter entirely independent of subjective value judgments and ethical issues concerning fairness or unfairness of tests and the uses to which they are put" (p. 375). Some scholars consider the characterization of bias as objective and independent of the value judgments associated with fair use of tests to be fundamentally incorrect (e.g., Willingham, 1999).

*Test score fairness* refers to the ways in which test scores are utilized, most often for various forms of consequential decision making, such as selection or placement. Jensen (1980) suggested that the term refers "to the ways in which test scores (whether of biased or unbiased tests) are used in any selection situation" (p. 376), arguing that fairness is a subjective policy decision based on philosophic, legal, or practical considerations rather than a statistical decision. Willingham (1999) described a test fairness manifold that extends throughout the entire process of test development including the consequences of test usage. Embracing the idea that fairness is akin to demonstrating the generalizability of test validity across population subgroups, Willingham noted that "the manifold of fairness issues is complex because validity is complex" (p. 223). Fairness is a concept that transcends a narrow statistical and psychometric approach.

Finally, *equity* refers to a social value associated with the intended and unintended consequences and impact of test score usage. Because of the importance of equal opportunity, equal protection, and equal treatment in mental health, education, and the workplace, Willingham (1999) recommended that psychometrics actively consider equity issues in test development. As Tiedeman (1978) noted, "Test equity seems to be emerging as a criterion for test use on a par with the concepts of reliability and validity" (p. xxviii). However, the expectation that tests can correct long-standing problems of equity in society has never been grounded in psychometric science.

## Internal Evidence of Fairness

The demonstration that a test has *equal internal integrity* across racial and ethnic groups has been described as a way to demonstrate test fairness (e.g., Mercer, 1984). The *internal* features of a test related to fairness generally include the test's theoretical underpinnings, item content and format, differential item and test functioning, reliability generalization, and measurement invariance. The two best-known procedures for evaluating test fairness include expert reviews of content bias and analysis of differential item functioning. This section discusses these and several additional sources of evidence of test fairness.

### *Item Bias and Sensitivity Review*

In efforts to enhance fairness, the content and format of psychological and educational tests commonly undergo subjective bias and sensitivity reviews one or more times during test development. In this review, independent representatives from diverse groups closely examine tests, identifying items and procedures that may yield differential responses for one group relative to another. Content may be reviewed for cultural, disability, ethnic, racial, religious, sex, and SES bias. For example, a reviewer may be asked a series of questions, including "Does the content, format, or structure of the test item present greater problems for students from some backgrounds than for others?" A comprehensive item bias review is available from Hambleton and Rodgers (1995), and useful guidelines to reduce bias in language are available from the American Psychological Association (1994).

Ideally there are two objectives in bias and sensitivity reviews: (1) eliminate biased material and (2) ensure balanced and neutral representation of groups within the test. Among the potentially biased elements of tests that should be avoided is

- material that is controversial, or emotionally charged, or inflammatory for any specific group;
- language, artwork, or material that is demeaning or offensive to any specific group;
- content or situations with differential familiarity and relevance for specific groups;
- language and instructions that have different or unfamiliar meanings for specific groups;
- information and/or skills that may not be expected to be within the educational background of all examinees; and
- format or structure of the item that presents differential difficulty for specific groups.

Among the prosocial elements that ideally should be included in tests are

- presentation of universal experiences in test material;
- balanced distribution of people from diverse groups;
- presentation of people in activities that do not reinforce stereotypes;
- item presentation in a sex-, culture-, age-, and race-neutral manner; and
- inclusion of individuals with disabilities or handicapping conditions.

In general, the content of test materials should be relevant and accessible for the entire population of examinees for whom the test is intended. For example, the experiences of snow and freezing winters are outside the range of knowledge of many Southern students, thereby introducing a potential geographic regional bias. Use of utensils such as forks may be unfamiliar to Asian immigrants who may instead use chopsticks. Use of coinage from the United States ensures that the test cannot be validly used with examinees from countries with different currency.

Tests should also be free of controversial, emotionally charged, or value-laden content, such as violence or religion. The presence of such material may prove distracting, offensive, or unsettling to examinees from some groups, detracting from test performance. For example, Lichtenberger and Kaufman (2009) documented the removal of emotionally evocative and clinically rich items from the Wechsler intelligence scales—for example, *beer-wine* from the Similarities subtest and *knife* and *gamble* from the Vocabulary subtest—because these items elicited responses that sometimes tapped psychological constructs irrelevant to intelligence per se.

*Stereotyping* refers to the portrayal of a group using only a limited number of attributes, characteristics, or roles. As a rule, stereotyping should be avoided in test development. Specific groups should be portrayed accurately and fairly, without reference to stereotypes or traditional roles regarding sex, race, ethnicity, religion, physical ability, or geographic setting. Group members should be portrayed as exhibiting a full range of activities, behaviors, and roles.

### Differential Item and Test Functioning

Are item and test statistical properties equivalent for individuals of comparable ability, but from different groups? *Differential test and item functioning* (DTIF, or DTF and DIF) refers to a family of statistical procedures aimed at determining whether examinees of the same ability but from different groups have different probabilities of success on a test or an item. The most widely used of DIF procedures is the Mantel-Haenszel technique (Holland & Thayer, 1988), which assesses similarities in item functioning across various demographic groups of comparable ability. Items showing significant DIF are usually considered for deletion from a test.

DIF has been extended by Shealy and Stout (1993) to a test score–based level of analysis known as differential test functioning, a multidimensional nonparametric IRT index of test bias. Whereas DIF is expressed at the item level, DTF represents a combination of two or more items to produce DTF, with scores on a valid subtest used to match examinees according to ability level. Tests may show evidence of DIF on some items without evidence of DTF, provided item bias statistics are offsetting and eliminate differential bias at the test score level.

Although psychometricians have embraced DIF as a preferred method for detecting potential item bias (McAllister, 1993), this methodology has been subjected to increasing criticism because of its dependence on internal test properties and its inherent circular reasoning. Hills (1999) noted that two decades of DIF research have failed to demonstrate that removing biased items affects test bias and narrows the gap in group mean scores. Furthermore, DIF rests on several assumptions including that items are unidimensional, that the latent trait is equivalently distributed across groups, that the groups being compared (usually racial, sex, or ethnic groups) are homogeneous, and that the overall test is unbiased. Camilli and Shepard (1994) observed: "By definition, internal DIF methods are incapable of detecting constant bias. Their aim, and capability, is only to detect relative discrepancies" (p. 17). Hunter and Schmidt (2000) have criticized DIF methodology, finding that most evidence of DIF may be explained by a failure to control for measurement error in ability estimates, violations of the DIF unidimensionality assumption, and/or reliance on spurious artifactual findings from statistical significance testing. Disparaging DIF methodology, they wrote, "[W]e know that the literature on item bias is unsound from a technical standpoint" (p. 157).

### Measurement Invariance

*Measurement invariance* in psychological measurement is concerned with systematic group consistency in the information provided by a test about the latent variable or variables to be measured. Although there are multiple potential ways to demonstrate measurement invariance, the demonstration of *factorial invariance* across racial and ethnic groups via confirmatory factor analyses is one way to provide evidence that a test's internal structure is invariant. Millsap (1997) observed, "When measurement bias is present, two individuals from different groups who are identical on the latent variable(s) of interest would be expected to score differently on the test" (p. 249).

A difference in the factor structure across groups provides some evidence for bias even though factorial invariance does not necessarily signify fairness (e.g., Meredith, 1993; Nunnally & Bernstein, 1994). Floyd and Widaman (1995) suggested that "[i]ncreasing recognition of cultural, developmental, and contextual influences on psychological constructs has raised interest in demonstrating measurement invariance before assuming that measures are equivalent across groups" (p. 296).

### Reliability Generalization

Earlier we described the methodology of reliability generalization as a meta-analytic methodology that can investigate test score reliability across samples (Vacha-Haase, 1998). Reliability generalization also has the capacity to provide evidence of test score fairness by demonstrating relatively little change in score reliabilities across racial, ethnic, linguistic, and gender subsamples. Demonstration of adequate measurement precision across groups suggests that a test has adequate accuracy for the populations in which it may be used. Geisinger (1998) noted that

> subgroup-specific reliability analysis may be especially appropriate when the reliability of a test has been justified on the basis of internal consistency reliability procedures (e.g., coefficient *alpha*). Such analysis should be repeated in the group of special test takers because the meaning and difficulty of some components of the test may change over groups, especially over some cultural, linguistic, and disability groups. (p. 25)

Differences in group reliabilities may be evident, however, when test items are substantially more difficult for one group than another or when ceiling or floor effects are present for only one group.

The temporal stability of test scores should also be compared across groups, using similar test-retest intervals, in order to ensure that test results are equally stable irrespective of race and ethnicity. Jensen (1980) suggested:

> If a test is unbiased, test-retest correlation, of course with the same interval between testings for the major and minor groups, should yield the same correlation for both groups. Significantly different test-retest correlations (taking proper account of possibly unequal variances in the two groups) are indicative of a biased test. Failure to understand instructions, guessing, carelessness, marking answers haphazardly, and the like, all tend to lower the test-retest correlation. If two groups differ in test-retest correlation, it is clear that the test scores are not equally accurate or stable measures of both groups. (p. 430)

### External Evidence of Fairness

Beyond the concept of internal integrity, Mercer (1984) recommended that studies of test fairness include evidence of *equal external relevance*. In brief, this determination requires the examination of relations between item/test scores and independent external criteria. External evidence of test score fairness has been accumulated in the study of comparative prediction of future performance (e.g., use of the SAT across racial groups to predict a student's ability to do college-level work). Fair prediction and fair selection are two objectives that are particularly important as evidence of test fairness, in part because they figure prominently in legislation and court rulings.

### Fair Prediction

Prediction bias can arise when a test differentially predicts future behaviors or performance across groups. Cleary (1968) introduced a methodology that evaluates comparative predictive validity between two or more salient groups. The Cleary rule states that a test may be considered fair if it has the same approximate regression equation (i.e., comparable slope and intercept) explaining the relationship between the predictor test and an external criterion measure in the groups undergoing comparison. A slope difference between the two groups conveys differential validity and relates that one group's performance on the external criterion is predicted less well than the other's performance. An intercept difference suggests a difference in the level of estimated performance between the groups, even if the predictive validity is comparable. It is important to note that this methodology assumes adequate levels of reliability for both the predictor and criterion variables. This procedure has several limitations that have been summarized by Camilli and Shepard (1994). The demonstration of equivalent predictive validity across demographic groups constitutes an important source of fairness that is related to validity generalization. Millsap (1997) demonstrated, however, that measurement invariance may be logically and statistically incompatible with invariant prediction, challenging the value of conventional approaches to prediction bias. Hunter and Schmidt (2000) went further in their appraisal of the fair prediction literature:

> For the past 30 years, civil rights lawyers, journalists, and others . . . have argued that when test scores are equal, minorities have higher average levels of educational and work performance, meaning that test scores underestimate the real world performance of minorities. Thousands of test bias studies have been conducted, and these studies have disconfirmed that hypothesis. The National Academy of Science . . . concluded that professionally developed tests are not predictively biased. (p. 151)

Based on these observations pertaining to predictive bias, Hunter and Schmidt concluded that "the issue of test bias is scientifically dead" (p. 151).

## Fair Selection

The consequences of test score use for selection and decision making in clinical, educational, and occupational domains constitute a source of potential bias. The issue of fair selection addresses the question: Do the use of test scores for selection decisions unfairly favor one group over another? Specifically, test scores that produce adverse, disparate, or disproportionate impact for various racial or ethnic groups may be said to show evidence of selection bias, even when that impact is construct relevant. Since enactment of the Civil Rights Act of 1964, demonstration of adverse impact has been treated in legal settings as prima facie evidence of test bias. Adverse impact occurs when there is a substantially different rate of selection based on test scores and other factors works to the disadvantage of members of a race, sex, or ethnic group.

Federal mandates and court rulings often have indicated that adverse, disparate, or disproportionate impact in selection decisions based on test scores constitutes evidence of unlawful discrimination, and differential test selection rates among majority and minority groups have been considered a bottom line in federal mandates and court rulings. In its Uniform Guidelines on Employment Selection Procedures (1978), the Equal Employment Opportunity Commission operationalized adverse impact according to the four-fifths rule, which states: "A selection rate for any race, sex, or ethnic group which is less than four-fifths (4/5) (or eighty percent) of the rate for the group with the highest rate will generally be regarded by the Federal enforcement agencies as evidence of adverse impact" (p. 126). Adverse impact has been applied to educational tests (e.g., the *Texas Assessment of Academic Skills*) as well as tests used in personnel selection. The U.S. Supreme Court held in 1988 that differential selection ratios can constitute sufficient evidence of adverse impact. The 1991 Civil Rights Act, Section 9, specifically and explicitly prohibits any discriminatory use of test scores for minority groups.

Since selection decisions involve the use of test cutoff scores, an analysis of costs and benefits according to decision theory provides a methodology for fully understanding the consequences of test score usage. Cutoff scores may be varied to provide optimal fairness across groups, or alternative cutoff scores may be utilized in certain circumstances. McArdle (1998) observed, "As the cutoff scores become increasingly stringent, the number of false negative mistakes (or costs) also increase, but the number of false positive mistakes (also a cost) decrease" (p. 174).

## LIMITS OF PSYCHOMETRICS

Psychological assessment is ultimately about the examinee. A test is merely a tool to understand the examinee, and psychometrics are merely rules to build and evaluate the tools. The tools themselves must be sufficiently sound (i.e., valid, reliable) and fair so that they introduce acceptable levels of error into the process of decision making. Some of the guidelines that have been described in this chapter for psychometrics of test construction and application help us not only to build better tools but to use these tools as skilled craftspersons.

As an evolving field of study, psychometrics still has some glaring shortcomings. A long-standing limitation of psychometrics is its systematic overreliance on internal sources of evidence for test validity and fairness. In brief, it is more expensive and more difficult to collect external criterion-based information, especially with special populations; it is simpler and easier to base all analyses on the performance of a normative standardization sample. This dependency on internal methods has been recognized and acknowledged by leading psychometricians. In discussing psychometric methods for detecting test bias, for example, Camilli and Shepard (1994) cautioned about circular reasoning: "Because DIF indices rely only on internal criteria, they are inherently circular" (p. 17). Similarly, psychometricians have been hesitant to consider attempts to extend the domain of validity into consequential aspects of test usage (e.g., Borsboom 2006a; Lees-Haley, 1996). We have witnessed entire testing approaches based on internal factor-analytic approaches and evaluation of content validity (e.g., McGrew & Flanagan, 1998), with comparatively little attention paid to the external validation of the factors against independent, ecologically valid criteria. This shortcoming constitutes a serious limitation of psychometrics, which we have attempted to address by encouraging use of both internal and external sources of psychometric evidence.

Another long-standing limitation is the tendency of test developers to wait until the test is undergoing standardization to establish its validity through clinical studies. A typical sequence of test development involves pilot studies, a content tryout, and finally a national standardization and supplementary studies (e.g., Robertson, 1992). In the stages of test development described by Loevinger (1957), the external criterion-based validation stage comes last in the process—after the test has effectively been built. A limitation in test development and psychometric practice is that many tests validate their effectiveness for a stated purpose only at the end of the process rather than at the beginning, as MMPI developers did over a half century ago by selecting items that discriminated between specific diagnostic groups (Hathaway & McKinley, 1943). The utility of a test for its intended application should be at least partially validated at the pilot study stage, prior to norming. Even better is an evidence-based validity argument, such as proposed by Mislevy and Haertel (2006), to explicitly link test construction with its intended application.

Finally, psychometrics has failed to directly address many of the applied questions of practitioners. Test results often do not readily lend themselves to functional decision making. For example, psychometricians have been slow to develop consensually accepted ways of measuring growth and maturation, reliable change (as a result of enrichment, intervention, or treatment), and atypical response patterns suggestive of lack of effort or dissimilation. There is a strong need for more innovations like the Bayesian nomogram, which readily lends itself to straightforward clinical application (e.g., Bianchi, Alexander, & Cash, 2009; Jenkins et al., 2011). In general, the failure of treatment validity and assessment–treatment linkage undermines the central purpose of testing.

Looking to the future, the emergence of evidence-based assessment (EBA) guidelines now appears inevitable, paralleling the numerous evidence-based treatment, instruction, and intervention effectiveness studies that have led to professional practice guidelines. While EBA has taken many different forms in the literature, Hunsley and Mash (2005) have anticipated that it will include standard psychometric indices of reliability and validity and also encompass treatment utility, diagnostic utility, and a range of additional factors, such as the economic and psychological costs associated with assessment error. Any forthcoming rules for EBA are likely to increase the accountability of test users (who will increasingly be required to use empirically supported measurements) and test developers (who will need to carefully determine the new mix of psychometric studies necessary to successfully meet professional needs). The powerful impact of a single psychometrically oriented review—Lilienfeld, Wood, and Garb's (2000) critical assessment of projective tests—may provide a hint of the magnitude of changes that may come with EBA.

## REFERENCES

Achenbach, T. M., & Rescorla, L. A. (2001). *Manual for the ASEBA school-age forms and profiles.* Burlington: University of Vermont, Research Center for Children, Youth, & Families.

American Psychological Association. (1994). *Publication manual of the American Psychological Association* (4th ed.). Washington, DC: Author.

American Psychological Association. (2002). Ethical principles of psychologists and code of conduct. *American Psychologist, 57,* 1060–1073.

Anastasi, A., & Urbina, S. (1997). *Psychological testing* (7th ed.). Upper Saddle River, NJ: Prentice-Hall.

Andrich, D. (1988). *Rasch models for measurement.* Thousand Oaks, CA: Sage.

Angoff, W. H. (1984). *Scales, norms, and equivalent scores.* Princeton, NJ: Educational Testing Service.

Banaji, M. R., & Crowder, R. C. (1989). The bankruptcy of everyday memory. *American Psychologist, 44,* 1185–1193.

Barrios, B. A. (1988). On the changing nature of behavioral assessment. In A. S. Bellack & M. Hersen (Eds.), *Behavioral assessment: A practical handbook* (3rd ed., pp. 3–41). New York, NY: Pergamon Press.

Bayley, N. (1993). *Bayley Scales of Infant Development, Second edition manual.* San Antonio, TX: Psychological Corporation.

Ben-Porath, Y. S., & Tellegen, A. (2008). *MMPI-2-RF: Manual for administration, scoring, and interpretation.* Minneapolis: University of Minnesota Press.

Beutler, L. E. (1998). Identifying empirically supported treatments: What if we didn't? *Journal of Consulting & Clinical Psychology, 66,* 113–120.

Beutler, L. E., & Clarkin, J. F. (1990). *Systematic treatment selection: Toward targeted therapeutic interventions.* Philadelphia, PA: Brunner/Mazel.

Beutler, L. E., & Harwood, T. M. (2000). *Prescriptive psychotherapy: A practical guide to systematic treatment selection.* New York, NY: Oxford University Press.

Bianchi, M. T., Alexander, B. M., & Cash, S. S. (2009). Incorporating uncertainty into medical decision making: An approach to unexpected test results. *Medical Decision Making, 29,* 116–124.

Binet, A., & Simon, T. (1911/1916). New investigation upon the measure of the intellectual level among school children. *L'Année Psychologique, 17,* 145–201. In E. S. Kite (Trans.), *The development of intelligence in children* (pp. 274–329). Baltimore, MD: Williams & Wilkins. (Original work published 1911)

Borsboom, D. (2006a). The attack of the psychometricians. *Psychometrika, 71,* 425–440.

Borsboom, D. (2006b). Can we bring out a velvet revolution in psychological measurement? A rejoinder to commentaries. *Psychometrika, 71,* 463–467.

Borsboom, D., Cramer, A. O. J., Kievit, R. A., Scholten, A. Z., & Franić, S. (2009). The end of construct validity. In R. W. Lissitz (Ed.), *The concept of validity: Revisions, new directions, and applications* (pp. 135–170). Charlotte, NC: Information Age.

Borsboom, D., Mellenbergh, G. J., & Van Heerden, J. (2004). The concept of validity. *Psychological Review, 111,* 1061–1071.

Bracken, B. A. (1987). Limitations of preschool instruments and standards for minimal levels of technical adequacy. *Journal of Psychoeducational Assessment, 4,* 313–326.

Bracken, B. A. (1988). Ten psychometric reasons why similar tests produce dissimilar results. *Journal of School Psychology, 26,* 155–166.

Bracken, B. A., & McCallum, R. S. (1998). *Universal Nonverbal Intelligence Test examiner's manual.* Itasca, IL: Riverside.

Brennan, R. L. (2010a). Evidence-centered assessment design and the Advanced Placement Program: A psychometrician's perspective. *Applied Measurement in Education, 23,* 392–400.

Brennan, R. L. (2010b). *Generalizability theory.* New York, NY: Springer-Verlag.

Brown, W. (1910). Some experimental results in the correlation of mental abilities. *British Journal of Psychology, 3,* 296–322.

Bruininks, R. H., Woodcock, R. W., Weatherman, R. F., & Hill, B. K. (1996). *Scales of Independent Behavior—Revised comprehensive manual.* Itasca, IL: Riverside.

Camilli, G., & Shepard, L. A. (1994). *Methods for identifying biased test items* (Vol. 4). Thousand Oaks, CA: Sage.

Campbell, D. T., & Fiske, D. W. (1959). Convergent and discriminant validation by the multitrait-multimethod matrix. *Psychological Bulletin, 56,* 81–105.

Campbell, D. T., & Stanley, J. C. (1963). *Experimental and quasi-experimental designs for research.* Chicago, IL: Rand McNally.

Campbell, S. K., Siegel, E., Parr, C. A., & Ramey, C. T. (1986). Evidence for the need to renorm the Bayley Scales of Infant Development based on the performance of a population-based sample of 12-month-old infants. *Topics in Early Childhood Special Education, 6,* 83–96.

Carroll, J. B. (1983). Studying individual differences in cognitive abilities: Through and beyond factor analysis. In R. F. Dillon & R. R. Schmeck (Eds.), *Individual differences in cognition* (pp. 1–33). New York, NY: Academic Press.

Cattell, R. B. (1986). The psychometric properties of tests: Consistency, validity, and efficiency. In R. B. Cattell & R. C. Johnson (Eds.), *Functional psychological testing: Principles and instruments* (pp. 54–78). New York, NY: Brunner/Mazel.

Chudowsky, N., & Behuniak, P. (1998). Using focus groups to examine the consequential aspect of validity. *Educational Measurement: Issues & Practice, 17,* 28–38.

Cizek, G. J., Bowen, D., & Church, K. (2010). Sources of validity evidence for educational and psychological tests: A follow-up study. *Educational and Psychological Measurement, 70,* 732–743.

Clark, L. A., & Watson, D. (1995). Constructing validity: Basic issues in objective scale development. *Psychological Assessment, 7,* 309–319.

Cleary, T. A. (1968). Test bias: Prediction of grades for Negro and White students in integrated colleges. *Journal of Educational Measurement, 5,* 115–124.

Cohen, J. (1992). A power primer. *Psychological Bulletin, 112,* 155–159.

Cone, J. D. (1978). The behavioral assessment grid (BAG): A conceptual framework and a taxonomy. *Behavior Therapy, 9,* 882–888.

Cone, J. D. (1988). Psychometric considerations and the multiple models of behavioral assessment. In A. S. Bellack & M. Hersen (Eds.), *Behavioral assessment: A practical handbook* (3rd ed., pp. 42–66). New York, NY: Pergamon Press.

Cook, T. D., & Campbell, D. T. (1979). *Quasi-experimentation: Design and analysis issues for field settings.* Chicago, IL: Rand McNally.

Cortina, J. M. (1993). What is coefficient alpha? An examination of theory and applications. *Journal of Applied Psychology, 78,* 98–104.

Costa, P. T. Jr., & McCrae, R. R. (2010). *NEO Inventories Professional Manual for NEO-PI-3, NEO FFI-3 & NEO PIR.* Lutz, FL: Psychological Assessment Resources.

Crocker, L. (2003). Teaching for the test: Validity, fairness, and moral action. *Educational Measurement: Issues and Practice, 22,* 5–11.

Crocker, L., & Algina, J. (1986). *Introduction to classical and modern test theory.* New York, NY: Holt, Rinehart.

Cronbach, L. J. (1957). The two disciplines of scientific psychology. *American Psychologist, 12,* 671–684.

Cronbach, L. J. (1971). Test validation. In R. L. Thorndike (Ed.), *Educational measurement* (2nd ed., pp. 443–507). Washington, DC: American Council on Education.

Cronbach, L. J., & Gleser, G. C. (1965). *Psychological tests and personnel decisions.* Urbana, IL: University of Illinois Press.

Cronbach, L. J., Gleser, G. C., Nanda, H., & Rajaratnam, N. (1972). *The dependability of behavioral measurements: Theory of generalizability scores and profiles.* New York, NY: Wiley.

Cronbach, L. J., & Meehl, P. E. (1955). Construct validity in psychological tests. *Psychological Bulletin, 52,* 281–302.

Daniel, M. H. (1999). Behind the scenes: Using new measurement methods on the DAS and KAIT. In S. E. Embretson & S. L. Hershberger (Eds.), *The new rules of measurement: What every psychologist and educator should know* (pp. 37–63). Mahwah, NJ: Erlbaum.

Daniel, M. H. (2007). *Test norming.* Retrieved from www.pearsonassessments.com/pai/ca/RelatedInfo/TestNorming.htm

Dimitrov, D. M. (2002). Reliability: Arguments for multiple perspectives and potential problems with generalization across studies. *Educational and Psychological Measurement, 62,* 783–801.

Efron, B., & Tibshirani, R. J. (1993). *An introduction to the bootstrap.* New York, NY: Chapman & Hall/CRC.

Elliott, C. D. (1990). *Differential Ability Scales: Introductory and technical handbook.* San Antonio, TX: Psychological Corporation.

Embretson, S. E. (1995). The new rules of measurement. *Psychological Assessment, 8,* 341–349.

Embretson, S. E. (1999). Issues in the measurement of cognitive abilities. In S. E. Embretson & S. L. Hershberger (Eds.), *The new rules of measurement: What every psychologist and educator should know* (pp. 1–15). Mahwah, NJ: Erlbaum.

Embretson, S. E. (2004). The second century of ability testing: Some predictions and speculations. *Measurement, 2,* 1–32.

Embretson, S. E., & Hershberger, S. L. (Eds.). (1999). *The new rules of measurement: What every psychologist and educator should know.* Mahwah, NJ: Erlbaum.

Ercikan, K., Arim, R., Law, D., Domene, J., Gagnon, F., & Lacroix, S. (2011). Application of Think Aloud Protocols for examining and confirming sources of differential item functioning identified by expert reviews. *Educational Measurement: Issues and Practice, 29(2),* 24–35.

Erdodi, L. A., Richard, D. C. S., & Hopwood, C. (2009). The importance of relying on the manual: Scoring error variance in the WISC-IV Vocabulary subtest. *Journal of Psychoeducational Assessment, 27,* 374–385.

Ericsson, K. A., & Simon, H. A. (1980). Verbal reports as data. *Psychological Review, 87,* 215–251.

Fan, X. (1998). Item response theory and classical test theory: An empirical comparison of their item/person statistics. *Educational and Psychological Measurement, 58,* 357–381.

Fan, X., & Thompson, B. (2001). Confidence intervals about score reliability coefficients, please: An EPM guidelines editorial. *Editorial and Psychological Measurement, 61,* 517–531.

Fiske, D. W., & Campbell, D. T. (1992). Citations do not solve problems. *Psychological Bulletin, 112,* 393–395.

Fleiss, J. L. (1981). Balanced incomplete block designs for inter-rater reliability studies. *Applied Psychological Measurement, 5,* 105–112.

Floyd, F. J., & Widaman, K. F. (1995). Factor analysis in the development and refinement of clinical assessment instruments. *Psychological Assessment, 7,* 286–299.

Flynn, J. R. (1984). The mean IQ of Americans: Massive gains 1932 to 1978. *Psychological Bulletin, 95,* 29–51.

Flynn, J. R. (1987). Massive IQ gains in 14 nations: What IQ tests really measure. *Psychological Bulletin, 101,* 171–191.

Flynn, J. R. (1994). IQ gains over time. In R. J. Sternberg (Ed.), *The encyclopedia of human intelligence* (pp. 617–623). New York, NY: Macmillan.

Flynn, J. R. (1999). Searching for justice: The discovery of IQ gains over time. *American Psychologist, 54,* 5–20.

Fox, M. C., Ericsson, K. A., & Best, R. (2011). Do procedures for verbal reporting of thinking have to be reactive? A meta-analysis and recommendations for best reporting methods. *Psychological Bulletin, 137,* 316–344.

Foy, P., & Joncas, M. (2004). TIMSS 2003 sampling design. In M. O. Martin, I. V. S. Mullis, & S. J. Chrostowski (Eds.), *Trends in*

*International Mathematics and Science Study (TIMSS) 2003 technical report* (pp. 109–122). Chestnut Hill, MA: TIMSS & PIRLS International Study Center, Boston College.

Frisby, C. L., & Kim, S. (2008). Using profile analysis via multidimensional scaling (PAMS) to identify core profiles from the WMS-III. *Psychological Assessment, 20,* 1–9.

Galton, F. (1879). Psychometric experiments. *Brain: A Journal of Neurology, 2,* 149–162.

Geisinger, K. F. (1998). Psychometric issues in test interpretation. In J. Sandoval, C. L. Frisby, K. F. Geisinger, J. D. Scheuneman, & J. R. Grenier (Eds.) *Test interpretation and diversity: Achieving equity in assessment* (pp. 17–30). Washington, DC: American Psychological Association.

Gignac, G. E., Bates, T. C., & Jang, K. (2007). Implications relevant to CFA model misfit, reliability, and the five-factor model as measured by the NEO FFI. *Personality and Individual Differences, 43,* 1051–1062.

Gorsuch, R. L. (1983a). *Factor analysis* (2nd ed.). Hillsdale, NJ: Erlbaum.

Gorsuch, R. L. (1983b). The theory of continuous norming. In R. L. Gorsuch (Chair), *Continuous norming: An alternative to tabled norms?* Symposium conducted at the 91st Annual Convention of the American Psychological Association, Anaheim, CA.

Gorsuch, R. L. (2010). Continuous parameter estimation model: Expanding our statistical paradigm. In G. H. Roid (Chair), *Continuous parameter estimation and continuous norming methods.* Symposium conducted at the 118th annual convention of the American Psychological Association, San Diego, CA.

Gorsuch, R. L., & Zachary, R. A. (1985). Continuous norming: Implication for the WAIS-R. *Journal of Clinical Psychology, 41,* 86–94.

Guilford, J. P. (1950). *Fundamental statistics in psychology and education* (2nd ed.). New York, NY: McGraw-Hill.

Guion, R. M. (1977). Content validity—The source of my discontent. *Applied Psychological Measurement, 1,* 1–10.

Gulliksen, H. (1950). *Theory of mental tests.* New York, NY: McGraw-Hill.

Hambleton, R., & Rodgers, J. H. (1995). *Item bias review.* (ERIC Clearinghouse on Assessment and Evaluation, EDO-TM-95-9). Washington, DC: Catholic University of America Department of Education.

Hambleton, R. K., Swaminathan, H., & Rogers, H. J. (1991). *Fundamentals of item response theory.* Newbury Park, CA: Sage.

Hathaway, S. R. & McKinley, J. C. (1943). *Manual for the Minnesota Multiphasic Personality Inventory.* New York, NY: Psychological Corporation.

Hayes, S. C., Nelson, R. O., & Jarrett, R. B. (1987). The treatment utility of assessment: A functional approach to evaluating assessment quality. *American Psychologist, 42,* 963–974.

Haynes, S. N., Richard, D. C. S., & Kubany, E. S. (1995). Content validity in psychological assessment: A functional approach to concepts and methods. *Psychological Assessment, 7,* 238–247.

Heinrichs, R. W. (1990). Current and emergent applications of neuropsychological assessment problems of validity and utility. *Professional Psychology: Research and Practice, 21,* 171–176.

Helmes, E., & Reddon, J. R. (1993). A perspective on developments in assessing psychopathology: A critical review of the MMPI and MMPI-2. *Psychological Bulletin, 113,* 453–471.

Herrnstein, R. J., & Murray, C. (1994). *The bell curve: Intelligence and class in American life.* New York, NY: Free Press.

Hertzog, M. A. (2008). Considerations in determining sample size for pilot studies. *Research in Nursing & Health, 31,* 180–191.

Hills, J. (1999, May 14). Re: Construct validity. *Educational Statistics Discussion List (EDSTAT-L).* Available e-mail: edstat-l@jse.stat.ncsu.edu

Hoelzle, J. B., & Meyer, G. J. (2008). The factor structure of the MMPI–2 Restructured Clinical (RC) scales. *Journal of Personality Assessment, 90,* 443–455.

Hogan, T. P., Benjamin, A., & Brezinski, K. L. (2000). Reliability methods: A note on the frequency of use of various types. *Educational and Psychological Measurement, 60,* 523–531.

Holland, P. W., & Thayer, D. T. (1988). Differential item functioning and the Mantel-Haenszel procedure. In H. Wainer & H. I. Braun (Eds.), *Test validity* (pp. 129–145). Hillsdale, NJ: Erlbaum.

Horn, J. L., Wanberg, K. W., & Appel, M. (1973). On the internal structure of the MMPI. *Multivariate Behavioral Research, 8,* 131–171.

Hopkins, C. D., & Antes, R. L. (1978). *Classroom measurement and evaluation.* Itasca, IL: F. E. Peacock.

Hopwood, C., & Richard, D. C. S. (2005). WAIS-III scoring accuracy is a function of scale IC and complexity of examiner tasks. *Assessment, 12,* 445–454.

Hunsley, J., & Mash, E. J. (2005). Introduction to the special section on developing guidelines for the evidence-based assessment (EBA) of adult disorders. *Psychological Assessment, 17,* 251–255.

Hunter, J. E., & Schmidt, F. L. (1990). *Methods of meta-analysis: Correcting error and bias in research findings.* Newbury Park, CA: Sage.

Hunter, J. E., & Schmidt, F. L. (2000). Racial and gender bias in ability and achievement tests: Resolving the apparent paradox. *Psychology, Public Policy & Law, 6,* 151–158.

Hunter, J. E., Schmidt, F. L., & Jackson, C. B. (1982). *Advanced meta-analysis: Quantitative methods of cumulating research findings across studies.* San Francisco, CA: Sage.

Ittenbach, R. F., Esters, I. G., & Wainer, H. (1997). The history of test development. In D. P. Flanagan, J. L. Genshaft, & P. L. Harrison (Eds.), *Contemporary intellectual assessment: Theories, tests, and issues* (pp. 17–31). New York, NY: Guilford Press.

Jackson, D. N. (1971). A sequential system for personality scale development. In C. D. Spielberger (Ed.), *Current topics in clinical and community psychology* (Vol. 2, pp. 61–92). New York, NY: Academic Press.

Jencks, C., & Phillips, M. (Eds.). (1998). *The Black-White test score gap.* Washington, DC: Brookings Institute.

Jenkins, M. A., Youngstrom, E. A., Washburn, J. J., & Youngstrom, J. K. (2011). Evidence-based strategies improve assessment of pediatric bipolar disorder by community practitioners. *Professional Psychology: Research and Practice, 42,* 121–129.

Jensen, A. R. (1980). *Bias in mental testing.* New York, NY: Free Press.

Johnson, N. L. (1949). Systems of frequency curves generated by methods of translation. *Biometrika, 36,* 149–176.

Julious, S. A. (2005). Sample size of 12 per group rule of thumb for a pilot study. *Pharmaceutical Statistics, 4,* 287–291.

Kalton, G. (1983). *Introduction to survey sampling.* Beverly Hills, CA: Sage.

Kelley, K., & Rausch, J. R. (2006). Sample size planning for the standardized mean difference: Accuracy in parameter estimation via narrow confidence intervals. *Psychological Methods, 11,* 363–385.

Kelley, T. L. (1927). *Interpretation of educational measurements.* New York, NY: Macmillan.

Knowles, E. S., & Condon, C. A. (2000). Does the rose still smell as sweet? Item variability across test forms and revisions. *Psychological Assessment, 12,* 245–252.

Kolen, M. J., Zeng, L., & Hanson, B. A. (1996). Conditional standard errors of measurement for scale scores using IRT. *Journal of Educational Measurement, 33,* 129–140.

Kuhn, T. (1970). *The structure of scientific revolutions* (2nd ed.). Chicago, IL: University of Chicago Press.

Lazarus, A. A. (1973). Multimodal behavior therapy: Treating the BASIC ID. *Journal of Nervous and Mental Disease, 156,* 404–411.

Lees-Haley, P. R. (1996). Alice in validityland, or the dangerous consequences of consequential validity. *American Psychologist, 51,* 981–983.

Lehtonen, R., & Pahkinen, E. (2004). *Practical methods for design and analysis of complex surveys* (2nd ed.). Hoboken, NJ: Wiley.

Levy, P. S., & Lemeshow, S. (1999). *Sampling of populations: Methods and applications.* New York, NY: Wiley.

Li, H., Rosenthal, R., & Rubin, D. B. (1996). Reliability of measurement in psychology: From Spearman-Brown to maximal reliability. *Psychological Methods, 1,* 98–107.

Lichtenberger, E. O., & Kaufman, A. S. (2009). *Essentials of WAIS-IV assessment.* Hoboken, NJ: Wiley.

Lilienfeld, S. O., Wood, J. M., & Garb, H. N. (2000). The scientific status of projective techniques. *Psychological Science in the Public Interest, 1,* 27–66.

Linacre, J. M., & Wright, B. D. (1999). *A user's guide to Winsteps/Ministep: Rasch-model computer programs.* Chicago, IL: MESA Press.

Linn, R. L. (1998). Partitioning responsibility for the evaluation of the consequences of assessment programs. *Educational Measurement: Issues & Practice, 17,* 28–30.

Lissitz, R. W. (Ed.) (2009). *The concept of validity: Revisions, new directions, and applications.* Charlotte, NC: Information Age.

Loevinger, J. (1957). Objective tests as instruments of psychological theory [Monograph]. *Psychological Reports, 3,* 635–694.

Loevinger, J. (1972). Some limitations of objective personality tests. In J. N. Butcher (Ed.), *Objective personality assessment* (pp. 45–58). New York, NY: Academic Press.

Lohman, D. F., & Lakin, J. (2009). Consistencies in sex differences on the Cognitive Abilities Test across countries, grades, test forms, and cohorts. *British Journal of Educational Psychology, 79,* 389–407.

Loken, E., & Rulison, K. L. (2010). Estimation of a four-parameter item response theory model. *British Journal of Mathematical and Statistical Psychology, 63,* 509–525.

Lombard, M., Snyder-Duch, J., & Bracken, C. C. (2002). Content analysis in mass communication: Assessment and reporting of intercoder reliability. *Human Communication Research, 28,* 587–604.

Lord, F. N., & Novick, M. (1968). *Statistical theories of mental tests.* New York, NY: Addison-Wesley.

Maruish, M. E. (Ed.) (1994). *The use of psychological testing for treatment planning and outcome assessment.* Hillsdale, NJ: Erlbaum.

McAllister, P. H. (1993). Testing, DIF, and public policy. In P. W. Holland & H. Wainer (Eds.), *Differential item functioning* (pp. 389–396). Hillsdale, NJ: Erlbaum.

McArdle, J. J. (1998). Contemporary statistical models for examining test-bias. In J. J. McArdle & R. W. Woodcock (Eds.), *Human cognitive abilities in theory and practice* (pp. 157–195). Mahwah, NJ: Erlbaum.

McCrae, R. R., Zonderman, A. B., Costa, P. T., Bond, M. H., & Paunonen, S. V. (1996). Evaluating replicability of factors in the revised NEO personality inventory: Confirmatory factor analysis versus Procrustes rotation. *Journal of Personality and Social Psychology, 70,* 552–566.

McGrew, K. S., Dailey, D. E. H., & Schrank, F. A. (2007). *Woodcock-Johnson III/Woodcock-Johnson III Normative Update score differences: What the user can expect and why (Woodcock-Johnson III Assessment Service Bulletin No. 9).* Rolling Meadows, IL: Riverside.

McGrew, K. S., & Flanagan, D. P. (1998). *The intelligence test desk reference (ITDR): Gf-Gc cross-battery assessment.* Boston, MA: Allyn & Bacon.

McGrew, K. S., & Woodcock, R. W. (2001). *Woodcock-Johnson III technical manual.* Itasca, IL: Riverside.

Mercer, J. R. (1984). What is a racially and culturally nondiscriminatory test? A sociological and pluralistic perspective. In C. R. Reynolds & R. T. Brown (Eds.), *Perspectives on bias in mental testing* (pp. 293–356). New York, NY: Plenum Press.

Meredith, W. (1993). Measurement invariance, factor analysis and factorial invariance. *Psychometrika, 58,* 525–543.

Messick, S. (1989a). Meaning and values in test validation: The science and ethics of assessment. *Educational Researcher, 18,* 5–11.

Messick, S. (1989b). Validity. In R. L. Linn (Ed.), *Educational measurement* (3rd ed., pp. 13–103). Washington, DC: American Council on Education and National Council on Measurement in Education.

Messick, S. (1995a). Standards of validity and the validity of standards in performance assessment. *Educational Measurement: Issues & Practice, 14,* 5–8.

Messick, S. (1995b). Validity of psychological assessment: Validation of inferences from persons' reponses and performances as scientific inquiry into score meaning. *American Psychologist, 50,* 741–749.

Meyer, P. (2010). *Reliability.* New York, NY: Oxford University Press.

Millon, T., Davis, R., & Millon, C. (1997). *MCMI-III: Millon Clinical Multiaxial Inventory-III manual* (3rd ed.). Minneapolis, MN: National Computer Systems.

Millsap, R. E. (1997). Invariance in measurement and prediction: Their relationship in the single-factor case. *Psychological Methods, 2,* 248–260.

Mislevy, R. J., & Haertel, G. (2006). Implications for evidence-centered design for educational assessment. *Educational Measurement: Issues and Practice, 25,* 6–20.

Mooney, C. Z., & Duval, R. D. (1993). *Bootstrapping: A nonparametric approach to statistical inference.* Newbury Park, CA: Sage.

Neisser, U. (1978). Memory: What are the important questions? In M. M. Gruneberg, P. E. Morris, & R. N. Sykes (Eds.), *Practical aspects of memory* (pp. 3–24). London, UK: Academic Press.

Neuendorf, K. A. (2002). *The content analysis guidebook.* Thousand Oaks, CA: Sage.

Newborg, J., Stock, J. R., Wnek, L., Guidubaldi, J., & Svinicki, J. (1984). *Battelle Developmental Inventory.* Itasca, IL: Riverside.

No Child Left Behind Act of 2001. Pub. L. No. 107–110, 20 U.S.C. § 6301 *et seq.* (2002).

Nunnally, J. C., & Bernstein, I. H. (1994). *Psychometric theory* (3rd ed.). New York, NY: McGraw-Hill.

Oakes, J. M., & Rossi, P. H. (2003). The measurement of SES in health research: current practice and steps toward a new approach. *Social Science & Medicine, 56,* 769–784.

Pearson, K. (1924). *The life, letters and labours of Francis Galton* (Vol. 2). *Researches of middle life.* London, UK: Cambridge University Press.

Peckham, R. F. (1972). Opinion, *Larry P.* v. *Riles. Federal Supplement 343,* 1306–1315.

Peckham, R. F. (1979). Opinion, *Larry P.* v. *Riles. Federal Supplement 495,* 926–992.

Pomplun, M. (1997). State assessment and instructional change: A path model analysis. *Applied Measurement in Education, 10,* 217–234.

Rasch, G. (1960). *Probabilistic models for some intelligence and attainment tests.* Copenhagen, Denmark: Danish Institute for Educational Research.

Reckase, M. D. (1998). Consequential validity from the test developer's perspective. *Educational Measurement: Issues & Practice, 17,* 13–16.

Reschly, D. J. (1997). Utility of individual ability measures and public policy choices for the 21st century. *School Psychology Review, 26,* 234–241.

Reschly, D. J., Myers, T. G., & Hartel, C. R. (2002). *Mental retardation: Determining eligibility for Social Security Benefits.* Washington, DC: National Academies Press.

Riese, S. P., Waller, N. G., & Comrey, A. L. (2000). Factor analysis and scale revision. *Psychological Assessment, 12,* 287–297.

Robertson, G. J. (1992). Psychological tests: Development, publication, and distribution. In M. Zeidner & R. Most (Eds.), *Psychological testing: An inside view* (pp. 159–214). Palo Alto, CA: Consulting Psychologists Press.

Roid, G. (2003). *Stanford-Binet Intelligence Scales* (5th ed.). *Interpretive manual: Expanded guide to the interpretation of SB5 test results.* Itasca, IL: Riverside.

Roid, G. H. (2010). Update and new evidence for continuous norming. In G. H. Roid (Chair), *Continuous parameter estimation and continuous norming methods.* Symposium conducted at the 118th annual convention of the American Psychological Association, San Diego, CA.

Rust, K. F., & Johnson, E. G. (1992). Sampling and weighting in the National Assessment. *Journal of Educational Statistics, 17,* 111–129.

Salvia, J., Ysseldyke, J., & Bolt, S. (2010). *Assessment in special and inclusive education* (11th ed.). Belmont, CA: Wadsworth.

Samejima, F. (1994). Estimation of reliability coefficients using the test information function and its modifications. *Applied Psychological Measurement, 18,* 229–244.

Schmidt, F. L., & Hunter, J. E. (1977). Development of a general solution to the problem of validity generalization. *Journal of Applied Psychology, 62,* 529–540.

Shealy, R., & Stout, W. F. (1993). A model-based standardization approach that separates true bias/DIF from group differences and detects test bias/DTF as well as item bias/DIF. *Psychometrika, 58,* 159–194.

Shrout, P. E., & Fleiss, J. L. (1979). Intraclass correlations: Uses in assessing rater reliability. *Psychological Bulletin, 86,* 420–428.

Sireci, S. G. (2009). Packing and unpacking sources of validity evidence: History repeats itself again. In R. W. Lissitz (Ed.), *The concept of validity: Revisions, new directions, and applications* (pp. 19–37). Charlotte, NC: Information Age.

Slaney, K. L., & Maraun, M. D. (2008). A proposed framework for conducting data-based test analysis. *Psychological Methods, 13,* 376–390.

Spearman, C. (1910). Correlation calculated from faulty data. *British Journal of Psychology, 3,* 171–195.

*Standards for educational and psychological testing.* (1999). Washington, DC: American Educational Research Association.

Stigler, S. M. (1999). *Statistics on the table: The history of statistical concepts and methods.* Cambridge, MA: Harvard University Press.

Stigler, S. M. (2010). Darwin, Galton and the statistical enlightenment. *Journal of the Royal Statistical Society: Series A (Statistics in Society), 173,* 469–482.

Streiner, D. L. (2003). Starting at the beginning: An introduction to coefficient alpha and internal consistency. *Journal of Personality Assessment, 80,* 99–103.

Suen, H. K. (1990). *Principles of test theories.* Hillsdale, NJ: Erlbaum.

Superfine, B. M. (2004). At the intersection of law and psychometrics: Explaining the validity clause of *No Child Left Behind. Journal of Law and Education, 33,* 475–514.

Swets, J. A. (1992). The science of choosing the right decision threshold in high-stakes diagnostics. *American Psychologist, 47,* 522–532.

Teasdale, T. W., & Owen, D. R. (2005). A long-term rise and recent decline in intelligence test performance: The Flynn effect in reverse. *Personality and Individual Differences, 39,* 837–843.

Tellegen, A., & Ben-Porath, Y. S. (2008). *MMPI-2-RF (Minnesota Multiphasic Personality Inventory-2): Technical manual.* Minneapolis: University of Minnesota Press.

Tellegen, A., Ben-Porath, Y. S., McNulty, J. L., Arbisi, P. A., Graham, J. R., & Kaemmer, B. (2003). *The MMPI-2 Restructured Clinical (RC) scales: Development, validation, and interpretation.* Minneapolis: University of Minnesota Press.

Terman, L. M. (1916). *The measurement of intelligence: An explanation of and a complete guide for the use of the Stanford revision and extension of the Binet Simon Intelligence Scale.* Boston, MA: Houghton Mifflin.

Terman, L. M. & Merrill, M. A. (1937). *Directions for administering: Forms L and M, Revision of the Stanford-Binet Tests of Intelligence.* Boston, MA: Houghton Mifflin.

Thompson, B. (Ed.) (2003). *Score reliability: Contemporary thinking on reliability issues.* Thousand Oaks, CA: Sage.

Thompson, B. (2004). *Exploratory and confirmatory factor analysis: Understanding concepts and applications.* Washington, DC: American Psychological Association.

Tiedeman, D. V. (1978). In O. K. Buros (Ed.), *The eight mental measurements yearbook.* Highland Park: NJ: Gryphon Press.

Tinsley, H. E. A., & Weiss, D. J. (1975). Interrater reliability and agreement of subjective judgments. *Journal of Counseling Psychology, 22,* 358–376.

Tulsky, D. S., Chiaravallotti, N. D., Palmer, B. W., & Chelune, G. J. (2003). The Wechsler Memory Scale (3rd ed.): A new perspective. In D. S. Tulsky et al. (Eds.), *Clinical interpretation of the WAIS-III and WMS-III* (pp. 93–139). New York, NY: Academic Press.

Tulsky, D. S., & Ledbetter, M. F. (2000). Updating to the WAIS-III and WMS-III: Considerations for research and clinical practice. *Psychological Assessment, 12,* 253–262.

Tulsky, D. [S.], Zhu, J., & Ledbetter, M. F. (1997). *WAIS-III/WMS-III technical manual.* San Antonio, TX: Psychological Corporation.

Turkheimer, E., Haley, A., Waldron, M., D'Onofrio, B., & Gottesman, I. I. (2003). Socioeconomic status modifies heritability of IQ in young children. *Psychological Science, 14,* 623–628.

Uniform guidelines on employee selection procedures. (1978). *Federal Register, 43,* 38296–38309.

Urbina, S. (2004). *Essentials of psychological testing.* Hoboken, NJ: Wiley.

Vacha-Haase, T. (1998). Reliability generalization: Exploring variance in measurement error affecting score reliability across studies. *Educational & Psychological Measurement, 58,* 6–20.

Vacha-Haase, T., Kogan, L. R., & Thompson, B. (2000). Sample compositions and variabilities in published studies versus those in test manuals: Validity of score reliability inductions. *Educational and Psychological Measurement, 60,* 509–522.

Vassend, O., & Skrondal, A. (2011). The NEO personality inventory revised (NEO-PI-R): Exploring the measurement structure and variants of the five-factor model. *Personality and Individual Differences, 50,* 1300–1304.

Vaughn, S., & Fuchs, L. S. (2003). Redefining learning disabilities as inadequate response to instruction: The promise and potential problems. *Learning Disabilities Research & Practice, 18*(3), 137–146.

Vogt, D. S., King, D. W., & King, L. A. (2004). Focus groups in psychological assessment: Enhancing content validity by consulting members of the target population. *Psychological Assessment, 16,* 231–243.

Wainer, H. (2010). 14 conversations about three things. *Journal of Educational and Behavioral Statistics, 35,* 5–25.

Walker, K. C., & Bracken, B. A. (1996). Inter-parent agreement on four preschool behavior rating scales: Effects of parent and child gender. *Psychology in the Schools, 33,* 273–281.

Wechsler, D. (1939). *The measurement of adult intelligence.* Baltimore, MD: Williams & Wilkins.

Wechsler, D. (1946). *The Wechsler-Bellevue intelligence scale: Form II. Manual for administering and scoring the test.* New York, NY: Psychological Corporation.

Wechsler, D. (1949). *Wechsler Intelligence Scale for Children manual.* New York, NY: Psychological Corporation.

Wechsler, D. (1991). *Wechsler Intelligence Scale for Children* (3rd ed.). San Antonio, TX: Psychological Corporation.

Wechsler, D. (1997). *Wechsler Memory Scale—Third Edition (WMS-III) administration and scoring manual.* San Antonio, TX: Psychological Corporation.

Wechsler, D. (2003). *WISC-IV technical and interpretive manual.* San Antonio, TX: Psychological Corporation.

Wechsler, D. (2008). *WAIS-IV technical and interpretive manual.* San Antonio, TX: Pearson.

Weed, N. C. (2006). Syndrome complexity, paradigm shifts, and the future of validation research: Comments on Nichols and Rogers, Sewell, Harrison, and Jordan. *Journal of Personality Assessment, 87,* 217–222.

Wilkins, C., & Rolfhus, E. (2004). *A simulation study of the efficacy of inferential norming compared to traditional norming* (Assessment Report). San Antonio, TX: Harcourt.

Wilkinson, L., & APA Task Force on Statistical Inference. (1999). Statistical methods in psychology journals: Guidelines and explanations. *American Psychologist, 54,* 594–604.

Willingham, W. W. (1999). A systematic view of test fairness. In S. J. Messick (Ed.), *Assessment in higher education: Issues of access, quality, student development, and public policy* (pp. 213–242). Mahwah, NJ: Erlbaum.

Wood, J. M., Nezworski, M. T. & Stejskal, W. J. (1996). The Comprehensive System for the Rorschach: A critical examination. *Psychological Science, 7,* 3–10.

Woodcock, R. W. (1999). What can Rasch-based scores convey about a person's test performance? In S. E. Embretson & S. L. Hershberger (Eds.), *The new rules of measurement: What every psychologist and educator should know* (pp. 105–127). Mahwah, NJ: Erlbaum.

Wright, B. D. (1999). Fundamental measurement for psychology. In S. E. Embretson & S. L. Hershberger (Eds.), *The new rules of measurement: What every psychologist and educator should know* (pp. 65–104). Mahwah, NJ: Erlbaum.

Wright, B. D. (2001). Separation, reliability, and skewed distributions. *Rasch Measurement Transactions, 14,* 786.

Wu, M. (2010). Measurement, sampling, and equating errors in large-scale assessments. *Educational Measurement: Issues and Practice, 29*(4), 15–27.

Zhu, J., Cayton, T., Weiss, L., & Gabel, A. (2008). *WISC-IV extended norms (WISC-IV technical report #7).* San Antonio, TX: Pearson Education. Retrieved from www.pearsonassessments.com/NR/rdonlyres/C1C19227-BC79–46D9-B43C-8E4A114F7E1F/0/WISCIV_TechReport_7.pdf

Zhu, J., & Chen, H. (2011). Utility of inferential norming with smaller sample sizes. *Journal of Psychological Assessment, 29*(6), 570–580.

Zieky, M. (1993). Practical questions in the use of DIF statistics in test development. In P. W. Holland & H. Wainer (Eds.), *Differential item functioning* (pp. 337–347). Hillsdale, NJ: Erlbaum.

CHAPTER 4

# Bias in Psychological Assessment

## An Empirical Review and Recommendations

CECIL R. REYNOLDS AND LISA A. SUZUKI

## UNDERSTANDING BIAS IN PSYCHOLOGICAL ASSESSMENT

Few issues in psychological assessment today are as polarizing among clinicians and laypeople as the use of standardized tests with minority examinees. For clients, parents, and clinicians, the central issue is one of long-term consequences that may occur when mean test results differ from one ethnic group to another—Blacks, Hispanics, American Indians, Asian Americans, and so forth. Important concerns include, among others, that psychiatric clients may be overdiagnosed, students disproportionately placed in special classes, and applicants unfairly denied employment or college admission because of purported bias in standardized tests.

Among researchers, polarization also is common. Here, too, observed mean score differences among ethnic groups are fueling the controversy, but in a different way. Alternative explanations of these differences seem to give shape to the conflict. Reynolds (2000a, 2000b) divided the most common explanations into four categories: (1) genetic influences; (2) environmental factors involving economic,

social, and educational deprivation; (3) an interactive effect of genes and environment; and (4) biased tests that systematically underrepresent minorities' true aptitudes or abilities. The last two of these explanations have drawn the most attention. Williams (1970) and Helms (1992) proposed a fifth interpretation of differences between Black and White examinees: The two groups have qualitatively different cognitive structures, which must be measured using different methods (Reynolds, 2000b).

The problem of cultural bias in mental tests has drawn controversy since the early 1900s, when Binet's first intelligence scale was published and Stern introduced procedures for testing intelligence (Binet & Simon, 1916/1973; Stern, 1914). The conflict is in no way limited to cognitive ability tests, but the so-called IQ controversy has attracted most of the public attention. A number of authors have published works on the subject that quickly became controversial (Gould, 1981; Herrnstein & Murray, 1994; Jensen, 1969). IQ tests have gone to court, provoked legislation, and taken thrashings from the popular media (Brown, Reynolds, & Whitaker, 1999; Reynolds, 2000a). In New York, the conflict has culminated in laws known as truth-in-testing legislation, which some clinicians say interferes with professional practice. In California, a ban

---

This chapter is based substantively on a chapter that appears in the prior edition of this text by Reynolds and Ramsay (2003).

was placed on the use of IQ tests for identification and placement of African American students.

In statistics, *bias* refers to systematic error in the estimation of a value. A biased test is one that systematically overestimates or underestimates the value of the variable it is intended to assess. If this bias occurs as a function of a nominal cultural variable, such as ethnicity or gender, cultural test bias is said to be present. On the Wechsler series of intelligence tests, for example, the difference in mean scores for Black and White Americans hovers around 15 points. If this figure represents a true difference between the two groups, the tests are not biased. If, however, the difference is due to systematic underestimation of the intelligence of Black Americans or overestimation of the intelligence of White Americans, the tests are said to be culturally biased.

Many researchers have investigated possible bias in intelligence tests, with inconsistent results. The question of test bias remained chiefly within the purview of scientists until the 1970s. Since then it has become a major social issue, touching off heated public debate (e.g., Brooks, 1997; Fine, 1975). Many professionals and professional associations have taken strong stands on the question. Van de Vijver and Tanzer (2004) presented a taxonomy of three kinds of bias:

1. *Construct bias* [e.g., overlap in definitions of the construct across cultures, "differential appropriateness of behaviors associated with the construct in different cultures" (p. 124), and poor sampling of relevant behaviors associated with the construct]
2. *Method bias* [i.e., bias pertaining to the sample (e.g., samples are not matched in terms of all relevant aspects, which is nearly impossible to achieve), instrument (e.g., differential familiarity with the items), or administration (e.g., ambiguous directions, tester/interviewer/observer effects)]
3. *Item bias* due to "poor item translation, ambiguities in the original item, low familiarity/appropriateness of the item content in certain cultures, or influence of culture specifics such as nuisance factors or connotations associated with the item wording" (p. 127).

A number of strategies are available to address bias in cross-cultural assessment (van de Vijver & Tanzer, 2004).

## MINORITY OBJECTIONS TO TESTS AND TESTING

Since 1968, the Association of Black Psychologists (ABP) has called for a moratorium on the administration of psychological and educational tests with minority examinees (Samuda, 1975; Williams, Dotson, Dow, & Williams, 1980). The ABP brought this call to other professional associations in psychology and education. The American Psychological Association (APA) responded by requesting that its Board of Scientific Affairs establish a committee to study the use of these tests with disadvantaged students. (See the committee's report, Cleary, Humphreys, Kendrick, & Wesman, 1975.)

The ABP published this policy statement in 1969 (cited in Williams et al., 1980):

The Association of Black Psychologists fully supports those parents who have chosen to defend their rights by refusing to allow their children and themselves to be subjected to achievement, intelligence, aptitude, and performance tests, which have been and are being used to (a) label Black people as uneducable; (b) place Black children in "special" classes and schools; (c) potentiate inferior education; (d) assign Black children to lower educational tracks than whites; (e) deny Black students higher educational opportunities; and (f) destroy positive intellectual growth and development of Black children. (pp. 265–266)

Subsequently, other professional associations issued policy statements on testing. Williams et al. (1980) and Reynolds, Lowe, and Saenz (1999) cited the National Association for the Advancement of Colored People (NAACP), the National Education Association, the National Association of Elementary School Principals, and the American Personnel and Guidance Association, among others, as organizations releasing such statements.

The ABP, perhaps motivated by action and encouragement on the part of the NAACP, adopted a more detailed resolution in 1974. The resolution described, in part, these goals of the ABP: (a) a halt to the standardized testing of Black people until culture-specific tests are made available, (b) a national policy of testing by competent assessors of an examinee's own ethnicity at his or her mandate, (c) removal of standardized test results from the records of Black students and employees, and (d) a return to regular programs of Black students inappropriately diagnosed and placed in special education classes (Williams et al., 1980). This statement presupposes that flaws in standardized tests are responsible for the unequal test results of Black examinees and, with them, any detrimental consequences of those results. Concerns continue despite the 2004 reauthorization of the Individuals with Disabilities Education Act, which indicates alternative methods can be used (e.g., Response to Intervention [RTI] to assess learning disabilities eliminating reliance upon an intelligence/achievement discrepancy formula. A study of African American psychology professionals indicated that concerns remain as to whether RTI will reduce the disproportionately high number of African Americans students in special education (Graves & Mitchell, 2011).

## ORIGINS OF THE TEST BIAS CONTROVERSY

Challenges of test bias have emerged given the emphasis placed on American societal values and beliefs, the nature of tests and testing, and conflicting views regarding definition.

### Social Values and Beliefs

The present-day conflict over bias in standardized tests is motivated largely by public concerns. The impetus, it may be argued, lies with beliefs fundamental to democracy in the United States. Most Americans, at least those of majority ethnicity, view the United States as a land of opportunity. Historically, this has meant that equal opportunity is extended to every person.

We want to believe that any child can grow up to be president. Concomitantly, we believe that everyone is created equal, that all people harbor the potential for success and achievement. This equality of opportunity seems most reasonable if everyone is equally able to take advantage of it. Concerns have arisen given debates among scholars as to whether intelligence is a fixed trait (i.e., corresponding test scores are stable over time) or whether intelligence is malleable (Ramsden et al., 2011; Suzuki & Aronson, 2005).

Parents and educational professionals have corresponding beliefs: The children we serve have an immense potential for success and achievement; the great effort we devote to teaching or raising children is effort well spent; my own child is intelligent and capable. The result is a resistance to labeling and alternative placement, which are thought to discount students' ability and diminish their opportunity. This terrain may be a bit more complex for clinicians, because certain diagnoses have consequences desired by clients. A disability diagnosis, for example, allows people to receive compensation or special services, and insurance companies require certain serious conditions for coverage.

### Character of Tests and Testing

The nature of psychological characteristics and their measurement is partly responsible for long-standing concern over test bias (Reynolds & Brown, 1984a). Psychological characteristics are internal, so scientists cannot observe or measure them directly but must infer them from a person's external behavior. By extension, clinicians must contend with the same limitation.

According to MacCorquodale and Meehl (1948), a psychological process is an *intervening variable* if it is treated only as a component of a system and has no properties beyond the ones that operationally define it. It is a *hypothetical construct* if it is thought to exist and to have properties beyond its defining ones. In biology, a *gene* is an example of a hypothetical construct. The gene has properties beyond its use to describe the transmission of traits from one generation to the next. Both intelligence and personality have the status of hypothetical constructs. The nature of psychological processes and other unseen hypothetical constructs are often subjects of persistent debate. (See Ramsay, 1998b, for one approach.) Intelligence, a highly complex, multifaceted psychological process, has given rise to disputes that are especially difficult to resolve (Reynolds, Willson, & Ramsey, 1999). Test development procedures (Ramsay & Reynolds, 2000a) are essentially the same for all standardized tests. Initially, the author of a test develops or collects a large pool of items thought to measure the characteristic of interest. Theory and practical usefulness are standards commonly used to select an item pool. The selection process is a rational one. That is, it depends on reason and judgment. A rigorous means to carry out the item selection process at this stage simply does not exist. At this stage, then, test authors have no generally accepted evidence that they have selected appropriate items.

A common second step is to discard items of suspect quality, again on rational grounds, to reduce the pool to a manageable size. Next, the test's author or publisher administers the items to a group of examinees called a *tryout sample*. Statistical procedures then help to identify items that seem to be measuring an unintended characteristic or more than one characteristic. The author or publisher discards or modifies these items.

Finally, examiners administer the remaining items to a large, diverse group of people called a standardization sample or *norming sample*. This sample should reflect every important characteristic of the population that will take the final version of the test. Statisticians compile the scores of the norming sample into an array called a *norming distribution*. In order to address concerns regarding racial and ethnic group representation in the norming sample, some test developers engage in racial and ethnic group oversampling (i.e., including larger numbers of individuals from different racial and ethnic groups above and beyond their proportional representation in the overall population). Supplemental norms may then be created for a particular racial/ethnic group. Tests such as the Wechsler scales often incorporate this oversampling procedure (cited in Suzuki, Kugler, & Aguiar, 2005).

Eventually, clients or other examinees take the test in its final form. The scores they obtain, known as *raw scores*, do not yet have any interpretable meaning. A clinician compares these scores with the norming distribution. The comparison is a mathematical process that results in new, *standard scores* for the examinees. Clinicians can interpret these scores, whereas interpretation of the original, raw scores would be difficult and impractical in the absence of a comparable norm group (Reynolds, Lowe, et al., 1999).

Standard scores are relative. They have no meaning in themselves but derive their meaning from certain properties—typically the mean and standard deviation (*SD*) of the norming distribution. The norming distributions of many ability tests, for example, have a mean score of 100 and a standard deviation of 15. A client might obtain a standard score of 127. This score would be well above average, because 127 is almost 2 SDs of 15 above the mean of 100. Another client might obtain a standard score of 96. This score would be a little below average, because 96 is about one third of a SD below a mean of 100.

Here the reason why raw scores have no meaning gains a little clarity. A raw score of, say, 34 is high if the mean is 30 but low if the mean is 50. It is very high if the mean is 30 and the SD is 2 but less high if the mean is again 30 and the SD is 15. Thus, a clinician cannot know how high or low a score is without knowing certain properties of the norming distribution. The standard score is the one that has been compared with this distribution, so that it reflects those properties. (See Ramsay & Reynolds, 2000a, for a systematic description of test development.)

Charges of bias frequently spring from low proportions of minorities in the norming sample of a test and correspondingly small influence on test results. Many norming samples include only a few minority participants, eliciting suspicion that the tests produce inaccurate scores—misleadingly low ones in the case of ability tests—for minority examinees. Whether this is so is an important question that calls for scientific study (Reynolds, Lowe et al., 1999).

Test development is a complex and elaborate process (Ramsay & Reynolds, 2000a). The public, the media, Congress, and even the intelligentsia find it difficult to understand. Clinicians, and psychologists outside the measurement field, commonly have little knowledge of the issues surrounding this process. Its abstruseness, as much as its relative nature, probably contributes to the amount of conflict over test bias. Physical and biological measurements such as height, weight, and even risk of heart disease elicit little controversy, although they vary from one ethnic group to another. As explained by Reynolds, Lowe et al. (1999), this is true in part because such measurements are absolute, in part because they can be obtained and verified in direct and relatively simple ways, and in part because they are free from the distinctive social implications and consequences of standardized test scores. Reynolds et al. correctly suggested that test bias is a special case of the uncertainty that accompanies all measurement in science. Ramsay (2000) and Ramsay and Reynolds (2000b) presented a brief treatment of this uncertainty incorporating Heisenberg's model.

## Divergent Ideas of Bias

Besides the character of psychological processes and their measurement, differing understandings held by various segments of the population also add to the test bias controversy. Researchers and laypeople view bias differently. Clinicians and other professionals bring additional divergent views. Many lawyers see bias as illegal, discriminatory practice on the part of organizations or individuals (Reynolds, 2000a; Reynolds & Brown, 1984a).

To the public at large, bias sometimes conjures up notions of prejudicial attitudes. A person seen as prejudiced may be told, "You're biased against Hispanics." For other laypersons, bias is more generally a characteristic slant in another person's thinking, a lack of objectivity brought about by the person's life circumstances. A sales clerk may say, "I think sales clerks should be better paid." "Yes, but you're biased," a listener may retort. These views differ from statistical and research definitions for bias as for other terms, such as *significant, association,* and *confounded.* The highly specific research definitions of such terms are unfamiliar to almost everyone. As a result, uninitiated readers often misinterpret research reports.

Both in research reports and in public discourse, the scientific and popular meanings of bias are often conflated, as if even the writer or speaker had a tenuous grip on the distinction. Reynolds, Lowe et al. (1999) have suggested that the topic would be less controversial if research reports addressing test bias as a scientific question relied on the scientific meaning alone.

## EFFECTS AND IMPLICATIONS OF THE TEST BIAS CONTROVERSY

The dispute over test bias has given impetus to an increasingly sophisticated corpus of research. In most venues, tests of reasonably high statistical quality appear to be largely unbiased. For neuropsychological tests, results are not definitive but so far they appear to indicate little bias. Studies examining psychophysiological approaches to intelligence have yielded results that may further elucidate the relationship between culture and cognitive functioning. Verney, Granholm, Marshall, Malcarne, and Saccuzzo (2005) found that measures of information processing efficiency were related to Caucasian American students' performance but not to a comparable sample of Mexican American students, suggesting differential validity in prediction. Both sides of the debate have disregarded most of these findings and have emphasized, instead, a mean difference between ethnic groups (Reynolds, 2000b).

In addition, publishers have released nonverbal tests that have been identified as culture-reduced measures of ability; practitioners interpret scores so as to minimize the influence of putative bias; and, finally, publishers revise tests directly, to expunge group differences. For minority group members, these revisions may have an undesirable long-range effect: to prevent the study and thereby the remediation of any bias that might otherwise be found. In addition, all tests involve some form of language and communication (Mpofu & Ortiz, 2009). Methods for detecting bias on nonverbal measures are the same as those for tests with verbal content. Information regarding bias studies on several nonverbal measures including the Comprehensive Test of Nonverbal Intelligence (CTONI; Hammill, Pearson, & Wiederholt, 1997), Leiter International Performance Scale-R (LIPS-R; Roid & Miller, 1997), and Universal Nonverbal Intelligence Test (UNIT: Bracken & McCallum, 1998) are evaluated in seminal texts (Maller, 2003). Results indicate that differences in performance by racial and ethnic groups are reduced on nonverbal measures.

The implications of these various effects differ depending on whether the bias explanation is correct or incorrect, assuming it is accepted. An incorrect bias explanation, if accepted, would lead to modified tests that would not reflect important, correct information and, moreover, would present the incorrect information that unequally performing groups had performed equally. Researchers, unaware or unmindful of such inequalities, would neglect research into the causes of these inequalities. Economic and social deprivation would come to appear less harmful and therefore more justifiable. Social programs, no longer seen as necessary to improve minority students' scores, might be discontinued, with serious consequences.

A correct bias explanation, if accepted, would leave professionals and minority group members in a relatively better position. We would have copious research correctly indicating that bias was present in standardized test scores. Surprisingly, however, the limitations of having these data might outweigh the benefits. Test bias would be a correct conclusion reached incorrectly.

Findings of bias rely primarily on mean differences between groups. These differences would consist partly of bias and partly of other constituents, which would project them upward or downward, perhaps depending on the particular groups involved. Thus, we would be accurate in concluding that bias was present but inaccurate as to the amount of bias and, possibly, its direction: that is, which of two groups it favored. Any modifications made would do too little or too much, creating new bias in the opposite direction.

The presence of bias should allow for additional explanations. For example, bias and *Steelean effects* (Steele & Aronson, 1995, 2004), in which fear of confirming a stereotype impedes minorities' performance, might both affect test results. Research indicates that stereotype threat may be viewed as a source of measurement bias (Wicherts, Dolan, & Hessen, 2005). Such additional possibilities, which now receive little attention, would receive even less. Economic and social deprivation, serious problems apart from testing issues, would again appear less harmful and therefore more justifiable. Efforts to improve people's scores through social programs would be difficult to defend, because this work presupposes that factors other than test bias are the causes of score differences. Thus, Americans' belief in human potential would be vindicated, but perhaps at considerable cost to minority individuals.

## POSSIBLE SOURCES OF BIAS

Minority and other psychologists have expressed numerous concerns over the use of psychological and educational tests with minorities. These concerns are potentially legitimate and substantive but are often asserted as true in the absence of scientific evidence. Reynolds, Lowe et al. (1999) have divided the most frequent of the problems cited into seven categories, described briefly here. Two categories, inequitable social consequences and qualitatively distinct aptitude and personality, receive more extensive treatments in the "Test Bias and Social Issues" section.

1. *Inappropriate content*. Tests are geared to majority experiences and values or are scored arbitrarily according to majority values. Correct responses or solution methods depend on material that is unfamiliar to minority individuals.
2. *Inappropriate standardization samples*. Minorities' representation in norming samples is proportionate but insufficient to allow them any influence over test development.
3. *Examiners' and language bias*. White examiners who speak standard English intimidate minority examinees and communicate inaccurately with them, spuriously lowering their test scores.
4. *Inequitable social consequences*. Ethnic minority individuals, already disadvantaged because of stereotyping and past discrimination, are denied employment or relegated to dead-end educational tracks. Labeling effects are another example of invalidity of this type.
5. *Measurement of different constructs*. Tests largely based on majority culture are measuring different characteristics altogether for members of minority groups, rendering them invalid for these groups.
6. *Differential predictive validity*. Standardized tests accurately predict many outcomes for majority group members, but they do not predict any relevant behavior for their minority counterparts. In addition, the criteria that tests are designed to predict, such as achievement in White, middle-class schools, may themselves be biased against minority examinees.
7. *Qualitatively distinct aptitude and personality*. This position seems to suggest that minority and majority ethnic groups possess characteristics of different *types*, so that test development must begin with different definitions for majority and minority groups.

Researchers have investigated these concerns, although few results are available for labeling effects or for long-term social consequences of testing. As noted by Reynolds, Lowe et al. (1999), both of these problems are relevant to testing in general rather than to ethnic issues alone. In addition, individuals as well as groups can experience labeling and other social consequences of testing. Researchers should investigate these outcomes with diverse samples and numerous statistical techniques. Finally, Reynolds, Lowe et al. suggest that tracking and special education should be treated as problems with education rather than assessment.

## WHAT TEST BIAS IS AND IS NOT

Scientists and clinicians should distinguish bias from *unfairness* and from *offensiveness*. Thorndike (1971) wrote, "The presence (or absence) of differences in mean score between groups, or of differences in variability, tells us nothing directly about fairness" (p. 64). In fact, the concepts of test bias and unfairness are distinct in themselves. A test may have very little bias, but a clinician could still use it unfairly to minority examinees' disadvantage. Conversely, a test may be biased, but clinicians need not—and must not—use it to unfairly penalize minorities or others whose scores may be affected. Little is gained by anyone when concepts are conflated or when, in any other respect, professionals operate from a base of misinformation.

Jensen (1980) was the author who first argued cogently that fairness and bias are separable concepts. As noted by Brown et al. (1999), fairness is a moral, philosophical, or legal issue on which reasonable people can legitimately disagree. By contrast, bias is an empirical property of a test, as used with two or more specified groups. Thus, bias is a statistically estimated quantity rather than a principle established through debate and opinion.

A second distinction is that between test bias and item *offensiveness*. In the development of many tests, a minority review panel examines each item for content that may be offensive to one or more groups. Professionals and laypersons alike often view these examinations as tests of bias. Such *expert reviews* have been part of the development of many prominent ability tests, including the Kaufman Assessment Battery for Children (K-ABC), the Wechsler Preschool and Primary Scale of Intelligence–Revised (WPPSI-R), and the Peabody Picture Vocabulary Test–Revised (PPVT-R). The development of personality and behavior tests also incorporates such reviews (e.g., Reynolds, 2001; Reynolds & Kamphaus, 1992). Prominent authors such as Anastasi (1988), Kaufman (1979), and Sandoval and Mille (1979) support this method as a way to enhance rapport with the public.

In a well-known case titled *PASE v. Hannon* (Reschly, 2000), a federal judge applied this method rather quaintly, examining items from the Wechsler Intelligence Scales for Children (WISC) and the Binet intelligence scales to personally determine which items were biased (Elliot, 1987). Here an authority figure showed startling naiveté and greatly exceeded his expertise—a telling comment on modern hierarchies of influence. Similarly, a high-ranking representative of the Texas Education Agency argued in a televised interview (October 14, 1997, KEYE 42, Austin, TX) that the Texas Assessment of Academic

Skills (TAAS), controversial among researchers, could not be biased against ethnic minorities because minority reviewers inspected the items for biased content.

Several researchers have reported that such expert reviewers perform at or below chance level, indicating that they are unable to identify biased items (Jensen, 1976; Sandoval & Mille, 1979; reviews by Camilli & Shepard, 1994; Reynolds, 1995, 1998a; Reynolds, Lowe et al., 1999). Since initial research by McGurk (1951), studies have provided little evidence that anyone can estimate, by personal inspection, how differently a test item may function for different groups of people.

Sandoval and Mille (1979) had university students from Spanish, history, and education classes identify items from the WISC-R that would be more difficult for a minority child than for a White child, along with items that would be equally difficult for both groups. Participants included Black, White, and Mexican American students. Each student judged 45 items, of which 15 were most difficult for Blacks, 15 were most difficult for Mexican Americans, and 15 were most nearly equal in difficulty for minority children, in comparison with White children.

The participants read each question and identified it as easier, more difficult, or equally difficult for minority versus White children. Results indicated that the participants could not make these distinctions to a statistically significant degree and that minority and nonminority participants did not differ in their performance or in the types of misidentifications they made. Sandoval and Mille (1979) used only extreme items, so the analysis would have produced statistically significant results for even a relatively small degree of accuracy in judgment.

For researchers, test bias is a deviation from examinees' real level of performance. Bias goes by many names and has many characteristics, but it always involves scores that are too low or too high to accurately represent or predict some examinee's skills, abilities, or traits. To show bias, then—to greatly simplify the issue—requires estimates of scores. Reviewers have no way of producing such an estimate.

Despite these issues regarding fairness and expert reviews, testing companies continue to employ these methods as part of the development process. For example, the Educational Testing Service (2002) provides *Standards for Quality and Fairness* and *International Principles for Fairness Review of Assessments*. These documents emphasize the importance of: treating people with respect; minimizing the effects of construct-irrelevant knowledge or skills; avoiding material that is unnecessarily controversial, inflammatory, offensive, or upsetting; using appropriate terminology; avoiding stereotypes; and representing diversity (Zieky, 2006).

While these procedures can suggest items that may be offensive, statistical techniques are necessary to determine test bias. Thus, additional procedures for fairness reviews include a focus on how to resolve disputes among reviewers, attention to test design, diverse input, provision of accommodations, differential item functioning, validation of the review process, and attention to how the test is used (Zieky, 2006).

## Culture Fairness, Culture Loading, and Culture Bias

A third pair of distinct concepts is cultural *loading* and cultural *bias*, the former often associated with the concept of culture fairness. Cultural loading is the degree to which a test or item is specific to a particular culture. A test with greater cultural loading has greater potential bias when administered to people of diverse cultures. Nevertheless, a test can be culturally loaded without being culturally biased.

An example of a culture-loaded item might be "Who was Eleanor Roosevelt?" This question may be appropriate for students who have attended U.S. schools since first grade with curriculum highlighting her importance as a historical figure in America. The cultural specificity of the question would be too great, however, to permit its use with European and certainly Asian elementary school students, except perhaps as a test of knowledge of U.S. history. Nearly all standardized tests have some degree of cultural specificity. Cultural loadings fall on a continuum, with some tests linked to a culture as defined very generally and liberally and others to a culture as defined very narrowly.

Cultural loading, by itself, does not render tests biased or offensive. Rather, it creates a potential for either problem, which must then be assessed through research. Ramsay (2000; Ramsay & Reynolds, 2000b) suggested that some characteristics might be viewed as desirable or undesirable in themselves but others as desirable or undesirable only to the degree that they influence other characteristics. Test bias against Cuban Americans would itself be an undesirable characteristic. A subtler situation occurs if a test is both culturally loaded and culturally biased. If the test's cultural loading is a cause of its bias, the cultural loading is then *indirectly* undesirable and should be corrected. Alternatively, studies may show that the test is culturally loaded but unbiased. If so, indirect undesirability due to an association with bias can be ruled out.

Some authors (e.g., Cattell, 1979) have attempted to develop culture-fair intelligence tests. These tests, however, are characteristically poor measures from a statistical standpoint (Anastasi, 1988; Ebel, 1979). In one study, Hartlage, Lucas, and Godwin (1976) compared Raven's Progressive Matrices (RPM), thought to be culture fair, with the WISC, thought to be culture loaded. The researchers assessed these tests' predictiveness of reading, spelling, and arithmetic measures with a group of disadvantaged, rural children of low socioeconomic status (SES). WISC scores consistently correlated higher than RPM scores with the measures examined.

The problem may be that intelligence is defined as adaptive or beneficial behavior within a particular culture. Therefore, a test free from cultural influence would tend to be free from the influence of intelligence—and to be a poor predictor of intelligence in any culture. As Reynolds, Lowe et al. (1999) observed, if a test is developed in one culture, its appropriateness to other cultures is a matter for scientific verification. Test scores should not be given the same interpretations for different cultures without evidence that those interpretations would be sound.

### Test Bias and Social Issues

Authors have introduced numerous concerns regarding tests administered to ethnic minorities (Brown et al., 1999). Many of these concerns, however legitimate and substantive, have little connection with the scientific estimation of test bias. According to some authors, the unequal results of standardized tests produce inequitable social consequences. Low test scores relegate minority group members, already at an educational and vocational disadvantage because of past discrimination and low expectations of their ability, to educational tracks that lead to mediocrity and low achievement (Chipman, Marshall, & Scott, 1991; Payne & Payne, 1991; see also "Possible Sources of Bias" section).

Other concerns are more general. Proponents of tests, it is argued, fail to offer remedies for racial or ethnic differences (Scarr, 1981), to confront societal concerns over racial discrimination when addressing test bias (Gould, 1995, 1996), to respect research by cultural linguists and anthropologists (Figueroa, 1991; Helms, 1992), to address inadequate special education programs (Reschly, 1997), and to include sufficient numbers of African Americans in norming samples (Dent, 1996). Furthermore, test proponents use massive empirical data to conceal historic prejudice and racism (Richardson, 1995). Some of these practices may be deplorable, but they do not constitute test bias. A removal of group differences from scores cannot combat them effectively and may even remove some evidence of their existence or influence.

Gould (1995, 1996) has acknowledged that tests are not statistically biased and do not show differential predictive validity. He has argued, however, that defining cultural bias statistically is confusing: The public is concerned not with statistical bias but with whether Black–White IQ differences occur because society treats Black people unfairly. That is, the public considers tests biased if they record biases originating elsewhere in society (Gould, 1995). Researchers consider them biased only if they introduce additional error because of flaws in their design or properties. Gould (1995, 1996) argued that society's concern cannot be addressed by demonstrations that tests are statistically unbiased. It can, of course, be addressed empirically.

Another social concern, noted briefly earlier, is that majority and minority examinees may have qualitatively different aptitudes and personality traits, so that traits and abilities must be conceptualized differently for different groups. If this is not done, a test may produce lower results for one group because it is conceptualized most appropriately for another group. This concern is complex from the standpoint of construct validity and may take various practical forms.

In one possible scenario, two ethnic groups can have different patterns of abilities, but the sums of their abilities can be about equal. Group A may have higher verbal fluency, vocabulary, and usage but lower syntax, sentence analysis, and flow of logic than Group B. A verbal ability test measuring only the first three abilities would incorrectly represent Group B as having lower verbal ability. This concern is one of construct validity.

Alternatively, a verbal fluency test may be used to represent the two groups' verbal ability. The test accurately represents Group B as having lower verbal fluency but is used inappropriately to suggest that this group has lower verbal ability per se. Such a characterization is not only incorrect; it is unfair to group members and has detrimental consequences for them that cannot be condoned. Construct invalidity is difficult to argue here, however, because this concern is one of test use.

## RELATED QUESTIONS

The next sections clarify what can be inferred from test score differences and the application of statistical methods to investigate test bias.

### Test Bias and Etiology

The etiology of a condition is distinct from the question of test bias. (For a review, see Reynolds & Kaiser, 1992.) In fact, the need to research etiology emerges only after evidence that a score difference is a real one, not an artifact of bias. Authors have sometimes inferred that score differences themselves indicate genetic differences, implying that one or more groups are genetically inferior. This inference is scientifically no more defensible—and ethically much less so—than the notion that score differences demonstrate test bias.

Jensen (1969) has long argued that mental tests measure, to some extent, the intellectual factor *g*, found in behavioral genetics studies to have a large genetic component. In Jensen's view, group differences in mental test scores may reflect largely genetic differences in *g*. Nonetheless, Jensen made many qualifications to these arguments and to the differences themselves. He also posited that other factors make considerable, though lesser, contributions to intellectual development (Reynolds, Lowe et al., 1999). Jensen's theory, if correct, may explain certain intergroup phenomena, such as differential Black and White performance on digit span measures (Ramsay & Reynolds, 1995).

### Test Bias Involving Groups and Individuals

Bias may influence the scores of individuals as well as groups on personality and ability tests. Therefore, researchers can and should investigate both of these possible sources of bias. An overarching statistical method called the general linear model permits this approach by allowing both *group* and *individual* to be analyzed as independent variables. In addition, item characteristics, motivation, and other nonintellectual variables (Reynolds, Lowe et al. 1999; Sternberg, 1980; Wechsler, 1975) admit of analysis through recoding, categorization, and similar expedients.

## EXPLAINING GROUP DIFFERENCES

Among researchers, the issue of cultural bias stems largely from well-documented findings, now seen in more than 100 years of research, that members of different ethnic groups have different levels and patterns of performance on many prominent cognitive ability tests. Intelligence batteries have generated some of the most influential and provocative of these findings (Elliot, 1987; Gutkin & Reynolds, 1981; Reynolds, Chastain, Kaufman, & McLean, 1987; Spitz, 1986). In many countries worldwide, people of different ethnic and racial groups, genders, socioeconomic levels, and other demographic groups obtain systematically different intellectual test results. Black–White IQ differences in the United States have undergone extensive investigation for more than 50 years. Jensen (1980), Shuey (1966), Tyler (1965), and Willerman (1979) have reviewed the greater part of this research. The findings occasionally differ somewhat from one age group to another, but they have not changed substantially in the past century. Scholars often refer to the racial and ethnic group hierarchy of intelligence that has remained in the same consistent order for decades. Overall estimates based on a mean of 100 and *SD* of 15 are often cited in this way: Whites 100, Black/African Americans 85, Hispanics midway between Whites and Blacks; Asians and Jews above 100 ("Mainstream Science on Intelligence," 1994). American Indians score at approximately 90 (McShane, 1980).

On average, Blacks differ from Whites by about 1.0 *SD*, with White groups obtaining the higher scores. The differences have been relatively consistent in size for some time and under several methods of investigation. An exception is a reduction of the Black–White IQ difference on the intelligence portion of the K-ABC to about .5 *SD*s, although this result is controversial and poorly understood. (See Kamphaus & Reynolds, 1987, for a discussion.) In addition, such findings are consistent only for African Americans. Other highly diverse findings appear for native African and other Black populations (Jensen, 1980).

Researchers have taken into account a number of demographic variables, most notably SES. The size of the mean Black–White difference in the United States then diminishes to .5 to .7 *SD*s (Jensen, 1980; Kaufman, 1973; Kaufman & Kaufman, 1973; Reynolds & Gutkin, 1981) but is robust in its appearance. It should be noted that mean score differences between Black and White Americans have lessened over the years. For example, IQ differences between Black and White 12-year-olds have dropped 5.5 points to 9.5 over the past three decades (Nisbett, 2009).

While group differences have often received attention in the literature, differences in general ability areas, such as verbal and spatial abilities, are also noted within particular racial and ethnic groups. For example, Suzuki, et al. (2005) conducted a preliminary analysis of Wechsler studies including American Indian samples between 1986 and 2003. A total of 63 studies included samples from the Navajo, Papago, Ojibwa, Inuit, and Eskimo communities. All studies revealed higher performance on nonverbal spatial reasoning tasks (e.g., Object Assembly and Block Design) in comparison to verbal subtests (e.g., Information and Vocabulary). The standard score difference between Verbal IQ and Performance IQ was approximately 17 points (SD 8.92). Explanation of these findings focused on the Verbal IQ being lower due to linguistic and cultural factors, thus leading authors to suggest that the Performance IQ may be more indicative of intellectual potential in American Indian communities. Hagie, Gallipo, and Svien (2003) examined American Indian students' patterns of performance across items on the Bayley Scales of Infant Development (BSID) and the WISC-III. The authors reported based on their analysis that "[i]ssues of poverty, remoteness, access to resources, and health care need to be considered before sweeping conclusions can be made about performance on nationally normed, standardized instruments" (p. 15). In addition, they concluded that these traditional measures may yield "distorted and inaccurate results due to cultural biases of test items and environmental concerns" (p. 24).

Asian groups, although less thoroughly researched than Black groups, have consistently performed as well as or better than Whites (Pintner, 1931; Tyler, 1965; Willerman, 1979), Asian Americans obtain average mean ability scores (Flynn, 1991; Lynn, 1995; Neisser et al., 1996; Reynolds, Willson, et al., 1999). It is important to note that most of the published studies in the past decade have focused on non–U.S. international Asian samples (Okazaki & Sue, 2000). The demand for intelligence tests like the Wechsler scales in Asia has led to the exporting of measures that are then normed and restandardized. For example, the WAIS has been translated and standardized in China, Hong Kong, India, Japan, Korea, Taiwan, Thailand, and Vietnam (Cheung, Leong, & Ben-Porath, 2003).

Matching is an important consideration in studies of ethnic differences. Any difference between groups may be due to neither test bias nor ethnicity but to SES, nutrition, home environment, and other variables that may be associated with test performance. Matching on these variables controls for their associations.

A limitation to matching is that it results in regression toward the mean. Black respondents with high self-esteem, for example, may be selected from a population with low self-esteem. When examined later, these respondents will test with lower self-esteem, having regressed to the lower mean of their own population. Their extreme scores—high in this case—were due to chance.

Clinicians and research consumers should also be aware that the similarities between ethnic groups are much greater than the differences. This principle holds for intelligence, personality, and most other characteristics, both psychological and physiological. From another perspective, the variation among members of any one ethnic group greatly exceeds the differences between groups. The large similarities among groups appear repeatedly in analyses as large, statistically significant constants and great overlap between different groups' ranges of scores.

Some authors (e.g., Schoenfeld, 1974) have disputed whether racial differences in intelligence are real or even researchable. Nevertheless, the findings are highly reliable from study to study, even when study participants identify their own race. Thus, the existence of these differences has gained wide acceptance. The differences are real and undoubtedly complex. The tasks remaining are to describe them thoroughly (Reynolds, Lowe et al., 1999) and, more difficult, to explain them in a causal sense (Ramsay, 1998a, 2000). Both the lower scores of some groups and the higher scores of others must be explained, and not necessarily in the same way.

Over time, exclusively genetic and environmental explanations have lost so much of their credibility that they can hardly be called current. Most researchers who posit that score differences are real now favor an interactionist perspective. This development reflects a similar shift in psychology and social science as a whole. However, this relatively recent consensus masks the subtle persistence of an earlier assumption that test score differences must have either a genetic or an environmental basis. The relative contributions of genes and environment still provoke debate, with some authors seemingly intent on establishing a predominantly genetic or a predominantly environmental basis. The interactionist perspective shifts the focus of debate from *how much* to *how* genetic and environmental factors contribute to a characteristic. In practice, not all scientists have made this shift. In 2005, Rushton and Jensen published a monograph focusing on the past 30 years of research on race differences in cognitive ability. The culture-only (0% genetic, 100% environmental) and hereditarian (50% genetic 50% environmental) perspectives were examined based on a variety of sources of evidence, including: worldwide distribution of test scores, *g* factor of mental ability, brain size and cognitive ability, transracial adoption studies, human origins research, and hypothesized environmental variables. Rushton and Jensen concluded that their extensive findings support a hereditarian explanation for race differences. A number of scholars, however, debated their findings and the interpretation of the data from a number of studies.

## CULTURAL TEST BIAS AS AN EXPLANATION

The bias explanation of score differences has led to the cultural test bias hypothesis (CTBH; Brown et al., 1999;

Reynolds, 1982a, 1982b; Reynolds & Brown, 1984b). According to the CTBH, differences in mean performance for members of different ethnic groups do not reflect real differences among groups but are artifacts of tests or of the measurement process. This approach holds that ability tests contain systematic error occurring as a function of group membership or other nominal variables that should be irrelevant. That is, people who should obtain equal scores obtain unequal ones because of their ethnicities, genders, socioeconomic levels, and the like.

For SES, Eells, Davis, Havighurst, Herrick, and Tyler (1951) summarized the logic of the CTBH in this way: If (a) children of different SES levels have experiences of different kinds and with different types of material, and if (b) intelligence tests contain a disproportionate amount of material drawn from cultural experiences most familiar to high-SES children, then (c) high-SES children should have higher IQ scores than low-SES children. As Eells et al. observed, this argument tends to imply that IQ differences are artifacts that depend on item content and "do not reflect accurately any important underlying ability" (p. 4) in the individual. Sattler (2008) noted that "poverty in and of itself is not necessary nor sufficient to produce intellectual deficits," although children growing up in this context may be exposed to "low level parental education, poor nutrition and health care, substandard housing, family disorganization, inconsistent discipline, diminished sense of personal worth, low expectations, frustrated aspirations, physical violence in their neighborhoods, and other environmental pressures" (pp. 137–138).

Since the 1960s, the CTBH explanation has stimulated numerous studies, which in turn have largely refuted the explanation. Lengthy reviews are available (e.g., Jensen, 1980; Reynolds, 1995, 1998a; Reynolds & Brown, 1984b). This literature suggests that tests whose development, standardization, and reliability are sound and well documented are not biased against native-born American racial or ethnic minorities. Studies do occasionally indicate bias, but it is usually small, and most often it favors minorities.

Results cited to support content bias indicate that item biases account for < 1% to about 5% of variation in test scores. In addition, it is usually counterbalanced across groups. That is, when bias against an ethnic group occurs, comparable bias favoring that group occurs also and cancels it out. When apparent bias is counterbalanced, it may be random rather than systematic and therefore not bias after all. Item or subtest refinements, as well, frequently reduce and counterbalance bias that is present.

No one explanation is likely to account for test score differences in their entirety. A contemporary approach

to statistics, in which effects of zero are rare or even nonexistent, suggests that tests, test settings, and nontest factors may all contribute to group differences. (See also Bouchard & Segal, 1985; Flynn, 1991; Loehlin, Lindzey, & Spuhler, 1975.)

Some authors, most notably Mercer (1979; see also Helms, 1992; Lonner, 1985), have reframed the test bias hypothesis over time. Mercer argued that the lower scores of ethnic minorities on aptitude tests can be traced to the Anglocentrism, or adherence to White, middle-class value systems, of these tests. Mercer's assessment system, the System of Multicultural Pluralistic Assessment (SOMPA), effectively equated ethnic minorities' intelligence scores by applying complex demographic corrections. The SOMPA was popular for several years. It is used less commonly today because of its conceptual and statistical limitations (Reynolds, Lowe et al., 1999). Gopaul-McNicol and Armour-Thomas (2002) proposed a biocultural assessment system incorporating psychometric assessment, psychometric potential assessment [i.e., "value added information about nascent potentials not yet fully developed or competencies not likely to be determined under standardized testing conditions" (p. 38)], ecological assessment (direct observation in the relevant contexts of the individual), and other intelligences assessment (cognitive strengths beyond the IQ test).

In addition, the Gf-Gc Cross-Battery Assessment Model (XBA; Flanagan, Ortiz, & Alfonso, 2007) takes into consideration a wider range of cognitive abilities enabling the evaluator to select from a range of potential tests, addressing broad and narrow ability areas, rather than relying on one battery of subtests (McGrew & Flanagan, 1998). As part of this model, the authors developed the Culture-Language Test Classifications (C-LTC; McGrew & Flanagan, 1998). The C-LTC is based on the degree of cultural loading (i.e., cultural specificity) and linguistic demand of various measures. The classification is based on examination of empirical data available as well as expert consensus procedures when data are not available. The Culture-Language Interpretive Matrix (C-LIM) is derived from this classification system and is represented by a matrix to assist the evaluator in test selection and interpretation (Ortiz & Ochoa, 2005). The model takes into consideration issues of acculturation and language proficiency.

## HARRINGTON'S CONCLUSIONS

Unlike such authors as Mercer (1979) and Helms (1992), Harrington (1968a, 1968b) emphasized the proportionate but small numbers of minority examinees in norming samples. Their low representation, Harrington (1968a, 1968b) argued, made it impossible for minorities to exert any influence on the results of a test. Harrington devised an innovative experimental test of this proposal.

Harrington (1975, 1976) used six genetically distinct strains of rats to represent ethnicities. He then composed six populations, each with different proportions of the six rat strains. Next, Harrington constructed six intelligence tests resembling Hebb-Williams mazes. These mazes, similar to the Mazes subtest of the Wechsler scales, are commonly used as intelligence tests for rats. Harrington reasoned that tests normed on populations dominated by a given rat strain would yield higher mean scores for that strain.

Groups of rats that were most numerous in a test's norming sample obtained the highest average score on that test. Harrington concluded from additional analyses of the data that a test developed and normed on a White majority could not have equivalent predictive validity for Blacks or any other minority group (1975, 1976).

Reynolds, Lowe et al. (1999) have argued that Harrington's generalizations break down in three respects. Harrington (1975, 1976) interpreted his findings in terms of predictive validity. Most studies have indicated that tests of intelligence and other aptitudes have equivalent predictive validity for racial groups under various circumstances and with many criterion measures.

A second problem noted by Reynolds, Lowe et al. (1999) is that Chinese Americans, Japanese Americans, and Jewish Americans have little representation in the norming samples of most ability tests. According to Harrington's model, they should score low on these tests. However, they score at least as high as Whites on tests of intelligence and of some other aptitudes (Gross, 1967; Marjoribanks, 1972; Tyler, 1965; Willerman, 1979). Jewish and Asian communities notably emphasize education. Thus, it can be hypothesized that there is congruence between the intelligence test and the cultural background of members of these communities. Therefore, their performance on these measures would be higher given that the cultural loading has been minimized (Valencia, Suzuki, & Salinas, 2001).

Finally, Harrington's (1975, 1976) approach can account for group differences in overall test scores but not for patterns of abilities reflected in varying subtest scores. For example, one ethnic group often scores higher than another on some subtests but lower on others. Harrington's model can explain only inequality that is uniform from subtest to subtest. The arguments of Reynolds, Lowe et al. (1999) carry considerable weight, because (a) they are grounded directly in empirical results rather than rational arguments, such as those made by Harrington, and (b) those results have been found with humans; results found with nonhumans cannot be generalized to humans without additional evidence.

Harrington's (1975, 1976) conclusions were overgeneralizations. Rats are simply so different from people that rat and human intelligence cannot be assumed to behave the same. Finally, Harrington used genetic populations in his studies. However, the roles of genetic, environmental, and interactive effects in determining the scores of human ethnic groups are still topics of debate, and an interaction is the preferred explanation. Harrington begged the nature-nurture question, implicitly presupposing heavy genetic effects.

The focus of Harrington's (1975, 1976) work was reduced scores for minority examinees, an important avenue of investigation. Artifactually low scores on an intelligence test could lead to acts of race discrimination, such as misassignment to educational programs or spurious denial of employment. This issue is the one over which most court cases involving test bias have been contested (Reynolds, Lowe, et al., 1999).

## MEAN DIFFERENCES AS TEST BIAS

A view widely held by laypeople and researchers (Adebimpe, Gigandet, & Harris, 1979; Alley & Foster, 1978; Hilliard, 1979, 1984; Jackson, 1975; Mercer, 1976; Padilla, 1988; Williams, 1974; Wright & Isenstein, 1977–1978) is that group differences in mean scores on ability tests constitute test bias. As adherents to this view contend, there is no valid, a priori reason to suppose that cognitive ability should differ from one ethnic group to another. However, the same is true of the assumption that cognitive ability should be the same for all ethnic groups and that any differences shown on a test must therefore be effects of bias. As noted by Reynolds, Lowe et al. (1999), an a priori acceptance of either position is untenable from a scientific standpoint.

Some authors add that the distributions of test scores of each ethnic group, not merely the means, must be identical before one can assume that a test is fair. Identical distributions, like equal means, have limitations involving accuracy. Such alterations correct for any source of score differences, including those for which the test is not responsible. Equal scores attained in this way necessarily depart from reality to some degree.

## Egalitarian Fallacy

Jensen (1980; Brown et al., 1999) contended that three fallacious assumptions were impeding the scientific study of test bias: (a) the *egalitarian fallacy*, that all groups were equal in the characteristics measured by a test, so that any score difference must result from bias; (b) the *culture-bound fallacy*, that reviewers can assess the culture loadings of items through casual inspection or armchair judgment; and (c) the *standardization fallacy*, that a test is necessarily biased when used with any group not included in large numbers in the norming sample. In Jensen's view, the mean-difference-as-bias approach is an example of the egalitarian fallacy.

A prior assumption of equal ability is as unwarranted scientifically as the opposite assumption. Studies have shown group differences for many abilities and even for sensory capacities (Reynolds, Willson et al., 1999). Both equalities and inequalities must be found *empirically*, that is, through scientific observation. An assumption of equality, if carried out consistently, would have a stultifying effect on research. Torrance (1980) observed that disadvantaged Black children in the United States have sometimes earned higher creativity scores than many White children. This finding may be important, given that Blacks are underrepresented in classes for gifted students. The egalitarian assumption implies that these Black children's high creativity is an artifact of tests, foreclosing on more substantive interpretations—and on possible changes in student placement.

Equal ability on the part of different ethnic groups is not a defensible egalitarian fallacy. A fallacy, as best understood, is an error in judgment or reasoning, but the question of equal ability is an empirical one. By contrast, an *a priori assumption* of either equal or unequal ability can be regarded as fallacious. The assumption of equal ability is most relevant, because it is implicit when any researcher interprets a mean difference as test bias.

The impossibility of proving a null hypothesis is relevant here. Scientists never regard a null hypothesis as proven, because the absence of a counterinstance cannot prove a rule. If 100 studies do not provide a counterinstance, the 101st study may. Likewise, the failure to reject a hypothesis of equality between groups—that is, a null hypothesis—cannot prove that the groups are equal. This hypothesis, then, is not falsifiable and is therefore problematic for researchers.

## Limitations of Mean Differences

As noted, a mean difference by itself does not show bias. One may ask, then, what (if anything) it does show. It indicates simply that two groups differ when means are taken to represent their performance. Thus, its accuracy depends on how well means, as opposed to other measures of the typical score, represent the two groups; on how well *any* measure of the typical score *can* represent the two groups; and on how well *differences* in typical scores, rather than in variation, asymmetry, or other properties, can represent the relationships between the two groups. Ramsay (2000) reanalyzed a study in which mean differences between groups had been found. The reanalysis showed that the two groups differed much more in variation than in typical scores.

Most important, a mean difference provides no information as to *why* two groups differ: because of test bias, genetic influences, environmental factors, a gene-environment interaction, or perhaps biases in society recorded by tests. Rather than answering this question, mean differences raise it in the first place. Thus, they are a starting point—but are they a good one? Answering this question is a logical next step.

A difference between group means is easy to obtain. In addition, it permits an easy, straightforward interpretation—but a deceptive one. It provides scant information, and none at all regarding variation, kurtosis, or asymmetry. These additional properties are needed to understand any group's scores.

Moreover, a mean difference is often an inaccurate measure of center. If a group's scores are highly asymmetric—that is, if the high scores taper off gradually but the low scores clump together, or vice versa—their mean is always too high or too low, pulled as it is toward the scores that taper gradually. Symmetry should never be assumed, even for standardized test scores. A test with a large, national norming sample can produce symmetric scores with that sample but asymmetric or *skewed* scores for particular schools, communities, or geographic regions. Results for people in these areas, if skewed, can produce an inaccurate mean and therefore an inaccurate mean difference. Even a large norming sample can include very small samples for one or more groups, producing misleading mean differences for the norming sample itself.

Finally, a mean is a point estimate: a single number that summarizes the scores of an entire group of people. A group's scores can have little skew or kurtosis but vary so widely that the mean is not typical of the highest and lowest scores. In addition to being potentially inaccurate, then, a mean can be unrepresentative of the group it purports to summarize.

Thus, means have numerous potential limitations as a way to describe groups and differences between groups. In addition to a mean, measures of shape and spread, sometimes called *distribution* and *variation*, are necessary. Researchers, including clinical researchers, sometimes may need to use different centroids entirely: medians, modes, or modified *M* statistics. Most basically, we always need a thoroughgoing description of each sample. Furthermore, it is both possible and necessary to test the characteristics of each sample to assess their representativeness of the respective population characteristics. This testing can be a simple process, often using group confidence intervals.

Once we know what we have found—which characteristics vary from group to group—we can use this information to start to answer the question *why*. That is, we can begin to investigate causation. Multivariate techniques are often suitable for this work. Bivariate techniques address only two variables, as the name implies. Thus, they are ill suited to pursue possible causal relationships, because they cannot rule out alternative explanations posed by additional variables (Ramsay, 2000).

Alternatively, we can avoid the elusive causal question *why* and instead use measurement techniques developed to assess bias. Reynolds (1982a; Reynolds & Carson, 2005) provides copious information about these techniques. Such procedures cannot tell us if group differences result from genetic or environmental factors, but they can suggest whether test scores may be biased. Researchers have generated a literature of considerable size and sophistication using measurement techniques for examining test bias. This chapter next considers the results of such research.

## RESULTS OF BIAS RESEARCH

Methods of detecting bias include using explicit procedures to determine content validity, oversampling of particular racial and ethnic groups, and employing statistical procedures to address potential concerns. Enhanced computer technology has also enabled implementation of alternative testing formats (e.g., item response theory) and other methods to determine equitable assessment across diverse racial and ethnic groups, taking into consideration testing procedures, scoring, and use of scores (Dana, 2005; Mpofu & Ortiz, 2009).

A review of 62 cultural bias studies conducted by Valencia et al. (2001) determined that most of the studies were conducted in the 1980s, with fewer studies being conducted in the 1990s due to the consistent finding that "prominent intelligence tests" like the WISC/WISC-R were found to be nonbiased. In addition, the studies were "overwhelmingly based on African American and Mexican American children" (p. 120). A substantial proportion of the studies did not control for SES, language dominance and proficiency, and sex of the participants in the bias evaluation. The majority of the studies 71% ($n = 44$) indicated nonbiased results while 29% ($n = 18$) were found to have mixed or biased findings. The next sections provide greater detail regarding the seminal review of test bias studies by Jensen (1980), which provided a major impetus for published research in the years that followed.

## Review by Jensen

Jensen (1980) compiled an extensive early review of test bias studies. One concern addressed in the review was rational judgments that test items were biased based on their content or phrasing. For scientists, *rational* judgments are those based on reason rather than empirical findings. Such judgments may seem sound or even self-evident, but they often conflict with each other and with scientific evidence.

A WISC-R item (also included on the WISC-IV) often challenged on rational grounds is "What is the thing to do if a boy/girl much smaller than yourself starts to fight with you?" Correct responses include "Walk away" and "Don't hit him back." CTBH proponents criticized this item as biased against inner-city Black children, who may be expected to hit back to maintain their status and who may therefore respond incorrectly for cultural reasons. Jensen (1980) reviewed large-sample research indicating that proportionately more Black children than White children responded correctly to this item. Miele (1979), who also researched this item in a large-*N* study, concluded that the item was easier for Blacks than for Whites. As with this item, empirical results often contradict rational judgments.

### Predictive and Construct Validity

Jensen (1980) addressed bias in predictive and construct validity along with situational bias. Bias in predictive validity, as defined by Jensen, is systematic error in predicting a criterion variable for people of different groups. This bias occurs when one regression equation is incorrectly used for two or more groups. The review included studies involving Blacks and Whites, the two most frequently researched groups. The conclusions reached by Jensen were that (a) a large majority of studies showed that tests were equally valid for these groups and that (b) when differences were found, the tests overpredicted the criterion performance of Black examinees when compared with White examinees. CTBH would have predicted the opposite result.

Bias in construct validity occurs when a test measures groups of examinees differently. For example, a test can be more difficult, valid, or reliable for one group than for another. Construct bias involves the test itself, whereas predictive bias involves a test's prediction of a result outside the test.

Jensen (1980) found numerous studies of bias in construct validity. Regarding difficulty, when item scores differed for ethnic groups or social classes, the differences were not consistently associated with the culture loadings of the tests. Score differences between Black and White examinees were larger on nonverbal than on verbal tests, contrary to beliefs that nonverbal tests are culture fair or unbiased. The sizes of Black–White differences were positively associated with tests' correlations with *g*, or general ability. In tests with several item types, such as traditional intelligence tests, the rank orders of item difficulties for different ethnic groups were very highly correlated. Items that discriminated most between Black and White examinees also discriminated most between older and younger members of each ethnic group. Finally, Blacks, Whites, and Mexican Americans showed similar correlations between raw test scores and chronological ages.

In addition, Jensen (1980) reviewed results pertaining to validity and reliability. Black, White, and Mexican American examinees produced similar estimates of internal consistency reliability. Regarding validity, Black and White samples showed the same factor structures. According to Jensen, the evidence was generally inconclusive for infrequently researched ethnic groups, such as Asian Americans and Native Americans.

### Situational Bias

Jensen's (1980) term *situational bias* refers to "influences in the test situation, but independent of the test itself, that may bias test scores" (p. 377). These influences may include, among others, characteristics of the test setting, the instructions, and the examiners themselves. Examples include anxiety, practice and coaching effects, and examiner dialect and ethnic group (Jensen, 1984). As Jensen (1980) observed, situational influences would not constitute test bias, because they are not attributes of the tests themselves. Nevertheless, they should emerge in studies of construct and predictive bias. Jensen concluded that the

situational variables reviewed did not influence group differences in scores.

Soon after Jensen's (1980) review was published, the National Academy of Sciences and the National Research Council commissioned a panel of 19 experts, who conducted a second review of the test bias literature. The panel concluded that well-constructed tests were not biased against African Americans or other English-speaking minority groups (Wigdor & Garner, 1982). Later, a panel of 52 professionals signed a position paper that concluded, in part: "Intelligence tests are not culturally biased against American blacks or other native-born, English-speaking peoples in the United States. Rather, IQ scores predict equally accurately for all such Americans, regardless of race and social class" ("Mainstream Science," 1994, p. A18). That same year, a task force of 11 psychologists, established by the APA Association, concluded that no test characteristic reviewed made a substantial contribution to Black–White differences in intelligence scores (Neisser et al., 1996). Thus, several major reviews have failed to support CTBH. (See also Reynolds, 1998a, 1999.)

## Review by Reynolds, Lowe, and Saenz

The next sections highlight the work of Reynolds, Lowe, and Saenz (1999) focusing on content, construct, and predictive validity in relation to issues of bias.

### Content Validity

*Content validity* is the extent to which the content of a test is a representative sample of the behavior to be measured (Anastasi, 1988). Items with content bias should behave differently from group to group for people of the same standing on the characteristic being measured. Typically, reviewers judge an intelligence item to have content bias because the information or solution method required is unfamiliar to disadvantaged or minority individuals, or because the test's author has arbitrarily decided on the correct answer, so that minorities are penalized for giving responses that are correct in their own culture but not in the author's culture.

The issue of content validity with achievement tests is complex. Important variables to consider include exposure to instruction, general ability of the group, and accuracy and specificity of the items for the sample (Reynolds, Lowe et al., 1999; see also Schmidt, 1983). Little research is available for personality tests, but cultural variables that may be found to influence some personality tests include beliefs regarding discipline and aggression, values related to education and employment, and perceptions concerning society's fairness toward one's group.

Camilli and Shepard (1994; Reynolds, 2000a) recommended techniques based on item-response theory to detect differential item functioning (DIF). DIF statistics detect items that behave differently from one group to another. A statistically significant DIF statistic, by itself, does not indicate bias but may lead to later findings of bias through additional research, with consideration of the construct meant to be measured. For example, if an item on a composition test were about medieval history, studies might be conducted to determine if the item is measuring composition skill or some unintended trait, such as historical knowledge. For smaller samples, a contingency table (CT) procedure is often used to estimate DIF. CT approaches are relatively easy to understand and interpret.

Freedle and Kostin (1997) used ethnic comparison to examine factors that may have impacted DIF values on the Scholastic Aptitude Test (SAT) and Graduate Record Exam (GRE) analogy items comparing Black and White examinees matched for total verbal score. African American examinees performed better than Whites on analogy items that had a social-personality content as opposed to a science content. The authors proposed two concepts, cultural familiarity and semantic ambiguity, to explain the persistent pattern of results indicating that Black examinees and other minority groups consistently perform differentially better on harder verbal items and differentially worse on easier items. The "easy" items contain more culturally specific content and can be viewed differently based on cultural and socioeconomic background. The "hard" items do not generally contain words that have variable definitions because they are familiar to those with higher levels of education. Freedle (2003) noted that African American and White examinees disagreed in how they responded to "common" words, such as "valuable," "justice," "progress," and "class" (p. 7). "Such words, when presented in restricted verbal context, can potentially be misinterpreted across racial groups" (Freedle, 2010, p. 396). These findings have been replicated by other scholars, indicating that SAT items function differently for African American and White subgroups (Santelices & Wilson, 2010).

Nandakumar, Glutting, and Oakland (1993) used a CT approach to investigate possible racial, ethnic, and gender bias on the Guide to the Assessment of Test Session Behavior (GATSB). Participants were boys and girls age 6 to 16 years, of White, Black, or Hispanic ethnicity. Only 10 of 80 items produced statistically significant DIFs,

suggesting that the GATSB has little bias for different genders and ethnicities.

In very-large-$N$ studies, Reynolds, Willson, and Chatman (1984) used a partial correlation procedure (Reynolds, 2000a) to estimate DIF in tests of intelligence and related aptitudes. The researchers found no systematic bias against African Americans or women on measures of English vocabulary. Willson, Nolan, Reynolds, and Kamphaus (1989) used the same procedure to estimate DIF on the Mental Processing scales of the K-ABC. The researchers concluded that there was little apparent evidence of race or gender bias.

Jensen (1976) used a chi-square technique (Reynolds, 2000a) to examine the distribution of incorrect responses for two multiple-choice intelligence tests, RPM and the Peabody Picture-Vocabulary Test (PPVT). Participants were Black and White children age 6 to 12 years. The errors for many items were distributed systematically over the response options. This pattern, however, was the same for Blacks and Whites. These results indicated bias in a general sense, but not racial bias. On RPM, Black and White children made different types of errors, but for few items. The researcher examined these items with children of different ages. For each of the items, Jensen was able to duplicate Blacks' response patterns using those of Whites approximately 2 years younger.

Scheuneman (1987) used linear methodology on GRE item data to show possible influences on the scores of Black and White test takers. Vocabulary content, true-false response, and presence or absence of diagrams were among the item characteristics examined. Paired, experimental items were administered in the experimental section of the GRE General Test, given in December 1982. Results indicated that certain characteristics common to a variety of items may have a differential influence on Blacks' and Whites' scores. These items may be measuring, in part, test content rather than verbal, quantitative, or analytical skill.

Jensen (1974, 1976, 1977) evaluated bias on the Wonderlic Personnel Test (WPT), PPVT, and RPM using correlations between $P$ decrements (Reynolds, 2000a) obtained by Black students and those obtained by White students. $P$ is the probability of passing an item, and a $P$ decrement is the size of the difference between $P$s for one item and the next. Thus, $P$-decrements represent an "analysis of the ordering of the difficulties of the items as a whole, and the degree to which such ordering remains constant across groups" (Reynolds & Carson, 2005, p. 803). Jensen also obtained correlations between the rank orders of item difficulties for Black and Whites. Results for rank orders and

*P* decrements, it should be noted, differ from those that would be obtained for the scores themselves.

The tests examined were RPM; the PPVT; the WISC-R; the WPT; and the Revised Stanford-Binet Intelligence Scale, Form L-M. Jensen (1974) obtained the same data for Mexican American and White students on the PPVT and RPM. Table 4.1 shows the results, with similar findings obtained by Sandoval (1979) and Miele (1979). The correlations showed little evidence of content bias in the scales examined. Most correlations appeared large. Some individual items were identified as biased, but they accounted for only 2% to 5% of the variation in score differences.

Hammill (1991) used correlations of *p* decrements to examine the Detroit Tests of Learning Aptitude (DTLA-3). Correlations exceeded .90 for all subtests, and most exceeded .95. Reynolds and Bigler (1994) presented correlations of *P* decrements for the 14 subtests of the Test of Memory and Learning (TOMAL). Correlations again exceeded .90, with most exceeding .95, for males and females and for all ethnicities studied.

Another procedure for detecting item bias relies on the partial correlation between an item score and a nominal variable, such as ethnic group. The correlation partialed out is that between total test score and the nominal variable. If the variable and the item score are correlated after the partialed correlation is removed, the item is performing differently from group to group, which suggests bias. Reynolds, Lowe et al. (1999) described this technique as a powerful means of detecting item bias. They noted, however, that it is a relatively recent application. Thus, it may have limitations not yet known.

Research on item bias in personality measures is sparse but has produced results similar to those with ability tests (Moran, 1990; Reynolds, 1998a, 1998b; Reynolds & Harding, 1983). The few studies of behavior rating scales

have produced little evidence of bias for White, Black, and Hispanic and Latin populations in the United States (James, 1995; Mayfield & Reynolds, 1998; Reynolds & Kamphaus, 1992).

Not all studies of content bias have focused on items. Researchers evaluating the WISC-R have defined bias differently. Few results are available for the WISC-III; future research should use data from this newer test. Prifitera and Saklofske (1998) addressed the WISC-III and ethnic bias in the United States. These results are discussed later in the "Construct Validity" and "Predictive Validity" sections.

Reynolds and Jensen (1983) examined the 12 WISC-R subtests for bias against Black children using a variation of the group by item analysis of variance (ANOVA). The researchers matched Black children to White children from the norming sample on the basis of gender and Full Scale IQ. SES was a third matching variable and was used when a child had more than one match in the other group. Matching controlled for *g*, so a group difference indicated that the subtest in question was more difficult for Blacks or for Whites.

Black children exceeded White children on Digit Span and Coding. Whites exceeded Blacks on Comprehension, Object Assembly, and Mazes. Blacks tended to obtain higher scores on Arithmetic and Whites on Picture Arrangement. The actual differences were very small, and variance due to ethnic group was less than 5% for each subtest. If the WISC-R is viewed as a test measuring only *g*, these results may be interpretable as indicating subtest bias. Alternatively, the results may indicate differences in Level II ability (Reynolds, Willson et al., 1999) or in specific or intermediate abilities.

Taken together, studies of major ability and personality tests show no consistent evidence for content bias. When

**TABLE 4.1  Ethnic Correlations for *P* Decrements and for Rank Orders of Item Difficulties**

| Scale | Black–White | | | | Mexican American–White | | | |
| --- | --- | --- | --- | --- | --- | --- | --- | --- |
| | Rank Orders | | *P* Decrements | | Rank Orders | | *P* Decrements | |
| PPVT (Jensen, 1974) | .99[a] | .98[b] | .79[a] | .65[b] | .98[a] | .98[b] | .78[a] | .66[b] |
| RPM (Jensen, 1974) | .99[a] | .99[b] | .98[a] | .96[b] | .99[a] | .99[b] | .99[a] | .97[b] |
| SB L-M (Jensen, 1976) | .96[c] | | | | | | | |
| WISC-R (Jensen, 1976) | .95[c] | | | | | | | |
| (Sandoval, 1979) | .98[c] | | .87[c] | | .99[c] | | .91[c] | |
| WISC (Miele, 1979) | .96[a] | .95[b] | | | | | | |
| WPT (Jensen, 1977) | .94[c] | | .81[c] | | | | | |

*Notes.* PPVT = Peabody Picture Vocabulary Test; RPM = Raven's Progressive Matrices; SB L-M = Stanford-Binet, Form LM; WISC-R = Wechsler Intelligence Scale for Children-Revised; WPT= Wonderlic Personnel Test; Sandoval, 1979 = Medians for 10 WISC-R subtests, excluding Coding and Digit Span.

[a]Males.

[b]Females.

[c]Males and females combined.

bias is found, it is small. Tests with satisfactory reliability, validity, and norming appear also to have little content bias. For numerous standardized tests, however, results are not yet available. Research with these tests should continue investigating possible content bias with differing ethnic and other groups.

## Construct Validity

Anastasi (1988) has defined construct validity as the extent to which a test may be said to measure a theoretical construct or trait. Test bias in construct validity, then, may be defined as the extent to which a test measures different constructs for different groups.

Factor analysis is a widely used method for investigating construct bias (Reynolds, 2000a). This set of complex techniques groups together items or subtests that correlate highly among themselves. When a group of items correlates highly together, the researcher interprets them as reflecting a single characteristic. The researcher then examines the pattern of correlations and induces the nature of this characteristic. Table 4.2 shows a simple example.

In the table, the subtests picture identification, matrix comparison, visual search, and diagram drawing have high correlations in the column labeled "Factor 1." Definitions, antonyms, synonyms, and multiple meanings have low correlations in this column but much higher ones in the column labeled "Factor 2." A researcher might interpret these results as indicating that the first four subtests correlate with factor 1 and the second four correlate with factor 2. Examining the table, the researcher might see that the subtests correlating highly with factor 1 require visual activity, and he or she might therefore label this factor Visual Ability. The same researcher might see that the subtests correlating highly with factor 2 involve the meanings of words, and he or she might label this factor Word Meanings. To label factors in this way, researchers must be familiar with the subtests or items, common responses to them, and scoring of these responses. (See also Ramsay &

**TABLE 4.2   Sample Factor Structure**

| Subtest | Factor 1 | Factor 2 |
|---|---|---|
| Picture Identification | .78 | .17 |
| Matrix Comparison | .82 | .26 |
| Visual Search | .86 | .30 |
| Diagram Drawing | .91 | .29 |
| Definitions | .23 | .87 |
| Antonyms | .07 | .92 |
| Synonyms | .21 | .88 |
| Multiple Meanings | .36 | .94 |

Reynolds, 2000a.) The results in Table 4.2 are called a *two-factor solution*. Actual factor analysis is a set of advanced statistical techniques, and the explanation presented here is necessarily a gross oversimplification.

Very similar factor analytic results for two or more groups, such as genders or ethnicities, are evidence that the test responses being analyzed behave similarly as to the constructs they represent and the extent to which they represent them. As noted by Reynolds, Lowe et al. (1999), such comparative factor analyses with multiple populations are important for the work of clinicians, who must know that a test functions very similarly from one population to another to interpret scores consistently.

Researchers most often calculate a coefficient of congruence or simply a Pearson correlation to examine factorial similarity, often called *factor congruence* or *factor invariance*. The variables correlated are one group's item or subtest correlations (shown in Table 4.2) with another's. A coefficient of congruence may be preferable, but the commonly used techniques produce very similar results, at least with large samples (Reynolds & Harding, 1983; Reynolds, Lowe et al., 1999). Researchers frequently interpret a value of .90 or higher as indicating factor congruity. For other applicable techniques, see Reynolds (2000a).

Extensive research regarding racial and ethnic groups is available for the widely used WISC and WISC-R. This work consists largely of factor analyses. Psychometricians are trained in this method, so its usefulness in assessing bias is opportune. Unfortunately, many reports of this research fail to specify whether exploratory or confirmatory factor analysis has been used. In factor analyses of construct and other bias, exploratory techniques are most common. Results with the WISC and WISC-R generally support factor congruity. For preschool-age children also, factor analytic results support congruity for racial and ethnic groups (Reynolds, 1982a).

Reschly (1978) conducted factor analyses comparing WISC-R correlations for Blacks, Whites, Mexican Americans, and Papagos, a Native American group, all in the southwestern United States. Reschly found that the two-factor solutions were congruent for the four ethnicities. The 12 coefficients of congruence ranged from .97 to .99. For the less widely used three-factor solutions, only results for Whites and Mexican Americans were congruent. The one-factor solution showed congruence for all four ethnicities, as Miele (1979) had found with the WISC.

Oakland and Feigenbaum (1979) factor-analyzed the 12 WISC-R subtests separately for random samples of normal Black, White, and Mexican American children from an urban school district in the northwestern United States.

Samples were stratified by race, age, sex, and SES. The researchers used a Pearson $r$ for each factor to compare it for the three ethnic groups. The one-factor solution produced $r$s of .95 for Black and White children, .97 for Mexican American and White children, and .96 for Black and Mexican American children. The remaining results were $r = .94$ to .99. Thus, WISC-R scores were congruent for the three ethnic groups.

Gutkin and Reynolds (1981) compared factor analytic results for the Black and White children in the WISC-R norming sample. Samples were stratified by age, sex, race, SES, geographic region, and community size to match 1970 U.S. Census Bureau data. The researchers compared one-, two-, and three-factor solutions using magnitudes of unique variances, proportion of total variance accounted for by common factor variance, patterns of correlations with each factor, and percentage of common factor variance accounted for by each factor. Coefficients of congruence were .99 for comparisons of the unique variances and of the three solutions examined. Thus, the factor correlations were congruent for Black and White children.

Dean (1979) compared three-factor WISC-R solutions for White and Mexican American children referred because of learning difficulties in the regular classroom. Analyzing the 10 main WISC-R subtests, Dean found these coefficients of congruence: .84 for Verbal Comprehension, .89 for Perceptual Organization, and .88 for Freedom from Distractibility.

Gutkin and Reynolds (1980) compared one-, two-, and three-factor principal-factor solutions of the WISC-R for referred White and Mexican American children. The researchers also compared their solutions to those of Reschly (1978) and to those derived from the norming sample. Coefficients of congruence were .99 for Gutkin and Reynolds's one-factor solutions and .98 and .91 for their two-factor solutions. Coefficients of congruence exceeded .90 in all comparisons of Gutkin and Reynolds's solutions to Reschly's solutions for normal Black, White, Mexican American, and Papago children and to solutions derived from the norming sample. Three-factor results were more varied but also indicated substantial congruity for these children.

DeFries et al. (1974) administered 15 ability tests to large samples of American children of Chinese or Japanese ancestry. The researchers examined correlations among the 15 tests for the two ethnic groups and concluded that the cognitive organization of the groups was virtually identical. Willerman (1979) reviewed these results and concluded, in part, that the tests were measuring the same abilities for the two groups of children.

Results with adults are available as well. Kaiser (1986) and Scholwinski (1985) have found the Wechsler Adult Intelligence Scale–Revised (WAIS-R) to be factorially congruent for Black and White adults from the norming sample. Kaiser conducted separate hierarchical analyses for Black and White participants and calculated coefficients of congruence for the General, Verbal, and Performance factors. Coefficients for the three factors were .99, .98, and .97, respectively. Scholwinski selected Black and White participants closely matched in age, sex, and Full Scale IQ, from the WAIS-R norming sample. Results again indicated factorial congruence.

Edwards and Oakland (2006) examined the factorial invariance of Woodcock-Johnson III (WJ-III) scores for African Americans and Caucasian American students in the norming sample. Results indicate that although their mean scores differ, the WJ-III scores have comparable meaning across groups, as evidenced by the consistent factor structure found for both groups.

Researchers have also assessed construct bias by estimating internal consistency reliabilities for different groups. *Internal consistency reliability* is the extent to which all items of a test are measuring the same construct. A test is unbiased with regard to this characteristic to the extent that its reliabilities are similar from group to group.

Jensen (1977) used Kuder-Richardson formula 21 to estimate internal consistency reliability for Black and White adults on the Wonderlic Personnel Test. Reliability estimates were .86 and .88 for Blacks and Whites, respectively. In addition, Jensen (1974) used Hoyt's formula to obtain internal consistency estimates of .96 on the PPVT for Black, White, and Mexican American children. The researcher then subdivided each group of children by gender and obtained reliabilities of .95 to .97. Raven's colored matrices produced internal consistency reliabilities of .86 to .91 for the same six race–gender groupings. For these three widely used aptitude tests, Jensen's (1974, 1976) results indicated homogeneity of test content and consistency of measurement by gender and ethnicity.

Sandoval (1979) and Oakland and Feigenbaum (1979) have extensively examined the internal consistency reliability of the WISC-R subtests, excluding Digit Span and Coding, for which internal consistency analysis is inappropriate. Both studies included Black, White, and Mexican American children. Both samples were large, with Sandoval's exceeding 1,000.

Sandoval (1979) estimated reliabilities to be within .04 of each other for all subtests except Object Assembly. This subtest was most reliable for Black children at .95, followed by Whites at .79 and Mexican Americans at .75.

Oakland and Feigenbaum (1979) found reliabilities within .06, again excepting Object Assembly. In this study, the subtest was most reliable for Whites at .76, followed by Blacks at .64 and Mexican Americans at .67. Oakland and Feigenbaum also found consistent reliabilities for males and females.

Dean (1979) assessed the internal consistency reliability of the WISC-R for Mexican American children tested by White examiners. Reliabilities were consistent with, although slightly larger than, those reported by Wechsler (1975) for the norming sample.

Results with the WISC-III norming sample (Prifitera, Weiss, & Saklofske, 1998) suggested a substantial association between IQ and SES. WISC-III Full Scale IQ was higher for children whose parents had high education levels, and parental education is considered a good measure of SES. The children's Full Scale IQs were 110.7, 103.0, 97.9, 90.6, and 87.7, respectively, in the direction of highest (college or above) to lowest (<8th grade) parental education level. Researchers have reported similar results for other IQ tests (Prifitera et al., 1998). Such results should not be taken as showing SES bias because, like ethnic and gender differences, they may reflect real distinctions, perhaps influenced by social and economic factors. Indeed, IQ is thought to be associated with SES. By reflecting this theoretical characteristic of intelligence, SES differences may support the construct validity of the tests examined.

Psychologists view intelligence as a developmental phenomenon (Reynolds, Lowe et al., 1999). Hence, similar correlations of raw scores with age may be evidence of construct validity for intelligence tests. Jensen (1976) found that these correlations for the PPVT were .73 with Blacks, .79 with Whites, and .67 with Mexican Americans. For Raven's colored matrices, correlations were .66 for Blacks, .72 for Whites, and .70 for Mexican Americans. The K-ABC produced similar results (Kamphaus & Reynolds, 1987).

A review by Moran (1990) and a literature search by Reynolds, Lowe et al. (1999) indicated that few construct bias studies of personality tests had been published. This limitation is notable, given large mean differences on the Minnesota Multiphasic Personality Inventory (MMPI), and possibly the MMPI-2. The MMPI is the most widely used and researched personality test in the world (e.g., Butcher, 2009). Patterns of score differences have been noted based on gender and ethnicity (Reynolds, Lowe et al.). In addition, to challenges of cultural bias, Groth-Marnat (2009) noted that score differences may reflect different personality traits, cultural beliefs, and experiences

of racial discrimination (e.g., anger, frustration). Other popular measures, such as the Revised Children's Manifest Anxiety Scale (RCMAS), suggest consistent results by gender and ethnicity (Moran, 1990; Reynolds & Paget, 1981).

To summarize, studies using different samples, methodologies, and definitions of bias indicate that many prominent standardized tests are consistent from one race, ethnicity, and gender to another. (See Reynolds, 1982b, for a review of methodologies.) These tests appear to be reasonably unbiased for the groups investigated.

## Predictive Validity

As the term implies, *predictive validity* pertains to *prediction* from test scores, whereas *content* and *construct validity* pertain to *measurement*. Anastasi (1988) defined predictive or criterion-related validity as "the effectiveness of a test in predicting an individual's performance in specified activities" (p. 145). Thus, test bias in predictive validity may be defined as systematic error that affects examinees' performance differentially depending on their group membership. Cleary et al. (1975) defined predictive test bias as constant error in an inference or prediction, or error in a prediction that exceeds the smallest feasible random error, as a function of membership in a particular group. Oakland and Matuszek (1977) found that fewer children were wrongly placed using these criteria than using other, varied models of bias. An early court ruling also favored Cleary's definition (*Cortez v. Rosen*, 1975).

Of importance, inaccurate prediction sometimes reflects inconsistent measurement of the characteristic being predicted rather than bias in the test used to predict it. In addition, numerous investigations of predictive bias have addressed the selection of employment and college applicants of different racial and ethnic groups. Studies also address prediction bias in personality tests (Moran, 1990; Monnot, Quirk, Hoerger, & Brewer, 2009). As the chapter shows, copious results for intelligence tests are available.

Under the definition presented by Cleary et al. (1975), the regression line formed by any predictor and criterion (e.g., total test score and a predicted characteristic) must be the same for each group with whom the test is used. A regression line consists of two parameters: a slope, $a$, and an intercept, $b$. Too great a group difference in either of these parameters indicates that a regression equation based on the combined groups would predict inaccurately (Reynolds, Lowe et al., 1999). A separate equation for each group then becomes necessary with the groups and characteristics for which bias has been found.

Hunter, Schmidt, and Hunter (1979) reviewed 39 studies, yielding 866 comparisons, of Black–White test score validity in personnel selection. The researchers concluded that the results did not support a hypothesis of differential or single-group validity. Several studies of the SAT indicated no predictive bias, or small bias against Whites, in predicting grade point average and other measures of college performance (Cleary, 1968; Cleary et al., 1975).

Reschly and Sabers (1979) examined the validity of WISC-R IQs in predicting the Reading and Math subtest scores of Blacks, Whites, Mexican Americans, and Papago Native Americans on the Metropolitan Achievement Tests (MAT). The MAT has undergone item analysis procedures to eliminate content bias, making it especially appropriate for this research: Content bias can be largely ruled out as a competing explanation for any invalidity in prediction. WISC-R IQs underpredicted MAT scores for Whites compared with the remaining groups. Overprediction was greatest for Papagos. The intercept typically showed little bias.

Reynolds and Gutkin (1980) conducted similar analyses for WISC-R Verbal, Performance, and Full Scale IQs as predictors of arithmetic, reading, and spelling. The samples were large groups of White and Mexican American children from the southwestern United States. Only the equation for Performance IQ and arithmetic achievement differed for the two groups. Here an intercept bias favored Mexican American children.

Likewise, Reynolds and Hartlage (1979) assessed WISC and WISC-R Full Scale IQs as predictors of Blacks' and Whites' arithmetic and reading achievement. The children's teachers had referred them for psychological services in a rural, southern school district. The researchers found no statistically significant differences for these children. Many participants, however, had incomplete data (34% of the total).

Prifitera et al. (1998) noted studies in which the WISC-III predicted achievement equally for Black, White, and Hispanic children. In one study, Weiss and Prifitera (1995) examined WISC-III Full Scale IQ as a predictor of Wechsler Individual Achievement Test (WIAT) scores for Black, White, and Hispanic children age 6 to 16 years. Results indicated little evidence of slope or intercept bias, a finding consistent with those for the WISC and WISC-R. Weiss, Prifitera, and Roid (1993) reported similar results.

Bossard, Reynolds, and Gutkin (1980) analyzed the 1972 Stanford-Binet Intelligence Scale when used to predict the reading, spelling, and arithmetic attainment of referred Black and White children. No statistically

significant bias appeared in comparisons of either correlations or regression analyses.

Reynolds, Willson, and Chatman (1985) evaluated K-ABC scores as predictors of Black and White children's academic attainment. Some of the results indicated bias, usually overprediction of Black children's attainment. Of 56 Potthoff comparisons (i.e., determining bias based on whether the regression equation relating two variables is constant across groups; Reynolds, 1982), however, most indicated no statistically significant bias. Thus, evidence for bias had low method reliability for these children.

In addition, Kamphaus and Reynolds (1987) reviewed seven studies on predictive bias with the K-ABC. Overprediction of Black children's scores was more common than with other tests and was particularly common with the Sequential Processing Scale. The differences were small and were mitigated by using the K-ABC Mental Processing Composite. Some underprediction of Black children's scores also occurred.

A series of very-large-$N$ studies reviewed by Jensen (1980) and Sattler (1974) compared the predictive validities of group IQ tests for different races. This procedure has an important limitation. If validities differ, regression analyses must also differ. If validities are the same, regression analyses may nonetheless differ, making additional analysis necessary (but see Reynolds, Lowe, et al., 1999). In addition, Jensen and Sattler found few available studies that followed this method of analysis on which to base their results. Lorge-Thorndike Verbal and Nonverbal IQs were the results most often investigated. The reviewers concluded that validities were comparable for Black and White elementary school children. Despite the fact that decades have passed since the publications by Jensen and Sattler, there still exists the need for researchers to broaden the range of group intelligence tests that they examine. Emphasis on a small subset of available measures continues to be a common limitation of test research.

Guterman (1979) reported an extensive analysis of the Ammons and Ammons Quick Test (QT), a verbal IQ measure, with adolescents of different social classes. The variables predicted were (a) social knowledge measures; (b) school grades obtained in Grades 9, 10, and 12; (c) Reading Comprehension Test scores on the Gates Reading Survey; and (d) Vocabulary and Arithmetic subtest scores on the General Aptitude Test Battery (GATB). Guterman found little evidence of slope or intercept bias with these adolescents, except one social knowledge measure, sexual knowledge, showed intercept bias.

Another extensive analysis merits attention, given its unexpected results. Reynolds (1978) examined seven major preschool tests: the Draw-a-Design and Draw-a-Child subtests of the McCarthy Scales, the Mathematics and Language subtests of the Tests of Basic Experiences, the Preschool Inventory–Revised Edition, and the Lee-Clark Readiness Test. Variables predicted were four MAT subtests: Word Knowledge, Word Discrimination, Reading, and Arithmetic. Besides increased content validity, the MAT had the advantage of being chosen by teachers in the district as the test most nearly measuring what was taught in their classrooms. Reynolds compared correlations and regression analyses for the following race-gender combinations: Black females versus Black males, White females versus White males, Black females versus White females, and Black males versus White males. The result was 112 comparisons each for correlations and regression analyses.

For each criterion, scores fell in the same rank order: White females < White males < Black females < Black males. Mean validities comparing pre- and posttest scores, with 12 months intervening, were .59 for White females, .50 for White males, .43 for Black females, and .30 for Black males. In spite of these overall differences, only three differences between correlations were statistically significant, a chance finding with 112 comparisons. Potthoff comparisons of regression lines, however, indicated 43 statistically significant differences. Most of these results occurred when race rather than gender was compared: 31 of 46 comparisons ($p < .01$). The Preschool Inventory and Lee-Clark Test most frequently showed bias; the Metropolitan Readiness Tests (MRT) never did. The observed bias overpredicted scores of Black and male children.

Researchers should investigate possible reasons for these results, which may have differed for the seven predictors but also by the statistical results compared. Either Potthoff comparisons or comparisons of correlations may be inaccurate or inconsistent as analyses of predictive test bias. (See also Reynolds, 1980.)

Brief screening measures tend to have low reliability compared with major ability and aptitude tests such as the WISC-III and the K-ABC. Low reliability can lead to bias in prediction (Reynolds, Lowe et al., 1999). More reliable measures, such as the MRT, the WPPSI, and the McCarthy Scales, have shown little evidence of internal bias. The WPPSI and McCarthy Scales have not been assessed for predictive bias with differing racial or ethnic groups (Reynolds, Lowe et al., 1999).

Reynolds (1980) examined test and subtest scores for the seven tests noted earlier when used to predict MAT scores for males and females and for diverse ethnic groups. The

researcher examined *residuals*—the differences between predicted scores and actual scores obtained by examinees. Techniques used were multiple regression to obtain residuals and race by gender ANOVA to analyze them.

ANOVA results indicated no statistically significant differences in residuals for ethnicities or genders and no statistically significant interactions. Reynolds (1980) then examined a subset of the seven-test battery. No evidence of racial bias appeared. The results indicated gender bias in predicting two of the four MAT subtests, Word Discrimination and Word Knowledge. The seven tests consistently underpredicted females' scores. The difference was small, on the order of .13 to .16 *SD*.

Bias studies are especially critical on personality tests used to diagnose mental disorders, although much of the research conducted on the most popular personality tests (e.g., MMPI-2) continues to focus on differences in scoring patterns between racial and ethnic groups (Suzuki, Onoue, & Hill, forthcoming). A study by Monnot et al. (2009) on male veteran inpatients revealed a "modest" pattern of predictive bias across numerous scales. The authors concluded that "[t]hese biases indicate both over- and underprediction of psychiatric disorders among African Americans on a variety of scales suggesting differential accuracy for the MMPI-2 in predicting diagnostic status between subgroups of male veteran inpatients seeking substance abuse treatment" (p. 145). By comparison, no evidence of overprediction of diagnosis was found for Caucasians across the test scores.

For predictive validity, as for content and construct validity, the results reviewed suggest little evidence of bias, whether differential or single-group validity. Differences are infrequent. Where they exist, they usually take the form of small overpredictions for lower-scoring groups, such as disadvantaged, low-SES, or ethnic minority examinees. These overpredictions are unlikely to account for adverse placement or diagnosis of these groups. On a grander scale, the small differences found may be reflections, but would not be major causes, of sweeping social inequalities affecting ethnic group members. The causes of such problems as employment discrimination and economic deprivation lie primarily outside the testing environment.

## Path Modeling and Predictive Bias

Keith and Reynolds (1990; see also Ramsay, 1997) have suggested path analysis as a means of assessing predictive bias. Figure 4.1 shows one of their models. Each arrow represents a path, and each oblong or rectangle represents a variable.

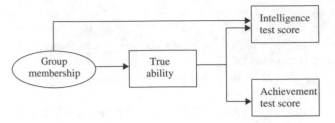

The arrow from group membership to intelligence test score represents bias

**Figure 4.1**  Path model showing predictive bias

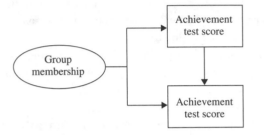

The arrow from group membership to predictor of school achievement represents bias

**Figure 4.2**  Revised path model showing predictive bias

The path from group membership to intelligence test score denotes bias. Its beta value, then, should be small. The absence of this path would represent bias of zero.

A limitation of this approach is that no true ability measures exist. Thus, a path model could not incorporate true ability unless it was measured by three or more existing variables. Figure 4.2 shows a proposed model that disposes of this limitation. Here true ability drops out, and a path leads from the predictor, *Achievement Test Score*, to the criterion, *School Achievement*. The path from group membership to the predictor denotes bias; as before, its beta value should be small. The absence of this path would, again, reflect zero bias.

## EXAMINER–EXAMINEE RELATIONSHIP

Contrary findings notwithstanding, many psychological professionals continue to assert that White examiners impede the test performance of minority group members (Sattler, 1988). Sattler and Gwynne (1982) reviewed 27 published studies on the effects of examiners' race on the test scores of children and youth on a wide range of cognitive tests. Participants were students in preschool through Grade 12, most from urban areas throughout the United States. Tests included the Wechsler Scales; the Stanford-Binet, Form L-M; the PPVT; the Draw-a-Man Test; the Iowa Test of Preschool Development; and others. In 23 of

these studies, examiner's race (Black or White) and test scores of racial groups (Black or White) had no statistically significant association. Sattler and Gwynne reported that the remaining four studies had methodological limitations, including inappropriate statistical tests and designs. Design limitations included lack of a comparison group and of external criteria to evaluate the validity of procedures used.

The question of possible examiner–examinee effects has taken numerous forms. Minority examinees might obtain reduced scores because of their *responses* to examiner–examinee differences. An examiner of a different race, for example, might evoke anxiety or fear in minority children. Research has lent little support to this possibility. Kaufman (1994), for example, found that Black populations obtained their highest scores on tests most sensitive to anxiety.

White examiners may be less effective than Hispanic American examiners when testing Hispanic American children and adolescents. This proposal, too, has received little support. Gerkin (1978) found that examiner's ethnicity (White or Hispanic American) and examiner's bilingual ability (monolingual or bilingual) had no statistically significant association with the WPPSI IQs or the Leiter International Performance Scale scores of children age 4, 5, and 6 years. Morales and George (1976) found that Hispanic bilingual children in Grades 1 to 3 obtained higher WISC-R scores with monolingual non-Hispanic examiners than with bilingual Hispanic examiners, who tested the children in both Spanish and English (Sattler, 1988; Reynolds, Lowe et al., 1999).

These findings suggest that examiner ethnicity has little adverse effect on minority scores. Examiners need to be well trained and competent, however, in administering standardized tests to diverse minority group members. Rapport may be especially crucial for minority examinees, and approaches that are effective with one ethnic group may be less so with another. The *Guidelines on Multicultural Education, Training, Research, Practice, and Organizational Change for Psychologists* adopted by the American Psychological Association (2002) noted that cultural competence in assessment requires multicultural understanding in the establishment of the relationship with the client and attending to potential measurement limitations including issues of test bias, fairness, and cultural equivalence. As usual, research in this area should continue. Neither researchers nor clinicians can assume that the results reviewed in this chapter typify all future results.

## HELMS AND CULTURAL EQUIVALENCE

As noted, Helms (1992) and other authors have reframed the CTBH approach over time. Helms has addressed the implicit biological and environmental philosophical perspectives used to explain racial and ethnic group differences in tested cognitive ability. Helms's position is that these perspectives stem from inadequate notions of culture and that neither perspective provides useful information about the cultural equivalence of tests for diverse ethnic groups. Assessment of cultural equivalence is necessary to account for minority groups' cultural, social, and cognitive differences from the majority. Helms (2006) noted the complexity of understanding the internalized racial and cultural experiences and environmental socialization that can impact test performance that are unrelated to intelligence and therefore comprise error. These factors may have a greater impact on the test performance of members of racial and ethnic minority groups in comparison to nonminority group members.

For Helms (1992), cultural equivalence should take seven forms (Butcher, 1982): (1) *functional equivalence*, the extent to which test scores have the same meaning for different cultural groups; (2) *conceptual equivalence*, whether test items have the same meaning and familiarity in different groups; (3) *linguistic equivalence*, whether tests have the same linguistic meaning to different groups; (4) *psychometric equivalence*, the extent to which tests measure the same thing for different groups; (5) *testing condition* equivalence, whether groups are equally familiar with testing procedures and view testing as a means of assessing ability; (6) *contextual equivalence*, the extent to which a cognitive ability is assessed similarly in different contexts in which people behave; and (7) *sampling equivalence*, whether comparable samples of each cultural group are available at the test development, validation, and interpretation stages.

Helms (1992) argued for the diversification of existing tests, the development of new standardized tests, and the formation of explicit principles, hypotheses, assumptions, and theoretical models for investigating cultural differences. In addition, Helms argued that existing frameworks—biological, environmental, and cultural—should be operationally defined.

For future research, Helms (1992) recommended (a) development of measures for determining interracial cultural dependence and levels of acculturation and assimilation in test items, (b) modification of test content to include items that reflect cultural diversity, (c) examination of incorrect responses, (d) incorporation of cognitive psychology into interactive modes of assessment, (e) use of theories to examine environmental content of criteria, and (f) separate racial group norms for existing tests. Researchers should interpret test scores cautiously, Helms suggested, until psychometricians develop more diverse procedures to address cultural concerns.

Helms's (1992) approach, or one like it, is likely to become a future trend. As observed by Reynolds, Lowe et al. (1999), however, much of the work recommended by Helms has been well under way for several decades. (For an extensive treatment, see Cronbach & Drenth, 1972; see also Hambleton, 1994; Van de Vijver & Hambleton, 1996.) Reynolds et al. contended that Helms coined new terms for old constructs and dismissed many studies already addressing the issues she raises. At best, they believe, Helms organized and continues to call attention to long-recognized empirical issues. She emphasized that test takers of color (i.e., African American, Latino/Latina, Asian American, and Native American) "are competing with White test takers whose racial socialization experiences are either irrelevant to their test performance or give them an undeserved advantage" (Helms, 2006, p. 855).

## TRANSLATION AND CULTURAL TESTING

The findings already reviewed do not apply to translations of tests. Use of a test in a new linguistic culture requires that it be redeveloped from the start. One reason for the early success of the Stanford-Binet Intelligence Scale was that Terman reconceptualized it for the United States, reexamining Binet's theory of intelligence, writing and testing new items, and renorming the scales (Reynolds, Lowe et al., 1999).

Terman's work was an exception to a rule of simple translation of the Binet Scales. Even today, few researchers are experienced in procedures for adapting tests and establishing score equivalence. Nonetheless, the procedures are available, and they increase the validity of the adapted tests (Hambleton & Kanjee, 1995). Adaptation of educational and psychological tests most frequently occurs for one of three reasons: to facilitate comparative ethnic studies, to allow individuals to be tested in their own language, or to reduce the time and cost of developing new tests.

Test adaptation has been commonplace for more than 90 years, but the field of cross-cultural and cross-national comparisons is relatively recent. This field has focused on development and use of adaptation guidelines (Hambleton, 1994), ways to interpret and use cross-cultural and cross-national data (Hambleton & Kanjee, 1995;

Poortinga & Malpass, 1986), and especially procedures for establishing item equivalence (Ellis, 1991; Hambleton, 1993; Poortinga, 1983; van de Vijver & Poortinga, 1991). Test items are said to be equivalent when members of each linguistic or cultural group who have the same standing on the construct measured by the tests have the same probability of selecting the correct item response.

A number of test adaptations can be based on the area of equivalence being addressed (i.e., conceptual, cultural, linguistic, or measurement) (van de Vijver & Leung, 2011). For example, cultural adaptations can be made in terms of terminological/factual driven, including accommodation of specific cultural or country characteristics, or norm driven, taking into consideration norms, values and practices. Language adaptations can be linguistic driven to accommodate structural differences in the language or pragmatics driven to address conventional language usage. Van de Vijver and Tanzer (2004) suggested the committee approach in which "[a] group of people, often with different areas of expertise (such as cultural, linguistic, and psychological) prepare a translation" (p. 123). The cooperative effort among this group improves the quality of the translation. Similarly, Geisinger (2005) outlined translation methods that incorporate a team of culturally sensitive translators "who not only translate the assessment device linguistically, but from a cultural perspective as well." This work is then evaluated by a "panel of others who are knowledgeable about the content covered by the assessment, fluent in both the original and target languages, and thoroughly experienced in the two cultures" (p. 197).

The designs used to establish item equivalence fall into two categories, judgmental and statistical. Judgmental designs rely on a person's or group's decision regarding the degree of translation equivalence of an item. Two common designs are forward translation and back translation (Hambleton & Bollwark, 1991). In the first design, translators adapt or translate a test to the target culture or language. Other translators then assess the equivalency of the two versions. If the versions are not equivalent, changes are made. In the second design, translators adapt or translate a test to the target culture or language as before. Other translators readapt the items back to the original culture or language. An assessment of equivalence follows. Judgmental designs are a preliminary approach. Additional checks, such as DIF or other statistical analyses, are also needed (Reynolds, Lowe et al., 1999).

Three statistical designs are available, depending on the characteristics of the sample. In the bilingual examinees design, participants who take both the original and the target version of the test are bilingual (Hambleton & Bollwark, 1991). In the source and target language monolinguals design, monolinguals in the original language take the original or back-translated version, and monolinguals in the target language take the target version (Ellis, 1991). In the third design, monolinguals in the original language take the original and back-translated versions.

After administration and scoring, statistical procedures are selected and performed to assess DIF. Procedures can include factor analysis, item response theory, logistic regression, and the Mantel-Haenszel technique. If DIF is statistically significant, additional analyses are necessary to investigate possible bias or lack of equivalence for different cultures or languages.

A study by Arnold, Montgomery, Castaneda, and Longoria (1994) illustrated the need to evaluate item equivalence. The researchers found that acculturation affected several subtests of the Halstead-Reitan neuropsychological test when used with unimpaired Hispanics. By contrast, Boivin et al. (1996) conducted a study with Lao children and identified variables such as nutritional development, parental education, and home environment that may influence scores on several tests, including the K-ABC, the Tactual Performance Test (TPT), and the computerized Tests of Variables of Attention (TOVA). These results suggested that tests can potentially be adapted to different cultures, although the challenges of doing so are formidable. Such results also showed that psychologists have addressed cultural equivalence issues for some time, contrary to the view of Helms (1992).

Hambleton and Zenisky (2011) offer a Review Form to evaluate the test translation and adaptation efforts. The form is comprised of 25 questions centering around five topics: General Translation Questions, Item Format and Appearance, Grammar and Phrasing, Passages and Other Item-Relevant Stimulus Materials (if relevant), and Cultural Relevance or Specificity. The Review Form reflects the complexity of the translation and adaptation process. For example, they cite research indicating that different font styles and typefaces can be a source of DIF.

## NATURE AND NURTURE

Part of the emotion surrounding the test bias controversy stems from its association in the human mind with the troubling notion of innate genetic inferiority. Given real differences, however, a genetic explanation is by no means inevitable. Absence of bias opens up the possibility of environmental causes as well, and explanations span the sociopolitical spectrum. Discrimination, economic disadvantage, exclusion from educational opportunity, personal development, social support, practical information, and achievement-oriented values—all become possible causes, if differences are real.

All sides of the nature–nurture debate depend on the existence of real differences. Therefore, the debate will prove irresolvable unless the test bias question is somehow answered. The reverse, however, is not true. Test bias research can continue indefinitely with the nature–nurture question unresolved. Psychometricians are attempting to disentangle the nature–nurture debate from the empirical investigation of test bias, but the separation is unlikely to be a neat one (Reynolds, Lowe et al., 1999).

## CONCLUSIONS AND RECOMMENDATIONS

The conclusion reached in most of the research reviewed above was that test bias did not exist. Today, the same research would lead to different conclusions. Test bias exists but is small, which raises questions about its importance. It most often overestimates or over predicts minority examinees' performance, so that its social consequences may be very different from those typically ascribed to it, and appropriate responses to it may differ from those typically made. Finally, just as purely genetic and environmental paradigms have given way, the interpretation of zero bias should cede to a better informed understanding that bias cannot be understood in isolation from other possible influences.

We recommend that rigorous examination of possible test bias and inaccuracy should continue, employing the latest and most diverse techniques. Nonetheless, we caution against labeling tests biased in the absence of, or in opposition to, reliable evidence. To do so is of questionable effectiveness in the struggle to identify and combat real discrimination and to ensure that everyone is treated fairly.

Discrimination is a legitimate and compelling concern. We do not argue that it is rare, unimportant, or remotely acceptable. We do, however, suggest from research findings that standardized test bias is not a major source of discrimination. Accordingly, resources meant to identify and alleviate discrimination might better be directed toward real-world causes rather than standardized tests. In addition, we question whether the goal of equal opportunity is served if possible evidence of discrimination, or of inequalities resulting from it, is erased by well-meaning test publishers or other professionals.

The issue of bias in mental testing, too, is an important concern with strong historical precedence in the social sciences and with formidable social consequences. The controversy is liable to persist as long as we entangle it with the nature–nurture question and stress mean differences in standardized test scores. Similarly, the use of aptitude and achievement measures is long-standing and widespread, extending back more than 2,000 years in some cultures and across most cultures today. It is unlikely to disappear soon.

The news media may be partly responsible for a popular perception that tests and testing are uniformly biased or unfair. As indicated by the findings reviewed here, the view that tests are substantially biased has little support at present, at least in cultures with a common language and a degree of common experience. In addition, public pressure has pushed the scientific community to refine its definitions of bias, scrutinize the practices used to minimize bias in tests, and develop increasingly sophisticated statistical techniques to detect bias (Reynolds, Lowe et al., 1999; Samuda, 1975). Finally, the findings reviewed here give indications that fair testing is an attainable goal, albeit a challenging one that demands skill and training.

Reynolds, Lowe et al. (1999) suggested four guidelines to help ensure equitable assessment:

1. Investigate possible referral source bias, because evidence suggests that people are not always referred for services on impartial, objective grounds.
2. Inspect test developers' data for evidence that sound statistical analyses for bias have been completed.
3. Conduct assessments with the most reliable measure available.
4. Assess multiple abilities and use multiple methods.

In summary, clinicians should use accurately derived data from multiple sources before making decisions about an individual.

Clinicians should be cognizant of a person's environmental background and circumstances. Information about a client's home, community, and the like must be evaluated in an individualized decision-making process. Likewise, clinicians should not ignore evidence that disadvantaged, ethnic minority clients with unfavorable test results are as likely to encounter difficulties as are middle-class, majority clients with unfavorable test results, given the same environmental circumstances. The purpose of the assessment process is to beat the prediction—to suggest hypotheses for interventions that will prevent a predicted failure or adverse outcome (Reynolds, Lowe et al., 1999). This perspective, although developed primarily around ability testing, is relevant to personality testing as well.

We urge clinicians to use tests fairly and in the interest of examinees, but we see little benefit in discarding standardized tests entirely. We recommend that test consumers evaluate each measure separately to ensure that results pertaining to bias are available and satisfactory. If results are unsatisfactory, local norming may produce less biased scores. If results are unavailable, additional testing may be possible, given samples of sufficient size. In addition, clinical practice and especially research should reflect an understanding of the conceptual distinctions, such as bias versus unfairness, described in this chapter.

A philosophical perspective emerging in the bias literature is that, before publication, test developers should not only demonstrate content, construct, and predictive validity but should also conduct content analysis in some form to ensure that offensive material is absent from the test. Expert reviews of test content can have a role, and the synergistic relationship between test use and psychometrics must be accommodated in an orderly manner before tests gain increased acceptance in society.

Nevertheless, informal reviews cannot meet the need to assess for bias. Test authors and publishers must demonstrate factorial congruence with all groups for whom a test is designed, to permit accurate interpretation. Comparisons of predictive validity with ethnic and gender groups are also important. Such research should take place during test development, a window during which measures can be altered using numerous item analysis procedures to minimize gender or ethnic bias. This practice has been uncommon, except with some recent achievement tests.

Greater attention to bias issues and personality tests are needed, though studies have emerged in recent years (e.g., Reynolds & Kamphaus, 1992; Suzuki & Ponterotto, 2008). Increased research is needed also for neuropsychological tests, for ability and achievement tests not yet investigated, for SES, and for minority examinees tested by majority examiners. Future results, it is expected, will continue to indicate consistency for different genders, races, ethnicities, and similar groups.

Finally, a clear consensus on fairness, and on steps to be taken to attain it, is needed between persons with humanitarian aims and those with scientific interest in test bias. Accommodation toward this end would ensure that everyone concerned with a given test was satisfied that it was unbiased and that the steps taken to achieve fairness could be held up to public scrutiny without reservation (Reynolds, Lowe et al., 1999). Test bias and fairness is a domain in great need of consensus, and this goal is attainable only with concessions on all sides.

## REFERENCES

Adebimpe, V. R., Gigandet, J., & Harris, E. (1979). MMPI diagnosis of black psychiatric patients. *American Journal of Psychiatry*, *136*, 85–87.

Alley, G., & Foster, C. (1978). Nondiscriminatory testing of minority and exceptional children. *Focus on Exceptional Children*, *9*, 1–14.

American Psychological Association. (2002). *Guidelines on Multicultural Education, Training, Research, Practice, and Organizational Change for Psychologists*. Retrieved from www.apa.org/pi/oema/resources/policy/multicultural-guidelines.aspx

Anastasi, A. (1988). *Psychological testing* (6th ed.). New York, NY: Macmillan.

Arnold, B., Montgomery, G., Castaneda, I., & Longoria, R. (1994). Acculturation and performance of Hispanics on selected Halstead-Reitan neuropsychological tests. *Assessment*, *1*, 239–248.

Binet, A., & Simon, T. (1973). *The development of intelligence in children*. New York, NY: Arno. (Original work published 1916)

Boivin, M., Chounramany, C., Giordani, B., Xaisida, S., Choulamountry, L., Pholsena, P., et al. (1996). Validating a cognitive ability testing protocol with Lao children for community development applications. *Neuropsychology*, *10*, 1–12.

Bossard, M., Reynolds, C. R., & Gutkin, T. B. (1980). A regression analysis of test bias on the Stanford-Binet Intelligence Scale. *Journal of Clinical Child Psychology*, *9*, 52–54.

Bouchard, T. J., & Segal, N. L. (1985). *Environment and IQ*. In B. Wolman (Ed.), *Handbook of intelligence* (pp. 391–464). New York, NY: Wiley-Interscience.

Bracken, B. A., & McCallum, R. S. (1998). *Universal Nonverbal Intelligence Test*. Itasca, IL: Riverside.

Brooks, A. P. (1997). TAAS unfair to minorities, lawsuit claims. *Austin American-Statesman*, p. A1.

Brown, R. T., Reynolds, C. R., & Whitaker, J. S. (1999). Bias in mental testing since "Bias in Mental Testing." *School Psychology Quarterly*, *14*, 208–238.

Butcher, J. N. (1982). Cross-cultural research methods in clinical psychology. In P. C. Kendall & J. N. Butcher (Eds.), *Black children: Social educational and parental environments* (pp. 33–51). Beverly Hills, CA: Sage.

Butcher, J. N. (2009). Clinical personality assessment: History, evolution, contemporary models, and practical applications. In J. N. Butcher (Ed.), *Oxford handbook of personality assessment* (pp. 5–21). New York, NY: Oxford University Press.

Camilli, G., & Shepard, L. A. (1994). *Methods for identifying biased test items*. Thousand Oaks, CA: Sage.

Cattell, R. B. (1979). Are culture fair intelligence tests possible and necessary? *Journal of Research and Development in Education*, *12*, 3–13.

Cheung, F. M., Leong, F. T. L., & Ben-Porath, Y. S. (2003). Psychological assessment in Asia: Introduction to the special section. *Psychological Assessment*, *15*, 243–247.

Chipman, S., Marshall, S., & Scott, P. (1991). Content effect on word-problem performance: A possible source of test bias? *American Educational Research Journal*, *28*, 897–915.

Cleary, T. A. (1968). Test bias: Prediction of grades of Negro and white students in integrated universities. *Journal of Educational Measurement*, *5*, 118–124.

Cleary, T. A., Humphreys, L. G., Kendrick, S. A., & Wesman, A. (1975). Educational uses of tests with disadvantaged students. *American Psychologist, 30*, 15–41.

Cortez v. Rosen (N.D. Cal., Docket No. C-73-388-SW, March 11, 1975).

Cronbach, L. J., & Drenth, P. J. D. (Eds.). (1972). *Mental tests and cultural adaptation*. The Hague, the Netherlands: Mouton.

Dana, R. H. (2005). *Multicultural assessment: Principles, application, and examples*. Mahwah, NJ: Erlbaum.

Dean, R. S. (1979, September). *WISC-R factor structure for Anglo and Hispanic children*. Paper presented at the annual meeting of the American Psychological Association, New York.

DeFries, J. C., Vandenberg, S. G., McClearn, G. E., Kuse, A. R., Wilson, J. R., Ashton, G. C., et al. (1974). Near identity of cognitive structure in two ethnic groups. *Science, 183*, 338–339.

Dent, H. E. (1996). Non-biased assessment or realistic assessment? In R. L. Jones (Ed.), *Handbook of tests and measurement for Black populations* (Vol. 1, pp. 103–122). Hampton, VA: Cobb & Henry.

Ebel, R. L. (1979). Intelligence: A skeptical view. *Journal of Research and Development in Education, 12*, 14–21.

Educational Testing Service. (2002). *Standards for quality and fairness and international principles for fairness review of assessments*. Retrieved from www.ets.org/Media/About_ETS/pdf/frintl.pdf

Eells, K., Davis, A., Havighurst, R. J., Herrick, V. E., & Tyler, R. W. (1951). *Intelligence and cultural differences: A study of cultural learning and problem-solving*. Chicago, IL: University of Chicago Press.

Edwards, O. W., & Oakland, T. D. (2006). Factorial invariance of Woodcock-Johnson III scores for African Americans and Caucasian Americans. *Journal of Psychoeducational Assessment, 24*(4), 358–366.

Elliot, R. (1987). *Litigating intelligence*. Dover, MA: Auburn House.

Ellis, B. B. (1991). Item response theory: A tool for assessing the equivalence of translated tests. *Bulletin of the International Test Commission, 18*, 33–51.

Figueroa, R. A. (1991). Bilingualism and psychometrics. *Diagnostique, 17*(1), 70–85.

Fine, B. (1975). *The stranglehold of the IQ*. Garden City, NY: Doubleday.

Flanagan, D. P., Ortiz, S. O., & Alfonso, V. C. (2007). *Essentials of cross-battery assessment* (2nd ed.). San Francisco, CA: Wiley.

Flynn, J. R. (1991). *Asian-Americans: Achievement beyond IQ*. Hillsdale, NJ: Erlbaum.

Freedle, R. O. (2003). Correcting the SATs ethnic and social class bias: A method for reestimating SAT scores. *Harvard Educational Review, 73*(1), 1–43.

Freedle, R. O. (2010). On replicating ethnic test bias effects: The Santelices and Wilson study. *Harvard Educational Review, 80*(3), 394–403.

Freedle, R. O., & Kostin, I. (1997). Predicting Black and White differential item functioining in verbal analogy performance. *Intelligence, 24*(3), 417–444.

Geisinger, K. F. (2005). The testing industry, ethnic minorities, and individuals with disabilities. In R. P. Phelps (Ed.) *Defending standardized testing* (pp. 187–204). Mahwah, NJ: Erlbaum.

Gerkin, K. C. (1978). Performance of Mexican-American children on intelligence tests. *Exceptional Children, 44*, 438–443.

Gopaul-McNicol, S. & Armour-Thomas, E. (2002). *Assessment and culture: Psychological tests with minority populations*. New York, NY: Academic Press.

Gould, S. J. (1981). *The mismeasure of man*. New York, NY: Norton.

Gould, S. J. (1995). Curveball. In S. Fraser (Ed.), *The bell curve wars: Race, intelligence, and the future of America* (pp. 11–22). New York, NY: Basic Books.

Gould, S. J. (1996). *The mismeasure of man* (rev. ed.). New York, NY: Norton.

Graves, S., & Mitchell, A. (2011). Is the moratorium over? African American psychology professionals' views on intelligence testing in response to changes in federal policy. *Journal of Black Psychology, 37*(4), 407–425.

Gross, M. (1967). *Learning readiness in two Jewish groups*. New York, NY: Center for Urban Education.

Groth-Marnat, G. (2009). *Handbook of psychological assessment* (5th ed.). Hoboken, NJ: Wiley.

Guterman, S. S. (1979). IQ tests in research on social stratification: The cross-class validity of the tests as measures of scholastic aptitude. *Sociology of Education, 52*, 163–173.

Gutkin, T. B., & Reynolds, C. R. (1980). Factorial similarity of the WISC-R for Anglos and Chicanos referred for psychological services. *Journal of School Psychology, 18*, 34–39.

Gutkin, T. B., & Reynolds, C. R. (1981). Factorial similarity of the WISC-R for white and black children from the standardization sample. *Journal of Educational Psychology, 73*, 227–231.

Hagie, M. U., Gallipo, P. L., & Svien, L. (2003). Traditional culture versus traditional assessment for American Indian students: An investigation of potential test item bias. *Assessment for Effective Intervention, 29*(1), 15–25.

Hambleton, R. K. (1993). Translating achievement tests for use in cross-national studies. *European Journal of Psychological Assessment, 9*, 54–65.

Hambleton, R. K. (1994). Guidelines for adapting educational and psychological tests: A progress report. *European Journal of Psychological Assessment, 10*, 229–244.

Hambleton, R. K., & Bollwark, J. (1991). Adapting tests for use in different cultures: Technical issues and methods. *Bulletin of the International Test Commission, 18*, 3–32.

Hambleton, R. K., & Kanjee, A. (1995) Increasing the validity of cross-cultural assessments: Use of improved methods for adaptations. *European Journal of Psychological Assessment, 11*, 147–157.

Hambleton, R. K., & Zenisky, A. L. (2011). Translating and adapting tests for cross-cultural assessments. In D. Matsumoto & F. J. R. van de Vijver (Eds.), *Cross-cultural research methods in psychology* (pp. 46–74). New York, NY: Cambridge University Press.

Hammill, D. D. (1991). *Detroit Tests of Learning Aptitude* (3rd ed.). Austin, TX: Pro-Ed.

Hammill, D. D., Pearson, N. A., & Wiederholt, J. L. (1997). *Comprehensive test of nonverbal intelligence*. Austin, TX: Pro-Ed.

Harrington, G. M. (1968a). Genetic-environmental interaction in "intelligence": I. Biometric genetic analysis of maze performance of *Rattus norvegicus*. *Developmental Psychology, 1*, 211–218.

Harrington, G. M. (1968b). Genetic-environmental interaction in "intelligence": II. Models of behavior, components of variance, and research strategy. *Developmental Psychology, 1*, 245–253.

Harrington, G. M. (1975). Intelligence tests may favor the majority groups in a population. *Nature, 258*, 708–709.

Harrington, G. M. (1976, September). *Minority test bias as a psychometric artifact: The experimental evidence*. Paper presented at the annual meeting of the American Psychological Association, Washington, DC.

Hartlage, L. C., Lucas, T., & Godwin, A. (1976). Culturally biased and culturally fair tests correlated with school performance in culturally disadvantaged children. *Journal of Consulting and Clinical Psychology, 32*, 325–327.

Helms, J. E. (1992). Why is there no study of cultural equivalence in standardized cognitive ability testing? *American Psychologist, 47*, 1083–1101.

Helms, J. E. (2006). Fairness is not validity or cultural bias in racial/group assessment: A quantitative perspective. *American Psychologist, 61*, 845–859.

Herrnstein, R. J., & Murray, C. (1994). *The bell curve*. New York, NY: Free Press.

Hilliard, A. G. III. (1979). Standardization and cultural bias as impediments to the scientific study and validation of "intelligence." *Journal of Research and Development in Education, 12*, 47–58.

Hilliard, A. G. III. (1984). IQ testing as the emperor's new clothes: A critique of Jensen's Bias in Mental Testing. In C. R. Reynolds & R. T. Brown (Eds.), *Perspectives on bias in mental testing* (pp. 139–169). New York, NY: Plenum Press.

Hunter, J. E., Schmidt, F. L., & Hunter, R. (1979). Differential validity of employment tests by race: A comprehensive review and analysis. *Psychological Bulletin, 86*, 721–735.

Jackson, G. D. (1975). Another psychological view from the Association of Black Psychologists. *American Psychologist, 30*, 88–93.

James, B. J. (1995). *A test of Harrington's experimental model of ethnic bias in testing applied to a measure of emotional functioning in adolescents*. (Unpublished doctoral dissertation). Texas A&M University, College Station.

Jensen, A. R. (1969). How much can we boost IQ and scholastic achievement? *Harvard Educational Review, 39*, 1–123.

Jensen, A. R. (1974). How biased are culture loaded tests? *Genetic Psychology Monographs, 90*, 185–224.

Jensen, A. R. (1976). Test bias and construct validity. *Phi Delta Kappan, 58*, 340–346.

Jensen, A. R. (1977). An examination of culture bias in the Wonderlic Personnel Test. *Intelligence, 1*, 51–64.

Jensen, A. R. (1980). *Bias in mental testing*. New York, NY: Free Press.

Jensen, A. R. (1984). Test bias: Concepts and criticisms. In C. R. Reynolds & R. T. Brown (Eds.), *Perspectives on bias in mental testing* (pp. 507–586). New York, NY: Plenum Press.

Kaiser, S. (1986). *Ability patterns of black and white adults on the WAIS-R independent of general intelligence and as a function of socioeconomic status*. (Unpublished doctoral dissertation). Texas A&M University, College Station.

Kamphaus, R. W., & Reynolds, C. R. (1987). *Clinical and research applications of the K-ABC*. Circle Pines, MN: American Guidance Service.

Kaufman, A. S. (1973). Comparison of the performance of matched groups of black children and white children on the Wechsler Preschool and Primary Scale of Intelligence. *Journal of Consulting and Clinical Psychology, 41*, 186–191.

Kaufman, A. S. (1979). *Intelligent testing with the WISC-R*. New York, NY: Wiley-Interscience.

Kaufman, A. S. (1994). *Intelligent testing with the WISC-III*. New York, NY: Wiley.

Kaufman, A. S., & Kaufman, N. L. (1973). Black-white differences on the McCarthy Scales of Children's Abilities. *Journal of School Psychology, 11*, 196–206.

Keith, T. Z., & Reynolds, C. R. (1990). Measurement and design issues in child assessment research. In C. R. Reynolds & R. W. Kamphaus (Eds.), *Handbook of psychological and educational assessment of children*. New York, NY: Guilford Press.

Loehlin, J. C., Lindzey, G., & Spuhler, J. N. (1975). *Race differences in intelligence*. San Francisco, CA: Freeman.

Lonner, W. J. (1985). Issues in testing and assessment in crosscultural counseling. *Counseling Psychologist, 13*, 599–614.

Lynn, R. (1995). Cross-cultural differences in intelligence and personality. In D. Sakolfske & M. Zeidner (Eds.), *The international handbook of personality and intelligence* (pp. 107–134). New York, NY: Plenum Press.

MacCorquodale, K., & Meehl, P. E. (1948). On a distinction between hypothetical constructs and intervening variables. *Psychological Review, 55*, 95–107.

Mainstream science on intelligence. (1994, December 13). *Wall Street Journal*, p. A18.

Maller, S. J. (2003). Best practices in detecting bias in nonverbal tests. In R. S. McCallum (Ed.) *Handbook of nonverbal assessment* (pp. 23–48). New York, NY: Plenum Press.

Marjoribanks, K. (1972). Ethnic and environmental influences on mental abilities. *American Journal of Sociology, 78*, 323–337.

Mayfield, J. W., & Reynolds, C. R. (1998). Are ethnic differences in diagnosis of childhood psychopathology an artifact of psychometric methods? An experimental evaluation of Harrington's hypothesis using parent report symptomatology. *Journal of School Psychology, 36*, 313–334.

McGrew, K. S., & Flanagan, D. P. (1998). *The intelligence test desk reference (ITDR): Gf-Gc Cross Battery Assessment*. Boston, MA: Allyn & Bacon.

McGurk, F. V. J. (1951). *Comparison of the performance of Negro and white high school seniors on cultural and noncultural psychological test questions*. Washington, DC: Catholic University of American Press.

McShane, D. (1980). A review of scores of American Indian children on the Wechsler Intelligence Scale. *White Cloud Journal, 2*, 18–22.

Mercer, J. R. (1976, August). *Cultural diversity, mental retardation, and assessment: The case for nonlabeling*. Paper presented at the Fourth International Congress of the International Association for the Scientific Study of Mental Retardation, Washington, DC.

Mercer, J. R. (1979). *System of Multicultural Pluralistic Assessment (SOMPA): Conceptual and technical manual*. San Antonio, TX: Psychological Corporation.

Miele, F. (1979). Cultural bias in the WISC. *Intelligence, 3*, 149–164.

Monnot, M. J., Quirk, S. W., Hoerger, M. & Brewer, L. (2009). Racial bias in personality assessment: Using the MMPI-2 to predict psychiatric diagnoses of African American and Caucasian chemical dependency inpatients. *Psychological Assessment, 21*(2), 137–151.

Morales, E. S., & George, C. (1976, September). *Examiner effects in the testing of Mexican-American children*. Paper presented at the annual meeting of the American Psychological Association, Washington, DC.

Moran, M. P. (1990). The problem of cultural bias in personality assessment. In C. R. Reynolds & R. W. Kamphaus (Eds.), *Handbook of psychological and educational assessment of children. Vol. 2: Personality, behavior, and context* (pp. 524–545). New York, NY: Guilford Press.

Mpofu, E., & Ortiz, S. O. (2009). Equitable assessment practices in diverse contexts. In E. L. Grigorenko (Ed.), *Multicultural psychoeducational assessment* (pp. 41–76). New York, NY: Springer.

Nandakumar, R., Glutting, J. J., & Oakland, T. (1993). Mantel-Haenszel methodology for detecting item bias: An introduction and example using the Guide to the Assessment of Test Session Behavior. *Journal of Psychoeducational Assessment, 11*(2), 108–119.

Neisser, U., Boodoo, G., Bouchard, T. J. Jr., Boykin, A. W., Brody, N., Ceci, S. J., et al. (1996). Intelligence: Knowns and unknowns. *American Psychologist, 51*, 77–101.

Nisbett, R. E. (2009). *Intelligence and how to get it: Why schools and cultures count*. New York, NY: Norton.

Oakland, T., & Feigenbaum, D. (1979). Multiple sources of test bias on the WISC-R and the Bender-Gestalt Test. *Journal of Consulting and Clinical Psychology, 47*, 968–974.

Oakland, T., & Matuszek, P. (1977). Using tests in nondiscriminatory assessment. In T. Oakland (Ed.), *Psychological and educational assessment of minority children*. New York, NY: Brunner/Mazel.

Okazaki, S., & Sue, S. (2000). Implications for test revisions for assessment with Asian Americans. *Psychological Assessment, 12*(30), 272–280.

Ortiz, S. O., & Ochoa, S. H. (2005). Advances in cognitive assessment of culturally linguistically diverse individuals. In D. P. Flanagan & P. L. Harrison (Eds.), *Contemporary intellectual assessment: Theories, tests and issues* (2nd ed., pp. 234–250). New York, NY: Guilford Press.

Padilla, A. M. (1988). Early psychological assessment of Mexican-American children. *Journal of the History of the Behavioral Sciences*, *24*, 113–115.

Payne, B., & Payne, D. (1991). The ability of teachers to identify academically at-risk elementary students. *Journal of Research in Childhood education*, *5*(2), 116–126.

Pintner, R. (1931). *Intelligence testing*. New York, NY: Holt, Rinehart, & Winston.

Poortinga, Y. H. (1983). Psychometric approaches to intergroup comparison: The problem of equivalence. In S. H. Irvine & J. W. Berry (Eds.), *Human assessment and cross-cultural factors* (pp. 237–258). New York, NY: Plenum Press.

Poortinga, Y. H., & Malpass, R. S. (1986). Making inferences from cross-cultural data. In W. J. Lonner & J. W. Berry (Eds.), *Field methods in cross-cultural psychology* (pp. 17–46). Beverly Hills, CA: Sage.

Prifitera, A., & Saklofske, D. H. (Eds.). (1998). *WISC-III clinical use and interpretation: Scientist-practitioner perspectives*. San Diego, CA: Academic Press.

Prifitera, A., Weiss, L. G., & Saklofske, D. H. (1998). The WISC-III in context. In A. Prifitera & D. H. Saklofske (Eds.), *WISC-III clinical use and interpretation: Scientist-practitioner perspectives* (pp. 1–37). San Diego, CA: Academic Press.

Ramsay, M. C. (1997, November). *Structural equation modeling and test bias*. Paper presented at the annual meeting of the Educational Research Exchange, Texas A&M University, College Station.

Ramsay, M. C. (1998a, February). *Proposed theories of causation drawn from social and physical science epistemology*. Paper presented at the annual meeting of the Education Research Exchange, Texas A&M University, College Station.

Ramsay, M. C. (1998b, February). *The processing system in humans: A theory*. Paper presented at the annual meeting of the Education Research Exchange, Texas A&M University, College Station.

Ramsay, M. C. (2000). *The putative effects of smoking by pregnant women on birthweight, IQ, and developmental disabilities in their infants: A methodological review and multivariate analysis*. (Unpublished doctoral dissertation). Texas A&M University, College Station.

Ramsay, M. C., & Reynolds, C. R. (1995). Separate digits tests: A brief history, a literature review, and a reexamination of the factor structure of the Test of Memory and Learning (TOMAL). *Neuropsychology Review*, *5*, 151–171.

Ramsay, M. C., & Reynolds, C. R. (2000a). Development of a scientific test: A practical guide. In G. Goldstein & M. Hersen (Eds.), *Handbook of psychological assessment* (3rd ed.). Amsterdam, the Netherlands: Pergamon Press.

Ramsay, M. C., & Reynolds, C. R. (2000b). Does smoking by pregnant women influence birth weight, IQ, and developmental disabilities in their infants? A methodological review and multivariate analysis. *Neuropsychology Review*, *10*, 1–49.

Ramsden, S., Richardson, F. M., Josse, G., Thomas, M. S., Ellis, C., Shakeshaft, C., et al. (2011). Verbal and nonverbal changes to the teenage brain. *Nature*, *479*, 113–116.

Reschly, D. J. (1978). WISC-R factor structures among Anglos, Blacks, Chicanos, and Native American Papagos. *Journal of Consulting and Clinical Psychology*, *46*, 417–422.

Reschly, D. J. (1997). Diagnostic and treatment utility of intelligence tests. In D. P. Flanagan, J. L. Genshaft, & P. L. Harrison (Eds.), *Contemporary intellectual assessment: Theories, tests, and issues* (pp. 437–456). New York, NY: Guilford Press.

Reschly, D. J. (2000). PASE v. Hannon. In C. R. Reynolds & E. Fletcher-Janzen (Eds.), *Encyclopedia of special education* (2nd ed., pp. 1325–1326). New York, NY: Wiley.

Reschly, D. J., & Sabers, D. (1979). Analysis of test bias in four groups with the regression definition. *Journal of Educational Measurement*, *16*, 1–9.

Reynolds, C. R. (1978). *Differential validity of several preschool assessment instruments for blacks, whites, males, and females*. (Unpublished doctoral dissertation). University of Georgia, Athens.

Reynolds, C. R. (1980). Differential construct validity of intelligence as popularly measured: Correlation of age and raw scores on the WISC-R for blacks, whites, males and females. *Intelligence: A Multidisciplinary Journal*, *4*, 371–379.

Reynolds, C. R. (1982a). Construct and predictive bias. In R. A. Berk (Ed.), *Handbook of methods for detecting test bias* (pp. 199–227). Baltimore, MD: Johns Hopkins University Press.

Reynolds, C. R. (1982b). The problem of bias in psychological assessment. In C. R. Reynolds & T. B. Gutkin (Eds.), *The handbook of school psychology* (pp. 178–208). New York, NY: Wiley.

Reynolds, C. R. (1995). Test bias in the assessment of intelligence and personality. In D. Saklofsky & M. Zeidner (Eds.), *International handbook of personality and intelligence* (pp. 545–576). New York, NY: Plenum Press.

Reynolds, C. R. (1998a). Cultural bias in testing of intelligence and personality. In A. Bellack & M. Hersen (Series Eds.) & C. Belar (Vol. Ed.), *Comprehensive clinical psychology: Vol. 10. Cross cultural psychology* (pp. 53–92). New York, NY: Elsevier Science.

Reynolds, C. R. (1998b). Need we measure anxiety separately for males and females? *Journal of Personality Assessment*, *70*, 212–221.

Reynolds, C. R. (1999). Cultural bias in testing of intelligence and personality. In M. Hersen & A. Bellack (Series Eds.) & C. Belar (Vol. Ed.), *Comprehensive clinical psychology: Vol. 10. Sociocultural and individual differences* (pp. 53–92). Oxford, UK: Elsevier Science.

Reynolds, C. R. (2000a). Methods for detecting and evaluating cultural bias in neuropsychological tests. In E. Fletcher-Janzen, T. L. Strickland, & C. R. Reynolds (Eds.), *Handbook of cross-cultural neuropsychology* (pp. 249–285). New York, NY: Kluwer Academic/Plenum Press.

Reynolds, C. R. (2000b). Why is psychometric research on bias in mental testing so often ignored? *Psychology, Public Policy, and Law*, *6*, 144–150.

Reynolds, C. R. (2001). *Professional manual for the Clinical Assessment Scales for the Elderly*. Odessa, FL: Psychological Assessment Resources.

Reynolds, C. R., & Bigler, E. D. (1994). *Test of Memory and Learning (TOMAL)*. Austin, TX: Pro-Ed.

Reynolds, C. R., & Brown, R. T. (1984a). Bias in mental testing: An introduction to the issues. In C. R. Reynolds & R. T. Brown (Eds.), *Perspectives on bias in mental testing* (pp. 1–39). New York, NY: Plenum Press.

Reynolds, C. R., & Brown, R. T. (1984b). *Perspectives on bias in mental testing*. New York, NY: Plenum Press.

Reynolds, C. R., & Carson, A. D. (2005). Methods for assessing cultural bias in tests. In C. L. Frisby & C. R. Reynolds (Eds.), *Comprehensive handbook of multicultural school psychology* (pp. 795–839). Hoboken, NJ: Wiley.

Reynolds, C. R., Chastain, R., Kaufman, A. S., & McLean, J. (1987). Demographic influences on adult intelligence at ages 16 to 74 years. *Journal of School Psychology*, *25*, 323–342.

Reynolds, C. R., & Gutkin, T. B. (1980, September). *WISC-R performance of blacks and whites matched on four demographic variables*. Paper presented at the annual meeting of the American Psychological Association, Montreal, Canada.

Reynolds, C. R., & Gutkin, T. B. (1981). A multivariate comparison of the intellectual performance of blacks and whites matched on four demographic variables. *Personality and Individual Differences*, *2*, 175–180.

Reynolds, C. R., & Harding, R. E. (1983). Outcome in two large sample studies of factorial similarity under six methods of comparison. *Educational and Psychological Measurement*, *43*, 723–728.

Reynolds, C. R., & Hartlage, L. C. (1979). Comparison of WISC and WISC-R regression lines for academic prediction with black and white referred children. *Journal of Consulting and Clinical Psychology*, *47*, 589–591.

Reynolds, C. R., & Jensen, A. R. (1983, September). *Patterns of intellectual performance among blacks and whites matched on "g."* Paper presented at the annual meeting of the American Psychological Association, Montreal, Canada.

Reynolds, C. R., & Kaiser, S. (1992). Test bias in psychological assessment. In T. B. Gutkin & C. R. Reynolds (Eds.), *The handbook of school psychology* (2nd ed., pp. 487–525). New York, NY: Wiley.

Reynolds, C. R., & Kamphaus, R. W. (1992). *Behavior Assessment System for Children (BASC): Manual*. Circle Pines, MN: American Guidance Service.

Reynolds, C. R., Lowe, P. A., & Saenz, A. (1999). The problem of bias in psychological assessment. In T. B. Gutkin & C. R. Reynolds (Eds.), *The handbook of school psychology* (3rd ed., 549–595). New York, NY: Wiley.

Reynolds, C. R., & Paget, K. (1981). Factor analysis of the Revised Children's Manifest Anxiety Scale for blacks, whites, males, and females with a national normative sample. *Journal of Consulting and Clinical Psychology*, *49*, 349–352.

Reynolds, C. R., Willson, V. L., & Chatman, S. P. (1984). Item bias on the 1981 revisions of the Peabody Picture Vocabulary Test using a new method of detecting bias. *Journal of Psychoeducational Assessment*, *2*, 219–221.

Reynolds, C. R., Willson, V. L., & Chatman, S. P. (1985). Regression analyses of bias on the Kaufman Assessment Battery for Children. *Journal of School Psychology*, *23*, 195–204.

Reynolds, C. R., Willson, V. L., & Ramsay, M. C. (1999). Intellectual differences among Mexican Americans, Papagos and Whites, independent of g. *Personality and Individual Differences*, *27*, 1181–1187.

Richardson, T. Q. (1995). The window dressing behind the bell curve. *School Psychology Review*, *24*, 42–44.

Roid, G. H., & Miller, L. J. (1997). *Leiter International Performance Scale-Revised: Examiner's manual*. Wood Dale, IL: Stoelting.

Rushton, J. P., & Jensen, A. R. (2005). Thirty years of research on race differences in cognitive ability. *Psychology, Public Policy, and Law*, *11*(2), 235–294.

Samuda, A. J. (1975). *Psychological testing of American minorities: Issues and consequences*. New York, NY: Dodd.

Santelices, M. V., & Wilson, M. (2010). Unfair treatment? The case of Freedle, the SAT, and the standardization approach to differential item functioning. *Harvard Educational Review*, *80*(1), 106–128.

Sandoval, J. (1979). The WISC-R and internal evidence of test bias with minority groups. *Journal of Consulting and Clinical Psychology*, *47*, 919–927.

Sandoval, J., & Mille, M. P. W. (1979). *Accuracy judgments of WISC-R item difficulty for minority groups*. Paper presented at the annual meeting of the American Psychological Association.

Sattler, J. M. (1974). *Assessment of children's intelligence*. Philadelphia, PA: Saunders.

Sattler, J. M. (1988). *Assessment of children* (3rd ed.). San Diego, CA: Author.

Sattler, J. M. (2008). *Assessment of children: Cognitive foundations* (5th ed.). San Diego, CA: Author.

Sattler, J. M., & Gwynne, J. (1982). White examiners generally do not impede the intelligence test performance of black children: To debunk a myth. *Journal of Consulting and Clinical Psychology*, *50*, 196–208.

Scarr, S. (1981). Implicit messages: A review of bias in mental testing. *American Journal of Education*, *89*(3), 330–338.

Scheuneman, J. D. (1987). An experimental, exploratory study of the causes of bias in test items. *Journal of Educational Measurement*, *29*, 97–118.

Schmidt, W. H. (1983). Content biases in achievement tests. *Journal of Educational Measurement*, *20*, 165–178.

Schoenfeld, W. N. (1974). Notes on a bit of psychological nonsense: "Race differences in intelligence." *Psychological Record*, *24*, 17–32.

Scholwinski, E. (1985). *Ability patterns of blacks and whites as determined by the subscales on the Wechsler Adult Intelligence Scale–Revised*. (Unpublished doctoral dissertation). Texas A&M University, College Station.

Shuey, A. M. (1966). *The testing of Negro intelligence* (2nd ed.). New York, NY: Social Science Press.

Spitz, H. (1986). *The raising of intelligence*. Hillsdale, NJ: Erlbaum.

Steele, C. M., & Aronson, J. (1995). Stereotype threat and the intellectual test performance of African Americans. *Journal of Personality and Social Psychology*, *69*, 797–811.

Steele, C. M., & Aronson, J. (2004). Stereotype threat does not live by Steele and Aronson alone. *American Psychologist*, *59*(1), 47–48.

Stern, W. (1914). *The psychological methods of testing intelligence*. Baltimore, MD: Warwick & York.

Sternberg, R. J. (1980). Intelligence and test bias: Art and science. *Behavioral and Brain Sciences*, *3*, 353–354.

Suzuki, L. A., & Aronson, J. (2005). The cultural malleability of intelligence and its impact on the racial/ethnic hierarchy. *Psychology, Public Policy, and Law*, *11*(2), 320–327.

Suzuki, L. A., Kugler, J. F., & Aguiar, L. J. (2005). Assessment practices in racial-cultural psychology. In R. T. Carter (Ed.) *Handbook of racial-cultural psychology and counseling: Training and practice* (Vol. 2, pp. 297–315). Hoboken, NJ: Wiley.

Suzuki, L. A., Onoue, M. A., & Hill, J. (forthcoming). Clinical assessment: A multicultural perspective. In K. Geisinger (Ed.), *APA handbook of testing and assessment in psychology*. Washington, DC: APA Books.

Suzuki, L. A., & Ponterotto, J. G. (Eds.) (2008). *Handbook of multicultural assessment: Clinical, psychological and educational applications* (3rd ed.). San Francisco, CA: Sage.

Thorndike, R. L. (1971). Concepts of culture-fairness. *Journal of Educational Measurement*, *8*, 63–70.

Torrance, E. P. (1980). Psychology of gifted children and youth. In W. M. Cruickshank (Ed.), *Psychology of exceptional children and youth*. Englewood Cliffs, NJ: Prentice-Hall.

Tyler, L. E. (1965). *The psychology of human differences*. New York, NY: Appleton-Century-Crofts.

Valencia, R. A., & Suzuki, L. A. (2001). *Intelligence testing with minority students: Foundations, performance factors and assessment issues*. Thousand Oaks, CA: Sage.

Valencia, R. A., Suzuki, L. A., & Salinas, M. (2001). Test bias. In R. R. Valencia & L. A. Suzuki, *Intelligence testing with minority students: Foundations, performance factors and assessment issues* (pp. 111–181). Thousand Oaks, CA: Sage.

van de Vijver, F., & Tanzer, N. K. (2004). Bias and equivalence in cross-cultural assessment: An overview. *European Review of Applied Psychology*, *54*(2), 119–135.

van de Vijver, F. J. R., & Hambleton, R. K. (1996). Translating tests: Some practical guidelines. *European Psychologists*, *1*, 89–99.

van de Vijver, F. J. R., & Poortinga, Y. H. (1991). Culture-free measurement in the history of cross-cultural psychology. *Bulletin of the International Test Commission*, *18*, 72–87.

van de Vijver, F. J. R., & Leung, K. (2011). Equivalence and bias: A review of concepts, models, and data analytic procedures. In D. Matsumoto and F. J. R. van de Vijver (Eds.) *Cross-cultural research methods in psychology* (pp. 17–45). New York, NY: Cambridge University Press.

Verney, S. P., Granholm, E., Marshall, S. P., Malcarne, V. L., & Saccuzzo, D. P. (2005). Culture-fair cognitive ability assessment: Information processing and psychophysiological approaches. *Assessment*, *12*, 303–319.

Wechsler, D. (1975). Intelligence defined and undefined: A relativistic appraisal. *American Psychologist*, *30*, 135–139.

Weiss, L. G., & Prifitera, A. (1995). An evaluation of differential prediction of WIAT achievement scores from WISC-III FSIQ across ethnic and gender groups. *Journal of School Psychology*, *33*, 297–304.

Weiss, L. G., Prifitera, A., & Roid, G. H. (1993). The WISC-III and fairness of predicting achievement across ethnic and gender groups. *Journal of Psychoeducational Assessment*, 35–42.

Wicherts, J. M., Dolan, C. V., & Hessen, D. J. (2005). Stereotype threat and group differences in test performance: A question of measurement invariance. *Journal of Personality and Social Psychology*, *89*(5), 696–719.

Wigdor, A. K., & Garner, W. R. (Eds.). (1982). *Ability testing: Uses, consequences, and controversies*. Washington, DC: National Academy of Sciences.

Willerman, L. (1979). *The psychology of individual and group differences*. San Francisco, CA: Freeman.

Williams, R. L. (1970). Danger: Testing and dehumanizing Black children. *Clinical Child Psychology Newsletter*, *9*, 5–6.

Williams, R. L. (1974). From dehumanization to black intellectual genocide: A rejoinder. In G. J. Williams & S. Gordon (Eds.), *Clinical child psychology: Current practices and future perspectives*. New York, NY: Behavioral Publications.

Williams, R. L., Dotson, W., Dow, P., & Williams, W. S. (1980). The war against testing: A current status report. *Journal of Negro Education*, *49*, 263–273.

Willson, V. L., Nolan, R. F., Reynolds, C. R., & Kamphaus, R. W. (1989). Race and gender effects on item functioning on the Kaufman Assessment Battery for Children. *Journal of School Psychology*, *27*, 289–296.

Wright, B. J., & Isenstein, V. R. (1977–1978). *Psychological tests and minorities* (DHEW Publication No. ADM 78–482). Rockville, MD: National Institutes of Mental Health.

Zieky, M. (2006). Fairness review in assessment. In S. M. Downing & T. M. Haladyna (Eds.), *Handbook of Test Development* (pp. 359–376). Mahwah, NJ: Erlbaum.

# CHAPTER 5

# Testing and Assessment
# in Cross-Cultural Psychology

KURT F. GEISINGER AND CARINA McCORMICK

Some say that the world is shrinking. We know that world-wide cable news programs and networks, the Internet, and satellites are making communications across cultures and around the world much easier, less expensive, and remarkably faster. *Cross-cultural psychology* studies the psychological differences associated with cultural differences. At one time, such research implied crossing the borders of countries, and to a large extent, it still does. However, as countries become more multicultural due to immigration (made much easier in Europe with the advent of the European Union), different cultures often exist within a country as well as in differing countries. Research in psychology, too, has been affected by these worldwide changes.

The world context has also shifted. The cultural makeup of the United States is certainly changing rapidly; recent U.S. Census Bureau analyses indicate the rapid increase in ethnic minorities, especially Hispanic Americans and Asian Americans, to the extent that the historical European American majority in American is likely to become a minority group within our lifetime. (See Geisinger, 2002, or Sandoval, 1998, for an elaboration of these data.) While the United States is experiencing population changes with a considerable increase in groups traditionally identified as ethnic minorities, so have other

parts of the world experienced these same population shifts. Many of these changes are occurring as "the direct consequence of cross-immigration and globalization of the economy" (Allen & Walsh, 2000, p. 63). Cultures change due to population changes caused by immigration and emigration, birth and death rates, and other factors, but they also change due to historical influences apart from population shifts. Countries that have suffered famine, aggression on the part of other nations, or other traumatic changes may experience significant cultural transformations as well as population changes. Historically, psychologists had studied human behavior within a single, broad culture, sometimes called *Euro-American culture* (Moreland, 1996; Padilla & Medina, 1996). Cross-cultural psychology has long been recognized as a relevant field, though; the *Journal of Cross-Cultural Psychology* has been published since 1970, but one might question the degree to which the concept of culture has been integrated into psychology. In more recent years, psychologists have begun to recognize the importance of culture to a greater extent; in 1995 the American Psychological Association began publishing the journal *Culture and Psychology*. Such an event may be seen as an indication of the increased recognition of the importance of culture in psychology. There is also an increasingly international presence within the field of cross-cultural psychology itself: "Cross-cultural psychology, while still dominated by Western views and psychologists, is

---

Reprinted from the International Test Commission Guidelines for Test Adaptation (International Test Commission, 2010).

no longer their exclusive preserve. What started as a Western-based attempt to understand the 'others' is now a field well-populated by these 'others'" (Berry, 1997, p. xiii).

According to Berry (1997), cross-cultural psychology seeks to systematically explore the relationships between cultural contexts and behavior of individuals in those cultures. He included ecological and societal factors within the realm of cultural variables. Likewise, he included as part of behavioral variables those that must be inferred from behavior, such as personality, attitudes, interests, and so on. The variables that are studied in cross-cultural psychology, as in all psychology, have traditionally been examined using standardized tests, interviews, and a variety of formal and informal assessments. In fact, Triandis, Malpass, and Davidson (1971) described cross-cultural psychology in this way: "Cross-cultural psychology includes studies of subjects from two or more cultures, using equivalent methods of measurement, to determine the limits within which general psychological theories do hold, and the kinds of modifications of these theories that are needed to make them universal" (p. 1, emphasis added; also cited in Berry, 1980, p. 4). The previous statement emphasizes the need for equivalent methods of measurement. If the findings of cross-cultural psychology are to have validity, then equivalent measurement is required. This point is the general theme of this chapter. It is argued that to note cross-cultural differences or similarities in terms of psychological variables and theories across cultures, one must have confidence that the measures used in research are equivalent measures, or at least are as similar as possible, in each culture.

When one is comparing two cultures with respect to any variable, there are a number of factors that can invalidate the comparison. For example, if one selects well-educated individuals from one culture and less well-educated persons from the second culture, whether both groups are representative of the education distribution in their respective countries or not, the comparison will be flawed in terms of internal validity, external validity, or both. However, one of the primary sources of invalidity, one that is often not understood as easily as the previous sampling example, relates to measurement instruments. When the two cultures to be compared do not employ the same language to communicate and have other cultural differences, the measures that are used in the comparison must of necessity be somewhat different. A number of the possible options are discussed and evaluated in this chapter. Cross-cultural psychologists and psychologists dealing with testing issues in applied use are provided

with some strategies for solving the measurement dilemmas that they face. Language is generally not the only disparity when making cross-cultural comparisons. Cultural differences in idioms, personal styles, experiences in test taking, and a plethora of other variables must also be considered in making cross-cultural or multicultural assessments. These factors are often more subtle than language differences.

Thus, there are theoretical reasons to examine testing within cross-cultural psychology. There are also applied reasons that testing is important in cross-cultural settings. Obviously, the applied uses of tests and assessments across cultures must rely on the theoretical findings from cross-cultural psychology. Tests and assessment devices have been found to have substantial validity in aiding in various kinds of decision making in some cultures. Thus, other cultures may wish to employ these measures, or adaptations of them, in what appear to be similar applied settings in cultures different from those where they were first developed and used.

Test development, test use, and other psychometric issues have long held an important role in cross-cultural psychology. The words *testing* and *assessment* are used interchangeably by some psychologists but differentially by others. When they are distinguished, testing involves the administration and scoring of a measurement instrument; assessment is a broader term that includes score and behavioral interpretation in the context of the culture or the individual being evaluated. Berry (1980) differentiated cross-cultural psychology from many other areas of psychology and aligned it closely to measurement and methodology by reflecting that "most areas of psychological enquiry are defined by their content; however, cross-cultural psychology is defined primarily by its method" (p. 1).

## Some Basic Distinctions in Cross-Cultural Measurement

Before beginning a formal discussion of testing in cross-cultural psychology, a few fundamental features must be differentiated. When one uses measures in two or more cultures, one engages in cross-cultural work. When one studies the various subcultures within a country, such as the United States, one performs multicultural analyses. The distinction is somewhat more complex, however, as described in the next section. Next, a fundamental distinction in cross-cultural psychology relates the concepts of etic and emic; these terms in some ways parallel the distinction between cross-cultural and multicultural analyses.

In brief, etic studies compare a variable across cultures whereas emic studies are performed within a single culture without comparison to another culture. Finally, a distinction between the use of tests in relatively pure research as opposed to the testing of individuals in real-life, often high-stakes, decisions is described.

### Concepts of Cross-Cultural and Multicultural

The differences between cross-cultural and multicultural are not entirely clear. Allen and Walsh (2000), for example, made the distinction that use of tests across cultural groups, such as in cross-national research, is a cross-cultural application of tests whereas the use of tests with individuals of differing ethnic minority (or perhaps cultural) status within a nation is a multicultural application of tests. They noted that there is often overlap between culture and minority group status. Clearly, the distinction blurs. Thus, the techniques used in cross-cultural psychology have great applicability to multicultural, psychological issues. The questions and concerns involved in adapting a test to make a comparison between U.S. and Mexican cultures, for example, are certainly applicable to the testing of Spanish-speaking Chicanos in the United States.

### Concepts of Etic and Emic

Linguists often use two important words in their work: phonetic and phonemic. According to Domino (2000), "Phonetic refers to the universal rules for all languages, while phonemic refers to the sounds of a particular language. From these terms, the word 'etic' and 'emic' were derived and used in the cross-cultural literature. Etic studies compare the same variable across cultures.... Emic studies focus on only one culture and do not attempt to compare cultures" (p. 296). These terms were originally coined by Pike (1967). Emics are behaviors that apply only in a single society or culture; etics are those that are seen as universal, or without the restrictions of culture. A complaint made about traditional psychology has been that it presumed that certain findings in the field are etics, even though they have not been investigated in nonwestern arenas (Berry, 1980; Moreland, 1996). Thus, some findings considered etics are pseudoetics (Triandis et al., 1971). The emic–etic distinction is one that has broad applicability to the adaptation of tests developed in America to other cultural spheres.

The emic–etic distinction also applies to the goals of and approaches to cross-cultural research: The first goal is to document valid principles that describe behavior in any one culture by using constructs that the people themselves conceive as meaningful and important; this is an emic analysis. The second goal of cross-cultural research is to make generalizations across cultures that take into account all human behavior. The goal, then, is theory building; that would be an etic analysis (Brislin, 1980, p. 391). In searching for emic findings, we are attempting to establish behavioral systems (or rules) that appear to hold across cultures. That is, we are endeavoring to verify that certain behavioral patterns exist universally. Etic studies look at the importance of a given behavior within a specific culture.

### Use of Tests and Assessments for Research and Applied Use

The goal of most cross-cultural psychologists and other researchers is the development of knowledge and the correlated development, expansion, and evaluation of theories of human behavior. Many applied psychologists, however, are more concerned with the use of assessments with specific individuals, whether in clinical practice, school settings, industrial applications, or other environments in which tests are effectively used. The difference in the use of tests in these settings is significant; differences in the type or nature of the tests that they need for their work, however, may well be trivial. If we assume that the psychological variable or construct to be measured is the same, differences required for such varied uses are likely to be minor. Both uses of tests, whether for research or application, require that the measure be assessed accurately and validly. Part of validity, it is argued, is that the measure is free from bias, including those biases that emerge from cultural and language differences. Some writers (e.g., Padilla, 2001; Padilla & Medina, 1996) have accentuated the need for valid and fair assessments, especially when the nature of the assessment is for high-stakes purposes such as admissions in higher education, placement into special education, employment, licensure, or psychodiagnosis.

## KEY ISSUES IN CROSS-CULTURAL AND MULTICULTURAL MEASUREMENT

Issues related to the use of measures in a culture different from the one for which they were originally intended have two primary and overlapping concerns: language and culture. Language may be considered as a part of culture or not. As an example, a question on an achievement test that assumes knowledge of culturally specific life aspects, such as sports, may not make sense going from the United States to Australia, even though they use the same language. Similarly, a question about Canadian geography may be truly foreign to many residents of the United States. Each of these constructs is discussed in the sections that follow.

## Role of Language

One of the primary ways that cultures differ is through language. In fact, in considering the level of acculturation of individuals, their language skills are often given dominant (and sometimes mistaken) importance. Even within countries and regions of the world where ostensibly the same language is spoken, accents can make oral communication difficult. Language skill is, ultimately, the ability to communicate. Generally, language skills may be considered along two dimensions: the oral and written dimension and the understanding and expression dimension.

Depending on the nature of the assessment to be performed, different kinds and qualities of language skills may be needed. Academically oriented, largely written language skills may require 6 to 8 years of instruction and use to develop, whereas the development of the spoken word for everyday situations is much faster (Cummins, 2000; Sandoval & Durán, 1998). These issues are of critical importance for the assessment of immigrants and their children (Cummins, 2000; Geisinger, 2002; Sandoval, 1998). Some cross-cultural comparisons are made using one language for both groups, even though the language may be the second language for one of the groups. In such cases, language skills may be a confounding variable. In the United States, the issue of language often obscures comparisons of Caucasians and Hispanics. Pennock-Roman (1992) demonstrated that English-language tests for admissions to higher education may not be valid for language minorities when their English-language skills are not strong.

Before making many assessments, we need to establish whether the individuals being tested have the requisite levels of language skills that will be used on the examination. Handel and Ben-Porath (2000) argued that such an assessment should be made prior to administration of the Minnesota Multiphasic Personality Inventory (MMPI-2) because studies have shown that it does not work as effectively with individuals whose language skills are not robust and that the validity of at least some of the scales is compromised if the respondent does not have adequate English reading ability. Butcher, Cabiya, Lucio, and Garrido (2007), however, have demonstrated that the MMPI works effectively in many cultures. Many school

systems and other agencies have developed tests of language skills, sometimes equating tests of English- and Spanish-language skills so that the scores are comparable (e.g., O'Brien, 1992; Yansen & Shulman, 1996).

Judd et al. (2009) pointed out that the optimal language of assessment may even vary for a single individual for different types of assessments. For example, for an individual who speaks Spanish at home but learned English in school, Spanish may be the preferred language for a test of emotions while English might be more appropriate for a test of academic skills. Bilingual assessment may also be a viable option for academic skills tests (other than those defined as reading English) in such circumstances (Judd et al., 2009). When decisions are being made about cognitive functioning, such as in learning disability diagnosis, it is especially crucial to avoid errors in judgment caused by improper test administration. In all cases, the reason for selecting the language of the test administered should be documented (Judd et al., 2009).

Culture and language are often very closely wedded. However, not all individuals who speak the same language come from the same culture or are able to take the same test validly. Also within the United States, the heterogeneous nature of individuals who might be classified as Hispanic Americans is underscored by the need for multiple Spanish-language translations and adaptations of tests (Handel & Ben-Porath, 2000). For example, the same Spanish-language measure may not be appropriate for Mexicans, individuals from the Caribbean, and individuals from the Iberian Peninsula. Individuals from different Latin American countries may also need different or at least modified instruments.

When a cross-cultural study involves two or more settings in which different languages are employed for communication, the quality and fidelity of the translation of tests, testing materials, questionnaires, interview questions, open-ended responses from test takers, and the like are critical to the validity of the study. It should be noted that the term *translation* is now rarely used within the context of testing; the term *test adaptation* is preferred because many of the changes needed include more than direct, literal translation. Differences in the wording of questions on a test, for example, can have a significant impact on both the validity of research results and the applicability of a measure in a practice setting. If items include idioms, the adaptation of those idioms is typically unlikely to convey the same meaning in the target language. The translation of tests from host language to target language has been a topic of major concern to cross-cultural psychologists and psychometricians involved in this work. A discussion of issues and approaches to the translation of testing materials appears later in this chapter.

## Role of Culture

One of the primary and most evident ways that cultures often differ is by spoken and written language. They also differ, of course, in many other ways. Individuals from two different cultures who take part in a cross-cultural investigation are likely to differ according to other variables that can influence testing and the study. Among these are speed of responding, the amount of education that they have received, the nature and content of that schooling, their levels of motivation, and how they interact with the examiner. All of these factors may influence the findings of cross-cultural studies.

Culture may be envisioned as an antecedent of behavior. Culture is defined as a set of contextual variables that have either a direct or an indirect effect on thought and behavior (Cuellar, 2000). Culture provides a context for all human behavior, thought, and other mediating variables, and it is so pervasive that it is difficult to imagine human behavior that might occur without reference to culture. As noted at the beginning of this chapter, one of the goals of cross-cultural psychology is to investigate and differentiate those behaviors, behavior patterns, personalities, attitudes, worldviews, and so on that are universal from those that are culture specific. (See van de Vijver & Poortinga, 1982.) "The current field of cultural psychology represents a recognition of the cultural specificity of all human behavior, whereby basic psychological processes may result in highly diverse performance, attitude, self-concepts, and world views in members of different cultural populations" (Anastasi & Urbina, 1997, p. 341). Personality has sometimes been defined as an all-inclusive characteristic describing one's patterns of responding to others and to the world. It is not surprising that so many anthropologists and cross-cultural psychologists have studied the influence of culture on personality—the effects of the pervasive environment on the superordinate organization that mediates behavior and one's interaction with the world.

For much of the history of western psychology, investigators and theorists believed that many basic psychological processes were universal, that is, that they transcended individual cultures (e.g., Moreland, 1996; Padilla & Medina, 1996). More psychologists now recognize that culture has the omnipresent impact. Malgady (1996) has extended this argument. He has stated that we should actually assume cultural *nonequivalence* rather than cultural equivalence. Of course, much of the work of cross-cultural psychologists and other researchers is determining whether our measures are equivalent and appropriate (not biased). Clearly, if we are unable to make parallel tests that are usable in more than one culture and whose scores are comparable in the varying cultures, we do not have an ability to compare cultures. Helms (1992), too, has questioned cultural relevance and appropriateness with a particular reference to intelligence testing, arguing that intelligence tests are oriented to middle-class, White Americans and are less appropriate to other subpopulations within our American culture.

What about working with individuals with similar-appearing psychological concerns in different cultures, especially where a useful measure has been identified in one culture? Can we use comparable, but not identical, psychological measures in different cultures? Indeed, we should probably use culture-specific measures, even though these measures cannot be used for cross-cultural comparisons (van de Vijver, 2000). If we use measures that have been translated or adapted from other cultures, we need to revalidate them in the new culture. In some circumstances, we may also need to use assessments of acculturation as well as tests of language proficiency before we use tests with clients requiring assessment. (See Geisinger, 2002, for a description of such an assessment paradigm.) Mpofu and Ortiz (2009) provided a matrix with which to evaluate multiple test scores from culturally and linguistically diverse individuals in order to determine the role that culture and language play in test scores. In general, if examinees demonstrate relatively higher scores on tests with low cultural and language demands than they do on tests with high cultural and language demands, there is evidence that these features are affecting their test scores. While evidence with a small but diverse sample by Kranzler, Flores, and Coady (2010) did not find strict support for the notion proposed by Flanagan, Ortiz, and Alfonso (2007) that subtests of cognitive batteries could be rank-ordered in terms of linguistic and cultural impact on difficulty, they nevertheless found considerable support that both linguistic and cultural differences matter and that using nonverbal tests probably makes the most sense for children with significant cultural and/or linguistic differences in the United States.

Intelligence tests are among the most commonly administered types of psychological tests. Kamin (1974) demonstrated in dramatic form how tests of intelligence administered in English were misused early in the 20th century in U.S. governmental decision making concerning the status of immigrants, despite lack of English-language proficiency of many of the examinees. In general, immigration policies were affected by analyses of the intelligence of immigrants from varying countries and regions of the world. Average IQs were computed from country and region of origin; these data were shared widely and generally were believed to be the results of innate ability, even though one of the strongest findings of the time was that the longer immigrants lived in the United States, the higher their levels of intelligence were (Kamin, 1974). The tests used for many of these analyses were the famous Army Alpha and Army Beta, which were early verbal and nonverbal tests of intelligence, respectively. It was obvious even then, at the time of World War I, that language could cause validity problems in the intelligence testing of those whose English was not proficient. Leaders in the intelligence-testing community have also attempted to develop tests that could be used cross-culturally without translation. These measures have often been called culture-free or culture-fair tests of intelligence.

## Culture-Free and Culture-Fair Assessments of Intelligence

Some psychologists attempted to develop so-called culture-free measures of intelligence. In the 1940s, for example, Cattell (1940) attempted to use very simple geometric forms that were not reliant on language to construct what he termed culture-free tests. These tests were based on a notion that Cattell (1963) conceptualized and later developed into a theory that intelligence could be decomposed into two types of ability: fluid and crystallized mental abilities. Fluid abilities were nonverbal and involved in adaptation and learning capabilities. Crystallized abilities were developed as a result of the use of fluid abilities while interacting with one's environment and were based on cultural assimilation (Sattler, 1992). These tests, then, were intended to measure only fluid abilities and, according to this theory, would hence be culture-free: that is, implicitly conceptually equivalent.

It was soon realized that it was not possible to eliminate the effects of culture from even these geometric-stimulus-based, nonverbal tests. According to Ritzier (1996):

> Even those designated as "culture-free" do not eliminate the effects of previous cultural experiences, both of impoverishment and enrichment. Language factors greatly affect performance, and some of the tasks used to measure intelligence have little or no relevance for cultures very different from the Anglo-European. (p. 125)

Nonlanguage tests may even be more culturally loaded than language-based tests. Larger group differences often have been found with nonverbal tests than with verbal ones. "Nonverbal, spatial-perceptual tests frequently require relatively abstract thinking processes and analytic cognitive styles characteristic of middle-class Western cultures" (Anastasi & Urbina, 1997, p. 344). In retrospect, "cultural influences will and should be reflected in test performance. It is therefore futile to try to devise a test that is free from cultural influences" (p. 342).

Noting these and other reactions, Cattell (Cattell & Cattell, 1963) tried to balance cultural influences and build what he termed culture fair tests. These tests also tend to use geometric forms of various types. The items frequently are complex patterns, classification tasks, or solving printed mazes; and although the tests can be paper-and-pencil based, they can also be based on performance tasks and thus avoid language-based verbal questions. They may involve pictures rather than verbal stimuli. Even such tests were not seen as fully viable:

> It is unlikely, moreover, that any test can be equally "fair" to more than one cultural group, especially if the cultures are quite dissimilar. While reducing cultural differentials in test performance, cross-cultural tests cannot completely eliminate such differentials. Every test tends to favor persons from the culture in which it was developed. (Anastasi & Urbina, 1997, p. 342)

> Some cultures place greater or lesser emphases upon abstractions, and some cultures value the understanding of contexts and situations more than Western cultures. (Cole & Bruner, 1971)

> [T]here is a substantial literature that suggests culture-fair tests like the Cattell fulfill not only theoretical and social concerns but practical needs as well.... Smith, Hays, and Solway (1977) compared the Cattell Culture-Fair Test and the WISC-R [Wechsler Intelligence Scale for Children-Revised] in a sample of juvenile delinquents, 53% of whom were black or Mexican-Americans.... The authors concluded that the Cattell is a better measure of intelligence for minority groups than the WISC-R, as it lessens the effect of cultural bias and presents a "more accurate" picture of their intellectual capacity. (Domino, 2000, p. 300)

Some of our top test developers continue to develop tests intended to be culture-fair (e.g., Bracken, Naglieri, & Bardos, 1999). Although such measures may not be so culture-fair that they would permit cross-cultural comparisons that would be free of cultural biases, they nevertheless have been used effectively in a variety of cultures and may be transported from culture to culture without many of the translation issues so inherent to most tests of ability that are used in more than one culture. Such tests should, however, be evaluated carefully for what some have seen as their middle-class, Anglo-European orientation. In addition, tests that heavily rely on patterns or figures laid out from left to right may disadvantage individuals from cultures in which text is read from right to left. Psychologists should also ask whether the construct represented in "culture-fair" tests adequately covers the range of traits the psychologists wish to measure. Mpofu and Ortiz (2009) raised a concern that nonverbal tests of intelligence assess only a narrow range of abilities and consequently may be insufficient for some assessment goals.

## Acculturation

According to Mpofu and Ortiz (2009), "Culture, or more accurately, level of acculturation, is one of the most important variables that affects test performance and which must be evaluated and understood so that results can be interpreted fairly" (p. 60). Berry and Sam (1997) defined *acculturation* as "how individuals, who developed in one cultural context, manage to adapt to new contexts" (p. 293) for reasons not limited to migration, including major political changes in the person's own country. Cuellar (2000) has described *acculturation* as a moderator variable between personality and behavior and *culture* as "learned behavior transmitted from one generation to the next" (p. 115). When an individual leaves one culture and joins a second, a transition is generally needed. This transition is, at least in part, acculturation. "Most psychological research defines the construct of acculturation as the product of learning due to contacts between the members of two or more groups" (Marin, 1992, p. 345). Learning the language of the new culture is only one of the more obvious aspects of acculturation. It also involves learning the history and traditions of the new culture, changing personally meaningful behaviors in one's life (including the use of one's language), and changing norms, values, worldview, and interaction patterns.

In practice settings, when considering the test performance of an individual who is not from the culture in which the assessment instrument was developed, one needs to consider the individual's level of acculturation. Many variables have been shown to be influenced by the level of acculturation in the individual being assessed. Sue, Keefe, Enomoto, Durvasula, and Chao (1996), for example, found that acculturation affected scales on the MMPI-2. It has also been shown that one's level of acculturation affects personality scales to the extent that these differences could lead to different diagnoses and, perhaps, hospitalization decisions (Cuellar, 2000).

Keitel, Kopala, and Adamson (1996) have provided guidelines for conducting ethical multicultural assessments. Included among these guidelines are assessing acculturation level, selecting tests appropriate for the culture of the test taker, administering tests in an unbiased fashion, and interpreting results appropriately and in a manner that a client can understand. Dana (2005) and Moreland (1996) concurred that acculturation should be assessed as a part of an in-depth evaluation. They suggested, as well, that the psychologist first assess an individual's acculturation and then use instruments appropriate for the individual's dominant culture. Too often, they feared, psychologists use instruments from the dominant culture and with which the psychologists are more likely to be familiar. They also proposed that psychologists dealing with clients who are not fully acculturated should consider test results with respect to the clients' test sophistication, motivation, and other psychological factors that may be influenced by their level of acculturation. Because of the importance of learning to deal with clients who are not from dominant cultures, it has been argued that in training psychologists and other human service professionals, practicums should provide students with access to clients from different cultures (Geisinger & Carlson, 1998; Keitel et al., 1996).

There are many measures of acculturation. Measurement is complex, in part because it is not a unidimensional characteristic (even though many measures treat it as such). A bidimensional model of acculturation, which accounts for both retention of the first culture while increasingly adhering to the new culture, is now generally preferred to a unidimensional model, which includes only changes favoring the new culture (Cabassa, 2003). Discussion of this topic is beyond the scope of this chapter; however, the interested reader is referred to Cuellar (2000), Cabassa (2003), or Marin (1992).

## ADAPTATION OF TESTS FOR CROSS-CULTURAL USE

The translation and adaptation of tests was one of the most discussed testing issues in the 1990s. The decade ended with a major conference held in Washington, DC, in 1999 called the International Conference on Test Adaptation: Adapting Tests for Use in Multiple Languages and Cultures. The conference brought together many of the leaders in this area of study for an exchange of ideas. Many of the presentations were published in Hambleton, Merenda, and Spielberger (2005), from which the current chapter frequently draws. In a decade during which many tests had been translated and adapted and some examples of poor testing practice had been noted, one significant development was the publication of the *Guidelines for Test Adaptation* by the International Test Commission (2010). These guidelines, which appear as the appendix to this chapter, summarize some of the best thinking on test adaptation. Further discussion of each guideline can be found in Hambleton (2005) and van de Vijver and Leung (1997a).

A major question in cross-cultural assessment is whether to create a new measure or adapt an existing measure. We begin our discussion with the assumption that the researcher is adapting an existing measure. We then follow up with information about creating a new measure, including the advantages and disadvantages of doing so.

## Adapting Existing Tests for Cross-Cultural Use

The process of adapting an existing instrument without changing the original instrument is called sequential development. The sequential development approach is commonly used (Harkness, van de Vijver, & Johnson, 2003). The language of the original measure (usually English) is considered the source language. From this source measure, the test is adapted into one or more target languages. However, certain changes may first be made to the original measure to facilitate adaptation.

### Decentering

Cultural decentering is the process of creating items that are appropriate for the different cultures involved in a project rather than linked to a single culture. When using an existing measure, cultural decentering involves altering the items so they are less anchored to the original culture. Those components of the test that are likely to be specific to the original culture are removed or altered. Thus, the cultural biases, both construct and method, are reduced. In addition, the wording of the original measure may be changed in a way that will enhance its translatability. The decentering process is usually performed by a team composed of multilingual, multicultural individuals who have knowledge of the construct to be measured and, perhaps, of the original measure (van de Vijver & Leung, 1997a). If decentering is successful, the two assessment instruments that result, one in each language, are both generally free of culture-specific language and content.

There are several reasons that cultural decentering is not frequently performed, however. First, of course, is that the process is time consuming and expensive. Second, data collected using the original instrument in the first language cannot be used as part of cross-cultural comparisons; only data from the two decentered methods may be used. This condition means that the rich history of validation and normative data that may be available for the original measure are likely to have little use, and the decentered measure in the original language must be used in regathering such information for comparative purposes. For this reason, this process is most likely to be used in comparative cross-cultural research when there is not plentiful supportive data on the original measure.

### Best Practice for Source Language Item Writing

Initial item writing that is targeted for cross-cultural translation is similar to decentering for item content. Once item content has been agreed on, certain procedures for rewording the source language measure can make the translation process smoother. Brislin (1980, p. 432) provided a list of general rules for developing research documents and instruments in English that are to be translated into target languages. Most appear as rules for good writing and effective communication, and they have considerable applicability. These 12 rules have been edited slightly for use here.

1. Use short, simple sentences of fewer than 16 words.
2. Employ active rather than passive words.
3. Repeat nouns instead of using pronouns.
4. Avoid metaphors and colloquialisms. Such phrases are least likely to have equivalents in the target language.
5. Avoid the subjunctive mood (e.g., verb forms with *could* or *would*).
6. Add sentences that provide context for key ideas. Reword key phrases to provide redundancy.
7. Avoid adverbs and prepositions telling where or when (e.g., *frequently, beyond, around*).
8. Avoid possessive forms where possible.
9. Use specific rather than general terms (e.g., the specific animal name, such as *cows, chickens,* or *pigs* rather than the general term *livestock*).
10. Avoid words indicating vagueness regarding some event or thing (*e.g., probably, frequently*).
11. Use wording familiar to the translators where possible.
12. Avoid sentences with two different verbs if the verbs suggest two different actions.

## Adapting Tests Items to Target Languages

When working from a test in the source language, the test will need to be translated or adapted into the target languages. The term *test adaptation* took prominence during the last decade of the 20th century; previously, the term *test translation* had been dominant. This change was based on the more widespread recognition that changes to tests were needed to reflect both cultural differences and language differences. The individuals who translate tests must perform a more difficult task than a simple translation. They frequently must adapt questions as well. That is, direct, literal translation of questions may not convey meaning because the behaviors mentioned in some or all of the items might not generalize across cultures. Therefore, those involved in adapting the original test to a new language and culture must remove or change those items that deal with behavior that does not generalize equivalently in the target culture. When translators find functionally equivalent behaviors to use to replace those that do not generalize across cultures, they are adapting, rather than translating, the test; for this reason, it is preferable to state that the test is *adapted* rather than translated (Geisinger, 1994; Hambleton, 1994). Of course, if the source items were created using decentering techniques and Brislin's guide to initial item writing, the need for changes other than direct translation may be lessened.

Because we expect that those performing the adaptations (many in the field continue to use the term *translations,* however) are highly trained in translation of the applicable material type (e.g., educational assessments, personality assessments), we do not attempt to provide a how-to guide for translation and adaptation itself. Rather, we focus on issues relevant to psychologists or decision makers involved in cross-cultural assessment. The selection and training of translators is a major factor in the success of the process, and Harkness (2003) provided good suggestions in this regard. For an excellent treatment on the translation and adaptation of tests, see Hambleton and Zenisky (2011) or Brislin (1980, 1986).

Changes made to items can be terminological or factual adaptation, such as titles of government officials; language-driven adaptation, such as when languages have different structures; convention-driven adaptation, such as changing to a right-to-left design for languages read right-to-left; and culture-driven adaptation, such as changing the wording to be more relevant in the target culture (Harkness, 2003). However, because items have been changed, they cannot be assumed to operate exactly like the unchanged items:

> Small changes... are not the same as insignificant changes. Therefore, adapted questions should be treated as new questions and not automatically compared with original versions and their performance. The equivalence of modified items must be test and demonstrated. (Harkness et al., 2003, p. 27)

This quotation is specifically aimed at survey translation, but we agree with the point made when applied to psychological and educational tests, both at the item level and the test level.

## Committee Approach

Rather than relying on single translators or evaluators, it is preferable to employ multiple translators to complete the process, either independently or with discussion. A translator working alone may not produce the best test in all cases; "[m]ultiple translators can protect against the dangers of a single translator and his or her preferences and peculiarities" (Hambleton, 2005, p. 10). Particularly effective are committees that work together during the adaptation process. In this method, a group of bilingual individuals translates the test from the original language to the target language (e.g., van de Vijver & Leung, 1997a). Like most committee processes, this procedure has advantages and disadvantages. A committee will be more expensive than a single translator. A committee may not work well together or may be dominated by one or more persons. Members of the committee are likely to catch mistakes of others on the committee, however (Brislin, 1980). It is also possible that committee members can cooperate and help each other, especially if their expertise is complementary (van de Vijver & Leung, 1997a). Alternatively, using what has been termed *parallel* or *split translation methods*, multiple translators work independently, their resulting translations are compared, and the final version is agreed on (Harkness, 2003). Whether individual translators or a committee is used, all translators need to be not only bilingual but also thoroughly familiar with both cultures, with the construct(s) measured on the test, and with general testing principles (e.g., Geisinger, 1994).

## Cross-Cultural Use of Testing Materials

Moreland (1996) called attention to the translation of test-taker responses and of testing materials. Using objective personality inventories, for example, in a new culture when they were developed in another requires substantial revisions in terms of language and cultural differences. It is relatively easy to use a performance-based (or "projective") device, such as the Rorschach inkblots, in a variety of languages. That is because such measures normally consist of nonverbal stimuli, which on first glance do not need translating in terms of language. However, pictures and stimuli that are often found in such measures may need to be changed to be consistent with the culture in which they are to be used. The images of stereotypic people may differ across cultures, as may other aspects of the stimuli that appear in the performance-based or projective techniques. Furthermore, it is critical in such a case that the scoring systems, including rubrics when available, be carefully translated as well. The same processes that are used to ensure that test items are acceptable in both languages must be followed if the responses are to be evaluated in equivalent manners.

### Back-Translation as an Evaluation of Translation Quality

Back-translation is frequently discussed in the test adaptation literature. As Harkness (2003) pointed out, back-translation is not actually an approach to translation but rather a method of evaluating the quality and accuracy of the translation. This technique is sometimes called the translation/back-translation technique and was an initial attempt to advance the test adaptation process beyond a direct test translation (Brislin, 1970; Werner & Campbell, 1970). In this approach, an initial translator or team of translators alters the test materials from the original language to the target language. Then a second translator or team, without having seen the original test, begins with the target language translation and renders this form back to the original language. At this point, the original test developer (or the individuals who plan to use the translated test, or their representatives) compare the original test with the back-translated version, both of which are in the original language. The quality of the translation is evaluated in terms of how accurately the back-translated version agrees with the original test. This technique was widely cited as the procedure of choice (e.g., Butcher & Pancheri, 1976) for several decades, and it has been very useful in remedying certain translation problems (van de Vijver & Leung, 1997a). It may be especially useful if the test user or developer lacks facility in the target language. It also provides an attempt to evaluate the quality of the translation.

However, it also has other disadvantages. Namely, the back-translation procedure never evaluates the target language item, which is where our primary concern should be (Harkness, 2003). In addition, the expectation of back-translation to original item equivalence ignores the complexities of different languages. "Languages are not isomorphic, . . . and we cannot expect that what goes

in will, indeed, come out. We also cannot assume that because something comes out 'right' this means that what we cannot read (and really want to know about) is also 'right'" (Harkness, 2003, p. 42). Harkness provided examples of items that would be mistranslated in the target language but could appear to be acceptable when evaluated only using back-translation.

Further, the orientation is on a language-only translation; there is no possibility of changes in the test to accommodate cultural differences. Thus, if there are culture-specific aspects of the test, this technique should generally not be used. In fact, this technique can lead to special problems if the translators know that their work will be evaluated through a back-translation procedure. In such an instance, they may use stilted language or wording to ensure an accurate back-translation rather than a properly worded translation that would be understood best by test takers in the target language. In short, "a translation-back translation procedure pays more attention to the semantics and less to connotations, naturalness, and comprehensibility" (van de Vijver & Leung, 1997a, p. 39).

### Additional Ways to Evaluate Adaptation Quality

Back translation continues to be used as one method to check the adequacy of an adaptation. In addition to back-translation, flawed though this method is, it is best to use another standardized procedure to evaluate test evaluation quality. Hambleton and Zenisky (2011) recommended a standardized procedure for evaluating each translated or adapted item. In fact, they provided a review form using criteria based on known problems for past studies of item translation. In a classification of test translation errors in an international test of mathematics and science, Solano-Flores, Backhoff, and Contreras-Niño (2009) identified 10 dimensions: Style, Format, Conventions, Grammar and Syntax, Semantics, Register, Information, Construct, Curriculum, and Origin. For example, *Register* relates to the use of terms in unintended ways, and *Origin* relates to copying flaws in the original item. As in the committee approach to adaptation, a committee can be used to evaluate the quality of the adaptation.

### Automated Translation

Computer translations of language are advancing rapidly; free services, such as Google Translate, even exist. In some future chapter such as this one, the author may direct that the first step is to have a computer perform the first translation of the test materials. Currently, though, technology has not yet advanced to this point; human review for cultural and language appropriateness continues to be needed. Consequently, we emphasize that automated translation alone should not be used for any test or instrument. Automated translation programs often yield the sort of direct translations that seem awkward and may be culturally inappropriate, as described in discussing the need for adaptation rather than simple direct translation. Using an example phrase provided by Hambleton (2005) for the French phrase "Je ne suis pas une valise," which means "I am not that stupid" (p. 11), Google Translate returned the literal translation of "I am not a suitcase." It is precisely these culturally rich ideas that require human judgment for the complex process of instrument translation. However, we expect continued improvements in automated translation programs.

## Developing New Measures for Cross-Cultural Use

Before beginning a cross-cultural assessment endeavor, the research team should ask whether a new instrument will be developed or whether an existing instrument could be used with adaptation (Harkness et al., 2003). Developing a new instrument that is thoughtfully designed for use in multiple cultures may be more suited to those cultures than one imported from a monocultural setting. Initially developing items by working together with participating countries "helps to culturally and linguistically decenter questions so that they are more likely to be functionally equivalent across languages and societies.... This is essential since the more the societies/groups being compared differ, the harder it is to achieve equivalence" (Smith, 2003, p. 86). Once the source language questionnaire has been decided on, the steps described for adaptation of an existing test are also applied with new measures, with the exception that the decentering process has already been taken into account. However, developing a new measure can be costly, and the tried and true research history of accepted instruments is lost.

Before building a test for use in more than one culture, one would need to ask how universal the constructs to be tested are (Anastasi & Urbina, 1997; van de Vijver & Poortinga, 1982). One would also have to decide how to perform validation research on the measure in the varying cultures. If one imagines a simple approach to collecting validation evidence (e.g., the criterion-related approach), one would need equivalent criteria in each culture. This requirement is often formidable, which helps explain why a more common model is to take an existing and generally much-used measure from one culture and language to attempt to adapt it to a second culture and language. However, when using an adapted version of an existing instrument, even if an instrument had accumulated considerable validity evidence in its original language, validation should be repeated in the new contexts in which the test is used.

When creating a new instrument, the development team can use parallel or sequential development to better incorporate the needs of different cultures and languages into the resultant measures. "Parallel development is time-consuming and requires conservable effort to coordinate feedback and version changes. At the same time, it is likely to result in instruments that function more effectively across cultures" (Harkness et al., 2003, p. 22). Tanzer (2005) provided an example of a measure successfully designed for cross-cultural use using simultaneous development and urged others to follow similar procedures rather than rely on translation of existing measures. The Programme for International Student Assessment (PISA) is another example of thoughtful multicultural considerations when creating a new instrument for cross-cultural use (documented in McQueen & Mendelovits, 2003). The test framework was developed jointly by participating countries, and participating countries provided representative texts in English or French to contribute to the item pool. Though all questions originated in English, draft items were submitted to all countries before they were finalized.

## Steps in the Translation and Adaptation Process

Geisinger (1994) elaborated 10 steps that should be involved in any test-adaptation process. In general, these steps are themselves an adaptation of any test-development project. Other writers have altered these procedural steps to some extent, but most modifications are quite minor. Each step is listed and annotated briefly next.

1. *Translate and adapt the measure.* "Sometimes an instrument can be translated or adapted on a question-by-question basis. At other times, it must be adapted and translated only in concept" (Geisinger, 1994, p. 306). This decision must be made based on the concept of whether the content and constructs measured by the test are free from construct bias. Translators must be knowledgeable about the content covered on the test, completely bilingual, expert about both cultures, and often able to work as part of a team.

2. *Review the translated or adapted version of the instrument.* Once the measure has been adapted, the quality of the new document must be judged. Back-translation

can be employed at this stage, but it may be more effective to utilize and empower individual or group reviews of the changed document. Geisinger (1994) suggested that members of the panel review the test individually in writing, share their comments with one another, and then meet to resolve differences of opinion and, perhaps, to rewrite portions of the draft test. The individual participants in this process must meet a number of criteria. They must be fluent in both languages and knowledgeable about both cultures. They must also understand the characteristics measured with the instrument and the likely uses to which the test is to be put. If they do not meet any one of these criteria, their evaluation may be flawed.

3. *Adapt the draft instrument on the basis of the comments of the reviewers.* The individuals involved in the translation or adaptation process need to receive the feedback that arose in Step 2 and consider the comments. There may be reasons not to follow some of the suggestions of the review panel (e.g., reasons related to the validity of the instrument), and the original test author, test users, and the translator should consider these comments.

4. *Pilot test the instrument.* It is frequently useful to have a very small number of individuals who can take the test and share concerns and reactions that they may have. They should be as similar as possible to the eventual test takers, and they should be interviewed (or should complete a questionnaire) after taking the test. They may be able to identify problems or ambiguities in wording, in the instructions, in timing, and so on. Any changes that are needed after the pilot test should be made, and if these alterations are extensive, the test may need to be pilot-tested once again.

5. *Field-test the instrument.* This step differs from the pilot test in that it involves a large and representative sample. If the population taking the test in the target language is diverse, all elements of that diversity should be represented and perhaps overrepresented. After collection of these data, the reliability of the test should be assessed and item analyses performed. Included in the item analyses should be analyses for item bias (both as compared to the original-language version and, perhaps, across elements of diversity within the target field-testing sample). Van de Vijver and Leung (1997a) described some of the analyses that should be performed on an item-analysis basis.

6. *Standardize the scores.* If desirable and appropriate, link or equate them with scores on the original version. If the sample size is large enough, it would be useful (and necessary for tests to be used in practice) to establish norms. If the field-test sample is not large enough, and the test is to be used for more than cross-cultural research in the target language, then collection of norm data is necessary. Scores may be linked back to the score scale of the original instrument, just as may be performed for any new form of a test. These procedures are beyond the scope of this chapter but may be found in Kolen and Brennan (2004).

7. *Perform validation research as needed.* The validation research that is needed includes at least research to establish the equivalence to the original measure. However, as noted earlier, the concepts of construct validation represent the ideal to be sought (Embretson, 1983). Some forms of appropriate revalidation are needed before the test can be used with clients in the target language. It is appropriate to perform validation research before the test is used in research projects as well.

8. *Develop a manual and other documents for users of the assessment device.* Users of this newly adapted instrument are going to need information so that they may employ it effectively. A manual that describes administration, scoring, and interpretation should be provided. To provide information that relates to interpretation, summarization of norms, equating (if any), reliability analyses, validity analyses, and investigations of bias should all be supplied. Statements regarding the process of adaptation should be also included.

9. *Train users.* New users of any instrument need instruction so that they can use it effectively. There may be special problems associated with adapted instruments because users may tend to use materials and to employ knowledge that they have of the original measure. Although transfer of training is often positive, negative consequences may result if there are differences between the language versions.

10. *Collect reactions from users.* Whether the instrument is to be used for cross-cultural research or with actual clients, it behooves the test adaptation team to collect the thoughts of users (and perhaps of test takers as well) and to do so on a continuing basis. As more individuals take the test, their different experiential backgrounds may identify concerns. Such comments may lead to changes in future versions of the target-language form.

## NATURE OF EQUIVALENCE

The very nature of cross-cultural psychology places a heavy emphasis on assessment. In particular, measures that are used to make comparisons across cultural groups need to measure the characteristic unvaryingly in two or more cultural groups. Of course, in some settings, this procedure may be rather simple; a comparison of American and British participants with regard to a variable such as depression or intelligence may not produce unusual concerns. The language, English, is of course largely the same for both groups. Minor adjustments in the spelling of words (e.g., behavioral becomes behavioural) would be needed first. Some more careful editing of the items composing scales would also be needed, however, to ensure that none of the items include content that has differing cultural connotations in the two countries. Questions about baseball or cricket, for example, could affect resultant comparisons. These examples are provided simply to present the nature of the issue. Cross-cultural psychologists have focused on the nature of equivalence and, in particular, have established qualitative levels of equivalence.

Many writers have considered the notion of equivalence in cross-cultural testing. Lonner (1979) is acknowledged often for systematizing our conception of equivalence in testing in cross-cultural psychology. He described four kinds of equivalence: linguistic equivalence, conceptual equivalence, functional equivalence, and metric equivalence (Nichols, Padilla, & Gomez-Maqueo, 2000). These were described in Geisinger (2003). Brislin (1993) provided a similar nomenclature with three levels of equivalence: translation, conceptual, and metric, leaving out functional equivalence, an important kind of equivalence, as noted by Berry (1980), Butcher and Han (1998), and Helms (1992). Van de Vijver and Leung (2011) operationalized four hierarchical levels of equivalence as well, encompassing construct inequivalence, structural or functional equivalence, metric or measurement unit equivalence, and scalar equivalence or full score comparability. It should be noted, however, that like the concepts of test reliability and validity, equivalence is not a property resident in a particular test or assessment device (van de Vijver & Leung, 1997b). Rather, the construct is tied to a particular instrument and the cultures involved. Equivalence is also time dependent, given the changes that may occur in cultures. For consistency with current literature, we follow the classification system outlined in van de Vijver and Leung (2011).

## Construct Inequivalence

The first level of equivalence in this hierarchy is actually one of inequivalence, a feature researchers hope to avoid. In evaluating whether construct inequivalence is present, we ask whether the instrument measures the same construct in different groups. If it does not measure the same construct in different groups, the measure is considered construct inequivalent (van de Vijver & Leung, 2011). No etic comparisons can be made in such a situation, because the comparison would be a classic apples-and-oranges contrast. This class of inequivalence relates to construct bias; we discuss this problem further when describing types of bias. Construct inequivalence sometimes occurs when constructs are so different in two or more cultures, or even absent in one culture, that cross-cultural measurement of the construct is impossible. For example, if an assessment of dieting behaviors intended for a country where food was overabundant was administered in a culture with severe food shortages, beliefs about food would likely be very different. In such case, it would be inappropriate to attempt to measure dieting behaviors in the second culture. In designing the PISA assessment for various educational comparisons, efforts were taken to involve representative countries in the definition of the test construct to ensure construct equivalence: The first task was therefore not to judge the appropriateness of an existing construct across languages and cultures but to develop a construct in consultation with representatives of participating groups (McQueen & Mendelovits, 2003).

For some constructs or measures, there are problems with equivalence that not even the best translations can overcome. For example, even when professional translators, content or psychological specialists, and test designers are involved, "direct translations of the tests are often not possible as psychological constructs may have relevance in one culture and not in another.... Just because the content of the items is preserved does not automatically insure that the item taps the same ability within the cultural context of the individual being tested" (Suzuki, Vraniak, & Kugler, 1996, p. 151). This lack of parallelism can be considered construct inequivalence. Brislin (1980) has also referred to this issue as *translatability,* that is, whether salient characteristics in the construct to be assessed can be translated.

## Functional, Structural, or Construct Equivalence

Once we have evidence that the same construct is measured by the instrument in both cultures, we then ask whether the construct is measured in the same way in both groups. This question determines whether requirements for functional or structural equivalence have been met. As defined by van de Vijver and Leung (1997b), structural equivalence is "the similarity of psychometric properties of data sets from different cultures" (p. 261), especially the correlations between items of a measure or correlations with outside variables. As described in the section on methods to evaluate score equivalence, many analyses can be used to evaluate this type of equivalence, including structural equation modeling, factor analysis, and multidimensional scaling (van de Vijver and Leung, 1997b). Technically, van de Vijver and Leung (2011) considered functional equivalence to be a specific category of structural equivalence, in which nomological networks are the same across cultures, showing similar patterns of correlations between variables. Fischer and Fontaine (2011) have provided detailed directions for various methods of testing structural equivalence.

In an earlier version (1997a) of van de Vijver and Leung's conceptualization, this level was also called *construct equivalence*. We find it easier to merge existing psychometric literature with the current cross-cultural literature using the term *construct equivalence* instead of *functional* or *structural equivalence* because it is closely related to the concept of *construct validity*. Cronbach and Meehl (1955) established the conceptual structure for construct validity with the model of a nomological network. The *nomological network* concept is based on our understanding of psychological constructs (hypothetical psychological variables, characteristics, or traits) through their relationships with other such variables. What psychologists understand about in vivo constructs emerges from how those constructs relate empirically to other constructs. In naturalistic settings, psychologists tend to measure two or more constructs for all participants in the investigation and to correlate scores among variables. Over time and multiple studies, evidence is amassed so that the relationships among variables appear known. From their relationships, the structure of these constructs becomes known and a nomological network can be imagined and charted: Variables that tend to be highly related are closely aligned in the nomological network, and those that are not related have no connective structure between them. The *construct validity* of a particular test, then, is the extent to which it appears to measure the theoretical construct or trait that it is intended to measure. This construct validity is assessed by determining the extent to which the test correlates with variables in the patterns predicted by the nomological network. When the test correlates with other variables with which it is expected to correlate, evidence of construct validation, called *convergent validation*, is found (Campbell & Fiske, 1959; Geisinger, 1992). Conversely, when a test does not correlate with a measure that the theory of the psychological construct suggests that it should not, positive evidence of construct validation, called *discriminant validation* (Campbell & Fiske, 1959), is also found. Of course, using parlance, we perceive these results as evidence of validity rather than validation per se.

Consider this simple example. *Intelligence* and *school performance* are constructs measured by both the Wechsler Intelligence Scale for Children–III (WISC-III) and grade point average (GPA)—in this instance, in the fourth grade. Numerous investigations in the United States provide data showing the two constructs to correlate moderately. The WISC-III is translated into French, and a similar study is performed with fourth graders in schools in Quebec, where a GPA measure similar to that in U.S. schools is available. If the correlation is similar between the two variables (intelligence and school performance), some degree of conceptual equivalence between the English and French versions of the WISC-III is demonstrated. If a comparable result is not found, however, it is unclear whether (a) the WISC-III was not properly translated and adapted to French; (b) the GPA in the Quebec study is different somehow from that in the American studies; (c) one or both of the measured constructs (intelligence and school performance) does not exist in the same fashion in Quebec as they do in the United States; or (d) the constructs simply do not relate to each other the way they do in the United States. Additional research would be needed to establish the truth in this situation.

Ultimately and theoretically, construct equivalence is achieved when a test that has considerable evidence of construct validity in the original or host language and culture is adapted for use in a second language and culture, and the target-language nomological network is highly similar to the original one. When such a nomological network has been replicated, it might be said that the construct validity of the test *generalizes* from the original test and culture to the target one. *Factor analysis* has long been used as a technique of choice for this equivalence evaluation (e.g., Ben-Porath, 1990). Techniques such as *structural equation modeling* are even more useful for such analyses (e.g., Kline, 2010), in which the statistical model representing the nomological network in the host culture can be applied and tested in the target culture. Additional information on these approaches is provided later in this chapter.

## Metric or Measurement Unit Equivalence

As defined by van de Vijver and Poortinga (2005), metric or measurement unit equivalence indicates that a measure that has been adapted for use in a target culture continues to have the same units of measurement in the two culture-specific forms but can have different zero-points (i.e., origins). That is, both forms of the measure must continue to yield assessments that follow an interval scale, and in addition, it must be the same interval scale. If a translated form of a test was studied using a sample in the target culture comparable to the original norm group and the new test form was found to have the same raw-score standard deviation as the original, this finding would be strong initial evidence of measurement unit equivalence. When measurement unit equivalence is supported, within-group differences can be examined, but individual differences cannot be directly examined across groups in the absence of scalar equivalence (van de Vijver & Poortinga, 2005).

## Scalar or Full Score Equivalence

Scalar equivalence assumes measurement unit equivalence and requires one additional finding: Not only must the units be equivalent, the zero-points of the scales must also be identical (van de Vijver & Leung, 2011). Thus, the units must both fall along the same ratio scale. The means do not need to be the same in both cultures, though, allowing for cultural differences. Only if criteria for scalar equivalence are met should cross-cultural conclusions be directly made (van de Vijver & Poortinga, 2005). However, scalar equivalence is difficult to prove with psychological measures (van de Vijver & Leung, 1997b). The discussion of metric equivalence by Moreland (1996), in which scores from the different forms must convey the same meaning, appears to be more related to the concept of scalar equivalence in the present conceptualization.

## NATURE OF BIAS

There have been many definitions of *test bias* (Flaugher, 1978; and see Reynolds & Suzuki, this volume). Messick's (e.g., 1989) conceptions of test bias are perhaps the most widely accepted and emerge from the perspective of construct validity. Messick portrayed *bias* as a specific source of test variance other than the valid variance associated with the desired construct. Bias is associated with some irrelevant variable, such as race, gender, or, in the case of cross-cultural testing, culture (or perhaps country of origin). Van de Vijver (2000) and his associates (van de Vijver & Leung, 1997a; van de Vijver & Poortinga, 2005) have perhaps best characterized bias within the context of cross-cultural assessment as "a generic term for all nuisance factors threatening the validity of cross-cultural comparisons" (van de Vijver & Leung, p. 10). There are many potential sources of bias, including but not limited to inadequate translation, differences in content interpretation, and failure to uphold administration standardization. Van de Vijver (2000) also described bias as "a lack of similarity of psychological meaning of test scores across cultural groups" (p. 88). Allen and Walsh (2000) provided a related definition: "Test bias exists . . . when an existing test does not measure the equivalent underlying psychological construct in a new group or culture, as was measured within the original group in which it was standardized" (p. 67).

As can be seen, the term *bias* is very closely related to *equivalence*. Van de Vijver (2000) described the distinction in this way: "Bias refers to the presence or absence of validity-threatening factors in such assessment, whereas equivalence involves the consequences of these factors on the comparability of test scores" (p. 89). In his various publications, van de Vijver has identified three groupings of bias: construct, method, and item bias. The next sections explain each one.

## Construct Bias

Measures that do not examine *identical* constructs across cultural groups exhibit *construct bias* (van de Vijver, 2000),which clearly is highly related to the notion of construct equivalence previously described. When the constructs underlying the measures vary across cultures, with culture-specific components of the construct present in some cultures, such evidence is not only likely to but it *should* result if both measures are to measure the construct validly in their respective cultures. Construct bias can occur when constructs only partially overlap across cultures, when there is a differential appropriateness of behaviors comprising the construct in different cultures, when there is a poor sampling of relevant behaviors constituting the construct in one or more cultures, or when there is incomplete coverage of all relevant aspects of the construct (van de Vijver, 2000).

The concept of construct bias has implications for both cross-cultural research and cross-cultural psychological practice. Cross-cultural or etic comparisons are unlikely to be very meaningful if the construct means something different in the two or more cultures, or if it is a reasonably valid representation of the construct in one culture but less so in the other. The practice implications in the target language emerge from the fact that the measure may not be valid as an instrument assessing culturally relevant constructs that may be of more consequence for diagnosis and treatment.

In regard to construct bias, the adequacy of sampling of the domain is critical. To establish comparable content relevance in two forms of a measure, each in a different language for a different cultural group, first one must gauge whether the content domain is the same or different in each case. In addition, one must establish that the domain is sampled with equivalent representativeness in all cases. Both of these determinations may be problematic. An example of construct bias can be seen in the following two brief examples. In many instances, inventories (such as personality inventories) are adapted from the original language to a second or target language. If the culture that uses the target language has culture-specific aspects of personality that either do not exist or are not as prevalent as in the original culture, these aspects certainly will not be able to be included in the target-language form of the assessment instrument. For a second example, imagine the translation of a fourth-grade mathematics test that, in its original country, is given to students who attend school 10 months of the year whereas, in the target country, the students attend for only 8 months. In such an instance, the two domains of mathematics taught in the fourth year of schooling are likely to be overlapping but not identical. Because the students from the original country have already attended three longer school years prior to this year, they are likely to begin at a more advanced level. Furthermore, given that the year is longer, they are likely to cover more material during the academic year, all other things being equal. In short, the domains are not likely to be identical. Finally, the representativeness of the domains must be considered.

## Method Bias

Van de Vijver (2000) has identified a number of types of method bias, including sample, instrument, and administration bias. The different issues composing this type of bias were given the name *method bias* because they relate to the kinds of topics covered in methods sections of journal articles. Method biases often affect performance on the assessment instrument as a whole (rather than affecting only components of the measure). Some of the types of method bias are described next.

### Sample Bias

In studies comparing two or more cultures, the samples from each culture may differ on variables related to test-relevant background characteristics. These differences may affect the comparison. Examples of such characteristics would include fluency in the language in which testing occurs, general education levels, and underlying motivational levels (van de Vijver, 2000). Imagine an essay test that is administered in a single language. Two groups are compared: Both have facility with the language, but one has substantially more ability. Regardless of the knowledge involved in the answers, it is likely that the group that is more facile in the language will provide better answers on average because of their ability to employ the language better in answering the question.

Häder and Gabler (2003) considered the methodology of sampling for multinational studies "a somewhat underdeveloped aspect of social research" (p. 117). When the purpose of the research is to make comparisons of scores between cultures or countries, strict adherence to a rigorous and fair sampling plan is essential. When sampling procedures differ across countries, these differences can be taken into account with weighting of the resultant data, but the inclusion probabilities must be carefully documented in order to calculate the needed weights (Häder & Gabler, 2003) appropriately. Acknowledging the necessity of straying from textbook sampling procedures, the authors stated, "The view taken here is that such departures, which are likely in cross-cultural studies, are acceptable departures provided probability samples and only probability samples are used" (p. 117).

Boehnke, Lietz, Schreier, and Wilhelm (2011) considered sampling and the purpose of the research to be interrelated. According to these authors, if the goal of research is to examine relationships between variables in different cultures rather than to make cross-cultural comparisons regarding the level of traits (such as with means or percents), probability sampling is not necessary. Indeed, in a review of studies published in the *Journal of Cross-Cultural Psychology*, Boenke et al. found that only 7% used probability sampling of individuals.

### Instrument Bias

Instrument bias is much like sample bias, but the groups being tested tend to differ in less generic ways that are more specific to the testing method itself, as when a test subject has some familiarity with the general format of the testing or some other form of test sophistication. Van de Vijver (2000) stated that the most common forms of this bias exist when groups differ by response styles in answering questions. For example, different cultures vary in the tendency of their members to disclose personal issues about themselves. When two cultures are compared, depending on who is making the comparison, it is possible that one group could look overly self-revelatory or the other too private. Harzing (2006) analyzed patterns of response bias and found certain response styles to be related to cultural values, consistent with previous research. Thus, one should examine the data carefully for evidence of response bias.

Another source of instrument bias is examinees' familiarity with the materials on the test. Imagine the use of a measure like the Thematic Apperception Test (TAT) in a cross-cultural comparison. Not only do the people pictured on many of the TAT cards not look like persons from some cultures, but the scenes themselves have a decidedly western orientation. Respondents from some cultures would obviously find such pictures more foreign and strange. Hambleton (2005) recommended that cross-cultural educational assessments use a variety of item types to reduce the effect of unfamiliarity with any one format, a recommendation followed in the design of PISA (McQueen & Mendelovitis, 2003). As noted previously, attempts to develop culture-fair or culture-free intelligence tests (e.g., Bracken et al., 1999; Cattell, 1940; Cattell & Cattell, 1963) often have used geometric figures rather than language in the effort to avoid dependence on language. Groups that differ in educational experience or by culture also may have differential exposure to geometric figures. This differential contact with the stimuli composing the test may bias the comparison in a manner that is difficult to disentangle from the construct of intelligence measured by the instrument. Geisinger (1994) recommended the use of enhanced test-practice exercises to attempt to reduce differences in test-format familiarity. Such exercises could be performed at the testing site or in advance of the testing, depending on the time needed to gain familiarity. These exercises may not, however, eliminate differences developed over years of testing.

### Administration Bias

The final type of method bias emerges from the interactions between test-taker or respondent and components of the administration, including the administrator and setting. Such biases could come from language problems on the part of an interviewer, who may be conducting the interview in a language in which he or she is less adept than might be ideal (van de Vijver & Leung, 1997a), or from inconsistently trained administrators. Additionally, if the administration setting differs across countries, such as at home in some cultures but in a psychologist's office in others, these differences can affect comparability of the results (van de Vijver & Leung, 2011).

Another example of administration bias may be seen in the multicultural testing literature in the United States. The theory of *stereotype threat* (Steele, 1997; Steele & Aronson, 1995) suggests that African Americans, when taking an individualized intellectual assessment or other similar measure that is administered by someone whom the test takers believe holds negative stereotypes about them, will perform at the level expected by the test administrator. Steele's theory holds that negative stereotypes can have a powerful influence on the results of important assessments—stereotypes that can influence test takers' performance and, ultimately, their lives. Sackett, Hardison, and Cullen (2004) have summarized considerable empirical research that conflict with this theoretical hypothesis of stereotype threat, however. Of course, in a world where there are many cultural tensions and cultural preconceptions, it is possible that this threat may apply to groups other than Whites and Blacks in the American culture. Van de Vijver (2000) concluded his chapter with the statement that with notable exceptions, responses to either interviews or most cognitive tests do not seem to be strongly affected by the cultural, racial, or ethnic status of administrators.

### Item Bias

Individual items that are translated or adapted from one language to another, as well as a single test used in multiple cultures, should be subjected to item bias analyses. Even when using a single assessment within a single country, individuals from different groups may have differential exposure to certain item content or formats, making the item easier or harder for members of that group, regardless of overall ability. Item bias or differential item functioning (DIF) analyses test whether a group is statistically disadvantaged on a certain item, after controlling for overall ability. Essentially, on a cognitive test, an item will demonstrate DIF for a particular group if it is more difficult for individuals of a certain level of overall ability than it is for members of the other group who have that same level of overall ability. Sireci, Patsula, and Hambleton (2005) distinguished between items that statistically demonstrate DIF and the term *item bias,* reserving "item bias" for situations where the reason for the difference can be shown to be construct irrelevant. Van de Vijver and Leung (1997a) preferred continuing to use the term *item bias,* however, to accentuate the notion that these issues, if not handled appropriately, may bias the results of measurement.

In addition to cultural differences in item content salience, adaptation to different languages has the potential to contribute to unfair differences between item difficulty for different groups. With adapted tests for cross-cultural use, evidence of DIF suggests either that the adaptation may have made an item easier or harder in the target language or that the question operates differently in the different cultural group. Items may demonstrate DIF because they deal with content that is not uniformly available to members of all cultures involved or because translations have not been adequately performed. Mpofu and Ortiz (2009) have reminded us, though, that DIF indices do not identify all problems with fairness. In particular, when all items are biased against members of a certain group, such as those for whom the language of testing is not their strongest language on a verbal ability test, DIF indices will likely not indicate bias because those with limited skills in the language of testing will likely perform worse on all items.

Differences in item difficulty can emerge from differences in wording, in content, in format, or in cultural relevance (Allalouf, Hambleton, & Sireci, 1999). There may be factors, such as item wording, that are *differentially more difficult* in one language than the other. A number of studies describe the kinds of item problems that lead to differential levels of difficulty (e.g., Allalouf et al., 1999; Budgell, Raju, & Quartetti, 1995; Hulin, 1987; Tanzer, Gittler, & Sim, 1994). Some of these findings may prove very useful for future test-translation projects and may even influence the construction of tests that are likely to be translated. For example, in an early study of Hispanics and Anglos taking the Scholastic Aptitude Test (now the SAT), Schmitt (1988) found that verbal items that used roots common to English and Spanish appeared to help Hispanics. Limited evidence suggested that words that differed in cognates (words that appear to have the same roots but have different meanings in both languages) and homographs (words spelled alike in both languages but with different meanings in the two) caused difficulties for Hispanic test takers. Allalouf et al. (1999) examined item bias in a verbal test for college admissions that had been translated from Hebrew to Russian. They found that most items identified as differentially more difficult emerged from word difficulty, especially in analogy items, because the translators chose easier words in Russian, thus making items less difficult. Budgell et al. (1995) used an expert committee to review the results of statistical analyses that identified items as biased; in many cases, the committee

could not provide logic as to why an item translated from English to French was differentially more difficult for one group or the other. This research and most other comparable research have not been able to identify reasons why individual groups have different success rates on different items.

For items requiring human scoring, *differences in scoring rubrics* can also lead to item bias. In developing scoring procedures for PISA, the development team used field test responses from different countries to modify the scoring rubrics in ways that made them more appropriate for the various cultures included in the test (McQueen & Mendelovits, 2003). Item bias has been studied primarily in cognitive measures: ability and achievement tests. Van de Vijver (2000) correctly notes that measures such as the Rorschach should also be evaluated for item bias. It is possible that members of different cultures could differentially interpret the cards on measures such as the Rorschach or the TAT.

Holland and Wainer (1993) have provided an excellent resource on DIF techniques in general, while van de Vijver and Leung (1997a), Sireci et al. (2005), and Sireci (2011) have specifically addressed the use of item bias techniques in areas cultural research. Kim, Cohen, and Park (1995) expanded traditional DIF to multiple groups, which could be especially useful in cross-cultural assessment. Allalouf et al. (1999), Budgell et al. (1995), and Ercikan (2002), have provided examples and guidance for evaluating DIF in cross-cultural assessment. Items that demonstrate DIF based on translation problems can then be revised with the goal of eliminating the DIF after revision (e.g., Allalouf, 2003).

## METHODS OF EVALUATING TEST EQUIVALENCE

Once a test has been adapted into a target language, it is necessary to establish that the test has the kinds of equivalence that are needed for proper test interpretation and use. Methodologists and psychometricians have worked for several decades on this concern, and a number of research designs and statistical methods are available to help provide data for this analysis, which ultimately inform the test-development team to make a judgment regarding test equivalence. Such research is essential for tests that are to be used with clients in settings that differ from that in which the test was originally developed and validated.

## Methods to Evaluate Score Equivalence

Historically, a number of statistical methods have been used to establish the comparability of scores emerging from translated tests or tests used cross-culturally. Four techniques are discussed in this section: exploratory factor analysis, structural equation modeling (including confirmatory factor analysis), regression analysis, and item-response theory. Allen and Walsh (2000) and van de Vijver and Leung (1997a) have provided a far more detailed description of these techniques.

### Exploratory, Replicatory Factor Analysis

Many psychological and educational tests have been subjected to *factor analysis,* a technique that has often been used in psychology in an exploratory fashion to identify dimensions or consistencies among the items composing a measure (Anastasi & Urbina, 1997). According to Sireci et al. (2005), "exploratory factor analysis is one of the oldest and most popular methods for evaluating whether different language versions of a test measure the same construct" (p. 96). To establish that the internal relationships of items or test components hold across different language versions of a test, a factor analysis of the translated version is performed. In an evaluation of structural equivalence, we would find evidence against a claim of structural equivalence if a measure that has been (a) factor analyzed in its original culture with the repeated finding of a four-factor solution and that is then (b) translated to another language and administered to a sample from the culture in which that language is spoken, with a factor analysis of the test results indicating a two-factor and therefore different solution.

A factor analysis normally begins with the correlation matrix of all the items composing the measure. The factor analysis looks for patterns of consistency or factors among the items. There are many forms of factor analysis, and techniques differ in many conceptual ways. Among the important decisions made in any exploratory factor analysis are determining the number of factors, deciding whether these factors are permitted to be correlated (*oblique*) or forced to be uncorrelated (*orthogonal*), and interpreting the resultant factors (e.g., Fabrigar, Wegener, MacCallum, & Strahan, 1999). In *rotation,* a component of the factor analysis, the dimensions are changed mathematically to increase interpretability.

The exploratory factor analysis that bears on the construct equivalence of two measures has been called *replicatory factor analysis* (RFA; Ben-Porath, 1990) and is a form of cross-validation. In this instance, the number of

factors and whether the factors are orthogonal or oblique are constrained to yield the same number of factors as in the original test. In addition, a rotation of the factors is made to attempt to maximally replicate the original solution; this technique is called *target rotation.* Once these procedures have been performed, analysts can estimate how similar the factors are across solutions. Van de Vijver and Leung (1997a) provide indices that may be used for this judgment (e.g., the *coefficient of proportionality*). Although RFA probably has been the most used technique for estimating congruence (van de Vijver & Leung, 1997a), it does suffer from a number of problems. One of these is simply that newer techniques, especially confirmatory factor analysis, can now perform a similar analysis while also testing whether the similarity is statistically significant through hypothesis testing. A second problem is that different researchers have not employed standard procedures and do not always rotate their factors to a target solution (van de Vijver & Leung, 1997a). Finally, many studies do not compute indices of factor similarity across the two solutions and make this discernment only judgmentally (van de Vijver & Leung, 1997a). Nevertheless, a number of outstanding researchers (e.g., Ben-Porath, 1990; Butcher, 1996) have recommended the use of RFA to establish equivalence and this technique has been widely used, especially in validation efforts for various adaptations of the frequently translated Minnesota Multiphasic Personality Inventory and the Eysenck Personality Questionnaire.

### Regression

Regression approaches generally are used to establish the relationships between the newly translated measure and measures with which it has traditionally correlated in the original culture. The new test can be correlated statistically with other measures, and the correlation coefficients that result may be compared statistically with similar correlation coefficients found in the original population. There may be one or more such correlated variables. When there is more than one independent variable, *multiple regression* is used. In this case, the adapted test serves as the dependent variable and the other measures as the independent variables. When multiple regression is used, the independent variables are used to predict the adapted test scores. Multiple regression weights the independent variables mathematically to optimally predict the dependent variable. The regression equation for the original test in the original culture may be compared with that for the adapted test; where there are differences between the two regression lines, whether in the slope or the intercept, or in some other manner, bias in the testing is often presumed.

If the scoring of the original- and target-language measures is the same, it is also possible to include cultural group membership in a multiple regression equation. Such a nominal variable is added as what has been called a *dummy-coded* variable. In such an instance, if the dummy-coded variable is assigned a weighting as part of the multiple regression equation, indicating that it predicts test scores, evidence of cultural differences across either the two measures or the two cultures may be presumed (van de Vijver & Leung, 1997a).

## Structural Equation Modeling, Including Confirmatory Factor Analysis

Structural equation modeling (SEM; Kline, 2010) is a more general and statistically sophisticated procedure that encompasses both factor analysis and regression analysis and does so in a manner that permits elegant hypothesis testing. SEM can be used to perform a type of factor analysis called *confirmatory factor analysis* (CFA). The distinction between exploratory and confirmatory methods of factor analysis is that in CFA the researcher determines the model in advance. Essentially, the results of factor-analytic studies of the measure in the original language are constrained on the adapted measure, data from the adapted measure are analyzed, and a goodness-of-fit statistical test is performed. In CFA, as in exploratory factor analysis (EFA), the researcher must make certain decisions about the analysis; in CFA, individual decisions about the components of the model can change the results or interpretation of the results and should be made thoughtfully. Brown (2006) provided guidance in conducting confirmatory factor analyses.

Regression approaches to relationships among a number of tests can also be studied with SEM. Elaborate models of relationships among other tests, measuring variables hypothesized and found through previous research to be related to the construct measured by the adapted test, also may be tested using SEM. In such an analysis, it is possible for a researcher to approximate the kind of nomological net conceptualized by Cronbach and Meehl (1955) and test whether the structure holds in the target culture as it does in the original culture. Such a test should be the ideal to be sought in establishing the construct equivalence of tests across languages and cultures. An example of the use of SEM for evaluating cross-cultural equivalence of attitudinal variables in two cultures is shown in Billiet (2003), in addition to many studies using SEM

to evaluate equivalence across groups in single culture research.

### Item-Response Theory

Item-response theory (IRT) is an alternative to classical psychometric true-score theory as a method for analyzing test data. Van de Vijver and Leung (1997a), Allen and Walsh (2000), and Drasgow and Probst (2005) have provided descriptions of the way that IRT can be used to compare items across two forms of a measure that differ by language. Although a detailed description of IRT is beyond the scope of this chapter, a brief explanation may provide a conceptual understanding of how the procedure is used, especially for cognitive tests. An item characteristic curve (ICC) is computed for each item. This curve has as the $x$-axis the overall ability level of test takers, and as the $y$-axis, the probability of answering the question correctly. Different IRT models have different numbers of parameters, with one-, two-and three-parameter models most common. These parameters correspond to difficulty, discrimination, and the ability to get the answer correct by chance, respectively. The ICC curves are plotted as normal ogive curves. When a test is adapted, each translated item may be compared across languages graphically by overlaying the two ICCs as well as by comparing the item parameters mathematically. Differences can be considered conceptually. This method, too, may be considered as one technique for identifying item bias.

## Methods to Establish Linkage of Scores

Once the conceptual equivalence of an adapted measure has been met, researchers and test developers often wish to provide measurement-unit and metric equivalence. For most measures, this requirement is met through the process of *test equating*. As noted throughout this chapter, merely translating a test from one language to another, even if cultural biases have been eliminated, does not ensure that the two different-language forms of a measure are equivalent. Conceptual or construct equivalence needs to be established first. Once such a step has been taken, then one can consider higher levels of equivalence. The mathematics of equating may be found in a variety of sources (e.g., Kolen & Brennan, 2004). However, translated measures would generally be "linked" rather than "equated" per se. The mathematical procedures are the same, but adapted tests do not meet the more stringent psychometric requirements to be considered "equated." Cook and Schmitt-Cascallar (2005) have provided an integration of research designs and analysis for linking scores of adapted tests. Research designs for such studies are abstracted in the next paragraphs.

Sireci (1997) clarified three experimental designs that can be used to link adapted forms to their original-language scoring systems and, perhaps, norms. He refers to them as (1) the separate-monolingual-groups design, (2) the bilingual-group design, and (3) the matched-monolingual-groups design. A brief description of each follows.

### Separate-Monolingual-Groups Design

In the separate-monolingual-groups design, two different groups of test takers are involved, one from each language or cultural group. Although some items may simply be assumed to be equivalent across both tests, data can be used to support this assumption. These items serve as what is known in equating as *anchor items*. IRT methods are then generally used to calibrate the two tests to a common scale, most typically the one used by the original-language test (Angoff & Cook, 1988; O'Brien, 1992; Sireci, 1997). Translated items must then be evaluated for invariance across the two different-language test forms; that is, they are assessed to determine whether their difficulty differs across forms. This design does not work effectively if the two groups actually differ, on average, on the characteristic that is assessed (Sireci, 1997); in fact, in such a situation, one cannot disentangle differences in the ability measured from differences in the two measures. The method also assumes that the construct measured is based on a single, unidimensional factor. Measures of complex constructs, then, are not good prospects for this method.

### Bilingual-Group Design

In the bilingual-group design, a single group of bilingual individuals takes both forms of the test in counterbalanced order. An assumption of this method is that the individuals in the group are all equally bilingual (i.e., equally proficient in each language). In Maldonado and Geisinger (2005), all participants first were tested in both Spanish and English competence to gain entry into the study. Even under such restrictive circumstances, however, a ceiling effect made a true assessment of equality impossible. The problem of finding equally bilingual test takers is almost insurmountable. Also, if knowledge of what is on the test in one language affects performance on the other test, it is possible to use two randomly assigned groups of bilingual individuals (where their level of language skill is equated via randomization). In such an instance, it is possible either to give each group one of the tests or to give each group one-half of the items (counterbalanced) from each test in a nonoverlapping manner (Sireci, 1997). Finally, one must question how representative the equally bilingual individuals are of the target population; thus, the external validity of the sample may be questioned. Sireci (2005) gave additional guidance for research designs in which bilingual test takers can give valuable information about the different versions of the adapted test. To the extent that the aforementioned problems with acquiring an appropriate bilingual sample are overcome, this design can be very useful because the trait or skill level of the examinees is the same across languages, thus isolating the cause of performance differences as caused by linguistic differences in the tests, by eliminating other possible causes.

### Matched-Monolingual-Groups Design

The matched-monolingual-groups design is conceptually similar to the separate monolingual-groups design, except that in this case the study participants are matched on the basis of some variable expected to correlate highly with the construct measured. By being matched in this way, the two groups are made more equal, which reduces error. "There are not many examples of the matched monolingual group linking design, probably due to the obvious problem of finding relevant and available matching criteria" (Sireci, 1997, p. 17). Nevertheless, the design is an extremely powerful one.

## CONCLUSION

Psychology has been critiqued as having a Euro-American orientation (Moreland, 1996; Padilla & Medina, 1996), Moreland wrote:

> Koch (1981) suggests that American psychologists are trained in scientific attitudes that Kimble (1984) has characterized as emphasizing objectivity, data, elementism, concrete mechanisms, nomothesis, determinism, and scientific values. Dana (1993) holds that multicultural research and practice should emanate from a human science perspective characterized by the opposite of the foregoing terms: intuitive theory, holism, abstract concepts, idiography, indeterminism, and humanistic values. (p. 53)

Moreland believed that this dichotomy was a false one. Nevertheless, he argued that a balance of the two approaches was needed to understand cultural issues more completely. One of the advantages of cross-cultural psychology is that it challenges many of our preconceptions of psychology. It is often said that one learns much about one's own language when learning a foreign tongue. The analogy for psychology is clear.

Assessment in cross-cultural psychology emphasizes an understanding of the context in which assessment occurs. The notion that traditional understandings of testing and assessment have focused solely on the individual can be tested in this discipline. Cross-cultural and multicultural testing help us focus upon the broader systems of which the individual is but a part.

Hambleton (1994) stated:

> The common error is to be rather casual about the test adaptation process, and then interpret the score differences among the samples or populations as if they were real. This mindless disregard of test translation problems and the need to validate instruments In the cultures where they are used has seriously undermined the results from many cross cultural studies. (p. 242)

This chapter has shown that tests that are adapted for use in different languages and cultures need to be studied for equivalence. Adequate cross-cultural measurement requires sophisticated translation techniques and an evaluation of the effectiveness of the translation. There are a variety of types of equivalence: structural or construct equivalence, measurement unit equivalence, and scalar equivalence, in addition to construct nonequivalence. Avoiding construct inequivalence requires that those translating the test be aware of cultural issues in the original test, in the construct, in the target culture, and in the resultant target test. Structural or construct requires a relentless adherence to a construct-validation perspective and the conduct of research using data from both original and target tests. Metric equivalence, too, involves careful analyses of the test data. The requirements of scalar equivalence may not be met in many situations regardless of how much we would like to use scoring scales from the original test with the target test.

If equivalence is one side of the coin, then bias is the other. Construct bias, method bias, and item bias can all influence the usefulness of a test adaptation in detrimental ways. The need for construct-validation research on adapted measures is reiterated; there is no more critical point in this chapter. In addition, however, it is important to replicate the construct validation that had been found in the original culture with the original test or, better yet, to research the applicability of the construct in the additional cultures before even writing the assessment items. Factor analysis, multiple regression, and structural equation

modeling permit researchers to assess whether construct equivalence is achieved.

The future holds much promise for cross-cultural psychology and for testing and assessment within that subdiscipline of psychology. There will be an increase in the use of different forms of tests in both the research and the practice of psychology. In a shrinking world, it is clearer that many psychological constructs are likely to hold for individuals around the world, or at least throughout much of it. Knowledge of research from foreign settings and in foreign languages is much more accessible than in the recent past. Thus, researchers may take advantage of theoretical understandings, constructs, and their measurement from leaders all over the world. However, the potential to engage in inadequate research is also increasing with these changes.

In applied settings, companies such as Microsoft are already fostering a world in which tests (such as for software literacy) are available in dozens of languages. Costs of test development are so high that adaptation and translation of assessment materials can make the possibility of professional assessment in a target language cost effective even in developing nations, where the benefits of psychological testing are likely to be highest. That is, the reduced costs of adapting a measure rather than constructing it anew benefit the countries where a target language measure might be used. The search for psychological universals will continue, as will the search for cultural and language limitations on these characteristics. Psychological constructs, both of major import and of more minor significance, will continue to be found that do not generalize to different cultures. The fact that the world is shrinking because of advances in travel and communications does not mean that we should assume it is necessarily becoming more western—more American. To do so is, at best, pejorative.

These times are exciting, both historically and psychometrically. The costs in time and money to develop new tests in each culture are often prohibitive. Determination of those aspects of a construct that are universal and those that are culturally specific is critical. Good procedures for adapting tests are available, and the results of these efforts can be evaluated. Testing can help society, and there is no reason for any country to hoard good assessment devices. Through the adaptation procedures discussed in this chapter, they can be shared. In addition, through the deliberate and principled use of cross-cultural assessment, researchers and the public can gain valuable insights from cross-cultural comparisons in situations where the evidence for equivalence supports such comparisons.

# APPENDIX

## Context

C.1 Effects of cultural differences which are not relevant or important to the main purposes of the study should be minimized to the extent possible.

C.2 The amount of overlap in the construct measured by the test or instrument in the populations of interest should be assessed.

## Test Development and Adaptation

D.1 Test developers/publishers should insure that the adaptation process takes full account of linguistic and cultural differences among the populations for whom adapted versions of the test or instrument are intended.

D.2 Test developers/publishers should provide evidence that the language use in the directions, rubrics, and items themselves as well as in the handbook are appropriate for all cultural and language populations for whom the test or instrument is intended.

D.3 Test developers/publishers should provide evidence that the choice of testing techniques, item formats, test conventions, and procedures are familiar to all intended populations.

D.4 Test developers/publishers should provide evidence that item content and stimulus materials are familiar to all intended populations.

D.5 Test developers/publishers should implement systematic judgmental evidence, both linguistic and psychological, to improve the accuracy of the adaptation process and compile evidence on the equivalence of all language versions.

D.6 Test developers/publishers should ensure that the data collection design permits the use of appropriate statistical techniques to establish item equivalence between the different language versions of the test or instrument.

D.7 Test developers/publishers should apply appropriate statistical techniques to (1) establish the equivalence of the different versions of the test or instrument, and (2) identify problematic components or aspects of the test or instrument which may be inadequate to one or more of the intended populations.

D.8 Test developers/publishers should provide information on the evaluation of validity in all target populations for whom the adapted versions are intended.

D.9 Test developers/publishers should provide statistical evidence of the equivalence of questions for all intended populations.

D.10 Non-equivalent questions between versions intended for different populations should not be used in preparing a common scale or in comparing these populations. However, they may be useful in enhancing content validity of scores reported for each population separately.

## Administration

A.1 Test developers and administrators should try to anticipate the types of problems that can be expected, and take appropriate actions to remedy these problems through the preparation of appropriate materials and instructions.

A.2 Test administrators should be sensitive to a number of factors related to the stimulus materials, administration procedures, and response modes that can moderate the validity of the inferences drawn from the scores.

A.3 Those aspects of the environment that influence the administration of a test or instrument should be made as similar as possible across populations of interest.

A.4 Test administration instructions should be in the source and target languages to minimize the influence of unwanted sources of variation across populations.

A.5 The test manual should specify all aspects of the administration that require scrutiny in a new cultural context.

A.6 The administrator should be unobtrusive and the administrator-examinee interaction should be minimized. Explicit rules that are described in the manual for administration should be followed.

## Documentation/Score Interpretations

I.1 When a test or instrument is adapted for use in another population, documentation of the changes should be provided, along with evidence of the equivalence.

I.2 Score differences among samples of populations administered the test or instrument should not be taken at face value. The researcher has the responsibility to substantiate the differences with other empirical evidence.

I.3 Comparisons across populations can only be made at the level of invariance that has been established for the scale on which scores are reported.

I.4 The test developer should provide specific information on the ways in which the socio-cultural and ecological contexts of the populations might affect performance, and should suggest procedures to account for these effects in the interpretation of results.

# REFERENCES

Allalouf, A. (2003). Revising translated differential item functioning items as a tool for improving cross-lingual assessment. *Applied Measurement in Education, 16*(1), 55–73.

Allalouf, A., Hambleton, R. K., & Sireci, S. G. (1999). Identifying the causes of DIF in translated verbal items. *Journal of Educational Measurement, 36,* 185–198.

Allen, J., & Walsh, J. A. (2000). A construct-based approach to equivalence: Methodologies for cross-cultural/multicultural personality assessment research. In R. H. Dana (Ed.), *Handbook of cross-cultural and multicultural personality assessment* (pp. 63–85). Mahwah, NJ: Erlbaum.

Anastasi, A., & Urbina, S. (1997). *Psychological testing* (7th ed.). Upper Saddle River, NJ: Prentice Hall.

Angoff, W. H., & Cook, L. L. (1988). *Equating the scores of the "Prueba de Aptitud Academica" and the "Scholastic Aptitude Test"* (Report No. 88–2). New York, NY: College Entrance Examination Board.

Ben-Porath, Y. S. (1990). Cross-cultural assessment of personality: The case of replicatory factor analysis. In J. N. Butcher & C. D. Spielberger (Eds.), *Advances in personality assessment* (Vol. 8, pp. 27–48). Hillsdale, NJ: Erlbaum.

Berry, J. W. (1980). Introduction to methodology. In H. C. Triandis & J. W. Berry (Eds.), *Handbook of cross-cultural psychology* (Vol. 2, pp. 1–28). Boston, MA: Allyn & Bacon.

Berry, J. W. (1997). Preface. In J. W. Berry, Y. H. Poortinga, & J. Padney (Eds.), *Handbook of cross-cultural psychology* (2nd ed., Vol. 1, pp. x–xv). Boston, MA: Allyn & Bacon.

Berry, J. W., & Sam, D. (1997). Acculturation and adaptation. In J. W. Berry, Y. H. Poortinga, & J. Padney (Eds.), *Handbook of cross-cultural psychology* (2nd ed., Vol. 3, pp. 291–326). Boston, MA: Allyn & Bacon.

Billiet, J. (2003). Cross-cultural equivalence with structural equation modeling. In J. A. Harkness, F. J. R. van de Vijver, and P. Ph. Mohler (Eds.), *Cross-cultural survey methods* (pp. 247–263). Hoboken, NJ: Wiley.

Boehnke, K., Lietz, P., Schreier, M., & Wilhlem, A. (2011). Sampling: The selection of cases for culturally comparative psychological research. In D. Matsumoto & F. J. R. van de Vijver (Eds.), *Cross-cultural research methods in psychology* (pp. 101–129). New York, NY: Cambridge University Press.

Bracken, B. A., Naglieri, J., & Bardos, A. (1999, May). *Nonverbal assessment of intelligence: An alternative to test translation and adaptation.* Paper presented at the International Conference on Test Adaptation, Washington, DC.

Brislin, R. W. (1970). Back translation for cross-cultural research. *Journal of Cross-Cultural Psychology, 1,* 185–216.

Brislin, R. W. (1980). Translation and content analysis of oral and written material. In H. C. Triandis & J. W. Berry (Eds.), *Handbook of cross-cultural psychology, Vol. 2: Methodology* (pp. 389–444). Needham Heights, MA: Allyn & Bacon.

Brislin, R. W. (1986). The wording and translation of research instruments. In W. J. Lonner & J. W. Berry (Eds.), *Field methods in cross-cultural research* (pp. 137–164). Newberry Park, CA: Sage.

Brislin, R. W. (1993). *Understanding culture's influence on behavior.* New York, NY: Harcourt Brace.

Brown, T. A. (2006). *Confirmatory factor analysis for applied research.* New York, NY: Guilford Press.

Budgell, G. R., Raju, N. S. & Quartetti, D. A. (1995). Analysis of differential item functioning in translated assessment instruments. *Applied Psychological Measurement, 19,* 309–321.

Butcher, J. N. (1996). Translation and adaptation of the MMPI-2 for international use. In J. N. Butcher (Ed.), *International adaptations of the MMPI-2* (pp. 393–411). Minneapolis: University of Minnesota Press.

Butcher, J. N., Cabiya, J., Lucio, E., & Garrido, M. (2007). *Assessing Hispanic clients using the MMPI-2 and MMPI-A.* Washington, DC: American Psychological Association.

Butcher, J. N., & Han, K. (1998). Methods of establishing cross-cultural equivalence. In J. N. Butcher (Ed.), *International adaptations of the MMPI-2: Research and clinical applications* (pp. 44–63). Minneapolis: University of Minnesota Press.

Butcher, J. N., & Pancheri, P. (1976). *A handbook of cross-cultural MMPI research.* Minneapolis, MN: University of Minnesota Press.

Cabassa, L. (2003). Acculturation: Where we are and where we need to go. *Hispanic Journal of Behavioral Sciences, 25,* 127–146.

Campbell, D. T., & Fiske, D. W. (1959). Convergent and discriminant validity by the multitrait-multimethod matrix. *Psychological Bulletin, 56,* 81–105.

Cattell, R. B. (1940). A culture-free intelligence test. *Journal of Educational Psychology, 31,* 176–199.

Cattell, R. B. (1963). Theory of fluid and crystallized intelligence: A critical experiment. *Journal of Educational Psychology, 54,* 1–22.

Cattell, R. B., & Cattell, A. K. S. (1963). *A culture-fair intelligence test.* Champaign, IL: Institute for Personality and Ability Testing.

Cole, M., & Bruner, J. S. (1971). Cultural differences and inferences about psychological processes. *American Psychologist, 26,* 867–876.

Cook, L. L., & Schmitt-Cascallar, A. P. (2005). Establishing score comparability for tests given in different languages. In R. K. Hambleton, P. F. Merenda, & C. D. Spielberger (Eds.), *Adapting educational and psychological tests for cross-cultural assessment* (pp. 139–169). Mahwah, NJ: Erlbaum.

Cronbach, L. J., & Meehl, P. E. (1955). Construct validity in psychological tests. *Psychological Bulletin, 52,* 281–302.

Cuellar, I. (2000). Acculturation as a moderator of personality and psychological assessment. In R. H. Dana (Ed.), *Handbook of cross-cultural and multicultural personality assessment* (pp. 113–130). Mahwah, NJ: Erlbaum.

Cummins, J. (2000). *Language, power, and pedagogy: Bilingual children in the crossfire.* Bristol, UK: Multilingual Matters.

Dana, R. H. (2005). *Multicultural assessment: Principles, applications, and examples.* Mahwah, NJ: Erlbaum.

Domino, G. (2000). *Psychological testing. An introduction.* Upper Saddle River, NJ: Prentice Hall.

Drasgow, F., & Probst, T. M. (2005) The psychometrics of adaptation: Evaluating measurement equivalence across languages and cultures. In R. K. Hambleton, P. F. Merenda, & C. D. Spielberger (Eds.), *Adapting educational and psychological tests for cross-cultural assessment* (pp. 171–192). Mahwah, NJ: Erlbaum.

Embretson, S. E. (1983). Construct validity: Construct representation versus nomothetic span. *Psychological Bulletin, 93,* 179–193.

Ercikan, K. (2002). Disentangling sources of differential item functioning in multilanguage assessments. *International Journal of Testing, 2*(3&4), 199–215.

Fabrigar, L. R., Wegener, D. T., MacCallum, R. C., & Strahan, E. J. (1999). Evaluating the use of exploratory factor analysis in psychological research. *Psychological Methods, 4,* 272–299.

Flanagan, D. P., Ortiz, S. O., & Alfonso, V. C. (2007). *Essentials of cross-battery assessment* (2nd ed.). Hoboken, NJ: Wiley.

Flaugher, R. J. (1978). The many definitions of test bias. *American Psychologist, 33,* 671–679.

Fischer, R., & Fontaine, J. R. J. (2011). Methods for investigating structural equivalence. In D. Matsumoto & F. J. R. van de Vijver (Eds.), *Cross-cultural research methods in psychology* (pp. 179–215). New York, NY: Cambridge University Press.

Geisinger, K. F. (1992). Fairness and selected psychometric issues in the psychological assessment of Hispanics. In K. F. Geisinger (Ed.), *Psychological testing of Hispanics* (pp. 17–42). Washington, DC: American Psychological Association.

Geisinger, K. F. (1994). Cross-cultural normative assessment: Translation and adaptation issues influencing the normative interpretation of assessment instruments. *Psychological Assessment, 6,* 304–312.

Geisinger, K. F. (2002). Testing the members of an increasingly diverse society. In J. F. Carlson & B. B. Waterman (Eds.), *Social and personal assessment of school-aged children: Developing interventions for educational and clinical use* (pp. 349–364). Boston, MA: Allyn & Bacon.

Geisinger, K. F. (2003). Testing and assessment in cross-cultural psychology. In J. R. Graham & J. A. Naglieri (Eds.), *Handbook of psychology, Volume 10: Assessment psychology* (pp. 95–117). Hoboken, NJ: Wiley.

Geisinger, K. F., & Carlson, J. F. (1998). Training psychologists to assess members of a diverse society. In J. Sandoval, C. L. Frisby, K. F. Geisinger, J. D. Schueneman & J. R. Grenier (Eds.), *Test interpretation and diversity: Achieving equity in assessment* (pp. 375–386). Washington, DC: American Psychological Association.

Häder, S., & Gabler, S. (2003). Sampling and estimation. In J. A. Harkness, F. J. R. van de Vijver, and P. Ph. Mohler (Eds.), *Cross-cultural survey methods* (pp. 117–134). Hoboken, NJ: Wiley.

Hambleton, R. K. (1994). Guidelines for adapting educational and psychological tests: A progress report. *European Journal of Psychological Assessment, 10,* 229–244.

Hambleton, R. K. (2005). Issues, designs, and technical guidelines for adapting tests in multiple languages and cultures. In R. K. Hambleton, P. F. Merenda, & C. D. Spielberger (Eds.) *Adapting educational and psychological tests for cross-cultural assessment* (pp. 3–38). Mahwah, NJ: Erlbaum.

Hambleton, R. K., Merenda, P. F., & Spielberger, C. D. (Eds.) (2005) *Adapting educational and psychological tests for cross-cultural assessment*. Mahwah, NJ: Erlbaum.

Hambleton, R. K., & Zenisky, A. L. (2011). Translating and adapting tests for cross-cultural assessments. In D. Matsumoto & F. J. R. van de Vijver (Eds.), *Cross-cultural research methods in psychology* (pp. 46–70). New York, NY: Cambridge University Press.

Handel, R. W., & Ben-Porath, Y. S. (2000). Multicultural assessment with the MMPI-2: Issues for research and practice. In R. H. Dana (Ed.), *Handbook of cross-cultural and multicultural personality assessment* (pp. 229–245). Mahwah, NJ: Erlbaum.

Harkness, J. A. (2003). Questionnaire translation. In J. A. Harkness, F. J. R. van de Vijver, and P. Ph. Mohler (Eds.), *Cross-cultural survey methods* (pp. 35–56). Hoboken, NJ: Wiley.

Harkness, J. A., van de Vijver, F. J. R., & Johnson, T. P. (2003). Questionnaire design in comparative resarch. In J. A. Harkness, F. J. R. van de Vijver, and P. Ph. Mohler (Eds.), *Cross-cultural survey methods* (pp. 19–34). Hoboken, NJ: Wiley.

Harzing, A. (2006). Response styles in cross-national survey research: A 26-country study. *Journal of Cross Cultural Management, 6,* 243–266.

Helms, J. E. (1992). Why is there no study of cultural equivalence in standardized cognitive ability testing? *American Psychologist, 47,* 1083–1101.

Holland, P. W., & Wainer, H. (Eds.). (1993). *Differential item functioning.* Hillsdale, NJ: Erlbaum.

Hulin, C. L. (1987). A psychometric theory of evaluations of item and scale translations: Fidelity across languages. *Journal of Cross-Cultural Psychology, 18,* 721–735.

International Test Commission. (2010). *International Test Commission guidelines for translating and adapting tests.* Retrieved from www.intestcom.org

Judd, T., et al. (2009). Professional considerations for improving the neuropsychological evaluation of Hispanics: NAN education paper. *Archives of Clinical Neuropsychology, 24,* 127–135.

Kamin, L. J. (1974). *The science and politics of IQ.* Potomac, MD: Erlbaum.

Kranzler, J. H., Flores, C. G., & Coady, M. (2010). Examination of the cross-battery approach for the cognitive assessment of children and youth from diverse linguistic and cultural backgrounds. *School Psychology Review, 39,* 431–446.

Keitel, M. A., Kopala, M., & Adamson, W. S. (1996). Ethical issues in multicultural assessment. In L. A. Suzuki, P. J. Meller, & J. G. Ponterotto (Eds.), *Handbook of multicultural assessment: Clinical, psychological and educational applications* (pp. 2848). San Francisco, CA: Jossey-Bass.

Kim, S. H., Cohen, A. S., & Park, T. H. (1995). Detection of differential item functioning in multiple groups. *Journal of Educational Measurement, 32,* 261–276.

Kline, R. B. (2010). *Principles and practice of structural equation modeling* (3rd ed.). New York, NY: Guilford Press.

Kolen, M. J., & Brennan, D. B. (2004). *Test equating, scaling, and linking: Methods and practices* (2nd ed.). New York, NY: Springer.

Kranzler, J. H., Flores, C. G., & Coady, M. (2010). Examination of the cross-battery approach for the cognitive assessment of children and youth from diverse linguistic and cultural backgrounds. *School Psychology Review, 39,* 431–446.

Lonner, W. J. (1979). Issues in cross-cultural psychology. In A. J. Marsella, R. Tharp, & T. Ciborowski (Eds.), *Perspectives on cross-cultural psychology* (pp. 17–45). New York, NY: Academic Press.

Maldonado, C. Y., & Geisinger, K. F. (2005). Conversion of the Wechsler Adult Intelligence Scale into Spanish: An early test adaptation effort of considerable consequence. In R. K. Hambleton, P. E. Merenda, & C. D. Spielberger (Eds.), *Adapting educational and psychological tests for cross-cultural assessment* (pp. 213–234). Hillsdale, NJ: Erlbaum.

Malgady, R. G. (1996). The question of cultural bias in assessment and diagnosis of ethnic minority clients: Let's reject the null hypothesis. *Professional Psychology: Research and Practice, 27,* 33–73.

Marin, G. (1992). Issues in the measurement of acculturation among Hispanics. In K. F. Geisinger (Ed.), *The psychological testing of Hispanics* (pp. 235–272). Washington, DC: American Psychological Association.

McQueen, J., & Mendelovits, J. (2003). PISA reading: Cultural equivalence in a cross-cultural study. *Language Testing, 20*(2), 208–224.

Messick, S. (1989). Validity. In R. L. Linn (Ed.), *Educational measurement* (3rd ed., pp. 13–104). New York, NY: American Council on Education/Macmillan.

Moreland, K. L. (1996). Persistent issues in multicultural assessment of social and emotional functioning. In L. A. Suzuki, P. J. Meller, & J. G. Ponterotto (Eds.), *Handbook of multicultural assessment: Clinical, psychological and educational applications* (pp. 51–76). San Francisco, CA: Jossey-Bass.

Mpofu, E., & Ortiz, S. O. (2009) Equitable assessment practices in diverse contexts. In E. L. Grigorenko (Ed.), *Multicultural psychoeducational assessment* (pp. 41–76). New York, NY: Springer.

Nichols, D. S., Padilla, J., & Gomez-Maqueo, E. L. (2000). Issues in the cross-cultural adaptation and use of the MMPI-2. In R. H. Dana (Ed.), *Handbook of cross-cultural and multicultural personality assessment* (pp. 247–266). Mahwah, NJ: Erlbaum.

O'Brien, M. L. (1992). A Rasch approach to scaling issues in testing Hispanics. In K. F. Geisinger (Ed.), *Psychological testing of Hispanics* (pp. 43–54). Washington, DC: American Psychological Association.

Padilla, A. M. (2001). Issues in culturally appropriate assessment. In L. A. Suzuki, & J. G. Ponterotto, & P. J. Meller (Eds.), *Handbook of multicultural assessment: Clinical, psychological and educational applications* (2nd ed., pp. 3–28). San Francisco, CA: Jossey-Bass.

Padilla, A. M., & Medina, A. (1996). Cross-cultural sensitivity in assessment: Using tests in culturally appropriate ways. In L. A. Suzuki, P. J. Meller, & J. G. Ponterotto (Eds.), *Handbook of multicultural assessment: Clinical, psychological and educational applications* (pp. 3–28). San Francisco, CA: Jossey-Bass.

Pennock-Roman, M. (1992). Interpreting test performance in selective admissions for Hispanic students. In K. F. Geisinger (Ed.), *The psychological testing of Hispanics* (pp. 99–136). Washington, DC: American Psychological Association.

Pike, K. L. (1967). *Language in relation to a unified theory of the structure of human behavior*. The Hague, The Netherlands: Mouton.

Ritzier, B. A. (1996). Projective techniques for multicultural personality assessment: Rorschach, TEMAS and the Early Memories Procedure. In L. A. Suzuki, P. J. Meller, & J. G. Ponterotto (Eds.), *Handbook of multicultural assessment: Clinical, psychological and educational applications* (pp. 115–136). San Francisco, CA: Jossey-Bass.

Sackett, P. R., Hardison, C. M., & Cullen, M. J. (2004). On interpreting stereotype threat as accounting for African American-White differences on cognitive tests. *American Psychologist, 59,* 7–13.

Sandoval, J. (1998). Test interpretation in a diverse future. In J. Sandoval, C. L. Frisby, K. F. Geisinger, J. D. Schueneman, & J. R. Grenier (Eds.), *Test interpretation and diversity: Achieving equity in assessment* (pp. 387–402). Washington, DC: American Psychological Association.

Sandoval, J., & Durán, R. P. (1998). Language. In J. Sandoval, C. L. Frisby, K. F. Geisinger, J. D. Schueneman, & J. R. Grenier (Eds.), *Test interpretation and diversity: Achieving equity in assessment* (pp. 181–211). Washington, DC: American Psychological Association.

Sattler, J. M. (1992). *Assessment of children* (revised and updated 3rd ed.). San Diego, CA: Author.

Schmitt, A. P. (1988). Language and cultural characteristics that explain differential item functioning for Hispanic examinees on the Scholastic Aptitude Test. *Journal of Educational Measurement, 25,* 1–13.

Sireci, S. G. (1997). Problems and issues in linking assessments across languages. *Educational Measurement: Issues and Practice, 16,* 12–17.

Sireci, S. G., (2005). Using bilinguals to evaluate the comparability of different language versions of a test. In R. K. Hambleton, P. F. Merenda, & C. D. Spielberger (Eds.), *Adapting educational and psychological tests for cross-cultural assessment* (pp. 117–138). Mahwah, NJ: Erlbaum.

Sireci, S. G. (2011). Evaluating test and survey items for bias across languages and cultures. In D. Matsumoto & F. J. R. van de Vijver (Eds.) *Cross-cultural research methods in psychology* (pp. 216–240). New York, NY: Cambridge University Press.

Sireci, S. G., Patsula, L., & Hambleton, R. (2005). Statistical methods for identifying flaws in the test adaptation process. In In R. K. Hambleton, P. F. Merenda, & C. D. Spielberger (Eds.) *Adapting educational and psychological tests for cross-cultural assessment* (pp. 171–192). Mahwah, NJ: Erlbaum.

Smith, T. (2003). Developing comparable questions in cross-national surveys. In J. A. Harkness, F. J. R. van de Vijver, and P. Ph. Mohler (Eds.), *Cross-cultural survey methods* (pp. 69–91). Hoboken, NJ: Wiley.

Smith, A. L., Hays, J. R., & Solway, K. S. (1977). Comparison of the WISC-R and Culture Fair Intelligence Test in a juvenile delinquent population. *Journal of Psychology, 77,* 179–182.

Solano-Flores, G., Backhoff, E., Contreras-Niño, L. A. (2009). Theory of test translation error. *International Journal of Testing, 9,* 78–91.

Steele, C. M. (1997). A threat in the air: How stereotypes shape intellectual identity and performance. *American Psychologist, 52,* 613–629.

Steele, C. M., & Aronson, J. (1995). Stereotype threat and the intellectual test performance of African Americans. *Journal of Personality and Social Psychology, 69,* 797–811.

Sue, S., Keefe, K., Enomoto, K., Durvasula, R., & Chao, R. (1996). Asian American and White college students' performance on the MMPI-2. In J. N. Butcher (Ed.), *International adaptations of the MMPI-2: Research and clinical applications* (pp. 206–220). Minneapolis: University of Minnesota Press.

Suzuki, L. A., Vraniak, D. A., & Kugler, J. F. (1996). Intellectual assessment across cultures. In L. A. Suzuki, P. J. Meller, & J. G. Ponterotto (Eds.), *Handbook of multicultural assessment: Clinical, psychological and educational applications* (pp. 141–178). San Francisco, CA: Jossey-Bass.

Tanzer, N. K. (2005). Developing tests for use in multiple languages and cultures: A plea for simultaneous development. In R. K. Hambleton, P. F. Merenda, & C. D. Spielberger (Eds.), *Adapting educational and psychological tests for cross-cultural assessment* (pp. 235–263). Mahwah, NJ: Erlbaum.

Tanzer, N. K., Gittler, G., & Sim, C. Q. E. (1994). Cross-cultural validation of item complexity in an LLTM-calibrated spatial ability test. *European Journal of Psychological Assessment, 11,* 170–183.

Triandis. H. C., Malpass, R. S., & Davidson, A. (1971). Cross-cultural psychology. In B. J. Siegel (Ed.), *Biennial review of anthropology* (pp. 1–84). Palo Alto, CA: Annual Reviews.

van de Vijver, F. J. R. (2000). The nature of bias. In R. H. Dana (Ed.), *Handbook of cross-cultural and multicultural personality assessment* (pp. 87–106). Mahwah, NJ: Erlbaum.

van de Vijver, F. J. R., & Leung, K. (1997a). *Methods and data analysis for cross-cultural research*. Thousand Oaks, CA: Sage.

van de Vijver, F. J. R., & Leung, K. (1997b). Methods and data analysis of comparative research. In J. W. Berry, Y. H. Poortinga, & J. Padney (Eds.), *Handbook of cross-cultural psychology* (2nd ed., Vol. 1, pp. 257–300). Boston, MA: Allyn & Bacon.

van de Vijver, F. J. R., & Leung, K. (2011). Equivalence and bias: A review of concepts, models, and data analytic procedures. In D. Matsumoto & F. J. R. van de Vijver (Eds.), *Cross-cultural research methods in psychology* (pp. 17–45). New York, NY: Cambridge University Press.

van de Vijver, F. J. R., & Poortinga, Y. H. (1982). Cross-cultural generalization and universality. *Journal of Cross-Cultural Psychology, 13,* 387–408.

van de Vijver, F. J. R., & Poortinga, Y. H. (2005). Conceptual and methodological issues in adapting tests. In R. K. Hambleton, P. F. Merenda, & C. D. Spielberger (Eds.), *Adapting educational and psychological tests for cross-cultural assessment* (pp. 39–63). Mahwah, NJ: Erlbaum.

Werner, O., & Campbell, D. T. (1970). Translating, working through interpreters, and the problem of decentering. In R. Narroll & R. Cohen (Eds.), *A handbook of cultural anthropology* (pp. 398–419). New York, NY: American Museum of Natural History.

Yansen, E. A., & Shulman, E. L. (1996). Language testing: Multicultural considerations. In L. A. Suzuki, P. J. Meller, & J. G. Ponterotto (Eds.). *Handbook of multicultural assessment: Clinical, psychological and educational applications* (pp. 353–394). San Francisco, CA: Jossey-Bass.

# CHAPTER 6

# Psychological Assessment in Treatment

MARK E. MARUISH

Society's need for behavioral health-care services provides an opportunity for trained providers of mental health and substance abuse services to become part of the solution to a major health-care problem. Each of the behavioral health professions has the potential to make a particular contribution to this solution. Not the least of these contributions are those that can be made by clinical psychologists. The use of psychological tests in the assessment of the human condition is one of the hallmarks of clinical psychology. The training and acquired level of expertise in psychological testing distinguishes the clinical psychologist from other behavioral health-care professionals. Indeed, expertise in test-based psychological assessment can be said to be *the* unique contribution that clinical psychologists make to the behavioral health-care field.

For decades, clinical psychologists and other behavioral health-care providers have come to rely on psychological assessment as a standard tool to be used with other sources of information for diagnostic and treatment planning purposes as well as for several other purposes. (See Meyer et al., 2001.) However, changes that have taken place during the past several years in the delivery of

health care in general and behavioral health-care services in particular have led to changes in the way in which third-party payers and clinical psychologists themselves think about and use psychological assessment in day-to-day clinical practice. Some have questioned the value of psychological assessment in the current time-limited, capitated service delivery arena, where the focus has changed from clinical priorities to fiscal priorities (Schaefer, Murphy, Westerveld, & Gewirtz, 2000; Sederer, Dickey, & Hermann, 1996). Others argue that it is in just such an arena that the benefits of psychological assessment can be most fully realized and contribute significantly to the delivery of cost-effective treatment for behavioral health disorders (Maruish, 2004). Consequently, psychological assessment could assist the health-care industry in appropriately controlling or reducing the utilization and cost of health care over the long term.

Psychological assessment has had to face many challenges over the past several decades. But as Butcher (2006) has noted, the continued use of psychological tests and assessment has been supported by many developments. These include:

- the recognition of how psychotherapy can be enhanced through therapeutic assessment techniques (Finn, 2007; see "Therapeutic Assessment Process" section);
- an important demonstration of the comparability of the validity and reliability of psychological test results

---

Portions adapted from M. E. Maruish (1999a) with permission from Erlbaum. Portions adapted from M. E. Maruish (1999b) with permission from Elsevier Science. Portions adapted from M. E. Maruish (2002b) with permission from Erlbaum.

with those of most medical results in medical settings (Meyer et al., 2001);

- the availability of many well-researched personality inventories, formal behavioral assessment methods, and behavioral rating scales;
- the availability and acceptance of computer-based psychological testing; and
- a broadening of the use of psychological testing to other applied settings such as forensic and personnel selection settings.

In developing this chapter for the first edition of this *Handbook,* I intended to provide students and practitioners of clinical psychology with an overview of how psychological assessment can be used in the treatment of behavioral health problems. In doing so, I discussed how psychological assessment is currently being used in the therapeutic environment and the many ways in which it might be used to the ultimate benefit of patients. In this second edition of the *Handbook,* I present an update to my original discussion, incorporating pertinent new research and thinking that has occurred during the past decade.

As a final introductory note, it is important for the reader to understand that the term *psychological assessment,* as it is used in this chapter, refers to the evaluation of a patient's mental health status using psychological tests or related instrumentation. Implicit here is the use of additional information from patient or collateral interviews, review of medical or other records, or other sources of relevant information about the patient as part of this evaluation, as has been described by numerous others (e.g., Groth-Marnat, 2009; Hunsley, 2009; Meyer et al., 2001; Smith & Archer, 2008).

## PSYCHOLOGICAL ASSESSMENT AS A TREATMENT ADJUNCT: AN OVERVIEW

In the past, the role of psychological assessment in therapeutic settings had been quite limited. Those who did not receive their clinical training within the past couple of decades were probably taught that the value of psychological assessment is found only at the front end of treatment. That is, they probably were instructed in the power and utility of psychological assessment as a means of assisting in the identification of symptoms and their severity, personality characteristics, and other aspects of the individual (e.g., intelligence, vocational interests) that are important in understanding and describing the patient at a specific point in time. Based on these data

and information obtained from patient and collateral interviews, medical records, and the individual's stated goals for treatment, a diagnostic impression was given and a treatment plan was formulated and placed in the patient's chart, to be reviewed, it is hoped, at various points during the course of treatment. In some cases, the patient's treatment was assigned to another practitioner within the same organization or referred out, with the patient never to be seen or contacted again, much less be reassessed by the one who performed the original assessment.

Fortunately, over the past several years, psychological assessment has come to be recognized for more than just its usefulness at the beginning of treatment. Consequently, its utility has been extended beyond being a mere tool for describing an individual's current state, to a means of facilitating the treatment and understanding behavioral health-care problems throughout and beyond the episode of care. There are now many commercially available and public domain measures that can be employed as tools to assist in clinical decision making, treatment monitoring, outcomes assessment, and, more directly, as a treatment technique in and of itself. Each of these uses contributes value to the therapeutic process.

## Psychological Assessment for Clinical Decision Making

Traditionally, psychological assessment has been used to assist psychologists and other behavioral health-care clinicians in making important clinical decisions. The types of decision making for which it has been used include those related to screening, diagnosis, treatment planning, and monitoring of treatment progress. Generally, screening may be undertaken to assist in either (a) identifying the patient's need for a particular service or (b) determining the likely presence of a particular disorder or other behavioral/emotional problems. More often than not, a positive finding on screening leads to a more extensive evaluation of the patient in order to confirm with greater certainty the existence of the problem or to further delineate the nature of the problem. The value of screening lies in the fact that it permits the clinician to quickly identify, with a fairly high degree of confidence, those who are likely to need care or at least require further evaluation.

Psychological assessment has long been used to obtain information necessary to determine the diagnoses of mental health patients. It may be used routinely for diagnostic purposes or to obtain information that can assist in differentiating one possible diagnosis from another in cases that present particularly complicated pictures. Indeed, even under current restrictions, managed care companies are likely to authorize payment for psychological assessment when a diagnostic question impedes the development of an appropriate treatment plan for one of its health plan members (United Behavioral Health, 2010).

In many instances, psychological assessment is performed in order to obtain information that is deemed useful in the development of a patient-specific treatment plan. Typically, this type of information is not easily (if at all) accessible through other means or sources. When combined with other information about the patient, information obtained from a psychological assessment can aid in understanding him or her, identifying the most important problems and issues that need to be addressed, and formulating recommendations about the best means of addressing them.

Another way psychological assessment plays a valuable role in clinical decision making is through treatment monitoring. Repeated assessment of the patient at regular intervals during the treatment episode can provide the clinician with valuable feedback regarding therapeutic progress, as has been demonstrated in several studies by Lambert and his colleagues. (See Lambert, 2010.) Depending on the findings, the therapist will be encouraged either to continue with the current therapeutic approach or, in the case of no change or an exacerbation of the problem, to modify or abandon the approach in favor of an alternate one.

### Psychological Assessment for Outcomes Assessment

Currently, one common reason for conducting psychological assessment in the United States is to assess the outcomes of behavioral health-care treatment. The initial interest in and focus on outcomes assessment can probably be traced to the continuous quality improvement (CQI) movement that was first implemented in business and industrial settings. The impetus for the movement was a desire to produce quality products in the most efficient manner, resulting in increased revenues and decreased costs.

In health care, outcomes assessment has multiple purposes, not the least of which is as a tool for marketing the care provider's or organization's services. Providers or organizations vying for lucrative contracts from third-party payers may be asked to present outcomes data demonstrating the effectiveness of their services. Equally important are data that demonstrate patient satisfaction with the services they have received. However, perhaps the most important potential use of outcomes data within provider organizations (although it is not always recognized as such) is the knowledge it can yield about what works and what does not. In this regard, outcomes data can serve as a means for ongoing evaluation of the quality of the treatment the clinician or organization provides. It is the knowledge obtained from outcomes data that, if acted on, can lead to improvement in the services the provider or organization offers. When used in this manner, outcomes assessment can become an integral component of an organization's CQI initiative.

More important, for the individual patient, outcomes assessment provides a means of objectively demonstrating how much improvement he or she has made from the time of treatment initiation to the time of treatment termination and in some cases extending to some time after termination. Feedback to this effect may serve to instill in the patient greater self-confidence and self-esteem or a more realistic view of where he or she is (from a psychological standpoint) at that point in time. It also may serve as an objective indicator to the patient of the need for continued treatment.

### Psychological Assessment as a Treatment Technique

The degree to which the patient is involved in the assessment process has changed. One reason for this can be found in the most recent revision of the ethical standards of the American Psychological Association (2002). This revision includes a mandate for psychologists to provide feedback to clients whom they assess. According to ethical standard 9.10, "psychologists take reasonable steps to ensure that explanations of results are given to the individual or designated representative unless the nature of the relationship precludes provision of an explanation of results" (p. 1072).

Finn and Tonsager (1992) offered other reasons for the interest in providing patients with assessment feedback. These include the recognition of patients' right to see their medical and psychiatric health-care records as well as clinically and research-based findings and impressions that suggest that *therapeutic assessment* (see "Therapeutic Assessment Process" section) facilitates patient care. Finn and Tonsager also referred to Finn and Butcher's (1991) summary of potential benefits that may accrue from providing test results feedback to patients about their results. These include increased feelings of self-esteem and hope, reduced symptomatology and feelings of isolation, increased self-understanding and self-awareness, and increased motivation to seek or be more actively involved in their mental health treatment. In addition, Finn and

Martin (1997) noted that the therapeutic assessment process provides a model for relationships that can result in increased mutual respect, lead to increased feelings of mastery and control, and decrease feelings of alienation.

Therapeutic use of assessment generally involves a presentation of assessment results (including assessment materials such as test protocols, profile forms, and other assessment summary materials) directly to the patient; an elicitation of the patient's reactions to them; and an in-depth discussion of the meaning of the results in terms of patient-defined assessment goals. In essence, assessment data can serve as a catalyst for the therapeutic encounter via (a) the objective feedback that is provided to the patient, (b) the patient self-assessment that is stimulated, and (c) the opportunity for patient and therapist to arrive at mutually agreed-on therapeutic goals.

The purpose of the foregoing was to present a broad overview of psychological assessment as a multipurpose behavioral health-care tool. Depending on the individual clinician or provider organization, psychological assessment may be employed for one or more of the purposes just described. The preceding overview should provide a context for better understanding the more in-depth and detailed discussion about each of these applications that follows.

## PSYCHOLOGICAL ASSESSMENT AS A TOOL FOR SCREENING AND DIAGNOSIS

One of the most apparent ways in which psychological assessment can contribute to economical and efficient behavioral health care is by using it to screen potential patients for the need of behavioral health-care services and to determine the likelihood that the problem identified is a particular disorder or problem of interest. Probably the most concise, informative treatment of the topic of the use of psychological tests in screening for behavioral health disorders is provided by Derogatis and Culpepper (2004). They clarified the nature and the use of screening procedures, stating that

> the screening process represents a relatively unrefined sieve that is designed to segregate the cohort under assessment into "positives," who presumably have the condition, and "negatives," who are ostensibly free of the disorder. Screening is not a diagnostic procedure per se. Rather, it represents a preliminary filtering operation that identifies those individuals with the highest probability of having the disorder in question for subsequent specific diagnostic evaluation. Individuals

found negative by the screening process are not evaluated further. (pp. 69–70)

The most important aspect of any screening procedure is the efficiency with which it can provide information useful to clinical decision making. In the area of clinical psychology, the most efficient and thoroughly investigated screening procedures involve the use of psychological assessment instruments. As implied by the preceding quotation, the power or utility of a psychological screener lies in its ability to determine, with a high level of probability, whether the respondent is or is not a member of a group with clearly defined characteristics. In daily clinical practice, the most commonly used screeners are those designed specifically to identify some aspect of psychological functioning or disturbance, or to provide a broad overview of the respondent's point-in-time mental status. Examples of screeners include the Beck Depression Inventory II (BDI-II; Beck, Steer, & Brown, 1996), the Symptom Checklist-90 Revised (SCL-90-R; Derogatis, 1994), and the Brief Symptom Inventory (BSI; Derogatis, 1992).

The establishment of a system for screening for a particular disorder or condition involves determining what it is one wants to screen in or screen out, at what level of probability one feels comfortable about making that decision, and how many incorrect classifications or what percentage of error one is willing to tolerate. Once one decides what one wishes to screen for, one must then turn to the instrument's classification efficiency statistics—sensitivity, specificity, positive predictive power (PPP), negative predictive power (NPP), and receiver operating characteristic (ROC) curves—for the information necessary to determine if a given instrument is suitable for the intended purpose(s). These statistics are discussed in detail elsewhere. (See Wasserman & Bracken, this volume.)

A note of caution is warranted when evaluating sensitivity, specificity, and the two predictive powers of a test. First, the cutoff score, index value, or other criterion used for classification can be adjusted to maximize either sensitivity or specificity. However, maximization of one will necessarily result in a decrease in the other, thus increasing the percentage of false positives (with maximized sensitivity) or false negatives (with maximized specificity). Second, unlike sensitivity and specificity, both PPP and NPP are affected and change according to the prevalence or base rate at which the condition or characteristic of interest (i.e., that which is being screened by the test) occurs within a given setting. As Elwood (1993) noted, the lowering of base rates results in lower PPPs, whereas increasing base rates results in higher PPPs. The opposite trend is true for NPPs. Elwood noted that this is an important consideration because clinical tests are frequently validated using samples in which the prevalence rate is .50, or 50%. Thus, it is not surprising to see a test's PPP drop in real-life clinical applications where the prevalence is lower.

## DIAGNOSIS

Key to the development of any effective plan of treatment for mental health and substance abuse patients is the ascertainment of an accurate diagnosis of the problem(s) for which the patient is seeking intervention. As in the past, assisting in the differential diagnosis of psychiatric disorders continues to be one of the major functions of psychological assessment (Meyer et al., 1998). As alluded to earlier, managed behavioral health-care organizations (MBHOs) are likely to authorize reimbursement of testing for this purpose when it "contributes necessary clinical information for differential diagnostic clarification" (United Behavioral Health, 2010, p. 2). Assessment with well-validated, reliable psychological test instruments can provide information that might otherwise be difficult (if not impossible) to obtain through psychiatric or collateral interviews, medical record reviews, or other clinical means. Obtaining this information is generally made possible through the inclusion of (a) test items representing diagnostic criteria from an accepted diagnostic classification system, such as the *Diagnostic and Statistical Manual of Mental Disorders, Fourth Edition, Text Revision* (*DSM-IV-TR*; American Psychiatric Association, 2000) or (b) scales that either alone or in combination with other scales have been empirically tied (directly or indirectly) to specific diagnoses or diagnostic groups.

In most respects, considerations related to the use of psychological testing for diagnostic purposes are the same as those related to their use for screening. In fact, information obtained from screening can be used to help determine the correct diagnosis for a given patient. As well, information from either source should be used only in conjunction with other clinical information to arrive at a diagnosis. The major difference between the two functions is that screening generally involves the use of a relatively brief instrument for the identification of patients with a specific diagnosis, a problem that falls within a specific diagnostic grouping (e.g., affective disorders), or a level of impairment that falls within a problematic range.

Moreover, it represents the first step in a process designed to separate those who do not exhibit indications of the problem being screened for from those with a higher probability of experiencing the target problem and thus warrant further evaluation for its presence. Diagnostic instruments such as those just described generally tend to be lengthier and to differentiate among multiple disorders or broad diagnostic groups (e.g., anxiety disorders versus affective disorders), or they are administered farther along in the evaluation process than is the case with screeners. In many cases, these instruments also allow for a formulation of description of personality functioning.

### Diagnosis-Specific Instruments

Many instruments are available that have been specifically designed to help identify individuals with disorders that meet a diagnostic classification system's criteria for the disorder(s). In the vast majority of the cases, these types of tests will be designed to detect individuals meeting the diagnostic criteria of *DSM-IV* or the 10th edition of the *International Classification of Diseases* (*ICD-10*; World Health Organization, 1992). Excellent examples of such instruments include: the Millon Clinical Multiaxial Inventory-III (MCMI-III; Millon, Millon, Davis, & Grossman, 2009); the Primary Care Evaluation of Mental Disorders (PRIME-MD; Hahn, Sydney, Kroenke, Williams, & Spitzer, 2004; Maruish, 2002b); the Patient Health Questionnaire (PHQ, the self-report version of the PRIME-MD; Hahn et al., 2004; Spitzer, Kroenke, Williams, & Patient Health Questionnaire Primary Care Study Group, 1999); and the Mini-International Neuropsychiatric Interview (MINI; Maruish, 2002b; Sheehan et al., 1998).

Like many of the instruments developed for screening purposes, most diagnostic instruments are accompanied by research-based diagnostic efficiency statistics—sensitivity, specificity, PPP, NPP, and overall classification rates—that provide the user with estimates of the probability of accurate classification of those having or not having one or more specific disorders. One typically finds classification rates of the various disorders assessed by any of these types of instrument to vary considerably. For example, the PPPs for those disorders as assessed by the PRIME-MD (Spitzer et al., 1994) range from 19% for minor depressive disorder to 80% for major depressive disorder. For the self-report version of the MINI (Sheehan et al., 1998), the PPPs ranged from 11% for dysthymia to 75% for major depressive disorder. Generally, NPPs and overall classification rates are found to be relatively high and show a lot less variability across diagnostic groups. For the PRIME-MD, overall accuracy rates ranged from 84% for anxiety not otherwise specified to 96% for panic disorder, whereas MINI NPPs ranged from 81% for major depressive disorder to 99% for anorexia. Thus, it would appear that one can feel more confident in the results from these instruments when they indicate that the patient does *not* have a particular disorder. Classification accuracy, of course, is going to vary from instrument to instrument and disorder to disorder. For diagnostic instruments such as these, it is important for the user to be aware of what the research has demonstrated as far the instrument's classification accuracy for *each individual disorder,* since accuracy may vary within and between measures.

## Personality Measures and Symptom Surveys

There are a number of instruments that, although not specifically designed to arrive at a diagnosis, can provide information that is suggestive of a diagnosis or diagnostic group (e.g., affective disorders) or can assist in the differential diagnosis of complicated cases. These include multiple instruments that list symptoms and other aspects of psychiatric disorders and ask respondents to indicate if or how much they are bothered by each of these or whether certain statements arc true or false as they apply to them. Generally, research on these instruments has found elevated scores on individual scales, or patterns or profiles of multiple elevated scale scores, to be associated with specific disorders or diagnostic groups. Thus, when present, these score profiles are suggestive of the presence of the associated type of pathology and bear further investigation. This information can be used either as a starting place in the diagnostic process or as additional information to support an already suspected problem.

Probably the best known of this type of instrument is the Minnesota Multiphasic Personality Inventory–2 (MMPI-2; Butcher, Graham, Ben-Porath, Tellegen, Dahlstrom, & Kaemmer, 2001). It has a substantial body of research indicating that certain elevated scale and subscale profiles or code types are strongly associated with specific diagnoses, groups of diagnoses, or problematic behaviors. (See Graham, 2000; Greene, 2000.) For example, an 8–9/9–8 two-point code type (Schizophrenia [Sc] and Hypomania [Ma] scales being the highest among the significantly elevated scales) is associated with schizophrenia, whereas the 4–9/9–4 code type is commonly associated with a diagnosis of antisocial personality disorder. Within the past few years, a revised and abbreviated version of the MMPI-2—the MMPI-2-RF (Minnesota Multiphasic

Personality Inventory-2 Restructured Form)—has been introduced (Ben-Porath & Tellegen, 2008; Tellegen & Ben-Porath, 2008). This latest version of the time-tested MMPI instrument was developed to examine the entire MMPI-2 item pool and "to identify potential targets for additional substantive scale construction that would result in a comprehensive set of scales yielding an efficient and exhaustive assessment of the salient, clinically relevant variables measurable with the MMPI-2 item pool" (Ben-Porath & Tellegen, 2008, p. 5).

Similarly, research on the Personality Assessment Inventory (PAI; Morey, 1991, 1999, 2004) has demonstrated typical patterns of PAI individual and multiple-scale configurations that also are diagnostically related. For one PAI profile cluster—prominent elevations on the Depression (DEP) and Suicidal Ideation (SUI) scales with additional elevations on the Schizophreniz (SCZ), Stress (STR), Nonsupport (NON), Boderline Features (BOR), Somatic Complaints (SOM), Anxiety (ANX), and Anxiety-Related Disorders (ARD) scales—the most frequently reported associated diagnoses were major depression (20%), dysthymia (23%), and anxiety disorder (23%). Sixty-two percent of those with a profile cluster consisting of prominent elevations on Alcohol Problems (ALC) and SOM with additional elevations on DEP, STR, and ANX were diagnosed with alcohol abuse or dependence.

In addition, other well-validated, single- or multiscale symptom checklists can also be useful for diagnostic purposes. They provide means of identifying symptom domains (e.g., anxiety, depression, somatization) that arc problematic for the patient, thus providing diagnostic clues and guidance for further exploration to the assessing psychologist.

The BDI-II and State-Trait Anxiety Inventory (STAI; Spielberger, Gorsuch, & Lushcne, 1970; Spielberger et al., 2004) are good examples of well-validated, single-scale symptom measures. Multiscale instruments include measures such as the SCL-90-R and the Symptom Assessment-45 Questionnaire (SA-45; Strategic Advantage, 1996). Regardless of the psychometric property of any given instrument for any disorder or symptom domain evaluated by that instrument, or whether it was developed for diagnostic purposes or not, one should never rely on test findings alone when assigning a diagnosis. As with any other psychological test instruments, diagnosis should be based on findings from the test and from other sources, including findings from other instruments, patient and collateral interviews, reviews of psychiatric and medical records (when available), and other pertinent documents.

## PSYCHOLOGICAL ASSESSMENT AS A TOOL FOR TREATMENT PLANNING

Psychological assessment can provide information that can greatly facilitate and enhance the planning of a specific therapeutic intervention for the individual patient. It is through the implementation of a tailored treatment plan that the patient's chances of problem resolution are maximized. The importance of treatment planning has received significant attention recently. (See Maruish, 2002a, 2004.)

The role that psychological assessment can play in planning a course of treatment for behavioral health-care problems is significant. Indeed, as Groth-Marnat (2009) indicated, "The ultimate goal of psychological assessment is to help solve problems by providing information and recommendations relevant to making the optimum decisions related to the client" (p. 535). Butcher (1990) indicated that information available from instruments such as the MMPI-2 not only can assist in identifying problems and establishing communication with the patient but can also help ensure that the plan for treatment is consistent with the patient's personality and external resources. In addition, psychological assessment may reveal potential obstacles to therapy, areas of potential growth, and problems that the patient may not be consciously aware of. Moreover, both Butcher (1990) and Appelbaum (1990) viewed testing as a means of quickly obtaining a second opinion. Other benefits of the results of psychological assessment identified by Appelbaum include assistance in identifying patient strengths and weaknesses, identification of the complexity of the patient's personality, and establishment of a reference point during the therapeutic episode. And as Strupp (cited in Butcher, 1990) has noted, "It will . . . save money and avoid misplaced therapeutic effort; it can also enhance the likelihood of favorable treatment outcomes for suitable patients" (pp. v–vi).

As has already been touched on, there are several ways in which psychological assessment can assist in the planning of treatment for behavioral health-care patients. The more common and evident contributions can be organized into four general categories: problem identification, problem clarification, identification of important patient characteristics, and prediction of treatment outcomes.

### Problem Identification

Probably the most common use of psychological assessment in the service of treatment planning is for problem identification. Often the use of psychological testing per se is not needed to identify what problems the patient is experiencing. He or she will either tell the clinician directly without questioning or admit his or her problem(s) while being questioned during a clinical interview. However, this is not always the case.

The value of psychological testing becomes apparent in those cases in which the patient is hesitant or unable to identify the nature of his or her problems. In addition, the nature of some of the more commonly used psychological test instruments allows for the identification of secondary, but significant, problems that might otherwise be overlooked. Note that the type of problem identification described here is different from that conducted during screening. (See earlier discussion.) Whereas screening is commonly focused on determining the presence or absence of a single problem, problem identification generally takes a broader view and investigates the possibility of the presence of multiple problem areas. At the same time, there also is an attempt to determine problem severity and the extent to which the problem area(s) affect the patient's ability to function.

### Problem Clarification

Psychological testing can often assist in the clarification of a known problem. Through tests designed for use with populations presenting problems similar to those of the patient, aspects of identified problems can be elucidated. Information gained from these tests can both improve the patient's and clinician's understanding of the problem and lead to the development of a better treatment plan. The three most important types of information that can be gleaned for this purpose are the severity of the problem, the complexity of the problem, and the degree to which the problem impairs the patient's ability to function in one or more life roles.

### Identification of Important Patient Characteristics

The identification and clarification of the patient's problems is of key importance in planning a course of treatment. However, numerous other types of patient information not specific to the identified problem can be useful in planning treatment and may be easily identified through the use of psychological assessment instruments. The vast majority of treatment plans are developed or modified with consideration to at least some of these nonpathological characteristics. The exceptions are generally found with clinicians or programs that take a one-size-fits-all approach to treatment.

Probably the most useful type of information that is not specific to the identified problem but can be gleaned from psychological assessment is the identification of patient characteristics that can serve as assets or areas of strength for the patient in working to achieve his or her therapeutic goals. For example, elevated scores on the PAI's Affective Instability (BOR-A) or Antisocial Behaviors (ANT-A) subscales suggest problems with the introspection and self-awareness that is required for most forms of psychological therapies (Morey, 2004).

Similarly, knowledge of the patient's weaknesses or deficits may affect the type of treatment plan that is devised. Greene and Clopton (2004) provided numerous types of deficit-relevant information from the MMPI-2 content scales that have implications for treatment planning. For example, a clinically significant score ($T > 64$) on the Anger scale should lead one to consider the inclusion of training in assertiveness or anger control techniques as part of the patient's treatment. Uneasiness in social situations, as suggested by a significantly elevated score on either the Low Self-Esteem or Social Discomfort scale, suggests that a supportive approach to the intervention would be beneficial, at least initially.

Moreover, use of specially designed scales and procedures can provide information related to the patient's ability to become engaged in the therapeutic process. For example, the Therapeutic Reactance Scale (Dowd, Milne, & Wise, 1991), the PAI's Treatment Rejection scale (RXR; Morey, 2004), and the MMPI-2 Negative Treatment Indicators content scale developed by Butcher and his colleagues (Butcher, Graham, Williams, & Ben-Porath, 1989) may be useful in determining whether the patient is likely to resist therapeutic intervention.

Other types of patient characteristics that can be identified through psychological assessment have implications for selecting the best therapeutic approach for a given patient and thus can contribute significantly to the treatment planning process. Moreland (1996), for example, pointed out how psychological assessment can assist in determining whether the patient deals with problems through internalizing or externalizing behaviors. He noted that, all other things being equal, internalizers would probably profit more from an insight-oriented approach than a behaviorally oriented approach. The reverse would be true for externalizers. Through their work over the years, Beutler and his colleagues (Beutler & Clarkin, 1990; Beutler, Malik, Talebi, Fleming, & Moleiro, 2004) as well as others (e.g., see Prochaska & Prochaska, 2004) have identified several other patient characteristics that are important

to matching patients and treatment approaches for maximized therapeutic effectiveness.

## Prediction of Treatment Outcomes

An important consideration in the development of a treatment plan has to do with the likely outcome of treatment. In other words, how likely is it that a given patient with a given set of problems or level of dysfunction will benefit from any of the treatment options that are available? In some cases, the question is: What is the probability that the patient will significantly benefit from *any* type of treatment? In many cases, psychological test results can yield empirically based predictions that can assist in answering these questions. In doing so, the most effective treatment can be implemented immediately, saving time, money, and potential exacerbation of problems that might result from implementation of a less than optimal course of care.

The ability to predict outcomes is going to vary from test to test and even within individual tests, depending on the population being assessed and what one would like to predict. For example, Chambless, Renneberg, Goldstein, and Gracely (1992) were able to detect predictive differences in MCMI-II identified (Millon, 1987) personality disorder patients seeking treatment for agoraphobia and panic attacks. Patients classified as having an MCMI-II avoidant disorder were more likely to have poorer outcomes on measures of depression, avoidance, and social phobia than those identified as having dependent or histrionic personality disorders. Also, paranoid personality disorder patients were likely to drop out before receiving 10 sessions of treatment. Hannan, Lambert, Harmon, Nielsen, Smart, and Shimokawa (2005) used results from the Outcome Questionnaire–45 (OQ-45) to develop a linear model for expected treatment response. This model was found to be 82% accurate in predicting a positive outcome and 100% accurate in predicting a negative outcome among the study subjects.

At the same time, in another study, Lima et al. (2005) investigated whether therapists' access to their patients' MMPI-2 scores resulted in incremental validity in the prediction of positive treatment outcome beyond that offered by other measures that were also administered to the patients. The investigators did not find this to be the case. In addition, Chisholm, Crowther, and Ben-Porath (1997) did not find any of the seven MMPI-2 scales they investigated to be particularly good predictors of early termination in a sample of university clinic outpatients. They did find that the MMPI-2 Depression

(DEP) and Anxiety (ANX) content scales were predictive of other treatment outcomes. Both were shown to be positively associated with therapist-rated improvement in current functioning and global psychopathology, with ANX scores also being related to therapist-rated progress toward therapy goals.

The reader is referred to Hunsley (2003) and Hunsley and Meyer (2003) for discussions regarding the importance of evaluating incremental validity of psychological assessment when considering psychological assessment findings for planning and other treatment-related purposes. Also, Meyer et al. (1998) have provided an excellent overview of the research supporting the use of objective and projective test results for outcomes prediction as well as for other clinical decision-making purposes. The use of patient profiling for the prediction of treatment outcome is discussed later in this chapter.

In closing this discussion of psychological assessment and treatment planning, it is important to mention Groth-Marnat's (2009) acknowledgment that the development of effective treatment recommendations requires more than the clinician being skilled in the area of test interpretation. It requires knowledge and skill in case management in the sense of making decisions regarding how restrictive treatment should be and the frequency and length of treatment, as well as knowing and making use of appropriate social and community resources. In addition, the clinician must be able to be flexible in his or her approach to the treatment that is recommended, taking into account the characteristics and specific circumstances of the patient.

## PSYCHOLOGICAL ASSESSMENT AS A TREATMENT INTERVENTION

The use of psychological assessment as an adjunct to or means of therapeutic intervention in and of itself has received more than passing attention (e.g., Butcher, 1990; Clair & Prendergast, 1994; Groth-Marnat, 2009). Martin (2009) referred to the rise of collaborative or therapeutic assessment as "the most important development in the recent history of assessment" (p. 24). "Therapeutic assessment" (TA) with the MMPI-2 received particular attention primarily through the work of Finn and his associates (Finn, 1996a, 1996b; Finn & Martin, 1997; Finn & Tonsager, 1992). Finn's approach appears to be particularly applicable with instruments or batteries of instruments that provide multidimensional information relevant to the concerns of patients seeking answers to questions related to their mental health status.

Other *collaborative assessment* approaches have been identified in the literature (e.g., see Fischer, 1994, 2001). However, because of the exposure it has received, the approach espoused by Finn will be presented here as a model for deriving direct therapeutic benefits from the psychological assessment experience.

### What Is Therapeutic Assessment?

In discussing the use of the MMPI-2 as a therapeutic intervention, Finn described a "semi-structured collaborative assessment approach" (2007) whose goal is to "gather accurate information about clients . . . and then use this information to help clients understand themselves and make positive changes in their lives" (Finn, 1996b, p. 3). Simply stated, TA may be considered an approach to the assessment of behavioral health patients in which the patient is not only the primary provider of information needed to answer questions but is also actively involved in formulating the questions that are to be answered by the assessment. Feedback regarding the results of the assessment is provided to the patient and is considered a primary, if not *the* primary, element of the assessment process. Thus, the patient becomes a partner in the assessment process; as a result, therapeutic and other benefits accrue.

### Therapeutic Assessment Process

Finn (1996b) originally outlined a three-step procedure for TA using the MMPI-2 in those situations in which the patient is seen *only* for assessment. More recently, he has expanded the formal TA process to a six-step procedure applicable to presentation of results from the MMPI-2 and other psychological tests (Finn, 2007; Finn & Martin, forthcoming; Fischer & Finn, 2008). A brief summary of each of the steps outlined by Finn and his colleagues follows.

#### Initial Contact

Although not listed as a step in the standard TA process in Finn (2007), Finn and Martin (forthcoming) identified the initial contact (usually by telephone) with the referring professional and, subsequently, with the patient as if it is a formal step. The referring party provides the questions he or she would like to have answered and other information. Subsequently, the assessor contacts the patient. In addition to scheduling the time and place for the assessment, the assessor asks the patient to think about questions he or she would like to have answered through the assessment.

## Step 1: Initial Session(s)

The initial session(s) with the patient serve multiple purposes. It provides the assessor an opportunity to build rapport with the patient and to present the assessment task as a collaborative one. The therapist gathers background information, addresses concerns, and provides the patient the opportunity to identify or otherwise clarify questions that he or she would like answered using the assessment data.

## Step 2: Standardized Testing Session(s)

Administration of standardized tests to the patient may take place during more than one session, thus avoiding having the patient feel overwhelmed with the process. Tests selected for administration and the order in which they are administered tend to be those that are focused more on answering the questions raised by the patient. These tests would be followed by administration of tests that would provide information related to the referring professional's questions. In addition to following standardized test administration procedures, the assessor would also engage in inquiry about certain aspects of the patient's responses relevant to the assessment questions and ask the patient about his or her thoughts about the testing.

## Step 3: Assessment Intervention Session(s)

These sessions, which take place after the completion of standardized testing, are used to further understand the patient by evoking emotions related to the problems that have been identified. The sessions provide an opportunity for the patient to observe problem behaviors, better understand them, and then work with the assessor to find a solution to them. Discussions during these sessions are related to the problems the patient is experiencing in his or her daily life. Various assessment materials (e.g., Thematic Apperception Test (TAT) cards) and other techniques may be employed to facilitate these sessions.

## Step 4: Summary/Discussion Session(s)

These sessions are used for the assessor and the patient to collaboratively discuss the findings of the assessment. The assessor first discusses the findings with the referring professional and collaboratively plans the summary/discussion session. Ideally, the session then takes place in the office of the referring professional with him or her also in attendance to provide emotional support to the patient. The session begins with the assessor proposing tentative answers—based on information obtained from the test findings and the assessment intervention sessions—to the questions the patient previously indicated as being important to address. The patient is then asked to respond to the proposed answers, giving examples of real-life experiences that support his or her level of agreement or disagreement with the assessor's propositions. These interactive sessions can end with the referring professional and the patient discussing how the patient can address the problems that were evaluated by the assessment.

## Step 5: Provision of Written Feedback

Following the summary/discussion session, the assessor writes a letter to the patient, summarizing the answers to the patient's questions.

## Step 6: Follow-Up Session(s)

As a final part of the TA process, the assessor arranges to meet with the patient again 3 to 6 months after the summary/discussion session. The purpose of this meeting is to provide the patient an opportunity to better understand what the results of the assessment mean and how they may relate to questions, concerns, or developments that have occurred recently. This step is found to be particularly useful to individuals who are not engaged in any ongoing psychotherapy.

## Empirical Support for Therapeutic Assessment

Noting the lack of direct empirical support for the therapeutic effects of sharing test results with patients, Finn and Tonsager (1992) investigated the benefits of providing feedback to university counseling center clients regarding their MMPI-2 results. Thirty-two participants underwent therapeutic assessment and feedback procedures similar to those described in text while on the counseling center's waiting list. Another 28 participants were recruited from the same waiting list to serve as a control group. Instead of receiving feedback, Finn and Tonsager's control group received nontherapeutic attention from the examiner. However, they were administered the same dependent measures as the feedback group at the same time that the experimental group received feedback. They were also administered the same dependent measures as the experimental group 2 weeks later (i.e., 2 weeks after the experimental group received the feedback) in order to determine if there were differences between the two groups on those dependent measures. These measures included a self-esteem questionnaire, a symptom checklist (the SCL-90-R), a measure of private and public self-consciousness, and a questionnaire assessing the subjects' subjective impressions of the feedback session.

The results of Finn and Tonsager's (1992) study indicate that compared to the control group, the feedback group demonstrated significantly less distress at the 2-week postfeedback follow-up and significantly higher levels of self-esteem and hope at both the time of feedback and the 2-week postfeedback follow-up. In other findings, feelings about the feedback sessions were positively and significantly correlated with changes in self-esteem from testing to feedback, both from feedback to follow-up and from testing to follow-up among those who were administered the MMPI-2. In addition, change in level of distress from feedback to follow-up correlated significantly with private self-consciousness (i.e., the tendency to focus on the internal aspects of oneself) but not with public self-consciousness.

M. L. Newman and Greenway (1997) provided support for Finn and Tonsager's findings in their study of 60 Australian college students. Clients given MMPI-2 feedback reported an increase in self-esteem and a decrease in psychological distress that could not be accounted for by their merely completing the MMPI-2. At the same time, changes in self-esteem or symptomatology were not found to be related to either the level or type of symptomatology at the time of the first assessment. Also, the clients' attitudes toward mental health professionals (as measured by the MMPI-2 Negative Treatment Indicators (TRT) scale) were not found to be related to level of distress or self-esteem. Newman and Greenway's results differed from those of Finn and Tonsager (1992) in that general satisfaction scores were not associated with change in self-esteem or change in symptomatology, nor was private self-consciousness found to be related to changes in symptomatology. Recognizing the limitations of their study, Newman and Greenway's recommendations for future research in this area included examination of the components of therapeutic assessment separately and the use of different patient populations and different means of assessing therapeutic change (i.e., use of both patient and therapist/third party report).

Several investigations of the effectiveness of TA have been reported since the publication of the first edition of this volume. (See, e.g., Little & Smith, 2009; Morey, Lowmaster, & Hopwood, 2010; Tharinger et al., 2009.) Perhaps the most significant among them is Poston and Hanson's (2010) meta-analysis of the effectiveness of TA and other therapeutic models of assessment involving collaborative feedback. This investigation, using findings from 17 published studies involving a total of 1,496 participants, yielded an overall effect size of 0.423 ($p <$ .01). Also, of the participants who engaged in psychological assessment as an intervention, 66% fell above the group mean on dependent variables of therapeutic benefit (e.g., reduced symptomatology) for control or comparison groups. The authors concluded: "If tests are used collaboratively—and if they are accompanied by personalized, highly involving feedback—then clients and treatment appear to benefit greatly" (p. 210).

## TREATMENT MONITORING

Monitoring treatment progress with psychological assessment instruments can prove to be quite valuable, especially with patients who are seen over relatively long periods of time. If the treatment is inefficient, inappropriate, or otherwise not resulting in the expected effects, changes in the treatment plan can be formulated and deployed. These adjustments may reflect the need for (a) more intensive or aggressive treatment (e.g., increased number of psychotherapeutic sessions each week, addition of a medication adjunct); (b) less intensive treatment (e.g., reduction or discontinuation of medication, transfer from inpatient to outpatient care); or (c) a different therapeutic approach (e.g., a change from psychodynamic therapy to cognitive-behavioral therapy). Regardless, any modifications require later reassessment of the patient to determine if the treatment revisions have affected patient progress in the expected direction. This process may be repeated any number of times. These in-treatment reassessments also can provide information relevant to the decision of when to terminate treatment.

### Monitoring Change

Methods for determining if statistically and clinically significant change has occurred from one point in time to another have been developed and can be used for treatment monitoring. Many of these methods are the same as those that can be used for outcomes assessment and are discussed later in this chapter (see "Outcomes Assessment" section). In addition, the reader is also referred to an excellent discussion of analyzing individual and group change data in F. L. Newman and Wong (2004) and F. L. Newman and Tejeda (2004), respectively.

*Patient profiling* is yet another approach to monitoring therapeutic change that can prove to be more valuable than looking at simple changes in test scores from one point in time to another. Patient profiling involves the generation of an expected curve of recovery over the course of psychotherapy based on the observed recovery of similar patients (Howard, Moras, Brill, Martinovich, & Lutz, 1996; Leon, Kopta, Howard, & Lutz, 1999). An individual recovery curve is generated from selected clinical characteristics (e.g., severity and chronicity of the problem, attitudes toward treatment, scores on treatment-relevant measures) present at the time of treatment onset. This curve enables the clinician to determine if the patient is on the expected track for recovery through the episode of care. Multiple measurements of the clinical characteristics during the course of treatment allow a comparison of the patient's actual test score with that which would be expected from similar individuals after the same number of treatment sessions. The therapist thus knows when the treatment is working and when it is not working so that any necessary adjustments in the treatment strategy can be made.

### Other Uses for Patient Profiling

Aside from its obvious treatment value, treatment monitoring data can support decisions regarding the need for continued treatment. This holds true whether the data are nothing more than a set of scores from a relevant measure (e.g., a symptom inventory) administered at various points during treatment or are actual and expected recovery curves obtained by Howard et al.'s (1996) patient profiling method. Expected and actual data obtained from patient profiling can easily point to the likelihood that additional sessions are needed or would be significantly beneficial for the patient. Combined with clinician impressions, these data can make a powerful case for the patient's need for additional treatment sessions or, conversely, for treatment termination.

Besides being used to support decisions regarding additional treatment sessions for patients already in treatment, patient profiling may also be useful in making initial treatment-related decisions. Leon et al. (1999) sought to determine whether patients whose actual response curve matched or exceeded (i.e., performed better than) the expectancy curve could be differentiated from those whose actual curve failed to match their expectancy curve on the basis of pretreatment clinical characteristics. They first generated patient profiles for 821 active outpatients and found a correlation of .57 ($p < .001$) between the actual and expected slopes. They then used half of the original sample to develop a discriminate function that

was able to significantly discriminate ($p < .001$) patients whose recovery was predictable (i.e., those with consistent actual and expected curves) from those whose recovery was not predictable (i.e., those with inconsistent curves). The discriminant function was based on 15 pretreatment clinical characteristics (including the subscales and items of the Mental Health Index, or MHI; Howard, Brill, Lueger, O'Mahoney, & Grissom, 1993) and was cross-validated with the other half of the original sample. In both subsamples, lower levels of symptomatology and higher levels of functioning were associated with those in the predictable group of patients.

The implications of these findings are quite powerful. According to Leon and his colleagues (1999):

> The patient profiling-discriminant approach provides promise for moving toward the reliable identification of patients who will respond more rapidly in psychotherapy, who will respond more slowly in psychotherapy, or who will demonstrate a low likelihood of benefiting from this type of treatment. (p. 703)

### Effects of Providing Feedback to the Therapist

Intuitively, one would expect that patient profiling information would result in positive outcomes for the patient. Is this really the case, though? Lambert, Whipple, Smart, Vermeesch, Nielsen, and Hawkins (1999) sought to answer this question by conducting a study to determine if patients whose therapists receive feedback about their progress (experimental group) would have better outcomes and better treatment attendance (an indicator of cost-effective psychotherapy) than those patients whose therapists did not receive this type of feedback (control group). The feedback provided to the experimental group's therapists came in the form of a weekly updated numerical and color-coded report based on the baseline and current total scores of the Outcome Questionnaire (OQ-45; Lambert, 2010; Lambert et al., 1996) and the number of sessions that the patient had completed. The feedback report also contained one of four possible interpretations of the patient's progress (not making expected level of progress, may have negative outcome or drop out of treatment, consider revised or new treatment plan, reassess readiness for change). The findings from this study were mixed and lent only partial support for benefits accruing from the use of assessment-based feedback to therapists. They also suggested that information provided in a feedback report alone is not sufficient to maximize its impact on the quality of care provided to a patient; that is, the information must be put to use.

Since the publication of the first edition of this volume, Lambert and his colleagues have published numerous investigations demonstrating the value of regularly tracking treatment progress and providing feedback to therapists and, in some cases, the patients themselves. It is beyond the scope of this chapter to provide a thorough review of these studies; however, the reader is referred to several publications (Lambert, 2010; Lambert, Harmon, Slade, Whipple, & Hawkins, 2005; Shimokawa, Lambert, & Smart, 2010) that provide analyses of findings from several studies, using various approaches (e.g., meta-analysis), to demonstrate the positive effect of providing feedback to therapists whose patients are not making the expected progress in treatment.

Notwithstanding their use as fodder for generating complex statistical predictions or for simple point-in-time comparisons, psychological test data obtained for treatment monitoring can provide an empirically based means of determining the effectiveness of mental health and substance abuse treatment during an episode of care. The value of psychological test data lies in the ability of these data to support ongoing treatment decisions that must be made using objective findings. Consequently, this type of data allows for improved patient care while supporting efforts to demonstrate accountability to the patient and interested third parties.

## OUTCOMES ASSESSMENT

The 1990s witnessed accelerating growth in the level of interest and development of behavioral health-care outcomes programs that has continued into the 21st century. The interest in and necessity for outcomes measurement and accountability in this era of managed care provide a unique opportunity for psychologists to use their training and skills in assessment (Maruish, 2002b, 2004). As noted by Reed and Eisman (2006):

> In principle, the assessment of outcomes could offer substantial benefit to health systems, practitioners, and consumers. Theoretically, outcomes assessment can support the identification of best practices and help to ensure that health care quality does not suffer in the interests of cost containment. (p. 24)

However, the extent to which psychologists and other trained professionals can benefit in their own practices or become key and successful contributors to an organization's outcomes initiative will depend on their understanding of what outcomes and their measurement and applications are all about.

In a survey conducted in 1995 by the Committee for the Advancement of Professional Practice (CAPP) of the American Psychological Association (APA), Phelps, Eisman, and Kohut (1998) found that assessment activity (unspecified) was the second most prevalent activity of their sample, occupying an average of 16% of the professional time of the nearly 16,000 respondents. They also found that 29% of the respondents were involved in outcomes assessment, with the highest rate of use of outcomes measures (40%) reported by psychologists in medical settings. To investigate the use of outcomes measures in clinical practice, Hatfield and Ogles (2004, 2007) conducted a survey of 2,000 licensed psychologists who were randomly drawn from APA members who had paid APA's special practice assessment fee. Among the 874 respondents, 37.1% reported that they used some outcomes assessment in their practice. Of these, 74.4% indicated that they used patient self-report measures, and 61.2% reported using clinician-completed measures.

This may in fact be a reason for findings by Mours, Campbell, Gathercoal, and Peterson (2009) regarding the training and use of psychotherapy outcome measures at psychology internship sites. Results from a survey of directors of 244 APA-accredited psychology internship programs revealed that while 47% of the sites used outcomes measures for assessment, 79% of the respondents agreed that using outcome assessment measures to evaluate client progress was important. Fifty-eight percent reported their use with each client, and 61% agreed that interns should receive training on these measures. Moreover, 97% of directors whose sites routinely used these measures indicated that they did so to track client progress.

### What Are Outcomes?

*Outcomes* is a term that refers to the results of the specific treatment that was rendered to a patient or group of patients. Along with structure and process, outcomes is one component of what Donabedian (1980, 1982, 1985) referred to as "quality of care." The first component is *structure,* which refers to various aspects of the organization providing the care, including how the organization is organized, the physical facilities and equipment, and the number and professional qualifications of its staff. *Process* refers to the specific types of services that are provided to a given patient (or group of patients) during a specific episode of care. These might include various tests and assessments (e.g., psychological tests, lab tests, magnetic resonance imaging), therapeutic interventions (e.g., group psychotherapy, medication), and discharge planning activities. *Outcomes*, however, refers to the results of the specific treatment that was rendered.

In considering the types of outcomes that might be assessed in behavioral health-care settings, a substantial number of clinicians would probably identify symptomatic change in psychological status as being the most important. However, no matter how important change in symptom status may have been in the past, psychologists and other behavioral health-care providers have come to realize that change in many other aspects of functioning identified by Stewart and Ware (1992) are equally important indicators of treatment effectiveness. As Sederer et al. (1996) have noted:

> Outcome for patients, families, employers, and payers is not simply confined to symptomatic change. Equally important to those affected by the care rendered is the patient's capacity to function within a family, community, or work environment or to exist independently, without undue burden to the family and social welfare system. Also important is the patient's ability to show improvement in any concurrent medical and psychiatric disorder.... Finally, not only do patients seek symptomatic improvement, but they want to experience a subjective sense of health and well being. (p. 2)

## Use of Outcomes Assessment in Treatment

Considerations and recommendations for the development and implementation of outcomes assessment by psychologists are discussed next. Although space limitations do not allow a comprehensive review of all issues and solutions, the information that follows touches on matters that are most important to psychologists who wish to incorporate outcomes assessment into their standard therapeutic routine.

### Measurement Domains

The specific aspects or dimensions of patient functioning that are measured as part of outcomes assessment will depend on the purpose for which the assessment is being conducted. Probably the most frequently measured variable is that of symptomatology or psychological/mental health status. After all, disturbance or disruption in this dimension is probably the most common reason why people seek behavioral health-care services in the first place. However, there are other reasons for seeking help. Common examples include difficulties in coping with various types of life transitions (e.g., a new job, a recent marriage

or divorce, other changes in the work or home environment), an inability to deal with the behavior of others (e.g., children, coworkers), or general dissatisfaction with life. Additional assessment of related variables may therefore be necessary or even take precedence over the assessment of symptoms or other indicators of psychological problems.

For some patients, measures of one or more specific psychological disorders or symptom clusters are at least as important as, if not more important than, overall symptom or mental health status. Here, if interest is in only one disorder or symptom cluster (e.g., depression), one may choose to measure only that particular set of symptoms using an instrument designed specifically for that purpose (e.g., the BDI-II would be used with depressed patients). For those interested in assessing the outcomes of treatment relative to multiple psychological dimensions, the administration of more than one disorder-specific instrument or a single, multiscale instrument that assesses all or most of the dimensions of interest would be required. Again, instruments such as the SCL-90-R can provide a quick, broad assessment of several symptom domains.

It is not always a simple matter to determine exactly what should be measured. However, careful consideration of the next questions should greatly facilitate the decision:

- Why did the patient seek services?
- What does the patient hope to gain from treatment?
- What are the patient's criteria for successful treatment?
- What are the clinician's criteria for the successful completion of the current therapeutic episode?
- What, if any, are the outcomes initiatives within the organization providing the service?

Note that the selection of the variables to be assessed may address more than one of the listed issues. Ideally, this is what should happen. However, one needs to ensure that the task of gathering outcomes data does not become too burdensome. The key is to identify the point at which both the amount of data that can be obtained from a patient or collaterals and the ease at which the data can be gathered are optimized.

### Measurement Methodology

Once the decision of *what* to measure has been made, one must then decide *how* it should be measured. In many cases, the most important data will be those that are obtained directly from the patient using self-report instruments. Underlying this assertion is the assumption that valid and reliable instrumentation, appropriate to the needs of the patient, is available to the clinician; the patient can read at the level required by the instruments; and the patient is motivated to respond honestly to the questions asked. Barring one or more of these conditions, other options should be considered.

Other types of data-gathering tools may be substituted for self-report measures. Rating scales completed by the clinician or other members of the treatment staff may provide information that is as useful as that elicited directly from the patient. In those cases in which the patient is severely disturbed, unable to give valid and reliable answers (as in the case of younger children), unable to read, or otherwise an inappropriate candidate for a self-report measure, clinical rating scales, such as the Brief Psychiatric Rating Scale (BPRS; Lachar, Espadas, & Bailley, 2004; Overall & Gorham, 1962) and the Child and Adolescent Functional Assessment Scale (CAFAS; Hodges, 1994, 2004), can serve as valuable substitutes for gathering information about the patient. Related to these instruments are parent-completed instruments for child and adolescent patients, such as the Child Behavior Checklist (CBCL; Achenbach, 1991; Achenbach & Rescorla, 2004) and the Personality Inventory for Children-2 (PIC-2; Lachar, 2004; Lachar & Gruber, 2001). Collateral rating instruments and parent-report instruments can also be used to gather information in addition to that obtained from self-report measures. When used in this manner, these instruments provide a mechanism by which the clinician, other treatment staff, and parents, guardians, or other collaterals can contribute data to the outcomes assessment endeavor.

It is beyond the scope of this chapter to provide a useful discussion pertaining to the selection of outcomes measures. Instead, the reader is directed to the works of Maruish (2002b, 2004), Lambert and his colleagues (Lambert & Hawkins, 2004; Ogles, Lambert & Fields, 2002), and Newman, Rugh, and Ciarlo (2004) for discussions and recommendations regarding this topic.

### When to Measure

There are no hard-and-fast rules or widely accepted conventions related to when outcomes should be assessed. The common practice is to assess the patient at least at treatment initiation and again at termination or discharge. Additional assessment of the patient on the variables of interest can take place at other points as part of postdischarge follow-up.

Many would argue that postdischarge or posttermination follow-up assessment provides the best or most important indication of the outcomes of therapeutic intervention.

In general, posttermination outcomes assessment should probably take place no sooner than 1 month after treatment has ended. When feasible, waiting 3 to 6 months to assess the variables of interest is preferred. A longer interval between termination and follow-up assessment should provide a more valid indication of the lasting effects of treatment effectiveness. Thus, comparison of the patient's status on the variables of interest at the time of follow-up with that found at the time of either treatment initiation or termination will provide an indication of the more *lasting* effects of the intervention. Generally, the variables of interest for this type of comparison include symptom presence and intensity, feeling of well-being, frequency of substance use, and social or role functioning.

Although it provides what is arguably the best and most useful outcomes information, a program of postdischarge follow-up assessment is also the most difficult to successfully implement. There must be a commitment of staff and other resources to track terminated or discharged patients; contact them at the appropriate times to schedule a reassessment; and process, analyze, report, and store the follow-up data. The task is made more difficult by frequently noted difficulties in locating terminated patients whose contact information has changed or convincing those who can be located to complete a task from which they will not directly benefit. However, those organizations and individual clinicians who are able to overcome these barriers will find the fruits of their efforts quite rewarding.

### Analysis of Outcomes Data

There are two general approaches to the analysis of treatment outcomes data. The first is by determining whether changes in patient scores on outcomes measures are statistically significant. The other is by establishing whether these changes are clinically significant. Use of standard tests of statistical significance is important in the analysis of group or population change data. Clinical significance is more relevant to change in the individual patient's scores.

The issue of clinical significance has received a great deal of attention in psychotherapy research during the past few decades. This is at least partially owing to the work of Jacobson and his colleagues (Jacobson, Follette, & Revenstorf, 1984, 1986; Jacobson & Truax, 1991) and others (e.g., Christensen & Mendoza, 1986; Speer, 1992; Wampold & Jenson, 1986). Their work came at a time when researchers began to recognize that traditional statistical comparisons do not reveal a great deal about the efficacy of therapy. In discussing the topic, Jacobson and

Truax (1991) broadly defined the clinical significance of treatment as "its ability to meet standards of efficacy set by consumers, clinicians, and researchers" (p. 12).

From their perspective, Jacobson and his colleagues (Jacobson et al., 1984; Jacobson & Truax, 1991) felt that clinically significant change could be conceptualized in one of three ways. Thus, for clinically significant change to have occurred, the measured level of functioning following the therapeutic episode would either (a) fall outside the range of the dysfunctional population by at least 2 standard deviations from the mean of that population, in the direction of functionality; (b) fall within 2 standard deviations of the mean for the normal or functional population; or (c) be closer to the mean of the functional population than to that of the dysfunctional population. Jacobson and Truax viewed option (c) as being the least arbitrary, and they provided different recommendations for determining cutoffs for clinically significant change, depending on the availability of normative data.

At the same time, these investigators noted the importance of considering the change in the measured variables of interest from pre- to posttreatment in addition to the patient's functional status at the end of therapy. To this end, Jacobson et al. (1984) proposed the concomitant use of a reliable change (RC) index to determine whether change is clinically significant. This index, modified on the recommendation of Christensen and Mendoza (1986), is nothing more than the pretest score minus the posttest score divided by the standard error of the difference of the two scores.

The demand to demonstrate the outcomes of treatment is pervasive throughout the health-care industry. Regulatory and accreditation bodies are requiring that providers and provider organizations show that their services are having a positive impact on the people they treat. Beyond that, the behavioral health-care provider also needs to know whether what he or she does works. Outcomes information derived from psychological assessment of individual patients allows the provider to know the extent to which he or she has helped each patient. At the same time, in aggregate, this information can offer insight about what works best for whom under what circumstances, thus facilitating program evaluation and the treatment of future patients.

## PSYCHOLOGICAL ASSESSMENT IN THE ERA OF MANAGED BEHAVIORAL HEALTH CARE

Numerous observers (e.g., Ficken, 1995; Maruish, 2004) have commented on how the advent of managed care

has limited the reimbursement for (and therefore the use of) psychological assessment. Certainly, no one would argue with this assertion. In an era of capitated behavioral health-care coverage, the amount of money available for behavioral health-care treatment is limited. MBHOs therefore require a demonstration that the amount of money spent for testing will result in a greater amount of treatment cost savings. Indeed, in order for the service to be authorized, one MBHO requires that psychological testing (a) provides information necessary for differential diagnosis, (b) provides information needed to develop an initial treatment plan or revise an existing plan, (c) is used when response to treatment is different than expected, or (d) is used to determine if the patient has the functional capacity to engage in treatment, and that other means of obtaining this information (e.g., clinical interview, review of relevant history) are insufficient (United Behavioral Health, 2010).

### Current Status

Where does psychological assessment currently fit into the daily scope of activities for practicing psychologists in this age of managed care? In a survey conducted in 1995 by the APA's CAPP (Phelps et al., 1998), almost 16,000 psychological practitioners responded to questions related to workplace settings, areas of practice concerns, and range of activities. Even though there were not any real surprises, there were several interesting findings. The principal professional activity reported by the respondents was psychotherapy, with 44% of the sample acknowledging involvement in this service. Assessment was the second most prevalent activity, with only 16% reporting this activity. In addition, the results showed that 29% were involved in outcomes assessment.

Taking a closer look at the impact that managed care has had on assessment, Piotrowski, Belter, and Keller (1998) surveyed 500 psychologists randomly selected from that year's *National Register of Health Service Providers in Psychology* in the fall of 1996 to investigate how managed care had affected assessment practices. One hundred thirty-seven usable surveys (32%) were returned. Sixty-one percent of the respondents saw no positive impact of managed care; and, consistent with the CAPP survey findings, 70% saw managed care as negatively affecting clinicians or patients. The testing practices of 72% of the respondents were affected by managed care, as reflected in their performing less testing, using fewer instruments when they did test patients, and having lower reimbursement rates. Overall, they reported less reliance on those tests requiring much clinician time—such as the Weschler scales, Rorschach, and Thematic Apperception Test—along with a move to briefer, problem-focused tests. The results of their study led Piotrowski et al. to describe many possible scenarios for the future of assessment, including providers relying on briefer tests or briefer test batteries, changing the focus of their practice to more lucrative types of assessment activities (e.g., forensic assessment), using computer-based testing, or, in some cases, referring testing out to another psychologist.

In yet another survey, Stout and Cook (1999) contacted 40 managed care companies regarding their viewpoints concerning reimbursement for psychological assessment. The good news is that the majority (70%) of these companies reported that they did reimburse for these services. At the same time, the authors pointed to the possible negative implications for the individuals whose health care coverage was provided by those other 12 or so companies that did not reimburse for psychological assessment. That is, these people may not be receiving the services they need because of missing information that might have been revealed through the assessment.

Piotrowski (1999) summed up the then-current state of psychological assessment:

> Admittedly, the emphasis on the standard personality battery over the past decade has declined due to the impact of brief therapeutic approaches with a focus on diagnostics, symptomatology, and treatment outcome. That is, the clinical emphasis has been on addressing referral questions and not psychodynamic defenses, character structure, and object relations. Perhaps the managed care environment has brought this issue to the forefront. Either way, the role of clinical assessment has, for the most part, changed. To the dismay of proponents of clinical methods, the future is likely to focus more on specific domain-based rather than comprehensive assessment. (p. 793)

These observations appear to be just as valid now as they were when first published.

Eisman et al. (2000) also provided an excellent overview of the numerous problems and limitations that psychologist may experience in using psychological assessment in managed care health systems. The overview is accompanied by recommendations for addressing these problems.

## Opportunities for Psychological Assessment

The foregoing representations of the state of psychological assessment in behavioral health-care delivery can be viewed as an omen of worse things to come. In my opinion, they are not. Rather, the limitations that are being imposed on psychological assessment and the demand for justification of its use in clinical practice represent part of health-care consumers' dissatisfaction with the way things were done in the past. In general, this author views the tightening of the purse strings as a positive move for both behavioral health care and the profession of psychology. It is a wake-up call to those who have contributed to the health-care crisis by uncritically performing costly psychological assessments, being unaccountable to the payers and recipients of those services, and generally not performing assessment services in the most responsible, cost-effective way possible. Psychologists need to evaluate how they have used psychological assessment in the past and then determine the best way to use it in the future.

Consequently, this is an opportunity for psychologists to reestablish the value of the contributions they can make to improve the quality of care delivery through their knowledge and skills in the area of psychological assessment. As has been shown throughout this chapter, there are many ways in which the value of psychological assessment can be demonstrated in traditional mental health and substance abuse treatment settings during this era of managed behavioral health care. However, the health-care industry is now beginning to recognize the value of psychological assessment in the more traditional *medical* arenas. This is where potential opportunities are just now beginning to be realized.

### Psychological Assessment in Primary Care Settings

The past three decades have witnessed a significant increase in the number of psychologists who work in general health-care settings (Groth-Marnat & Edkins, 1996). This can be attributed to several factors, including the realization that psychologists can improve a patient's physical health by helping to reduce overutilization of medical services and prevent stress-related disorders, offering alternatives to traditional medical interventions, and enhancing the outcomes of patient care. The recognition of the financial and patient-care benefits that can accrue from the integration of primary medical care and behavioral health care has resulted in the implementation of various types of integrated behavioral health programs in primary care settings. Kaplan, Patterson, and Groessl (2004) also acknowledged the increasing role of psychologists in primary care medicine and noted that the role will become bigger in the future. Regardless of the extent to which these services are merged, these efforts attest to the belief that any steps toward integrating behavioral health-care services—including psychological testing and assessment—in primary care settings represents an improvement over the more traditional model of segregated service delivery.

The alliance of primary and behavioral health-care providers is not a new phenomenon; it has existed in one form or another for decades. As Goldstein, Bershadsky, and Maruish (2000) pointed out:

1. A large portion of patients who seek services from primary care providers experience significant psychological distress or symptomatology.
2. Primary care providers, in general, are not sufficiently skilled to identify or provide appropriate treatment to these patients.
3. Consequently, patients with behavioral health problems consume a large portion of the available primary care resources.
4. Identifying and adequately treating the behavioral health problems of primary care patients in the primary care setting has been shown to result in significant cost savings.
5. Consultation, liaison, and educational services offered by behavioral health professionals can be instrumental in ensuring the success of these intervention efforts in the primary care setting. (p. 735)

Thus, it is not difficult to demonstrate that clinical psychologists and other trained behavioral health-care professionals can uniquely contribute to efforts to fully integrate their services in primary care settings through the establishment and use of psychological assessment services. Information obtained from psychometrically sound, self-report tests and other assessment instruments (e.g., clinician rating scales, parent-completed instruments) can assist the primary care provider in several types of clinical decision-making activities, including screening for the presence of mental health or substance abuse problems, planning a course of treatment, and monitoring patient progress. Testing can also be used to assess the outcomes of treatment that has been provided to patients with mental health or substance abuse problems, thus assisting in determining what works for whom. Pollak (2010) indicated that the future of psychological assessment will depend, in part, on how successful professional psychology is in integrating it into primary care.

### Psychological Assessment in Disease Management Programs

Beyond the primary care setting, the medical populations for which psychological assessment can be useful are quite varied and may even be surprising to some. Todd

(1999) observed that "[t]oday, it is difficult to find any organization in the healthcare industry that isn't in some way involved in disease management.... This concept has quickly evolved from a marketing strategy of the pharmaceutical industry to an entrenched discipline among many managed care organizations" (p. xi). It is here that opportunities for the application of psychological screening and other assessment activities are just beginning to be realized.

What is *disease management* or (as some prefer) disease state management? Gurnee and DaSilva (1999, p. 12) described it as "an integrated system of interventions, measurements, and refinements of health care delivery designed to optimize clinical and economic outcomes within a specific population.... [S]uch a program relies on aggressive prevention of complications as well as treatment of chronic conditions." The focus of these programs is on a systems approach that treats the entire disease rather than its individual components, such as is the case in the more traditional practice of medicine. The payoff comes in improvement in the quality of care offered to participants in the program as well as real cost savings.

Where can psychological assessment fit into these programs? In some MBHOs, for example, there is a drive to work closer with health plan customers in their disease management programs for patients facing diabetes, asthma, and recovery from cardiovascular diseases. This has resulted in a recognition on the part of the health plans of the value that MBHOs can bring to their programs, including the expertise in selecting or developing assessment instruments and developing an implementation plan that can help identify and monitor medical patients with comorbid behavioral health problems. These and other medical disorders are frequently accompanied by depression and anxiety that can significantly affect quality of life, morbidity, and, in some cases, mortality. Early identification and treatment of comorbid behavioral health problems in patients with chronic medical diseases can thus dramatically affect the course of the disease and the toll it takes on the patient. In addition, periodic (e.g., annual) monitoring of the patient can be incorporated into the disease management process to help ensure that there has been no recurrence of the problem or development of a different behavioral health problem over time.

### A Concluding Note

It is difficult to imagine that any behavioral health-care organization—managed or otherwise—would not find value in at least one or two of the previously described applications. The issue becomes whether there are funds for these applications. These might include funds for assessment materials, reimbursing network providers or other third-party contractors (e.g., disease management companies) for their assessment work, an in-house staff position to conduct or oversee the implementation of this work, or any combination of the three. Regardless, it is highly unlikely that any MBHO is going to spend money on any service that is not considered essential for the proper care of patients unless that service can demonstrate value in short-term or long-term money savings or offset costs in other ways. The current restrictions for authorizing assessment are a reflection of this fact. As Dorfman (2000) succinctly put it:

> Until the value of testing can be shown unequivocally, support and reimbursement for evaluation and testing will be uneven with [MBHOs] and frequently based on the psychologist's personal credibility and competence in justifying such expenditures. In the interim, it is incumbent on each psychologist to be aware of the goals and philosophy of the managed care industry, and to understand how the use of evaluation and testing with his or her patients not only is consistent with, but also helps to further, those goals. To the extent that these procedures can be shown to enhance the value of the managed care product by ensuring quality of care and positive treatment outcome, to reduce treatment length without sacrificing that quality, to prevent overutilization of limited resources and services, and to enhance patient satisfaction with care, psychologists can expect to gain greater support for their unique testing skill from the managed care company. (pp. 24–25)

## FUTURE DIRECTIONS

The ways in which psychologists and other behavioral health-care clinicians conduct the types of psychological assessment described in this chapter underwent dramatic changes during the 1990s and continue to change in this new millennium. Some of those involved in the delivery of psychological assessment services may wonder (with some fear and trepidation) where the recently legislated health-care reform will lead the behavioral health-care industry and, in particular, how their ability to practice will be affected in the years to come. At the same time, others are eagerly awaiting the inevitable advances in technology and other resources that will come with the passage of time. What ultimately will occur is open to speculation. However, close observation of the practice of psychological assessment and the various industries that support it has led this author to arrive at a few predictions

as to where the field of psychological assessment is headed and the implications for patients, clinicians, and provider organizations.

### What the Field Is Moving Away From

One way of discussing what the field is moving toward is to first talk about what it is moving away from. In the case of psychological assessment, two trends are becoming quite clear. First, as just noted, the use of (and reimbursement for) psychological assessment has gradually been curtailed over the past several years. In particular, this has been the case with regard to indiscriminate administration of lengthy and expensive psychological test batteries. Payers have demanded evidence that the knowledge gained from the administration of these instruments in fact contributes to the delivery of cost-effective, efficient care to patients. This author sees no indications that this trend will stop.

Second, as the Piotrowski et al. (1998) findings suggest, the form of assessment commonly used is moving away from lengthy, multidimensional objective instruments (e.g., MMPI) or time-consuming projective techniques (e.g., Rorschach) that previously represented the standard in practice. The type of assessment authorized now usually involves the use of brief, inexpensive, problem-oriented instruments that have demonstrated validity for the purpose for which they will be used. Indeed, Mours et al.'s (2009) survey of APA internship training directors found that the BDI was the most prevalent (71.8%) standardized outcomes measure used at their training sites. This reflects a time-limited, problem-oriented approach to the treatment of modern behavioral health care. Today, the clinician may no longer be able to afford to spend a great deal of time in assessment if the patient is allowed only a limited number of payer-authorized sessions. Thus, brief instruments will continue to be more commonly employed for problem identification, progress monitoring, and outcomes assessment in the foreseeable future.

### Trends in Instrumentation

As for the types of instrumentation that will be used, one can probably expect continuation of emerging trends. Accompanying the increasing focus on outcomes assessment is recognition by payers and patients that positive change in several areas of functioning is at least as important as change in level of symptom severity when evaluating treatment effectiveness. For example, employers are interested in the patient's ability to resume the functions of his or her job, whereas family members are probably concerned with the patient's ability to resume his or her role as spouse or parent. Increasingly, measurement of the patient's functioning in areas other than psychological or mental status has come to be included as part of behavioral health-care outcomes systems. Instruments such as the Behavior and Symptom Identification Scale (BASIS-32; Eisen, Grob, & Klein, 1986; Eisen, Normand, Belanger, Gevorkian, & Irvin, 2004) and the OQ-45 (Lambert, Gregerson, & Burlingame, 2004) are good examples of such tools that can help meet these needs, as are the SF-36v2 Health Survey (SF-36v2; Maruish, 2011) and the SF-12v2 Health Survey (SF-12v2; Maruish, 2012). Probably the most visible indication of this is the incorporation of the SF-36v2 or SF-12v2 in both medical and behavioral health-care studies. One will likely see more non–symptom-oriented instruments, especially those emphasizing social and occupational role functioning, in increasing numbers over the next several years.

Other types of instrumentation will also become prominent. These may well include measures of specific variables that support outcomes and other assessment initiatives undertaken by individual health plans and provider organizations. What one organization or provider believes is important, or what payers determine is important for reimbursement or other purposes, will dictate what is measured. Instrumentation may also include measures that will be useful in predicting outcomes or even health-care expenses (see Fleishman, Cohen, Manning, & Kosinski, 2006) for individuals seeking specific psychotherapeutic services from those organizations.

### Trends in Technology

As has always been the case, someone has had the foresight to develop applications of several current technological advances used every day to the practice of psychological testing. Just as at one time the personal computer held the power of facilitating the testing and assessment process, Internet, faxback, and interactive voice response (IVR) technologies are being developed to make the assessment process easier, quicker, and more cost effective. (See Maruish, 2004; Maruish & Turner-Bowker, 2009.)

#### Internet Technology

The Internet has changed the way we do many things, so its use for the administering, scoring, and interpreting the results of psychological instruments should not be a surprise to anyone. The process here is straightforward. The clinician accesses the website on which the desired instrumentation resides. The desired test is selected for administration, and then the patient completes the test online. There is also the option of having the patient complete a paper-and-pencil version of the instrument and then having administrative staff enter the responses into the program. The data are scored and entered into the website's database, and a report is generated and transmitted back to the clinician and/or patient through the Internet. Turnaround time on receiving the report will be only a matter of minutes. The archived data can later be used for any of a number of purposes. The most obvious, of course, is reporting of aggregated data on a scheduled basis. Data from repeated testing can be used for treatment monitoring and report card generation. These data can also be used for psychometric test development or other statistical purposes.

The advantages of an Internet-based assessment system are rather clear-cut. This system allows for online administration of tests that include item response theory (IRT) or other branching logic for item selection. Any instruments available through a website can be easily updated and made available immediately to users, which is not the case with disk-distributed software for which updates and fixes are sometimes long in coming. The results of a test administration can be made available almost immediately. In addition, data from multiple sites can be aggregated and used for normative comparisons, test validation and risk adjustment purposes, generation of recovery curves, and any number of other statistically based activities that require large data sets.

There are only a couple of major disadvantages to an Internet-based system. The first and most obvious is the fact that it requires access to the Internet. Not all clinicians have Internet access. The second disadvantage has to do with the general Internet data security issue. However, it appears that the access and security issues are becoming less of a concern as the use of the Internet in the workplace becomes more of the standard and advances in Internet security software and procedures continue to take place.

#### Faxback Technology

The development of facsimile and faxback technology that has taken place over the past two decades has opened an important application for psychological testing. The process for implementing faxback technology is fairly simple. Paper-and-pencil answer sheets developed specifically for those tests available through the faxback system are completed by the patient. The answer sheet for a given test contains numbers or other types of code that tell the scoring and reporting software which test is being submitted. When the answer sheet is completed, it is faxed in—usually through a toll-free number that the scoring service has provided—to the central scoring facility, where data entry is checked for accuracy and then entered into a database and scored. A report is generated and faxed back to the clinician and/or patient within minutes. At the scoring end of the process, the whole system remains paperless. Later, the stored data can be used in the same ways as those gathered by an Internet-based system.

Like Internet-based systems, faxback systems allow for immediate access to software updates and fixes. Also, its paper-and-pencil administration format allows for more flexibility as to where and when a patient can be tested. Like Internet-based testing, a disadvantage has to do with security issues.

### IVR Technology

One of the more recent applications of new technology to the administration, scoring, and reporting of results of psychological tests can be found in the use of interactive voice response, or IVR, systems. Almost everyone is familiar with the IVR technology. When one places a phone call to order products, address billing problems, or find out what the balance is their checking accounts, one is often asked to provide information to an automated system in order to facilitate the meeting of his or her requests. This is IVR, and its applicability to test administration, data processing, and data storage should be obvious. What may not be obvious is that the data can later be accessed and used.

IVR technology is attractive from many standpoints. It requires no extra equipment beyond a touch-tone telephone for administration. It is available for use 24 hours a day, 7 days a week. One does not have to be concerned about the patient's reading ability, although oral comprehension levels need to be taken into account when determining which instruments are appropriate for administration via IVR or any audio administration format. As with Internet-based assessment, the system is such that IVR-based item selection or other branching logic can be used in the administration of the instrument. Updates and fixes are easily implemented system wide. Also, the ability to store data allows for comparison of results from previous testings, aggregation of data for statistical analyses, and all the other data analytic capabilities available through faxback- and Internet-based assessment.

As for the downside of IVR assessment, probably the biggest issue is that in many instances the patient must be the one to initiate the testing. Control of the testing is turned over to a party that may or may not be amenable to assessment. With less cooperative patients, this may mean costly follow-up efforts to encourage full participation in the process.

Dillman and his colleagues (Dillman, 2000; Dillman, Smyth, & Christian, 2009) and Maruish and Turner-Bowker (2009) have provided excellent guidance on the development of Internet, fax, and IVR systems for the administration of surveys. As such, these discussions can also provide sets of criteria that can assist the clinician in evaluating any of these technologies when they are used for the administration, scoring, and reporting the results from administration of psychological assessment instruments.

Overall, the developments in instrumentation and technology that have taken place over the past several years suggest two major trends. First, there will always be a need for the commercially published, multidimensional assessment instruments in which most psychologists received training. These instruments can efficiently provide the type of information that is critical in forensic, employment, or other evaluations that generally do not involve ongoing treatment-related decision making. However, use of these types of instruments will become the exception rather than the rule in day-to-day, in-the-trenches clinical practice. Instead, brief, valid, problem-oriented instruments will continue to gain prominence in the psychologist's armamentarium of assessment tools.

As for the second trend, it appears that the Internet will eventually become the primary medium for automated test administration, scoring, and reporting. Access to the Internet will soon become universal, expanding the possibilities for in-office and off-site assessment and making test administration simple, convenient, and cost effective for patients and psychologists.

## REFERENCES

Achenbach, T. M. (1991). *Manual for the Child Behavior Checklist/4–18 and 1991 Profile*. Burlington: University of Vermont, Department of Psychiatry.

Achenbach, T. M., & Rescorla, L. A. (2004). The Achenbach System of Empirically Based Assessment (ASEBA) for Ages 1.5 to 18 years. In M. E. Maruish (Ed.), *The use of psychological testing for treatment planning and outcomes assessment* (3rd ed.; pp. 179–213). *Vol. 2. Instruments for children and adolescents*. Mahwah, NJ: Erlbaum.

American Psychiatric Association. (2000). *Diagnostic and statistical manual of mental disorders* (4th ed., text revision). Washington, DC: Author.

American Psychological Association. (2002). Ethical principles of psychologists and code of conduct. *American Psychologist, 57*, 1060–1073.

Appelbaum, S. A. (1990). The relationship between assessment and psychotherapy. *Journal of Personality Assessment, 54,* 791–801.

Beck, A. T., Steer, R. A., & Brown, G. K. (1996). *Manual for the Beck Depression Inventory-II.* San Antonio, TX: Psychological Corporation.

Ben-Porath, Y. S., & Tellegen, A. (2008). *MMPI-2-RF (Minnesota Multiphasic Personality Inventory-2 Restructured Form) manual for administration, scoring, and interpretation.* Minneapolis: University of Minnesota Press.

Beutler, L. E., & Clarkin, J. (1990). *Systematic treatment selection: Toward targeted therapeutic interventions.* New York, NY: Brunner/Mazel.

Beutler, L. E., Malik, M., Talebi, H., Fleming, J., & Moleiro, C. (2004). Use of psychological tests/instruments for treatment planning. In M. E. Maruish (Ed.), *The use of psychological testing for treatment planning and outcomes assessment* (3rd ed.) Vol. 1, *General considerations* (pp. 111–145). Mahwah, NJ: Erlbaum.

Butcher, J. N. (1990). *The MMPI-2 in psychological treatment.* New York, NY: Oxford University Press.

Butcher, J. N. (2006). Assessment in clinical psychology: A perspective on the past, present challenges, and future prospects. *Clinical Psychology: Science and Practice, 13,* 205–209.

Butcher, J. N., Graham, J. R., Ben-Porath, Y. S., Tellegen, A. M., Dahlstrom, W. G., & Kaemmer, B. (2001). *MMPI-2: Manual for administration and scoring* (rev. ed.). Minneapolis: University of Minnesota Press.

Butcher, J. N., Graham, J. R., Williams, C. L., & Ben-Porath, Y. (1989). *Development and use of the MMPI-2 content scales.* Minneapolis: University of Minnesota Press.

Chambless, D. L., Renneberg, B., Goldstein, A., & Gracely, E. J. (1992). MCMI-diagnosed personality disorders among agoraphobic outpatients: Prevalence and relationship to severity and treatment outcome. *Journal of Anxiety Disorders, 6,* 193–211.

Chisholm, S. M., Crowther, J. H., & Ben-Porath, Y. S. (1997). Selected MMPI-2 scales' ability to predict premature termination and outcome from psychotherapy. *Journal of Personality Assessment, 69,* 127–144.

Christensen, L., & Mendoza, J. L. (1986). A method of assessing change in a single subject: An alteration of the RC index [Letter to the Editor]. *Behavior Therapy, 17,* 305–308.

Clair, D., & Prendergast, D. (1994). Brief psychotherapy and psychological assessments: Entering a relationship, establishing a focus, and providing feedback. *Professional Psychology: Research and Practice, 25,* 46–49.

Derogatis, L. R. (1992). *BSI: Administration, scoring and procedures manual—II.* Baltimore, MD: Clinical Psychometric Research.

Derogatis, L. R. (1994). *SCL-90-R Symptom Checklist-90-R: Administration, scoring, and procedures manual—II.* Baltimore, MD: Clinical Psychometric Research.

Derogatis, L. R., & Culpepper, W. J. (2004). Screening for psychiatric disorders. *The use of psychological testing for treatment planning and outcomes assessment* (3rd ed.), *Vol. 1, General considerations* (pp. 65–109). Mahwah, NJ: Erlbaum.

Dillman, D. A. (2000). *Mail and Internet surveys: The tailored design method* (2nd ed.). New York, NY: Wiley.

Dillman, D. A., Smyth, J. D., & Christian, L. M. (2009). *Internet, mail, and mixed-mode surveys: The tailored design method* (3rd ed.). Hoboken, NJ: Wiley.

Donabedian, A. (1980). *Explorations in quality assessment and monitoring. Vol. 1, The definition of quality and approaches to its assessment.* Ann Arbor, MI: Health Administration Press.

Donabedian, A. (1982). *Explorations in quality assessment and monitoring. Vol. 2, The criteria and standards of quality.* Ann Arbor, MI: Health Administration Press.

Donabedian, A. (1985). *Explorations in quality assessment and monitoring. Vol. 3, The methods and findings in quality assessment: An illustrated analysis.* Ann Arbor, MI: Health Administration Press.

Dorfman, W. I. (2000). Psychological assessment and testing under managed care. In A. J. Kent & M. Hersen (Eds.), *A psychologist's proactive guide to managed mental health care* (pp. 23–39). Mahwah, NJ: Erlbaum.

Dowd, E. T., Milne, C. R., & Wise, S. L. (1991). The therapeutic Reactance Scale: A measure of psychological reactance. *Journal of Counseling and Development, 69,* 541–545.

Eisen, S. V., Grob, M. C., & Klein, A. A. (1986). BASIS: The development of a self-report measure for psychiatric inpatient evaluation. *Psychiatric Hospital, 17,* 165–171.

Eisen, S. V., Normand, S. T., Belanger, A. J., Gevorkian, S., & Irvin, E. A. (2004). BASIS-32 and the Revised Behavior and Symptom Identification Scale (BASIS-R). In M. E. Maruish (Ed.), *The use of psychological testing for treatment planning and outcomes assessment* (3rd ed.), *Vol. 3, Instruments for adults* (pp. 79–113). Mahwah, NJ: Erlbaum.

Eisman, E. J., Dies, R. R., Finn, S. E., Eyde, L. D., Kay, G. G., Kubiszyn, T. W.,...Moreland, K. L. (2000). Problems and limitations in using psychological assessment in the contemporary health care delivery system. *Professional Psychology: Research and Practice, 31,* 131–140.

Elwood, R. W. (1993). Psychological tests and clinical discrimination: Beginning to address the base rate problem. *Clinical Psychology Review, 13,* 409–419.

Ficken, J. (1995). New directions for psychological testing. *Behavioral Health Management, 20,* 12–14.

Finn, S. E. (1996a). Assessment feedback integrating MMPI-2 and Rorschach findings. *Journal of Personality Assessment, 67,* 543–557.

Finn, S. E. (1996b). *Manual for using the MMPI-2 as a therapeutic intervention.* Minneapolis: University of Minnesota Press.

Finn, S. E. (2007). *In our clients' shoes: Theory and techniques of therapeutic assessment.* Mahwah, NJ: Erlbaum.

Finn, S. E., & Butcher, J. N. (1991). Clinical objective personality assessment. In M. Hersen, A. E. Kazdin, & A. S. Bellack (Eds.), *The clinical psychology handbook* (2nd ed., pp. 362–373). New York, NY: Pergamon Press.

Finn, S. E., & Martin, H. (1997). Therapeutic assessment with the MMPI-2 in managed health care. In J. N. Butcher (Ed.), *Objective personality assessment in managed health care: A practitioner's guide* (pp. 131–152). Minneapolis: University of Minnesota Press.

Finn, S. E., & Martin, H. (forthcoming). Therapeutic assessment: Using psychological testing as brief therapy. In K. F. Geisinger (Ed.), *APA Handbook of Testing and Assessment in Psychology. Vol. 2.* Washington, DC: American Psychological Association.

Finn, S. E., & Tonsager, M. E. (1992). Therapeutic effects of providing MMPI-2 test feedback to college students awaiting therapy. *Psychological Assessment, 4,* 278–287.

Fischer, C. T. (1994). *Individualizing psychological assessment.* Mahwah, NJ: Erlbaum.

Fischer, C. T. (2001). Collaborative exploration as an approach to personality assessment. In K. J., Schneider, J. F. T. Bugenthal, & J. F. Pierson (Eds.), *The handbook of humanistic psychology: Leading edges in theory, research and practice* (pp. 525–538). Thousand Oaks, CA: Sage.

Fischer, C. T., & Finn, S. E. (2008). Developing the life meaning of psychological test data. In R. P. Archer & S. R. Smith (Eds.), *Personality assessment* (pp. 379–404) New York, NY: Routledge Taylor & Francis.

Fleishman, J. A., Cohen, J. W., Manning, W. G., & Kosinski, M. (2006). Using the SF-12 health status measure to improve predictions of medical expenditures. *Medical Care, 44*(5), I-54–I-63.

Goldstein, L., Bershadsky, B., & Maruish, M. E. (2000). The INOVA behavioral healthcare pilot project. In M. E. Maruish (Ed.), *Handbook of psychological assessment in primary care settings* (pp. 735–760). Mahwah, NJ: Erlbaum.

Graham, J. R. (2000). *MMPI-2: Assessing personality and psychopathology* (3rd ed.). New York, NY: Oxford University Press.

Greene, R. L. (2000). *The MMPI-2: An interpretive manual* (2nd ed.). Boston, MA: Allyn & Bacon.

Greene, R. L., & Clopton, J. R. (2004). Minnesota Multiphasic Personality Inventory-2 (MMPI-2). In M. E. Maruish (Ed.), *The use of psychological testing for treatment planning and outcomes assessment* (3rd ed.), *Vol. 3. Instruments for adults* (pp. 449–477). Mahwah, NJ: Erlbaum.

Groth-Marnat, G. (2009). *Handbook of psychological assessment* (5th ed.). Hoboken, NJ: Wiley.

Groth-Marnat, G., & Edkins, G. (1996). Professional psychologists in general medical settings: A review of the financial efficacy of direct treatment interventions. *Professional Psychology: Research and Practice, 2,* 161–174.

Gurnee, M. C., & DaSilva, R. V. (1999). Constructing disease management programs. In S. Heffner (Ed.), *Disease management sourcebook 2000: Resources and strategies for program design and implementation* (pp. 12–18). New York, NY: Faulkner and Gray.

Hahn, S. R., Sydney, E., Kroenke, K., Williams, J. B. W., & Spitzer, R. L. (2004). Evaluation of mental disorders with the Primary Care Evaluation of Mental Disorders and Patient Health Questionnaire. In M. E. Maruish (Ed.), *The use of psychological testing for treatment planning and outcomes assessment* (3rd ed.), *Vol. 3, Instruments for adults* (pp. 235–291). Mahwah, NJ: Erlbaum.

Hannan, C., Lambert, M. J., Harmon, C., Nielsen, S. L., Smart, D. W., & Shimokawa, K. (2005). A lab test and algorithms for identifying clients at risk for treatment failure. *Journal of Clinical Psychology, 61,* 155–163.

Hatfield, D. R., & Ogles, B. M. (2004). The use of outcome measures by psychologists in clinical practice. *Professional Psychology: Research and Practice, 35,* 485–491.

Hatfield, D. R., & Ogles, B. M. (2007). Why some clinicians use outcomes measures and other do not. *Administration Policy in Mental Health & Mental Health Services Research, 34,* 283–291.

Hodges, K. (1994). *Child and Adolescent Functional Assessment Scale.* Ypsilanti: Eastern Michigan University.

Hodges, K. (2004). The Child and Adolescent Functional Assessment Scale. In M. E. Maruish (Ed.), *The use of psychological testing for treatment planning and outcomes assessment* (3rd ed.), *Vol. 2, Instruments for children and adolescents* (pp. 405–441). Mahwah, NJ: Erlbaum.

Howard, K. I., Brill, P. L., Lueger, R. J., O'Mahoney, M. T., & Grissom, G. R. (1993). *Integra outpatient tracking assessment.* Philadelphia, PA: Compass Information Services.

Howard, K. I., Moras, K., Brill, P. B., Martinovich, Z., & Lutz, W. (1996). Evaluation of psychotherapy: Efficacy, effectiveness, and patient progress. *American Psychologist, 51,* 1059–1064.

Hunsley, J. (2003). Introduction to the special section on incremental validity and utility of clinical assessment. *Psychological Assessment, 15,* 443–445.

Hunsley, J. (2009). Introduction to the special issue on developments in psychological measurement and assessment. *Canadian Psychology, 50,* 117–119.

Hunsley, J., & Meyer, G. J. (2003). The incremental validity of psychological testing and assessment: Conceptual, methodological, and statistical issues. *Psychological Assessment, 15,* 446–455.

Jacobson, N. S., Follette, W. C., & Revenstorf, D. (1984). Psychotherapy outcome research: Methods for reporting variability and evaluating clinical significance. *Behavior Therapy, 15,* 336–352.

Jacobson, N. S., Follette, W. C., & Revenstorf, D. (1986). Toward a standard definition of clinically significant change [Letter to the Editor]. *Behavior Therapy, 17,* 309–311.

Jacobson, N. S., & Truax, P. (1991). Clinical significance: A statistical approach defining meaningful change in psychotherapy research. *Journal of Consulting and Clinical Psychology, 59,* 12–19.

Kaplan, R. M., Patterson, T. L., & Groessl, E. J., (2004). Outcome assessment for resource allocation in primary care. In R. G. Frank, S. H. McDaniel, J. H. Bray, & M. Heldring (Eds.), *Primary care psychology* (pp. 293–315). Washington, DC: American Psychological Association.

Lachar, D. (2004). Personality Inventory for Children, Second Edition (PIC-2), Personality Inventory for Youth (PIY), and Student Behavior Survey (SBS). In M. E. Maruish (Ed.), *The use of psychological testing for treatment planning and outcomes assessment* (3rd ed.), *Vol. 2, Instruments for children and adolescents* (pp. 141–178). Mahwah, NJ: Erlbaum.

Lachar, D., Espadas, A., & Bailley, S. E. (2004). The Brief Psychiatric Rating Scale: Contemporary applications. In M. E. Maruish (Ed.), *The use of psychological testing for treatment planning and outcomes assessment* (3rd ed.), *Vol. 3, Instruments for adults* (pp. 153–190). Mahwah, NJ: Erlbaum.

Lachar, D., & Gruber, C. P. (2001). *Personality Inventory for Children-2 (PIC-2) manual.* Los Angeles, CA: Western Psychological Services.

Lambert, M. J. (2010). *Prevention of treatment failure: The use of measuring, monitoring, and feedback in clinical practice.* Washington, DC: American Psychological Association.

Lambert, M. J., Gregerson, A. T., & Burlingame, G. M. (2004). The Outcome Questionnaire–45. In M. E. Maruish (Ed.), *The use of psychological testing for treatment planning and outcomes assessment* (3rd ed.), *Vol. 3, Instruments for adults* (pp. 191–234). Mahwah, NJ: Erlbaum.

Lambert, M. J., Hansen, N. B., Umphress, V., Lunnen, K., Okiishi, J., Burlingame, G, . . . Reisinger, C. W. (1996). *Administration and scoring manual for the Outcome Questionnaire (OQ 45.2).* Wilmington, DE: American Professional Credentialing Services.

Lambert, M. J., Harmon, C., Slade, K., Whipple, J. L., & Hawkins, E. J. (2005). Providing feedback to psychotherapists on their patients' progress: Clinical results and practice suggestions. *Journal of Clinical Psychology, 61,* 165–174.

Lambert, M. J., & Hawkins, E. J. (2004). Use of psychological tests for assessing treatment outcomes. In M. E. Maruish (Ed.), *The use of psychological testing for treatment planning and outcomes assessment* (3rd ed.), *Vol. 1, General considerations* (pp. 171–195). Mahwah, NJ: Erlbaum.

Lambert, M. J., Whipple, J. L., Smart, D. W., Vermeesch, D. A., Nielsen, S. L., & Hawkins, E. J. (1999). *The effects of providing therapists with feedback on patient progress during psychotherapy: Are outcomes enhanced?* Manuscript submitted for publication.

Leon, S. C., Kopta, S. M., Howard, K. I., & Lutz, W. (1999). Predicting patients' responses to psychotherapy: Are some more predictable than others? *Journal of Consulting and Clinical Psychology, 67,* 698–704.

Lima, E. N., Stanley, S., Kaboski, B., Reitzel, L. R., Richey, J. A., Castro, Y., et al. (2005). The incremental validity of the MMPI-2: When does therapist access not enhance treatment outcome? *Psychological Assessment, 17,* 462–468.

Little, J. A., & Smith, S. R. (2009, March). *Collaborative assessment, supportive psychotherapy, or treatment a usual: An analysis of ultrabrief individualized intervention with psychiatric inpatients.* Paper presented at the annual meeting of the Society for Personality Assessment, Chicago, IL.

Martin, H. (2009). A bright future for psychological assessment. *Psychotherapy Bulletin, 44* (4), 23–26.

Maruish, M. E. (1999a). Introduction. In M. E. Maruish (Ed.), *The use of psychological testing for treatment planning and outcomes assessment* (2nd ed., pp. 1–39). Mahwah, NJ: Erlbaum.

Maruish, M. E. (1999b). Therapeutic assessment: Linking assessment and treatment. In M. Hersen, A. Bellack (Series Eds.), & C. R. Reynolds (Vol. Ed.), *Comprehensive clinical psychology: Volume 4, Assessment* (pp. 563–600). New York, NY: Elsevier Science.

Maruish, M. E. (2002a). *Essentials of treatment planning.* Hoboken, NJ: Wiley.

Maruish, M. E. (2002b). *Psychological testing in the age of managed behavioral health care.* Mahwah, NJ: Erlbaum.

Maruish, M. E. (2004). Introduction. In M. E. Maruish (Ed.), *The use of psychological testing for treatment planning and outcomes assessment* (3rd ed.), *Vol. 1, General considerations* (pp. 1–64). Mahwah, NJ: Erlbaum.

Maruish, M. E. (Ed.). (2011). *User's manual for the SF-36v2 Health Survey* (3rd ed.). Lincoln, RI: QualityMetric Incorporated.

Maruish, M. E. (Ed.). (2012). *User's manual for the SF-12v2 Health Survey* (3rd ed.). Lincoln, RI: QualityMetric Incorporated.

Maruish, M. E., & Turner-Bowker, D. M. (2009). *A guide to the development of certified modes of Short Form survey administration.* Lincoln, RI: QualityMetric.

Meyer, G. J., Finn, S. E., Eyde, L. D., Kay, G. G., Kubiszyn, T. W., Moreland, K. L.,...Dies, R. R. (1998). *Benefits and costs of psychological assessment in healthcare delivery: Report of the Board of Professional Affairs Psychological Assessment Work Group, Part I.* Washington, DC: American Psychological Association.

Meyer, G. J., Finn, S. E., Eyde, L. D., Kay, G. G., Moreland, K. L, Dies, R. R.,...Reed, G. M. (2001). Psychological testing and psychological assessment: A review of evidence and issues. *American Psychologist, 56,* 128–165.

Millon, T. (1987). *Manual for the MCMI-II.* Minneapolis, MN: National Computer Systems.

Millon, T., Millon, C., Davis, R., & Grossman, S. (2009). *MCMI-III Millon Clinical Multiaxial Inventory–III manual* (4th ed.). Minneapolis, MN: NCS Pearson.

Moreland, K. L. (1996). How psychological testing can reinstate its value in an era of cost containment. *Behavioral Healthcare Tomorrow, 5,* 59–61.

Morey, L. C. (1991). *The Personality Assessment Inventory professional manual.* Odessa, FL: Psychological Assessment Resources.

Morey, L. C. (1999). Personality Assessment Inventory. In M. E. Maruish (Ed.), *The use of psychological testing for treatment planning and outcomes assessment* (2nd ed., pp. 1083–1121). Mahwah, NJ: Erlbaum.

Morey, L. C. (2004). The Personality Assessment Inventory. In M. E. Maruish (Ed.), *The use of psychological testing for treatment planning and outcomes assessment* (3rd ed.), *Vol. 3, Instruments for adults* (pp. 509–551). Mahwah, NJ: Erlbaum.

Morey, L. C., Lowmaster, S. E., & Hopwood, C. J. (2010). A pilot study of manual assisted cognitive therapy with a therapeutic assessment augmentation for borderline personality disorder. *Psychiatry Research, 178,* 531–535.

Mours, J. M., Campbell, C. D., Gathercoal, K. A., & Peterson, M. (2009). Training in the use of psychotherapy outcome assessment measures at psychology internship sites. *Training and Education in Professional Psychology, 3,* 169–176.

Newman, F. L., Rugh, D., & Ciarlo, J. A. (2004). Guidelines for selecting psychological instruments for treatment planning and outcomes assessment. In M. E. Maruish (Ed.), *The use of psychological testing for treatment planning and outcomes assessment* (3rd ed.), *Vol. 1, General considerations* (pp. 197–214). Mahwah, NJ: Erlbaum.

Newman, F. L., & Tejeda, M. J. (2004). Selecting statistical procedures for progress and outcome assessment: The analysis of group data.

In M. E. Maruish (Ed.), *The use of psychological testing for treatment planning and outcomes assessment* (3rd ed.), *Vol. 1, General considerations* (pp. 291–333). Mahwah, NJ: Erlbaum.

Newman, F. L., & Wong, S. E. (2004). Progress and outcomes assessment of individual patient data: Selecting single-subject design and statistical procedures. In M. E. Maruish (Ed.), *The use of psychological testing for treatment planning and outcomes assessment* (3rd ed.), *Vol. 1, General considerations* (pp. 273–289). Mahwah, NJ: Erlbaum.

Newman, M. L., & Greenway, P. (1997). Therapeutic effects of providing MMPI-2 test feedback to clients at a university counseling service: A collaborative approach. *Psychological Assessment, 9,* 122–131.

Ogles, B. M., Lambert, M. J., & Fields, S. A. (2002). *Essentials of outcome assessment.* Hoboken, NJ: Wiley.

Overall, J. E., & Gorham, D. R. (1962). The Brief Psychiatric Rating Scale. *Psychological Reports, 10,* 799–812.

Phelps, R., Eisman, E. J., & Kohut, J. (1998). Psychological practice and managed care: Results of the CAPP practitioner survey. *Professional Psychology: Research and Practice, 29,* 31–36.

Piotrowski, C. (1999). Assessment practices in the era of managed care: Current status and future directions. *Journal of Clinical Psychology, 55,* 787–796.

Piotrowski, C., Belter, R. W., & Keller, J. W. (1998). The impact of "managed care" on the practice of psychological testing: Preliminary findings. *Journal of Personality Assessment, 70,* 441–447.

Pollak, J. (2010). Psychological testing: A look back; a look ahead. *National Psychologist, 19*(5), 8, 10.

Poston, J. M., & Hanson, W. E. (2010). Meta-analysis of psychological assessment as a therapeutic intervention. *Psychological Assessment, 22,* 203–212.

Prochaska, J. O., & Prochaska, J. M. (2004). Assessment as intervention within the Transtheoretical Model. In M. E. Maruish (Ed.), *The use of psychological testing for treatment planning and outcomes assessment* (3rd ed.), *Vol. 1, General considerations* (pp. 147–170). Mahwah, NJ: Erlbaum.

Reed, G. M., & Eisman, E. J. (2006). Uses and misuses of evidence: Managed care, treatment guidelines, and outcomes measurement in professional practice. In C. D. Goodheart, A. E. Kazdin, & R. J. Sternberg (Eds.), *Evidence-based psychotherapy: Where practice and research meet* (pp. 13–35). Washington, DC: American Psychological Association.

Schaefer, M., Murphy, R., Westerveld, M., & Gewirtz, A. (2000, August). *Psychological assessment and managed care: Guidelines for practice with children and adolescents.* Continuing education workshop presented at the annual meeting of the American Psychological Association, Washington, DC.

Sederer, L. I., Dickey, B., & Hermann, R. C. (1996). The imperative of outcomes assessment in psychiatry. In L. I. Sederer & B. Dickey (Eds.), *Outcomes assessment in clinical practice* (pp. 1–7). Baltimore, MD: Williams & Wilkins.

Sheehan, D. V., Lecrubier, Y., Sheehan, K. H., Amorim, P., Janavs, J., Weiller, E.,...Dunbar, G. C. (1998). The Mini-International Neuropsychiatric Interview (M.I.N.I.): The development and validation of a structured diagnostic interview for DSM-IV and ICD-10. *Journal of Clinical Psychiatry, 59*(Suppl. 20), 22–33.

Shimokawa, K., Lambert, M. J., & Smart, D. W. (2010). Enhancing treatment outcome of patients at risk of treatment failure: Meta-analytic and mega-analytic review of a psychotherapy quality assurance system. *Journal of Consulting and Clinical Psychology, 78,* 298–311.

Smith, S. R., & Archer, R. P. (2008). Introducing personality assessment. In R. P. Archer & S. R. Smith (Eds.), *Personality assessment* (pp. 1–35). New York, NY: Routledge Taylor & Francis.

Speer, D. C. (1992). Clinically significant change: Jacobson and Truax (1991) revisited. *Journal of Consulting and Clinical Psychology, 60,* 402–408.

Spielberger, C. D., Gorsuch, R. L., & Lushene, R. D. (1970). *STAI: Manual for the State-Trait Anxiety Inventory.* Palo Alto, CA: Consulting Psychologists Press.

Spielberger, C. D., Reheiser, E. C., Owen, A. E., & Sydeman, S. J. (2004). Measuring psychological vital signs of anxiety, anger, depression, and curiosity in treatment planning and outcomes assessment. In M. E. Maruish (Ed.), *The use of psychological testing for treatment planning and outcomes assessment* (3rd ed.), *Vol. 3, Instruments for adults* (pp. 421–447). Mahwah, NJ: Erlbaum.

Spitzer, R. L., Kroenke, K., Williams, J. B., & Patient Health Questionnaire Primary Care Study Group (1999). Validation and utility of a self-report version of PRIME-MD: The PHQ primary care study. *Journal of the American Medical Association, 282,* 1737–1744.

Spitzer, R. L., Williams, J. B., Kroenke, K., Linzer, M., duGruy, F. V., Hahn, S. R., . . . Johnson, J. G. (1994). Utility of a new procedure for diagnosing mental disorders in primary care: The PRIME–MD 1000 study. *Journal of the American Medical Association, 272,* 1749–1756.

Stewart, A. L., & Ware, J. E. Jr. (1992). *Measuring functioning and well-being.* Durham, NC: Duke University Press.

Stout, C. E., & Cook, L. P. (1999). New areas for psychological assessment in general health care settings: What to do today to prepare for tomorrow. *Journal of Clinical Psychology, 55,* 797–812.

Strategic Advantage, Inc. (1996). *Symptom Assessment-45 Questionnaire manual.* Minneapolis, MN: Author.

Tellegen, A., & Ben-Porath, Y. S. (2008). *MMPI-2-RF (Minnesota Multiphasic Personality Inventory-2 Restructured Form) technical manual.* Minneapolis: University of Minnesota Press.

Tharinger, D. J., Finn, S. E., Gentry, L., Hamilton, A., Fowler, J., Matson, M., . . . Walkowiak, J. (2009). Therapeutic assessment with children: A pilot study of treatment acceptability and outcome. *Journal of Personality Assessment, 91,* 238–244.

Todd, W. E. (1999). Introduction: Fulfilling the promise of disease management: Where are we today? Where are we headed? In S. Heffner (Ed.), *Disease management sourcebook 2000: Resources and strategies for program design and implementation* (pp. xi–xxiii). New York, NY: Faulkner and Gray.

United Behavioral Health. (2010). *2010 psychological and neuropsychological testing guidelines.* Retrieved from https://www.ubhonline.com/html/psychTesting/pdf/psychNeuropsychTestGuidelines.pdf

Wampold, B. E., & Jenson, W. R. (1986). Clinical significance revisited [Letter to the Editor]. *Behavior Therapy, 17,* 302–305.

World Health Organization. (1992). *International classification of diseases* (10th rev.). Geneva, Switzerland: Author.

CHAPTER 7

# Computerized Personality Assessment

JAMES N. BUTCHER

Computers have been an integral part of psychological assessment since the 1950s although initially only in the scoring and processing of research information. Over the past 60 years, their applications in mental healthcare and forensic settings have broadened, and computers have become important and necessary components to assessment. The benefits of computers to the field of psychology continue to expand as technology becomes more advanced, allowing for more sophisticated operations, including integrative test interpretation, which once was the sole domain of humans. How can an electronic and nonintuitive machine perform a complex cognitive process such as psychological test interpretation, a task that requires extensive knowledge and experience and a modicum of intuition?

The theoretical rationale underlying automated psychological test interpretation was provided in 1954 when Meehl published a monograph in which he debated the merits of actuarial or statistical (objective) decision-making methods versus relying on more subjective or clinical strategies. Meehl's analysis of the relative strengths of actuarial prediction over clinical judgment led to the conclusion that decisions based upon objectively applied interpretive

I would like to express my appreciation to Carolyn Williams, who provided editorial suggestions.

rules were ultimately more valid than judgments based on subjective strategies. Subsequently, Dawes, Faust, and Meehl (1989) and Grove and Meehl (1996) have reaffirmed the finding that objective assessment procedures are equal or superior to subjective interpretation methods. In a meta-analysis of 136 studies, Grove, Zald, Lebow, Smith, and Nelson (2000) reviewed the existing research and concluded that the advantage in accuracy for statistical prediction over clinical prediction was approximately 10%.

In spite of the common foundations and comparable rationales that actuarial assessment and computerized assessment share, they are not strictly the same. Computer-based test interpretation (CBTI) can be either clinical or actuarial in foundation. It is an actuarial task only if its interpretive output is determined strictly by statistical rules that have been demonstrated empirically to exist between the input and the output data. A computer-based system for describing or predicting events that are not actuarial in nature might base its interpretations on the work of a clinician (or even an astrologer) who hypothesizes relationships using theory, practical experience, or even lunar phases and astrology charts.

In the field of psychological assessment, it is important that the validity of computerized assessment instruments be demonstrated if they are to be relied on for making crucial dispositions or decisions that can affect people. Psychological tests are often used in high-stakes assessments, that is, those involving personnel selection, job placement, not guilty by reason of insanity pleas, or personal injury litigation in which disabled people might be denied compensation. Unfortunately, new psychological tests are published without an empirical database to support or allow us to verify their conclusions. A number of professional guidelines pertinent to computer-based assessment have been published: The Committee on Professional Standards of the American Psychological Association (APA) (1984) cautioned psychologists who used interpretive reports in business and school settings against using computer-derived narrative test summaries in the absence of adequate data to validate their accuracy. The APA Ethics Code (2002, 2010) also cautioned that psychologists base the opinions contained in their recommendations, reports, and diagnostic or evaluative statements, including forensic testimony, on information and techniques sufficient to substantiate their "findings" (p. 493).

The need for maintaining high standards in psychological assessment involving computer or Internet-based assessment is described in this chapter. Several sources provide further information (Bersoff & Hofer, 2008; British Psychological Society Psychological Testing Centre, 2002; Coyne, 2006; Naglieri, Drasgow, Schmit, Handler, Profitera, Margolis, & Velasquez, 2004).

## WAYS COMPUTERS ARE USED IN CLINICAL ASSESSMENT

In the history of psychological assessment, the various computer-based test applications evolved differently. The relatively more routine tasks (i.e., scoring) were implemented first, and the applications of more complex tasks, such as interpretation, required several decades to become available.

### Scoring and Data Analysis

The earliest computer-based applications of psychological tests involved scoring and data processing in research. Almost as soon as large mainframe computers became available for general use in the 1950s, researchers began to use them to process test development information. In the early days, data were input for scoring by key entry, paper tape, or cards. Today optical readers or scanners are used widely but not exclusively. It is also common to find procedures in which the respondent enters his or her responses directly into the machine using a keyboard or in connection with the Internet. Allard, Butler, Faust, and Shea (1995) found that computer scoring was more reliable than manual scoring of test responses.

### Profiling and Charting of Test Results

In the 1950s, some commercial services for scoring psychological tests for both research and clinical purposes emerged. These early services typically provided summary scores for the test protocols; in some cases, they provided a profile graph with the appropriate levels of the scale elevation designated. Initially, the technology of computer graphics of the time did not allow for complex visual displays or graphing a profile by connecting the dots, and the practitioner needed to connect the dots manually to complete the profile.

### Listing of Possible Interpretations

As computer use became more widespread, its potential advantage to the process of profiling of scores and assigning meaning to significantly elevated scores came to be recognized and computer-based assessment quickly evolved into report generation (Bartram, 2006). A research group at Mayo Clinic in Rochester, MN, developed a computer program that actually provided rudimentary interpretations for the Minnesota Multiphasic Personality Inventory (MMPI) results of patients being seen at the hospital (Rome et al., 1962). The interpretive program was comprised of 110 statements or descriptions that were based on empirical correlates for particular MMPI scale elevations. The program simply listed the most relevant statements for each client's profile. This system was in use for many years to assess psychopathology of patients undergoing medical examinations at the Mayo Clinic.

In 1963 Piotrowski completed a very elaborate computer program for Rorschach interpretation (Exner, 1987). The program was based on his own interpretive logic and included hundreds of parameters and rules. Because the program was too advanced for the computer technology available at that time, Piotrowski's program never became very popular. However, it was a precursor of modern computer programs for calculating scores and indexes and generating interpretations of Rorschach data.

### Evolution of More Complex Test Interpretation and Report Generation

It was not long until others saw the broader potential in computer-based test interpretation. Fowler (1969) developed a computer program for the drug company Hoffman-La Roche Laboratories that not only interpreted the important scales of the MMPI but also combined the interpretive statements into a narrative report. Several other computer-based systems became available in the years that followed—for example, the Caldwell Report (Caldwell, 1996) and the Minnesota Report (Butcher, 1982).

Exner (1987) and Weiner (2004, 2007) provided a computer-based interpretation system for the Rorschach that included a more advanced interpretation system for Rorschach variables that has come to be widely used in clinical assessment. Exner (2005) provided cautions about using computer-based interpretive programs. He noted that "interpretative statements are only empirically based hypotheses that must be reviewed and evaluated carefully by the user" and that a computer program "cannot think, and it cannot integrate data at a level higher than that for which it has been programmed. The complexity and uniqueness of each human makes it essentially impossible for any program to be developed that would account for all of the idiosyncratic features that mark the individual" (p. 3).

### Adapting the Administration of Test Items

Computer administration has been widely used as a means of obtaining response data from clients. This response format has many advantages over traditional manual processing methods—particularly the potential time saved, elimination of the possibility that respondents would make errors while filling out handwritten answer sheets, and elimination of the possibility that clinicians and technicians would make errors while hand-scoring items.

The flexibility of the computer offers the option of adapting the test to suit the needs and preferences of the test taker instead of simply administering all the items in the test. The administration of test items in a paper-and-pencil inventory requires that the test taker respond to each and every question regardless of whether it applies. Psychologists have been interested in modifying the administration of test items to fit the respondent—that is, to tailor a test administration to be analogous to an interview. For example, in an interview, if a question such as *are you married?* is answered *no,* all subsequent questions take this response into account and are branched away from seeking responses to items pertinent to being married. In other words, the items are administered in an adapted or tailored manner for the specific test taker.

The comparability and validity of this method (known as computer- adaptive testing, or CAT) have been explored in several studies (e.g., Butcher, Keller, & Bacon, 1985). The method of adapting the administration to tailor-make the test to the client follows strategies such as Item

Response Theory (IRT; see discussions by Bartram, 2006; Lord, 1980). Roper, Ben-Porath, and Butcher (1995) examined an adaptive version of the MMPI-2. Three versions of the MMPI-2 were administered to 571 undergraduate psychology students: a booklet version, a CAT version, and a conventional computerized version. Each participant took the same format twice, took the booklet and CAT versions (in counterbalanced order), or took the conventional and CAT versions (again, in counterbalanced order).

There were few statistically significant differences in the resulting mean scale scores between the booklet and CAT formats. A number of researchers have conducted evaluations of IRT-based personality test administration (Aguado, Rubio, Hontangas, & Hernandez, 2005; Ben-Porath, Slutske, & Butcher, 1989; Butcher et al., 1985; Chuah, Drasgow, & Roberts, 2006; Forbey & Ben-Porath, 2007; Forbey, Ben-Porath, & Gartland, 2009; Forbey, Handel, & Ben-Porath, 2000; Hol, Vorst, & Mellenbergh, 2008; Reise & Henson, 2000; Walter, Becker, Bjorner, Fliege, Klapp, & Rose, 2007).

CATs using IRT have also shown potential problems compared with the full form of tests. Simms and Clark (2005) found that an IRT-based computer-adaptive procedure significantly reduced the number of items administered (37%), although the adapted version was somewhat less effective in predicting variables for some scales. Ortner (2008) showed significant differences in average gained person parameters for three out of seven scales between the adaptive versions as well as differences in average reaction times for answering the items. Results indicated context effects as a problem for using CAT to measure personality. Archer, Tirrell, and Elkins (2001) conducted an empirical study on an abbreviated MMPI-A that they considered to have impact on CAT versions. They reported that relatively lower congruency of profile configural patterns when individual profiles are compared as derived from a full administration of the MMPI-A and as prorated from a short-form administration, raising cautions about shortening psychological tests through adaptation.

Computer adaptation strategies such as IRT generally perform more effectively if the item pool of the scale is homogeneous in content—that is, if the scale is comprised of highly correlated items on a single dimension. Some measures, such as the MMPI-2 clinical scales, are heterogeneous and composed of multiple distinct item sets in order to predict complex diagnostic problems. Thus, these measures are not well suited to IRT procedures. Other computer-administered procedures have been shown to work more effectively than IRT in abbreviating heterogeneous scales (Butcher et al., 1985). This approach was referred to as the "countdown strategy," and it was shown to be effective when the assessment goal of testing is classifying a client into one of two groups. The logic of the strategy is very straightforward: If one wishes to classify an individual using a particular cutting score on the scale, then one need only administer the number of items needed to rule out classification in one group to positively establish membership in the other. For example, if the instrument is 30 items long and a score of 20 is needed to be classified as falling into the criterion category, a subject who fails to endorse any of the first 11 items cannot attain a score that would classify him or her as meeting the criterion, even if he or she answered all of the remaining items in the deviant direction. The countdown approach, in this case, suggests that only the first 11 items would need to be administered in order to positively classify this individual into the nondeviant group. Of course, if our hypothetical examinee endorses any of the first 11 items, more items will need to be administered.

Overall, even though the IRT-based studies have been shown to lower the number of items required to estimate the full-scale score, this application is difficult to justify in situations in which important recommendations or decisions are made about people, such as in court, personnel screening, or clinical treatment settings. The saving of item administration time is of considerable less importance than having an accurate, fuller assessment.

One problem with CATs is that the scales become abbreviated and thus are impacted by lower scale reliability. In general, abbreviated versions of psychological tests have been questioned. Emons, Sijtsma, and Meijer (2007) found that shortened tests were found to classify at most 50% of a group consistently. They found that the results were much better for tests that contained 20 or 40 items.

## Decision Making by Computer

Available computer interpretation systems, even the most sophisticated report-generating programs, are essentially look-up, list-out programs—that is, they provide canned interpretations that have been stored in the computer to be called up when various test scores and indexes are obtained. As Bartram (2006) pointed out, despite the increasing sophistication of computer-based assessment systems in the testing field, the application almost always involved the implementation of older paper-and-pencil tests.

The computer does not actually make decisions but simply follows instructions (often very complex and detailed ones) about the statements or paragraphs that are to be printed out. The use of computers to actually make decisions or simulate what the human brain does in making decisions—an activity that has been referred to as *artificial intelligence*—has not been fully accomplished in the assessment field. One program that comes closest to having the computer actually make the decisions is the Minnesota Personnel Screening Report (Butcher, 2002). In this system, the computer has been programmed with decision rules defining an array of test scores and decisions (e.g., *manages stress well*). The computer program determines the scores and indexes and then decides which of the summary variables are most appropriate for the range of scores obtained.

Butcher (1988) investigated the usefulness of this computer-based MMPI assessment strategy for screening in personnel settings. A group of 262 airline pilot applicants were evaluated by both expert clinicians and by computer-based decision rules. The overall level of adjustment of each applicant was rated by experts (using only an MMPI profile) on a Likert-type scale with three categories: *adequate, problems possible,* and *problems likely.* The computer-based decision rules were also used to make determinations about the applicants. Here the categories of *excellent, good, adequate, problems possible,* and *poor* were used to classify the profiles. The results showed high agreement between the computer-based decisions and those made by clinicians in rating overall adjustment. Over 50% of individuals falling into the adequate category based on the computer-based rules were given ratings of adequate by the clinicians. There was agreement between the computer rules and clinician judgment on the possibility of problems being present in 26.7% of cases. Over 60% of individuals rated as poor by the computer rules were given problems likely ratings by the clinicians. This study indicated that there could be substantial agreement between clinicians and the computer when an objectively interpreted test is used. The study did not, however, provide information on the external validity of either approach because no criteria were available to allow for an assessment of the relative accuracy of either method.

## EQUIVALENCE OF COMPUTER-ADMINISTERED TESTS AND TRADITIONAL METHODS

Several authorities have raised questions about the equivalence of computer-based assessment methods and traditional psychological testing procedures. Hofer and Green (1985), for example, pointed out that there are several conditions related to computerized test administration that could produce noncomparable results. Some people might be uncomfortable with computers and feel awkward dealing with them; this would make the task of taking tests on a computer different from standard testing procedures. Moreover, factors such as the type of equipment used and the nature of the test material (i.e., when item content deals with sensitive and personal information) might make respondents less willing (or more willing) to reveal their true feelings to a computer than to a human being. These situations might lead to atypical results for computerized assessment compared to a traditional format. Another possible disadvantage of computer assessment is that computer-generated interpretations may be excessively general in scope and not specific enough for practical use. Finally, there is a potential for computer-based results to be misused because they might be viewed as more scientific than they actually are, simply because they came out of a computer (Butcher, 1987; Butcher, Perry, & Dean, 2009). It is therefore important that the issues of measurement comparability and, of course, validity of the interpretation be addressed. The next section addresses the comparability of CATs and paper-and-pencil measures or other traditional methods of data collection.

## Comparability of Psychiatric Screening by Computer and Clinical Interview

Several studies have reported on adaptations of psychiatric interviews for computer-based screening. Research has shown that clients in mental health settings report feeling comfortable with providing personal information through computer assessment (e.g., Hile & Adkins, 1997). Moreover, research has shown that computerized assessment programs were generally accurate in being able to diagnose the presence of behavioral problems. Ross, Swinson, Larkin, and Doumani (1994) used the Computerized Diagnostic Interview Schedule (C-DIS) and a clinician-administered Structural Clinical Interview for the *Diagnostic and Statistical Manual of Mental Disorders–Third Edition–Revised* (*DSM-III-R*; SCID) to evaluate 173 clients. They reported the congruence between the two instruments to be acceptable except for substance abuse disorders and antisocial personality disorder, in which the levels of agreement were poor. The C-DIS was able to rule out the possibility of comorbid disorders in the sample with approximately 90% accuracy.

Farrell, Camplair, and McCullough (1987) evaluated the capability of a computerized interview to identify the presence of target complaints in a clinical sample. Both a face-to-face, unstructured intake interview and the interview component of a computerized mental health

information system, the Computerized Assessment System for Psychotherapy Evaluation and Research (CASPER), were administered to 103 adult clients seeking outpatient psychological treatment. Results showed relatively low agreement (mean $r = .33$) between target complaints as reported by clients on the computer and as identified by therapists in interviews. However, 9 of the 15 complaints identified in the computerized interview were found to be significantly associated with other self-report and therapist-generated measures of global functioning.

## Comparability of Standard and Computer-Administered Questionnaires

The comparability of computer and standard administrations of personality questionnaires has been widely researched (e.g., Honaker, Harrell, & Buffaloe, 1988; Jemelka, Wiegand, Walker, & Trupin, 1992; Lambert, Andrews, Rylee, & Skinner, 1987; Merten and Ruch, 1996; Pinsoneault, 1996; Roper et al., 1995; Schuldberg, 1988; Watson, Juba, Anderson, & Manifold, 1990; Wilson, Genco, & Yager, 1985).

The question of whether computer-administered and paper and pencil forms are equivalent was pretty much laid to rest by a comprehensive meta-analysis (Finger & Ones, 1999). Their analysis included 14 studies, all of which included computerized and standard formats of the MMPI or MMPI-2, that had been conducted between 1974 and 1996. They reported that the differences in $T$ score means and standard deviations between test formats across the studies were negligible. Correlations between forms were consistently near 1.00. Based on these findings, the authors concluded that computer-administered inventories are comparable to booklet-administered forms. Recently, Naus, Philipp, and Samsi (2009) conducted an equivalency study in the administration of paper-and-pencil, computer, and Internet formats using the Quality of Life Scale, the Beck Depression Scale, and the Neuroticism-Extroversion-Openness Inventory (NEO) personality scale. Although some significant differences were obtained on the NEO between computer-administered and paper-and-pencil formats, the researchers generally found that the computer administration format was an efficient way to conduct research.

## COMPUTER-BASED PERSONALITY NARRATIVES

Computer-based psychological interpretation systems usually provide a comprehensive interpretation of relevant test variables, along with scores, indexes, critical item responses, and other pertinent test information. (For further discussions, see: Butcher, 2009, 2010, 2011; Coyne, 2006; Weiner & Greene, 2008.) The narrative report for a computer-based psychological test interpretation is often designed to read like a psychological report that has been prepared by a practitioner. However, psychological tests differ with respect to the amount of valid and reliable information available about them and consequently differ in terms of the time required to program the information into an effective interpretive system. Of course, if more research is available about a particular instrument, the more likely it is that the interpretations will be accurate. Instruments that have been widely researched, such as the MMPI and MMPI-2 (which have a research base of more than 19,000 articles) will likely have a more defensible interpretive system than will a test that has little or no research base. Test users need to be aware of the fact that some commercially available test interpretation systems are published with minimal established validity research to support the interpretations. Simply being commercially available by computer and widely marketed does not ensure the validity of a test.

### Steps in the Development of a Narrative Report

In developing a computer-based narrative report, the system developer typically follows several steps:

- Develops a systematic strategy for storing and retrieving relevant test information. This initial phase of development sets out the rationale and procedure for incorporating the published research findings into a coherent theme.
- Designs a computer program that scores the relevant scales and indexes and presents the information in a consistent and familiar form. This step may involve development of a program that accurately plots test profiles.
- Writes a dictionary of appropriate and validated test behaviors or correlates that can serve as the narrative database. The test index definitions stored into memory can vary in complexity, ranging from discrete behaviors (e.g., if Scale 1 receives a $T$ score greater than 70, print: *Reports many physical symptoms*) to extensive descriptors (e.g., if Scale 2 receives a $T$ score greater than 65, print: *This client has obtained a significant scale elevation on the depression scale. It is likely that he is reporting extensive mental health*

*symptoms including depression, worry, low self-esteem, low energy, feelings of inadequacy, lacking in self-confidence, social withdrawal, and a range of physical complaints*). The dictionary of stored test information can be quite extensive, particularly if the test on which it is based has a broad research base. For example, a comprehensive MMPI-2-based interpretive system would likely include hundreds of pages of stored behavioral correlates.

- Specifies the interpretive algorithms for combining test indexes and dictionary text. This component of the interpretive system is the engine for combining the test indexes to use in particular reports and locating the appropriate dictionary text relevant for the particular case.
- Organizes the narrative report in a logical and user-friendly format.
- Determines what information is available in the test being interpreted and organizes the information into a structure that maximizes the computer-generated hypotheses.
- Tests the system extensively before it is offered to the public. This may involve generating sample reports that test the system with a broad range of possible test scores and indexes.
- Eliminates internal contradictions within the system. This phase involves examining a broad range of reports on clients with known characteristics in order to modify the program to prevent contradictory or incorrect statements from appearing in the narrative (e.g., stating that a patient's response style is characterized by underreporting and overreporting).
- Revises the system periodically to take into account new research on the test instrument.

### Responsibilities of Users of Computer-Based Reports

Users of computer-based psychological reports assume specific responsibilities (see Atlis, Hahn, & Butcher, 2006; Butcher et al., 2009; Butcher,1987, 2009), and these responsibilities are especially important when the reports are used in forensic evaluations in which the resulting interpretations can adversely impact an individual if incorrect decisions are made.

Computer report users need to take into consideration the next points:

- It is important to ensure that appropriate custody of answer sheets and generated test materials be maintained (i.e., kept in a secure place). Practitioners should see to it that the client's test materials are properly labeled and securely stored so that records can be identified if circumstances call for recovery at a later date—for example, in a court case.

- The practitioner should closely follow computer-based validity interpretations because clients in both clinical and forensic cases may have motivation to distort their answers in order to present a particular pattern in the evaluation.

- It is up to the practitioner to ensure that there is an appropriate match between the prototypal report generated by the computer and background and other test information available about a particular client. Does the narrative report match the test scores generated by the scoring program? (Please refer to the note at the end of the sample computerized narrative report presented in the appendix to this chapter.) It is customary for reports to contain language that stresses the importance of the practitioner making sure that the case matches the report.

- The practitioner must integrate congruent information from the client's background and other sources into evaluation based on test results. Computer-based reports are by necessity general personality or clinical descriptions based on prototypes.

- It is the responsibility of the practitioner using computer-based test interpretations to account for any possible discrepancies between the report and other client data.

## Illustration of a Computer-Based Narrative Report

Although the output of various interpretive systems can vary from one service to another or from one test to another, the Minnesota Report for the MMPI-2 offers a fairly representative example of what one might expect when using computerized interpretation services. The MMPI-2 responses for the case of Susan K. were submitted to be interpreted by computer. The resulting report is presented in the appendix to this chapter.

Susan K., a 38-year-old divorced woman, a mother of one child who is 10 years old, was admitted to a private inpatient psychiatric program after she attempted suicide. Her parents, who accompanied her to the hospital, reported that she has been severely depressed for several months following her divorce. Although she had been in outpatient psychiatric treatment for 2 years and was being treated with antidepressant medication on an outpatient basis, she showed little improvement in her mood. Ms. K. has a history of outpatient mental health treatment for

mood disorders on three occasions since she was 22 years of age.

Ms. K. graduated from high school and had worked as a checkout clerk in a large retail store and became an assistant manager. She was married at the age of 18 and worked periodically at the store. She was divorced a year before her suicide attempt and was receiving both financial and emotional support from her parents during this period. The stress she was experiencing after her divorce intensified her depression, and her medication failed to provide relief for her symptoms.

The MMPI-2 was administered to her a week after she was admitted to the hospital as a component of her intake evaluation. Although her MMPI-2 test results showed some extreme responding to items that are infrequently endorsed (scale F), her symptom profiles were considered valid and reflected severe mental health problems she was experiencing. See the appendix for Ms. K's MMPI-2 profiles, test scores, and computer-based narrative report. Ms. K.'s extensive endorsement of mental health symptoms in the MMPI-2 reflected her severe affective disorder, low morale, and inability to deal effectively with problems she is facing. The Minnesota Report narrative described her low personality functioning and pointed out the need for intensive treatment to assist her in managing her adjustment problems.

During her hospitalization, Ms. K. was treated with electroconvulsive therapy (ECT) along with both individual and group therapy. She responded positively to the treatment and was discharged from the inpatient facility after 2 months of follow-up treatment. She continued in outpatient treatment after her discharge. Her mood substantially improved following her therapy, and she was able to return home and was able to resume work.

## VALIDITY RESEARCH ON COMPUTERIZED NARRATIVE REPORTS

Interpretive reports generated by computer-based psychological assessment systems need to have demonstrated validity even if the instruments on which the interpretations are based are supported by research literature. Computerized outputs are typically one step removed from the test index-validity data relationships from the original test; therefore, it is important to demonstrate that the inferences included in the computerized report are reliable and valid in the settings where they are used. Some computer interpretation programs now in use also provide comprehensive personality assessment by combining test findings into narrative descriptions and conclusions. Butcher, Perry, and Atlis (2000) and Butcher et al. (2009) reviewed the validity research for computer-based interpretation systems. Information from their evaluations are summarized in the following sections. In discussing computer-based assessment, it is useful to subdivide computerized reports into two broad categories: descriptive summaries and consultative reports. Descriptive summaries (e.g., for the 16 Personality Factor Test [16PF]) are usually on a scale-by-scale basis without integration of the results into a narrative. Consultative reports (e.g., those for the MMPI-2) provide detailed analysis of the test data and emulate as closely as possible the interpretive strategies of a trained human consultant.

## Narrative Reports in Personality Assessment

The validity of computerized reports has been extensively studied in both personality testing and psychiatric screening (computer-based diagnostic interviewing). Research aimed at exploring the accuracy of narrative reports has been conducted for several computerized personality tests, such as the Rorschach Inkblot Test (e.g., Harris, Niedner, Feldman, Fink, & Johnson, 1981; Prince & Guastello, 1990), the 16PF (e.g., Guastello & Rieke, 1990; O'Dell, 1972), the Marital Satisfaction Questionnaire (Hoover & Snyder, 1991), and the Millon Clinical Multiaxial Inventory (MCMI; Moreland & Onstad, 1987; Rogers, Salekin, & Sewell, 1999). Moreland (1987) surveyed results from the most widely studied computer-based personality assessment instrument, the MMPI. Evaluation of diagnostic interview screening by computer (e.g., Structured Diagnostic Interview for DSM-IV) has also been reported (First, 1994). Moreland (1987) provided an overview of studies that investigated the accuracy of computer-generated MMPI narrative reports. Some studies compared computer-generated narrative interpretations with evaluations provided by human interpreters. One methodological limitation of this type of study is that the clinician's interpretation might not be valid and accurate (Moreland, 1987). For example, Labeck, Johnson, and Harris (1983) asked three clinicians (each with at least 12 years of clinical experience) to rate the quality and the accuracy of code-type interpretations generated by an automated MMPI program. (The clinicians did not rate the fit of a narrative to a particular patient, however.) Results indicated that the MMPI code-type, diagnostic, and overall profile interpretive statements were consistently rated by the expert judges as strong interpretations. The narratives

provided by automated MMPI programs were judged to be substantially better than average when compared to the blind interpretations of similar profiles that were produced by the expert clinicians. The researchers, however, did not specify how they judged the quality of the blind interpretation and did not investigate the possibility that statements in the blind interpretation could have been so brief and general (especially when compared to a two-page narrative CBTI) that they could have artificially inflated the ratings of the CBTI reports. In spite of these limitations, this research design was considered useful in evaluating the overall congruence of computer-generated decision and interpretation rules.

Shores and Carstairs (1998) evaluated the effectiveness of the Minnesota Report in detecting faking. They found that the computer-based reports detected fake-bad profiles in 100% of the cases and detected fake-good profiles in 94% of the cases. The primary way researchers have attempted to determine the accuracy of computer-based tests is through the use of raters (usually clinicians) who judge the accuracy of computer interpretations based on their knowledge of the client (Moreland, 1987). For example, a study by Butcher and colleagues (1998) explored the utility of computer-based MMPI-2 reports in Australia, France, Norway, and the United States. In all four countries, clinicians administered the MMPI-2 to their patients being seen for psychological evaluation or therapy; they used a booklet format in the language of each country. The tests were scored and interpreted by the Minnesota Report using the American norms for MMPI-2. Practitioners familiar with the clients rated the information available in each narrative section as *insufficient, some, adequate, more than adequate,* or *extensive.* In each case, the clinicians also indicated the percentage of accurate descriptions of the patient and were asked to respond to open-ended questions regarding ways to improve the report. Relatively few raters found the reports inappropriate or inaccurate. In all four countries, the Validity Considerations, Symptomatic Patterns, and Interpersonal Relations sections of the Minnesota Report were found to be the most useful sections in providing detailed information about the patients, compared with the Diagnostic Considerations section. Over two thirds of the records were considered to be highly accurate, which indicated that clinicians judged 80% to 100% of the computer-generated narrative statements in them to be appropriate and relevant. Overall, in 87% of the reports, at least 60% of the computer-generated narrative statements were believed to be appropriate and relevant to understanding the client's clinical picture.

J. E. Williams and Weed (2004) conducted a study in which test users were randomly assigned to rate either a single authentic CBTI report on one of their clients or a single CBTI report generated from a modal MMPI-2 profile for their clinical setting. They reported that 257 authentic and modal CBTI reports were rated by 41 clinicians on 10 dimensions. They found that each of the authentic reports received substantially higher ratings than the modal reports, with ratings of perceived accuracy and opinion confirmation best differentiating between authentic and modal reports.

Although such field studies are valuable in examining the potential usefulness of computer-based reports for various applications, there are limitations to their generalizability. Moreland (1985) concluded that this type of study has limitations, in part because estimates of interrater reliability are usually not practical. Raters usually are not asked to provide descriptions of how their judgments were made, and the appropriateness of their judgments was not verified with information from the patients themselves and from other sources (e.g., physicians or family members). Moreland suggested that in assessing the validity of computer-generated narrative reports, raters should evaluate individual interpretive statements because global accuracy ratings may limit the usefulness of ratings in developing the CBTI system.

Eyde, Kowal, and Fishburne (1991) followed Moreland's recommendations in a study that investigated the comparative validity of the narrative outputs for several CBTI systems. They used case histories and self-report questionnaires as criteria against which narrative reports obtained from seven MMPI computer interpretation systems could be evaluated. Each of the clinicians rated six protocols. Some of the cases were assigned to all raters; they consisted of an African American patient and a Caucasian patient who were matched for a 7–2 (Psychasthenia-Depression) code-type and an African American soldier and a Caucasian soldier who had all clinical scales in the subclinical range ($T = 70$). The clinicians rated the relevance of *each sentence* presented in the narrative CBTI as well as the global accuracy of each report. Some CBTI systems studied showed a high degree of accuracy (The Minnesota Report was found to be most accurate of the seven.) However, the overall results indicated that the validity of the narrative outputs varied, with the highest accuracy ratings being associated with narrative lengths in the short to medium range. The longer reports tended to include less accurate statements. For different CBTI systems, results for both sentence-by-sentence and global ratings were consistent, but they differed for the clinical and subclinical normal profiles. The subclinical normal cases had a high percentage (*Mdn* 50%) of unrateable sentences, and the 7–2 profiles had a low percentage (*Mdn* 14%) of sentences that could not be rated. One explanation for such differences may come from the fact that the clinical cases were inpatients for whom more detailed case histories were available. Because the length of time between the preparation of the case histories and the administrations of the MMPI varied from case to case, it was not possible to control for changes that a patient might have experienced over time or as a result of treatment.

One possible limitation of the published accuracy-rating studies is that it is usually not possible to control for a phenomenon referred to as the P. T. Barnum effect (e.g., Meehl, 1956) or Aunt Fanny effect (e.g., Tallent, 1958), which suggests that a narrative report may contain high base-rate descriptions that apply to virtually anybody. One factor to consider is that personality variables, such as extraversion, introversion, and neuroticism (Furnham, 1989), as well as the extent of private self-consciousness (Davies, 1997), also have been found to be connected to individuals' acceptance of Barnum feedback.

Research on the Barnum rating effect has shown that participants can usually detect the nature of the overly general feedback if asked the appropriate questions about it (Furnham & Schofield, 1987; Layne, 1979). However, this criticism might not be appropriate for clinical studies because this research has most often been demonstrated for situations involving acceptance of positive statements in self-ratings in normally functioning individuals. For example, research also has demonstrated that people typically are more accepting of favorable Barnum feedback than they are of unfavorable feedback (Dickson & Kelly, 1985; Furnham & Schofield, 1987; Snyder & Newburg, 1981), and people have been found to perceive favorable descriptions as more appropriate for themselves than for people in general (Baillargeon & Danis, 1984). Dickson and Kelly (1985) suggested that test situations, such as the type of assessment instruments used, can be significant in eliciting acceptance of Barnum statements. However, Baillargeon and Danis (1984) found no interaction between the type of assessment device and the favorability of statements. Research has suggested that people are more likely to accept Barnum descriptions that are presented by persons of authority or expertise (Lees-Haley, Williams, & Brown, 1993). However, the relevance of this interpretation to studies of testing results has been debated.

Some researchers have made efforts to control for Barnum-type effects on narrative CBTIs by comparing the accuracy of ratings to a stereotypical client or an average subject and by using multireport-multirating intercorrelation matrices (Moreland, 1987) or by examining differences in perceived accuracy between bogus and real reports (Moreland & Onstad, 1987; O'Dell, 1972). Several studies have compared bogus with genuine reports and found them to be statistically different in judged accuracy. In one study, for example, Guastello, Guastello, and Craft (1989) asked college students to complete the Comprehensive Personality Profile Compatibility Questionnaire (CPPCQ). One group of students rated the real computerized test interpretation of the CPPCQ, and another group rated a bogus report. The difference between the accuracy ratings for the bogus and real profiles (57.9% and 74.5%, respectively) was statistically significant. In another study (Guastello & Rieke, 1990), undergraduate students enrolled in an industrial psychology class evaluated a real computer-generated Human Resources Development Report (HRDR) of the 16PF and a bogus report generated from the average 16PF profile of the entire class. Results indicated no statistically significant difference between the ratings for the real reports and the bogus reports (which had mean accuracy ratings of 71.3% and 71.1%, respectively). However, when the results were analyzed separately, four out of five sections of the real 16PF output had significantly higher accuracy ratings than did the bogus report. Contrary to these findings, Prince and Guastello (1990) found no statistically significant differences between descriptions of a bogus and real CBTI interpretations when they investigated a computerized version of the Exner Rorschach interpretation system.

Moreland and Onstad (1987) asked clinical psychologists to rate genuine MCMI computer-generated reports and randomly generated reports. The judges rated the accuracy of the reports based on their knowledge of the client as a whole as well as the global accuracy of each section of the report. Five out of seven sections of the report exceeded chance accuracy when considered one at a time. Axis I and Axis II sections demonstrated the highest incremental validity. There was no difference in accuracy between the real reports and the randomly selected reports for the Axis IV psychosocial stressors section. The overall pattern of findings indicated that computer reports based on the MCMI can exceed chance accuracy in diagnosing patients (Moreland & Onstad, 1987, 1989).

Overall, research concerning computer-generated narrative reports for personality assessment typically has found that the interpretive statements contained in them are comparable to clinician-generated statements. Research also points to the importance of controlling for the degree of generality of the reports' descriptions in order to reduce the confounding influence of the Barnum effect (Butcher et al., 2000).

## Evaluation of Computerized Structured Interviews

Research on computer-assisted psychiatric screening initially involved the development of logic-tree decision models to assist the clinician in arriving at clinical diagnoses (Erdman, Klein, & Greist, 1985). Logic-tree systems are designed to establish the presence of symptoms specified in diagnostic criteria and to arrive at a particular diagnosis (First, 1994). For example, the DTREE is a program that was designed to guide the clinician through the diagnostic process (First, 1994) and provide the clinician with diagnostic consultation both during and after the assessment process. A narrative report is provided that includes likely diagnoses as well as an extensive narrative explaining the reasoning behind diagnostic decisions included. Research on the validity of logic-tree programs typically compares diagnostic decisions made by a computer and diagnostic decisions made by clinicians. In an initial evaluation, First et al. (1993) used the use of DTREE in an inpatient setting by comparing case conclusions by expert clinicians with the results of DTREE output. A second logic-tree program in use is a computerized version of the World Health Organization (WHO) Composite International Diagnostic Interview (CIDI-Auto). Peters and Andrews (1995) conducted an investigation of the validity of the CIDI-Auto in the *DSM-III-R* diagnoses of anxiety disorders, finding generally variable results ranging from low to high accuracy for the CIDI-Auto administered by computer. However, there was only modest overall agreement for the procedure. A brief version of the CIDI has been used recently to assess *DSM-IV* disorders (see Pez et al., 2010; Røysamb et al., 2011).

In one study, 37 psychiatric inpatients completed a structured computerized interview assessing their psychiatric history (Carr, Ghosh, & Ancill, 1983). The computerized interview agreed with the case records and clinician interview on 90% of the information. Most patients (88%) considered the computer interview to be no more demanding than a traditional interview, and about one third reported that computer interview was easier. Some patients felt that their responses to the computer were more accurate than those provided to interviewers.

The computer program in this study elicited about 9.5% more information than did traditional interviews. Psychiatric screening research has more frequently involved evaluating computer-administered versions of the DIS (Blouin, Perez, & Blouin, 1988; Erdman et al., 1992; Greist et al., 1987; Mathisen, Evans, & Meyers, 1987; Wyndowe, 1987). Research has shown that, in general, patients tend to hold favorable attitudes toward computerized DIS systems, although diagnostic validity and reliability are questioned when such programs are used alone (First, 1994).

## PAST LIMITATIONS AND UNFULFILLED DREAMS

So far I have explored the development of computer-based assessment strategies for clinical decision making, described how narrative programs are developed, and examined their equivalence and accuracy or validity. In this section I provide a summary of the overall progress and limitations of computer-based assessment and indicate some directions that further studies should go to advance the field.

### Assessments Have Not Maximally Incorporated the Flexibility and Graphic Capabilities of Computers in Presenting Test-Based Stimuli

Psychologists have not used to a great degree the extensive powers of the computer in presenting stimuli to test takers. Much could be learned from the computer game industry about presenting items in an interesting manner. With the power, graphic capability, and flexibility of the computer, it is possible to develop more sophisticated, real-world stimulus environments than are currently available in computer-administered methods. For example, the test taker might be presented with a virtual environment and be asked to respond appropriately to the circumstances presented.

Assessment stimuli could be improved in quality, effectiveness and interest value by incorporating more contemporary technology—particularly graphic displays and voice-activated systems—rather than simply item administration. Although the technology exists for computer-based assessment of some complex motor activities, CATs are extremely expensive to develop and maintain. For example, airlines use complex flight simulators that mimic the flight environment extremely well. Similar procedures

could be employed in the assessment of cognitive functioning; however, the psychotechnology is lacking for developing more sophisticated uses. The research development in the computer assessment field has not kept up with the rapid electronic technology that allows developing test administration strategies along the lines of the virtual reality environment. A great deal more could be done in this area to provide more realistic and interesting stimulus situations to test takers. At present, stimulus presentation of personality test items simply follows the printed booklet form. A statement is printed on the screen and the client simply presses a *yes* or *no* key. Many response behaviors that are important to test interpretation are not incorporated in computer-based interpretation at present (e.g., stress-oriented speech patterns, facial expressions, or the behavior of the client during testing). Further advancements from the test development side need to come to fruition in order to take fuller advantage of the present and future computer technology.

### Computer-Based Reports Are Not Stand-Alone Clinical Evaluations

Even after almost 50 years in development, most computer-based interpretive reports are still considered to be broad, generic descriptions rather than integrated, stand-alone psychological reports. Computer-generated reports should be considered as potentially valuable adjuncts to clinical judgment rather than stand-alone assessments that are used in lieu of an evaluation of a skilled clinician (Fowler, 1969). The reports are essentially listings of the most likely test interpretations for a particular set of test scores—an electronic dictionary of interpretive hypotheses that have been stored in the computer to be called out when those variables are obtained for a client.

Many people would not, however, consider this feature to be a limitation of the computer-based system; they actually prefer this more limited role as the major goal rather than development of final-product reports for an instrument that emerges from an automated system. There has been no clamoring in the field for computer-based finished-product psychological reports.

### Computer-Based Assessment Systems Often Fail to Consider Client Uniqueness

Matarazzo (1986) criticized computerized test interpretation systems because of their seeming failure to recognize the uniqueness of the test takers—that is, computer-based reports are often amorphous descriptions of clients that do not tap the uniqueness of the individual's personality.

It is true that computer-based reports seem to read a lot alike when one sees a number of them for different patients in a particular setting. This sense of sameness has two sources. First, computerized reports are the most general summaries for a particular test score pattern and do not contain much in the way of low-frequency and specifically tailored information. Second, it is natural for reports to contain similar language because patients in a particular setting *are* alike when it comes to describing their personality and symptoms. For example, patients in a chronic pain program tend to cluster into four or five MMPI-2 profile types—representing a few scales, such as Hypochondriasis (Hs), Hysteria (Hy), Depression (D), and Psychasthenia (Pt; Keller & Butcher, 1991). Patients seen in an alcohol treatment setting tend to cluster into about four scales, usually Paranoia (Pd), D, Pt, and Hypomania (Ma). Reports across different settings are more recognizably different. It should be noted that attempting to tailor test results to unique individual characteristics is a complex process and may not always increase test validity because it is then necessary to include low base rate or rare hypotheses into the statement library.

### Use of Computer-Based Reports in Clinical Practice Might Dilute Responsibility in the Psychological Assessment

Matarazzo (1986) pointed out that the practice of having unsigned computer-based reports creates a problem: a failure of responsibility for the diagnostic evaluation. According to Matarazzo, no one feels directly accountable for the contents of reports when they come from computers. In most situations today, this is not considered a problem because computer-based narrative reports are clearly labeled *professional-to-professional consultations*. The practitioner chooses to (or not to) incorporate the information from the report into his or her own signed evaluation report. Computer-based reports are presented as likely relevant hypotheses and labeled as consultations; they are not sold as stand-alone assessment evaluations. In this way, computerized interpretation systems are analogous to electronic textbooks or reference works: They provide a convenient lookup service. They are not finished products.

### Computer-Based Reporting Services Do Not Maximally Use the Vast Powers of the Computer in Integrating Test Results From Different Sources

It is conceptually feasible to develop an integrated diagnostic report—one that incorporates such elements or components as

- behavioral observations;
- personal history;
- personality data from an omnibus personality measure such as the MMPI-2;
- intellectual-cognitive abilities such as those reported by the Wechsler scales or performance on a neuropsychological battery such as the Reitan Neuropsychological Battery;
- life events;
- current stressors; and
- substance use history.

Moreover, it would be possible (and some research supports its utility) to administer this battery adaptively (i.e., tailored to the individual client), reducing the amount of testing time by eliminating redundancy. However, although a fully integrated diagnostic system that incorporates different measures from different domains is conceptually possible, it is not a practical or feasible undertaking for a number of reasons. First, there are issues of copyright with which to contend. Tests are usually owned and controlled by different—often competing—commercial publishers. Obtaining cooperation between such groups to develop an integrated system is unlikely. Second, there is insufficient research information on integrated interpretation with present-day measures to guide their integration into a single report that is internally consistent.

The idea of having the computer substitute for the psychologist's integrative function has not been widely proclaimed as desirable and in fact has been lobbied against. Matarazzo (1986), for example, cautioned that computerized testing must be subjected to careful study in order to preserve the integrity of psychological assessment. Even though decision-making and interpretation procedures may be automated with computerized testing, personal factors must still be considered in some way. Styles (1991) investigated the importance of a trained psychologist during computerized testing with children. Her study of Raven's Progressive Matrices demonstrated the need for the psychologist to establish and maintain rapport and interest prior to, during, and after testing. These factors were found to have important effects on the reliability and validity of the test data, insofar as they affected test-taking attitudes, comprehension of test instructions, on-task behavior, and demeanor.

## Tests Should Not Be Used for Tasks Different From Those for Which They Were Designed and Their Validity Research Supports

If a test has not been developed for or validated in a particular setting, computer-based applications of it in that setting are not warranted. Even though computer-based psychological tests have been validated in some settings, their validity and appropriateness for all settings is not guaranteed. In their discussion of the misuse of psychological tests, Wakefield and Underwager (1993) cautioned against the use of computerized test interpretations of the MCMI and MCMI-II, which were designed for clinical populations, in other settings, such as for forensic evaluations. The danger of misusing data applies to all psychological test formats, but the risk seems particularly high when one considers the convenience of computerized outputs—that is (as noted by Garb, 1998), some of the consumers of computer interpretation services are nonpsychologists who are unlikely to be familiar with the validation research on a particular instrument. It is important for scoring and interpretation services to provide computer-based test results only to qualified users.

## Research Evaluations of Computer-Based Systems Have Been Slow to Appear for Some Assessment Methods

The problems with computer-based assessment research have been widely discussed (Butcher, 1987a; Maddux & Johnson, 1998; Moreland, 1985). Moreland (1985), for example, concluded that the existing research on computer-based interpretation has been limited because of several methodological problems, including small sample sizes, inadequate external criterion measures to which one can compare the computer-based statements, lack of information regarding the reports' base-rate accuracy, failure to assess the ratings' reliability across time or across raters, failure to investigate the internal consistency of the reports' interpretations, and issues pertaining to the report raters (e.g., lack of familiarity with the interpretive system employed), lack of expertise in the area of interest, and possible bias secondary to the theoretical orientation of the rater. Snyder, Widiger, and Hoover (1990) expressed concerns over computer-based

interpretation systems, concluding that the literature lacks rigorously controlled experimental studies that examine methodological issues. They recommended that future studies include representative samples of both computer-based test consumers and test respondents and use characteristics of each as moderator variables in analyzing reports' generalizability.

In fairness to computer-based assessment, there has been more research into validity and accuracy for this approach than there has been for the validity of interpretation by human interpreters—that is, for clinical interpretation strategies. Extensive research on some computer-assisted assessments has shown that automated procedures can provide valid and accurate descriptions and predictions. Research on the accuracy of some computer-based systems (particularly those based on the MMPI and MMPI-2, which have been subjected to more scrutiny) has shown promising results with respect to accuracy. However, reliability and utility of computer-based interpretations vary as a function of the instruments and the settings included, as illustrated by Eyde et al. (1991) in their extensive study of the accuracy of computer-based reports.

Computer-based applications need to be evaluated carefully. Computer system developers have not always been sensitive to the requirement of validation of procedures.

It is important, particularly in high-stakes assessments, for the test user to be aware of the validity and reliability of the scales that are being interpreted in the computer system. Computers assure only convenience and speed in processing test material—not validity and reliability of the measures being interpreted. The effectiveness of the scales used in the evaluation need to be independently established. Having a computer-based personality test evaluation is no guarantee that the information presented in the report is valid and reliable.

## Commercial Distribution of a Computer Interpretation System Does Not Guarantee Validity or Acceptance of Test Reports

Computerized test reports can be commercially available and widely promoted before their underlying validity has been generally accepted by test experts or their widespread adoption by test users in clinical settings. A recent example is the MMPI-2-RF, a new test (Ben-Porath & Tellegen, 2008a) and accompanying computerized interpretive system (Ben-Porath & Tellegen, 2008b) that relies on the broad-based acceptability of the

MMPI-2, which was established through decades of research and clinical practice. However, as Greene (2011) pointed out:

> The "MMPI-2" in the MMPI-2-RF is a misnomer because the only relationship to the MMPI-2 is its use of a subset of the MMPI-2 item pool, its normative group, and similar validity scales. The MMPI-2-RF should *not* be conceptualized as a revised or restructured form of the MMPI-2, but as a *new* self-report inventory that chose to select its items from the MMPI-2 item pool and to use its normative group. As a new self-report inventory, it makes little sense to have used items that are over 70 years old (Humm & Wadsworth, 1935; Hathaway & McKinley, 1940) and a normative group (Butcher et al., 1989) that is over 20 years old.... Clinicians who choose to use the MMPI-2-RF should realize that they have forsaken the MMPI-2 and its 70 years of clinical and research history, and they are learning a new self-report inventory. (p. 22)

Before using the MMPI-2-RF and its computerized interpretive system, clinicians must carefully evaluate this new measure. Greene (2011) described two substantive losses of research and clinical experience for those contemplating use of the MMPI-2-RF and its interpretive system:

> First, the absence of the MMPI-2 clinical scales from the MMPI-2-RF makes it impossible to utilize code type interpretation that has been the core of the MMPI/MMPI-2 interpretation for over 50 years. Second, none of the MMPI-2 content and supplementary scales can be scored on the MMPI-2-RF, and so all of this research and clinical usage also is lost. (p. 22)

The MMPI-2-RF contains 338 of the 567 MMPI-2 items grouped into 50 new scales. Its foundation is the controversial MMPI-2 Restructured Clinical (RC) Scales (Ben-Porath & Tellegen, 2008a, 2008b; Tellegen & Ben-Porath, 2008). The RC Scales were introduced five years before the publication of the MMPI-2-RF as supplements to the interpretation of the MMPI-2 Clinical Scales (Tellegen, Ben-Porath, McNulty, Arbisi, Graham, & Kaemmer, 2003). No mention was made in 2003 of plans to replace the MMPI-2 Clinical Scales with the RC Scales in a new version of the instrument. During the 5 year period prior to the release of the MMPI-2-RF, multiple researchers pointed out flaws in the conceptualization and design of the research program underlying the development of MMPI-2 RC Scales, supplied empirical demonstrations that the RC Scales did not provide unique information beyond extant MMPI-2 scales, and showed that the RC Scales were less sensitive

to psychopathology than the original MMPI-2 Clinical Scales (e.g., Butcher, Hamilton, Rouse, & Cumella, 2006; Gordon, 2006; Nichols, 2006; Rogers, Sewell, Harrison, & Jordan, 2006; Rouse, Greene, Butcher, Nichols, & Williams, 2008).

In addition to problems with replacing the MMPI-2 Clinical Scales with the RC Scales, the new MMPI-2-RF and its interpretive system have a number of other shortcomings, including low reliability for several of the newly introduced scales, as reported by its developers (Tellegen & Ben-Porath, 2008). If scales included in a computerized interpretative report have reliability coefficients as low as those reported in Tellegen and Ben-Porath (2008), the test results and interpretation may not be reproducible upon retesting. Examples of MMPI-2-RF scales with low reliability include the Helplessness (HLP) scale (its reported reliability coefficients were only .39 for men and .50 for women in the normative sample), the Behavior-Restricting Fears (BRF) scale (.44 for men and .49 for women), and Suicidal/Death Ideation (SUI; .41 for men .34 for women).

Another major departure from the MMPI-2 is the exclusive use of nongendered T-scores for deriving interpretive statements for the MMPI-2-RF computerized system. (See Butcher & Williams, 2009, for a discussion.) From the earliest days of the use of the MMPI measures, gender differences in responses to the items have been observed. Therefore, norms compared women to women and men to men to eliminate the potential for gender bias. However, the computerized reports for the MMPI-2-RF, like the test itself, use a combined gender normative sample developed by eliminating the responses of 324 women from the MMPI-2 normative sample. The implications of using a combined gender comparison group rather than the established gender-specific T-scores were not adequately investigated prior to the release of this new test. Nor does the MMPI-2-RF Technical Manual (Tellegen & Ben-Porath, 2008) provide descriptive statistics by sex for raw scores that would allow users to evaluate the impact of any differential response rates for men and women to the items on the new scales included in the instrument. Nowhere is the potential for gender bias more evident than in the case of the controversial Fake Bad Scale (FBS, renamed Symptom Validity Scale in late 2007) developed by Lees-Haley, English, and Glenn (1991) and included in the MMPI-2-RF validity scales. Numerous reports in the literature, including from the scale's proponents, report gender differences in item responses, with women obtaining higher raw scores than men (e.g., Butcher, Arbisi, Atlis, & McNulty 2003; Dean et al., 2008; Greiffenstein,

Fox, & Lees-Haley, 2007). Use of nongendered T-scores to interpret a scale with established item response differences between men and women increases the potential for a biased assessment.

The controversy over the use of the FBS is not limited to concerns about gender bias. Other major problems include the unclear interpretive guidelines provided by various proponents of the scale, the inclusion of frequently occurring somatic and posttraumatic stress disorder symptoms on a scale purported to measure the overreporting of symptoms, and the resulting high false positive rates for invalid test results (i.e., inaccurate determinations that patients are misrepresenting legitimate somatic and/or cognitive problems). These issues have been described in a number of articles (Butcher et al., 2003; Butcher, Gass, Cumella, Kally, & Williams, 2008; Butcher & Williams, 2009; Gass, Williams, Cumella, Butcher, & Kally, 2010; C. L. Williams, Butcher, Gass, Cumella, & Kally, 2009). In addition, a case illustration of the negative consequences for a woman hospitalized for a serious eating disorder, mislabeled as malingering based on the guidelines provided at the time the FBS was added to the MMPI-2 computerized scoring program, is provided in C. L. Williams and colleagues (2009). The developers of the MMPI-2-RF interpretive system included the FBS-r in their Validity Scales Profile. They clearly indicated that both FBS and FBS-r can be used to identify overreporting of somatic and/or cognitive problems, even in patients with objectively documented and serious medical problems. (See Ben-Porath, Graham, & Tellegen, 2009; Ben-Porath & Tellegen, 2008a.)

Clinicians must gain a thorough understanding of the underlying research of any new measures used for clinical decision making. These include studies and critiques by experts other than the test developers, their colleagues, and students. Such an examination is needed before using newly released computerized interpretive systems in their practices. Simply relying on a name that links a new interpretive system to a widely accepted standard, as seen in the example of the MMPI-2-RF, is not sufficient. The MMPI-2-RF and its interpretive system represent a significant departure from the empirical basis of the MMPI-2—resulting in major misgivings by a number of test experts and users about its utility in clinical decision making.

### Errors in Computer-Scored Psychological Tests

Scoring errors have plagued some commercial test companies and have resulted in extensive problems for test takers. A recent review by Eyde, Robertson, and Krug (2010) found a number of incidents in which computer-based reporting services produced erroneous results. Eyde et al. pointed out:

> Each year, the millions of test takers and test users who rely on standardized test results for a variety of purposes—college and professional school admissions, high school graduation, certification of elementary and secondary student achievement, and vocational competence and licensure, among others—share a common expectation: that the systems used by testing agencies to process, score, and report results produce accurate, error-free results. A review of the evidence from the past 25 years, a period in which both the number of test takers and the number of large-scale testing programs have increased drastically, indicates that this expectation has not always been met. (Toch, 2006)

Psychologists using computer-based tests results need to verify the quality of the products to assure that decisions that affect clients are accurate.

## OFFERING PSYCHOLOGICAL ASSESSMENT SERVICES VIA THE INTERNET

The Internet is revolutionizing the way psychologists conduct behavioral research. The broad expansion of the Internet and its potential for behavioral research has been well described. (See discussions in Gosling & Johnson, 2010.) However, the expansion of psychological assessment services through the Internet brings a number of special problems that have not been sufficiently dealt with by psychologists. For example, Tippins (2009) has pointed out that the use of Internet-based tests in personnel assessment is highly vulnerable to cheating. There have been concerns that Internet application of tests may not be equivalent to standard administration. An APA task force (Naglieri et al., 2004) recommended that the test administration of a previously developed paper-and-pencil test be shown to be equivalent to originally developed measures before it is made available on the Internet. In this section I address several important issues that need to be considered before making psychological tests available on the Internet. I examine several of the potential problems in more detail below.

### Test Security

The question of test security has several facets.

- One must ensure that the test items are secure and not made available to the public. Most psychologists are aware that test items are considered protected items and should not be made public to prevent the test from being compromised. Making test items available to the general public would undermine the value of the test for making important decisions. The security of materials placed on the Internet has been questioned (Naglieri et al., 2004; Rothstein & Goffin, 2006). There have been numerous situations in which hackers have gotten into highly secure files of banks, the State Department, and so forth. It is important for test security to be ensured before items are made available through the Internet. However, Bartram (2006) has pointed out that there is great value in using the Internet for assessment in clinical practice today to obtain information from clients in a time-efficient manner if appropriate authentication procedures are followed.

- Some psychological tests are considered to require higher levels of expertise and training to interpret and are not made available to psychologists without clear qualifications to use them. Many psychological tests—particularly those involved in clinical assessment—require careful evaluation of user qualifications. Wide availability of tests on the Internet could result in access to the test for nonqualified test users.

- Most psychological tests are copyrighted and cannot be copied. Making test items available through the Internet increases the likelihood that copyright infringement will occur. Of course, there are ways of controlling access to test materials in a manner similar to the way they are controlled in traditional clinical practice—that is, the tests would be available only to practitioners who would administer them in controlled office settings. The item responses could then be sent to the test scoring-interpreting service through the Internet for processing. The results of the testing could then be returned to the practitioner electronically in a coded manner that would not be accessible to nonauthorized persons.

### Assurance That the Test Norms Are Appropriate for Internet Application

Most psychological tests are normed in a controlled environment—that is, by having the normative population taking the test in a standard, carefully monitored test situation. Relatively few traditional personality tests were normed through an Internet-administered format. (One exception to this was the Dutch-language version of the MMPI-2; see Sloore, Derksen, de Mey, & Hellenbosch, 1996.) Consequently, for many tests, availability to clients

through the Internet would represent a test administration environment very different from the one for which they were developed. It is imperative for psychologists to ensure that the Internet-based test has been appropriately normed and validated.

### Assurance That the Individual Taking the Test Has the Cooperative Response Set Present in the Normative Sample

Response sets for Internet administration versus standard administration have not been widely studied. It would be important to ensure that Internet administration would not produce results different from those of standard administration. As noted earlier, computer-administered versus booklet-administered tests have been empirically studied. Although recent studies of the comparability of Internet and paper-and-pencil administration shows likely comparability (Coles, Cook & Blake, 2007), some reviewers have raised possible problems with the different response sets that can occur with Internet administration (Rothstein & Goffin, 2006). If Internet administration involves development procedures that are different from those of typical computer administration, these conditions should be evaluated to ensure comparability.

### Internet Test Version Needs to Have Reliability and Validity Demonstrated

It is important to ensure that the scores for the test being administered through the Internet are equivalent to those on which the test was originally developed and that the correlates for the test scores apply equally well for the procedure when the test administration procedures are altered. Psychological test distributors need to develop procedures to ensure that the problems noted here do not occur. As previously noted, it is possible that although the tests are processed through the Internet, they could still be administered and controlled through individual clinicians—that is, it is possible that the problems described here could be resolved by limiting access to the test in much the same way that credit card numbers are currently protected. Practitioners who wish to process their test results through the Internet could administer the test to the client in their office and then enter the client's responses into the computer from their own facility keyboard or scanner before accessing the Internet server. In this manner, the clinician (who has been deemed a qualified test user and is eligible to purchase the test) can assume the responsibility for test security as well as determine which psychological tests meet the essential criteria for the test application involved.

A number of psychologists have predicted a strong future for Internet-based psychological assessments with continued growth and development in a broad range of applications. (See discussions by Bartram, 2006; Breithaupt, Mills, & Melican, 2006.) However, Breithaupt et al. (2006) pointed out that the onus is on the community of testing professioals to make available appropriate and timely information on the design and scoring of their assessments.

## ACCEPTANCE AND ETHICS OF COMPUTER-BASED PSYCHOLOGICAL ASSESSMENT

After almost 50 years, where does computer-based psychological assessment stand in the field of professional psychology in terms of user acceptance? Survey evidence shows that applied psychologists have substantially endorsed computer-based psychological assessment, although, as a group, clinicians are seemingly reluctant to endorse or use new technological developments in their practice (McMinn, Buchanan, Ellens, & Ryan, 1999). The actual use of computer-scored test results is unclear. One earlier survey of practitioners found that 67.8% of respondents used computer scoring of psychological tests and 43.8% also used computer-derived reports in their practice (Downey, Sinnett, & Seeberger, 1998). However, Camara, Nathan, and Puente (2000) reported that only about 10% of neuropsychologists and clinical psychologists score tests by computer.

When computer-based assessment was in its infancy, there was a concern that ethical problems could result from handing over a professionally sensitive task like personality assessment to computers. Some authorities (e.g., Matarazzo, 1986) expressed concerns that individual clinicians might defer important clinical decisions to computers, thereby ignoring the client in the assessment process. Such reliance on machines to provide clinical assessments could result in unethical and irresponsible judgments on the part of the practitioner. However, these arguments were answered by Fowler and Butcher (1986), who noted that psychologists use computer-based psychological reports not as a final polished report but as one source of information that is available to the practitioner who is responsible for decisions made about clients. Most authorities in the computer-based area as

well as several professional organizations that have provided practical guidelines for computer-based assessment have supported the ethical use of computer-based psychological assessment (see American Educational Research Association, American Psychological Association, and National Council on Measurement in Education, 1999; American Psychological Association, 1986, British Psychological Society Psychological Testing Centre, 2002; Coyne, 2006).

How do present-day clinicians feel about the ethics of computerized assessment? The earlier concerns over computer-based test usage seem to have waned considerably with the growing familiarity with computerized assessment. For example, in the survey concerning computer-based test use by McMinn et al. (1999), most respondents thought that use of computer-based assessment was an ethical practice.

## SUMMARY

Computer-based psychological assessment has come far since it began over 50 years ago. As a group, assessment practitioners have generally accepted computerized testing. Many clinicians use some computer scoring, computer-based interpretation, or both. Most practitioners today consider computer-assisted test interpretation to be an ethical professional activity. Computers have been important to the field of applied psychology almost since they were introduced, and the application of computerized methods has expanded over the past several decades. Since that time, the application of computerized methods has broadened both in scope and in depth.

The merger of computer technology and psychological test interpretation has not, however, been a perfect relationship. Past efforts at computerized assessment have not gone far enough in making optimal use of the flexibility and power of computers for making complex decisions. At present, most interpretive systems largely perform a lookup, list-out function—a broad range of interpretations is stored in the computer for various test scores and indexes, and the computer simply lists out the stored information for appropriate scale score levels. Computers are not involved as much in decision making.

Computerized applications are limited to some extent by the available psychological expertise and psychotechnology. To date, computer–human interactions are confined to written material. Potentially valuable information, such as critical nonverbal cues (e.g., speech patterns, vocal tone, and facial expressions), is not currently incorporated in computer-based assessments. Furthermore, the response choices are usually provided to the test taker in a fixed format (e.g., true–false).

On the positive side, the earlier suggestion made by some researchers that computer-administered and traditional administration approaches were nonequivalent has not been supported by more recent findings. Research has supported the view that computer-administered tests are essentially equivalent to booklet-administered instruments.

In spite of what have been described as limitations and unfulfilled hopes, computer-based psychological assessment is an enormously successful endeavor. Research thus far appears to point to the conclusion that computer-generated reports should be viewed as valuable adjuncts to clinical judgment rather than as substitutes for skilled clinicians.

Computer-based assessment has brought accountability and reliability into the assessment field. It is apparent that whatever else computerized assessment has done for the field of psychology, it clearly has focused attention on objective and accurate assessment in the fields of clinical evaluation and diagnosis.

## APPENDIX
## PROFILE VALIDITY

Her extremely elevated F score and low VRIN scale score suggest that her endorsement of extreme items is the result of careful item responding rather than a random response pattern. She apparently understood the item content and endorsed the symptoms as descriptive of her current functioning.

Her self-description as extremely disturbed requires further consideration because she claimed many more extreme psychological symptoms than most patients do. Several possibilities require further evaluation. It is possible that she is exaggerating her symptoms in order to gain attention or services. Sometimes an individual involved in litigation will produce this exaggerated profile. If an exaggerated response set cannot be explained by life circumstances, it may be that her extreme responding is the result of unusually severe psychological problems.

Some patients being admitted to an inpatient psychiatric facility produce extremely elevated F scale scores as a result of confusion, disorganization, or decompensation. It appears that this individual consistently endorsed a number of extreme symptoms that should be further evaluated as possibly important problem areas.

## SYMPTOMATIC PATTERNS

This report was developed using the Hs, D, and Sc scales as the prototype. The client's MMPI-2 clinical profile suggests that she is presently experiencing many psychological problems. She is probably an extremely depressed and ineffective individual who is exhibiting personality deterioration at this time. She is likely to be quite confused and disoriented and to have inappropriate or blunted affect. She may appear tense, anxious, agitated, or hostile at times. Individuals with this profile are typically experiencing extreme physical symptoms, depressed mood, and cognitive disorganization. Symptoms of severe psychosis, such as delusions or hallucinations, are likely to be present.

She appears to feel very insecure. Her life adjustment is chronically poor and she may drift from job to job or place to place. Social withdrawal is characteristic of her behavior. She has a great many vague physical concerns and may have somatic delusions.

In addition, the following description is suggested by the client's scores on the content scales. She endorsed a number of items suggesting that she is experiencing low morale and a depressed mood. She reports a preoccupation with feeling guilty and unworthy. She feels that she deserves to be punished for wrongs she has committed. She feels regretful and unhappy about life, and she seems plagued by anxiety and worry about the future. She feels hopeless at times and feels that she is a condemned person. She endorsed response content that reflects low self-esteem and long-standing beliefs about her inadequacy. She has difficulty managing routine affairs, and the items she endorsed suggest a poor memory, concentration problems, and an inability to make decisions. She appears to be immobilized and withdrawn and has no energy for life. She views her physical health as failing and reports numerous somatic concerns. She feels that life is no longer worthwhile and that she is losing control of her thought processes.

According to her response content, there is a strong possibility that she has seriously contemplated suicide. She acknowledged having suicidal thoughts recently. Although she denies suicidal attempts in the past, given her current mood, an evaluation of suicidal potential appears to be indicated. She may feel somewhat estranged and alienated from people. She is suspicious of the actions of others, and she may tend to blame them for her negative frame of mind. Her high elevation on the Pd scale may result from a sense of social alienation. (Her response content does not reflect antisocial behavior or practices.)

Her attitudes toward rules and societal norms should be further evaluated. She is rather high-strung and believes that she feels things more, or more intensely, than others do. She feels quite lonely and misunderstood at times.

Long-term personality factors identified by her PSY-5 scale elevations may help provide a clinical context for the symptoms she is presently experiencing. She shows a meager capacity to experience pleasure in life. Persons with high scores on INTR (Introversion/Low Positive Emotionality) tend to be pessimistic.

## PROFILE FREQUENCY

Profile interpretation can be greatly facilitated by examining the relative frequency of clinical scale patterns in various settings. The client's high-point clinical scale score (D) occurred in 7.0% of the MMPI-2 normative sample of women. However, only 4.4% of the women had D scale peak scores at or above a T score of 65, and only 2.1% had well-defined D spikes. This high MMPI-2 profile configuration (2-8/8-2) is very rare in samples of normals,

MMPI-2 VALIDITY PATTERN

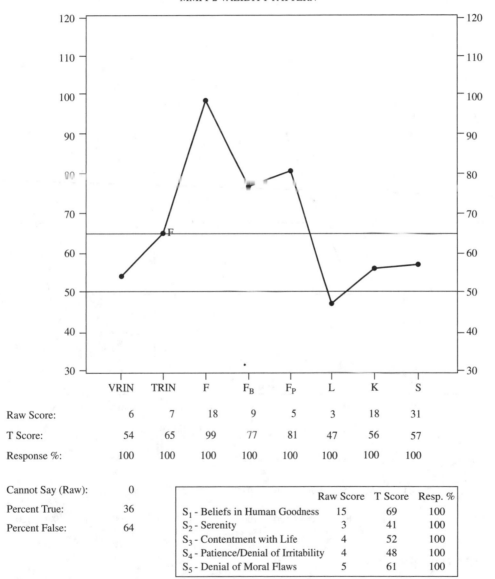

|  | VRIN | TRIN | F | F$_B$ | F$_P$ | L | K | S |
|---|---|---|---|---|---|---|---|---|
| Raw Score: | 6 | 7 | 18 | 9 | 5 | 3 | 18 | 31 |
| T Score: | 54 | 65 | 99 | 77 | 81 | 47 | 56 | 57 |
| Response %: | 100 | 100 | 100 | 100 | 100 | 100 | 100 | 100 |

| | Raw Score | T Score | Resp. % |
|---|---|---|---|
| Cannot Say (Raw): 0 | | | |
| Percent True: 36 | | | |
| Percent False: 64 | | | |
| S$_1$ - Beliefs in Human Goodness | 15 | 69 | 100 |
| S$_2$ - Serenity | 3 | 41 | 100 |
| S$_3$ - Contentment with Life | 4 | 52 | 100 |
| S$_4$ - Patience/Denial of Irritability | 4 | 48 | 100 |
| S$_5$ - Denial of Moral Flaws | 5 | 61 | 100 |

occurring in less than 1% of the MMPI-2 normative sample of women.

This high-point MMPI-2 score is very frequent among various samples of inpatient women. In the Graham and Butcher (1988) sample, the D scale occurred as the high point in 12.2% of the females (all of the cases were at or above a T score of 65, and 8.4% were well defined in that range). In the Pearson inpatient sample, the high-point clinical scale score on D occurred in 25.4% of the women. Moreover, 24.3% had the D scale spike at or over a T score of 65, and 13.8% produced well-defined D scale peak scores in that range.

Her high MMPI-2 profile configuration (2-8/8-2) was found in 4.6% of the females in the Graham and Butcher (1988) sample and in 4.0% of the females in the Pearson inpatient sample.

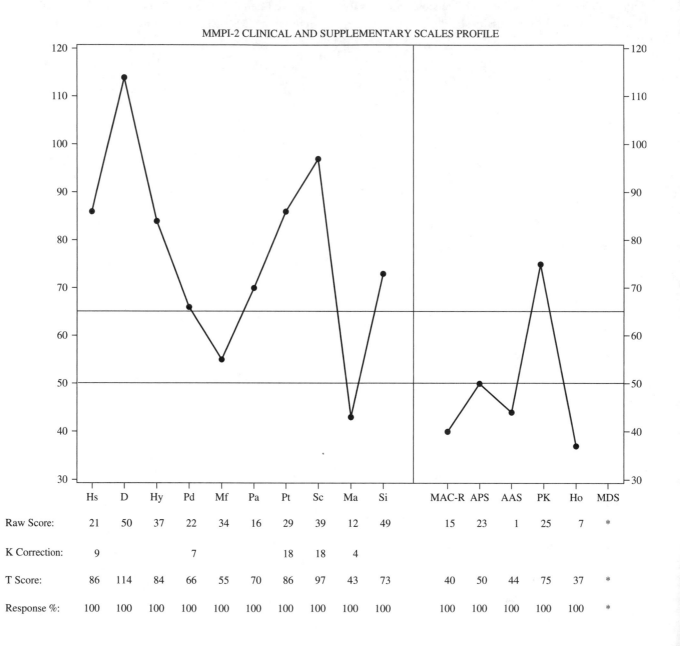

### MMPI-2 CLINICAL AND SUPPLEMENTARY SCALES PROFILE

| | Hs | D | Hy | Pd | Mf | Pa | Pt | Sc | Ma | Si | MAC-R | APS | AAS | PK | Ho | MDS |
|---|---|---|---|---|---|---|---|---|---|---|---|---|---|---|---|---|
| Raw Score: | 21 | 50 | 37 | 22 | 34 | 16 | 29 | 39 | 12 | 49 | 15 | 23 | 1 | 25 | 7 | * |
| K Correction: | 9 | | | 7 | | | 18 | 18 | 4 | | | | | | | |
| T Score: | 86 | 114 | 84 | 66 | 55 | 70 | 86 | 97 | 43 | 73 | 40 | 50 | 44 | 75 | 37 | * |
| Response %: | 100 | 100 | 100 | 100 | 100 | 100 | 100 | 100 | 100 | 100 | 100 | 100 | 100 | 100 | 100 | * |

Welsh Code:    2**8*173"06'4+-5/9: F*"'+-K/L:

Profile Elevation: 80.8

*MDS scores are reported only for clients who indicate that they are married or separated.

## PROFILE STABILITY

The relative elevation of her clinical scale scores suggests that her profile is not as well defined as many other profiles. There was no difference between the profile type used to develop the present report (involving Hs, D, and Sc) and the next highest scale in the profile code. Therefore, behavioral elements related to elevations on Pt should be considered as well. For example, intensification of anxiety, negative self-image, and unproductive rumination could be important in her symptom pattern.

## INTERPERSONAL RELATIONS

The client has not developed effective ways of dealing with others and feels very inadequate and socially alienated. Individuals with this profile type tend not to marry. Individuals with this profile are quite self-absorbed and find marital relationships problematic. Marital breakup is not uncommon.

She is a very introverted person who has difficulty meeting and interacting with other people. She is shy and emotionally distant. She tends to be very uneasy, rigid, and overcontrolled in social situations. Her shyness is probably symptomatic of a broader pattern of social withdrawal. Personality characteristics related to social introversion tend to be stable over time. Her generally reclusive behavior, introverted lifestyle, and tendency toward interpersonal avoidance may be prominent in any future test results.

The client's scores on the content scales suggest the following additional information concerning her interpersonal relations. Her social relationships are likely

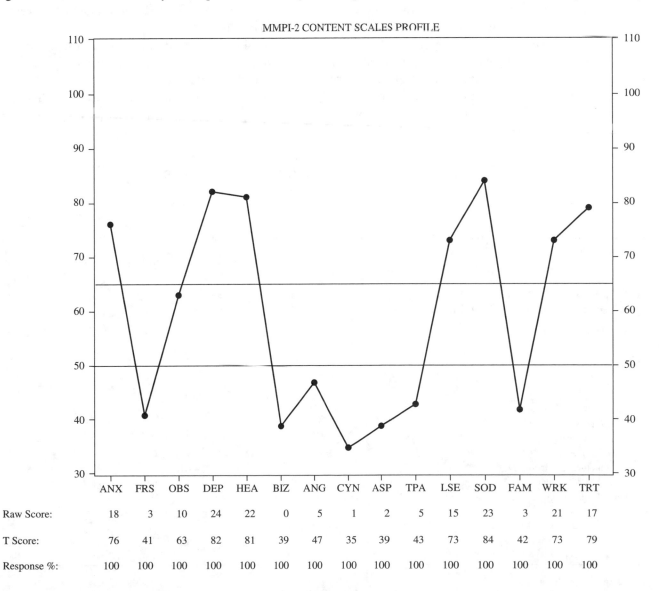

MMPI-2 CONTENT SCALES PROFILE

| | ANX | FRS | OBS | DEP | HEA | BIZ | ANG | CYN | ASP | TPA | LSE | SOD | FAM | WRK | TRT |
|---|---|---|---|---|---|---|---|---|---|---|---|---|---|---|---|
| Raw Score: | 18 | 3 | 10 | 24 | 22 | 0 | 5 | 1 | 2 | 5 | 15 | 23 | 3 | 21 | 17 |
| T Score: | 76 | 41 | 63 | 82 | 81 | 39 | 47 | 35 | 39 | 43 | 73 | 84 | 42 | 73 | 79 |
| Response %: | 100 | 100 | 100 | 100 | 100 | 100 | 100 | 100 | 100 | 100 | 100 | 100 | 100 | 100 | 100 |

to be viewed by others as problematic. She may be visibly uneasy around others, sits alone in group situations, and dislikes engaging in group activities.

## DIAGNOSTIC CONSIDERATIONS

The client can probably be diagnosed as having a Schizophrenic Disorder, possibly of a Disorganized or Undifferentiated type. Her scores on the content scales indicate that her acknowledged tendency toward experiencing depressed mood should be taken into consideration in any diagnostic formulation.

## TREATMENT CONSIDERATIONS

Individuals with this MMPI-2 clinical profile are experiencing significant adjustment problems for which they need treatment. This individual appears to have attitudes and beliefs centering on somatic symptoms that are chronic, intractable, and possibly delusional. Her vague physical problems, social alienation, and general lack of trust in others make it difficult for her to view her problems objectively. Severe personality deterioration is apparent, and her treatment prognosis is likely to be poor.

Psychotherapy alone is not likely to be effective because she would probably have difficulty establishing a therapeutic relationship. Her unusual thinking related to her bodily processes may also make her difficult to approach through psychological treatment methods. Psychotropic medications are usually considered the treatment of choice for individuals with this profile, but behavioral management or psychosocial therapy might also be attempted to decrease her somatic complaints and increase her interpersonal adjustment.

The client's scores on the content scales seem to indicate low potential for change. She may feel that her problems are not addressable through therapy and that she is not likely to benefit much from psychological treatment at this time. Her apparently negative treatment attitudes may need to be explored early in therapy if treatment is to be successful.

In any intervention or psychological evaluation program involving occupational adjustment, her negative work attitudes could become an important problem to overcome. She has a number of attitudes and feelings that could interfere with work adjustment.

## ADDITIONAL SCALES

|  | Raw Score | T Score | Resp % |
|---|---|---|---|
| **Personality Psychopathology Five (PSY-5) Scales** | | | |
| Aggressiveness (AGGR) | 0 | 30 | 100 |
| Psychoticism (PSYC) | 3 | 50 | 100 |
| Disconstraint (DISC) | 6 | 39 | 100 |
| Negative Emotionality/Neuroticism (NEGE) | 16 | 57 | 100 |
| Introversion/Low Positive Emotionality (INTR) | 30 | 99 | 100 |
| **Supplementary Scales** | | | |
| Anxiety (A) | 26 | 68 | 100 |
| Repression (R) | 30 | 86 | 100 |
| Ego Strength (Es) | 20 | 30 | 100 |
| Dominance (Do) | 14 | 42 | 100 |
| Social Responsibility (Re) | 24 | 59 | 100 |
| **Harris-Lingoes Subscales** | | | |
| Depression Subscales | | | |
| Subjective Depression ($D_1$) | 29 | 101 | 100 |
| Psychomotor Retardation ($D_2$) | 12 | 84 | 100 |
| Physical Malfunctioning ($D_3$) | 9 | 93 | 100 |
| Mental Dullness ($D_4$) | 13 | 97 | 100 |
| Brooding ($D_5$) | 9 | 83 | 100 |
| Hysteria Subscales | | | |
| Denial of Social Anxiety ($Hy_1$) | 1 | 35 | 100 |
| Need for Affection ($Hy_2$) | 10 | 63 | 100 |

|  | Raw Score | T Score | Resp % |
|---|---|---|---|
| Lassitude-Malaise ($Hy_3$) | 13 | 91 | 100 |
| Somatic Complaints ($Hy_4$) | 7 | 65 | 100 |
| Inhibition of Aggression ($Hy_5$) | 4 | 54 | 100 |
| Psychopathic Deviate Subscales |  |  |  |
| Familial Discord ($Pd_1$) | 3 | 56 | 100 |
| Authority Problems ($Pd_2$) | 3 | 53 | 100 |
| Social Imperturbability ($Pd_3$) | 1 | 35 | 100 |
| Social Alienation ($Pd_4$) | 7 | 65 | 100 |
| Self-Alienation ($Pd_5$) | 5 | 58 | 100 |
| Paranoia Subscales |  |  |  |
| Persecutory Ideas ($Pa_1$) | 3 | 57 | 100 |
| Poignancy ($Pa_2$) | 5 | 65 | 100 |
| Naivete ($Pa_3$) | 8 | 65 | 100 |
| Schizophrenia Subscales |  |  |  |
| Social Alienation ($Sc_1$) | 11 | 81 | 100 |
| Emotional Alienation ($Sc_2$) | 5 | 86 | 100 |
| Lack of Ego Mastery, Cognitive ($Sc_3$) | 5 | 74 | 100 |
| Lack of Ego Mastery, Conative ($Sc_4$) | 9 | 85 | 100 |
| Lack of Ego Mastery, Defective Inhibition ($Sc_5$) | 2 | 53 | 100 |
| Bizarre Sensory Experiences ($Sc_6$) | 9 | 81 | 100 |
| Hypomania Subscales |  |  |  |
| Amorality ($Ma_1$) | 2 | 54 | 100 |
| Psychomotor Acceleration ($Ma_2$) | 5 | 50 | 100 |
| Imperturbability ($Ma_3$) | 1 | 37 | 100 |
| Ego Inflation ($Ma_4$) | 1 | 37 | 100 |
| Social Introversion Subscales (Ben-Porath, Hostetler, Butcher & Graham) |  |  |  |
| Shyness/Self-Consciousness ($Si_1$) | 12 | 68 | 100 |
| Social Avoidance ($Si_2$) | 8 | 74 | 100 |
| Alienation–Self and Others ($Si_3$) | 6 | 52 | 100 |
| **Content Component Scales (Ben-Porath & Sherwood)** |  |  |  |
| Fears Subscales |  |  |  |
| Generalized Fearfulness ($FRS_1$) | 1 | 48 | 100 |
| Multiple Fears ($FRS_2$) | 2 | 37 | 100 |
| Depression Subscales |  |  |  |
| Lack of Drive ($DEP_1$) | 11 | 95 | 100 |
| Dysphoria ($DEP_2$) | 6 | 79 | 100 |
| Self-Depreciation ($DEP_3$) | 3 | 61 | 100 |
| Suicidal Ideation ($DEP_4$) | 2 | 77 | 100 |
| Health Concerns Subscales |  |  |  |
| Gastrointestinal Symptoms ($HEA_1$) | 3 | 75 | 100 |
| Neurological Symptoms ($HEA_2$) | 8 | 83 | 100 |
| General Health Concerns ($HEA_3$) | 6 | 87 | 100 |
| Bizarre Mentation Subscales |  |  |  |
| Psychotic Symptomatology ($BIZ_1$) | 0 | 44 | 100 |
| Schizotypal Characteristics ($BIZ_2$) | 0 | 41 | 100 |
| Anger Subscales |  |  |  |
| Explosive Behavior ($ANG_1$) | 1 | 47 | 100 |
| Irritability ($ANG_2$) | 3 | 49 | 100 |
| Cynicism Subscales |  |  |  |
| Misanthropic Beliefs ($CYN_1$) | 0 | 34 | 100 |
| Interpersonal Suspiciousness ($CYN_2$) | 1 | 40 | 100 |
| Antisocial Practices Subscales |  |  |  |
| Antisocial Attitudes ($ASP_1$) | 1 | 36 | 100 |
| Antisocial Behavior ($ASP_2$) | 1 | 51 | 100 |

|  | Raw Score | T Score | Resp % |
|---|---|---|---|
| Type A Subscales |  |  |  |
| Impatience (TPA$_1$) | 4 | 58 | 100 |
| Competitive Drive (TPA$_2$) | 1 | 40 | 100 |
| Low Self-Esteem Subscales |  |  |  |
| Self-Doubt (LSE$_1$) | 7 | 71 | 100 |
| Submissiveness (LSE$_2$) | 5 | 69 | 100 |
| Social Discomfort Subscales |  |  |  |
| Introversion (SOD$_1$) | 16 | 85 | 100 |
| Shyness (SOD$_2$) | 6 | 65 | 100 |
| Family Problems Subscales |  |  |  |
| Family Discord (FAM$_1$) | 2 | 42 | 100 |
| Familial Alienation (FAM$_2$) | 0 | 41 | 100 |
| Negative Treatment Indicators Subscales |  |  |  |
| Low Motivation (TRT$_1$) | 9 | 86 | 100 |
| Inability to Disclose (TRT$_2$) | 3 | 60 | 100 |

Uniform T scores are used for Hs, D, Hy, Pd, Pa, Pt, Sc, Ma, the content scales, the content component scales, and the PSY-5 scales. The remaining scales and subscales use linear T scores.

# REFERENCES

Allard, G., Butler, J., Faust, D., & Shea, M. T. (1995). Errors in hand scoring objective personality tests: The case of the Personality Diagnostic Questionnaire-Revised (PDQ). *Professional Psychology, 2*(6), 304–308.

Aguado, D., Rubio, V. J., Hontangas, P. M., & Hernandez, J. M. (2005). Psychometric properties of an emotional adjustment computerized adaptive test [Propiedades psicometricas de un test Adaptativo Informatizado para la medicion del ajuste emocional]. *Psicothema, 17*(3), 484–491.

American Educational Research Association, American Psychological Association, & National Council on Measurement in Education. (1999). *Standards for educational and psychological testing*. Washington, DC: American Educational Research Association.

American Psychological Association. (1986). *Guidelines for computer-based tests and interpretations*. Washington, DC: Author.

American Psychological Association. (2002). Ethical principles of psychologists and code of conduct. *American Psychologist, 47*, 1597–1611.

American Psychological Association Ethics Code Amendments (2010). Amendments to the 2002 "Ethical principles of psychologists and code of conduct." *American Psychologist, 65*(5), 493.

American Psychological Association, Committee on Professional Standards. (1984). Casebook for providers of psychological services. *American Psychologist, 39*, 663–668.

Archer, R. P., Tirrell, C. A., & Elkins, D. E. (2001). Evaluation of an MMPI-A short form: Implications for adaptive testing. *Journal of Personality Assessment, 76*(1), 76–89.

Atlis, M. M., Hahn, J., & Butcher, J. N. (2006). Computer-based assessment with the MMPI-2. In J. N. Butcher (Ed.), *MMPI-2: The practitioner's handbook* (pp. 445–476). Washington, DC: American Psychological Association.

Baillargeon, J., & Danis, C. (1984). Barnum meets the computer: A critical test. *Journal of Personality Assessment, 48*, 415–419.

Bartram, D. (2006). Testing on the Internet: Issues, challenges and opportunities in the field of occupational assessment. In D. Bartram & R. K. Hambleton (Eds.), *Computer-based testing and the Internet* (pp. 13–37). Hoboken, NJ: Wiley.

Ben-Porath, Y. S., Graham, J. R. & Tellegen, A. (2009). *The MMPI-2 Symptom Validity (FBS) scale development, research findings, and interpretive recommendations*. Minneapolis: University of Minnesota Press.

Ben-Porath, Y. S., Slutske, W. S., & Butcher, J. N. (1989). A real-data simulation of computerized adaptive administration of the MMPI. *Psychological Assessment: A Journal of Consulting and Clinical Psychology, 1*(1), 18–22.

Ben-Porath, Y. S., & Tellegen, A. (2008a). *MMPI-2RF: Manual for administration, scoring, and interpretation*. Minneapolis: University of Minnesota Press.

Ben-Porath, Y. S., & Tellegen, A. (2008b). *MMPI-2RF user's guide for reports*. Minneapolis: University of Minnesota Press.

Bersoff, D. N. & Hofer, P. J. (2008). Legal issues in computerized psychological testing. In D. N. Bersoff (Ed.), *Ethical conflicts in psychology* (4th ed., pp. 303–305). Washington, DC: American Psychological Association.

Blouin, A. G., Perez, E. L., & Blouin, J. H. (1988). Computerized administration of the Diagnostic Interview Schedule. *Psychiatry Research, 23*, 335–344.

Breithaupt, K. J., Mills, C. N. & Melican, G. J. (2006). Facing the opportunities of the future. In D. Bartram & R. K. Hambleton (Eds.) *Computer-based testing and the Internet* (pp. 219–251). Hoboken, NJ: Wiley.

British Psychological Society Psychological Testing Centre. (2002). *Guidelines for the development and use of computer-based assessments*. Leicester, UK: British Psychological Society.

Butcher, J. N. (1982). *User's guide for the MMPI-2 Minnesota Report: Adult clinical system*. Minneapolis, MN: National Computer Systems.

Butcher, J. N. (Ed.). (1987). *Computerized psychological assessment*. New York, NY: Basic Books.

Butcher, J. N. (1988). *Personality profile of airline pilot applicants*. Unpublished manuscript, University of Minnesota, Department of Psychology, MMPI-2 Workshops.

Butcher, J. N. (2002). *User's guide to the Minnesota Report: Revised personnel report* (3rd Edition). Minneapolis, MN: National Computer Systems.

Butcher, J. N. (2009). How to use computer-based reports. In J. N. Butcher (Ed.). *Oxford handbook of personality assessment* (pp. 693–706). New York, NY: Oxford University Press.

Butcher, J. N. (2010). Personality assessment from the 19th to the early 21st century: Past achievements and contemporary challenges. *Annual Review of Clinical Psychology, 6,* 1–20.

Butcher, J. N. (2011). *A beginner's guide to the MMPI-2* (3rd ed.). Washington, DC: American Psychological Association.

Butcher, J. N., Arbisi, P. A., Atlis, M., & McNulty, J. (2003). The construct validity of the Lees-Haley Fake Bad Scale (FBS): Does this scale measure malingering and feigned emotional distress? *Archives of Clinical Neuropsychiatry, 18,* 473–485.

Butcher, J. N., Berah, E., Ellersten, B., Miach, P., Lim, J., Nezami, E.,..., Almagor, M. (1998). Objective personality assessment: Computer-based MMPI-2 interpretation in international clinical settings. In C. Belar (Ed.), *Comprehensive clinical psychology: Sociocultural and individual differences* (pp. 277–312). New York, NY: Elsevier.

Butcher, J. N., Dahlstrom, W. G., Graham, J. R., Tellegen, A., & Kaemmer, B. (1989). *Manual for the restandardized Minnesota Multiphasic Personality Inventory: MMPI-2. An administrative and interpretive guide.* Minneapolis: University of Minnesota Press.

Butcher, J. N., Gass, C. S., Cumella, E., Kally, Z., & Williams, C. L. (2008). Potential for bias in MMPI-2 assessments using the Fake Bad Scale (FBS). *Psychological Injury and Law, 1,* 191–209.

Butcher, J. N., Hamilton, C. K., Rouse, S. V. & Cumella, E. J. (2006). The deconstruction of the Hy scale of MMPI-2: Failure of RC3 in measuring somatic symptom expression. *Journal of Personality Assessment, 87*(1), 199–205.

Butcher, J. N., Keller, L., & Bacon, S. (1985). Current developments and future directions in computerized personality assessment. *Journal of Consulting and Clinical Psychology, 53,* 803–815.

Butcher, J. N., Perry, J., & Atlis (2000). Validity and utility of computer-based test interpretation. *Psychological Assessment, 12,* 6–18.

Butcher, J. N., Perry, J., & Dean, B. L. (2009). Computer based assessment. In J. N. Butcher (Ed.), *Oxford handbook of personality assessment* (pp. 163–182). New York, NY: Oxford University Press.

Butcher, J. N., & Williams, C. L. (2009). Personality assessment with the MMPI-2: Historical roots, international adaptations, and current challenges. *Applied Psychology: Health and Well-Being, 2,* 105–135.

Caldwell, A. B. (1996). *Forensic questions and answers on the MMPI/MMPI-2.* Los Angeles, CA: Caldwell Reports.

Camara, W. J., Nathan, J. S., & Puente, A. E. (2000). Psychological test usage: Implications in professional psychology. *Professional Psychology: Research and Practice, 31,* 141–154.

Carr, A. C., Ghosh, A., & Ancill, R. J. (1983). Can a computer take a psychiatric history? *Psychological Medicine, 13,* 151–158.

Chuah, S. C., Drasgow, F., & Roberts, B. W. (2006). Personality assessment: Does the medium matter? No. *Journal of Research in Personality, 40,* 359–376.

Coles, M. E., Cook, L. M., & Blake, T. R. (2007). Assessing obsessive compulsive symptoms and cognitions on the Internet: Evidence for the comparability of paper and Internet administration. *Behaviour Research and Therapy, 45*(9), 2232–2240.

Coyne, I. (2006). International guidelines on computer-based and Internet-delivered testing. *International Journal of Testing, 6*(2), 143–171.

Davies, M. F. (1997). Private self-consciousness and the acceptance of personality feedback: Confirmatory processing in the evaluation of general vs. specific self-information. *Journal of Research in Personality, 31,* 78–92.

Dawes, R. M., Faust, D., & Meehl, P. E. (1989). Clinical versus actuarial judgment. *Science, 24,* 1668–1674.

Dean, A. C., Boone, K. R., Kim, M. S., Curiel, A. R., Martin, D. J., Victor, T. L.,... Lang, Y. K. (2008). Examination of the impact of ethnicity on the Minnesota Multiphasic Personality Inventory-2 (MMPI-2) Fake Bad Scale. *Clinical Neuropsychologist, 1,* 1–7.

Dickson, D. H., & Kelly, I. W. (1985). The "Barnum effect" in personality assessment: A review of the literature. *Psychological Reports, 57,* 367–382.

Downey, R. B., Sinnett, E. R., & Seeberger, W. (1998). The changing face of MMPI practice. *Psychological Reports, 83*(3, Pt 2), 1267–1272.

Emons, W. H. M., Sijtsma, K., & Meijer, R. R. (2007). On the consistency of individual classification using short scales. *Psychological Methods, 12*(1), 105–120.

Erdman, H. P., Klein, M. H., & Greist, J. H. (1985). Direct patient computer interviewing. *Journal of Consulting and Clinical Psychology, 53,* 760–773.

Erdman, H. P., Klein, M. H., Greist, J. H., Skare, S. S., Husted, J. J., Robins, L. N.,..., Miller, J. P. (1992). A comparison of two computer-administered versions of the NMIH Diagnostic Interview schedule. *Journal of Psychiatric Research, 26,* 85–95.

Exner, J. E. Jr. (1987). Computer assistance in Rorschach interpretation. In J. N. Butcher (Ed.), *Computerized psychological assessment: A practitioner's guide* (pp. 218–235). New York, NY: Basic Books.

Exner, J. E. Jr. (2005). Comment on "science and soul." *Rorschachiana, 27*(1), 3.

Eyde, L., Kowal, D. M., & Fishburne, F. J. (1991). The validity of computer-based test interpretations of the MMPI. In T. B. Gutkin & S. L. Wise (Eds.), *The computer and the decision-making process* (pp. 75–123). Hillsdale, NJ: Erlbaum.

Eyde, L. D., Robertson, G. J. & Krug, S. E. (2010). *Responsible test use: Case studies for assessing human behavior* (2nd ed.). Washington, DC: American Psychological Association.

Farrell, A. D., Camplair, P. S., & McCullough, L. (1987). Identification of target complaints by computer interview: Evaluation of the computerized assessment system for psychotherapy evaluation and research. *Journal of Consulting and Clinical Psychology, 55,* 691–700.

Finger, M. S., & Ones, D. S. (1999). Psychometric equivalence of the computer and booklet forms of the MMPI: A meta-analysis. *Psychological Assessment, 11,* 58–66.

First, M. B. (1994). Computer-assisted assessment of DSM-III-R diagnosis. *Psychiatric Annals, 24,* 25–29.

First, M. B., Opler, L. A., Hamilton, R. M., Linder, J., Linfield, L. S., Silver, J. M., Toshav, N. L.,... Spitzer, R. L. (1993). Evaluation in an inpatient setting of DTREE, a computer-assisted diagnostic assessment procedure. *Comprehensive Psychiatry, 34,* 171–175.

Forbey, J. D., & Ben-Porath, Y. S. (2007). Computerized adaptive personality testing: A review and illustration with the MMPI-2 computerized adaptive version. *Psychological Assessment, 19*(1), 14–24.

Forbey, J. D., Ben Porath, Y. S., & Gartland, D. (2009). Validation of the MMPI-2 computerized adaptive version (MMPI-2-CA) in a correctional intake facility. *Psychological Services, 6*(4), 279–292.

Forbey, J. D., Handel, R. W., & Ben-Porath, Y. S. (2000). A real-data simulation of computerized adaptive administration of the MMPI-A. *Computers in Human Behavior, 16*(1), 83–96.

Fowler, R. D. (1969). Automated interpretation of personality test data. In J. N. Butcher (Ed.), *MMPI: Research developments and clinical applications* (pp. 325–342). New York, NY: McGraw-Hill.

Fowler, R. D., & Butcher, J. N. (1986). Critique of Matarazzo's views on computerized testing: All sigma and no meaning. *American Psychologist, 41,* 94–96.

Furnham, A. (1989). Personality and the acceptance of diagnostic feedback. *Personality and Individual Differences, 10,* 1121–1133.

Furnham, A., & Schofield, S. (1987). Accepting personality test feedback: A review of the Barnum effect. *Current Psychological Research and Reviews, 6,* 162–178.

Garb, H. N. (1998). *Studying the clinician: Judgment research and psychological assessment*. Washington, DC: American Psychological Association.

Gass, C. S., Williams, C. L., Cumella, E., Butcher, J. N. & Kally, Z. (2010). Ambiguous measures of unknown constructs: The MMPI-2 Fake Bad Scale (aka Symptom Validity Scale, FBS, FBS-r). *Psychological Injury and the Law, 3*(1), 81–85, doi:10.1007/s12207-009-9063-2

Gordon, R. M. (2006). False assumptions about psychopathology, hysteria and the MMPI-2 restructured clinical scales. *Psychological Reports, 98,* 870–872.

Gosling, S. D., & Johnson, J. A. (Eds). (2010). *Advanced methods for conducting online behavioral research*. Washington, DC: American Psychological Association.

Greene, R. L. (2011). *MMPI-2/MMPI-2-RF: An interpretive manual* (3rd ed.). Boston, MA: Allyn & Bacon.

Greiffenstein, M. F., Fox, D., & Lees-Haley, P. R. (2007). The MMPI-2 Fake Bad Scale in detection of noncredible brain injury claims. In K. Boone (Ed.), *Detection of noncredible cognitive performance* (pp. 210–235). New York, NY: Guilford Press.

Greist, J. H., Klein, M. H., Erdman, H. P., Bires, J. K., Bass, S. M., Machtinger, P. E., & Kresge, D. G. (1987). Comparison of computer- and interviewer-administered versions of the Diagnostic Interview Schedule. *Hospital and Community Psychiatry, 38,* 1304–1310.

Grove, W. M., & Meehl, P. E. (1996). Comparative efficiency of information (subjective, impressionistic) and formal (mechanical, algorithmic) prediction procedures: The clinical-statistical controversy. *Psychology, Public Policy, and Law, 2,* 293–323.

Grove, W. M., Zald, D. H., Lebow, B., Smith, E., & Nelson, C. (2000). Clinical versus mechanical prediction: A meta-analysis. *Psychological Assessment, 12,* 19–30.

Guastello, S. J., Guastello, D., & Craft, L. (1989). Assessment of the Barnum effect in computer-based test interpretations. *Journal of Psychology, 123,* 477–484.

Guastello, S. J., & Rieke, M. L. (1990). The Barnum effect and validity of computer-based test interpretations: The Human Resource Development Report. *Psychological Assessment, 2,* 186–190.

Harris, W. G., Niedner, D., Feldman, C., Fink, A., & Johnson, J. N. (1981). An on-line interpretive Rorschach approach: Using Exner's comprehensive system. *Behavior Research Methods and Instrumentation, 13,* 588–591.

Hathaway, S. R., & McKinley, J. C. 1940. A multiphasic personality schedule (Minnesota): I. Construction of the schedule. *Journal of Psychology, 10,* 249–54

Hile, M. G., & Adkins, R. E. (1997). Do substance abuse and mental health clients prefer automated assessments? *Behavior Research Methods, Instruments, and Computers, 29,* 146–150.

Hofer, P. J., & Green, B. F. (1985). The challenge of competence and creativity in computerized psychological testing. *Journal of Consulting and Clinical Psychology, 53,* 826–838.

Hol, A. M., Vorst, H. C. M. & Mellenbergh, G. J. (2008). Computerized adaptive testing of personality traits. *Journal of Psychology, 216,* 12–21.

Honaker, L. M., Harrell, T. H., & Buffaloe, J. D. (1988). Equivalency of Microtest computer MMPI administration for standard and special scales. *Computers in Human Behavior, 4,* 323–337.

Hoover, D. W., & Snyder, D. K. (1991). Validity of the computerized interpretive report for the Marital Satisfaction Inventory. *Psychological Assessment: A Journal of Consulting and Clinical Psychology, 3,* 213–217.

Humm, D. G., & Wadsworth, G. W. Jr. 1935. The Humm-Wadsworth Temperament Scale. *American Journal of Psychiatry, 92,* 163–200.

Jemelka, R. P., Wiegand, G. A., Walker, E. A., & Trupin, E. W. (1992). Computerized offender assessment: Validation study. *Psychological Assessment, 4,* 138–144.

Keller, L. S., & Butcher, J. N. (1991). *Use of the MMPI-2 with chronic pain patients*. Minneapolis, MN: University of Minnesota Press.

Labeck, L. J., Johnson, J. H., & Harris, W. G. (1983). Validity of a computerized on-line MMPI interpretive system. *Journal of Clinical Psychology, 39,* 412–416.

Lambert, M. E., Andrews, R. H., Rylee, K., & Skinner, J. (1987). Equivalence of computerized and traditional MMPI administration with substance abusers. *Computers in Human Behavior, 3,* 139–143.

Layne, C. (1979). The Barnum effect: Rationality versus gullibility? *Journal of Consulting and Clinical Psychology, 47,* 219–221.

Lees-Haley, P. R., English, L. T., & Glenn, W. J. (1991). A Fake Bad Scale on the MMPI-2 for personal injury claimants. *Psychological Reports, 68,* 203–210.

Lees-Haley, P. R., Williams, C. W., & Brown, R. S. (1993). The Barnum effect and personal injury litigation. *American Journal of Forensic Psychology, 11,* 21–28.

Lord, F. M. (1980). *Application of Item Response Theory to practical testing problems*. Hillsdale, NJ: LEA Press.

Maddux, C. D., & Johnson, L. (1998). Computer assisted assessment. In H. B. Vance (Ed.), *Psychological assessment in children* (2nd ed., pp. 87–105). New York, NY: Wiley.

Matarazzo, J. D. (1986). Computerized clinical psychological interpretations: Unvalidated plus all mean and no sigma. *American Psychologist, 41,* 14–24.

Mathisen, K. S., Evans, F. J., & Meyers, K. M. (1987). Evaluation of the computerized version of the Diagnostic Interview Schedule. *Hospital and Community Psychiatry, 38,* 1311–1315.

McMinn, M. R., Buchanan, T., Ellens, B. M., & Ryan, M. (1999). Technology, professional practice, and ethics: Survey findings and implications. *Professional Psychology: Research and Practice, 30,* 165–172.

Meehl, P. E. (1954). *Clinical versus statistical prediction: A theoretical analysis and a review of the evidence*. Minneapolis: University of Minnesota Press.

Meehl, P. E. (1956). Wanted—a good cookbook. *American Psychologist, 11,* 263–272.

Merten, T., & Ruch, W. (1996). A comparison of computerized and conventional administration of the German versions of the Eysenck Personality Questionnaire and the Carroll Rating Scale for depression. *Personality and Individual Differences, 20,* 281–291.

Moreland, K. L. (1985). Validation of computer-based interpretations: Problems and prospects. *Journal of Consulting and Clinical Psychology, 53,* 816–825.

Moreland, K. L. (1987). Computerized psychological assessment: What's available. In J. N. Butcher (Ed.), *Computerized psychological assessment: A practitioner's guide* (pp. 64–86). New York, NY: Basic Books.

Moreland, K. L., & Onstad, J. A. (1987). Validity of Millon's computerized interpretation system of the MCMI: A controlled study. *Journal of Consulting and Clinical Psychology, 55,* 113–114.

Moreland, K. L., & Onstad, J. A. (1989). Yes, our study could have been better: Reply to Cash, Mikulka, and Brown. *Journal of Consulting and Clinical Psychology, 57,* 313–314.

Naglieri, J., Drasgow, F., Schmit, M., Handler, L., Profitera, A., Margolis, A. & Velasquez, R. (2004). Psychological testing on the Internet: New problems, old issues. *American Psychologist, 59,* 150–162.

Naus, M. J., Philipp, L. M., & Samsi, M. (2009). From paper to pixels: A comparison of paper and computer formats in psychological assessment. *Computers in Human Behavior, 25*(1), 1–7.

Nichols, D. S. (2006). The trials of separating bath water from baby: A review and critique of the MMPI-2 Restructured Clinical scales. *Journal of Personality Assessment, 87,* 121–138.

O'Dell, J. W. (1972). P. T. Barnum explores the computer. *Journal of Consulting and Clinical Psychology, 38,* 270–273.

Ortner, T. M. (2008). Effects of changed item order: A cautionary note to practitioners on jumping to computerized adaptive testing for personality assessment. *International Journal of Selection and Assessment, 16*(3), 249–257.

Peters, L., & Andrews, G. (1995). Procedural validity of the computerized version of the Composite International Diagnostic Interview (CIDI—Auto) in the anxiety disorders. *Psychological Medicine: A Journal of Research in Psychiatry and the Allied Sciences, 25*(6), 1269–1280.

Pez, O., Gilbert, F., Bitfoi, A., Carta, M. G., Jordanova, V., Garcia-Mahia, C., . . . Kovess-Masfety, V., 2010). Validity across translations of short survey psychiatric diagnostic instruments: CIDI—SF and CIS—R versus SCID—I/NP in four European countries. *Social Psychiatry and Psychiatric Epidemiology, 45*(12), 1149–1159.

Pinsoneault, T. B. (1996). Equivalency of computer-assisted and paper and pencil administered versions of the Minnesota Multiphasic Personality Inventory-2. *Computers in Human Behavior, 12,* 291–300.

Prince, R. J., & Guastello, S. J. (1990). The Barnum effect in a computerized Rorschach interpretation system. *Journal of Psychology, 124,* 217–222.

Reise, S. P., & Henson, J. M. (2000). Computerization and adaptive administration of the NEO PI-R. *Assessment, 7*(4), 347–364.

Rogers, R., Salekin, R. T., & Sewell, K. W. (1999). Validation of the Millon Clinical Multiaxial Inventory for Axis II disorders: Does it meet *Daubert* standard? *Law and Human Behavior, 23,* 425–443.

Rogers, R., Sewell, K. W., Harrison, K. S., & Jordan, M. J. (2006). The MMPI-2 Restructured Clinical Scales: A paradigmatic shift in scale development. *Journal of Personality Assessment, 87,* 139–147.

Rome, H. P., Swenson, W. M., Mataya, P., McCarthy, C. E., Pearson, J. S., Keating, F. R., & Hathaway, S. R. (1962). Symposium on automation techniques in personality assessment. *Proceedings of the Staff Meetings of the Mayo Clinic, 37,* 61–82.

Roper, B. L., Ben-Porath, Y. S., & Butcher, J. N. (1995). Comparability and validity of computerized adaptive testing with the MMPI-2. *Journal of Personality Assessment, 65,* 358–371.

Ross, H. E., Swinson, R., Larkin, E. J., & Doumani, S. (1994). Diagnosing comorbidity in substance abusers: Computer assessment and clinical validation. *Journal of Nervous and Mental Disease, 182,* 556–563.

Rothstein, M. G., & Goffin, R. D. (2006). The use of personality measures in personnel selection: What does current research support? *Human Resource Management Review, 16*(2), 155–180.

Rouse, S. V., Greene, R. L., Butcher, J. N., Nichols, D. S., & Williams, C. L (2008). What do the MMPI-2 Restructured Clinical Scales reliably measure? Answers from multiple research settings. *Journal of Personality Assessment, 90,* 435–442.

Røysamb, E., Kendler, K. S., Tambs, K., Ørstavik, R. E., Neale, M. C., Aggen, S. H., . . . Reichborn-Kjennerud, T. (2011). The joint structure of DSM-IV Axis I and Axis II disorders. *Journal of Abnormal Psychology, 120*(1), 198–209. doi:10.1037/a0021660

Schuldberg, D. (1988). The MMPI is less sensitive to the automated testing format than it is to repeated testing: Item and scale effects. *Computers in Human Behaviors, 4,* 285–298.

Shores, A., & Carstairs, J. R. (1998). Accuracy of the Minnesota Report in identifying fake-good and fake-bad response sets. *Clinical Neuropsychologist, 12,* 101–106.

Simms, L. J., & Clark, L. A. (2005). Validation of a computerized adaptive version of the schedule for nonadaptive and adaptive personality (SNAP). *Psychological Assessment, 17*(1), 28–43.

Sloore, H., Derksen, J., de Mey, H., & Hellenbosch, G. (1996). The Flemish/Dutch version of the MMPI-2: Development and adaptation of the inventory for Belgium and the Netherlands. In J. N. Butcher (Ed.), *International adaptations of the MMPI-2: Research and clinical applications* (pp. 329–349). Minneapolis: University of Minnesota Press.

Snyder, C. R., & Newburg, C. L. (1981). The Barnum effect in a group setting. *Journal of Personality Assessment, 45,* 622–629.

Snyder, D. K., Widiger, T. A., & Hoover, D. W. (1990). Methodological considerations in validating computer-based test interpretations: Controlling for response bias. *Psychological Assessment, 2,* 470–477.

Styles, I. (1991). Clinical assessment and computerized testing. *International Journal of Man-Machine Studies, 35,* 133–150.

Tallent, N. (1958). On individualizing the psychologist's clinical evaluation. *Journal of Clinical Psychology, 14,* 243–245.

Tellegen, A., & Ben-Porath, Y. S. (2008). *MMPI-2-RF technical manual*. Minneapolis: University of Minnesota Press.

Tellegen, A., Ben-Porath, Y. S., McNulty, J., Arbisi, P., Graham, J. R., & Kaemmer, B. (2003). *MMPI-2: Restructured clinical (RC) scales*. Minneapolis: University of Minnesota Press.

Tippins, N. T. (2009). Where is the unproctored Internet testing train headed now? *Industrial and Organizational Psychology: Perspectives on Science and Practice, 2*(1), 69–76.

Toch, T. (2006). *Margins of error: The education testing industry in the No Child Left Behind era*. Washington, DC: Education Sector.

Wakefield, H., & Underwager, R. (1993). Misuse of psychological tests in forensic settings: Some horrible examples. *American Journal of Forensic Psychology, 11,* 55–75.

Walter, O. B., Becker, J., Bjorner, J. B., Fliege, H., Klapp, B. H. & Rose, M. (2007). Development and evaluation of a computer adaptive tool for "Anxiety." *Quality of Life Research, 16,* 143–155.

Watson, C. G., Juba, M., Anderson, P. E., & Manifold, V. (1990). What does the Keane et al. PTSD scale for the MMPI measure? *Journal of Clinical Psychology, 46,* 600–606.

Weiner, I. B. (2004). Rorschach assessment: Current status. In M. J. Hilsenroth & D. L. Segal (Eds.), *Comprehensive handbook of psychological assessment, Vol. 2: Personality assessment* (pp. 343–355). Hoboken, NJ: Wiley.

Weiner, I. B. (2007). Rorschach assessment in forensic cases. In A. M. Goldstein (Ed.), *Forensic psychology: Emerging topics and expanding roles* (pp. 127–153). Hoboken, NJ: Wiley.

Weiner, I. B., & Greene, R. L. (2008). *Handbook of personality assessment*. Hoboken, NJ: Wiley.

Williams, C. L., Butcher, J. N., Gass, C. S., Cumella, E., & Kally, Z. (2009). Inaccuracies about the MMPI-2 Fake Bad Scale in the reply by Ben-Porath, Greve, Bianchini, and Kaufmann (2009). *Psychological Injury and Law, 2,* 182–197.

Williams, J. E., & Weed, N. C. (2004). Relative user ratings of MMPI-2 computer-based test interpretations. *Assessment, 11*(4), 316–329.

Wilson, F. R., Genco, K. T., & Yager, G. G. (1985). Assessing the equivalence of paper-and-pencil vs. computerized tests: Demonstration of a promising methodology. *Computers in Human Behavior, 1,* 265–275.

Wyndowe, J. (1987). The microcomputerized Diagnostic Interview Schedule: Clinical use in an outpatient setting. *Canadian Journal of Psychiatry, 32,* 93–99.

# CHAPTER 8

# Ethical Issues in Psychological Assessment

CELIANE REY-CASSERLY AND GERALD P. KOOCHER

Psychological assessment is unique among the services provided by professional psychologists. Unlike psychotherapy, in which clients may come seeking help for themselves, psychological evaluation services are seldom performed solely at the request of a single individual. In the most common circumstances, people are referred to psychologists for assessment by third parties with questions about school performance, suitability for potential employment, disability status, competence to stand trial, or differential clinical diagnosis. The referring parties are invariably seeking answers to questions with varying degrees of specificity, and these answers may or may not be scientifically addressable via the analysis of psychometric data. In addition, the people being tested may benefit (e.g., obtain remedial help, collect damages, or gain a job offer) or suffer (e.g., lose disability benefits, lose custody of a child, or face imprisonment) as a consequence of the assessment, no matter how competently it is carried out.

Psychological assessment is founded on a scientific base and has the capacity to translate human behavior, characteristics, and abilities into numbers or other forms that lend themselves to description and comparison across individuals and groups of people. Many of the behaviors studied in the course of an evaluation appear to be easily comprehensible to the layperson unfamiliar with test development and psychometrics (e.g., trace a path through a maze, perform mental arithmetic, repeat digits, or copy geometric shapes)—thereby implying that the observed responses must have some inherent validity for some purpose. Even common psychological assessment tasks that may be novel to most people (e.g., Put these blocks together quickly to match this pattern. What does

this inkblot look like to you?) are imbued by the general public with some implied valuable meaning. After all, some authority suggested that the evaluation be done, and the person conducting the evaluation is a licensed expert. Unfortunately, the statistical and scientific underpinnings of the best psychological assessments are far more sophisticated than most laypersons and more than a few psychologists understand them to be. When confronted with an array of numbers or a computer-generated test profile, some people are willing to uncritically accept these data as simple answers to incredibly complex questions. This is the heart of the ethical challenge in psychological assessment: the appropriate use of psychological science to make decisions with full recognition of its limitations and the legal and human rights of the people whose lives are influenced.

In attempting to address the myriad issues that challenge psychologists undertaking to conduct assessments in the most ethically appropriate manner, it is helpful to think in terms of the prepositions *before, during,* and *after.* Some ethical considerations are best addressed before the assessment is begun; others come into play as the data are collected and analyzed; and still other ethical issues crop up after the actual assessment is completed. This chapter explores the ethical problems inherent in psychological assessment using the same sequence. In the beginning—prior to meeting the client and initiating data collection—it is important to consider several questions: What is being asked for and by whom (i.e., who is the client, and what use does that person hope to make of the data)? Is the proposed evaluator qualified to conduct the evaluation and interpret the data obtained? What planning is necessary to ensure the adequacy of the assessment? What instruments are available and most appropriate for use in this situation?

As one proceeds to the actual evaluation and prepares to undertake data collection, other ethical issues come to the fore. Has the client (or his or her representative) been given adequate informed consent about both the nature and intended uses of the evaluation? Is it clear who will pay for the evaluation, what is included, and who will have access to the raw data and report? What are the obligations of the psychologist with respect to optimizing the participants' performance and ensuring validity and thoroughness in documentation? When the data collection is over, what are the examiner's obligations with respect to scoring, interpreting, reporting, documenting procedures, and explaining the data collected?

Finally, after the data are collected and interpreted, what are the ongoing ethical responsibilities of the psychologist with respect to maintenance of records, allowing access to the data, and providing feedback or follow-up services? What is appropriate conduct when one psychologist is asked to review and critique another psychologist's work? How should one respond upon discovery of apparent errors or incompetence of a colleague in the conduct of a now-completed evaluation?

Guidance on ethical decision making is available in the area of psychological assessment in the Ethical Principles of Psychologists and Code of Conduct of the American Psychological Association (APA, 2010), which was most recently revised in 2002 and amended in 2010. Other resources include the Standards for Educational and Psychological Testing (American Educational Research Association, American Psychological Association, & National Council of Measurement in Education, 1999), a jointly sponsored document that is currently undergoing revision, and the Principles for Professional Ethics geared towards school psychology practitioners (National Association of School Psychologists, 2010). The APA ethics code applies to the professional conduct of members and student affiliates of the APA. This chapter focuses on key ethical foundations and refers to the APA ethics code when relevant. We also identify areas of controversy and, whenever possible, discuss likely policy decisions based on the code.

## IN THE BEGINNING

Psychological assessment requires careful planning and attention to a range of ethical issues from the outset. Relevant domains include specifying the psychologist's obligations, informing clients about the nature of the assessment, evaluating one's own competence to perform a specific assessment, planning an assessment strategy grounded in scientific evidence, and addressing issues of culture and diversity.

## Who Is the Client?

The first step in undertaking the evaluator role is often seductively automatic. The simple act of accepting the referral and setting up the appointment may occur almost automatically; not much thought may be devoted to the question of what specific duties or professional obligations are owed to which parties. Is the client simply the person to be evaluated, or are there layers of individuals and institutions to whom the psychologist owes some degree of professional obligation? For example, is the person to be evaluated a legally competent adult? If not—as in the case of children or dependent adults—the party seeking the evaluation may be a parent, guardian, government agency, institution, or other legally responsible authority. The evaluator must pause to consider what rights each layer of authority has in terms of such factors as the ability to compel cooperation of the person to be assessed, the right of access to test data and results, and the right to dictate components of the evaluation or the manner in which it is conducted. Sometimes there is uniform agreement by all parties, and no conflicts of interest take place. In other circumstances, the person being evaluated may have had little choice in the matter or may wish to reserve the right to limit access to results of the evaluation. In still other instances, there may be direct conflicts between what one party is seeking and the objectives of another party with some degree of client status.

Evaluations conducted in the context of the educational system provide a good example of the complex layers of client status that can be involved. Suppose that a schoolchild is failing and an assessment is requested by the child's family to qualify for services and for use in preparation of an individualized educational plan (IEP) as specified under state or federal special education laws. If a psychologist employed by the public school system undertakes the task, that evaluator certainly owes a set of professional duties (e.g., competence, fairness, etc.) to the child, to the adults acting on behalf of the child (i.e., parents or guardians), to the employing school system, and—by extension—to the citizens of the community who pay school taxes. In the best of circumstances, there may be no problem—that is to say, the evaluation will identify the child's needs, parents and school will agree, and an appropriate effective remediation or treatment component for the IEP will be put in place.

The greater ethical challenge occurs when parents and school authorities disagree and apply pressure to the evaluator to interpret the data in ways that support their conflicting demands. One set of pressures may apply when the psychologist is employed by the school, and another may apply when the evaluation is funded by the parents or another third party. From an ethical perspective, there should be no difference in the psychologist's behavior. The psychologist should offer the most scientifically and clinically sound recommendations drawn from the best data while relying on competence and personal integrity without undue influence from external forces.

Similar conflicts in competing interests occur frequently within the legal system and the business world—a person may agree to psychological assessment with a set of hopes or goals that may be at variance or in direct conflict with the data or the outcomes desired by another party in the chain of people or institutions to whom the evaluator may owe a professional duty. Consider defendants whose counsel hope that testing will support insanity defenses, plaintiffs who hope that claims for psychological damages or disability will be supported, or job applicants who hope that test scores will prove that they are the best qualified. In all such instances, it is critical that the psychologist conducting the assessment strive for the highest level of personal integrity while clarifying the assessment role and its implications to all parties to whom a professional duty is owed.

Other third parties (e.g., potential employers, the courts, and health insurers) are involved in many psychological assessment contexts. In some cases, when the psychologist is an independent practitioner, the third party's interest is in making use of the assessment in some sort of decision (e.g., hiring or school placement); in other cases, the interest may simply be contract fulfillment (e.g., an insurance company may require that a written report be prepared as a condition of the assessment procedure). In still other situations, the psychologist conducting the evaluation may be a full-time employee of a company or agency with a financial interest in the outcome of the evaluation (e.g., an employer hoping to avoid a disability claim or a school system that wishes to avoid expensive special education placements or services). For all these reasons, it is critical that psychologists clearly conceptualize and accurately represent their obligations to all parties.

## Informed Consent

The Ethical Principles of Psychologists and Code of Conduct (American Psychological Association, 2010) added a proposed standard referring specifically to obtaining informed consent for psychological assessment in the 2002 major revision (Standard 9.03 Informed consent in assessments). The issue of consent is also discussed extensively in the professional literature in areas of consent to treatment (Grisso & Appelbaum, 1998) and consent for research participation (Knudson, 2001; National Commission for the Protection of Human Subjects of Biomedical and Behavioral Research, 1979), but references to consent in the area of psychological assessment have been quite limited and are only recently expanding such that there is now a position paper recommending best practices for neuropsychological assessment (Johnson-Greene, 2005). Johnson-Greene, Hardy-Morais, Adams, Hardy, and Bergloff (1997) reviewed this issue and proposed a set of recommendations for providing informed consent to clients. These authors also proposed that written documentation of informed consent be obtained; the APA ethical principles allow but do not require this step. We believe that psychologists would be wise to establish consistent routines and document all discussions with clients related to obtaining consent, explaining procedures, and describing confidentiality and privacy issues. A wise psychologist will obtain written informed consent in situations that may have forensic implications, such as personal injury lawsuits and child custody litigation. Johnson-Greene (2005) outlined a detailed flowchart that specifies steps in the process.

Psychologists are expected to explain the nature of the evaluation, clarify the referral questions, and discuss the goals of the assessment, in language the client can readily understand. It is also important to be aware of the limitations of the assessment procedures and discuss these procedures with the client. To the extent possible, the psychologist also should be mindful of the goals of the client, clarify misunderstandings, and correct unrealistic expectations. For example, parents may seek a psychological evaluation with the expectation that the results will ensure that their child will be eligible for a gifted and talented program; accident victims may anticipate that the evaluation will document their entitlement to damages; and job candidates may hope to become employed or qualify for advancement. These hopes and expectations may come to pass, but one cannot reasonably comment on the outcome before valid data are in hand.

Whether the assessment takes place in a clinical, employment, school, or forensic setting, some universal principles apply. The nature of assessment must be described to all parties involved before the evaluation is performed. This includes explaining the purpose of the evaluation, who will have access to the data or findings, who is responsible for payment, and what any relevant limitations are on the psychologist's duties to the parties. In employment contexts, for example, the psychologist is usually hired by a company and may not be authorized to provide feedback to the employee or candidate being assessed. Similarly, in some forensic contexts, the results of the evaluation ultimately may be open to the court or other litigants over the objections of the person being assessed. In each case, it is the psychologist's responsibility to recognize the various levels of people and organizations to whom a professional duty may be owed and to clarify the relationship with all parties at the outset of the assessment activity.

The key elements of consent are information, understanding, and voluntariness. First, do the people to be evaluated have all the information that might reasonably influence their willingness to participate? Such information includes the purpose of the evaluation, who will have access to the results, and any costs or charges to them. Second, is the information presented in a manner that is comprehensible to the client? This includes use of appropriate language, vocabulary, and explanation of any terms that are confusing to the client. Finally, is the client willing to be evaluated? There are often circumstances in which an element of coercion may be present. For example, the potential employee, admissions candidate, criminal defendant, or person seeking disability insurance coverage might prefer to avoid mandated testing. Prospective assessment clients might reluctantly agree to testing in such a context because they have no other choice if they wish to be hired, gain admission, be found not criminally responsible, or adjudicated disabled, respectively. Conducting such externally mandated evaluations does not pose ethical problems as long as the nature of the evaluation and obligations of the psychologist are carefully delineated at the outset. It is not necessary that the person being evaluated be happy about the prospect—he or she must simply understand and agree to the assessment and associated risks, much like people referred for a colonoscopy or exploratory surgery. Additional issues of consent and diminished competence come into play when a psychologist is called on to evaluate a minor child, an individual with dementia, or other persons with reduced mental capacity as a result of significant physical or mental disorder. When such an evaluation is undertaken primarily for service to the client (e.g., as part of

treatment planning), the risks to the client are usually minimal. However, if the data might be used in legal proceedings (e.g., a competency hearing) or in any way that might have significant potentially adverse future consequences that the client is unable to competently evaluate, a surrogate consent process should be used—that is to say, a parent or legal guardian ought to be involved in granting permission for the evaluation. Obtaining such permission helps to address and respect the vulnerabilities and attendant obligations owed to persons with reduced personal decision-making capacities.

## Test User Competence

Before agreeing to undertake a particular evaluation, the clinician should be competent to provide the particular service to the client, but evaluating such competence varies with the eye of the beholder. In the 2002 APA Ethics Code, competence was added as a standard; previously it had been included as a general principle. Competence and adequacy of training and experience in psychological assessment have been described as central ethical issues in psychological assessment (Bush, Grote, Johnson Greene, & Macartney-Filgate, 2008; Society for Personality Assessment, 2006). The five general principles of the 2002 APA Ethics Code—Beneficence and Nonmaleficence; Fidelity and Responsibility; Integrity; Justice; Respect for People's Rights and Dignity—are all relevant in the area of competence.

Psychologists often face situations that require skills that exceed their competence, such as forensic assessments or evaluation of specific populations. Psychologists are ethically bound not to promote the use of psychological assessment techniques by unqualified persons, except when such use is conducted for training purposes with appropriate supervision. Ascertaining what constitutes competence or qualifications in the area of psychological assessment has been a difficult endeavor due to the complex nature of assessment, the diverse settings and contexts in which psychological assessments are performed, and the differences in background and training of individuals providing psychological assessment services. Psychological assessment is described as a complex area of specific expertise that requires intensive and ongoing education and training for ethical and competent practice (Society for Personality Assessment, 2006). Is a doctoral degree in clinical, counseling, or school psychology required? How about testing conducted by licensed counselors or by individuals with master's degrees in psychology? Are some physicians competent to use psychological tests? After all, Hermann Rorschach was a psychiatrist, and so was J. Charnley McKinley, one of the two originators of the Minnesota Multiphasic Personality Inventory (MMPI). Henry Murray, a nonpsychiatric physician, co-developed the Thematic Apperception Test (TAT) with Christiana Morgan, who had no formal training in psychology.

Historically, the APA addressed this issue only in a very general manner in the Ethical Principles and Code of Conduct for Psychologists. In the earliest versions of the Ethical Standards of Psychologists (American Psychological Association, 1953), the ethical distribution and sale of psychological tests was to be limited to unspecified "qualified persons." A system of categorization of tests and concordant qualifications that entailed three levels of tests and expertise was subsequently developed. Vocational guidance tools, for example, were at the low end in terms of presumed required expertise. At the high end of required competence were tests designed for clinical assessment and diagnoses such as intelligence and personality assessment instruments. The rationale involved in this scheme was based on the need to understand statistics, psychopathology, and psychometrics in order to accurately draw clinical inference or make actuarial predictions based on the test data. Although the three-tier system is no longer discussed in APA ethical standards, it was adopted by many test publishers, and variations continue in use. When attempting to place orders for psychological test materials, would-be purchasers are often asked to list their credentials, cite a professional license number, or give some other indication of presumed competence. Decisions about the actual sale are generally made by the person processing the order—often a clerk who has little understanding of the issues and considerable incentive to help the test publisher make the sale. Weaknesses and inconsistencies in the implementation of these criteria are discussed in a Canadian study (Simmer, 1994). Controlling the sale and distribution of psychological tests through documentation of credentials can only go so far in today's world. Test materials can be found on the Internet, and coaching clients on psychological tests can occur in forensic settings (LoBello & Zachar, 2007; Victor & Abeles, 2004).

Further efforts to delineate qualifications of test users included the lengthy efforts of the Test User Qualifications Working Group (TUQWG) sponsored by an interdisciplinary group, the Joint Committee on Testing Practices, which was convened and funded by the APA. To study competence problems, this group of professionals and academics attempted to quantify and describe factors associated with appropriate test use by using a data-gathering (as opposed to a specification of qualifications) approach (Eyde, Moreland, Robertson, Primoff, & Most, 1988; Eyde, Robertson, Krug, Moreland, Robertson, Shewan, Harrison, Porch, Hammer, & Primoff, 1993; Moreland, Eyde, Robertson, Primoff, & Most, 1995).

International concerns regarding competent test use—perhaps spurred by expansion of the European Economic Community and the globalization of industry—prompted the British Psychological Society (BPS) to establish a certification system that delineates specific competencies for the use of tests in employment settings (British Psychological Society, 2011). Under this system, the user who demonstrates competence in test use is certified and listed in an official register (Register of Competence in Psychological Testing). Professionals aspiring to provide psychological assessment services must demonstrate competence with specific tests to be listed. The BPS is currently revising these standards and is in the process of creating the new Register of the British Psychological Society's Qualifications in Test Use to align with European standards. The International Test Commission adopted test-use guidelines describing required knowledge, competence, and skills (Bartram, 2001). The European Federation of Psychologists' Associations has further refined this competency based approach in the employment setting (Bartram, 2011).

Within the United States, identifying test user qualifications and establishing competence in test use have been complicated by political and practical issues, including the potential for nonprofit professional groups to be accused of violating antitrust laws, the complexity of addressing the myriad settings and contexts in which tests are used, and the diversity of experience and training in assessment among the professionals who administer and interpret psychological tests. Further complicating matters is the trend in recent years for many graduate programs in psychology to deemphasize psychological assessment theory and practice in required course work, producing many licensed doctoral psychologists who are unfamiliar with contemporary measurement theory (Aiken, West, & Millsap, 2008; Aiken et al., 1990).

In October 1996, the APA formed the Task Force on Test User Qualifications to develop more specific guidelines in the area of test user qualifications and competence. Members of the task force were selected to represent the various settings and areas of expertise in psychological assessment (clinical, industrial/organizational, school, counseling, educational, forensic, and neuropsychological). Instead of focusing on qualifications in terms of professional degrees or licenses, the task force elected to delineate a core set of competencies in psychological assessment and then describe more specifically the knowledge and skills expected of test users in specific contexts. The core competencies included not only knowledge of psychometric and measurement principles and appropriate test administration procedures but also appreciation of the factors affecting tests' selection and interpretation in different contexts and across diverse individuals.

Other essential competencies listed by the task force included familiarity with relevant legal standards and regulations relevant to test use, including civil rights laws, the Americans with Disabilities Act (ADA), and the Individuals with Disabilities Education Act (IDEA). Public commentary in response to the task force's preliminary report emphasized the variety of settings and purposes involved and generally argued against a focus on degrees and licenses as providing adequate assurance of competence. The task force delineated the purposes for which tests are typically used (e.g., classification, description, prediction, intervention planning, and tracking) and described the competencies and skills required in specific settings (e.g. employment, education, career-vocational counseling, health care, and forensic). Its recommendations were drafted as aspirational guidelines describing the range of knowledge and skills for optimal test use in various contexts. The task force report also expressed the hope that the guidelines would serve to bolster the training of future psychologists in the area of assessment. The final report of the task force was approved by the APA Council of Representatives in August 2000 (Turner, DeMers, Fox, & Reed, 2001).

The chief ethical problems in this area involve matters of how to objectively determine one's own competence and how to deal with the perceived lack of competence in others whose work is encountered in the course of professional practice. The key to the answer lies in peer consultation. Discussion with colleagues, teachers, and clinical supervisors is the best way to assess one's emerging competence in assessment and focus on additional training needs. Following graduation and licensing, continuing professional education and peer consultation are the most effective strategies for assessing and maintaining one's own competence. When in doubt, presenting samples of one's work to a respected senior colleague for review and critique is a useful strategy. If one's competence is ever challenged before a court, ethics committee, or licensing board, the expert testimony of senior colleagues will be used in an effort to prove incompetence or negligence. By consulting with such colleagues

regularly, one can be continuously updated on any perceived problems with one's own work and minimize the risk of criticism in this regard.

Dealing with the less-than-adequate work of others poses a different set of ethical concerns. At times psychologists may become aware of inadequate assessment work or misuse of psychological tests by colleagues or individuals from other professions (e.g., physicians or nonpsychologist counselors). Such individuals may be unaware of appropriate testing standards or may claim that they disagree with or are not bound by them. Similarly, some psychologists may attempt to use assessment tools they are not qualified to administer or interpret. The context in which such problems come to light is critical in determining the most appropriate course of action. The ideal circumstance is one in which the presumed malefactor is amenable to correcting the problem as a result of an informal conversation, assuming that you have the consent of the party who has consulted you to initiate such a dialogue. Ideally, a professional who is the recipient of an informal contact expressing concern about matters of assessment or test interpretation will be receptive to and interested in remedying the situation. When this is not the case, the client who has been improperly evaluated should be advised about potential remedies available through legal and regulatory channels.

If one is asked to consult as a potential expert witness in matters involving alleged assessment errors or inadequacies, one has no obligation to attempt informal consultation with the professional who rendered the report in question. In most cases, such contact would be ethically inappropriate because the client of the consulting expert is not the person who conducted the assessment. In such circumstances, the people seeking an expert opinion will most likely be attorneys intent on challenging or discrediting a report deemed adverse to their clients. The especially complex issues raised when there are questions of challenging a clinician's competence in the area of neuropsychological assessment have been effectively discussed by Grote, Lewin, Sweet, and van Gorp (2000).

## Planning the Evaluation

As an essential part of accepting the referral, the psychologist should clarify the questions to be answered in an interactive process that refines the goals of the evaluation in the context of basic assessment science and the limitations of available techniques; this is especially important when the referral originates with nonpsychologists or others who may be unaware of the limitations of testing or may have unrealistic expectations regarding what they may learn from the test data.

## Selection of Instruments

In attempting to clarify the ethical responsibilities of psychologists conducting assessments, the APA's ethics code states that psychologists should base their assessments, recommendations, reports, opinions, and diagnostic or evaluative statements on information and techniques sufficient to substantiate their findings (American Psychological Association, 2010). The psychologist should have a sound knowledge of the available instruments for assessing the particular construct related to the assessment questions. This knowledge should include an understanding of the psychometric properties of the instruments being employed (e.g., their validity, reliability, and normative base) as well as an appreciation of how the instrument can be applied in different contexts or with different individuals across age levels, cultures, languages, and other variables (Wong, 2006). It is also important for psychologists to differentiate between the instrument's strengths and weaknesses such that the most appropriate and valid measure for the intended purpose is selected. For example, so-called floor and ceiling constraints can have special implications for certain age groups. When evaluating children with significant intellectual impairment, many instruments can have limited ability to discriminate among children with significant impairments at the youngest age level of the normative data (Flanagan & Alfonso, 1995). In evaluating such children, the use of other instruments with lower floor capabilities would be more appropriate.

## Adequacy of Instruments

Consistent with the APA ethics code (American Psychological Association, 2010) psychologists are expected to develop, administer, score, interpret, or use assessment techniques, interviews, tests, or instruments only in a manner and for purposes that are appropriate in light of the research on or evidence of the usefulness and proper application of the techniques in question. Psychologists who develop and conduct research with tests and other assessment techniques are expected to use appropriate psychometric procedures and current scientific or professional knowledge in test design, standardization, validation, reduction or elimination of bias, and recommendations for use of the instruments. The ethical responsibility of justifying the appropriateness of the assessment is firmly on the psychologist who uses the particular instrument. Although a test publisher has some related obligations, the APA ethics code can be enforced only against individuals who are APA members, not corporations. The reputations of test publishers will invariably rise or fall based on the quality of the tools they develop and distribute. When preparing new assessment techniques for publication, a test manual that includes the data necessary for psychologists to evaluate the appropriateness of the tool for their work is of critical importance (American Educational Research Association, American Psychological Association, & National Council of Measurement in Education, 1999). The psychologist must have the clinical and scientific skill needed to evaluate the data provided by the publisher. The test selection strategy employed by the psychologist needs to be informed by the available evidence that supports the intended use (Adams & Luscher, 2003; Wong, 2006).

## Appropriate Assessment in a Multicultural Society

In countries with a citizenry as diverse as that of the United States, psychologists are invariably confronted with the challenge of people who by reason of race, culture, language, or other factors are not well represented in the normative base of frequently used assessment tools. The Reynolds and Suzuki chapter in this volume considers these issues in detail. Such circumstances demand consideration of a multiplicity of issues. When working with diverse populations, psychologists are expected to use assessment instruments whose validity and reliability have been established for that particular population. When such instruments are not available, psychologists are expected to take care to interpret test results cautiously and with regard to the potential bias and potential misuses of such results. When appropriate tests for a particular population have not been developed, psychologists who use existing standardized tests may ethically adapt the administration and interpretation procedures only if the adaptations have a sound basis in the scientific and experiential foundation of the discipline. Psychologists have an ethical responsibility to document any such adaptations and clarify their probable impact on the findings. Psychologists are expected to use assessment methods in a manner appropriate to an individual's language preference, competence, and cultural background, unless the use of an alternative language is relevant to the purpose of the assessment. Furthermore, competence in multicultural issues is critical for practice in psychological assessment (Brickman, Cabo, & Manly, 2006).

## Getting Around Language Barriers

Some psychologists incorrectly assume that the use of an interpreter will compensate for a lack of fluency in the language of the person being tested. Aside from the obvious nuances involved in vocabulary, the meaning of specific instructions can vary widely. For example, some interpreters may tend to simplify instructions or responses rather than give precise linguistic renditions. At other times, the relative rarity of the language may tempt an examiner to use family or community members when professional interpreters are not readily available. Such individuals may have personal motives that could lead to alterations in the meaning of what was actually said, or their presence may compromise the privacy of the person being assessed. Psychologists using the services of an interpreter must assure themselves of the adequacy of the interpreter's training, obtain the informed consent of the client to use that particular interpreter, and ensure that the interpreter will respect the confidentiality of test results and test security. In addition, any limitations on the data obtained via the use of an interpreter must be discussed in presenting the results of the evaluation. Psychologists also need to have an understanding of the impact of bilingual background on performance on psychological tests (Mindt, Arentoft, Germano, D'Aquila, Scheiner, Pizzirusso, Sandoval, & Gollan, 2008).

Some psychologists mistakenly assume that they can compensate for language or educational barriers by using measures that do not require verbal instructions or responses. When assessing individuals of diverse cultural and linguistic backgrounds, it is not sufficient to rely solely on nonverbal procedures and assume that resulting interpretations will be valid. Many human behaviors, ranging from the nature of eye contact; speed, spontaneity, and elaborateness of response; and persistence on challenging tasks, may be linked to social or cultural factors independent of language or semantics. It has been demonstrated, for example, that performance on nonverbal tests can be significantly affected both by culture and educational level (Manly, Jacobs, Sano, Bell, Merchant, Small, & Stern, 1999; Ostrosky-Solís, Ramirez, & Ardila, 2004).

## What Is in a Norm?

Psychologists must have knowledge of the applicability of the instrument's normative basis to the client. Are the norms up to date and based on people who are compatible with the client? If the normative data do not apply to the client, the psychologist must be able to discuss the limitations in interpretation. In selecting tests for specific populations, it is important that the scores be corrected not only with respect to age but also with respect to educational level (Greenaway, Smith, Tangalos, Geda, & Ivnik, 2009; Heaton, Grant, & Matthews, 1991). For example, the assessment of dementia in an individual with an eighth-grade education would demand very different considerations from those needed for a similar assessment in a person who has worked as a college professor.

Psychologists should select and interpret tests with an understanding of how specific tests and the procedures they entail interact with the specific individual undergoing evaluation. Several tests purporting to evaluate the same construct (e.g., general cognitive ability) put varying demands on the client and can place different levels of emphasis on specific abilities. For example, some tests used with young children have different expectations for the amount of language used in the instructions and required of the child in a response. A child with a specific language impairment may demonstrate widely discrepant scores on different tests of intelligence as a function of the language load of the instrument because some tests place a premium on verbal skills (Kamphaus, Dresden, & Kaufman, 1993).

It is important to remember that psychologists must not base their assessment, intervention decisions, or recommendations on outdated data or test results. Similarly, psychologists must not base such decisions or recommendations on test instruments and measures that are obsolete. Test kits can be expensive, and more than a few psychologists rationalize that there is no need to invest in a newly revised instrument when they already own a perfectly serviceable set of materials of the previous edition. Adopting new versions of tests requires careful consideration and understanding of the changes of the instruments in question (Bush, 2010). In some instances, a psychologist may reasonably use an older version of a standardized instrument, but he or she must have an appropriate and valid rationale to justify the practice and document this in the report. For example, a psychologist may wish to assess whether there has been deterioration in a client's condition and may elect to use the same measure as used in prior assessments, such as the Wechsler Adult Intelligence Scales–Third Edition (WAIS-III), even if a newer improved version such as the WAIS-IV is now available. The chapter in this volume by Wasserman and Bracken discusses psychometric issues relevant to such comparisons.

## Bases for Assessment

The current APA ethics code holds that psychologists typically provide opinions on the psychological characteristics of individuals only after conducting an examination of the individuals that is adequate to support the psychologists' statements or conclusions. This provision is confusing in some contexts. At times such an examination is not practical (e.g., when a psychologist serving as an expert witness is asked to offer hypothetical opinions regarding data sets collected by others). Another example would occur when a psychologist is retained to provide confidential assistance to an attorney. Such help might be sought to explore the accuracy of another's report or to help the attorney frame potential cross-examination questions to ask the other side's expert. In such situations, psychologists document the efforts they made to obtain their own data (if any) and clarify the potential impact of their limited information on the reliability and validity of their opinions.

The key to ethical conduct in such instances is to take great care to appropriately limit the nature and extent of any conclusions or recommendations. Related areas of the APA ethics code include Standards 2.01 (Boundaries of competence), 9.01 (Bases for assessments), and 9.06 (Interpreting assessment results). When psychologists conduct record review and an individual examination is not warranted or necessary for their opinions, they explain this situation and describe the bases on which they formulated this opinion in their conclusions and recommendations. This same issue is addressed in Section 9 (Assessment) of the ethics code. Subsection b of 9.01 (Bases for assessments) indicates that when, despite reasonable efforts, examination of an individual is impractical, "psychologists document the efforts they made and the result of those efforts, clarify the probable impact of their limited information on the reliability and validity of their opinions, and appropriately limit the nature and extent of their conclusions or recommendations" (American Psychological Association, 2010). Subsection c addresses the issue of record review without individual examination. This practice is especially common in the forensic arena; attorneys often want their own expert to examine the complete data set and may not wish to disclose the identity of the expert to the other side. This circumstance of being able to ethically offer an opinion with limitations—absent a direct assessment of the client—is also germane with respect to requests for the release of raw test data, as discussed later in this chapter (see Release of Data).

## CONDUCTING THE EVALUATION

The requirements for and components of informed consent—including contracting details (i.e., who is the client, who is paying for the psychologist's services, and who will have access to the data)—were discussed earlier in this chapter. We proceed with a discussion of the conduct of the evaluation on the assumption that adequate informed consent has been obtained.

### Conduct of the Assessment

A conducive climate is critical to collection of valid test data. In conducting their assessments, psychologists strive to create appropriate rapport with clients by helping them to feel physically comfortable and emotionally at ease, as appropriate to the context. The psychologist should be well prepared and work to create a suitable testing environment. Most psychological tests are developed with the assumption that the test takers' attitudes and motivations are generally positive. For example, attempting to collect test data in a noisy, distracting environment or asking a client to attempt a lengthy test (e.g., an MMPI-2) while seated uncomfortably with a clipboard balanced on one knee and the answer form on another would be inappropriate. With the increasing use of computer-administered tests, psychologists need to be aware of the test taker's experience and facility with a computer. Particularly in older individuals, lack of comfort with this response method can compromise performance and affect validity of the testing (Bush, Naugle, & Johnson-Greene, 2002).

The psychologist should also consider and appreciate the attitudes of the client and address any issues raised in this regard. Some test takers may be depressed or apathetic in a manner that retards their performance, whereas others may engage in dissimulation, hoping to fake bad (i.e., falsely appear to be more pathological) or to fake good (i.e., conceal psychopathology). If there are questions about a test taker's motivation, ability to sustain adequate concentration, or problems with the test-taking environment, the psychologist should attempt to resolve these issues and is expected to discuss how these circumstances ultimately affect test data interpretations in any reports that result from the evaluation. Similarly, in circumstances in which subtle or obvious steps by clients to fake results appear to be under way, it is important for psychologists to note these steps and consider additional instruments or techniques useful in detecting dissimulation. It has become standard practice in forensic neuropsychological assessments to include measures of effort as part of the assessment (Heilbronner, Sweet, Morgan, Larrabee, & Millis, 2009; Iverson, 2006, 2008; Sweet & Morgan, 2009).

Another factor that can affect the test-taking environment is the presence of third-party observers during the interview and testing procedures. In forensic evaluations, psychologists are occasionally faced by a demand from attorneys to be present as observers. Having a third-party observer present can compromise the ability of the psychologist to follow standardized procedures and can affect the validity and reliability of the data collection (Gavett, Lynch, & McCaffrey, 2005; McCaffrey, Fisher, Gold, & Lynch, 1996; McSweeny, Becker, Naugle, Snow, Binder, & Thompson, 1998). The National Academy of Neuropsychology and the American Academy of Clinical Neuropsychology have taken a position that third-party observers should be excluded from evaluations (American Academy of Clinical Neuropsychology, 2001; Axelrod, Barth, Faust, Fisher, Heilbronner, Larrabee, Pliskin, & Silver, 2000). In addition, it is clearly inappropriate to record testing sessions without a client's knowledge and consent (Bush, Pimental, Ruff, Iverson, Barth, & Broshek, 2000). A reasonable alternative that has evolved in sexual abuse assessment interviewing, in which overly suggestive interviewing by unskilled clinicians or the police is a well-known problem, can include video recording or remote monitoring of the process when appropriate consent is granted. Such recording can have a mixed effect. It can be very useful in demonstrating that a competent evaluation was conducted, but it can also provide a strong record for discrediting poor-quality work.

## Data Collection and Report Preparation

Psychologists are expected to conduct assessments with explicit knowledge of the procedures required and to adhere to the standardized test administration prescribed in the relevant test manuals. In some contexts—particularly in neuropsychological assessment, in which a significant number and wide range of instruments may be used—technicians are sometimes employed to administer and score tests as well as to record behaviors during the assessment. In this situation, it is the neuropsychologist who is responsible for assuring adequacy of the training of the technician, selecting test instruments, and interpreting findings (Axelrod et al., 2000b; Hall, Howerton, & Bolin, 2005). Even in the case of less sophisticated evaluations (e.g., administration of common IQ or achievement testing in public school settings), psychologists charged with signing official reports are responsible for assuring

the accuracy and adequacy of data collection, including the training and competence of other personnel engaged in test administration. This responsibility is especially relevant in circumstances in which classroom teachers or other nonpsychologists are used to proctor group-administered tests. Preparation of a report is a critical part of a psychological assessment, and the job is not complete until the report is finished; this sometimes leads to disputes when payment for assessment is refused or delayed. Psychologists are not ethically required to prepare a report if payment is refused; however, if a completed report is needed for critical decision making regarding a client's welfare, it is not ethically appropriate to withhold the report. Many practitioners require advance payment or a retainer as a prerequisite for undertaking a lengthy evaluation. In some instances, practitioners who have received partial payment that covers the time involved in record review and data collection will pause prior to preparing the actual report and await additional payment before writing the report. Such strategies are not unethical per se but should be carefully spelled out and agreed to as part of the consent process before the evaluation is begun. Ideally, such agreements should be made clear in written form to avoid subsequent misunderstandings. In contexts where third-party reimbursement is used, the procedures codes for psychological testing include the professional time spent integrating findings and preparing the report. In these circumstances, the preparation of the report is part of the service billed and needs to be produced in a timely manner.

## Automated Test Scoring and Interpretation

The psychologist who signs the report is responsible for its contents, including the accuracy of the data scoring and validity of the interpretation. When interpreting assessment results—including automated interpretations—psychologists must take into account the purpose of the assessment, the various test factors, the client's test-taking abilities, and the other characteristics of the person being assessed (e.g., situational, personal, linguistic, and cultural differences) that might affect psychologists' judgments or reduce the accuracy of their interpretations. If specific accommodations for a client (e.g., extra time, use of a reader, or availability of special assistive technology) are employed in the assessment, these accommodations must be described; automated testing services cannot do this. Although mechanical scoring of objective test data is often more accurate than hand scoring, machines can and do make errors. Psychologists who make use of an automated scoring system should check the mechanically generated results carefully. Psychologists are ethically responsible for indicating any significant reservations they have about the accuracy or limitations of their interpretations in the body of their reports, including any limitations on automated interpretative reports that may be a part of the case file. For example, psychologists who obtain computer-generated interpretive reports of MMPI-2 protocols may choose to use some or all of the information so obtained in their personally prepared reports. These individually prepared reports should indicate whether a computer-assisted or interpretive report was used and explain any modified interpretations made or confirm the validity of the computerized findings, as appropriate. A summary of criteria helpful in evaluating psychological assessment reports (Koocher, 2005) is presented in Table 8.1. The psychological assessment report needs to be understandable to

TABLE 8.1  Assessing the Quality of a Psychological Assessment

| Criterion | Quality Indicators |
| --- | --- |
| Referral questions and context | Does the report explain the reason for referral and state the assessment questions to be addressed? |
| | Does the report note that the client or legal guardian was informed about the purpose of and agreed to the assessment? |
| | Is the relevant psychological ecology of the client mentioned (e.g., recently divorced, facing criminal charges, candidate for employment)? |
| | If the evaluation is being undertaken at the request of a third party (e.g., a court, an employer, or a school), does the examiner note that the client was informed of the limits of confidentiality and whether a release was obtained? |
| Current status/behavioral observations | Has the examiner described the client's behavior during the interview, especially with respect to any aspects that might relate to the referral questions or the validity of the testing (e.g., mood, ability to form rapport, concentration, mannerisms, medication side effects, language problems, cooperation, phenotype, or physical handicaps)? |
| | Has the examiner described any deviations from standard testing administration or procedures? |
| Listing of instruments used | Is a complete list (without jargon or abbreviations) of the tests administered presented, including the dates administered? |
| | Does the report explain the nature of any unusual instruments or test procedures used? |
| | If more than one set of norms or test forms exists for any given instrument, does the psychologist indicate which forms or norms were used? |
| Reliability and validity | Does the psychologist comment specifically on whether the test results in the present circumstances can be regarded as reasonably accurate (e.g., the test administration was valid and the client fully cooperative)? |
| | If mediating factors apply, are these discussed in terms of reliability and validity implications? |
| | Are the tests used valid for assessing the aspects of the client's abilities in question? (This should be a special focus of attention if the instrument used is nonstandard or is being used in a nonstandard manner.) |
| Data presentation | Are scores presented and explained for each of the tests used? (If an integrated narrative or description is presented, does it report on all the aspects assessed, such as intellectual functioning, personality structure, etc.?) |
| | Are the meanings of the test results explained in terms of the referral questions asked? |
| | Are examples or illustrations included if relevant? |
| | Are technical terms and jargon avoided? |
| | Does the report note whether the pattern of scores (e.g., variability in measuring similar attributes across instruments) is a consistent or heterogeneous one? |
| | For IQ testing, are subtest scatter and discrepancy scores mentioned? |
| | For personality testing, does the psychologist discuss self-esteem, interpersonal relations, emotional reactivity, defensive style, and areas of focal concern? |
| Summary | If a summary is presented, does it err by surprising the reader with material not mentioned earlier in the report? |
| | Is it overly redundant? |
| Recommendations | If recommendations are made, do these flow logically from the test results mentioned and discussed earlier? |
| | Do the recommendations mention all relevant points raised as initial referral questions? |
| Diagnosis | If a diagnosis is requested or if differential diagnosis was a referral question, does the report specifically address this point? |
| Authentication | Is the report signed by the individual(s) who conducted the evaluation? |
| | Are the credentials/title of each person noted (e.g., Mary Smith, PhD, Staff Psychologist, or John Doe, MS, Psychology Intern)? |
| | If the examiner is unlicensed or a trainee, is the report cosigned by a qualified licensed supervisor? |
| Feedback | Is a copy of the report sent to the person who made the referral? |
| | Is some mechanism in place for providing feedback to the client, consistent with the context of testing and original agreement with the client? |

the intended audience while being thorough and professional in wording and tone (Adams & Luscher, 2003). Material presented in the report should be relevant to the referral question at hand; psychologists refrain from including sensitive or personal information that is not germane or could cause inadvertent harm to the test taker or family (Michaels, 2006).

## AFTER THE EVALUATION

Following completion of their evaluations and reports, psychologists often receive requests for additional clarification, feedback, release of data, or other information and materials related to the evaluation. Release of confidential client information is addressed in the ethics code and highly regulated under many state and federal laws, but many other issues arise when psychological testing is involved.

## Feedback Requests

Psychologists are expected to provide explanatory feedback to the people they assess unless the nature of the client relationship precludes provision of an explanation of results (Standard 9.10, Explaining assessment results). Providing feedback should be seen as a critical component of the assessment process that can have a significant therapeutic impact with respect to treatment and helping the client understand interventions recommended (Poston & Hanson, 2010). Examples of relationships in which feedback might not be owed to the person tested would include some organizational consulting, preemployment or security screening, and some forensic evaluations. In every case the nature of feedback to be provided and any limitations must be clearly explained to the person being assessed in advance of the evaluation. Ideally, any such limitations are provided in both written and oral form at the outset of the professional relationship. In normal circumstances, people who are tested can reasonably expect an interpretation of the test results and answers to questions they may have in a timely manner. Copies of actual test reports may also be provided as permitted under applicable law.

## Requests for Modification of Reports

On some occasions, people who have been evaluated or their legal guardians may request modification of a psychologist's assessment report. One valid reason for altering or revising a report would be to allow for the correction of factual errors. Another appropriate reason

might involve release of information on a need-to-know basis for the protection of the client. For example, suppose that in the course of conducting a psychological evaluation of a child who has experienced sexual abuse, a significant verbal learning disability is uncovered. This disability is fully described in the psychologist's report. In an effort to secure special education services for the learning problem, the parents of the child ask the psychologist to tailor a report for the school focusing only on matters relevant to the child's educational needs—that is to say, the parents would prefer that information on the child's sexual abuse is not included in the report sent to the school's learning disability assessment team. Such requests to tailor or omit certain information gleaned during an evaluation may be honored as long as doing so does not tend to mislead or misrepresent the relevant findings. In addition, errors of fact can occur, and steps should be taken to rectify these when they arise. In these situations, it is preferable to add an addendum to the report, noting the error and making the correction.

Psychologists must also be mindful of their professional integrity and obligation to fairly and accurately represent relevant findings. A psychologist may be approached by a case management firm with a request to perform an independent examination and to send a draft of the report so that editorial changes can be made. This request presents serious ethical considerations, particularly in forensic settings. Psychologists are ethically responsible for the content of all reports issued over their signature. One can always listen to requests or suggestions, but professional integrity and oversight of one's work cannot be delegated to another. Reports should not be altered to conceal crucial information, mislead recipients, commit fraud, or otherwise falsely represent findings of a psychological evaluation. The psychologist has no obligation to modify a valid report at the insistence of a client if the ultimate result would misinform the intended recipient.

## Release of Data

Who should have access to the data on which psychologists predicate their assessments? This issue comes into focus most dramatically when the conclusions or recommendations resulting from an assessment are challenged. In such disputes, the opposing parties often seek review of the raw data by experts not involved in the original collection and analyses. The purpose of the review might include actual rescoring of raw data or reviewing interpretations of scored data. In this context, test data may refer to any test protocols, transcripts of responses, record forms, scores, and notes regarding an individual's responses to test items in any medium (American Psychological Association, 2010). The ethics code makes a distinction between test data and test materials; test materials refer to manuals, instruments, test questions, and so on. Under long-standing accepted ethical practices, psychologists may release test data to a psychologist or another qualified professional after being authorized by a valid release or court order. In the 2002 revision of the ethics code (American Psychological Association, 2010), the previously generic prohibition around releasing test data was changed to take into account situations in which there is a conflict between legal requirements and the ethical standards. This change has engendered significant controversy in the field, particularly since some states specifically include prohibitions of release of tests in their licensing regulations. Under the Health Information Portability and Accountability Act of 1996 (HIPAA) regulations, patients have access to their records, including their psychological assessment reports and test data. Psychologists are exhorted to generally refrain from releasing test data to persons who are not qualified to use such information, except (a) as required by law or court order, (b) to an attorney or court based on a client's valid release, or (c) to the client as appropriate (American Psychological Association, 2010). Psychologists may also refrain from releasing test data to protect a client from harm or to protect test security.

In recent years, psychologists have worried about exactly how far their responsibility goes in upholding such standards. It is one thing to express reservations about a release, but it is quite another matter to contend within the legal system. For example, if a psychologist receives a valid release from the client to provide the data to another professional, is the sending psychologist obligated to determine the specific competence of the intended recipient? Is it reasonable to assume that any other psychologist is qualified to evaluate all psychological test data? If psychologists asked to release data are worried about possible harm or test security, must they retain legal counsel at their own expense to vigorously resist releasing the data? The Clinical Neuropsychology division of the APA collaborated with other neuropsychology organizations on a position statement to provide guidance to psychologists with respect to this issue (Attix, Donders, Johnson-Greene, Grote, Harris, & Bauer, 2007).

## Test Security

The current APA ethics code requires that psychologists make reasonable efforts to maintain the integrity and security of copyright-protected tests and other assessment techniques consistent with law and with their contractual obligations (American Psychological Association, 2010). Most test publishers also elicit such a pledge from those seeking to purchase test materials. Production of well-standardized test instruments represents a significant financial investment to the publisher. Breaches of such security can compromise the publisher's proprietary rights and vitiate the utility of the test to the clinician by enabling coaching or otherwise inappropriate preparation by test takers.

What is a reasonable effort as envisioned by the authors of the ethics code? Close reading of the code indicates that psychologists may rely on other elements of the code in maintaining test security. In that context, psychologists have no intrinsic professional obligation to contest valid court orders or to resist appropriate requests for disclosure of test materials—that is to say, the psychologists are not obligated to litigate in the support of a test publisher or to protect the security of an instrument at significant personal cost. When in doubt, a psychologist always has the option of contacting the test publisher. If publishers who sold tests to the psychologist eliciting a promise that the test materials be treated confidentially wish to object to requested or court-ordered disclosure, they should be expected to use their own financial and legal resources to defend their own copyright-protected property.

Psychologists must also pay attention to the laws that apply in their own practice jurisdiction(s). For example, Minnesota has a specific statute that prohibits a psychologist from releasing psychological test materials to individuals who are unqualified or if the psychologist has reason to believe that releasing such material would compromise the integrity of the testing process. Such laws can provide additional protective leverage but are rare exceptions.

An editorial in the *American Psychologist* (American Psychological Association, 1999) discussed test security in the context of both scholarly publishing and litigation, suggesting that potential disclosure must be evaluated in light of both ethical obligations of psychologists and copyright law. The editorial also recognized that the psychometric integrity of psychological tests depends on the test taker's not having prior access to study or not being coached on the test materials. National neuropsychology organizations have published position papers on test security and disclosure (Attix, Donders, Johnson-Greene, Grote, Harris, & Bauer, 2007; Axelrod et al., 2000a). There has been significant concern among neuropsychologists about implications for the validity of tests intended to assess malingering if such materials are freely circulated among attorneys and clients. Both the *American Psychologist* editorial and these position papers ignore the implications of this issue with respect to preparation for high-stakes testing and the testing industry, as discussed in detail later in this chapter (see Special Issues). Authors who plan to publish information about tests should always seek permission from the copyright holder of the instrument and not presume that the fair use doctrine will protect them from subsequent infringement claims. When sensitive test documents are subpoenaed, psychologists should also ask courts to seal or otherwise protect the information from unreasonable public scrutiny (Kaufmann, 2009).

## SPECIAL ISSUES

In addition to the basic principles described earlier in this chapter (i.e., the preparation, conduct, and follow-up of the actual assessment), some special issues pertain to psychological testing. These issues include automated or computerized assessment services, high-stakes testing, and teaching of psychological assessment techniques. Many of these topics fall under the general domain of the testing industry.

### Testing Industry

Psychological testing is big business. Test publishers and other companies offering automated scoring systems or national testing programs are significant business enterprises. Over the past decade, test publishers have consolidated and control even larger market share. With the introduction of educational standards and benchmarks in public schools, large-scale testing has increased substantially. The spread of consumerism in America has seen increasing criticism of the testing industry (Haney, Madaus, & Lyons, 1993). Most of the ethical criticism leveled at the larger companies fall into the categories of marketing, sales to unauthorized users, and the problem of so-called impersonal services. Publishers claim that they do make good-faith efforts to police sales so that only qualified users obtain tests. They note that they cannot control the behavior of individuals in institutions where tests are sent. Because test publishers must advertise in the media provided by organized psychology (e.g., the *APA Monitor*) to influence their prime market, most major firms are especially responsive to letters of concern from psychologists and APA committees. At the same time, such companies are quite readily prepared to cry antitrust fouls when professional organizations become too critical of their business practices.

### Automated Testing Services

Automated testing services and software can be a major boon to psychologists' practices and can significantly enhance the accuracy and sophistication of diagnostic decision making, but there are important caveats to observe. The APA ethics code (section 9.09 Test scoring and interpretation services) states that "psychologists who offer assessment or scoring services to other professionals should accurately describe the purpose, norms, validity, reliability, and applications of the procedures and any special qualifications applicable to their use" (American Psychological Association, 2010). Psychologists who use such scoring and interpretation services (including automated services) are urged to select them based on evidence of the validity of the program and analytic procedures. In every case, it is the psychologist who is responsible for applying and interpreting psychological assessments appropriately, regardless of whether automated services or computer programs are used.

One key difficulty in the use of automated testing is the aura of validity conveyed by the adjective *computerized* and its synonyms. Aside from the long-standing debate within psychology about the merits of actuarial versus clinical prediction, there is often a kind of magical faith that numbers and graphs generated by a computer program somehow equate with increased validity of some sort. Too often, skilled clinicians do not fully educate themselves about the underpinnings of various analytic models. Even when a clinician is so inclined, the copyright holders of the analytic program are often reluctant to share too much information, lest they compromise their property rights.

In the end, the most reasonable approach is to use automated scoring and interpretive services as only one component of an evaluation and to carefully probe any apparently discrepant findings. Interpretations provided by an automated scoring program can be seen as hypotheses to be considered in the context of the entire assessment and integrated into the overall formulation as relevant. This suggestion will not be a surprise to most competent psychologists, but unfortunately they are not the only users of these tools. Many users of such tests are nonpsychologists with little understanding of the interpretive subtleties. Some take the computer-generated reports at face value as valid and fail to consider important factors that make their client unique. A few users are simply looking for a quick and dirty source of data to help them make a decision in the absence of clinical acumen. Other users inflate the actual cost of the tests and scoring services to enhance their own billings. When making use of such tools, psychologists should have a well-reasoned strategy for incorporating them in the assessment and should interpret them with well-informed caution.

### Do-It-Yourself Tests

Executing a Google search on "psychological testing" in June 2011 yielded more than 6 million hits. When asked to address the ethics of psychological testing on the Internet, most members of the psychological community will think first about matters of data integrity, validity, security, or similar professional issues (Barak & English, 2002; Naglieri, Drasgow et al., 2004; Rapp, 2006). Others have expressed worries about test security after finding sales of obsolete and unwanted test materials on Internet auctions (LoBello & Zachar, 2007). During one 3-month interval of monitoring eBay, Lobello and Zachar found 82 tests or partial tests for sale online.

Members of the public have increasingly become fascinated with do-it-yourself (DIY) tests available online. Such self-care products can confuse and compromise perceptions of the public face of psychology. Tests have circulated on the Internet for years, purporting to assess physical conditions (e.g., risk for assorted diseases). Increasingly, one can find psychological mass screening tools (e.g., for attention deficit disorder, early Alzheimer's disease, or depression) or actual versions of IQ and personality assessments. Often the tests appear on Internet sites associated with the advertisement of services for the problem that the test purports to assess. The ethical issues regarding DIY tests mirror criticisms of some self-help books. These include insufficient regulation or professional oversight of test validity, potential for misuse and errors in interpretation, and absence of in-person support counseling (Kier & Molinari, 2004).

Some of the online instruments seemed grounded in meaningful research while others present more ambiguous constructs. For example, one site apparently based at the University of Pennsylvania under the auspices of a former APA president purports to assist participants in determining whether they have authentic happiness, leading to the question of whether inauthentic happiness represents delusional thinking. That site requires a personalized log-on and appears intended for data collection and marketing related to other "authentic happiness" products. Other sites with no clear expert connections offer a wide range of online testing opportunities, including personality assessment based on color preferences and the ability to assess one's possible racial biases. (See Koocher & Keith-Spiegel, 2008). We encourage approaching DIY

psychological assessment with the same trepidation one might apply to DIY cardiac surgery and root canal procedures.

### High-Stakes Testing

The term *high-stakes tests* refers to cognitively loaded instruments designed to assess knowledge, skill, and ability with the intent of making employment, academic admission, graduation, or licensing decisions. For a number of public policy and political reasons, these testing programs face considerable scrutiny and criticism (Garrison, 2009; Haney, Madaus, & Lyons, 1993; Sackett, Schmitt, Ellingson, & Kabin, 2001). Such testing includes the SAT, Graduate Record Examination (GRE), state examinations that establish graduation requirements, and professional or job entry examinations. Such tests can provide very useful information but are also subject to misuse and a degree of tyranny in the sense that individuals' rights and welfare are easily lost in the face of corporate advantage and political struggles about accountability in education.

In May 2001 the APA issued a statement on such testing titled "Appropriate Use of High Stakes Testing in Our Nation's Schools." The statement noted that the measurement of learning and achievement are important and that tests—when used properly—are among the most sound and objective ways to measure student performance. However, when tests' results are used inappropriately, they can have highly damaging unintended consequences. High-stakes decisions, such as high school graduation or college admissions, should not be made on the basis of a single set of test scores that provide only a snapshot of student achievement. Such scores may not accurately reflect a student's progress and achievement, and they do not provide much insight into other critical components of future success, such as motivation and character. The APA statement (2001) noted:

> When test results substantially contribute to decisions made about student promotion or graduation, there should be evidence that the test addresses only the specific or generalized content and skills that students have had an opportunity to learn.
>
> When a school district, state, or some other authority mandates a test, the intended use of the test results should be clearly described. It is also the responsibility of those who mandate the test to monitor its impact—particularly on racial- and ethnic-minority students or students of lower socioeconomic status—and to identify and minimize potential negative consequences of such testing.

In some cases, special accommodations for students with limited proficiency in English may be necessary to obtain valid test scores. If students with limited English skills are to be tested in English, their test scores should be interpreted in light of their limited English skills. For example, when a student lacks proficiency in the language in which the test is given (students for whom English is a second language, for example), the test could become a measure of their ability to communicate in English rather than a measure of other skills.

Likewise, special accommodations may be needed to ensure that test scores are valid for students with disabilities. Not enough is currently known about how particular test modifications may affect the test scores of students with disabilities; more research is needed. As a first step, test developers should include students with disabilities in field testing of pilot tests and document the impact of particular modifications (if any) for test users. (p. 2)

The statement also recommends that test results be reported by sex, race-ethnicity, income level, disability status, and degree of English proficiency.

One adverse consequence of high-stakes testing is that some schools will almost certainly focus primarily on teaching-to-the-test skills acquisition. Students prepared in this way may do well on the test but find it difficult to generalize their learning beyond that context and be unprepared for critical and analytic thinking in subsequent learning environments. Some testing companies, such as the Educational Testing Service (developers of the SAT), at one time claimed that coaching or teaching to the test would have little meaningful impact and still publicly attempt to minimize the potential effects of coaching or teaching to the test. Currently, however, coaching and test preparation are commonplace. A recent book addresses issues related to high-stakes testing in education in the K–12 context such as measurement concerns and applications to special populations (Bovaird, Geisinger, & Buckendahl, 2011).

## Teaching Psychological Testing

Psychologists teaching assessment have a unique opportunity to shape their students' professional practice and approach to ethics by modeling how ethical issues are actively integrated into the practice of assessment (Yalof & Brabender, 2001). Ethical standards in the areas of education and training are relevant (Standard 7.01 Design of education and training programs): "Psychologists who are responsible for education and training programs take reasonable steps to ensure that the

programs are designed to provide appropriate knowledge and proper experiences to meet the requirements for licensure, certification and other goals for which claims are made by the program" (American Psychological Association, 2010). Course content and training methods can vary widely in professional psychology programs (Childs & Eyde, 2002); however, the primary responsibility is to ensure competence in assessment practice by providing the requisite education and training.

A review of studies evaluating the competence of graduate students and practicing psychologists in administration and scoring of cognitive tests demonstrated that errors occur frequently and at all levels of training (Alfonso & Pratt, 1997). The review also noted that relying only on practice assessments as a teaching methodology does not ensure competent practice. The authors concluded that teaching programs that include behavioral objectives and that focus on evaluating specific competencies are generally more effective. This approach is also more concordant with the APA guidelines for training in professional psychology (American Psychological Association, 1996) and current competency-based approaches to education and training (Assessment of Competency Benchmarks Work Group, 2007).

The use of children and students' classmates as practice subjects in psychological testing courses raises ethical concern (Rupert, Kozlowski, Hoffman, Daniels, & Piette, 1999). In other teaching contexts, the potential for violations of privacy are significant in situations in which graduate students are required to take personality tests for practice. Yalof and Brabender (2001) addressed ethical dilemmas in personality assessment courses with respect to using the classroom for in vivo training. They argued that students' introduction to ethical decision making in personality assessment occurs in assessment courses with practice components. In this type of course, students experience firsthand how ethical problems are identified, addressed, and resolved. The authors noted that the instructor's demonstration of how the ethical principles are highlighted and explored can enable students to internalize a model for addressing such dilemmas in the future. Four particular concerns are described: (1) the students' role in procuring personal experience with personality testing, (2) identification of participants with which to practice, (3) the development of informed consent procedures for assessment participants, and (4) classroom presentations. This discussion does not provide universally applicable concrete solutions to ethical problems; however, it offers a consideration of the relevant ethical principles that any adequate solution must incorporate.

## RECOMMENDATIONS

In an effort to summarize the essence of good ethical practice in psychological assessment, we offer this set of suggestions:

- Clients to be tested (or their parents or legal guardians) must be given full informed consent about the nature of the evaluation, payment for services, access to results, and other relevant data prior to initiating the evaluation.
- Psychologists should be aware of and adhere to published professional standards and guidelines relevant to the nature of the particular type of assessment they are conducting.
- Different types of technical data on tests exist—including reliability and validity data—and psychologists should be sufficiently familiar with such data for any instrument they use so that they can justify and explain the appropriateness of the selection.
- Those administering psychological tests are responsible for ensuring that the tests are administered and scored according to standardized instructions.
- Test users should be aware of potential test bias or client characteristics that might reduce the validity of the instrument for that client and context. When validity is threatened, psychologists should specifically address the issue in their reports.
- No psychologist is competent to administer and interpret all psychological tests. It is important to be cautiously self-critical and to agree to undertake only those evaluations that fall within one's training and sphere of competence.
- The validity and confidence of test results relies to some degree on test security. Psychologists should use reasonable caution in protecting the security of test items and materials.
- Automated testing services create a hazard to the extent that they may generate data that are inaccurate for certain clients or that are misinterpreted by improperly trained individuals. Psychologists operating or making use of such services should take steps to minimize such risks.
- Clients have a right to feedback and to have confidentiality of data protected to the extent agreed on at the outset of the evaluation or in subsequent authorized releases.
- Test users should be aware of the ethical issues that can develop in specific settings and should consult with other professionals when ethical dilemmas arise.

## REFERENCES

Adams, H. E., & Luscher, K. A. (2003). Ethical considerations in psychological assessment. In W. T. O'Donohue & K. E. Ferguson (Eds.), *Handbook of professional ethics for psychologists: Issues, questions, and controversies* (pp. 275–284). Thousand Oaks, CA: Sage.

Aiken, L. S., West, S. G., & Millsap, R. E. (2008). Doctoral training in statistics, measurement, and methodology in psychology: Replication and extension of Aiken, West, Sechrest, and Reno's (1990) survey of PhD programs in North America. *American Psychologist, 63*(1), 32–0. doi:10.1037/0003–066x.63.1.32

Aiken, L. S., West, S. G., Sechrest, L., Reno, R. R., Roediger, H. L., Scarr, S., . . . Sherman, S. J. (1990). Graduate training in statistics, methodology, and measurement in psychology: A survey of PhD programs in North America. *American Psychologist, 45*(6), 721–734. doi:10.1037/0003–066x.45.6.721

Alfonso, V. C., & Pratt, S. I. (1997). Issues and suggestions for training professionals in assessing intelligence. In D. P. Flanagan, J. L. Genshaft & P. L. Harrison (Eds.), *Contemporary intellectual assessment: Theories, tests, and issues* (pp. 326–344). New York, NY: Guilford Press.

American Academy of Clinical Neuropsychology. (2001). Policy statement on the presence of third party observers in neuropsychological assessments. *Clinical Neuropsychologist, 15*(4), 433–439.

American Educational Research Association, American Psychological Association, & National Council of Measurement in Education. (1999). *Standards for educational and psychological testing*. Washington, DC: Author.

American Psychological Association. (1953). *Ethical standards of psychologists*. Washington, DC: Author.

American Psychological Association. (1996). *Guidelines and principles for accreditation of programs in professional psychology*. Washington, DC: Author.

American Psychological Association. (1999). Test security: Protecting the integrity of tests. *American Psychologist, 54*(12), 1078. doi:10.1037/0003–066x.54.12.1078

American Psychological Association. (2010). Ethical principles of psychologists and code of conduct (2002, Amended June 1, 2010). Retrieved from www.apa.org/ethics/code/index.aspx

Assessment of Competency Benchmarks Work Group. (2007). *Assessment of competency benchmarks work group: A developmental model for defining and measuring competetence in professional psychology*. Washington, DC: American Psychological Association.

Attix, D. K., Donders, J., Johnson-Greene, D., Grote, C. L., Harris, J. G., & Bauer, R. M. (2007). Disclosure of neuropsychological test data: official position of Division 40 (Clinical Neuropsychology) of the American Psychological Association, Association of Postdoctoral Programs in Clinical Neuropsychology, and American Academy of Clinical Neuropsychology. *Clinical Neuropsychologist, 21*(2), 232–238. doi:10.1080/13854040601042928

Axelrod, B., Barth, J., Faust, D., Fisher, J., Heilbronner, R., Larrabee, G., . . . Silver, C. (2000). Presence of third party observers during neuropsychological testing: Official statement of the National Academy of Neuropsychology. *Archives of Clinical Neuropsychology, 15*(5), 379–380.

Axelrod, B., Heilbronner, R., Barth, J., Larrabee, G., Faust, D., Pliskin, N., . . . Silver, C. (2000a). Test security: Official position statement of the National Academy of Neuropsychology. *Archives of Clinical Neuropsychology, 15*(5), 383–386.

Axelrod, B., Heilbronner, R., Barth, J., Larrabee, G., Faust, D., Pliskin, N., . . . Silver, C. (2000b). The use of neuropsychology test technicians in clinical practice: Official statement of the National Academy of Neuropsychology. *Archives of Clinical Neuropsychology, 15*(5), 381–382.

Barak, A., & English, N. (2002). Prospects and limitations of psychological testing on the Internet. *Journal of technology in human services, 19*, 65–89.

Bartram, D. (2001). International guidelines for test use. *International Journal of Testing, 1*(2), 93–114. doi:10.1207/s15327574ijt0101_3

Bartram, D. (2011). Contributions of the EFPA Standing Committee on Tests and Testing to standards and good practice. *European Psychologist, 16*(2), 149–159. doi:10.1027/1016–9040/a000093

Bovaird, J. A., Geisinger, K. F., & Buckendahl, C. W. (Eds.). (2011). *High-stakes testing in education: Science and practice in K-12 settings*. Washington, DC: American Psychological Association.

Brickman, A. M., Cabo, R., & Manly, J. J. (2006). Ethical issues in cross-cultural neuropsychology. *Applied Neuropsychology, 13*(2), 91–100.

British Psychological Society. (2011). Psychological Testing Centre. Retrieved from www.psychtesting.org.uk/

Bush, S. S. (2010). Determining whether or when to adopt new versions of psychological and neuropsychological tests: Ethical and professional considerations. *Clinical Neuropsychologist, 24*(1), 7–16.

Bush, S. S., Grote, C. L., Johnson-Greene, D. E., & Macartney-Filgate, M. (2008). A panel interview on the ethical practice of neuropsychology. *Clinical Neuropsychologist, 22*(2), 321–344. doi:10.1080/13854040601139187

Bush, S. S., Naugle, R., & Johnson-Greene, D. (2002). Interface of information technology and neuropsychology: Ethical issues and recommendations. *Clinical Neuropsychologist, 16*(4), 536–547.

Bush, S. S., Pimental, P. A., Ruff, R. M., Iverson, G. L., Barth, J. T., & Broshek, D. K. (2009). Secretive recording of neuropsychological testing and interviewing: official position of the National Academy of Neuropsychology. *Archives of Clinical Neuropsychology, 24*(1), 1–2.

Childs, R. A., & Eyde, L. D. (2002). Assessment training in clinical psychology doctoral programs: What should we teach? What do we teach? *Journal of Personality Assessment, 78*(1), 130–144. doi:10.1207/s15327752jpa7801_08

Eyde, L. D., Moreland, K. L., Robertson, G. J., Primoff, E. S., & Most, R. B. (1988). Test user qualifications: A data-based approach to promiting good test use. Issues in scientific psychology (Report of the Test User Qualifications Working Group of the Joint Committee on Testing Practices). Washington, DC: American Psychological Association.

Eyde, L. D., Robertson, G. J., Krug, S. E., Moreland, K. L., Robertson, A. G., Shewan, C. M., ... Primoff, E. S. (1993). *Responsible test use: Case studies for assessing human behavior*. Washington, DC: American Psychological Association.

Flanagan, D. P., & Alfonso, V. C. (1995). A critical review of the technical characteristics of new and recently revised intelligence tests for preschool children. *Journal of Psychoeducational Assessment, 13*(1), 66–90. doi:10.1177/073428299501300105

Garrison, M. J. (2009). *A measure of failure: The political origins of standardized testing*. Albany: State University of New York Press.

Gavett, B. E., Lynch, J. K., & McCaffrey, R. J. (2005). Third party observers: The effect size is greater than you might think. *Journal of Forensic Neuropsychology, 4*(2), 49–64. doi:10.1300/J151v04n02_05

Greenaway, M. C., Smith, G. E., Tangalos, E. G., Geda, Y. E., & Ivnik, R. J. (2009). Mayo older americans normative studies: Factor analysis of an expanded neuropsychological battery. *Clinical Neuropsychologist, 23*(1), 7–20. doi:792026144 [pii] 10.1080/13854040801891686

Grisso, T., & Appelbaum, P. S. (1998). *Assessing competence to consent to treatment: A guide for physicians and other health professionals*. New York, NY: Oxford University Press.

Grote, C. L., Lewin, J. L., Sweet, J. J., & van Gorp, W. G. (2000). Responses to perceived unethical practices in clinical neuropsychology: Ethical and legal considerations. *Clinical Neuropsychologist, 14*(1), 119–134.

Hall, J. D., Howerton, D. L., & Bolin, A. U. (2005). The use of testing technicians: Critical issues for professional psychology. *International Journal of Testing, 5*(4), 357–375.

Haney, W. M., Madaus, G. F., & Lyons, R. (1993). *The fractured marketplace for standardized testing*. Norwell, MA: Kluwer.

Heaton, R. K., Grant, I., & Matthews, C. (1991). *Comprehensive norms for an expanded Halstead-Reitan neuropsychological battery: Demographic corrections, research findings, and clinical applications*. Odessa, FL: Psychological Assessment Resources.

Heilbronner, R. L., Sweet, J. J., Morgan, J. E., Larrabee, G. J., & Millis, S. R. (2009). American Academy of Clinical Neuropsychology consensus conference statement on the neuropsychological assessment of effort, response bias, and malingering. *Clinical Neuropsychologist, 23*(7), 1093–1129.

Iverson, G. L. (2006). Ethical issues associated with the assessment of exaggeration, poor effort, and malingering. *Applied Neuropsychology, 13*(2), 77–90. doi:10.1207/s15324826an1302_3

Iverson, G. L. (2008). Assessing for exaggeration, poor effort, and malingering in neuropsychological assessment. In A. M. Horton Jr. & D. Wedding (Eds.), *The neuropsychology handbook* (3rd ed., pp. 125–182). New York, NY: Springer.

Johnson-Greene, D. (2005). Informed consent in clinical neuropsychology practice Official statement of the National Academy of Neuropsychology. *Archives of Clinical Neuropsychology, 20*(3), 335–340.

Johnson-Greene, D., Hardy-Morais, C., Adams, K. M., Hardy, C., & Bergloff, P. (1997). Informed consent and neuropsychological assessment. Ethical considerations and proposed guidelines. *Clinical Neuropsychologist, 11*, 454–460.

Kamphaus, R. W., Dresden, J., & Kaufman, A. S. (1993). Clinical and psychometric considerations in the cognitive assessment of preschool children. In J. L. Culbertson & D. J. Willis (Eds.), *Testing young children: A reference guide for developmental, psychoeducational, and psychosocial assessments.* (pp. 55–72). Austin, TX: Pro-Ed.

Kaufmann, P. M. (2009). Protecting raw data and psychological tests from wrongful disclosure: a primer on the law and other persuasive strategies. *Clinical Neuropsychologist, 23*(7), 1130–1159.

Kier, F. J., & Molinari, V. (2004). Do-it-yourself testing for mental illness: Ethical issues, concerns, and recommendations. *Professional Psychology: Research and Practice, 35*, 261–267. doi:10.1037/0735–7028.35.3.261

Knudson, P. L. (2001). Ethical principles in human subject research. *Archives of Medical Research, 32*(5), 473–474. doi:S018844 0901003113 [pii]

Koocher, G. P. (2005). Assessing the quality of a psychological testing report. In G. P. Koocher, J. C. Norcross & S. S. Hill, III (Eds.), *Psychologists' Desk Reference* (2nd ed., pp. 117–119). New York, NY: Oxford University Press.

Koocher, G. P., & Keith-Spiegel, P. C. (2008). *Ethics in psychology and the mental health professions: Standards and cases* (3rd ed.). New York, NY: Oxford University Press.

LoBello, S. G., & Zachar, P. (2007). Psychological test sales and Internet auctions: Ethical considerations for dealing with obsolete or unwanted test materials. *Professional Psychology: Research and Practice, 38*(1), 68–70. doi:10.1037/0735–7028.38.1.68

Manly, J. J., Jacobs, D. M., Sano, M., Bell, K., Merchant, C. A., Small, S. A., & Stern, Y. (1999). Effect of literacy on neuropsychological test performance in nondemented, education-matched elders. *Journal of the International Neuropsychological Society, 5*(3), 191–202.

McCaffrey, R. J., Fisher, J. M., Gold, B. A., & Lynch, J. K. (1996). Presence of third parties during neuropsychological evaluations: Who is evaluating whom? *Clinical Neuropsychologist, 10,* 435–449.

McSweeny, A. J., Becker, B. C., Naugle, R. I., Snow, W. G., Binder, L. M., & Thompson, L. L. (1998). Ethical issues related to the presence of third party observers in clinical neuropsychological evaluations. *Clinical Neuropsychologist, 12*(4), 552–559. doi:10.1076/clin.12.4.552.7245

Michaels, M. H. (2006). Ethical considerations in writing psychological assessment reports. *Journal of Clinical Psychology, 62*(1), 47–58.

Mindt, M. R., Arentoft, A., Germano, K. K., D'Aquila, E., Scheiner, D., Pizzirusso, M., . . . Gollan, T. H. (2008). Neuropsychological, cognitive, and theoretical considerations for evaluation of bilingual individuals. *Neuropsychology Review, 18*(3), 255–268.

Moreland, K. L., Eyde, L. D., Robertson, G. J., Primoff, E. S., & Most, R. B. (1995). Assessment of test user qualifications: a research-based measurement procedure. *American Psychologist, 50,* 14–23.

Naglieri, J. A., Drasgow, F., Schmit, M., Handler, L., Prifitera, A., Margolis, A., & Velasquez, R. (2004). Psychological testing on the Internet: new problems, old issues. *American Psychologist, 59*(3), 150–162. doi:10.1037/0003–066X.59.3.1502004–14611–001 [pii]

National Association of School Psychologists. (2010). Principles for professional ethics. Retrieved from www.nasponline.org/standards/2010standards.aspx

National Commission for the Protection of Human Subjects of Biomedical and Behavioral Research. (1979). *The Belmont Report: Ethical principles and guidelines for the protection of human subjects of research.* Washington, DC: U.S. Government Printing Office.

Ostrosky-Solís, F., Ramirez, M., & Ardila, A. (2004). Effects of culture and education on neuropsychological testing: A preliminary study with indigenous and nonindigenous population. *Applied Neuropsychology, 11*(4), 186–193. doi:10.1207/s15324826an1104_3

Poston, J. M., & Hanson, W. E. (2010). Meta-analysis of psychological assessment as a therapeutic intervention. *Psychological Assessment, 22*(2), 203–212. doi:10.1037/a0018679

Rapp, J. H. (2006). Computer-based testing and the Internet: Issues and advances. *International Journal of Testing, 6,* 195–200.

Rupert, P. A., Kozlowski, N. F., Hoffman, L. A., Daniels, D. D., & Piette, J. M. (1999). Practical and ethical issues in teaching psychological testing. *Professional Psychology: Research and Practice, 30*(2), 209–214. doi:10.1037/0735–7028.30.2.209

Sackett, P. R., Schmitt, N., Ellingson, J. E., & Kabin, M. B. (2001). High-stakes testing in employment, credentialing, and higher education: Prospects in a post-affirmative-action world. *American Psychologist, 56*(4), 302–318. doi:10.1037/0003–066x.56.4.302

Simmer, M. L. (1994). *Draft of final report of the Professional Affairs Working Group on Test Publishing Industry Safegueards.* Ottawa, Canada: Canadian Psychological Association.

Society for Personality Assessment. (2006). Standards for Education and Training in Psychological Assessment Position of the Society for Personality Assessment. *Journal of Personality Assessment, 87*(3), 355–357.

Sweet, J. J., & Morgan, J. E. (2009). Neuropsychology and the law: Malingering assessment in perspective. In J. J. Sweet & J. E. Morgan (Eds.), *Neuropsychology of malingering casebook.* (pp. 3–8). New York, NY: Psychology Press.

Turner, S. M., DeMers, S. T., Fox, H. R., & Reed, G. (2001). APA's guidelines for test user qualifications: An executive summary. *American Psychologist, 56*(12), 1099–1113. doi:10.1037/0003–066x.56.12.1099

Victor, T. L., & Abeles, N. (2004). Coaching clients to take psychological and neuropsychological tests: A clash of ethical obligations. *Professional Psychology: Research and Practice, 35*(4), 373–379.

Wong, T. M. (2006). Ethical controversies in neuropsychological test selection, administration, and interpretation. *Applied Neuropsychology, 13*(2), 68–76.

Yalof, J., & Brabender, V. (2001). Ethical dilemmas in personality assessment courses: Using the classroom for in vivo training. *Journal of Personality Assessment, 77,* 203–213.

# CHAPTER 9

# Education and Training in Psychological Assessment

LEONARD HANDLER AND JUSTIN D. SMITH

## INTRODUCTION

We begin this chapter by citing a very brief history of assessment use in the United States, written by Hale Martin (2009). In "A Bright Future for Psychological Assessment," Martin stated:

> With the rise of managed care over the past 20 years, psychological assessment has seen hard times. From what some saw as an over-emphasis on assessment in the 1970s and 1980s . . . the pendulum has swung to . . . under-use of assessment in serving clients. . . . However there are those who persevered in practicing assessment, believing that it offered responsible and effective service to some clients. Much of their work was done outside the confines of managed care because insurance reimbursement was time-consuming to arrange and poorly compensated. In reaction to this difficult time for assessment, many training programs around the country de-emphasized training in assessment. . . . There have been developments in assessment that bode well for its future. (p. 23)

Martin highlighted two such developments: research to improve testing instruments has continued unabated, and the new collaborative and therapeutic assessment paradigm, which we discuss later in this chapter.

The approach to teaching personality assessment described in this chapter emphasizes the importance of viewing assessment as an interactive process, the interaction of teacher and student, and the interaction of patient and assessor. The process emphasizes the use of critical thinking and continued questioning of approaches to assessment and to their possible interpretations. Throughout the chapter we have emphasized the integration of research and clinical application. It is the authors' opinion that assessment should be a central part of any doctoral curriculum that prepares students to do applied work.

## DIFFERENCES BETWEEN TESTING AND ASSESSMENT

Unfortunately, many people use the terms *testing* and *assessment* synonymously, but actually they mean quite different things. *Testing* refers to the process of administering, scoring, and perhaps interpreting individual test scores by applying a descriptive meaning based on normative, nomothetic data. The focus here is on the individual test itself. *Assessment*, however, consists of a process in which a number of tests, obtained from the use of multiple methods, are administered and the results of these tests are integrated among themselves, along with data obtained from observations, history, information from other professionals, and information from other sources—friends, relatives, legal sources, and so on. All of these data are integrated to produce, typically, an in-depth understanding of the individual, focused on the reasons the person was referred for assessment. This process is person focused or problem issue focused (Handler & Meyer, 1998). The issue is not, for example, what the person scored on the Minnesota Multiphasic Personality Inventory-2 (MMPI-2), or what the Rorschach Structural Summary yielded, but, rather, what we can say about the patient's symptomatology, personality structure, and dynamics and how we can answer the referral questions. Tests typically are employed in the assessment process, but much more information and much more complexity are involved in the assessment process than in the simple act of testing itself. Many training programs teach testing but describe it as assessment. The product produced with this focus is typically a report that presents data from each test separately, with little or no integration or interpretation. Often one can make no valid clear-cut conclusions from interpreting tests individually, because the results of other test and nontest data often modify interpretations or conclusions concerning the meaning of specific test signs or results on individual tests. In fact, the data indicate that a clinician who uses a single method will develop an incomplete or biased understanding of the patient (Meyer, Riethmiller, Brooks, Benoit, & Handler, 2000).

## WHY TEACH AND LEARN PERSONALITY ASSESSMENT?

We have documented the many reasons personality assessment should be taught in doctoral training programs and highlighted as an important and respected area of study.

## Learning Assessment Teaches Critical Thinking and Integrative Skills

We believe that the best reason to highlight personality assessment courses in the doctoral training curriculum concerns the importance of teaching critical thinking skills through the process of learning to integrate various types of data. In most training programs until this point, students have amassed a great deal of information from discrete courses by reading, attending lectures, and discussion. However, in order to learn to do competent assessment work, students must learn to organize and integrate information from many diverse courses, to bring these and other skills to bear in transversing the scientist–practitioner bridge, linking nomothetic and ideographic data. These critical thinking skills, systematically applied to the huge task of data integration, provide students with a template that can be used in other areas of psychological functioning (e.g., psychotherapy, or research application).

## Assessment Allows the Illumination of a Person's Experience

Sometimes assessment data allow us to observe a person's experience as he or she is being assessed. This issue is important because it is possible to generalize from these experiences to similar situations in psychotherapy and to the patient's environment. For example, when a 40-year-old man first viewed Card II of the Rorschach, he produced a response that was dysphoric and poorly defined, suggesting possible problems with emotional control, because Card II is the first card containing color that the patient encounters. He said, "A bloody wound." After a minute he said, "A rocket, with red flames, blasting off." This response, in contrast to the first one, was of good form quality. These responses illuminate the man's style of dealing with troubling emotions: He becomes angry and quickly and aggressively leaves the scene with a dramatic show of power and force. Next, the patient gave this response: "Two people, face to face, talking to each other, discussing." One could picture the sequence of intrapsychic and interpersonal events in the series of these responses. First, it is probable that the person's underlying depression is close to the surface and is poorly controlled. With little pressure it breaks through and causes him immediate but transitory disorganization in his thinking and in the ability to manage his emotions. He probably recovers quickly and is quite capable, after a release of anger and removing himself from the situation, of reestablishing an interpersonal connection. Later in therapy this man enacted just such a pattern of action in his work situation, his relationships with family members and with the therapist, who was able to understand the pattern of behavior and could help the patient understand it.

The good assessor also attends to the facilitating and creative aspects of personality, and the harmonious interplay of intrapsychic and external forces, as the individual copes with day-to-day life issues (Handler & Meyer, 1998). It is possible to create a portrait of a person's experience, such as the woman who saw "a tattered, torn butterfly, slowly dying" on Card I of the Rorschach or a reclusive, schizoid man, who saw "a mushroom" on the same card. When the therapist asked, "If this mushroom could talk, what would it say?" the patient answered, "Don't step on me! Everyone likes to step on them and break them!" The response allowed the therapist to understand this reserved and quiet man's experience of the therapist, who quickly altered his approach and became more supportive and affiliative.

## Assessment Can Illuminate Underlying Conditions

Responses to assessment stimuli allow us to look beyond a person's pattern of self presentation, possibly uncooling underlying emotional problems. For example, a 21-year-old male did not demonstrate any overt signs of gross pathology in his initial intake interview. His Rorschach record was also unremarkable for any difficulties until Card X, to which he gave this response: "It looks like someone crying for help, all bruised and scarred, with blood running down their face." The student who was doing the assessment quickly changed her stance with this young man, providing him with rapid access to treatment.

## Assessment Facilitates Treatment Planning

Treatment planning can focus and shorten treatment, resulting in benefits to the patient and to third-party payers. Informed treatment planning can also prevent hospitalization and provide more efficient and effective treatment. Assessment can enhance the likelihood of a favorable treatment outcome and can serve as a guide during the course of treatment (Applebaum, 1990).

## Assessment Facilitates the Therapeutic Process

Asking the new patient to participate in an assessment before beginning treatment would seem to result in greater dropout than would a simple intake interview because it may seem to be just another bothersome hurdle the patient must jump over to receive services. However, recent data indicate that the situation is just the opposite (Ackerman, Hilsenroth, Baity, & Blagys, 2000). Perhaps the assessment procedure allows clients to slide into therapy in a less personal manner, desensitizing them to the stresses of the therapy setting. Bram (2010) provided an exemplary case example of the way in which the Rorschach facilitates a therapeutic relationship, which then aids in treatment planning and outcome assessment.

## Assessment Process Itself Can Be Therapeutic

Recently several psychologists have provided data that demonstrate the therapeutic effects of the assessment process itself, when it is conducted in a facilitative manner. The work of Finn (1996a, 1996b, 2007; Finn & Tonsager, 1992), Fischer (1994), Handler (2006), and J. D. Smith, Handler, and colleagues (e.g., J. D. Smith, Wolf, Handler, & Nash, 2009; J. D. Smith, Handler, & Nash, 2010) have indicated that assessment typically results in the production of therapeutic results when conducted following collaborative principles. The first author has developed a therapeutic assessment approach that is ongoing in the treatment process with children and adolescents to determine whether therapeutic assessment changes are long lasting. Further discussion of collaborative and therapeutic approaches to assessment appears in the section of this chapter titled "Therapeutic and Collaborative Approaches to Assessment."

## Assessment Provides Professional Identity

There are many mental health specialists who do psychotherapy (e.g., psychologists, psychiatrists, social workers, marriage and family counselors, ministers), but only psychologists are trained to do assessment. Possession of this skill allows us to be called on to provide evaluations by other professionals in the mental health area as well as by school personnel, physicians, attorneys, the court, government, and even by business and industry.

## Personality Assessment Helps Psychologists Arrive at a Diagnosis

Assessment provides information to make a variety of diagnostic statements, including a *Diagnostic and Statistical Manual* (*DSM*) diagnosis. Whether the diagnosis includes descriptive factors, cognitive and affective factors, interaction patterns, level of ego functions, process aspects, object relations factors, or other dynamic aspects of functioning, it is an informed and comprehensive diagnosis, with or without a diagnostic label.

## Assessment Is Used in Work-Related Settings

There is a huge literature on the use of personality assessment in the workplace. Many studies deal with vocational choice or preference, using personality assessment instruments (e.g., Krakowski, 1984; Rezler & Buckley, 1977), and there is a large literature in which personality assessment is used as an integral part of the study of individuals in work-related settings and in personnel selection and promotion (Barrick & Mount, 1991; Tett, Jackson, & Rothstein, 1991).

## Assessment Is Used in Forensic and Medical Applications

Psychologists are frequently asked to evaluate people for a wide variety of domestic legal problems. Assessments are often used in criminal cases to determine the person's ability to understand the charges brought against him or her or to determine whether the person is competent to stand trial, or is malingering to avoid criminal responsibility. Convicted offenders are often assessed in correctional facilities to determine their mental health needs, the appropriateness of being housed in a facility or unit with programs for inmates with mental illnesses, and their potential risk for suicide, violence, and being targeted or victimized by fellow offenders. Assessment is also used in domestic issues, such as fitness to parent. Readers should see the chapter by Ogloff and Douglas in this volume for a discussion of forensic assessment.

## Assessment Procedures Are Used in Research

Assessment techniques are used to test a variety of theories or hypothesized relationships. Psychologists search among a large array of available tests for assessment tools to quantify the variables of interest to them. There are now at least three excellent journals in the United States as well as some excellent journals published abroad that are devoted to research in assessment.

## Assessment Is Used to Evaluate the Effectiveness of Psychotherapy

In the future, assessment procedures will be important to ensure continuous improvement of psychotherapy through more adequate treatment planning and outcome assessment.

Maruish (2004) discussed the application of test-based assessment in Continuous Quality Improvement, a movement to plan treatment and systematically measure improvement. Psychologists can play a major role in the future delivery of mental health services because their assessment instruments can quickly and economically highlight problems that require attention and can assist in selecting the most cost-effective, appropriate treatment (Maruish, 2004). Such evidence will also be necessary to convince legislators that psychotherapy services are effective. Maruish believed that our psychometrically sound measures, which are sensitive to changes in symptomatology and are administered pre- and posttreatment, can help psychology demonstrate treatment effectiveness. The chapter by Maruish in this volume discusses the topic of assessment and treatment in more detail.

## Assessment Is Important in Risk Management

Assessment can substantially reduce many of the potential legal liabilities involved in the provision of psychological services (Bennett, Bryant, VandenBos, & Greenwood, 1990; Schutz, 1982) in which providers might perform routine baseline assessments of their psychotherapy patients' initial level of distress and of personality functioning (Meyer et al., 2001).

## PROBLEMS OF LEARNING PERSONALITY ASSESSMENT: THE STUDENT SPEAKS

The first assessment course typically focuses on teaching students to give an array of tests. Advanced courses are either didactic or are taught by the use of a group process model in which hypothesis generation and data integration are learned. With this model, *depression*, *anxiety*, *ambivalence*, and similar words take on new meaning for students when they are faced with the task of integrating personality assessment data. These words not only define symptoms seen in patients; they also define students' experiences.

Early in their training, students are often amazed at the unique responses given to the most obvious test stimuli. Training in assessment is about experiencing for oneself what it is like to be with patients in a variety of situations, both fascinating and unpleasant, and what it is like to get a glimpse of someone else's inner world. Fowler (1998) described students' early experience in learning assessment with the metaphor of being in a "psychic nudist colony" (p. 33). With this metaphor he is referring to students' realization that much of what they say or do in assessment class reveals to others and to themselves otherwise private features of their personality. Despite the feeling that one can no longer ensure the privacy of one's inner world, or perhaps because of this, the first few years of training in personality assessment can become an incredibly profound educational experience. If nothing else, students can learn something many of them could perhaps learn nowhere else—what it is like to feel examined and assessed from all angles, sometimes against their will. This approach to learning certainly allows students to become more empathic and sensitive to their patients' insecurities throughout the assessment procedure. Likewise, training in assessment has the potential to greatly enrich one's ability to be present with clients during psychotherapy. Trainees learn how to observe subtleties in behavior, how to sit through uncomfortable moments with their patients, and how to endure scrutiny by them as well. Such learning is enhanced if students learn assessment in a safe environment, such as a group learning class, to be described later in this chapter in the section titled "Problems of Learning Personality: The Student Speaks." However, with the use of this model, there is the strange sense that our interpretation of the data may also say something about ourselves and our competence in relation to our peers. Are we revealing part of our inner experience that we would prefer to keep hidden?

Although initially one cannot escape scrutiny, eventually there is no need to do so. With proper training, students will develop the ability to separate their personal concerns and feelings from those of their patients, which is an important step in becoming a competent clinician. Much of their ignorance melts away as they develop increased ability to be excited about their work in assessment. This then frees students to wonder about their own contributions to the assessment experience. They wonder what they are projecting onto the data that might not belong there. Fortunately, in the group learning model, students have others to help keep them in check. Hearing different views of the data helps to keep personal projections at a minimum and helps students recognize the many different levels at which the data can be understood. It is certainly a more enriching experience when students are allowed to learn from different perspectives than it is when one is left on one's own to digest material taught in a lecture.

The didactic approach leaves much room for erroneous interpretation of the material once students are on their own and are trying to make sense of the test data discussed in class.

This style of learning encourages students to be more dependent on the instructor's method of interpretation, whereas group learning fosters the interpretative abilities of individual students by giving each a chance to confirm or to disconfirm the adequacy of his or her own hypothesis building process. This is an important step in the development of students' personal assessment styles, which is missed in the didactic learning model. Furthermore, in the didactic learning model it is more difficult for the instructor to know if the pace of teaching or the material being taught is appropriate for the skill level of the students, whereas the group learning model allows the instructor to set a pace matched to their abilities and expectations for learning. During their experience in a group learning environment students emphasize that what became increasingly more important over time was the emotional support they received from learning in a group environment. Some students feel more at ease consulting with their peers rather than the teacher.

After several classes in personality assessment and after doing six or seven practice assessments, students typically feel they are beginning to acquire the skills necessary to complete an assessment, until their supervisor asks them to schedule a feedback session with the patient. Suddenly, newfound feelings of triumph and mastery turn again into fear and confusion because students find it awkward and discomforting to be put in a position of having to reveal to the patient negative aspects of his or her functioning. How do new students communicate such disturbing and seemingly unsettling information to another person? How can the patient ever understand what it has taken the student 2 to 3 years to even begin to understand? Students fear that it will surely devastate someone to hear he or she has a thought disorder or inadequate reality testing. However, when the emphasis of assessment (as in a therapeutic assessment approach) is on the facilitation of the client's questions about him- or herself, in addition to the referral question(s), this seemingly hopeless bind becomes much less of a problem. This approach makes the patient an active participant in the feedback process.

## PROBLEMS OF TEACHING PERSONALITY ASSESSMENT: THE INSTRUCTOR SPEAKS

The problems encountered in teaching the initial assessment course, in which the emphasis is on learning the administration and scoring of various instruments, are different from those involved in teaching an advanced course, in which assessment of patients is the focus and the primary issue is integration of data. It must be made clear that the eventual goal is to master the integration of diverse data.

The instructor should provide information about many tests while still giving students enough practice with each instrument. However, there may be time only to demonstrate some tests or have students read about others. The instructor should introduce each new test by describing its relevance to an assessment battery and discussing what it offers that other tests do not offer. Instructors should resist students' efforts to ask for cookbook interpretations. Students often ask what each variable means. The response to the question of meaning is a point where the instructor can begin shifting from a test-based approach to one in which each variable is seen in context with many others.

Learning to do assessment is inherently more difficult for students than learning to do psychotherapy, because the former activity does not allow for continued evaluation of hypotheses. In contrast, the therapeutic process allows for continued discussion, clarification, and reformulation of hypotheses, over time, with the collaboration of the patient. This problem is frightening to students, because they fear making interpretive errors in this brief contact with the patient. More than anything else, they are concerned that their inexperience will cause them to harm the patient. Their task is monumental: They must master test administration while also being empathic to patient needs, and their learning curve must be rapid. At the same time they must also master test interpretation and data integration, report writing, and the feedback process.

Sometimes students feel an allegiance to the patient, and the instructor might be seen as callous because he or she does not feel this personal allegiance or identification. Students' attitudes in this regard must be explored in a patient, in a nonconfrontational manner. Otherwise, the students might struggle to maintain their allegiance with the patient and might turn against learning assessment. Many students also resist learning assessment because of the requirement to rely on intuitive processes, albeit those of disciplined intuition, and the fear of expressing their own conflicts in this process rather than explaining those of the patient. The students feel frightened of newfound responsibilities of evaluating, diagnosing, and committing themselves to paper concerning the patients. As one former student put it, "Self-doubt, anxiety, fear, and misguided optimism are but a few defenses that cropped up during our personality assessment seminar" (Fowler, 1998, p. 34).

Typically, students avoid committing themselves to sharply crafted, specific interpretations, even though they are told by the instructor that these are only hypotheses to try out. Instead, they resort to vague Barnum statements, statements true of most human beings (e.g., "This patient typically becomes anxious when under stress"). Students also often refuse to recognize pathology, even when it is blatantly apparent in the test data. They feel the instructor is overpathologizing the patient. The instructor should not challenge these defenses directly but instead should explore them in a patient, supportive manner, helping to provide additional clarifying data and trying to understand the source of the resistance. Time must also be made available outside the classroom for consultation with the instructor or assessment supervisors. Most of all, students who are just learning to integrate test data need a great deal of encouragement and support of their efforts.

## LEARNING TO INTERVIEW

All too often the importance of interviewing is ignored in doctoral training programs. Sometimes it is taken for granted that a student will already know how to approach a person who comes for assessment. In the old days this was the role of the social worker, who then passed the patient on for assessment. We prefer the system in which the person who does the assessment also does the interview before any tests are given, since the interview is part of the assessment. In this way rapport can be built, so that the actual testing session is less stressful. Just as important, however, is that the assessor will have a great deal of information and impressions that can be used as a reference in the interpretation of the other data. Test responses take on additional important meaning when seen in reference to history data.

There are many ways to teach interviewing skills. In the interviewing class taught by the first author (Handler), students first practice using role-playing and psychodrama techniques.

Then they conduct videotaped interviews with student volunteers, and their interviews are watched and discussed by the class. Students learn to identify latent emotions produced in the interview, to handle their anxiety in productive ways, to manage the interviewee's anxiety, to go beyond mere chitchat with the interviewee, and to facilitate meaningful conversation. Students also learn to examine relevant life issues of the people they interview; to conceptualize these issues and describe them in a report; to ask open-ended questions rather than closed-ended questions, which can be answered with a brief yes or no; to reflect the person's feelings; and to encourage more open discussion.

## IMPORTANT OF RELIABILITY AND VALIDITY

# IMPORTANCE OF RELIABILITY AND VALIDITY

It is essential when teaching students about the use of assessment instruments that one also teaches them the importance of sound psychometric properties for any measure used. By learning what qualities make an instrument useful and meaningful, students can be more discerning when confronted with new instruments or modifications of traditional measures. "In the absence of additional interpretive data, a raw score on any psychological test is meaningless" (Anastasi & Urbina, 1998, p. 67). This statement attests to the true importance of gathering appropriate normative data for all assessment instruments. Likewise, information concerning the reliability of a measure is essential in understanding each individual score that is generated. If the measure has been found to be reliable, this then allows the examiner increased accuracy in the interpretation of variations in scores, such that differences between scores are more likely to result from individual differences than from measurement error (Nunnally & Bernstein, 1994). Furthermore, reliability is essential for an instrument to be valid.

The assessment instruments considered most useful are those that accurately measure the constructs they intend to measure, demonstrating both *sensitivity*, the true positive rate of identification of the individual with a particular trait or pattern, and *specificity*, the true negative rate of identification of individuals who do not have the personality trait being studied. In addition, the overall correct classification, or hit rate, indicates how accurately test scores classify both individuals who meet the criteria for the specific trait and those who do not. A measure can demonstrate a high degree of sensitivity but low specificity, or an inability to correctly exclude those individuals who do not meet the construct definition. When this occurs, the target variable is consistently correctly classified, but other variables that do not truly fit the construct definition are also included in the categorization of items. As a result, many false positives will be included along with the correctly classified variables, and the precision of the measure suffers. Therefore, it is important to consider both the sensitivity and the specificity of any measure being used in order to better understand the meaning of their findings. For a more detailed discussion of these issues, see the chapter by Wasserman and Bracken in this volume.

# TEACHING AN INTRODUCTORY COURSE IN PERSONALITY ASSESSMENT

Given that students have had an adequate course in psychometrics, the next typical step in training is an introductory course in assessment, in which they learn the many details of test administration, scoring, and initial interpretation. Assessment is taught quite differently in doctoral programs throughout the country. As mentioned previously, in some programs testing is actually taught, but the course is labeled assessment, and it might be taught entirely as a survey course; students do little or no practice testing, scoring, or interpretation (e.g., Childs & Eyde, 2002; Hilsenroth & Handler, 1995). We believe this is a grave error, because each assessment course builds on the previous one(s). A great deal can be learned about assessment from reading textbooks and test manuals, but there is no substitute for practical experience.

Some doctoral training programs require only one assessment course in which there is actual practice with various tests. Many other programs have two courses in their curriculum but require only one, whereas other programs require two courses. In some programs only self-report measures are taught, and in others only "projective measures" (now referred to as "performance based" tests) are taught. In some programs optional courses are available, and in others no such opportunities exist. The variability of the required and optional personality assessment courses in training programs is astounding, especially since assessment is a key area of proficiency, required by the American Psychological Association (APA) for program accreditation. In our opinion, students cannot become well grounded in assessment unless they learn interviewing skills and have taken both an introductory course focused on the administration and scoring of individual tests and an advanced course focused on the integration of assessment data and their communication to referral sources and to the person who took the tests. Many times the required assessment courses are determined by a prevailing theoretical emphasis in the program. In these settings, assessment techniques chosen for study are limited to those instruments that are believed to fit the prevailing point of view. This is unfortunate, because students should be exposed to a wide variety of instruments and approaches to personality assessment and because no instrument belongs to a particular theoretical approach; each test can be interpreted from a wide variety of theoretical viewpoints.

Some programs do not include the training of students in assessment as one of their missions, despite the APA requirement. Instead, they believe that the responsibility for teaching personality assessment lies with the internship site. Relegating this important area of clinical experience to the internship is a bad idea, because students learn under a great deal of pressure in these settings, pressure far greater than that of graduate school. Learning assessment in this type of pressured environment is truly a trial by fire. Most students do not know the history of the testing and assessment movement and the relevance of assessment to clinical psychology. We recommend that this information be shared with students, along with the long list of reasons to learn assessment, which was discussed earlier in this chapter.

The necessary emphasis on each test as a separate entity in the first course must eventually give way to a more integrated approach. In addition, although it is necessary to teach students to administer tests according to standardized instructions, they must also be introduced to the idea that in some cases it will not be possible or perhaps advisable to follow standardized instructions. Although they should be urged to follow the standardized procedures whenever possible, modifying instructions sometimes can help students understand the patient better; test scores derived in a nonstandardized manner are not necessarily invalid.

We believe that it is important to draw students' attention to the similarities and differences among the tests, emphasizing the details of the stimuli, the ability of different tests to tap similar factors, the style of administration, and so on. Students should be taught the relevance of the variables they are measuring and scoring for each test. Otherwise, their administration is often rote and meaningless. For example, it makes little sense for students to learn to do a Rorschach Inquiry if they are not first acquainted with the relevance of the variables scored. Therefore, conceptualization of the perceptual, communicative, and representational aspects of perceiving the inkblots, and any other stimuli, for that matter, must first be discussed.

In our opinion, the most important function of this first course is to discuss the reasons each test was chosen to be studied and to help students become proficient in the administration, scoring, and initial interpretation of each test. Once students have mastered test administration, the instructor should begin to emphasize the establishment of rapport with the patient, which involves knowing the directions well enough to focus on the patient rather than on one's manual. The introductory course usually has an assigned laboratory section, in which students practice with volunteer subjects to improve proficiency. Checkouts with volunteer subjects or with the instructor are routine. Students must be able to administer the tests smoothly and in an error-free manner and then score them properly before moving on to the next course.

In many programs students are required to administer, score, and begin to interpret several of each test they are learning. The number of practice protocols varies considerably, but it is typical to require two or three, depending on each student's level of proficiency. In the classroom there should be discussion of the psychometric properties and the research findings for each test and a discussion of the systematic administration and scoring errors produced by students. Additionally, students should be taught that each type of data collected in an assessment has its strengths and its weaknesses. For example, observational and history data are especially helpful in assessment, but these sources can also be quite misleading. Anyone who has done marital therapy or custody evaluations has experienced a situation in which each spouse's story sounds quite plausible, but the husband and the wife tell opposite stories. Such are the limitations of history and observational data. People typically act differently in different situations, and they interpret their behaviors and intentions, and the behaviors and intentions of others, from their own biased vantage points. It soon becomes obvious that additional methods of understanding people are necessary in order to avoid these types of errors described. Adding test data to the history and observational data should increase the accuracy of the assessment and can allow access to other key variables involved in knowing another person. However, test-derived data also contain sources of error, and at times they are also distorted by extratest effects or by impression management attempts. Many tests include systematic methods of determining test-taking attitude and the kind and degree of impression management attempted. Students should be taught that no assessment method is error-free and no test, by itself, is comprehensive. Therefore, it is important to use a number of assessment methods and a number of different types of tests and to aggregate and integrate them in order to answer referral questions adequately and to obtain a meaningful picture of the person assessed.

## TEACHING AN ADVANCED COURSE IN PERSONALITY ASSESSMENT

What follows is a description of an advanced course in personality assessment much like the one taught by the first author (Handler). We present this model to the reader for consideration because it is based on data culled from work on creative reasoning processes and is supported by research. We have added the use of integration approaches based on the use of metaphor, as well as an approach with which to facilitate empathic attunement with the patient. To this experiential approach we have also added an approach that asks the interpreter to imagine interacting with the person who produced the test results.

A second important reason we have used the following description as a suggested model is that it can be used with any test battery the instructor wishes to teach, because the approach is not test specific. We suggest that the reader attempt to use this model in communicating integrative and contextual approaches to assessment teaching, modifying and tailoring the approach to fit individual needs and style. Nevertheless, we recognize that this approach will not be suitable in its entirety for some clinicians who teach personality assessment. Readers should feel free to use any part or parts of this model that are consistent with their theoretical point of view and their preferred interpretive style. We believe the approach described here can be of use to those with an emphasis on intuition, as well as to those who prefer a more objective approach, because the heart of the approach to data integration is the use of convergent and divergent reasoning processes. This approach can be applicable to self-report data as well as to performance-based test data. Indeed, in the class described, the first author models the same approaches to the interpretation of the MMPI-2 and the Personality Assessment Inventory (PAI), for example, that we do to the Rorschach and the Thematic Apperception Test (TAT).

In this second course, students typically begin assessing patients. They must now focus on using their own judgment and intuitive skills to make interpretations and to integrate data. The task now, as we proceed, is the use of higher-level integrative approaches to create an accurate picture of the person they are assessing. The instructor should describe the changed focus and the difficult and complex problem of interpretation, along with the assurance that students will be able to master the process. Nevertheless, students are typically quite anxious, because interpretation places novel demands on them; for the first time they are being placed in a position of authority as experts and are being called on to use themselves as an assessment tool. They have difficulty in the integration of experiential data and objective data, such as test scores and ratios. The complexity of the data is often overwhelming, and this pressure often leads students to search instead for cookbook answers.

With no attention to the interpretive process, students make low-level interpretations; they stay too close to the data, and therefore little meaningful integration is achieved. Hypotheses generated from this incomplete interpretive process are mere laundry lists of disconnected and often meaningless technical jargon. An approach is needed that systematically focuses on helping students develop meaningful interpretations and on the integration of these interpretations to produce a meaningful report (Handler, Fowler, & Hilsenroth, 1998).

Emphasis is now placed on the communication of the experiential and cognitive aspects involved in the process of interpretation. Students are told that the interpretive process is systematized at each step of their learning, that each step will be described in detail, and that the focus will be on the development of an experience-near picture of the person assessed. First students observe the instructor making interpretations from assessment data. In the next step the focus is on group interpretation, to be described. Next, the student does the interpretation and integration with the help of a supervisor and then writes a report, free of technical jargon, responding to the referral questions. Reports are returned to the students with detailed comments about integration, style, accuracy, and how well the referral questions were answered. The students rewrite or correct their reports and return them to the instructor for review.

The group interpretation focuses on protocols collected by students in their clinical setting. Only the student who did the assessment knows the referral issue, the history, and any other relevant information. The remainder of the class and the instructor are ignorant of all details (only age and gender are supplied).

Tests typically included in many test batteries include the Wechsler Adult Intelligence Scale, Fourth Edition (WAIS-IV), the Wechsler Intelligence Scale for Children (WISC-IV), the Symptom Checklist-90-Revised (SCL-90-R), the MMPI-2 or the MMPI-2-RF (Reconstructive Form), the Personality Assessment Inventory (PAI), the Bender Gestalt, a sentence completion test, figure drawings (Draw-A-Person Test [DAP]), the Rorschach, the TAT, a variety of self-report depression and anxiety measures, and early memories. However, instructors might add or delete tests depending on their interests and those of the students. Although this is much more than a full battery, these tests are included to give students wide exposure to available instruments.

Rather than seeking only one isolated interpretation for a specific test response, students are able to see that several interpretations might fit the data and that although one of these might be the best choice as a hypothesis, it is also possible that several interpretations can fit the data simultaneously. This approach is especially useful in preventing students from ignoring possible alternatives and in helping them avoid the problem of confirmatory bias: ignoring data that do not fit the hypothesis and selecting data that confirm the initial hypothesis. Gradually, the students interpret larger and larger pieces of data by searching for additional possibilities, because they understand that it is premature to focus on certainty.

The second interpretive method based on creativity research is called convergent thinking. It asks how different bits of information can be brought together so that they reflect something unique and quite different from any of the pieces but are related to those pieces. Convergent thinking has been measured by the Remote Associates Test (RAT; Mednick & Mednick, 1967), in which the respondent is asked to come up with a word that is related in some way to three other presented stimulus words. For example, for these three words, "base," "round," and "dance," the correct answer is "ball." The interpretive process concerns "seeing relationships among seemingly mutually remote ideas" (Mednick & Mednick, 1967, p. 4). This is essentially the same type of task that is required in effective assessment interpretation, in which diverse pieces of data are fitted together to create an interpretive hypothesis. Burley and Handler (1997) found that the RAT significantly differentiated good and poor DAP interpreters.

A helpful teaching heuristic in the interpretive process is the use of the metaphor (Hilsenroth, 1998), in which students are taught to offer an interpretive response as if it were an expression of the patient's experience. They are asked to summarize the essential needs, wishes, expectations, major beliefs, and unresolved issues of the patient through the use of a short declarative statement, typically beginning with "I wish," "I feel," "I think," "I want," or "I am." This "metaphor of the self" facilitates interpretation because it allows for a quick and easy way to frame the response to empathize vicariously with the patient. When this approach is combined with the cognitive approaches of divergent and convergent thinking, students generate meaningful hypotheses not only about self-experience but also about how others might experience the patient in other settings. To facilitate this latter approach, students are asked how they would feel interacting with a patient who gave a certain response if they met the person at a party or in some other interpersonal setting (Potash, 1998).

At first students focus on individual findings, gradually branching out to include patterns of data from a series of responses, and finally integrating these interpretations across various tests. Initial attempts at interpretation are little more than observations, couched as interpretations, such as "This response is an F−"; or "She drew her hands behind her back"; or "He forgot to say how the person was feeling in this TAT story." The student is surprised when the instructor states that the interpretation was merely an observation. To discourage this descriptive approach, the instructor typically asks the student to tell all the things that such an observation could mean, thereby encouraging divergent thinking.

At the next level, students typically begin to shift their interpretations to a somewhat less descriptive approach, but the interpretations are still test based rather than being psychologically relevant. Examples of this type of interpretation are "She seems to be experiencing anxiety on this card" and "The patient seems to oscillate between being too abstract and too concrete on the WAIS-III." Again, the instructor asks the student to generate a psychologically relevant interpretation concerning the meaning of this observation in reference to the person's life issues or in reference to the data we have already processed.

Efforts are made to sharpen and focus interpretations. Other students are asked to help by attempting to clarify and focus a student's overly general interpretation, and often a discussion ensues among several students to further define the original interpretation. The instructor focuses the questions to facilitate the process. The task here is to model the generation of detailed, specific hypotheses that can be validated once we have completed all the interpretation and integration of the data. Whenever a segment of the data begins to build a picture of the person tested, students are asked to separately commit themselves to paper in class by writing a paragraph that summarizes and integrates the data available so far. The act of committing their interpretations to paper forces students to focus and to be responsible for what they write. They are impressed with each other's work and typically find that several people have focused on additional interpretations they had not noticed.

Anyone who uses this teaching format will inevitably encounter resistance from students who have been trained to stick closely to empirical findings. Sometimes a student will feel the class is engaging in reckless and irresponsible activities and/or that others are saying negative and harmful things about people, without evidence. It is necessary to patiently but persistently work through these defensive barriers. It is also sometimes frightening for students to experience blatant pathology so closely that it becomes necessary to back away from an interpretation and, perhaps, to condemn the entire process.

The instructor should be extremely supportive and facilitative, offering hints when a student feels stuck and a helpful direction when the student cannot proceed further. The entire class becomes a protective and encouraging environment, offering suggestions, ideas for rephrasing, and a great deal of praise for effort expended and for successful interpretations. It is also important to empower students, reassuring them that they are on the correct path and that even at this early stage they are doing especially creative work. Students are also introduced to relatively new material concerning the problem of test integration. The work of Beutler and Berren (1995), Beutler & Groth-Marnat, 2005, Finn (1996a, 2007), Ganellen (1996), Handler and Hilsenroth (1998), Meyer (1997), and Weiner (2003) has focused on different aspects of this issue.

Once the entire record is processed and a list of specific hypotheses is recorded, the student who did the assessment tells the class about the patient, including history, presenting problem(s), pattern and style of interaction, and so forth. Each hypothesis generated is classified as "correct," "incorrect," or "cannot say," because of lack of information. Typically, correct responses range from 90% to 95%, with only one or two "incorrect" hypotheses and one or two "cannot say" responses.

In this advanced course students might complete two or three reports. They should continue to do additional supervised assessments in their program's training clinic and, later, in their clinical placements throughout the remainder of their university training.

## IMPROVING ASSESSMENT RESULTS THROUGH MODIFICATION OF ADMINISTRATION PROCEDURES

Students learning assessment are curious about ways to improve the accuracy of their interpretations, but they nevertheless adhere strictly to standardized approaches to administration, even when, in some situations, these approaches result in a distortion of findings. They argue long, hard, and sometimes persuasively that it is wrong to modify standardized procedures, for any reason. However, we believe that at certain times changing standardized instructions will often yield data that are a more accurate measure of the individual than would occur with reliance on standardized instructions. For example, a rather suspicious man was being tested with the WAIS. He stated that an orange and a banana were not alike and continued in this fashion for the other pairs of items. The examiner then reassured him that there really was a way in which the pairs of items were alike and that there was no trick involved. The patient then responded correctly to almost all of the items, earning an excellent score. When we discuss this alteration in the instructions, students express concern about how the examiner would score the subtest results. The response of the instructor is that the students

are placing the emphasis in the wrong area: They are more interested in the test and less in the patient. If the standardized score was reported, it would also not give an accurate measure of this patient's intelligence or of his emotional problems. Instead, the change in instructions can be described in the report, along with a statement that says something like "The patient's level of suspicion interferes with his cognitive effectiveness, but with some support and assurance he can give up this stance and be more effective."

Students are also reluctant to modify standardized instructions by merely adding additional tasks after standardized instructions are followed. For example, the first author typically recommends that students ask patients what they thought of each test they took, how they felt about it, what they liked and disliked about it, and so on. This approach helps in the interpretation of the test results by clarifying the attitude and approach the patient took to the task, which perhaps have affected the results. The first author has designed a systematic Testing of the Limits procedure, based on the method first employed by Bruno Klopfer (Klopfer, Ainsworth, Klopfer, & Holt, 1954). In this method the patient is questioned to amplify the meanings of his or her responses and to gain information about his or her expectations and attitudes about the various tests and subtests. This information helps put the responses and the scores in perspective. For example, when a patient gave the response "A butterfly coming out of an iceberg" to Card VII of the Rorschach, he was asked, after the test had been completed, "What's that butterfly doing coming out of that iceberg?" The patient responded, "That response sounds kind of crazy; I guess I saw a butterfly and an iceberg. I must have been nervous; they don't actually belong together." This patient recognized the cognitive distortion he apparently experienced and was able to explain the reason for it and correct it. Therefore, this response speaks to a less serious condition, compared with a patient who could not recognize that he or she had produced the cognitive slip. Indeed, later on, the patient could typically recognize when he had made similar cognitive misperceptions, and he was able to correct them, as he had done in the assessment.

## TEACHING STUDENTS HOW TO CONSTRUCT AN ASSESSMENT BATTERY

Important sources of information will of course come from an interview with the patient and possibly with members of his or her family. Important history data and observations from these contacts form a significant core of data, enriched, perhaps, by information derived from other case records and from referral sources. In our clinical setting patients take the SCL-90-R before the intake interview. This self-report instrument allows the interviewer to note those physical and emotional symptoms or problems the patients endorse as particularly difficult problems for them. This information is typically quite useful in structuring at least part of the interview. The construction of a comprehensive assessment battery is typically the next step.

What constitutes a comprehensive assessment battery differs from setting to setting. Certainly, adherents of the Five-Factor Model would constitute an assessment battery differently from someone whose theoretical focus is object relations. However, there are issues involved in assessment approaches that are far more important than one's theoretical orientation. No test is necessarily tied to any one theory. Rather, it is the clinician interpreting the test who may imbue it with a particular theory.

It is difficult to describe a single test battery that would be appropriate for everyone, because referral questions vary, as do assessment settings and their requirements; physical and emotional needs, educational and intellectual levels, and cultural issues might require the use of somewhat different instruments. Nevertheless, there are a number of guiding principles used to help students construct a comprehensive assessment battery, which can and should be varied, given the issues just described. Beutler and Berren (1995) compared test selection and administration in assessment to doing research. They viewed each test as an "analogue environment" to be presented to the patient. In this process the clinician should ask which types of environments should be selected in each case. The instructions of each test or subtest are the clinician's way of manipulating these analogue environments and presenting them to the patient. Assessment is typically a stressful experience because the examiner constantly asks the patient to respond in a certain manner or in a certain format, as per the test instructions. When the format is unstructured, there is sometimes less stress because the patient has many options in the way in which he or she can respond. However, there are marked differences in the ways that people experience this openness. For some people a vague or open format is gratifying, and for others it is terrifying. For this reason it is helpful to inquire about the patient's experience with each format, to determine its effect.

Beutler and Berren (1995) made another important point in reference to test selection: Some tests are measures of enduring internal qualities (traits) whereas others tap more transitory aspects of functioning (states), which differ for an individual from one situation to another. The clinician's job is to determine which test results are measuring states and which reflect traits. When a specific test in some way resembles some aspects of the patient's actual living environment, we can assume that the patient's response will be similar to his or her response in the real-world setting (Beutler & Berren, 1995; Beutler & Groth-Marnat, 2005). The assessor can often observe these responses, which we call stylistic aspects of a person's personality.

One question to be answered is whether this approach is typical of the patient's performance in certain settings in the environment, whether it is due to the way in which the person views this particular task (or the entire assessment), or whether it is due to one or more underlying personality problems, elicited by the test situation itself. It is in part for this reason that students are taught to carefully record verbatim exactly what the patient answers, the extratest responses (e.g., side comments, emotional expressions, etc.), and details of how each task was approached.

Important aspects of test choice are the research that supports the instrument, the ease of administration for the patient, and the ability of the test to tap specific aspects of personality functioning that other instruments do not tap. We discuss choosing a comprehensive assessment battery next.

## Choosing a Comprehensive Battery

First, an intellectual measure should be included in a comprehensive battery, even if the person's intelligence level appears obvious, because it allows the assessor to estimate whether there is emotional interference in cognitive functioning. For this we recommend the WAIS-IV or the WISC-IV, although the use of various short forms is acceptable if time is of importance. For people with language problems of one type or another, or for people whose learning opportunities have been atypical for any number of reasons (e.g., poverty, dyslexia, etc.), a nonverbal intelligence test might be substituted for an IQ measure. The Wechsler tests also offer many clues concerning personality functioning, from the pattern of interaction with the examiner, the approach to the test, the patient's attitude while taking it, response content, to the style and approach to the subtest items and the response to success or failure. If these issues are not relevant for the particular referral questions, the examiner could certainly omit this test.

Additionally, one or more self-report inventories should be included, two if time permits. The MMPI-2 is an extremely well-researched instrument that can provide a great deal more information than the patient's self-perception. Students are discouraged from using the descriptive printout and instead are asked to interpret the test using a more labor-intensive approach, examining the scores on the many supplementary scales and integrating them with the clinical scales. The PAI is also recommended because it yields estimates of adaptability and emotional health that are not defined merely as the absence of pathology, because it has several scales concerning treatment issues and because it is very psychometrically sound. Other possible inventories include the Millon Clinical Multiaxial Inventory-III (MCMI-III), because it focuses on Axis II disorders, and the SCL-90-R or its abbreviated form, because it yields a comprehensive picture concerning present physical and emotional symptoms the patient endorses. A host of other possible self-report measures can be used, depending on the referral issues (e.g., the Beck Depression Inventory and the Beck Anxiety Inventory).

Several performance-based tests are suggested, again depending on the referral questions and the presenting problems. It is helpful to use an array of projective (performance-based) tests that vary on a number of dimensions, to determine whether there are different patterns of functioning with different types of stimuli. We recommend a possible array of stimuli that range from those that are very simple and specific (e.g., the Bender Gestalt [BG] Test) to the opposite extreme, the DAP test, because it is the only test in the battery in which there is no external guiding stimulus. Between these two extremes are the TAT, in which the stimuli are relatively clear-cut, and the Rorschach, in which the stimuli are vague and unstructured.

Although the research concerning the symbolic content in the interpretation of the BG is rather negative, the test nevertheless allows the assessor a view of the person's stylistic approach to the rather simple task of copying the stimuli. The Rorschach is a multifaceted measure that may be used in an atheoretical manner, using the Comprehensive System (Exner, 2003), or it may be used in association with a number of theoretical approaches, including self psychology, object relations, ego psychology, and even Jungian psychology. In addition, many of the variables scored in the Exner system could very well be of interest to psychologists with a cognitive-behavioral approach. The Rorschach is a good choice as a projective (performance-based) instrument because it is

multidimensional, tapping many areas of functioning, and because there has been a great deal of recent research that supports its validity (e.g., Ganellen, 1999; Kubeszyn et al., 2000; Meyer & Archer, 2001; Meyer & Handler, 1997; Meyer et al., 2000; B. L. Smith et al., 2005; Viglione, 1999; Viglione & Hilsenroth, 2001; Weiner, 2001). There are also several well-validated Rorschach content scoring systems that were generated from research and have found application in clinical assessment as well (e.g., the Mutuality of Autonomy Scale, Urist, 1977; the Holt Primary Process Scale, Holt, 1977; the Rorschach Oral Dependency Scale [ROD], Bornstein, 1993; Masling, Rabie, & Blondheim, 1967; and the Lerner Defense Scale, Lerner & Lerner, 1980).

The TAT is another instrument frequently used by psychologists that can be used with a variety of theoretical approaches. The TAT can be interpreted using content, style, and coherence variables. There are several interpretive systems for the TAT, but the systematic work of Cramer (1996, 2006) and Westen (1991a, 1991b) seems most promising.

One assessment technique that might be new to some psychologists is the early memories technique, in which the assessor asks the patient for a specific early memory of mother, father, first day of school, eating or being fed, of a transitional object, and of feeling snug and warm (Fowler, Hilsenroth, & Handlerstet, 1995, 1996). This approach, which can also be used as part of an interview, has demonstrated utility for predicting details of the therapeutic relationship, and it correlates with a variety of other measures of object relations. The approach can be used with a wide variety of theoretical approaches, including various cognitive approaches (Bruhn, 1990, 1992).

Additional possible tests include various drawing tests (e.g., the DAP test and the Kinetic Family Drawing Test [K-F-D]). The research findings for these tests are not consistently supportive (Handler, 1996; Handler & Habenicht, 1994). However, many of the studies are not well conceived or well controlled (Handler & Habenicht, 1994; Riethmiller & Handler, 1997a, 1997b). The DAP and/or the K-F-D are nevertheless recommended because they are the only tests in which there is no standard stimulus to be placed before the patient. This lack of structure allows the examiner to observe organizing behavior in situations with no real external structure. Therefore, the DAP taps issues concerning the quality of internal structuring. Poor results are often obtained if the person tested has problems with identity or with the ability to organize self-related issues. Also, drawing tests are helpful if the person being assessed is not very verbal or communicative, because a minimum of talking is required in the administration. They are also quick and easy to administer and have been demonstrated to be excellent instruments to reflect changes in psychotherapy (e.g., Handler, 1996; Robins, Blatt, & Ford, 1991; Yama, 1990).

A sentence completion test (there are many different types) is a combination of a self-report measure and a projective test. The recommended version is the Miale-Holsopple Sentence Completion Test (Holsopple & Miale, 1954). Patients are asked to complete a series of sentence stems in any way they wish. Most of the items are indirect, such as "Closer and closer there comes...," "A wild animal...," and "When fire starts...." Sentence completion tests also provide information to be followed up in an interview. The assessor can also create sentence stems to address the client's specific issues identified or hypothesized in previous testing.

## ASSESSMENT AND CULTURAL DIVERSITY

No assessment education is complete without an understanding of the cultural and subcultural influences on assessment data. This is an important issue because often the effects of cultural variables may be misinterpreted as personality abnormality. Therefore, traditional tests might be inappropriate for some people, and for others adjustments in interpretation should be made by reference to cultural or subcultural norms. Students should recognize that it is unethical to use typical normative findings to evaluate members of other cultures unless data are available suggesting cross-cultural equivalence. Byrne and colleagues (2009) also discussed the litany of methodological and empirical considerations of cross-cultural assessment and presented the implications for assessment training. The reader should also refer to the chapter by Geisinger and McCormick in this volume on testing and assessment in cross-cultural psychology.

In many cases traditional test items are either irrelevant to the patient or have a different meaning from that intended. Often, merely translating a test into the patient's language is not adequate because the test items or even the test format may still be inappropriate. Knowledge of various subgroups obtained from reading, consulting with colleagues, and interacting with members of the culture goes a long way to sensitize a person to the problems encountered in personality assessment with members of that subgroup. It is also important to understand the significant differences among various ethnic and cultural groups in what is considered normal or typical behavior. Cultural factors play a critical role in the expression of psychopathology; unless this context is understood, it is not possible to make an accurate assessment of the patient. The instructor should introduce examples of variations in test performance from members of different cultural groups.

Another problem concerning culturally competent personality assessment is the importance of determining the degree of acculturation the person being assessed has made to the prevailing mainstream culture. This analysis is necessary to determine what set of norms the assessor might use in the interpretive process. Although it is not possible to include readings about assessment issues for all available subcultures, it is possible to include research on the subgroups the student is likely to encounter in his or her training. A number of important resources are available to assist students in doing competent multicultural assessments (e.g., Dana, 2000a, 2000b). Allen (1998) reviewed personality assessment with American Indians and Alaska Natives; Lindsey (1998) reviewed such work with African American clients; Okazaki (1998) reviewed assessment with Asian Americans; and Cuéllar (1998) reviewed cross-cultural assessment with Hispanic Americans.

## TEACHING ETHICAL ISSUES OF ASSESSMENT

As students enter the field and become professional psychologists, they must have a clear understanding of how legal and ethical responsibilities affect their work. However, Plante (1995) found that ethics courses in graduate training programs tend to focus little on practical strategies for adhering to ethical and legal standards once students begin their professional careers.

One way to reduce the risks associated with the practice of assessment is to maintain an adequate level of competency in the services one offers (Plante, 1999). *Competency* generally refers to the extent to which a psychologist is appropriately trained and has obtained up-to-date knowledge in the areas in which he or she practices. This principle assumes that professional psychologists are aware of the boundaries and limitations of their competence. Determining this is not always easy, because there are no specific guidelines for measuring competence or indicating how often training should be conducted. To reduce the possibility of committing ethical violations, the psychologist should attend continuing education classes and workshops at professional conferences and local psychology organizations.

The APA (1992) publication titled *Ethical Principles of Psychologists and Code of Conduct* also asserts that psychologists who use assessment instruments must use them appropriately, based on relevant research on the administration, scoring, and interpretation of the instrument. Another important book that deals with various aspects of test administration and feedback to clients is a volume titled *Standards for Educational and Psychological Testing* (American Educational Research Association, the APA, and the National Council on Measurement in Education, 2004). To adhere to various assessment principles, psychologists using assessment instruments must be aware of the data concerning reliability, validity, and standardization of the instruments. Consideration of normative data is essential when interpreting test results. There may be occasions when an instrument has not been tested with a particular group of individuals and, as a result, normative data do not exist for that population. If this is the case, use of the measure with an individual of that population is inappropriate.

Information regarding the psychometric properties of an instrument and its intended use must be provided in the test manual to be in accordance with the ethical standards of publication or distribution of an assessment instrument (Koocher & Keith-Spiegel, 1998). Anyone using the instrument should read the manual thoroughly and understand the measure's limitations before using it. "The responsibility for establishing whether the test measures the construct or reflects the content of interest is the burden of both the developers and the publishers," (Koocher & Keith-Spiegel, 1998, p. 147), but the person administering it is ultimately responsible for knowing this information and using it appropriately. The reader should refer to the chapter by Rey-Casserly and Koocher in this volume, on ethical issues in psychological assessment, for a more detailed discussion of this topic.

## THERAPEUTIC AND COLLABORATIVE APPROACHES TO ASSESSMENT

The collaborative/therapeutic assessment paradigm has gained in popularity in the past decade since this chapter was first published. Previously, therapeutic assessment was included in a section titled "Personality Assessment in the Future," but it is safe to say that it has established itself as a distinct area of assessment psychology and has found a home in a number of training programs. Finn and Tonsager's (1997) landmark paper highlighted differences between the goals and guiding principles of "traditional,

information-gathering" models of assessment with the therapeutic and collaborative assessment paradigm articulated by Finn (2007), Fischer (1994), and Handler (2006). The usual goal of traditional assessment is a communication *about* the client. In therapeutic approaches, the goal is for clients to learn about themselves and experience new aspects of their personality, which can be used to facilitate therapeutic change (Finn & Tonsager, 1997). Another defining characteristic of therapeutic assessment is the way in which psychological tests are used. Traditional assessment typically emphasizes standardized test scores that can be translated into nomothetic predictions about clients' behaviors outside the testing situation (Finn & Tonsager, 1997). Alternatively, Finn (2007) proposed the use of psychological tests as "empathy magnifiers" to help assessors understand the client's "dilemmas of change." Test data are considered useful if they result in mutual learning and provide the client and assessor an opportunity for dialogue concerning the client's subjective experiences of the testing situation (Finn & Tonsager, 1997). Test results and the testing situation provide a stimulus for collaborative dialogue regarding the client's stated concerns and reasons for seeking a psychological assessment. Observation, background information, formal test results, patient input during testing, and the therapeutic relationship are then used by the assessor in devising an intervention using particular assessment stimuli or procedures to bring client's life issues into the room. In vivo elicitation of clients' problems facilitates exploration of these issues, including identifying the factors that are necessary and sufficient to produce the problem behavior—what elicits it, what reinforces it, and what maintains it. Finn (2007) has dubbed this procedure the Assessment Intervention, which can be a stand-alone session that follows standardized testing, or immediately following the administration of a test. The goal of the assessor is to then help the client in developing a new awareness of the problem in order to produce more positive outcomes in the future.

The empirical support for therapeutic assessment principles and techniques has similarly grown in recent years. The process of providing feedback in a therapeutic manner has received perhaps the most empirical support. Students often have more difficulty with assessment feedback than with any other aspect of assessment. Curry and Hanson's (2010) national survey of assessment psychologists revealed that approximately one third of respondents felt that predoctoral course work, pratica, and internship were of no help in preparing them to provide feedback from assessment procedures. Beginning and even novice assessors are often anxious about providing feedback to patients regarding undesirable aspects of their personality. In the initial session of a therapeutic assessment, clients are invited to collaboratively generate questions with the assessor that they would like to have answered. When preparing feedback, Finn (2007) uses the concept of "Levels" of information to gauge the potential impact of assessment findings and the likelihood that the client will be able to integrate feedback into his or her existing self-view. The collaborative presentation and discussion of assessment findings has been found to result in therapeutic benefits for clients (Finn, 2007; Finn & Martin, 1997; Finn & Tonsager, 1992; Hanson, Claiborn, & Kerr, 1997; Newman, 2004; Newman & Greenway, 1997). The Finn and Tonsager (1992) study randomly assigned patients to either a group receiving therapeutic feedback of MMPI-2 results or examiner attention. The group receiving therapeutic feedback reported significant improvements in symptomatic distress and self-esteem and were also more hopeful immediately following the feedback and at a 2-week follow-up. Newman (2004) compared a group of adolescents receiving brief (2-hour) MMPI-2 therapeutic feedback to a group receiving five 1-hour sessions of traditional psychotherapy. Participants in both groups reported a significant decrease in depression, hopelessness, and loneliness. Those in the therapeutic MMPI-2 feedback group additionally reported significantly improved symptomatic distress and self-esteem. Poston and Hanson (2010) found robust support for the effectiveness of therapeutic approaches to feedback in a recent meta-analysis of 17 studies.

Research has also demonstrated that participation in a therapeutic assessment enhances utilization of subsequent psychological services: In comparison to a traditional assessment group, Ougrin, Ng, and Low (2008) found that adolescents referred to the emergency room because they engaged in self-harming behaviors who received a therapeutic assessment were more likely to attend their first community follow-up appointment (75% versus 40%) and were twice as likely to continue to engage in community services (62% versus 30%); Michel (2002) found support for therapeutic assessment resulting in greater engagement in treatment by adolescent patients and their families in an inpatient hospital for severe eating disorders. Hilsenroth and colleagues have demonstrated a relationship between therapeutic assessment procedures and the therapeutic alliance. In comparison to a traditional assessment, patients receiving a therapeutic assessment had a stronger therapeutic alliance with their assessor (Ackerman et al., 2000). Ackerman and colleagues also found that clients involved in a therapeutic assessment were more likely

to complete the assessment and follow through with recommendations compared to clients receiving traditional assessment. Similarly, therapeutic alliance to the assessor was found to predictive of the therapeutic alliance the client later develops with his or her therapist (Hilsenroth, Peters, & Ackerman, 2004). In this study, patients receiving therapeutic assessment were found to have stronger therapeutic alliance to their subsequent therapist compared to those having received traditional assessment.

Finn and colleagues (e.g., Finn, 2007; Finn & Tonsager, 1997) developed the semistructured Therapeutic Assessment (TA) model. The model is a value-driven, six-step process comprised of (1) the assessment question and relationship-building phase; (2) the test administration phase; (3) the intervention phase; (4) the summary/discussion phase; (5) the written communication of feedback phase; and (6) the follow-up period (Finn, 2007, 2009). The TA model has been employed successfully with individual adult clients (Aschieri & Smith, under review; Finn, 2003, 2007; Peters, Handler, White, & Winkel, 2008) and couples (Finn, 2007; Uhinki, 2001).

Finn, Tharinger, and colleagues adapted the TA model to be used with children and families (Tharinger, Finn, Wilkinson, & Schaber, 2007; Tharinger, Krumholz, Austin, & Matson, 2011) and adolescent clients (Tharinger, Gentry, & Finn, forthcoming). The child and adolescent TA models emphasize a systemic conceptualization of the problem behaviors and include extensive participation from parents and other family members in nearly all aspects of the assessment process. With children, parents are invited to observe the test administration procedures, assist in the interpretation of test results, and participate in a family intervention session (Tharinger et al., 2008). In addition to therapeutic feedback provided to the parents (Tharinger, Finn, Hersh et al., 2008), the child is routinely given feedback in the form of a personalized story or fable (Tharinger, Finn, Wilkinson, et al., 2008). The systemic emphasis of the child and adolescent TA models aids families in developing an awareness of familial factors that contribute to, and even perpetuate, the youth's problem behaviors and provides them with alternative ways of interacting with and understanding the child. J. D. Smith, Finn, Swain, and Handler (2010) demonstrated the effective use of the child TA model in a children's hospital setting for a psychosomatic presentation. An overview of the child TA model and a review of the current research base can be found in J. D. Smith (2010).

Research suggests that the child TA model is an effective, consumer-friendly brief intervention: In an aggregate group study Tharinger et al. (2009) assessed the comprehensive model with 14 families with preadolescent children referred for emotional and behavioral problems. Children and mothers experienced reduced symptomatology and family conflict and increased communication and family cohesion following the TA. Participants were enthusiastically engaged and reported satisfaction with the services, suggesting consumer acceptability. Families also reported that the ability to observe the assessment of their child, a central practice in the child TA model, was one of the most impactful aspects of the assessment. TA practitioners can utilize a behind-the-mirror or video link observation arrangement, if available, or parents can be invited to observe the testing in the room with the child and assessor.

J. D. Smith, Handler, Nash, and colleagues (2010) employed an experimental time-series design to assess the effectiveness of the child TA model. J. D. Smith, Wolf, Handler, and Nash (2009) demonstrated statistically significant improvements in the child's aggression and oppositionality, as well as family distress, as a result of TA. J. D. Smith, Nicholas, Handler, and Nash (2011) found that TA resulted in greater self-esteem, fewer depressive symptoms, and enhanced social interactions after the family of a 12-year-old with internalizing symptoms completed a TA. This study also found that the family intervention session (Tharinger, Finn, Austin et al., 2008), a distinctive component of the child TA model, coincided with a change in the trajectory of the child's and family's reported symptoms, in that the slope of improvement seemed to have shifted as a result of this brief systemic intervention. J. D. Smith, Handler, and Nash (2010) provided support for the efficacy of TA for preadolescent boys with oppositional defiant disorder using a replicated single-case time-series design. In this study, three families demonstrated significant improvement across multiple domains after participating in a TA. However, each family improved at different time points during the TA or after a 2-month follow-up period. These findings suggest both the potential for differential response to specific components and the robust nature of the comprehensive TA model.

Although training in traditional assessment may be in decline, the advent of TA collaborative assessment practices seems to have stimulated a resurgence of psychological assessment practices. Students seem to enjoy learning and practicing TA because of the way in which assessment blends with therapy to facilitate change in patients. Echoing the conclusions of Curry and Hanson (2010), we believe graduate and internship programs should include therapeutic and collaborative models of assessment in training curricula. The techniques and principles of TA

provide students with a paradigm for assessment practices that is accessible, effective, and reduces the anxiety of delivering difficult feedback to patients. Clinical case studies by Finn (2003), by Peters et al. (2008), and an edited casebook by Finn, Fischer, and Handler (2012) demonstrate the utility and effectiveness of the TA approach when delivering feedback that is both difficult and modifies the client's previously held self-view. Finn's TA model additionally offers a semistructured model trainees might find particularly useful during training. Based on the results of their meta-analysis, Poston and Hanson (2010) wrote that "those who engage in *assessment and testing as usual* may miss out . . . on a golden opportunity to effect client change and enhance clinically important treatment processes" (p. 210; emphasis in original).

## LEARNING THROUGH DOING: PROFICIENCY THROUGH SUPERVISED PRACTICE

Something interesting happens when a student discusses data with his or her supervisor. The supervisee often says and does things that reveal information about the nature and experience of the client being assessed, in metaphors used to describe assessment experiences, slips of the tongue when discussing a client, or an actual re-creation of the dynamics present in the relationship between client and assessor in the supervisory relationship. This reenactment has come to be known as parallel process (e.g., Deering, 1994; Whitman & Jacobs, 1998), defined by Deering (1994) as "an unconscious process that takes place when a trainee replicates problems and symptoms of patients during supervision" with the purpose "of causing the supervisor to demonstrate how to handle the situation" (p. 1). If the supervisor and supervisee can become aware of the presence of parallel process in the supervision, it can be a powerful diagnostic and experiential tool. It is important for the supervisor to note when students act in a way that is not characteristic of their usual behavior; often this is the first clue that parallel process is occurring (Sigman, 1989). Students sometimes take on aspects of their clients' personality, especially when they identify with some facet of a patient's experience or character style.

The supervisor should always strive to model the relationship with the supervisee after that which he or she would want the supervisee to have with the client. With this approach, the supervisor becomes an internalized model or standard for the trainee. Supervisors often serve as the template for how to behave with a client during assessment because many students have no other opportunities to observe seasoned clinicians at their work. It is also important to remember that problems in the supervisor–supervisee relationship can trickle down into the supervisee–client relationship, so issues such as power, control, competition, and inferiority may arise between the supervisee and the client as well if these emotions happen to be present in the supervision relationship. Nevertheless, given the inevitable occurrence of parallel process, going over data with the student is not sufficient supervision or training. The supervisory relationship itself should be used to facilitate student growth and development. There must also be a good alliance between the supervisor and the student and a sense of confidence from both parties involved that each has sound judgment and good intentions toward the assessment process and the client.

It is important for the supervisor to encourage a sense of hopefulness in the student that will translate into hope for the client that this new information will be helpful. Otherwise, it is difficult for students to know or at least to believe that what they are doing is meaningful. When the characteristics of trust, confidence, collaboration, and hopefulness are not present in the supervision relationship, this should be discussed during the supervision hour. It is crucial that the relationship be examined when something impedes the ability to form a strong alliance.

## ASSESSMENT TEACHING IN GRADUATE SCHOOL: A REVIEW OF THE SURVEYS

A survey of the literature for the first edition of this chapter suggested that training in assessment was still being emphasized in clinical training programs (e.g., Belter & Piotrowski, 1999; Piotrowski, 1999), but this trend may be shifting. There is also evidence that those in academic positions view assessment as less important than other areas of clinical training (Kinder, 1994; Retzlaff, 1992) and that assessment training in graduate programs is being taught by adjunct faculty rather than those faculty holding academic positions (Eyde & Childs, 2000). Those instruments that have consistently received the most attention during graduate training are MMPI, Rorschach, Wechsler scales, and TAT (e.g., Belter & Piotrowski, 1999; Hilsenroth & Handler, 1995). Some concern, however, has been expressed about the level of training being conducted in the area of projective assessment (e.g., Hershey, Kopplin, & Cornell, 1991; Hilsenroth & Handler, 1995; Rossini & Moretti, 1997). Watkins, Campbell, and Manus (1990) found that clinical psychologists in academia generally

believe that performance-based tests "projective techniques" are less important assessment approaches now than they have been in the past and that they are not grounded in empirical research.

Academic training often emphasizes so-called objective assessment over performance-based techniques. Clinical training directors surveyed by Rossini and Moretti (1997) reported that the amount of formal instruction or supervision being conducted in the use of the TAT was little to none, and Hilsenroth and Handler (1995) and Mihura and Weinle (2002) found that graduate students were often dissatisfied with the quality and degree of training they received in the Rorschach. It is apparent that although training in assessment is emphasized in most graduate programs, it does not mean that students are well prepared, especially in the area of performance-based assessment, which data show is an area of assessment that has been in decline since 1960 (Norcross, Karpiak, & Santoro, 2005). Specific qualities and approaches to training may vary widely from program to program and may not meet the needs of applied settings and internship programs. Much of the literature reflects the discrepancy between graduate training in assessment and internship needs (e.g., Brabender, 1992; Shemberg & Leventhal, 1981). Furthermore, given the report by Camara, Nathan, and Puente (2000), who found that the most frequently used instruments by professional psychologists are the WAIS/WISC, the MMPI-2, the Rorschach, BG, and the TAT, it is clear that the discrepancy between training and application of assessment goes beyond that of internship needs and includes real-world needs as well.

## ASSESSMENT ON INTERNSHIP: REPORT OF A SURVEY

Clemence and Handler (2001) sought to examine the expectations that internship training directors have for students and to ascertain the specific psychological assessment methods most commonly used at internship programs in professional psychology. Questionnaires designed to access this information were mailed to all 563 internships listed in the 1998–1999 Association of Psychology Postdoctoral and Internship Centers Directory. Only two sites indicated that no patients are assessed, and 41% responded that testing instruments are used with the majority of their patients. Each intern is required to administer an average of 27 full battery or 33 partial battery assessments per year, far exceeding the number of batteries administered by most students during their graduate training.

Piotrowski and Belter (1999) also found the four most commonly used assessment instruments at internship facilities to be the MMPI-2/MMPI-A (86%), the WAIS (83%), the Rorschach (80%), and the TAT (76%). In the Clemence and Handler study, 99% of the internships surveyed reported offering training in assessment, and three approaches to training in personality assessment were most commonly endorsed by training directors: intellectual assessment (79%), interviewing (76%), and psychodynamic personality assessment (64%). These three methods seem to be the predominant training approaches used by the sites included in the survey. This finding suggests that these are important directions for training at the graduate level, as well.

Of the topics being offered in the area of assessment training, report writing is most often taught (92%); 86% of the rotations conduct training in advanced assessment, 84% in providing feedback to clients, 74% in providing feedback to referral sources, 56% in introductory assessment, and 44% in the study of a specific test. This breakdown may reflect the priorities internship training directors place on areas of assessment or the areas in which students are less prepared upon leaving graduate school.

Piotrowski and Belter (1999) surveyed 84 APA-approved internship programs and found that 87% of their respondents required interns to participate in assessment seminars. If the demand for training is as critical as these surveys seem to indicate, it is curious that graduating students do not appear to be especially well prepared in this area. Training in basic assessment should be the job of graduate training programs, not internship sites, whose primary function should be in providing supervised practical experience in the field. From our findings and other surveys (Petzel & Berndt, 1980; Stedman, 1997), it appears that internship training directors prefer students who have been properly trained in a variety of assessment approaches, including self-report, performance based, and intelligence testing.

## POSTGRADUATE ASSESSMENT TRAINING

Although assessment practice during internship helps to develop skills, it is important to continue to refine these skills and add to them and to continue reading the current research literature in assessment. There are many opportunities to attend workshops that focus on particular tests or on the development of particular assessment skills. For example, there is a series of workshops available at various annual meetings of professional groups devoted to assessment, taught by assessment experts. This is an excellent way to build skills and to learn about the development of new instruments. Also, workshops, often offered for continuing education credit, are available throughout the year and are listed in the *APA Monitor*.

## PSYCHOLOGICAL ASSESSMENT IN HEALTH-CARE SETTINGS

The health-care field is beginning to appreciate the benefits of assessment in the evaluation of psychological and behavioral factors related to the treatment outcomes of medical procedures. Assessment in health-care settings emphasizes a biopsychosocial approach, in which assessment can target emotional factors along with the physical problems that are involved in the person's total functioning. Psychological assessment has become an integral part of this movement in health psychology (Handler & Meyer, 1998). Based on a meta-analysis, Meyer, et al. (2001) concluded that psychological testing is equivalent if not superior to medical diagnostic tests in their ability to predict treatment outcome. Similarly, the World Health Organization found psychopathology to be a stronger predictor of disability than disease severity (Ormel et al., 1994). Currently, many medical teams mandate that a psychosocial evaluation be performed prior to certain medical procedures, including bariatric surgery, bone marrow transplant, and solid organ transplant (Levenson & Olbrisch, 1993).

Assessments of medical patients generally adhere to the traditional biopsychosocial model of care (Engel, 1977), but strong evidence supports the superiority of the *collaborative* biopsychosocial model. In the collaborative model, psychologists and physicians jointly assess patients and draw conclusions from psychological and medical factors related to outcome (Gatchel, Peng, Peters, Fuchs, & Turk, 2007). Regardless of the assessment approach, psychologists evaluate the patient's current psychological functioning in order to inform the medical team of the ways in which this could affect recovery. In order to accomplish this task, assessors utilize various psychometric personality, symptom, neuropsychological, and transplant-specific assessment instruments (for a review of commonly used tests, see Collins & Labott, 2007) as well as a clinical interview. In the remainder of this section we focus on the applications and practice of psychological assessment for the medical management of chronic pain and for invasive surgical procedures.

An estimated 80% of physician visits are for the complaint of pain (Gatchel & Turk, 1996). Severe pain has been shown to be associated with a host of negative emotional conditions, mainly depression and anxiety (Pincus, Burton, Vogel, & Field, 2002; Van Dorsten, 2006). Based on a review of the literature, Van Dorsten and Weisberg (2011) concluded that depression poses the most significant threat to pain management treatment outcomes. Depression rates in patients reporting pain may reach as high as 2 to 3 times the prevalence rate of adults in the community (Bair, Robinson, Katon, & Kroenke, 2003; Reid, Engles-Horton, Weber, Kerns, Rogers, & O'Connor, 2002). The presence of anxiety is also associated with negative treatment outcome for pain (Granot & Farber, 2005; Mannion et al., 2007). Examinations of the comorbidity of pain and anxiety indicate an equally problematic relationship. In a study of 85,088 community adults, compared to those without pain, respondents with complaints of pain in multiple sites were roughly equally likely to also meet diagnostic criteria for a mood disorder or an anxiety disorder (Gureje, Von Korff, Kola, Demyttenaere, He, & Posada-Villa, 2008).

Research suggests that physicians accurately diagnose only 35% to 50% of major depressive disorder cases (Coyne, Schwenk, & Fechner-Bates, 1995), which suggests a distinct role for assessment psychologists in healthcare settings. Psychologists can identify risk factors for poor response to medical intervention through assessments procedures, which can then be used to inform subsequent medical and psychological care of the patient, as well as make empirically derived decisions regarding the risks of benefits of costly, elective surgical procedures.

Personality factors, including dysfunction and disorders, have also been associated with outcomes of medical pain management. Gatchel and Weisberg (2000) provided a comprehensive discussion of this topic. Within the chronic pain population, personality disorder prevalence is between 31% and 59% higher than in other medical populations and the general population (Weisberg, 2000). Given the high comorbidity of anxiety and depression in pain patients, Van Dorsten and Weisberg (in press) suggested that psychologists take into account acute emotional distress at the time of personality assessment with this population, particularly when treatment recommendations will be based on personality factors. Dorsten and Weisberg's review (in press) suggested that the MMPI-2 and the NEO Personality Inventory are the most commonly used personality measures in the assessment of chronic pain.

Psychosocial variables have been found to be a significant predictor of outcome following life-saving invasive surgical procedures (e.g., solid organ and bone marrow

transplant), and elective invasive procedures, such as bariatric and spine surgery. Psychiatric disorders are common among patients seeking transplant (for a comprehensive review, see Dew, Switzer, DiMartini, Matukaitis, Fitzgerald, & Kormos, 2000), with estimates of Axis I prevalence at 60%, Axis II at 32%, and comorbid Axis I and Axis II disorders at 25% (Chacko, Harper, Gotto, & Young, 1996). Bariatric surgery candidates had similarly high rates of psychiatric disorder diagnoses: one third carrying a mood disorder, one fifth with an anxiety disorder, and over one half having at least one current psychiatric diagnosis. Some evidence suggests that the presence of a psychiatric condition contributes to poorer surgical outcomes across the board. Bruns and Disorbio's (2009) systematic review suggested that depression, anxiety, and somatization were among the strongest psychosocial predictors of poor outcome. and have been empirically linked to surgical outcome. The high rates of psychiatric comorbidities among medical patients awaiting transplant necessitate comparison groups from medical populations. Normative data have been published with specific transplant populations, such as cardiac, kidney, liver, and bone marrow. In the case of bone marrow transplant, which is used to treat malignant and nonmalignant diseases, affective functioning, assessed by psychologists using psychometric tests (e.g., MMPI-2 and Beck Depression Inventory), were found to predict survival status and quality of life following transplant.

## ASSESSMENT AND MANAGED CARE ISSUES

Restrictions by managed care organizations (MCOs) have affected the amount of assessment clinicians are able to conduct (e.g., Eisman et al., 2000; Piotrowski, 1999). Piotrowski, Belter, and Keller (1998) found that 72% of psychologists in applied settings are conducting less assessment in general and are using fewer assessment instruments, especially lengthy assessment instruments, due to restrictions by MCOs. Likewise, Phelps, Eisman, and Kohout (1998) found that 79% of licensed psychologists felt that managed care had a negative impact on their work, and Acklin (1996) reported that clinicians are limiting their use of traditional assessment measures and are relying on briefer, problem-focused procedures.

With the growing influence of MCOs in mental health settings, it is inevitable that reimbursement practices will eventually affect training in assessment techniques and approaches (Piotrowski, 1999). We hope this will not be the case because of the many important training functions facilitated in assessment training, mentioned earlier in this chapter. Also, since we are training for the future, we must train students for the time when managed care will not dictate assessment practice. If, as we indicated earlier, assessment serves important training functions, it should continue to be enthusiastically taught, especially for the time when managed care will be merely a curiosity in the history of assessment. However, managed care has served us well in some ways, because we have sharpened and streamlined our approach to assessment and our instruments. We have focused anew on issues of reliability and validity of our measures, not merely in nomothetic research but in research that includes reference to a test's positive predictive power, negative predictive power, sensitivity, and specificity to demonstrate the validity of our measures. Psychologists have turned more and more to assessment in other areas, such as therapeutic assessment, disability assessment, assessment in child custody, and other forensic applications. The Society for Personality Assessment has reported an increase in membership and in attendance at annual meetings. We are optimistic that good evaluations, done in a competent manner and meaningfully communicated to the patient and referral source, will always be in great demand. Nevertheless, an investigation concerning the impact of managed care on assessment at internship settings found that there has been a decrease in the training emphasis of various assessment techniques; 43% of directors reported that managed care has had an impact on their program's assessment curriculum (Piotrowski & Belter, 1999). It is important to remember that MCOs do not dictate our ethical obligations; the interests of our clients do. It is the ethical psychologist's responsibility to persistently request compensation for assessment that can best serve the treatment needs of the client. However, even if psychologists are denied reimbursement, it does not mean they should not do assessments when they are indicated. Therefore, options for meeting both financial needs of the clinician and health-care needs of the client should be considered. One solution may be the integration of assessment into the therapy process. Techniques such as the Early Memories Procedure, sentence completion tasks, brief questionnaires, and figure drawings may be incorporated into the therapy without requiring a great deal of additional contact or scoring time.

## POLITICS IN PERSONALITY ASSESSMENT

For many years there has been a very active debate, and sometimes even animosity and expressions of derision,

between those who preferred a more objective approach to personality assessment (read self-report and MMPI) and those who preferred a more subjective approach (read projective tests and Rorschach). This schism was fueled by researchers and teachers of assessment. Each group disparaged the other's instruments, viewing them as irrelevant at best and essentially useless, while championing the superiority of its own instruments (e.g., Holt, 1970; Meehl, 1956).

This debate seems ill advised to us, and it should be described in this way to students, in order to bring assessment integration practices to the forefront. These misleading attitudes have unfortunately been transmitted to graduate students by instructors and supervisors over many years. Gradually, however, the gulf between the two seemingly opposing approaches has narrowed. Clinicians have come to use both types of tests, but the great deal of misperception about each type interferes with productive integration and impairs clinicians' efforts to do assessment rather than testing. Perhaps in the future teachers of personality assessment will make fewer and fewer pejorative remarks about each other's preferred instruments and will concentrate more and more on the focal issue of test integration.

Another issue is the place of assessment in the clinical psychology curriculum. For many years graduate curricula contained many courses in assessment. The number of courses has gradually been reduced, in part because the curricula have become crowded with important courses mandated by the APA, such as professional ethics, biological bases of behavior, cognitive and affective aspects of behavior, social aspects of behavior, history and systems, psychological measurement, research methodology, techniques of data analysis, individual differences, human development, and psychopathology, as well as courses in psychotherapy and in cultural and individual diversity (Committee on Accreditation, Education Directorate, & American Psychological Association, 1996). Courses have also been added because they have become important for clinical training (e.g., child therapy, marital therapy, health psychology, neuropsychology, hypnosis). Therefore, there is sometimes little room for assessment courses. To complicate matters even more, some instructors question the necessity of teaching assessment at all. Despite the published survey data, we know of programs that have no identified courses in assessment, and programs in which only one type of measure (e.g., self-report, interview, or projective measures) is taught. While most programs do have courses in assessment, the content of some courses does not prepare students to do effective assessment.

Sometimes the courses offered are merely survey courses, or courses in which the student administers and scores one of each type of test. With the impact of cognitive therapy there have been radical changes in the ways in which some training programs teach assessment, seemingly without knowledge of the significant improvements in assessment research and practice that have taken place in the past 20 years or so. There seems to be a "Throw the baby out with the bathwater" approach, whereby traditional instruments are derided and replaced primarily with self-report measures. This is an important issue because it has major implications for teaching assessment in graduate school and in internship settings. For example, Wetzler (1989) describes a hospital-based assessment approach in which a general broadly focused assessment has been replaced with a so-called focal approach, using self-report instruments. These changes, he indicates, have come about because of shorter hospitalization stays, and because what he calls "the standard battery" (Rapaport, Gill, & Schafer, 1968) is no longer appropriate. He believes the questions that need to be answered in this acute problem setting cannot be adequately addressed using the "traditional" assessment approach. He lists a number of reported dissatisfactions with "traditional assessment" procedures, which include the problem that "test findings do not respond to [the] referral questions." His solution is to replace "traditional assessment" with "focal assessment," which includes the use of observer rating scales, self-report inventories, and a number of questionnaires derived from psychological research rather than from clinical observation or theory. He describes focal tests as specialized instruments considering specific areas of psychopathology, which have a much narrower focus and are "more concrete and descriptive, focused on surface symptoms and behavior, with clearly defined criteria for scoring, and with normative data available."

We do not agree with a number of Wetzler's conclusions; we believe the approach he described comes closer to the definition we used earlier of testing than it does to assessment, since only self-report measures are employed, and test scores are emphasized rather than the development of integrated findings. The overemphasis on the validity of test scores does not take into account the validity of their use in a particular clinical setting without the concomitant understanding of the patient's feelings and his or her experience of being hospitalized, as well as other important issues that would make these disembodied test scores more meaningful. What is lacking is an understanding of and an appreciation for the patient's contextual world, which we emphasize in our teaching. We have no way of knowing whether the patient responded to these instruments in a meaningful manner. Validity of the instrument may be only an illusion in many cases, in which patients take a test with perhaps questionable motivation and a nonfacilitative orientation. Wetzler's approach to assessment is a prototype of other similar approaches that are convenience driven, test driven, and technician driven; it is a most dangerous approach, in which the role of the assessor is primarily to choose the right test, and the test scores are said to provide the appropriate answers.

Earlier in this chapter we emphasized that psychologists should be well trained in the area of psychometrics and in the limitations of tests, especially issues related to of reliability and validity. In testing, one seeks the assistance of confidence limits of the results, but in assessment, one determines the validity of the results of the test scores by taking into account a host of variables determined from interview data, from observations of the patient during the assessment, and from the similarities and differences among the various assessment findings. It is doubtful whether the proper evaluation of the test scores can be accomplished in the focused approach. More to the point, however, is the criticism that there is actually a rigid adherence to a traditional battery. Our survey of test use in internship settings suggests otherwise; internship directors reported that a wide variety of tests are employed in assessment in their setting. We do not recommend or teach adherence to a traditional test battery, although these assessment devices are among those recommended for use, for reasons discussed in this chapter. We believe innovations in assessment should be employed to improve the validity of the assessment procedure and to improve the delivery of assessment services to those who request them. If the referral questions are not answered in an assessment, it is the fault of the assessor, who has not paid attention to the referral issue or who has not sufficiently clarified the referral issue with the person requesting the assessment.

To describe an approach we believe is more typical of assessment rather than testing, also in a hospital setting, we review the approaches of Blais and Eby (1998), in which psychologists have even more stringent demands on them to provide focal answers, often within a day. Blais and Eby trained their internship students to assist the referring physician in clarifying referral questions. After a brief discussion with the nurse in charge of the patient, a review of the patient's chart, or both, the student is to select the appropriate tests and procedures to answer the referral questions, taking into account the necessary turnaround time and both the physical and psychological limitations of the patient.

In a training case example in which the turnaround time was less than a day, Blais and Eby (1998) described a battery that included a seven-subtest short form of the WAIS-R, the Rorschach, four TAT cards, and the PAI. The brief WAIS-R took less than 30 minutes to administer. Since the patient was described by the staff as extremely guarded, projective testing was viewed as crucial. The Rorschach and the TAT were chosen, the latter to identify the patient's object relations and core interpersonal themes, and both tests served to determine the degree of suicidal ideation. The PAI was chosen rather than the MMPI-2 because it is significantly shorter and the patient had poor physical stamina, and because it can be scored as a short form, using only 199 of its 344 items. It also contained several treatment planning scales that could possibly provide important information relevant to a referral question about treatment.

Although the battery described for this individual patient did include the traditional tests, batteries designed for other patients might not include *any* of the traditional tests. In addition, these tests were employed not because they were traditional but, rather, because each offered something that the other measures did not offer. Also, the manner in which they are scored is directly tied to a large body of research, including, in the case of the Rorschach, extensive normative findings and reliability and validity data. The Rorschach was scored using the Comprehensive System (Exner, 2003), which includes a well-validated suicide constellation measure along with a host of other scores of importance to the referral issue, and with the Lerner Defense Scale (P. Lerner and Lerner, 1980). The TAT was scored as well, using the Social Cognition and Object Relations Scale (SCORS) system, a research-based interpretive system that measures eight aspects of object relations (Westen, 1991a, 1991b). The data were integrated into a picture of the patient's current psychological functioning and categorized according to thought quality, affect, defenses, and relationship to self and others, all issues directly related to the referral questions. Verbal report was given to the referring psychiatrist by telephone well before rounds the next morning, along with treatment recommendations.

The assessment approach designed by Blais and Eby (1998) is an example of a hospital-based assessment that demonstrates that traditional tests can be employed with quite rapid turnaround time and that a test battery that includes traditional tests need not be rigidly fixed. In their approach, the clinicians responded flexibly and actively in the assessment process, integrating data from several different sources and responding in an efficient and rapid

manner to focalized referral issues generated from several sources. In Wetzler's (1989) approach, the response was to develop a test-focused approach rather than a person-focused approach. Sharing the information in this section of our chapter with students helps to impress them with the importance of taking a person-focused approach to personality assessment.

## PERSONALITY ASSESSMENT IN THE FUTURE

In this section we describe several changes we foresee in personality assessment teaching and practice as well as changes we would like to see.

### The Assessment of Psychological Health and the Rise of Positive Psychology

Psychological assessment has typically been tied to the medical model, in which health is defined as the absence of pathology rather than as an aggregate of positive psychological traits that differentiate the psychologically healthy person from others (e.g., Adler, 1958; Erikson, 1963; Maslow, 1954; Rogers, 1961). Seligman and Csikszentmihalyi (2000) have suggested using the term *positive psychology* instead. Such variables as playfulness, the ability to self-soothe and to be soothed by others, psychological-mindedness, flexibility, and the ability to establish intimacy and to express tenderness in relationships are important variables to consider. Seligman has discussed the concept of optimism, and several of the variables discussed by the Big Five theorists, such as openness to experience (McCrae, 1996), surgency, and agreeableness (Goldberg, 1992) describe positive aspects of personality functioning. The surgency factor includes such concepts as extroversion, energy level, spontaneity, assertiveness, sociability, and adventurousness. The agreeableness factor includes interpersonal warmth, cooperativeness, unselfishness, and generosity. In the future we expect to see a number of scoring systems to measure the variables described in this chapter using traditional tests as well as a number of new tests specially designed to tap positive psychology variables. The *Journal of Personality Assessment* published a special series, The Assessment of Psychological Health (Handler & Potash, 1999), which included a discussion of four variables that were measured using traditional tests: optimism, creativity, playfulness, and transitional relatedness. Handler and Potash (1999) suggested that in the future students should be taught to routinely measure these variables and discuss them in feedback.

## Assessment on the Internet

Schlosser (1991) envisioned a future in which computers would present test takers with stimuli ranging from verbal items to moving projective stimuli, including stimuli with synthesized smells. He conceived of the use of virtual reality techniques, computer-generated simulations in which images, sounds, and tactile sensations would be produced to create a synthetic, three-dimensional representation of reality. Twenty years later we found that a great deal of testing (not assessment) is being done on the Internet, but we have not yet approached Schlosser's vision. This procedure offers the psychologist a number of fascinating opportunities, but it also presents a number of professional and ethical problems. Much research needs to be done to determine the effects of differences in the interpersonal setting with this more artificial Internet approach for various clinical populations. Just because the interaction simulates the traditional approach does not mean the experience of the assessor and the patient will be similar to that of the traditional approach.

These issues seem modest to some psychologists, who even now offer screening tests for depression, anxiety, sexual disorders, attention-deficit disorder, and various personality disorders. Students should be made aware that such blunt feedback of test results does not meet APA ethics requirements. There is also a long list of other ethical issues in this approach that should be discussed in class, because these problems will face students in the future. Buchanan (2002) and Naglieri, et al. (2004) have provided broad discussions of the benefits and limitations of Web-based assessment. Nevertheless, Internet testing promises to be a great help for people who for one reason or another cannot get to a psychologist's office to be tested or for people in rural communities in which there are no such services available.

## Expanded Conception of Intelligence

Wechsler's definition of intelligence—"the aggregate or global capacity to act purposefully, think rationally, and to deal effectively with [the] environment" (1958, p. 7)—is hardly reflected in his intelligence tests. The definition implies that being interpersonally effective and thinking clearly are important intellectual variables. However, these and other variables suggested by Wechsler's definition are personality variables as well. Thus, it appears that personality variables and so-called intelligence variables overlap to some extent. Indeed, Daniel Goleman, in his book *Emotional Intelligence* (1995), highlighted the importance of emotional and social factors as measures of intelligence. He described an expanded model of what it means to be intelligent, emphasizing such variables as being able to motivate oneself and persist in the face of frustration; the ability to control impulses; the ability to delay gratification; the ability to regulate one's moods and to keep distress from interfering with thought processes; the ability to empathize and to hope. Other researchers in the area of intelligence have discussed similar issues. For example, Gardner (1993) and Salovey (Mayer & Salovey, 1993; Salovey & Mayer, 1989–1990) have discussed the importance of interpersonal intelligence, defined as "the ability to understand other people; what motivates them, how they work; how to work cooperatively with them" (Goleman, 1995, p. 39), and intrapersonal intelligence, defined as "the capacity to form an accurate, veridical model of oneself and to be able to use that model to operate effectively in life" (Goleman, 1995, p. 43). Mayer, Caruso, & Solovey (2000) focused on four areas of emotional intelligence: perception, facilitation, understanding, and management of emotions. Bar-On and Parker (2000) have compiled a handbook of emotional intelligence, in which they also include the concepts of alexithymia and what they term *practical intelligence*. Nevertheless, researchers and test constructors seem to focus on a more traditional definition of intelligence variables. Although clinical psychologists take these important variables into account in describing personality functioning, they do not typically construct intelligence tests with these interpersonal and intrapersonal variables in mind. Although there are now measures of emotional intelligence available for adults (e.g., the Bar-On Emotional Quotient Inventory; Bar-On, 1997) and for children (e.g., the Emotional Intelligence Scale for Children; Sullivan, 1999), emotional intelligence measures have yet to be integrated as parts of more traditional tests measuring other intelligence factors. However, their use in the future will undoubtedly go a long way toward a more integrated view of human functioning than exists in the somewhat arbitrary split between the concepts of intelligence and personality.

## REFERENCES

Ackerman, S., Hilsenroth, M., Baity, M., & Blagys, M. (2000). Interaction of therapeutic process and alliance during psychological assessment. *Journal of Personality Assessment*, 75, 82–109.

Acklin, M. (1996). Personality assessment and managed care. *Journal of Personality Assessment*, 66, 194–201.

Adler, A. (1958). *What life should mean to you*. New York, NY: Capricorn.

Allen, J. (1998). Personality assessment with American Indians and Alaska Natives: Instrument considerations and service delivery style. *Journal of Personality Assessment*, 70, 17–42.

American Educational Research Association, American Psychological Association, and the National Council on Measurement in Education. (2004). *Standards for educational and psychological testing*. Washington, DC: Author.

American Psychological Association. (1992). Ethical principles of psychologists and code of conduct. *American Psychologist, 47*, 1597–1611.

Anastasi, A., & Urbina, S. (1998). *Psychological testing* (7th ed.). Upper Saddle River, NJ: Prentice Hall.

Applebaum, S. (1990). The relationship between assessment and psychotherapy. *Journal of Personality Assessment, 54*, 79–80.

Aschieri, F., & Smith, J. D. (under review). The effectiveness of an adult Therapeutic Assessment: A single-case time-series experiment.

Bair, M. J., Robinson, R. L., Katon, W. J., & Kroenke, K. (2003). Depression and pain comorbidity: A literature review. *Archives of Internal Medicine, 163*, 2433–2445.

Bar-On, R. (1997). *The Bar On Emotional Quotient Inventory*. North Tonawanda, NY: Multi-Health Systems.

Bar-On, R., & Parker, J. (Eds.). (2000). *The handbook of emotional intelligence*. San Francisco, CA: Jossey-Bass.

Barrick, M., & Mount, M. (1991). The big five personality dimensions and job performance: A meta-analysis. *Personnel Psychology, 44*, 1–26.

Belter, R., & Piotrowski, C. (1999). Current status of master's-level training in psychological assessment. *Journal of Psychological Practice, 5*, 1–5.

Bennett, B. E., Bryant, B. K., VandenBos, G. R., & Greenwood, A. (1990). *Professional liability and risk management*. Washington, DC: American Psychological Association.

Beutler, L., & Berren, M. (1995). *Integrative assessment of adult personality*. New York, NY: Guilford Press.

Beutler, L., & Groth-Marnat, G. (2005). *Integrative assessment of adult personality* (2nd ed.). New York, NY: Guilford Press.

Blais, M., & Eby, M. (1998). Jumping into fire: Internship training in personality assessment. In L. Handler & M. Hilsenroth (Eds.), *Teaching and learning personality assessment* (pp. 485–500). Mahwah, NJ: Erlbaum.

Bornstein, R. (1993). *The dependent personality*. New York, NY: Guilford Press.

Brabender, V. (1992, March). *Graduate program training models*. Paper presented at the meeting of the Society for Personality Assessment, Washington, DC.

Bram, A. D. (2010). The relevance of the Rorschach and patient–examiner relationship in treatment planning and outcome assessment. *Journal of Personality Assessment, 92*(2), 91–115.

Bruhn, A. (1990). *Earliest childhood memories, Vol. 1: Theory and application to clinical practice*. New York, NY: Praeger.

Bruhn, A. (1992). The early memories procedure: A projective test of autobiographical memory. *Journal of Personality Assessment, 58*, 1–25.

Bruns, D., & Disorbio, J. M. (2009). Assessment of biopsychosocial risk factors for medical treatment: A collaborative approach. *Journal of Clinical Psychology in Medical Settings, 16*, 127–147.

Buchanan, T. (2002). Online assessment: Desirable or dangerous? *Professional Psychology: Research and Practice, 33*(2), 148–154.

Burley, T., & Handler, L. (1997). Personality factors in the accurate interpretation of projective tests: The Draw-A-Person Test. In E. Hammer (Ed.), *Advances in projective test interpretation* (pp. 359–380). Springfield, IL: Charles C Thomas.

Byrne, B. M., Oakland, T., Leong, F. T. L., van de Vijver, F. J. R., Hambleton, R. K., Cheung, F. M., & Bartram, D. (2009). A critical analysis of cross-cultural research and testing practices: Implications for improved education and training in psychology. *Training and Education in Professional Psychology, 3*(2), 94–105.

Camara, W., Nathan, J., & Puente, A. (2000). Psychological test usage: Implications in professional psychology. *Professional Psychology: Research and Practice, 31*, 141–154.

Chacko, R. C., Harper, R. G., Gotto, J., & Young, J. (1996). Psychiatric interview and psychometric predictors of cardiac transplant survival. *American Journal of Psychiatry, 153*, 1607–1612.

Childs, R., & Eyde, L. (2002). Assessment training in clinical psychology doctoral programs: What should we teach? What do we teach? *Journal of Personality Assessment, 78*(1), 130–144.

Clemence, A., & Handler, L. (2001). Psychological assessment on internship: A survey of training directors and their expectations for students. *Journal of Personality Assessment, 76*, 18–47.

Collins, C. A., & Labott, S. M. (2007). Psychological assessment of candidates for solid organ transplantation. *Professional Psychology: Research and Practice, 38*(2), 150–157.

Committee on Accreditation, Education Directorate, & American Psychological Association. (1996). *Guidelines and principles for accreditation of programs in professional psychology, January 1, 1996*. Washington, DC: American Psychological Association.

Coyne, J. C., Schwenk, T. L., & Fechner-Bates, S. (1995). Nondetection of depression by primary care physicians reconsidered. *General Hospital Psychiatry, 17*, 3–12.

Cramer, P. (1996). *Storytelling, narrative and the Thematic Apperception Test*. New York, NY: Guilford Press.

Cramer, P. (2006). *Protecting the self: Defense mechanisms in action*. New York, NY: Guilford Press.

Cuéllar, I. (1998). Cross-cultural clinical psychological assessment of Hispanic Americans. *Journal of Personality Assessment, 70*, 71–86.

Curry, K. T., & Hanson, W. E. (2010). National survey of psychologists' test feedback training, supervision, and practice: A mixed methods study. *Journal of Personality Assessment, 92*(1), 327–336.

Dana, R. H. (2000a). Culture and methodology in personality assessment. In I. Cueller & F. A. Paniagua (Eds.), *Handbook of multicultural mental health* (pp. 97–120). San Diego, CA: Academic Press.

Dana, R. H. (Ed.). (2000b). *Handbook of cross-cultural and multicultural personality assessment*. Mahwah, NJ: Erlbaum.

Deering, C. (1994). Parallel process in the supervision of child psychotherapy. *American Journal of Psychotherapy, 48*, 102–108.

Dew, M. A., Switzer, G. E., DiMartini, A. F., Matukaitis, J., Fitzgerald, M. G., & Kormos, R. L. (2000). Psychosocial assessments and outcomes in organ transplantation. *Progress in Transplantation, 10*, 239–261.

Eisman, E. J., Dies, R. R., Finn, S. E., Eyde, L. D., Kay, G. G., Kubiszyn, T. W.,... Moreland, K. L. (2000). Problems and limitations in using psychological assessment in the contemporary health care delivery system. *Professional Psychology: Research and Practice, 31*(2), 131–140.

Engel, G. (1977). The need for a new medical model: A challenge for biomedicine. *Science, 196*, 129–136.

Erikson, E. (1963). *Childhood and society* (2nd ed.). New York, NY: Wiley.

Exner, J. E. Jr. (2003). *The Rorschach: A comprehensive system* (4th ed.). Hoboken, NJ: Wiley.

Eyde, L. D., & Childs, R. A. (2000). Qualifications of assessment faculty in clinical psychology doctoral programs: An analysis of American Psychological Association membership data. *Professional Psychology: Research and Practice, 31*(2), 165–169.

Finn, S. E. (1996a). Assessment feedback integrating MMPI-2 and Rorschach findings. *Journal of Personality Assessment, 67*(3), 543–557.

Finn, S. [E.] (1996b). *A manual for using the MMPI-2 as a therapeutic intervention*. Minneapolis, MN: University of Minnesota Press.

Finn, S. E. (2003). Therapeutic assessment of a man with "ADD." *Journal of Personality Assessment, 80*(2), 115–129.

Finn, S. E. (2007). *In our client's shoes: Theory and techniques of Therapeutic Assessment*. Mahwah, NJ: Erlbaum.

Finn, S. E. (2009). Core values in Therapeutic Assessment. Excerpt from the Therapeutic Assessment website, www.therapeutic assessment.com

Finn, S. [E.], Fischer, C., & Handler, L. (2012). *A guide to Collaborative/Therapeutic Assessment*. Hoboken, NJ: Wiley.

Finn, S. [E.], & Martin, H. (1997). Therapeutic assessment with the MMPI-2 in managed healthcare. In J. Butcher (Ed.), *Objective psychological assessment in managed healthcare: A practitioner's guide* (pp. 131–152). New York, NY: Oxford University Press.

Finn, S. [E.], & Tonsager, M. (1992). The therapeutic effects of providing MMPI-2 test feedback to college students awaiting psychotherapy. *Psychological Assessment, 4*, 278–287.

Finn, S. E., & Tonsager, M. E. (1997). Information-gathering and therapeutic models of assessment: Complementary paradigms. *Psychological Assessment, 9*(4), 374–385.

Fischer, C. (1994). *Individualizing psychological assessment*. Hillsdale, NJ: Erlbaum.

Fowler, J. (1998). The trouble with learning personality assessment. In L. Handler & M. Hilsenroth (Eds.), *Teaching and learning personality assessment* (pp. 31–44). Mahwah, NJ: Erlbaum.

Fowler, J., Hilsenroth, M., & Handler, L. (1995). Early memories: An exploration of theoretically derived queries and their clinical utility. *Bulletin of the Menninger Clinic, 59*, 79–98.

Fowler, J., Hilsenroth, M., & Handler, L. (1996). A mulitmethod approach to assessing dependency: The early memory dependency probe. *Journal of Personality Assessment, 67*, 399–413.

Ganellen, R. (1996). *Integrating the Rorschach and the MMPI-2 in personality assessment*. Mahwah, NJ: Erlbaum.

Ganellen, R. (1999). Weighing the evidence for the Rorschach's validity: A response to Wood et al. *Journal of Personality Assessment, 77*, 1–15.

Gardner, H. (1993). *Multiple intelligences: The theory in practice*. New York, NY: Basic Books.

Gatchel, R. J., Peng, Y. B., Peters, M. L., Fuchs, P. N., & Turk, D. C. (2007). The biopsychosocial approach to chronic pain: Scientific advances and future directions. *Psychological Bulletin, 133*, 581–624.

Gatchel, R. J., & Turk, D. C. (1996). *Psychological approaches to pain management: A practitioners handbook*. New York, NY: Guilford Press.

Gatchel, R. J., & Weisberg, J. N. (2000). *Personality characteristics of patients with pain*. Washington, DC: American Psychological Association.

Goldberg, L. (1992). The development of markers for the Big-Five factor structure. *Psychological Assessment, 4*, 26–42.

Goleman, D. (1995). *Emotional intelligence*. New York, NY: Bantam.

Granot, M., & Ferber, S. G. (2005). The roles of pain catastophizing and anxiety in the prediction of postoperative pain intensity: A prospective study. *Clinical Journal of Pain, 21*, 439–445.

Gureje, O., Von Korff, M., Kola, L., Demyttenaere, K., He, Y., & Posada-Villa, J. (2008). The relation between multiple pain and mental disorders: Results for the World Mental Health Surveys. *Pain, 135*, 82–91.

Handler, L. (1996). The clinical use of the Draw-A-Person Test (DAP), the House-Tree-Person Test and the Kinetic Family Drawing Test. In C. Newmark (Ed.), *Major psychological assessment techniques* (2nd ed., pp. 206–293). Needham Heights, MA: Allyn & Bacon.

Handler, L. (2006). The use of therapeutic assessment with children and adolescents. In S. R. Smith & L. Handler (Eds.), *The clinical assessment of children and adolescents: A practitioner's handbook* (pp. 53–72). Mahwah, NJ: Erlbaum.

Handler, L., Fowler, J., & Hilsenroth, M. (1998). Teaching and learning issues in an advanced course in personality assessment. In L. Handler & M. Hilsenroth (Eds.), *Teaching and learning personality assessment* (pp. 431–452). Mahwah, NJ: Erlbaum.

Handler, L., & Habenicht, D. (1994). The Kinetic Family Drawing Technique: A review of the literature. *Journal of Personality Assessment, 62*, 440–464.

Handler, L., & Hilsenroth, M. (1998). *Teaching and learning personality assessment*. Mahwah, NJ: Erlbaum.

Handler, L., & Meyer, G. (1998). The importance of teaching and learning personality assessment. In L. Handler & M. Hilsenroth (Eds.), *Teaching and learning personality assessment* (pp. 3–30). Mahwah, NJ: Erlbaum.

Handler, L., & Potash, H. (1999). The assessment of psychological health [Introduction, Special series]. *Journal of Personality Assessment, 72*, 181–184.

Hanson, W., Claiborn, C., & Kerr, B. (1997). Differential effects of two test interpretation styles in counseling: A field study. *Journal of Counseling Psychology, 44*, 400–405.

Hershey, J., Kopplin, D., & Cornell, J. (1991). Doctors of psychology: Their career experiences and attitudes toward degree and training. *Professional Psychology: Research and Practice, 22*, 351–356.

Hilsenroth, M. (1998). Using metaphor to understand projective test data: A training heuristic. In L. Handler & M. Hilsenroth (Eds.), *Teaching and learning personality assessment* (pp. 391–412). Mahwah, NJ: Erlbaum.

Hilsenroth, M., & Handler, L. (1995). A survey of graduate students' experiences, interests, and attitudes about learning the Rorschach. *Journal of Personality Assessment, 64*, 243–257.

Hilsenroth, M. J., Peters, E. J., & Ackerman, S. J. (2004). The development of therapeutic alliance during psychological assessment: Patient and therapist perspectives across treatment. *Journal of Personality Assessment, 83*(3), 332–344.

Holsopple, J., & Miale, F. (1954). *Sentence completion: A projective method for the study of personality*. Springfield, IL: Charles C Thomas.

Holt, R. (1970). Yet another look at clinical and statistical prediction: Or, is clinical psychology worthwhile? *American Psychologist, 25*, 337–349.

Holt, R. (1977). A method for assessing primary process manifestations and their control in Rorschach responses. In M. Rickers-Ovsiankina (Ed.), *Rorschach psychology* (pp. 375–420). Huntington, NY: Kreiger.

Kinder, B. (1994). Where the action is in personality assessment. *Journal of Personality Assessment, 62*, 585–588.

Klopfer, B., Ainsworth, M., Klopfer, W., & Holt, R. (1954). *Development in the Rorschach technique* (Vol. 1). New York, NY: World Book.

Koocher, G., & Keith-Spiegel, P. (1998). *Ethics in psychology: Professional standards and cases* (2nd ed.). New York, NY: Oxford University Press.

Krakowski, A. (1984). Stress and the practice of medicine: III. Physicians compared with lawyers. *Psychotherapy and Psychosomatics, 42*, 143–151.

Kubeszyn, T., Meyer, G., Finn, S., Eyde, L., Kay, G., Moreland, K., . . . Eisman, E. (2000). Empirical support for psychological assessment in health care settings. *Professional Psychology: Research and Practice, 31*(2), 119–130.

Lerner, P., & Lerner, H. (1980). Rorschach assessment of primitive defenses in borderline personality structure. In J. Kwarer, H. Lerner, P. Lerner, & A. Sugarman (Eds.), *Borderline phenomena and the Rorschach test* (pp. 257–274). New York, NY: International Universities Press.

Levenson, J. L., & Olbrisch, M. E. (1993). Psychosocial evaluation of organ transplant candidates: A comparative survey of process, criteria, and outcomes in heart, liver, and kidney transplantation. *Psychosomatics, 34*, 314–323.

Lindsey, M. (1998). Culturally competent assessment of African American clients. *Journal of Personality Assessment*, *70*, 43–53.

Mannion, A. F., Elfering, A., Staerkle, R., Junge, A., Grob, D., Dvorak, J., & et al. (2007). Predictors of multidimensional outcome after spinal surgery. *European Spine Journal*, *16*, 777–786.

Martin, H. (2009). A bright future for psychological assessment. *Psychotherapy Bulletin*, *44*, 23–26.

Maruish, M. E. (Ed.). (2004). *The use of psychological testing for treatment planning and outcomes assessment*. Mahwah, NJ: Erlbaum.

Masling, J., Rabie, L., & Blondheim, S. (1967). Relationships of oral imagery to yielding behavior and birth order. *Journal of Consulting Psychology*, *32*, 89–91.

Maslow, A. (1954). *Motivation and personality*. New York, NY: Harper & Row.

Mayer, J., Caruso, D., & Salovey, P. (2000). Selecting a measure of emotional intelligence: The case for ability scales. In R. Bar-On & J. Parker (Eds.), *The handbook of emotional intelligence* (pp. 320–342). San Francisco, CA: Jossey-Bass.

Mayer, J., & Salovey, P. (1993). The intelligence of emotional intelligence. *Intelligence*, *7*, 433–442.

McCrae, R. (1996). Social consequences of experiential openness. *Psychological Bulletin*, *120*, 323–337.

Mednick, S., & Mednick, M. (1967). *Examiner's manual: Remote Associates Test*. Boston, MA: Houghton Mifflin.

Meehl, P. (1956). Wanted: A good cookbook. *American Psychologist*, *11*, 263–272.

Meyer, G. (1997). On the integration of personality assessment methods: The Rorschach and the MMPI-2. *Journal of Personality Assessment*, *68*, 297–330.

Meyer, G., & Archer, R. (2001). The hard science of Rorschach research: What do we know and where do we go? *Psychological Assessment*, *13*(4), 486–502.

Meyer, G., Finn, S., Eyde, L., Kay, G., Moreland, K., Dies, R., ... Reed, J. (2001). Psychological testing and psychological assessment: A review of evidence and issues. *American Psychologist*, *56*, 128–165.

Meyer, G., & Handler, L. (1997). The ability of the Rorschach to predict subsequent outcome: A meta-analytic analysis of the Rorschach Prognostic Rating Scale. *Journal of Personality Assessment*, *69*(1), 1–38.

Meyer, G., Riethmiller, R., Brooks, R., Benoit, W., & Handler, L. (2000). A replication of Rorschach and MMPI-2 convergent validity. *Journal of Personality Assessment*, *74*(2), 175–215.

Michel, D. M. (2002). Psychological assessment as a therapeutic intervention in patients hospitalized with eating disorders. *Professional Psychology: Research and Practice*, *33*(5), 470–477.

Mihura, J. L., & Weinle, C. A. (2002). Rorschach training: Doctoral students' experiences and preferences. *Journal of Personality Assessment*, *79*(1), 39–52.

Naglieri, J. A., Drasgow, F., Schmit, M., Handler, L., Prifitera, A., Margolis, A., & Velasquez, R. (2004). Psychological testing on the Internet: New problems, old issues. *American Psychologist*, *59*(3), 150–162.

Newman, M. L. (2004). *Psychological assessment as brief psychotherapy: Therapeutic effects of providing MMPI—A test feedback to adolescents*. (Unpublished doctoral dissertation). La Trobe University, Australia.

Newman, M. L., & Greenway, P. (1997). Therapeutic effects of providing MMPI-2 test feedback to clients at a university counseling service: A collaborative approach. *Psychological Assessment*, *9*, 122–131.

Norcross, J. C., Karpiak, C. P., & Santoro, S. O. (2005). Clinical psychologists across the years: The Division of Clinical Psychology from 1960 to 2003. *Journal of Clinical Psychology*, *61*(12), 1467–1483.

Nunnally, J., & Bernstein, I. (1994). *Psychometric theory* (3rd ed.). New York, NY: McGraw-Hill.

Okazaki, S. (1998). Psychological assessment of Asian-Americans: Research agenda for cultural competency. *Journal of Personality Assessment*, *70*, 54–70.

Ormel, J., VonKorff, M., Ustun, T. B., Pini, S., Korten, S., & Oldehinkel, T. (1994). Common mental disorders and disability across cultures. Results from the WHO Collaborative Study on Psychological Problems in General Health Care. *Journal of the American Medical Association*, *272*, 1741–1748.

Ougrin, D., Ng, A. V., & Low, L. (2008). Therapeutic assessment based on cognitive-analytic therapy for young people presenting with self-harm: Pilot study. *Psychiatric Bulletin*, *32*, 423–426.

Peters, E. J., Handler, L., White, K., & Winkel, J. (2008). "Am I going crazy, doc?": A self psychology approach to Therapeutic Assessment. *Journal of Personality Assessment*, *90*(5), 421–434.

Petzel, T., & Berndt, D. (1980). APA internship selection criteria: Relative importance of academic and clinical preparation. *Professional Psychology*, *11*, 792–796.

Phelps, R., Eisman, E., & Kohout, J. (1998). Psychological practice and managed care: Results of the CAPP practitioner study. *Professional Psychology: Research and Practice*, *29*, 31–36.

Pincus, T., Burton, K., Vogel, S., & Field, A. P. (2002). A systematic review of psychological factors as predictors of chronicity/disability in prospective cohorts of low back pain. *Spine*, *27*, 109–120.

Piotrowski, C. (1999). Assessment practices in the era of managed care: Current status and future directions. *Journal of Clinical Psychology*, *55*, 787–796.

Piotrowski, C., & Belter, R. W. (1999). Internship training in psychological assessment: Has managed care had an impact? *Assessment*, *6*, 381–389.

Piotrowski, C., Belter, R., & Keller, J. (1998). The impact of managed care on the practice of psychological testing: Preliminary findings. *Journal of Personality Assessment*, *70*, 441–447.

Plante, T. (1995). Training child clinical predoctoral interns and postdoctoral fellows in ethics and professional issues: An experiential model. *Professional Psychology: Research and Practice*, *26*, 616–619.

Plante, T. (1999). Ten strategies for psychology trainees and practicing psychologists interested in avoiding ethical and legal perils. *Psychotherapy*, *36*, 398–403.

Poston, J. M., & Hanson, W. E. (2010). Meta-analysis of psychological assessment as a therapeutic intervention. *Psychological Assessment*, *22*(2), 203–212.

Potash, H. (1998). Assessing the social subject. In L. Handler & M. Hilsenroth (Eds.), *Teaching and learning personality assessment* (pp. 137–148). Mahwah, NJ: Erlbaum.

Rapaport, D., Gill, M., & Schafer, R. (1968). In R. Holt (Ed.), *Diagnostic psychological testing* (2nd ed.). New York, NY: International Universities Press.

Reid, M. C., Engles-Horton, L. L., Weber, M. B., Kerns, R. D., Rogers, E. L., & O'Connor, P. G. (2002). Use of opiod medications for chronic non-cancer pain syndromes in primary care. *Journal of General Internal Medicine*, *17*, 173–179.

Retzlaff, P. (1992). Professional training in psychological testing: New teachers and new tests. *Journal of Training and Practice in Professional Psychology*, *6*, 45–50.

Rezler, A., & Buckley, J. (1977). A comparison of personality types among female student health professionals. *Journal of Medical Education*, *52*, 475–477.

Riethmiller, R., & Handler, L. (1997a). The great figure drawing controversy: The integration of research and practice [Special series]. *Journal of Personality Assessment*, *69*, 488–496.

Riethmiller, R., & Handler, L. (1997b). Problematic methods and unwarranted conclusions in DAP research: Suggestions for improved procedures [Special series]. *Journal of Personality Assessment*, *69*, 459–475.

Robins, C., Blatt, S., & Ford, R. (1991). Changes on human figure drawings during intensive treatment. *Journal of Personality Assessment*, *57*, 477–497.

Rogers, C. (1961). *On becoming a person: A therapist's view of psychotherapy*. Boston, MA: Houghton Mifflin.

Rossini, E., & Moretti, R. (1997). Thematic Apperception Test (TAT) interpretation: Practice recommendations from a survey of clinical psychology doctoral programs accredited by the American Psychological Association. *Professional Psychology: Research and Practice*, *28*, 393–398.

Salovey, P., & Mayer, J. (1989–1990). Emotional intelligence. *Imagination, Cognition, and Personality*, *9*, 185–211.

Schlosser, B. (1991). The future of psychology and technology in assessment. *Social Science Computer Review*, *9*, 575–592.

Schutz, B. (1982). *Legal liability in psychotherapy: A practitioner's guide to risk management*. San Fransisco, CA: Jossey-Bass.

Seligman, M., & Csikszentmihalyi, M. (2000). Positive psychology: An introduction. *American Psychologist*, *55*, 5–14.

Shemberg, K., & Leventhal, D. B. (1981). Attitudes of internship directors towards preinternship training and clinical models. *Professional Psychology*, *12*, 639–646.

Sigman, S. (1989). Parallel process at case conferences. *Bulletin of the Menninger Clinic*, *53*, 340–349.

Smith, B. L., Boss, A. L., Brabender, V., Evans, B. F., Handler, L., Mihura, J. L., & Nichols, D. (2005). The status of the Rorschach in clinical and forensic practice: An official statement by the board of trustees of the Society of Personality Assessment. *Journal of Personality Assessment*, *85*(2), 219–237.

Smith, J. D. (2010). Therapeutic Assessment with children and families: Current evidence and future directions. *Report on Behavioral and Emotional Disorders in Youth*, *10*(2), 39–43.

Smith, J. D., Finn, S. E., Swain, N. F., & Handler, L. (2010). Therapeutic Assessment in pediatric and primary care psychology: A case presentation of the model's application. *Families, Systems, & Health*, *28*(4), 369–386.

Smith, J. D., Handler, L., & Nash, M. R. (2010). Therapeutic Assessment for preadolescent boys with oppositional-defiant disorder: A replicated single-case time-series design. *Psychological Assessment*, *22*(3), 593–602.

Smith, J. D., Nicholas, C. R. N., Handler, L., & Nash, M. R. (2011). Examining the clinical effectiveness of a family intervention session in Therapeutic Assessment: A single-case experiment. *Journal of Personality Assessment*, *93*(3), 204–212.

Smith, J. D., Wolf, N. J., Handler, L., & Nash, M. R. (2009). Testing the effectiveness of family Therapeutic Assessment: A case study using a time-series design. *Journal of Personality Assessment*, *91*(6), 518–536.

Stedman, J. (1997). What we know about predoctoral internship training: A review. *Professional Psychology: Research and Practice*, *28*, 475–485.

Sullivan, A. (1999, July). The Emotional Intelligence Scale for Children. *Dissertation Abstracts International*, *60*(01), 0068A.

Tett, R., Jackson, D., & Rothstein, M. (1991). Personality measures as predictors of job performance: A meta-analytic review. *Personnel Psychology*, *44*, 703–742.

Tharinger, D., Finn, S., Austin, C., Bailey, K., Parton, V., & Fisher, M. (2008). Family sessions in psychological assessment with children: Goals, techniques and clinical utility. *Journal of Personalityy Assessment*, *90*, 547–558.

Tharinger, D. J., Finn, S. E., Austin, C. A., Gentry, L. B., Bailey, K. E., Parton, V. T., & Fisher, M. E. (2008). Family sessions in psychological assessment with children: Goals, techniques, and clinical utility. *Journal of Personality Assessment*, *90*(6), 547–558.

Tharinger, D. J., Finn, S. E., Gentry, L., Hamilton, A. M., Fowler, J. L., Matson, M., Walkowiak, J. (2009). Therapeutic Assessment with children: A pilot study of treatment acceptability and outcome. *Journal of Personality Assessment*, *91*(3), 238–244.

Tharinger, D. J., Finn, S. E., Hersh, B., Wilkinson, A. D., Christopher, G., & Tran, A. (2008). Assessment feedback with parents and pre-adolescent children: A collaborative approach. *Professional Psychology: Research and Practice*, *39*(6), 600–609.

Tharinger, D. J., Finn, S. E., Wilkinson, A. D., DeHay, T., Parton, V. T., Bailey, K. E., & Tran, A. (2008). Providing psychological assessment feedback to children through individualized fables. *Professional Psychology: Research and Practice*, *39*(6), 610–618.

Tharinger, D. J., Finn, S. E., Wilkinson, A. D., & Schaber, P. M. (2007). Therapeutic assessment with a child as a family intervention: A clinical and research case study. *Psychology in the Schools*, *44*(3), 293–309.

Tharinger, D. J., Gentry, L. B., & Finn, S. E. (Forthcoming). Therapeutic Assessment with adolescents and their parents: A comprehensive model. In C. R. Reynolds (Ed.), *Oxford handbook of psychological assessment of children and adolescents*. New York, NY: Oxford University Press.

Tharinger, D. J., Krumholz, L., Austin, C., & Matson, M. (2011). The development and model of Therapeutic Assessment with children: Application to school-based assessment. In M. A. Bray & T. J. Kehle (Eds.), *Oxford handbook of school psychology* (pp. 224–259). New York, NY: Oxford University Press.

Uhinki, A. (2001). Experiences of the therapeutic assessment with couples. *Journal of Projective Psychology and Mental Health*, *8*(1), 15–18.

Urist, J. (1977). The Rorschach test and the assessment of object relations. *Journal of Personality Assessment*, *41*, 3–9.

Van Dorsten, B. (2006). Psychological considerations in preparing patients for implantation procedures. *Pain Medicine*, *7*, 47–57.

Van Dorsten, B., & Weisberg, J. N. (2011). Psychological comorbidities in patients with pain. In S. Pagoto (Ed.), *Handbook of comorbid psychological and physical illness: A behavioral medicine perspective*. New York, NY: Springer. doi:10.1007/978-1-4419-0029-6

Viglione, D. (1999). A review of the recent research addressing the utility of the Rorschach. *Psychological Assessment*, *11*(3), 251–265.

Viglione, D., & Hilsenroth, M. (2001). The Rorschach: Facts, fictions, and the future. *Psychological Assessment*, *13*, 452–471.

Watkins, C. E. Jr., Campbell, V., & Manus, M. (1990). Personality assessment training in counseling psychology programs. *Journal of Personality Assessment*, *55*, 380–383.

Wechsler, D. (1958). *The measurement and appraisal of adult intelligence* (4th ed.). Baltimore, MD: Williams & Wilkins.

Weiner, I. [B.] (2001). Advancing the science of psychological assessment: The Rorschach Inkblot Method. *Psychological Assessment*, *13*(4), 423–432.

Weiner, I. B. (2003). *Principles of Rorschach interpretation* (2nd ed.). Mahwah, NJ: Erlbaum.

Weisberg, J. N. (2000). Personality and personality disorders in chronic pain. *Current Review of Pain*, *4*(1), 60–70.

Westen, D. (1991a). Clinical assessment of object relations using the Thematic Apperception Test. *Journal of Personality Assessment*, *56*, 56–74.

Westen, D. (1991b). Social cognition and object relations. *Psychological Bulletin*, *109*, 429–455.

Wetzler, S. (1989). Parameters of psychological assessment. In S. Wetzler & M. Katz (Eds.), *Contemporary approaches to psychological assessment* (pp. 3–15). New York, NY: Brunner/Mazel.

Whitman, S., & Jacobs, E. (1998). Responsibilities of the psychotherapy supervisor. *American Journal of Psychotherapy*, *52*, 166–175.

Yama, M. (1990). The usefulness of human figure drawings as an index of overall adjustment inferred from human figure drawings. *Journal of Personality Assessment*, *54*, 78–86.

PART II

# Assessment Settings

CHAPTER 10

# Psychological Assessment in Adult Mental Health Settings

MARTIN SELLBOM, BRANDEE E. MARION, AND R. MICHAEL BAGBY

## WHY CONDUCT PSYCHOLOGICAL ASSESSMENTS?

We conceptualize psychological assessment as a problem-solving process in which psychological tests, interviews, and other sources of data function as tools used to answer questions (e.g., to address a referral request) and resolve perplexities (e.g., to assist in differential diagnosis; Maloney & Ward, 1976). The primary purpose of psychological assessments in adult inpatient and outpatient mental health settings is to evaluate patients' cognitions, affect, behaviors, personality traits, strengths, and weaknesses in order to make judgments, diagnoses, predictions, and treatment recommendations (Maruish, 2008). The functional utility of psychological assessments, we believe, lies in the ability to provide information about not only the clients' symptoms but also their stable personality characteristics, defensive patterns, identifications, interpersonal styles, self-concepts, and beliefs (B. L. Smith, 1998). Furthermore, comprehensive assessments address the factors that led to the problems and difficulties that presumably initiated the referral (Wakefield, 1998). Thus, the general goals of psychological assessment include providing an accurate description of the client's problems, determining what interpersonal and environmental factors precipitated and are sustaining the problems, and making predictions concerning outcome with or without intervention (Aiken, 2000; Beutler, Malik, Talebi, Fleming, & Moleiro, 2004). In addition, assessments can support or

challenge clinical impressions and previous working diagnoses as well as identify obstacles to therapy (Appelbaum, 1990; Clarkin & Mattis, 1991; Hurt, Reznikoff, & Clarkin 1991; Maruish, 1994, 2008).

Finally, assessments can also provide assistance in developing and evaluating the effectiveness of a treatment plan consistent with the client's personality and external resources as well as allowing the client to find out more about him- or herself (Butcher, 1990; Finn, 2007). As clients continue to adapt and deal with their symptoms after their discharge, assessments can guide discharge planning and subsequent treatment.

## FOUNDATIONS OF PSYCHOLOGICAL ASSESSMENT IN MENTAL HEALTH SETTINGS

Psychological assessments must be founded on specific theoretical premises that guide the assessment process. The history of psychological assessment is quite extensive, resulting in many theoretical stances upon which assessments can be based. It is our belief, however, that psychological assessment of adults in mental health settings is based on two founding premises: assessments must be evidence based and multimodal.

### Evidence-Based Assessment

Psychological assessment in mental health settings must be evidence based. That is, a client's psychiatric symptoms must be systematically assessed in relation to the text revision of the fourth edition of the *Diagnostic and Statistical Manual of Mental Disorders* (*DSM-IV-TR*; American Psychiatric Association, 2000) criteria for particular disorders. This criteria analysis is then supplemented with results from empirically validated psychological tests and structured interviews. The client's responses on these measures are used to indicate likely diagnoses and appropriate treatment implications based on empirical research. Consequently, an evidence-based approach to psychological assessment requires empirical support for any conclusions or recommendations, as opposed to relying solely on clinical impression and judgment.

The evidence-based approach was initially practiced in general medicine and recently has been incorporated in psychology. Evidence-based medicine (EBM) integrates clinical expertise with external evidence based on systematic research, while considering the values and expectations of patients or clients (Gambrill, 1999). Within the medical community, EBM is defined as a set of strategies designed to ensure that the clinicians form opinions and base subsequent decisions on the best available external evidence (Elstein, 2004; Geddes, 1997). Thus, decisions pertaining to the client are made in light of the most up-to-date information available. The steps involved in EBM include a precise definition of the clinical problem, an efficient search for the best available evidence, critical appraisal of the evidence, and integration of the research findings with clinical expertise (Geddes, 1997; Olson, 1996). At each stage of EBM, recent developments in clinical findings and information technology are harnessed and utilized (Geddes, 1997). As physicians have acknowledged that no single authority has comprehensive scientific knowledge, the EBM approach is viewed as an improvement over the authoritative knowledge approach to practicing medicine (Kennell, 1999).

With the movement toward an evidence-based approach comes greater accountability for the content and quality of psychological assessments (Barlow, 2005). Instead of administering a standard assessment battery to clients, this approach encourages psychologists to conduct an evaluation that is tailored to each individual client's presenting problem, specific symptoms, and other characteristics that could affect their ability or willingness to perform on a task or disclose information. An evidence-based psychological assessment should be as efficient as possible, using methods with sufficient levels of reliability and validity to provide the psychologist and client with the information they need to address the referral question (Barlow, 2005).

McFall (2005) indicated that to be able to conduct such evaluations, psychologists must first examine the tools at their disposal, focusing on both theory and utility. First, a sound theoretical model provides a solid foundation on which to base a psychological assessment and allows the psychologist to draw informative conclusions about a client. It is vital that each method or instrument adequately and accurately captures the theory or construct that it is supposed to measure. For example, if the goal of a particular assessment is to determine whether an individual has a depressive disorder, the psychologist would have to know which constructs or symptoms to assess to answer this question. These constructs should evidence both convergent validity (positive relationships to conceptually similar constructs [e.g., sadness and anhedonia]; e.g., Joiner, Walker, Pettit, Perez, & Cukrowicz, 2005) and divergent validity (no relationship to conceptually distinct constructs [e.g., anger and fear]). If a component of an assessment does not provide information relevant to the goal of answering the referral question, it is not appropriate for use in an evidence-based approach.

Second, McFall (2005) also emphasized the importance of evaluating the utility of psychological assessment methods and instruments. When a component of a psychological assessment adds information above and beyond what can be gained from other components, it is said to have incremental validity (Sechrest, 1963). It is not merely sufficient that the component provides unique information; it is necessary that it provides unique information that is relevant to the referral question. If a method or instrument provides significant incremental validity when predicting conceptually relevant criteria, it is contributing useful information to the assessment. McFall (2005) expressed the concern that there is not a widely accepted benchmark for determining the meaningfulness of such contributions.

Hunsley and Mash (2005) highlighted two other major concerns for evidence-based assessments: gaps in psychometric data, and training and practice. First, there is not enough information available about all psychological assessments to determine their utility with all individuals. It is important to ensure that an assessment has adequate reliability and validity for use with each particular client, taking into account the measure's normative sample (e.g., such variables as age, gender, and race). Second, many of the methods that have previously shown utility in evidence-based approaches are underrepresented in both clinical training and practice. Increasing demands by third parties (e.g., insurance companies) for evidence-based assessments may influence some clinicians to move toward these practices (Barlow, 2005). It is vital that clinicians receive the necessary training to evaluate and implement such practices.

We agree with Hunsley and Mash (2007) that clinical decision making is always a concern in any psychological assessment. Even if all of the methods and instruments are evidence based, a certain degree of clinical judgment must be exercised in order for the psychologist to synthesize all of the information into an overall picture of the client. Faust and Ziskin (1988) highlighted some advantages and disadvantages of clinical judgment. Clinical judgment can be beneficial to the assessment process in terms of gaining information (e.g., clinical impressions as to the nature of clients' difficulties and distresses) that cannot be obtained from an evidence-based approach. Moreover, many clinicians contend that their clinical impressions and judgments are rarely disputed by empirical test results; they may even shun actuarial-based data for fear that the data themselves will involve significant error, thereby leading to misdiagnosis of a client. Consequently many clinicians rely on their own experience and judgment rather than actuarial-based data when making diagnoses and treatment recommendations. However, the validity of such judgments is often low, thereby placing the client at potential risk for underdiagnosis, overdiagnosis, or misdiagnosis. Clinicians often overvalue supportive evidence and undervalue evidence contrary to their hypotheses, and tend to find evidence of abnormality in those they assess, regardless of whether they have any psychopathology. However, using an evidence-based approach does reduce the propensity for a psychologist's bias or judgment to affect an assessment.

Though we advocate for the use of evidence-based practice (EBP), critics have raised some valid concerns that warrant consideration. As stated previously, some individuals (e.g., McFall, 2005) question the lack of research standards for determining the utility of a practice, such as the lack of a widely accepted benchmark for determining incremental validity. The American Psychological Association's (APA) Presidential Task Force on Evidence-Based Practice (2006) has attempted to address these concerns by providing some guidelines for what constitutes appropriate research evidence for EBPs. Some clinicians are also concerned about the use of EBPs placing too many restrictions on clinical decision making (Nathan, 1998; Wilson, 2010). The APA's Task Force (2006) emphasized the importance of clinical decision making by stating that the clinician must choose which practices are suitable for each individual client, even when using EBPs. On a related note, many clinicians are also wary of the restrictions that may be imposed by third parties (e.g., insurance companies),

which may not provide financial support for practices that do not meet the criteria for EPB or for those practices that simply have not been studied in enough detail yet. With the progression of EBPs in psychology, it is our hope that some of these issues will be addressed so that more clinicians may feel comfortable with using the EBPs that are most appropriate for each individual client. Thus, it is vital that research continue to develop and test evidence-based approaches for a variety of diagnoses and contexts.

## Multimodal Assessment

The approach to psychological assessment in mental health settings should also be multimodal. One assessment tool is not sufficient to tap into complex human processes. Moreover, given that empirical support is critical to the validity of a psychological assessment, it is just as essential that there is concordance among the results from the client's history, structured interview, self-report inventories, and clinical impression. Because the results and interpretations are obtained from several sources, the multimodal approach increases reliability of the information gathered and helps corroborate hypotheses (Hertzman, 1984; cf. McFall, 2005). Moreover, this approach draws on the strengths of each test and reduces the limitations associated with each one. A multimodal approach has the benefit of relying on shared methods and thus minimizing any potential biases associated with specific assessment methods or particular instruments. Finn and Butcher (1991) noted that self-report inventories are imperfect and the results should not be seen as definitive conclusions but rather as hypotheses that should be compared with information from other sources. A diagnosis can be made with more confidence when several independent sources of information converge than when inferences are based on a single source. When various sources are inconsistent, however, this may also provide important information about the test taker. (See Weiner, this volume.) For example, some individuals might not have the insight to report difficulties that are brought to light using performance-based testing. Moreover, the multimodal approach prevents the influence of a single perspective from biasing the results (Beutler, Wakefield, & Williams, 1994).

## GOALS OF PSYCHOLOGICAL ASSESSMENT

An evidence-based and multimodal approach to psychological assessment enables the clinician to attain the main goals of assessment, namely clarifying diagnosis and providing treatment recommendations. Whereas other authors have emphasized additional assessment goals, such as insight into a client's personality, interpersonal style, and underlying drives, we think that the goals of clarifying diagnosis and guiding treatment are the mainstays of psychological assessment in mental health settings and, in fact, incorporate many of the other goals.

## Diagnostic Clarification

A primary reason for conducting psychological assessments of adults in a mental health setting is to make or clarify a diagnosis based on the client's presenting symptomatology, which will likely require significant consideration of differential diagnosis. However, the either/or implication of differential diagnosis is problematic. Often clients manifest criteria of several disorders simultaneously, or they may manifest symptoms that do not meet criteria for a specific disorder despite the fact that their behaviors and cognitions are maladaptive (Westen & Arkowitz-Westen, 1998). Thus, clinicians may find it beneficial to use multiple diagnostic impressions and, if possible, determine which disorder is generating the most distress and requires immediate attention. Making or clarifying one or more diagnoses can benefit the clinician in many ways, including enhanced communication between clinicians about clients who share certain features, enhanced communication between a clinician and the client through feedback, helping put the client's symptoms into a manageable and coherent form for the client, giving the client some understanding of his or her distress, guiding treatment, and enhancing research that, in turn, should feed back into clinical knowledge (Westen, 1998). Nonetheless, difficulties of psychological diagnosis should also be mentioned.

Diagnosis itself is a complex process that involves a myriad of complicated data. Diagnostic formulation incorporates the relationship between the presenting problem and the client's personality, acute versus chronic dimension of the pathology, the presence of various levels and types of pathology and their interconnections, and the impact of diagnostic features on the development of intervention strategies and prognostic formulations. In essence, the diagnosis of the problem is not a discrete final step but rather a process that begins with the referral question and continues through the collecting of data from interviews and test results (Maloney & Ward, 1976). Furthermore, diagnostic formulation is dependent on the *DSM-IV-TR* (and the forthcoming fifth edition of the *DSM* [*DSM-5*]) for guidance in terms of meeting criteria on multiple dimensions.

Unfortunately, there are problems inherent in making a diagnosis based on the *DSM-IV-TR,* because the *DSM-IV-TR* itself has certain limitations.

1. It is based on a medical model and does not consider underlying processes or liabilities (i.e., it is concerned only with the signs and associations of the disorder).
2. The *DSM-IV-TR* is categorical in nature, even though human nature, mental illness, and mental health are distributed dimensionally. Failure to recognize both adaptive and maladaptive levels and constellations of symptoms and traits may provide an incomplete or inaccurate picture of an individual's functioning (Lowe & Widiger, 2009; Widiger, Livesly, & Clark, 2009). Overlapping category boundaries (or poor discriminant validity; McFall, 2005) frequently result in multiple diagnoses and the problem of comorbidity (Barron, 1998; Brown & Barlow, 2009). Moreover, a categorical approach does not provide as powerful predictions about etiology, pathology, prognosis, and treatment as a dimensional approach (Gunderson, Links, & Reich, 1991).
3. The *DSM-IV-TR* does not address etiological contributions to disorders and how they affect the manifestation and outcome of disorders (Joyce, 2008).
4. The Axis I and Axis II disorder criteria represent a consensual opinion of a committee of experts that labeled a particular pattern of symptoms of a disorder rather than relying on extensive empirical evidence and ensuring the collection of data from a variety of sources (cf. Clark, 2005).
5. The *DSM-IV-TR* is skewed toward the nomothetic end of the spectrum, resulting in static diagnoses whose operational definitions may be inaccurate, unsupported by research findings, and camouflage questionable construct validity (Barron, 1998).
6. The *DSM-IV-TR* requires a specific number of symptoms to achieve a specific diagnosis, which disregards individuals with subthreshold symptoms regardless of level of impairment and may result in false negatives (Beals et al., 2004; Karsten, Hartman, Ormel, Nolen, & Pennix, 2010).

Other criticisms of the *DSM-IV-TR* include excessive focus on reliability at the expense of validity, arbitrary cutoff points (Karsten et al., 2010), proliferation of personality disorders, and questionable validity of the personality disorder clusters (Besteiro-González, Lemos-Giráldez, & Muñiz, 2004; Blatt & Levy, 1998).

Although criticized for its significant limitations, the *DSM-IV-TR* does have some notable strengths. It provides a common language in which to describe psychopathology and personality (Widiger, 2005), attempts to address the heterogeneity of clinical presentation of symptoms by adopting a polythetic approach (Clarkin & Levy, 2003), and includes several axes to take social, medical, and economic factors into account. In summary, the *DSM-IV-TR* is a descriptive nosology, ostensibly unbound to a specific theory of development, personality organization, etiology, or theoretical approach (Barron, 1998). It has shown utility as a diagnostic framework that is applicable for use in a wide number of contexts by clinicians and researchers from various theoretical orientations. These merits of the *DSM-IV-TR*, particularly in the absence of another comprehensive diagnostic system, suggest that assessment of psychological disorders should adhere to this multiaxial system.

Clinicians who practice in adult mental health settings should also become aware of the significant changes likely to occur in the forthcoming *DSM-5*. Although it is beyond the scope of this chapter to cover all the changes in detail, we provide some highlights. Regier, Narrow, Kuhl, and Kupfer (2009) outlined the conceptual development for the *DSM-5*, which emphasizes greater incorporation of dimensional conceptualizations of psychopathology, providing further distinction between the assessment of symptoms and impairment, the need to address the various manifestations of disorders across the developmental stages of the life span, and enhancing differential manifestations of disorders as conditioned by gender and cultural characteristics. Regier et al. (2009) also indicated that the *DSM-5* allows for ample opportunity to incorporate neuroscientific advances in pathophysiology, genetics, pharmacogenomics, structural and functional imaging, and neuropsychology into the understanding and expression of mental disorders.

There are two major advances or shifts that clinicians working in adult mental health settings should be particularly aware of. First, the American Psychiatric Association task force (2011) proposed a cross-cutting assessment domain, which focuses on general dimensions of psychopathology that are not specific to any particular syndrome or are associated with any set of diagnostic criteria. Rather, these are domains that may be relevant to treatment planning, prognosis, and understanding diagnostic comorbidity—a phenomenon highly relevant in adult mental health settings. Examples of cross-cutting domains include measurement of depressed mood, anxiety, substance use, or sleep problems for all patients seen in a mental health center. These can be used to determine general maladjustment as change subsequent to treatment.

A second major revision relevant to adult mental health settings concerns the personality disorders. The task force (American Psychiatric Association, 2011) proposed a radical shift away from the 10 diagnostic categories in the *DSM-IV-TR* to an entirely dimensional approach. They are recommending six broad personality trait domains onto which patients will be mapped—each with 4 to 10 specific facets. The proposed domains are negative emotionality, detachment, antagonism, disinhibition, compulsivity, and schizotypy. Once the patient's personality profile has been generated, it will be compared to and mapped onto one of five personality disorder prototypes: antisocial/psychopathic, borderline, obsessive-compulsive, avoidant, and schizotypal. There will not be any prototypes reflecting histrionic, paranoid, schizoid, or dependent personality disorders. If the personality profile does not match any of the five proposed personality disorder types, a diagnosis of "PD Trait Specified" will be assigned. Finally, the patient will be tested on measures of self- and interpersonal functioning. The patient will also have to exhibit some form of self-oriented and/or interpersonal impairment to warrant a diagnosis (American Psychiatric Association, 2011). Thus, clinicians who frequently evaluate or treat patients with personality psychopathology will have to accommodate these changes and consider new assessment devices. It should be noted that the Minnesota Multiphasic Personality Inventory-2 (MMPI-2; Butcher, Graham, Ben-Porath, Tellegen, Dahlstrom, & Kaemmer, 2001) and its Restructured Form (MMPI-2-RF; Ben-Porath & Tellegen, 2008) have a set of scales that measure the Personality Psychopathology-Five (Harkness, McNulty, & Ben-Porath, 1995)—a set of personality pathology constructs that map onto the proposed *DSM-5* domains remarkably well (e.g., Harkness, Finn, McNulty, & Shields, 2011; Krueger et al., 2011; Widiger & Simonsen, 2005).

## Guide for Treatment

A second and potentially more important goal of psychological assessments of adults in a mental health setting is to offer a guide for treatment by developing an individualized treatment plan for the client (and family). A psychological assessment offers the opportunity to link symptomatology, personality attributes, and other information with certain treatment modalities or therapeutic targets. Therefore, giving treatment recommendations allows psychologists to proceed past the level of diagnosis and provide suggestions about how to deal with the diagnosed disorder. Ideally, an outline of treatment recommendations should include short-term and long-term goals to address both acute and chronic symptoms; procedures to reach the goals; possible obstacles and aids to treatment; and client prognosis (Groth-Marnat, 2009; Hertzman, 1984; Maloney & Ward, 1976).

In addition to diagnosis, treatment planning should take into account other information about the client, as well as their history and environment. Client variables which can affect treatment selection include: symptom severity, readiness to change, personality traits, comorbidity, and interpersonal functioning (Clarkin & Levy, 2003). In particular, *patient enabling factors* refer to patient dimensions that are important for treatment planning and engaging in particular forms of psychological intervention (Clarkin & Mattis, 1991). For example, the patient's defensive structure, coping style, interpersonal sensitivity, and basic tendencies and characteristics may dictate the most appropriate psychological intervention (Beutler & Clarkin, 1990; Clarkin & Levy, 2003; Harkness & Lilienfeld, 1997). Further sources of information include the client's psychiatric and medical history, psychological mindedness, current levels of stress, motivation levels, and history of prior treatments, as well as physical condition, age, sex, intelligence, education, occupational status, and family situation (Clarkin & Levy, 2003; Halleck, 1991).

This information is relevant to treatment planning in two ways. First, demographic variables and a history of prior treatments can dictate or modify current treatment modalities. Second, other variables might help formulate certain etiological models that can in turn guide treatment (Halleck, 1991). Thus, information from various sources obtained in a psychological assessment can be integrated to provide treatment recommendations as well as to predict the prognosis of the client and expected effects of treatment.

Psychological tests have been widely used to guide treatment. Unfortunately, the information they provide is not necessarily useful in guiding the choice of specific therapeutic modality. However, test scores can guide treatment recommendations. For example, symptom severity, stage of client resolution, recurrent interpersonal themes, level of resistance to treatment, and coping styles can be obtained from various psychological tests, and all serve as indicators for the focus and prognosis of psychotherapeutic procedures (Beutler et al., 2004).

Some omnibus inventories also provide information relevant to treatment planning. In particular, clients' scores on the MMPI-2 validity scales offer predictions about treatment based on factors such as compliance, level of insight, current psychological status, risk of premature termination of therapy, and level of motivation (Graham, 2012). Both individual scores and profiles of scores on the content and clinical scales, as well as endorsement of critical items, can be used for treatment planning, including determining needs to be met, issues with which to deal, and structure and style of therapy (Greene & Clopton, 2004). Similarly, the Personality Assessment Inventory (PAI; Morey, 1991) can guide treatment recommendations by providing information about a client's level of functional impairment, potential for self-harm, risk of danger to others, chemical dependency, traumatic stress reaction, and likelihood of need for medication (Morey & Henry, 1994). Furthermore, the PAI contains a number of scales that have shown utility as either positive or negative indicators of potential for psychotherapy (e.g., Morey & Quigley, 2002). Positive indicators include level of perceived distress, positive attitude toward treatment, capacity to utilize psychotherapy, availability of social supports, and ability to form a therapeutic alliance. These suitability indicators should then be weighed against negative indicators, including having disorganized thought processes, being nonpsychologically minded, and being characterologically unsuited for therapy (Morey & Henry, 1994).

Fischer and Finn (2008) described the importance of involving the client in the process. They stressed the value of delivering the test results and treatment plan information in a manner that is understandable to the client. The client must be able to comprehend the treatment plan and its goals. By explaining how the clinician formed the treatment plan and on what information conclusions were based, the clinician may be able to assist the client in gaining insight into his or her problems. This individualized and detailed approach to conveying information to clients can serve to increase their positive feelings regarding the assessment and treatment plan.

## PSYCHOLOGICAL ASSESSMENT TOOLS

Next we detail various types of psychological assessment instruments that are available to clinicians in adult mental health settings, how to best select such tests, and how to integrate test results.

### Types of Psychological Assessment Instruments

Any diagnosis or treatment recommendation should be based on a configuration of impressions from client history, collateral sources (e.g., other persons, records), and the results of several psychological tests. Various types of assessment tools that can guide the psychological assessment when used in collaboration with other sources of data are discussed next.

## Interviews

Clinical interviews provide comprehensive and detailed analysis of clients' past and current psychological symptomatology. Furthermore, they offer insight into clients' personality features, coping styles, interpersonal styles, and behaviors. Interviews help the clinician generate and evaluate hypotheses and then select appropriate psychological tests to clarify diagnostic impressions. Consequently, clinical interviews play a central role in the assessment process (Craig, 2009; Maruish, 2008). Interviews can be unstructured, semistructured, or structured. Unstructured interviews are often conducted to obtain a clinical impression (person-centered) view of the client, build rapport, clarify symptomatology, and test for discrepancies between self- and other reports. They allow for greater depth and insight into the nature of the client's problems, behaviors, and other modes of functioning—and many times help gather information not typically accessible via other means (Mohr & Beutler, 2003). Interpretation of the client's responses relies primarily on the expertise of the clinician. In contrast, semistructured and structured interviews are often scored and interpreted against some criterion standard or normative data. Thus, they provide the potential for greater objectivity and less bias in interpretation. Examples of semistructured and structured interviews include the Structured Clinical Interview for DSM-IV Axis I (SCID-I/P; First, Gibbon, Spitzer, & Williams, 2002) and Axis II disorders (SCID-II; First, Gibbon, Spitzer, Williams, & Benjamin, 1997), and the Diagnostic Interview for Personality Disorders (DIPD; Zanarini, Frankenburg, Chauncey, & Gunderson, 1987). A primary advantage of such diagnostic interviews is that the questions ensure that certain criteria are directly questioned, such as whether a syndrome has persisted for a minimum period of time (DSM-IV-TR; American Psychiatric Association, 2000). Thus, diagnosis follows directly from the results.

Whereas interviews often provide a plethora of information and help with both diagnostic clarification and treatment recommendation, their clinical utility is reduced by limitations typically associated with such techniques. For example, results of interviews are solely based on the client's self-report and are therefore subject to client overreporting, underreporting, or memory distortions. Moreover, the dynamics of directly interviewing clients engender potential biases in clients' responses, as a result of their need to present themselves favorably to the clinician or as a plea for help. Thus, interviews should be supplemented with objective tests in order to assess client response style and to confirm diagnosis.

## Self-Report Inventories

We advocate the use of self-report inventories primarily in three ways: (1) to assess the frequency and intensity of psychiatric symptoms; (2) to provide corroborating information for a clinical diagnosis; and (3) to assess enduring traits that predict future behaviors, symptoms, or treatment implications. Self-report inventories vary in the degree of expertise required to accurately evaluate and interpret the results. These tests may have fixed, precise scoring standards and may be scored manually or by computer or require interpretation by the clinician (Aiken, 2000). Often many of these tests are based on certain criterion groups of people with known symptoms or characteristics, so that the selection of the test items suggests these symptoms.

The self-report modality has several advantages—namely, empirical validity, brevity, low cost, and generalized utility in various settings. As well, many self-report inventories (e.g., MMPI-2, PAI, Beck Depression Inventory) are empirically based and have been extensively researched, providing a sound basis on which to evaluate their reliability and validity along with other psychometric criteria. (See also Ben-Porath, this volume.) Moreover, the respondent completing these tests is the person who is actually experiencing the psychological symptoms. Thus, the client is directly expressing his or her actual experience and state of distress. However, disadvantages of this modality also include client bias, conscious or unconscious distortion of responses (although many contemporary self-report inventories have scales designed to assess such response bias), and the inflexibility of the tests to alter the types of questions depending on the client's responses. Consequently, self-report inventories should be used to supplement, not supplant, interview and behavioral observation data.

## Performance-Based Techniques

Although these are still commonly referred to as projective tests by some, we prefer the less archaic and more descriptively accurate label of performance-based tests. (See Meyer & Kurtz, 2006.) These techniques, such as the Rorschach Inkblot Method and Thematic Apperception Test (TAT), are unstructured, disguised, and reflect omnibus measurement. Although certain administration and scoring systems allow for the quantification of response scoring, extensive training is typically required (cf. Groth-Marnat, 2009). There has been substantial research supporting the validity of reliably scored Rorschach indices (cf. Meyer & Viglione, 2008; Board of Trustees for the Society for Personality Assessment, 2005); however, most performance-based tests fail to meet conventional standards of empirically based assessments as outlined earlier (e.g., Aiken, 2000; Lilienfeld, Wood, & Garb, 2001). Possible obstacles to the clinical utility of these tests include low validity coefficients of the instruments, the influence of situational factors on client's responses, and clinician subjectivity in scoring and interpreting responses. Thus, the lack of objectivity in scoring and the paucity of representative normative data on many performance-based tests, in our opinion, limit their use with an adult clinical population. Their use is also limited because they may require more time to administer, score, and interpret than many self-report inventories, and the assessment procedure is usually under strict time constraints.

It is important to note that both self-report inventories and performance-based techniques, by themselves, typically are insufficient to answer referral questions, make differential diagnoses, or decide on treatment recommendations. These three tasks can be performed effectively only if the clinician develops a conceptual model of the client based on a hypothetical deductive reasoning approach (Maloney & Ward, 1976) and if the clinician utilizes multiple assessment tools, including tests, interviews, and other sources of data. Clinicians seem to be polarized as to whether they should use performance-based tests or rely solely on objectively scored instruments. With the exception of a selected group of indices from a reliably scored Rorschach administration, it is our opinion within the context of evidence-based assessment that performance techniques are not appropriate for use in adult mental health settings.

### Cognitive Testing

Many clinicians, including us, believe that it is important to determine client cognitive status and a basic estimate of intellectual functioning. Comprehensive neuropsychological assessments are typically beyond the scope of most clinicians in adult mental health settings and are usually conducted by clinical neuropsychologists in larger medical centers (e.g., academic medical centers, Veterans Affairs medical centers). Clinicians should, however, obtain basic screens for intellectual functioning; in addition to determining potential impairment in such area (e.g., borderline intellectual functioning), such screens also provide the clinician with further information for client

conceptualization and treatment planning. For instance, an individual with an IQ of 85 very likely experiences the world much differently from an individual with an IQ of 130 (cf. Finn, 2007), and decisions about what type of treatment might best fit such individuals would likely be different.

As with other psychological test instruments, we advocate for using those that meet criteria for evidence-based assessment. It is particularly important to pay attention to reliability information with high-stakes decisions regarding intellectual functioning (e.g., a diagnosis of mental retardation), given the serious implications such decisions might have for clients. Furthermore, in some settings clients may be motivated to put forth poor effort on cognitive testing. When such motivations are expected, particularly in light of an external incentive, symptom validity tests (such as the Test of Memory Malingering [Tombaugh, 1996]) may be necessary to ascertain appropriate effort.

### Choosing the Tests to Use

In order to choose which tests to use, clinicians must be familiar with the effectiveness and efficiency of the tests that could help answer the referral question (Olin & Keatinge, 1998). Clinicians should also select tests that, together, measure a variety of dimensions and are of importance for making treatment recommendations (Beutler et al., 1994) and meet criteria for evidence-based assessment (Barlow, 2005; Hunsley & Mash, 2005, 2007; McFall, 2005).

Four major considerations important in selecting which tests to administer are the test's psychometric properties, clinical utility, client factors, and clinician variables (Hunsley & Mash, 2005). The first two speak to the ability of the psychological tests to answer the referral question based on an evidence-based approach, whereas the latter two consider factors such as client ethnicity, age, level of education, functional capacity, motivation, and clinician experience, all of which may confound test results or interpretation. One must also take into account the client's ability to speak the language in which the tests are written. For example, if the client speaks Italian and is being assessed in an English-speaking setting, the clinician can utilize versions of some self-report questionnaires that have been translated into Italian and later validated. It may also be necessary to use a translator and modified versions of interviews and other self-report questionnaires. Furthermore, the client's ability to remain focused for extended periods of time must be taken into account. In addition, the length of time required to complete the test must be considered. The utility of the results must be weighed against the time to administer the test and to score and interpret the results.

During the assessment, the clinician may decide to add, eliminate, or modify some tests if the client appears to have a limited attention span or cognitive ability or to be functionally illiterate. In addition, the emphasis of the assessment may change depending on the symptoms the client describes and the clinician's impression. The assessment tools might change accordingly. Finally, a number of tests contain so-called validity scales designed to measure inconsistent responding, response biases, exaggeration of psychopathology, and/or overreporting of cognitive deficits. Consequently, the clinician should pay careful attention to the validity scales included in tests, such as the MMPI-2 and the PAI. These tests allow the clinician to determine whether the client is presenting an accurate picture of his or her symptoms.

## Choosing the Number of Tests

Although the multimodal approach to assessment encourages the use of more than one test, it does not specify the exact number of tests clinicians should use. The clinician must prevent the assessment from becoming too cumbersome yet still obtain enough information to provide an empirically supported diagnosis (cf. McFall, 2005). Those tests selected should assess for the presence of the primary disorder or problem as well as other disorders that either share similar essential features or typically cooccur (Olin & Keatinge, 1998). Although it is less time consuming and costly to use fewer tests, taking a multimodal approach and using several tests with demonstrated validity allows for cross-validation, assessment of a client's responses to different situations, identification of previously unrecognized problems, and provision of a more comprehensive evaluation (Olin & Keatinge, 1998). There may be instances in which a focal assessment is more appropriate than a comprehensive one; however, given fewer time and financial restraints, a comprehensive assessment tailored to the individual is usually considered better practice. On a note of caution, clinicians can give too many tests, which can result in interpreting chance effects as real (O'Neill, 1993).

An important issue in multimodal assessment that should influence the number of tests to use is incremental validity (Hunsley & Meyer, 2003; McFall, 2005). Dating back to Meehl (1959) and Sechrest (1963), incremental validity has typically been concerned with the amount of additional information gained with every additional test or predictor added. Although some research has reported extensively on incremental validity of test scales within omnibus personality inventories, such as the MMPI-2 (see e.g., Barthlow, Graham, Ben-Porath, & McNulty, 1999; Sellbom, Graham, & Schenk, 2006), there has been less research concerning the incremental benefits of adding additional assessment procedures in psychological assessment, and most such research has been conducted in personnel selection. (See Hunsley & Meyer, 2003, for a review.) Thus, in light of empirically based and multimodal assessment (McFall, 2005), we encourage clinicians to review the research literature to determine the extent to which various tests may offer incremental utility in clinical decision making.

## Integration and Interpretation of Tests

After each of the test results has been discerned, it is important to interpret and integrate the results. Blais and Smith (2008) described the assessment process as deconstructing the individual to learn more about his or her individual parts (e.g., levels of single personality traits); the integration of test results is like putting these pieces back together to interpret them in the context of the client as a whole. Most psychologists are well trained in psychometrics; however, their training frequently lacks focus on developing and writing an integrative interpretation, which is the part of an assessment that actually serves to provide a global picture of the client.

Test interpretation involves integrating all the information from the various test results into a cohesive and plausible account. Proficient integration of the tests should explain the presenting problem, answer the referral question, and offer additional information to clarify diagnoses and guide treatment. The results of any test should be cross-referenced with other test results, interview findings, current behaviors, and client history to search for convergence of symptoms, personality traits, coping and interpersonal styles, environmental situations, and any other pertinent information that will guide diagnosis and treatment recommendations. Discrepancies between results can also provide valuable information. For example, discrepancies between self-report and performance-based tests may provide valuable information about differences between explicit content and implicit processes of an individual's personality (Blais & Smith, 2008).

O'Neill (1993) described three levels of test interpretation that can help the clinician gain insight into the nature of the client's psychological status. Level 1, the concrete level, involves interpretation that is limited to the subtest and subscale scores and does not draw conclusions beyond the scores. Level 2, the mechanical level, is concerned with the pattern of subscales and subtests, particularly significant differences between scores. Level 3, the individualized level, involves interpreting the test results in the context of a larger picture, incorporating specific details that are particularly characteristic of the client. This last level offers the best clinical interpretation of the client and helps guide treatment goals.

It is important to have a framework in which to integrate assessment results in order to avoid simply interpreting individual test scores (Blais & Smith, 2008). Focusing on a theory can assist in arranging test results in a structure that helps conceptualize the client as a whole and predict how the person might feel and react in certain situations (Sugarman, 1991).

In general, the primary goal of test integration is to discover what O'Neill has termed the "internal connection" (1993); that is, to use the test results in conjunction with the client's behavior and history to arrive at an understanding of the client's current state of psychological functioning. Furthermore, integrating the test results helps the clinician make objective observations, infer internal psychological states, make generalized descriptions about the client's behavior and functioning, and give probable explanations for the client's psychological difficulties. Essentially, analysis of test results and integration and interpretation of the tests enable the clinician to make inferences and, ultimately, decisions concerning the most appropriate care for the client.

## ASSESSMENT PROCEDURE IN ADULT MENTAL HEALTH SETTINGS

A psychological assessment in an adult mental health setting can be of intermediate or extensive depth. The range of information required, the sampling of a number of areas of a client's life, series of psychological tests, and multiple sources of information, all systematically collected and interpreted, testify to the breadth and complexity of psychological assessment in such settings. This, in turn, generates a plethora of information and recommendations. Olin and Keatinge (1998) have proposed an 11-step model for the assessment procedure:

1. Determine the information needed to answer the referral question(s).
2. Identify who is to be involved.
3. Obtain informed consent and releases.
4. Collect and examine medical records.
5. Identify what is to be measured.
6. Identify and select appropriate measures.
7. Administer assessment and modify as needed.
8. Score measures and analyze and interpret results.
9. Seek consultation if necessary.
10. Write the report.
11. Provide feedback to appropriate parties.

We believe that these recommendations are well taken within the empirically based assessment framework (Hunsley & Mash, 2005, 2007; McFall, 2005), and we also advocate for the integrative approach suggested by Blais and Smith (2008) and others described earlier.

Next, we provide some general information about typical components of psychological assessments in mental health settings. Throughout the discussion, we also describe our general view and opinions about how to execute each of the components. We recognize that there is not one single method of conducting a psychological assessment in any setting; rather, we present one model that we believe aligns with the empirically based and multimodal assessment approach advocated for earlier.

## Referral Question

Referral questions are the foundation of any psychological assessment. They provide the rationale for conducting an evaluation and dictate the types of questions to ask and the selection of psychological tests to be employed. Typically, as the examiner starts to clarify the referral question, the process of collecting and interpreting data and formulating hypotheses has already begun (Maloney & Ward, 1976). In essence, the referral question sets the focus of the assessment, which in turn shapes the information gathered. The assessment process thus involves linking the information with the problem (referral question) by a configural web of explanations (O'Neill, 1993).

Although psychological assessment can address a variety of referral questions, there are several questions that psychologists commonly encounter in assessing mental health patients. Examples of typical referral questions include: clarify a previous working diagnosis or the referring physician's impression of the client; differentiate the client's symptom presentation; identify the cause of the client's symptoms; and determine what characterological features may be interfering with the client's ability to engage in treatment.

We believe that it is important to initially contact the referral source (typically a psychiatrist or case worker in mental health settings) from the outset to ensure that the referral question is clear and to gather additional impressions. Moreover, the potential use of the test results (e.g., disability insurance, workplace competency) must be clarified and given careful consideration. The clinician must take into account what type of professional made the referral and tailor the report to that person's discipline and level of expertise. We typically also review the patient's medical records (if immediately accessible) so as to have clearer insight into the nature of the person's problems.

## Preliminary Information

Like any detective work, a psychological assessment involves amassing preliminary information that will further guide the nature of the assessment. Preliminary information about the client's history and current psychological state can be obtained from many sources. Often the clients themselves are asked to provide this information, because it is helpful to understand their impressions of their history and current problems. This general information is typically gained using an unstructured interview format. However, clients may have memory distortions or biases and may wish to portray themselves in an overly positive or negative manner. Therefore, it is important to be able to rely on collateral sources of information as well, including records and third-party interviews, to corroborate or supplement client self-report (Mohr & Beutler, 2003).

First, records can often provide a good and sometimes more objective (relative to client's and other vested parties' self-statements) history of the clients experiences and functioning to further provide a context within which the client is conceptualized. Medical and mental health records should be examined, because they contain pertinent information regarding clients' psychiatric histories, medications, previous treatments, and working diagnoses. Sometimes school and other educational records can be important to provide further objective information to offer a more detailed context in terms of developmental factors and the course of potential long-lasting behavioral or emotional difficulties.

Second, reliance on third-party sources can many times be beneficial in understanding the client. Discussions with the clients' past and current mental health professionals may provide additional insight into the client's mental health problems. Sometimes it is advisable to obtain information from family members or close friends of the clients. This is particularly useful if the clinician suspects that the clients are not portraying themselves in an accurate manner and if the clinician desires insight into the

clients' interactions in other environments; other times clients are not sufficiently introspective to fully understand or describe their problems. However, clinicians should also consider that individuals close to a client might also have their own biases and motives.

## Assessment Procedure

The assessment procedure can be divided into different domains of assessment, all of which we discuss in the next sections. These domains include informed consent, presenting symptoms and problems, psychosocial background information, clinical interview (including mental status exam and behavioral observations), diagnostic clarification, and personality processes (including coping skills, self-concept, and interpersonal functioning).

### Informed Consent

Psychologists have an ethical obligation (except under rare circumstances, such as court-ordered evaluations) to obtain informed consent prior to any psychological evaluations (American Psychological Association, 2002). Thus, before beginning any psychological assessment, we recommend first explaining the process to the client, including who requested the assessment, what is expected of the client, who will have access to the assessment results, and what the client can hope to gain by participating. The clinician may often paraphrase the question posed by the referral source in order to help the client clearly understand the reason for the referral. The clinician should obtain verbal and written informed consent to use the results from the assessment to address the specific reasons for the referral. Patients are given the opportunity to pose any of their questions.

### Presenting Problems and Symptoms

As part of a psychological assessment, it is obviously imperative to gather information directly from the client about his or her current problems. First and foremost, the psychologist should record the client's chief complaint, including current signs and symptoms of presentation. Equally important is recording symptom chronology, which includes symptom onset and progress as well as changes in behavior, emotional state, mentation, and personality from the time the client was last considered well until the current assessment (Mohr & Beutler, 2003). This should be followed by noting the relevant preceding events, the length and severity of the problem, precipitants and effects, patterns of recurrence, and past psychological treatments (Halleck, 1991; Hertzman, 1984).

In addition, a history of the client's previous hospitalizations and medications should be obtained. Moreover, assessing the client's current life situation, including family, living and working environment, and stressors, and how these aspects contribute to the client's symptomatology, will help clarify the manner in which the client's symptoms developed and are being maintained.

### Psychosocial Background History

Obtaining information pertaining to the client's developmental, family, emotional, academic, vocational, social, economic, legal, cultural, and medical history is also an essential feature of psychological assessment (Groth-Marnat, 2009; Maruish, 2008; Mohr & Beutler, 2003). Such information provides an understanding of the subtleties of the client's problems and the context in which they exist (e.g., Mohr & Beutler, 2003). Furthermore, this information can help inform diagnosis, identify and clarify stressors, and guide treatment.

Developmental and family history should include attainment of developmental milestones, relationships among family members, history of childhood abuse, and a family history of mental illness (Maruish, 2008). Social history should contain information about past and current friendships, intimate relationships, sexual history, religious participation, social support, and hobbies and activities. A basic appraisal of the client's academic and vocational history should include details about the client's problematic academic areas, special education, grades (including courses failed or skipped), best and worst subjects, highest level of education completed, school behavior, extracurricular activities, attendance, occupational history, current occupational status, and relationships with coworkers and employers. A legal history pertains to any difficulties the client has had with the law, and an economic history relates to the client's financial status and stability. With respect to cultural history, information should be obtained about the client's feelings of closeness, distance, or alienation from his or her cultural group and about the beliefs and meanings associated with the culture. Finally, a medical history should cover previous head injuries, serious accidents or illnesses, surgeries, past and current medical problems, and medications (Halleck, 1991; Hertzman, 1984; Olin & Keatinge, 1998). This list is by no means exhaustive but rather provides a guideline for discovering information that may be pertinent to the client's current psychological state.

### Clinical Interview

By "clinical interview" here, we refer to the unstructured interview process by which psychologists collect additional information from the clients pertaining to their difficulties. This "clinical" piece is in addition to the presenting problems and symptoms and client history, which are also generated via a combination of unstructured interviews and collateral data.

The unstructured clinical interview is often used to determine which psychological symptoms require further inquiry and to test for discrepancies between the client's self-report and other information sources. In essence, such an interview assists us in generating and testing (i.e., confirming, invalidating, or moderating) hypotheses about the client. In addition, the clinical interview enables us to conduct firsthand observations and evaluations of the client's coping and interpersonal styles (cf. Groth-Marnat, 2009). These psychological features provide essential data that are used to assess the client's overall functioning. Additionally, a specific component of this process involves noting the client's behaviors. Often the assessment situation represents a microcosm of the client's behavioral and psychological functioning. Thus, observation of the client is an essential source of information, since it represents a sample of the patient's pattern of functioning and can reveal some of the problems that brought the client to the assessment in the first place (Kellerman & Burry, 1981).

Additional information should be obtained by conducting a Mental Status Exam (MSE; Maruish, 2008). The MSE originated from medical interviews and is now commonly part of psychological assessments. It is a summary of the client's current emotional and cognitive states and provides information about the client's current level of functioning and severity of impairment (Trzepacz & Baker, 1993). Information obtained from the MSE is vital in that it describes the client's level of functioning at the time of testing. Key sections in the MSE include appearance, mood, affect, behavior and activity, intellectual functioning, language, orientation, memory, attention, thought processes (form and content), perception, dangerousness (including suicidal and homicidal ideation), degree of impulse control, insight, judgment, and emotional state (Groth-Marnat, 2009; Trzepacz & Baker, 1993). The presence of normal and the absence of abnormal processes should be noted, as well as any observations of unusual, strange, or significant thoughts, emotions, or behaviors.

### Diagnostic Clarification

Diagnostic clarification of mental disorders organizes the presenting symptomatology into a framework in which the nature, severity, and extent of the client's problems can be understood and addressed. Many clinicians depend on the medical chart and clinical interview to make diagnoses. However, the ideal practice is to use an empirically based and multimodal approach relying on several sources of information, including the collateral sources, unstructured interview, structured clinical interviews, and psychological test instruments. Reliable diagnosis must always rest on clear operational or behavioral criteria that can be assessed by the clinician. We recommend that all assessment tools used be subjected to extensive empirical testing, meet acceptable standards for reliability and validity, and provide actuarial-based data (Hunsley & Mash, 2005). Currently, the *DSM-IV-TR* manual is the basis on which diagnoses are met, and clients must meet a certain number of criteria of specific severity and duration in order to receive a diagnosis. Furthermore, although it is beyond the scope of this chapter to cover evidence-based assessment for all different types of mental disorders, we recommend specific reading for anxiety disorders (Antony & Rowa, 2005), depressive disorders (Joiner et al., 2005), and personality disorders (Widiger & Samuel, 2005).

In clarifying diagnosis, typically it is appropriate to begin with an unstructured interview as a means to survey the client's past experiences and complaints. We recommend, however, that such interviews be followed with more structured tools, such as the SCID-I (First, Spitzer, Gibbon, & Williams, 2002) and SCID-II (First, Gibbon, Spitzer, Williams, & Benjamin, 1997), to guide diagnostic clarification because they are derived directly from the *DSM-IV-TR*. Both versions of the SCID systematically and comprehensively assess for the symptoms and syndromes of major mental illnesses; the results afford clinical diagnoses based on objective and evidence-based information. In particular, both versions of the SCID allow the clinician to make differential diagnoses among overlapping and conflicting symptoms and to examine whether a client's presenting symptomatology is better accounted for by another disorder or a medical condition. However, we are aware of the time constraints placed on the assessment process. Thus, we recommend first using the SCID-I/P screener to screen briefly for the presence or absence of anxiety, substance abuse, and eating disorders. We also recommend that, prior to administering the SCID-II, the psychologist administers the personality questionnaire version of SCID-II and follows up with interview modules for those specific disorders the client meets criteria on the SCID-II-PQ. Furthermore, interviews are particularly useful to clarify personality disorder diagnoses, because this format allows clinicians to discern the chronology of clients' symptoms and the effect these symptoms have made on their interpersonal relationships and their daily

functioning and to determine how clients' characterological patterns are currently affecting their psychological functioning.

From the multimodal assessment perspective, we believe that interviews should be supplemented by the results of both omnibus and specific psychological tests. Examples of omnibus tests of general symptom impairment and personality traits include such inventories as the MMPI-2 and PAI. Although a variety of other tests are used to examine the presence of potential psychopathology, we focus on the MMPI-2 because it is the instrument that is most widely used in adult mental health settings (e.g., Camara, Nathan, & Puente, 2000) and is unrivaled in the amount of empirical data to support its use (e.g., Butcher & Rouse, 1996). Furthermore, the Rorschach Inkblot Method has some evidence of reliability and validity (e.g., Rosenthal, Hiller, Bornstein, Berry, & Brunell-Neuleib, 2001), at least for certain scores, but there has not yet been extensive empirical research to indicate that Rorschach information has incremental validity relative to other omnibus measures, such as the MMPI-2 or the PAI, to warrant the amount of time that it takes to administer and score the instrument. Consequently, we do not focus on the Rorschach here but acknowledge that many clinicians find it acceptable to use in adult mental health settings (cf. Board of Trustees for the Society for Personality Assessment, 2005).

The MMPI-2 is often used to clarify coexisting diagnoses, validate the clinical impression of a client from the structured interviews, assess emotional functioning, and obtain information about the client's level of psychopathology. The MMPI-2 is an excellent example of a carefully developed psychological test with attention to details of reliability, validity, and normative information (e.g., Graham, 2012). Moreover, it provides a great deal of information in a variety of areas of client functioning. An alternative version of the MMPI-2, the MMPI-2 Restructured Form (MMPI-2-RF; Ben-Porath & Tellegen, 2008) has been released. This 338-item version of the MMPI-2 was designed to take advantage of the clinically useful variance of the MMPI-2 item pool in an efficient and psychometrically up-to-date manner. The test's scales are organized in a hierarchical format that corresponds well to contemporary models of personality and psychopathology. There is a substantial amount of empirical data already supporting its use (Tellegen & Ben-Porath, 2008; see Tellegen, Ben-Porath, & Sellbom, 2009, for a review on the core set of scales—the Restructured Clinical scales). Although more empirical data are being published as we write this chapter, we believe that this instrument can be a viable alternative to the MMPI-2 in adult mental health settings, particularly for the clarification of diagnosis.

We also believe that psychologists should consider psychological test instruments that target specific types of psychopathology when potentially implicated, especially when tailoring the assessment to an individual client (cf. McFall, 2005). In fact, there is practically a test designed for every disorder or psychological difficulty. These tests may provide incremental validity or consensual validity to omnibus tests. Examples of such specific tests are the State-Trait Anxiety Inventory (Spielberger, 1983), the Beck Anxiety Inventory (BAI; Beck, Epstein, Brown, & Steer, 1988), the Hamilton Anxiety Rating Scale (Hamilton, 1959), the Post-traumatic Stress Disorder Symptom Scale (Foa, Riggs, Dancu, & Rothbaum, 1993), the Trauma Symptom Inventory (Briere, 1995), the Maudsley Obsessional-Compulsive Inventory (Hodgson & Rachman, 1977), the Beck Depression Inventory (Beck, Ward, Mendelson, Mock, & Erbaugh,1961), the Hamilton Rating Scale for Depression (Hamilton, 1960), the Suicide Risk Assessment Scale (Motto, 1985), and the Alcohol Use Inventory (Wanberg, Horn, & Foster, 1977). However, the clinician must consider the efficiency of using specific measures given that many omnibus tests are able to assess a variety of specific disorders and psychological difficulties.

### Personality Profile, Coping, Self-Concept, and Interpersonal Styles

Clients' personality profiles, coping styles, self-concept, and interpersonal patterns provide insightful and extended information that is directly pertinent to diagnosis and treatment recommendations (Blais & Smith, 2008). Information gleaned from these areas of a client's psychological functioning serves four purposes.

1. It clarifies diagnosis. Examination of interpersonal and coping patterns associated with particular disorders can often assist with differential diagnosis.
2. The information, especially that which relates to a client's personality style, offers added insight and clarification of personality disorder diagnoses, including clarification of symptom criteria, intensity and duration of symptoms, and the pervasiveness of clients' symptoms in their everyday functioning.
3. This information can provide insight into the extent of a client's distress, the manner in which a client attempts to handle and adjust to difficulties, the effect that the symptoms have on significant people in the client's life, and the degree to which the symptoms are affecting the client's life.

4. Integration of the information helps summarize the client's functioning, problems, and strengths; clarifies the nature of the problem; and encapsulates the client's functioning as well as the role that the client's symptoms play in his or her daily functioning. This insight, in turn, is a powerful tool in guiding treatment recommendations.

Several omnibus inventories can assess clients' personality profiles, coping styles, self-concept, and interpersonal patterns. As mentioned earlier, we tend to prefer the MMPI-2 instruments because of the substantial empirical base underlying their use. The new MMPI-2-RF could be particularly useful in this regard, as it includes very specific, nonoverlapping scales measuring various aspects of self-concept and interpersonal functioning. Other empirically supported instruments that assess personality functioning include the revised NEO Personality Inventory (NEO PI-R; Costa & McCrae, 1992) and Structured Interview for the Five Factor Model of Personality (SIFFM; Trull & Widiger, 1997). These tests are empirically validated measures of clients' enduring attributes, stylistic characteristics, and general personality structure. Of course, one critical issue is whether the client has the capacity to read at an appropriate grade level for these self-report inventories. If the reading level is not adequate, audio-recorded versions of the MMPI-2 can be used in addition to the interview-based SIFFM.

### Treatment Implications and Recommendations

Finally, the information obtained from clinical unstructured and structured interviews, psychological test results, behavioral observations, and additional information from collateral sources is integrated and interpreted to generate a conceptual formulation of the client and a set of coherent treatment recommendations (Blais & Smith, 2008). In effect, the initial problems of the client "have been given a context that serves as a . . . map in which the relevant details of the problem can be made visible and related to each other" (Kellerman & Burry, 1981, p. 4). This integration provides the most valid indicator of whether the client is suffering from a disorder and, if so, the type of disorder (Wakefield, 1998). Each detail of the client's symptoms, behaviors, and history is encapsulated into larger concepts that are then organized in relation to one another. Thus, the presenting problem is demonstrated to be part of a larger system that includes the client's history, personality, coping style, and interpersonal pattern of relating to others. This integration reveals the meaning of the presenting symptoms and provides both information and guidelines in the treatment of the initial problem (Beutler et al., 2004). Again, we stress that the integration and interpretation of a client's psychological status must be validated by empirical data.

As previously stated, the conceptualization of each client, including his or her diagnoses, symptoms, behaviors, and characterological patterns, is used to provide treatment recommendations. The nature of the recommendations depends on the client and on the referral question. Based on our experience, treatment recommendations tend to focus on several areas, including recommending a medication review, commencing a certain therapeutic intervention or changing current treatment, or discussing suitability for therapy. Additional information tends to pertain to the client's prognosis and preexisting factors as well as precautions and restrictions.

## THERAPEUTIC ASSESSMENT

When conducting psychological evaluations in adult mental health settings, it is important and ethically indicated that clients receive feedback about their test results. Stephen Finn and colleagues (e.g., Finn, 1996, 2007; Finn & Martin, 1997) have taken this further and developed a semistructured psychological intervention based on psychological assessment labeled Therapeutic Assessment (TA). TA grew out of the less structured approach of collaborative assessment (e.g., Fischer, 1994). It has substantial roots in humanistic psychology, in that it is collaborative and client centered (Finn, 2007). Furthermore, the approach is also insight oriented as the therapists' goal is many times to help the client obtain new ways of understanding him- or herself. Indeed, Finn (2007) reported that a major theoretical building block comes from Swann's self-verification theory (Swann, 1996, 1997), which posits that individuals are very likely to reject information that is inconsistent with their self-schemas; therefore, when a psychologist conducts a feedback session with clients regarding psychological test data, Finn recommended that this process is guided by the presentation and discussion of information that is gradually more discrepant to how the clients perceive themselves (Finn, 1996, 2007). This topic is discussed in more detail later in this section, under the fourth step of TA.

TA is a stepwise process that begins with an initial session during which the goals of the psychological assessment are discussed in a collaborative fashion (Finn, 2007). One of the major goals of this session (in addition to building a therapeutic alliance) is to help the client generate questions that he or she would like to see answered. Moreover, sometimes clients are referred by another mental health professional who might also have specific referral questions. All such questions are established before the psychological assessment begins. Finn (2007) reported that the second step typically involves a standardized assessment session in which psychological test instruments are administered. These instruments should be tailored to the client's questions, but some tests, such as the MMPI-2/MMPI-2-RF, are almost always administered.

After the testing sessions have been completed, the therapist reviews all of the interview and test information to generate a conceptual formulation of the client. Often information about clients is uncovered that they will likely perceive as threatening to their self-schemas and will probably reject unless enough behavioral evidence can be generated. Finn and Martin (1997) therefore recommended conducting an assessment intervention session that provides the opportunity to study assessment findings in vivo which can afford clients the possibility to discover them on their own. Such sessions also provide the opportunity to potentially test out possible interventions and give clients an experience in implementing more adaptive solutions (Finn, 2007). Finn (2003) has provided an excellent example of an assessment intervention session. He conducted a TA with a client ("David") who had been referred for possible attention-deficit disorder. Based on psychological testing, it became evident that David did not have a cognitive disorder. Rather, it was more likely that emotional flooding was the primary cause for his attention difficulties. During the assessment intervention session, Finn exposed David to emotional arousing situations (via the TAT) and asked to him do a digit span test immediately following his responses to the TAT. After subsequent iterations, David started to realize that his attention problems were the worst when he was emotionally aroused, whereas his performance on the digit span was in the average range when he was relaxed. Thus, David was beginning to make the connection between emotional flooding and his attention difficulties based on this in vivo exposure. Such behavioral information can be invaluable when discussing the test results with clients.

The fourth step in TA is the summary and discussion session in which the assessment findings are discussed with the client with a particular aim to answer the client's questions formulated during the initial session (Finn, 2007). Because of self-verification theory discussed earlier, Finn (1996) recommended that assessment findings be presented in order of least threatening to clients' self-schemas. More specifically, he recommended three levels of discussion. Level 1 refers to assessment findings that clients readily accept and are very likely incorporated into their self-schemas. Level 2 findings are those that clients may not have considered before and likely modify self-schema, but they are unlikely to be threatening. Finally, Level 3 findings are those that are highly novel or discrepant with how clients views themselves and will likely mobilize some defense mechanisms. These findings will be difficult for clients to incorporate immediately, and they may reject them outright at first. The assessment intervention sessions just discussed can be helpful to make such information less threatening and more accessible.

After the TA has been completed, Finn (2007) recommended writing a letter to the client that details the summary and discussion session in understandable language. He also recommended inviting the client to revise the letter—in a way "co-editing the new story that emerged from the assessment" (p. 11). Finn and others have presented examples of such letters (e.g., Finn, 2003, 2007; J. D. Smith & Handler, 2009; Wygant & Fleming, 2008). Finally, Finn (2007) recommended follow-up sessions with clients who desire such sessions, especially if they have not continued with psychotherapy after the TA was completed.

In sum, TA has the potential to be a powerful and brief intervention technique in adult mental health settings, and we strongly recommend that clinicians consider its use. The empirical evidence for TA is growing; so far it has focused on time-series case designs (e.g., J. D. Smith, Handler, & Nash, 2010) and group effectiveness and efficacy trials in children, adults, and families (e.g., Finn & Tonsager, 1992; Newman & Greenway, 1997; Ougrin, Ng, & Low, 2008; Tharinger et al., 2009; see also Poston & Hanson, 2010, for a meta-analysis of the effectiveness of psychological assessment as an intervention more broadly).

### Issues Specific to the Psychological Assessment of Inpatients in the Mental Health Setting

Five issues regarding psychological assessment are particularly relevant to assessing inpatients in adult mental health settings.

1. *Time constraints may unfortunately dictate the depth and breadth of psychological assessments.* Clinicians find themselves having to triage because of the cost of keeping inpatients at the facility and the fact that clients often stay for short periods of time. Consequently, a comprehensive, in-depth assessment that measures all aspects of a client's psychological functioning, including current symptomatology, history, chronic difficulties, coping patterns, interaction styles, personality, and environmental factors, is rarely done. However, we believe that despite the time constraints, a psychological assessment should be as inclusive and comprehensive as possible, in order to best answer the referral question, make a diagnosis, and provide accurate treatment recommendations. To demand any less than this can cause great risk, detriment, and harm to the client.

2. *It is important to note that the severity of clients' psychopathology may affect their self-reports, both within the interview and on psychological tests.* Many clients who are in an acute state of distress tend to generalize and overpathologize their symptoms, to the extent that results from various instruments, such as the MMPI-2, become invalid. It is important for the clinician to tease apart the most salient problems from the client's tendency to use the psychological assessment as a cry for help.

3. *Comorbidity of psychological disorders is high within the adult clinical popul*ation (e.g., Brown, Campbell, Lehman, Grisham, & Mancill, 2001). Another problem is determining which disorder should be addressed first in treatment, particularly since the symptomatology, etiology, and environmental factors influencing one disorder may also present in another disorder. Of particular concern to the adult inpatient population is the high prevalence of substance abuse or dependence disorders in conjunction with another mental disorder. Clinicians assessing inpatients should always assess for possible substance abuse, because this affects the treatment plan and likely prognosis and outcome for the client.

4. *Another critical area to assess is the client's risk of harm to self and others, particularly with respect to suicidal ideation.* This matter should not be taken lightly. Any suicidal ideation, plan, or intent should be documented and the appropriate measures taken to decrease the risk of harm. Furthermore, it is important that the clinician examine specific stressors, events, or other variables that are likely to increase a patient's risk of suicide.

5. *In psychiatry, an analysis of the influence of the environment on a patient's symptomatology is indispensable.* Research suggests that the environment (both positive and negative) exerts an impact on symptom occurrence, development, and maintenance (Clarkin & Mattis, 1991; Halleck, 1991). The environment also

exerts a long-term influence on the patient's experiences and behaviors that in turn can contribute to his or her current psychological state or can develop into certain personality dimensions that complicate symptomatology (Halleck, 1991). The relationship between environment and symptoms is acknowledged in the *DSM-IV-TR* Axis IV. Even more important, understanding a patient's social, developmental, and familial history can guide therapeutic interventions.

It is our opinion that adult inpatients are experiencing a greater number of, and often more intense, psychosocial problems, particularly in the areas of interpersonal difficulty, financial constraints, and employment difficulties, than adult outpatients. This observation highlights the multidimensional nature of psychopathology, specifically that people's surrounding environmental situations and constraints often influence the onset, severity, maintenance, and outcome of their psychological symptoms. As previously mentioned, psychosocial difficulties must be given strong consideration and value in a psychological assessment.

## CONCLUSION

Formulation has been defined as the process by which we systematically, comprehensibly, and objectively assemble and integrate available information to arrive at an understanding of what is happening with the patient (Hertzman, 1984). It is essentially a working hypothesis on which we base our diagnoses and treatment recommendations. Hertzman (1984) recommended integrating the patient's symptoms, functions with which the symptoms interfere, history, premorbid personality structure, external stressors, and defenses and coping styles into a working formulation, which in turn guides diagnostic impression and treatment suggestions.

An effective psychological assessment should be based on empirically established techniques, use a multimodal approach, and have high clinical utility (Hunsley & Mash, 2005, 2007; McFall, 2005). All of the information obtained about a client's symptomatology, personality, and coping and interpersonal styles within a psychological assessment should be used to guide treatment recommendations.

In light of some of the concerns raised previously, the use of EBPs for psychological assessment may need to continue to change in the future. For example, third parties (e.g., insurance providers) may support only the use of evidence-based assessments and may continue to provide coverage for only a limited number of assessments for each individual. One way to address this issue may be to administer a brief (and perhaps even nonvalidated) symptom measure to provide basic information. This could lay the groundwork for determining what testing is needed, and reduce unnecessary expenditure of money and time. In addition, Maruish (2002) highlighted important ideas regarding psychological testing with regard to managed health care, such as how to increase the chance that assessments will be covered. Future research in this area is needed to address such issues as the efficacy of using only a limited number of assessments per individual and what should be done for individuals for whom no specific EBP is evident (e.g., individuals from a particular population or with a particular set of symptoms). Finally, in light of our recommendations for a multimodal assessment approach, additional research addressing incremental validity is needed. It is important to demonstrate which combinations of psychological assessment procedures have the best utility for different types of questions and purposes.

## REFERENCES

American Psychiatric Association. (2000). *Diagnostic and statistical manual of mental disorders* (4th ed., text rev.). Washington, DC: Author.

American Psychiatric Association. (2011). *Proposed draft revisions to DSM disorder and criteria*. Arlington, VA: Author. Retrieved from www.dsm5.org/Pages/Default.aspx

American Psychological Association. (2002). Ethical principles of psychologists and code of conduct. Washington, DC: Author.

American Psychological Association, Presidential Task Force on Evidence-Based Practice (2006). Evidence-based practice in psychology. *American Psychologist*, *61*, 271–285.

Aiken, L. R. (2000). *Psychological testing and assessment* (10th ed.). Needham Heights, MA: Allyn & Bacon.

Antony, M. M., & Rowa, K. (2005). Evidence-based assessment of anxiety disorders in adults. *Psychological Assessment*, *17*, 256–266.

Appelbaum, S. A. (1990). The relationship between assessment and psychotherapy. *Journal of Personality Assessment*, *54*, 791–801.

Barlow, D. H. (2005). What's new about evidence-based assessment? *Psychological Assessment*, *17*, 308–311.

Barron, J. (1998). *Making diagnosis meaningful: Enhancing evaluation and treatment of psychological disorders*. Washington, DC: American Psychological Association.

Barthlow, D. L., Graham, J. R., Ben-Porath, Y. S., & McNulty, J. L. (1999). Incremental validity of the MMPI-2 content scales in an outpatient mental health setting. *Psychological Assessment*, *11*, 39–47.

Beals, J., Novins, D. K., Spicer, P., Orton, H. D., Mitchell, C. M., Barón, A. E., & Manson, S. M. (2004). Challenges in operationalizing the *DSM-IV* clinical significance criterion. *Archives of General Psychiatry*, *61*, 1197–1207.

Beck, A. T., Epstein, N., Brown, G., & Steer, R. A. (1988). An inventory for measuring clinical anxiety: Psychometric properties. *Journal of Consulting and Clinical Psychology*, *56*, 893–897.

Beck, A. T., Ward, C. H., Mendelson, M., Mock, J., & Erbaugh, J. (1961). An inventory for measuring depression. *Archives of General Psychiatry*, *4*, 561–571.

Ben-Porath, Y. S., & Tellegen, A. (2008). *Minnesota Multiphasic Personality Inventory–2 Restructured Form: Manual for administration, scoring, and interpretation*. Minneapolis: University of Minnesota Press.

Besteiro-González, J. L., Lemos-Giráldez, S., & Muñiz, J. (2004). Neuropsychological, psychophysiological, and personality assessment of *DSM-IV* clusters of personality disorders. *Eurpoean Journal of Psychological Assessment*, *20*, 99–105.

Beutler, L. E., & Clarkin, J. F. (1990). *Systematic treatment selection*. New York, NY: Brunner/Mazel.

Beutler, L. E., Malik, M., Talebi, H., Fleming, J., & Moleiro, C. (2004). Use of psychological tests/instruments for treatment planning. In M. E. Maruish (Ed.), *The use of psychological testing for treatment planning and outcomes assessment: Volume 1* (3rd. ed., pp. 111–145). Hillsdale, NJ: Erlbaum.

Beutler, L. E., Wakefield, P., & Williams, R. E. (1994). Use of psychological tests/instruments for treatment planning. In M. E. Maruish (Ed.), *The use of psychological testing for treatment planning and outcome assessment* (pp. 55–74). Hillsdale, NJ: Erlbaum.

Blais, M. A., and Smith, S. R. (2008). Improving the integrative process in psychological assessment: Data organization and report writing. In R. P. Archer & S. R. Smith (Eds.), *Personality assessment* (pp. 405–439). New York, NY: Routledge/Taylor Francis.

Blatt, S. J., & Levy, K. N. (1998). *A psychodynamic approach to the diagnosis of psychopathology*. Washington, DC: American Psychological Association.

Board of Trustees for the Society for Personality Assessment. (2005). The status of the Rorschach in clinical and forensic practice: An official statement by the Board of Trustees for the Society for Personality Assessment. *Journal of Personality Assessment*, *85*, 219–237.

Briere, J. (1995). *Trauma Symptom Inventory Professional manual*. Odessa, FL: Psychological Assessment Resources.

Brown, T. A., & Barlow, D. H. (2009). A proposal for a dimensional classification system based on the shared features of the *DSM-IV* anxiety and mood disorders: Implications for assessment and treatment. *Psychological Assessment*, *21*, 256–271.

Brown, T. A., Campbell, L. A., Lehman, C. L., Grisham, J. R., & Mancill, R. B. (2001). Current and lifetime comorbidity of the *DSM-IV* anxiety and mood disorders in a large clinical sample. *Journal of Abnormal Psychology*, *110*, 585–599.

Butcher, J. N. (1990). *The MMPI-2 in psychological treatment*. New York, NY: Oxford University Press.

Butcher, J. N., Graham, J. R., Ben-Porath, Y. S., Tellegen, A., Dahlstrom, W. G., & Kaemmer, B. (2001). *Minnesota Multiphasic Personality Inventory—2: Manual for Administration and Scoring* (2nd ed.). Minneapolis: University of Minnesota Press.

Butcher, J. N., & Rouse, S. V. (1996). Personality: Individual differences and clinical assessment. *Annual Review of Psychology*, *47*, 87–111.

Camara, W. J., Nathan, J. S., & Puente, A. E. (2000). Psychological test usage: Implications in professional psychology. *Professional Psychology: Research and Practice*, *31*, 141–154.

Clark, L. (2005). Temperament as a unifying basis for personality and psychopathology. *Journal of Abnormal Psychology*, *114*, 505–521. doi:10.1037/0021–843X.114.4.505

Clarkin, J. F., & Levy, K. N. (2003). The influence of client variables on psychotherapy. In M. J. Lambert (Ed.), *Bergin and Garfield's handbook of psychotherapy and behavior change* (pp. 194–226). Hoboken, NJ: Wiley.

Clarkin, J. F., & Mattis, S. (1991). Psychological assessment. In L. I. Sederer (Ed.), *Inpatient psychiatry: Diagnosis and treatment* (3rd ed., pp. 360–378). Baltimore, MD: Williams & Wilkens.

Costa, P. T. Jr., & McCrae, R. R. (1992). *Revised NEO Personality Inventory: Professional manual*. Odessa, FL: Psychological Assessment Resources.

Craig, R. J. (2009). The clinical interview. In J. N. Butcher (Ed.), *Oxford handbook of personality assessment* (pp. 201–225). New York, NY: Oxford University Press.

Elstein, A. S. (2004). On the origins and development of evidence-based medicine and medical decision making. *Inflammation Research*, *53*, 184–189.

Faust, D., & Ziskin, J. (1988). The expert witness in psychology and psychiatry. *Science*, *241*, 31–35.

Finn, S. E. (1996). *Manual for using the MMPI-2 as a therapeutic intervention*. Minneapolis: University of Minnesota Press.

Finn, S. E. (2003). Therapeutic assessment of a man with "ADD." *Journal of Personality Assessment*, *80*, 115–129.

Finn, S. E. (2007). *In our clients' shoes: Theory and techniques of therapeutic assessment*. Mahwah, NJ: Erlbaum.

Finn, S. E., & Butcher, J. N. (1991). Clinical objective personality assessment. In M. Hersen, A. E. Kazdin, & A. S. Bellack (Eds.), *The clinical psychology handbook* (2nd ed., pp. 362–373). New York, NY: Pergamon Press.

Finn, S. E., & Martin, H. (1997). Therapeutic assessment with the MMPI-2 in managed health care. In J. N. Butcher (Ed.), *Objective psychological assessment in managed health care: A practitioner's guide* (pp. 131–152). New York, NY: Oxford University Press.

Finn, S. E., & Tonsager, M. E. (1992). Therapeutic effects of providing MMPI-2 test feedback to college students awaiting therapy. *Psychological Assessment*, *4*, 278–287.

First, M. B., Gibbon, M., Spitzer, M. D., Williams, J. B. W., & Benjamin, L. (1997). *Users' guide for the Structured Clinical Interview for DSM-IV Axis II Personality Disorders (SCID-II)*. Washington, DC: American Psychiatric Press.

First, M. B., Spitzer, R. L., Gibbon, M., & Williams, J. B. W. (2002). *Structured Clinical Interview for DSM-IV-TR Axis I disorders, Research Version, non-patient edition (SCID-I/NP)*. New York, NY: Biometrics Research, New York State Psychiatric Institute.

Fischer, C. T. (1994). *Individualizing psychological assessment*. Mahwah, NJ: Erlbaum.

Fischer, C. T., & Finn, S. E. (2008). Developing the life meaning of psychological test data: Collaborative and therapeutic approaches. In R. P. Archer & S. R. Smith (Eds.), *Personality assessment* (pp. 379–404). New York, NY: Routledge/Taylor Francis.

Foa, E. B., Riggs, D. S., Dancu, C. V., & Rothbaum, B. O. (1993). Reliability and validity of a brief instrument for assessing post-traumatic stress disorder. *Journal of Traumatic Stress*, *6*, 459–473.

Gambrill, E. (1999). Evidence-based clinical behavior analysis, evidence-based medicine and the Cochrane collaboration. *Journal of Behavior Therapy and Experimental Psychiatry*, *30*, 1–14.

Geddes, J. (1997). Using evidence about clinical effectiveness in everyday psychiatric practice. *Psychiatric Bulletin*, *21*, 390–393.

Graham, J. R. (2012). *MMPI-2: Assessing personality and psychopathology* (5th ed.). New York, NY: Oxford University Press.

Greene, R. L., & Clopton, J. R. (2004). Minnesota Multiphasic Personality Inventory–2. In M. E. Maruish (Ed.), *The use of psychological testing for treatment planning and outcomes assessment: Volume 3* (3rd ed., pp. 449–477). Mahwah, NJ: Erlbaum.

Groth-Marnat, G. (2009). The five assessment issues you meet when you go to heaven. *Journal of Personality Assessment*, *91*, 303–310.

Gunderson, J. G., Links, P. S., & Reich, J. H. (1991). Competing models of personality disorders. *Journal of Personality Disorders*, *5*, 60–68.

Halleck, S. L. (1991). *Evaluation of the psychiatric patient: A primer*. New York, NY: Plenum Press.

Hamilton, M. (1959). The assessment of anxiety states by rating. *British Journal of Medical Psychology*, *32*, 50–55.

Hamilton, M. (1960). A rating scale for depression. *Journal of Neurology, Neurosurgery and Psychiatry*, 23, 56–62.

Harkness, A. R., Finn, J. A., McNulty, J. L., Shields, S. M. (2011). The Personality Psychopathology–Five (PSY-5): Recent constructive replication and assessment literature review. *Psychological Assessment*. Advanced online publication.

Harkness, A. R., & Lilienfeld, S. O. (1997). Individual differences science for treatment planning: Personality traits. *Psychological Assessment*, 9, 349–360.

Harkness, A. R., McNulty, J. L., & Ben-Porath, Y. S. (1995). The Personality Psychopathology Five (PSY-5): Constructs and MMPI-2 scales. *Psychological Assessment*, 7, 104–114.

Hertzman, M. (1984). *Inpatient psychiatry: Toward rapid restoration of function*. New York, NY: Human Sciences Press.

Hodgson, R. J., & Rachman, S. (1977). Obsessional compulsive complaints. *Behavior Therapy*, 15, 389–395.

Hunsley, J., & Mash, E. J. (2005). Introduction to the special section on developing guidelines for the evidence-based assessment (EBA) of adult disorders. *Psychological Assessment*, 17, 251–255.

Hunsley, J., & Mash, E. J. (2007). Evidence-based assessment. *Annual Review of Clinical Psychology*, 3, 29–51.

Hunsley, J., & Meyer, G. J. (2003). The incremental validity of psychological testing and assessment: Conceptual, methodological, and statistical issues. *Psychological Assessment*, 15, 446–455.

Hurt, S. W., Reznikoff, M., & Clarkin, J. F. (1991). *Psychological assessment, psychiatric diagnosis, and treatment planning*. Philadelphia, PA: Brunner/Mazel.

Joiner, T. E., Walker, R. L., Pettit, J. W., Perez, M., & Cukrowicz, K. C. (2005). Evidence-based assessment of depression in adults. *Psychological Assessment*, 17, 267–277.

Joyce, P. R. (2008). Classification of mood disorders in DSM-V and DSM-VI. *Australian and New Zealand Journal of Psychiatry*, 42, 851–862.

Karsten, J., Hartman, C. A., Ormel, J., Nolen, W. A., & Pennix, B. W. J. H. (2010). Subthreshold depression based on functional impairment better defined by symptom severity than by number of *DSM-IV* symptoms. *Journal of Affective Disorders*, 123, 230–237.

Kellerman, H., & Burry, A. (1981). *Handbook of psychodiagnostic testing: Personality analysis and report writing*. New York, NY: Grune & Stratton.

Kennell, J. H. (1999). Authoritative knowledge, evidence-based medicine, and behavioral pediatrics. *Journal of Developmental and Behavioral Pediatrics*, 20, 439–445.

Krueger, R. F., Eaton, N. R., Clark, L. A., Watson, D., Markon, K. E., Derringer, J., . . . Lively, W. J. (2011). Deriving an empirical structure of personality pathology for *DSM-5*. *Journal of Personality Disorders*, 25, 170–191.

Lilienfeld, S. O., Wood, J. M., & Garb, H. N. (2001). What's wrong with this picture? *Scientific American*, 284, 80–87.

Lowe, J. R., & Widiger, T. A. (2009). Clinicians' judgments of clinical utility: A comparison of *DSM-IV* with dimensional models of general personality. *Journal of Personality Disorders*, 23, 221–229.

Maloney, M. P., & Ward, M. P. (1976). *Psychological assessment: A conceptual approach*. New York, NY: Oxford University Press.

Maruish, M. E. (1994). Introduction. In M. E. Maruish (Ed.), *The use of psychological testing for treatment planning and outcome assessment* (pp. 3–21). Hillsdale, NJ: Erlbaum.

Maruish, M. E. (2002). *Psychological testing in the age of managed behavioral health care*. Mahwah, NJ: Erlbaum.

Maruish, M. E. (2008). The clinical interview. In R. P. Archer & S. R. Smith (Eds.), *Personality assessment* (pp. 37–80). New York, NY: Routledge/Taylor Francis.

McFall, R. M. (2005). Theory and utility—Key themes in evidence-based assessment: Comment on the special section. *Psychological Assessment*, 17, 312–323.

Meehl, P. E. (1959). Some ruminations on the validation of clinical procedures. *Canadian Journal of Psychology/Revue canadienne de psychologie*, 13, 102–128.

Meyer, G. J., & Kurtz, J. E. (2006). Advancing personality assessment terminology: Time to retire "objective" and "projective" as personality test descriptors. *Journal of Personality Assessment*, 87, 223–225.

Meyer, G. J., & Viglione, D. J. (2008). An introduction to Rorschach assessment. In R. P. Archer & S. R. Smith (Eds.), *Personality assessment* (pp. 281–336). New York, NY: Routledge/Taylor Francis.

Mohr, D., & Beutler, L. E., (2003). The integrative clinical interview. In L. E. Beutler & G. Groth-Marnat (Eds.), *Integrative assessment of adult personality* (2nd ed., pp. 82–122). New York, NY: Guilford Press.

Morey, L. C. (1991). *The Personality Assessment Inventory professional manual*. Odessa, FL: Psychological Assessment Resources.

Morey, L. C., & Henry, W. (1994). Personality Assessment Inventory. In M. E. Maruish (Ed.), *The use of psychological testing for treatment planning and outcome assessment* (pp. 185–216). Hillsdale, NJ: Erlbaum.

Morey, L. C., & Quigley, B. D. (2002). The use of the Personality Assessment Inventory (PAI) in assessing offenders. *International Journal of Offender Therapy and Comparative Criminology*, 46, 333–349.

Motto, J. A. (1985). Preliminary field testing of a risk estimator for suicide, suicide and life threatening behavior. *American Journal of Psychiatry*, 15(3), 139–150.

Nathan, P. E. (1998). Practice guidelines: Not yet ideal. *American Psychologist*, 53, 290–299.

Newman, M. L., & Greenway, P. (1997). Therapeutic effects of providing MMPI-2 test feedback to clients at a university counseling service: A collaborative approach. *Psychological Assessment*, 9, 122–131.

O'Neill, A. M. (1993). *Clinical inference: How to draw meaningful conclusions from tests*. Brandon, VT: Clinical Psychology.

Olin, J. T., & Keatinge, C. (1998). *Rapid psychological assessment*. New York, NY: Wiley.

Olson, E. A. (1996). Evidence-based practice: A new approach to teaching the integration of research and practice in gerontology. *Educational Gerontology*, 22, 523–537.

Ougrin, D., Ng, A. V., & Low, J. (2008). Therapeutic assessment based on cognitive-analytic therapy for young people presenting with self-harm: Pilot study. *Psychiatric Bulletin*, 32, 423–426. doi:10.1192/pb.bp.107.018473

Poston, J. M., & Hanson, W. E. (2010). Meta-analysis of psychological assessment as a therapeutic intervention. *Psychological Assessment*, 22, 203–212. doi:10.1037/a0018679

Regier, D. A., Narrow, W. E., Kuhl, E. A., and Kupfer, D. J. (2009). The conceptual development of *DSM-V*. *American Journal of Psychiatry*, 166, 645–650.

Rosenthal, R., Hiller, J. B., Bornstein, R. F., Berry, D. T., & Brunell-Neuleib, S. (2001). Meta-analytic methods, the Rorschach, and the MMPI. *Psychological Assessment*, 13, 449–451.

Sechrest, L. (1963). Incremental validity: A recommendation. *Educational and Psychological Measurement*, 23, 1963.

Sellbom, M., Graham, J. R., & Schenk, P. W. (2006). Incremental validity of the MMPI-2 Restructured Clinical (RC) Scales in a private practice sample. *Journal of Personality Assessment*, 86, 196–205.

Smith, B. L. (1998). Psychological testing, psychodiagnosis, and psychotherapy. In J. W. Barron (Ed.), *Making diagnosis meaningful: Enhancing evaluation and treatment of psychological disorders* (pp. 227–245). Washington, DC: American Psychological Association.

Smith, J. D., & Handler, L. (2009). "Why do I get in trouble so much?": A family therapeutic assessment case study. *Journal of Personality Assessment*, 91, 197–210. doi:10.1080/00223890902794101

Smith, J. D., Handler, L., & Nash, M. R. (2010). Therapeutic assessment for preadolescent boys with oppositional defiant disorder: A replicated single-case time-series design. *Psychological Assessment*, *22*, 593–602. doi:10.1037/a0019697

Spielberger, C. D. (1983). *Manual for the State-Trait Anxiety Inventory*. Palo Alto, CA: Consulting Psychological Press.

Sugarman, A. (1991). Where's the beef? Putting personality back into personality assessment. *Journal of Personality Assessment*, *56*, 130–144.

Swann, W. B. (1996). *Self-traps: The elusive quest for higher self-esteem*. New York, NY: Freeman/Times Books/ Holt.

Swann, W. B. (1997). The trouble with change: Self-verification and allegiance to the self. *Psychological Science*, *8*, 177–180. doi:10.1111/j.1467–9280.1997.tb00407.x

Tellegen, A., & Ben-Porath, Y. S. (2008). *The Minnesota Multiphasic Personality Inventory—2 Restructured Form: Technical manual*. Minneapolis: University of Minnesota Press.

Tellegen, A., Ben-Porath, Y. S., & Sellbom, M. (2009). Construct validity of the MMPI-2 Restructured Clinical (RC) scales: Reply to Rouse, Greene, Butcher, Nichols, and Williams. *Journal of Personality Assessment*, *91*, 211–221.

Tharinger, D. J., Finn, S. E., Gentry, L., Hamilton, A., Fowler, J., Matson, M., ... Walkowiak, J. (2009). Therapeutic assessment with children: A pilot study of treatment acceptability and outcomes. *Journal of Personality Assessment*, *91*, 238–244. doi:10.1080/00223890902794275

Tombaugh, T. N. (1996). *Test of Memory Malingering*. Toronto, ON: MultiHealth Systems.

Trull, T. J., & Widiger, T. A. (1997). *Structured Interview for the Five-Factor Model of Personality (SIFFM): Professional manual*. Odessa, FL: Psychological Assessment Resources.

Trzepacz, P. T., & Baker, R. W. (1993). *The psychiatric mental status examination*. New York, NY: Oxford University Press.

Wakefield, J. C. (1998). Meaning and melancholia: Why the *DSM-IV* cannot (entirely) ignore the patient's intentional system. In J. W. Barron (Ed.), *Making diagnosis meaningful: Enhancing evaluation and treatment of psychological disorders* (pp. 29–72). Washington, DC: American Psychological Association.

Wanberg, K. W., Horn, J. L., & Foster, F. M. (1977). A differential assessment model for alcoholism: The scales of the Alcohol Use Inventory. *Journal of Studies on Alcohol*, *38*, 512–543.

Westen, D. (1998). Case formulation and personality diagnosis: Two processes or one? In J. W. Barron (Ed.), *Making diagnosis meaningful: Enhancing evaluation and treatment of psychological disorders* (pp. 111–137). Washington, DC: American Psychological Association.

Westen, D., & Arkowitz-Westen, L. (1998). Limitations of Axis II in diagnosing personality pathology in clinical practice. *American Journal of Psychiatry*, *155*, 1767–1771.

Widiger, T. A. (2005). Classification and diagnosis: Historical development and contemporary issues. In J. E. Maddux & B. A. Winstead (Eds.), *Psychopathology: Foundations for a contemporary understanding* (pp. 63–83). Mahwah, NJ: Erlbaum.

Widiger, T. A., Lively, W. J., & Clark, L. A. (2009). An integrative dimensional classification of personality disorder. *Psychological Assessment*, *21*, 243–255.

Widiger, T. A., & Samuel, D. B. (2005). Evidence-based assessment of personality disorders. *Psychological Assessment*, *17*, 278–287.

Widiger, T. A., & Simonsen, E. (2005). Alternative dimensional models of personality disorder: Finding a common ground. *Journal of Personality Disorders*, *19*, 110–130.

Wilson, K. (2010). Evidence-based medicine: The good the bad and the ugly: A clinician's perspective. *Journal of Evaluation in Clinical Practice*, *16*, 398–400.

Wygant, D. B., & Fleming, K. P. (2008). Clinical utility of MMPI-2 Restructured Clinical (RC) scales in therapeutic assessment: A case study. *Journal of Personality Assessment*, *90*, 110–118.

Zanarini, M., Frankenburg, F. R., Chauncey, D. L., & Gunderson, J. G. (1987). The Diagnostic Interview for personality disorders: Interrater and test-retest reliability. *Comprehensive Psychiatry*, *28*, 467–480.

# CHAPTER 11

# Psychological Assessment in Child Mental Health Settings

NANCY HOWELLS WROBEL AND DAVID LACHAR

Although most children receive mental health services because some concern has been raised regarding their emotional and behavioral adjustment, those mental health services are provided in a variety of settings by a variety of professionals. Core evaluation and treatment services may be provided by educational or health-care organizations through outpatient clinics, inpatient facilities, or residential care agencies. Such services may be supported by an annual institutional budget from which resources are allocated on some rational basis, or each service may be available only to the extent to which associated expenses can be reimbursed. The latter consideration is always of central importance in private practice settings that provide the majority of fee-based or insurance reimbursed mental health care. Psychological assessment services may be routinely integrated into intake evaluation, treatment planning, and subsequent outcome review or may be obtained on a referral basis.

Routine psychological assessment in child mental health settings focuses on the identification and quantification of symptom dimensions and problem behaviors and the collection of information relevant to the development of treatment strategies. In contrast, psychological assessment provided in response to referral may incorporate any of the varied testing methodologies appropriate for the understanding of youth. Of necessity, routine assessment is designed to be cost and time efficient, requiring relatively narrowly defined skills that are easily acquired. The information provided in such routine assessments must be easily understood and applied by the variety of mental health professionals who evaluate and treat children, adolescents and their families. This chapter provides a detailed discussion of the forms of psychological assessment that can be either applied routinely or integrated into assessments designed to answer specific diagnostic inquiries.

Psychological assessment services requested by referral are usually provided by, or under the supervision of, doctoral-level psychologists with specialized training who are certified or licensed to provide mental health services independently. For example, the training necessary to provide assessment with performance measures or neuropsychological assessment requires specific graduate or postgraduate coursework and considerable supervised clinical experience delivered within structured practica, internships, and postdoctoral fellowships. Referral for psychological assessment is often requested to achieve an effective differential diagnosis. Such referrals are made following the collection of a complicated and contradictory history obtained from parent and child interview or subsequent to completion of an ineffective course of treatment. While psychologists have long viewed assessment as a unique and valuable contribution to mental health treatment, a need for continued guidance on evidence based assessment practices has been recognized (Mash & Hunsley, 2005).

Surveys of senior doctoral psychologists who maintain specific professional memberships often associated with the use of psychological testing or who conduct research using psychological tests provide some insight regarding valued tests and test-related procedures. Two of these surveys, conducted in 1990 and 2000, focused on the provision of assessment services to adolescents (Archer, Maruish, Imhof, & Piotrowski, 1991; Archer & Newsom, 2000). The first of these surveys noted the prominence of the Wechsler intelligence scales, Rorschach Inkblot Method (RIM), Bender-Gestalt Test, Thematic Apperception Test (TAT), Sentence Completion Test, and Minnesota Multiphasic Personality Inventory (MMPI), often (84%) also administered in a standard battery. The latter of these surveys suggests the continuing prominence of all but the Bender-Gestalt, the growing use of parent and teacher rating scales, and the influence of managed care in discouraging the use of the most labor-intensive procedures in psychological testing. Consistent with these trends, a more recent listing of top-ranked tests, according to counselor self-reports, suggests that use of performance measures such as the Rorschach has declined, while the use of the Millon Inventories has become more common (Koocher, Norcross, & Hill, 2005). Not surprisingly, a contemporary review of child and adolescent assessment practice concluded that measures that require the most time and specific training, such as the Rorschach and TAT, demonstrated reductions in their application. While these authors contributed another voice in warning about the potential negative effect of managed care guidelines on assessment practice, we also question whether current negative economic realities have placed additional service demands on psychologists, further eroding opportunities to provide comprehensive assessment efforts (Cashel, 2002). Unfortunately, such surveys identify neither the degree to which youth receiving mental health services are evaluated using psychological tests nor the context and efficacy of such applications (e.g., differential diagnosis, treatment planning, outcome assessment). Both managed care constraints and the movement toward evidence-based practice have encouraged greater use of briefer, more symptom-specific measures (Mash et al., 2005; Piotrowski, 1999).

## MENTAL HEALTH EVALUATION OF YOUTH

This chapter focuses on the ways in which the evaluation of the adjustment of children and adolescents benefits from the use of objective rating scales and questionnaires. The routine use of such procedures within mental health settings supports the primary mission of evaluation and treatment, although other assessment techniques also make a positive contribution in this regard.

The evaluation of cognitive, academic, and neuropsychological dysfunction and the assessment of family status and other contextual variables represent important components in current psychological assessment (Heffer, Barry, & Garland, 2009). Such efforts are applied to gain a fuller understanding of a child's adjustment and appreciation of the impact of the context of behaviors as well as aiding in efforts to arrive at an accurate differential diagnosis, to support treatment planning, and to monitor ongoing efforts. The evaluation of child and adolescent adjustment may also benefit from the additional application of performance measures (cf. Exner & Weiner, 1995; G. E. Roberts, 2005). The case examples in Lachar and Gruber (2001) demonstrate the considerable contribution that performance measures, psychoeducational evaluation, and neuropsychological assessment may make to the understanding of child adjustment, although any examination of the issues involved in such applications would merit separate chapters. The overall goal of this chapter is to examine the routine application of objective methods in youth evaluation and treatment and to discuss in some depth the issues related to such application.

## Characteristics of Children and Adolescents

The evaluation of youth is substantially different from the comparable evaluation of adults by mental health professionals. Children function in uniform social contexts and consistently perform in standard contexts. That is, they are routinely observed by parents and other guardians and, once they reach the age of 5 years, spend a substantial amount of their lives in the classroom and pursuing school-related activities. Many behavioral expectations are related to a child's specific age, and childhood is characterized by the attainment of a succession of developmental, academic, and social goals. Children and adolescents typically are not self-referred for mental health services but are referred by parents and teachers. Problems in child adjustment usually are defined and identified by adults, not by the child. These adults are routinely involved in assessment and treatment, because treatment efforts routinely incorporate modification of the home and classroom environments (cf. Heffer et al., 2009; LaGreca, Kuttler, & Stone, 2001).

### Developmental and Motivational Issues

#### Dimensions and Content of Adjustment Problems

The same or quite similar core presenting symptoms and problems may be associated with different diagnoses.

Presenting problems such as inattention may suggest the presence of attention-deficit/hyperactivity disorder (ADHD), depression, anxiety, defective reality testing, a learning disability, or an acquired cognitive deficit. The same core disability may be demonstrated by quite different symptoms and behaviors at different ages, problem behaviors may change substantially with maturation, and problems may appear as a consequence of a prior untreated condition.

### Psychosocial Development

An appreciation of typical child development as well as the course of various disorders across developmental levels is essential in child assessment (Barry & Pickard, 2008). Such an appreciation is also required in determining the appropriate mode of assessment for a child. Young children traditionally have been characterized as unable to contribute meaningfully to the assessment process through the completion of self-report questionnaires (Ammerman & Hersen, 1993). Children under the age of 10 typically have not been viewed as reliable reporters of their own behaviors (Edelbrock, Costello, Dulcan, Kalas, & Conover, 1985). More recent works have questioned the contribution of child self-report in young children in that they may not provide information that contributes beyond that already provided by the parent (De Los Reyes & Kazdin, 2005; Smith, 2007). Relevant challenges to test construction and test application most certainly include normative limitations of a child's age-appropriate language comprehension and reading skills. The task of self-evaluation and self-description may also be compromised by a fundamental developmental immaturity in the understanding of the principles of psychosocial adjustment. Although the cognitive capacity to label feelings may be present in young school-age children, the capacity to self-report and to evaluate one's social and emotional self is only emergent in later childhood. Additionally, a child's interpretation of test items may vary from the intended meaning of the test developer, thus presenting a challenge to test validity (Smith & Handler, 2007).

### Intrinsic Motivation

In contrast to adults who request services from mental health professionals, children and adolescents seldom request such assistance. Children are unlikely to find the completion of a self-description of adjustment consistent with their expectations and are unlikely to experience completion of such a questionnaire as positive. It is quite reasonable to anticipate that most youth will not be motivated to contribute information that is useful in the diagnostic process. In the mental health setting, youth contribution to a formal test-based assessment process may be even more problematic. Youth frequently are referred to mental health professionals because they have been unwilling or unable to comply with the requests of adults. Such youth frequently also present with cognitive or academic disabilities that represent additional obstacles to the use of formal assessment techniques.

## UNIQUE CHALLENGES OF THE MENTAL HEALTH SETTING

### Assessment of Comorbid Conditions

*Comorbidity*, the simultaneous occurrence of two or more unrelated conditions is very commonly observed in youth evaluated in mental health settings. This expectation of comorbid conditions should be seriously considered in the conduct of initial evaluations. Comprehensive multidimensional evaluations of adjustment and therefore the use of tests that simultaneously assess multiple dimensions of problematic adjustment (or multiple unidimensional tests that provide comparable information) are employed by mental health professionals because of the nature of the problems of the youth they evaluate. Children and adolescents troubled by multiple disorders are most likely to be assessed by a mental health professional because the probability of referral of such a child is determined by the combined likelihood of the referral for each separate disorder (Caron & Rutter, 1991). Meta-analytic examination of comorbidity (Angold, Costello, & Erkani, 1999) in children contradicts the notion that high rates of comorbidity in children are merely a result of "referral bias" or rater expectancies but rather may reflect significantly frequent cooccurrence of major disorders and symptom sets. It is therefore always reasonable to assume that conditions other than the one presented as the primary problem are contributing to the referral process and influencing current adjustment; this possibility must be considered in the selection of assessment procedures. In addition, it is important to consider the developmental implications of current conditions, in that the presence of specific unresolved problems may increase the subsequent likelihood of other specific conditions.

It is important to be alert to the possible presence of the various conditions that are frequently comorbid in youth seen by mental health professionals. Considerable effort has been applied in identifying frequent patterns of comorbidity. For example, as many as 87% of children with ADHD have been found to have at least one other diagnosable psychiatric disorder and up to two thirds may have two additional diagnoses (Teeter, Eckert, Nelson, Platten, Semrud-Clikeman, & Kamphaus, 2009). Measurement and treatment of these other disorders are often of comparable importance to the assessment and treatment of ADHD itself (Cantwell, 1996; Pelham, Fabiano, & Massetti, 2005). Such comorbid conditions may delineate meaningful subgroups of children with ADHD (Biederman, Newcorn, & Sprich, 1991; Jensen et al., 2001; Jenson, Martin, & Cantwell, 1997). Citing findings from the Multisite Multimodal Treatment Study of Children with Attention-deficit/Hyperactivity Disorder (MTA), Jensen and Members of the MTA Cooperative Group (2002) identified three subgroups with clear treatment implications including: ADHD with internalizing disorders; ADHD with oppositional defiant disorder (ODD) or conduct disorder (CD); and ADHD with both anxiety and ODD/CD. Even studies of nonreferred samples demonstrate that the majority of children with ADHD also qualify for an additional *disruptive behavior disorder* (e.g., ODD or CD). These patterns of comorbidity are more common in those with hyperactive and impulsive or combined ADHD symptoms (Willcutt, Pennington, Chhabildas, Friedman, & Alexander, 1999) and are more common in boys than girls. These comorbidities are also associated with increased severity and persistence of symptoms and have negative implications for future family and societal adjustment (Jensen et al., 1997). Comorbidity of ADHD, externalizing disorders, and executive function deficits suggest a common biological risk (Coolidge, Thede, & Young, 2000).

*Internalizing disorders* (anxiety, depression) are frequently diagnosed in children with ADHD, particularly the inattentive or combined types (Willcutt, Pennington, Chhabildas, Friedman, & Alexander, 1999); this pattern of problems appears to have important implications for treatment effectiveness. MTA data supports the notion that children with comorbid internalizing symptoms respond equally well to behavioral and medication treatment modes, while children with comorbid internalizing and externalizing symptoms received optimal benefit from combined treatment (Jensen et al., 2001). Jensen et al. (1997) noted that underachievement, Tourette's syndrome, bipolar disorder (BPD), and a variety of medical conditions should also be considered as possibly comorbid when ADHD has been established as a current diagnosis. (See also Pliszka, 1998.) Comorbidity rates for BPD and ADHD are substantial, with one third of children

and adolescents with BPD diagnoses having concurrent ADHD (Masi, Perugi, Millepiedi, Mucci, Bertini, & Pfanner, 2006), and particularly high (over 90%) in referred preschoolers with BPD (Wilens et al., 2003). ADHD is also a frequent comorbidity in childhood-onset schizophrenia (Ross, Heinlein, & Tregellas, 2006).

CD and ODD demonstrate substantial comorbidity in epidemiological studies and obtain rates of comorbidity in excess of 90% in referred samples. Some authors have even considered these two diagnostic categories not to be independent phenomenon, yet reviews suggest that there is sufficient evidence to view ODD as a distinct disorder (Loeber, Burke, Lahey, Winters, & Zera, 2000), with unique risks. Early-onset ODD has been accompanied by substantial risk of secondary disorders, including mood, impulse control, and substance abuse disorders (Nock, Kazdin, Hiripi, & Kessler, 2007). The majority of referred children with CD or ODD also meet the diagnostic criterion for ADHD, and the presence of ADHD influences the severity of externalizing symptoms (Loeber et al., 2000; Powell, Lochman, Jackson, Young, & Yaros, 2009). Comorbid internalizing conditions are less frequent, although gender may play a role. Girls are more likely than boys to have a comorbid internalizing condition at any age. The cooccurrence of depression is more likely in preadolescence for boys, and such comorbidity in girls increases significantly with age. Indeed, the majority of referred youth (except for adolescent boys) with CD have one or more additional diagnoses (Offord, Boyle, & Racine, 1991). Comorbid depression is more likely in CD cases than in those with ODD (Wolff & Ollendick, 2006). Comorbid anxiety may be associated with fewer CD symptoms of aggression, whereas comorbid depression is associated with increased risk for suicidal behavior (Loeber & Keenan, 1994). CD is also often associated with substantial academic underachievement (Hinshaw, Lahey, & Hart, 1993; Kern & State, 2008). Although a relationship between low IQ and CD diminishes when researchers control for ADHD, reading disorders do appear to be related to CD (Burke, Loeber, & Birmaher, 2002). The conjoint presence of CD and depression may represent an even greater risk for a variety of problems than is represented by each condition alone. These problems may include substance dependence, academic problems, problematic social competence and peer relationships, a predisposition not to experience positive emotions, treatment seeking, treatment resistance, and increased long-term negative implications (Marmorstein & Iacono, 2001). Depression and externalizing problems appear to interact, with the combination of disorders resulting in a remarkably high rate of alcohol abuse and psychological reactance, and this interaction supports tailoring treatment by utilizing a dimensional approach to diagnosis (Evans & Frank, 2004).

The comorbidity of depression and anxiety is substantial (up to 70%) in clinically referred youth (Brady & Kendall, 1992; Zahn-Waxler, Klimes-Dougan, & Slattery, 2000). Indeed, substantial evidence exists that anxiety and depression are part of a broader construct of emotional distress in children and adolescents (Finch, Lipovsky, & Casat, 1989; King, Ollendick, & Gullone, 1991), with the distinction of the two occurring more so in adulthood. Anxiety may more frequently appear before depression, and their joint occurrence suggests a higher degree of disability. Many of these youth have a comorbid externalizing disorder (cf. Zahn-Waxler et al., 2000). A high level of comorbidity between anxiety and externalizing disorders is evident particularly in younger children and in males with social phobia (Marmorstein, 2007).

Multidimensional inventories may be especially valuable in the assessment of children with a known disability. For example, comorbid conditions in youth classified as mentally impaired are common (Whitaker & Read, 2006) yet typically underdiagnosed (Nanson & Gordon, 1999). This phenomenon is so prevalent that unique descriptive labels have been proposed. *Diagnostic overshadowing* is the tendency for clinicians to overlook additional psychiatric diagnoses once the presence of intellectual impairment has been established (Spengler, Strohmer, & Prout, 1990); *masking* is the process by which the clinical characteristics of a mental disorder are assumed instead to be features of developmental delay (cf. Pearson et al., 2000). Careful analysis of existing studies suggests that comorbidity rates for mentally impaired children are highest for anxiety disorders and pervasive developmental disorder yet also are high for behavioral problems that may or may not fit a diagnostic category (Whitaker & Read).

Application of cluster analysis to the classification of multidimensional profiles illustrates the prevalence of symptom comorbidity among referred children and adolescents (cf. Caudle, 2008). In a study of 1,523 referred youth, a 13-cluster solution identified nine comorbid symptom patterns among Personality Inventory for Children, Second Edition (PIC-2) profiles representing 57% of this sample. Problem dimensions represented by PIC-2 subscales most associated with the pervasive evidence of other comorbid problems included disruptive and inattentive behavior, noncompliance, and conflict with peers. Substantial comorbidity was also demonstrated for dimensions that represented cognitive and adaptive limitations,

problematic anger, and depression. This methodological approach to the identification of symptom patterns was supported through evidence of pattern stability as well as through demonstration of the relation between these profile types and demographic variables, diagnosis, and independent clinician, teacher, and student description.

## Problem Intensity and Chronicity

Referral to a mental health professional, whether for hospitalization or residential care or for outpatient evaluation at a clinic or other tertiary referral center, ensures the presence of a high proportion of difficult and complicated cases that will include high levels of comorbidity (Achenbach, 2005; Caron & Rutter, 1991). Such referrals often represent a pattern of maladjustment that does not remit over time and that is also resistant to primary corrective efforts in the home or the school, or through consultation with a pediatrician or family physician. An extended symptomatic course suggests the presence of conditions that are secondary to primary chronic problems (e.g., primary disruptive behavior contributes to peer rejection that results in social isolation that leads to dysphoria). Chronicity and intensity of current adjustment problems represent an assessment challenge to establish the historical sequence of problem emergence and the consequences of previous intervention efforts. Such a history may seduce a clinician into making significant diagnostic leaps of inference that may not be warranted. Such errors may be avoided through systematic use of a multidimensional instrument during the intake process. When current problems have a significant history, the significant adults who will participate in the assessment process (parents, teachers) are likely to bring with them a high degree of emotional commitment to problem resolution. Such informant intensity may decrease the clarity of their contribution as a questionnaire informant to the assessment. Psychiatric diagnosis requires attention not just to the presence or absolute number of symptoms but also to their intensity and the resulting nature and level of impairment. In some cases reported symptoms may exist, but the degree of actual impairment may be in question. In the case of symptoms such as those found in ADHD, for example, a large proportion of children may demonstrate a significant number of symptoms, yet some may not demonstrate significant impairment in functioning (Lewandowski, Lovett, & Gordon, 2009). Again, a multidimensional approach allows a more precise evaluation of the degree of impairment across cognitive, behavioral, and social spheres.

## Referral Process

Youth generally come to mental health settings only because they are referred for specific services, although other evaluations may be conducted at school or in the physician's office secondary to some routine, setting-specific observation or other data-gathering process. Some consideration of the referral process provides insight into the challenges inherent in assessments conducted by mental health professionals. Requests for mental health evaluation often originate with a request by a professional or from a setting that is distant from the mental health professional, allowing less-than-complete communication. The mental health professional or mental health service delivery agency cannot assume that the detail that accompanies the request for service is either sufficient or accurate. Rather, at least one adult has been motivated to initiate this referral and at least one or more focused concerns may be communicated to some degree.

In other instances the referral for an evaluation may come from a behavioral health managed care company and may represent only the information provided by a parent who has called the number on the back of an insurance card. In such instances the referral assures the clinician of some financial reimbursement for services rendered but provides no independent meaningful clinical information. That is, the clinician must first document presence, then type, pattern, and severity. In such cases, the clinician must be especially vigilant regarding potential errors in focus—that is, assuming that specific behaviors represent one problem while they actually represent another (i.e., similar behaviors reflect dissimilar problems).

## Challenge of Managed Care

Maruish (2002), although focusing on mental health services for adults, provided a balanced discussion of the changes in psychometric practice that have accompanied behavioral health benefits management. Requests for psychological testing must be preauthorized if these services will be reimbursed. A delay in obtaining authorization may be of particular concern with high-risk groups, such as adolescents, who may deteriorate, become noncompliant, or leave a facility before the assessment can be authorized (Eisman et al., 2000). Approval of testing requests will be most successful when psychological testing is proposed to support the development of a differential diagnosis and a plan of treatment. Collection of this information is consistent with an emphasis on the application

of treatments with proven effectiveness (M. C. Roberts & Hurley, 1997). Psychological testing routinely applied without focus or supporting such goals as the development of an understanding of "the underlying personality structure," as well as administration of collections of tests that incorporate duplicative or overlapping procedures, are inconsistent with the goals and philosophy of managed care. This review process may reduce the use of psychological testing and limit more time-consuming procedures while supporting the use of brief, easily scored measures and checklists (Piotrowski, Belter, & Keller, 1998).

In contrast, the objectives and general philosophy of managed care are consistent with the application of objective multidimensional measures in the evaluation and treatment of children and adolescents. These goals include the efficient and rapid definition of current problems, the development of an effective treatment program, the monitoring of such intervention, and the evaluation of treatment effectiveness. Of greatest efficiency will be the application of procedures that generate information that supports all of these goals. The information generated by objective ratings and questionnaires are time and cost effective and provide information that can be easily assimilated by the significant adults in a child's life, therapists with various training backgrounds, and the organizations that ultimately monitor and control mental health resources.

It is of particular concern for child mental health providers that some diagnoses, most notably ADHD, are viewed by managed care organizations as best diagnosed through a trial of medication or a brief interview (Eisman et al., 2000; Groth-Marnat, 1999). It is useful to contrast contemporary descriptions of effective diagnostic and psychological assessment procedures to the expectation that the information necessary for accurate diagnosis and treatment planning can be obtained in a 1-hour clinical interview or medication trial. Cantwell (1996) outlined the necessary diagnostic components in the evaluation of ADHD. These components include: (a) a comprehensive interview with all parenting figures to review current symptoms and developmental, medical, school, family, social, medical, and mental health history; (b) a developmentally appropriate interview with the child that incorporates screening for comorbid disorders; (c) a medical evaluation; (d) assessment of cognitive ability and academic achievement; (e) application of both broad-spectrum and more narrowly focused parent and teacher rating scales; and (f) other adjunct assessments, such as speech and language assessment. Cordell (1998) described the range of psychological assessment services often requested by a child psychiatry service. She provided outlines of assessment protocols for preschoolers, preteens, and adolescents. Each of these protocols requires three to five sessions for a total of up to 6 hours of patient contact.

The assessment methods that are the focus of this chapter may be applied to meet the goals of managed care. In routine (not crisis) evaluation, parents may be mailed a teacher rating form to be completed and returned before the intake interview. Parents may be asked to complete a questionnaire in a similar fashion. Completion of such rating forms not only provides valuable independent assessment of the child but also represents a sample of positive parent behavior. This compliant behavior may predict an increased likelihood of parent attendance at the first scheduled appointment. This is an important consideration, because an acutely distressed parent may make an appointment for mental health services yet not appear if the specific conditions that generated the distress resolve before the scheduled appointment.

When a parent completes a questionnaire to describe the child before the intake interview, this additional information can add an efficient focus to the topics subsequently discussed. Because of the central role of family and school in child treatment, the feedback to parents and teachers from these measures is usually accepted with little if any resistance. When these profiles are inconsistent with the global opinions that have motivated the mental health consultation, the presentation and discussion of such results may facilitate realignment of parent or teacher opinion and the development of an alliance with the therapist.

## CONDUCT OF ASSESSMENT BY QUESTIONNAIRE AND RATING SCALE

In contrast to the models proposed by managed care, contemporary models of the assessment of psychiatric disorders in youth are likely to be comprehensive and are increasingly expected to be evidence based (Archer, 2005; Mash & Hunsley, 2005). For example, although early approaches to the behavioral assessment of CD focused on identifying the parenting skills deficits conceptualized as causative and therefore in need of primary remediation, the increased understanding of the developmental aspects of this disorder has substantially influenced assessment. McMahon (1987) noted:

As our knowledge of the multiple factors influencing the development, manifestation, and maintenance of conduct disorders has grown, it has become apparent that a proper assessment of the conduct disordered child must make use of the multiple methods (e.g., behavioral rating scales, direct observation, interviews) completed by multiple informants (parents, teachers, the children themselves) concerning the child's behavior in multiple settings (e.g., home, school). Furthermore, it is essential that the familial and extra-familial contexts in which the conduct disordered child functions be assessed as well. (p. 246)

This assessment process is often described as *sequential* (Mash & Lee, 1993). The presence of specific problems is first established. Multidimensional inventories can make an efficient and effective contribution to this process. Each problem must be placed in its developmental and historical context and assessed in relation to recent experiences. Such information is most efficiently gathered by a focused and tailored interview. Once a treatment plan is developed, its effectiveness should be monitored through additional assessment. Repetition of baseline assessment procedures or the use of more focused or narrowly defined questionnaires during and at the completion of treatment can be applied in the support of this process. Such efforts can support modification of ongoing treatment, quantify change at termination, and estimate stability of such improvement by follow-up survey, all of which are consistent with the current view that evidence-based assessment is an integral part of evidence-based treatment (Achenbach, 2005).

### Example of a Family of Multidimensional, Multisource Measures

#### Personality Inventory for Children, Second Edition

First published in 1977, the Personality Inventory for Children questionnaire, completed by parent or other guardian, was completely revised in 2001 (Lachar & Gruber, 2001). It has been described as "one of the earliest and remains among the most well known of parent rating scales...the grandparent of many modern rating scales" (Kamphaus & Frick, 2002, p. 152). The current version, the Personality Inventory for Children, Second Edition (PIC-2), incorporates changes such as psychometric improvements and the addition of improved validity scales (Frick, Barry, & Kamphaus, 2010). It is provided in two formats. The first format consists of a reusable 275-statement administration booklet and a separate answer sheet for the recording of parent responses to booklet statements. Various answer sheets can be scored by hand with templates, or the recorded responses (true/false) can be entered for processing into a personal computer; answer sheets may also be mailed or faxed to the test publisher for processing. A multiscale profile (the PIC-2 Behavioral Summary) interpreted using guidelines presented in the test manual (Lachar & Gruber, 2001) is obtained by completion of the first 96 items, which takes about 15 minutes. A second, similarly interpreted comprehensive profile (the Standard Format) and responses to a critical item list may be obtained by completing the entire administration booklet, which takes about 40 minutes or less. The second published format provides the 96 statements of the PIC-2 Behavioral Summary and a simple, efficient method to generate and profile its 12 scores. The PIC-2 gender-specific $T$-score values are derived from a contemporary national sample of parent descriptions of youth 5 to 18 years of age.

Table 11.1 lists the components of these two profiles and some of their associated psychometric characteristics. PIC-2 statements are written at a low- to mid-fourth-grade reading level and represent current and previous behaviors, feelings, accomplishments, and interactions, both common to and relatively infrequent among youth evaluated by mental health professionals. These statements reflect both variations in problem frequency and severity. PIC-2 adjustment scales were constructed using an iterative procedure. Potential scale items were first assigned to initial dimensions on the basis of previous scale structure or manifest statement content, whereas final item-scale assignment reflected a demonstrated strong and primary correlation with the dimension on which it was finally assigned. The 9 nonoverlapping scales of the standard profile were further refined with the assistance of factor analysis to construct 21 subscales of greater content homogeneity applied to facilitate scale interpretation. The PIC-2 Behavioral Summary profile presents 8 core scales and 4 composites or combinations of these values designed to efficiently measure change in symptomatic status through readministration. Each of these core scales consists of 12 statements selected from the full-length standard form to support treatment planning and to measure behavioral change. Each short scale correlates .92 to .96 with its full-length equivalent.

A significant element of the PIC-2 Standard Format profile is the provision of three response validity scales. The first of these scales (Inconsistency) consists of 35 pairs of statements. Because each pair of statements is highly correlated, two of the four possible pairs of responses (true-true and false-false, or true-false and false-true) are classified as inconsistent and their presence adds a unit weight to the Inconsistency scale raw score that can range from 0 to 35. Review of examples of inconsistent response pairs clarifies this concept; for example, "My child has many friends. (True)/My child has very few friends. (True)"; "My child often disobeys me. (True)/My child often breaks the rules. (False)." An elevated $T$ score on this scale ($T > 69$) suggests that the parent who completed the PIC-2 failed to attend sufficiently to, or to achieve adequate comprehension of, PIC-2 statement content.

The second validity scale, Dissimulation, evaluates the likelihood that the responses to PIC-2 statements represent an exaggeration of current problems in adjustment, or the description of nonexistent problems and symptoms. These scale items were identified through an analytic process in which three samples were compared: a normative sample, a referred sample, and a sample in which parents were asked to describe their asymptomatic children as if they were in need of mental health services (i.e., a malingering sample). The average endorsement rate for these 35 items was 6.3% in normative, 15.3% in referred, and 54.5% in directed malingered protocols. Elevation of Dissimulation may reflect the presence of informant distress that may distort youth description.

The third validity scale, Defensiveness, includes 12 descriptions of infrequent or highly improbable positive attributes ("My child always does his/her homework on time." [True]) and 12 statements that represent the denial of common child behaviors and problems ("My child has some bad habits." [False]). Scale values above $59T$ suggest that significant problems may be minimized or denied on the PIC-2 profile. The PIC-2 manual provides interpretive guidelines for seven patterns of these three scales that classified virtually all cases (99.8%) in a study of 6,370 protocols.

### Personality Inventory for Youth

The Personality Inventory for Youth (PIY) and the PIC-2 are closely related in that the majority of PIY items were derived from rewriting content-appropriate PIC items into a first-person format. As demonstrated in Table 11.2, the PIY profile is very similar to the PIC-2 Standard Format profile. PIY scales were derived in an iterative fashion with 270 statements assigned to one of nine clinical scales and to three validity response scales (Inconsistency, Dissimulation, and Defensiveness). As in the PIC-2, each nonoverlapping scale is further divided into two or three more homogenous subscales to facilitate interpretation. PIY materials include a reusable administration booklet and a separate answer sheet that can be scored by hand

**TABLE 11.1  PIC-2 Adjustment Scales and Subscales and Selected Psychometric Performance**

| SCALE or Subscale (abbreviation) | Items | α | $r_{tt}$ | Subscale Representative Item |
|---|---|---|---|---|
| | | STANDARD FORMAT PROFILE | | |
| COGNITIVE IMPAIRMENT (COG) | 39 | .87 | .94 | |
| Inadequate Abilities (COG1) | 13 | .77 | .95 | My child seems to understand everything that is said. |
| Poor Achievement (COG2) | 13 | .77 | .91 | Reading has been a problem for my child. |
| Developmental Delay (COG3) | 13 | .79 | .82 | My child could ride a tricycle by age five years. |
| IMPULSIVITY AND DISTRACTABILITY (ADH) | 27 | .92 | .88 | |
| Disruptive Behavior (ADH1) | 21 | .91 | .87 | My child cannot keep attention on anything. |
| Fearlessness (ADH2) | 6 | .69 | .86 | My child will do anything on a dare. |
| DELINQUENCY (DLQ) | 47 | .95 | .90 | |
| Antisocial Behavior (DLQ1) | 13 | .88 | .83 | My child has run away from home. |
| Dyscontrol (DLQ2) | 17 | .91 | .91 | When my child gets mad, watch out! |
| Noncompliance (DLQ3) | 17 | .92 | .87 | My child often breaks the rules. |
| FAMILY DYSFUNCTION (FAM) | 25 | .87 | .90 | |
| Conflict Among Members (FAM1) | 15 | .83 | .90 | There is a lot of tension in our home. |
| Parent Maladjustment (FAM2) | 10 | .77 | .91 | One of the child's parents drinks too much alcohol. |
| REALITY DISTORTION (RLT) | 29 | .89 | .92 | |
| Developmental Deviation (RLT1) | 14 | .84 | .87 | My child needs protection from everyday dangers. |
| Hallucinations and Delusions (RLT2) | 15 | .81 | .79 | My child thinks others are plotting against him/her. |
| SOMATIC CONCERN (SOM) | 28 | .84 | .91 | |
| Psychosomatic Preoccupation (SOM1) | 17 | .80 | .90 | My child is worried about disease. |
| Muscular Tension and Anxiety (SOM2) | 11 | .68 | .88 | My child often has back pains. |
| PSYCHOLOGICAL DISCOMFORT (DIS) | 39 | .90 | .90 | |
| Fear and Worry (DIS1) | 13 | .72 | .76 | My child will worry a lot before starting something new. |
| Depression (DIS2) | 18 | .87 | .91 | My child hardly ever smiles. |
| Sleep Disturbance/Preoccupation with Death (DIS3) | 8 | .76 | .86 | My child thinks about ways to kill himself/herself. |
| SOCIAL WITHDRAWAL (WDL) | 19 | .81 | .89 | |
| Social Introversion (WDL1) | 11 | .78 | .90 | Shyness is my child's biggest problem. |
| Isolation (WDL2) | 8 | .68 | .88 | My child often stays in his/her room for hours. |
| SOCIAL SKILL DEFICITS (SSK) | 28 | .91 | .92 | |
| Limited Peer Status (SSK1) | 13 | .84 | .92 | My child is very popular with other children. |
| Conflict with Peers (SSK2) | 15 | .88 | .87 | Other children make fun of my child's ideas. |
| | | BEHAVIORAL SUMMARY PROFILE | | |
| SHORT ADJUSTMENT SCALES | | | | |
| Impulsivity and Distractibility-Short (ADH-S) | 12 | .88 | .87 | |
| Delinquency-Short (DLQ-S) | 12 | .89 | .85 | |
| Family Dysfunction-Short (FAM-S) | 12 | .82 | .86 | |
| Reality Distortion-Short (RLT-S) | 12 | .82 | .87 | |
| Somatic Concern-Short (SOM-S) | 12 | .73 | .85 | |
| Psychological Discomfort-Short (DIS-S) | 12 | .81 | .97 | |
| Social Withdrawal-Short (WDL-S) | 12 | .76 | .88 | |
| Social Skill Deficits-Short (SSK-S) | 12 | .82 | .89 | |
| COMPOSITE SCALES | | | | |
| Externalizing (EXT-C) | 24 | .94 | .89 | |
| Internalizing (INT-C) | 36 | .89 | .89 | |
| Social Adjustment (SOC-C) | 24 | .86 | .89 | |
| Total Score (TOT-C) | 96 | .95 | .89 | |

*Note:* Scale and subscale alpha (α) values based on a referred sample $n = 1,551$. One-week clinical retest correlation ($r_{tt}$) sample $n = 38$.
Selected material from the PIC-2 copyright © 2001 by Western Psychological Services. Reprinted by permission of the publisher, Western Psychological Services, 12031 Wilshire Boulevard, Los Angeles, California, 90025, U.S.A., www.wpspublish.com. Not to be reprinted in whole or in part for any additional purpose without the expressed, written permission of the publisher. All rights reserved.

**TABLE 11.2  PIY Clinical Scales and Subscales and Selected Psychometric Performance**

| SCALE or Subscale (abbreviation) | Items | α | $r_{tt}$ | Subscale Representative Item |
|---|---|---|---|---|
| COGNITIVE IMPAIRMENT (COG) | 20 | .74 | .80 | |
| Poor Achievement and Memory (COG1) | 8 | .65 | .70 | School has been easy for me. |
| Inadequate Abilities (COG2) | 8 | .67 | .67 | I think I am stupid or dumb. |
| Learning Problems (COG3) | 4 | .44 | .76 | I have been held back a year in school. |
| IMPULSIVITY AND DISTRACTABILITY (ADH) | 17 | .77 | .84 | |
| Brashness (ADH1) | 4 | .54 | .70 | I often nag and bother other people. |
| Distractibility and Overactivity (ADH2) | 8 | .61 | .71 | I cannot wait for things like other kids can. |
| Impulsivity (ADH3) | 5 | .54 | .58 | I often act without thinking. |
| DELINQUENCY (DLQ) | 42 | .92 | .91 | |
| Antisocial Behavior (DLQ1) | 15 | .83 | .88 | I sometimes skip school. |
| Dyscontrol (DLQ2) | 16 | .84 | .88 | I lose friends because of my temper. |
| Noncompliance (DLQ3) | 11 | .83 | .80 | Punishment does not change how I act. |
| FAMILY DYSFUNCTION (FAM) | 29 | .87 | .83 | |
| Parent-Child Conflict (FAM1) | 9 | .82 | .73 | My parent(s) are too strict with me. |
| Parent Maladjustment (FAM2) | 13 | .74 | .76 | My parents often argue. |
| Marital Discord (FAM3) | 7 | .70 | .73 | My parents' marriage has been solid and happy. |
| REALITY DISTORTION (RLT) | 22 | .83 | .84 | |
| Feelings of Alienation (RLT1) | 11 | .77 | .74 | I do strange or unusual things. |
| Hallucinations and Delusions (RLT2) | 11 | .71 | .78 | People secretly control my thoughts. |
| SOMATIC CONCERN (SOM) | 27 | .85 | .76 | |
| Psychosomatic Syndrome (SOM1) | 9 | .73 | .63 | I often get very tired. |
| Muscular Tension and Anxiety (SOM2) | 10 | .74 | .72 | At times I have trouble breathing. |
| Preoccupation with Disease (SOM3) | 8 | .60 | .59 | I often talk about sickness. |
| PSYCHOLOGICAL DISCOMFORT (DIS) | 32 | .86 | .77 | |
| Fear and Worry (DIS1) | 15 | .78 | .75 | Small problems do not bother me. |
| Depression (DIS2) | 11 | .73 | .69 | I am often in a good mood. |
| Sleep Disturbance (DIS3) | 6 | .70 | .71 | I often think about death. |
| SOCIAL WITHDRAWAL (WDL) | 18 | .80 | .82 | |
| Social Introversion (WDL1) | 10 | .78 | .77 | Talking to others makes me nervous. |
| Isolation (WDL2) | 8 | .59 | .77 | I almost always play alone. |
| SOCIAL SKILL DEFICITS (SSK) | 24 | .86 | .79 | |
| Limited Peer Status (SSK1) | 13 | .79 | .76 | Other kids look up to me as a leader. |
| Conflict with Peers (SSK2) | 11 | .80 | .72 | I wish that I were more able to make and keep friends. |

*Note:* Scale and subscale alpha (α) values based on a clinical sample $n = 1,178$. One-week clinical retest correlation ($r_{tt}$) sample $n = 86$. Selected material from the PIY copyright © 1995 by Western Psychological Services. Reprinted by permission of the publisher, Western Psychological Services, 12031 Wilshire Boulevard, Los Angeles, California, 90025, U.S.A., www.wpspublish.com. Not to be reprinted in whole or in part for any additional purpose without the expressed, written permission of the publisher. All rights reserved.

with templates, processed by personal computer, or mailed to the test publisher to obtain a narrative interpretive report, profile, and responses to a critical item list. PIY items were intentionally written at a low readability level, and a low- to mid-fourth-grade reading comprehension level is adequate for understanding and responding to the PIY statements. When students have at least an age-9 working vocabulary, but do not have a comparable level of reading ability, or when younger students have limited ability to attend and concentrate, an audiotape recording of the PIY items is available and can be completed in less than 1 hour. Scale raw scores are converted to $T$ scores using contemporary gender-specific norms from students in grades 4 through 12, representing ages 9 through 19 (Lachar & Gruber, 1995).

## Student Behavior Survey

The Student Behavior Survey (SBS) is a teacher rating form developed through reviewing established teacher rating scales and by writing new statements that focused on content appropriate to teacher observation (Lachar, Wingenfeld, Kline, & Gruber, 2000). Unlike ratings that can be scored on parent or teacher norms (Naglieri, LeBuffe, & Pfeiffer, 1994), the SBS items demonstrate a specific school focus. Fifty-eight of its 102 items specifically refer to in-class or in-school behaviors and judgments that can be rated only by school staff (Wingenfeld, Lachar, Gruber, & Kline, 1998). SBS items provide a profile of 14 scales that assess student academic status and work habits, social skills, parental participation in the educational process,

**TABLE 11.3    SBS Scales, Their Psychometric Characteristics, and Sample Items**

| Scale Name | Items | α | $r_{tt}$ | $r_{1,2}$ | Example of Scale Item |
|---|---|---|---|---|---|
| Academic Performance (AP) | 8 | .89 | .78 | .84 | Reading Comprehension |
| Academic Habits (AH) | 13 | .93 | .87 | .76 | Completes class assignments |
| Social Skills (SS) | 8 | .89 | .88 | .73 | Participates in class activities |
| Parent Participation (PP) | 6 | .88 | .83 | .68 | Parent(s) encourage achievement |
| Health Concerns (HC) | 6 | .85 | .79 | .58 | Complains of headaches |
| Emotional Distress (ED) | 15 | .91 | .90 | .73 | Worries about little things |
| Unusual Behavior (UB) | 7 | .88 | .76 | .62 | Says strange or bizarre things |
| Social Problems (SP) | 12 | .87 | .90 | .72 | Teased by other students |
| Verbal Aggression (VA) | 7 | .92 | .88 | .79 | Argues and wants the last word |
| Physical Aggression (PA) | 5 | .90 | .86 | .63 | Destroys property when angry |
| Behavior Problems (BP) | 15 | .93 | .92 | .82 | Disobeys class or school rules |
| Attention-Deficit/Hyperactivity (ADH) | 16 | .94 | .91 | .83 | Waits for his/her turn |
| Oppositional Defiant (OPD) | 16 | .95 | .94 | .86 | Mood changes without reason |
| Conduct Problems (CNP) | 16 | .94 | .90 | .69 | Steals from others |

*Note:* Scale alpha (α) values based on a referred sample $n = 1,315$. Retest correlation ($r_{tt}$) 5- to 11-year-old student sample ($n = 52$) with average rating interval of 1.7 weeks. Interrater agreement ($r_{1,2}$), sample $n = 60$ fourth- and fifth-grade, team-taught or special-education students.

and problems such as aggressive or atypical behavior and emotional stress (see Table 11.3). Norms that generate linear *T* scores are gender specific and derived from two age groups: 5 to 11 and 12 to 18 years.

SBS items are presented on one two-sided form. The rating process takes 15 minutes or less. Scoring of scales and completion of a profile are straightforward clerical processes that take only a couple of minutes. The SBS consists of two major sections. The first section, Academic Resources, includes four scales that address positive aspects of school adjustment, whereas the second section, Adjustment Problems, generates seven scales that measure various dimensions of problematic adjustment. Unlike the PIC-2 and PIY statements, which are completed with a true or false response, SBS items are mainly rated on a 4-point frequency scale. Three additional disruptive behavior scales each consist of 16 items nominated as representing phenomena consistent with the characteristics associated with one of three major disruptive disorder diagnoses: ADHD, combined type; ODD; and CD (*Diagnostic and Statistical Manual, Fourth Edition DSM-IV*; [American Psychiatric Association, 2000]; Pisecco, Lachar, Gruber, Gallen, Kline, & Huzinec, 1999).

### Behavioral Summary

This most recent version of these three multidimensional questionnaires was developed to maximize efficient application and interpretation (Lachar & Gruber, 2009). Each measure is completed by marking responses on one two-sided page that is then converted either manually to scale scores using each form's internal guides with the resulting raw scores plotted on a profile form or by item response entry with unlimited-use software. The Behavioral Summary includes the teacher assessment already described in some detail as well as parent and student questionnaires, parallel in both dimensions and item content. Parent and student forms each provide eight substantive 12-item scales (Impulsivity & Distractibility; Defiance; Family Problems; Atypical Behavior; Somatic Concern; Emotional Problems; Social Withdrawal; Social Skill Deficits), two validity scales (Inconsistent Responding, Exaggeration), three composite scales (Externalization; Internalization; Social Adjustment), and a total score. Scale and item content facilitates measurement of change and provided software allows concurrent scale and item comparisons between two teachers, two parents, or between parent and child descriptions. In a similar fashion, the results of the same informant, obtained at two different times, can easily be compared to estimate symptomatic change.

### Multidimensional Assessment

The overwhelming merits of objective multidimensional questionnaires reflect the reality that there is no reasonable alternative to their use in baseline evaluation of children seen in mental health settings (Lachar, 1993, 1998). Such questionnaires employ consistent stimulus and response demands, measure a variety of useful dimensions, and generate a profile of scores standardized using the same normative reference. The clinician may therefore reasonably assume that differences obtained among dimensions reflect variation in content rather than some difference in technical or stylistic characteristic between independently constructed unidimensional measures (e.g., true-false versus multiple-choice format, application of regional versus national norms, or statement sets that require different minimum reading requirements). In addition, it is more likely that interpretive materials will be provided in an integrated fashion and the clinician need not select or accumulate information from a variety of sources for each profile dimension.

Selection of a multidimensional instrument that documents problem presence *and* absence demonstrates that the clinician is sensitive to the challenges inherent in the referral process and the likelihood of comorbid conditions, as previously discussed. This action also demonstrates that the clinician understands that the accurate assessment of a variety of child and family characteristics that are independent of diagnosis may yet be relevant to treatment design and implementation. For example, the PIY *FAM1* subscale (Parent-Child Conflict) may be applied to estimate whether a child's parents should be considered a treatment resource or a source of current conflict. Similarly, the PIC-2 and PIY *WDL1* subscale (Social Introversion) may be applied to predict whether an adolescent will easily develop rapport with his or her therapist or whether the process of developing rapport should be one of the first therapeutic objectives.

## Multisource Assessment

The collection of standardized observations from different informants is quite natural in the evaluation of children and adolescents. Despite growing use of child self-report by psychologists and concerns about discrepant information from various sources, pediatricians and other professionals continue to rely heavily on informants (Konold & Pianta, 2007). Application of multisource assessment has inherent strengths yet presents the clinician with several challenges. Considering parents or other guardians, teachers or school counselors, and the students themselves as three distinct classes of informant, each brings unique strengths to the assessment process. Significant adults in a child's life are in a unique position to report on behaviors that they—not the child—find problematic. Youth are in a unique position to report on their thoughts and feelings. Adult ratings on these dimensions must of necessity reflect, or be inferred from, child language and behavior. Parents are in a unique position to describe a child's development and history as well as observations that are unique to the home. Teachers observe students in an environment that allows for direct comparisons with same-age classmates as well as a focus on cognitive and behavioral characteristics prerequisite for success in the classroom and the acquisition of knowledge. Collection of independent parent and teacher ratings also contributes to comprehensive assessment by determining classes of behaviors that are unique to a given setting or that generalize across settings (Mash & Terdal, 1997).

Studies suggest that parents and teachers may be the most attuned to a child's behaviors that they find to be disruptive, and informant agreement is somewhat higher for externalizing symptoms (cf. De Los Reyes & Kazdin, 2005; Loeber & Schmaling, 1985), but informants are less consistent in the report of internalizing disorders (Cantwell, 1996). More recent reviews and meta-analytic studies have suggested logically that more observable symptoms are more consistently reported across informants (De Los Reyes & Kazdin, 2005), regardless of whether the problems are traditionally classified as externalizing or internalizing. Thus, low to moderate correspondence between informant reports of depression and anxiety may reflect the lower degree of observability relative to externalizing behaviors. Symptoms and behaviors that reflect the presence of depression may be more frequently endorsed in questionnaire responses and in standardized interviews by children than by their mothers (cf. Barrett et al., 1991; Moretti, Fine, Haley, & Marriage, 1985). In normative studies, mothers endorse more problems than their spouses or the child's teacher (cf. Abidin, 1995; Duhig, Renk, Epstein, & Phares, 2000; Goyette, Conners, & Ulrich, 1978). Measured parent agreement may be related to the amount of time that a father spends with his child (Fitzgerald, Zucker, Maguin, & Reider, 1994), but disagreement may also be a function of parent psychological symptoms or aspects of the parent–child relationship (Treutler & Epkins, 2003). Maternal depression, for example, may distort parent report in a negative direction. Teacher ratings have (Burns, Walsh, Owen, & Snell, 1997), and have not, separated ADHD subgroups (Crystal, Ostrander, Chen, & August, 2001). Perhaps this inconsistency demonstrates the complexity of drawing generalizations from one or even a series of studies. The ultimate evaluation of this diagnostic process must consider the dimension assessed, the observer or informant, the specific measure applied, the patient studied, and the setting of the evaluation.

An influential meta-analysis by Achenbach, McConaughy, and Howell (1987) demonstrated that poor agreement historically has been obtained on questionnaires or rating scales among parents, teachers, and students, although relatively greater agreement among sources was obtained for descriptions of externalizing behaviors. One source of informant disagreement between comparably labeled questionnaire dimensions may be revealed by the direct comparison of scale content, in terms of items as well as anchors (Carlston & Ogles, 2006). Scales similarly named may not incorporate the same content, whereas scales with different titles may correlate because of parallel content. The application of standardized interviews often resolves this issue when the questions asked and the criteria for evaluating responses obtained are consistent across informants. When standardized interviews are independently conducted with parents and with children, more agreement is obtained for visible behaviors and when the interviewed children are older (Lachar & Gruber, 1993). Yet, even when scales or interview questions are held consistent, informants may lend a unique perspective on symptoms (Baldwin & Dadds, 2007; Carlston & Ogles, 2006).

Informant agreement and the investigation of comparative utility of classes of informants continue to be a focus of considerable effort (cf. Des Los Reyes, 2011; Smith, 2007; Youngstrom, Loeber, & Stouthamer-Loeber, 2000) and further "theory-guided" research involving principles of observer bias is suggested (De Los Reyes & Kazdin, 2005). The opinions of mental health professionals and parents as to the relative merits of these sources of information have been surveyed (Loeber, Green, & Lahey, 1990; Phares, 1997). Indeed, even parents and their adolescent children have been asked to suggest the reasons for their disagreements. One identified causative factor was the deliberate concealment of specific behaviors by youth from their parents (Bidaut-Russell, Reich, Robins, Compton, & Mattison, 1995). Certainly, children's motivation may impact the degree to which their self-reported symptoms are consistent with other sources (Reuterskiöld, Öst, & Ollendick, 2008). Considering that youth seldom refer themselves for mental health services, routine assessment of their motivation to provide full disclosure would seem prudent.

The parent-completed Child Behavior Checklist (CBCL; Achenbach, 1991a) and student-completed Youth Self-Report (YSR; Achenbach, 1991b), as symptom checklists with parallel content and derived dimensions, have facilitated the direct comparison of these two sources of diagnostic information. The study by Handwerk, Larzelere, Soper, and Friman (1999) is at least the 21st such published comparison, joining 10 other studies of samples of children referred for evaluation or treatment. These studies of referred youth have consistently demonstrated that the CBCL provides more evidence of student maladjustment than does the YSR. In contrast, 9 of the 10 comparable studies of nonreferred children (classroom-based or epidemiological surveys) demonstrated the opposite relationship: The YSR documented more problems in adjustment than did the CBCL. One possible explanation for these findings is that children referred for evaluation often demonstrate a defensive response set, whereas nonreferred children do not (Lachar, 1998).

Because the YSR does not incorporate response validity scales, a recent study of the effect of defensiveness on YSR profiles of inpatients applied the PIY Defensiveness scale to assign YSR profiles to defensive and nondefensive groups. (See Wrobel, Lachar, Wrobel, Morgan, Gruber, & Neher, 1999, for studies of this scale.) The substantial influence of measured defensiveness was demonstrated for five of eight narrow-band and all three summary measures of the YSR. For example, only 10% of defensive YSR protocols obtained an elevated ($>63T$) Total Problems score, whereas 45% of nondefensive YSR protocols obtained a similarly elevated Total Problems score (Lachar, Morgan, Espadas, & Schomer, 2000). The magnitude of this difference was comparable to the YSR versus CBCL discrepancy obtained by Handwerk et al. (1999; i.e., 28% of YSR versus 74% of CBCL Total Problems scores were comparably elevated). However, youth may reveal specific problems on a questionnaire that they denied during a clinical or structured interview.

## Clinical Issues in Application

### Priority of Informant Selection

When different informants are available, who should participate in the assessment process, and what priority should be assigned to each potential informant? Efforts have been made to prescribe which informant is best for a particular problem or age of child (Smith, 2007), yet discrepancies in past research findings and practices make it difficult to find the golden rule. Given the ambiguity at present, it makes a great deal of sense first to call on the person who expresses initial or primary concern regarding child adjustment—that is, the guardian, the teacher, or the student. This person should be motivated to participate in the systematic quantification of problem behaviors and other symptoms of poor adjustment. The nature of the problems and the unique dimensions assessed by certain informant-specific scales may also influence the selection process. If the teacher has not referred the child, report of classroom adjustment should also be obtained when the presence of disruptive behavior is of concern or when academic achievement is one focus of assessment. In these cases, such information may document the degree to which problematic behavior is situation specific and the degree to which academic problems either accompany other problems or may result from inadequate motivation. When an intervention is to be planned, all proposed participants should be involved in the assessment process.

### Disagreements Among Informants

Even estimates of considerable informant agreement derived from study samples are not easily applied as the clinician processes the results of one evaluation at a time. Although the clinician may be reassured when all sources of information converge and are consistent in the conclusions drawn, resolving inconsistencies among informants often provides information that is important to the diagnostic process or to treatment planning. Certain behaviors may be situation specific or certain informants may provide inaccurate descriptions that have been compromised by denial, exaggeration, or some other inadequate response. Disagreements among family members can be especially important in the planning and conduct of treatment. Parents may not agree about the presence or the nature of the problems that affect their child, and a youth may be unaware of the effect that his or her behavior has on others or may be unwilling to admit to having problems. In such cases, early therapeutic efforts must focus on such discrepancies in order to facilitate progress (cf. Achenbach, 2011).

### Multidimensional Versus Focused Assessment

Adjustment questionnaires vary in format from those that focus on the elements of one symptom dimension or diagnosis (i.e., depression, ADHD) to more comprehensive questionnaires. The most finely articulated of these instruments rate current and past phenomena to measure a broad variety of symptoms and behaviors, such as externalizing symptoms or disruptive behaviors, internalizing symptoms of depression and anxiety, and dimensions of social and peer adjustment. These questionnaires may also provide estimates of cognitive, academic, and adaptive adjustment as well as dimensions of family function that may be associated with problems in child adjustment and treatment efficacy. Considering the unique challenges characteristic of evaluation in mental health settings discussed earlier, it is thoroughly justified that every intake or baseline assessment should employ a multidimensional instrument.

Questionnaires selected to support the planning and monitoring of interventions and to assess treatment effectiveness must take into account a different set of considerations. Response to scale content must be able to represent

behavioral change, and scale format should facilitate application to the individual and summary to groups of comparable children similarly treated. Completion of such a scale should represent an effort that allows repeated administration, and the scale selected must measure the specific behaviors and symptoms that are the focus of treatment. Treatment of a child with a single focal problem may require the assessment of only this one dimension. In such cases, a brief depression or articulated ADHD questionnaire may be appropriate. If applied within a specialty clinic, similar cases can be accumulated and summarized with the same measure. Application of such scales to the typical child treated by mental health professionals is unlikely to capture all dimensions relevant to treatment.

## SELECTION OF PSYCHOLOGICAL TESTS

### Evaluating Scale Performance

#### Consult Published Resources

Although clearly articulated guidelines have been offered (cf. Newman, Ciarlo, & Carpenter, 1999), selection of optimal objective measures for either a specific or a routine assessment application may not be an easy process. An expanded variety of choices has become available in recent years, and the demonstration of their value is an ongoing effort. Manuals for published tests vary in the amount of detail that they provide. The reader cannot assume that test manuals provide comprehensive reviews of test performance or even offer adequate guidelines for application. Because of the growing use of such questionnaires, guidance may be gained from graduate-level textbooks (cf. Frick et al., 2010; Mash & Hunsley, 2007; Matson, Andrasik, & Matson, 2010; Merrell, 2010); handbooks (e.g., Reitman, 2008; Smith & Handler, 2007) and monographs designed to review a variety of specific measures (cf. Maruish, 1999). An introduction to more established measures, such as the MMPI adapted for adolescents (MMPI-A; Butcher et al., 1992), can be obtained by reference to chapters and books (e.g., Archer, 1999, 2005; Graham, 2006).

### Estimate of Technical Performance: Reliability

*Test performance* is judged by the adequacy of demonstrated reliability and validity. It should be emphasized from the onset that reliability and validity are not characteristics that reside in a test but describe a specific test application (e.g., assessment of depression in hospitalized adolescents). A number of statistical techniques are applied in the evaluation of scales of adjustment that were first developed in the study of cognitive ability and academic achievement. The generalizability of these technical characteristics may be less than ideal in the evaluation of psychopathology because the underlying assumptions made may not be achieved.

The core of the concept of *reliability* is performance consistency; the classical model estimates the degree to which an obtained scale score represents the true phenomenon, rather than some source of error (Gliner, Morgan, & Harmon, 2001). At the item level, reliability measures internal consistency of a scale—that is, the degree to which scale item responses agree. Because the calculation of internal consistency requires only one set of responses from any sample, this estimate is easily obtained. Unlike an achievement subscale in which all items correlate with each other because they are supposed to represent a homogenous dimension, the internal consistency of adjustment measures will vary by the method used to assign items to scales. Scales developed by the identification of items that meet a nontest standard (*external* approach) will demonstrate less internal consistency than will scales developed in a manner that takes the content of the relation between items into account (*inductive* or *deductive* approach; Burisch, 1984). An example is provided by comparison of the two major sets of scales for the MMPI-A (Butcher et al., 1992). Of the 10 profile scales constructed by empirical keying, 6 obtained estimates of internal consistency below 0.70 in a sample of referred adolescent boys. In a second set of 15 scales constructed with primary concern for manifest content, only 1 scale obtained an estimate below 0.70 using the same sample. Internal consistency may also vary with the homogeneity of the adjustment dimension being measured, the items assigned to the dimension, and the scale length or range of scores studied, including the influence of multiple scoring formats.

Scale reliability is usually estimated by comparison of repeated administrations. It is important to demonstrate stability of scales if they will be applied in the study of an intervention. Most investigators use a brief interval (e.g., 7–14 days) between measure administrations. The assumption is made that no change will occur within this interval. It has been our experience, however, with both the PIY and PIC-2 that small reductions are obtained on several scales at retest, while the Defensiveness scale *T* score increases by a comparable degree on retest. In some clinical settings, such as an acute inpatient unit, it would be impossible to calculate test–retest reliability estimates in which an underlying change would not be expected.

In such situations, *interrater comparisons*, when feasible, may be more appropriate. In this design it is assumed that each rater has had comparable experience with the youth to be rated and that any differences obtained would therefore represent a source of error across raters. Two clinicians could easily participate in the conduct of the same interview and then independently complete a symptom rating (cf. Lachar et al., 2001). However, interrater comparisons of mothers to fathers, or of pairs of teachers, assume that each rater has had comparable experience with the youth—such an assumption is seldom met.

### Estimate of Technical Performance: Validity

Of major importance is the demonstration of scale *validity* for a specific purpose. A valid scale measures what it was intended to measure (Morgan, Gliner, & Harmon, 2001). Validity may be demonstrated when a scale's performance is consistent with expectations (*construct* validity) or predicts external ratings or scores (*criterion* validity). The foundation for any scale is *content* validity, that is, the extent to which the scale represents the relevant content universe for each dimension. Test manuals should demonstrate that items belong on the scales on which they have been placed and that scales correlate with each other in an expected fashion. In addition, substantial correlations should be obtained between the scales on a given questionnaire and similar measures of demonstrated validity completed by the same and different raters. Valid scales of adjustment should separate meaningful groups (*discriminant* validity) and demonstrate an ability to assign cases into meaningful categories.

Examples of such demonstrations of scale validity are provided in the SBS, PIY, PIC-2, and Behavioral Summary manuals: When normative and clinically and educationally referred samples were compared on the 14 SBS scales, 10 obtained a difference that represented a large effect, whereas 3 obtained a medium effect. When the SBS items were correlated with the 11 primary academic resources and adjustment problems scales in a sample of 1,315 referred students, 99 of 102 items obtained a substantial and primary correlation with the scale on which it was placed. These 11 nonoverlapping scales formed three clearly interpretable factors that represented 71% of the common variance: externalization, internalization, and academic performance. The SBS scales were correlated with six clinical rating dimensions ($n = 129$), with the scales and subscales of the PIC-2 in referred ($n = 521$) and normative ($n = 1,199$) samples, and with the scales and subscales of the PIY in a referred ($n = 182$) sample.

The SBS scales were also correlated with the four scales of the Conners' Teacher Ratings Scale, Short Form, in 226 learning-disabled students and in 66 students nominated by their elementary school teachers as having most challenged their teaching skills over the previous school year. SBS scale discriminant validity was also demonstrated by comparison of samples defined by the Conners' Hyperactivity Index. Similar comparisons were also conducted across student samples that had been classified as intellectually impaired ($n = 69$), emotionally impaired ($n = 170$), or learning disabled ($n = 281$; Lachar, Wingenfeld, et al., 2000).

Estimates of PIY validity were obtained through the correlations of PIY scales and subscales with MMPI clinical and content scales ($n = 152$). The scales of 79 PIY protocols completed during clinical evaluation were correlated with several other self-report scales and questionnaires: Social Support, Adolescent Hassles, State-Trait Anxiety, Reynolds Adolescent Depression, Sensation-Seeking scales, State-Trait Anger scales, and the scales of the Personal Experience Inventory. PIY scores were also correlated with adjective checklist items in 71 college freshmen and chart-derived symptom dimensions in 86 adolescents hospitalized for psychiatric evaluation and treatment (Lachar & Gruber, 1995).

When 2,306 normative and 1,551 referred PIC-2 protocols were compared, the differences on the 9 adjustment scales represented a large effect for 6 scales and a moderate effect for the remaining scales. For the PIC-2 subscales, these differences represented at least a moderate effect for 19 of these 21 subscales. Comparable analysis for the PIC-2 Behavioral Summary demonstrated that these differences were similarly robust for all of its 12 dimensions. Factor analysis of the PIC-2 subscales resulted in 5 dimensions that accounted for 71% of the common variance: Externalizing Symptoms, Internalizing Symptoms, Cognitive Status, Social Adjustment, and Family Dysfunction. Criterion validity was demonstrated by correlations between PIC-2 values and 6 clinician rating dimensions ($n = 888$), the 14 scales of the teacher-rated SBS ($n = 520$), and the 24 subscales of the self-report PIY ($n = 588$). In addition, the PIC-2 manual provides evidence of discriminant validity by comparing PIC-2 values across 11 *DSM-IV* diagnosis-based groups ($n = 754$; Lachar & Gruber, 2001). In the Behavioral Summary manual (Lachar & Gruber, 2009), parent-, student-, and teacher-report scales classified as either externalizing or internalizing demonstrated validity through the presentation of multitrait, multimethod convergent and discriminant analysis.

## Interpretive Guidelines: The Actuarial Process

The effective application of a profile of standardized adjustment scale scores can be a daunting challenge for a clinician. The standardization of a measure of general cognitive ability or academic achievement provides the foundation for score interpretation. In such cases, a score's comparison to its standardization sample generates the IQ for the test of general cognitive ability and the grade equivalent for the test of academic achievement. In contrast, the same standardization process that provides $T$-score values for the raw scores of scales of depression, withdrawal, or noncompliance does not similarly provide interpretive guidelines. Although this standardization process facilitates direct comparison of scores from scales that vary in length and rate of item endorsement, there is not an underlying theoretical distribution of, for example, depression to guide scale interpretation in the way that the normal distribution supports the interpretation of an IQ estimate. Standard scores for adjustment scales represent the likelihood of a raw score within a specific standardization sample. A depression scale $T$ score of 70 can be interpreted with certainty as an infrequent event in the standardization sample. Although a specific score is infrequent, the prediction of significant clinical information, such as likely symptoms and behaviors, degree of associated disability, seriousness of distress, and the selection of a promising intervention, cannot be derived from the standardization process that generates a standard score of $70T$.

Comprehensive data that demonstrate criterion validity can also be analyzed to develop actuarial, or empirically based, scale interpretations. Such analyses first identify the fine detail of the correlations between a specific scale and nonscale clinical information and then determine the range of scale standard scores for which this detail is most descriptive. The content so identified can be integrated directly into narrative text or provide support for associated text (cf. Lachar & Gdowski, 1979). Table 11.4 provides an example of this analytic process for each of the 21 PIC-2 subscales. The PIC-2, PIY, SBS, and Behavioral Summary manuals present actuarially based narrative interpretations for these inventory scales and the rules for their application.

## Review for Clinical Utility

A clinician's careful consideration of the content of an assessment measure is an important exercise. As previously discussed (Lachar, 1993), item content, statement and response format, and scale length facilitate or limit scale application. *Content validity* as a concept reflects the

**TABLE 11.4   Examples of PIC-2 Subscale External Correlates and Their Performance**

| Subscale | Subscale External Correlate (source) | R | Rule | Performance |
|----------|--------------------------------------|-----|------|-------------|
| COG1 | Specific intellectual deficits (clinician) | .30 | >69T | 18%/47% |
| COG2 | Poor mathematics (teacher) | .51 | >59T | 18%/56% |
| COG3 | Vineland Communication (psychometric) | .60 | >59T | 32%/69% |
| ADH1 | Teachers complain that I can't sit still (self) | .34 | >59T | 23%/47% |
| ADH2 | Irresponsible behavior (clinician) | .44 | >59T | 26%/66% |
| DLQ1 | Expelled/suspended from school (clinician) | .52 | >59T | 6%/48% |
| DLQ2 | Poorly modulated anger (clinician) | .58 | >59T | 23%/80% |
| DLQ3 | Disobeys class or school rules (teacher) | .49 | >59T | 27%/70% |
| FAM1 | Conflict between parents/guardians (clinician) | .34 | >59T | 14%/43% |
| FAM2 | Parent divorce/separation (clinician) | .52 | >59T | 24%/76% |
| RLT1 | Wide Range Achievement Test Arithmetic (psychometric) | .44 | >59T | 14%/61% |
| RLT2 | Auditory hallucinations (clinician) | .31 | >79T | 4%/27% |
| SOM1 | I often have stomachaches (self) | .24 | >69T | 26%/52% |
| SOM2 | I have dizzy spells (self) | .27 | >59T | 24%/44% |
| DIS1 | I am often afraid of little things (self) | .26 | >69T | 19%/39% |
| DIS2 | Becomes upset for little or no reason (teacher) | .33 | >59T | 25%/56% |
| DIS3 | Suicidal threats (clinician) | .39 | >69T | 8%/34% |
| WDL1 | Shyness is my biggest problem (self) | .28 | >69T | 12%/60% |
| WDL2 | Except for going to school, I often stay in the house for days at a time (self) | .31 | >69T | 21%/48% |
| SSK1 | Avoids social interaction in class (teacher) | .31 | >59T | 19%/42% |
| SSK2 | I am often rejected by other kids (self) | .36 | >69T | 17%/46% |

*Note:* $r$ = point biserial correlation between external dichotomous rating and PIC-2 $T$ score; Rule = incorporate correlate content above this point; Performance = frequency of external correlate below and above rule; Dichotomy established as follows: Self-report (True–False), Clinician (Present–Absent), Teacher (average, superior/below average, deficient; never, seldom/sometimes, usually), Psychometric (standard score > 84/standard score < 85).

adequacy of the match between questionnaire elements and the phenomena to be assessed. It is quite reasonable for the potential user of a measure to first gain an appreciation of the specific manifestations of a designated delinquency or psychological discomfort dimension. Test manuals should facilitate this process by listing scale content and relevant item endorsement rates. Questionnaire content should be representative and include frequent and infrequent manifestations that reflect mild, moderate, and severe levels of maladjustment. A careful review of scales constructed solely by factor analysis will identify manifest item content that is inconsistent with expectation; review across scales may identify unexpected scale overlap when items are assigned to more than one dimension. Important dimensions of instrument utility associated with content are instrument readability and the ease of scale administration, completion, scoring, and interpretation.

It is useful to identify the typical raw scores for normative and clinical evaluations and to explore the amount and variety of content represented by scores that are indicative of significant problems. It will then be useful to determine the shift in content when such raw scores representing significant maladjustment are reduced to the equivalents of standard scores within the normal range. Questionnaire application can be problematic when its scales are especially brief, are composed of statements that are rarely endorsed in clinical populations, or apply response formats that distort the true raw-score distribution. Many of these issues can be examined by looking at a typical profile form. For example, CBCL standard scores of 50T often represent raw scores of only 0 or 1. When clinically elevated baseline CBCL scale values are reduced to values within normal limits on retest, treatment effectiveness and the absence of problems would appear to have been demonstrated. Actually, the shift from baseline to post-treatment assessment may represent the process in which as few as three items that were first rated as a 2 (*very true* or *often true*) at baseline remain endorsed but are rated as a 1 (*somewhat* or *sometimes true*) on retest (cf. Lachar, 1993).

## SELECTED ADJUSTMENT MEASURES FOR YOUTH ASSESSMENT

An ever-increasing number of assessment instruments may be applied in the assessment of youth adjustment.

This chapter concludes by providing a survey of some of these instruments. Because of the importance of considering different informants, all four families of parent-, teacher-, and self-report measures are described in some detail. In addition, several multidimensional, single-informant measures are described. Each entry has been included to demonstrate the variety of measures that are available. Although each of these objective questionnaires is available from a commercial test publisher, no other specific inclusion or exclusion criteria have been applied. This section concludes with an even more selective description of a few of the many published measures that restrict their assessment of adjustment or may be specifically useful to supplement an otherwise broadly based evaluation of the child. Such measures may contribute to the assessment of youth seen in a specialty clinic or support treatment planning or outcome assessment.

## Other Families of Multidimensional, Multisource Measures

Considering their potential contribution to the assessment process, a clinician would benefit from gaining sufficient familiarity with at least one parent-report questionnaire, one teacher rating form, and one self-report inventory. Four integrated families of these measures have been developed over the past decade. Some efficiency is gained from becoming familiar with one of these sets of measures rather than selecting three independent measures. Manuals describe the relations between measures and provide case studies that apply two or all three measures. Competence in each class of measures is also useful because it provides an additional degree of flexibility for the clinician. The conduct of a complete multi-informant assessment may not be feasible at times (e.g., teachers may not be available during summer vacation) or may prove difficult for a particular mental health service (e.g., the youth may be under the custody of an agency or a hospital setting may distance the clinician from parent informants). In addition, the use of self-report measures may be systematically restricted by child age or some specific cognitive or motivational characteristics that could compromise the collection of competent questionnaire responses. Because of such difficulties, it is also useful to consider the relationship between the individual components of these questionnaire families. Some measures are complementary and focus on informant-specific content, whereas others make a specific effort to apply duplicate content and therefore represent parallel forms. One of these measure families, consisting of the PIC-2, the PIY, and the SBS (and the abbreviated and focused versions in the Behavioral Summary),

has already been described in some detail. The PIC-2, PIY, and SBS are independent comprehensive measures that both emphasize informant-appropriate and informant-specific observations and provide the opportunity to compare similar dimensions across informants.

### Behavior Assessment System for Children—Second Edition

The Behavior Assessment System for Children—Second Edition (BASC-2) family of multidimensional scales includes the Parent Ratings Scales (PRS), Teacher Rating Scales (TRS), and Self-Report of Personality (SRP), which are conveniently described in one integrated manual (C. R. Reynolds & Kamphaus, 2004). Two additional instruments, the Structured Developmental History and the Student Observation System, are also available as supplements to these scales. BASC-2 ratings on the parent, teacher, and self-report measures are marked directly on self-scoring pamphlets or on one-page forms that allow the recording of responses for subsequent computer entry. The TRS and PRS have separate forms for age groupings including preschool (2–5), child (6–11), and adolescent (12–21). Each of these forms is relatively brief (TRS: 100–139 items, 10–15 minutes; PRS: 134–160 items, 10–20 minutes). The SRP provides separate forms for children (8–11), adolescents (12–21), and young adults (18–25, attending postsecondary school). Written at a third-grade reading level, the SRP takes 20 to 30 minutes to complete. The PRS and TRS items, in the form of mainly short, descriptive phrases, are rated on a 4-point frequency scale (*never*, *sometimes*, *often*, and *almost always*), while SRP items in the form of short, declarative statements are rated as either true or false. Final BASC-2 items were assigned through multistage iterative item analyses to only one narrow-band scale measuring clinical dimensions or adaptive behaviors; these scales are combined to form composites. All forms include content scales, which are described by the test authors as more "specific or syndrome oriented," such as Bullying or Anger Control. The PRS and TRS forms emphasize across-informant similarities; the SRP has been designed to complement parent and teacher reports as a measure focused on mild to moderate emotional problems and clinically relevant self-perceptions, rather than overt behaviors and externalizing problems, with the exception of hyperactivity.

The PRS composites and component scales are Internalizing Problems (Anxiety, Depression, Somatization), Externalizing Problems (Hyperactivity, Aggression, and Conduct Problems), and Adaptive Skills (Adaptability,

Social Skills, Functional Communication, Leadership, and Activities of Daily Living). The Behavioral Symptoms Index (BSI) reflects more global symptoms (Hyperactivity, Aggression, Depression, Atypicality, Withdrawal, and Attention Problems). The TRS Internalizing and Externalizing Problems composites, the BSI, and their component scales parallel the PRS structure. The TRS presents items that are unique to the classroom by including a Study Skills scale in the Adaptive Skills composite and a Learning Problems scale that is combined with the Attention Problems Scale to form the School Problems composite. The BASC-2 manual suggests that clinical scale elevations for all three measures are potentially significant over $59T$, with scores of 70 or above being clinically significant, and that adaptive scores gain importance under $41T$, with scores below 30 representing clinically significant maladaptive behavior. The SRP composites and their component scales are School Problems (Attitude to School, Attitude to Teachers, Sensation Seeking), Internalizing Problems (Atypicality, Locus of Control, Social Stress, Anxiety, Depression, Sense of Inadequacy, Somatization), Personal Adjustment (Relations with Parents, Interpersonal Relations, Self-Esteem, Self-Reliance), and Inattention/Hyperactivity (Attention Problems, Hyperactivity). All three measures include validity scales representing the F, Consistency, and Response Pattern Indexes. The SRP includes two additional validity scales, L and V, which assesses whether a student is attending to and understanding content. Psychometric characteristics of the validity scales are not presented in the manual.

### Conners' Rating Scales—3

The Conners' parent and teacher scales were first used in the 1960s in the study of pharmacological treatment of disruptive behaviors. The current published Conners' Rating Scales—3 (CRS-3; Conners, 2008) require selection of one of four response alternatives to brief phrases (parent, teacher) or short sentences (adolescent): 0 = Not True at All (Never, Seldom), 1 = Just a Little True (Occasionally), 2 = Pretty Much True (Often, Quite a Bit), and 3 = Very Much True (Very Often, Very Frequent). All three rating scales are available in long and short forms. These revised scales continue their original focus on disruptive behaviors (especially ADHD), adding *DSM-IV* Symptom Scales for these problems, and strengthening their assessment of related or comorbid disorders. The Conners' Parent Rating Scale—3 (Conners-3P. Long Form) derives from 110 items. Six factor-derived nonoverlapping scales were generated and confirmed from the ratings of the regular-education

students (i.e., the normative sample): Hyperactivity/ Impulsivity, Learning Problems, Aggression, Peer Relations, and Family Relations. In addition, *DSM-IV* Symptom Scales include: ADHD Hyperactive/Impulsive, ADHD Inattentive, ADHD Combined, Oppositional Defiant Disorder, and Conduct Disorder. A rationally derived scale entitled Inattention is also included. Both this scale and the teacher rating are written at a fourth- to fifth-grade level and can be applied to children ages 6 to 18. Although there are substantial improvements in the latest edition of the Conners Scales and some "good initial evidence" of validity (Frick et al., 2010), the CRS-3 awaits validation research independent of the authors. A review of the considerable literature generated using the original CPRS (Conners' Parent Rating Scale) did not demonstrate its ability to discriminate among psychiatric populations, although it was able to separate psychiatric patients from normal youth (Gianarris, Golden, & Greene, 2001). More recent studies involving the CPRS-R indicated that both teacher and parent ratings were sensitive to treatment-related behavioral changes (Biederman, Gao, Rogers, & Spencer, 2006), yet the utility of the scales in discriminating ADHD subtypes was viewed as moderate (Hale, Howe, DeWitt, & Coury, 2001), and comorbidity contributed to complication and errors in diagnosis for both the parent and teacher ratings (Charach, Chen, Hogg-Johnson, & Schachar, 2009). Perhaps future reviews of the CRS-3 will demonstrate additional discriminant validity when the revised versions are further evaluated.

The Conners' Teacher Rating Scale—3 (Conners-3T) consists of only 115 items, representing a greater consistency with the Parent Rating in length and derived scales relative to the prior version, allowing improved comparison across informants. For parent and teacher ratings, the normative sample ranges from 6 to 18 years, whereas the self-report scale is normed for ages 8 to 18. The current revision of the Conners Scales provides standard linear $T$ scores, which are now available both by gender and by age at 1-year intervals. This represents a substantial improvement over the previous versions, which were calculated at 3-year intervals. Combined gender norms are also available. Conners (1999) also described a serious administration artifact, in that the parent and teacher scores typically drop on their second administration. Pretreatment baseline therefore should always consist of a second administration to avoid this artifact. The test author has provided more specific guidelines for interpretation of $T$-scores relative to past editions of the scales. Scores ranging from 60 to 64 are considered "High Average" and reflect a need for careful consideration as they fall between typical and atypical, while scores between 65 and 69 are viewed as "Elevated" and thus reflect more "significant concerns." Those over 70 are viewed as "Very Elevated" and most likely represent atypical behavior. The Self-Report Rating Scale (Conners -3SR), Long Form, consists of 59 items, written at a third-grade reading level. This measure, which provides parallel scales, can be used to assess children and adolescents ages 8 to 18. Shorter versions and several indices have been derived from these three questionnaires. These additional forms contribute to the focused evaluation of ADHD treatment and would merit separate listing under the later section "Selected Focused (Narrow) or Ancillary Objective Measures." Of interest in the current version is the addition of validity scales titled Negative Impression and Inconsistency Index. Also added are items described as Screener Items (Anxiety, Depression), Impairment Items (Schoolwork/Grades, Friendships/Relationships, Home Life), and Critical Items (Severe Conduct).

### Child Behavior Checklist (6–18); Teacher's Report Form; Youth Self-Report

The popularity of the CBCL and related instruments in research application since the CBCL's initial publication in 1983 has influenced thousands of research projects; the magnitude of this research application has had a significant influence on the study of child and adolescent psychopathology. The 1991 revision, documented in five monographs totaling more than 1,000 pages, emphasized consistencies in scale dimensions and scale content across child age, gender, and respondent or setting (Achenbach, 1991a, 1991b, 1991c, 1991d, 1993). In 2001, revisions of the Child Behavior Checklist (CBCL), along with the accompanying Teacher Report Form (TRF) and Youth Self-Report (YSR), were published (Achenbach & Rescorla, 2001). This revision included replacement of problem items and updated analysis of data collected on a new general population and clinical sample. The major component of the current parent, teacher, and self-report forms is a common set of 112 behavior problems described in one to eight words ("Overtired," "Argues a lot," "Feels others are out to get him/her"). Items are rated as 0 = Not True, 1 = Somewhat or Sometimes True, or 2 = Very True or Often True, although several items require individual elaboration when these items are positively endorsed. These 112 items generate eight narrow-band and three composite scale scores similarly labeled for each informant, although some item content varies. Composite Internalizing Problems consists of Withdrawn/Depressed, Somatic Complaints, and Anxious/Depressed and composite Externalizing Problems consists of Rule Breaking Behavior and Aggressive Behavior; Social Problems, Thought Problems, and Attention Problems contribute to a summary Total scale along with the other five narrow-band scales.

The 2001 forms provide standard scores based on national samples. Although the CBCL and the YSR are routinely self-administered in clinical application, the CBCL normative data were obtained through interview of the informants, and the first four items of the YSR were read to the participants. This process of collecting items by interview may have inhibited affirmative response to checklist items. For example, three of eight parent informant scales obtained average normative raw scores of less than 2, with restricted scale score variance, while the YSR results indicated a higher mean and greater variance for the corresponding scales. It is important to note that increased problem behavior scale elevation reflects increased problems, although $T$ scores are truncated for Syndrome and *DSM* scales, which do not extend below $50T$ (Frick et al., 2010). $T$ scores are assigned to scale raw scores using normalized $T$s which facilitates comparison across scales, but the interpretive meaning of checklist $T$ scores has been questioned due to this approach (Frick et al., 2010; Lachar, 1998). The gender-specific CBCL norms are provided for two age ranges (6–11 and 12–18). The TRF norms are also gender-specific and provided for two age ranges (6–11 and 12–18). The YSR norms are gender-specific, incorporate the entire age range of 11 to 18 years, and require a fifth-grade reading ability. Narrow-band scores between the 93rd and 97th percentile, or 65 to $69T$, are designated as borderline; values above the 97th percentile, $70T$ or higher, represent the clinical range. Composite scores of 60 to $63T$ are designated as borderline, whereas values above $63T$ represent the clinical range. While base rates for syndrome and composite scales may vary between countries, there has been empirical support for the use of the CBCL in diverse cultural groups (Ivanova et al., 2007; Verhulst et al., 2003).

The other main component of these forms measures adaptive competence using a less structured approach. The CBCL competence items are organized by manifest content into three narrow scales (Activities, Social, and School), which are then summed into a total score. Parents are asked to list and then rate (frequency, performance level) child participation in sports, hobbies, organizations, and chores. Parents also describe the child's friendships, social interactions, performance in academic subjects, need for special assistance in school, and history of retention in grade. As standard scores for these scales increase with demonstrated ability, a borderline range is suggested at 31 to $35T$ and the clinical range is designated as less than 31*T*. The ranges for the Total Competence scale are designated at a higher level, with the clinical range cutpoint being 37, which incorporates those in the 10th percentile or lower. Some evidence for validity has been provided in their comparison to the PIC in ability to predict adaptive level as defined by the Vineland Adaptive Behavior Scales (Pearson & Lachar, 1994). Youth ethnicity and social and economic opportunities may affect CBCL competence scale values (Drotar, Stein, & Perrin, 1995).

In comparison to the CBCL, the TRF measures of competence are derived from very limited data: an average rating on a 1-to-5 ratings scale of academic performance based on as many as six academic subjects identified by the teacher, individual 7-point ratings on four topics (how hard working, behaving appropriately, amount learning, and how happy), and a summary score derived from these four items. The TRF designates a borderline interpretive range for the mean academic performance and the summary score of 37 to 40*T*, with the clinical range less than 37*T*. The TRF avoids the measurement of a range of meaningful classroom observations to maintain structural equivalence with the CBCL. The YSR provides seven adaptive competency items that parallel the items on the CBCL and are scored for Activities, Social, and a Total Competence scale. Reference to the YSR manual is necessary to score these multipart items, which tap competence and levels of involvement in sports, activities, organizations, jobs, and chores. Items also provide self-report of academic achievement, interpersonal adjustment, and level of socialization. Scales Activities and Social are classified as borderline at 30 to 33*T* with the clinical range less than 30*T*. The YSR Total Competence scale is classified as borderline at 37 to 40*T* with the clinical range at less than 37*T*. The strengths and weaknesses of these forms have been presented in some detail elsewhere (Frick et al., 2010). The CBCL, TRF, and YSR provide quickly administered and easily scored parallel problem-behavior measures that facilitate direct comparison. The forms do not provide validity scales, and the test manuals provide neither evidence of scale validity nor interpretive guidelines.

## Multisource Single-Dimension Measure

### Children's Depression Inventory, Second Edition

The CDI 2 (Kovacs, 2011) is a focused measure that may be used in the early identification of developmentally appropriate symptoms and the monitoring of treatment effectiveness, and may contribute to the diagnostic process. Originally a self-report measure only, the CDI 2 now provides a multi-informant approach, with the development of the Parent Report (CDI 2:P) and Teacher Report (CDI 2:T). The CDI 2:SR child self-report represents a unique format because children are required to select one statement from each of 28 statement triads to describe their past 2 weeks. The first option is scored a 0 (symptom absence), the second a 1 (definite but not disabling symptom), and the third a 2 (disabling symptom). It may therefore be more accurate to characterize the CDI 2 as a task requiring the child to read 81 short statements and make a selection from statement triplets. Although cited in the manual as being written at a first-grade level, reports on the earlier version (CDI; Kovacs, 1992) suggest that a more accurate estimation may be a third-grade reading level (Sitarenios & Stein, 2004). The Total score combines the dysphoric affect and neurovegetative aspects of depression summarized by the Emotional Problems Scale and the functional consequences reflected by the Functional Problems Scale. Four factor-derived subscales include Negative Mood/Physical Symptoms, Negative Self-Esteem, Ineffectiveness, and Interpersonal Problems. Also available is a 12-item short form that correlates .89 to the Total score and yields an alpha coefficient of .80, demonstrating internal consistency. Regional norms generate a profile of gender- and age-specific (7–12 and 13–17 years) *T* scores, in which values in the 60s (especially those above 65*T*) in children referred for evaluation are clinically significant (Sitarenios et al., 2004). Although considerable emphasis has been placed on the accurate description of the CDI as a good indicator of self-reported distress and not a diagnostic instrument, the manual and considerable literature focus on classification based on a total raw score cutoff (Fristad, Emery, & Beck, 1997; Kovacs, 2011). The parent and teacher ratings (CDI:P, 17 items; CDI:T, 12 items) were developed to measure symptoms of depression, which could either be verbalized or visible. Parents and teachers rate the items on a 4-point scale, and results include a Total Score as well as Emotional Problems and Functional Problems subscales. Discriminant function analysis predicting clinical versus nonclinical status supported the incremental validity of the parent and teacher forms, and all three forms provided unique variance (Kovacs, 2003).

## Selected Single-Source Multidimensional Measures

### Minnesota Multiphasic Personality Inventory—Adolescent

The Minnesota Multiphasic Personality Inventory (MMPI) has been found to be useful in the evaluation of adolescents for more than 50 years (cf. Hathaway & Monachesi,

1953), although many questions have been raised as to the adequacy of this inventory's content, scales, and the application of adult norms (cf. Lachar, Klinge, & Grisell, 1976). In 1992 a fully revised version of the MMPI custom designed for adolescents, the MMPI-A, was published (Butcher et al., 1992). Although the traditional empirically constructed validity and profile scales have been retained, scale item content has been somewhat modified to reflect contemporary and developmentally appropriate content (e.g., the *F* scale was modified to meet statistical inclusion criteria for adolescents). In addition, a series of 15 content scales has been constructed that take advantage of new items that reflect peer interaction, school adjustment, and common adolescent concerns: Anxiety, Obsessiveness, Depression, Health Concerns, Alienation, Bizarre Mentation, Anger, Cynicism, Conduct Problems, Low Self-Esteem, Low Aspirations, Social Discomfort, Family Problems, School Problems, and Negative Treatment Indicators (Williams, Butcher, Ben-Porath, & Graham, 1992).

The MMPI-A normative sample for this 478-statement true–false questionnaire consists of 14- to 18-year-old students collected in eight U.S. states. Inventory items and directions are written at the sixth-grade level. The MMPI-A has also incorporated a variety of test improvements associated with the revision of the MMPI for adults: the development of uniform *T* scores and validity measures of response inconsistency that are independent of specific dimensions of psychopathology. Substantive scales are interpreted as clinically significant at values above 65*T*, while scores of 60 to 65*T* may be suggestive of clinical concerns. The frequency of within-normal-limits profiles obtained from adolescents with notable pathology has been a concern (Archer, 2005). Recent investigations aimed at increasing predictive accuracy of the measure have explored ways to improve the sensitivity of the MMPI-A. Alterations to the normative sample and variations in interpretive ranges used did not appear to result in significant improvement, and clinicians are advised to use 65*T* as the cutoff for classification for greatest accuracy (Fontaine, Archer, Elkins, & Johansen, 2001; Hand, Archer, Handel, & Forbey, 2007). Archer (1999) also concluded that the MMPI-A continues to represent a challenge for many of the adolescents who are requested to complete it and requires extensive training and expertise to ensure accurate application. These opinions are voiced in a survey (Archer & Newsom, 2000).

### Adolescent Psychopathology Scale

This 346-item inventory was designed to be a comprehensive assessment of the presence and severity of psychopathology in adolescents ages 12 to 19. The Adolescent Psychopathology Scale (APS; W. M. Reynolds, 1998) incorporates 25 scales modeled after Axis I and Axis II *DSM-IV* criteria. The APS is unique in the use of different response formats depending on the nature of the symptom or problem evaluated (e.g., True–False; Never or almost never, Sometimes, Nearly all the time) and across different time periods depending on the dimension assessed (e.g., past 2 weeks, past month, past 3 months, in general). One computer-generated profile presents 20 Clinical Disorder scales (such as Conduct Disorder, Major Depression), whereas a second profile presents 5 Personality Disorder scales (such as Borderline Personality Disorder), 11 Psychosocial Problem Content scales (such as Interpersonal Problem, Suicide), and 4 Response Style Indicators. Linear *T* scores are derived from a mixed-gender representative standardization sample of 7th- to 12-grade students ($n = 1,827$), although gender-specific and age-specific score conversions can be selected. The 12-page administration booklet requires a third-grade reading level and is completed in 1 hour or less. APS scales obtained substantial estimates of internal consistency and test–retest reliability (median values in the .80s); mean scale score differences between APS administrations separated by a 14-day interval were small (median = 1.8*T*). The detailed organized manuals provide a sensible discussion of scale interpretation and preliminary evidence of scale validity. Additional study will be necessary to determine the relationship between scale *T*-score elevation and diagnosis and clinical description for this innovative measure. W. M. Reynolds (2000) also developed a 20-minute, 115-item APS short form that generates 12 clinical scales and 2 validity scales. These shortened and combined versions of full-length scales were selected because they were judged to be the most useful in practice.

### Beck Youth Inventories for Children and Adolescents, Second Edition

Recently published and updated, and characterized by the ultimate of simplicity, the Beck Youth Inventories (BYI; Beck, Beck, & Jolly, 2001; BYI-II; Beck, Beck, Jolly, & Steer, 2005) consist of five separately printed 20-item scales that can be completed individually or in any combination. The updated version expands the application from the original 7- to 14-year-old range up to 18 years. The child selects one of four frequency responses to statements written at the second-grade level: Never, Sometimes, Often, Always. Raw scores are converted to gender-specific linear *T*-scores for ages 7 to 10, 11 to 14, and 15 to 18. The manual notes that 7-year-olds and students in second grade may need to have the scale items read to them and that children and youth of any age may be assisted with reading if deemed necessary. For the scales Depression (BDI: "I feel sorry for myself"), Anxiety (BAI: "I worry about the future"), Anger (BANI: "People make me mad"), Disruptive Behavior (BDBI: "I break the rules"), and Self-Concept (BSCI: "I feel proud of the things I do"), the manual provides estimates of internal consistency ($\alpha = .86–.95$, median $= .91$) and 7- to 8-day temporal stability ($r_{tt} = .74–.93$). Both consistency and stability of test results tend to be higher for older children. Three studies of scale validity are also described. Substantial correlations were obtained between each BYI scale and a parallel established scale (BDI and Children's Depression Inventory, $r = .72$ for children, $r = .67$ for adolescents; BAI and Revised Children's Manifest Anxiety Scale, $r = .70$ for children, $r = .64$ for adolescents; BSCI and Piers-Harris Children's Self-Concept Scale, $r = .61$ for children, $r = .77$ for adolescents; BDBI and Conners-Wells' Self-Report Conduct Problems, $r = .69$ for children, $r = .76$ for adolescents; BANI and Conners-Wells' Self-Report AD/HD Index, $r = .73$ for children, $r = .64$). Each BYI scale significantly separated matched samples of special education and normative children, with the special-education sample obtaining higher ratings on Depression, Anxiety, Anger, and Disruptive Behavior and lower ratings on Self-Concept. In a comparable analysis with an outpatient sample, three out of five scales obtained a significant difference from matched controls and a fourth approached significance. A secondary analysis demonstrated that outpatients who obtained a diagnosis of a mood disorder rated themselves substantially lower on Self-Concept and substantially higher on Depression and Anger in comparison to other outpatients. Additional study will be necessary to establish BYI-II diagnostic utility and sensitivity to symptomatic change.

## Millon Adolescent Clinical Inventory

The Millon Adolescent Clinical Inventory (MACI; Millon, 1993; Millon, Millon, Davis, & Grossman, 2006), a 160-item true–false questionnaire, may be scored for 12 Personality Patterns, 8 Expressed Concerns, and 7 Clinical Syndromes dimensions as well as 4 validity measures including 3 modifying indices (Disclosure, Desirability, and Debasement) and a 2-item Reliability scale. Gender-specific raw score conversions, or Base Rate scores, are provided for age ranges 13 to 15 and 16 to 19 years. Scales were developed in multiple stages, with item composition reflecting theory, *DSM-IV* structure, and item-to-scale performance. Facet scales representing 3 subdomains of

each of the Personality Pattern Scales have been derived, with items selected on rational and theoretical grounds. The 27 substantive scales require 888 scored items and therefore demonstrate considerable item overlap, even within scale categories. For example, the most frequently placed item among the Personality Patterns scales is "I've never done anything for which I could have been arrested"—an awkward double-negative as a scored statement. The structures of these scales and the effect of this characteristic are basically unknown because scales, or classes of scales, were not submitted to factor analysis. Additional complexity is contributed by the weighting of items (3, 2, or 1) to reflect assigned theoretical or demonstrated empirical importance. Given the additional complexity of validity adjustment processes, it is accurate to state that it is possible to hand-score the MACI, although any reasonable application requires computer processing. Base rate scores range from 1 to 115, with specific importance given to values 75 to 84 and above 84. These values are tied to "target prevalence rates" derived from clinical consensus and anchor points that are discussed in this manual with minimal clarifying examples. These scores are supposed to relate in some fashion to performance in clinical samples; no representative standardization sample of nonreferred youth was collected for analysis. Base rate scores are designed to identify the pattern of problems, not to demonstrate the presence of adjustment problems. MACI scores demonstrate adequate internal consistency and temporal stability. Except for some minimal correlational evidence purported to support validity, no evidence of scale performance is provided in the manual, although dimensions of psychopathology and scale intent are discussed in detail. Manual readers reasonably expect test authors to demonstrate the wisdom of their psychometric decisions. No evidence is provided to establish the value of item weighting, the utility of correction procedures, or the unique contribution of scale dimensions. For example, a cursory review of the composition of the 12 Personality Patterns scales revealed that the majority of the 22 Forceful items are also placed on the dimension labeled Unruly. These dimensions correlate .75 and may not represent unique dimensions. Analyses should demonstrate whether a 13-year-old's self-description is best represented by 27 independent (versus nested) dimensions. A manual should facilitate the review of scale content by assigned value and demonstrate the prevalence of specific scale elevations and their interpretive meaning. The authors note that use of the test with nonclinical samples is inappropriate and may result in "erroneous information." Clearly the

MACI should not be used for screening or in settings in which some referred youth may not subsequently demonstrate significant problems. A review of recent literature involving the MACI suggests that there is increased support for its use with juvenile forensic populations (Baum, Archer, Forbey, & Handel, 2009).

## Selected Focused (Narrow) or Ancillary Objective Measures

### Monitoring Treatment Progress

**BASC-2 Progress Monitor (C. R. Reynolds & Kamphaus, 2009).** Scales in this multi-informant set of tools are designed to evaluate the effectiveness of treatments used for Externalizing and ADHD Problems, Internalizing Problems, Social Withdrawal, and Adaptive Skills from ages 2 to 21. Teacher and Parent forms are available for ages 2 to 5 (preschool) and grades K to 12. A self-report Student form can be used from grades 3 to 12; it is written at a fourth-grade level. These brief forms take 5 minutes to complete.

### Attention Deficit Hyperactivity

**Brown Attention-Deficit Disorder Scales for Children and Adolescents (BADDS; Brown, 2001).** This series of brief parent-, teacher-, and self-report questionnaires evaluates dimensions of ADHD that reflect cognitive impairments and symptoms beyond current *DSM-IV* criteria. As many as six subscales may be calculated from each form: Activation ("Seems to have exceptional difficulty getting started on tasks or routines [e.g., getting dressed, picking up toys]"); Focus/Attention ("Is easily sidetracked; starts one task and then switches to a less important task"); Effort ("Do your parents or teachers tell you that you could do better by trying harder?"); Emotion/Affect ("Seems easily irritated or impatient in response to apparently minor frustrations"); Memory ("Learns something one day, but doesn't remember it the next day"); and Action ("When you're supposed to sit still and be quiet, is it really hard for you to do that?"). Three item formats and varying gender-specific age-normative references are provided: 44-item parent and teacher forms normed by gender for ages 3 to 5 and 6 to 7; 50-item parent, teacher, and self-report forms normed by gender for ages 8 to 9 and 10 to 12; and a 40-item self-report form (also used to collect collateral responses) for ages 12 to 18. All forms generate an ADD Inattention Total score, and the multi-informant questionnaires also provide an ADD Combined Total score. The BADDS manual provides an informative discussion of ADHD and a variety of

psychometric studies. Subscales and composites obtained from adult informants demonstrated excellent internal consistency and temporal stability, although estimates derived from self-report data were less robust. Children with ADHD obtained substantially higher scores when compared to controls. Robust correlations were obtained for BADDS dimensions both across informants (parent-teacher, parent-child, teacher-child) and between BADDS dimensions and other same-informant measures of ADHD (CBCL, TRF, BASC Parent and Teacher Monitors, CPRS-R Short Form, CTRS-R Short Form). This manual does not provide evidence that BADDS dimensions can separate different clinical groups and quantify treatment effects.

### Internalizing Symptoms

**Revised Children's Manifest Anxiety Scale: Second Edition (RCMAS-2; C. R. Reynolds & Richmond, 2008).** Response of *Yes–No* to 49 statements generate a focused Total Anxiety score that incorporates three clinical subscales (Physiological Anxiety, Worry, Social Anxiety); the two validity scales include Defensiveness and an Inconsistent Responding Index. Standard scores derived from an ethnically diverse sample of approximately 2,300 protocols are gender and age specific (6–8; 9–14; and 15–19 years). Independent response to scale statements requires a second-grade reading level. Items were originally selected for the RCMAS if they obtained an endorsement rate between .30 and .70 and correlated at least .40 with the total score. Item-total correlations with the RCMAS-2 are comparable, with some slightly lower. Anxiety is considered extremely problematic with a total score that exceeds 70*T*; symptoms of anxiety are considered moderate if subscale elevations are over 60, but remains below 70*T* (Gerard & Reynolds, 1999; C. R. Reynolds & Richmond, 2008).

### Family Adjustment

**Marital Satisfaction Inventory—Revised (MSI-R; Snyder, 1997).** When the marital relationship becomes a potential focus of treatment, it often becomes useful to define areas of conflict and the differences manifest by comparison of parent descriptions. The MSI-R includes 150 true–false items comprising two validity scales (Inconsistency, Conventionalization), 1 global scale (Global Distress), and 10 scales that assess specific areas of relationship stress (Affective Communication, Problem-Solving Communication, Aggression, Time Together, Disagreement About Finances, Sexual Dissatisfaction, Role Orientation, Family History of Distress, Dissatisfaction with Children, Conflict over Child Rearing). Items are presented on a self-scoring form or by personal computer, and one profile facilitates direct comparison of paired sets of gender-specific normalized $T$ scores that are subsequently applied in evaluation, treatment planning, and outcome assessment. Empirically established $T$-score ranges suggesting adjustment problems are designated on the profile (usually scores above $59T$). The geographically diverse, representative standardization sample included more than 2,000 married adults. Because of substantial scale internal consistency (median $\alpha = .82$) and temporal stability (median 6-week $r_{tt} = .79$), a difference between spouse profiles or a shift on retest of as little as 6 $T$-points represents a meaningful and stable phenomenon. Evidence of scale discriminant and actuarial validity has been summarized in detail (Snyder & Aikman, 1999).

**Parenting Stress Index (PSI), Third Edition (Abidin, 1995).** This unique 120-item questionnaire measures excessive stressors and stress within families of children age 1 to 12 years. Description is obtained by parent selection from five response options to statements often presented in the form of strongly agree, agree, not sure, disagree, strongly agree. A profile of percentiles from maternal response to the total mixed-gender normative sample includes a Child Domain score (subscales Distractibility/Hyperactivity, Adaptability, Reinforces Parent, Demandingness, Mood, Adaptability) and a Parent Domain score (subscales Competence, Isolation, Attachment, Health, Role Restriction, Depression, Spouse), which are combined into a Total Stress composite. Additional measures include a Life Stress scale of 19 *Yes–No* items and a Defensive Responding scale. Interpretive guidelines are provided for substantive dimensions at 1 standard deviation above and for Defensiveness values at 1 standard deviation below the mean. A 36-item short form provides three subscales: Parental Distress, Parent-Child Dysfunctional Interaction, and Difficult Child. These subscales are summed into a Total Stress score; a Defensiveness Responding scale is also scored.

## CURRENT STATUS AND FUTURE DIRECTIONS

Multidimensional, multi-informant objective assessment makes a unique contribution to the assessment of youth adjustment. This chapter argues that this form of assessment is especially responsive to the evaluation of the evolving child and compatible with the current way in which mental health services are provided to youth.

Trends toward evaluation of comorbid conditions and variation in child behavior across settings are well documented and support the use of such instruments (Heffer et al., 2009; Mash & Hunsley, 2007). The growing popularity of these instruments in clinical practice (cf. Archer & Newsom, 2000), however, has not stimulated comparable efforts in research that focuses on instrument application. Objective measures of youth adjustment would benefit from the development of a research culture that promotes the study and demonstration of measure validity. Current child clinical literature predominantly applies objective measures in the study of psychopathology and does not focus on the study of test performance as an important endeavor. The journals that routinely publish studies on test validity (e.g., *Psychological Assessment*, *Journal of Personality Assessment*, *Assessment*) seldom present articles that focus on instruments that measure child or adolescent adjustment. An exception to this observation is the MMPI-A, for which research efforts have been influenced by the substantial research culture of the MMPI and MMPI-2 (cf. Archer, 2005).

Considerable effort will be required to establish the construct and actuarial validity of popular child and adolescent adjustment measures. It is not sufficient to demonstrate that a distribution of scale scores separates regular-education students from those referred for mental health services to establish scale validity. Indeed, the absence of such evidence may not exclude a scale from consideration, because it is possible that the measurement of some normally distributed personality characteristic, such as social introversion, may contribute to the development of a more effective treatment plan. Once a child is referred for mental health services, application of a screening measure is seldom of value. The actuarial interpretive guidelines of the PIC-2, PIY, SBS, and Behavioral Summary have established one standard of the significant scale score by identifying the minimum $T$-score elevation from which useful clinical information may be reliably predicted. Although other paradigms might establish such a minimum scale score standard as it predicts the likelihood of significant disability or caseness, scale validity will be truly demonstrated only when a measure contributes to the accuracy of routine decision making that occurs in clinical practice. Such decisions include the successful solution of a representative differential diagnosis (cf. Forbes, 1985) or the selection of an optimal plan of treatment (cf. Voelker, Lachar, & Gdowski, 1983).

Similarly, traditional evidence of scale reliability is an inadequate standard of scale performance as applied to clinical situations in which a scale is sequentially administered over time. To be applied in the evaluation of treatment effectiveness, degree of scale score change must be found to accurately track some independent estimate of treatment effectiveness (cf. Sheldrick, Kendall, & Heimberg, 2001). Of relevance here will be the consideration of scale score range and the degree to which a ceiling or floor effect restricts scale performance.

Considering that questionnaire-derived information may be obtained from parents, teachers, and the child, it is not unusual that the study of agreement among informants continues to be of interest (cf. De Los Reyes, 2011). In this regard, it will be more useful to determine the clinical implications of the results obtained from each informant rather than the magnitude of correlations that are so easily derived from samples of convenience (cf. Hulbert, Gdowski, & Lachar, 1986). Rather than attributing obtained differences solely to situation specificity or even measurement error, other explanations should be explored. For example, evidence suggests that considerable differences between informants may be attributed to the effects of response sets, such as respondent defensiveness. Perhaps the study of informant agreement has little value in increasing the contribution of objective assessment to clinical application. Rather, it may be more useful for research to apply paradigms that focus on the *incremental validity* of applications of objective assessment. Beginning with the information obtained from an intake interview, a parent-derived profile could be collected and its additional clinical value determined. In a similar fashion, one could evaluate the relative individual and combined contribution of parent and teacher description in making a meaningful differential diagnosis, say, between ADHD and ODD. The feasibility of such psychometric research should increase as routine use of objective assessment facilitates the development of clinical databases at clinics and inpatient units.

# REFERENCES

Abidin, R. R. (1995). *Parenting Stress Index, third edition, professional manual*. Odessa, FL: Psychological Assessment Resources.

Achenbach, T. M. (1991a). *Integrative guide for the 1991 CBCL/4–18, YSR, and TRF profiles*. Burlington: University of Vermont, Department of Psychiatry.

Achenbach, T. M. (1991b). *Manual for the Child Behavior Checklist/4–18 and 1991 Profile*. Burlington: University of Vermont, Department of Psychiatry.

Achenbach, T. M. (1991c). *Manual for the Teacher's Report Form and 1991 Profile*. Burlington: University of Vermont, Department of Psychiatry.

Achenbach, T. M. (1991d). *Manual for the Youth Self-Report and 1991 Profile*. Burlington: University of Vermont, Department of Psychiatry.

Achenbach, T. M. (1993). *Empirically based taxonomy: How to use syndromes and profile types derived from the CBCL/4–18, TRF, and YSR*. Burlington: University of Vermont, Department of Psychiatry.

Achenbach, T. M. (2005). Advancing assessment of children and adolescents: Commentary on evidence-based assessment of child and adolescent disorders. *Journal of Clinical Child and Adolescent Psychology, 34,* 541–547.

Achenbach, T. M. (2011) Commentary: Definitely more than measurement error: But how should we understand and deal with informant discrepancies? *Journal of Clinical and Adolescent Psychology, 40,* 80–86.

Achenbach, T. M., McConaughy, S. H., & Howell, C. T. (1987). Child/adolescent behavioral and emotional problems: Implications of cross-informant correlations for situational specificity. *Psychological Bulletin, 101,* 213–232.

Achenbach T. M., & Rescorla L. (2001). *Manual for ASEBA School-Age Forms & Profiles*. Burlington, VT: University of Vermont, Research Center for Children, Youth, & Families.

American Psychiatric Association (2000). *The diagnostic and statistical manual of mental disorders* (4th ed., text revision). Washington, DC: Author.

Ammerman, R. T., & Hersen, M. (1993). Developmental and longitudinal perspectives on behavior therapy. In R. T. Ammerman & M. Hersen (Eds.), *Handbook of behavior therapy with children and adults* (pp. 3–9). Boston, MA: Allyn & Bacon.

Angold, A., Costello, E. J., & Erkanli, A. (1999). Comorbidity. *Journal of Child Psychology and Psychiatry, 40,* 57–87.

Archer, R. P. (1999). Overview of the Minnesota Multiphasic Personality Inventory—Adolescent (MMPI-A). In M. E. Maruish (Ed.), *The use of psychological testing for treatment planning and outcomes assessment* (2nd ed., pp. 341–380). Mahwah, NJ: Erlbaum.

Archer, R. P. (2005). *MMPI-A: Assessing adolescent psychopathology* (3rd ed.). Mahwah, NJ: Erlbaum.

Archer, R. P., Maruish, M., Imhof, E. A., & Piotrowski, C. (1991). Psychological test usage with adolescent clients: 1990 survey findings. *Professional Psychology: Research and Practice, 22,* 247–252.

Archer, R. P., & Newsom, C. R. (2000). Psychological test usage with adolescent clients: Survey update. *Assessment, 7,* 227–235.

Baldwin, J. S., & Dadds, M. R. (2007). Reliability and validity of parent and child versions of the multidimensional anxiety scale for children in community samples. *Journal of the American Academy of Child & Adolescent Psychiatry, 46,* 252–260.

Barrett, M. L., Berney, T. P., Bhate, S., Famuyiwa, O. O., Fundudis, T., Kolvin, I., & Tyrer, S. (1991). Diagnosing childhood depression. Who should be interviewed—parent or child? The Newcastle child depression project. *British Journal of Psychiatry, 159*(Suppl. 11), 22–27.

Barry, C. T. & Pickard, J. D. (2008). Developmental issues. In M. Hersen (ed. in chief), D. Reitman (Vol. Ed.), *Handbook of psychological assessment, case conceptualization, and treatment. Vol. 2. Children and adolescents* (pp. 76–100). Hoboken, NJ: Wiley.

Baum, L. J., Archer, R. P., Forbey, J. D., & Handel, R. W. (2009). A review of the Minnesota Multiphasic Personality Inventory-Adolescent (MMPI-A) and the Millon Adolescent Clinical Inventory (MACI) with an emphasis on juvenile justice samples. *Assessment, 16,* 384–400.

Beck, J. S., Beck, A. T., & Jolly, J. B. (2001). *Beck Youth Inventories of Emotional and Social Impairment manual*. San Antonio, TX: Psychological Corporation.

Beck, J. S., Beck, A. T., Jolly, J. B., & Steer, R. A. (2005). *Beck Youth Inventories manual* (2nd ed.). San Antonio, TX: Pearson.

Bidaut-Russell, M., Reich, W., Cottler, L. B., Robins, L. N., Compton, W. M., & Mattison, R. E. (1995). The Diagnostic Interview Schedule for Children (PC-DISC v.3.0): Parents and adolescents suggest reasons for expecting discrepant answers. *Journal of Abnormal Child Psychology*, *23*, 641–659.

Biederman, J., Gao, H., Rogers, A. K., & Spencer, T. J. (2006). Comparison of parent and teacher reports of attention-deficit/hyperactivity disorder symptoms from two placebo-controlled studies of atomoxetine in children. *Biological Psychiatry*, *60*, 1106–1110.

Biederman, J., Newcorn, J., & Sprich, S. (1991). Comorbidity of attention deficit hyperactivity disorder with conduct, depressive, anxiety, and other disorders. *American Journal of Psychiatry*, *148*, 564–577.

Brady, E. U., & Kendall, P. C. (1992). Comorbidity of anxiety and depression in children in children and adolescents. *Psychological Bulletin*, *111*, 244–255.

Brown, T. E. (2001). *Brown Attention-Deficit Disorder Scales for Children and Adolescents manual*. San Antonio, TX: Psychological Corporation.

Burisch, M. (1984). Approaches to personality inventory construction. *American Psychologist*, *39*, 214–227.

Burke, J. D., Loeber, R., & Birmaher, B. (2002). Oppositional defiant disorder and conduct disorder: A review of the past 10 years, part II. *Journal of the American Academy of Child & Adolescent Psychiatry*, *41*, 1275–1293.

Burns, G. L., Walsh, J. A., Owen, S. M., & Snell, J. (1997). Internal validity of attention deficit hyperactivity disorder, oppositional defiant disorder, and overt conduct disorder symptoms in young children: Implications from teacher ratings for a dimensional approach to symptom validity. *Journal of Clinical Child Psychology*, *26*, 266–275.

Butcher, J. N., Williams, C. L., Graham, J. R., Archer, R. P., Tellegen, A., Ben-Porath, Y. S., & Kaemmer, B. (1992). *Minnesota Multiphasic Personality Inventory—Adolescent: Manual for administration, scoring, and interpretation*. Minneapolis. University of Minnesota Press.

Cantwell, D. P. (1996). Attention deficit disorder: A review of the past 10 years. *Journal of the American Academy of Child and Adolescent Psychiatry*, *35*, 978–987.

Carlston, D., & Ogles, B. (2006). The impact of items and anchors on parent-child reports of problem behavior. *Child & Adolescent Social Work Journal*, *23*, 24–37.

Caron, C., & Rutter, M. (1991). Comorbidity in child psychopathology: Concepts, issues, and research strategies. *Journal of Child Psychology and Psychiatry*, *32*, 1063–1080.

Cashel, M. L. (2002). Child and adolescent psychological assessment: Current clinical practices and the impact of managed care. *Professional Psychology: Research and Practice*, *33*, 446–453.

Caudle, D. D. (2008). *Cluster analysis of children referred for evaluation using the Personality Inventory for Children, Second Edition*. (Unpublished doctoral dissertation). University of Houston, TX.

Charach, A., Chen, S., Hogg-Johnson, S., & Schachar, R. J. (2009). Using the Conners' Teacher Rating Scale—revised in school children referred for assessment. *Canadian Journal of Psychiatry /La Revue Canadienne de Psychiatrie*, *54*, 232–241.

Coolidge, F. L., Thede, L. L., & Young, S. E. (2000). Heritability and the comorbidity of attention deficit hyperactivity disorder with behavioral disorders and executive function deficits: A preliminary investigation. *Developmental Neuropsychology*, *17*, 273–287.

Conners, C. K. (1999). Conners' Rating Scales–Revised. In M. E. Maruish (Ed.), *The use of psychological testing for treatment planning and outcome assessment* (2nd ed., pp. 467–495). Mahwah, NJ: Erlbaum.

Conners, C. K. (2008). *Conners, 3rd edition (CRS-3) manual*. North Tonawanda NY: Multi-Health Systems.

Cordell, A. (1998). Psychological assessment of children. In W. M. Klykylo, J. Kay, & D. Rube (Eds.), *Clinical child psychiatry* (pp. 12–41). Philadelphia, PA: W. B. Saunders.

Crystal, D. S., Ostrander, R., Chen, R. S., & August, G. J. (2001). Multimethod assessment of psychopathology among *DSM-IV* subtypes of children with attention-deficit/hyperactivity disorder: Self-, parent, and teacher reports. *Journal of Abnormal Child Psychology*, *29*, 189–205.

De Los Reyes, A. (2011). Introduction to the special section: More than measurement error: Discovering meaning behind informant discrepancies in clinical assessment of children and adolescents. *Journal of Clinical Child and Adolescent Psychology*, *40*, 1–9.

De Los Reyes, A., & Kazdin, A.E. (2005). Informant discrepancies in the assessment of childhood psychopathology: a critical review, theoretical framework, and recommendations for further study. *Psychological Bulletin*, *131*, 483–509.

Drotar, D., Stein, R. E., & Perrin, E. C. (1995). Methodological issues in using the Child Behavior Checklist and its related instruments in clinical child psychology research. *Journal of Clinical Child Psychology*, *24*, 184–192.

Duhig, A. M., Renk, K., Epstein, M. K., & Phares, V. (2000). Interparental agreement on internalizing, externalizing, and total behavior problems: A meta-analysis. *Clinical Psychology: Science and Practice*, *7*, 435–453.

Edelbrock, C., Costello, A. J., Dulcan, M. K., Kalas, D., & Conover, N. (1985). Age differences in the reliability of the psychiatric interview of the child. *Child Development*, *56*, 265–275.

Eisman, E. J., Dies R. R., Finn, S. E., Eyde, L. D., Kay, G. G., Kubiszyn, T. W., ... Moreland, G. J. (2000). Problems and limitations in using psychological assessment in the contemporary health care delivery system. *Professional Psychology: Research and Practice 2000*, *31*, 131–140.

Evans, A. S., & Frank, S. J. (2004). Adolescent depression and externalizing problems: Testing two models of comorbidity in an inpatient sample. *Adolescence*, *39*, 1–18.

Exner, J. E. Jr., & Weiner, I. B. (1995). *The Rorschach: A comprehensive system: Vol. 3* (2nd ed.). *Assessment of children and adolescents*. New York, NY: Wiley.

Finch, A. J., Lipovsky, J. A., & Casat, C. D. (1989). Anxiety and depression in children and adolescents: Negative affectivity or separate constructs. In P. C. Kendall & D. Watson (Eds.), *Anxiety and depression: Distinctive and overlapping features* (pp. 171–202). New York, NY: Academic Press.

Fitzgerald, H. E., Zucker, R. A., Maguin, E. T., & Reider, E. E. (1994). Time spent with child and parental agreement about preschool children's behavior. *Perceptual and Motor Skills*, *79*, 336–338.

Fontaine, J. L., Archer, R. P., Elkins, D. E., & Johansen, J. (2001). The effects of MMPI-A T-score elevation on classification accuracy for normal and clinical adolescent samples. *Journal of Personality Assessment*, *76*, 264–281.

Forbes, G. B. (1985). The Personality Inventory for Children (PIC) and hyperactivity: Clinical utility and problems of generalizability. *Journal of Pediatric Psychology*, *10*, 141–149.

Frick, P. J., Barry, C. T., & Kamphaus, R. W. (2010). *Clinical assessment of child and adolescent personality and behavior* (3rd ed.). New York, NY: Springer.

Fristad, M. A., Emery, B. L., & Beck, S. J. (1997). Use and abuse of the Children's Depression Inventory. *Journal of Consulting and Clinical Psychology*, *65*, 699–702.

Gerard, A. B., & Reynolds, C. R. (1999). Characteristics and applications of the Revisd Children's Manifest Anxiety Scale (RCMAS). In M. E. Maruish (Ed.), *The use of psychological testing for treatment planning and outcomes assessment* (2nd ed., pp. 323–340). Mahwah, NJ: Erlbaum.

Gianarris, W. J., Golden, C. J., & Greene, L. (2001). The Conners' Parent Rating Scales: A critical review of the literature. *Clinical Psychology Review*, *21*, 1061–1093.

Gliner, J. A., Morgan, G. A., & Harmon, R. J. (2001). Measurement reliability. *Journal of the American Academy of Child and Adolescent Psychiatry*, 40, 486–488.

Goyette, C. H., Conners, C. K., & Ulrich, R. F. (1978). Normative data on Revised Conners' Parent and Teacher Rating Scales. *Journal of Abnormal Child Psychology*, 6, 221–236.

Graham, J. R. (2006). *MMPI-2: Assessing personality and psychopathology* (4th ed.). New York, NY: Oxford University Press.

Groth-Marnat, G. (1999). Current status and future directions of psychological assessment: Introduction. *Journal of Clinical Psychology*, 55, 781–785.

Hale, J. B., How, S. K., Dewitt, M. B., & Coury, D. L. (2001). Discriminant validity of the Conners' Scales for ADHD subtypes. *Current Psychology: A Journal for Diverse Perspectives on Diverse Psychological Issues*, 20, 231–249.

Hand, C. G., Archer, R. P., Handel, R. W., & Forbey, J. D. (2007). The classification accuracy of the Minnesota Multiphasic Personality Inventory—Adolescent: Effects of modifying the normative sample. *Assessment*, 14, 80–85

Handwerk, M. L., Larzelere, R. E., Soper, S. H., & Friman, P. C. (1999). Parent and child discrepancies in reporting severity of problem behaviors in three out-of-home settings. *Psychological Assessment*, 11, 14–23.

Hathaway, S. R., & Monachesi, E. D. (1953). *Analyzing and predicting juvenile delinquency with the MMPI*. Minneapolis: University of Minnesota Press.

Heffer, R. W., Barry, T. D., & Garland, B. H. (2009). History, overview, and trends in child and adolescent psychological assessment. In M. L. Matson (Ed.), *Assessing childhood psychopathology and developmental disabilities* (pp. 3–29). New York, NY: Springer Science + Business Media.

Hinshaw, S. P., Lahey, B. B., & Hart, E. L. (1993). Issues of taxonomy and comorbidity in the development of conduct disorder. *Development and Psychopathology*, 5, 31–49.

Hulbert, T. A., Gdowski, C. L., & Lachar, D. (1986). Interparent agreement on the Personality Inventory for Children: Are substantial correlations sufficient? *Journal of Abnormal Child Psychology*, 14, 115–122.

Ivanova, M. Y., Achenbach, T. M., Dumenci, L., Rescorla, L. A., Almqvist, F., Weintraub, S.,... Verhulst, F. C. (2007). Testing the 8-syndrome structure of the child behavior checklist in 30 societies. *Journal of Clinical Child and Adolescent Psychology*, 36, 405–417.

Jensen, P. S., Hinshaw, S. P., Kraemer, H. C., Lenora, N., Newcorn, J. H., Abikoff, H. B.,... Vitiello, B. (2001). ADHD comorbidity findings from the MTA study: Comparing comorbid subgroups. *Journal of the American Academy of Child & Adolescent Psychiatry*, 40, 147–158.

Jensen, P. S., Martin, D., & Cantwell, D. P. (1997). Comorbidity in ADHD: Implications for research, practice, and *DSM-IV*. *Journal of the American Academy of Child and Adolescent Psychiatry*, 36, 1065–1079.

Jensen, P. S., & Members of the MTA Cooperative Group. (2002). ADHD comorbidity findings from the MTA study: New diagnostic subtypes and their optimal treatments. In J. J. Hudziak (Ed.), *Defining psychopathology in the 21st century: DSM-V and beyond*. (pp. 169–192). Arlington, VA: American Psychiatric Publishing.

Kamphaus, R. W., & Frick, P. J. (2002). *Clinical assessment of child and adolescent personality and behavior* (2nd ed.). Boston, MA: Allyn & Bacon.

Kern, L., & State, T. (2008). Oppositional defiant and conduct disorders. In D. Reitman (Ed.), *Handbook of psychological assessment, case conceptualization, and treatment, vol. 2: Children and adolescents* (pp. 292–316). Hoboken, NJ: Wiley.

King, N. J., Ollendick, T. H., & Gullone, E. (1991). Negative affectivity in children and adolescents: Relations between anxiety and depression. *Clinical Psychology Review*, 11, 441–459.

Konold, T. R., & Pianta, R. C. (2007). The influence of informants on ratings of children's behavioral functioning: A latent variable approach. *Journal of Psychoeducational Assessment*, 25, 222–236.

Koocher, G. P., Norcross, J. C., & Hill, S. S. (Eds.). (2005). *Psychologists' desk reference* (2nd ed.). New York, NY: Oxford University Press.

Kovacs, M. (1992). *Children's Depression Inventory (CDI) manual*. Toronto, Canada: Multi-Health Systems.

Kovacs, M. (2003). *Children's Depression Inventory (CDI) Technical Manual Update*. Toronto, Canada: Multi-Health Systems.

Kovacs, M. (2011). *Children's Depression Inventory* (2nd ed.) *(CDI-2) manual*. North Tonawanda, NY: Multi-Health Systems.

Lachar, D. (1993). Symptom checklists and personality inventories. In T. R. Kratochwill & R. J. Morris (Eds.), *Handbook of psychotherapy for children and adolescents* (pp. 38–57). Needham Heights, MA: Allyn & Bacon.

Lachar, D. (1998). Observations of parents, teachers, and children: Contributions to the objective multidimensional assessment of youth. In A. S. Bellack & M. Hersen (Series Eds.), & C. R. Reynolds (Vol. Ed.), *Comprehensive clinical psychology: Vol. 4*, *Assessment* (pp. 371–401). New York, NY: Pergamon Press.

Lachar, D., & Gdowski, C. L. (1979). *Actuarial assessment of child and adolescent personality: An interpretive guide for the Personality Inventory for Children profile*. Los Angeles, CA: Western Psychological Services.

Lachar, D., & Gruber, C. P. (1993). Development of the Personality Inventory for Youth: A self-report companion to the Personality Inventory for Children. *Journal of Personality Assessment*, 61, 81–98.

Lachar, D., & Gruber, C. P. (1995). *Personality Inventory for Youth (PIY) manual: Administration and interpretation guide. Technical guide*. Los Angeles, CA: Western Psychological Services.

Lachar, D., & Gruber, C. P. (2001). *Personality Inventory for Children, Second Edition (PIC-2). Standard Form and Behavioral Summary manual*. Los Angeles, CA: Western Psychological Services.

Lachar, D., & Gruber, C. P. (2009). *The Behavioral Summary manual*. Los Angeles, CA: Western Psychological Services.

Lachar, D., Klinge, V., & Grisell, J. L. (1976). Relative accuracy of automated MMPI narratives generated from adult-norm and adolescent-norm profiles. *Journal of Consulting and Clinical Psychology*, 46, 1403–1408.

Lachar, D., Morgan, S. T., Espadas, A., & Schomer, O. (2000, August). *Effect of defensiveness on two self-report child adjustment inventories*. Paper presented at the 108th annual meeting of the American Psychological Association, Washington, DC.

Lachar, D., Randle, S. L., Harper, R. A., Scott-Gurnell, K. C., Lewis, K. R., Santos, C. W.,... Morgan, S. T. (2001). The Brief Psychiatric Rating Scale for Children (BPRS-C): Validity and reliability of an anchored version. *Journal of the American Academy of Child and Adolescent Psychiatry*, 40, 333–340.

Lachar, D., Wingenfeld, S. A., Kline, R. B., & Gruber, C. P. (2000). *Student Behavior Survey manual*. Los Angeles, CA: Western Psychological Services.

LaGreca, A. M., Kuttler, A. F., & Stone, W. L. (2001). Assessing children through interviews and behavioral observations. In C. E. Walker & M. C. Roberts (Eds.), *Handbook of clinical child psychology* (3rd ed., pp. 90–110). Hoboken, NJ: Wiley.

Lewandowski, L., Lovett, B. & Gordon, M. (2009). Measures of symptom severity and impairment. In S. Goldstein and J. Naglieri (Eds.), *Assessing impairment: From theory to practice*. (pp. 5–14). New York, NY: Springer, 2009.

Loeber, R., Burke, J. D., Lahey, B. B., Winters, A., & Zera, M. (2000). Oppositional defiant and conduct disorder: A review of the past 10 years, part I. *Journal of the American Academy of Child & Adolescent Psychiatry*, *39*, 1468–1484.

Loeber, R., Green, S. M., & Lahey, B. B. (1990). Mental health professionals' perception of the utility of children, mothers, and teachers as informants on childhood psychopathology. *Journal of Clinical Child Psychology*, *19*, 136–143.

Loeber, R., & Keenan, K. (1994). Interaction between conduct disorder and its comorbid conditions: Effects of age and gender. *Clinical Psychology Review*, *14*, 497–523.

Loeber, R., & Schmaling, K. B. (1985). The utility of differentiating between mixed and pure forms of antisocial child behavior. *Journal of Abnormal Child Psychology*, *13*, 315–336.

Marmorstein, N. R. (2007). Relationships between anxiety and externalizing disorders in youth: The influences of age and gender. *Journal of Anxiety Disorders*, *21*(3), 420–432.

Marmorstein, N. R., & Iacono, W. G. (2001). An investigation of female adolescent twins with both major depression and conduct disorder. *Journal of the American Academy of Child and Adolescent Psychiatry*, *40*, 299–306.

Maruish, M. E. (1999). *The use of psychological testing for treatment planning and outcomes assessment* (2nd ed.) Mahwah, NJ: Erlbaum.

Maruish, M. E. (2002). *Psychological testing in the age of managed behavioral health care*. Mahwah, NJ: Erlbaum.

Mash, E. J., & Hunsley, J. (2005). Evidence-based assessment of child and adolescent disorders: Issues and challenges. *Journal of Clinical Child and Adolescent Psychology*, *34*, 362–379.

Mash, E. J., & Hunsley, J. (2007). Assessment of child and family disturbance. A developmental-systems approach. In R. A. Barkley (Ed.), *Assessment of childhood disorders* (4th ed., pp. 3–50). New York, NY: Guilford Press.

Mash, E. J., & Lee, C. M. (1993). Behavioral assessment with children. In R. T. Ammerman & M. Hersen (Eds.), *Handbook of behavior therapy with children and adults* (pp. 13–31). Boston, MA: Allyn & Bacon.

Mash, E. J., & Terdal, L. G. (1997). Assessment of child and family disturbance: A behavioral-systems approach. In E. J. Mash & L. G. Terdal (Eds.), *Assessment of childhood disorders* (3rd ed., pp. 3–69). New York, NY: Guilford Press.

Masi, G., Perugi, G., Toni, C., Millepiedi, S., Mucci, M., Bertini, N., & Pfanner, C. (2006). Attention-deficit hyperactivity disorder—bipolar comorbidity in children and adolescents. *Bipolar Disorders*, *8*, 373–381.

Matson, J. L., Andrasik, F., & Matson, M. L., eds. (2010). *Assessing childhood psychopathology and developmental disabilities*. New York, NY: Springer.

McMahon, R. J. (1987). Some current issues in the behavioral assessment of conduct disordered children and their families. *Behavioral Assessment*, *9*, 235–252.

Merrell, K. W. (2010). *Behavioral, social, and emotional assessment of children and adolescents* (2nd ed.). New York, NY: Routledge.

Millon, T. (1993). *Millon Adolescent Clinical Inventory (MACI) manual*. Minneapolis, MN: National Computer Systems.

Millon, T., Millon, C., Davis, R., & Grossman, S. (2006). *Millon Adolescent Clinical Inventory (MACI) manual* (2nd ed.). Minneapolis, MN: NCS Pearson.

Moretti, M. M., Fine, S., Haley, G., & Marriage, K. (1985). Childhood and adolescent depression: Child-report versus parent report information. *Journal of the American Academy of Child Psychiatry*, *24*, 298–302.

Morgan, G. A., Gliner, J. A., & Harmon, R. J. (2001). Measurement validity. *Journal of the American Academy of Child and Adolescent Psychiatry*, *40*, 729–731.

Naglieri, J. A., LeBuffe, P. A., & Pfeiffer, S. I. (1994). *Devereux Scales of Mental Disorders manual*. San Antonio, TX: Psychological Corporation.

Nanson, J. L., & Gordon, B. (1999). Psychosocial correlates of mental retardation. In V. L. Schwean & D. H. Saklofske (Eds.), *Handbook of psychosocial characteristic of exceptional children* (pp. 377–400). New York, NY: Kluwer Academic/Plenum Press.

Newman, F. L., Ciarlo, J. A., & Carpenter, D. (1999). Guidelines for selecting psychological instruments for treatment planning and outcome assessment. In M. E. Maruish (Ed.), *The use of psychological testing for treatment planning and outcomes assessment* (2nd ed., pp. 153–170). Mahwah, NJ: Erlbaum.

Nock, M. K., Kazdin, A. E., Hiripi, E., & Kessler, R. C. (2007). Lifetime prevalence, correlates, and persistence of oppositional defiant disorder: Results from the national comorbidity survey replication. *Journal of Child Psychology and Psychiatry*, *48*, 703–713.

Offord, D. R., Boyle, M. H., & Racine, Y. A. (1991). The epidemiology of antisocial behavior in childhood and adolescence. In D. J. Pepler & K. H. Rubin (Eds.), *The development and treatment of childhood aggression* (pp. 31 54). Hillsdale, NJ: Erlbaum.

Pearson, D. A., & Lachar, D. (1994). Using behavioral questionnaires to identify adaptive deficits in elementary school children. *Journal of School Psychology*, *32*, 33–52.

Pearson, D. A., Lachar, D., Loveland, K. A., Santos, C. W., Faria, L. P., Azzam, P. N., . . . Cleveland, L. A. (2000). Patterns of behavioral adjustment and maladjustment in mental retardation: Comparison of children with and without ADHD. *American Journal on Mental Retardation*, *105*, 236–251.

Pelham, W. E. Jr., Fabiano, G. A., & Massetti, G. M. (2005). Evidence-based assessment of attention deficit hyperactivity disorder in children and adolescents. *Journal of Clinical Child and Adolescent Psychology*, *34*, 449–476.

Phares, V. (1997). Accuracy of informants: Do parents think that mother knows best? The influence of informants on ratings of children's behavioral functioning: A latent variable approach. *Journal of Psychoeducational Assessment*, *25*, 222–236.

Piotrowski, C. (1999). Assessment practices in the era of managed care: Current status and future direction. *Journal of Clinical Psychology*, *55*, 787–796.

Piotrowski, C., Belter, R. W., & Keller, J. W. (1998). The impact of "managed care" on the practice of psychological testing: Preliminary findings. *Journal of Personality Assessment*, *70*, 441–447.

Pisecco, S., Lachar, D., Gruber, C. P., Gallen, R. T., Kline, R. B., & Huzinec, C. (1999). Development and validation of disruptive behavior *DSM-IV* scales for the Student Behavior Survey (SBS). *Journal of Psychoeducational Assessment*, *17*, 314–331.

Pliszka, S. R. (1998). Comorbidity of attention-deficit/hyperactivity disorder with psychiatric disorder: An overview. *Journal of Clinical Psychiatry*, *59*(Suppl. 7), 50–58.

Powell, N. R., Lochman, J. E., Jackson, M. F., Young, L., & Yaros, A. (2009). Assessment of conduct problems. In M. L. Matson (Ed.), *Assessing childhood psychopathology and developmental disabilities*. (pp. 185–207). New York, NY: Springer Science.

Reitman, D. (Vol. Ed.). (2008). *Children and adolescents*, Vol. 2. In M. Hersen (Ed. in Chief), D. Reitman (Vol. Ed.), *Handbook of psychological assessment, case conceptualization, and treatment*. Hoboken, NJ: Wiley.

Reuterskiöld, L., Öst, L., & Ollendick, T. (2008). Exploring child and parent factors in the diagnostic agreement on the anxiety disorders interview schedule. *Journal of Psychopathology and Behavioral Assessment*, *30*, 279–290.

Reynolds, C. R., & Kamphaus, R. W. (2004). *Behavior Assessment System for Children, 2nd edition (BASC-2) manual*. Minneapolis, MN: NCS Pearson.

Reynolds, C. R., & Kamphaus, R. W. (2009). *BASC-2 monitor manual*. Circle Pines, MN: NCS Pearson.

Reynolds, C. R., & Richmond, B. O. (2008). *Revised Children's Manifest Anxiety Scale, 2nd ed. (RCMAS-2) manual*. Los Angeles, CA: Western Psychological Services.

Reynolds, W. M. (1998). *Adolescent Psychopathology Scale (APS): Administration and interpretation manual*. Odessa, FL: Psychological Assessment Resources.

Reynolds, W. M. (2000). *Adolescent Psychopathology Scale–Short Form (APS-SF) professional manual*. Odessa, FL: Psychological Assessment Resources.

Roberts, G. E. (2005) *Roberts Apperception Test for Children: 2 (Roberts-2)*. Los Angeles, CA: Western Psychological Services.

Roberts, M. C., & Hurley, L. (1997). *Managing managed care*. New York, NY: Plenum Press.

Ross, R. G., Heinlein, S., & Tregellas, H. (2006). High rates of comorbidity are found in childhood-onset schizophrenia. *Schizophrenia Research*, *88*(1–3), 90–95.

Sheldrick, R. C., Kendall, P. C., & Heimberg, R. G. (2001). The clinical significance of treatments: A comparison of three treatments for conduct disordered children. *Clinical Psychology: Science and Practice*, *8*, 418–430.

Sitarenios, G., & Stein, M. (2004). Use of the Children's Depression Inventory. In M. E. Maruish (Ed.), *The use of psychological testing for treatment planning and outcomes assessment, Vol. 2: Instruments for Children and Adolescents* (3rd ed., pp. 1–37). Mahwah, NJ: Erlbaum.

Smith, S. R. (2007). Making sense of multiple informants in child and adolescent psychopathology: a guide for clinicians. *Journal of Psychoeducational Assessment*, *25*, 139–149.

Smith, S. R., & Handler, L. (2007). *The clinical assessment of children and adolescents: A practitioner's handbook*. Mahwah, NJ: Erlbaum.

Snyder, D. K. (1997). *Manual for the Marital Satisfaction Inventory—Revised*. Los Angeles, CA: Western Psychological Services.

Snyder, D. K., & Aikman, G. G. (1999). Marital Satisfaction Inventory—Revised. In M. E. Maruish (Ed.), *The use of psychological testing for treatment planning and outcomes assessment* (2nd ed., pp. 1173–1210). Mahwah, NJ: Erlbaum.

Spengler, P. M., Strohmer, D. C., & Prout, H. T. (1990). Testing the robustness of the diagnostic overshadowing bias. *American Journal on Mental Retardation*, *95*, 204–214.

Teeter, P. A., Eckert, L., Nelson, A., Platten, P., Semrud-Clikeman, M., & Kamphaus, R. W. (2009). Assessment of behavior and personality in the neuropsychological diagnosis of children. In E. Fletcher-Janzen (Ed.), *Handbook of clinical child neuropsychology* (3rd ed., pp. 349–381). New York, NY: Springer Science + Business Media.

Treutler, C. M., & Epkins, C. C. (2003). Are discrepancies among child, mother, and father reports on children's behavior related to parents' psychological symptoms and aspects of parent-child relationships? *Journal of Abnormal Child Psychology*, *31*, 13–27.

Verhulst, F. C., Achenbach, T. M., van, d. E., Erol, N., Lambert, M. C., Leung, P.W.L., Silva, M. A., Zilber, N., & Zubrick, S. R. (2003). Comparisons of problems reported by youths from seven countries. *American Journal of Psychiatry*, *160*, 1479–1485.

Voelker, S., Lachar, D., & Gdowski, C. L. (1983). The Personality Inventory for Children and response to methylphenidate: Preliminary evidence for predictive utility. *Journal of Pediatric Psychology*, *8*, 161–169.

Whitaker, S., & Read, S. (2006). The prevalence of psychiatric disorders among people with intellectual disabilities: An analysis of the literature. *Journal of Applied Research in Intellectual Disabilities*, *19*, 330–345.

Wilens, T. E., Biederman, J., Forkner, P., Ditterline, J., Morris, M., Moore, H., . . . Wozniak, J. (2003). Patterns of comorbidity and dysfunction in clinically referred preschool and school-age children with bipolar disorder. *Journal of Child and Adolescent Psychopharmacology*, *13*, 495–505.

Willcutt, E. G., Pennington, B. F., Chhabildas, N. A., Friedman, M. C., & Alexander, J. (1999). Psychiatry comorbidity associated with *DSM-IV* ADHD in a nonreferred sample of twins. *Journal of the American Academy of Child & Adolescent Psychiatry*, *38*, 1355–1362.

Williams, C. L., Butcher, J. N., Ben-Porath, Y. S., & Graham, J. R. (1992). *MMPI-A content scales. Assessing psychopathology in adolescents*. Minneapolis: University of Minnesota Press.

Wingenfeld, S. A., Lachar, D., Gruber, C. P., & Kline, R. B. (1998). Development of the teacher-informant Student Behavior Survey. *Journal of Psychoeducational Assessment*, *16*, 226–249.

Wolff, J. C., & Ollendick, T. H. (2006). The comorbidity of conduct problems and depression in childhood and adolescence. *Clinical Child and Family Psychology Review*, *9*(3–4), 201–220.

Wrobel, T. A., Lachar, D., Wrobel, N. H., Morgan, S. T., Gruber, C. P., & Neher, J. A. (1999). Performance of the Personality Inventory for Youth validity scales. *Assessment*, *6*, 367–376.

Youngstrom, E., Loeber, R., & Stouthamer-Loeber, M. (2000). Patterns and correlates of agreement between parent, teacher, and male adolescent ratings of externalizing and internalizing problems. *Journal of Consulting and Clinical Psychology*, *68*, 1038–1050.

Zahn-Waxler, C., Klimes-Dougan, B., & Slattery, M. J. (2000). Internalizing problems of childhood and adolescence: Prospects, pitfalls, and progress in understanding the development of anxiety and depression. *Development and Psychopathology*, *12*, 443–466.

# CHAPTER 12

# Psychological Assessment in School Settings

JEFFERY P. BRADEN

Psychological assessment in school settings is in many ways similar to psychological assessment in other settings. This may be due in part because the practice of modern psychological assessment began with an application to schools (Fagan, 1996). However, the practice of psychological assessment in school settings may be discriminated from practices in other settings by three characteristics: populations, problems, and procedures (American Psychological Association, 1998).

The primary population targeted by psychological assessment in school settings is children and, secondarily, the parents, families, and educators of those children. In the United States, schools offer services to preschool children with disabilities as young as 3 years of age and are obligated to provide services to individuals up to 21 years of age. Furthermore, schools are obligated to educate all children, regardless of their physical, behavioral, or cognitive disabilities or gifts. Because public schools are free and attendance is compulsory for children, schools are more likely than private or fee-for-service settings to serve individuals who are minority and poor and have language and cultural differences. Consequently, psychological assessment must respond to the diverse developmental, cultural, linguistic, disability, and individual differences reflected in school populations.

The primary problems targeted by psychological assessment in school settings are those of learning and school adjustment. Although psychologists must also assess and respond to other developmental, social, emotional, and behavioral issues, the primary focus behind most psychological assessment in schools is understanding and ameliorating learning problems. Children and families presenting psychological problems unrelated to learning are generally referred to services in nonschool settings. Also, school-based psychological assessment addresses problem prevention, such as reducing academic or social failure. Whereas psychological assessment in other settings is frequently not invoked until a problem is presented, psychological assessment in schools may be used to prevent problems from occurring.

The procedures most common to psychological assessment in school settings are relevant to the populations and problems served in schools. Therefore, school-based psychologists emphasize assessment of academic achievement and student learning, use interventions that emphasize educational or learning approaches, and use consultation to implement interventions. Because children experience problems in classrooms, playgrounds, homes, and other settings that support education, interventions to address problems are generally implemented in the setting where the problem occurs. School-based psychologists generally do not provide direct services (e.g., play therapy) outside of educational settings. Consequently, psychologists in school settings consult with teachers, parents, and other educators to implement interventions. Psychological assessment procedures that address student learning, psychoeducational interventions, and intervention implementation mediated via consultation are emphasized to a greater degree in schools than in other settings.

The remainder of this chapter addresses aspects of psychological assessment that distinguish practices in school-based settings from practices in other settings. The chapter is organized into three major sections: assessment purposes, current practices, and future trends of psychological assessment in schools.

## PURPOSES OF PSYCHOLOGICAL ASSESSMENT IN SCHOOLS

There are generally six distinct, but related, purposes that drive psychological assessment. These are:

1. screening,
2. diagnosis,
3. intervention,
4. evaluation,
5. selection, and
6. certification.

Psychological assessment practitioners may address all of these purposes in their school-based work.

### Screening

Psychological assessment may be useful for detecting psychological or educational problems in school-aged populations. Typically, psychologists employ screening instruments to detect students at risk of various psychological disorders, including depression, suicide, academic failure, social skills deficits, academic competence, and other forms of maladaptive behaviors. Thus, screening is most often associated with selected or targeted prevention programs. (See Coie et al., 1993, and Reiss & Price, 1996, for a discussion of contemporary prevention paradigms and taxonomies.)

The justification for screening programs relies on three premises: (1) individuals at significantly higher than average risk for a problem can be identified prior to onset of the problem; (2) interventions can eliminate later problem onset or reduce the severity, frequency, and duration of later problems; and (3) the costs of the screening and intervention programs are justified by reduced fiscal or human costs. In some cases, psychologists justify screening with the additional argument that interventions are more effective if initiated prior to or shortly after problem onset than if they are delivered later.

Three lines of research validate the assumptions supporting screening programs in schools. First, school-age children who exhibit later problems often may be identified with reasonable accuracy via screening programs, although the value of screening varies across problem types (Durlak, 1997). Second, there is a substantial literature base to support the efficacy of prevention programs for children (Durlak, 1997; Weissberg & Greenberg, 1998). Third, prevention programs are consistently cost effective and usually pay dividends of greater than 3:1 in cost-benefit analyses (Durlak, 1997).

Although support for screening and prevention programs is compelling, there are also concerns about the value of screening using psychological assessment techniques. For example, the consequences of screening mistakes (i.e., false positives and false negatives) are not always well understood. Furthermore, assessment instruments typically identify children as at risk rather than identifying the social, educational, and other environmental conditions that put them at risk. The focus on the child as the problem (i.e., the "disease" model) may undermine necessary social and educational reforms. (See Albee, 1998.) Screening may also be more appropriate for some conditions (e.g., suicide, depression, social skills deficits) than for others (e.g., smoking), in part because students may not be motivated to change (Norman, Velicer, Fava, & Prochaska, 2000). Placement in special programs or remedial tracks may reduce, rather than increase, students' opportunity to learn and develop. Therefore, the use of psychological assessment in screening and prevention programs should consider carefully the consequential validity of the assessment process and should ensure that inclusion in or exclusion from a prevention program is based on more than a single screening test score (see Standard 13.7, pp. 146–147, American Educational Research Association, American Psychological Association, & National Council on Measurement in Education, 1999).

Schools also use screening tools to identify and correct early academic failure, especially in the area of reading. There have been dramatic developments in detection of early reading failure, including Dynamic Indicators of Basic Early Literacy Skills (DIBELS), which successfully identifies difficulties in subsequent reading performance (e.g., Roehrig, Petscher, Nettles, Hudson, & Torgesen, 2008). Schools use regular (two to four times per year) assessments in other academic domains, sometimes known as benchmarks, for early identification and correction of academic failure, although the practice remains controversial for younger children, where child-centered philosophies and approaches to education conflict with assessment of curriculum mastery (Wyse & Torrance, 2009). However, there has been a substantial increase in screening assessments to identify educational problems in most western schools, particularly at the early primary (preschool–grade 3) level.

## Diagnosis

Psychological assessment procedures play a major, and often decisive, role in diagnosing psychoeducational problems. Generally, diagnosis serves two purposes: establishing eligibility for services and selecting interventions. The use of assessment to select interventions is discussed in the next section. Eligibility for special educational services in the United States is contingent on receiving a diagnosis of a psychological or psychoeducational disability. Statutory legislation (e.g., the Americans with Disabilities Act) is generally silent on eligibility criteria, meaning diagnosis is most often done by medical professionals outside the schools. In contrast, entitlement legislation (e.g., the Individuals with Disabilities Education Improvement Act, 2004; IDEIA) provides legislative and regulatory procedures schools must follow to establishing eligibility for services. Although statutory and entitlement legislation share many diagnostic categories (e.g., learning disability, mental retardation), they differ with regard to specificity and recognition of other diagnoses. For example, entitlement legislation identifies "severely emotionally disturbed" as a single category consisting of a few broad diagnostic indicators, whereas medical nosologies (e.g., American Psychiatric Association, 2000) differentiate more types and varieties of emotional disorders. However, whereas psychological and medical nosologies recognize attention deficit disorder (ADD) as a unique disorder, IDEIA does not.

IDEIA also introduced another major change in diagnosing eligibility for special education services: Response to Intervention (RTI) (Batsche et al., 2005). Essentially, psychologists can invoke interventions and assess the student's response to those interventions as a mechanism for establishing eligibility for services. Should a student respond successfully to an intervention, the psychologist's focus shifts from establishing student eligibility to implementing the intervention in the classroom, as evidence that the student's needs may be served in the general education classroom is sufficient to demonstrate ineligibility for services. That is, if the student's needs can be adequately met by acceptable classroom modifications, the student cannot be eligible for special education under the IDEIA (but could be identified as having a disability under ADA/504). Conversely, a student's failure to respond is necessary, and may be sufficient (particularly in response to multiple evidence-based interventions implemented with high integrity), to establish eligibility for special education services. The RTI approach emphasizes in vivo over in vitro assessment procedures, although significant issues of reliability and interpretation of results

remain unresolved (Braden & Shernoff, 2008). The process and use of RTI methods is discussed in greater detail later in this chapter.

## Intervention

Assessment is often invoked to help professionals select an intervention from among an array of potential interventions (i.e., treatment matching). The fundamental assumption is that the knowledge produced by a psychological assessment improves treatment or intervention selection. Although most psychologists would accept the value for treatment matching at a general level of assessment, the notion that psychological assessment results can guide treatment selection is more controversial with respect to narrower levels of assessment. For example, determining whether a student's difficulty with written English is caused by severe mental retardation, deafness, lack of exposure to English, inconsistent prior instruction, or a language processing problem would help educators select interventions ranging from operant conditioning approaches, placement in a program using American Sign Language, English as a Second Language (ESL) programs, general writing instruction with some support, or speech therapy.

However, the utility of assessment to guide intervention is less clear at narrower levels of assessment. For example, knowing that a student has a reliable difference between one or more cognitive subtest or composite scores, or fits a particular personality category or learning style profile, may have little value in guiding intervention selection. In fact, some critics (e.g., Gresham & Witt, 1997) have argued that there is no incremental utility for assessing cognitive or personality characteristics beyond recognizing extreme abnormalities (and such recognition generally does not require the use of psychological tests). Indeed, some critics argue that data-gathering techniques such as observation, interviews, records reviews, and curriculum-based assessment of academic deficiencies (coupled with common sense) are sufficient to guide treatment matching (Gresham & Witt, 1997; Reschly & Grimes, 1995). Others argue that knowledge of cognitive processes and, in particular, of neuropsychological processes is useful for treatment matching (e.g., Das, Naglieri, & Kirby, 1994; Naglieri, 1999; Naglieri & Das, 1997). This issue is discussed later in the chapter under "RTI Approaches."

## Evaluation

Psychologists may use assessment to evaluate the outcome of interventions, programs, or other educational and psychological processes. Evaluation implies an expectation for a certain outcome, and the outcome is usually a change or improvement (e.g., improved reading achievement, increased social skills). Increasingly, the public and others concerned with psychological services and education expect students to show improvement as a result of attending school or participating in a program. Psychological assessment and, in particular, assessment of student learning help educators decide whether and how much students improve as a function of a curriculum, intervention, or program. Furthermore, this information is increasingly of interest to public and lay audiences concerned with accountability. (See Elmore & Rothman, 1999; McDonnell, McLaughlin, & Morrison, 1997.)

Evaluation comprises two related purposes: formative evaluation (e.g., ongoing progress monitoring to make instructional decisions, providing feedback to students) and summative evaluation (e.g., assigning final grades, making pass/fail decisions, awarding credits). Psychological assessment is helpful for both purposes. Formative evaluation may focus on students (e.g., curriculum-based measurement of academic progress; changes in frequency, duration, or intensity of social behaviors over time or settings) but may also focus on the adults involved in an intervention. Psychological assessment can be helpful for assessing treatment acceptability (i.e., the degree to which those executing an intervention find the procedure acceptable and are motivated to comply with it) (Fairbanks & Stinnett, 1997), treatment integrity (i.e., adherence to a specific intervention or treatment protocol) (Wickstrom, Jones, LaFleur, & Witt, 1998), and goal attainment (the degree to which the goals of the intervention are met) (MacKay, Somerville, & Lundie, 1996). Because psychologists in educational settings frequently depend on others to conduct interventions, they must evaluate the degree to which interventions are acceptable, and whether interventions were executed with integrity, before drawing conclusions about intervention effectiveness. Likewise, psychologists should use assessment to obtain judgments of treatment success from adults in addition to obtaining direct measures of student change to make formative and summative decisions about student progress or outcomes.

## Selection

Psychological assessment for selection is a historic practice that has become controversial. Students of intellectual assessment may remember that Binet and Simon developed the first practical test of intelligence to help Parisian educators select students for academic or vocational programs. The use of psychological assessment to select—or assign—students to educational programs or tracks was a major function of U.S. school-based psychologists in the early to mid-1900s (Fagan, 2000). However, the general practice of assigning students to different academic tracks (called "tracking") fell out of favor with educators, due in part to the perceived injustice of limiting students' opportunity to learn. Furthermore, the use of intellectual ability tests to assign students to tracks was deemed illegal by a U.S. federal district court, although later judicial decisions have upheld the assignment of students to different academic tracks if those assignments are based on direct measures of student performance (Reschly, Kicklighter, & McKee, 1988). Therefore, the use of psychological assessment to select or assign students to different educational tracks is allowed if the assessment is nonbiased and is directly tied to the educational process. However, many educators view tracking as ineffective and immoral (Oakes, 1992), although recent research suggests that tracking may have beneficial effects for all students, including those in the lowest academic tracks (Figlio & Page, 2000). The selection activities likely to be supported by psychological assessment in schools include determining eligibility for special education (discussed previously under diagnosis), programs for gifted children, and academic honors and awards (e.g., National Merit Scholarships).

## Certification

Psychological assessment rarely addresses certification, because psychologists are rarely charged with certification decisions. An exception to this rule is certification of student learning, or achievement testing. Schools must certify student learning for graduation purposes and increasingly for other purposes, such as promotion to higher grades or retention for an additional year in the same grade.

Historically, teachers make certification decisions with little use of psychological assessment. Teachers generally certify student learning based on their assessment of student progress in the course via grades. However, grading practices vary substantially among teachers and are often unreliable within teachers, because teachers struggle to reconcile judgments of student performance with motivation and perceived ability when assigning grades (McMillan & Workman, 1999). Also, critics of public education have expressed grave concerns regarding teachers' expectations and their ability and willingness to hold students to high expectations (Ravitch, 1999).

In response to critics' concerns and U.S. legislation (e.g., Title I of the Elementary and Secondary Education Act), schools have dramatically increased the use and importance of standardized achievement tests to certify student knowledge. Because states often attach significant student consequences to their standardized assessments of student learning, these tests are called high-stakes tests. (See Heubert & Hauser, 1999; cf. Braden & Tayrose, 2008). About half of the states in the United States currently use tests in whole or in part for making promotion and graduation decisions (National Governors Association, 1998); consequently, psychologists should help schools design and use effective assessment programs. Because these high-stakes tests are rarely given by psychologists and because they do not assess more "psychological" attributes such as intelligence or emotion, a discussion of high-stakes achievement tests could be excluded from this chapter. However, I include them here and in the section on achievement testing, because these assessments are playing an increasingly prominent role in schools and in the lives of students, teachers, and parents. (See Wang, Beckett, & Brown, 2006, for a discussion.)

## CURRENT STATUS AND PRACTICES OF PSYCHOLOGICAL ASSESSMENT IN SCHOOLS

The primary use of psychological assessment in U.S. schools is for the diagnosis and classification of educational disabilities. Surveys of school psychologists (e.g., Lewis, Truscott, & Volker, 2008) show that most school psychologists are trained in assessment of intelligence, achievement, and social-emotional disorders, and their use of these assessments comprise the largest single activity they perform. Consequently, most school-based psychological assessment is initiated at the request of an adult, usually a teacher, for the purpose of deciding whether the student is eligible for special services.

However, psychological assessment practices range widely according to the competencies and purposes of the psychologist. Most of the assessment technologies that school psychologists use fall within these six categories:

1. Interviews and records reviews
2. Observational systems
3. Checklists and self-report techniques
4. Projective techniques
5. Standardized tests
6. RTI approaches

Methods to measure academic achievement are addressed in a separate section of this chapter.

### Interviews and Records Reviews

Most assessments begin with interviews and records reviews. Assessors use interviews to: define the problem or concerns of primary interest; learn about their history (when the problems first surfaced, when and under what conditions problems are likely to occur); determine whether there is agreement across individuals, settings, and time with respect to problem occurrence; and discover what individuals have done in response to the problem. Interviews serve two purposes: They are useful for generating hypotheses and for testing hypotheses. Unstructured or semistructured procedures are most useful for hypothesis generation and problem identification; structured protocols are most useful for refining and testing hypotheses.

Structured interview protocols used in school settings are usually driven by instructional theory or by behavioral theory. For example, interview protocols in an instructional consultation model elicit information about the instructional practices the teacher uses in the classroom (Benn, Jones, & Rosenfield, 2008). This information can be useful in identifying more and less effective practices and in developing hypotheses that the assessor can evaluate through further assessment. Behavioral theories also guide structured interviews. The practice of functional assessment of behavior (see Gresham, Watson, & Skinner, 2001) first identifies one or more target behaviors. These target behaviors are typically defined in specific, objective terms and are by their frequency, duration, and intensity. The interview protocol then elicits information about environmental factors that occur before, during, and after the target behavior. This approach is known as the ABCs of behavior assessment, in that assessors seek to define the antecedents (A), consequences (C), and concurrent factors (B) that control the frequency, duration, or intensity of the target behavior. Assessors then use their knowledge of the environment–behavior links to develop interventions to reduce problem behaviors and increase appropriate behaviors.

Examples of functional assessment procedures include systems developed by Munk and Repp (1994) and by Kratochwill and Stoiber (2002). However, functional assessment of behavior is different from functional analysis of behavior. Whereas a functional assessment generally relies on interview and observational data to identify links between the environment and the behavior, a functional analysis requires that the assessor actually manipulate suspected links (e.g., antecedents or consequences) to test the environment–behavior link. Functional analysis procedures are described in greater detail in RTI assessment approaches later in this chapter.

Assessors also review permanent products in a student's record to understand his or her medical, educational, and social history. Among the information most often sought in a review of records is the student's school attendance history, prior academic achievement, the perspectives of previous teachers, and whether and how problems were defined in the past. Although most records reviews are informal, formal procedures exist for reviewing educational records (e.g., Walker, Block-Pedego, Todis, & Severson, 1991). Some of the key questions addressed in a records review include whether the student has had adequate opportunity to learn (e.g., are current academic problems due to lack of or poor instruction?), and whether problems are unique to the current setting or year. Also, salient social (e.g., custody problems, foster care) and medical conditions (e.g., otitis media, attention deficit disorder) may be identified in student records. However, assessors should avoid focusing on less salient aspects of records when defining problems (e.g., birth weight, developmental milestones), as such a focus may undermine effective problem solving in the school context (Gresham, 1994). Analysis of students' permanent products (rather than records about the student generated by others) is discussed in the section on curriculum-based assessment methodologies.

Together, interviews and records reviews help define the problem and provide a historical context for the problem. Assessors use interviews and records reviews early in the assessment process, because these procedures focus and inform the assessment process. However, assessors may return to interview and records reviews throughout the assessment process to refine and test their definition and hypotheses about the student's problem. Also, psychologists may meld assessment and intervention activities into interviews, such as in behavioral consultation procedures (Bergan & Kratochwill, 1990) in which consultants use interviews to define problems, analyze problem causes, select interventions, and evaluate intervention outcomes.

## Observational Systems

Most assessors will use one or more observational approaches as the next step in a psychological assessment. Although assessors may use observations for purposes other than individual assessment (e.g., classroom behavioral screening, evaluating a teacher's adherence to an intervention protocol), the most common use of an observation is as part of a diagnostic assessment. (See Shapiro & Kratochwill, 2000.) Assessors use observations to refine their definition of the problem, generate and test hypotheses about why the problem exists, develop interventions within the classroom, and evaluate the effects of an intervention.

Observation is recommended early in any diagnostic assessment process, and many states in the United States require classroom observation as part of a diagnostic assessment. Most assessors conduct informal observations early in a diagnostic assessment because they want to evaluate the student's behavior in the context where the behavior occurs. This allows the assessor to corroborate different views of the problem, compare the student's behavior to peers (i.e., determine what is typical for that classroom), and detect features of the environment that might contribute to the referral problem.

Observation systems can be informal or formal. The informal approaches are, by definition, idiosyncratic and vary among assessors. Most informal approaches rely on narrative recording, in which the assessor records the flow of events and then uses the recording to help refine the problem definition and develop hypotheses about why the problem occurs. These narrative qualitative records provide rich data for understanding a problem but are rarely sufficient for problem definition, analysis, and solution.

As is true for interview procedures, formal observation systems are typically driven by behavioral or instructional theories. Behavioral observation systems use applied behavioral analysis techniques for recording target behaviors. These techniques include sampling by events or intervals and attempt to capture the frequency, duration, and intensity of the target behaviors. One system that incorporates multiple observation strategies is the Ecological Behavioral Assessment System for Schools (Greenwood, Carta, & Dawson, 2000); another is !Observe (Martin, 1999). Both use laptop or handheld computer technologies to record, summarize, and report observations and allow observers to record multiple facets of multiple behaviors simultaneously. Other methods may also be used to supplement data collection and interpretation (Nock & Kurtz, 2005).

Formal observational systems help assessors by virtue of their precision, the ability to monitor change over time and circumstances, and their structured focus on factors relevant to the problem at hand. Formal observation systems often report fair to good interrater reliability but often fail to report stability over time. Stability is an important issue in classroom observations, as observer ratings are generally unstable if based on three or fewer observations. (See Plewis, 1988.) Poor stability of ratings suggests that teacher behaviors are not consistent. Behavioral observation systems overcome this limitation via frequent use (e.g., observations are conducted over multiple sessions); observations based on a single session are susceptible to instability but may attempt to overcome this limitation via interviews of the teacher and student. Together, informal and formal observation systems are complementary processes in identifying problems, developing hypotheses, suggesting interventions, and monitoring student responses to classroom changes (Nock & Kurtz, 2005).

## Checklists and Self-Report Techniques

School-based psychological assessment also solicits information directly from informants in the assessment process. In addition to interviews, assessors use checklists to solicit teacher and parent perspectives on student problems. Assessors may also solicit self-reports of behavior from students to help identify, understand, and monitor the problem.

Schools use many of the checklists popular in other settings with children and young adults. Checklists to measures a broad range of psychological problems include the Child Behavior Checklist (CBCL) (Achenbach, 1991a, 1991b), Devereux Rating Scales (Naglieri, LeBuffe, & Pfeiffer, 1993a, 1993b), and the Behavior Assessment System for Children Second Edition (BASC-2) (Kamphaus & Reynolds, 2007). However, school-based assessments also use checklists oriented more specifically to schools, such as the SCALES (for hyperactivity) (Ryser & McConnell, 2002), and the Social Skills Improvement System—Rating System (SSRS) (Gresham & Elliott, 2008).

The majority of checklists focus on quantifying the degree to which the child's behavior is typical or atypical with respect to age or grade-level peers. These judgments can be particularly useful for diagnostic purposes, in which the assessor seeks to establish clinically unusual behaviors. In addition to identifying atypical social-emotional behaviors such as internalizing or externalizing problems, assessors use checklists such as the Scales of Independent Behavior (Bruininks, Woodcock, Weatherman, & Hill, 1996) to rate adaptive and maladaptive behavior. Also, some instruments (e.g., the Adaptive Behavior Assessment System, Second Edition, Harrison & Oakland, 2003) combine semistructured parent or caregiver interviews with teacher checklists to rate adaptive behavior. Checklists are most useful for quantifying the degree to which a student's behavior is atypical, which in turn is useful for differential diagnosis of handicapping conditions.

For example, diagnosis of severe emotional disturbance implies elevated maladaptive or clinically atypical behavior levels, whereas diagnosis of mental retardation requires depressed adaptive behavior scores.

The Academic Competence Evaluation Scale (ACES; DiPerna & Elliott, 2000) and the Devereux Student Strengths Assessment (DESSA; LeBuffe, Shapiro, & Naglieri, 2009) are exceptions to the rule that checklists quantify abnormality. Teachers use the ACES to rate students' academic competencies and strengths, which is more directly relevant to academic achievement and classroom performance than measures of social-emotional or clinically unusual behaviors. The ACES includes a self-report form to corroborate teacher and student ratings of academic competencies. Assessors can use the results of the teacher and student forms of the ACES with the Academic Intervention Monitoring System (AIMS; S. N. Elliott, DiPerna, & Shapiro, 2001) to develop interventions to improve students' academic competence. The DESSA lends itself to measuring resilience and other assets for social-emotional interventions and supports.

Self-report techniques invite students to provide open- or close-ended response to items or probes. Many checklists (e.g., the CBCL, BASC-2, ACES, SSRS) include a self-report form that invites students to evaluate the frequency or intensity of their own behaviors. These self-report forms can be useful for corroborating the reports of adults and for assessing the degree to which students share perceptions of teachers and parents regarding their own behaviors. Triangulating perceptions across raters and settings is important because the same behaviors are not rated identically across raters and settings. In fact, the agreement among raters, and across settings, can vary substantially (Achenbach, McConaughy, & Howell, 1987). That is, most checklist judgments within a rater for a specific setting are quite consistent, suggesting high reliability. However, agreement between raters within the same setting, or agreement within the same rater across setting, is much lower, suggesting that many behaviors are situation specific and that there are strong rater effects for scaling (i.e., some raters are more likely to view behaviors as atypical than other raters).

Other self-report forms exist as independent instruments to help assessors identify clinically unusual feelings or behaviors. Self-report instruments that seek to measure a broad range of psychological issues include the Feelings, Attitudes and Behaviors Scale for Children (Beitchman, 1996) and the Adolescent Psychopathology Scale (W. M. Reynolds, 1998). Most personality inventories address adolescent populations, because younger children may not be able to accurately or consistently complete personality inventories due to linguistic or developmental demands. Other checklists solicit information about more specific problems, such as social support (Malecki & Elliott, 1999), anxiety (March, 1997), depression (W. M. Reynolds, 2008), internalizing disorders (Merrell & Walters, 1998), and self-concept (Piers, Herzberg, & Harris, 2002).

One form of a checklist or rating system that is unique to schools is the peer nomination instrument. Peer nomination methods invite students to respond to items such as "Who in your classroom is most likely to fight with others?" or "Who would you most like to work with?" to identify maladaptive and prosocial behaviors. Peer nomination instruments (e.g., the Oregon Youth Study Peer Nomination Questionnaire, Capaldi & Patterson, 1989) are generally reliable and stable over time (Coie, Dodge, & Coppotelli, 1982). Peer nomination instruments allow school-based psychological assessment to capitalize on the availability of peers as indicators of adjustment rather than relying exclusively on adult judgments or self-report ratings.

The use of self-report and checklist instruments in schools is generally similar to their use in nonschool settings. That is, psychologists use self-report and checklist instruments to quantify and corroborate clinical abnormality. However, some instruments lend themselves to large-scale screening programs for prevention and early intervention purposes (e.g., the Reynolds Adolescent Depression Scale) and thus allow psychologists in school settings the opportunity to intervene prior to onset of serious symptoms. Unfortunately, this is a capability that is not often realized in practice.

### Projective Techniques

Psychologists in schools use instruments that elicit latent emotional attributes in response to unstructured stimuli or commands to evaluate social-emotional adjustment and abnormality. The use of projective instruments is most relevant for diagnosis of emotional disturbance, in which the psychologist seeks to evaluate whether the student's atypical behavior extends to atypical thoughts or emotional responses.

Most school-based assessors favor projective techniques requiring lower levels of inference. For example, the Rorschach tests are used less often than drawing tests. Draw-A-Person or human figure drawings are especially popular in schools because they solicit responses that are common (e.g., children are often asked to draw),

require little language mediation or other culturally specific knowledge, can be group administered for screening purposes, and the same drawing can be used to estimate mental abilities and emotional adjustment. Although human figure drawings have been popular for many years, their utility is questionable, due in part to questionable psychometric characteristics (Motta, Little, & Tobin, 1993). However, more recent scoring systems have reasonable reliability and demonstrated validity for evaluating mental abilities (e.g., Naglieri, 1988; C. R. Reynolds & Hickman, 2004) and emotional disturbance (Naglieri, McNeish, & Bardos, 1991). The use of projective drawing tests is controversial, with some arguing that psychologists are prone toward unwarranted interpretations (Smith & Dumont, 1995) and others arguing that the instruments inherently lack sufficient reliability and validity for clinical use (Motta et al., 1993). However, others offer data supporting the validity of drawings when scored with structured rating systems (e.g., Naglieri & Pfeiffer, 1992), suggesting that the problem may lie more in unstructured or unsound interpretation practices than in drawing tests per se. Other projective assessments used in schools include the Rotter Incomplete Sentences Test (Rotter, Lah, & Rafferty, 1992), which induces a projective assessment of emotion via incomplete sentences (e.g., "I am most afraid of _____"). General projective tests, such as the Thematic Apperception Test (TAT; Murray & Bellak, 1973), can be scored for attributes such as achievement motivation (e.g., Novi & Meinster, 2000). There are also apperception tests that use educational settings (e.g., the Education Apperception Test; Thompson & Sones, 1973) or were specifically developed for children (e.g., the Children's Apperception Test; Bellak & Bellak, 1992). Despite these modifications, apperception tests are not widely used in school settings. Furthermore, psychological assessment in schools has tended to reduce projective techniques, favoring instead more objective approaches to measuring behavior, emotion, and psychopathology.

### Standardized Tests

Psychologists use standardized tests primarily to assess cognitive abilities and academic achievement. Academic achievement is considered in its own section later in this chapter. Also, standardized assessments of personality and psychopathology using self-report and observational ratings were described in a previous section. Consequently, this section describes standardized tests of cognitive ability.

Standardized tests of cognitive ability may be administered to groups of students or to individual students by an examiner. Group-administered tests of cognitive abilities were popular for much of the previous century as a means for matching students to academic curricula. Indeed, Binet and Simon (1914) developed the first practical test of intelligence to help Parisian schools match students to academic or vocational programs, or "tracks." However, the practice of assigning students to academic programs or tracks based on intelligence tests is no longer legally defensible (Reschly et al., 1988). Consequently, the use of group-administered intelligence tests has declined in schools. However, some schools continue the practice to help screen for giftedness and cognitive delays that might affect schooling. Instruments that are useful in group-administered contexts include the Otis-Lennon School Ability Test (Pearson, 2003), the Naglieri Nonverbal Ability Test (Naglieri, 1993), the Raven Matrices Tests (Raven, 1992a, 1992b), and the Draw-A-Person (Naglieri, 1988; C. R. Reynolds & Hickman, 2004). Note that, with the exception of the Otis-Lennon School Ability Test, most of these screening tests use culture-reduced items. The reduced emphasis on culturally specific items makes them more appropriate for younger and ethnically and linguistically diverse students. Although culture-reduced, group-administered intelligence tests have been criticized for their inability to predict school performance, there are studies that demonstrate strong relationships between these tests and academic performance (e.g., Naglieri & Ronning, 2000).

The vast majority of cognitive ability assessments in schools use individually administered intelligence test batteries. The most popular batteries include the Weschler Intelligence Scale for Children—Fourth Edition (WISC-IV; Wechsler, 2004), the Stanford Binet Intelligence Test—Fifth Edition (SB5; Roid, 2003), the Woodcock-Johnson Cognitive Battery—Third Edition (WJ III COG; Woodcock, McGrew, & Mather, 2000b), and the Cognitive Assessment System (CAS; Naglieri & Das, 1997). Psychologists may also use Wechsler Scales for preschool (Wechsler, 2003) and young adult (Wechsler, 2008) assessments and may use other, less popular, assessment batteries, such as the Differential Ability Scales Second Edition (DAS-2; C. D. Elliott, 2007) or the Kaufman Assessment Battery for Children Second Edition (KABC-II; Kaufman & Kaufman, 2004a) on occasion.

Two approaches to assessing cognitive abilities other than broad intellectual assessment batteries are popular in schools: nonverbal tests and computer-administered tests. Nonverbal tests of intelligence seek to reduce prior learning and, in particular, linguistic and cultural differences by using language- and culture-reduced test items. (See Braden & Athanasiou, 2005.) Many nonverbal tests of intelligence also allow for nonverbal responses and may be administered via gestures or other nonverbal or language-reduced means. Nonverbal tests include the Universal Nonverbal Intelligence Test (UNIT; Bracken & McCallum, 1998), the Comprehensive Test of Nonverbal Intelligence (CTONI; Hammill, Pearson, & Wiederholt, 1997), and the Leiter International Performance Scale—Revised (LIPS-R; Roid & Miller, 1997). The technical properties of these tests is usually good to excellent, although they typically provide less data to support their validity and interpretation than do more comprehensive intelligence test batteries (Athanasiou, 2000).

Computer-administered tests promise a cost- and time-efficient alternative to individually administered tests. Three examples are the General Ability Measure for Adults (Naglieri & Bardos, 1997), the Multidimensional Aptitude Battery (Jackson, 1984), and the Computer Optimized Multimedia Intelligence Test (TechMicro, 2000). In addition to reducing examiner time, computer-administered testing can improve assessment accuracy by using adaptive testing algorithms that adjust the items administered to most efficiently target the examinee's ability level. However, computer-administered tests are typically normed only on young adult and adult populations, and many examiners are not yet comfortable with computer technologies for deriving clinical information. Therefore, these tests are not yet widely used in school settings but are likely to become more popular in the future.

Intelligence test batteries use a variety of item types, organized into tests or subtests, to estimate general intellectual ability. Batteries produce a single composite based on a large number of tests to estimate general intellectual ability and typically combine individual subtest scores to produce composite or factor scores to estimate more specific intellectual abilities. Most batteries recommend a "successive" approach to interpreting the myriad of scores the battery produces. (See Sattler, 2001.) The successive approach reports the broadest estimate of general intellectual ability first and then proceeds to report narrower estimates (e.g., factor or composite scores based on groups of subtests), followed by even narrower estimates (e.g., individual subtest scores). Assessors often interpret narrower scores as indicators of specific, rather than general, mental abilities. For each of the intellectual assessment batteries listed, Table 12.1 describes the estimates of general intellectual ability, the number of more

**TABLE 12.1    Intelligence Test Battery Scores, Subtests, and Availability of Conormed Achievement Tests**

| Instrument | General Ability | Cognitive Factors | Tests or Subtests | Conormed Achievement Tests |
|---|---|---|---|---|
| CAS | 1 (Full Scale Score) | 4 cognitive | 12 | Yes (22 tests on the Woodcock-Johnson-Revised Achievement Battery) |
| DAS-2 | 1 (General Conceptual Ability) | 7 cognitive | 22 | Yes (School Readiness for young children) |
| KABC-II | 2 (Mental Processing Index or Fluid Cognitive Index, depending on model) | 4 or 5 cognitive (depending on model) | 20 | Yes (K-TEA2) |
| SB5 | 1 (Composite Score) | 5 cognitive | 15 | No |
| WISC-IV | 1 (Full Scale IQ) | 4 cognitive factor scores | 14 | Yes (15 tests on the Wechsler Individual Achievement Test—Third Edition) |
| WJ III COG | 3 (Brief, Standard, & Extended General Intellectual Ability) | 7 cognitive, 5 clinical | 20 | Yes (22 tests on the Achievement Battery) |

specific score composites, the number of individual subtests, and whether the battery has a conormed achievement test.

The practice of drawing inferences about a student's cognitive abilities from constellations of test scores is usually known as profile analysis (Sattler, 2001), although it is more precisely called ipsative analysis (Kamphaus, Reynolds, & Vogel, 2009). The basic premise of profile interpretation is that individual subtest scores vary, and the patterns of variation suggest relative strengths and weaknesses within the student's overall level of general cognitive ability. Test batteries support ipsative analysis of test scores by providing tables that allow examiners to determine whether differences among scores are reliable (i.e., unlikely given that the scores are actually equal in value) or unusual (i.e., rarely occur in the normative sample). Many examiners infer unusual deficits or strengths in a student's cognitive abilities based on reliable or unusual differences among cognitive test scores, despite evidence that this practice is not well supported by statistical or logical analyses (Watkins, Glutting, & Youngstrom, 2005; but see Naglieri, 2000).

Although examiners use intelligence test scores primarily for diagnosing disabilities in students, it is not clear that psychoeducational assessment practices and technologies are accurate for making differential diagnoses (MacMillan, Gresham, Bocian, & Siperstein, 1997). Decision-making teams reach decisions about special education eligibility that are only loosely related to differential diagnostic taxonomies (Gresham, MacMillan, & Bocian, 1998), particularly for diagnosing mental retardation, behavior disorders, and learning disabilities (Bocian,

Beebe, MacMillan, & Gresham, 1999; Gresham, MacMillan, & Bocian, 1996; MacMillan, Gresham, & Bocian, 1998). Although many critics of traditional psychoeducational assessment believe intellectual assessment batteries cannot differentially diagnose learning disabilities primarily because defining learning disabilities in terms of score discrepancies is an inherently flawed practice, others argue that better intellectual ability batteries are more effective in differential diagnosis of learning disabilities (Naglieri, 2000, 2001).

Differential diagnosis of noncognitive disabilities, such as emotional disturbance, behavior disorders, and attention deficit disorder, is also problematic (Kershaw & Sonuga-Barke, 1998). That is, diagnostic conditions may not be as distinct as educational and clinical classification systems imply. Also, intellectual ability scores may not be useful for distinguishing among some diagnoses. Therefore, the practice of differential diagnosis, particularly with respect to the use of intellectual ability batteries for differential diagnosis of learning disabilities, is a controversial—yet ubiquitous—practice.

**Response-to-Intervention Approaches**

An alternative to differential diagnosis in schools emphasizes students' responses to interventions as a means of diagnosing educational disabilities. (See Batsche et al., 2005; Gresham, 2001.) The logic of the approach is based on the assumption that the best way to differentiate students with disabilities from students who have not yet learned or mastered academic skills is to intervene with the students and evaluate their response to the intervention. Students without disabilities are likely to respond well to the intervention (i.e., show rapid progress), whereas students with disabilities are unlikely to respond well (i.e., show slower or no progress). Studies of students with diagnosed disabilities suggest that they indeed differ from nondisabled peers in their initial levels of achievement (low) and their rate of response (slow; Speece & Case, 2001).

The primary benefit of an RTI approach is shifting the assessment focus from diagnosing and determining eligibility for special services to improving the student's academic skills (Batsche et al., 2005). This benefit is articulated within the problem-solving approach to psychological assessment and intervention in schools (Tilley, 2008). In the problem-solving approach, a problem is the gap between current levels of performance and desired levels of performance (Shinn, 2008). The definitions of current and desired performance emphasize precise, dynamic measures of student performance such as rates of behavior. The assessment is aligned with efforts to intervene and evaluating the student's response to those efforts. Additionally, an RTI approach can identify ways in which the general education setting can be modified to accommodate the needs of a student, as it focuses efforts on closing the gap between current and desired behavior using pragmatic, available means.

The problems with the RTI are logical and practical. Logically, it is not possible to diagnose based on response to a treatment unless it can be shown that only people with a particular diagnosis fail to respond. In fact, individuals with and without disabilities respond to many educational interventions (Swanson & Hoskyn, 1998), so the premise that only students with disabilities will fail to respond is unsound. Practically, RTI judgments require accurate and continuous measures of student performance, the ability to select and implement sound interventions, and the ability to ensure that interventions are implemented with reasonable fidelity or integrity. Of these requirements, the assessor controls only the accurate and continuous assessment of performance. Selection and implementation of interventions is often beyond the assessor's control, as nearly all educational interventions are mediated and delivered by other adults (e.g., teachers, assistants, parents). Protocols for assessing treatment integrity exist (Roach & Elliott, 2008), although treatment integrity protocols are rarely implemented when evaluating educational interventions (Gresham, MacMillan, Beebe, & Bocian, 2000).

Although there are significant gaps regarding both the internal logic and the evidence base needed to support RTI (Braden & Shernoff, 2008), the shift in U.S. federal legislation from a diagnosis/eligibility model of special education services to an RTI model has encouraged the development and practice of RTI assessment approaches, to the point where some states mandate RTI methods as a necessary but not sufficient condition for diagnosing mild educational disabilities. Therefore, it is no longer a question of whether psychologists in schools should move toward implementation of RTI but how they will do so.

## Summary

The current practices in psychological assessment are, in many cases, similar to practices used in nonschool settings. Assessors use instruments for measuring intelligence, psychopathology, and personality that are shared by colleagues in other settings, and do so for similar purposes. Much of contemporary assessment is driven by the need to differentially diagnose disabilities so that students can qualify for special education. However, psychological assessment in schools is more likely to use screening instruments, observations, peer-nomination methodologies, and RTI approaches than psychological assessment in other settings. As the mechanisms that allocate special services shift from differential diagnosis to intervention-based decisions, psychological assessment in schools is also shifting away from traditional clinical approaches toward ecological, intervention-based models for assessment (Reschly, 2008).

## ASSESSMENT OF ACADEMIC ACHIEVEMENT

Until recently, the assessment of academic achievement would not merit a separate section in a chapter on psychological assessment in schools. In the past, teachers and educational administrators were primarily responsible for assessing student learning, except for differentially diagnosing a disability. However, recent changes in methods for assessing achievement, and changes in the decisions made from achievement measures, have pushed assessment of academic achievement to center stage in many schools. This section describes the traditional methods for assessing achievement (i.e., individually administered tests used primarily for diagnosis) and new methods for assessing achievement. The section concludes with a review of the standards and testing movement that has increased the importance of academic achievement assessment in schools. Specifically, the topics in this section include individually administered achievement tests, curriculum-based assessment and measurement, and large-scale tests and standards-based educational reform.

## Individually Administered Tests

Much like individually administered intellectual assessment batteries, individually administered achievement batteries provide a collection of tests to broadly sample various academic achievement domains. Among the most popular achievement batteries are the Woodcock-Johnson Achievement Battery—Third Edition (WJ III ACH; Woodcock, McGrew, & Mather, 2000a), the Wechsler Individual Achievement Test—Third Edition (WIAT-III; Pearson, 2009), and the Kaufman Test of Educational Achievement—Second Edition (KTEA-II; Kaufman & Kaufman, 2004b).

The primary purpose of individually administered academic achievement batteries is to quantify student achievement in ways that support diagnosis of educational disabilities. Therefore, these batteries produce standard scores (and other norm-reference scores, such as percentiles and stanines) that allow examiners to describe how well the student scores relative to a norm group. Often examiners use scores from achievement batteries to verify that the student is experiencing academic delays or to compare achievement scores to intellectual ability scores for the purpose of diagnosing learning disabilities. Because U.S. federal law identifies seven areas in which students may experience academic difficulties due to a learning disability, most achievement test batteries include tests to assess those seven areas. Table 12.2 lists the tests within each academic achievement battery that assesses the seven academic areas identified for learning disability diagnosis.

Interpretation of scores from achievement batteries is less hierarchical or successive than for intellectual assessment batteries. That is, individual test scores are often used to represent an achievement domain. Some achievement test batteries combine two or more test scores to produce a composite. For example, the WJ III ACH combines scores from Passage Comprehension and Reading Vocabulary tests to produce a Reading Comprehension cluster score. However, many achievement batteries use a single test to assess a given academic domain, and scores are rarely combined across academic domains to produce more general estimates of achievement.

Occasionally examiners will use specific instruments to assess academic domains in greater detail. Examples of more specialized instruments includes the Test of Irregular Word Reading Efficiency (TIWRE; Reynolds & Kamphaus, 2007), Test of Early Mathematics Ability—Third Edition (Ginsberg & Baroody, 2003), and Test of Adolescent and Adult Language, Fourth Edition (Hammill, Brown, Larsen, & Wiederholt, 2007). Examiners are likely to use these tests to supplement an achievement test battery or to get additional information that could be useful in refining and understanding of the problem or developing an academic intervention. Specialized tests can help examiners go beyond a general statement (e.g., math skills are low) to more precise problem statements (e.g., the student has not yet mastered regrouping procedures for

**TABLE 12.2   Alignment of Achievement Test Batteries to the Seven Areas of Academic Deficit Identified in Federal Legislation**

| Academic Area | KTEA-II | WIAT-III | WJ III ACH |
| --- | --- | --- | --- |
| Listening Comprehension | Listening Comprehension | Listening Comprehension | Understanding Directions, Oral Comprehension |
| Oral Expression | Oral Expression | Oral Expression | Story Recall, Picture Vocabulary |
| Reading Skills | Phonological Awareness, Nonsense Word Decoding, Letter and Word Recognition | Early Reading Skills, Word Reading, Pseudoword Decoding, Oral Reading Fluency | Letter-Word Identification, Word Attack, Reading Fluency |
| Reading Comprehension | Reading Comprehension | Reading Comprehension | Passage Comprehension, Reading Vocabulary |
| Math Skills | Mathematics Computation | Numerical Operations, Math Fluency—Addition, Math Fluency—Subtraction, Math Fluency—Multiplication | Calculation, Math Fluency |
| Math Applications | Mathematics Concepts and Applications | Math Problem Solving | Applied Problems, Quantitative Concepts |
| Written Expression | Written Expression, Spelling* | Sentence Composition, Essay Composition, Alphabet Writing Fluency,* Spelling* | Writing Samples |

*A related but indirect measure of the academic area.

multidigit arithmetic problems). Some achievement test batteries (e.g., the WIAT-III) also supply error analysis protocols to help examiners isolate and evaluate particular skills within a domain.

One domain not listed among the seven academic areas in federal law that is of increasing interest to educators and assessors is the domain of phonemic awareness. Phonemic awareness comprises the areas of grapheme-phoneme relationships (e.g., letter–sound links), phoneme manipulation, and other skills needed to analyze and synthesize print to language. Reading research increasingly identifies phonemic awareness as a major factor in reading failure and recommends early assessment and intervention to enhance phonemic awareness skills (National Reading Panel, 2000). Consequently, assessors serving younger elementary students may seek and use instruments to assess phonemic awareness. Although most measures of phonemic awareness were not standardized and were experimental in nature (Yopp, 1988), recent emphasis on reading assessment and intervention has led to a variety of well-standardized phonemic awareness instruments, which are included in many achievement test batteries.

## Curriculum-Based Assessment and Measurement

Although standardized achievement tests are useful for quantifying the degree to which a student deviates from normative achievement expectations, such tests have been criticized. Among the most persistent criticisms are these six:

1. Lack of alignment with important learning outcomes
2. Inability to provide formative evaluation
3. Inability to describe student performance in ways that are understandable and linked to instructional practices
4. Lack of responsiveness to the varying instructional models that teachers use
5. Inability to administer, score, and interpret in classrooms
6. Inability to communicate to teachers and students what is important to learn (Shinn, 2008)

Curriculum-based assessment (CBA) (see Idol, Nevin, & Paolucci-Whitcomb, 1996) and curriculum-based measurement (CBM) (see Shinn, 2008) approaches seek to respond to these criticisms. Most CBA and CBM approaches use materials selected from the student's classroom to measure student achievement and therefore overcome issues of alignment (i.e., unlike standardized batteries, the content of CBA/CBM is directly drawn from

the specific curricula used in the school), links to instructional practice, and sensitivity and flexibility to reflect what teachers are doing. Also, most CBM approaches recommend brief (1–3 minute) assessments two or more times per week in the student's classroom, which allows CBM to overcome issues of contextual value (i.e., measures are taken and used in the classroom setting) and allows for formative evaluation (i.e., decisions about what is and is not working). Therefore, CBA and CBM approaches to assessment provide technologies that are embedded in the learning context by using classroom materials and observing behavior in classrooms.

The primary distinction between CBA and CBM is the intent of the assessment. Generally, CBA intends to provide information for instructional planning (e.g., deciding what curricular level best meets a student's needs). In contrast, CBM intends to monitor the student's progress in response to instruction. Progress monitoring is used to gauge the outcome of instructional interventions (i.e., deciding whether the student's academic skills are improving). Thus, CBA methods provide teaching or planning information, whereas CBM methods provide testing or outcome information. The metrics and procedures for CBA and CBM are similar but differ as a function of the intent of the assessment.

The primary assumption driving CBA is instructional matching. Therefore, the assessor varies the difficulty of the probes, so that the assessor can identify the ideal balance between instruction that is too difficult and instruction that is too easy for the student. CBA identifies three levels of instructional match:

1. *Frustration level*. Task demands are too difficult; the student will not sustain task engagement and will generally not learn because there is insufficient understanding to acquire and retain skills.
2. *Instructional level*. Task demands balance task difficulty, so that new information and skills are presented and required, with familiar content or mastered skills, thus encouraging students to sustain their engagement in the task. Instructional level provides the best trade-off between new learning and familiar material.
3. *Independent/Mastery level*. Task demands are sufficiently easy or familiar to allow the student to complete the tasks with no significant difficulty. Although mastery-level materials support student engagement, they do not provide much new or unfamiliar task demands and therefore result in little learning.

Instructional match varies as a function of the difficulty of the task and the support given to the student. That is, students can tolerate more difficult tasks when they have direct support from a teacher or other instructor, but students require lower levels of task difficulty in the absence of direct instructional support.

CBA uses direct assessment using behavioral principles to identify when instructional demands are at frustration, instruction, or mastery levels. The behavioral principles that guide CBA and CBM include: (a) defining behaviors in their smallest meaningful unit of behavior (e.g., a word read aloud in context); (b) objectivity and precision of assessment (e.g., counting the frequency of a specific behavior); and (c) repeated measurement over time.

CBA protocols define instructional match between the student and the material in terms of these objective measures of performance. For example, a passage in which a student recognizes less than 93% of the words is deemed to be at frustration level. Likewise, a third-grade student reading aloud at a rate of 82 words per minute, with 3 errors per minute, is deemed to be reading a passage that is at instructional level; a passage that the student could read aloud at a rate of more than 100 words/min. with 5 errors would be deemed to be at the student's mastery level. Table 12.3 provides examples of how assessors can use CBA and CBM metrics to determine the instructional match for task demands in reading and mathematics.

Whereas assessors vary the type and difficulty of task demands in a CBA approach to identify how best to match instruction to a student, CBM approaches require assessors to hold task type and difficulty constant and interpret changes in the metrics as evidence of improving student skill. Thus, assessors might develop a set of 20 reading passages or 20 probes of mixed mathematics problem types of similar difficulty levels and then randomly

and repeatedly administer these probes to a student over time to evaluate academic progress. In most instances, the assessor would chart the results of these 1- or 2-minute samples of behavior to create a time series. Increasing rates of desired behavior (e.g., words read aloud per minute) and stable or decreasing rates of errors (e.g., incorrect words per minute) indicate an increase in a student's skills.

Figures 12.1 and 12.2 present oral reading fluency rates for a student. Figure 12.1 plots the results of eight 1-minute reading probes, indicating the number of words the student read correctly and the number read incorrectly in 1 minute. The assessor calculated the median words/minute correct for the eight data points and placed an X in the middle of the collected (baseline) data series. The assessor then identified an instructional goal—that is, that the student would read 100 words per minute correctly within 30 days. The line connecting the student's current median performance and the assessor's goal is an aim line, or the rate of improvement needed to ensure the student meets the goal. Figure 12.2 shows the intervention selected to achieve the goal (choral reading), and the chart reflecting the student's progress toward the goal. Given the tendency for the student's progress to fall below the aim line, the assessor concluded that this instructional intervention was not sufficient to meet the performance goal. Assuming that the assessor determined that the choral reading approach was conducted appropriately, these results would lead the assessor to select a more modest goal or a different intervention.

CBA and CBM approaches promise accurate instructional matching and continuous monitoring of progress to enhance instructional decision making. Also, school

**TABLE 12.3 Sample Values of Curriculum-Based Metrics for Instructional Matching in Reading and Mathematics**

| Academic Skill | Support Level | Frustration | Instruction | Mastery |
|---|---|---|---|---|
| Proportion of unique known words in a passage | Independent | 0–92% | 93–96% | 97–100% |
| | Supported | 0–69% | 70–85% | 86–100% |
| Oral reading rate Grades 1–2 | Independent | 0–39 words/min. *or* more than 4 errors/min. | 40–60 words/min. *and* 4 or less errors/min. | More than 60 words/min. *and* 4 or fewer errors/min. |
| Oral reading rate Grades 3–6 | Independent | 0–69 words/min. *or* more than 6 errors/min. | 70–100 words/min. *and* 6 or less errors/min. | More than 100 words/min. *and* 6 or less errors/min. |
| Proportion of mathematics problems correct | Supported | 0–74% | 75–90% | 91–100% |
| Correct digits/min. Grades 1–3 | Independent | 0–9 | 10–19 | 20 or more |
| Correct digits/min. Grades 4 & up | Independent | 0–19 | 20–39 | 40 or more |

*Sources*: Data in this table are based on Fuchs, Fuchs, and Deno (1982), Shapiro (1988), and Braden, Kovaleski, and Prasse (1996).

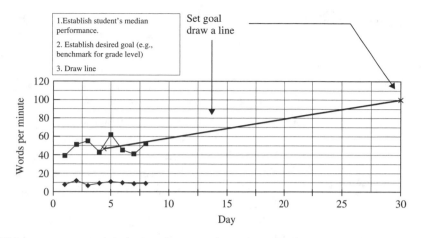

**Figure 12.1**   Using CBM to set current and desired performance for oral reading fluency

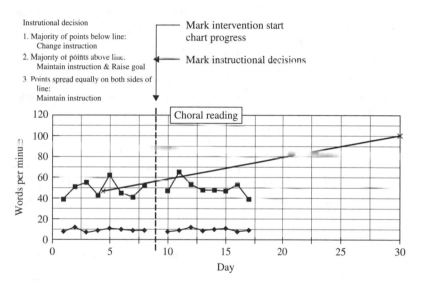

**Figure 12.2**   Using CBM to make instructional decisions using an aim line and progress monitoring

districts can develop CBM norms to provide scores similar to standardized tests (see Shinn, 2008) for screening and diagnostic purposes (although it is expensive to do so). Generally, research supports the value of these approaches. They are reliable and consistent within individuals (Hintze, Owen, Shapiro, & Daly, 2000), although there is some evidence of slight ethnic and gender bias (Kranzler, Miller, & Jordan, 1999). The validity of CBA/CBM measures is supported by correspondence to standardized achievement measures and other measures of student learning (e.g., Hintze, Shapiro, Conte, & Basile, 1997; Kranzler, Brownell, & Miller, 1998) and evidence that teachers value CBA methods more than standardized achievement tests (Eckert & Shapiro, 1999). Most important, CBA matching and CBM monitoring of mathematics performance yields more rapid increases in

academic achievement among mildly disabled students than among peers who were not provided with CBM monitoring (Allinder, Bolling, Oats, & Gagnon, 2000; Stecker & Fuchs, 2000).

However, CBA/CBM has some limitations. One such limitation is the limited evidence supporting the positive effects of CBA/CBM for reading achievement (Nolet & McLaughlin, 1997; Peverly & Kitzen, 1998). Others criticize CBA/CBM for failing to reflect constructivist, cognitively complex, and meaning-based learning outcomes and for having some of the same shortcomings as standardized tests (Mehrens & Clarizio, 1993). Still, CBA and CBM promise to align assessment with learning and intervention more directly than standardized tests of achievement and lend themselves to continuous progress monitoring in ways that traditional tests cannot match.

## Large-Scale Tests and Standards-Based Educational Reform

Educators have used large-scale assessments or group tests to measure academic achievement for decades. Historically, a school district would give a test at one or more elementary and middle school grades, report the scores to its school board and community, and use the results for self-evaluations (e.g., adequacy of curriculum). However, beginning in the late 1980s, the local, informal use of large-scale achievement tests gave way to standards-based education reform.

The logic of standards-based education reform is straightforward: Establish standards for what students should know and do, select assessments to evaluate the degree to which students meet these standards, and report results back to educational stakeholders (e.g., students, teachers, parents, administrators) with the expectation that educators would use assessment results to guide educational reforms. (See Ravitch, 1999; Thomas B. Fordham Foundation, 1998; cf. Ravitch, 2011). Standards-based reforms at the state and federal levels introduced two key changes from previous educational practices: (1) that standards would be high and (2) that test results have formal consequences for schools, states, and possibly individual students and teachers.

The impetus for these changes was reflected in federal funding of public education. Title I of the Elementary and Secondary Education Act (ESEA) requires states to adopt "challenging educational standards" and to institute assessment procedures to judge whether schools are demonstrating continuous progress in preparing elementary, junior high, and high school students to meet these standards. Because every state accepts Title I ESEA funding, all states have large-scale assessment programs in three or more grades (*Education Week*, 2001). The 2001 ESEA reauthorization expanded the testing requirement to include annual testing in reading and mathematics in grades 3 to 8 and increase accountability requirements for states (Bush, 2001).

Prior to the No Child Left Behind Act of 2001, most states met federal requirements to annually assess student achievement by purchasing one of the "Big Three" group achievement tests: the Iowa Tests of Basic Skills (ITBS; Hoover, Hieronymus, Frisbie, & Dunbar, 2003), the Stanford Achievement Tests—Tenth Edition (SAT-10; Harcourt Assessment, 2003), or the TerraNova—Third Edition (CTB/McGraw-Hill, 2009), However, the current trend is to customize tests to match specific state curricula. For example, California, Arizona, and Florida use a customized version of the SAT-10 for their annual testing programs. Some states (e.g., North Carolina) develop their own tests specifically tailored to their educational standards. All but a few states use group achievement tests composed primarily of selected response (i.e., multiple-choice) items as their primary accountability mechanism, although many states also include a constructed response essay in their assessments. A few states (e.g., Kentucky, Vermont) developed portfolio assessment systems, but those assessments were largely replaced by standardized, selected response tests for economic and psychometric reasons (*Education Week*, 2001).

In addition to increasing their use of large-scale achievement tests, states are also increasing the consequences associated with test results. Consequences have moved from low-stakes uses, such as simply reporting results to the public, to high-stakes uses, such as tracking, retention, promotion, and graduation (Braden & Tayrose, 2008). The increased importance of test scores for students has inspired professional psychology and education organizations to produce policies to guide the appropriate and effective uses of large-scale tests for high-stakes decisions (e.g., American Educational Research Association, 2000; American Educational Research Association, American Psychological Association, National Council on Measurement in Education, 1999; American Psychological Association, 2001). These policies encourage the use of multiple data sources (rather than a single test score), improving students' opportunities to learn, and adopting effective alternatives to grade retention for students not meeting standards.

The increased use of large-scale achievement tests to stimulate standards-based reforms and educational accountability is not without critics. Although there have been episodes of parent-supported boycotts of testing (Schrag, 2000), surveys of parents show generally strong support for tests as a tool for systemic accountability and even for making high-stakes decisions (Driesler, 2001). Within the educational community, critics (e.g., Labaree, 2000; Nave, Miech, & Mosteller, 2000) have argued against state standards, although most critics focus their criticism on large-scale achievement tests as a tool for educational reform (e.g., Kohn, 2000; Wiggins, 1989). Yet others argue that standards are antithetical to profound individual differences among students (Coffman, 1993), whereas others counter that individual differences can be reconciled with high achievement standards (Tomlinson, 2000). The specific value of standardized achievement tests as a tool for instructional reform is increasingly controversial, especially as those who initially supported standards and testing have concluded testing has done more harm than good (e.g., Ravitch, 2011).

## Summary

Assessment of academic achievement is often informal and conducted primarily by teachers in classrooms with little or no input from psychologists. However, individually administered academic achievement test batteries have a strong diagnostic focus, and are typically used only by assessment specialists. Curriculum-based assessment and measurement technologies are increasingly popular with professionals concerned with intervening in classroom settings to improve student performance. Finally, the use of large-scale assessment techniques and, in particular, group achievement test batteries is increasing among states as they seek to comply with federal legislation and spur standards-based educational reforms. Except for individually administered achievement test batteries, psychological assessors traditionally have delegated assessment of student achievement to nonspecialists. This may change, as educational systems will increasingly require knowledge of assessment principles, procedures, and practices to make appropriate high stakes decisions. Experts in psychological assessments within schools may help systems acquire the capacity for understanding and using assessment procedures wisely (Braden, 2007).

## FUTURE OF PSYCHOLOGICAL ASSESSMENT IN SCHOOLS

In addition to describing the current practice of psychological assessment in schools, I will prognosticate about the future of assessment. The future is a child of the present, and consequently, predictions will reflect trends already evident in contemporary practice. The four trends I discuss with respect to their impact on the future are

1. aligning assessment to scientific advances,
2. accountability and value-added assessment,
3. accommodating diverse learners in assessment, and
4. assessment utility.

### Aligning Assessment to Scientific Advances

The trend to align assessment with scientific advances means developing and using assessment instruments and procedures that reflect the field's knowledge of psychology. This trend is already evident in the assessment of intelligence. For example, newer intelligence test batteries (e.g., SB5, WJ III, WISC-IV) have all moved to align their structure and interpretation with hierarchical intelligence theories much more than their predecessors. All of these new intelligence test batteries embrace a hierarchical taxonomy of mental abilities, in which general intellectual ability is a superordinate construct, and under which various mental abilities are organized into increasingly narrow cognitive processes (e.g., Carroll, 2005). This model is increasingly promoted as a unifying framework for cognitive assessment (e.g., Flanagan, 2000; McGrew, Keith, Flanagan, & Vanderwood, 1997). However, at least one alternative model, based on Luria's neuropsychological framework, is embodied in two tests of intelligence: the CAS and the KABC-II. It is not yet clear whether Luria's framework is viable for assessing individual differences in cognitive abilities and, if so, whether the CAS successfully represents the framework with practical assessment technologies (Keith, Kranzler, & Flanagan, 2001; cf. Naglieri, 1999).

Aligning assessment to scientific advances in the affective domain will most likely mean pushing instruments and classification systems toward an empirical approach to defining psychopathology (e.g., Achenbach & McConaughy, 1996). That is, assessment instruments and procedures are likely to focus on broad dimensions of externalizing versus internalizing disorders and will be less likely to adopt diagnostic categories developed for adults and extended into childhood (e.g., American Psychiatric Association, 2000). Additionally, the trend away from projective measures in favor of observational and checklist approaches, which is already evident in school-based practices, is likely to continue so that projective measures will be increasingly marginalized in school-based assessment practice.

A way in which scientific advances will affect assessment comes from outside psychology: the domain of technology. Clearly, computer-assisted assessment is already making inroads into school-based assessment practices. This trend will continue, not only for supporting the scoring and interpretation of traditional assessment tools (e.g., the WJ III can be scored only with the assistance of a computer) but also in the administration of assessment instruments. To date, computer-based assessment of students has been slow to develop because of technological limitations and the relative inability of younger students to use computers. Those barriers will fall as computers become more available and easier to use (e.g., popular game consoles now allow users to interface with computers through body motions). Three aspects of computer-administered assessments are likely to develop: (1) computer-assisted technologies for selecting a set of items customized to the student's ability level (increasing assessment efficiency), (2) repeated assessments of student performance to provide progress monitoring and support instructional decision making (e.g., using the computer to administer and score oral reading rate from student speech), and (3) increased use of computers to assess domains that cannot be assessed with assessor-driven technologies (e.g., correct decision speed, Nettelbeck, 1998, or functional magnetic resonance imaging techniques to track neural activity).

### Accountability and Value-Added Assessments

The educational accountability movement has brought about two important changes in the focus and use of test results. The first is that, although students take standardized tests, the results are increasingly used to evaluate not the student but the educational institution to which the student belongs. The large-scale assessments mandated in No Child Left Behind are silent on the use of results to make decisions about schools but are explicit about the use of results to identify schools "in need of improvement." Similar trends are evident in western European countries; for example, the United Kingdom collects and reports data on a variety of student attainments and attributes to help the public identify successful and less successful schools (Office for Standards in Education, Children's Services, and Skills, n.d.). The shift from evaluating students for selection to evaluating students as a means of school accountability is still rare across the globe (e.g., the testing systems in India and China are still primarily focused on student selection, not school evaluation), but it is increasing, especially in western countries.

The second major trend in accountability assessment is an increased emphasis on value-added methods of analyzing data. Essentially, value-added approaches seek to identify how much students learn independent of factors outside of school control. Such factors include prior levels of achievement, ethnicity, and socioeconomic status, which are generally entered as covariates in a multivariate analysis to statistically control their influence on educational outcomes. By controlling for these variables, differences among schools should more accurately reflect the degree to which they enhance student learning (i.e., add value). Although the value-added approach is fraught with many significant challenges (e.g., Rubin, Stuart, & Zanutto, 2004), its intuitive appeal to statistically eliminate differences among schools due to student demographics is highly appealing. Indeed, value-added approaches to measuring schools are already under way in some states with approval from the U.S. Department of Education, and so it is likely that value-added methods will be included in the next reauthorization of ESEA. Finally, the application of value-added approaches to evaluating educational institutions is not limited to primary and secondary education. Institutions of higher education have also come under withering criticism, as value-added approaches to measuring growth in critical thinking show that a large minority (40%) of college students show no discernible growth even after years of full-time study (Arum & Roska, 2011).

### Accommodating Diverse Learners in Assessment

At the present time, procedures for accommodating diverse learners in assessments are largely a subjective process driven by examiner judgments. As scientific advances and educational standards more clearly define the constructs to be assessed, assessment instruments and processes will need to be more rigorous in adequately assessing constructs without capturing construct-irrelevant influences on test scores introduced by student diversity. Historically, test authors and publishers have addressed issues of ethnic and gender diversity directly but generally have avoided or only indirectly addressed issues of linguistic differences and disabilities in their assessment procedures. This will begin to change, in part because the proportion of students speaking languages other than English is rapidly increasing and in part because of pressures to include all students (including those with language differences or disabilities) in educational accountability programs.

Research on these topics is still fairly limited, although the available results are intriguing. For example, research suggests that some accommodations either fail to help or even hinder the performance of students who are English language learners (Abedi, Lord, Hofstetter & Baker, 2000) or who have disabilities (S. N. Elliott, Kratochwill, & McKevitt, 2001). Therefore, test publishers will need to consider ways in which tests can be constructed (e.g., multiple language forms) or adapted (e.g., accommodations) to help assessors accurately assess the constructs targeted. Consequently, it is likely that test publishers will offer increasingly diverse arrays of assessment forms (e.g., formal language translations) as they publish tests, and the directions accompanying tests are likely to be more explicit regarding ways in which assessors can (and cannot) accommodate diverse student needs without compromising the validity of the assessment. One example of this trend is the specification of the skills targeted by each of the subtests in the SB5 and those that are needed to provide access but that themselves are not intended to be assessed (Braden & Elliott, 2003). This information allows examiners to identify whether a given change to an assessment is likely to be a valid accommodation or an inappropriate test modification that would invalidate the test results. Similar efforts are likely to accompany future revisions of existing and new tests as a means of helping assessors adapt tests to the needs of test takers.

## Assessment Utility

The final issue that is likely to influence psychological assessment in schools is the increasing expectation that assessment has utility for advancing student outcomes. Benefits to students may be realized in many ways, including selecting, implementing, or monitoring interventions. In school contexts, treatment utility may also be understood to include instructional utility—that is, the value of assessment for selecting, implementing, or monitoring instruction.

Contemporary methods of assessment using individually administered tests of intelligence and emotion contribute to diagnosis but do not contribute to intervention or treatment. Although interpretive protocols promise utility for selecting interventions or treatments (e.g., Sattler, 2001), there is no evidence that these tests have treatment utility (Braden & Shaw, 2009). The use of assessment for treatment selection is warranted when two conditions are met: when the cost (human and financial) of assessment is less than the treatment, and when there are substantially different treatment responses among individuals with similar problems (Braden & Kratochwill, 1997). It is not clear that these conditions are met for most academic and social problems experienced in school settings (e.g., the same instructional intervention tends to work regardless of diagnostic category) (Braden & Shaw, 2009; Kavale, 1990). However, some newer approaches to assessment may provide better value for treatment matching (e.g., Naglieri & Gottling, 1997; Naglieri & Johnson, 2000). Although it may be debated whether tests of latent psychological traits, such as cognitive abilities or emotional status, will ever contribute to treatment selection (Gresham & Witt, 1997), the notion that assessment should contribute to treatment utility is becoming a shared expectation that will challenge those who develop assessments (e.g., Naglieri & Das, 1997) to demonstrate how their assessments contribute to treatment utility.

The other two aspects of treatment utility (i.e., implementing and monitoring interventions) will also receive greater attention in the future. Currently, methods for evaluating the degree to which teachers or others adhere to an intervention protocol (i.e., treatment integrity) are limited to global, indirect, qualitative approaches (Sterling-Turner, Watson, Wildman, Watkins, & Little, 2001). It is likely that protocols for evaluating treatment integrity will increase in sophistication and will be aligned with the movement to ensure interventions have demonstrated effectiveness for helping students (Roach & Elliott, 2008). All treatments are not equal in quality or outcome; likewise, psychologists will be under increasing pressure from internal and external sources to ensure that they select and implement evidence based interventions for the students they serve. (See Stoiber & Kratochwill, 2001.) Assessment procedures and techniques must provide more compelling evidence to show that they respond to these pressures than do most current approaches, particularly diagnostic assessment instruments. Some early examples of assessment-to-intervention protocols include the ACES and AIMS (DiPerna & Elliott, 2000; S. N. Elliott, Braden, & White, 2001) and the Process Assessment of the Learner (PAL) (Berninger, 2001). Future developments will expand these efforts, most likely by including treatment integrity protocols. However, the available technology for evaluating treatment integrity is not yet well developed, is resource intensive, and will require collaboration across disciplines that have not regularly influenced each other (Schulte, Easton, & Parker, 2009). Furthermore, it is not clear that educators will welcome the scrutiny inherent in evaluations of their adherence to intervention protocols.

The final way in which assessment may have treatment utility is via progress monitoring. The tools for progress monitoring appear to be present or nearly so in the form of observational systems, ratings of nonacademic behaviors and skills, and CBM metrics. The largest changes in progress monitoring will come from two influences already discussed in this section: technology and alignment to educational standards. Technology will most likely improve observational and rating recording systems, allow for more natural administration and scoring of progress monitoring (e.g., allow students to write or say their responses), and incorporate academic content aligned to educational standards.

Treatment utility will also be enhanced by the alignment and integration of assessment techniques and processes. Current assessment procedures lack alignment and integration. For example, diagnostic instruments are qualitatively different from the assessment approaches used for assessing treatment integrity, and these in turn are different from progress-monitoring techniques. An exception to this general conclusion is the alignment and integration of techniques and processes that use CBA for instructional matching (treatment selection), followed by CBM for progress monitoring. Future methods of assessment in schools will align assessment, so that procedures used early in the problem identification process contribute meaningfully and directly to intervention selection, monitoring treatment integrity, and evaluating treatment outcomes. Also, these processes will be integrated into unified systems of assessment. It is likely that this integration will proceed by adding modules to existing instruments, so that assessors can add functions as needed. For example, modules that add treatment integrity and progress monitoring to ACES/AIMS or PAL approaches are likely targets for integrating and aligning assessment across problem identification, intervention, and evaluation stages. Once again, in school contexts, interventions could include treatments (special procedures to solve atypical problems), interventions (changes in the environment to accommodate individual differences among students), or instruction (methods of teaching to enhance learning).

## Summary

The near future of psychological assessment in schools is likely to respond to already-existing pressures. These pressures come from within the field of psychology (e.g., aligning procedures to scientific advances and evidence based evaluations of interventions) and from without (e.g., technology, educational accountability, student diversity). In most cases, I have identified trends that have already elicited new instruments, approaches, or changes in assessments. However, changes in assessment practices will not occur unless the pressures maintaining current practices and procedures also change.

## REFERENCES

Abedi, J., Lord, C., Hofstetter, C., & Baker, E. (2000). Impact of accommodation strategies on English language learners' test performance. *Educational Measurement: Issues and Practice, 19*(3), 16–26.

Achenbach, T. M. (1991a). *Child Behavior Checklist & Profile for ages 4–18*. Burlington, VT: Child Behavior Checklist.

Achenbach, T. M. (1991b). *Youth Self-Report Form & Profile for ages 11–18*. Burlington, VT: Child Behavior Checklist.

Achenbach, T. M., & McConaughy, S. H. (1996). Relations between *DSM-IV* and empirically based assessment. *School Psychology Review, 25*(3), 329–341.

Achenbach, T. M., McConaughy, S. H., & Howell, C. T. (1987). Child/adolescent behavioral and emotional problems: Implications of cross-informant correlations for situational specificity. *Psychological Bulletin, 101*(2), 213–232.

Albee, G. (1998). The politics of primary prevention. *Journal of Primary Prevention, 19*, 117–127.

Allinder, R. M. Bolling, R. M., Oats, R. G., & Gagnon, W. A. (2000). Effects of teacher self-monitoring on implementation of curriculum-based measurement and mathematics computation achievement of students with disabilities. *Remedial and Special Education, 21*(4), 219–226.

American Education Research Association. (2000). *AERA position statement concerning high-stakes testing preK–12 education*. Washington, DC: Author.

American Educational Research Association, American Psychological Association, & National Council on Measurement in Education. (1999). *Standards for educational and psychological testing* (3rd ed.). Washington, DC: Author.

American Psychiatric Association. (2000). *Diagnostic and statistical manual of mental disorders: DSM-IV-TR (4th ed., text revision)*. Washington, DC: Author.

American Psychological Association. (1998). *Archival description of school psychology*. Washington, DC: Author.

American Psychological Association. (2001). *Appropriate use of high-stakes testing in our nation's schools*. Washington, DC: Author.

Arum, R., & Roska, J. (2011). *Academically adrift: Limited learning on college campuses*. Chicago, IL: University of Chicago Press.

Athanasiou, M. S. (2000). Current nonverbal assessment instruments: A comparison of psychometric integrity and test fairness. *Journal of Psychoeducational Assessment, 18*(3), 211–229.

Batsche, G., Elliott, J., Graden, J., Grimes, J., Kovaleski, J., Prasse, D., et al. (2005). *Response to Intervention: Policy considerations and implementation*. Alexandria, VA: National Association of State Directors of Special Education.

Beitchman, J. H. (1996). *Feelings, Attitudes and Behaviors Scale for Children*. North Tonawanda, NY: Multi-Health Systems.

Bellak, L., & Bellak, S. S. (1992). *Children's Apperception Test*. Larchmont, NY: C.P.S.

Benn, A., Jones, G. W., & Rosenfield, S. (2008). Analysis of instructional consultants' questions and alternatives to questions during the Problem Identification Interview. *Journal of Educational & Psychological Consultation, 18*(1), 54–80.

Bergan, J. R., & Kratochwill, T. R. (1990). *Behavioral consultation and therapy*. New York, NY: Plenum Press.

Berninger, V. W. (2001). *Process Assessment of the Learner*. San Antonio, TX: Pearson.

Binet, A., & Simon, T. (1914). *Mentally defective children*. London, UK: E. Arnold.

Bocian, K. M., Beebe, M. E., MacMillan, D. L., & Gresham, F. M. (1999). Competing paradigms in learning disabilities classification by schools and the variations in the meaning of discrepant achievement. *Learning Disabilities Research and Practice, 14*(1), 1–14.

Bracken, B. A., & McCallum, R. S. (1998). *Universal Nonverbal Intelligence Test*. Rolling Meadows, IL: Riverside.

Braden, J. P. (2007). Using data from high-stakes testing in program planning and evaluation. *Journal of Applied School Psychology, 23*(2), 129–150.

Braden, J. P., & Athanasiou, M. S. (2005). A comparative review of nonverbal measures of intelligence. In D. P. Flanagan & P. L. Harrison (Eds.), *Contemporary intellectual assessment: Theories, tests and issues* (2nd ed., pp. 557–577). New York, NY: Guilford Press.

Braden, J. P. & Elliott, S. N. (2003). Accommodations on the Stanford-Binet Intelligence Scales, Fifth Edition. In G. Roid, *Interpretive manual for the Stanford-Binet (Fifth Edition) Intelligence Scales* (pp. 135–143). Itasca, IL: Riverside.

Braden, J. P., Kovaleski, J. F., & Prasse, D. P. (1996). *Facilitator's training manual*. Chicago, IL: Chicago Public Schools.

Braden, J. P., & Kratochwill, T. R. (1997). Treatment utility of assessment: Myths and realities. *School Psychology Review*, *26*(3), 475–485.

Braden, J. P., & Shaw, S. R. (2009). Intervention validity of cognitive assessment: Knowns, unknowables, and unknowns. *Assessment for Effective Intervention 34*(2), 106–115.

Braden, J. P., & Shernoff, E. S. (2008). Evidence-based interventions: Why the need? In R. J. Morris & N. M. Mather (eds.) *Evidence-based interventions for students with learning and behavioral challenges* (pp. 9–30). Mahwah, NJ: Erlbaum.

Braden, J. P., & Tayrose, M. P. (2008). Best practices in educational accountability: High stakes testing and educational reform. In A. Thomas & J. Grimes (Eds.), *Best practices in school psychology* (5th ed., pp. 575–588). Silver Spring, MD: National Association of School Psychologists.

Bruininks, R. H., Woodcock, R. W., Weatherman, R. F., & Hill, B. K. (1996). *Scales of Independent Behavior—Revised*. Rolling Meadows, IL: Riverside.

Bush, G. W. (2001). *No child left behind*. Washington, DC: Office of the President of the United States.

Capaldi, D. M., & Patterson, G. R. (1989). *Psychometric properties of fourteen latent constructs from the Oregon Youth Study*. New York, NY: Springer-Verlag.

Carroll, J. B. (2005). The three-stratum theory of cognitive abilities. In D. P. Flanagan & P. L. Harrison (Eds.), *Contemporary intellectual assessment: Theories, tests, and issues* (pp. 69–75). New York, NY: Guilford Press.

Coffman, W. E. (1993). A king over Egypt, which knew not Joseph. *Educational Measurement: Issues and Practice*, *12*(2), 5–8.

Coie, J. D., Dodge, K. A., & Coppotelli, H. (1982). Dimensions and type of status: A cross age perspective. *Developmental Psychology*, *18*, 557–570.

Coie, J. D., et al. (1993). The science of prevention. A conceptual framework and some directions for a national research program. *American Psychologist*, *48*, 1013–1022.

CTB/McGraw-Hill. (2009). *TerraNova—Third Edition*. Monterey, CA: Author.

Das, J. P., Naglieri, J. A., & Kirby, J. R. (1994). *Assessment of cognitive processes: The PASS theory of intelligence*. Boston, MA: Allyn & Bacon.

DiPerna, J. C., & Elliott, S. N. (2000). *Academic competence evaluation scales*. San Antonio, TX: Pearson.

Driesler, S. D. (2001). Whiplash from backlash? The truth about public support for testing. *National Council on Measurement in Education Newsletter*, *9*(3), 3–5.

Durlak, J. A. (1997). *Successful prevention programs for children and adolescents*. New York, NY: Plenum.

Eckert, T. L., & Shapiro, E. S. (1999). Methodological issues in analog acceptability research: Are teachers' acceptability ratings of assessment methods influenced by experimental design? *School Psychology Review*, *28*(1), 5–16.

*Education Week*. (2001). *Quality counts 2001: A better balance: Standards, tests, and the tools to succeed*. Bethesda, MD: Author.

Elliott, C. D. (2007). *Differential Ability Scales—Second Edition*. San Antonio, TX: Pearson.

Elliott, S. N., Braden, J. P., & White, J. L. (2001). *Assessing one and all: Educational accountability for students with disabilities*. Reston, VA: Council for Exceptional Children.

Elliott, S. N., DiPerna, J. C., & Shapiro, E. S. (2001). *Academic intervention monitoring system*. San Antonio, TX: Psychological Corporation.

Elliott, S. N., Kratochwill, T. R., & McKevitt, B. C. (2001). Experimental analysis of the effects of testing accommodations on the scores of students with and without disabilities. *Journal of School Psychology*, *39*(1), 3–24.

Elmore, R. F., & Rothman, R. (Eds.) (1999). *Testing, teaching, and learning: A guide for states and school districts*. (Committee on Title I Testing and Assessment, National Research Council). Washington, DC: National Academy Press. Retrieved from www.nap.edu/catalog/9609.html

Fagan, T. K. (1996). Witmer's contribution to school psychological services. *American Psychologist*, *51*(3), 241–243.

Fagan, T. K. (2000). Practicing school psychology: A turn-of-the-century perspective. *American Psychologist*, *55*(7), 754–757.

Fairbanks, L. D., & Stinnett, T. A. (1997). Effects of professional group membership, intervention type, and diagnostic label on treatment acceptability. *Psychology in the Schools*, *34*(4), 329–335.

Figlio, D. N., & Page, M. E. (2000). *School choice and the distributional effects of ability tracking: Does separation increase equality?* (Working Paper No. W8055). Cambridge, MA: National Bureau of Economic Research. Retrieved from http://papers.nber.org/papers/W8055

Flanagan, D. P. (2000). Wechsler-based CHC cross-battery assessment and reading achievement: Strengthening the validity of interpretations drawn from Wechsler test scores. *School Psychology Quarterly*, *15*(3), 295–329.

Fuchs, L. S., Fuchs, D., & Deno, S. L. (1982). Reliability and validity of curriculum-based informal reading inventories. *Reading Research Quarterly*, *18*(1), 6–26.

Ginsberg, H. P., & Baroody, A. J. (2003). *Test of Early Mathematics Ability—Third Edition*. Austin, TX: Pro-Ed.

Greenwood, C. R., Carta, J. J., & Dawson, H. (2000). Ecobehavioral Assessment Systems Software (EBASS), A system for observation in education settings. In T. Thompson & D. Felce (Eds.), *Behavioral observation: Technology and applications in developmental disabilities* (pp. 229–251). Baltimore, MD: Paul H. Brookes.

Gresham, F. M. (1994). *Behavioral profiles of students considered at-risk using school records*. (ERIC Document Reproduction Service No. ED393024).

Gresham, F. M. (2001, August). *Responsiveness to intervention: An alternative approach to the identification of learning disabilities*. Paper presented at the Learning Disabilities Summit, Building a Foundation for the Future, Office of Special Education Programs, Washington, DC.

Gresham, F. M., & Elliott, S. N. (2008). *Social Skills Improvement System—Rating Scales*. Minneapolis, MN: Pearson.

Gresham, F. M., MacMillan, D. L., Beebe, F. M. E., & Bocian, K. M. (2000). Treatment integrity in learning disabilities intervention research: Do we really know how treatments are implemented? *Learning Disabilities—Research and Practice*, *15*(4), 198–205.

Gresham, F. M., MacMillan, D. L., & Bocian, K. M. (1996). Learning disabilities, low achievement, and mild mental retardation: More alike than different? *Journal of Learning Disabilities*, *29*(6), 570–581.

Gresham, F. M., MacMillan, D. L., & Bocian, K. M. (1998). Agreement between school study team decisions and authoritative definitions in classification of students at-risk for mild disabilities. *School Psychology Quarterly*, *13*(3), 181–191.

Gresham, F. M., Watson, T. S., & Skinner, C. H. (2001). Functional behavioral assessment: Principles, procedures, and future directions. *School Psychology Review*, *30*(2), 156–172.

Gresham, F. M., & Witt, J. C. (1997). Utility of intelligence tests for treatment planning, classification, and placement decisions: Recent empirical findings and future.

Hammill, D. D., Brown, V. L., Larsen, S. C., & Wiederholt, J. L. (2007). *Test of Adolescent and Adult Language—Fourth Edition*. Austin, TX: Pro-Ed.

Hammill, D. D., Pearson, N. A., & Wiederholt, J. L. (1997). *Comprehensive Test of Nonverbal Intelligence*. Austin, TX: Pro-Ed.

Harcourt Assessment. (2003). *Stanford Achievement Test—10th ed.* San Antonio, TX: Pearson.

Harrison, P. L., & Oakland, T. (2003). *Adaptive Behavior Assessment System—Second Edition.* Los Angeles, CA: Western Psychological Services.

Heubert, J. P. & R. M. Hauser (Eds.) (1999). *High stakes: Testing for tracking, promotion, and graduation.* Washington, DC: National Academy Press.

Hintze, J. M., Owen, S. V., Shapiro, E. S., & Daly, E. J. (2000). Generalizability of oral reading fluency measures: Application of G theory to curriculum-based measurement. *School Psychology Quarterly, 15*(1), 52–68.

Hintze, J. M., Shapiro, E. S., Conte, K. L., Basile, I. M. (1997). Oral reading fluency and authentic reading material: Criterion validity of the technical features of CBM survey-level assessment. *School Psychology Review, 26*(4), 535–553.

Hoover, H. D., Hieronymus, A. N., Frisbie, D. A., & Dunbar, S. B. (2003). *Iowa Tests of Basic Skills—Revised.* Rolling Meadows, IL: Riverside.

Idol, L., Nevin, A., & Paolucci-Whitcomb, P. (1996). *Models of curriculum-based assessment: A blueprint for learning* (2nd ed.). Austin, TX: Pro-Ed.

Individuals with Disabilities Education Act. Amendments of 2004, 20 U.S.C. §§ 1400 et seq.

Jackson, D. N. (1984). *Multidimensional Aptitude Battery.* Port Huron, MI: Sigma Assessment Systems.

Kamphaus, R. W., & Reynolds, C. R. (2007). *Behavior Assessment System for Children—Second Edition (BASC-2), Behavioral and Emotional Screening System (BESS).* Bloomington, MN: Pearson.

Kamphaus, R. W., Reynolds, C. R., & Vogel, K. K. (2009). Intelligence testing. In J. L. Matson, F. Andrasik, & M. L. Matson (Eds.), *Assessing child psychopathology and developmental disabilities* (pp. 91–115). New York, NY: Springer-Verlag.

Kaufman, A. S., & Kaufman, N. L. (2004a). *Kaufman Assessment Battery for Children, Second Edition.* San Antonio, TX: Pearson.

Kaufman, A. S., & Kaufman, N. L. (2004b). *Kaufman Test of Educational Achievement, Second Edition.* San Antonio, TX: Pearson.

Kavale, K. (1990). The effectiveness of special education. In T. B. Gutkin & C. R. Reynolds (Eds.), *The handbook of school psychology* (2nd ed., pp. 868–898). New York, NY: Wiley.

Keith, T. Z., Kranzler, J. H., & Flanagan, D. P. (2001). What does the Cognitive Assessment System (CAS) measure? Joint confirmatory factor analysis of the CAS and the Woodcock-Johnson Tests of Cognitive Ability (3rd ed.). *School Psychology Review, 30*(1), 89–119.

Kershaw, P., & Sonuga-Barke, E. (1998). Emotional and behavioural difficulties: Is this a useful category? The implications of clustering and comorbidity—the relevance of a taxonomic approach. *Educational and Child Psychology, 15*(4), 45–55.

Kohn, A. (2000). Burnt at the high stakes. *Journal of Teacher Education, 51*(4), 315–327.

Kranzler, J. H., Brownell, M. T., & Miller, M. D. (1998). The construct validity of curriculum-based measurement of reading: An empirical test of a plausible rival hypothesis. *Journal of School Psychology, 36*(4), 399–415.

Kranzler, J. H., Miller, M. D., & Jordan, L. (1999). An examination of racial/ethnic and gender bias on curriculum-based measurement of reading. *School Psychology Quarterly, 14*(3), 327–342.

Kratochwill, T. R. & Stoiber, K. C. (2002). *Functional Assessment and Intervention System: Improving school behavior.* San Antonio, TX: Psychological Corporation.

Labaree, D. F. (2000). Resisting educational standards. *Phi Delta Kappan, 82*(1), 28–33.

LeBuffe, P. A., Shapiro, V. B., & Naglieri, J. A. (2009). *Devereux Student Strengths Assessment.* Lewisville, NC: Kaplan Early Learning Co.

Lewis, M. F., Truscott, S. D., & Volker, M. A. (2008). Demographics and professional practices of school psychologists: A comparison of NASP members and non-NASP school psychologists by telephone survey. *Psychology in the Schools, 45*(6), 467–482.

MacKay, G., Somerville, W., & Lundie, J. (1996). Reflections on goal attainment scaling (GAS), Cautionary notes and proposals for development. *Educational Research, 38*(2), 161–172.

MacMillan, D. L., Gresham, F. M., & Bocian, K. M. (1998). Discrepancy between definitions of learning disabilities and school practices: An empirical investigation. *Journal of Learning Disabilities, 31*(4), 314–326.

MacMillan, D. L., Gresham, F. M., Bocian, K. M., & Siperstein, G. N. (1997). The role of assessment in qualifying students as eligible for special education: What is and what's supposed to be. *Focus on Exceptional Children, 30*(2), 1–18.

Malecki, C. K., & Elliott, S. N. (1999). Adolescents' ratings of perceived social support and its importance: Validation of the Student Social Support Scale. *Psychology in the Schools, 36*(6), 473–483.

March, J. S. (1997). *Multidimensional Anxiety Scale for Children.* North Tonawanda, NY: Multi-Health Systems.

Martin, S. (1999). !Observe: *A behavior recording and reporting software program.* Longmont, CO: Sopris West.

McDonnell, L. M., McLaughlin, M. J., & Morison, P. (Eds.) (1997). *Educating one and all: Students with disabilities and standards-based reform* (Committee on Goals 2000 and the Inclusion of Students with Disabilities, National Research Council). Washington, DC: National Academy Press. Retrieved from www.nap.edu/catalog/5788.html

McGrew, K. S., Keith, T. Z., Flanagan, D. P., & Vanderwood, M. (1997). Beyond "g": The impact of "Gf-Gc" specific cognitive abilities research on the future use and interpretation of intelligence test batteries in the schools. *School Psychology Review, 26*(2), 189–210.

McMillan, J. H., & Workman, D. (1999). *Teachers' classroom assessment and grading practices: Phase I and II.* Richmond, VA: Metropolitan Educational Research Consortium. (ERIC Document Reproduction Service No. 442840).

Mehrens, W. A. & Clarizio, H. F. (1993). Curriculum-based measurement: Conceptual and psychometric considerations. *Psychology in the Schools, 30*(3), 241–254.

Merrell, K. W., & Walters, A. S. (1998). *Internalizing Symptoms Scale for Children.* Austin, TX: Pro-Ed.

Motta, R. W., Little, S. G., Tobin, M. I. (1993). The use and abuse of human figure drawings. *School Psychology Quarterly, 8*(3), 162–169.

Munk, D. D., & Repp, A. C. (1994). The relationship between instructional variables and problem behavior: A review. *Exceptional Children, 60*(5), 390–401.

Murray, H. A., & Bellak, L. (1973). *Thematic Apperception Test.* San Antonio, TX: Psychological Corporation.

Naglieri, J. A. (1988). *Draw A Person—A quantitative scoring system.* San Antonio, TX: Psychological Corporation.

Naglieri, J. A. (1993). *Naglieri Nonverbal Abilities Test.* San Antonio, TX: Psychological Corporation.

Naglieri, J. A. (1999). How valid is the PASS theory and CAS? *School Psychology Review, 28*(1), 145–162.

Naglieri, J. A. (2000). Can profile analysis of ability test scores work? An illustration using the PASS theory and CAS with an unselected cohort. *School Psychology Quarterly, 15*(4), 419–433.

Naglieri, J. A. (2001). Using the Cognitive Assessment System (CAS) with learning-disabled children. In A. S. Kaufman & N. L. Kaufman (Eds.), *Specific learning disabilities and difficulties in children and adolescents: Psychological assessment and evaluation. Cambridge child and adolescent psychiatry* (pp. 141–177). New York, NY: Cambridge University Press.

Naglieri, J. A., & Bardos, A. N. (1997). *General Ability Measure for Adults.* Minnetonka, MN: NCS Assessments.

Naglieri, J. A., & Das, J. P. (1997). *Das-Naglieri Cognitive Assessment System.* Rolling Meadows, IL: Riverside.

Naglieri, J. A., & Gottling, S. H. (1997). Mathematics instruction and PASS cognitive processes: An intervention study. *Journal of Learning Disabilities, 30*(5), 513–520.

Naglieri, J. A., & Johnson, D. (2000). Effectiveness of a cognitive strategy intervention in improving arithmetic computation based on the PASS theory. *Journal of Learning Disabilities, 33*(6), 591–597.

Naglieri, J. A., LeBuffe, P. A., & Pfeiffer, S. I. (1993a). *Devereux Behavior Rating Scale—School Form—Adolescents.* San Antonio, TX: Pearson.

Naglieri, J. A., LeBuffe, P. A., & Pfeiffer, S. I. (1993b). *Devereux Behavior Rating Scale—School Form—Children.* San Antonio, TX: Pearson.

Naglieri, J. A., McNeish, T. J., & Bardos, A. N. (1991). *Draw a Person: Screening procedure for emotional disturbance.* Austin, TX: Pro-Ed.

Naglieri, J. A., & Pfeiffer, S. I. (1992). Validity of the Draw a Person—Screening Procedure for Emotional Disturbance with a socially-emotionally disturbed sample. *Journal of Consulting and Clinical Psychology: Psychological Assessment, 4,* 156–159.

Naglieri, J. A., & Ronning, M. E. (2000). The relationship between general ability using the Naglieri Nonverbal Ability Test (NNAT) and Stanford Achievement Test (SAT) reading achievement. *Journal of Psychoeducational Assessment, 18*(3), 230–239.

National Governors Association. (1998). *High school exit exams: Setting high expectations.* Washington, DC: Author.

National Reading Panel. (2000). *Teaching children to read: An evidence-based assessment of the scientific research literature on reading and its implications for reading instruction.* (National Institute of Child Health and Human Development NIH Pub. No. 00–4769). Bethesda, MD: U.S. Department of Health and Human Services.

Nave, B., Miech, E., & Mosteller, F. (2000). A lapse in standards: Linking standards-based reform with student achievement. *Phi Delta Kappan, 82*(2), 128–132.

Nettelbeck, T. (1998). Jensen's chronometric research: Neither simple nor sufficient but a good place to start. *Intelligence, 26*(3), 233–241.

Nock, M. K., & Kurtz, S. S. (2005). Direct behavioral observation in school settings: Bringing science to practice. *Cognitive and Behavioral Practice, 12*(3), 359–370.

Nolet, V. & McLaughlin, M. (1997). Using CBM to explore a consequential basis for the validity of a state-wide performance assessment. *Diagnostique, 22*(3), 146–163.

Norman, G. J., Velicer, W. F., Fava, J. L., & Prochaska, J. O. (2000). Cluster subtypes within stage of change in a representative sample of smokers. *Addictive Behaviors, 25*(2), 183–204.

Novi, M. J., & Meinster, M. O. (2000). Achievement in a relational context: Preferences and influences in female adolescents. *Career Development Quarterly, 49,* 73–84.

Oakes, J. (1992). Can tracking research inform practice? Technical, normative, and political considerations. *Educational Researcher, 21*(4), 12–21.

Office for Standards in Education, Children's Services, and Skills. (n.d.). Retrieved from www.ofsted.gov.uk/schools

Pearson. (2003). *Otis-Lennon School Ability Test—Eighth Edition.* San Antonio, TX: Author.

Pearson. (2009). *Wechsler Individual Achievement Test—Third Edition.* San Antonio, TX: Author.

Peverly, S. T., & Kitzen, K. R. (1998). Curriculum-based assessment of reading skills: Considerations and caveats for school psychologists. *Psychology in the Schools, 35*(1), 29–47.

Piers, E. V., Herzberg, D. S., & Harris, D. B. (2002). *Piers-Harris Children's Self Concept Scale* (2nd ed.). Los Angeles, CA: Western Psychological Services.

Plewis, I. (1988). Estimating generalizability in systematic observation studies. *British Journal of Mathematical and Statistical Psychology, 41*(1), 53–62.

Raven, J. C. (1992a). *Raven's Coloured Progressive Matrices.* San Antonio, TX: Pearson.

Raven, J. C. (1992b). *Raven's Progressive Matrices.* San Antonio, TX: Pearson.

Ravitch, D. (1999). Student performance: The national agenda in education. In M. Kanstoroom & C. E. Finn (Eds.), *New directions: Federal education policy in the twenty-first century.* Washington, DC: Thomas B. Fordham Foundation & the Manhattan Policy Institute.

Ravitch, D. (2011). Dictating to the schools: A look at the effect of the Bush and Obama administration on schools. *Education Digest, 76*(8), 4–9.

Reiss, D., & Price, R. H. (1996). National research agenda for prevention research. The National Institute of Mental Health report. *American Psychologist, 51,* 1109–1115.

Reschly, D. J. (2008). School psychology paradigm shift and beyond. In A. Thomas & J. Grimes (Eds.), *Best practices in school psychology* (5th ed.), pp. 3–16. Silver Spring, MD: National Association of School Psychologists.

Reschly, D. J., & Grimes, J. P. (1995). Best practices in intellectual assessment. In A. Thomas & J. Grimes (Eds.), *Best practices in school psychology* (3rd ed.), Bethesda, MD: National Association of School Psychologists.

Reschly, D. J., Kicklighter, R. H., & McKee, P. (1988). Recent placement litigation. Part III: Analysis of differences in Larry P., Marshall, and S-1 and implications for future practices. *School Psychology Review, 17,* 37–48.

Reynolds, C. R., & Hickman, J. A. (2004). *Draw-A-Person Intellectual Ability Test for Children, Adolescents, and Adults.* Austin, TX: Pro-Ed.

Reynolds, C. R., & Kamphaus, R. W. (2007). *Test of irregular word reading efficiency.* Lutz, FL: Psychological Assessment Resources.

Reynolds, W. M. (1998). *Adolescent Psychopathology Scale.* Lutz, FL: Psychological Assessment Resources.

Reynolds, W. M. (2008). *Reynolds Adolescent Depression Scale—Second Edition.* Lutz, FL: Psychological Assessment Resources.

Roach, A. T., & Elliott, S. N. (2008). Best practices in facilitating and evaluating intervention integrity. In A. Thomas & J. Grimes. (Eds.): *Best practices in school psychology* (5th ed.), pp. 195–208. Silver Spring, MD: National Association of School Psychologists.

Roehrig, A. D., Petscher, Y., Nettles, S. M., Hudson, R. F., & Torgesen, J. K. (2008). Accuracy of the DIBELS oral reading fluency measure for predicting third grade reading comprehension outcomes. *Journal of School Psychology, 46*(3), 343–366.

Roid, G. H. (2003). *Stanford-Binet Intelligence Scales, Fifth Edition.* Rolling Meadows, IL: Riverside.

Roid, G. H. & Miller, L. J. (1997). *Leiter International Performance Scale—Revised.* Wood Dale, IL: Stoeling.

Rotter, J. B., Lah, M. I., & Rafferty, J. E. (1992). *Rotter Incomplete Sentences Blank—Second Edition.* San Antonio, TX: Pearson.

Rubin, D. B., Stuart, E. A., & Zanutto, E. L. (2004). A potential outcomes view of value-added assessment in education. *Journal of Educational and Behavioral Statistics, 29*(1), 103–116.

Ryser, G., & McConnell, K. (2002). *SCALES for diagnosing attention-deficit hyperactivity disorder: Examiner's manual.* Austin, TX: Pro-Ed.

Sattler, J. M. (2001). *Assessment of children: Cognitive applications* (4th ed.). La Mesa, CA: Author.

Schrag, P. (2000). High stakes are for tomatoes. *Atlantic Monthly, 286*(2). Retrieved from www.theatlantic.com/issues/2000/08/schrag.htm

Schulte, A. C., Easton, J. E., & Parker, J. (2009). Advances in treatment integrity research: Multidisciplinary perspectives on the conceptualization, measurement, and enhancement of treatment integrity. *School Psychology Review*, *38*(4), 460–475.

Shapiro, E. S. (1988). Preventing academic failure. *School Psychology Review*, *17*(4), 601–613.

Shapiro, E. S., & Kratochwill, T. K. (Eds.). (2000). *Conducting school-based assessments of child and adolescent behavior*. New York, NY: Guilford Press.

Shinn, M. R. (2008). Best practices in using curriculum-based measurement in a problem-solving model. In A. Thomas & J. Grimes (Eds.), *Best practices in school psychology* (5th ed., pp. 243–262). Silver Spring, MD: National Association of School Psychologists.

Smith, D., & Dumont, F. (1995). A cautionary study: Unwarranted interpretations of the Draw-A-Person Test. *Professional Psychology: Research and Practice*, *26*, 298–303.

Speece, D. L., & Case, L. P. (2001). Classification in context: An alternative approach to identifying early reading disability. *Journal of Educational Psychology*, *93*(4), 735–749.

Stecker, P. M., & Fuchs, L. S. (2000). Effecting superior achievement using curriculum-based measurement: The importance of individual progress monitoring. *Learning Disabilities: Research and Practice*, *15*(3), 128–134.

Sterling-Turner, H. E., Watson, T. S., Wildman, M., Watkins, C., & Little, E. (2001). Investigating the relationship between training type and treatment integrity. *School Psychology Quarterly*, *16*(1), 56–67.

Stoiber, K. C., & Kratochwill, T. R. (2001). Evidence-based intervention programs: Rethinking, refining, and renaming the new standing section of *School Psychology Quarterly*. *School Psychology Quarterly*, *16*(1), 1–8.

Swanson, H. L., & Hoskyn, M. (1998). Experimental intervention research on students with learning disabilities: A meta-analysis of treatment outcomes. *Review of Educational Research*, *68*(3), 277–321.

TechMicro. (2000). *Computer Optimized Multimedia Intelligence Test*. New York, NY: Author.

Thomas B. Fordham Foundation. (1998). *A nation still at risk: An educational manifesto*. Washington, DC: Author. (ERIC Document Reproduction Service ED429988)

Thompson, J. M., & Sones, R. A. (1973). *Education Apperception Test*. Los Angeles, CA: Western Psychological Services.

Tilley, D. W. (2008). The evolution of school psychology to science-based practice: Problem solving and the three-tiered model. In A. Thomas & J. Grimes (Eds.), *Best practices in school psychology* (5th ed., pp. 17–28). Silver Spring, MD: National Association of School Psychologists.

Tomlinson, C. A. (2000). Reconcilable differences: Standards-based teaching and differentiation. *Educational Leadership*, *58*(1), 6–11.

Walker, H. M., Block-Pedego, A., Todis, B., & Severson, H. H. (1991). *School archival records search*. Longmont, CO: Sopris West.

Wang, L., Beckett, G. H., & Brown, L. (2006). Controversies of standardized assessment in school accountability reform: A critical synthesis of multidisciplinary research evidence. *Applied Measurement in Education*, *19*(4), 305–328.

Watkins, M. W., Glutting, J. J., & Youngstrom, E. A. (2005). Issues in subtest profile interpretation. In D. P. Flanagan & P. L. Harrison (Eds.), *Contemporary intellectual assessment: Theories, tests, and issues* (2nd ed., pp. 251–268). New York, NY: Guilford Press.

Wechsler, D. (2003). *Wechsler Preschool and Primary Scale of Intelligence—Third Edition*. San Antonio, TX: Pearson.

Wechsler, D. (2004). *Wechsler Intelligence Scale for Children—Fourth Edition*. San Antonio, TX: Pearson.

Wechsler, D. (2008). *Wechsler Adult Intelligence Scale—Third Edition*. San Antonio, TX: Pearson.

Weissberg, R. P., & Greenberg, M. T. (1998). School and community competence-enhancement and prevention programs. In W. Damon (Ed.), *Handbook of child psychology: Child psychology in practice* (Vol. 4, pp. 877–954). New York, NY: Wiley.

Wickstrom, K. F., Jones, K. M., LaFleur, L. H., & Witt, J. C. (1998). An analysis of treatment integrity in school-based behavioral consultation. *School Psychology Quarterly*, *13*(2), 41–54.

Wiggins, G. (1989). A true test: Toward more authentic and equitable assessment. *Phi Delta Kappan*, *70*(9), 703–713.

Woodcock, R. W., McGrew, K. S., & Mather, N. (2000a). *Woodcock-Johnson Tests of Achievement*. Rolling Meadow, IL: Riverside.

Woodcock, R. W., McGrew, K. S., & Mather, N. (2000b). *Woodcock-Johnson Tests of Cognitive Ability*. Rolling Meadow, IL: Riverside.

Wyse, D., & Torrance, H. (2009). The development and consequences of national curriculum assessment for primary education in England. *Educational Research*, *51*(2), 213–228

Yopp, H. (1988). The validity and reliability of phonemic awareness tests. *Reading Research Quarterly*, *23*, 159–177.

# CHAPTER 13

# Psychological Assessment in Medical Settings

JERRY J. SWEET, STEVEN M. TOVIAN, LESLIE M. GUIDOTTI BRETING, AND YANA SUCHY

Historically, medical settings have provided a fertile environment for formal psychological assessment. In fact, primarily as a consequence of the large number of training opportunities provided by Veterans Affairs hospitals, a majority of clinical psychologists have had internship and other levels of training within medical settings. Moreover, the specialties of clinical health psychology and clinical neuropsychology had their genesis and seminal growth within medical settings. Within a wide range of medical settings, formal assessment activities by psychologists have become so commonplace as to now be taken for granted by physician colleagues who have trained recently in major urban American medical schools. That is, recently trained physicians now expect to have psychological assessment resources available within the hospital systems in which they practice because these resources were present within the institutions in which they were trained.

In this chapter we discuss and delineate general and specific issues that are important to psychological assessment activities in medical settings. Included in the topics discussed are unique aspects of the environment and unique assessment issues, assessment with specific medical populations, and opportunities for psychologists practicing assessment in medical settings. Unless otherwise specified, our use of the term *psychological assessment* encompasses all traditional (e.g., personality, intellectual, academic) and specialized (e.g., health illness coping styles, specific neuropsychological) testing. We endeavor to be explicit when issues pertain only to a subset of formal psychological assessment procedures.

## UNIQUE GENERAL ASPECTS OF THE MEDICAL ENVIRONMENT THAT AFFECT PSYCHOLOGICAL PRACTICE

In general, there are a number of characteristics of medical settings that influence—and in some instances even guide—practice activities of psychologists. These characteristics include:

- the organizational structure of some medical setting (e.g., hospitals),
- the predominant power and authority conferred to the doctor of medicine (MD) or doctor of osteopathic medicine (DO),
- the increased pressure for accountability associated with physical health care,
- opportunities for clinical collaboration with physicians,
- multidisciplinary aspects of health care in some medical settings,
- possible involvement in medical education, and
- possible involvement in medical and/or translational research.

We consider each of these factors individually.

### Organizational Structure

The decision-making power and authority of hospitals and other medical service delivery institutions is structured—like most large businesses—in a hierarchical administrative tree. Although in the past many of the top leadership positions in hospitals were occupied by physicians, currently the vast majority are filled by individuals who have earned a master's of business administration (MBA or equivalent) degree, specializing in hospital administration or health services administration. The chief administrators (e.g., chairman of the board, chief executive officer, chief financial officer, president, vice president) make business decisions, such as those related to marketing, limiting expenses and developing revenues from day-to-day operations, and planning for future growth. As the administrative structure reaches downward to clinical departments and then to clinical programs, the leadership is much more likely to have had training in a health-care delivery field (e.g., nursing or medicine) and to be licensed clinicians as well as administrators. The important decisions regarding targeting of health-care problems and effective delivery and quality control of relevant services occur at this level. Although a sharing of financial responsibility occurs throughout the administrative structure of hospitals, it is a relatively recent event at most health-care institutions that individual health-care providers, who occupy the lowest level of the administrative tree and therefore have the least amount of power and authority, are held accountable for a personal budget of expenses and revenue. This latter event has caused a paradigm shift with regard to the clinical expectations and daily activities of practitioners, including psychologists, within large organized medical settings, such as hospitals. Essentially, there is now a clear burden for a practitioner to earn the equivalent of salary and benefits, *plus* a substantial amount that is typically defined by top administrators, through collection of real dollars in order to justify the practitioner's clinical position. The influence of this environment extends to psychologists practicing assessment in medical settings.

## Power and Authority Conferred to Physicians

Although their amount of unquestioned power is decreasing with the passage of time, individuals who have earned an MD or DO continue to be at the top of that part of the administrative tree that governs clinicians providing services within medical settings. For example, in a multidisciplinary rehabilitation program, the top leadership position is almost always an MD or DO. This physician is referred to as a medical director and is conferred a position of decision-making power over other individuals—even fellow physicians and others licensed as independent practitioners who do not require medical supervision. Although some notable exceptions can be identified (i.e., psychologists sometimes serve as clinical directors with

a purview over physicians), most psychologists working in medical settings work in some sense under a medical director, who may or may not appreciate the unique aspects of psychological service provision. Moreover, awareness and knowledge of specialty assessment services delivered by psychologists may be limited.

The past decade has produced a move toward competency-based assessment in psychology education and clinical practice (American Psychological Association (APA) Task Force on the Assessment of Competencies, 2006), which began most notably with the convening of the 2002 Competencies Conference, Future Directions in Education and Credentialing in Professional Psychology (Kaslow et al., 2004). Medical settings, especially hospitals, have some unique characteristics that affect the provision of care, including psychological and neuropsychological assessments.

First, and perhaps foremost, is that the provision of care within hospitals and some other medical settings requires credentialing and privileging of the provider—that is, each provider must have his or her professional *credentials* (e.g., degree programs, formal nondegree course work, certifications of training or competence, etc.) placed under peer review that allows a determination of which *privileges* (e.g., professional procedures associated with the individual's field of study and practice, such as personality testing or neuropsychological testing) the person will be allowed to perform while working within a given facility. In other words, a psychologist may not simply enter and provide services in a medical facility merely because someone has referred a patient. In most instances, credentialing and privileging at a medical facility implies that the provider will provide services intermittently or with some regularity. However, when a one-time evaluation is requested, temporary privileges can usually be granted expeditiously. These requirements are an expectation of agencies such as the Joint Commission on Accreditation of Healthcare Organizations (JCAHO). Therefore, it is important to note that merely being hired as an employee of a medical facility is not enough to begin practicing within the facility; credentialing and privileging must still take place, even for a full-time employee of the institution. The facility must still document that an adequate review of credentials and an appropriate granting of privileges for the practice of psychology have taken place. As more psychologists have been hired within medical facilities, more sophisticated and specific credentialing and privileging procedures have been created and entrusted to psychologists, rather than medical staff. Thus, currently this intended *peer* review process is more likely to be a review by one's true peers (other practicing psychologists) than it has been in the past.

It is quite understandable therefore that Kaslow, Dunn, and Smith (2008) would view securing hospital privileges as part of the medical or professional staff as the first step toward practicing clinically as a professional within hospital settings. Consequently, hospital system bylaws are essential in providing the opportunity to be credentialed and granted privileges in health-care facilities, which is of paramount importance to psychologists. The actual clinical services that a practitioner is authorized to provide in a hospital are commensurate with the psychologist's training and experience, which become embodied in the specific privileges granted to the individual by the hospital. A true *peer* review process for psychologists requires that the reviewers are psychologists. The related review processes include examination of academic and professional credentials, continuing education, and competency. Other areas of consideration by the reviewers of an individuals' application typically include history of lawsuits, adequacy of malpractice insurance, disciplinary history with licensing boards, and problems at other hospitals (Rozensky, 2006). In some academic medical centers, an academic appointment to the medical school may be required of individuals who are granted professional staff appointment.

Psychologists are now routinely granted a broad range of assessment and intervention privileges in hospitals, with a recent study finding that 66% of psychologists had hospital privileges (Robiner, Dixon, Miner, & Hong, 2010). This study also pointed out that many psychologists lack an understanding of hospital privileges and that there is a need for greater education in this area. An example of current experience with hospital privileges for psychological assessment is illustrated in Table 13.1. The table demonstrates that many psychologists have general assessment privileges; as one might expect, privileges for more specialized assessment activities are granted less frequently, which parallels the privileging of generalist and specialist physicians.

## Pressure for Accountability Associated With Physical Health Care

American society has come to believe that when it comes to medical care, a negative outcome—regardless of whether it is associated with quality care—potentially may raise the issue of accountability. With impressive developments in science and technology that have fostered true medical advances has come unyielding optimism that nearly all illnesses can and should be controlled or ameliorated with early diagnosis followed by appropriate, good care. This perspective is an understandable outgrowth of rapid progress in recent decades and represents a human attribute that drives us incessantly toward higher accomplishments. The other side of the coin consists of perfectionistic expectations that errors can be reduced to zero and that effectiveness can be maximized at all times. As health-care practitioners who work closely with physicians, psychologists are placed under the same expectations of accountability. One has only to explore litigation against psychologists to understand that although the damages may or may not be as visible as those resulting from use of a scalpel, accountability for psychological diagnostic and treatment activities are just as real as for more seemingly tangible medical fields, such as dermatology. Within medical settings, accountability for accuracy of providers individually and clinical procedures in general often is readily apparent among health-care workers operating in close proximity. This close accountability for efficacious outcomes is applied in the same manner for psychological assessment outcomes of an individual provider and—for better or worse—will be readily apparent to the nonpsychologists working alongside psychologists within a medical setting.

### Board Certification: Embracing the Gold Standard of Physicians

Board certification is the general expectation that is held for physicians within the medical setting when presenting one's credentials, and it is common practice in the medical field to list one's specialty. Surprisingly, however, only a small percentage of psychologists are actually board certified, in contrast to the field of medicine in which the vast majority of physicians maintain one or more board certifications under the auspices of the American Board of Medical Specialties (ABMS). This may be primarily due to psychologists' view that board certification is unnecessary. In order for psychologists to fit within the medical setting, however, they too should meet the standards of becoming board certified in their specialty area. The parallel organization to ABMS is the American Board of Professional Psychology (ABPP). ABPP has been board certifying practicing psychologists since 1947 (Nezu, Finch, & Simon, 2009). The current ABPP president, Dr. Nadine Kaslow, envisions that by 2020, voluntary certification will be an expected credentialing step for specialty practitioners within psychology (Kaslow, 2010). Being board certified signals the attainment of competence within a specialty and reflects an expected level of professionalism within that specialty (Elman, Illfelder-Kaye,

**TABLE 13.1  Psychologists' Hospital Privileges for Assessments**

| Privilege | Total Yes % | Yes, I can Provide this Service as a Core or Generic Privilege % | Yes, I can Provide this Service as a Specialized Privilege % | No, I have not Requested this Privilege % | No, I have Requested but have been Denied this Privilege % | Psychologists are Never Granted this Privilege in My Hospital % | Unsure/NA % | n |
|---|---|---|---|---|---|---|---|---|
| Diagnostic Interview | 98.9 | 90.9 | 8.0 | 0.4 | 0.0 | 0.0 | 2.5 | 275 |
| General psychological assessment (with testing) | 94.9 | 75.1 | 19.8 | 2.9 | 0.4 | 0.0 | 3.7 | 273 |
| Psychoeducational evaluation | 65.7 | 52.5 | 13.2 | 20.0 | 0.0 | 3.0 | 13.2 | 265 |
| Substance abuse/chemical dependence | 43.8 | 34.2 | 9.6 | 31.9 | 0.0 | 4.2 | 20.8 | 260 |
| Clinical neuropsychological assessment | 43.0 | 20.4 | 22.6 | 46.8 | 0.4 | 0.8 | 10.2 | 265 |
| Disability determination or worker compensation evaluation | 37.6 | 31.9 | 5.7 | 32.3 | 0.0 | 7.6 | 22.4 | 263 |
| Forensic evaluation | 36.9 | 29.2 | 7.7 | 33.8 | 0.0 | 8.1 | 22.3 | 260 |
| Career counseling and vocational assessment | 25.6 | 20.3 | 5.1 | 34.4 | 0.0 | 10.2 | 30.9 | 256 |
| Child custody evaluation | 16.3 | 12.8 | 3.5 | 45.3 | 0.0 | 10.9 | 28.3 | 258 |
| Wada test | 9.9 | 4.2 | 5.7 | 43.1 | 0.0 | 16.0 | 31.3 | 262 |
| Mean across assessment privileges | 47.3 | 37.2 | 10.1 | 29.1 | 0.1 | 6.1 | 18.6 | |

*Source:* From "Hospital Privileges for Psychologists in the Era of Competencies and Increased Accountability," by W. N. Robiner, K. E. Dixon, J. L. Miner, and B. A. Hong, 2010, *Journal of Clinical Psychology in Medical Settings, 17*(4), 301–314. Reproduced courtesy of the publisher.

& Robiner, 2005). There are now 14 different specialties that one can become board certified in under the ABPP.

## Opportunities for Clinical Collaboration With Physicians

Within medical settings, psychologists can encounter numerous unique opportunities for collaboration with physician colleagues. Physicians are more than just a referral source for patients; psychologists working in medical settings with physicians can encounter opportunities to work more closely together for the purpose of providing a wider range of services or perhaps reaching a more diverse medical population than would otherwise be seen for psychological services. For example, the close monitoring of mental status changes in patients with acute medical conditions—such as those found in patients hospitalized with delirium, onset of central nervous system infections, or cerebrovascular stroke—makes for a close clinical collaboration that is not present in outpatient private practice settings. These sorts of close clinical relationships have at times led to improved clinical service delivery that would not have occurred otherwise. For example, monitoring via repeat neuropsychological screenings of patients suffering from brain involvement of AIDS during intense inpatient medical treatment often provides earlier indication of treatment effectiveness than would be possible using only traditional medical markers of brain function. Similarly, psychological screening of candidates for surgical procedures, ranging from high-risk, resource-draining procedures (e.g., organ transplantation) to common surgeries, the outcomes of which are known to be affected by psychosocial variables, has increased the frequency of positive outcomes. Finally, from a very different perspective, when one considers the medical cost offset literature (cf. Sobel, 2000), which has demonstrated that appropriate psychological assessment and intervention can produce savings on what would have been unnecessary medical assessment and treatment, it is apparent that utilization of psychological assessment services has a meaningful impact in reducing health-care costs. Although it is often overlooked, this latter point is perhaps a unique contribution of psychological services to overall improved health care, an effect produced as a direct by-product of close collaboration between physicians and psychologists.

## Multidisciplinary Aspects of Current Health Care in Medical Settings

Perhaps nowhere has there been more opportunity for psychologists than in multidisciplinary clinical programs, which are almost invariably housed within medical settings and staffed partly by physicians. These programs have grown from the recognition that in order to provide the best care for some medical conditions, the special skills of more than one field are needed. For example, a psychologist working within a hospital may have the opportunity to become part of a multidisciplinary inpatient oncology program, thereby assessing and treating patients who are more acutely ill or who have progressed to the point in their illness that outpatient care is no longer feasible. This multidisciplinary type of endeavor may involve physicians from multiple specialties and specialists from other disciplines, such as physical therapy, speech therapy, and nursing. Similar examples of common real-life collaborations between psychologists in medical settings and various health-care professionals can be seen with multidisciplinary rehabilitation, cardiac disorders, epilepsy, neurodegenerative disorders (e.g., Parkinson's disease, Alzheimer's disease), stroke, traumatic brain injury, chronic pain treatment, dental problems, and organ transplant programs. Within these programs, psychologists often play a key role—in a well-integrated fashion with other specialists—in evaluating and treating psychosocial, cognitive, and family problems associated with the respective medical disorder.

## Unique Opportunities for Professional Learning and Growth

Accompanying opportunities for meaningful and close collaborative involvement with physicians are opportunities for professional learning and growth in what would be considered nontraditional areas for psychologists. For example, neuropsychologists may be able to participate in invasive diagnostic procedures, such as the Wada procedure (i.e., assessment of localization of language and memory during intracarotid sodium amytal injection to each hemisphere of the brain) that takes place in the surgical room. The Wada procedure is often relevant for patients who are under consideration for surgical intervention in areas of the brain where loss of language may occur, such as surgery for temporal lobe epilepsy. These types of sophisticated, highly specialized assessment opportunities take place only in medical settings.

## Possible Involvement in Medical Education

Some medical settings—particularly hospitals and medical centers associated with university medical schools—provide psychologists practicing assessment with opportunities to become involved in the educational process of physicians in training. In fact, psychologists have been well represented in physician training programs for many years. More than three decades ago a survey revealed that 98% of all medical schools in the United States employed psychologists, at a ratio of 1 psychologist for every 24 medical students (Gentry & Matarazzo, 1981). In 2002, personal communication with B. Hong, president of the Association of Medical School Psychologists (AMSP), indicated that there are approximately 4,000+ full-time psychologists on faculty at medical schools in the United States and Canada (Tovian, Rozensky, & Sweet, 2003). Psychologists are also frequently relied on in medical schools to teach students interview skills during the first 2 years. Psychologists have assumed central roles in undergraduate and graduate medical education over the past several decades (Eckleberry-Hunt, Van Dyke, Stucky, & Misch, 2009). The professional identity of psychologists in medical schools crystallized with the formation of the Association of Medical School Professors of Psychology, an organization that subsequently evolved into the Association of Medical School Psychologists and most recently is now called the Association of Psychologists in Academic Health Centers (APAHC) and achieved the status of an official section within Division 12 (Clinical Psychology) of the American Psychological Association. This organization adopted the *Journal of Clinical Psychology in Medical Settings* as its official publication. In addition, several health-care specialty areas (including health psychology, neuropsychology, rehabilitation, and pediatric health psychology) represented by their respective divisions in APA formed the Interdivisional Healthcare Committee (IHC), the purpose of which is to establish a common agenda for promoting professional, educational, and scientific goals of health-care psychology (Glueckauf, 1999).

In a different vein, involvement in assessment activities within academic medical settings is likely to bring clinical involvement with medical students and residents who are struggling academically. Such involvement may be in the form of assessment of apparent psychological difficulties, possible substance abuse, or possible learning disability.

### Possible Involvement in Medical Research

With the recent research initiative on translational projects and related funding opportunities through the National Institutes of Health (NIH), there is now more opportunity and encouragement for psychologists to engage in collaborative research with physicians. Some medical settings and some collaborations between psychologists and physicians offer unique medical research opportunities. For example, a neuropsychologist may contribute to medical research by assessing patients' psychological and cognitive functioning before and after the implementation of pharmacological or surgical intervention. Specifically, neuropsychologists may conduct pre- and postoperative evaluations of patients suspected of normal-pressure hydrocephalus. There may also be an opportunity to work with patients to evaluate their neuropsychological status immediately before and after surgical intervention for an intractable movement disorder or intractable epilepsy. In this manner, the assessment instruments of neuropsychologists may provide the most salient outcome measure for patients assigned to different types of surgical interventions in an attempt to determine the most effective treatment of a medical disorder. In addition, quality-of-life measures from health psychology have also been utilized in medical treatment outcome studies of cancer patients (and other medical patients) in an attempt to objectify the possible psychosocial benefits of medical interventions to prolong life.

## UNIQUE PSYCHOLOGICAL ASSESSMENT ISSUES WITHIN MEDICAL SETTINGS

Here, we individually consider these factors that can affect the assessment practices of psychologists in medical settings: reimbursement, ethical-legal, logistics, and special instrumentation. The reader should note that, in some instances, these factors create a favorable effect, whereas in other instances they create an untoward effect for clinicians as compared to those not practicing in medical settings.

### Reimbursement

Although obtaining reimbursement for services legitimately rendered has become more difficult for all healthcare providers in recent years, there have been particular issues and emphases for those practicing within medical settings. These factors fundamentally all relate to characteristics and expectations of payer sources.

#### Evolution of "Managed Care" Into "Accountable Care"

On the heels of the initial managed care era of the 1980s and 1900s, Piotrowski (1999) presented evidence that "managed care policies are having an onerous influence on the majority of practicing clinicians, particularly in the area of assessment" (p. 792). For psychologists practicing assessment in medical settings, initial managed care presented a mixed picture of challenges and some advantages. Among the advantages of practicing within medical settings was an associated easier access to managed care panels that were intent on offering a continuum of care that included outpatient and inpatient services from the entire range of health-care disciplines, including psychology. The restriction of access to patients by exclusion of some psychologists from managed care panels was significant enough to cause the APA to engage in lawsuits against some managed care companies (Nessman & Herndon, 2000). When psychologists providing clinical services are fully integrated into larger medical practice groups, inclusion in managed care panels seemed to be facilitated. Individual clinicians not associated with large groups of providers of medical care (e.g., hospitals, independent physician associations) within a given economic geography may not appear as attractive to insurance company gatekeepers, who may prefer to sign up the entire continuum of care in one major agreement with a well-established medical institution. This seemed particularly true in well-populated, urban areas, within which large medical delivery systems already had earned a positive reputation that made for very favorable marketing once signed up by a particular managed care organization.

Moreover, as they were accepted by the managed care company for inclusion on provider panels and therefore accessible to their subscribers, psychologists in large, well-organized medical settings also benefited from the available infrastructure of their employer's organization. Burdensome tasks for clinicians were common with the initial iteration of managed care. Psychologists practicing in large medical settings, such as hospitals, likely had a better support system for the incredibly time-consuming tasks of (a) completion of unrelenting paperwork associated with initial applications and maintenance of panel memberships, (b) accurate completion of extensive and obfuscated precertification procedures, and (c) effective submission and resubmission of proper service delivery and billing documentation. Barisa (2010) has provided a summary of current tips for working with managed care patients.

On the negative side of the ledger, psychologists practicing within the organized multidisciplinary practice group of a medical setting may be required to accept panel inclusion for managed care plans that provide relatively better reimbursement rates for physicians than do carved-out (i.e., separately administered and often separately owned) behavioral health plans that often reimburse psychologists. Providing services to patients with carved-out insurance can be problematic, inasmuch as psychologists are more frequently reimbursed from the behavioral health portion rather than the medical portion of health insurance benefits. In fact, particularly discouraging is the fact that carved-out behavioral health plans may proactively discourage thorough and formal psychological assessments, preferring a less expensive, routine diagnostic interview; a few have at times had a blanket prohibition against neuropsychological evaluations, and some do not ever cover testing for learning disabilities. When a patient's primary care services have been paid from a different portion of his or her health insurance coverage, there can be instances of no reimbursement being available for some psychological and neuropsychological assessment services—a situation that can prove very awkward in maintaining a good working relationship with a referral source.

Whatever the successes or failures of psychologists within initial managed care programs, the overall impact of initial approaches was not effective in reducing overall national health-care costs, which have continued to increase at unsustainable rates. Thus, other health-care containment solutions have been sought. Even though not yet visible to most health-care practitioners, a larger evolution within health care reimbursement systems is currently under way. Accountable health-care organizations (ACOs) are about to enter the national health-care marketplace out of necessity (McClellan, McKethan, Lewis, Roski, & Fisher, 2010). ACOs will likely become the primary force that drives health-care reimbursement in the United States, though that may take as many as 10 years to occur. There are two key differences between the initial managed care era and the evolving accountable care era: (a) Managed care was largely promoted and led by insurance companies and politicians, whereas the accountable care era requires medical leadership and health-care professionals to be actively involved in the development of the structure, mechanisms, and delivery; and (b) managed care largely involved reimbursement restrictions on the basis of access and volume allowed, whereas in ACOs, reimbursement (including incentives for higher reimbursement) is greatly affected by quality, engendering the phrase *pay for performance*. In the emerging era of ACOs, health-care organizations and providers will increasingly move from a position of being responsible only for providing clinical care (i.e., carrying the risk for clinical outcomes) to a position of being clinically responsible and also partially financially responsible (i.e., sharing the risk with insurers for financial outcomes). No one can yet predict how this health-care evolution will affect delivery of assessment services by psychologists.

*Medicare*

With the rapidly aging population, the need for more assessments of dementia and prior to presurgical interventions may prove to be necessary. It is estimated that by the year 2020, 18% of the United States population (approximately 52 million people) will be over the age of 65. Therefore, understanding how Medicare functions is imperative for psychologists. Within each region of the United States, Medicare establishes what it considers to be acceptable (i.e., reimbursable) clinical care and the billing procedures required in order to obtain partial reimbursement of standard charges for clinical services. Although the specifics are well known to vary from region to region (e.g., the maximum number of hours for neuropsychological assessment per patient that can be considered without special documentation), there are some general overarching issues in all Medicare regions. For example, the most important consideration in providing psychological assessments to Medicare patients is the documentation of *medical necessity*. In most instances, the documentation of medical necessity is provided by the fact that a physician generated the referral. When bills are submitted, the referring physician's unique physician identifier number (UPIN) is submitted along with patient and provider identification and billing charges.

However, Medicare can deem certain clinical procedures identified by current procedural terminology (CPT) codes—often linked to certain diagnoses, identified by International Classification of Diseases (ICD) codes—as not medically necessary, even with physician referral. For example, in the Illinois and Wisconsin Medicare region, neuropsychological evaluation is considered *not* medically necessary if the diagnosis is adjustment disorder, not otherwise specified; therefore, the billing would not be reimbursed. Despite the fact that the diagnosis cannot be known in advance, providers must take responsibility for understanding the Medicare rules and policies concerning psychological and neuropsychological assessments within their region. Such procedures as the Minnesota Multiphasic Personality Inventory–Second Edition (MMPI-2) must be billed using a psychological test procedure code, even if contained within a neuropsychological testing battery. As a final example, a mental status procedure, such as the Mini Mental Status Examination (MMSE), is considered part of a diagnostic interview and should not be billed with a neuropsychological assessment code. Those who fail to follow such rules run the risk of rejected bills at the minimum and audits and possible legal and financial penalties at the maximum.

A second major issue pertaining to Medicare and especially relevant to psychological assessment in medical settings is the *incident to* provision. Basically, with regard to clinical psychology, this provision requires that when providing psychological assessment or treatment to hospitalized patients, the licensed psychologist whose name appears on the bill must provide all services submitted to Medicare for partial reimbursement. That is, the time and associated charges for testing assistants who are in the employ of the psychologist and who provide part of the services to a Medicare *inpatient* will not be reimbursed. This problem can be substantial for busy hospital-based consultation programs. In fact, survey data indicate that in 2010, 61.7% of board-certified neuropsychologists (American Board of Clinical Neuropsychology, ABPP-other, and American Board of Professional Neuropsychology) used assistants in carrying out formal evaluations (Sweet, Giuffre Meyer, Nelson, & Moberg, 2011). From a broader and larger sample of the memberships of Division 40 and the American Academy of Clinical Neuropsychology (AACN) in 2010, the same study found that 51% of clinical neuropsychologists were using assistants (Sweet et al., 2011).

*Payer Mix*

As noted previously, psychologists working in medical settings such as hospitals and other types of formal healthcare organizations may be part of large health-care provider groups. As such, individual members may be forced to take referrals from a variety of payer sources, including those for whom there is very poor reimbursement for psychological and neuropsychological assessment services as defined by managed care contracts and/or those for whom there is no reimbursement possible at all. Unlike clinicians in private practice, providers working in institutions are likely to not have the choice of so-called cherry picking (i.e., accepting referrals with ability to pay most or all of billing charges while declining to see patients with little or no insurance coverage). Similarly, a recent national survey of clinical neuropsychologists (Sweet et al., 2011) showed a lower proportion of forensic cases, which are known to pay full fee, and self-pay cases among those providing assessment services in medical institutions compared to private practice. As discussed in the section regarding managed care, loss of freedom to decline patients can be a negative incentive for psychologists who practice as employees or affiliates to provider groups in some medical settings.

## Consultation-Liaison and Emergency Referrals

Some of the formal assessment services provided within medical settings are associated with a degree of timeliness that requires special consideration not normally seen outside of medical settings. Psychologists providing assessment services within medical settings may be asked to interrupt their daily activities to provide very rapid response to an inpatient. For example, a brief baseline neuropsychological screening of a patient scheduled for imminent surgery may be requested, or the abrupt change of mental status in a hospitalized cardiac patient with heretofore normal neurological status may bring in requests for rapid consultations from neurology, psychiatry, and neuropsychology. Such requests are unique to medical settings in their requirements of extremely rapid assessment and feedback to the referral source. There is no time for insurance carriers to authorize services in advance of this type of clinical psychological assessment.

## Financial Efficacy of Assessment

As the expenditure of health-care monies has come under closer scrutiny, questions regarding containing costs of insurance coverage for psychological assessment have grown to include demonstration of financial efficacy. Ambrose (1997) described some of the scant research regarding this issue; Groth-Marnat (1999) proposed seven rational strategies that can be used to enhance financial efficacy of clinical assessment. Given the increased pressure for rapid services, efficiency of service delivery (often related to needing to see more patients within the same amount of time), and cost containment within institutional medical settings, Groth-Marnat's recommendations seem particularly well suited to psychological assessment within medical settings. These recommendations were:

- Focus on domains most relevant for treatment planning and outcomes.
- Use formal assessment for risk management.
- Target conditions most likely to result in financial efficacy.
- Use computer-assisted assessment.
- Use time-efficient instruments.
- More closely link assessment, feedback, and intervention.
- Integrate treatment planning, monitoring progress, and evaluating outcome.

With these considerations in mind, Groth-Marnat (1999) suggested that research pertaining to financial efficacy of formal psychological assessment include specific impacts on cost benefit (financial gain resulting from an expenditure), cost effectiveness (gains in such areas as quality of life [QOL] and wellness that cannot easily be expressed in monetary units), cost offset (expenses reduced by utilizing a less expensive procedure in place of one that is more expensive), and cost containment (general efforts to reduce costs through limiting procedures covered or frequency of service utilization). The question is not whether there is empirical support for psychological assessment activities in health-care settings (Kubiszyn et al., 2000; Meyer et al., 2001); it is whether these activities can be justified on an economic basis. It is not difficult to imagine that although relevant financial efficacy research data will be very helpful in answering this question at the national level, the most salient information may be that which is gathered at the local level and targeted to specific service delivery systems. In this latter regard, the prominence of the scientist-practitioner approach, a mainstay of individual and programmatic service delivery of clinical psychologists in medical settings (Rozensky, Sweet, & Tovian, 1997; Sweet, Rozensky, & Tovian, 1991), seems ideally suited to the task. An entire book has been dedicated specifically to cost outcome research and assessments by clinical neuropsychologists (Prigatano & Pliskin, 2003). Additionally, evidence suggests that psychological evaluations have the potential to produce significant cost offsets in medical settings. Cost offset has been examined most frequently in the chronic pain population (Blount et al., 2007; Bruns, 2009). The American Academy of Clinical Neuropsychology Foundation (AACNF) has emphasized the importance of outcome studies on cost effectiveness and has developed the AACNF Outcome Studies Grant Program to fund these studies.

The differences between cost-effectiveness, cost-utility, cost-benefit, and cost-offset analysis in relation to how they relate to psychology practice have been delineated (Goodheart, 2010; Kaplan & Groessl, 2002). Cost effectiveness examines the monetary value of resources used in relation to clinically based health outcomes. Cost utility examines the monetary value of resources used in relation to quality-of-life health outcomes. Cost benefit examines the monetary value of resources used in relation to the monetary value of resources saved in an effort to reduce overutilization of health-care services. Cost offset examines the monetary value of resources used in relation to when a service saves money independent of any health benefits. Results of research examining the economic effect that a specific psychological practice or assessment has can vary greatly depending on what analytical approach is used. Therefore, it is important to know the differences between these types of economical analyses in order to best apply them to clinical practice.

## Ethical and Legal Issues

### Ability to Give Informed Consent for Assessment

*Informed consent* is defined by the 2002 APA ethics code, section 3.10 (American Psychological Association, 2002), as:

> When psychologists conduct research or provide assessment, therapy, counseling, or consulting services in person or via electronic transmission or other forms of communication, they obtain the informed consent of the individual or individuals using language that is reasonably understandable to that person except when conducting such activities is mandated by law or governmental regulation or as otherwise provided in this Ethics Code. (p. 1065)

The APA ethics code was revised in 2002; under section 9 there are many revisions pertinent to informed consent for assessment purposes (see American Psychological Association, 2002). The revised ethics code also now describes instances in which informed consent is not necessary (section 9.03), which includes when the purpose of testing is to evaluate decisional capacity or is mandated by law or governmental regulations. Concerns regarding the need for documenting informed consent for assessment—as has been more common with treatment—have been well articulated and appear cogent. (See Johnson-Greene, Hardy-Morais, Adams, Hardy, & Bergloff, 1997, for a discussion pertaining to neuropsychological assessment.) Yet unique aspects of medical settings increase the likelihood that ethical guidelines may conflict with patient-related situations that may be uncommon—or even nonexistent—in other practice settings. First, within medical settings, there are more likely to be seriously ill patients whose conditions may impair or at least bring into question their ability to give consent for diagnostic testing and treatment. As the APA has moved toward more explicit guidelines and expectations regarding the need for informed written consent for treatment *and* assessment, the ethical dilemma for practitioners engaged in assessments with seriously ill patients has increased meaningfully. For example, when a medical inpatient becomes a management problem and also refuses treatment, it is appropriate for physicians to call on colleagues, such as clinical psychologists and neuropsychologists, to better determine the problem and related solutions. A medical inpatient who is not able to understand the dire consequences of refusing treatment that would correct the underlying medical situation and also return the patient to competent cognitive status may not have the legal right to refuse the treatment agreed on by physicians and responsible family members. However, what if the assessment that objectively would document the cognitive incapacity and the need for others to judge the medical necessity of treatment is not possible because the patient also will not cooperate in providing written informed consent? Is a psychologist vulnerable to legal or ethics action if the assessment is carried out without informed consent? At present, there is no completely satisfying answer for this difficult situation. When informed consent cannot be obtained because the patient is either uncooperative due to delirium or not competent to be truly informed due to dementia, many practitioners rely on the direction and approval of close family members before proceeding. The notion of considering and including family members in a process of medical decision making rests on a philosophical position that views informed consent as a collaborative decision-making *process* in which values and thinking related to informed consent "are not the hidden and privileged property of the individual" (Kuczewski, 1996, p. 35). The direction of decisions derived in such a process is best documented in writing, with an endorsing signature of a family member, if possible. However, it is also noteworthy that inpatient services will at times be requested when it appears that no patient family member is available to sign consent for the evaluation or for the release of information. Under such circumstances, the psychologist may have no choice but to document in writing that consent could not be obtained, before proceeding. This topic brings us to the next section, which is related.

### Competency Issues in Medical Settings

Inpatient medical settings are more likely than any other type of outpatient clinical setting to involve questions pertaining to competency. Competency is a legal concept, not a medical concept, which—in order to be established as present or absent by legal standards—relies on observations, opinions, and data from health-care providers. Melton, Petrila, Poythress, and Slobogin (1997) noted multiple delineations of competency pertaining to criminal matters, including competency to: consent to search or seizure, confess, plead guilty, waive the right to counsel, refuse an insanity defense, testify, and be sentenced and executed. These authors also noted numerous civil competencies, which have more bearing in psychological assessment with medical inpatients. These are competency to make treatment decisions, competency to consent to research, and testamentary competency. Although the latter two types have relevance, competency to make treatment decisions is perhaps the most salient within medical settings (e.g., Feenan, 1996; Pollack & Billick, 1999) and in particular for psychologists performing inpatient psychological assessments. Setting aside the legal discussion of relevant constructs, the sum of which surpasses the space limitations of this chapter, competence to accept or refuse treatment fundamentally requires:

> At a minimum the clinician will want to learn the patient's understanding of the nature and purpose of the treatment; its risks and benefits; and the nature, risks, and benefits of alternative treatments. Under the "appreciation" and "reasonable process" test of competency, it will also be important to determine the patient's reasons for consenting or refusing consent. (Melton et al., 1997, p. 355)

The notion of whether a patient is capable of understanding relevant facts and circumstances is part of virtually all types of competency and is the fundamental reason that psychologists are often called on to provide quantitative evidence of cognitive capacities when issues regarding competency arise. To serve this purpose, psychological test data pertaining to verbal reasoning, learning and memory, and other cognitive domains can be used—in conjunction with information and observations of physicians and others—to assist a judge in establishing the legal presence of competence or incompetence (e.g., Marson, Chatterjee, Ingram, & Harrell, 1996; Marson & Harrell, 1999; Marson, Hawkins, McInturff, & Harrell, 1997). A variety of specific quantified cognitive measures have been constructed for the purpose of addressing issues of competency in medical settings (e.g., Billick, Bella, & Burgert, 1997; Etchells et al., 1999; Glass, 1997; Grisso, Appelbaum, & Hill-Fotouhi, 1997; Holzer, Gansler, Moczynski, & Folstein, 1997; Marson et al., 1997).

Whereas it has been advocated that children and adolescents—within the limits of cognitive and social development—be involved in medical decision making (McCabe, 1996), minors may not have an absolute right to consent to or refuse medical treatment (cf. Williams, Harris, Thompson, & Brayshaw, 1997). That is, although it may be best from a psychological standpoint to involve children and adolescents in decision making regarding their own medical care, legal standards ultimately bestow final authority to parents or legal guardians.

From both legal and medical perspectives, lack of competence to participate in informed consent and make decisions with regard to treatment has implications for helping patients make decisions regarding advanced directives,

such as health-care power of attorney and a living will (Ahmed, 1998; Chen & Grossberg, 1997). These decisions require adequate cognitive capacity. For that reason, patients with medical conditions in which illness progression is likely to lead to cognitive incapacity should be educated early regarding the importance of completing advance directives and taking care of personal financial matters (including a legal will that requires that legal standards of testamentary competence be met) while it is still possible to do so. More recently, with the rapidly aging population and the challenges of assessment of older adults came the need for a *Handbook for Psychologists on the Assessment of Older Adults with Diminished Capacity*, which was published by the American Bar Association and the APA Committee on Aging in 2008. This text reviewed psychological assessment of six civil capacities, including informed consent capacity for medical decisions.

Another important arena for psychologists that has been explored in relation to competency is forensic assessment. There are five components of legal competencies, which include functional abilities, causal inferences, person–context interactions, judgment, and disposition (Grisso, 2003). Of these five components, Grisso has stated that psychological assessment for competency most often examines the person's functional abilities, which includes examining what the person understands, knows, believes, or can do.

## Unique Quality-of-Life Versus Death Issues

With the advent of sophisticated medical technology that can prolong life, occasionally at the cost of QOL, some seriously ill patients within medical settings may bring the need for very complex decisions to physicians, psychologists, and other health-care professionals. With examples such as choosing to forgo dialysis for renal disease (Moss, 2001; O'Hare, Rodriguez, Hailpern, Larson, & Tamura, 2010) and determining a consensual threshold beyond which slowing the progression of Alzheimer's disease may not serve the patient (Hughes, 2000) and hastened death requests associated with terminal illness (Farberman, 1997; Hendin, 1999), it seems that the choice to discontinue life-prolonging treatment becomes an issue worthy of consideration. Psychologists working in certain specialty programs, especially as technology to keep very ill patients alive continues to improve, can expect to be involved with other health-care professionals in attempting to establish the presence or absence of certain factors (e.g., treatable depression, serious cognitive compromise) in an individual case. In part, the contribution of the psychologist in assisting with this differential diagnosis may come from formal psychological assessment. For example, Smithline, Mader, and Crenshaw (1999) demonstrated that on the basis of formal intellectual testing, as many as 20% to 32% patients with acute myocardial infarction probably had insufficient capacity to give informed consent to participate in emergency medicine research. Without formal psychological testing, only 8% of these patients were suspected of having insufficient capacity for informed consent.

### Limits of Confidentiality

Medical settings may present unique concerns regarding confidentiality. Whether inpatient or outpatient, numerous medical settings involve multiple clinicians and sometimes multiple disciplines. Patients and other health-care professionals outside of psychology may or may not understand the realities of confidentiality with regard to such settings. For example, multidisciplinary outpatient clinics and inpatient medical settings often maintain, at the specific direction of the JCAHO, a single centralized chart, wherein all medical, nursing, and mental health records are stored. For psychologists providing formal assessment services within such settings, there may be a pressure to store psychological test results in this single patient chart, even though state law and professional guidelines and ethics standards may require storage in a separate chart. In order to maintain adequate test security of the test forms, questions, and answers as well as to protect unnecessary disclosure by another party (e.g., medical records department staff) of detailed personal and psychological information, a separate psychological testing record should be maintained. To accomplish this task, clinic, hospital, and office support staffs need to be educated about the special circumstances pertaining to storage and maintenance of psychological test records. When applicable (e.g., when a formal psychological test report is to be placed in a common inpatient hospital chart), patients should be informed of the degree to which psychological test information may be accessed by others. Alternatively, the psychologist can proactively adopt policies to safeguard against unimpeded access; for example, psychological test reports can be provided only to the referral source rather than placed in a common file.

Some unique ethical and legal issues associated with medical settings relate to the dying patient. In the course of an assessment of an inpatient whose terminal condition has just been discovered, the patient might ask a psychologist for information that has not yet been shared with him or her by the rest of the health-care team. Or the dying patient may divulge important and previously unknown psychological information that would be destructive to the rest of the family if that information were shared and divulged by the health-care team, the members of which in turn may not understand the patient's reactions without being informed of the provocative information. Alternatively, what should a psychologist do if while evaluating a dying patient, the patient confesses to serious illegal activities that would almost certainly result in prosecution, *if* he or she survived?

In some states, mental health records are subject to different regulations to protect the patient's confidentiality. Increasingly, medical systems are moving toward electronic medical records, which can ultimately increase opportunities for an integrated record and increase of communication between psychologists and physicians. Electronic medical records pose a specific problem regarding confidentiality of mental health information and therefore should be accessible only to treating mental health care professionals, with a special firewall blocking other physicians from access to them. One example of this mental health firewall creating difficulty is when an information-sharing need arises, as when physicians collaborate in patient care as part of a concussion program, but are unable to access the psychologist or neuropsychologists report in the electronic medical record. Psychologists are required to provide their patients with additional information regarding the protection of their medical records, based on the HIPAA (Health Information Portability and Accountability Act) Privacy Rule, which created national standards to protect individuals' medical records and personal health-care information.

### Limits of Recommendations for Medical Patients

Medical patients have a variety of assessment and treatment needs, some of which are addressed by psychologists and others of which are either outside the scope of psychological practice or not part of the services requested by the physician referral source. Practices that are outside the scope of training and licensure may appear at first glance to be clear-cut. However, conflicts can arise when referral questions raised by the referral source are not within the individual psychologist's expertise (e.g., frequent questions from physicians regarding the psychologist's suggested choice of medication after an assessment-based recommendation is made for an antidepressant medication evaluation). Whether the psychologist has considerable relevant expertise pertaining to such a scenario determines the limits of responses that can be made, all of which must be within current licensing limits.

Conflict may also arise when the referral question and assessment-based recommendations for the patient do not match. For example, if an assessment pertaining only to impaired memory uncovers suicidal ideation and a suicidal plan, presumably no one would suggest that the psychologist should not recommend appropriate treatment, regardless of the specialty or original referral interests of the referring physician. However, in less emergent circumstances, when asked to assess a particular facet of an individual (e.g., psychological readiness for surgery intended to relieve chronic back pain), if additional unrelated needs are identified (e.g., a long-standing learning disability that obstructs a lifelong dream of obtaining a college degree), should treatment recommendations related to the latter issue be included, even if they are not relevant to the reason for the consultation and not within the purview of the referral source? To elaborate further, psychological assessment services within medical settings are often delivered when the psychologist is in the role of a consultant to another health-care professional, most often a physician. In such a situation, the purview and associated latitude of recommendations appear more limited than they would be if the psychologist were being consulted directly by a patient who held the expectation that the psychologist would be in the role of primary responsibility for the broad range of caring for the patient's psychological needs.

## Logistics

The amount of time within which a psychologist provides assessment services to patients is quite different on an inpatient unit than it is in outpatient practice. In fact, three separate time intervals are considered critical to the provision of responsive inpatient services: (a) starting with the referral being received, time to begin the evaluation; (b) time to complete the evaluation; and (c) time to provide feedback (usually in the form of a written report) regarding the evaluation findings. Currently, as a result of shortened hospital stays, the total time available for all three phases of completing a psychological or neuropsychological evaluation of an inpatient often is less than 3 days. Barring difficulties that cannot be controlled, such as patient unavailability and patient lack of cooperation, it is not uncommon in our own hospital system to complete all three phases within 1 to 2 days. It is important for the inpatient process to occur quickly, which requires that the clinician can be notified immediately of the consult (e.g., by being paged) and can respond quickly to the consult, carry out the assessment, and convey the summary of the

evaluation in a timely manner. In order for this to occur, many psychologists conduct a shorter evaluation and write a briefer report than is typically associated with outpatient evaluations.

## Special Instruments and Issues

Assessments in some medical settings require particular attention to the possibilities that (a) the patient may have limited ability to respond, (b) the patient may be seriously ill and possibly infectious, and (c) the nature of the case may require unusual or special testing procedures, equipment, or both. These types of issues are usually not found outside of medical settings. The presence of such issues requires that the psychologist performing assessments (a) maintain a wide array of testing options in order to be able to assess even the most frail medically ill patients at bedside in their hospital rooms; (b) be aware of universal precautions (generally accepted practices for preventing the spread of infection within hospitals) and the possible need to disinfect or dispose of test materials if they become contaminated; and (c) be able to foresee and employ assessment techniques for patients who may be recently or chronically physically, sensorily, or cognitively handicapped. Given the greater acuity of illness currently required to satisfy admission requirements to inpatient hospital programs and the shorter length of hospital stays, decreasing numbers of these patients are suitable for traditional standardized testing instruments.

## ASSESSMENT WITHIN A BIOPSYCHOSOCIAL MODEL

In medicine, the goals of clinical diagnosis are to identify the ongoing disease process and to formulate a plan to deal with the disease. When psychosocial factors are added to the medical symptomatology, the patient cannot be seen as a single entity that carries a group of predictable or constant symptoms requiring evaluation. Rather, psychosocial factors interact with the patient's premorbid personality to create a changing pattern. Under these circumstances, clinical analysis must not only systematically evaluate these varied elements but also clarify their interrelationships and changes over time. Current behaviors and attitudes are assessed in conjunction with the physical basis of the presenting problem. Premorbid background is delineated in an effort to clarify the person's baseline and the historical context for the medical condition. Moreover, using the biopsychosocial model (Belar & Deardorff, 2009; Engel,

1977; Nicassio & Smith, 1995) clinical health psychology has been able to move from an ineffectual model supporting mind–body duality to a model that considers influences of culture, environment, behavior, and beliefs on physiology and symptomatology. This model is not an end point in understanding medical patients, but it can serve as an organizing schema for identifying diagnostic questions. Within this approach an attempt is made to assess the interaction of the *type* of data collected (affective, behavioral, cognitive, or physiological information) with the *source* from which the data can be collected (the patient, his or her environment, or both).

The goal of a psychologist performing assessments in medical settings is to contribute to a broader understanding of the patient. This information can include an understanding of the patient within his or her physical and social environment; the patient's relative psychological assets and weaknesses; evidence of psychopathology contributing to, in reaction to, or separate from the physical disease process; the patient's response or predicted response to both illness and the medical or surgical treatment regimen; and identification of the coping skills being used by the patient and family (Belar & Deardorff, 2009). In addition, the psychologist can be especially helpful to the health-care team, the patient, and the patient's family in assessing the complicated questions surrounding issues of malingering, factious disorders, the interaction of psychological disorders and medical disorders, or the problems of the *worried well* (i.e., individuals who are healthy but nevertheless have health concerns that lead to medical consultation) seen in the medical setting (Rozensky et al., 1997).

More recently, with the changes in health care, insurance reform, managed care, and reimbursement policies pressures have been placed on psychologists to diversify. With the changes in the primary care setting some have proposed new models, such as the *chronic illness model* or *integrated care model*. The integrated care model incorporates primary care physicians with psychologists working off of a biopsychosocial model, rather than a strict biomedical model, and stressing team-based care (Bluestein & Cubic, 2007). Some clinical psychology internship programs, such as Eastern Virginia Medical School, have started to include training about integrated care and experience in primary care settings. (See Bluestein & Cubic, 2007, for a description of the training model.) Liu and colleagues (2003) have found the integrated care model to be cost effective even in large health-care systems.

## General Issues

### Modalities

Assessment information comes from a variety of sources. These sources include interviews, questionnaires and inventories (self-reporting), self-monitoring, direct observation of behavior, and psychophysiological measurement. Each measurement modality must be evaluated uniquely to identify which sources lead to the most valid and relevant information.

The interview provides the foundation of the assessment process. Interviewing the medical patient requires the basic skills needed in evaluating patients in any setting. Basic to all effective interviewing, the clinician must be able to empathize and develop rapport, gather information relevant to the referral question, make adjustments as a function of process issues and patient characteristics, understand the importance of timing in the disease process and medical treatment intervention, and utilize a theoretical framework to guide the assessment process. More information on the interview process and other modalities in assessment with medical patients can be found in Behel and Rybarczyk (2010); Hersen and Turner (1994); Pinkerton, Hughes, and Wenrich (1982); and Van Egren and Striepe (1998).

Self-report measures are advantageous when external observers cannot achieve sufficient access to that which is being measured (e.g., affect or attitude), cost is crucial, staff time is at a premium, or trained clinicians are not available. Clinical observer rating scales and interviews are usually preferred in situations in which clinical judgment is essential (e.g., diagnosis), the disease process or disability has robbed the patient of the ability to report accurately (e.g., delirium or dementia), or sophisticated clinical decisions are required (e.g., neuropsychological testing). Clinical experience has demonstrated that certain constructs (e.g., QOL) are best measured via self-report; other measurement tasks have been determined to often require judgment from clinical observers (e.g., diagnostic assessment from the *Diagnostic and Statistical Manual of Mental Disorders, Fourth Edition, Text Revision*; American Psychiatric Association, 1994). Other aspects of psychological assessment (e.g., psychological distress) may be approached through either modality (Derogatis, Fleming, Sudler, & DellaPietra, 1995).

### Timing

Another important general issue involves the specific point in time that an assessment occurs. The natural history of many medical conditions may include specific events that place stress on patients' coping abilities. Medical interventions also have noxious side effects that cause psychological effects. Baseline assessment prior to the introduction of any significant treatment intervention would be useful. In addition, it would be ideal if psychological assessments could coincide with major medical diagnostic evaluations and interventions so that information on a patient's psychological state could be integrated with the overall clinical picture and treatment plan. Finally, with many chronic illnesses, a comprehensive yearly psychological assessment focusing on QOL, coping efficacy, and possible psychological distress completed during scheduled medical visits could yield crucial information as the illness, the treatments, or both change over time.

## Normative Standards

Crucial to effective psychological assessment of medically ill patients is the selection of the most appropriate normative standards, or *norms*, to use as referents (e.g., general population norms or illness-specific population norms) when using self-report inventories. The identification of appropriate norms is based on the nature of the comparison that the psychologist wishes to make and the specific question that is addressed. If the basic question is whether the patient's psychological distress has reached clinical proportions, the general population norm may be used because it is much more likely to have well-established so-called caseness criteria associated with it. Comparison with a general norm addresses this question: Does this patient have a psychological problem of sufficient clinical magnitude to require a therapeutic intervention? Alternatively, if the referral question concerns the quality of a patient's adjustment to the illness at a particular stage in comparison with the typical patient, an illness-specific norm is indicated (Derogatis et al., 1995). Therefore, referral questions involving psychological distress and psychiatric disorder are often sufficiently salient to generalize across groups of patients. Adjustment to a particular illness is a construct that is much more illness-specific and may require the psychologist to interpret adjustment profiles in terms of specific illness stages.

Some variables, such as QOL, are best assessed in a manner that combines normative data from both general and illness-specific populations. Quality-of-life measures often generate a very broad-spectrum continuum—from a status reflecting optimum health, social functioning, and so forth, to one of indicating serious deterioration of

well-being at the other end. In addition, specific medical disorders often involve specific symptoms, problems, and disabilities that require detailed assessment. Investigators assessing QOL (Derogatis et al., 1995; Mayou, 1990) often use a modular strategy combining both norms. In this paradigm, the illness-specific module may be treated as an additional domain of the general inventory instrument or as a distinct, individual measure.

## Assessment Measures

In their review of psychological assessment, Derogatis et al. (1995) identified five constructs or attributes to measure in patients with medical disease: (1) well-being or affect balance, (2) psychological distress, (3) cognitive functioning, (4) psychosocial adjustment to illness, and (5) personality or health-related constructs. To this end, the authors recommended several screening instruments to delineate whether the patient has a psychological disorder requiring treatment or influencing medical treatment. Screening instruments are not diagnostic tests per se; rather, they represent an attempt to describe whether the patient has a high probability of having a certain condition in question (positive) or a low probability of the condition (negative). Those with positive screening can be further evaluated. The screening instrument should both be reliable (i.e., consistent in its performance from one administration to the next—sensitivity) and have predictive validity (i.e., capable of identifying those with the disorder and eliminating those who do not).

Several examples of psychological and cognitive screening measures and a neuropsychological battery are presented in Tables 13.2, 13.3, and 13.4. The examples presented are not intended to be exhaustive. Instead, they represent some of the most popular and frequently cited in literature reviews on assessment in medical settings (Demakis, Mercury, & Sweet, 2000; Keefe & Blumenthal, 1982; Rozensky et al., 1997; Sweet et al., 1991). For more information on most of these measures, the reader is advised to consult Maruish (2000) and Derogatis et al. (1995). With regard to Table 13.3, Sweet et al. (1991) recommended that neuropsychological screening batteries be used with cases involving differential psychiatric versus neurological diagnosis, including patients with subtle to mild dementia, who require more extensive diagnostic information and more complex case management. These authors recommended that more comprehensive neuropsychological batteries be used with (a) rehabilitation cases, such as stroke and head injury; (b) neurological

**TABLE 13.2   Examples of Affect, Personality, Psychopathology, Interview, and Adjustment Measures Used Within Medical Settings**

**Affect Measures**

Beck Anxiety Inventory (BAI)

Beck Depression Inventory—II (BDI-II)

Beck Hopelessness Scale (BHS)

Center for Epidemiological Studies Depression Scale (CES-D)

Geriatric Depression Scale (GDS)

State-Trait Anxiety Inventory (STAI)

State-Trait Anger Expression Inventory—2 (STAXI-2)

**Personality Measures**

Millon Clinical Multiaxial Inventory—III (MCMI-III)

Minnesota Multiphasic Personality Inventory—2 (MMPI-2)

Minnesota Multiphasic Personality Inventory-2-Restructured Form (MMPI-2-RF)

Personality Assessment Inventory (PAI)

**Brief Measures of Psychopathology Symptoms**

Brief Symptom Inventory (BSI)

Illness Behavior Questionnaire (IBQ)

Symptom Checklist—90—Revised (SCL-90-R)

**Structured Clinical Interviews**

Schedule for Affective Disorders and Schizophrenia (SADS)

Structured Clinical Interview for *DSM IV-TR* (SCID)

**Psychological Adjustment to Illness**

Battery for Health Improvement—2 (BHI-2)

Millon Behavioral Medicine Diagnostic (MBMD)

Multidimensional Health Locus of Control (MHLC)

Psychological Adjustment to Illness—Self-Report (PAIS-SR)

SF-36 Health Survey

Sickness Impact Profile (SIP)

Ways of Coping Inventory (WOC)

**Quality of Life**

Quality of Life Inventory (QOLI)

*Source*: Adapted from Rozensky, Sweet, & Tovian (1997).

**TABLE 13.3   Examples of Measures Used for Neuropsychological Referrals Within Medical and Psychiatric Settings**

**Dementia and Delirium Rating Scales**

Delirium Rating Scale (DelRS)

Mattis Dementia Rating Scale—2 (DRS-2)

Mini-Mental State Exam (MMSE)

**Screening Batteries**

California Verbal Learning Test—Second Edition (CVLT-II)

Finger Tapping

Multilingual Aphasia Examination (MAE)

Repeatable Battery for the Assessment of Neuropsychological Status (RBANS)

Ruff Figural Fluency

Shipley-2

Stroop Color-Word Test

Trail Making

Wechsler Adult Intelligence Scale-IV Digit Symbol

Wechsler Memory Test—Fourth Edition (WMS-IV), select subtests

**Comprehensive Batteries**

Beck Anxiety Inventory (BAI)

Beck Depression Inventory—II (BDI-II)

Beck Hopelessness Scale (BHS)

Boston Naming Test (BNT)

California Verbal Learning Test—Second Edition (CVLT-II)

Gordon Diagnostic System (Vigilance, Distractibility)

Grooved Pegboard

Halstead-Reitan Battery

Minnesota Multiphasic Personality Inventory—2 (MMPI-2)

Minnesota Multiphasic Personality Inventory-2-Restructured Form (MMPI-2-RF)

Multilingual Aphasia Examination (Visual Naming, COWA)

Paced Auditory Serial Addition Test

Personality Assessment Inventory (PAI)

Ruff Figural Fluency Test

Shipley-2

Stroop Color-Word Test

Test of Nonverbal Intelligence—Third Edition (TONI-3)

Wechsler Adult Intelligence Scale—Fourth Edition (WAIS-IV)

Wechsler Memory Scale—Fourth Edition (WMS-IV)

Wide Range Achievement Test—Fourth Edition (WRAT-4)

Wisconsin Card Sorting Test (WCST)

*Source*: Adapted from Rozensky, Sweet, & Tovian (1997).

cases that may involve progression of a brain disorder across time, such as early cases of multiple sclerosis, systemic lupus erythematosus, or AIDS, and those that require baseline and interval testing in which a relatively diverse and unpredictable set of deficits is possible, as in cerebrovascular disease; (c) presurgical multidisciplinary evaluation of epilepsy cases; (d) learning disability cases; and (e) attention deficit hyperactivity disorder cases. Forensic neuropsychological cases also require a comprehensive battery (cf. Sweet, 1999). Additionally, tests that involve stand-alone electronic devices (i.e., Gordon Diagnostic System) or tests administered via computerized software (i.e., Victoria Symptom Validity Test; Immediate Postconcussion Assessment of Cognitive Testing) are a growing area of assessment development. For example, the Immediate Postconcussion Assessment of Cognitive Testing (ImPACT) computer-based neurocognitive test battery was designed specifically for sport-related concussion (Podell, 2004).

**TABLE 13.4   Examples of Measures Used Within Psychiatric Settings**

**Objective Personality Measures**

Millon Clinical Multiaxial Inventory—III (MCMI-III)

Minnesota Multiphasic Personality Inventory—2 (MMPI-2)

Minnesota Multiphasic Personality Inventory-2-Restructured Form (MMPI-2-RF)

Narcissistic Personality Inventory

Neuroticism, Extraversion, Openness Personality Inventory—Revised (NEO-PI-R)

Personality Assessment Inventory (PAI)

**Posttraumatic Stress Disorder Measures**

Clinician Administered Posttraumatic Stress Disorder Scale—Forms 1 & 2 (CAPS-1 & 2)

University of Pennsylvania Posttraumatic Stress Disorder Inventory

Impact of Event Scale—Revised

**Additional Self-Report Measures**

Alcohol Use Disorders Identification Test (AUDIT)

Beck Anxiety Inventory (BAI)

Beck Depression Inventory—II (BDI-II)

Beck Hopelessness Scale (BHS)

Dissociative Experiences Scale (DES)

Drug Abuse Screening Test (DAST-20)

Eating Disorders Inventory—2 (EDI-2)

State-Trait Anger Expression Inventory—2 (STAXI-2)

State-Trait Anxiety Inventory (STAI)

Yale-Brown Obsessive Compulsive Scale (Y-BOCS)

**Structured Clinical Interviews**

Schedule for Affective Disorders and Schizophrenia (SADS)

Structured Clinical Interview for *DSM-IV* (SCID)

*Source*: Adapted from Rozensky, Sweet, & Tovian (1997).

## Types of Referrals

The nature of a referral question depends on the psychologist's role in the specific medical program or setting (e.g., consultant or full service) and the referral source. Belar and Geisser (1995) outlined three broad areas of assessment: differential diagnosis, provision of treatment, and treatment planning. Differential diagnosis involves assessment of significant psychological contributions to illness. Assessment of the need for treatment can include assessment of patient readiness to undergo a procedure, need for treatment for a particular problem, reevaluation for readiness for the procedure after treatment is completed, and need for concurrent treatment to facilitate a favorable outcome. An example of such a referral would involve whether a patient is a good candidate for cardiac transplant despite being a smoker. In this instance, evaluation,

recommendation of smoking cessation intervention, and reevaluation after a period of smoking abstinence may be appropriate.

A final referral area involves assessment that provides an understanding of the concomitants of a chronic disease, the sequelae of a particular event, or reaction to illness, so as to facilitate either medical or psychological treatment planning. Examples include identifying problems of adherence to diabetic regimens, assessing individual and family coping strategies in a depressed cancer patient, and delineating cognitive deficits in a brain tumor patient to help in planning for appropriate support services.

Camic and Knight (2004) outlined guidelines to be used by medical staff who make assessment referrals. Referral sources are encouraged to refer when emotional or behavioral responses (a) interfere with the ability to seek appropriate treatment or to cooperate with necessary medical procedures, (b) cause greater distress than does the disease itself or increase disease-related impairment, (c) interfere with activities of daily living, or (d) result in curtailing of usual sources of gratification or result in disorganization so severe and inappropriate that it results in misinterpretation and distortion of events. Referrals of medical patients are also encouraged when psychological dysfunction is significant from the patient history (e.g., history of suicide attempt, substance abuse).

### Surgical Interventions

Positive psychological outcome of surgery is directly correlated with patients' ability to understand the proposed procedure, recognize its necessity, and tolerate the stress and discomfort associated with the procedure. Several problems, however, can require psychological evaluation and can serve as reasons for referral: a dysfunctional relationship with the surgeon or staff secondary to personality disorder, inability to understand and give consent, severe panic and refusal of surgery, and exacerbation of a preexisting psychiatric problem (e.g., depression, suicide risk).

There are two primary groups of determinants in the psychological adaptation of a patient to surgery. The first group consists of such variables as the patient's specific combination of salient medical variables (i.e., surgery site, reason for surgery), functional deficits resulting from surgery, rehabilitation potential, and the surgeon's psychological management of the patient. The second group consists of patient-related variables, such as the meaning that the patient attaches to the need for surgery and the site of the surgery, perception of the surgical consequences, the patient's psychological ability to tolerate a stressful event, and the relationship between patient and surgeon (Jacobsen & Holland, 1989).

Some degree of presurgery apprehension is normal. Patients with traumatic pasts (e.g., sexual or physical abuse) or premorbid psychiatric disorders can be among the most vulnerable to an abnormal level of fear. In addition to fear, patients can feel hopeless, angry, helpless, and depressed. In assessing the presurgery patient, the psychologist needs to consider salient factors associated with a particular site (e.g., mastectomy, which often involves cancer, altered body image, fear of loss of sexual attractiveness; cardiac surgery, with possible altered lifestyle postsurgery and the fact that the heart is viewed as synonymous with life).

Salient interview issues for the presurgery patient involve identifying the exact nature of the symptoms experienced (e.g., cognitive, affective, and somatic components). Interview questions should differentiate several possible characteristics:

- Avoidance often seen in phobias
- Flashbacks of previous medical, physical, or sexual trauma, all characteristic of a posttraumatic stress disorder (PTSD)
- Nervousness and anxiety for 6 months or more, often seen in generalized anxiety disorders
- Attacks of panic, fear, and dread for no apparent reason, characteristic of panic disorders
- A maladaptive response to a severe stressor, often seen in adjustment disorders

The interview can also highlight past compliance (or lack thereof) with medical personnel and medical regimen, the patient's perception of situational demands from surgery and sense of personal control, meanings attributed to the procedure and organ site, knowledge of pre- and postoperative procedures, and desire to obtain information about the procedure.

In addition to measures used to assess brief cognitive functioning, psychopathology, and affect, it may be useful to consider questionnaires pertaining to coping (e.g., Ways of Coping; Folkman & Lazarus, 1980) and locus of control (e.g., Multidimensional Health Locus of Control; Wallston, Wallston, & DeVellis, 1978) in presurgery assessment.

A spectrum of postoperative central nervous system dysfunctions, both acute and persistent, has been documented after cardiac surgical procedures, including stroke, subtle neurological signs, and overt neuropsychological impairment (Newman et al., 2001). In fact, Murkin, Newman, Stump, and Blumenthal (1995) summarized a group consensus statement from experts, highlighting the need for a standardized core battery of neuropsychological tests to be employed with cardiac surgery patients. The group consensus also indicated that mood state assessment should be evaluated concurrently because neuropsychological performance can be influenced by mood state. Although it is arguable whether the panel in its specific test recommendations achieved its stated purposes (i.e., identifying specific tests relevant to the postsurgical phenomenon documented in the literature that would minimize practice effects due to necessary repeat testing), the goals were sound. Although supplementary tests could be added as deemed appropriate, it was envisioned that a core battery could provide a basis for rational comparison across clinical outcome studies and eventually allow combination of study results by meta-analysis. The need for a core battery can also be relevant to other chronic illnesses such as diabetes, in which cognitive and affect changes occur over time (Strachan, Frier, & Deary, 1997).

### Organ Transplant Surgery

It is beyond the scope of this chapter to present a detailed discussion of the medical and psychological conditions of potential transplant patients. It is important to note, however, that consideration of organ transplantation is often precipitated by a major medical crisis with a chronic medical condition, and the possibility of death during and shortly after transplantation remains salient. Recent advances in bone marrow, renal, hepatic (liver), and cardiac transplantation have made organ transplantation a viable medical practice. (See Olbrisch, Benedict, Ashe, & Levenson, 2002, for a review.)

Organ transplantation remains extremely stressful for patients and their families and involves the allocation of scarce resources (Zipel et al., 1998). As of March 2011 there were 110,500 candidates waiting for donor organs nationwide (Organ Procurement and Transplantation Network, 2011). Noncompliant patient behavior following transplant surgery can endanger a graft and result in death. Serious psychopathology, including schizophrenia, major affective disorders, and certain personality disorders, may interfere with optimal self-care. Toward this end, psychological assessment goals with transplant patients may include (a) determining contraindications to transplant, (b) establishing baselines of affect and cognitive and coping skills for future reference or comparison, (c) identifying psychosocial problems and beginning preoperative intervention, and (d) establishing patient ability to understand the realities of program involvement and postsurgical rehabilitation (Olbrisch, Levenson, & Hamer, 1989).

Rozensky et al. (1997) have outlined a protocol for the assessment of transplant patients as well as psychological contraindications for transplantations. The interview can focus on issues involving knowledge of the transplantation experience and procedures, desire for and reservations about transplantation, adherence and compliance with medical regimen, premorbid health habits (e.g., weight control, exercise, substance abuse), and family reactions. In addition, the Psychological Adjustment to Illness Scale—Self-Report (PAIS-SR), with scoring norms using coronary heart disease patients and dialysis patients, can be helpful in assessing current adjustment to illness and predicting posttransplant patient compliance.

Several authors have assessed psychopathology in both pre- and postcardiac transplantation using diagnostic interviews with *DSM-IV* formats (Kay & Bienenfeld, 1991; Kuhn, Brennan, Lacefield, Brohm, Skelton, & Gray, 1990; Olbrisch & Levenson, 1991). From these data it appears that approximately 75% of candidates are accepted for cardiac transplant with no significant psychosocial contraindications, approximately 20% of candidates are accepted with preconditions (i.e., specific criteria to be met prior to acceptance, such as completion of weight loss or smoking cessation programs), and 5% are refused on psychosocial grounds. Olbrisch et al. (1989) summarized the ethical problems in the application of psychosocial criteria to transplant assessment—namely, allocating scarce organs and expensive care and technology to those patients likely to derive maximum benefit and longevity. The authors noted that ethical problems can involve confusing psychosocial factors predictive of survival with judgments of an individual's social worth (not regarded by most as acceptable grounds for choosing candidates), unjust decisions resulting from inconsistencies in the application of psychosocial criteria across transplantation centers, and use of criteria that are of questionable reliability and validity.

Olbrisch et al. (1989) developed the Psychosocial Assessment of Candidates for Transplantation (PACT) rating scale to objectify and allow scientific study of clinical decision making criteria in psychosocial assessment of transplantation candidates. Normed on 47 cardiac and liver transplant patients, the PACT was shown to have high interrater reliability, with 96% overall agreement between raters on whether to perform a transplant on a given patient. Less than 5% of all pairs of ratings disagreed by more than one category. The scale shows promise for studying the pretransplant psychosocial evaluation in process and can aid in learning how different programs weight various factors in selecting patients and how these decisions predict clinical outcome. Sears, Rodrigue, Sirois, Urizar, and Perri (1999) attempted to extend psychometric norms for precardiac transplant evaluations using several cognitive measures, affective functioning and adjustment measures, coping strategies, and quality-of-life measures.

Studies examining the QOL in heart and lung transplant recipients before and after surgery found correlations between extreme pretransplant anxiety levels and poorer posttransplant QOL (Cohen, Littlefield, Kelly, Maurer, & Abbey, 1998; Deshields, Mannen, Tait, & Bajaj, 1997). Stilley, Miller, Gayowski, and Marino (1999) found in a study of 73 candidates for liver transplant that past history of substance abuse correlated with more distress and less adaptable coping styles after transplantation.

There continues to be tremendous variability in the measures used for psychological and neuropsychological evaluations prior to transplant (Olbrisch et al., 2002). This continues to be an area in need of further investigation in order to establish empirically supported assessment guidelines.

### Bariatric Surgery

Obesity in the United States has reached epidemic proportions. At least 69 million Americans are considered significantly overweight and another 51 million are morbidly obese (body mass index > 40 and at least 100 pounds overweight) (Ritz, 2006). Recent medical advances have led to surgical treatment for the morbidly obese patient. Surgical stomach reconfiguration (i.e., gastric bypass) and constriction (e.g., lap band) have become the recommended treatments for bariatric surgery. Ritz (2006) noted that a presurgical psychological evaluation can assist the surgeon and other members of the surgical team: (a) assess the candidate's psychological readiness for surgery; (b) determine strategies to help the patient prepare for surgery; (c) develop individual treatment plans to help the patient make permanent lifestyle changes in eating behavior and exercise activities that are a necessary part of the treatment protocol; and (d) provide documentation for insurers to verify the suitability of the patient for bariatric surgery.

Franks and Kaiser (2008) recommended that the structured interview in an evaluation for bariatric surgery include questions about the patient's: (a) motivation for surgery; (b) expectations and goals about life following surgery; (c) knowledge about the surgery, including risks and benefits; (d) lifestyle and dietary changes the candidate has already made; and (e) personal strengths and liabilities affecting the candidate's possible responses to treatment.

In addition to behavioral observation during the evaluation, Franks and Kaiser (2008) also recommended the inclusion of questions about the candidate's (a) history of sexual or physical abuse; (b) alcohol, tobacco, or drug abuse; (c) history of surgeries; (d) family and social support; and (e) willingness to use available support.

Despite the variability of measures used prior to bariatric surgery, the authors of this chapter recommend that the assessment include some measure of:

- general psychopathology (i.e., MMPI-2-RF);
- enduring personality traits or characterological problems seen in medical populations (i.e., MBMD, BHI-2);
- affective symptoms (i.e., BDI-2, BAI, SCL-90);
- behavioral problems such as substance abuse potential, impulsivity, suicide ideation, problems of attention, coping style, motivation for treatment, and likelihood to comply with treatment and adhere to self-management guidelines (MMPI-2-RF, MBMD); and
- maladaptive eating attitudes and behaviors (i.e., EDI-2).

Both the MMPI-2-RF and MBMD, for example, have been normed with bariatric samples, and comparison scores can be provided.

### Spine Surgery

For the patient with chronic, intractable back pain, spine surgery offers the prospect of dramatic improvement. After careful patient selection and preparation, technically sophisticated surgical techniques such as nerve blocks, disk stabilizing procedures, and in-dwelling pain medication pumps, to name a few, can offer these patients some modicum of relief. Psychological assessment can provide information to help: (a) identify patients for whom psychological factors make it unlikely that spine surgery will be effective; (b) prepare patients to undergo the rigors of spine surgery; and (c) improve rehabilitation outcomes for chronic back pain patients (Block, Gatchel, Deardoff, & Guyer, 2003). The careful selection and assessment of back pain patients and the biopsychosocial aspects of pain treatment increase the probability of successful surgery. Block and his colleagues (2003) recommended a structured presurgery interview with measures involving assessment of personality and possible psychopathology (i.e., MMPI-2, MMPI-2-RF), affective states including depression, anxiety, and anger (i.e., BDI-2, BAI), coping strategies (i.e., Ways of Coping, Coping Strategies Questionnaire), and pain sensitivity measures (i.e., West Haven-Yale Multidimensional Pain Inventory [WHYMPI], Pain Patient Profile).

### Genetics

As the medical field continues to advance, further developments are made in terms of genetics and genetic testing. The current genetic predictive testing is largely limited to high-risk individuals for certain diseases, such as Huntington's disease and breast cancer. However, it is predicted that within the next decade there will be over 10 genetic tests for more common medical conditions. This advancement in science will bring about a new role for psychologists to play in terms of assessing a person's psychological functioning prior to genetic testing and neuropsychological testing to determine if the person is competent to consent to the procedure and then cognitively able to understand the results of such a test.

Patenaude, Guttmacher, and Collins (2002) outlined core competencies for psychologists working in the area of genetic testing. The authors also highlighted the significant roles psychologists can play in assessing and helping individuals with genetic concerns to cope with issues of vulnerability, optimize family interactions, and improve health behaviors. To this end, Cella and colleagues (2002) have developed the Multidimensional Impact of Cancer Risk Assessment Questionnaire (MICRA), which assists in identifying groups of vulnerable genetic testing participants after genetic testing for the BRCA-gene for breast cancer has been completed. The MICRA Questionnaire assesses several emotional factors, including distress, uncertainty, and positive outlook in post–genetic-tested cancer patients.

### Psychiatric Conditions

Patients with psychiatric conditions will be seen by psychologists in medical settings when they develop medical symptoms or because psychiatric treatment facilities exist within or adjacent to medical treatment facilities. The most recent prevalence rates from 2005 in the general population for any psychiatric disorder and any substance abuse-dependence disorder were estimated to be 46.4% and 14.6%, respectively. Prevalence rates for any anxiety disorder and any affective disorder for the same year were estimated to be 28.8% and 20.8%, respectively. Lifetime prevalence rates for these conditions were estimated to be 25% and 19%, respectively (Maruish, 2000). As summarized by Maruish (2000), there are significant comorbidity rates of depression with cancer (18%–39%), myocardial infarction (15%–19%), rheumatoid arthritis (13%), Parkinson's disease (10%–37%), stroke (22%–50%), and diabetes (5%–11%). The author also summarized studies that indicate between 50% and 70% of visits to primary care physicians have a psychosocial basis. These figures highlight the need for psychological assessment and screening of psychiatric disorders in medical settings.

Toward this end, the most frequently used instruments for screening and treatment planning, monitoring, and outcome assessment are measures of psychopathological symptomatology. These instruments were developed to assess behavioral health problems that typically prompt people to seek treatment. Frequently used psychopathology instruments are summarized in Table 13.4 and are reviewed in more detail by Rozensky et al. (1997), Sweet and Westergaard (1997), and Maruish (2000).

There are several types of measures of psychological-psychiatric symptoms. The first category is comprised of comprehensive multidimensional measures. These instruments are typically lengthy, multiscale, standardized instruments that measure and provide a graphic profile of the patient on several psychopathological symptom domains (e.g., anxiety, depression) or disorders (schizophrenia, antisocial personality disorder). Summary indexes provide a global picture of the individual with regard to his or her psychological status or level of distress. Probably the most widely used and recognized example of these multidimensional measures is the restandardized version of the MMPI-2 (Butcher, Graham, Ben-Porath, Tellegen, Dahlstrom, & Kaemmer, 2001).

The MMPI-2-RF (Restructured Form) represents an important development in multidimensional measures for both psychiatric symptoms and reactions to medical problems. The MMPI-2-RF is a 338-item, restructured version of the MMPI-2 developed as a subset of the MMPI-2 item pool with norms based on MMPI-2 samples. The MMPI-2-RF contains 51 scales, including 9 validity scales; 3 higher-order and 9 restructured scales assessing behavioral, thought, and affective dysfunction; 5 somatic/cognitive scales assessing complaints involving malaise, gastrointestinal, head pain, neurological, and cognitive complaints; 20 specific problem-area scales involving internalizing, externalizing, interpersonal, and interest domains; and 5 scales updated from the MMPI-2 involving major dimensions of personality pathology (Ben-Porath & Tellegen, 2008). The MMPI-2-RF is considered a broadband measure of personality and psychopathology that can be implemented in psychiatric and medical settings or wherever the MMPI-2 has been used. The MMPI-2-RF provides important information on patients' test-taking approaches, symptoms of psychopathology,

personality traits, and behavior proclivities. The MMPI-2-RF also provides improved efficiency (less patient time to complete compared to the MMPI-2), protocol validity, enhanced construct validity, expanded focus on somatic complaints, as well as comparison groups in medical settings (Binford & Liljequist, 2008; Thomas & Locke, 2010).

Ben-Porath and Tellegan (2008) report applications of the MMPI-2-RF in medical settings that include norms on chronic pain patients; chronic fatigue patients; life-threatening illness groups; presurgical screening on spine, bariatric, and organ transplant patients; and assessment of health-related behaviors involving coronary heart disease and smoking cessation. The authors also report applications of the MMPI-2-RF in neuropsychology assessments involving rehabilitation, disability claims, and personal injury litigation.

Multidimensional instruments can serve a variety of purposes that facilitate therapeutic interventions in medical and behavioral health-care settings. They may be used on initial patient contact to screen for the need for service and simultaneously offer information that is useful for treatment planning. These instruments might also be useful in identifying specific problems that may be unrelated to the patient's chief complaints (e.g., poor interpersonal relations). In addition, they generally can be administered numerous times during the course of treatment to monitor the patient's progress toward achieving established goals and to assist in determining what adjustments (if any) are needed to the intervention. In addition, pre- and post-treatment use of such instruments can provide individual treatment outcome data.

In a second category, abbreviated multidimensional measures are similar to the MMPI-2 and other comprehensive multidimensional measures in many respects. First, they contain multiple scales for measuring a variety of symptoms and disorders. They may also allow for the derivation of an index that can indicate the patient's general level of psychopathology or distress. In addition, they may be used for screening, treatment planning and monitoring, and outcome assessment, just like the more comprehensive instruments. These instruments, however, differ by their shorter length and ease by which they are administered and scored. Their brevity does not allow for an in-depth assessment, but this is not the purpose for which they were designed. Probably the most widely used of these brief instruments are Derogatis's family of symptom checklists, which include the Symptom Checklist-90-Revised (SCL-90-R) and the Brief Screening Inventory (BSI; Derogatis et al., 1995; Derogatis & Spencer, 1982).

The major advantage of the abbreviated multiscale instruments is the ability to survey—quickly and broadly—psychological symptom domains and disorders. Their value is evident in settings in which time and costs available for assessment are limited. These instruments provide a lot of information quickly and are much more likely to be completed by patients than are their lengthier counterparts. This is an important consideration if one is monitoring treatment or assessing outcomes, which requires at least two or more assessments to obtain the necessary information. Ironically, disadvantages of these instruments also relate primarily to decreased items: potential absence of or reduced effectiveness of validity scale items, decreased reliability, and, as noted earlier, restricted range of clinical content.

A third category consists of disorder-specific measures, which are designed to measure one specific disorder or family of disorders (e.g., anxiety, depression, suicidality, substance abuse). These instruments are usually brief, requiring 5 to 10 minutes to complete. They were thoroughly reviewed by Maruish (2000).

### Neuropsychological Dysfunction

Neuropsychological tests are designed to provide information related to the presence and degree of cognitive impairment resulting from brain disease, disorder, or trauma; in some instances, they also can provide information pertaining to diagnosis and etiology. The results of these tests also are used, for example, to draw inferences about the extent to which an impairment interferes with the patient's daily functioning, ability to return to work, and competency to consent to treatment. There are numerous psychometrically sound neuropsychological measures. (See Mitrushina, Boone, Razani, & D'Elia, 2005, or Strauss, Sherman, & Spreen, 2006, for a comprehensive review.) Some instruments assess only specific areas of functioning (e.g., immediate visual memory, naming ability). Others assess broader areas of functioning (e.g., a battery of memory measures that assesses immediate, intermediate, and long-term verbal and nonverbal memory). Still others are part of a battery of measures that aim to provide a more comprehensive assessment of neuropsychological functioning (e.g., a battery that include tests of memory, language, academic skills, abstract thinking, nonverbal auditory perception, sensorimotor skills). Examples of neuropsychological screening measures as well as examples of comprehensive batteries can be found in Table 13.3.

The top two referral sources for neuropsychologists are psychiatrists and neurologists (Sweet, Moberg, & Suchy,

2000). The typical referral question stemming from a psychiatric setting concerns discriminating between an emotionally based (or psychological) and a brain-based (or neurological) disorder. It is important to avoid the inaccurate and out-of-date conceptualization of functional versus organic as well as either/or dichotomous questions—that is, neurologically disordered individuals can also be psychologically disordered (e.g., depressed), and individuals with significant psychiatric disorders can develop neurological disorders.

Neurology patients are referred for assessment for a variety of reasons, including to (a) establish functioning before and after surgery or other medical intervention, (b) track recovery or deterioration of a known neurological disorder, (c) assist in differentiating psychiatric and neurological disorder, (d) assist in assigning relative contributions of multiple known disorders to clinical presentation, and (e) assist in identifying difficult diagnostic conditions for which there is little or no abnormality on neurological examination or medical diagnostic procedures. Patients with a wide range of neurological disorders are referred for neuropsychological evaluation; these disorders include traumatic brain injury, cortical degenerative diseases (e.g., Alzheimer's disease), subcortical degenerative diseases (e.g., Parkinson's disease), demyelinating disease (e.g., multiple sclerosis), cerebrovascular disease (hemorrhagic and thromboembolic stroke), primary and secondary brain tumors, seizure disorders, and brain infections (e.g., herpes simplex encephalitis).

Neuropsychological assessment referrals of patients in outpatient or inpatient rehabilitation typically are motivated by the need of the multidisciplinary rehabilitation team to understand each patient's emotional status and capacity. The two most common acute neurological conditions that lead to subsequent rehabilitation during which patients may be referred for neuropsychological evaluation are cerebrovascular stroke and traumatic brain injury. Another increasingly common reason for referral to a neuropsychologist is assessment of cognitive change following cancer treatment, such as chemotherapy, or after cardiac surgery. In fact, both of these topics have developed into collaborative research for neuropsychologists and physicians. Further discussion of the nature of referral questions from psychiatry, neurology, and rehabilitating medicine with neuropsychological assessment may be found in Rozensky et al. (1997). Demakis et al. (2000) reviewed neuropsychological screening measures and referral issues in general medicine and primary care.

A specific neuropsychological assessment referral that has become increasingly common is that of concussion or mild traumatic brain injury (mTBI), and, in particular, sport-related concussion. Research has indicated that as many as 3.8 million sport-related traumatic brain injuries may occur annually in the United States, and the incidence between sports widely varies (Guskiewicz & Mihalik, 2011). Specifically, a minimum of 1.5 million concussion injuries occur in American football in the United States alone (Bailes & Cantu, 2001). Neuropsychological assessment in sport-related concussion has become recognized as essential in providing the only quantitative measurement of injury effects. A National Academy of Neuropsychology position paper recommended "neuropsychological evaluation for the diagnosis, treatment, and management of sports-related concussion at all levels of play," which is now a mandate in the National Football League (NFL), National Hockey League, and in many other professional organizations of sport (Moser et al., 2007, pp. 910).

The assessment of PTSD and/or mTBI has recently become a referral focus of psychologists and neuropsychologists. This area of assessment has grown the most within the Veterans Affairs (VA) system due to the high number of Operation Iraqi Freedom and Operation Enduring Freedom veterans returning with these symptoms and complaints. When assessing patients for PTSD and mTBI, the potential for secondary gain should routinely be considered and addressed often through measures of symptom validity and symptom overreporting. (See Elhai, Sweet, Guidotti Breting, & Kaloupek, 2012 for a review.) A few of the assessment measures that have been found to be useful in the PTSD and mTBI population are the MMPI-2 (Butcher et al., 2001), PAI (Morey, 1991), Trauma Symptom Inventory (TSI; Briere, 1995), Victoria Symptom Validity Test (VSVT; Slick, Hopp, Strauss, & Thompson, 1997), and the Test of Memory Malingering (TOMM; Tombaugh, 1997).

## Psychosomatic Disorders

When patients are referred because one or more careful medical workups identify no clear physical findings, their physicians may proceed with diagnosis by exclusion. Because no somatic cause is found, it is hoped that psychological assessment will identify psychosocial or psychological factors that could be causing or maintaining the somatic symptoms. Such patients can also be referred to as experiencing "health anxiety" (Abramowitz & Braddock, 2008). Health anxiety or somatoform conditions involve physiologic, cognitive, and behavioral processes that can exert varying negative influences on one another. There is a tendency for somatic patients to be referred for

psychological evaluation as a last resort. Rozensky et al. (1997) outlined approaches to inform referral sources in making a referral for psychological evaluation as well as introducing the assessment to the somatoform patient to avoid increased resistance. The authors also supported a comprehensive evaluation utilizing specific interview questions, self-monitoring by the patient, and several questionnaires found in Table 13.2.

Bucholz, Dinwiddie, Reich, Shayka, and Cloninger (1993) reviewed three separate screening proposals for somatization disorder. They did not find any one proposal to be superior to the others; rather, selection of screening criteria should be dependent on the intended application. One of the screening proposals included in this review was proposed by Swartz, Hughes, and George (1986) as a brief screening index to identify patients with probable somatoform disorders. The index can be used in an interview format or by review of patient records. The patient's physical complaints are categorized according to 11 symptoms: abdominal pain, abdominal gas, diarrhea, nausea, vomiting, dizziness, fainting, weakness, feeling sickly, pain in extremities, and chest pain. To confirm a probable somatoform diagnosis, the patient must have at least 5 of the 11 symptoms *without* demonstrable medical findings.

Katon, Von Korff, Lipscomb, Russo, Wagner, & Polk (1990), focusing on the prognostic value of somatic symptoms, used the SCL-90-R to provide an operational definition of high distressed—high utilizers. The investigators observed linear increases in SCL-90-R dimension scores of Somatization, Depression, and Anxiety as they moved progressively through the somatic symptom groups from low to high.

Kellner, Hernandez, and Pathak (1992) related distinct dimensions of the SCL-90-R to different aspects of hypochondriasis. The authors observed high levels of the SCL-90-R Somatization and Anxiety scores to be predictive of hypochondriacal fears and beliefs, whereas elevations on Depression were not. Fear of disease correlated most highly with the SCL-90-R Anxiety score, but the false conviction of having a disease was more highly correlated with somatization.

Abramowitz and Braddock (2008) provided an extensive review of several inventories and measures developed to assess somatoform conditions and hypochondriasis. From the authors' reviews, the Short Health Anxiety Inventory (SHAI; Salkovskis, Rimes, Warwick, & Clark, 2002) is a desirable tool because it is fairly brief and assesses health concerns independent of whether the individual is actually medically ill. The measure has good reliability and validity in assessing the feared likelihood of becoming ill as well as the feared negative consequences of becoming ill.

### Alcohol and Substance Abuse

It is well documented that alcohol abuse and substance abuse are often comorbid with anxiety and depressive disorders. Many measures assess alcohol and substance use and abuse or have a scale examining these issues, such as the MMPI-2, MMPI-2-RF, PAI, and MCMI-III. Johnson, Brems, and Fisher (1996) compared psychopathology levels of substance abusers not receiving substance abuse treatment with those in treatment. They found SCL-90-R scores to be significantly higher for the majority of subscales for the treatment versus the non-treatment group. Drug abusers in treatment were found to have more psychological symptoms than were those not in treatment, except on the Hostility and Paranoid Ideation Scales, on which the nontreatment group had higher levels. The authors suggested that the presence of a comorbid condition is associated with a greater likelihood that drug abusers will seek treatment.

The Self-Administered Alcoholism Screening Test (SAAST) is a 37-item questionnaire that has been shown to have good reliability and validity when administered to a variety of patient samples. Patient acceptance has also been good when the use of alcohol is viewed as a health-care issue. Patient endorsement of test items on the SAAST has been an excellent starting point or screening prior to a clinical interview (Davis, 2000). The Alcohol Use Disorders Identification Test (AUDIT; Allen, Reinert, & Volk, 2001) is a brief self-report measure used for alcohol abuse screening. Test items address alcohol intake, alcohol dependence, and adverse consequences of drinking. The audit was developed through a collaborative effort through the World Health Organization. The DAST-20 (Skinner, 1982) was developed to screen for the abuse of illegal, over-the-counter, and prescribed drugs. It is not for the assessment of alcohol abuse. The DART-20 asks 20 questions that categorizes possible drug abuse over a continuum from "low abuse" to "severe abuse."

### Trauma and Sexual Abuse

Sexual abuse and physical abuse are factors associated with medical problems that are often overlooked. Individuals who experience such abuse also experience significant emotional distress and personal devaluation, which can lead to a chronic vulnerability and can compromise the effective treatment of their medical conditions. Many individuals who have been sexually abused exhibit clinical manifestations of anxiety or depressive disorders, without a clear understanding of the contribution made by their victim experiences (Derogatis & Savitz, 2000).

Some investigators have established the utility of the BSI in work with patients who have been sexually abused. Frazier and Schauben (1994) investigated the stressors experienced by college-age females in adjusting to the transition of college life. Significant correlations were found between the magnitude of stress and levels of psychological symptoms on the BSI. Survivors of sexual abuse had significantly higher total scores on the BSI. Coffey, Leitenberg, Henning, Turner, and Bennett (1996) also investigated the consequences of sexual abuse in 192 women with a history of childhood sexual abuse. Women who had been sexually abused revealed a higher total distress score on the BSI than did women in a nonabused control group, and a greater proportion of their BSI subscale scores fell in clinical ranges.

Toomey, Seville, Mann, Abashian, and Grant (1995) assessed a heterogeneous group of chronic pain patients and observed that those patients with a history of sexual abuse scored higher on the SCL-90-R than did nonabused patients. Similar findings were reported by Walker et al. (1995), who found that female patients with chronic pelvic pain had significantly higher symptomatic distress levels than did a patient group (tubal ligation) without pain. The mean score for chronic pelvic pain sufferers fell in the 60th percentile of psychiatric outpatient norms on the SCL-90-R. The pain group also revealed a significantly greater incidence of somatization disorders, phobias, sexual dysfunction, and sexual abuse as compared to the no-pain group. These studies suggest chronic pain may be another condition that is associated with sexual abuse.

## Quality of Life and Outcomes Research

Andrews, Peters, and Tesson (1994) indicated that most of the definitions of QOL describe a multidimensional construct encompassing physical, affective, cognitive, social, and economic domains. QOL scales are designed to evaluate—from the patient's point of view—the extent to which the patient feels satisfied with his or her level of functioning in the aforementioned life domains. Objective measures of QOL focus on the environmental resources required to meet one's need and can be completed by someone other than the patient. Subjective measures of QOL assess the patient's satisfaction with the various aspects of his or her life and thus must be completed by the patient. Andrews et al. (1994) indicated distinctions between QOL and health-related quality of life (HRQL) and between generic and condition-specific measures of QOL. QOL measures differ from HRQL measures in that the former assess the whole aspect of one's life, whereas the latter assesses quality of life as it is affected by a disease or disorder or by its treatment. Generic measures are designed to assess aspects of life that are generally relevant to most people; condition-specific measures are focused on aspects of the lives of particular disease-disorder populations. QOL scales also provide a means to gauge treatment success. One of the more widely used QOL measures is the Medical Outcomes Study Short Form Health Status (SF-36; Ware, 1993). The scale consists of 36 items, yielding scores on eight subscales: physical functioning, social functioning, body pain, general mental health, role limitations due to emotional problems, role limitations due to physical functioning, vitality, and general health perception. New scoring algorithms yielded two summary scales: one for physical functioning and one for mental functioning (Wetzler, Lum, & Bush, 2000).

Wallander, Schmitt, and Koot (2001) provided a thorough review of QOL issues, instruments, and applications with children and adolescents. Much of what they proposed is clearly applicable to QOL measurement in adult patients. The authors concluded that QOL is an area that has growing importance but has suffered from methodological problems and has relied on untested instruments and on functional measurement to the neglect of the subjective experience. They offered a set of coherent guidelines about QOL research in the future and support the development of broadly constructed, universal QOL measures, constructed using people with and without identified diseases, rather than disease-specific QOL measures.

Given the expanding interest in assessing QOL and treatment outcomes for the patient, it is not surprising to see an accompanying interest in assessing the patient's (and in some cases, the patient's family's) satisfaction with services received. Satisfaction should be considered a measure of the overall treatment process, encompassing the patient's (and at times, others') view of how the service was delivered, the capabilities and the attentiveness of the service provider, the perceived benefits of the service, and various other aspects of the service the patient received. Whereas QOL may measure the result of the treatment rendered, program evaluation may measure how the patient felt about the treatment he or she received (Maruish, 2000).

## TYPES OF MEDICAL SETTINGS

During the past decade, there has been an increasing interest in the assessment of health status in medical and behavioral health-care delivery systems. Initially, this interest was shown primarily within those settings that focused on the treatment of physical diseases and disorders. In recent years, psychologists have recognized the value of assessing the general level of health as well. Measures of health status and physical functioning can be classified into one of two groups: generic and condition-specific (Maruish, 2000). An example of a generic measure assessing psychological adjustment to illness would be the PAIS-SR (Derogatis et al., 1995). Several of these measures are listed in Table 13.2 and are reviewed by Derogatis et al. (1995) and Rozensky et al. (1997). Condition-specific measures have been available for a number of years and are used with specific medical disorders, diseases, or conditions. Some of these measures are discussed within this section and listed in Table 13.5.

TABLE 13.5  Examples of Illness- or Condition-Specific Measures Used Within Medical Settings

| Disorder | Measure |
| --- | --- |
| Cancer | Cancer Behavior Inventory (CBI) |
| | Cancer Inventory of Problem Situations (CIPS) |
| | Mental Adjustment to Cancer Scale |
| | Profile of Mood States for Cancer (PMS-C) |
| Dentistry | Dental Anxiety Scale |
| Diabetes mellitus | Diabetic Adjustment Scale (DAS) |
| | Problem Areas in Diabetes (PAID) |
| Epilepsy | Quality of Life in Epilepsy (QOLIE) |
| Genetic Testing | Multidimensional Impact of Cancer Risk Assessment (MICRA) |
| HIV | Health-Related Quality of Life (HRQOL) |
| Pain | McGill Pain Questionnaire (MPQ) |
| | Measure of Overt Pain Behavior |
| | Pain Patient Profile (P-3) |
| | West Haven-Yale Multidimensional Pain Inventory (WHYMPI) |
| Rheumatoid arthritis | Arthritis Impact Measurement Scales |
| Sleep | Functional Outcomes of Sleep Questionnaire (FOSQ) |
| | Insomnia Severity Index (ISI) |
| | Pittsburgh Sleep Quality Index (PSQI) |
| Spinal cord injury | Psychosocial Questionnaire for Spinal Cord Injured Persons |
| Traumatic brain injury | Glasgow Coma Scale |
| | Portland Adaptability Inventory |
| | Rancho Los Amigos Scale |

## General Medical Settings and Primary Care

As the primary care physician becomes the gatekeeper in many managed care and capitated health-care organizations and systems, several instruments have been developed to meet the screening and assessment needs of the primary care physician. The Primary Care Evaluation of Mental Disorders (PRIME-MD; Hahn, Kroenke, Williams, & Spitzer, 2000) is a diagnostic instrument designed specifically for use in primary care by internists and other practitioners. The PRIME-MD contains separate modules addressing the five most common categories of psychopathology seen in general medicine: mood disorders, anxiety disorders, alcohol abuse and dependence, eating disorders, and somatoform disorders. The PRIME-MD has been shown to be valid and reliable, is acceptable to patients, and is often selected as a research tool by investigators (Hahn et al., 2000). The central function of the PRIME-MD is detection of psychopathology and treatment planning. However, it can also be used in episodic care, in subspecialty consultations, and in consultation-liaison psychiatry and health psychology assessments.

The COMPASS for Primary Care (COMPASS-PC; Grissom & Howard, 2000) is also a valid and reliable instrument designed for internists and primary care physicians. Within the instrument's 68 items are three major scales—Current Well-Being (CWB), Current Symptoms (CS), and Current Life Functioning (CLF). The four-item CWB scale includes items on distress, energy and health, emotional and psychological adjustment, and current life satisfaction. The 40-item CS scale contains at least three symptoms from each of seven diagnoses—depression, anxiety, obsessive-compulsive disorder, adjustment disorder, bipolar disorder, phobia, and substance abuse disorders. The 24-item CLF represents six areas of life functioning—self-management, work-school-homemaker, social and leisure, intimacy, family, and health (Grissom & Howard, 2000). Like the PRIME-MD, the COMPASS-PC can be easily administered over various intervals of treatment.

The Health-Related Quality of Life (HRQOL; Hays, Cunningham, Beck, Shapiro, & Ettl, 1995) is used in general health-care settings to measure concepts such as health perception, social functioning, level of energy, pain sensitivity, leisure and social activities, sexual functioning, family life, and friendships. Although the tool was standardized on patients with HIV, it has been used with patients with other chronic diseases and to measure overall life satisfaction in patients who are not experiencing significant illness. Some of the brief instruments discussed earlier are also appropriate for general medical settings. These include the QPD, SCL-90-R, and the SF-36. Linton (2004) has cautioned that to provide psychological assessment services most effectively, care must be taken to understand the unique nature of the primary care patient and the unique constraints of the primary care milieu. The psychologist in primary care must maintain appropriate professional testing standards and at the same time recognize the need for speed and the need to focus on functional abilities more than on diagnostic purity. Integrating assessment practice into the primary care environment poses challenges in selecting appropriate tools, developing appropriate procedures, and communicating results appropriately.

## Specialty Areas

In their review of adaptation to chronic illness and disability, Livneh and Antonak (1997) discussed frequently used general measures of adaptation to illness, such as the PAIS-SR (Derogatis et al., 1995). The authors also discussed several unidimensional, general measures of adaptation to disability. Numerous condition-specific measures have been developed in various medical specialty areas. For example, several measures of adaptation to specific conditions have been developed in oncology (Shapiro et al., 2001), in cardiology (Derogatis & Savitz, 2000), in rehabilitation medicine (Cushman & Scherer, 1995), for AIDS-HIV patients (Derogatis & Savitz, 2000), for sleep disorders (Rozensky et al., 1997), for diabetes (Rubin & Peyrot, 2001), for pain treatment (Cushman & Scherer, 1995), for geriatric patients (Scogin, Rohen, & Bailey, 2000), in emergency medicine (Rozensky et al., 1997), in neurology (Livneh & Antonak, 1997), and in renal dialysis (Derogatis & Savitz, 2000). Examples of these measures are listed in Table 13.5.

When considering general measures of adaptation or condition-specific measures, the determination of which to use can be based on the specific referral question posed to the psychologist. If the referral question involves whether the patient's psychological distress is significant enough to warrant clinical intervention, a general measure of adaptation will be clinically useful and sufficient. However, if the referral question concerns the quality of a patient's adjustment to a specific illness at a particular stage of that illness compared with the typical patient with that illness, a condition-specific measure—if available—may be more meaningful. QOL constructs combine normative data from both general and illness-specific populations. Researchers such as Derogatis et al. (1995) support the use of a modular strategy, combining general instruments with modules developed from illness-specific samples. In this way, an illness-specific measure can be used as an additional domain of the general instrument or as a distinct, stand-alone measure.

For example, sleep disorders, including insomnia and daytime sleepiness, are considered public health problems. In the primary care setting, sleep disturbance is the second most frequent compliant after pain problems. In addition, the prevalence of excessive daytime sleepiness is reported to affect 31% of the adult population (Nadolski, 2005). It is beyond the scope of this chapter to discuss sleep disorders. The reader should refer to texts by Pressman and Orr (1997) and to articles by Ahmed and Thorpy (2007) for more information. The Epworth Sleepiness Scale (Johns, 1991) is a validated, self-report assessment of daytime sleepiness that can be used as an effective screening test. The Functional Outcomes of Sleep Questionnaire (FOSQ), the Insomnia Severity Index (ISI), and the Pittsburgh Sleep Quality Index (PSQI) also remain validated measures for targeting possible insomnia (Pressman & Orr, 1997). A targeted, detailed medical history, physical examination, sleep diaries, and sleep laboratory assessment should follow any sleep disorder inventory or scale.

## SUMMARY

As can be seen from the broad range of topics covered within this chapter, psychological assessment in medical settings is diverse and can in some instances be highly specialized. The individuals practicing in these settings may prefer the professional identity of clinical psychologist, clinical health psychologist, or clinical neuropsychologist. All three of these specialists have a place in performing formal assessments within medical settings, with the latter two being more specialized with regard to particular medical populations and specific medical disorders. With regard to training and employment, medical settings have played an important historical role in the development of psychological assessment and will likely continue to do so in the future.

## FUTURE DIRECTIONS

Future developments in the area of psychological assessment in medical settings will center around such concepts as specificity, brevity, and normative standards for particular medical populations. Assessments will be targeted to address specific outcome and QOL questions rather than general psychological status and will be utilized across large health-care systems as well as with specific disease entities. This goal will require more precise development of specific normative standards for specific, well-defined patient groups and subgroups. Because of economic pressures, including the need to see patients for less time and to see a greater number of patients, there will continue to be pressure on test authors and publishers to create short forms and shorter instruments. As the former trend continues to take place, we must bear in mind the psychometric costs associated with accompanying threats to validity (Smith, McCarthy, & Anderson, 2000). Psychological assessment will become incorporated in cost utility analysis, as outcomes involving patient adjustment, well-being, and QOL become more central and quantifiable as part of the economic dimensions of treatment (Kopta, Howard, Lowry, & Beutler, 1994). Brevity, cost efficiency, minimal intrusiveness, and broader applicability will be salient concepts in the design of future assessment systems (Derogatis et al., 1995).

Although it has been recommended for many years that clinician-based judgments yield to actuarial or mechanical judgments (cf. Grove, Zald, Lebow, Snitz, & Nelson, 2000), and without question there has been a useful trend in this direction of at least partial reliance on empirically derived decision aids, we do not foresee a time in the near future when clinicians will abrogate their assessment roles completely to actuarial or mechanical methods. This position is *not* based on philosophical or scientific disagreement with the relevant decision-making literature; rather, it is based on the belief that there will not be a sufficient number of appropriate mechanical algorithms for years to come (cf. Kleinmuntz, 1990).

Computer-administered assessment, as well as planning for treatment and prevention, will likely be an important component of the future in psychological assessment in medical settings, as has been suggested regarding psychological assessment in general. (See Butcher, this volume; Butcher, Perry, & Atlis, 2000; Garb, 2000; Snyder, 2000.) Maruish (2000) sampled several computerized treatment and prevention programs involving depression, obsessive-compulsive disorders, smoking cessation, and alcohol abuse. Symptom rating scales, screening measures, diagnostic interviews, and QOL and patient satisfaction scales already have been or can easily be computerized, making administration of these measures efficient and cost effective. As computer technology advances with interactive voice response (IVR), new opportunities for even more thorough evaluation exist. However, as computer usage and technology develop, so do concerns about patient confidentiality, restricting access to databases, and the integration of assessment findings into effective treatment interventions. Similarly, Rozensky et al. (1997) predicted that there will be less emphasis placed on the diagnosis of psychopathology and more focus on those computerized assessment procedures that directly enhance planning and evaluating treatment strategies. Moreover, as telemedicine or telehealth develops, psychological assessment will need to be an integral part of patient and program evaluation as distance medicine technologies improve continuity of care. With the increasing cost of health care, more efforts have been focused on telemedicine and examining the economics of this type of medicine (Dávalos, French, Burdick, & Simmons, 2009).

Assessment in medical settings will likely continue to become even more specialized in the future. With this trend, more attention will be paid—both within the discipline and by test publishers—to test user qualifications and credentials (cf. Moreland, Eyde, Robertson, Primoff, & Most, 1995). In this same vein, more specific guidelines will be developed to aid in dealing with difficult ethical and legal dilemmas associated with assessment practices with medical patients, as is already evident within clinical neuropsychology (e.g., Johnson-Greene et al., 1997; Sweet, Grote, & van Gorp, 2002).

Illness and disability necessitate change, resulting in continuous modification in coping and adjustment by the patient, his or her family, and medical personnel (Derogatis et al., 1995). Psychology's ability to document accurately the patient's response to disease and treatment-induced change is crucial to achieving an optimal treatment plan. Psychological assessment can be an integral part of the patient's care system and will continue to contribute crucial information to the patient's treatment regimen. Carefully planned, programmatic, integrated assessments of the patient's psychological coping and adjustment will always serve to identify problematic patients as well as those well-adjusted patients who are entering problematic phases of illness and treatment. Assessments that identify taxed or faltering coping responses can signal the need for interventions designed to avert serious adjustment problems, minimize deterioration of well-being, and restore patient QOL. Cost-effectiveness of medical interventions will continue to be enhanced by appropriate use of psychological assessment in medical settings.

## REFERENCES

Abramowitz, J. S., & Braddock, A. E. (2008). *Psychological treatment of health anxiety and hypochondriasis: A biopsychosocial approach*. Cambridge, MA: Hogrefe.

Ahmed, I., & Thorpy, M. J. (2007). Classification of sleep disorders. *Neurology, 13*, 13–30.

Ahmed, M. (1998). Psychological and legal aspects of mental incompetence. *Texas Medicine, 94*, 64–67.

Allen, J. P., Reinert, D. F., & Volk, R. J. (2001). The alcohol use disorders identification test: An aid to recognition of alcohol problems in primary care patients. *Preventive Medicine, 33*, 428–433.

Ambrose, P. Jr. (1997). Challenges for mental health service providers: The perspective of managed care organizations. In J. Butcher (Ed.), *Personality assessment in managed health care* (pp. 61–72). New York, NY: Oxford University Press.

American Bar Association and American Psychological Association Committee on Aging. (2008). *A handbook for psychologists: Assessment of the older adult with diminished capacity*. Retrieved from www.apa.org/pi/aging/programs/assessment/capacity-psychologist-handbook.pdf

American Psychiatric Association. (1994). Diagnostic and statistical manual of mental disorders (4th ed.). Washington, DC: Author.

American Psychological Association. (2002). Ethical Principals of Psychologists and Code of Conduct. Retrieved from www.apa.org/ethics/code/index.aspx

American Psychological Association Task Force on the Assessment of Competencies. (2006). *Report of the Assessment of Competency Benchmarks Work Group*. Washington, DC: Author. Retrieved from http://apa.org/ed/resources/competency-revised.pdf

Andrews, G., Peters, L., & Tesson, M. (1994). *The measurement of consumer outcomes in mental health*. Canberra, Australia: Australian Government Publishing Service.

Bailes, J. E., & Cantu, R. C. (2001). Head injury in athletes. *Neurosurgery, 48*, 26–45.

Barisa, M. T. (2010). *The business of neuropsychology: A practical guide*. Part of the Oxford Workshop Series: American Academy of Clinical Neuropsychology. New York, NY: Oxford University Press.

Behel, J. M., & Rybarczyk, B. (2010). Interviewing in health psychology and medical settings. In D. L. Segal & M. Hersen (Eds.), *Diagnostic interviewing* (pp. 495–516). Chicago, IL: Springer.

Belar, C., & Deardorff, W. (2009). *Clinical health psychology in medical settings: A practitioner's guidebook* (2nd ed.). Washington, DC: American Psychological Association.

Belar, C., & Geisser, M. (1995). Roles of the clinical health psychologist in the management of chronic illness. In P. Nicassio & T. Smith (Eds.), *Managing chronic illness: A biopsychosocial perspective* (pp. 33–58). Washington, DC: American Psychological Association.

Ben-Porath, Y. S., & Tellegan, A. (2008). *Minnesota Multiphasic Personality Inventory-2-Restructured Form: Manual for administration, scoring, and interpretation*. Minneapolis: University of Minnesota Press.

Billick, S., Bella, P., & Burgert, W. (1997). Competency to consent to hospitalization in the medical patient. *Journal of the American Academy of Psychiatry and Law, 25*, 191–196.

Binford, A., & Liljequist, L. (2008). Behavioral correlates of selected MMPI-2 Clinical, Content, and Restructured Clinical scales. *Journal of Personality Assessment, 60*, 608–614.

Block, A. R., Gatchel, R. J., Deardorff, W. W., & Guyer, R. D. (2003). *The psychology of spine surgery*. Washington, DC: American Psychological Association.

Blount, A., Schoenbaum, M., Kathol, R., Rollman, B. L., Thomas, M., O'Donohue, W., & Peck, C. J. (2007). The economics of behavioral health sciences in medical settings: A summary of the evidence. *Professional Psychology: Research and Practice, 38*, 290–297.

Bluestein, D., & Cubic, B. A. (2007). Psychologists and primary care physicians: A training model for creating collaborative relationships. *Journal of Clinical Psychology in Medical Settings, 16*, 101–112.

Briere, J. (1995). *Trauma Symptom Inventory professional manual*. Odessa, FL: Psychological Assessment Resources.

Bruns, D. (2009). *Psychological evaluations and cost offset for medical patients*. Retrieved from www.healthpsych.com/tools/presurgical_briefing_sheet.pdf

Bucholz, K. K., Dinwiddie, S. H., Reich, T., Shayka, J. J., & Cloninger, C. R. (1993). Comparison of screening proposals for somatization disorder empirical analyses. *Comprehensive Psychiatry, 34*, 59–64.

Butcher, J. N., Graham, J. R., Ben-Porath, Y. S., Tellegen, A., Dahlstrom, W. G., & Kaemmer, B. (2001). *MMPI-2 (Minnesota Multiphasic Personality Inventory-2): Manual for administration, scoring, and interpretation* (revised ed.). Minneapolis: University of Minnesota Press.

Butcher, J. N., Perry, J., & Atlis, M. (2000). Validity and utility of computer-based test interpretation. *Psychological Assessment, 12*, 6–18.

Camic, P., & Knight, S. (2004). *Clinical handbook of health psychology*. Cambridge, MA: Hogrefe & Huber.

Cella, D., Peterman, Tellegen, A., Chang, C. H., Wanzel, L., Marcus, A. C., ... Lerman, C. (2002). A brief assessment of concerns associated with genetic testing for cancer: The Multidimensional Impact of Cancer Risk Assessment (MICRA) questionnaire. *Health Psychology, 21*, 564–572.

Chen, F., & Grossberg, G. (1997). Issues involved in assessing competency. *New Directions for Mental Health Services, 76*, 71–83.

Coffey, P., Leitenberg, H., Henning, K., Turner, T., & Bennett, R. T. (1996). The relation between methods of coping during adulthood with a history of childhood sexual abuse and current psychological adjustment. *Journal of Consulting and Clinical Psychology, 64*, 1090–1093.

Cohen, L., Littlefield, C., Kelly, P., Maurer, J., & Abbey, S. (1998). Predictors of quality of life and adjustment after lung transplantation. *Chest, 113*, 633–644.

Cushman, L. A., & Scherer, M. J. (Eds.). (1995). *Psychological assessment in medical rehabilitation*. Washington, DC: American Psychological Association.

Dávalos, M. E., French, M. T., Burdick, A. E., & Simmons, S. C. (2009). Economic evaluation of telemedicine: Review of the literature and research guidelines for benefit-cost analysis. *Telemedicine and e-health, 15*, 933–949.

Davis, L. (2000). Self-administered alcohol screening test (SAAST). In M. Maruish (Ed.), *Handbook of psychological assessment in primary care settings* (pp. 537–554). Mahwah, NJ: Erlbaum.

Demakis, G. J., Mercury, M. G., & Sweet, J. J. (2000). Screening for cognitive impairments in primary care settings. In M. E. Maruish (Ed.), *Handbook of psychological assessment in primary care settings* (pp. 555–582). Mahwah, NJ: Erlbaum.

Derogatis, L. R., Fleming, M. P., Sudler, N. C., & DellaPietra, L. (1995). Psychological assessment. In P. M. Nicassio & T. W. Smith (Eds.), *Managing chronic illness: A biopsychosocial perspective* (pp. 59–116). Washington, DC: American Psychological Association.

Derogatis, L. R., & Savitz, K. L. (2000). The SCL-90-R and Brief Symptoms Inventory (BSI) in primary care. In M. E. Maruish (Ed.), *Handbook of psychological assessment in primary care settings* (pp. 297–334). Mahwah, NJ: Erlbaum.

Derogatis, L. R., & Spencer, P. M. (1982). *BSI administration and procedures manual*. Baltimore, MD: Clinical Psychometric Research.

Deshields, T. L., Mannen, K., Tait, R. C., & Bajaj, V. (1997). Quality of life in heart transplant candidates. *Journal of Clinical Psychology in Medical Settings, 4*, 327–341.

Eckleberry-Hunt, J., Van Dyke, A., Stucky, K., & Misch, P. (2009). Attaining medical staff membership and privileges for psychologists: A case study. *Professional Psychology: Research and Practice, 40*, 579–585.

Elhai, J. D., Sweet, J. J., Guidotti Breting, L. M. & Kaloupek, D. (2012). Considerations for PTSD and mTBI assessment in contexts where reporting validity is threatened. In J. Vasterling, R. Bryant, & T. Keane (Eds.), *PTSD and mild traumatic brain injury*. New York, NY: Guilford Press.

Elman, N., Illfelder-Kaye, J., & Robiner, W. (2005). Professional development: A foundation for psychologist competence. *Professional Psychology: Research and Practice, 36*, 367–375.

Engel, G. L. (1977). The need for a new medical model: A challenge for biomedicine. *Science, 196*, 129–136.

Etchells, E., Darzins, P., Silberfeld, M., Singer, P., McKenny, J., Naglie, G., Katz, M., ... Strang, D. (1999). Assessment of patient capacity to consent to treatment. *Journal of General Internal Medicine, 14*, 27–34.

Farberman, R. (1997). Terminal illness and hastened death requests: The important role of the mental health professional. *Professional Psychology: Research and Practice, 28*, 544–547.

Feenan, D. (1996). Capacity to decide about medical treatment. *British Journal of Hospital Medicine, 56*, 295–297.

Folkman, S., & Lazarus, R. (1980). An analysis of coping in a middle-aged community sample. *Journal of Health and Social Behavior, 21*, 219–239.

Franks, S. F., & Kaiser, K. A. (2008). Predictive factors in bariatric surgery outcomes: What is the role of the preoperative psychological evaluation? *Primary Psychiatry, 15*, 74–83.

Frazier, P. A., & Schauben, L. J. (1994). Stressful life events and psychological adjustment among female college students. *Measurement and Evaluation in Counseling and Development, 27*, 280–292.

Garb, H. (2000). Computers will become increasingly important for psychological assessment: Not that there's anything wrong with that! *Psychological Assessment, 12*, 31–39.

Gentry, W., & Matarazzo, J. (1981). Medical psychology: Three decades of growth and development. In C. Prokop & L. Bradley (Eds.), *Medical psychology: Contributions to behavioral medicine* (pp. 6–19). New York, NY: Academic Press.

Glass, K. (1997). Refining definitions and devising instruments: Two decades of assessing mental competence. *International Journal of Law and Psychiatry, 20*, 5–33.

Glueckauf, R. L. (1999). Interdivisional Healthcare Committee: Speaking with one voice on cross-cutting issues in health care psychology. *Journal of Clinical Psychology in Medical Settings, 6*, 171–182.

Goodheart, C. D. (2010). Economics and psychology practice: What we need to know and why. *Professional Psychology: Research and Practice, 41*, 189–195.

Grisso, T. (2003). *Evaluating competencies: Forensic assessments and instruments* (2nd ed.). New York, NY: Kluwer Academic/Plenum Press.

Grisso, T., Appelbaum, P., & Hill-Fotouhi, C. (1997). The MacCAT-T: A clinical tool to assess patients' capacities to make treatment decisions. *Psychiatric Services, 48*, 1415–1419.

Grissom, G. R., & Howard, K. I. (2000). Directions and COMPASSPC. In M. E. Maruish (Ed.), *Handbook of psychological assessment in primary care settings* (pp. 255–276). Mahwah, NJ: Erlbaum.

Groth-Marnat, G. (1999). Financial efficacy of clinical assessment: Rational guidelines and issues for future research. *Journal of Clinical Psychology, 55*, 813–824.

Grove, W., Zald, D., Lebow, B., Snitz, B., & Nelson, C. (2000). Clinical versus mechanical prediction: A meta-analysis. *Psychological Assessment, 12*, 19–30.

Guskiewicz, K. M., & Mihalik, J. P. (2011). Biomechanics of sport concussion: Quest for the elusive injury threshold. *Exercise and Sports Sciences Reviews, 39*, 4–11.

Hahn, S. R., Kroenke, K., Williams, J. B. W., & Spitzer, R. L. (2000). Evaluation of mental disorders with the PRIME-MD. In M. E. Maruish (Ed.), *Handbook of psychological assessment in primary care settings* (pp. 191–254). Mahwah, NJ: Erlbaum.

Hays, R. D., Cunningham, W. E., Beck, C. K., Shapiro, M. F., & Ettl, M. K. (1995). Health-related quality of life in HIV disease. *Assessment*, *2*, 363–380.

Hendin, H. (1999). Suicide, assisted suicide, and medical illness. *Journal of Clinical Psychiatry*, *60*, 46–52.

Hersen, M., & Turner, S. (1994). *Diagnostic interviewing* (2nd ed.). New York, NY: Plenum Press.

Holzer, J., Gansler, D., Moczynski, N., & Folstein, M. (1997). Cognitive functions in the informed consent evaluation process: A pilot study. *Journal of the American Academy of Psychiatry and Law*, *25*, 531–540.

Hughes, J. C. (2000). Ethics and anti-dementia drugs. *International Journal of Geriatric Psychiatry*, *15*, 538–543.

Jacobsen, P., & Holland, J. (1989). Psychological reactions to cancer surgery. In J. Holland & J. Rowland (Eds.), *Handbook of psychosocial oncology: Psychological care of the patient with cancer* (pp. 117–133). New York, NY: Oxford University Press.

Johns, M. W. (1991). A new method of measuring daytime sleepiness: The Epworth Sleepiness Scale. *Sleep*, *14*, 541–548.

Johnson, M. E., Brems, C., & Fisher, D. G. (1996). Self-reported levels of psychopathology and drug abusers not currently in treatment. *Journal of Psychopathology and Behavioral Assessment*, *18*, 21–34.

Johnson-Greene, D., Hardy-Morais, C., Adams, K., Hardy, C., & Bergloff, P. (1997). Informed consent and neuropsychological assessment: Ethical considerations and proposed guidelines. *Clinical Neuropsychologist*, *11*, 454–460.

Kaplan, R. M., & Groessl, E. J. (2002). Applications of cost-effectiveness methodologies in behavioral medicine. *Journal of Consulting and Clinical Psychology*, *70*, 482–493.

Kaslow, N. J. (2010). A message from the president: Envisioning the Future of ABPP. *Specialist*, *29*, 1, 4–5.

Kaslow, N. J., Borden, K. A., Collins, F. L., Forrest, L., Illfelder-Kaye, J., Nelson, P. D., . . . Willmuth, M. E. (2004). Competencies conference: Future directions in education and credentialing in professional psychology. *Journal of Clinical Psychology*, *60*, 699–712.

Kaslow, N. J., Dunn, S. E., & Smith, C. O. (2008). Competencies for psychologists in academic health centers (AHCs). *Journal of Clinical Psychology in Medical Settings*, *15*, 18–27.

Katon, W., Von Korff, M., Lin, E., Lipscomb, P., Russo, J., Wagner, E., & Polk, E. (1990). Distressed high users of medical care: DSM-III-R diagnosis and treatment needs. *General Hospital Psychiatry*, *12*, 355–362.

Kay, J., & Bienenfeld, D. (1991). The clinical assessment of the cardiac transplant candidate. *Psychosomatics*, *32*, 78–87.

Keefe, F. J., & Blumenthal, J. A. (Eds.). (1982). *Assessment strategies in behavioral medicine*. New York, NY: Grune & Stratton.

Kellner, R., Hernandez, J., & Pathak, D. (1992). Hypochondriacal fears and their relationship to anxiety and somaticization. *British Journal of Psychiatry*, *160*, 525–532.

Kleinmuntz, B. (1990). Why we still use our heads instead of formulas: Toward an integrative approach. *Psychological Bulletin*, *107*, 296–310.

Kopta, S. M., Howard, L. I., Lowry, J. L., & Beutler, L. E. (1994). Patterns of symptomatic recovery in psychotherapy. *Journal of Consulting and Clinical Psychology*, *62*, 1009–1016.

Kubiszyn, T., Meyer, G., Finn, S., Eyde, L., Kay, G., Moreland, K., . . . Eismean, E. (2000). Empirical support for the psychological assessment in clinical health care settings. *Professional Psychology: Research and Practice*, *31*, 119–130.

Kuczewski, M. (1996). Reconceiving the family: The process of consent in medical decision making. *Hastings Center Report*, *26*, 30–37.

Kuhn, W., Brennan, A., Lacefield, P., Brohm, J., Skelton, V., & Gray, L. (1990). Psychiatric distress during stages of the heart transplantation protocol. *Journal of Heart Transplant*, *9*, 25–29.

Liu, C. F., Cedrick, S. C., Chaney, E. F., Heagerty, P., Felker, B., Hasenburg, N., et al. (2003). Cost effectiveness of collaborative care for depression in a primary care veteran population. *Psychiatric Services*, *54*, 698–704.

Linton, J. C. (2004). Psychological assessment in primary care. In L. J. Haas (Ed.), *Handbook of primary care psychology* (pp. 35–48). New York, NY: Oxford Press.

Livneh, H., & Antonak, R. F. (1997). *Psychosocial adaptation to chronic illness and disability*. Gaithersburg, MD: Aspen.

Marson, D., Chatterjee, A., Ingram, K., & Harrell, L. (1996). Toward a neurologic model of competency: Cognitive predictors of capacity to consent in Alzheimer's disease using three different legal standards. *Neurology*, *46*, 666–672.

Marson, D., & Harrell, L. (1999). Executive dysfunction and loss of capacity to consent to medical treatment in patients with Alzheimer's disease. *Seminars in Clinical Neuropsychiatry*, *4*, 41–49.

Marson, D., Hawkins, L., McInturff, B., & Harrell, L. (1997). Cognitive models that predict physician judgments of capacity to consent in mild Alzheimer's disease. *Journal of the American Geriatric Society*, *45*, 458–464.

Marson, D., McInturff, B., Hawkins, L., Bartolucci, A., & Harrell, L. (1997). Consistency of physician judgments of capacity to consent in mild Alzheimer's disease. *Journal of the American Geriatric Society*, *45*, 453–457.

Maruish, M. E. (Ed.). (2000). *Handbook of psychological assessment in primary care settings*. Mahwah, NJ: Erlbaum.

Mayou, R. (1990). Quality of life in cardiovascular disease. *Psychotherapy and Psychosomatics*, *54*, 99–109.

McCabe, M. (1996). Involving children and adolescents in medical decision making: Developmental and clinical considerations. *Journal of Pediatric Psychology*, *21*, 505–516.

McClellan, M., McKethan, A., Lewis, J., Roski, J., & Fisher, E. (2010). A national strategy to put accountable care into practice. *Health Affairs*, *29*, 982–990.

Melton, G., Petrila, J., Poythress, N., & Slobogin, C. (Eds.). (1997). *Psychological evaluations for the courts: A handbook for mental health professionals and lawyers* (2nd ed.). New York, NY: Guilford Press.

Meyer, G., Finn, S., Eyde, L., Kay, G., Moreland, K., Dies, R., . . . Reed, G. (2001). Psychological testing and psychological assessment: A review of evidence and issues. *American Psychologist*, *56*, 128–165.

Mitrushina, M. N., Boone, K. B., Razani, L. J., & D'Elia, L. F. (Eds.). (2005). *Handbook of normative data for neuropsychological assessment* (2nd ed.). New York, NY: Oxford University Press.

Moreland, K., Eyde, L., Robertson, G., Primoff, E., & Most, R. (1995). Assessment of test user qualifications: A research-based measurement procedure. *American Psychologist*, *50*, 14–23.

Morey, L. C. (1991). *Personality Assessment Inventory: Professional manual*. Lutz, FL: Psychological Assessment Resources.

Moser, R. S., Iverson, G. L., Echemendia, R. J., Lovell, M. R., Schatz, P., Webbe, F. M., . . . the NAN Policy and Planning Committee. (2007). Neuropsychological evaluation in the diagnosis and management of sports-related concussion. *Archives of Clinical Neuropsychology*, *22*, 909–916.

Moss, A. H. (2001). Shared decision-making in dialysis: the new RPA/ASN guideline on appropriate initiation and withdrawal of treatment. *American Journal of Kidney Disease*, *37*, 1081.

Murkin, J. M., Newman, S. P., Stump, D. A., & Blumenthal, J. A. (1995). Statement of consensus on assessment of neurobehavioral outcomes after cardiac surgery. *Annals of Thoracic Surgery*, *59*, 1289–1295.

Nadolski, N. (2005). Diagnosing and treating insomnia. *Plastic Surgical Nursing*, *25*, 167–173.

Nessman, A., & Herndon, P. (2000). New Jersey settlement offers strong protection for psychologists. *Monitor on Psychology*, *31*, 20–21.

Newman, M., Kirchner, J., Phillips-Bute, B., Gaver, V., Grocott, H., Jones, R., . . . Blumenthal, J. (2001). Longitudinal assessment of neurocognitive function after coronary-artery bypass surgery. *New England Journal of Medicine*, *344*, 395–402.

Nezu, C. M., Finch, A. J. Jr., & Simon, N. P. (Eds.). (2009). *Becoming board certified by the American Board of Professional Psychology*. New York, NY: Oxford University Press.

Nicassio, P. M., & Smith, T. W. (1995). *Managing chronic illness: A biopsychosocial perspective*. Washington, DC: American Psychological Association.

O'Hare, A. M., Rodriguez, R. A., Hailpern, S. M., Larson, E. B., & Tamura, M. K. (2010). Regional variation in health care intensity and treatment practices for end-stage renal disease in older adults. *Journal of the American Medical Association*, *304*, 180–186.

Olbrisch, M. E., Benedict, S. M., Ashe, K., & Levenson, J. L. (2002). Psychological assessment and care of organ transplant patients. *Journal of Consulting and Clinical Psychology*, *70*, 771–783.

Olbrisch, M. E., & Levenson, J. (1991). Psychosocial evaluation of heart transplant candidates: An international survey of process, criteria, and outcome. *Journal of Heart and Lung Transplantation*, *10*, 948–955.

Olbrisch, M. E., Levenson, J., & Hamer, R. (1989). The PACT: A rating scale for the study of clinical decision-making in psychosocial screening of organ transplant candidates. *Clinical Transplantation*, *3*, 1–6.

Organ Procurement and Transplantation Network. (2011). U.S. Department of Health and Human Services. Retrieved from http://optn transplant.hrsa.gov

Patenaude, A. F., Guttmacher, A. E., & Collins, F. S. (2002). Genetic testing and psychology: New roles, new responsibilities. *American Psychologist*, *57*, 271–282.

Pinkerton, S. S., Hughes, H., & Wenrich, W. W. (1982). *Behavioral medicine: Clinical applications*. New York, NY: Wiley.

Piotrowski, C. (1999). Assessment practices in the era of managed care: Current status and future directions. *Journal of Clinical Psychology*, *55*, 787–796.

Podell, K. (2004). Computerized assessment of sports-related injury. In M. R. Lovell, J. T. Barth, & M. W. Collins (Eds.). Traumatic brain injury in sports (pp. 375–393). Lisse, the Netherlands: Swets & Zeitlinger.

Pollack, M., & Billick, S. (1999). Competency to consent to treatment. *Psychiatric Quarterly*, *70*, 303–311.

Pressman, M. R., & Orr, W. C. (1997). *Understanding sleep: The evaluation and treatment of sleep disorders*. Washington, DC: American Psychological Association.

Prigatano, G. P. & Pliskin, N. H. (2003). *Clinical neuropsychology and cost outcome research*. New York, NY: Psychology Press.

Ritz, S. (2006). The bariatric psychological evaluation: A heuristic for determining the suitability of the morbidly obese patient for weight loss surgery. *Bariatric Nursing and Surgical Patient Care*, *1*, 97–105.

Robiner, W. N., Dixon, K. E., Miner, J. L., & Hong, B. A. (2010). Hospital privileges for psychologists in the era of competencies and increased accountability. *Journal of Clinical Psychology in Medical Settings*, *17*, 301–314.

Rozensky, R. (2006). Clinical psychology in medical settings: Celebrating our past, enjoying the present, building our future. *Journal of Clinical Psychology in Medical Settings*, *13*, 343–352.

Rozensky, R., Sweet, J., & Tovian, S. (1997). *Psychological assessment in medical settings*. New York, NY: Plenum Press.

Rubin, R. R., & Peyrot, M. (2001). Psychological issues and treatments for people with diabetes. *Journal of Clinical Psychology*, *57*, 457–478.

Salkovskis, P. M., Rimes, K. A., Warwick, H. M., & Clark, D. M. (2002). The Health Anxiety Inventory: Development and validation of scales for the measurement of health anxiety and hypochondriasis. *Psychological Medicine*, *32*, 843–853.

Scogin, F., Rohen, N., & Bailey, E. (2000). Geriatric Depression Scale. In M. E. Maruish (Ed.), *Handbook of psychological assessment in primary care settings* (pp. 491–508). Mahwah, NJ: Erlbaum.

Sears, S. F., Rodrigue, J. R., Siros, B. C., Urizar, G. C., & Perri, M. G. (1999). Extending psychometric norms for pre-cardiac transplantation evaluations: The Florida cohort, 1990–1996. *Journal of Clinical Psychology in Medical Settings*, *6*, 303–316.

Shapiro, S. L., Lopez, A. M., Schwartz, G. E., Bootzin, R., Figueredo, A. J., Braden, C. J., & Kurker, S. F. (2001). Quality of life and breast cancer: Relationship to psychosocial variables. *Journal of Clinical Psychology*, *57*, 501–520.

Skinner, H. A. (1982). *The Drug Abuse Screening Test (DAST): Guidelines for administration and scoring*. Toronto, Canada: Addiction Research Foundation.

Slick, D. J., Hopp, G., Strauss, E., & Thompson, G. B. (1997). *Victoria Symptom Validity Test version 1.0 professional manual*. Odessa, FL: Psychological Assessment Resources.

Smith, G., McCarthy, D., & Anderson, K. (2000). On the sins of short-form development. *Psychological Assessment*, *12*, 102–111.

Smithline, H., Mader, T., & Crenshaw, B. (1999). Do patients with acute medical conditions have the capacity to give informed consent for emergency medicine research? *Academic Emergency Medicine*, *6*, 776–780.

Snyder, D. (2000). Computer-assisted judgment: Defining strengths and liabilities. *Psychological Assessment*, *12*, 52–60.

Sobel, D. (2000). Mind matters, money matters: The cost effectiveness of mind/body medicine [Editorial]. *Journal of the American Medical Association*, *284*, 1705.

Stilley, C. S., Miller, D. J., Gayowski, T., & Marino, I. R. (1999). Psychological characteristics of candidates for liver transplantation: Differences according to history of substance abuse and UNOS listing. *Journal of Clinical Psychology*, *55*, 1287–1297.

Strachan, M. W., Frier, B. M., & Deary, I. J. (1997). Cognitive assessment in diabetes: The need for consensus. *Diabetic Medicine*, *14*, 421–422.

Strauss, E., Sherman, E. M. S., & Spreen, O. (2006). *A compendium of neuropsychological tests: Administration, norms, and commentary* (3rd ed.). New York, NY: Oxford University Press.

Swartz, M., Hughes, D., & George, L. (1986). Developing a screening index for community studies of somaticization disorder. *Journal of Psychiatric Research*, *20*, 335–343.

Sweet, J. (Ed.). (1999). *Forensic neuropsychology: Fundamentals and practice*. Lisse, the Netherlands: Swets & Zeitlinger.

Sweet, J., Giuffre Meyer, D., Nelson, N. W., & Moberg, P. J. (2011). The TCN/AACN 2010 "Salary Survey": Professional practices, beliefs, and incomes of U.S. neuropsychologists. *Clinical Neuropsychologist*, *25*, 12–61.

Sweet, J., Grote, C., & van Gorp, W. (2002). Ethical issues in forensic neuropsychology. In S. Bush & M. Drexler (Eds.), *Ethical issues in clinical neuropsychology* (pp. 103–133). Lisse, the Netherlands: Swets & Zeitlinger.

Sweet, J., Moberg, P., & Suchy, Y. (2000). Ten-year follow-up survey of clinical neuropsychologists: Part I. Practices and beliefs. *Clinical Neuropsychologist*, *14*, 18–37.

Sweet, J., Rozensky, R., & Tovian, S. (Eds.). (1991). *Handbook of clinical psychology in medical settings*. New York, NY: Plenum Press.

Sweet, J., & Westergaard, C. (1997). Evaluation of psychopathology in neuropsychological assessment. In G. Goldstein & T. Incagnoli (Eds.), *Contemporary approaches in neuropsychological assessment* (pp. 325–358). New York, NY: Plenum Press.

Thomas, M. L., & Locke, D. E. C. (2010). Psychometric Properties of the MMPI-2-RF Somatic Complaints (RC1) Scale. *Psychological Assessment, 22*, 492–503.

Tombaugh, T. (1997). The Test of Memory Malingering (TOMM): Normative data from cognitively intact and cognitively impaired individuals. *Psychological Assessment, 9*, 260–268.

Toomey, T. C., Seville, J. L., Mann, J. D., Abashian, S. W., & Grant, J. R. (1995). Relationship of sexual and physical abuse to pain description, psychological distress, and health care utilization in a chronic pain sample. *Clinical Journal of Pain, 11*, 307–315.

Tovian, S. M., Rozensky, R. H., & Sweet, J. J. (2003). A decade of clinical psychology in medical settings: The short longer view. *Journal of Clinical Psychology in Medical Settings, 10*, 1–8.

Van Egren, L., & Striepe, M. I. (1998). Assessment approaches in health psychology: Issues and practical considerations. In P. M. Camic & S. J. Knight (Eds.), *Clinical handbook of health psychology: A practical guide to effective interventions* (pp. 17–52). Seattle, WA: Hogrefe and Huber.

Walker, E. A., Katon, W. J., Hansom, J., Haerrop-Griffiths, J., Holm, L., Jones, M. L., . . . Russo, J. (1995). Psychiatric diagnoses and sexual victimization in women with chronic pelvic pain. *Psychosomatics, 36*, 531–540.

Wallander, J. L., Schmitt, M., & Koot, H. M. (2001). Quality of life measurement in children and adolescents: Issues, instruments and applications. *Journal of Clinical Psychology, 57*, 571–586.

Wallston, K., Wallston, B., & DeVellis, R. (1978). Development of the Multidimensional Health Locus of Control (MHLC) scale. *Health Education Monographs, 6*, 160–170.

Ware, J. E. (1993). *SF-36 Health Survey: Manual and interpretation guide*. Boston, MA: New England Medical Center, the Health Institute.

Wetzler, H. P., Lum, D. L., & Bush, D. M. (2000). Using the SF-36 Health Survey in primary care. In M. E. Maruish (Ed.), *Handbook of psychological assessment in primary care settings* (pp. 583–622). Mahwah, NJ: Erlbaum.

Williams, L., Harris, A., Thompson, M., & Brayshaw, A. (1997). Consent to treatment by minors attending accident and emergency departments: Guidelines. *Journal of Accident and Emergency Medicine, 14*, 286–289.

Zipel, S., Lowe, B., Paschke, T., Immel, B., Lange, R., Zimmerman, R., Herzog, W., & Bergman, G. (1998). Psychological distress in patients awaiting heart transplantation. *Journal of Psychosomatic Research, 45*, 465–470.

CHAPTER 14

# Psychological Assessment in Industrial/ Organizational Settings

RICHARD J. KLIMOSKI AND TORREY R. WILKINSON

This chapter is built on a broad view of assessment regarding its use in work organizations. A major thrust of the chapter is to to focus on constructs that allow for the inferences about the possession of either job-relevant individual differences (as predictors) or assessments of an employee's job performance itself (as criteria). Although our emphasis is on describing the activities and tools of psychologists in industry, it should be made clear at the outset that the bulk of individual assessments in work settings is being conducted by others—managers, supervisors, trainers, human resource (HR) professionals—albeit often under the guidance of practicing psychologists or using assessment techniques that the latter designed or have implemented on behalf of the company.

The chapter has been updated relative to developments that have occurred in the field of psychological assessment in work settings since the volume was initially published. However, because these developments have been more evolutionary than revolutionary, we have kept the structure of this chapter relatively similar to the original. The major changes that we address reflect the challenges of managing people employed by companies in a largely service economy, one that increasingly has a global or international dimension. The technical changes that we highlight reflect the emergence of more sophisticated analytic tools that have been adopted by researchers which allow for developing and testing more refined models of the way that individual difference factors help us to predict and understand work place behavior and performance.

## HISTORICAL ROOTS

Psychologists have been active in the assessment of individuals in work settings for almost a century. Since the early 1900s, corporate managers looked for ways that the field could contribute to the solution of business problems, especially enhancing worker performance and reducing accidents. For example, Terman (1917) was asked to evaluate candidates for municipal positions in California. He used a shortened form of the Stanford-Binet and several other tests to look for patterns against past salary and occupational level (Austin, Scherbaum, & Mahlman, 2000). The approaches used and the tools and techniques developed clearly reflected prevailing thinking among researchers of the time. Spearman's views on generalized intelligence and measurement error had an influence on techniques that ultimately became the basis of the standardized instruments popular in work applications. When the laboratory experimental method was found valuable for theory testing, it was not long before it was adapted to the assessment of job applicants for the position of street railway operators (Munsterberg, 1913). Vocational interest blanks designed for guiding students into careers were adapted to the needs of personnel selection in industry.

The practice of assessment in work organizations was also profoundly affected by activities and developments during the great wars fought by the United States. Many of the personnel and performance needs of the military during both the first and second world wars were met by contributions of psychologists recruited from the academy. The work of Otis (cited in Strong, 1918) on the (then) new idea of the multiple-choice test was found extremely valuable in solving the problem of assessing millions of men called to duty for their suitability and, once enlisted, for their assignments to specific work roles. The Army's Alpha test, based on the work of Otis and others, was itself administered to 1,700,000 individuals. Tools and techniques for the assessment of job performance were refined or developed to meet the needs of the military relative to evaluating the impact of training and determining the readiness of officers for promotion. After the First World War, these innovations were diffused into the private sector, often by officers turned businessmen or by psychologists no longer employed in government. Indeed, the creation of the *Journal of Applied Psychology* in 1917 and the demand for practicing psychologists in industry are seen as outgrowths of the success of assessment operations in the military (Schmitt & Klimoski, 1991).

In a similar manner, conceptual and psychometric advances occurred as a result of psychologies involvement in government or military activities. During the Second World War, over 1,700 psychologists were involved in the research, development, or implementation of assessment procedures in an effort to deal with such things as absenteeism, personnel selection, training (especially leader training), and soldier morale (Capshew, 1999). Moreover, given advances in warfare technology, new problems had to be addressed in such areas as equipment design (especially user interfaces), overcoming the limitations of the human body (as in high-altitude flying), and managing work teams. Technical advances in survey methods (e.g., the Likert scale) found immediate applications in the form of soldier morale surveys or studies of farmers and their intentions to plant and harvest foodstuffs critical to the war effort.

A development of particular relevance to this chapter was the creation of assessment procedures for screening candidates for unusual or dangerous assignments, including submarine warfare and espionage. The multimethod, multisource philosophy of this approach eventually became the basis for the assessment center method used widely in industry for selection and development purposes (Howard & Bray, 1988). Finally, when it came to the defining of performance itself, Flanagan's (1954) work on the critical incident method was found invaluable. Eventually, extensions of the approach could be found in applied work on the assessment of training needs and even the measurement of service quality.

Over the years, the needs of the military and of government bureaus and agencies have continued to capture the attention of academics and practitioners, resulting in innovations of potential use to industry. This interplay has also encouraged the development of a large and varied array of measurement tools or assessment platforms. The Army General Classification test has its analogue in any number of multi-aptitude test batteries. Techniques for measuring the requirements of jobs, such as Functional Job Analysis or the Position Analysis Questionnaire, became the basis for assessment platforms like the General Aptitude Test Battery (GATB) or, more recently, the Occupational Information Network (O*Net; Peterson, Mumford, Borman, Jeanneret, & Fleishman, 1999). Scales to measure job attitudes (Smith, Kendall, & Hulin, 1969), organizational commitment (Mowday, Steers, & Porter, 1979), or work adjustment (Dawis, 1991) found wide application, once developed. Moreover, there is no shortage of standard measures for cognitive and noncognitive individual attributes (Impara & Plake, 1998).

Still another illustration of the importance of cultural context on developments in industry can be found in the implementation of civil rights legislation in America in the 1960s and 1970s (and, a little later, the Americans with Disabilities Act (1990)). This provided new impetus to changes in theory, research designs, and assessment practices in work organizations. The litigation of claims under these laws has also had a profound effect on the kinds of measures found to be acceptable for use. Among other things, this movement called for assessment tools and practices to be made more accessible to people with disabilities and to those with limited English-language skills.

As a final example of the interplay among society, policy, and assessments in industry, we would point out relatively recent trends to assess or to predict "dysfunctional" or "counterproductive" worker behaviors (Spector, Bauer, & Fox, 2010). Examples include such things as theft on the job, drug abuse, and betrayal of trust. The finding that such behaviors are not merely the opposite of desirable ("citizenship") behaviors (Dalal, 2005) has caused practitioners to spend effort to find valid and reliable ways to measure and predict their occurrence.

## NATURE OF ASSESSMENT IN INDUSTRIAL AND ORGANIZATIONAL SETTINGS

Most individuals are aware of at least some of the approaches used for individual assessment by psychologists.

For example, it is quite common to see mention in the popular press of psychologists' use of interviews and questionnaires in support of any number of practice areas (e.g., family counseling). Individual assessment in work organizations involves many of these same approaches, but there are some characteristic features worth stressing at the outset. Specifically, with regard to assessments in work settings, we highlight their multiple (and at times conflicting) purposes, the types of factors measured, the approach used, and the role that assessment must play to ensure business success.

## Distinctive Features of Assessments in Industry

Three features of the approach favored by many of those doing assessment work in industry are worth highlighting. The first has been noted already in that many assessment platforms are built on careful development and backed up by empirical evidence. It is not recommended that an assessment technique be adopted or a particular practitioner's services be used without empirical evidence of appropriateness for that particular organization.

A second distinctive feature is that most assessments of individuals in work contexts are not conducted by psychologists. Instead, managers, supervisors, trainers, and even peers are typically involved in evaluating individuals on the factors of interest. This said, for larger firms, practicing psychologists may participate in the design of assessment tools and programs (e.g., a structured interview protocol for assessing job applicants), or they may train company personnel on how to use them. This would be less likely for smaller firms, which might retain a psychologist or use one on an as-needed basis (e.g., to assist in the selection of a managing partner in a law firm) to use assessment tools that he or she has found valid in other applications.

A final distinction between assessment in industry and other psychological assessments is that quite often assessments are conducted on a large number of individuals at the same time or over a short period of time. For example, when the fire and safety service of Nassau County, New York, sought to recruit and select about 1,000 new police officers, it had to arrange for 25,000 applicants to sit for the qualifying exam at one time (Schmitt, 1997). This not only has implications for the kinds of assessment tools that can be used but affects such mundane matters as choice of venue (in this case, a sports arena was needed to accommodate all applicants) and how to manage test security (Halbfinger, 1999).

## Marketplace and the Business Case

Assessment practices in the workplace have been implemented in order to accomplish several objectives. These often revolve around the desire to address the challenges of effective human resource management.

### Business Necessity

Assessments in work organizations are conducted for the purpose of increasing the efficiency and effectiveness of business operations. Thus, they might be performed in order to design, develop, implement, or evaluate the impact of a business policy or practice. In this regard, the firm uses assessment information (broadly defined) to index such things as the level of skill or competency (or its obverse, their deficiencies) of its employees or their level of satisfaction (because this might presage quitting). As such, the information so gathered ends up serving an operational feedback function for the firm. It can also serve to address the issue of how well the firm is conforming to its own business plans (Katz & Kahn, 1978).

Organizations find it important to assess individuals as part of their risk management obligation and personnel administration functions. Most conspicuous is the use of assessments for selecting new employees (trying to identify who will work hard, perform well, and not steal), ensuring a nondiscriminatory workplace (Klimoski & Donahue, 1997), or conducting performance appraisals. The latter, in turn, serve as the basis for compensation or promotion decisions (Murphy & Cleveland, 1995; Saks, Schmitt, & Klimoski, 2000). Assessments of an individual's level of work performance can become the basis for the termination of employment, thus, the firm has a business need to use valid assessments as the basis for making all appropriate and defensible personnel judgments.

Most models of organizational effectiveness make it clear that the capacity to acquire, retain, and efficiently use key resources, including human resources, is essential. Unemployment levels rise and fall in the United States, each causing major implications in the workplace. In either circumstance, the demand for skilled workers is often high, and intense competition can be seen for workers with critical skills (e.g., information technology, science, mathematics). Talent identification and acquisition is one of the most difficult challenges faced by both public and private organizations today. Adding to this challenge is the proliferation of new Internet-based services that give more information than ever to current and prospective employees regarding the HR needs and practices of various organizations as well as a more accurate sense of their own market value. Clearly, there are intense competitive pressures to recruit, select, and retain good employees, and those responsible for the design and management of platforms for individual assessment must contribute to meeting such pressures.

Demands for efficiency and skilled workers are common across both the private and public sectors. However, additional demands and considerations must be taken into account in the nonprofit sector. Assessment at the local, state, and federal government levels brings an extra layer of complexity due to political pressures, union involvement, skyrocketing costs, shrinking budgets, privacy and security concerns, and the criticality of certain jobs (e.g., public safety professionals; Barrett, Doverspike, & Young, 2010). Similar to employment selection procedures, assessment psychologists must ensure that promotions follow federal merit based regulations regarding fair-and-open competition for all positions and abstain from preselecting employees for particular management positions or succession management or development programs. Given today's highly litigious environment, assessment psychologists must be keenly aware of recent legal issues, stakeholder demands, and perceptions of test fairness and data security in selection, promotion, and development circumstances.

### Worker Well-Being

Assessments in industry can also be performed with the goal of meeting the needs of the individual worker. The assessment of individual training needs, for example, can become the basis for a specific worker's training and development experiences. In a related manner, assessments may be gathered to guide the worker relative to his or her career. Whether done in the context of an organizationally managed career-path planning program or done by the worker on his or her own initiative, such competency assessments relative to potential future jobs or different careers are ultimately in the service of the worker. Assessment information may be used to help workers find suitable employment in different firms, a need precipitated by such things as a corporate restructuring effort or downsizing or as an outcome of an acquisition or a merger. Thus, job preferences and skills typically are evaluated as part of an outplacement program.

Assessments are at the core of counseling and coaching activities in the workplace. These activities can be part of a larger corporate program for enhancing the capabilities of the workforce. Often special assessments are conducted because the individual worker is in difficulty. This may be manifested in a career plateau, poor job performance,

excessive absenteeism, interpersonal conflict on the job, or symptoms of depression or substance abuse. In the latter cases, such assessments may be part of an employee assistance program specifically set up to help workers deal with personal issues or problems. Alternatively, certain individuals might be selected to participate in a coaching arrangement because they are seen as having high potential (Silzer & Church, 2009). In this case, the employee (often already a manager) receives the benefits of a personalized program of development based on assessments of strengths, weaknesses, and goals at the outset of the relationship between a coach and the employee (Bono, Purvanova, Towler, & Peterson, 2009).

### Assessments as Criterion Measures

In the course of more than 100 years of practice, specialists conducting personnel research have concluded that good criterion measures are hard to develop. This may be due in part to the technical requirements for such measures, or it may simply be a reflection that the human attributes and the performances of interest are, by their very nature, quite complex. When it comes to criterion measures, this complexity is most clearly noted in the fact that these are almost always treated as multidimensional.

The notion of dimensionality itself is seen most clearly in measures of job performance (Borman & Motowidlo, 1993; Spector et al., 2010). Research has supported the value of thinking of worker performance as one of three categories. The term *task performance* is used to refer to the usual domain of performance measurement. *Contextual performance* reflects such things as helping behaviors, "civic duty," self-development, or behaviors that reflect "good sportsmanship." These collectively are frequently referred to as "employee citizenship behaviors" (Podsakoff & MacKensie, 1997). Finally, one can often find reasons to measure a third category characterized as *counterproductive worker behaviors*. When we want to measure and assess worker performance for research purposes, we must be clear which of these is important to the company and proceed accordingly.

### Assessments as Predictors

In applied research, we are not just in need of a valid assessment of worker performance. In fact, we are most often doing such research because we want to identify or develop better assessments for the purpose of making good organizational decisions (e.g., selection or promotion). As such, the challenge involved is both conceptual and psychometric in nature.

Thus, assessments for purposes of applied research may not differ much in terms of the specific features of the tools themselves. For example, something as common as a work sample test may be the tool of choice to gather data for validation or for making selection decisions. However, when one is adopted as the source of criterion scores, it implies a requirement for special diligence from the organization in terms of assessment conditions, additional time or resources, and high levels of skill on the part of the practitioner (Campbell, 1990).

In summary, individual assessment in work settings is both similar to and different from many other contexts in which such assessments take place. Although the skills and techniques involved would be familiar to most psychologists, those responsible for making use of assessment information or data obtained in work settings must be sensitive and appropriate to the applied problems of interest and the needs of particular stakeholders.

## PROFESSIONAL AND TECHNICAL CONSIDERATIONS

As described in the overview section, professionals who conduct assessments in industrial settings do so based on the work context. A job analysis provides information on the tasks, duties, and responsibilities carried out by the job incumbents as well as the knowledge, skills, and abilities (KSAs) needed to perform the job well (Saks et al., 2000). Job analysis information helps us conduct selection and promotion assessments by determining if there is a fit between the skills needed for the job and those held by the individual and if the individual has the potential to perform well on the important KSAs. We can also use job analysis information for career management by providing the individual and the career counselor or coach with information about potential jobs or careers. The individual can then be assessed using various skill and interest inventories to determine fit. Job analysis information can also be used for classification and placement to determine which position within an organization best matches the skills of the individual. We discuss the purpose, application, and tools for assessments in the next section. In this section we focus on how organizations use job analysis tools to develop assessment tools to make organizational decisions.

### Role of Assessment Data for Inferences in Organizational Decisions

Guion (1998) pointed out that one major purpose of research on assessments in industrial/organizational settings is to evaluate how well these assessments help us make personnel decisions. The process he described is prescriptive and plays out especially well for selection purposes. The reader should be aware that descriptively several constraints, such as a small number of cases, the rapid pace at which jobs change, and the time it takes to carry out the process, make this approach difficult. Guion therefore suggested that assessment practices should be guided by theory, but so too should practice inform theory.

### Technical Parameters

We are using the term *technical parameters* to describe some of the key psychometric attributes that practitioners require from any assessment tool used to gather information on individuals in work settings. Practitioners often use these attributes to evaluate the claims of tools being proposed for use; thus, these attributes can serve as a way to vet the large number of assessment products or services currently available.

#### Reliability

Most readers are aware of the various forms of reliability and how they contribute to inferences in assessments. These are discussed in detail in other chapters in this volume. This section notes the forms of reliability used in industrial settings.

The kind of reliability sought should be appropriate to the application of the assessment. Of particular importance to industrial settings is interrater reliability. For example, in the context of structured interviews or assessment centers, if raters (or judges) do not agree on an individual's score, this should serve as a warning that the assessment platform should be reviewed. For the most part, organizations look at internal consistency reliability more than test–retest or parallel forms. In many industrial settings, with the exception of large organizations that conduct testing with many individuals on a regular basis, it is often asserted that time constraints limit the evaluation of the latter forms of reliability.

#### Validity

All test validation involves inferences about psychological constructs (Schmitt & Landy, 1993). We are interested not simply in whether an assessment predicts performance but whether the inferences we make with regard to these relationships are correct. Binning and Barrett (1989) laid out an approach for assessing the validity (job-relatedness of a predictor) of personnel decisions based on the many inferences we make in validation.

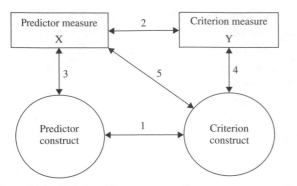

**Figure 14.1** Relationships among predictor constructs, predictor measures, criterion constructs, and criterion measures.

Guion's (1998) simplification of Binning and Barrett's (1989) presentation is described in Figure 14.1 to illustrate the relationships among predictor constructs, predictor measures, criterion constructs, and criterion measures. Line 1 shows that the relationship between the predictor construct (e.g., conscientiousness) is related to the criterion construct (some form of job behavior such as effective customer service) or a result of the behavior. Relationship 2 is the only inference that is empirically testable. It is the statistical relationship between the predictor measure, a test of conscientiousness such as the Hogan Personality Inventory (HPI; R. T. Hogan & Hogan, 1995), and the criterion measure (some measured criteria of job performance such as scores on a multisource feedback assessment). Tests of inferences 3 and 4 are used in construct validation. Relationship 3 shows whether the predictor measure (HPI) is a valid measure of the predictor construct (conscientiousness). Relationship 4 assesses whether the criterion measure (multisource feedback scores) is effectively measuring the performance of interest (e.g., effective customer service). Finally, relationship 5 is the assessment of whether the predictor measure (conscientiousness) is related to the criterion construct of interest (customer service) in a manner consistent with its presumed relationship to the criterion measure. Relationship 5 is dependent on the inferences we make about our job analysis data and those that we make about our predictor and construct relationships.

Although the importance of establishing construct validity is now well established in psychology, achieving the goal of known construct validity in the assessments used in work contexts continues to be elusive. Political considerations come into play in establishing validity in industrial settings. Austin, Klimoski, and Hunt (1996) pointed out that "validity is necessary but not sufficient for effective long-term selection systems" (p. 179). They suggest that in addition to the technical considerations already discussed, procedural justice or fairness and feasibility-utility also be considered. For example, in union environments, optimizing all three standards may be a better strategy than maximizing one set.

*Fairness*

Industrial/organizational psychologists view fairness as a technical issue (Cascio, 1993), a social justice issue (Austin et al., 1996), and a public policy issue (American Educational Research Association, American Psychological Association, & National Council on Measurement in Education, 1999). In industrial/organizational settings, the technical issues of differential validity and differential prediction are assessed for fairness. Differential validity exists when there are differences in subgroup validity coefficients. If a measure that is valid only for one subgroup is used for all individuals regardless of group membership, the measure may discriminate unfairly against the subgroup for which it is invalid. Job performance and test performance must be considered because unfair discrimination cannot be said to exist if unfair test performance is associated with inferior job performance by the same group. Differential prediction exists when there are slope and intercept differences between minority and nonminority groups. For example, Cascio (1993) pointed out that a common differential prediction exists when the prediction system for the nonminority group slightly overpredicts minority group performance. In this case, minorities would tend not to do as well on the job as their test scores would indicate.

As Austin et al. (1996) pointed out, fairness is also related to the social justice of how the assessment is administered. They argued that the perceptions of neutrality of decision makers, respect given to test takers, and trust in the system are important for the long-term success of assessments. In fact, Gilliland (1993) argued that procedural justice can be decomposed into three components: formal characteristics of procedures, the nature of explanations offered to stakeholders, and the quality of interpersonal treatment as information comes out. These issues must be considered for there to be acceptability of the process.

It cannot be stressed enough that there is no consensus on what is fair. Fairness is defined in a variety of ways and is subject to several interpretations (American Educational Research Association et al., 1999). Cascio (1993) pointed out that personnel practices, such as testing, must be considered in the total system of personnel decisions and that each generation should consider the policy implications of testing. The critical consideration is not whether to use tests but rather *how* to use them (Cronbach, 1984).

## Utility

When conducted properly, psychological assessments can result in substantial economic gains from improved decisions about individuals and programs. *Selection utility* is the dollar or output gain realized from administering a valid personnel selection assessment. This term has special meaning in the assessment of individuals in industry because it involves the analysis of the interplay among the predictive power of assessment tools and the selection ratio. In general, even a modest correlation coefficient can have utility if there is a favorable selection ratio. Assessments in this context must be evaluated against the cost and potential payoff to the organization. Utility theory does just that. It provides decision makers with information on the costs, benefits, and consequences of all assessment options.

Through utility analysis, an organization can decide whether a structured interview or a cognitive ability test is more valid and more cost effective. Based on 85 years of personnel selection research, Schmidt and Hunter (1998) estimated that the typical savings from increasing the validity of a selection test for a medium complexity job is approximately $18,000 per year, or an increase of 9% productivity. This is the average increase in output per hire as a direct result of increasing the validity of the selection method and must be multiplied for every person hired. In addition, because this figure is realized annually, it must be multiplied by each year an employee remains with the company. Refer to Schmidt and Hunter (1998) for an in-depth discussion of validity coefficients for the prediction of job performance and job training for some of the most common selection methods.

## Legal Considerations

Employment laws exist to prohibit unfair discrimination in employment and to provide equal employment opportunity for all. Unfair discrimination occurs when employment decisions are based on race, sex, religion, ethnicity, age, or disability rather than on job-relevant knowledge, skills, abilities, and other characteristics. Employment practices that unfairly discriminate against people are called unlawful or discriminatory employment practices.

The increased use of psychological assessments for selection and promotion purposes has resulted in greater scrutiny by the courts (Ashe & Lundquist, 2010). Those endeavoring to conduct individual assessments in industry must consider the laws that apply in their jurisdiction.

With the increasingly global society, assessment psychologists must also consider laws in other countries. In the United States, case law and professional standards and acts must be followed. The next paragraphs describe some of the standards, acts, and court rulings that must be considered.

*Title VII of the Civil Rights Act of 1964* (as amended in 1972) prohibits unfair discrimination in all terms and conditions of employment based on race, color, religion, sex, and national origin.

- *The Pregnancy Discrimination Act* amended Title VII to prohibit discrimination against a woman based on pregnancy, childbirth or medically related conditions.
- "Limited English Proficiency" (LEP)—Executive Order 13166, Improving Access to Services for Persons with Limited English Proficiency requires federal agencies and those in receipt of federal financial assistance to provide LEP individuals with meaningful access to programs and activities.

The *Age Discrimination in Employment Act of 1967* (ADEA) prohibits discrimination against employees or applicants age 40 or older in all aspects of the employment process.

The *Fair Credit Reporting Act* (FCRA) of 1970, Sections 604, 606, and 615, as amended, primarily protects a consumer's privacy in credit reporting. In an employment context, the FCRA sets national standards for employers that use third-party companies, such as a "consumer reporting agencies," to conduct background checks, credit reports and so forth. Under the FCRA, an employer must seek written permission from an applicant before conducting a background check and must notify a potential applicant when the information gathered from the report has a negative impact on an employment decision.

The *Equal Employment Opportunity Commission* (EEOC), established in 1972, is responsible for enforcing federal laws prohibiting employment discrimination.

The *Uniform Guidelines on Employee Selection Procedures of 1978* (Equal Employment Opportunity Commission, Civil Service Commission, U.S. Department of Labor, & U.S. Department of Justice, 1978) incorporate a set of principles governing the use of employee selection procedures (i.e., any measure, combination of measures, or procedure used as a basis for any employment decision) according to applicable laws and provide a framework for employers to determine the proper use of tests and other selection procedures. A basic principle of the guidelines is that it is unlawful to use a test or selection procedure that creates adverse impact, unless justified. When there is no charge of adverse impact, the guidelines do not require that one show the job-relatedness of assessment procedures; however, they strongly encourage one to use only job-related assessment tools. Demonstrating the job-relatedness of a test is the same as establishing that the test may be validly used as desired. Demonstrating the business necessity of an assessment involves showing that its use is essential to the safe and efficient operation of the business and that there are no alternative procedures available that are substantially equally valid to achieve business results with lesser adverse impact. The EEOC identified three ways employers can show their tests and other selection processes are job-related and consistent with business necessity:

1. *Criterion-related validity*: proof that there is a relationship between test scores and job performance on a sample of employees
2. *Content validity*: proof that the content of a test (or other selection procedure) represents important aspects of job performance
3. *Construct validity*: proof that the test measures a trait or characteristic that is important to successful job performance

The *Americans with Disabilities Act of 1990* (ADA) requires that qualified individuals with disabilities be given equal opportunity in all aspects of employment. Employers must provide reasonable accommodation to persons with disabilities when doing so would not pose undue hardship.

*Title I of the Civil Rights Act of 1991* specifically requires demonstration of both job relatedness and business necessity. The act also prohibits score adjustments, the use of different cutoff scores for different groups of test takers, or the alteration of employment-related tests based on the demographics of test takers.

Standards for Educational and Psychological Testing (American Educational Research Association et al., 1999) and principles for validation and use of Personnel Selection Procedures (1987) are guidelines for individuals developing, evaluating, and using assessments in employment, counseling, and clinical settings. Even though they are guidelines, they are consistent with applicable regulations.

*Genetic Information Nondiscrimination Act of 2008* (GINA) prohibits insurers and employers from discriminating against individuals, employees, or applicants on the basis of genetic information. *Genetic information* includes information about an individual's genetic tests and the genetic tests of an individual's family members as well as information about any disease, disorder, or condition of those family members (i.e., an individual's family medical history). Specifically, this act pertains to the collection of information in health risk assessments when determining employee eligibility and insurance plan coverage.

In *Ricci v. DeStefano*, 530 F. 3d 87, 2009, the Supreme Court found that the City of New Haven violated Title VII when it disregarded a firefighter's exam that resulted in the promotion only of White and Hispanic applicants, but no Black applicants. The city disregarded the test results because it feared a lawsuit due to the racially disparate impact of the test on black applicants. The Court created a new standard in which an employer must "*demonstrate a strong basis in evidence that, had it not taken the action, it would have been liable under the disparate-impact statute*" (emphasis added; quote taken from Justice Anthony Kennedy, writing for the majority, on June 29, 2009 at the U.S. Supreme Court).

## PURPOSE, FOCUS, AND TOOLS FOR ASSESSMENT IN INDUSTRIAL/ ORGANIZATIONAL SETTINGS

This section describes how assessments in industrial/ organizational settings are used, the focus of those assessments, and the major tools used to conduct them. The reader may notice that the focus of the assessment may be similar for different assessment purposes. For example, personality may be the focus of both a selection test and a developmental assessment. Table 14.1 provides the

**TABLE 14.1   Illustrations of the Interface Between the Purpose and Focus of Assessments**

|  | Selection | Promotion | Development |
|---|---|---|---|
| Cognitive ability | X | X | X |
| Personality |  | X | X |
| Teamwork skills | X | X | X |
| Physical abilities |  | X | X |
| Job-specific knowledge and skills | X |  | X |
| Honesty and integrity | X |  | X |
| Interpersonal skills | X | X | X |
| Interests |  |  | X |
| Learning orientation | X | X | X |
| Training and experience | X | X | X |
| Leadership | X | X | X |
| Job performance |  | X |  |
| Job satisfaction |  | X |  |
| Job engagement |  | X |  |
| Service orientation | X | X | X |

linkage of these components and can serve as a preview of the material to follow.

It should be noted that, while it is not the focus of this chapter, many individual assessments are valuable for modeling and improving work organizations. Individual data can be aggregated and serve as organizational diagnostic information. This allows assessment psychologists and organizational development experts to make inferences regarding the health, climate or culture of the organization. For example, aggregating job performance assessments at the position level can reveal a need for training; aggregating individual data on worker personality or value profiles may provide insights on the organization's culture or the type of new worker that might fit in well with this culture. While individual assessments can be important for organizational change and diagnosis, in the next section we concentrate on the key purpose, measurement focus and tools of assessments using the individual as the unit of analysis.

## Purpose

Assessment information may be gathered by organizations in order to facilitate any one of a number of business related human resource management practices. These include selecting individuals who will succeed as employees, promoting the best people, and conducting training and development programs that will show the results that are required.

### Selection and Good Employee "Fit"

Selection is relevant to organizations when there are more qualified applicants than positions to be filled. The organization must decide who among those applicants can perform best on the job and should therefore be hired. That decision is based on the prediction that the person hired will be more satisfactory than the person rejected (Cascio, 1993). The goal of selection is thus to capitalize on individual differences in order to select those persons who possess the greatest amount of characteristics judged important for job success. A particular assessment is chosen because it proves to be a valid measure of the attributes that are important for a particular job (Landy, 1989; Saks et al., 2000). One or more predictors are selected that presumably relate to the criteria (performance on the job). These predictor constructs become the basis for an assessment test. For example, if we identified that cognitive ability is an important predictor for performance in the job of customer service representative, we would develop a test that measures the construct of cognitive ability.

The use of assessment tools for selection varies depending on the job performance domain and the level of individual we are selecting. For example, because routine work (e.g., assembly line) is more structured than work that is more complex, more dynamic, and less programmed (e.g., consulting) and because teamwork requires more interpersonal skills than does individually based work, selection assessments vary greatly for different jobs. Additionally, the level of the position dictates the type of assessment we would use. Selection for a chief executive officer would probably involve several interviews, whereas selection for a secretary might involve a typing test, an interpersonal skills test, and an interview.

While the use of appropriate and valid selection systems is likely to have major payoffs for the company, the applicants or candidate will benefit as well. Such systems increase the likelihood that there will be a good fit between future workers' abilities, skills, and interests and the demands of the job to which they would be placed if they were hired. In this regard, such systems represent a win-win for both parties (Kallenberg, 2008).

### Promotion

In organizational settings, it is not uncommon to use tools such as a job knowledge test or multisource ratings on the individual's performance over the past year to estimate readiness. In the context of school, a more direct assessment of potential might be the Standardized Aptitude Test, which determines the person's potential to perform well in college (Anastasi & Urbina, 1996). At work, specially designed assessments might be administered specifically to focus on managerial or sales potential (e.g., J. Hogan & Hogan, 1986).

When we are conducting an assessment of performance, we are generally determining an individual's achievement at the time of the assessment. When we are considering an individual for a promotion, however, we must also determine those traits or qualities thought to be critical for success on the new job. Psychologists are often faced with the pressure of developing promotion instruments that are based (largely) on past performance. However, a new job involving a major change of duties requires additional qualities and qualifications. In the circumstances, assessments should focus on measuring those attributes that reflect potential rather than simply past performance.

Another challenge in the promotion arena is that organizations often intend to use yearly performance appraisals to determine if a candidate should be promoted. However, there is often little variance between candidates on these appraisals. It is well documented that managers, as raters, provide high ratings to ensure workplace harmony. The result is that records will show little difference among candidates, thus making them a poor basis on which to make promotion decisions. Other tools, which involve the use of multiple, trained raters used in conjunction with the performance appraisal, might be used to remedy this problem.

## Development

Development is a systematic process initiated by an organization to improve the knowledge, skills, abilities or attitudes of its employees (Kraiger, 2003). Assessments for the purpose of development are conducted so that individuals can have a realistic assessment of their strengths and weaknesses (Cascio, 1991) as well as their values, interests, and lifestyles (Brunkan, 1991). Multisource ratings, personality, interest, and observed leadership assessments as well as assessment centers and simulations are often used for this purpose. Typically the data obtained are shared with an employee to identify those areas on which he or she could develop further. However, assessments for development may be driven by the specific developmental options that are available in the organization. In this regard, the challenge is not just to determine what needs to be improved but to establish, a priori, that the person being developed will likely profit from these efforts (McCall, 2010).

Useful developmental insights for employees can come from assessments that allow for the demonstration of actual behavior, such as an assessment center or simulation. Simulations engage participants in mission-focused scenarios that demand fast-paced decisions, test limits, and result in realistic consequences. They elicit real-time skills, attitudes, and behaviors that can be judged as appropriate or inappropriate for the context of the organization. Simulations provide moments of insight based on the consequences of their behavior played out in real-life situations, and feedback based on this behavior helps employees see and accept areas for development more rapidly. However, simulations bring to light only some of the individual employee's strengths or weaknesses. In this regard, it is often useful to supplement simulation data with information regarding the person's typical behavior while on the job. Here tools such as personal diaries, self-ratings on carefully designed inventories, or peer (even subordinate) assessments gathered for purposes of development are useful.

## Focus and Tools

The focus of assessments in industrial settings involves any number of possible constructs. The set is as large as the number of individual difference factors that have been identified by researchers at a given point in time. In this section, we highlight those constructs that are robust and referenced consistently in the literature on promoting a more effective workplace. Where the information is available, this section also summarizes specific assessment tools and findings on the validity of these measures in predicting job performance. We suggest that the reader refer to Table 14.2 for examples of tools linked to each type of assessment.

## Cognitive Ability

The literature has established that cognitive ability, and specifically general mental ability, is a suitable predictor of many types of performance in the work setting. The work conducted for the Army Project A has shown that general mental ability consistently provides the best prediction of task proficiency (e.g., McHenry, Hough, Toquam, Hanson, & Ashworth, 1990). Hunter and Hunter's (1984) meta-analysis showed that validity for general mental ability is .58 for professional-managerial jobs, .56 for high-level complex technical jobs, .51 for medium-complexity jobs, .40 for semiskilled jobs, and .23 for unskilled jobs. Additionally, Schmidt and Hunter's (1998) meta-analysis showed that scores on cognitive ability measures predict task performance for all types of jobs and that general mental ability often combines with other predictors (e.g. a work sample test) to provide substantial multivariate validity and utility evidence. They found that cognitive ability tests (e.g., Wonderlic Personnel Test, 1992) are robust predictors of performance and job-related learning and argued that because cognitive ability is so robust, it should be referred to as a primary measure for hiring decisions and that other measures should be referred to as supplementary.

Despite these strong correlations, there is evidence that cognitive ability is more predictive of task performance (formally recognized as part of the job) than of contextual performance (activities such as volunteering, persisting, cooperating). While cognitive ability is a powerful predictor of job performance, for a variety of reasons (e.g., poor academic preparation) there exist consistent mean ethnic differences in applicant scores for jobs of all complexity levels (Roth, Bevier, Bobko, Switzer, & Tyler, 2001). Used alone, cognitive ability tests will results in disparate hiring rates by race. Adding other predictive assessments,

**TABLE 14.2   Example Tools Associated With the Focus of the Assessment**

| Focus | Example Tools |
|---|---|
| Cognitive ability | Wonderlic Personnel Test (Wonderlic, 1992) |
| | General Aptitude Test Battery (Nelson Education, 1986) |
| | Critical Reasoning Test Battery (SHL, 2000) |
| | Watson-Glaser Critical Thinking Appraisal (Pearson, 1965) |
| Personality | Hogan Personality Inventory (Hogan Assessment Systems, 1995) |
| | Hogan Development Survey (Hogan Assessment Systems, 1996) |
| | 16Personality Factor (16PF) (Cattell, Cattell, & Cattell, 1993) |
| | California Personality Inventory (Consulting Psychologists Press, 1957) |
| | NEO-Personality Inventory (Costa & McCrae, 1992) |
| Teamwork skills | Teamwork KSA Test (Stevens & Campion, 1994) |
| Physical abilities | *Handbook of Human Abilities* (Fleishman & Reilly, 1992) |
| | Candidate Physical Agility Test (International Association of Fire Fighters and International Association of Fire Chiefs, 1997) |
| Job-specific knowledge and skills | Work sample tests, such as those developed for specific trades |
| | Job knowledge tests |
| Honesty and integrity | Reliability scale of the Hogan Personnel Selection Series |
| Interpersonal skills | Goldberg's measure of interpersonal characteristics |
| | Structured interviews[1] |
| | Assessment centers[2] |
| Interests | Vocational Preference Inventory (Holland, Fritsche, & Powell, 1994) |
| | Self-Directed Search (Holland, 1985) |
| | Strong Vocational Interest Inventory (Consulting Psychologists Press, 1927) |
| Leadership | Leadership Forecast Series (Hogan Assessment Systems) |
| | DiSC (InScape) |
| | Myers-Briggs Type Inventory (Consulting Psychologists Press) |
| | Fundamental Interpersonal Relations Orientation (FIRO)-B (CPP) |
| | Achieving Styles Inventory (Connective Leadership Institute) |
| | Multifactor Leadership Questionnaire (Bass & Avolio, 1996) |
| | Leadership Practices Inventory (Kouzes & Posner, 2002) |
| | Simulations |
| Learning orientation | Learning Orientation Questionnaire (The Training Place) |
| Training and experience | Owens Biographical Questionnaire (Owens & Schoenfeldt, 1979) |
| Mechanical Aptitude Test (Ramsay Corp.) | |
| Multisource assessment | Leadership Versatility Index (Kaplan DeVries) |
| | Leadership Circle Profile (Leadership Circle) |
| | Benchmarks (Center for Creative Leadership) |
| Job satisfaction | Minnesota Satisfaction Questionnaire (Hirschfeld, 2000) |
| | Job Descriptive Index (Smith et al., 1969) |
| | Faces (Kunin, 1955) |
| Job engagement | Valtera Engagement Survey (Valtera, 2011) |
| | Individual Directions Inventory (Mahoney, 1991) |
| Service orientation | Caliper First Step (Caliper) |
| | Customer Service Skills (Learning Resources) |

[1] In addition to assessing interpersonal skills, structured interviews assess a variety of competencies (e.g., leadership skills, technical skills, and teamwork skills).

[2] In addition to assessing interpersonal skills, assessment centers assess a variety of competencies (e.g., leadership skills, technical skills, and teamwork skills).

such as personality, to a selection battery may reduce this disparity.

### Personality

As we expand the criterion domain (Borman & Moto-widlo, 1993) to include contextual performance, we see greater importance laid on personality constructs. Although there is controversy over just how to define personality operationally (Klimoski, 1993), R. Hogan and Kaiser (2010) have argued that the definition includes two components: the impressions that one makes on others resulting in one's reputation and the internal factors that define one's behavior and identity. These authors argued that confusion in the personality literature often results from not distinguishing between these two definitions.

Mount and Barrick (1995) suggested that the emergence of the five-factor structure of personality led to empirical research that found "meaningful and consistent" (p. 23) relationships between personality and job performance. Researchers have found a great deal of evidence to support the notion that different components of the five-factor model (FFM; also known as the "Big Five") predict various dimensions of performance. The FFM components are agreeableness, extroversion, emotional stability, conscientiousness, and openness to experience. Research has shown that these factors predict various dimensions of job performance and are useful constructs to assess in selection. For example, J. J. Hogan and Holland's (2003) meta-analysis of the relationship between personality and job performance resulted in observed validity coefficients from the scales of the HPI (an instrument based on the FFM) of .15 for Learning Approach (a measure of openness) to .25 for Adjustment (a measure of emotional stability). More recently, Oh, Wang & Mount (2011) report on the potential value of using observer-generated rather than self-report data on FFM measures. In their meta-analysis they obtained correlations with job performance ranging from .31 (for the conscientiousness dimension) to .17 (for emotional stability) when up to 3 observers provided ratings. McHenry et al. (1990) found that scores from ability tests provided the best prediction for job-specific and general task proficiency (i.e., task performance), whereas temperament or personality predictors showed the highest correlations with such criteria as giving extra support, supporting peers, and exhibiting personal discipline (i.e., contextual performance). Although the FFM is prevalent at this time, it is only one of many personality schema. Others include the 16 Personality Factor Questionnaire (16PF; Cattell, Cattell, & Cattell, 1993) and a nine-factor model (Hough, 1992).

The factor of personality that has received the most attention is conscientiousness. Mount and Barrick's (1995) meta-analysis found that although conscientiousness predicted overall performance (both task and contextual), its relationships with the specific criterion determined by motivational effort (employee reliability and effort) were stronger. Organ and Ryan (1995) found significant relationships between conscientiousness and the altruism component of organizational citizenship behavior (OCB). Schmidt and Hunter's (1998) meta-analysis showed a .31 correlation between conscientiousness and overall job performance, leading them to conclude that in addition to general mental ability and job experience, conscientiousness is the "central determining variable of job performance" (p. 272).

The FFM of personality has also been shown to be predictive of an individual's performance in the context of working in a team (an issue we discuss in the next section). For example, a meta-analysis conducted by Mount, Barrick, and Stewart (1998) found that conscientiousness, agreeableness, and emotional stability were positively related to overall performance in jobs involving interpersonal interactions. Emotional stability and agreeableness were strongly related to performance in jobs that involve teamwork. Beyond job and team performance, personality also predicts leadership (Judge, Bono, Illies, & Gerhardt, 2002), absenteeism (Ones, Viswesvaran, & Schmidt, 2003), counterproductive work behavior (Berry, Ones, & Sackett, 2007), job satisfaction (Judge, Heller, & Mount, 2002), and life expectancy (Roberts, Kuncel, Shiner, Caspi, & Goldberg, 2007). Additionally, personality assessment in the workplace is useful for developmental feedback and career guidance.

Several tools are available to measure personality. Some focus on the FFM of personality (e.g., Big Five Factor Markers, Goldberg, 1992; NEO-PI, Costa & McCrae, 1992; Mini-Markers, Saucier, 1994; HPI, R. T. Hogan & Hogan, 1995), whereas others focus on a broader set of personality characteristics (e.g., 16PF; Cattell et al., 1993). Personality measures add incremental validity over cognitive ability tests (Schmidt & Hunter, 1998) and reduce the occurrence of adverse impact, making them a wise choice for assessments in work settings.

### Teamwork Skills

Individuals working in organizations today are increasingly finding themselves working in teams with people who have different sets of functional expertise (Hollenbeck, LePine, & Ilgen, 1996). This change from a clearly defined set of individual roles and responsibilities to an arrangement in which the individual is required to exhibit both technical expertise and an ability to assimilate quickly into a team is due to the speed and amount of information entering and exiting an organization. No individual has the ability to effectively integrate all of this information; thus, teams have been introduced as a solution (Amason, Thompson, Hochwarter, & Harrison, 1995).

Although an organization may be interested in overall team performance, it is important to focus on individuals' performance within the team (individual-in-team performance) so that we know how to select and appraise employees. Hollenbeck et al. (1996) pointed out that certain types of individuals will assimilate into teams more easily than others. It is these individuals whom we would want to select for a team. In the case of individual-in-team performance, we would suggest that both a contextual and a teamwork analysis be conducted. The contextual analysis provides the framework for team staffing by looking at (a) the reason for selection, whether it is to fill a vacancy, staff a team, or transform an organization from individual to team-based work; and (b) the team's functions (as described by Katz & Kahn, 1978), whether they are productive/technical, related to boundary management, adaptive, maintenance oriented, or managerial/executive. Additionally, the team analysis focuses on the team's role, its division of labor, and the function of the position. The results have implications for the knowledge, skills, and other attributes needed for the job (Klimoski & Zukin, 1998).

Several industrial/organizational psychologists have investigated the KSAs and personality dimensions important for teamwork. Stevens and Campion (1994) studied several teams and argued that two major categories of KSAs are important for teamwork: interpersonal and self-management. These researchers found that teamwork KSAs (i.e., conflict resolution, collaborative problem solving, communication, goal setting and performance management, planning, and task coordination) predicted on-the-job teamwork performance of teams in a southeastern pulp processing mill and a cardboard processing plant. Cannon-Bowers and Salas (1997) also reported that a configuration of knowledge, skills, and attitudes are typically required to perform effectively as a member of a team. However, the specific combination will depend on the nature of team task or mission. To assess individual-in-team performance, we suggest both a contextual and a teamwork analysis be conducted, as described earlier in this chapter.

## Physical Abilities

Physical abilities are important for jobs in which strength, endurance, and balance are important (Guion, 1998), such as mail carrier, power line repairer, and police officer. Fleishman and Reilly (1992) have developed a taxonomy of these abilities. Measures developed to assess these abilities have predicted work sample criteria effectively (R. T. Hogan, 1991). However, they must be used with caution because they can cause discrimination. The key here is that the level of that ability must be job relevant. Physical ability tests can be used only when they are genuine prerequisites for the job.

In jobs where physical strength (e.g., endurance or speed) is critical to job performance, tools have been developed to assess the various types of physical abilities. Fleishman and Reilly's (1992) work in this area identified nine major physical ability dimensions along with scales for the analysis of job requirements for each dimension that are anchored with specific examples. More recently the field has focused on more global constructs, such as strength and fitness, often assessed with job-related simulations to evaluate candidates and to establish their suitability for physically demanding work (Henderson, 2010).

## Job-Specific Knowledge and Skills

The Occupational Information Network (O*NET) system of occupational information (Peterson, Mumford, Borman, Jeanneret, & Fleishman, 1995) suggests that skills can be categorized as basic, cross-functional, and occupation specific. Basic skills are developed over a long period of time and provide the foundation for future learning. Cross-functional skills are useful for a variety of occupations and might include such skills as problem solving and resource management. Occupational (or job-specific) skills focus on those tasks required for a specific occupation. It is not surprising that research has shown that job knowledge has a direct effect on one's ability to do one's job. In fact, Schmidt, Hunter, and Outerbridge's (1986) path analysis found a direct relationship between job knowledge and performance. Cognitive ability had an indirect effect on performance through job knowledge. Findings like this suggest that, under certain circumstances, job knowledge may be a more direct predictor of performance than cognitive ability.

Work sample tests are used to measure job-specific knowledge and skill and are hands-on job simulations that must be performed by applicants. These tests assess one's procedural knowledge base. For example, as part of a work sample test, an applicant might be required to repair a series of defective electric motors. Often used to hire skilled workers, such as welders and carpenters (Schmidt & Hunter, 1998), these assessments must be used with applicants who already know the job. Schmidt and Hunter found that work sample tests show a 24% increase in validity over that of cognitive ability tests.

Job knowledge tests are also used to assess job-specific knowledge and skills. Like work sample tests, these assessments cannot be used to hire or evaluate inexperienced employees. They are often constructed by the hiring organization on the basis of a job analysis. Although they can be developed internally, doing so is often costly and time consuming. Those purchased off the shelf are less expensive and have only slightly lower validity than those developed by the organization. Job knowledge tests increase the validity over cognitive ability measures by 14%.

### Honesty and Integrity

The purpose of honesty/integrity assessments is to avoid hiring people prone to counterproductive behaviors. Sackett, Burris, and Callahan (1989) classify the measurement of these constructs into two types of tests. The first type is overt tests, which directly assess attitudes toward theft and dishonesty. They typically have two sections: one deals with attitudes toward theft and other forms of dishonesty (beliefs about the frequency and extent of employee theft, perceived ease of theft, and punitiveness toward theft); the other deals with admissions of theft. The second type consists of personality-based tests, which are designed to predict a broad range of counterproductive behaviors such as substance abuse (Camera & Schneider, 1994; Ones & Viswesvaran, 1998b).

Schmidt and Hunter (1998) found that these types of assessments show greater validity and utility than do work samples. The reliability scale of the Hogan Personnel Selection Series (J. Hogan & Hogan, 1989) was designed to measure "organizational delinquency" and includes items dealing with hostility toward authority, thrill seeking, conscientiousness, and social insensitivity. Ones, Dilchert, Viswesvaran, and Judge (2007) reported that integrity tests possess impressive criterion-related validity. Both overt and personality-based integrity tests correlated with measures of broad counterproductive behaviors, such as violence on the job, tardiness, and absenteeism. Reviews of validity of these instruments show no evidence of adverse impact against women or racial minorities (Sackett & Harris, 1984; Sackett et al., 1989).

### Interpersonal Skills

The skills related to social perceptiveness are the focus of the work by Goleman (1995) on emotional intelligence and the works on social intelligence (e.g., M. E. Ford & Tisak, 1983; Zaccaro, Gilbert, Thor, & Mumford, 1991). Goleman (1995) argued that empathy and communication skills, as well as social and leadership skills, are important for success at work (and at home). Organizations assess individuals on emotional intelligence for both selection and developmental purposes. Another interpersonal skill that is used in industrial settings is social intelligence, which is defined as "acting wisely in human relations" (Thorndike, 1920) and one's ability to "accomplish relevant objectives in specific social settings" (M. E. Ford & Tisak, 1983, p. 197). In fact, Zaccaro et al. (1991) found that social intelligence is related to sensitivity to social cues and situationally appropriate responses. Socially intelligent individuals can better manage interpersonal interactions.

Interpersonal skills can be assessed in interviews by asking candidates to respond to questions on how they handled past experiences dealing with difficult interpersonal interactions. Interpersonal skills may also be assessed through assessment centers where participants are placed in situations, like the leaderless group discussion, in which their ability to interact with others is assessed by trained raters.

Employment interviews can be structured or unstructured (Huffcutt, Roth, & McDaniel, 1996). Unstructured interviews have no fixed format or set of questions, and there is no format for scoring responses. Structured interviews include questions that are determined by a careful job analysis, and they have set questions and a set approach to scoring. Structured interviews have greater validity and show a 24% increase in validity over cognitive ability (Schmidt & Hunter, 1998). Although there is no one universally accepted structured interview tool, depending on how structured the interview is, it might be based on detailed protocols so that candidates are asked the same questions and assessed against the same criteria. Interviewers are trained to ensure consistency between candidates (Judge, Higgins, & Cable, 2000). Landy (1976) found that interviews of prospective police officers were able to assess communication skills and personal stability. Arvey and Campion (1982) summarized evidence that the interview was suitable for determining sociability.

In assessment centers, participants are observed participating in various exercises, such as leaderless group discussions, supervisor/subordinate simulations, and business games. The average assessment center includes seven exercises and lasts 2 days (Gaugler, Rosenthal, Thornton, & Bentson, 1987). Assessment centers can be used for both selection and development. The purpose and design of the assessment center should be explicit such that one for development must focus on competencies that can be developed while one for selection may include measures of constructs that are difficult to develop (e.g., cognitive ability, personality; Howard & Thomas, 2010). Assessment centers have substantial validity but only moderate incremental validity over cognitive ability because they are so highly correlated. Although assessment centers lack incremental validity, organizations use them because they provide a wealth of information useful for individual development.

## Interests

Psychologists in industrial settings use interest inventories to assist individuals with job placement, career development, and career transition. Interests are useful in job placement and career coaching relationships to determine the best occupational fit for an individual because individual differences in interests predict occupational membership criteria as well as vocational success and satisfaction (R. T. Hogan & Hogan, 1996). Additionally, organizations undergoing major restructuring may have new positions available; interest inventories can help employees determine what new positions might be a fit for them (although they may still have to develop new skills to succeed in those new positions). Organizations going through mergers, acquisitions, and/or downsizing might also use interest inventories as part of their outplacement services to assist employees in finding new positions outside of the current organization.

Tools such as Holland's Vocational Preference Inventory (Holland et al., 1994) and Self-Directed Search (Holland, 1985) and the Strong Interest Inventory (Harmon, Hansen, Borgen, & Hammer, 1994) are used to help individuals going through a career change. Interest inventories are often validated against their ability to predict occupational membership criteria and satisfaction with a job (R. T. Hogan & Blake, 1996). There is evidence that interest inventories predict occupational membership criteria (e.g., Cairo, 1982; Hansen, 1986); however, results are mixed with regard to whether there is a significant relationship between interests and job satisfaction (e.g., Cairo, 1982; Worthington & Dolliver, 1977). These results may exist because job satisfaction is affected by many factors, such as pay, security, and supervision. Additionally, there are individual differences in the expression of interests with a job. More recently, Van Iddekinge, Putka, and Campbell (2011) showed that an interest inventory can be constructed for a specific application in a particular organization (U.S. Army) and add substantial value to

its HR management efforts. The authors reported good and incremental validity over using just personality measures when predicting a diverse set of criteria including job knowledge, job performance, and, especially, intentions to reenlist ($r = .25-.46$). The interest inventory also helped to better assess the reenlistment prospects of women and minorities. Regardless of their ability to predict these criteria, interest inventories have been useful in helping individuals determine the next steps in their career development.

## Learning Orientation

Psychologists in industry also assess one's ability to learn, readiness to learn, motivation for learning (i.e., mastery or performance), learning style, or the information that one has learned. Learning ability might be assessed for the purpose of determining potential success in a training effort or on the job (and therefore for selection). Individuals differ in their preference for how information is presented, and understanding their learning style (e.g., lecture, computer based, etc.) can assist trainers in developing learning programs suited to different audiences (Kraiger, 2003). Assessing the impact of individual differences in the amount of learning that results from attending a training course can help an organization determine whether a proposed new course should be used for a broader audience. Tools used to assess learning can range from knowledge tests to cognitive structures or to behavioral demonstration of competencies under standardized circumstances (J. K. Ford, 1997).

## Training and Experience

Organizations often use training and experience information to determine if the individual, based on his or her past, has the KSAs necessary to perform in the job of interest. This information is mostly used for selection. An applicant might describe his or her training and experience through an application form, a questionnaire, a resume, or some combination of these. It is important to point out that the assessment of these things is often not simple. For example, years working on a job may not produce personal or professional growth. Thus, it is important to systematically delve into what the individual personally accomplished (Tesluk & Jacobs, 1998).

Schneider and Schneider (1994) pointed out that there are two assumptions of experience and training rating techniques: (1) They are based on the notion that a person's past behaviors are a valid predictor of what the person is likely to do in the future; and (2) as individuals gain more experience in an occupation, they are more committed to it and will be more likely to perform well in it. There are various approaches to conducting these ratings. One approach is the point method, in which raters assign points to candidates based on the type and length of a particular experience depending on the results of a job analysis. The empirical literature of point method approaches suggests that they have sufficient validity. McDaniel, Schmidt, and Hunter's (1988) meta-analysis found a corrected validity coefficient of .15 for point method–based experience and training ratings.

Questionnaires on biographical data (biodata) contain questions about life experiences, such as involvement in student organizations and offices held. The logic for using biodata is based on the behavioral consistency theory, which suggests that past performance is the best predictor of future performance. Items are chosen because they have been shown to predict some criteria of job performance. Historical data, such as attendance and accomplishments, are included in these inventories. Research indicates that biodata measures correlate substantially with cognitive ability and that they may offer little or no incremental validity over merely using the former when attempting to predict job performance (but not necessarily other criteria, such as creativity). This finding has led some psychologists to suggest that biodata reflect indirect measures of cognitive ability. Although some biodata inventories are available for general use, most organizations develop tools in-house that are suitable to their specific needs. An example tool discussed as a predictor of occupational attainment (Snell, Stokes, Sands, & McBride, 1994) is the Owens Biographical Questionnaire (Owens & Schoenfeldt, 1979).

### Leadership

Having the right leader in key executive and management positions has become increasingly important with globalization. Currently, there are a large number of workers approaching retirement and not enough of a replacement pool to fill their leadership positions. Therefore, identifying, selecting, placing, and developing leaders to fill these gaps have become increasingly important. Leadership assessments are often used in organizations to identify potential leaders with the right KSAs to be placed in advanced development programs for rapid succession to the executive ranks. Leadership assessments are also used to diagnose leaders needing further development in their current roles and to predict their potential and need for development for future leadership roles. Tools used to assess leadership include self-assessments, multisource

questionnaires, structured interviews, assessment centers, and simulations.

Leadership assessments are used to predict success in future leadership positions and diagnose areas for development (Howard & Thomas, 2010). Some tools can be used for both prediction and diagnosis, such as the Leadership Forecast Series (J. Hogan & Hogan, 1986), while others are useful for development only (e.g., Myers Brigs Type Indicator, Fundamental Interpersonal Relationship Orientation-B, DiSC). Additionally, leadership assessments can be self-report, rely on multisource feedback, or place potential leaders in real-life situations for professional observers to test their performance (i.e., in an assessment center or simulation).

Simulations are a growing trend in leadership assessment and development. Simulations place leaders in real-life scenarios where they face challenges requiring decision making and risk taking. Simulation scenarios may include a media interview where leaders are challenged to defend their organization's mistakes (Howard & Thomas, 2010) or computer models that require a leader or team to manage the purchasing, sales, and lending decisions of a fictitious company (Salas, Wildman, & Piccolo, 2009). Simulations allow for faster skill development due to their ability to provide a complex model of reality where leaders can practice their skills and trained observers can assess, or computer-based simulations can capture, the performance for immediate feedback (Avolio & Hannah, 2008). Research has shown that simulations can successfully predict later managerial performance (Howard & Thomas, 2010) and also serve to increase respondent interest, involvement, and enthusiasm toward the learning material (Keys & Wolfe, 1990). Because simulations mimic real-life job responsibilities and challenges, they give candidates a realistic job preview, which may lead some to self-select out of the hiring or succession process (Zielinski, 2011).

### Job Performance

Job performance information is frequently used for compensation or promotion decisions as well as to refer an individual to an employee assistance program (if job performance warrants the need for counseling). In these situations, job performance is measured to make personnel decisions for the individual. In typical validation studies, job performance is the criterion, and measures discussed earlier (e.g., training and experience, personality, cognitive ability) are used as predictors.

Measures of job performance are often in the form of multisource assessment platforms that can be used for promotions, salary increases, reductions in force, development, and research purposes. Multisource assessments are based on evaluations gathered about a target participant from two or more rating sources, including self, supervisors, peers, direct reports, internal customers, external customers, and vendors or suppliers. These tools are often referred to as 360-degree feedback assessments due to the collection of ratings from individuals with multiple perspectives above, below, and equal to the target's organizational level. The ratings are based on KSAs related to the job and must be gathered from properly chosen raters who have had adequate opportunity to observe the target's on-the-job behavior. Results of multisource assessments can be either provided purely for development or shared with the supervisor as input to a personnel decision (Dalessio, 1998). The problem with the latter is that often the quality of ratings is poorer when the various sets of raters (especially peers) know that their evaluations will be used for important personnel decisions (e.g., Murphy & Cleveland, 1995); thus, the multisource assessment paradigm typically is not recommended for selection or promotion decisions (Howard & Thomas, 2010). However, multisource assessments can be powerful tools in development programs because they uncover discrepancies between self and other ratings that can be useful for creating self-awareness and prioritizing developmental actions.

### Service Orientation

The United States has continued to move toward a service economy since World War II with services accounting for nearly three quarters of the gross national product. Additionally, customer service has a strong influence on the sales and bottom lines of organizations (Ryan & Ployhart, 2003). As a result, the assessment of service orientation has increased along with the importance of customer service. Service orientation has been characterized as a predisposition of employees to behave in a friendly, pleasant, and empathetic manner when interacting with other people (Ryan & Ployhart, 2003). Because customer service skills are applicable to a wide variety of jobs, including administrative and managerial positions, organizations are increasingly assessing individual characteristics necessary to succeed in service jobs (Martin & Fraser, 2002).

Service orientation assessments seek to determine an employee's predisposition across a variety of administrative and managerial positions to be cooperative, dependable, courteous, considerate and tactful when interacting with customers. Not surprisingly, the Big Five personality factors of Extraversion and Conscientiousness have been shown to relate to sales performance in service jobs

(Barrick & Mount, 1991). Service orientation assessments, such as the Service Orientation Index (SOI) in the HPI, can help organizations predict worker success in jobs requiring interaction with their customers (R. Hogan, Hogan, & Busch 1984).

### Job Satisfaction

Job satisfaction is one of the most frequently studied variables in industrial/organizational psychology due to its modest ability to predict job performance and employee retention (Judge, Thoreson, Bono, & Patton, 2001). Researchers attest that a stronger relationship may exist but is difficult to uncover due to differences in the conceptualization and measurement of the job satisfaction construct. Recent research demonstrates that job satisfaction includes both a cognitive and an affective component, yet job satisfaction assessments typically measure only one of these components (Kaplan, Warren, Barsky, & Thoresen, 2009). Kaplan et al. (2009) have recommended that assessment psychologists and practitioners take time to conduct a detailed analysis of the desired outcomes before choosing a job satisfaction measure.

Measures of job satisfaction are used to predict job performance and employee retention. The majority of job satisfaction measures, such as the Minnesota Satisfaction Questionnaire (Hirschfeld, 2000) and the Job Descriptive Index (Smith et al., 1969), assess the cognitive components of workers' judgments and beliefs about work. Research conducted by Kaplan et al. (2009) concluded that Kunin's Faces scale (1955) was unique in its ability to tap the affective component (i.e., how a person feels about their job) of job satisfaction.

### Job Engagement

Job engagement measures are used by psychologists and organizations to assess employees' level of satisfaction and motivation to stay with the organization. Employees who are less engaged in their job are more likely to consider leaving or have high rates of absenteeism (Rich, LePine, & Crawford, 2010; Schaufeli & Bakker, 2004). Interestingly, recent research has shown that engagement does not decrease during economic recessions but rather increases, most likely as a result of decreased job mobility (Deal, Stawiski, & Gentry, 2010). Surveys and assessments of job engagement, such as the Individual Directions Inventory (Mahoney, 1991), can help organizations determine if changes need to be made to increase employee commitment and retention by adjusting compensation and benefits packages, training and development opportunities, advancement opportunities, or the work itself.

### Psychological Workups

It is not uncommon for psychologists to serve as the de facto assessment tools when they are hired by an organization to evaluate candidates for personnel decisions (e.g., hiring). Ryan and Sackett (1987) pointed out that typically the input for such a psychologist's decision could come from several sources (such as those already discussed) but that the final evaluation is made by the psychologist. In this regard, the consulting psychologist often develops a proprietary assessment battery, which, when used over time, provides a model on which to base recommendations and diagnoses. Client firms often do not see the data on candidates but trust the consultant to administer, score, and integrate the raw material.

## MAJOR CHALLENGES

It should be clear that the scope of individual assessment activities in work contexts is quite large. Similarly, many individuals and professions are involved in this activity. It follows, then, that what constitutes an important issue or a problem is likely to be tied to stakeholder needs and perspective. In deference to this, we briefly examine in this section issues that can be clustered around major stakeholder concerns related to business necessity, social policy, and technical or professional matters.

### Business Considerations

Several business-related factors will shape the approach used by practitioners when it comes to when, where, and how assessments are conducted in organizations.

### Business Strategy

To be successful, organizations need to manage human resources effectively, but the magnitude of this requirement and the options open are strongly affected by business conditions and business strategy. At the most fundamental level, the nature and quality of employees required will depend on economic conditions. In times of an expanding economy, both the firm and its competitors will try to rapidly hire, promote, and retain the best people. When business conditions are poor, the challenge is often to use assessment data to identify and find ways to retain the most competent and critical people. Similarly, the nature of the product or service of the firm often dictates

the level of investment required in people and for managing assessment activities. For example, in educational institutions or consulting firms, labor costs will be a major part of the cost structure of the firm. For heavy industry (e.g., steel making), these costs will be much less.

Business strategy also plays into the kind of human capital that will be needed by the firm. Increasingly, many businesses are moving into the global marketplace for their products or services. This creates new challenges for assessment relative to making adjustments in tests or measures developed in the United States (and written in the English language) without destroying their validity or utility overseas. (For an example, see Hülsheger, Maier, & Stumpp, 2007.) Firms must also identify those who will be successful in expatriate positions or who will be competent to manage host country (national) subordinates. Similarly, many companies have discovered that to be competitive, they must become more innovative. This implies the need to find ways to assess (or predict) the creative capabilities of current or future workers. Finally, several authors have highlighted the need to be aware of changes in the legal environment from an international perspective (Sackett et al., 2008).

### Build It or Buy It

At one time in the United States, many large corporations had their own HR research units. They would be located in the HR function, staffed by psychologists, and responsible for designing, developing, and implementing assessment programs. Today, most firms have elected to purchase such services. By using an outside firm, the company is presumably getting state-of-the-art methods and models for assessment. Moreover, the outside firm usually has greater insight regarding normative practices in the industry (and even normative assessment data). However, by going outside, the company may have increased its costs.

The challenges facing a company that wishes to buy assessment services are numerous. For instance, it is often difficult to ascertain the professional qualifications of the numerous firms offering services. This is especially true when a consulting firm has a strong internal champion for its services. The temptation to latch on to the latest tool or technique may also be irresistible. There is ample evidence that many management practices, including assessment programs, have a fadlike quality: they are adopted for their popularity at the moment (Abrahamson, 1996), regardless of their suitability. Finally, there is the very real possibility that the outside firm would not take a stewardship role and gather appropriate statistical evidence to ensure that the assessment program meets technical and legal requirements. Were a consultant to recommend a local validation study or adverse impact analysis, the extra costs, time, and effort may cause the firm to decline this activity. A focus on the short-term bottom line may disadvantage the company if the externally provided assessment program were to be legally challenged in the future.

## Maintaining Quality

As noted, most assessments in industry are carried out by individuals who are neither psychologists nor measurement specialists (e.g., psychometricians). Although it is also true that many kinds of assessments may not require a PhD to administer, it still is imperative that the firm ensure that those responsible for gathering and interpreting data are qualified to do so. This aspect of due diligence is increasingly difficult as a result of the increased public access to tests and the reluctance of test publishers (due to financial pressures) to ensure test user qualifications. It is also exacerbated by the increased use of computer- and Internet-based test systems, which make it logistically easy for even a novice to offer services.

## Privacy

Assessment data are often paid for by the firm and archived in a worker's personnel file. Thus, frequently there is a great deal of tension regarding just how long information should be retained and, importantly, who should have access. Increasingly, such records are available electronically as companies go to Web-based HR systems. Access to such systems, although protected, can rarely be guaranteed. Moreover, there are an increasing number of instances in which third parties can demand to see such data if they are seen as material to litigation.

Certain kinds of assessment methods are viewed as more problematic from a privacy perspective. At this time, most applicants will accept and tolerate being assessed on ability and performance tests. They will usually see a job interview as a reasonable intrusion into their affairs. However, such approaches as drug testing, honesty testing, and polygraph testing usually create concerns on the part of applicants and employees alike (e.g., Anderson, Salgado, & Hülsheger, 2010). Assessments with regard to physical or mental disability, even when they are not prohibited by the ADA, are also likely to lead to perceptions of abuse of power and invasion of privacy (Linowes & Spencer, 1996).

## Technical Considerations

The practice of psychological assessments in industrial and organizational settings continues to evolve as new conceptual frameworks emerge, alternative assessment technologies become available, or research uncovers the value of alternative approaches. Some examples of the dynamism of this field are presented next.

### Noncognitive Measures

There has been a major shift in thinking about the appropriateness of noncognitive measures because they have shown to contribute to effective HR management programs in work organizations. Early reviews of the usefulness of interest and personality inventories were quite critical (Guion & Gottier, 1965), and with good reason. Many of the inventories used had been designed for the assessment of psychopathology (e.g., the Minnesota Multiphasic Personality Inventory [MMPI]). Moreover, the application of a particular scale was often made without regard to a careful analysis of the requirements of the job (Day & Silverman, 1989). In contrast, greater attention to these technical issues in recent years has resulted in great advances and the increased use of personality and interest measures in personnel work. The empirical record has now convinced most critics (e.g., Schmidt & Hunter, 1998) that noncognitive measures truly can add value over cognitive measures when it comes to predicting success on the job. However, much more research is needed.

The conceptualization of noncognitive measures can be problematic. As noted in an earlier section reviewing technical parameters, it is now quite common to make use of inventories that are based on meta-analytic research (e.g., Digman, 1990; Goldberg, 1990; Saucier, 1994) that gives support to the existence of and importance for five key constructs. However, the Big Five dimensions are only one approach to conceptualizing and measuring the personality domain. Additional work needs to be done to ascertain when this set of robust factors is a better way to conceptualize and measure noncognitive assessment needs than scales that might be more focused on the problem at hand. Additionally, there is the issue of the appropriateness of using more clinically oriented noncognitive measures found in individual coaching or the diagnosis of behavior or performance problems at work. The validity and relative utility of these measures are not well understood. For a recent review on some of these issues, the reader is advised to review Hough and Oswald (2008).

The use of noncognitive measures in high-stakes settings, such as screening for employment, has also revealed a key weakness: their susceptibility to being faked (McFarland & Ryan, 2000; Ones, Viswesvaran, & Reiss, 1996). Applicants or candidates for promotion who are being assessed on personality measures are likely to try to look good. Very often the measures themselves are transparent to the applicant in the sense that he or she can imagine the right answers to questions, those that would give an advantage in the scoring. The issue of faking (or intentional distortion) has been investigated for many years (Ones et al., 1996). However, in the past the emphasis has been on response formats that were felt to make it difficult for someone to deliberately mislead the administrator. Formats like the forced-choice tetrad or the weighted checklists were invented for this purpose (Saks et al., 2000). Although there is evidence that these formats can help to mitigate the problem, this approach has not been a major breakthrough. Instead, research is currently under way to try to provide an understanding of faking as a phenomenon in and of itself. Thus, the newer focus includes examining such things as the level of awareness that the test taker may have about his or her behavior as investigators try to distinguish between distortion that is motivated or that which is based on lack of self-insight. Similarly, the role of contextual forces is being examined to understand those situations that may promote honesty. Paradoxically, there is also a question of the implications of faking for estimating the future job behavior or performance of one who does so. In this regard, some might argue that faking in a high-stakes situation is more of a manifestation of adaptability than dishonesty and thus might actually imply more, than less, likelihood for being a successful worker. Finally, there is uncertainty regarding the implications of applicant faking for personnel decisions based on data from those measures (e.g., personality). Such things as the prevalence and nonrandom distribution of faking behavior in the applicant pool should make a difference here, but the evidence is not conclusive (Ones & Viswesvaran, 1998). Clearly there is much research that remains to be done.

### Technology-Mediated Testing

Previous sections of this chapter have highlighted the variety of ways that individual assessments in work organizations can be carried out. Traditionally, the individual of interest is assessed when in physical proximity to the assessor. In contrast, current practice is moving toward technology-mediated interaction. The technology involved can vary, depending on the application. In the past, assessment processes were mediated by such mundane technologies as the telephone and fax machine. In the case of the former, the candidate might be asked to dial in to a number to be talked through a series of questions. The person could respond by using the dial matrix as a keypad, following instructions that translated the standard dial to a scoring matrix. Despite such primitive arrangements,

many organizations were able to achieve a cost savings and improve the speed of decisions while still maintaining test security and standardized administration. By and large, however, the computer is currently the technology of choice.

Burke (1993) identified and contrasts computer-based testing (CBT) and computer-adaptive testing (CAT) as two major advances in computerized psychological testing. The former builds on optical scanning technology and the capacity for computers not only to summarize responses but, using carefully developed algorithms, to provide interpretations. As the movement toward the online administration of tests converges with developments in the areas of Item Response Theory (IRT) and CAT, new technical issues arise and must be resolved (Green, Bock, Humphreys, Linn, & Reckase, 1994; Kingsbury, 1990). Burke (1993) highlighted such issues as resolving the best way to develop work attribute–job performance matrices on which to base computer algorithms, establishing the construct equivalence of tests across CAT versions and in relationship to conventional forms, and determining criterion-related validity. Finally, although there is some support for the belief that CAT might represent an improvement in test security (Bunderson, Inouye, & Olsen, 1989), it is possible that a test taker motivated to do so would have an easier time recalling specific test items and communicating them to future test takers.

As noted, a relatively recent development is for practitioners to make use of Web-based assessment practices. To be certain, there are many compelling reasons to support this movement, including cost and flexibility considerations. However, full implications of moving to Internet alternatives to traditional proctored testing have yet to be worked out. Some of the issues that have been identified relate to the extent that this practice allows for (or even encourages) cheating, affects validity, or has a negative impact on the applicant relative to their impression of their future employer. Some legal challenges have also been postulated, as the practice of Internet-based assessments may have a potential negative impact on protected classes of applicants (Tippins, 2009).

### Validity

The process of establishing construct validity is one of building a case that the measure is appropriate based on a variety of types of evidence obtained from multiple cases and over numerous settings. Analytic tools and approaches, such as factor analysis; scaling; rational methods; multimethod, multitrait analysis; validity generalization; path analysis; and even the experimental method, can be used (Schmitt & Landy, 1993). Although data from one study or analyzed by one technique may be less than conclusive, there is reassurance in replication and in finding expected or predicted patterns. Thus, the conceptual models and techniques needed to infer that an assessment tool does indeed measure what it is intended to are readily available.

Nevertheless, the problem of construct validity persists. For example, biodata or life history information has been found useful for predicting job outcomes, but the construct nature of such measures is often obscure or overlooked (Mael & Hirsch, 1993; Mumford, Costanza, Connelly, & Johnson, 1996). Similarly, the assessment center method has been adopted by many firms as a way to estimate the developmental needs of workers (usually couched in terms of traitlike constructs). However, the evidence for the construct validity of such applications is weak (Klimoski, 1993; Klimoski & Brickner, 1987).

The problem is likely to become worse, given many of the competitive pressures on companies and practitioners. For example, there is a great emphasis on satisfying the client. Often this means providing custom work within a short time frame, leaving few options for careful development work. Even if there is some scale or test development, given the proprietary nature of such work products, traditional ways of ascertaining the quality of a test (e.g., requesting and reviewing a technical report) are often thwarted by the lack of publicly verifiable research. Similarly, many managerial decisions about whom to hire for professional assessment work or just what assessment approach to use are unduly influenced by popular culture and testimonials; rarely are they based on rigorous evidence of validity or utility (Abrahamson, 1996).

On a different tack, a more diverse workforce, with English as a second language and the tendency for firms to become multinational, also presents challenges. The successful cross-translation of material is difficult at best. When this must be done for assessment tools, the challenges to construct validity are quite great. Similarly, as practitioners attempt to be responsive to applicants covered under the ADA, variation in testing conditions or test format would seem to have a major, but frequently underexamined, impact on construct validity (Klimoski & Palmer, 1994).

Finally, there are current debates regarding the use of alternative validation models given the changing nature of the workplace (Murphy, 2009). In particular, with business conditions changing rapidly, traditional validation strategies (as outlined earlier) may not be feasible. By the time the results of a study are in, the nature of the work to be performed, the nature of good performance, or even the nature of the applicant pool may have changed dramatically. Moreover, for small or emerging businesses,

the traditional approach to validating assessments is also problematic. But there is no consensus on how best to deal with these circumstances. Alternative approaches, such as synthetic validation, which is "a logical process of inferring validity between components of a job and tests that are needed to perform those components" (Johnson, Steel, Scherbaum, Hoffman, Jeanneret, & Foster, 2010, p. 306), have as many detractors as proponents. For example, advocates (e.g., Oswald and Hough, 2010) would argue that when one does not have the conditions suitable for a traditional validity study, it would be appropriate to "synthesize" a selection test battery from published evidence regarding what is known to be the valid predictors of the performance components (tasks, behaviors, or duties) of the job in question. They reason that assessments based on the sum of the parts (assembled subtests) would be a good approximation of what a new and conventional study would find when it comes to identifying the kind of predictors that would be appropriate and valid. Others, however, disagree (Murphy, 2010).

### Social Policy Considerations

The work of psychologists in industrial and organizational settings is usually open to public scrutiny. For that reason, practitioners must constantly be sensitive to issues of fairness and transparency.

### Fairness

Regardless of the approach used or the purpose, the issue of the fairness of assessments in the context of work is a major social policy issue facing practitioners. Indeed, much of the work on noncognitive predictors has been stimulated by the goal of finding valid measures that do not have adverse impact (Ryan, Ployhart, & Friedel, 1998). One approach to this problem is to investigate the bases for inferior performance of subgroups, often using cognitive psychology tools (DeShon, Smith, Chan, & Schmitt, 1998; Sternberg & Wagner, 1993). Here the goal is to ascertain the state of mind or the test-taking strategy used by individuals, with the aim of assisting them in changing their approach if it is dysfunctional.

Another approach is to examine the perceived fairness of assessment tools. Here the goal is to understand how fair the test is in the eyes of the test taker because this affects motivation to do well and to challenge the outcome of the assessment (Chan, Schmitt, Sacco, & DeSchon, 1998; Gilliland, 1994). An emerging body of research documents when and why assessment practices, at least for purposes of selection, will or will not be perceived as unfair (Anderson et al., 2010).

It has already been noted that the ADA presents fairness challenges. Applicants or workers covered under the ADA have the right to request an accommodation to allow them to perform to their potential in an assessment event. However, what is reasonable from the firm's point of view may be viewed as unfair by the test taker. Ironically, even when the company and the worker can agree on disability-mitigating adjustments to the assessment platform, other workers and even supervisors may see this as an injustice because they had to meet the standard, and frequently more strenuous, testing conditions (Klimoski & Donahue, 1997).

Finally, some of the most frequently used approaches to measuring or establishing test bias are now being debated. For example, the regression-based approach (also called the Cleary model), where criterion data are regressed on test scores along with a dichotomous demographic grouping variable (black/white) to reveal the possibility of different intercepts and slopes, has been critiqued for numerous shortcomings, especially with regard to its assumptions. Critics have even asserted that the method has been overrelied on and that it may have been interpreted improperly by those wishing to evaluate tests for bias in work settings (Meade & Tonidandel, 2010).

### Openness and Transparency

Given the importance of doing well on assessments as a way to obtain desirable work outcomes, it is not surprising that there are tremendous pressures to make the nature of tests, test content, and assessment protocols more public. Of course, over the years, there have always been arrangements for informing both representatives of the firm and prospective test takers about the measure. More recently, however, there are increasing demands for public disclosure of such things as the exact items or exercises, response options, and even item operating characteristics. This trend has been accelerated by the availability of social dialogue and ease of information search on the Internet. There are few barriers to those who might want to express their opinions (or even share experiences or information) on accessible electronic platforms, such as personal blogs, Wikipedia, or Facebook. Details on items can be made known to millions of people in a matter of seconds and at little cost. Needless to say, full disclosure would quickly compromise a test and dramatically affect its validity and utility. Yet more fully understanding the legitimate demands of the assessment protocol might allow qualified applicants (for example) to better prepare for the experience and allow them to maximize their ability to perform well. Thus, the challenge is to find ways of meeting the legitimate needs of stakeholders and to ensure the accountability of firms to professional practice while maintaining the integrity of the assessment program.

Although these issues are not exhaustive, they highlight the fact that the field must continue to confront new challenges. The field of practice is driven not only by developments in theory but also by forces surrounding the business enterprise. For that reason, those who provide psychological services to work organizations must not only respond but must also contribute to major societal changes in the economy, public policy, popular culture, and business practices.

## ANTICIPATING THE FUTURE

It is always risky to try to predict what the future might bring relative to the assessment of individuals in industry. Certainly, there may be major breakthroughs when it comes to assessment theory or methods. For example, there are those who feel that research on brain chemistry and neural mechanisms will lead to better and more valid assessments of some aspects of individual differences (e.g., attitudes, preferences, and decision-making propensities). Similarly, there is the possibility that legal challenges to certain assessment practices or new regulations or legislation will require changes in how we conduct ourselves as professionals. Concerns around ensuring homeland security also have implications for both theory and practice regarding the assessment of individuals who represent a risk to a company or to society. Due to current limitations in this area, we would expect an increase in U.S. government investments for new and useful approaches. This, in turn, may produce changes in our field.

In many respects, we anticipate few major disruptions in many of the trends mentioned in this chapter. Notably, likely more organizations will use outside firms to meet most of their assessment needs for such applications as selection and leader development. We also expect to see more use of technology-mediated approaches to assessment, but perhaps with a bit more emphasis on simulations, or games, designed to examine the behavior of individuals in very realistic yet controlled settings. This would aid in narrowing the gap between those advocating a construct versus a content approach to assessment.

We also feel that organizational context will continue to play a major role in the nature and use of assessments. Public sector organizations will continue to have different requirements than publicly traded organizations, and both will differ from privately held firms. Location in the organization's life cycle will make a difference as start-ups will use different approaches to assessment than mature or even declining businesses. Scale will also matter. Large firms have both different resources and different needs from small ones, and there will continue to be industry-sector differences (e.g., manufacturing, financial sector, entertainment, extraction). We predict that practitioners who specialize probably will be more successful than those who seek to be generalists.

In summary, we believe that the need for valid and efficient approaches to individual assessment will continue to exist in the future. Moreover, only when practitioners adopt such assessment approaches will the needs of employees and their companies for a safe, satisfying, and productive workplace be met. This, in turn, should contribute to a more prosperous society in the coming decades.

# REFERENCES

Abrahamson, E. (1996). Management fashion. *Academy of Management Review*, *21*, 254–285.

Amason, A. C., Thompson, K. R., Hochwarter, W. A., & Harrison, A. W. (1995). Conflict: An important dimension in successful management teams. *Organizational Dynamics*, *23*, 20–35.

American Educational Research Association, American Psychological Association, & National Council on Measurement in Education. (1999). *Standards for educational and psychological testing*. Washington, DC: American Educational Research Association.

Anastasi, A., & Urbina, S. (1996). *Psychological testing* (7th ed.). New York, NY: Macmillan.

Anderson, N., Salgado, J. F., & Hülsheger, U. R. (2010). Applicant reactions in selection: Comprehensive meta-analysis into reaction generalization versus situational specificity. *International Journal of Selection and Assessment*, *18*, 291–304.

Arvey, R. D., & Campion, J. E. (1982). Biographical trait and behavioral sampling predictors of performance in a stressful life situation. *Personnel Psychology*, *35*, 281–321.

Ashe, R. L., & Lundquist, K. K. (2010). The legal environment for assessment. In J. C. Scott & D. H. Reynolds (Eds.), *Handbook of workplace assessment: Evidence-based practices for selecting and developing organizational talent* (pp. 643–669). San Francisco, CA: Jossey-Bass.

Austin, J. T., Klimoski, R. J., & Hunt, S. T. (1996). Dilemmatics in public sector assessment: A framework for developing and evaluating selection systems. *Human Performance*, *3*, 177–198.

Austin, J. T., Scherbaum, C. A., & Mahlman, R. A. (2000). History of research methods in industrial and organizational psychology: Measurement, design analysis. In S. Rogelberg (Ed.), *Handbook of research methods in industrial and organizational psychology* (pp. 5–26). Malden, MA: Basil Blackwell.

Avolio, B. J., & Hannah, S. T. (2008). Developmental readiness: Accelerating leader development. *Consulting Psychology Journal: Practice and Research*, *60*, 331–347.

Barrett, G. V., Doverspike, D., & Young, C. M. (2010). The special case of public sector police and fire selection. In J. C. Scott & D. H. Reynolds (Eds.), *Handbook of workplace assessment: Evidence-based practices for selecting and developing organizational talent* (pp. 437–462). San Francisco, CA: Jossey-Bass.

Barrick, M. R., & Mount, M. K. (1991). The Big Five personality dimensions and job performance. *Personnel Psychology*, *44*, 1–26.

Bass, B. M., & Avolio, B. J. (1996). *The multifactor leadership questionnaire report*. Palo Alto, CA: Mind Garden.

Berry, C. M., Ones, D. S., & Sackett, P. R. (2007). Interpersonal deviance, organizational deviance, and their correlates. *Journal of Applied Psychology*, *92*, 410–424.

Binning, J. F., & Barrett, G. V. (1989). Validity of personnel decisions: A conceptual analysis of the inferential and evidential bases. *Journal of Applied Psychology*, *74*, 478–494.

Bono, J. R., Purvanova, R. K., Towler, A. J., & Peterson, D. B. (2009). A survey of executive coaching practices. *Personnel Psychology*, *62*, 361–404.

Borman, W. C., & Motowidlo, S. J. (1993). Expanding the criterion domain to include elements of contextual performance. In N. Schmitt & W. C. Borman (Eds.), *Personnel selection in organizations* (pp. 71–98). San Francisco, CA: Jossey-Bass.

Brunkan, R. J. (1991). Psychological assessment in career development. In C. P. Hansen & K. A. Conrad (Eds.), *A handbook of psychological assessment in business* (pp. 237–257). New York, NY: Quorum.

Bunderson, C. V., Inouye, D. K., & Olsen, J. B. (1989). The four generations of computerized educational measurement. In R. L. Linn (Ed.), *Educational measurement* (3rd ed.). New York, NY: American Council on Education and Macmillan.

Burke, M. J. (1993). Computerized psychological testing: Impacts on measuring predictor constructs and future job behavior. In N. Schmitt & W. C. Borman (Eds.), *Personnel selection in organizations* (pp. 203–239). San Francisco, CA: Jossey-Bass.

Cairo, P. C. (1982). Measured interests versus expressed interests as predictors of long-term occupational membership. *Journal of Vocational Behavior*, *20*, 343–353.

Camera, W., & Schneider, D. L. (1994). Integrity tests: Facts and unresolved issues. *American Psychologist*, *49*, 112–119.

Campbell, J. P. (1990). An overview of the army selection and classification project (Project A). *Personnel Psychology*, *43*, 231–240.

Cannon-Bowers, J. A., & Salas, E. (1997). Teamwork competencies: The intersection of team member knowledge, skills, and attitudes. In H. F. O'Neil (Ed.), *Workforce readiness: Competencies and effectiveness* (pp. 151–174). Hillsdale, NJ: Erlbaum.

Capshew, J. H. (1999). *Psychologists on the march: Science, practice and professional identity*. Cambridge, United Kingdom: Cambridge University Press.

Cascio, W. F. (1991). *Applied psychology in personnel management* (4th ed.). Englewood Cliffs, NJ: Prentice-Hall.

Cascio, W. F. (1993). Assessing the utility of selection decisions: Theoretical and practical considerations. In N. Schmitt & W. C. Borman (Eds.), *Personnel selection in organizations* (pp. 71–98). San Francisco, CA: Jossey-Bass.

Cattell, R. B., Cattell, A. K., & Cattell, H. F. (1993). *Sixteen Personality Factors Practical Questionnaire* (5th ed.). Champaign, IL: Institute for Personality and Abilities Testing.

Chan, D., Schmitt, N., Sacco, J. M., & DeShon, R. P. (1998). Understanding pretest and posttest reactions to cognitive ability and personality tests. *Journal of Applied Psychology*, *83*, 471–485.

Consulting Psychologists Press (1957). Palo Alto, CA: CPP; www.cpp.com

Costa, P. T., & McCrae, R .R. (1992). *NEO PI-R. Professional manual*. Odessa, FL: Psychological Assessment Resources.

Cronbach, L. J. (1984). Essentials of psychological testing (4th ed.). New York, NY: Harper & Row.

Dalal, R. S. (2005). A meta-analysis of the relationship of organizational citizenship behavior and counter productive work behavior. *Journal of Applied Psychology*, *90*, 1241–1255.

Dalessio, A. T. (1998). Using multisource feedback for employee development and personnel decisions. In J. W. Smither (Ed.), *Performance appraisal: State of the art in practice* (pp. 278–330). San Francisco, CA: Jossey-Bass.

Dawis, R. (1991). Vocational interests, values and preferences. In M. Dunnette & L. Hough (Eds.), *Handbook of industrial and organizational psychology* (2nd ed., pp. 833–872). Palo Alto, CA: Consulting Psychologists Press.

Day, D. V., & Silverman, S. B. (1989). Personality and job performance: Evidence of incremental validity. *Personnel Psychology*, *42*, 25–36.

Deal, J. J., Stawiski, S., & Gentry, W. A. (2010). *Employee engagement: Has it been a bull market?* A Center for Creative Leadership Report sponsored by Booz Allen Hamilton. Greensboro, NC: Center for Creative Leadership.

DeShon, R. P., Smith, M. R., Chan, D., & Schmitt, N. (1998). Can racial differences in cognitive test performance be reduced by presenting problems in a social context? *Journal of Applied Psychology*, *83*, 438–451.

Digman, J. M. (1990). Personality structure: Emergence of the Five-Factor Model. *Annual Review of Psychology*, *41*, 417–440.

Equal Employment Opportunity Commission, Civil Service Commission, U.S. Department of Labor, & U.S. Department of Justice. (1978). Uniform guidelines on employee selection procedures. *Federal Register*, *43*, 38290–38315.

Flanagan, J. C. (1954). The Critical Incident Technique. *Psychological Bulletin*, *51*, 327–358.

Fleishman, E. A., & Reilly, M. E. (1992). *Handbook of human abilities: Definitions, measurements and job task requirements*. Palo Alto, CA: Consulting Psychologists Press.

Ford, J. K. (1997). *Improving training effectiveness in work organizations*. Mahwah, NJ: Erlbaum.

Ford, M. E., & Tisak, M. S. (1983). A further search for social intelligence. *Journal of Educational Psychology*, *75*, 196–206.

Gaugler, B. B., Rosenthal, D. B., Thornton, G. C., & Bentson, C. (1987). Meta-analysis of assessment center validity. *Journal of Applied Psychology*, *72*, 493–511.

Gilliland, S. W. (1993). The perceived fairness of selection systems: An organizational justice perspective. *Academy of Management Review*, *18*, 694–734.

Gilliland, S. W. (1994). Effects of procedural and distributive justice on reactions to selection systems. *Journal of Applied Psychology*, *79*, 791–804.

Goldberg, L. R. (1990). An alternative "description of personality": The Big Five factor structures. *Journal of Personality and Social Psychology*, *59*, 1216–1229.

Goldberg, L. R. (1992). The development of markers for the Big- Five structure. *Psychological Assessment*, *4*, 26–42.

Goleman, D. (1995). *Emotional intelligence*. New York, NY: Bantam Books.

Green, B. F., Bock, R. D., Humphreys, L. G., Linn, R. L., & Reckase, M. D. (1994). Technical guidelines for assessing computer adaptive tests. *Journal of Educational Measurement*, *21*, 347–360.

Guion, R. M. (1998). *Assessment, measurement, and prediction for personnel decisions*. Mahwah, NJ: Erlbaum.

Guion, R. M., & Gottier, R. F. (1965). Validity of personality measures in personnel selection. *Personnel Psychology*, *18*, 135–164.

Halbfinger, D. M. (1999, March 21). Police and applicants have big stake in test. *New York Times*, p. I40.

Hansen, J. C. (1986). Strong Vocational Interest Blank/Strong Campbell Interest Inventory. In W. B. Walsh & S. H. Osipow (Eds.), *Advances in vocational psychology, Vol. 1: The assessment of interests* (pp. 1–29). Hillsdale, NJ: Erlbaum.

Harmon, L. W., Hansen, J. C., Borgen, F. H., & Hammer, A. L. (1994). *Strong Interest Inventory: Applications and technical guide*. Palo Alto, CA: Consulting Psychologists Press.

Henderson, N. D. (2010). Predicting long term firefighter performance from cognitive and physical ablity measures. *Personnel Psychology*, *63*, 999–1039.

Hirschfeld, R. R. (2000). Does revising the intrinsic and extrinsic subscales of the Minnesota Satisfaction Questionnaire Short Form make a difference? *Educational and Psychological Measurement*, *60*, 255–270.

Hogan Assessment Systems (1995). Tulsa, OK: Hogan Assessments; www.hoganassessments.com

Hogan Assessment Systems (1996). Tulsa, OK: Hogan Assessments; www.hoganassessments.com

Hogan, J., & Hogan, R. T. (1986). *Hogan Personnel Selection Series manual*. Minneapolis, MN: National Computer Systems.

Hogan, J., & Hogan, R. T. (1989). How to measure employee reliability. *Journal of Applied Psychology*, *74*, 273–279.

Hogan, J., & Holland, B., (2003). Using theory to evaluate personality and job-performance relations. *Journal of Applied Psychology*, *88*, 100–112.

Hogan, R. T. (1991). Personality and personality management. In M. D. Dunnette & L. M. Hough (Eds.), *Handbook of industrial and organizational psychology* (Vol. 2, pp. 873–919). Palo Alto, CA: Consulting Psychologists Press.

Hogan, R. T., & Blake, R. J. (1996). Vocational interests: Matching self concept with work environment. In K. R. Murphy (Ed.), *Individual difference and behavior in organizations* (pp. 89–144). San Francisco, CA: Jossey-Bass.

Hogan, R. T., & Hogan, J. (1995). *Hogan Personality Inventory manual*. Tulsa, OK: Hogan Selection Systems.

Hogan, R. T., & Hogan, J. (1996) *Hogan Motives, Values and Preferences Inventory manual*. Tulso, OK: Hogan Selection Systems.

Hogan, R. T., Hogan, J., & Busch, C. M. (1984). How to measure service orientation. *Journal of Applied Psychology*, *69*, 167–176.

Hogan, R. T., & Kaiser, R. B. (2010). Personality. In J. C. Scott & D. H. Reynolds (Eds.), *Handbook of workplace assessment: Evidence-based practices for selecting and developing organizational talent* (pp. 437–462). San Francisco, CA: Jossey-Bass.

Holland, J. L. (1985). *Professional manual Self-Directed Search*. Odessa, FL: Psychological Assessment Resources.

Holland, J. L., Fritsche, B. A., & Powell, A. B. (1994). *The Self- Directed Search (SDS): Technical manual*. Odessa, FL: Psychological Assessment Resources.

Hollenbeck, J. R., LePine, J. A., & Ilgen, D. R. (1996). Adapting to roles in decision-making teams. In K. R. Murphy (Ed.), *Individual differences and behavior in organizations* (pp. 300–333). San Francisco, CA: Jossey-Bass.

Hough, L. M. (1992). The "Big Five" personality variables—construct confusion: Description versus prediction. *Human Performance*, *5*(1&2), 139–155.

Hough, L. M., & Oswald, F. L. (2008). Personality testing and I-O psychology: Reflections, progress and prospects. *Industrial and Organizational Psychology: Perspectives on Science and Practice*, *1*, 272–290.

Howard, A., & Bray, D. W. (1988). Managerial lives in transition: Advancing age and changing times. New York, NY: Guilford Press.

Howard, A., & Thomas, J. N. (2010). Executive and managerial assessment. In J. C. Scott & D. H. Reynolds (Eds.), *Handbook of workplace assessment: Evidence-based practices for selecting and developing organizational talent* (pp. 395–436). San Francisco, CA: Jossey-Bass.

Huffcutt, A. I., Roth, P. L., & McDaniel, M. A. (1996). A meta-analytic investigation of cognitive ability in employment interview evaluations: Moderating characteristics and implications for incremental validity. *Journal of Applied Psychology*, *81*, 459–473.

Hülsheger, U. R., Maier, G. W. & Stumpp, T. (2007). Validity of general mental ability for the prediction of job performance and training success in Germany: A meta-analysis. *International Journal of Selection and Assessment*, *15*, 3–18.

Hunter, J. E., & Hunter, R. F. (1984). Validity and utility of alternative predictors of job performance. *Psychological Bulletin*, *96*, 72–98.

Impara, J. C., & Plake, B. S. (1998). *13th annual mental measurement yearbook*. Lincoln, NE: Buros Institute for Mental Measurement.

Johnson, J. W., Steel, P., Scherbaum, C. A., Hoffman, C. C., Jeanneret, P. R., & Foster, J. (2010). Validation is like motor oil: Synthetic is better. *Industrial and Organizational Psychology Perspectives*, *3*, 305–328.

Judge, T. A., Bono, J. E., Ilies, R., & Gerhardt, M. W. (2002). Personality and leadership: A qualitative and quantitative review. *Journal of Applied Psychology*, *87*, 765–780.

Judge, T. A., Heller, D., & Mount, M. K. (2002). Five-Factor Model of personality and job satisfaction: A meta-analysis. *Journal of Applied Psychology*, *87*, 530–541.

Judge, T. A., Higgins, C. A., & Cable, D. M. (2000). The employment interview: A review of recent research and recommendations for future research. *Human Resources Management Review*, *10*, 383–406.

Judge, T. A., Thoresen, C. J., Bono, J. E., & Patton, G. K. (2001). The job satisfaction-job performance relationship: A qualitative and quantitative review. *Psychological Bulletin*, *127*, 376–407.

Kallenberg, L. (2008). The mis-matched worker: When people don't fit their job. *Academy of Management Perspectives*, *22*, 24–40.

Kaplan, S. A., Warren, C. R., Barsky, A. P., & Thoresen, C. J. (2009). A note on the relationship between affect(ivity) and differing conceptualizations of job satisfaction: Some unexpected meta-analytic findings. *European Journal of Work and Organizational Psychology*, *18*(1), 29–54.

Katz, D., & Kahn, R. L. (1978). The social psychology of organizations. New York, NY: Wiley.

Keys, B., & Wolfe, J. (1990). The role of management games and simulations in education and research. *Journal of Management*, *16*(2), 307–336.

Kingsbury, G. G. (1990). Adapting adaptive testing with the MicroCAT testing system. *Educational Measurement*, *9*, 6–29.

Klimoski, R. J. (1993). Predictor constructs and their measurement. In N. Schmitt & W. C. Borman (Eds.), Personnel selection in organizations (pp. 71–98). San Francisco, CA: Jossey-Bass.

Klimoski, R. J., & Brickner, M. (1987). Why do assessment centers work? Puzzle of assessment center validity. *Personnel Psychology*, *40*, 243–260.

Klimoski, R. J., & Donahue, L. M. (1997). HR Strategies for integrating individuals with disabilities into the workplace. *Human Resources Management Review*, *7*(1), 109–138.

Klimoski, R. J., & Palmer, S. N. (1994). Psychometric testing and reasonable accommodation for persons with disabilities. In S. M. Bruyere & J. O'Keeffe (Eds.), *Implications of the Americans with Disabilities Act for psychology* (pp. 37–83). Washington, DC: American Psychological Association.

Klimoski, R. J., & Zukin, L. B. (1998). Selection and staffing for team effectiveness. In E. Sundstrom (Ed.), *Supporting work team effectiveness* (pp. 63–94). San Francisco, CA: Jossey-Bass.

Kouzes and Posner (2002). *The leadership challenge* (3rd ed.). San Francisco: Jossey Bass.

Kraiger, K. (2003). Perspectives on training and development. In W. C. Borman, D. R. Ilgen, & R. J. Klimoski (Eds.), *Handbook of psychology: Volume 12, Industrial and organizational psychology* (pp. 171–192). Hoboken, NJ: Wiley.

Kunin, T. (1955). The construction of a new type of attitude measure. *Personnel Psychology*, *8*, 65–78.

Landy, F. J. (1976). The validity of the interview in police officer selection. *Journal of Applied Psychology*, *61*, 193–198.

Landy, F. J. (1989). *The psychology of work behavior* (4th ed.). Pacific Grove, CA: Brooks/Cole.

Linowes, D. F., & Spencer, R. C. (1996). Privacy in the workplace in perspective. *Human Resources Management Review*, *613*, 165–181.

Mael, F., & Hirsch, A. (1993). Rainforest empiricism and quasi-rationality: Two approaches to objective biodata. *Personnel Psychology*, *46*, 719–738.

Mahoney, M. J. (1991). *Human change processes: The scientific foundations of psychotherapy*. New York, NY: Basic Books.

Martin, L. A., & Fraser, S. L. (2002). Customer service orientation in managerial and non-managerial employees: An exploratory study. *Journal of Business and Psychology*, *16*, 477–484.

McCall, M. W. (2010). Recasting leadership development. *Industrial and Organizational Psychology*, *3*, 3–19.

McDaniel, M. A., Schmidt, F. L., & Hunter, J. E. (1988). A meta-analysis of the validity of methods for rating training and experience in personnel selection. *Personnel Psychology*, *41*, 283–314.

McFarland, L. A., & Ryan, A. M. (2000). Variance in faking across non-cognitive measures. *Journal of Applied Psychology*, *85*, 812–821.

McHenry, J. J., Hough, L. M., Toquam, J. L., Hanson, M. A., & Ashworth, S. (1990). Project A validity results: The relationship between predictors and criterion domains. *Personnel Psychology*, *43*, 335–354.

Meade, A. W., & Tonidandel, S. (2010). Not seeing clearly with Cleary: What test bias analyses do and do not tell us. *Industrial and Organizational Psychology: Perspectives on Science and Practice*, *3*, 192–205.

Mount, M. K., & Barrick, M. R. (1995). The Big Five personality dimensions: Implications for research and practice in human resources management. *Research in Personnel and Human Resources Management*, *13*, 153–200.

Mount, M. K., Barrick, M. R., & Stewart, G. L. (1998). Five-factor model of personality and performance in jobs involving interpersonal interactions. *Human Performance*, *11*, 145–165.

Mowday, R. T., Steers, R. M., & Porter, L. W. (1979). The measurement of organizational commitment. *Journal of Vocational Behavior*, *14*, 224–247.

Mumford, M. D., Costanza, D. P., Connelly, M. S., & Johnson, J. F. (1996). Item generation procedures and background data scales: Implications for construct and criterion-related validity. *Personnel Psychology*, *49*, 361–398.

Munsterberg, H. L. (1913). *Psychology and industrial efficiency*. Boston, MA: Houghton-Mifflin.

Murphy, K. R. (2009). Content validation is useful for many things, but validity isn't one of them. *Industrial and Organizational Psychology Perspectives*, *2*, 45–465.

Murphy, K. R. (2010). Synthetic validity: A great idea whose time never came. *Industrial and Organizational Psychology Perspectives*, *3*, 356–359.

Murphy, K. R., & Cleveland, J. N. (1995). *Understanding performance appraisal: Social, organizational, and goal-based perspectives*. Thousand Oaks, CA: Sage.

Nelson Education, (1986). Scarborough, Ontario: Nelson Education; www.nelson.com

Oh, I., Wang, G., & Mount, M. K. (2011). Validity of observer ratings of the five-factor model of personality traits: A meta-analysis. *Journal of Applied Psychology*, *96*(4), 762–773.

Ones, D. S., Dilchert, S., Viswesvaran, C., & Judge, T. A. (2007). In support of personality assessment in organizational settings. *Personnel Psychology*, *60*, 995–1027.

Ones, D. S., & Viswesvaran, C. (1998). The effects of social desirability and faking on personality and integrity assessment for personnel selection. *Human Performance*, *11*, 245–269.

Ones, D. S., Viswesvaran, C., & Reiss, A. D. (1996). Role of social desirability in personality testing for personnel selection: The red herring. *Journal of Applied Psychology*, *81*, 660–679.

Ones, D. S., Viswesvaran, C., & Schmidt, F. L. (2003). Personality and absenteeism. *European Journal of Personality*, *17*(Suppl.), 519–538.

Organ, D., & Ryan, K. (1995). A meta-analytic review of the attitudinal and dispositional predictors of organizational citizenship behavior. *Personnel Psychology*, *48*, 775–802.

Oswald, F. L., & Hough, L. M. (2010). Validity in a jiffy: How synthetic validations contributes to personnel selection. *Industrial and Organizational Psychology Perspectives*, *3*, 329–334.

Owens, W. A., & Schoenfeldt, L. F. (1979). Toward a classification of persons. *Journal of Applied Psychology*, *65*, 569–607.

Pearson (1965). Pearson Assessment and Information, San Antonio, TX; www.pearsonassessments.com

Peterson, N. G., Mumford, M. D., Borman, W. C., Jeanneret, P. R., & Fleishman, E. A. (1995). *Development of Prototype Occupational Information Network (O*NET)*. (Vols. 1–2). Salt Lake City: Utah Department of Employment Security.

Peterson, N. G., Mumford, M. D., Borman, W. C., Jeanneret, P. R., & Fleishman, E. A. (1999). *An occupational information system for the 21st century: The development of the O*Net*. Washington, DC: American Psychological Association.

Podsakoff, P. M., & MacKensie, S. B. (1997). Impact of organizational citizenship behavior on organizational performance: A review and suggestions for further research. *Human Performance*, *10*, 133–151.

Rich, B. L., LePine, J. A., & Crawford, E. R. (2010). Job engagement: Antecedents and effects on job performance. *Academy of Management Journal*, *53*, 617–635.

Roberts, B. R., Kuncel, N. R., Shiner, R., Caspi, A., & Goldberg, L. R. (2007). The power of personality: The comparative validity of personality traits, socio-economic status, and cognitive ability for predicting important life outcomes. *Perspectives on Psychological Science*, *2*, 313–345.

Roth, P. L., BeVier, C. A., Bobko, P., Switzer, F. S. III, & Tyler, P. (2001). Ethnic group differences in cognitive ability in employment and educational settings: A meta-analysis. *Personnel Psychology*, *54*, 297–330.

Ryan, A. M., & Ployhart, R. E. (2003). Customer service behavior. In W. C. Borman, D. R. Ilgen, & R. J. Klimoski (Eds.), *Handbook of psychology: Volume 12, Industrial and organizational psychology* (pp. 377–397). Hoboken, NJ: Wiley.

Ryan, A. M., Ployhart, R. E., & Friedel, L. A. (1998). Using personality testing to reduce adverse impact: A cautionary note. *Journal of Applied Psychology*, *83*, 298–307.

Ryan, A. M., & Sackett, P. R. (1987). A survey of individual assessment practices by I/O psychologists. *Personnel Psychology*, *40*, 455–488.

Sackett, P. R., Burris, L. R., & Callahan, C. (1989). Integrity testing for personnel selection. *Personnel Psychology*, *42*, 491–529.

Sackett, P. R., & Harris, M. M. (1984). Honesty testing for personnel selection: A review and critique. *Personnel Psychology*, *37*, 221–245.

Sackett, P. R., Myors, B., Lievens, F., et al. (2008). International perspectives on the legal environment for selection. *Industrial Organizational Psychology Perspectives*, *1*, 206–246.

Saks, A. M., Schmitt, N. W., & Klimoski, R. J. (2000). *Research, measurement and evaluation of human resources*. Scarborough, Ontario: Thompson Learning.

Salas, E., Wildman, J. L., & Piccolo, R. F. (2009). Using simulation-based training to enhance management education. *Academy of Management Learning and Education*, *8*(4), 559–573.

Saucier, G. (1994). Mini-markers: A brief version of Goldberg's unipolar Big-five markers. *Journal of Personality Assessment*, *63*, 506–516.

Schaufeli, W. B., & Bakker, A. B. (2004). Job demands, job resources, and their relationship with burnout and engagement: A multi-sample study. *Journal of Organizational Behavior*, *25*, 293–315.

Schmidt, F. L., & Hunter, J. E. (1998). The validity and utility of selection methods in personnel psychology: Practical and theoretical implications of 85 years of research findings. *Psychological Bulletin*, *2*, 262–274.

Schmidt, F. L., Hunter, J. E., & Outerbridge, A. N. (1986). The impact of job experience and ability on job knowledge, work sample performance, and supervisory ratings of job performance. *Journal of Applied Psychology*, *71*, 432–439.

Schmitt, N. (1997, April). *Panel discussion: Police selection in Nassau County*. Presentation at the annual Society for Industrial and Organizational Psychology, St. Louis, MI.

Schmitt, N., & Klimoski, R. J. (1991). *Research methods for human resources management*. Cincinnati, OH: South-Western.

Schmitt, N., & Landy, F. J. (1993). The concept of validity. In N. Schmitt & W. C. Borman (Eds.), *Personnel selection in organizations* (pp. 275–309). San Francisco, CA: Jossey-Bass.

Schneider, B., & Schneider, J. L. (1994). Biodata: An organizational focus. In G. S. Stokes & M. D. Mumford (Eds.), *Biodata handbook: Theory, research, and use of biographical information in selection and performance prediction* (pp. 423–450). Palo Alto, CA: CPP Books.

SHL (2000). Chantilly, VA: SHL; www.shl.com

Silzer, R., & Church, A. H. (2009). The pearls and perils of identifying potential. *Industrial and Organizational Psychology*, *2*, 377–412.

SIOP (2003). *Principles for the validation and use of personnel selection procedures*. Bowling Green, OH: Society for Industrial and Organizational Psychology; www.siop.org

Smith, P. C., Kendall, L. M., & Hulin, C. L. (1969). *The measurement of satisfaction in work and retirement: A strategy for the study of attitudes*. Chicago, IL: Rand-McNally.

Snell, A. F., Stokes, G. S., Sands, M. M., & McBride, J. R. (1994). Adolescent life experiences as predictors of occupational attainment. *Journal of Applied Psychology*, *79*, 131–141.

Spector, P. E., Bauer, J. A., & Fox, S. (2010). Measurement artifacts in the assessment of counterproductive work behavior and organizational citizenship behavior: Do we know what we think we know? *Journal of Applied Psychology*, *95*, 781–790.

Sternberg, R. J., & Wagner, R. K. (1993). The g-centric view of intelligence and performance is wrong. *Current Directions in Psychological Science*, *2*, 1–5.

Stevens, M. J., & Campion, M. A. (1994). The knowledge, skill, and ability requirements for teamwork: Implications for human resource management. *Journal of Management*, *20*, 503–530.

Strong, E. K. (1918). Work of the Committee of Classification of Personnel. *Journal of Applied Psychology*, *2*, 130–139.

Terman, L. M. (1917). A trial of mental and pedagogical tests in a civil service examination for policemen and firemen. *Journal of Applied Psychology*, *1*, 17–29.

Tesluk, P. E., & Jacobs, R. J. (1998). Toward an integrated model of work experience. *Personnel Psychology*, *51*, 321–355.

Thorndike, E. L. (1920). Equality in difficulty of alternative intelligence examinations. *Journal of Applied Psychology*, *4*, 283–288.

Tippins, N. T. (2009). Internet alternatives to traditional proctored testing: Where are we now? *Industrial and Organizational Psychology: Perspectives on Science and Practice*, *2*, 2–10.

Valtera Engagement Survey (2011). Rolling Meadows, Ill: Valtera; www.valtera.com

Van Iddekinge, C. H., Putka, D. J., & Campbell, J. P. (2011). Reconsidering vocational interests for personnel selection: The validity of an interest-based test in relation to job knowledge, job performance and continence intentions. *Journal of Applied Psychology*, *96*, 1, 13–33.

Wonderlic Personnel Test. (1992). *Wonderlic Personnel Test user's manual*. Libertyville, IL: Author.

Worthington, E. L., & Dolliver, R. H. (1977). Validity studies of the Strong vocational interest inventories. *Journal of Counseling Psychology*, *24*, 208–216.

Zaccaro, S. J., Gilbert, J. A., Thor, K. K., & Mumford, M. D. (1991). Leadership and social intelligence: Linking social perceptiveness and behavioral flexibility to leader effectiveness. *Leadership Quarterly*, *2*, 317–342.

Zielinski, D. (2011). Effective assessments. *HR Magazine*, *56*(1).

# CHAPTER 15

# Forensic Psychological Assessments

JAMES R. P. OGLOFF AND KEVIN S. DOUGLAS

It has now been 10 years since the American Psychological Association (APA) Council of Representatives, in August 2001, voted to recognize forensic psychology as a specialty area of psychology. This was done following a petition from the American Academy of Forensic Psychology and the American Psychology Law Society/Division 41 of APA to have forensic psychology recognized as a specialty area (Forensic Psychology Specialty Council, 2000). Other jurisdictions, including, for example, Australia, also recognize forensic psychology as a specialty area of psychology (Psychology Board of Australia, 2010).

While this recognition was timely, psychology's first entrance to the courts in the United States occurred in the early 1900s (Ogloff, 2000). At that time, expert witnesses in psychology appeared in court in their capacity as experimental rather than clinical psychologists (Ogloff, Tomkins, & Bersoff, 1996). This is because clinical psychology as a discipline did not exist at that time. Following the end of World War II in the 1940s and 1950s, an enormous growth in clinical psychology saw clinical psychologists entering the courts as expert witnesses (Ogloff et al., 1996).

Although clinical psychologists gave evidence sporadically in cases in the United States as early as the 1940s (e.g., *People v. Hawthorne*, 1940), it was in 1962 (*Jenkins v. U.S.*) that the United States Court of Appeals for the District of Columbia clearly recognized clinical psychologists as experts in courts. This was an important case for psychology generally and for forensic psychology in particular. In *Jenkins v. U.S.*, the trial court judge instructed the jury to disregard a psychologist's testimony, holding that psychologists were not qualified to diagnose mental illness. The U.S. Court of Appeals, sitting *en banc* (i.e., with all of the appellate judges together), held that a psychologist's lack of medical training could not, in and of itself, be used to justify an automatic disqualification of psychological testimony. Instead, the court asserted that consideration of whether a psychologist could testify required the court to look at the knowledge and experience of a particular witness and the probative value of his or her opinion.

Following *Jenkins*, courts around the United States and other countries began to recognize clinical psychologists as expert witnesses in a variety of cases (Ferguson & Ogloff, 2011; Melton, Petrila, Poythress, & Slobogin, 2007; Ogloff et al., 1996; Viljoen, Roesch, Ogloff, & Zapf, 2003). Although the road to recognition was long and often bumpy, psychologists are now generally seen by the courts and others in the legal system as competent, independent, mental health professionals (Melton et al., 2007).

As psychologists were recognized as experts by the courts, the field of forensic psychology emerged. The development of forensic psychology included the emergence of doctoral training programs in forensic psychology as well as numerous journals and professional associations (Grisso, 1987, 1991; Helmus, Babchishin, Camilleri, & Olver, 2011; Ogloff, 1990, 2000, 2004; Ogloff et al., 1996; Otto & Heilbrun, 2003; Otto, Heilbrun, & Grisso, 1990). Twenty-five years ago, Melton (1987) wrote that law and psychology—and forensic psychology—was "psychology's growth industry" (p. 681). Melton's prognostication has been realized. Driven largely by the inherent challenge in the work and partly out of economic necessity due to factors like managed health care, increasingly more psychologists find themselves conducting forensic assessments. (See Otto & Heilbrun, 2003, for a review of many important developments that have occurred in forensic psychology since the 1980s.)

Forensic psychology and, in particular, forensic psychological assessments literally imply that the assessments will be employed in the legal system. Given their very serious nature, many unique issues arise in clinical forensic work (Melton, Petrila, Poythress, & Slobogin, 2007; Ogloff, 1999a). A review of the field of forensic psychology, or the many issues that arise in forensic assessments, is beyond the scope of this chapter. Many of the issues that we discuss in this chapter are covered in a more general context in Volume 11 of this series, which is dedicated entirely to forensic psychology. Due to the growth of forensic psychology and because of the large number of "mainstream" clinical psychologists who are conducting forensic assessment, though, we provide some foundational information about forensic psychology and highlight some of the contemporary issues that exist in this field. Finally, we also look to the future to identify possible issues that will arise.

By way of background, we define forensic psychology and discuss where forensic psychology fits within clinical psychology. We also note the interface between forensic psychology and law and outline criminal and civil topics addressed by forensic psychologists. As forensic assessments are grounded in law, it is important to briefly review the legal contours of forensic assessments as well as the legal admissibility of forensic assessments into evidence.

Among the contemporary issues in forensic psychological assessments that are reviewed in this chapter are clinical versus actuarial prediction models in assessments of risk for violence, the legally informed practitioner model, roles and limits of general psychological testing in forensic contexts, legal specificity, and training and credentialing in forensic psychology.

## DEFINING CLINICAL FORENSIC PSYCHOLOGY

Historically, forensic psychology has evolved as a broad field that includes any application of psychology to the legal field (Brigham, 1999; Ogloff, 2000). This broad definition is still used in some places in the world, including parts of the United Kingdom, continental Europe, Australia, and New Zealand. This wide-ranging construal of

the field includes everything from psychological research into legal matters such as eyewitness memory or jury decision making to applied clinical areas including psychological assessment of defendants for court. For the purposes of this chapter, we rely on a narrower, applied definition:

> Forensic psychology will be defined as the professional practice by psychologists within the areas of clinical psychology, counseling psychology, neuropsychology, and school psychology, when they are engaged regularly as experts and represent themselves as such, in an activity primarily intended to provide professional psychological expertise to the legal system. (Forensic Psychology Specialty Council, 2000, p. 2)

While still broad, this working definition focuses on the applied clinical aspects of forensic psychology. It is sometimes referred to as clinical forensic psychology, but for the sake of simplicity, in this chapter the term *forensic psychology* is be employed. Importantly, the definition does not include the work done by experimental psychologists who work in the field of psychology and law (e.g., eyewitness testimony, jury research, etc.). As we are discussing forensic assessment, the definition focuses us on assessments conducted by professional psychologists for the courts or legal system more broadly construed. Although broad, the definition does not encompass the practice of those clinical, counseling, neuropsychologists, or school psychologists whose work only occasionally makes its way into the legal system.

## Where Forensic Psychology Fits Within Clinical Psychology

Generally speaking, forensic assessments can be construed as specialized clinical psychological assessments (Melton et al., 2007; Otto & Heilbrun, 2003). As such, forensic assessments build on the foundational training, knowledge, and experience of clinical psychology. Given the range and depth of specialized knowledge in clinical forensic psychology, though, we must emphasize that a significant degree of expertise is required to conduct forensic assessments competently (Ogloff, 1999a). Others have noted, correctly, that forensic evaluations that were conducted by psychologists in the past did not differ from general clinical assessments (Grisso, 1987; Heilbrun, Rogers, & Otto, 2002). Sadly, this is still the case in many places where general clinical psychologists (or other psychologists) end up conducting assessments. As the field of forensic psychology and the expertise that underpins our work has evolved, though, the methods, instruments, and general skills of forensic psychologists have emerged as differing significantly from those of general clinical psychologists (Heilbrun et al., 2002).

The development of forensic psychology as an area of specialization within psychology has been evidenced, for example, by the development of *Specialty Guidelines for Forensic Psychologists* (Committee on Ethical Guidelines for Forensic Psychologists, 1991, 2011) that were promulgated by the American Psychology-Law Society and the American Academy of Forensic Psychology in 1991 and revised in 2011. The *Specialty Guidelines* were adopted by the APA Council of Representatives on August 3, 2011. The official version is available at www.ap-ls .org/aboutpsychlaw/SGFP_Final_Approved_2011.pdf and is in press in *American Psychologist*. Moreover, as already noted, the APA Council and other professional bodies and jurisdictions have recognized forensic psychology as a specialty area within psychology.

Psychological assessments are introduced into evidence in the courts or the legal system in one of two general ways. First, psychological assessments may be drawn into a legal context unexpectedly when the psychologist did not originally prepare the assessment for a legal purpose. For example, a clinical psychologist may have conducted an assessment on an individual for employment-related purposes. At some point in the future, the assessment could be subpoenaed or otherwise compelled by the court after the individual is in an automobile accident and the assessment is considered relevant as evidence of pre-morbid cognitive functioning. Such assessments cannot properly be referred to as forensic assessments because they are completed for some other purpose outside of the forensic context. Therefore, the psychologists conducting the assessments are not forensic psychologists and would not be held to the standards of the *Specialty Guidelines* (Committee on Ethical Guidelines for Forensic Psychologists, 2011).

Second, psychological assessments can be obtained by parties in a case, ordered by courts, or otherwise requested specifically for legal purposes. These assessments—in which the psychologist specifically sets out in an assessment to address some legal question—are properly referred to as forensic assessments. The psychologist conducting them would be required to adhere to the requirements of the APA Ethical Principles of Psychologists and Code of Conduct (American Psychological Association, 2002). In 2010 the APA Council of Representatives adopted amendments to the 2002 Ethical Principles of Psychologists and Code of Conduct (American Psychological Association, 2010). When referring to the 2002 ethics code, we have, where appropriate, taken the 2010 amendments into consideration. In addition, to the extent that the *Specialty Guidelines* are seen as establishing a standard of care in forensic psychology, those doing forensic assessments are advised to follow them (Ogloff, 1999a).

According to the *Specialty Guidelines*:

> The goals of these *Guidelines* are to improve the quality of forensic psychological services; enhance the practice and facilitate the systematic developments of forensic psychology; encourage a high level of quality in professional practice; and encourage forensic practitioners to acknowledge and respect the rights of those they serve. (Committee on Ethical Guidelines for Forensic Psychologists, 2011, p. 1)

The *Specialty Guidelines* expressly note that they are "intended for use by psychologists when engaged in the practice of forensic psychology" (p. 1). It is important to emphasize that the *Guidelines* are applicable to all psychologists, irrespective of specialty area, when they engage in forensic psychology practice. To this end, the *Specialty Guidelines* specify that

> forensic psychology refers to the professional practice by any psychologist working within any sub-discipline of psychology (e.g., clinical, developmental, social, cognitive) when applying the scientific, technical, or specialized knowledge of psychology to the law to assist in addressing legal, contractual, and administrative matters. Application of the Guidelines does not depend on the practitioner's typical areas of practice or expertise, but rather on the service provided in the case at hand. (Committee on Ethical Guidelines for Forensic Psychologists, 2011, p. 1)

These provisions are very important since they specify that all psychologists whose work takes them into the realm of forensic psychology may be held to the standard of practice of a forensic psychologist, irrespective of the psychologist's usual work or roles. Critically, the *Specialty Guidelines* emphasize that they are not applicable to the work of psychologists, even if it is done within the legal system, so long as the work is not specifically forensic in nature, as defined.

## NEED FOR PROFESSIONAL COMPETENCE IN FORENSIC PSYCHOLOGY

Regardless of their role, all psychologists, including forensic psychologists, are still obligated to comply with general ethical guidelines, principles, and standards. The *Specialty Guidelines* are

> aspirational in intent. They are intended to facilitate the continued systematic development of the profession and facilitate a high level of practice by psychologists. Guidelines are not intended to be mandatory or exhaustive and may not be applicable to every professional situation. They are not definitive, and they are not intended to take precedence over the judgment of psychologists. (Committee on Ethical Guidelines for Forensic Psychologists, 2011, p. 2)

Psychologists are *obligated* to adhere to the standards provided in the Ethical Principles of Psychologists and Code of Conduct (2002); the *Specialty Guidelines* are aspirational in nature. Nonetheless, the *Specialty Guidelines* can be seen as contributing to the establishment of a standard of care in forensic psychology. Indeed, they specifically note that while they are "intended for use by psychologists when engaged in the practice of forensic psychology . . . [they] may also provide guidance on professional conduct to the legal system, and other organizations and professions" (Committee on Ethical Guidelines for Forensic Psychologists, 2011, p. 1).

While a review of the ethical principles that govern forensic psychology is not necessary here, it is important to emphasize that those psychologists who conduct forensic assessments are obligated to ensure that they are competent in their work (APA Ethical Standard 2.01; Ogloff, 1999a). Although this might appear obvious, in our experience it is surprising how many clinical psychologists (and other psychologists) begin doing forensic assessments without proper training or experience, only to find themselves experiencing difficulties either by virtue of their lack of appropriate experience or by becoming the subject of an ethics complaint. Of course, psychologists are ethically obligated to be professionally competent in any realm in which they work. For example, the APA ethics code requires that "psychologists provide services, teach, and conduct research with populations and in areas only within the boundaries of their competence, based on their education, training, supervised experience, consultation, study, or appropriate professional experience" (APA Standard 2.01). Therefore, psychologists whose work includes forensic practice must have professional competence in forensic psychology generally (Specialty Guideline 2—Competence). Furthermore, if the psychologist engages in psychological services that require more specialized training, he or she must also demonstrate professional competence in that area of subspecialty (e.g., assessment and treatment of sexual offenders, forensic neuropsychological assessment).

As noted in the ethics code of the APA (Ethical Standard 2—Competence; see also Specialty Guideline 2—Competence), generally speaking, professional competence in an area of specialization may be obtained and demonstrated by a combination of education and training, supervised experience by a registered psychologist with expertise in the area of specialization; and reading and research in the area of specialization. There is no clear rule about what constitutes professional competence in any given area; however, if challenged, the psychologist bears the burden of demonstrating his or her competence.

In addition to matters concerning the boundaries of their professional competence, forensic psychologists are obligated to have a fundamental understanding of the legal and professional standards in their area, and they must understand the legal rights of the parties with whom they come into contact to ensure that they do not unwittingly abrogate those rights (Specialty Guideline 2.04—Knowledge of the Legal System and the Legal Rights of Individuals). While it is certainly not necessary for a forensic psychologist to have a law degree, forensic psychologists are ethically obligated to ensure that they become thoroughly familiar with the law that is relevant to their areas of practice.

## SCOPE OF FORENSIC PSYCHOLOGICAL ASSESSMENTS

Given that every law, no matter how simple or complex, has but one purpose—to control human behavior—it should come as no surprise that the range of topics in which forensic assessments can be requested is broad (Ogloff, 2001). We present the major divisions of law here and discuss briefly the topics in which forensic psychologists might be retained to conduct assessments. Most readers will have some familiarity with the general areas of law; therefore, this review focuses on the areas most relevant to forensic psychology. Law is generally divided into several areas defined by the nature of issues that emerge. (See Rose, 2001, for a discussion of the divisions of law relevant to forensic psychology; see Melton et al., 2007, for a comprehensive review of these areas that are relevant to forensic psychology.) The most common division in law is between criminal law and civil law. Criminal law is an area of law that is considered to be public law because crimes are considered to be acts against the public good. In the United States, for example, when one is charged with committing a crime, the case is referred to as "the people," "the state," or "the commonwealth" against the defendant. In many jurisdictions within the Commonwealth of Nations, such as Britain, Canada, or Australia, for example, cases are referred to as "the Queen" or "Regina" against the defendant since Queen Elizabeth II is the head of state of nations in the commonwealth.

Within criminal law, there are many matters in which a forensic psychologist could be requested to conduct an assessment. Such matters include pretrial assessments— such as competency or fitness to stand trial and mental state at the time of the offense evaluations, presentence evaluations, and other court-ordered or quasi-legal assessments. In criminal matters, psychologists can be retained by the prosecution, the defense, or, in some cases, the court itself. Criminal matters can involve either adult or juvenile defendants, although the specific legal issues that arise and the relevant legal standards will likely differ between these populations.

Beyond criminal law, there is a large area of law known as civil law. Unlike criminal law, civil law is an area of "private law" because civil law has developed to resolve conflicts between private parties or companies. Civil law includes the enforcement of contracts and the resolution of private "wrongs" between individuals or companies. Such wrongs can include matters such as trespass, personal injury, libel or slander, false imprisonment, conversion, and others. In such matters, the legal dispute is between two or more people or corporations that have turned to the courts to resolve the dispute in a fair and impartial manner. Unlike criminal law, then, civil lawsuits name the two or more parties or corporations that are in dispute (e.g., *Jones v. Gonzales*). Forensic assessments can be required in these areas for establishing the extent of personal injury (e.g., cognitive impairment or emotional harm), worker's compensation, capacity to make a will, and other matters.

The final major area of law in which forensic psychologists are routinely called on to conduct assessments is family law and children's law. Family law concerns marriage and divorce, custody of children, division of assets, and financial maintenance for the support of family members (or former family members). Psychologists are retained most commonly to conduct assessments to assist courts in deciding matters like the custody of and access to children or of matters related to the apprehension of children from their parents by child protective service agencies. Infrequently, psychologists may be asked to conduct assessments of parties in family disputes for matters such as capacity to marry. In some jurisdictions family law includes assessments of children for child protection matters (e.g., assessing children to determine whether they have been abused or neglected and what sort of damage

they may have experienced). In other jurisdictions this is known as children's law.

## LEGAL CONTOURS OF FORENSIC ASSESSMENTS

The primary purpose of most forensic assessments is to assist legal decision-makers to come to a legal decision. Of course, as reviewed above, there are myriad legal decisions to which forensic psychological assessments may contribute relevant information. The common thread that runs throughout these diverse areas of law, and, subsequently, forensic assessment, is that legal decisions must be made. The legal decision-maker may be judicial (e.g., a judge or jury) or quasi-judicial (administrative tribunal) in nature, and the source of authority may arise from statute, quasi-statute (regulations; by-laws), or common law.

Regardless of the nature and source of the legal decision that must be made, there are specific legal criteria that will be the basis for the decision. In a very real sense, the legal criteria may be considered the referral questions that underlie the request for forensic assessment. For example, a statute may require that to be found incompetent to stand trial, defendants, on account of mental impairment or mental disorder, are unable to understand the nature of the charges against them, to understand the outcome and implications of the case, or to be able to communicate with and instruct their lawyers. The psychologist conducting a competence-to-stand-trial assessment must address each of the legal criteria to provide the court with the information necessary for the judge (or in some jurisdictions the jury) to decide whether the defendant is competent to stand trial. As this example shows, the forensic assessment must be linked to the elements of law that requires the assessment to be completed.

Like any referral question, then, it is ultimately the legal criteria that the forensic psychological assessment must inform. Given this reality, forensic assessments may be considered *inherently legal in nature*. In many situations, such assessments are mandated by the same legal source (i.e., statute or regulation) that gives the legal decision maker jurisdiction to decide the issue. In others, the authority is permissive—for example, litigants may choose to offer expert evidence to the court, although such evidence is not required by statute.

As discussed earlier in this chapter, the legal context of forensic psychological assessment is largely what sets it apart from other types of psychological assessments. The practical implication of this situation is that the law dictates, to a lesser or greater degree depending on the issue, the areas that must be addressed in a forensic psychological assessment. This places some constraints on the freedom that clinicians have in determining what their assessments should cover. Moreover, assessments that either do not address the legal criteria or stray too far beyond the legal questions being asked are not helpful to the courts. The goal for any forensic assessment is to provide an optimal fit between the legal requirements and the corresponding psychological assessment, such that the findings of the assessment optimally map onto the legal criteria that will guide the decision maker's conclusions.

For forensic clinicians and researchers to provide legally informed assessments and clinical research, it is necessary for them to be knowledgeable about the law that is relevant to their assessments. As discussed earlier, ethical guidelines from the APA (2002), the Canadian Psychological Association (2000), and all other ethics codes require that psychologists have knowledge of the context in which they practice. For forensic psychologists, this context is the law.

## Psycholegal Content Analysis: A Method and an Example

Forensic assessment is advanced through a procedure that may be called *psycholegal content analysis* (Ogloff, Roberts, & Roesch, 1993). Assessment questions are derived from legal standards and requirements, and, to the extent that these legal standards vary, so too may the assessment questions. Further, to the extent that these legal-assessment questions vary, so too ought the research corpus vary to be responsive to the legal-assessment task. This is especially important according to a scientist-practitioner approach, as will be described.

A psycholegal content analysis requires the following steps. First, the source of the legal authority governing the forensic assessment question—typically a statute—is identified. Statutory principles or requirements provided by that authority that are relevant for the assessment should then be distilled. If there are other legal mechanisms that expand on the original legal authority—typically legal cases that interpret the statute—these are analyzed for, again, principles that are relevant to the assessment task. Once these assessment-relevant legal principles are distilled and organized, the psychological knowledge or strategies that map onto these legal principles can be discerned. Concerning assessment-related research, study questions can be devised that inform the assessment questions, which themselves have been informed by assessment-related legal principles. In essence, this method combines traditional legal research with psychological traditions of clinical assessment and empirical study. Here the clinical assessment procedures and research study questions are informed, shaped, or determined by the legal parameters or principles.

Melton et al. (2007) provide numerous illustrations of how clinical-forensic assessments ought to be informed by prevailing relevant legal standards. They have provided both legal and psychological analysis throughout their comprehensive analysis of psychology's application to law. Their book, *Psychological Evaluations for the Courts* (3rd ed.), discusses the legal context as well as psychological task for numerous applications of psychology and psychiatry to law (e.g., competence, family law, criminal responsibility, civil commitment, violence prediction). In general, they reasoned that it is essential for forensic tests and assessment measures to inform the specific legal judgment that is called for; tests that were not developed or validated within legal contexts and according to legal principles, they argued, should be used with great caution in forensic assessment arenas. As well, in places they highlight the difficulties for clinical practice posed by varying legal definitions and standards across jurisdictions and settings.

The area of violence risk assessment is illustrative of the parameters set by law on forensic assessment. Melton et al. (2007) pointed out that "dangerousness," legally, can been satisfied in various settings and jurisdictions by extremely diverse outcome criteria. For instance, harm to property or causing emotional harm may satisfy criteria in some settings and in some jurisdictions (i.e., involuntary civil commitment), whereas in other settings (i.e., death penalty cases, dangerous offender cases, Heilbrun, Ogloff, & Picarello, 1999, or sexually violent predator cases, Mercado, Calkins & Ogloff, 2007), the outcome criterion is serious physical violence or risk of sexual offending (Mercado et al., 2007). These differing legal criteria have implications for the forensic assessment that is carried out and the research that can be used to support the assessment procedures.

Heilbrun (1997) discussed in some depth how different legal contexts have different implications for the most appropriate clinical and scientific approaches to violence risk assessment. For instance, in some settings, such as involuntary civil commitment, the immediate goal may be to maximize the accuracy of the prediction whereas in others, such as graduated release of those found not guilty by reason of insanity, the goal may orient more toward ongoing management. Clearly, the legal questions that arise under these two legal contexts call for different assessment strategies and, correspondingly, different research strategies to inform the clinical endeavors.

As Heilbrun (1997) explained, clinicians faced with management-related legal questions (i.e., can this person's risk reasonably be managed in the community, and under what circumstances?) may be faced with a somewhat different task if the legal question is more heavily weighted toward pure prediction. Similarly, researchers interested in evaluating risk assessment strategies that pertain to one or the other legal context likely will choose different approaches (i.e., the use of survival analysis with time-dependent covariates in the former and receiver operating characteristic analyses in the latter).

As previously noted, Heilbrun's (1997) analysis used two legal contexts to illustrate his points (civil commitment and release of insanity acquittees). An additional level of complexity is introduced when making cross-jurisdictional comparisons of legal context on top of such legally substantive comparisons. For instance, does the legal setting for civil commitment in, say, California, mirror that in Florida? How similar are either of these to the regimes in the Canadian provinces of Ontario or British Columbia? For example, Douglas and Koch (2001) have described how the statutory criteria for involuntary civil commitment vary tremendously across Canadian jurisdictions alone in terms of risk-relevant requirements. In turn, this means that the nature of forensic assessment of violence risk across these jurisdictions also will vary. In the United States, there are 50 states across which statutory and case law requirements for civil commitment may vary.

The main points to be taken from this discussion are that (1) the law either shapes or sets the parameters of forensic assessment and (2) both clinical-forensic assessment and assessment-related research need to be informed by the differing legal requirements that bear on an assessment question (i.e., violence risk assessment), both with respect to different legal areas (e.g., civil commitment versus release of insanity acquittees) and to different legal jurisdictions.

## Admissibility of Forensic Assessments Into Evidence

Although a comprehensive review of the admissibility of psychological evidence is beyond the scope of this chapter, it is important to highlight the relevant legal criteria that courts consider when deciding whether the evidence of a psychologist will be admissible as expert opinion evidence. The specific rules of evidence vary across states and in federal court. Although the Federal Rules of Evidence (FRE; 2010) is federal law in the United States, many states have incorporated at least some portion of the FRE into their evidence legislation. As with any law that relates to their work, readers should determine the specific local laws that are relevant to the admissibility of expert testimony. In interpreting the FRE, attention will be paid to *Daubert v. Merrell Dow Pharmaceuticals, Inc.* (1993) and *Kuhmo Tire Co. v. Carmichael* (1999), two of the U.S. Supreme Court decisions that have considered the standard of acceptance for the admission of scientific evidence.

To be admissible, the psychological evidence must first be found by the court to be relevant. That means that the information provided by the psychological assessment must be related to some matter at issue in the case. In addition, the court must be assured that the probative value of the psychologist's evidence is not outweighed by its prejudicial value. This means that the value of the expert's testimony in assisting the jury or court to answer a question at issue will not be unduly outweighed by the expert's influence on the jury or court.

After the court has determined whether the expert testimony is relevant and that its probative weight outweighs its prejudicial value, the court can turn to a direct review of the expert testimony itself. The relevant provisions of the FRE governing expert testimony include FRE 702 (testimony by experts), FRE 703 (bases of opinion testimony by experts), FRE 704 (opinion on ultimate issue), FRE 705 (disclosure of facts or data underlying expert opinion), and FRE 706 (court-appointed experts).

For expert testimony to be admissible under FRE 702, three requirements must be satisfied: (1) the judge or jury must require the assistance of the expert's testimony; (2) the expert must be qualified, by knowledge, skill, experience, training or education, to offer an opinion; and (3) if "(1) the testimony is based upon sufficient facts or data, (2) the testimony is the product of reliable principles and methods, and (3) the witness has applied the principles and methods reliably to the facts of the case." In addition, FRE 702 specifies that the expert's testimony may be in the form of an opinion. Unlike all other witnesses who give evidence in trials, only experts are permitted to state their opinions about matters at issue in the case. Other witnesses must report only "fact-based" information—that is, information about which they have firsthand knowledge (e.g., what they have seen, what they have heard). Due to their expertise and the fact that their evidence is required to assist the judge or jury, experts are permitted to provide both fact-based information and opinion evidence. This rule is sometimes called the opinion rule, signifying that the expert may provide the court with an opinion since the information about which the expert has a unique understanding requires an expert to form an opinion.

Considerable controversy has surrounded the question of how a court determines whether the information presented by experts was reasonably relied on by experts in a particular field. Prior to the adoption of the FRE, and in some states even following, courts relied on the "*Frye* test" (*Frye v. U.S.*, 1923) to determine whether the scientific evidence on which expert testimony is based should be admitted into evidence at trial. To satisfy the *Frye* test, an expert witness who offered opinion evidence had to demonstrate not only that the methods relied upon are generally accepted, but that they are used in the relevant areas of the expert's area of expertise, and that the techniques he or she employed comported with the state of the art in the field.

The *Frye* test enjoyed widespread use and endorsement by federal and state courts until Congress adopted the FRE in 1976. Thereafter, considerable controversy arose regarding the extent to which the test for the admissibility of novel scientific evidence in *Frye* remained applicable, with different courts arriving at different conclusions. In 1993 the U.S. Supreme Court resolved the controversy by holding in *Daubert v. Merrell Dow Pharmaceuticals* that the *Frye* test's general acceptance requirement "is not a necessary precondition to the admissibility of scientific evidence under the Federal Rules of Evidence" (p. 597). In *Daubert* (1993), two infants and their parents brought a lawsuit against a pharmaceutical company, arguing that the mothers' prenatal ingestion of the drug Bendectin caused serious birth defects in the infants. During the trial, the testimony of an expert concluded that the corpus of scientific test results on the drug did not show that it was a significant risk factor for birth defects. As a result, the trial court decided in favor of the drug company. On appeal, the U.S. Court of Appeal for the Ninth Circuit relied on the *Frye* test and affirmed the lower court's decision. In overruling the decision, the U.S. Supreme Court held that nothing in the FRE incorporated *Frye*'s general acceptance rule and that "a rigid 'general acceptance' requirement would be at odds with the 'liberal thrust' of the Federal Rules and their 'general approach' of relaxing the traditional barriers to 'opinion' testimony" (Federal Rules of Evidence, 2010, p. 588).

Some states still employ the *Frye* test to ensure that the expert testimony is based on principles that are generally accepted by the field in which it is offered. Other jurisdictions have adopted the approach set out in *Daubert*. Moreover, jurisdictions outside the United States have also wrestled with this matter and have developed their own relevant rules of evidence. As with other points of law, therefore, psychologists should acquaint themselves with the standard of the admissibility of expert evidence that is in force in their jurisdiction.

In footnote 11 of their decision, the Supreme Court in *Daubert* provided further guidance that an assessment of scientific knowledge, as is mentioned in FRE 702, "entails a preliminary assessment of whether the reasoning or methodology underlying the testimony is scientifically valid" (p. 592). In addition, the Court noted that scientific validity asks the question "does the principle support what it purports to show?" (p. 590). In 1999 the U.S. Supreme Court explicitly expanded its ruling in *Daubert* to federal judges' consideration of all expert evidence (*Kuhmo Tire Co. v. Carmichael*, 1999). In 2010 the FRE were updated. The current rules, as discussed, take into account the evolution of the jurisprudence surrounding the admissibility of expert evidence.

Once the court is sure that the techniques on which the proposed expert testimony is based are valid, it must decide whether the proposed witness is qualified as an expert in the area in question (FRE 702). A witness may qualify as an expert based on his or her training or education, knowledge, skill, or experience. Typically, it is not difficult for psychologists to qualify as experts providing that they demonstrate sufficient training and knowledge about techniques that are employed in a particular area. It must be noted that the term *expert*, as it is used by the courts, does not pertain to some general expertise acquired by professional training but rather specific expertise pertaining to a particular matter at issue before the courts. Therefore, while one may be a properly licensed and experienced psychologist, for example, without specialized training, supervision, and experience, one would not be recognized by the courts as an expert for the purposes of giving an opinion about, say, risk for violence.

The final FRE specifically governing the admissibility of expert testimony involves the expert's opinion on the ultimate issue (FRE 704). Ultimate issue opinions directly address the legal question being asked (e.g., was the deceased competent to make a will, did the deceased die as the result of an accident or did she commit suicide?). Authorities from the legal and mental health disciplines have debated whether experts should offer opinions that are similar to, or parallel, the ultimate legal issue (Melton et al., 2007). Regardless of this debate, FRE 704 provides that "testimony in the form of an opinion or inference otherwise admissible is not objectionable because it embraces an ultimate issue to be decided by the trier of fact."

There is one major exception to allowing expert testimony on ultimate issue testimony. In 1984 Congress amended FRE 704(b) in response to the verdict in the *Hinckley* case in which the would-be assassin of President Reagan, John Hinckley, Jr., was found not guilty by reason of insanity. The amendment precludes experts in a criminal case from testifying whether they believe the defendant had the mental state or condition required to satisfy an element of the crime, or a defense to the crime. This section remains in force despite the U.S. Supreme Court's decisions in *Daubert* (1993) and *Kuhmo Tire* (1999) and has survived the 2010 revisions to the FRE.

In summary, to be admissible, expert psychological testimony must be relevant to the issues in the case, and its probative value must outweigh its prejudicial impact. If these two general requirements are met, expert psychological testimony will be admissible if it can be demonstrated that (a) an issue at question is beyond the understanding of the judge or jury and the decision reached by the judge or jury would benefit as the result of special expertise, (b) the technique or methods employed in the assessment are accepted by the field, and (c) the proffered witness has expertise with respect to the question at issue. Additionally, the FRE allow experts to base their testimony on their observations (in and out of court) or information introduced outside of court. Experts need reveal the underlying sources for their opinion only if requested to do so upon cross-examination. Finally, the psychologist must be aware of the standard for the admissibility of expert opinion evidence that is employed in the jurisdiction in which he or she practices psychology.

## CONTEMPORARY ISSUES IN FORENSIC ASSESSMENT

So far the information provided in this chapter has provided a broad overview of forensic psychological assessments. In this section, we review a number of contemporary issues that are affecting forensic psychologists: clinical versus actuarial predictions; legally informed practitioner model; roles and limits of general psychological testing in forensic contexts; legal specificity in our work; and training in forensic contexts.

### Clinical Versus Actuarial Predictions Revisited

The clinical-actuarial prediction debate has a long and heated history in the fields of clinical, counseling, educational, industrial-organizational, military, and other branches of psychology (Heilbrun, 2009). Although addressed in Weiner's chapter in this volume, we discuss its manifestation within forensic assessment because it has some unique aspects in this field (Hart, Michie, & Cooke, 2007; Rice, Harris, & Hilton, 2010). We use the area of violence risk assessment to illustrate our points.

There is little doubt that actuarial prediction tends to outperform unstructured clinical prediction in terms of validity indices. Of course, the early work of the late Paul Meehl (1954) and his subsequent work with colleagues (Grove & Meehl, 1996; Grove, Zald, Lebow, Snitz, & Nelson, 2000) have supported this position consistently for some time. In the field of violence risk assessment, the debate continues with respect to violence risk assessment instruments. Some instruments adopt pure actuarial decision-making procedures, citing Meehl's and colleagues' work in their support. (See, e.g., Quinsey, Harris, Rice, & Cormier, 2006.) Other instruments are developed that require *structured professional judgment*. (See, e.g., Douglas, Ogloff, & Hart, 2003; Douglas & Webster, 1999; Webster, Douglas, Eaves, & Hart, 1997.)

In the latter case, there is warranted concession that unstructured clinical opinion that "relies on an informal, 'in the head,' impressionistic, subjective conclusion, reached (somehow) by a human clinical judge" (Grove & Meehl, 1996, p. 294) has little evidence, empirical or conceptual, to support its use. However, research evidence shows that a *structured* approach to risk assessment can perhaps overcome some of the weaknesses (i.e., low interrater reliability and validity) inherent in the "impressionistic" nature of global clinical opinion while increasing predictive validity (Douglas, Ogloff, & Hart, 2003; Douglas & Reeves, 2010). Further, as Hart (1998) described, particularly in the field of risk assessment, the clinical task is much broader than prediction, including issues related to prevention and management of violence risk. For this reason, the clinical task has come to be called, in recent times, violence risk *assessment* rather than violence *prediction* per se.

The argument is that structured clinical assessment can achieve a more individualized and comprehensive assessment than can actuarial prediction, while still achieving a respectable level of interrater reliability and validity. Further, instruments that adopt structured professional judgment procedures tend to have been developed rationally or analytically rather than empirically. In theory, this method of developing the instruments should enhance their generalizability to the numerous contexts in which risk assessment is required and minimize the problems of validity shrinkage inherent in the application of empirically derived actuarial instruments to novel settings or purposes.

Research on three such violence risk assessment measures has supported the predictive validity of the clinical opinions that they call for. Relatively early in its implementation, Douglas and Ogloff (2003) tested the interrater reliability and predictive validity of violence risk judgments made with the Historical Clinical Risk—20; HCR-20 violence risk assessment scheme (Webster et al., 1997). Like all structured professional judgment risk measures, the HCR-20 is an analytically or logically developed guide intended to structure professional decisions about violence risk through encouraging the consideration of 20 key violence risk factors dispersed across three scales: Historical (H), Clinical (C), and Risk Management (R) (Webster et al., 1997). The risk factors identified by the HCR-20 have been found in the literature to relate to an individual's likelihood to engage in violent criminal behavior. The H scale focuses on past, mainly static risk factors; the C on current aspects of mental status and attitudes; and the R on future situational features.

Research by Douglas and Ogloff (2003) has shown that the interrater reliability of structured professional judgments regarding the patients' risk for violence risk was good or substantial. Violence risk judgments were also found to be significantly predictive of postrelease community violence. A direct comparison of the structured professional judgment approach and an actuarial approach, both using the HCR-20, showed that the structured professional violence judgments added incremental validity to the HCR-20 scored actuarially. These results showed that clinical judgment, if made within a structured context, can contribute in meaningful ways to the clinical practice of violence risk assessment.

Similar results have been found for two additional violence risk instruments. Investigating the predictive validity of the Sexual Violence Risk—20 (SVR-20; Boer, Hart, Kropp, & Webster, 1997), de Vogel, de Ruiter, van Beek, and Mead (2004) completed the SVR-20 on a sample of sexual offenders. The SVR-20, modeled on the HCR-20, provides a list of the factors that have been found to predict risk for sexual offending and sexual violence. De Vogel and colleagues compared the summed total of items (i.e., actuarial prediction) and the ratings of high, medium, and low risk (i.e., structured professional judgment). They found that the structured professional judgment approach provided incremental validity over the scored items on the scales of sexual violence risk. Finally, Kropp and Hart (2000) evaluated the structured clinical judgments produced by the Spousal Assault Risk Assessment guide (SARA; Kropp, Hart, Webster, & Eaves, 1999), a further example of the structured professional judgment

model of risk assessment. Kropp and Hart used a sample of 102 male probationers who had been convicted of offenses involving spousal assault and referred by the courts to attend domestic violence treatment. They found that structured professional judgments based on the SARA summary risk ratings of low, moderate, and high risk outperformed the summation of SARA items (actuarial prediction) in terms of their respective relationships to spousal assault recidivism. Kropp and Hart also reported good interrater reliability indices for the final risk judgments.

Taken together, research investigating the structured professional judgment based on the HCR-20, the SVR-20/Risk for Sexual Violence Protocol (Hart et al., 2003), and the SARA, supports both the interrater reliability and predictive validity of the instruments. There is some emerging support, therefore, for the supposition that a structured professional judgment approach to violence risk assessment, if carried out in a structured, operationalized, and measurable manner, can be reliable and valid, as well as potentially more comprehensive and responsive to idiographic concerns, than is actuarial prediction.

## Legally Informed Practitioner Model

As is well known, clinical psychology adopted the scientist-practitioner "Boulder" model of training and practice more than 60 years ago. This model of practice does have its critics, and it is a persisting source of professional disagreement and argument to this day (Beutler, Williams, Wakefield, & Entwistle, 1995; Fensterheim & Raw, 1996; Goldfried & Wolfe, 1996; Hayes, 1996; Kanfer, 1990; Nezu, 1996; Singer, 1990; Sobell, 1996; Stricker, 1992; Stricker & Trierweiler, 1995; Webster & Cox, 1997). The details of this debate cannot be addressed adequately in this chapter, but it is an operating assumption of this chapter that the scientist-practitioner model remains the theoretical cornerstone of doctoral training in clinical psychology. As such, clinical-forensic psychology, as a subfield of clinical psychology more broadly, subscribes to its tenets. Therefore, forensic assessment, as a particular activity within clinical-forensic psychology, also rests on the scientist-practitioner model. While we favor the scientist-practitioner model as the choice for those who conduct forensic assessments, we should note that we recognize at the outset that those trained in the scholar-practitioner tradition can become competent forensic psychologists.

Both scientist-practitioner and scholar-practitioner doctoral training programs require students to obtain systematic training and supervised experience in psychological assessment and psychological intervention. Training programs subscribing to the scientist-practitioner model, typically leading to the PhD degree, require students to complete a doctoral thesis or dissertation consisting of an empirical research project. By contrast, training programs based on the scholar-practitioner model that lead to the PsyD degree do not require students to complete empirical research. Instead, these programs require that students obtain expertise in reading, interpreting, and critically analyzing empirical research. Our emphasis here is that, particularly due to the inherently technical nature of forensic assessments, a strong background in experimental methods is an asset to those who conduct forensic assessments. Therefore, rather than focusing on the particular doctoral degree a psychologist has, consideration of suitability for practicing forensic psychology should be based on the individual's ability to understand the empirical research and to incorporate it into his or her work.

There are some modifications to and limitations of the scientist-practitioner and scholar-practitioner models in forensic assessment. First, the models must be conceptualized to be situated within a legal context. In essence, this makes the optimal model of training and practice in forensic psychology a legally informed scientist or scholar-practitioner model.

This reality has implications for the meaning of the science employed in clinical-forensic psychology. Some of these implications are similar to the issues discussed with respect to the "psycholegal content analysis" presented earlier. That is, we discussed how practice must be conducted to inform legal criteria. Similarly, if science is to inform clinical decision making, it too must find some inspiration within the law. In other fields of psychology, a scientist's questions may be limited only by his or her imagination. In forensic psychology, there is an overriding limiting factor—the law and the legal standards that can be derived from the particular legal question being asked in an assessment. This is not to say that *all* forensic psychological science must *always* line up exactly with legal issues. We would not advocate constraining scientific inquiry in such a manner. And, in fact, there is abundant "nonforensic," primary research that is very applicable and of great benefit to the forensic field. For instance, research on the effects of trauma, on violence, and on major mental disorders are all of import to forensic psychological science and practice. However, it is imperative that, in addition to maximizing the utility of this research as it pertains to forensic assessment, researchers *also* design studies that map as closely as possible onto quite strict legal criteria or standards. This necessity explains

the existence, for example, of research on the psychometric properties of competency measures whose items are defined largely by the legal definition of the term *incompetent* in the particular setting (i.e., incompetent to stand trial; incompetent to manage one's estate or affairs) and jurisdiction.

In some ways, this type of research has an additional evaluative component as part of the validation procedure. Content and construct-related validities must take into account legal definitions and outcome criteria that are meant to be represented in the measure. If a measure of competence, for instance, does not tap a major facet of the legal construct (i.e., ability to instruct counsel), its validity is questionable in this regard, despite the possible existence of otherwise excellent psychometric properties.

In addition to the "regular" components of the scientist-practitioner model, then, there is an additional, and sometimes superordinate, layer. As such, not only does research have to be carried out that is clinically meaningful and informative, and not only does clinical practice have to reciprocate by relying on this research as much as is reasonable, but *both* science *and* practice also must follow the lead of the law. It is likely that clinical practice has less flexibility than does science for straying from legal standards. All forensic practice, and much forensic research, however, must be mindful of the law.

Several further aspects of the legally informed practitioner model need explanation. First, the addition of the law to the models of clinical training imposes an inherent limitation on their theoretical utility and, perhaps, on the accumulation of clinical-scientific knowledge that gathers under it. Tomorrow, a high-level court could decide that, for example, all pieces of civil commitment legislation of a certain ilk are unconstitutional and in need of drastic revision. What happens to the established base of science and practice that developed to assist decision makers in this context? Research and practice must evolve alongside evolutions in the law. Research can become dated and clinical practice antiquated not only through the passage of time but through the passage of law.

A further limitation of the legally informed practitioner model within the forensic context involves the limitations placed on research methodology. Certain important issues can never be studied in an ideal methodological manner because of the pragmatic constraints of the law. For instance, nearly all research on violence risk assessment, the prediction of violence, and correlates of violence has been carried out on truncated research samples. That is, certain persons will never be included in research samples simply because they will never or only rarely be released from prisons or other institutions. Risk assessment studies that attempt to study postrelease community violence are forced to use only persons who have actually been released. However, when the clinical task of risk assessment is undertaken, this research is applied to *all* persons appearing for release.

Another example of a methodological shortcoming is the absence of gold standards for validation. For instance, research on criminal competencies is undertaken to maximize the utility of clinical determinations of competence. There is no inherent gold standard of comparison to validate the decisions that competence instruments yield. If an instrument yields a decision of "competent" but a judge declared a petitioner "incompetent," this does not mean that the instrument was wrong. Rather, it could be that the judge did not understand the psychological and clinical aspects that were entered into evidence in support of the petitioner's motion for a finding of incompetence. Although these instruments do use judicial decision as part of the formal validation procedure, they must also rely heavily on content validity and inference. That is, the measures must dissect the legal requirements for competence, construct items that tap these legal requirements, and provide thresholds at which inferences are drawn about whether persons understand what they need to about the legal and court process in order to be found competent.

To summarize, then, three main points can be made about the legally informed practitioner model as it manifests in forensic assessment: (1) Practice and scientific freedom must be constrained, in part, by the legal questions that are being posed; (2) the field must at times readjust itself and its scientific and clinical approaches in response to changes in the law; and (3) legal practicalities sometimes preclude optimal methodological approaches to a topic of inquiry.

## Roles and Limits of General Psychological Testing in Forensic Contexts

In much of this chapter, we have discussed the importance of aligning clinical assessment and research with legal requirements. This logic applies as well to psychological testing that is carried out in forensic contexts. In this section, we discuss specifically the use of psychological assessment instruments and tests as applied to forensic contexts. Following the theme of the legal specificity and parameters of forensic assessment, we discuss issues surrounding the use of "regular" psychological tests in forensic assessment as well as the development and use of tests that are intended to be forensic in nature.

By way of background, Heilbrun et al. (2002) have proposed a simple yet effective typology of psychological measures relevant to forensic assessment. These include forensic assessment instruments, forensically relevant instruments, and clinical instruments. While measures from each category can be useful for assisting with a forensic assessment, the specific nature and utility of each category of psychological measure varies. Similarly, the way in which the measures should be used in assessments vary.

A *forensic assessment instrument* is one that "is directly relevant to a specific legal standard and its included capacities that are needed for the individual being evaluated to meet that legal standard" (Heilbrun et al., 2002, p. 128). Examples of specific legal standards are criminal competence to stand trial, criminal responsibility ("insanity"), and competent to manage one's estate. An example of a forensic assessment instrument is the MacArthur Competence Assessment Tool-Criminal Adjudication (MacCAT-CA; Poythress, Monahan, Bonnie, & Hoge, 1999; Poythress, Nicholson, Otto, Edens, Bonnie, Monahan, & Hoge, 1999). The MacCAT-CA was developed to guide mental health professionals who are assessing a defendant's competency to stand trial. The instrument is specifically designed to assess the legal standards for competency to stand trial as set out by the U.S. Supreme Court (*Dusky v. United States*, 1960). As Heilbrun et al. (2002) pointed out, there has been a proliferation of instruments intended to be used in forensic settings. The development of forensic assessment instruments and forensically relevant instruments can be seen as an important development, in that it should, in principle, compensate for some of the pitfalls of using clinical measures for forensic assessments.

*Forensically relevant instruments* are those that do not address specific legal standards, but "clinical constructs that are sometimes pertinent to legal standards" (Heilbrun et al., 2002, p. 130). Examples may include measures of psychopathy (via the Hare Revised Psychopathy Checklist [PCL-R]; Hare, 2003) or measures of violence risk (such as the HCR-20 [Webster et al., 1997]). Concerning risk assessment measures, some argument may be made that many uses of these instruments actually should be placed in the forensic assessment instrument category, since often they are applied to specific legal standards pertaining to risk for future violence.

Heilbrun et al. (1999) called the third type of instrument, comprised of traditional psychological instruments, *clinical measures*. The implications of using these types of instruments in forensic assessment are discussed next.

Assessment questions in clinical psychology are usually informed through the use of psychological instruments. Such instruments typically were developed to inform decisions about common or traditional psychological constructs, such as intelligence, memory, depression, or anxiety. A problem emerges when these instruments (e.g., the Wechsler Adult Intelligence Scale—Fourth Edition [WAIS-IV]; Wechsler, 2009; or the Minnesota Multiphasic Personality Inventory-2 [MMPI-2], Butcher, Dahlstrom, Graham, Tellegen, & Kaemmer, 2001) are applied to forensic assessments. The underpinning of the problem lies in the fact that forensic constructs and questions rarely map directly onto traditional psychological constructs (Heilbrun et al., 2002; Otto & Heilbrun, 2003). As such, there is a schism between general psychological instruments, on one hand, and forensic psychological assessment questions, on the other. Traditional psychological instruments were not designed for the purpose of answering questions pertaining to legal constructs such as insanity, competence, or risk for certain types of violence. While they may perform well and as they were designed to with respect to general psychological assessment questions among forensic samples (i.e., what is the intelligence of a particular forensic patient), their ability to inform specific forensic questions is tenable (how does an IQ score inform a decision about competence?).

Research has supported the problems inherent in using traditional psychological instruments to answer forensic or legal questions. First, there is simply not much research that addresses the validity of traditional psychological instruments as applied to forensic questions (Heilbrun et al., 2002; Melton et al., 2007). Second, existing research does not provide strong support for their use in forensic assessments *to answer specifically forensic questions*. For instance, as reviewed by Heilbrun et al. (2002) and Rogers and Shuman (2000), the MMPI/MMPI-2 is commonly used in insanity evaluations, despite relatively few studies on its application to this task. (See Ogloff, 1995, for a review of the legal applications of the MMPI/MMPI-2.) Existing studies tend not to provide stable estimates of profiles indicative of *legal insanity*. While the MMPI-2, or some other measure such as the Personality Assessment Inventory (PAI; Morey, 1991), may have adequate research support with respect to its ability to detect *clinical* "insanity" or psychopathology (i.e., the presence of delusions or hallucinations), there is far from a one-to-one correspondence between clinical and legal "insanity." To the extent that the constructs tapped by the MMPI-2, the PAI, or comprehensive structured assessments, fail to align with the legal construct of insanity, the application of such measures for legal or forensic purposes is questionable.

This state of affairs is neither terribly surprising nor detrimental to the general validity of such measures as the MMPI-2 or WAIS-IV. Neither was designed with legal constructs in mind. Hence, in psychometric terms, they were not built to include construct coverage of legal questions such as insanity or violence risk. They do not include items that were meant to tap legal constructs. This situation is akin to a depression measure failing to include items designed to tap the physical signs and symptoms of depression. Such an instrument would have inadequate construct coverage, and its psychometric properties, in particular its validity indices, would suffer accordingly. Similarly, the validity indices of traditional psychological measures tend to suffer when applied to specific forensic or legal constructs or criteria.

In response to the difficulties associated with using traditional psychological measures in forensic assessments, commentators have provided some guidance for the use of tests in forensic psychological assessment. Earlier we discussed the importance of legal context to forensic assessment generally. Similarly, there has been discourse pertaining to the link between legal context and psychological instrumentation. Heilbrun et al. (2002) referred to the importance of correspondence between a (forensic) assessment measure and the legal construct to which it purportedly applies. This correspondence is an important part of the development and validation of forensic instruments. Heilbrun et al. discussed "legal status" as a "population-specific influence" on the development and validation of forensic instruments. In essence, they pointed out, forensic instruments (and, consequently, assessments) should be used only within legal settings for which they have been developed and validated. Similarly, writing about the importance of legal context for the practice of forensic assessment generally, Heilbrun (1992) and others (e.g., Melton et al., 2007) have argued that psychological tests used in such assessments must be germane to the legal issue at hand. As such, as Heilbrun et al. (2002) pointed out, the law is an important source of authority for the development of forensic instruments.

Grisso (1987), in discussing the "necessary research" (p. 834) to establish forensic psychological assessment as a credible and legally informative vehicle, discussed several law-related research avenues that could forward such a goal. These included pure legal analyses of specific questions (i.e., criminal responsibility), application of basic psychological principles to legal questions, research on the applicability of traditional psychological measures (i.e., MMPI-2) to legal issues, as well as the development of "specialized assessment instruments" (p. 835) that link directly to legal questions. These ideas overlap with the notion of psycholegal content analysis presented earlier.

In terms of providing a methodology for constructing forensic instruments, Grisso (2003) provided an example based on the assessment of criminal competency. According to Grisso (2003), the first stage of devising and validating a method for assessing criminal competencies is to translate legal standards into functional abilities. Then psychological test construction and validation procedures can be applied to these functional abilities. For example, if the legal standard for competency to stand trial requires, among other things, that the defendant is able to communicate with his or her lawyer, the first task of a psychologist assessing the defendant's competency is to determine what functional abilities the defendant must have to communicate with a lawyer. These functional abilities could include, for example, such things as being able to speak or otherwise communicate and being able to assist the lawyer by discussing the evidence and the weaknesses of the testimony to be given by prospective witnesses.

## Legal Specificity

In all areas of psychological assessment, it is beneficial to have referral questions that are as specific as possible. This helps to guide the nature and course of the assessment and prevent unnecessary "fishing expeditions." This admonition is particularly apt in forensic assessment. The law—in particular courts—are loathe to address more than is required for them to answer the legal question at stake. The reason for this is sensible. The adversarial legal system in which we live allows opposing parties to litigate their legal questions in front of judges and juries, in effect educating the court about the particular legal issue(s) in question. For a legal decision-maker to address more than what was argued is undesirable because the parties did not have a chance to address or argue the peripheral matters, and hence the decision-maker was not presented with evidence pertaining to these peripheral matters.

Following the logic presented above, it is undesirable for a forensic assessment, which often will be used to educate a legal decision-maker, either to address unduly broad referral questions, or to stray beyond the referral questions that were asked. Unduly broad referral questions are those that do not provide the forensic evaluator with sufficient information to proceed with an assessment. For example, without knowing exactly at what stage the defendant is in the legal process and the exact legal matters that are at

issue to require a forensic assessment, the forensic clinician can do little more that provide something akin to a traditional psychological assessment. Straying beyond the referral question results in the clinician raising issues or addressing matters that extend beyond the particular legal matter being considered. The following is an example of an actual excerpt from a report prepared by a forensic practitioner who was asked to conduct an assessment to determine whether the defendant's mental state at the time of the offense might be grounds for raising the insanity defense:

> It does not appear that Mr. S. was suffering from any psychosis at the time of the assault. He may have been under the influence of various drugs and alcoholic beverages, which he reported consuming at that time. There is no clinical basis for an insanity defense here. Mr. S. is one of the most dangerous persons I have ever examined; the only appropriate disposition would be a lengthy prison sentence. (Melton et al., 2007, p. 361)

In this case, the report introduced information that is off the legal point into the legal arena, without due cause, and without a priori notice that such information would be justiciable (i.e., at issue in the trial). This irrelevant information introduces an element of uncertainty into the legal forum, one that could unfairly affect the process or the result of the legal endeavor.

Apart from the rather picayune legal point just mentioned, psychologists should refrain from going beyond the legal referral question when preparing reports of forensic assessments because the reports that are prepared in legal cases, more so than virtually any other area of clinical practice, have a long shelf life. Thus, extraneous information that appears in a report prepared for a particular purpose can be used, sometimes years later, in a manner that can be harmful to the person who was assessed.

While it is important that forensic assessments address the legal questions for which they were requested, psychologists are generally advised to use extreme caution if asked to *answer* the legal question that is asked. In law, this is referred to as answering the ultimate issue (Melton et al., 2007). The ultimate issue in a case is the question the judge or jury is asked to decide. For example, in a case involving a custody dispute, the ultimate issue is generally what living arrangements would be in the child's best interests. Therefore, a psychologist who offered an opinion about which living arrangement would be in the child's best interests would be answering the ultimate issue. As discussed in the context of the guidelines for expert testimony, FRE 704 allows experts to give an opinion concerning the ultimate issue. Recall that, as discussed with reference to the admissibility of expert evidence earlier in this chapter, FRE 704(b) prohibits experts in a criminal case from testifying whether they believe the defendant had the mental state or condition required to satisfy an element of the crime or a defense to the crime. However, forensic mental health professionals should nonetheless be cautious when deciding to answer the ultimate issue. If the expert is allowed to answer the ultimate opinion, he or she is basically telling the jury or judge how to decide the case. Formerly, ultimate issue testimony was barred in courts (Melton et al., 2007). While the current rules of evidence are not as strict, psychologists generally should refrain from answering the ultimate issue both because doing so can usurp the power of the court or jury and because, most often, the ultimate legal issue does not correspond directly to the relevant psychological construct. For example, there is no construct in psychiatry or psychology that corresponds directly to competency to stand trial.

Despite the convincing arguments against providing an ultimate opinion, forensic psychologists are regularly asked by attorneys and judges to state whether they think, for example, that a defendant is competent to stand trial. Any reluctance to answer the question as asked—that is, to state the ultimate opinion—may be met with suspicion or criticism by the attorneys or the judge that the psychologists are not doing their jobs as expert witnesses. Rather than simply providing the answer to the ultimate issue, we recommend that psychologists take care to ensure that they discuss the psychological information that is relevant to the underlying legal principles that pertain to the construct being addressed. Taking the competency to stand trial case as an example, we would not recommend that psychologists simply express an opinion that a defendant is, or is not, "competent to stand trial." Rather, we suggest that psychologists provide the court with relevant psychological information that relates to the legal criteria in the competency to stand trial. For example, a psychologist could discuss the relevant psychological information that relates to how the defendant's mental state will affect his or her ability to communicate with counsel or to understand the nature of the legal proceedings. (See Roesch, Ogloff, & Golding, 1993.)

Another important issue concerns the absolute necessity of avoiding the role of "advocate" in forensic assessment practice. Terms such as *hired gun* or *whore of the court* are well-known monikers used to describe the forensic evaluator who will find certain results, given the right price. Of course, such practice is unethical and will undermine not only the credibility of the individual assessor in a given case but the profession of psychology as well. Despite the pressure that psychologists might experience, either explicitly or implicitly, from the parties that hire them, it is critical that they do not adopt the position of advocate. Rather, psychologists should most properly take on the role of impartial educators. That is, even when hired by one side or another, the proper role of the forensic evaluator is to impartially arrive at a conclusion based on assessment findings, and to deliver this conclusion, along with any uncertainties.

## Training in Forensic Assessment

As noted in the introduction to this chapter, along with the emergence of forensic psychology has come the development of graduate training programs in the area (see, e.g., Freeman & Roesch, 1992; Grisso, Sales, & Bayless, 1982; Hafemeister, Ogloff, & Small, 1990; Ogloff, 1990; Ogloff & Schuller, 2001; Ogloff et al., 1996; Roesch, Grisso, & Poythress, 1986; Tomkins & Ogloff, 1990). As with other aspects of the developing field, little attention has been given to the training needs and opportunities in the field. Part of the concern for the lack of attention directed to training in legal psychology has been rectified with the "National Invitational Conference on Education and Training in Law and Psychology" that took place at Villanova Law School in 1995. The "Villanova Conference," as it has come to be known, was attended by approximately 60 invited people from across the field of legal psychology. The overarching purpose of the conference was to develop an agenda for legal psychology training into the 21st century. A description of the conference can be found in an article written by Bersoff, Goodman-Delahunty, Grisso, Hans, Poythress and Roesch (1997).

People have debated whether psychologists who work in the law and psychology field need to be trained formally in law. (See Grisso et al., 1982; Hafemeister et al., 1990; Ogloff et al., 1996; Tomkins & Ogloff, 1990.) This debate has culminated in consideration of the joint degree programs where students can obtain both a law degree and a PhD. Arguments against dual degree training have emphasized the costs of such training and the fact that most people who work in legal psychology, as clinicians or researchers, focus on one or two specific areas of the law. Those who support dual degree programs, by contrast, argue that while all legal psychologists do not require formal training in law, there are considerable advantages to pursuing formal training in law and psychology (Hafemeister et al., 1990). Foremost among these advantages is the ability of psychologists with law degrees to have a sophisticated understanding of the law. Indeed, many psychologists with little appreciation of law have jumped into the field only to produce work that is of questionable validity. (See Hafemeister et al., 1990.) We want to emphasize here that while it would not be necessary—or even a good idea—for all forensic psychologists to obtain a law degree, it is nevertheless critical that forensic psychologists obtain a clear understanding, if not true expertise, in the law that relates to their work.

Most forensic psychologists working today obtained their forensic training and experience largely on their own. With the growth in the field, the recent recognition of forensic psychology as a specialty area, and the development of knowledge and sophisticated assessment techniques in the field, there will be continued growth in formal training programs in the field. Information about various training programs and internship opportunities in forensic psychology may be found on the website of the American Psychology Law Society (www.ap-ls.org).

There are several models and methods by which forensic psychologists are now being trained to work in the area (Ogloff & Schuller, 2001). In the mentor model, graduate students learn their skills by working and conducting research with individual faculty members who do research and/or practice in the field of law and psychology. While this model affords students with individualized training, they typically receive little formal training in the broad area of the field and are unlikely to have a critical mass of colleagues with whom they can converse and collaborate.

Ogloff and Schuller (2001) refer to the second model as the limited focus training model. In this model, students study and train in a department in which there is more than one person working in the field of law and psychology. Alternatively, they may study in a department with one person in the field but have access to psychologists in institutions (e.g., jails or prisons, forensic hospitals) who help enrich their training experiences. Programs of this ilk provide students with a wider range of training experiences than students trained by way of the mentor model. Again, though, it is generally difficult for prospective students to identify psychology departments that do offer some informal training by relying on one or two people in the field.

Another model includes the actual programs in law and psychology or forensic psychology. There are several of these programs available, and that number is gradually growing. Although the programs vary considerably in their detail and focus, they do provide students with an overview of the field of law and psychology as well as advanced courses, research experiences, and practical or applied training in some area of the field. Some of the courses allow graduate students in psychology to take one or more courses in law schools. At least one program, at the University of Nebraska-Lincoln, allows students the option of completing a nonprofessional degree in law, called the master of legal studies. This degree requires students to complete approximately one third of the course that a law student usually takes. The clear advantage of the programs in law and psychology, beyond the opportunity to complete a range of relevant courses in the field, is that students have the benefit of being part of a critical mass of students and faculty with common interests. Often the learning and training experiences are enriched by the expanded opportunities a program can afford them.

A final training model, which has been adopted in a few universities in North America, is a joint or dual degree program in law and psychology or forensic psychology (Ogloff, 1999b). In these programs, students have the opportunity of pursuing a law degree (a juris doctor or JD in the United States and a bachelor of laws degree or LL.B. in Canada) as well as a PhD or PsyD in psychology simultaneously. Although these programs are very demanding since they require students to complete all of the requirements for both the law degree and PhD, they do allow for students to become experts in the law.

Beyond developing training programs, considerable discussion is occurring in the field about whether forensic psychology programs should be accredited. In addition, commentators have noted that there still are few well-established training programs in forensic psychology (Otto & Heilbrun, 2003). Otto and Heilbrun (2003) also noted that there are few accredited internships with specialized training in forensic psychology and even fewer postdoctoral fellowships available. It is our view that with the rapid growth and development in the field, forensic programs will continue to emerge and at some point some form of accreditation might be developed.

## FUTURE CONCERNS

Throughout this chapter we have defined the newly recognized area of specialty practice: forensic psychology. We noted the growth of forensic psychology, and we reviewed some of the contemporary issues in the field. In the remainder of this chapter, we would like to highlight some of the concerns regarding forensic assessments that will need to be addressed in the future. This list is by no means exhaustive, but in our view the matters identified here are among the most pressing ones. The matters we highlight can be broken into two general topics: the need for quality control in forensic assessment and areas requiring future development (i.e., civil forensic assessment and forensic assessments with youth, women, and visible minorities).

## Quality Control in Forensic Assessment

In the good old days, most psychologists viewed forensic psychology as an unattractive and unappealing field. Our comment about the good old days is written somewhat facetiously; however, along with the recent attraction of the field of forensic psychology has come a plethora of related problems. Chief among the problems that we see in the field is the fact that many of the psychologists who are making their way into the forensic field are poorly trained and inexperienced, and do not do a good job overall. While this statement is damning, it points to a very serious problem. Given the force of the law in the lives of the people with whom forensic psychologists work, extreme care must be taken to ensure that our work is competent. As Otto and Heilbrun (2003) noted:

> That some psychologists are motivated to enter the forensic arena because of economic concerns is not, in itself, problematic. Those psychologists who actively seek to increase their forensic knowledge, skills, and abilities through continuing education, supervision, and other methods are to be commended and supported. It becomes problematic, however, when some psychologists, in response to financial concerns, enter and practice in the forensic arena unprepared. Psychological expertise, forensic or otherwise, is not developed overnight. By its very nature forensic work is likely to be subjected to a greater degree of scrutiny than other kinds of psychological services, and there is some support for the claim that this is occurring over time. (p. 11)

While we are sympathetic to the economic pressures that psychologists feel, particularly in light of the impact of managed care on the delivery of health-care services, psychologists must ensure that they are competent before entering forensic practice. Unfortunately, across North America, licensing bodies report that complaints arising from assessments and practice in the forensic arena are among the most frequent they see (Ogloff, 1999a). While forensic psychologists can expect a greater risk of being the focus of an ethics complaint, simply because of the adversarial nature of the law, the fact is that there is substance to a large proportion of the complaints that are lodged. To the extent that psychologists are not policing themselves appropriately, then, the question arises of whether we should not move toward a model of credentialing and certification in forensic psychology.

Otto and Heilbrun (2003) discussed the advances in credentialing and certification that have emerged in forensic psychology. In particular, they noted that as many as nine states have some program of credentialing psychologists who conduct criminal forensic assessments. In addition, increasing numbers of forensic psychologists are seeking board certification. Preeminent among these credentialing boards is the American Board of Forensic Psychology, which employs a stringent process of reviewing an individual's training, experience, and knowledge prior to granting the individual diplomate status. Sadly, a number of newer boards are emerging that grant diplomate or fellow status without careful scrutiny. Such boards are referred to unkindly as vanity boards; generally speaking, psychologists gain little from gaining recognition from such a board (Hanson, 2000; Otto & Heilbrun, 2003).

We are reluctant to advocate that all forensic psychologists ought to be board certified or otherwise specially credentialed. Indeed, little if any evidence exists to show that forensic psychologists who are board certified or otherwise recognized as specialists are more competent than other forensic psychologists or whether credentialed forensic psychologists are more ethical. Nonetheless, board certification through a rigorous process can at least provide some assurance that the forensic psychologist meets some accepted threshold of training, experience, and knowledge in the field. As discussed earlier in this chapter, the onus falls on the individual psychologist who enters the forensic area to ensure that he or she is competent in every sense of the word. As with developments in training programs, we can expect that more forensic psychologists will seek board certification or equivalent recognition.

## Areas Requiring Future Development

Given that forensic psychology can be seen as being in the developmental stage of adolescence (Grisso, 1991)—or perhaps early adulthood now—it is not surprising that many areas of forensic assessment require further development or refinement. Here we focus on two topics that are in great need of more attention at this time: the entire area of civil forensic assessments and the need to focus more attention on forensic assessments conducted with youth, women, and visible minorities.

### Civil Forensic Assessments

Traditionally, forensic psychologists have worked primarily in the criminal field. Indeed, most often when people think of forensic psychologists, they think of psychologists who work with criminals. Today, while more forensic psychologists do work in noncriminal areas of law, the focus of the research and development of instruments and techniques in practice still is on topics within criminal law. Without a doubt, though, many more people are affected by civil law than are ever affected by criminal law (Melton et al., 2007; Ogloff, 2001). As a result, forensic psychologists would do well to learn about civil law topics for which psychology has some relevance. More important, of course, psychologists need to develop more instruments that are relevant to civil law topics and to develop assessment techniques to address these matters. As discussed previously, there are several topics in civil law that require further development.

### Forensic Assessments With Youth, Women, and Visible Minorities

Perhaps because of our historical focus on criminal behavior, much of the research and practice in forensic psychology has focused on males—and adult males at that. Moreover, despite the overrepresentation of some visible minorities in the criminal justice system, relatively little attention has been paid in forensic assessments to questions about the validity of forensic assessments for populations other than White adult males (Ogloff, 2001).

Although the number of forensic assessment instruments has increased dramatically over the past 25 years (Heilbrun et al., 2002; Melton et al., 2007; Otto & Heilbrun, 2003), surprisingly little attention has been paid to the validation of such tests for the diverse populations with which the instruments are sometimes used. To simply employ an instrument across populations, regardless of age of the person being assessed, race, or gender, is inappropriate. At the very least, then, forensic psychologists need to be assured that the tests they are employing are valid and that there are normative data available for the population from which the person being assessed is drawn. In the extreme, using instruments that have not been normed on the population from which the person being assessed comes is evidence of incompetence, and the results of the assessments will have questionable validity.

As the refinement of legal standards for the admissibility of expert psychological testimony have developed following the *Daubert* decision (1993), the focus of inquiry by courts has moved from the general acceptance of a measure within the field to an examination of the scientific foundation of the instruments. This, again, increases the need for forensic psychologists to ensure that the psychometric instruments and clinical techniques they employ in their assessments are empirically validated.

## CONCLUSION

This is an exciting point in time for the field of forensic psychology. Forensic psychology had its current genesis in the 1960s (Ogloff, forthcoming) and was formally recognized as a specialty area of practice within psychology 10 years ago. Today the need is greater than it ever has been to ensure that forensic psychology meets the highest standards of the discipline. Unlike most other areas of psychology, forensic psychology's reliance on the law places unique demands on the field. In particular, the legal standards that govern the assessments that forensic psychologists perform establish the parameters of the assessments. Thus, forensic psychologists must be thoroughly knowledgeable about the areas of law in which they work.

As the field of forensic psychology has developed, several contemporary issues have received some attention. In particular, forensic psychologists must not rely solely on clinical experience when conducting assessments, nor should they limit their assessments to purely actuarial measures. Rather, we advocate the use of structured clinical decision making. This technique involves some reliance on actuarial instruments and, more important, empirically supported evidence in developing clinical decisions. Given its reliance on empirically validated instruments and techniques, we support the scientist-practitioner model in forensic psychology.

In addition, we recognize the need for forensic psychologists to be knowledgeable about the law in the areas in which they work. While general psychological testing has some utility for forensic assessments, gone are the days when "standard" psychological assessments could satisfy the demands of the legal system for our work. As we noted, it is critical to use the legal criteria that underlie a forensic assessment referral as guidelines for the assessment. At the same time, though, we caution against having forensic psychologists offer their opinions about the ultimate legal issue being addressed by the court or other legal decision makers. In addition, it is critical that forensic psychologists do not fall into the trap of becoming advocates or hired guns for the party that employed them. Finally, the emergence of forensic psychology has seen some development of forensic training programs. At the present time, there are not enough comprehensive programs to meet the needs of the field. Over time, too, it will become necessary to explore the possibility of accrediting specialized forensic clinical training programs.

Moving beyond the issues that have emerged in the fields, we highlighted two major areas that present future concerns. First, with the literal explosion of the field of forensic psychology, it has become increasingly important to ensure that some quality control mechanism is developed. While we do not advocate a strict model of board certification, we do recognize the value of such a credentialing mechanism. Moreover, we caution readers to avoid becoming recognized by the increasingly notorious vanity boards.

Of considerable importance in forensic assessment is the need to move beyond the criminal law field and to develop specialized forensic assessment techniques and instruments that will be valid for use in the expansive areas of civil law. Finally, surprisingly little attention has been paid to validating assessment instruments and methods for use with diverse populations, including youth, women, and visible minorities.

We in the field of forensic psychology have accomplished a great deal in a relatively short time. Interested readers need only review the premier books that were in print in the mid-1980s (e.g., Grisso, 1986; Melton et al., 1987) and compare the information in them with the more recent volumes (e.g., Grisso, 2003; Melton et al., 2007) to see how far we have come in so little time. Along with the growth in the field has come several contemporary issues and future concerns that must be addressed. From our perspective, the field of forensic clinical assessment is particularly challenging and rewarding, and we look eagerly toward the future developments that we shall experience in the field.

## REFERENCES

American Psychological Association. (2002). Ethical principles of psychologists and code of conduct. *American Psychologist, 57,* 1060–1073.

American Psychological Association. (2010). 2010 amendments to the 2002 "Ethical Principles of Psychologists and Code of Conduct." *American Psychologist, 65,* 493.

Bersoff, N., Goodman-Delahunty, J., Grisso, T., Hans, V., Poythress, N. & Roesch, R. (1997). Training in law and psychology: Models from the Villanova Conference. *American Psychologist, 52,* 1301–1310.

Beutler, L. R., Williams, R. E., Wakefield, P. J., & Entwistle, S. R. (1995). Bridging scientist and practitioner perspectives in clinical psychology. *American Psychologist, 50.* 984–994.

Boer, D. P., Hart, S. D., Kropp, P. R., & Webster, C. D. (1997). *Manual for the Sexual Violence Risk—20: Professional guidelines for assessing risk of sexual violence.* Vancouver, BC: British Columbia Institute Against Family Violence.

Brigham, J. (1999). What is forensic psychology anyway? *Law and Human Behavior, 23,* 273–298.

Butcher, J. N., Dahlstrom, N. G., Graham, J. R., Tellegen, A., & Kaemmer, B. (2001). *MMPI-2: Manual for administration and scoring* (2nd ed.). Minneapolis: University of Minnesota Press.

Canadian Psychological Association. (2000). *Canadian code of ethics for psychologists.* Ottawa, Canada: Author.

Committee on Ethical Guidelines for Forensic Psychologists. (1991). Specialty guidelines for forensic psychologists. *Law and Human Behavior, 15,* 655–665.

Committee on Ethical Guidelines for Forensic Psychologists. (2011). Specialty guidelines for forensic psychologists. American Psychological Association. www.ap-ls.org/aboutpsychlaw/SGFP_Final_Approved_2011.pdf

*Daubert v. Merrell Dow Pharmaceuticals, Inc.,* 727 F. Supp. 570 (S.D. Cal. 1989), *aff'd,* 951 F.2d 1128 (9th Cir. 1990), *vacated,* 509 U.S. 579 (1993).

de Vogel, V., de Ruiter, C., van Beek, D., & Mead, G. (2004). Predictive validity of the SVR-20 and the Static-99 in a Dutch sample of treated sex offenders. *Law and Human Behavior, 28,* 235–251.

Douglas, K. S., & Koch, W. J. (2001). Civil commitment and civil competencies: Psychological issues. In R. Schuller & J. R. P. Ogloff (Eds.), *Introduction to psychology and law: Canadian perspectives* (pp. 353–374). Toronto, Ontario, Canada: University of Toronto Press.

Douglas, K. S., & Ogloff, J. R. P. (2003). Evaluation of the structured professional judgment model of violence risk assessment among forensic psychiatric patients. *Psychiatric Services, 54,* 1372–1379.

Douglas, K. S., Ogloff, J. R. P., & Hart, S. D. (2003). Evaluation of the structured professional judgment model of violence risk assessment among forensic psychiatric patients. *Psychiatric Services, 54,* 1372–1379.

Douglas, K. S., & Reeves, K. A. (2010). Historical-Clinical-Risk Management-20 (HCR-20) Violence Risk Assessment Scheme: Rationale, application, and empirical overview. In R. K. Otto & K. S. Douglas (Eds.), *Handbook of violence risk assessment* (pp. 161–183). New York, NY: Routledge.

Douglas, K. S., & Webster, C. D. (1999). Predicting violence in mentally and personality disordered individuals. In R. Roesch, S. D. Hart, & J. R. P. Ogloff (Eds.), *Psychology and law: The state of the discipline* (pp. 175–239). New York, NY: Plenum Press.

*Dusky v. United States,* 362 U.S. 402 (1960).

Federal Rules of Evidence, 28 United States Code (2010).

Fensterheim, H., & Raw, S. D. (1996). Psychotherapy research is not psychotherapy practice. *Clinical Psychology: Science and Practice, 3,* 168–171.

Ferguson, M., & Ogloff, J. R. P. (2011). Criminal responsibility evaluations: Role of psychologists in assessment. *Psychiatry, Psychology and Law, 18,* 79–94.

Forensic Psychology Specialty Council. (2000, September). *Petition for forensic psychology as an APA specialization.* Presented to the Committee for the Recognition of Specialties and Proficiencies in Professional Psychology, American Psychological Association, Washington, DC.

Freeman, R. J., & Roesch, R. (1992). Psycholegal education: Training for forum and function. In D. K. Kagehiro & W. S. Laufer (Eds.), *Handbook of psychology and law* (pp. 567–576). New York, NY: Springer-Verlag.

*Frye v. U.S.,* 293 F. 1013 (D.C. Cir. 1923).

Goldfried, M. R., & Wolfe, B. E. (1996). Psychotherapy practice and research. *American Psychologist, 51,* 1007–1016.

Grisso, T. (1986). *Evaluating competencies: Forensic assessments and instruments.* New York, NY: Plenum Press.

Grisso, T. (1987). The economic and scientific future of forensic psychological assessment. *American Psychologist, 42,* 831–839.

Grisso, T. (1991). A developmental history of the American Psychology-Law Society. *Law and Human Behavior, 15,* 213–230.

Grisso, T. (2003). *Evaluating competencies: Forensic assessments and instruments* (2nd ed.). New York, NY: Plenum Press.

Grisso, T., Sales, B. D., & Bayless, S. (1982). Law-related courses and programs in graduate psychology departments. *American Psychologist*, *37*, 267–278.

Grove, W. M., & Meehl, P. E. (1996). Comparative efficiency of informal (subjective, impressionistic) and formal (mechanical, algorithmic) prediction procedures: The clinical-statistical controversy. *Psychology, Public Policy, and Law*, *2*, 293–323.

Grove, W. M., Zald, D. H., Lebow, B. S., Snitz, B. E., & Nelson, C. (2000). Clinical versus mechanical prediction: A meta-analysis. *Psychological Assessment*, *12*, 19–30.

Hafemeister, T., Ogloff, J. R. P., & Small, M. A. (1990). Training and careers in law and psychology: The perspectives of students and graduates of dual degree programs. *Behavioral Sciences and the Law*, *8*, 263–283.

Hanson, M. (2000). Expertise to go. *American Bar Association Journal*, *108*, 44–52.

Hare, R. D. (2003). *Manual for the Hare Psychopathy Checklist—Revised* (2nd ed.). Toronto, Ontario, Canada: Multi-Health Systems.

Hart, S. D. (1998). The role of psychopathy in assessing risk for violence: Conceptual and methodological issues. *Legal and Criminological Psychology*, *3*, 121–137.

Hart, S. D., Kropp, P. R., Laws, D. R., Klaver, J., Logan, C., & Watt, K. A. (2003). *The Risk for Sexual Violence Protocol (RSVP): Structured professional guidelines for assessing risk of sexual violence*. Burnaby, BC, Canada: Mental Health, Law, and Policy Institute, Simon Fraser University.

Hart, S. D., Michie, C., & Cooke, D. J. (2007). Precision of actuarial risk assessment instruments: Evaluating the "margins of error" of group v. individual predictions of violence. *British Journal of Psychiatry*, *190*, 60–65.

Hayes, S. C. (1996). Creating the empirical clinician. *Clinical Psychology: Science and Practice*, *3*, 179–181.

Heilbrun, K. (1992). The role of psychological testing in forensic assessment. *Law and Human Behavior*, *16*, 257–272.

Heilbrun, K. (1997). Prediction versus management models relevant to risk assessment: The importance of legal decision-making context. *Law and Human Behavior*, *21*, 347–359.

Heilbrun, K. (2009). *Principles of forensic mental health assessment*. New York, NY: Kluwer.

Heilbrun, K., Ogloff, J. R. P., & Picarello, K. (1999). Dangerous offender statutes: Implications for risk assessment. *International Journal of Psychiatry and Law*, *22*, 393–415.

Heilbrun, K., Rogers, R., & Otto, R. K. (2002). Forensic assessment: Current status and future directions. In J. R. P. Ogloff (Ed.), *Taking psychology and law into the twenty-first century* (pp. 119–146). New York, NY: Kluwer Academic/Plenum Press.

Helmus, L., Babchishin, K. M., Camilleri, J. A., & Olver, M. E. (2011). Forensic psychology opportunities in Canadian graduate programs: An update of Simourd and Wormith's (1995) survey. *Canadian Psychology*, *52*, 122–127.

*Jenkins v. U.S.*, 307 F.2d 637 (D.C. Cir. 1962) (*en banc*).

Kanfer, F. H. (1990). The scientist-practitioner connection: A bridge in need of constant attention. *Professional Psychology: Research and Practice*, *21*, 264–270.

Kropp, P. R., & Hart, S. D. (2000). The Spousal Assault Risk Assessment (SARA) Guide: Reliability and validity in adult male offenders. *Law and Human Behavior*, *24*, 101–118.

Kropp, P. R., Hart, S. D., Webster, C. D., & Eaves, D. (1999). *Manual for the Spousal Assault Risk Assessment Guide* (3rd ed.). Toronto, ON: Multi-Health Systems.

*Kuhmo Tire Co. v. Carmichael*, 67 U.S.L.W. 4179, 119 S.Ct. 1167 (1999).

Meehl, P. E. (1954). *Clinical versus statistical prediction*. Minneapolis: University of Minnesota Press.

Melton, G. B. (1987). Training in psychology and law. In I. D. Weiner & A. K. Hess (Eds.), *Handbook of forensic psychology* (pp. 681–697). New York, NY: Wiley.

Melton, G. B., Petrila, J., Poythress, N., & Slobogin, C. (1987). *Psychological evaluations for the courts: A handbook for attorneys and mental health professionals*. New York, NY: Guilford Press.

Melton, G. B., Petrila, J., Poythress, N., & Slobogin, C. (2007). *Psychological evaluations for the courts: A handbook for attorneys and mental health professionals* (3rd ed.). New York, NY: Guilford Press.

Mercado, C., Calkins, & Ogloff, J. R. P. (2007). Risk and the preventive detention of sex offenders in Australia and the United States. *International Journal of Law and Psychiatry*, *30*, 49–59.

Morey, L. C. (1991). *Personality Assessment Inventory: Professional manual*. Tampa, FL: Psychological Assessment Resources.

Nezu, A. M. (1996). What are we doing to our patients and should we care if anyone else knows? *Clinical Psychology: Science and Practice*, *3*, 160–163.

Ogloff, J. R. P. (1990). Law and psychology in Canada: The need for training and research. *Canadian Psychology*, *31*, 61–73.

Ogloff, J. R. P. (1995). The legal basis of forensic applications of the MMPI-2. In Y. S. Ben-Porath, J. R. Graham, G. Hall, R. D. Hirschman, & M. Zaragoza (Eds.), *Forensic Applications of the MMPI-2* (pp. 18–47). Thousand Oaks, CA: Sage.

Ogloff, J. R. P. (1999a). Ethical and legal contours of forensic psychology. In R. Roesch, S. D. Hart, & J. R. P. Ogloff (Eds.), *Psychology and law: The state of the discipline* (pp. 405–422). New York, NY: Kluwer Academic/Plenum Press.

Ogloff, J. R. P. (1999b). Graduate training in law and psychology at Simon Fraser University. *Professional Psychology: Research and Practice*, *30*, 99–103.

Ogloff, J. R. P. (2000). Two steps forward and one-step backward: The law and psychology movement(s) in the 20th century. *Law and Human Behavior*, *24*, 457–483.

Ogloff, J. R. P. (2001). Jingoism, dogmatism and other evils in legal psychology: Lessons learned in the 20th century. In R. Roesch, R. Corrado, & R. Dempster (Eds.), *Psychology in the courts: International advances in knowledge* (pp. 1–20). Amsterdam, the Netherlands: Harwood Academic.

Ogloff, J. R. P. (2004). Invited introductory remarks to the special issue on forensic psychology. *Canadian Journal of Behavioral Science*, *36*, 84–86.

Ogloff, J. R. P. (forthcoming). A century of psychology and law: Successes, challenges, and future opportunities. In Paul Martin et al. (Eds.), *The IAAP handbook of applied psychology*. London, UK: Wiley-Blackwell.

Ogloff, J. R. P., Roberts, C. F., & Roesch, R. (1993). The insanity defense: Legal standards and clinical assessment. *Applied and Preventive Psychology*, *2*, 163–178.

Ogloff, J. R. P., & Schuller, R. (2001). Law and psychology: Looking towards the future. In R. Schuller & J. R. P. Ogloff (Eds.), *An introduction to law and psychology: Canadian perspectives* (pp. 356–373). Toronto, Ontario, Canada: University of Toronto Press.

Ogloff, J. R. P., Tomkins, A. J., & Bersoff, D. N. (1996). Education and training in law/criminal justice: Historical foundations, present structures, and future developments. *Criminal Justice and Behavior*, *23*, 200–235.

Otto, R. K., & Heilbrun, K. (2003). The practice of forensic psychology: A look towards the future in light of the past. *American Psychologist*, *58*, 5–19.

Otto, R. K., Heilbrun, K., & Grisso, T. (1990). Training and credentialing in forensic psychology. *Behavioral Sciences and the Law*, *8*, 217–232.

*People v. Hawthorne* (1940), 291 N.W. 205.

Poythress, N., Monahan, J., Bonnie, R., & Hoge, S. K. (1999). *MacArthur Competence Assessment Tool—Criminal Adjudication*. Odessa, FL: Psychological Assessment Resources.

Poythress, N., Nicholson, R., Otto, R. K., Edens, J. F., Bonnie, R. J., Monahan, J., & Hoge, S. K. (1999). *Professional manual for the MacArthur Competence Assessment Tool—Criminal Adjudication*. Odessa, FL: Psychological Assessment Resources.

Psychology Board of Australia. (2010). *Guidelines on area of practice endorsements*. Melbourne, Australia: Author.

Quinsey, V. L., Harris, G. T., Rice, G. T., & Cormier, C. A. (2006). *Violent offenders: Appraising and managing risk* (2nd ed.). Washington, DC: American Psychological Association.

Rice, M. E., Harris, G. T., & Hilton, N. Z. (2010). The Violence Risk Appraisal Guide and Sex Offender Risk Appraisal Guide for violence risk assessment and the Ontario Domestic Assault Risk Assessment and Domestic Violence Risk Appraisal Guide for wife assault risk assessment. In R. K. Otto & K. S. Douglas (Eds.), *Handbook of violence risk assessment* (pp. 223–256). New York, NY: Routledge.

Roesch, R., Grisso, T., & Poythress, N. G. (1986). Training programs, courses, and workshops in psychology and law. In M. F. Kaplan (Ed.), *The impact of social psychology on procedural justice* (pp. 83–108). Springfield, IL: Charles C. Thomas.

Roesch, R., Ogloff, J. R. P., Golding, S. L. (1993). Competency to stand trial: Legal and clinical issues. *Applied and Preventive Psychology*, *2*, 43–51.

Rogers, R., & Shuman, D. W. (2000). *Conducting insanity evaluations*. New York, NY: Guilford Press.

Rose, V. G. (2001). An introduction to law and the Canadian legal system. In R. Schuller & J. R. P. Ogloff (Eds.), *An introduction to law and psychology: Canadian perspectives* (pp. 26–41). Toronto, ON: University of Toronto Press.

Singer, J. L. (1990). The scientific basis of psychotherapy practice: A question of values and ethics. *Psychotherapy: Theory, Research, and Practice*, *17*, 372–383.

Sobell, L. C. (1996). Bridging the gap between scientists and practitioners: The challenge before us. *Behavior Therapy*, *27*, 297–320.

Stricker, G. (1992). The relationship of research to clinical practice. *American Psychologist*, *47*, 543–549.

Stricker, G., & Trierweiler, S. J. (1995). The local clinical scientist: A bridge between science and practice. *American Psychologist*, *50*, 995–1002.

Tomkins, A. J., & Ogloff, J. R. P. (1990). Training and career options in psychology and law. *Behavioral Sciences and the Law*, *8*, 205–216.

*United States v. Hinckley*, 525 F. Supp. 1342 (D.C. 1981).

Viljoen, J. L., Roesch, R., Ogloff, J. R. P. and Zapf, P. A. (2003). The role of Canadian psychologists in conducting fitness and criminal responsibility evaluations. *Canadian Psychology*, *44*, 369–381.

Webster, C. D., & Cox, D. N. (1997). Integration of nomothetic and ideographic positions in risk assessment: Implications for practice and the education of psychologists and other mental health professionals. *American Psychologist*, *52*, 1245–1246.

Webster, C. D., Douglas, K. S., Eaves, D., & Hart, S. D. (1997). *HCR-20: Assessing the Risk for Violence* (Version 2). Vancouver, British Columbia, Canada: Mental Health, Law, and Policy Institute, Simon Fraser University.

Wechsler, D. (2009). *Wechsler Adult Intelligence Scale—Fourth Edition*. San Antonio, TX: Psychological Corporation.

# CHAPTER 16

# Psychological Assessment in Correctional Settings

EDWIN I. MEGARGEE

In the 10 years since the first edition of this chapter was written (Megargee, 2003), there have been many important developments in correctional assessment. New standards for mental health care in correctional facilities have been issued by the National Commission on Correctional Health Care (NCCHC; 2008c) and the International Association for Correctional and Forensic Psychology (IACFP; 2010). Several of the standardized cognitive, intellectual, and personality tests I discussed in the last edition have undergone substantive revisions. Some that I described then have fallen into disuse and others have taken their place. A new, fourth generation of risk assessment devices has appeared. The most recent instruments are now designed to be used in evidence-based practice to guide rehabilitative treatment interventions as well as management decisions (Andrews & Bonta, 2010; Brennan, Dieterich, & Ehret, 2009).

The number of adult men and women under some form of correctional supervision has grown from 5.7 million when this chapter was first written to 7.3 million in 2008, the most recent year for which data are available, a 28% increase (Sabol, West, & Cooper, 2010). Of these men and women, 4,270,917 were reported to be on probation, 785,556 in jails, 1,518,559 in state or federal prisons, and 828,169 on parole. In addition,

The author is grateful to Amy Cadalbert of Pearson Assessments for providing manuals for the Beta III, GAMA, and WAIS-IV and to Kirk Heilbrun and Randy Otto for supplying reprints and citations. Jill Mercer greatly assisted in the preparation of the manuscript.

Puzzanchera (2009) reported that nearly 2.2 million juveniles were arrested in 2007. Corrections is clearly a growth industry.

At every stage of the criminal justice system, crucial decisions must be made regarding each alleged offender. Police officers must decide whether to arrest people who are behaving illegally and/or deviantly. For those who are arrested, it must be decided whether they should be released or detained, diverted or prosecuted. Should their cases be handled by the regular criminal courts or, in some jurisdictions, by specialized mental health or substance abuse courts (Munetz & Griffin, 2006)? For those who are convicted of criminal offenses, judges must decide whether they should be admonished, fined, placed on probation, enrolled in appropriate treatment or rehabilitation programs, sentenced to terms of confinement, or, in the case of capital crimes, even put to death (Cunningham & Reidy, 1999; Small & Otto, 1991). Assessments, both formal and informal, are a vital aspect of this decision making (Megargee & Carbonell, 1995; Munetz & Griffin, 2006).

Those sentenced to terms of confinement must be evaluated to determine the settings, programs, interventions, and change agents best suited to their particular needs. Most will later need to be reassessed to determine who should be released on parole, retained for the duration of their sentences, or, in the case of certain sex offenders, confined beyond the expiration of their sentences for the protection of the community. Psychological evaluations, often including risk and needs assessments, are a critical factor in many of these decisions.

In addition to the assessments utilized in criminal justice decision making, psychological screenings and evaluations are required in institutional settings to enable authorities to fulfill their mandate to care for the physical and mental health and well-being of the prisoners entrusted to their care. In addition to a medical evaluation, each new admission to a jail or prison must be screened for mental illness and other psychological disorders, intellectual deficiencies, and developmental disabilities. Those identified as being likely to have such difficulties must be referred for more extensive evaluations to identify those who (a) are dangerous to themselves or others, (b) at risk of victimization, or (c) require mental health or other interventions. Psychological assessment plays a crucial role in many of these determinations.

## PART ONE: SCREENING AND ASSESSMENT AT VARIOUS STAGES OF THE CORRECTIONAL SYSTEM

Although the correctional system deals almost exclusively with people accused or convicted of committing crimes, it is comprised of several separate and distinct segments. Each has its own tasks and issues, and each is subject to different legal constraints. They include jails, probation services, correctional institutions of various types, and postrelease services such as parole. In this section, I discuss assessment issues in each of these settings.

### Standards for Health Care in Institutional Settings

Prisoners are, literally, a captive population. Unlike free-world clients, inmates cannot shop around for mental health services. Because prisoners are totally dependent on correctional staff for their health-care needs, a number of professional health-care organizations have formulated standards and guidelines regarding the nature and the extent of the psychological and other health-care services that should be afforded offenders confined in jails, prisons, and juvenile detention facilities. They include the American Correctional Association (ACA; 2010), the ACA and Commission on Accreditation (2002), the American Psychiatric Association (2000), the American Psychological Association (APA; 2002), the IACFP (2010), and the NCCHC (2004, 2008a, 2008b, 2008c). I focus on the standards set forth by the IACFP and the NCCHC since they most directly concern the delivery of mental health services to incarcerated inmates.

### General Provisions

The IACFP (2010) Standards contain certain general provisions that apply to assessment in all institutional settings. They specify that the administration of psychological services, including assessment, should be under the direction and supervision of doctoral-level licensed psychologists who are experienced in the delivery of psychological services in correctional settings. The number of such individuals and whether they are employed on a full- or part-time basis varies depending on the size of the facility and the nature of the population.

With millions of people being processed by correctional facilities each year, it is obviously impossible for such highly qualified practitioners to carry out all the assessment procedures that are needed. Instead, they must (a) formulate and implement protocols for psychological screening, (b) supervise assessments conducted by master's level psychologists, psychology interns, and paraprofessional mental health staff members, and (c) train other correctional staff members to recognize the signs and symptoms of mental disorders (Anno, 1991).

The IACFP (2010) Standards stipulate that psychological assessments should comply with the ethical standards of the APA (2002) as well as the laws applying in that locality. Specifically, correctional psychologists should "limit their functioning to areas of demonstrated professional competence" (p. 770). With regard to assessment, this means that correctional psychologists should not administer or supervise the administration of unfamiliar assessment techniques. Moreover, they should understand any problems associated with the administration and interpretation of familiar techniques in correctional settings, such as how the test scores might be influenced by deception or malingering, and the norms, base rates, and cutting scores found among criminal offenders in their particular correctional setting.

If fully qualified correctional psychologists do not administer psychological assessments personally, they are responsible for supervising the evaluations carried out by others; such assessments should be performed only by properly trained personnel. Under no circumstances should inmates or offenders be used to administer, score, process, or file other offenders' tests or mental health information.

A primary ethical concern in correctional psychology is "Who is the client?" (Monahan, 1980). Although correctional psychologists work *with* offenders, they work *for* the correctional system. Psychologists must make sure that offenders understand their obligations to the system as well as the offender, especially their duty to disclose information bearing on the security of the institution and the safety of the staff or inmates and their obligation to warn any potential victims who may be at risk (VandeCreek & Knapp, 1989). Inmates should also be informed about all limits on confidentiality, how the information they provide may be used, and who may have access to their data. If the evaluation is not court ordered, they should also be informed of their right not to participate (Vanderhoff, Jeglic, & Donovick, 2011). Before formal assessments, such disclosure should be made in writing as well as verbally and the offenders asked to sign a form acknowledging receipt of this information.

There should be written documentation of all mental health information and the results of all tests and evaluations. These data and reports should be placed in secure confidential files that are maintained by the mental health service and kept separate from other agency records. Information in the file should be provided to other correctional staff on a need-to-know basis under the supervision of a mental health staff member, and all such access documented (IACFP, 2010).

Within these general parameters, there are specific problems, issues, and guidelines for assessments conducted in different settings.

### Jails

Jails are local facilities that are typically under the jurisdiction of the county sheriff. They range in size and resources from small rural lockups to huge metropolitan facilities with thousands of inmates. The Cook County (Chicago) jail, for example, processes over 100,000 people annually (ACA, 2006). When someone is arrested, the local jail is typically that person's first point of contact with the correctional system.

Few, if any, clinical populations are as heterogeneous as the accused and convicted offenders encountered in county jails. They come from all walks of life, ranging from society's affluent to its effluent. All conceivable ethnicities and nationalities are represented, and, although they speak a variety of languages, English is not always one of them. Testing is further complicated by the fact that their academic and reading skills may be minimal or nonexistent.

The offenders encountered in jails approach assessment with different motivations and perspectives. Some may be malingering, hoping to be declared incompetent or legally insane. Others may try to impress the examiner with their exemplary mental health, hoping it will facilitate their release to the community.

Deinstitutionalization of the mentally ill has shifted much of the burden for coping with psychiatric patients from state and local psychiatric hospitals to jails (Torrey et al., 1992). As Kennedy (1993) noted, "many ex-patients become prisoners for relatively petty yet socially troublesome behavior related to their psychiatric condition" (p. 309). Problems include mental illness, substance abuse, and homelessness (McNiel, Binder, & Robinson, 2005). Such individuals are often unable to make bail, and, if released on their own recognizance, often fail to show up for court appearances, behaviors that increase their likelihood of being incarcerated. Using the Structured Clinical Interview for the fourth edition of the *Diagnostic and Statistical Manual of Mental Disorders* (*DSM-IV*), Steadman, Osher, Robbins, Case, and Samuels (2009) diagnosed 14.5% of the men and 31.0% of the women detained in five northeastern jails as having manifested serious mental disorders such as bipolar, major depression, and schizophrenic spectrum disorders within the past month, a prevalence more than double that reported the previous decade for the Cook County jail by Teplin (1990, 1996). Indeed, according to the IACFP (2010), "The Los Angeles and Cook County jails have been referenced as America's leading institutions for housing mentally ill individuals for a number of years" (p. 754). Suicide is another concern. The rate of suicide among people in custody is two to nine times higher than that in the community; of all those in custody, the highest rates are found among defendants awaiting trial (Rowan, 1998).

**Functions.** Jails are expected to serve three basic functions. First, they serve as a clearinghouse and referral source for arrested individuals. After an arrest, decisions must be made as to who can be released and who should be detained pending arraignment. Any detainees with urgent physical or mental problems must be identified and treated in house or referred elsewhere (Anno, 1991).

After arraignment, the second function of the jail is to provide for the secure detention of accused offenders who cannot make bail or who are not granted bail because they pose a flight risk. Such defendants can remain in the jail awaiting trial for weeks or even months, so additional assessment and screening are necessary to decide where and with whom they should be placed and to determine what services and programs they should be afforded. This latter task is complicated by the fact that the correctional system is not supposed to attempt to rehabilitate unconvicted individuals who, at this point in the proceedings, are not considered guilty of any crime (National Advisory Commission on Criminal Justice Standards and Goals, 1973).

The third and final function of the jail is to serve as a correctional facility for those convicted of misdemeanors and sentenced to periods of confinement of less than a year. This requires further screening to identify those offenders with special needs for physical or mental health care or interventions (Anno, 1991). Assessment is also needed to help formulate a management and treatment plan for each convicted offender, to guide his or her placement within the facility, and to determine the type of programming that is most appropriate.

In addition to these three basic functions, local jails may also house convicted felons awaiting transfer to state correctional facilities and temporary detainees, such as people suspected of being illegal immigrants awaiting processing by the U.S. Immigration and Customs Enforcement Service (ICE).

**Mental Health Staffing.**   Given the round-the-clock need for mental as well as physical screening of new arrivals, it is more difficult to provide adequate psychological services in jails than in any other component of the criminal justice system. Smaller facilities often cannot afford the services of a full-time licensed psychologist. Even if a jail has adequate financial resources, those in rural or isolated areas may not be able to find well-qualified practitioners, especially ones having correctional experience.

The IACFP Standards adjust expected staffing levels to the size of the jail. Jails with an average daily population (ADP) of 10 or less should have a licensed psychologist on call. Those with an ADP of 11 to 75 inmates are expected to have a licensed contract psychologist in the facility at least 8 hours a week; those with an ADP of 76 to 125 should have one on site at least 16 hours a week; and those with an ADP greater than 125 should have at least one full-time licensed psychologist for every 125 inmates (2010, p. 768).

It is difficult for most jails, especially small facilities in rural areas, to meet these levels. Jails are probably the most underfunded of all the elements in the criminal justice system. Sheriffs typically focus more on law enforcement than on corrections, and jails are often hard put to meet the basic physical and security needs of their inmates. Except in the case of the most flagrant and acutely disturbed inmates, mental health services may be regarded as a luxury. Even in those jails that do meet the recommended staffing guidelines, the inmate-to-psychologist ratio is often so high that the best use of the psychologists' time is assessing offenders and training paraprofessionals to recognize the signs and symptoms of mental disorders so they can refer disturbed inmates for further evaluation.

**Assessment.**   People arrive at the jail directly from the street at all hours of the day and night. Often they are in acute need of physical or mental health care. Acute mental health problems can include psychosis, agitation, anger, depression, intoxication, and drug withdrawal. The first requirement in jails is screening new admissions for physical and mental conditions requiring immediate intervention and identifying those who pose a threat to others or to themselves. The IACFP Standards (2010) state:

> Standard screening includes inquiries into past and present mental health difficulties including treatment and psychotropic medications, suicidal ideation, gestures, or attempts, substance dependence or abuse, and current mental status including behavioral observations, mood, cognitive function, stressors, measures of daily functioning (e.g. appetite, sleeping, and activity level), and any medical concerns. (p. 784)

Such reception screening should be done by qualified mental health personnel or appropriately trained staff members as part of the booking process, before any new admission is placed with any other inmates (IACFP, 2010).

The NCCHC provides intake and mental health evaluation forms that appropriately trained reception personnel can use to screen new admissions to jails (NCCHC, 2008a) and prisons (NCCHC, 2008b), while the ACA has developed a self-instructional course designed to train correctional officers to recognize the signs of suicide and intervene appropriately (Rowan, 1998). Screening data should be entered on a standard form to be placed in the inmate's confidential mental health service file. When needed, referrals should be made for a more comprehensive mental health evaluation.

Inmates referred for additional psychological assessment should be evaluated by qualified mental health personnel within 2 weeks. This should include reviewing intake records and referral information, contacting the individual's prior therapists or personal physician for information regarding his or her mental health history, conducting an extensive diagnostic interview, and writing and filing a brief report. Although not specifically called for by the Standards, psychological testing is also appropriate if qualified personnel are available to administer and interpret the tests. If signs of a major mental illness are found, the inmate should be placed in a separate area where closer supervision is possible. The psychologist should formulate a treatment plan that can be carried out in the jail by mental health staff members or, if release is imminent, by referral to a family physician or an appropriate mental health resource in the community (IACFP, 2010).

### Probation

Despite the fact that probation is the most common form of correctional supervision in the United States, there is less written about probation in the correctional psychology literature than there is about any other component of corrections.

**Functions.** When a juvenile or adult defendant pleads guilty or is convicted of committing a crime, the court often considers community supervision as an option, especially for younger offenders with benign criminal histories who are charged with relatively minor, nonviolent offenses. Probationers are expected to report to their supervising probation officers (POs) at regular intervals and abide by other conditions of probation, which may include: attending school; maintaining gainful employment; abstaining from alcohol; avoiding criminal associates; participating in various forms of treatment, such as anger management or substance abuse programs; and, obviously, refraining from further criminal activity. Successful completion of probation may get the original offense expunged from the probationer's record, but failure to comply with the terms of probation may mean that the offender is remanded into custody and sentenced on the original charges.

The clients encountered in a probation service often differ from those found in a jail. The most disturbed and acutely ill individuals should have been referred to the mental health system, and the felons should have been sent to prison. The adult clients have generally been advised by their attorneys to cooperate with their psychologists. Malingering is rare, but psychologists must be prepared for positive dissimulation.

**Mental Health Staffing.** Neither the IACFP nor the NCCHC Standards specify mental health staffing levels in community settings such as probation or parole. Some probation departments employ their own staff psychologists. Others employ private practitioners on a contract or consulting basis. Many refer clients to their county's community mental health service centers for psychological assessment and treatment. In the latter instance, clients must sign releases if the community center is to be authorized to communicate its findings and recommendations to their POs.

**Assessment.** Individual assessment is often a primary function of correctional psychologists in probation services. When a juvenile is accused or an adult is convicted of a criminal offense, the court may order a probation report to assist in sentencing. The investigating PO compiles a detailed case history based on interviews with the defendant and with other relevant sources, such as family members, teachers, and employers. As part of this investigation, the PO may request a psychological evaluation. This may focus on *diagnosis* (What is wrong with this person? Why is she running away from home, doing drugs, not attending school? Why is he stealing cars, getting into fights?) or *prognosis* (If we place this person on probation, will he or she make us look bad? Will she pass more bad checks? Will he keep hitting his wife?)

After a defendant has been placed on probation, a supervising PO may request a psychological evaluation to assist in management or treatment planning. (Should I set strict limits or be supportive? Will this probationer benefit from group therapy?)

The first step for the psychologist is to meet with the PO and clarify the reason for the referral. Often the psychologist can answer the referral question using information the PO has already collected. This not only takes care of the referral but also helps train the PO.

If an individual appraisal is indicated, it helps to have as much case history information as possible, including the prosecution's description of the current offense (the "DA's short story"), the prior criminal history (rap sheet), and whatever information the PO has been able to glean from the defendant's family, teachers, or employers. The observations of jail and custodial personnel are a useful source of information about clients who may have been detained. If time permits, and the client signs a release, reports from other mental health personnel who may have previously conducted evaluations are also helpful. The choice of assessment techniques should be geared to the issues raised by the referral question. In addition to a clinical interview, individual intelligence, achievement, and personality tests are often indicated.

In addition to these individual evaluations, an increasing number of probation agencies in Canada and the United Kingdom, as well as in the United States, are screening clients using risk and needs assessment instruments specifically designed for that purpose. These instruments, which are designed to appraise the likelihood of various types of reoffending, are used to determine which probationers need more or less intensive supervision and to guide correctional interventions, with the end goal of rehabilitating offenders (Andrews & Bonta, 2010;

Brennan, Dieterick, & Oliver, 2006). They are discussed in Part Two of this chapter.

### Prisons and Correctional Institutions

Much of the empirical research on correctional assessment has taken place in prisons and correctional institutions. As a captive population with an abundance of time on their hands, prisoners are much more available for research than probationers or parolees.

**Functions.** The basic function of prisons is to confine convicted felons in a secure setting for the period of time specified by the sentencing judge. While they are incarcerated, the courts have held that prisoners (as well as pretrial detainees) have a constitutional right to adequate and sufficient medical care under the Eighth Amendment's prohibition against "cruel and unusual punishments" (*Estelle v. Gamble*, 429 U.S. 97, 1976, cited by Kay, 1991, p. 3). The courts have further held that this includes mental, as well as physical, health care since "there is no underlying distinction between the right to medical care for physical ills and its psychological or psychiatric counterpart" (*Bowring v. Godwin*, 551 F. 2d 44, 47, 4th Cir. 1977, quoted by Kay, 1991, p. 15).

Prisons are expected to do much more than confine inmates and preserve their health. Various segments of society also expect prisons to incapacitate, punish, educate, work, and reform inmates while deterring criminal behavior in other potential offenders, a melange of demands that may be mutually exclusive.

To accomplish these goals, further assessment is required. To protect society and incapacitate offenders, correctional institutions must place them in settings that are sufficiently secure that they cannot or will not abscond or escape. However, the courts have also held that prisoners are entitled to the "least restrictive custody level that is commensurate with their own safety and the safety of other inmates, staff, and the community" (Solomon & Camp, 1993, p. 9). This means determining the security and supervision levels required by each inmate (Levinson, 1988). Further evaluations are needed to formulate management and treatment plans designed to educate, rehabilitate, or reform offenders. Moreover, limited resources may require establishing priorities for inmates' access to treatment programs.

**Mental Health Staffing.** IACFP (2010) Standards for prisons stipulate that there should be at least one licensed, doctoral-level, full-time psychologist with correctional experience on staff who is responsible for the delivery of psychological services at each correctional facility and at the headquarters of a multisite system. In ordinary correctional institutions, the expected ratio is one full-time psychologist for every 150 to 160 inmates. In specialized treatment units, such as those for drug-dependent or mentally ill inmates, the ratio should be one for every 50 to 75 adult offenders. As in jails, it is expected that the qualified mental health professionals will train line staff to recognize the signs of mental illness, potential suicide, or mental retardation and refer such inmates for more extensive mental health evaluations.

**Assessment.** After sentencing, offenders are typically held in the local jail until they can be transferred, along with copies of their legal, medical, and psychological records, to the federal or state correctional system, generally to a facility that is set aside for admission and classification. At the classification center, newly admitted inmates should immediately be screened for signs of mental illness, developmental disabilities, and suicide by qualified health-care professionals. Those referred for a comprehensive evaluation should be individually assessed within 14 days or sooner (IACFP, 2010). Patients found to require acute mental health services beyond those available at that institution should be transferred to an appropriate facility where such treatment can be provided (NCCHC, 2008b, 2008c).

Within the first 2 weeks to a month (IACFP, 2010), a standard individual mental health assessment should be conducted. The IACFP Standards (2010) state:

> Such routine evaluations may be brief and include (but not necessarily limited to) behavioral observations, record and file review, group testing to screen for emotional and intellectual abnormalities, and a brief written report of initial findings placed in the confidential mental health service's files. Referral for more intensive individual assessment is made on the basis of the results. (p. 786)

That report should note any indications that the inmate desires help and include an outline of a recommended treatment plan.

The NCCHC's (2008b) Prison Standards specify that the initial mental health assessment should include a structured interview that inquires into the client's (a) history of inpatient and outpatient psychiatric treatment, suicidal or violent behavior, victimization, special education placement, cerebral trauma or seizures, and sex offenses; (b) the current status of psychotropic medications, suicidal ideation, drug or alcohol use, and orientation to person place and time; and (c) emotional response to incarceration. It also includes a screening for intellectual functioning focusing on mental retardation and developmental or learning disabilities. Based on the results of this initial screening, referrals may be made for more thorough appraisals of mental health status, personality functioning, or intellectual and cognitive skills.

In addition to these assessments, prison psychologists also conduct formal and informal evaluations in response to requests and referrals by other staff members, such as caseworkers, teachers, and correctional officers, and respond to requests for mental health services ("copouts") by the inmates themselves. Both IACFP and NCCHC Standards also call for monitoring mentally ill inmates and those placed in disciplinary segregation.

**Classification.**   Classification is the next major assessment task in correctional institutions. In 1973 the National Advisory Commission on Criminal Justice Standards and Goals called for the immediate implementation of comprehensive classification systems at all levels of the criminal justice system, arguing that

> classification can make handling large numbers of offenders more efficient through a grouping process based on needs and problems. From an administrative standpoint, classification systems can provide for more orderly processing and handling of individuals. From a financial standpoint, classification schemes can enable administrators to make more efficient use of limited resources and to avoid providing resources for offenders who do not require them. (p. 201)

The courts agreed. In *Palmigiano v. Garrahy* (443 F. Supp. 956, D.R.I. 1977, cited by Solomon & Camp, 1993), the court held that "[c]lassification is essential to the operation of an orderly and safe prison system. It enables the institution to gauge the proper custody level of an inmate, to identify the inmate's educational, vocational and psychological needs, and to separate non-violent inmates from the more predatory" (p. 5).

The efficacy of such classification was demonstrated by Bohn (1979), who used a classification system based on the Minnesota Multiphasic Personality Inventory (MMPI; Hathaway & McKinley, 1943) to guide dormitory assignments in a federal correctional institution for youthful offenders. By separating the most predatory inmates from those assessed as most likely to be victimized, he achieved a 46% reduction in serious assaults.

### Parole

The vast majority of the prisoners in state and federal institutions are eventually returned to the community. Of the 683,106 individuals discharged from state prisons in 2008, 165,568 (24.2%) were released unconditionally, most upon expiration of their sentences. The remaining 505,168 (75.8%) were conditionally released, most to some form of community supervision, such as parole or halfway houses (Sabol et al., 2010).

**Functions.**   The function of parole agencies is to provide supervision and assistance to felons released to the community before the expiration of their sentences. Many parolees are placed in halfway houses, working in the community or attending classes by day and participating in therapeutic group activities in the evening.

In addition to monitoring parolees' behavior, parole officers are supposed to help them make the difficult transition from institutional to community life. This can include assisting them in getting housing, employment, education, and health care. Most parolees are released subject to certain specified conditions similar to those for probationers. If they do not abide by these conditions and/or commit additional crimes, their parole can be revoked and they are returned to prison to serve the balance of their sentence.

**Mental Health Staffing.**   As noted earlier, neither the IACFP nor the NCCHC Standards specify mental health staffing levels for parole agencies.

**Assessment.**   Psychological assessments may be requested to help determine if prison inmates are ready for parole and, if so, what conditions should be imposed. As with initial classification, correctional psychologists have devised a number of objective devices to predict both general and violent recidivism, as well as sexual predation. Some of these instruments are described and discussed in Part Two.

Once an offender has been paroled, the supervising parole officer may request a psychological assessment to assist in management or treatment. In these cases, the task is similar to that of psychologists in probation settings. In evidence-based agencies, formal structured risk and needs assessments may be made to determine the level of supervision required and to guide the types of interventions that may be needed (Andrews & Bonta, 2010; Goodloe, 2009). Some instruments used in these evaluations are discussed in Part Two.

### Useful Screening and Assessment Instruments

If the correctional system is to reform or rehabilitate inmates, each offender's mental health, emotional, educational, and vocational status and needs must be appraised and individual management and treatment programs formulated. Psychological assessments are needed to identify prisoners requiring mental health interventions, including those who are depressed, psychotic, emotionally disturbed, or prone to self-injurious behavior as well as those with problems centering on alcohol and substance abuse. In addition to assessing offenders' needs for treatment, program planning involves estimating each inmate's likely response to and ability to benefit from various types of interventions. In systems with limited mental health resources, each inmate's priority for treatment, based on diagnosis and prognosis, must also be determined. Cognitive appraisals are also needed to evaluate each offender's need for and ability to profit from educational programming. These decisions can be based in part on the educational history; there is no need to place college graduates in a general equivalency diploma (GED) program. However, given the extent of social promotion, a high school diploma does not necessarily guarantee literacy, so intelligence and achievement tests may also be necessary. As with mental health treatment, when educational resources are limited, it may be necessary to determine offenders' priorities for education based on their ability and motivation.

In this section, I discuss standardized psychological tests that are widely used in correctional settings to assess (a) mental illness and emotional adjustment, (b) intellectual and cognitive functioning, and (c) educational achievement.

### Mental Health Assessment

As noted earlier, many prisoners require mental health treatment and care. Steadman et al. (2009) documented serious mental illness in 16.9% (men 14.5%, women 31%) of the jail population. In addition to those entering with serious psychiatric disorders, Anno (1991) estimated another 15% to 20% of a prison's inmates require mental health services or interventions at some time during their incarceration.

As noted earlier, all new inmates should receive a mental health screening within the first week (IACFP, 2010) or two (NCCHC, 2008a, 2008b) after admission. This initial screening should be followed by more extensive evaluations of inmates who appear to show signs of mental illness or appear at risk for self-injury or suicide. Two wideband personality inventories, the Minnesota Multiphasic Personality Inventory-2 (MMPI-2; Butcher, Dahlstrom, Graham, Tellegen, & Kaemmer, 1989) and the Millon Clinical Multiaxial Inventory-III (MCMI-III; Millon & Millon, 2006), are useful in such appraisals.

**Minnesota Multiphasic Personality Inventory-2.** The MMPI-2 is a 567-item, true-false personality inventory that was originally devised to differentiate psychiatric patients from "normals," that is non-clinical respondents. Over the years, however, the MMPI-2 and its predecessor, the original MMPI, (Hathaway & McKinley, 1943) have been applied in a broad array of settings and populations. With over 14,000 articles and books published, the MMPI and MMPI-2 are the world's most thoroughly researched personality assessment devices (Butcher, 1999; 2006; Graham, 2006). They are also the most widely used personality inventories in both forensic (Archer, Buffington-Vollum, Stredny, & Handel, 2006; Viljoen, McLachlan, & Vincent, 2010), and correctional settings (Boothby & Clements, 2000) where they have been used for over 70 years. Well-established correctional norms and cutting scores are available and the correlates of the scales among criminal offenders have been thoroughly studied over the years (Megargee, 2006; Megargee, Mercer, & Carbonell, 1999). (A new instrument, the MMPI-2-RF [Ben-Porath & Tellegen, 2008], has been introduced recently. Although research with the MMPI-RF is proceeding apace, it is a different instrument [Greene, 2011] whose usefulness in correctional settings remains to be determined.)

Megargee (2006) has provided detailed instructions for administration in correctional settings. While MMPI-2 administration is not difficult, it must be done properly to achieve optimal results. The MMPI-2 should be administered in its entirety; so-called short forms result in the loss of important data, such as the Content and Supplementary scales. A sixth-grade reading level is needed to complete MMPI-2, so it is best to administer it after reading ability has been established. Audiotaped forms are available for poor readers. For inmates who are not proficient in English, the MMPI-2 is available in a number of other languages.

The MMPI-2 has four types of scales: validity, clinical, supplementary, and content. The eight validity scales enable the user to identify offenders who are (a) answering nonresponsively, (b) malingering (faking bad), or (c) dissembling (faking good). In assessing MMPI-2 validity in correctional settings, it is important to consult appropriate offender norms (Megargee, 2006; Megargee et al., 1999). For example, because of their deviant lifestyles and atypical experiences, criminal offenders answering truthfully may get elevations on the Infrequency (F) scale that would be regarded as invalid in free-world settings.

The 10 clinical, 15 supplementary, and 15 content scales assess a broad array of traits and behaviors. Because of the large number of scales, computerized scoring is advisable. Raw scores on the scales are converted into T-scores and plotted on profile sheets.

Many of these measures are relevant to mental health evaluations, needs assessments, and treatment planning in correctional settings. For example, elevations on MMPI-2 Scales 1 (Hs, Hypochondriasis), 3 (Hy, Hysteria), and HEA (Health Concerns) identify offenders who are likely to use sick call frequently. Clinical scale 2 (D, Depression) and content scale DEP (Depression) identify those who are depressed, and Scales 7 (Pt, Psychasthenia) and ANX (Anxiety) are associated with anxiety. Scales 4 (Pd, Psychopathic Deviate), 9 (Ma, Hypomania), and ASP (Antisocial Practices) reflect authority problems, antisocial behavior, and acting out. Scales ANG (Anger) and O-H (Overcontrolled Hostility) identify offenders who may have problems dealing with anger issues. Scales 4, MDS (Marital Distress Scale), and FAM (Family Problems) identify offenders who may be alienated or estranged from their families. Elevated scores on Scales MAC-R (MacAndrew Alcoholism Scale-Revised) and AAS (Addiction Admission Scale) suggest alcohol and/or substance abuse. Scales 6 (Pa, Paranoia), 8 (Sc; Schizophrenia), and BIZ (Bizarre Mentation) identify those who may have mental disorders that require further assessment. Scales 5 (Mf, Masculinity-Femininity), 0 (Si; Social Introversion), and SOD (Social Discomfort) are associated with passivity, introversion, and awkward interpersonal relations that may lead to exploitation by more predatory inmates in prison settings (Graham, 2006; Megargee, 2006).

Whereas most measures used in correctional settings assess only negative characteristics, MMPI-2 can also indicate positive attributes. Offenders with moderate elevations on Scale 0 are unlikely to be defiant or cause problems for those in authority; those high on Scale Re (Responsibility) should be more mature and cooperative than most; and those with elevations on Scale Do (Dominance) should manifest leadership (Megargee, 2006).

A unique advantage in the correctional use of the MMPI-2 is the ability to utilize the empirically derived offender classifications system developed by this author and others (Megargee & Bohn with Meyer & Sink, 1979; Megargee, Carbonell, Bohn & Sliger, 2001). Identified through cluster analyses of criminal offenders' original MMPI profiles, the system is comprised of 10 types labeled with neutral, alphabetic names. Independent studies applying similar clustering procedures to the MMPIs of male and female offenders in various settings have demonstrated the reliability of the typology, consistently

replicating most of the 10 groups (Goeke, Tosi, & Eshbaugh, 1993; Mrad, Kabacoff, & Duckro, 1983; Nichols, 1979/1980; Shaffer, Pettigrew, Blouin, & Edwards, 1983).

Independent investigators have reported the successful application of the MMPI-based classification system among male and female offenders in probation, parole, and correctional settings. Within correctional institutions, it has been utilized in federal, state, military, and local facilities with security levels ranging from minimum to maximum. It has also been applied in halfway houses, community restitution centers, forensic mental health units, and local jails. The specialized populations to which the system has been applied include death row inmates, presidential threateners, and mentally disordered sex offenders (Megargee, 1994; Sliger, 1992; Zager, 1988).

Once the 10 types were identified, we determined their characteristics entirely through empirical research in offender populations. Our original MMPI research delineating the attributes of male offenders has been replicated with MMPI-2 (Megargee, 1994; Megargee et al., 2001), and a number of studies have extended the system to female offenders (Megargee, 1997; Megargee et al., 2001; Sliger, 1997). In addition, almost 100 independent investigations have further explored the attributes and behaviors of the 10 types in various criminal justice settings (Megargee et al., 2001).

Based on the patterns of empirically observed differences, individual descriptions of the characteristics of each of the 10 MMPI-2-based types were written that discussed their modal family backgrounds, their social and demographic characteristics, their patterns of childhood and adult adjustment, and their educational, vocational, and criminal histories. In addition, a number of studies have examined how the types differ in their adjustment to prison, which ones are most likely to be disruptive or cause trouble, which are most likely to do well or poorly in educational or vocational programming, and which are most likely to succeed or fail on parole. Strategies for management and treatment have been formulated that address the optimal setting, change agent, and treatment program for each type (Megargee & Bohn, 1977; Megargee et al., 1979; Megargee et al., 2001). While the system is designed primarily for needs assessment, Bohn (1979) obtained a 46% reduction in serious assaults over a 2-year period when he used it for internal classification to separate the more predatory inmates from those most likely to be victimized.

One of the advantages of an MMPI-2-based system is that it can reflect changes in offenders over time in a way that systems based on the criminal history or current offense cannot. Studies have shown that many offenders' classifications do change over the course of their sentences. Doren and Megargee's (1980) research indicated that these differences reflect changes in the client rather than unreliability in the system. If a year or more has passed since the last MMPI-2, it is advisable to readminister the MMPI-2 and reclassify the offender if important programming or treatment decisions are to be made. The rules for classifying male and female offenders' MMPI-2 profiles can be found in Megargee et al. (2001, Appendices D, E, and F.)

Although it was once described as representing the "state of the art in correctional classification" (Gearing, 1981, pp. 106–107), the almost 40-year-old MMPI-2-based system is now best viewed as an empirically derived and validated tool for interpreting the MMPI-2 profiles of criminal offenders.

**Millon Clinical Multiaxial Inventory-III.** After the MMPI and the Wechsler Adult Intelligence Scale, Fourth Edition (WAIS-IV; Wechsler, Coalson, & Raiford, 2008), the MCMI-III (T. Millon & Millon, 2006) is the third most frequently used assessment instrument in correctional settings (Boothby & Clements, 2000). Like the MMPI, the MCMI was originally constructed to assess constructs relevant to psychiatric nosology. However, while the MMPI was aimed at differentiating psychiatric patients from normals, the MCMI was designed to be used in clinical settings to discriminate among different types of psychiatric patients, especially those with Axis II personality disorders (T. Millon & Green, 1989). Despite this clinical focus, the MCMI-III and its predecessors, the original MCMI (T. Millon, 1977) and the MCMI-II (T. Millon, 1987), have been utilized in correctional settings since the 1970s (C. Millon, 1997).

The MCMI-III is a standardized, 175-item self-report inventory for adults age 18 and older. Its brevity is an advantage in correctional settings, but it comes at the expense of considerable item overlap, with many items being scored on two or more scales resulting in high scale intercorrelations. Items on the MCMI-III scales are given weights of 1 or 2 points depending on their importance for the specific scale on which they are keyed. Raw scores are converted to base rate (BR) scores, which are based on the prevalence of each characteristic or syndrome in the normative population. BR scores of 85 or more indicate a feature is clearly present; 75 indicates that some aspects of the characteristic should be found (Groth-Marnat, 1997). The scoring, item content,

and normative populations of the MCMI-III differ from earlier forms of the test, and some authorities question whether validity studies conducted with the MCMI and MCMI-II apply to the MCMI-III (Rogers, Salekin, & Sewell, 1999).

Like its predecessors, the development of the MCMI-III scales was coordinated with the then-current *DSM,* in this case *DSM-IV* (American Psychiatric Association, 1994) and was strongly influenced by T. Millon's evolutionary theory of psychopathology (T. Millon & Davis, 1996, 1997; T. Millon & Green, 1989). The more conversant test users are with these approaches, the easier they will find the task of interpreting the MCMI-III (Groth-Marnat, 1997).

The basic MCMI-III is comprised of 24 clinical scales, divided into two groups. The first group consists of 10 *DSM-IV* Axis I scales, subdivided into 7 scales designed to assess Clinical Syndromes (Anxiety, Scale A; Somatoform, Scale H; Bipolar: Manic; Scale N; Dysthymia, Scale D; Alcohol Dependence, Scale B; Drug Dependence, Scale T; and Post-Traumatic Stress Disorder, Scale R) and 3 scales constructed to assess Severe Clinical Syndromes (Thought Disorder, Scale SS; Major Depression, Scale CC; and Delusional Disorder, Scale PP).

The second group is comprised of 14 Axis II scales, subdivided into 11 scales designed to assess Clinical Personality Patterns (Schizoid, Scale 1; Avoidant, Scale 2A; Depressive, Scale 2B; Dependent, Scale 3; Histrionic, Scale 4; Narcissistic, Scale 5; Antisocial, Scale 6A; Sadistic-Aggressive, Scale 6B; Compulsive, Scale 7; Negativistic/Passive-Aggressive, Scale 8A; and Masochistic/Self-defeating, Scale 8B) as well as 3 scales designed to assess Severe Personality Pathology (Schizotypal, Scale S; Borderline, Scale C; and Paranoid, Scale P) (T. Millon & Millon, 2009). While a number of instruments, including the MMPI-2 and MMPI-2-RF, have scales assessing Axis I disorders, the MCMI-III is unique in its emphasis on these Axis II disorders that are so prevalent in correctional populations (Stoner, 2008). Anderson and Capozzoli (2011) recently estimated that nearly 80% of the prisoners at the California Medical Facility at Vacaville manifested evidence of an Axis II diagnosis of antisocial personality disorder.

In addition to the 24 clinical scales, the MCMI-III has a Validity Index, consisting of four very unusual items, to detect random or careless responding, and three Modifying Indices, the Disclosure (X), Desirability (Y), and Debasement (Z) Scales, designed to identify problematic and potentially invalidating response sets (Groth-Marnat, 1997; T. Millon & Green, 1989).

A unique feature of the MCMI-III is the availability of a Corrections Report specifically designed to be used in the intake screening of prison inmates (T. Millon & Millon, 2009). Whereas the standard MCMI-III was normed on psychiatric patients, the norms for the Corrections Report are based entirely on 1,676 male and female prison inmates, 75% of whom were tested on intake. The BR scores were based on these data and on correctional psychologists' estimates of the prevalence of the various disorders among prison inmates.

The Correctional Summary, which is an addendum to the standard MCMI-III interpretive report, provides additional interpretive information judged by a pool of 48 correctional psychologists to be useful in correctional settings, especially during initial admission screening. Using a weighted combination of scale scores, respondents are evaluated as high, moderate, or low in their probable needs for (a) mental health intervention, (b) substance abuse treatment, and (c) anger management services. These assessments were cross-validated in a longitudinal study that related the assessments to clinicians' evaluations (concurrent) and of subsequent inmate behavior (predictive validity). Not surprisingly, concurrent validities were higher than predictive validities, and the mental health and substance abuse scales were higher than the anger management scales (T. Millon & Millon, 2009; Retzleff, Stoner, & Kleinsasser, 2002).

Inmates are also evaluated on six correctionally relevant dimensions: Reaction to Authority, Escape Risk, Disposition to Malinger, Response to Crowding/Isolation, Amenability to Treatment/Rehabilitation, and Suicidal Tendencies. The Summary notes, "These judgments are based primarily on clinical and theoretical hypotheses that derive from scores and profiles obtained on the MCMI-III test" (T. Millon & Millon, 2009, p. 50). No evidence of the validity of these assessments is presented.

Although the MCMI family of inventories was devised to discriminate among various groups of psychiatric patients, the test authors have put considerable time and effort into adapting the MCMI-III to correctional use. Serious questions have been raised over the validity of the MCMI-III, and its forensic use has been hotly and sometimes acrimoniously debated (Dyer & McCann, 2000; Retzleff, 2000; Rogers et al., 1999, 2000; Shutte, 2001). Little evidence has yet accrued on the MCMI-III's correctional measures. While the indices forecasting the need for mental health and substance abuse interventions appear promising, previous research with other instruments has demonstrated the difficulty of using personality tests to forecast low-BR behaviors that are strongly influenced by situational factors, such as violence, escape from prison, and suicide (Megargee, 1970).

### Intelligence Screening and Evaluation

As noted earlier, the National Commission's (2008b) Prison Standards stipulate that a brief intellectual assessment should be part of the postadmission mental health evaluation. The primary purpose of this screening assessment is to identify developmentally disabled inmates who may be victimized or exploited by predatory prisoners. The Standards recommend "that inmates identified as possibly retarded on group tests of intelligence or brief intelligence screening instruments be further evaluated by a comprehensive, individually administered instrument such as the Wechsler Adult Intelligence Scale (WAIS)" (p. 65).

A second purpose of appraising intelligence is to assist staff in formulating management and treatment plans with particular reference to the inmates' abilities to benefit from educational and vocational programming.

In this section, I describe two brief screening instruments, the Beta III (Kellogg & Morton, 1999) and the General Ability Measure for Adults (GAMA; Naglieri & Bardos, 1997), which are frequently utilized in correctional settings, as well as the WAIS-IV, which should be used for more comprehensive evaluations. All three have been normed on national samples stratified on age, gender, ethnicity, educational level, and geographic region according to the most recent census. All are suitable for administration to individuals ranging in age from their late teens to their early 90s.

**Beta III.** The Beta III (Kellogg & Morton, 1999) is a brief screening instrument used to assess the nonverbal general intelligence of adults aged 16 through 90. Although it can be used in the general population, it is particularly useful with individuals who have language difficulties or who are relatively illiterate. It can be administered individually or to groups in either English or Spanish. Prisons are cited as a specific area of application, and prisoners are among the clinical samples on which the instrument was normed and validated.

The Beta III is a direct descendant of the Army Beta examination that was used to screen illiterate recruits in World War I. In 1934, Kellogg and Morton revised the content to make the instrument suitable for civilian use, producing the "Revised Beta," also known as "Beta I." In 1946, Lindner and Gurvitz restandardized the Revised Beta to produce Wechsler-style deviation IQs.

In 1978, Kellogg and Morton published a major revision of Beta I. Beta II had updated item content, simpler instructions to ensure easier comprehension, and improved sampling that was more representative of the U.S. population.

Several studies investigated the Revised Beta in prison settings. In a study conducted at a federal correctional institution (FCI), 922 youthful male offenders obtained a mean Revised Beta IQ of 101.6 with a standard deviation of 13.6 (Megargee et al., 1979). In other studies using the same FCI population, Levine (1969) and Steuber (1975) obtained correlations of 0.25 and 0.26 respectively with prison teachers' averaged ratings of the offenders' motivation, effort, stability, and achievement in GED courses. However, Levine (1969) discovered that Revised Beta IQs did not predict success in two vocational training courses.

Two studies (Hiltonsmith, Hayman, & Kleinman, 1984; Spruill & May, 1988) found that the Revised Beta yielded lower IQs among minority and low-functioning prisoners than the WAIS-R, especially when administered in a group setting, thereby overestimating the incidence of mental retardation in this population. It is, therefore, advisable to follow up a suspiciously low Beta IQ with a more comprehensive, individually administered WAIS-IV evaluation.

The current version of the test, Beta III (Kellogg & Morton, 1999), features modernized and updated materials that give the instrument a more contemporary, professional appearance. Outdated and possibly biased items and one subtest were replaced, and the upper age range was extended from 64 to 89 in order to improve the test's utility and validity in a variety of settings including corrections. The means at the various age levels were reanchored to 100 to counteract the Flynn effect of upwardly creeping mean IQs in recent decades.

Beta III administrators should have a bachelor's degree in psychology or a related discipline. Because the test booklets have no written directions, examiners must read the instructions to the respondents exactly. On each subtest, they first read general instructions for the task and then direct the examinees to a series of practice problems, answering their questions and ensuring they understand the nature of the task. Once the examinees start each subtest, no more questions are allowed. Time is of the essence, and strict timing, preferably with a stopwatch, is essential.

The Beta III has five subtests, several of which are quite similar to Performance subtests on the WAIS III.

1. Coding (2 minutes) consists of a series of symbols, such as circles, squares and triangles, with empty boxes beneath them. Consulting a key in which a different number is associated with each symbol, the examinees must write as many correct numbers below the symbols as they can in the allotted time.
2. Picture Completion (2.5 minutes) consists of a series of pictures of objects, each of which has a part missing. Examinees must draw in the missing part to complete the picture.
3. Clerical Checking (2 minutes) has a series of pairs of pictures, numbers or symbols. The test taker must circle = or ≠ to indicate whether they are the same or different.
4. Picture Absurdities (3 minutes) presents respondents with four pictures. They must put an X on the one that has something wrong with it.
5. Matrix Reasoning (5 minutes) consists of a series of three pictures. From a group of five pictures, examinees must choose the one that should be the fourth picture in the series.

Although all five tests correlate positively with one another, with $rs$ ranging from .40 to .61, they fall into two general groups. Picture Completion, Picture Absurdities, and Matrix Reasoning correlate higher with each other than they do with Coding and Clerical Checking. The former group is thought to measure fluid or nonverbal reasoning while the latter group assesses processing speed (Kellogg & Morton, 1999). The subtest scores are combined into the Beta III IQ.

The Beta III Manual reports that the overall test–retest reliability over 2 to 12 weeks was 0.91. Average IQs increased 7 points on retest, thereby showing a practice effect. Because it is a timed test, internal consistency was not reported.

In the general sample, Beta III IQs correlated .67 with WAIS-III Verbal IQs (VIQ), .80 with Performance IQs (PIQ), and .77 with Full Scale IQs (FSIQ). Significant positive correlations with several other nonverbal and performance-based tests are also reported in the manual (Kellogg & Morton, 1999). Correlations with external criteria of intelligence are not reported.

In two prison samples comprising 388 inmates, the test developers obtained a mean Beta IQ of 97.3. Ages ranged from 17 to 68 and age-level IQs ranged from 90.5 to 105.4, with the youngest offenders having the highest mean scores.

**General Ability Measure for Adults.**   Like the Beta III, the GAMA (Naglieri & Bardos, 1997) is marketed as a brief screening measure for use in prisons. Unlike the Beta III, prison inmates were not among the groups used in its development or norming. The GAMA provides a measure of general intellectual ability using minimal verbal content. It was normed on adults ages 18 to 96 and can be self-administered or administered by an examiner in either a group or an individual setting.

The GAMA has 66 items consisting of attractive blue and yellow diagrams, each of which has six possible multiple-choice responses. There are four scales:

1. The Matching scale items present respondents with a series of stimulus diagrams. From an array of six similar diagrams, they must select the one that matches each stimulus item in color, shape, and configuration.
2. The Analogies subtest presents respondents with logic problems of the nature "A is to B as C is to (?)" using diagrams instead of letters. Respondents must choose the correct answer from six possible diagrams.
3. Sequences presents test takers with an interrupted sequence of five diagrams showing a figure that is being rotated or otherwise "moved" through space. In each sequence, the middle (third) diagram is missing. Test takers must select the one design that correctly completes the sequence from an array of six possibilities.
4. Construction presents respondents with fragments of shapes. From an array of six completed figures, they must choose the one diagram that could be built with the fragments.

The GAMA can be scored by hand or by computer, and tables are available for converting raw scores to scaled scores for each of 11 age levels ranging from 18 to 19 at the lower end to 80 or more at the upper end. Although the tasks are nonverbal, a third-grade reading level is needed to follow the directions. (A Spanish version is available for those who should be tested in that language.) Respondents have 25 minutes to complete the 66 GAMA items.

Split-half internal consistency coefficients, averaged over the 11 age groups and corrected by the Spearman Brown formula, ranged from .65 to .90, and test–retest coefficients over 2 to 6 weeks ranged from .38 to .74 (Naglieri & Bardos, 1997). Practice effects were evident on all of the retest means except Matching. Lassiter and Matthews (1999) reported only limited temporal stability with coefficients ranging from only .30 to .40 over a similar period. They too obtained significantly higher scores on retest. The magnitudes of these reliability coefficients suggest that psychologists should discuss the confidence limits when reporting GAMA scores.

Naglieri and Bardos (1997) reported that GAMA IQs correlated .65 with WAIS-R VIQs, .74 with PIQs, and .75 with FSIQs IQs. Independent studies have yielded similar correlations (Lassiter, Bell, Hutchinson, & Matthews, 2001; Lassiter, Leverett, & Safa, 2000), although one indicated that the GAMA IQs were lower than the WAIS-III results (Zafiris & Bardos, 2009).

Independent studies show that GAMA IQs also correlate significantly with scores on a number of other intelligence measures (Davis, Bardos, & Woodward, 2006; Lassiter, Matthews, Bell, & Maher, 2002; Leverett, Matthews, Lassiter, & Bell, 2001; Matthews, Lassiter, & Habedenk, 2001). Ispas, Iliescu, Ilie, and Johnson (2010) also reported that GAMA predicted employees' job performance with $r$s ranging from .27 to .50.

Regarding the cross-cultural applicability of the GAMA, Bardos and his colleagues reported using the GAMA in Mexico (Bardos & Johnson, 2007) and Greece (Patrogiannis, Bardos, & Politko, 1999) with satisfactory results.

Given the multiplicity of ethnicities, low reading levels, and poor English-language skills often encountered among criminal offenders, the GAMA appears to have potential as a brief, nonverbal intellectual screening device for correctional settings, with low-scoring offenders being referred for a more complete individual examination with WAIS-IV. Since the GAMA has been marketed for use in prisons for the last decade, studies investigating its utility in correctional settings are overdue.

While it may be true that "a rose is a rose is a rose," it is not true that an IQ is an IQ is an IQ. Beta III and GAMA IQs are related to one another but they are not identical, nor is either equivalent to a WAIS-IV FSIQ. Correctional psychologists should determine for themselves which screening instruments work best in their particular populations. Once they have settled on a given measure, they should determine how well that instrument's scores forecast the criteria they hope to predict, such as success in GED or vocational training programs.

**Wechsler Adult Intelligence Scale, Fourth Edition.** The WAIS-IV (Wechsler et al., 2008), an individually administered comprehensive intelligence test, is the latest edition of the cognitive test for adults most widely used in forensic, correctional, and free-world settings (Boothby & Clements, 2000; Viljoen et al., 2010). The WAIS-IV is a direct descendent of the original Wechsler-Bellevue Intelligence Scale (Wechsler, 1939), which introduced the concepts of Verbal and Performance as well as Full Scale deviation IQs. In 1955 the Wechsler Adult Intelligence

Scale (WAIS) was published (Wechsler, 1955), followed by the Wechsler Adult Intelligence Scale—Revised (WAIS-R; Wechsler, 1981) and the Wechsler Adult Intelligence Scale, Third Edition (WAIS-III; Wechsler, 1997). As we have seen, the National Commission recommends that prisoners suspected of being mentally retarded or developmentally disabled on the basis of intake screening be tested with the current form of the WAIS (NCCHC, 2008b).

WAIS-IV differs in several significant ways from WAIS-III. According to the WAIS-IV research directors, there is enhanced measurement of fluid reasoning, working memory, and processing speed. The instrument has been made more user friendly by reducing testing time, increasing the clarity and consistency of the instructions, and adding more sample responses to verbal subtests. The instructions were made more appropriate for older adults by increasing the directions and decreasing the vocabulary level to ensure understanding of each task. In addition, there is reduced emphasis on motor demands and speedy performance. Visual stimuli are larger, and auditory concerns are addressed (Raiford & Coalson, 2008).

Four WAIS-III subtests were deleted, 3 new subtests were added, and 12 WAIS-III subtests retained with modifications to the item content, administration, and scoring. The most striking change is the elimination of the familiar VIQs and PIQs that characterized all the previous Wechsler scales. In their place are four "Index Scales," that are "based on current intelligence theory and supported by clinical research and factor analytic results" (Wechsler et al., 2008, p. 8).

The Verbal Comprehension Index (VCI) Scale, which replaces the old VIQ, is based on three core subtests, Similarities, Vocabulary, and Information, with Comprehension available as a supplemental subtest. These subtests assess verbal abilities that require reasoning, comprehension, and conceptualization.

The Perceptual Reasoning Index (PRI) Scale, which replaces the old PIQ, is also based on three core subtests, Block Design, Matrix Reasoning, and Visual Puzzles, with Figure Weights and Picture Completion available as supplemental subtests. These subtests reflect nonverbal reasoning and perceptual organization.

The Working Memory Index (WMI) Scale is comprised of two core subtests, Digit Span and Arithmetic, with Letter–Number Sequencing available as a supplemental scale. These subtests assess simultaneous and sequential processing, attention, and concentration.

The Processing Speed Index (PSI) Scale is based on two core subtests, Symbol Search and Coding, with Cancellation available as a supplemental scale. These measure the speed of mental and graphomotor processing.

These four measures, VCI, PRI, WMI, and PSI, are combined into the WAIS-IV FSIQ, which reflects all four types of mental functioning. A General Ability Index (GAI) based only on the VCI and PRI subtests is also available for clinicians desiring a closer approximation to the old WAIS-III FSIQ.

In addition to the subtests, indices, and FSIQ, the WAIS-IV provides eight Process Scores, one for Block Design, six for Digit Span, and one for Letter–Number Sequencing, that "are designed to provide more detailed information on the cognitive abilities that contribute to examinees' subtest performance" (Wechsler et al., 2008, p. 10).

The WAIS-IV Manual is clear, detailed, and comprehensive. However, administering the WAIS-IV correctly requires training and practice. Incompetent administration not only yields questionable results but may also prevent a better-qualified examiner from obtaining a valid WAIS-IV for months thereafter (House, 1996).

Whereas earlier versions of the WAIS utilized patterns of subtest scores and discrepancies between VIQ and PIQ to make inferences regarding personality patterns, neurological functioning, possible clinical diagnoses, and even patterns of criminal behavior (DeWolfe & Ryan, 1984; Groth-Marnat, 1997; House, 1996), such usage has fallen out of favor and is not suggested in the WAIS-IV Manual (Wechsler et al., 2008). When neurological impairment is suspected, clinicians should consider administering the Wechsler Memory Scale IV (WMS-IV; Wechsler, Holdnack, & Drozdick, 2009), which was developed alongside of and conormed with WAIS-IV. With regard to personality adjustment, the MMPI-2 and MCMI are much more informative than the WAIS-IV.

The Manual reports test–retest coefficients over periods ranging from 8 to 81 days (average 22 days) for each age level. Over the entire age spectrum, the coefficients of stability for the 10 core subtests range from .74 to .90 with a median of .82; for the five supplemental subtests, from .77 to .86 with a median of .78; for the four indices, from .87 to .96 with a median of .875; and for the FSIQ, .96.

Validity of the WAIS-IV is based on correlations with numerous other measures, most notably WAIS-III, on confirmatory factor analyses, and on patterns of scores in various clinical and diagnostic groups (Wechsler et al., 2008). Thus far, it does not appear that the validity of the WAIS-IV in correctional samples has been investigated. Writing from a neuropsychological perspective, Loring and Bauer (2010) cautioned against plugging the new scores into algorithms developed using the WAIS-III. While I expect that the WAIS-IV will become the gold standard for the appraisal of adult intelligence, until actual data have been accumulated attesting to its applicability in correctional settings, correctional psychologists, too, should err on the side of caution when interpreting WAIS-IV results.

### Educational Screening

Although most correctional psychologists are trained in clinical psychology, in correctional settings they may also have to undertake some assessments that would fall to counseling or school psychologists in the free world. One such task is assessing offenders' needs for educational programming.

Intelligence tests, especially nonverbal and performance measures, are supposed to reflect intellectual ability rather than achievement. On an individual test such as WAIS-IV, it is possible to obtain an above-average IQ without being able to read. In assessing offenders' needs for educational programming, it is essential to evaluate their current educational level and skills.

Obviously, the best way to determine how many years of formal education an offender has completed is to check the presentence investigation report. Unfortunately, the number of grades attended may not reflect adults' actual skills in reading, mathematics, or language. Aiken (2000) reported that "at least one out of every four employees is functionally illiterate and must 'bluff it out' in performing a job requiring reading skills" (p. 118). The National Literacy Survey established that prisoners as a group are even more educationally handicapped than their free-world counterparts (National Center for Education Statistics, 1994). For this reason, many offenders' educational skills should be independently assessed.

**Test of Adult Basic Education.** The Test of Adult Basic Education (TABE; CTB/McGraw-Hill, 1987) is a flexible test of basic adult education skills. Originally designed for use in GED programs and community colleges, it is now used in a number of correctional settings. The TABE comes in two forms (5/6 and 7/8) and five levels: Literacy (L; grades 0.0–1.9); Easy (E; grades 1.6–3.9); Medium (M; grades 3.6–6.9); Difficult (D; grades 6.6–8.9); and Advanced (A; grades 8.6–12.9). Relatively brief Locator tests are used to diagnose which level is appropriate for an offender in each content area.

Form 5/6 covers seven content areas: Reading Vocabulary, Reading Comprehension, Mathematics Computation, Mathematics Concepts and Applications, Language

Expression, Language Mechanics, and Spelling. Form 7/8 covers Reading, Mathematics Computation, Applied Mathematics, Language, and Spelling. Any subtest can be administered independently.

For basic screening, Form 7/8's Reading and Mathematics subtests can be administered in less than 1 hour. The full TABE battery takes about 3 hours; a condensed TABE "Survey" requires 90 minutes; and the Locator takes about 35 minutes (CTB/McGraw-Hill, 1987). The choice of instrument depends on how detailed an educational evaluation is needed.

The test materials were prepared by teachers and drawn from adult basic education texts from around the country. The TABE is often administered to minorities, so great pains were taken to eliminate ethnic biases (Rogers, 1998). The basic evidence of validity is how the test was constructed and its manifest content. Correlations with external criteria such as grades or GED scores are not provided (Beck, 1998; Rogers, 1998).

Although more technical data are needed, the TABE provides correctional users with a broad array of testing options. In concept and design, it reflects common educational practices (Lissitz, 1992). An especially attractive feature of Form 7/8 for corrections use is that norms are provided based on 1,500 adult and juvenile offenders (Beck, 1998).

### Malingering on Intellectual and Achievement Measures

The basic assumption in free-world ability and achievement testing is that those being evaluated are motivated to perform at their best. Unfortunately, this is not always the case in assessing criminal offenders, so correctional psychologists must be alert to possible malingering.

Unlike personality assessment devices, intelligence and achievement tests do not have validity scales that reflect fake-bad tendencies, so appraisal of malingering must be based on other criteria. Correctional psychologists should keep the purpose of any assessment in mind and ask themselves if poorly performing offenders might think it is advisable to appear intellectually challenged. Although forensic assessment is beyond the scope of this chapter, correctional psychologists might find themselves evaluating offenders who are trying to establish a basis for a challenge to their criminal responsibility or legal competency. To take an extreme example, a death row inmate has an obvious incentive for being evaluated as not competent for execution (Small & Otto, 1991). A marked discrepancy between the intellectual level indicated by the case history and the results of intelligence testing is another red flag.

Although there has been relatively little research on criminal offenders' malingering on intelligence and achievement tests, researchers in other settings have examined the factors associated with deliberately poor performance on these measures. Some of the earliest studies were designed to detect draftees trying to evade induction into the armed services by feigning mental illness. More recent research has focused on patients feigning neurological disorders and memory deficits in conjunction with damage suits.

Schretelen (1988) reviewed 11 studies, many of which used individual intelligence tests, such as the WAIS. He reported that the most reliable signs of malingering were absurd or grossly illogical answers, approximations, and inconsistent performance across tests or subtests. He concluded: "At this point, examination of response 'scatter' appears to be the most powerful and well validated detection strategy. It is based on the finding that fakers tend to fail items genuine patients pass, and pass items genuine patients fail" (p. 458). However, Schretelen noted that this guideline is difficult to apply on brief scales and those where the items are arranged hierarchically in order of difficulty.

Schretelen also noted that it was easier to detect malingering from a battery of tests than it was from any single measure. If, for example, an intelligence test is administered in conjunction with MMPI-2, and the MMPI-2's validity scales suggest malingering, it would be prudent to question the intelligence test results as well.

**Symptom Validity Testing.** Originally developed to assist in the diagnosis of conversion reactions (Pankratz, 1979) and later applied to those feigning neurological and memory impairment (Rees, Tombaugh, Gansler, & Moczynski, 1998; Tombaugh, 1997), symptom validity testing (SVT) has been applied to correctional assessment by Hiscock and her associates (Hiscock, Rustemier, & Hiscock, 1993; Hiscock, Laymen, & Hiscock, 1994). In SVT, suspected malingerers are administered a forced-choice, two-alternative test that may appear challenging but that actually is very easy. Hiscock employed two very easy 72-item tests, one of General Knowledge and the other of Moral Reasoning. A typical item on the General Knowledge test was "Salt water is found in: (a) lakes or (b) oceans."

On two-choice tests, a person answering randomly should get half the items correct merely on the basis of chance. On SVT instruments, malingering is indicated by a score that is significantly lower than chance performance.

Hiscock et al. (1994) found that when male prisoners were instructed to take her tests as if they were poorly educated and could not tell the difference between right and wrong, 71% scored below chance on the General Knowledge test and 60% scored below chance on the Moral Reasoning measure; none of a control sample of offenders who took the tests under standard instructions scored this low. Coaching inmates on how to fake successfully reduced the hit rates to 60% on the General Knowledge test and 43% on Moral Reasoning, showing that the SVT technique works best on unsophisticated offenders.

### Evaluating the Use of Standardized Tests in Corrections

The standardized psychological tests discussed in this section were all developed and validated in free-world settings and subsequently applied to corrections. With the exception of the MMPI-2, whose utilization with criminal offenders has been studied for more than 60 years, correctional research on these instruments has generally been limited to obtaining normative data on various offender samples.

Much more needs to be done. Specifically, the relation of personality, ability, and educational measures to relevant correctional criteria in both community and institutional settings needs to be empirically determined. What patterns of psychometric signs or cutting scores, if any, predict adjustment to prison, need for medication, amenability to treatment, response to supervision, or success on parole or probation? Which measures differentiate potential predators from victims? What ability or achievement levels are required for various educational or vocational training programs or work assignments? How will different offenders respond to various treatment approaches, change agents, or correctional settings?

For the most part, the few instruments that venture to address questions such as these have done so on the basis of inferences extrapolated from free-world or clinical samples rather than on criterion data obtained in criminal justice settings. Given the importance of the decisions made in correctional assessment, empirical research investigating these issues is urgently needed.

## PART TWO: CLASSIFICATION AND RISK ASSESSMENT

Part One focused on assessments used to evaluate mental health, intelligence, and educational achievement using instruments and methods developed in other settings and applied to corrections. In Part Two I describe procedures and techniques specifically created to assess correctional issues, such as the classification of prison inmates, parole decision making, risk and needs assessment, and the diagnosis of antisocial behavior patterns and psychopathy. I begin by describing the issues involved in these assessments and delineating several different approaches used to address them. I conclude by describing six widely used instruments.

## Classification

"External" classification focuses on assigning prison inmates to the most appropriate facilities in a multisite system. Robert Levinson, an architect of the classification system used by the Federal Bureau of Prisons, wrote, "The goal of this first stage of the classification process is to designate new arrivals to the least restrictive correctional institution that appropriately matches the offenders' needs for security and control" (1988, p. 25). The latter elements are operationally defined by architectural features, such as the presence or absence of walls, fences, gun towers, sally ports, and corridor grills, and by the amount of supervision afforded each offender. In all but the smallest states, security levels for male prisoners typically range from maximum-security penitentiaries, through medium-security correctional institutions, down to minimum-security open camps. The federal system and many states also have forensic mental health facilities for prisoners with severe mental disorders. Women, who comprise only 7% of the incarcerated population, have a narrower range of facilities available (ACA, 2006; Sabol et al., 2010).

After external classification has determined offenders' custody and security levels and assigned offenders to the most appropriate correctional facilities, "internal classification" is used to further subdivide each institution's population into homogeneous subgroups for housing and management. According to Levinson (1988):

> [I]nternal classification is the final stage in the classification process. It is a systematic method that identifies homogeneous prisoner subgroups within a single institution's population. Although the degree of variation among one facility's inhabitants is smaller than that found in the total prison system, every institution has a range of inmates—from the predators at one extreme to their prey at the other end of the continuum. Various labels are used to define these individuals: thugs, toughs, wolves, agitators, con-artists, in contrast to weak sisters, sheep, dependents, victims, and other expressions less acceptable in polite society. (p. 27)

The goal of internal classification is to separate these groups in order to reduce the incidence of problematic and disruptive behavior within the institution.

Other factors that influence management and housing decisions are the amount of supervision each offender is likely to need, offenders' sense of responsibility and response to supervision, the approach correctional officers should take in working with them, and whether they will respond better to strict discipline or a more casual correctional atmosphere (Wright, 1986, 1988). Assignment to a special residential program such as a drug treatment unit is another consideration.

## Risk and Needs Assessments

*Risk assessment* refers to estimating the likelihood that offenders will engage in undesirable behaviors, the most common being institutional misconduct, recidivism, violence, and sexual reoffending. In addition to being an important consideration in prison classification, risk assessment is central to whether low-risk offenders can be placed in community-based supervision programs such as probation, parole, or halfway houses. High-risk offenders may be retained until their sentences expire or even longer in the case of certain mentally disordered sex offenders (MDSOs) (Cohen, 2008).

*Needs assessment* in this context refers to the appraisal of potentially changeable criminogenic factors that might be altered to lessen the likelihood of future undesirable behaviors. Such evaluations are used to guide the level of supervision required, the specific problems that should be addressed, and the nature of interventions that might be used to rehabilitate offenders, especially in community correctional agencies (Andrews & Bonta, 2003, 2010; Andrews, Bonta, & Hoge, 1990; Bonta, 1996).

Following the framework originally proposed by Bonta (1996), researchers have found it convenient to differentiate four "generations" of approaches to risk assessment (Brennan et al., 2009; Fass, Heilbrun, DeMatteo, & Fretz, 2008; Hanson & Morton-Bourgon, 2009).

### Generation 1: Subjective Appraisal and Judgment

The earliest and most ubiquitous approach to risk assessment was the subjective judgment of experienced caseworkers, correctional psychologists, and upstanding citizens. Parole board members in both the United Kingdom and the United States often based their decisions on their individual evaluations of each offender (Glaser, 1987; Tidmarsh, 1997). For example, the British Prison Service's "Wakefield" model used expert clinical judgment to decide the amount of time ("tariff") that each convicted lifer should serve (Clark, 1994).

Unstructured clinical risk assessment has been criticized as being overly subjective and potentially influenced by illusory correlation, stereotypes, and hindsight bias (Towl & Crighton, 1995). This was illustrated by Cooper and Werner's (1990) investigation of the abilities of 10 psychologists and 11 caseworkers to predict institutional violence based on 17 variables in a sample of 33 male federal prisoners, 8 of whom (24%) were violent and 25 of whom (76%) were not. They found that interjudge reliabilities were quite low, averaging only .23 among pairs of judges. Accuracy was appalling; the psychologists' predictive accuracy averaged only −.08 (range = −.25 to +.22), while the caseworkers' mean accuracy was +.08 (range = −.14 to +.34). The main reason for the inaccuracy appeared to be illusory correlation, with judges often using cues that proved to be unrelated to the criterion.

According to James Austin (1993), the executive vice president of the National Council on Crime and Delinquency:

> Prior to the development of objective prison classification systems in the late 1970s and through the 1980s, classification decisions were largely based on the subjective judgment of corrections professionals who relied on experience and intuition. Although agencies sometimes specified criteria to be considered by classification staff, the relative importance of each factor was left to the subjective judgment of each staff person or the uncharted consensus of a classification committee. Such informal criteria may have had little or no relationship to actual prison behavior and, generally, served to perpetuate myths regarding offender conduct. (pp. 108–109)

Subjective classification procedures were impossible to document, which resulted in a lack of oversight and accountability. One result was chronic "overclassification," with prisoners being assigned to more restrictive conditions of confinement than were necessary. In a series of cases, the courts held that unstructured subjective classifications were too often arbitrary, capricious, inconsistent, and invalid (Austin, 1993; Solomon & Camp, 1993). In *Laaman v. Helgemoe* (437 F. Supp. 318, D.N.H. 1977, quoted by Solomon & Camp, 1993, p. 9), the court ruled that classification systems "cannot be arbitrary, irrational, or discriminatory." In Alabama the court took over the entire correctional system and ordered every inmate reclassified (Fowler, 1976). Despite these drawbacks, subjective appraisals are still widely employed, even when clinicians have been provided with data from well-validated predictive devices (Hilton & Simmons, 2001).

### Generation 2: Objective Risk Assessment Based on Static Variables

Objective or standard risk-assessment instruments were created to minimize the subjectivity and unreliability associated with purely clinical decision making. Objective tools evaluate each offender on the same set of pre-specified criteria. Generation 2 instruments use relatively "static" predictors that do not change over the course of a sentence, such as: criminal history; age at first arrest; the nature of the current offense; the length of the current sentence; previous violence; history of alcohol, substance use, or mental illness; family background; vocational history; and the like, along with the usual demographic variables. Instruments devised in forensic psychiatric settings appear to use a broader array of information than those derived in prisons.

Generation 2 instruments differ with regard to how the salient factors are selected. Authors of "rational" objective schemes draw on psychological theory, clinical intuition, and correctional experience to select an array of variables that they believe to be predictive of misconduct, violence, or recidivism. "Actuarial" schemes are empirically derived by comparing the past histories of criterion groups, such as recidivists versus nonrecidivists, to determine which variables significantly differentiate them. Whichever approach is used to select potential predictors, every proposed scheme should be cross-validated before being implemented. Many promising variables and systems fail to hold up when applied to new samples or when transferred to different settings (Brennan, 1987; Hanson & Bussiere, 1998; Towl & Crighton, 1995). The simpler the system, the more likely it is to win staff acceptance (Brennan, 1993).

Criminal histories, mental health files, interviews, questionnaires, and, occasionally, scores on psychometric instruments such as Hare's (2003) Psychopathy Checklists are among the favorite sources for obtaining the information required to score the various Generation 2 devices. Typically, the presence or absence of each variable is noted and summary scores are tallied using checklists, score cards, decision trees, or regression equations.

How those scores are used in decision making is another issue in risk assessment. Actuarial or mechanical systems leave no room for subjectivity by specifying cutting scores or decision functions in advance. As with the selection of variables to consider, cutting scores may be established rationally or empirically. Adjusted actuarial schemes allow the clinician to override formula-based decisions, perhaps in consideration of some extraneous variable not included on the checklist (Meehl, 1957). Finally, in structured professional judgment, experienced clinicians make subjective decisions based on the objective data (Hanson & Morton-Bourgon, 2009).

### Generation 3: Objective Risk Assessment Using Dynamic as Well as Static Variables

Generation 3 instruments sample a broader array of factors and are more likely then Generation 2 measures to be rooted in psychological theory, typically social learning approaches (Brennan et al., 2009). Whereas Generation 2 schemes depend exclusively on static variables, Generation 3 instruments also consider dynamic factors that can change over time in prisons and in the community. They can include such factors as response to supervision, treatment or medication compliance, current employment, educational achievement, and criminogenic attitudes (Bonta, 1996; Douglas & Skeem, 2005). Like Generation 2 devices, Generation 3 schemes and their decision functions can constructed either clinically or actuarially. A recent meta-analysis by Campbell, French, and Gendreau (2009) indicated that the static factors in Generation 2 instruments were better at predicting institutional violence while the dynamic variables in Generation 3 devices were better at forecasting violent recidivism.

Since Meehl's (1954) germinal work on the relative merits of clinical versus statistical prediction, numerous analyses and meta-analyses in dozens of fields, including medicine, education, and psychology, have attested to the superiority of structured objective over unstructured subjective prediction techniques (Ægisdóttir et al., 2006; Grove & Meehl, 1996; Grove, Zald, Lebow, Snitz, & Nelson, 2000). Risk assessment is no exception. In their recent metareview, Singh and Fazel (2010) surveyed 9 extensive reviews and 31 meta-analyses covering 2,232 studies of 126 predictive schemes published from 1995 through 2009, while Hanson and Morton-Bourgon (2009) conducted a meta-analysis of 118 studies predicting reoffending among sex offenders. In both reviews, actuarial schemes did best and unstructured clinical decision making did the poorest, with adjusted actuarial and structured professional judgment falling in between. Hanson and Morton-Bourgon found moderate to large effect sizes for the actuarial measures in their study while Singh and Fazel reported that none of the major risk assessment techniques they surveyed was clearly or consistently superior to the others. They also did not find consistent differences between Generation 2 and 3 techniques.

### Generation 4: Needs Assessment as a Guide to Rehabilitation

The introduction of Generation 4 schemes coincided with a paradigm shift in North American corrections away from solely punishment-based, just-deserts models toward a renewed emphasis on reform, rehabilitation, and reentry (Andrews & Bonta, 2010). With the introduction of dynamic factors, objective predictive devices could be used not only to assist in management decisions but also to indicate how much supervision offenders might require and to identify issues that should be dealt with in treatment. With repeated assessments of dynamic factors, caseworkers could chart offenders' progress in institutional or community settings (Campbell et al., 2009).

Operating from a social learning perspective that assumes criminal behavior is learned and maintained within a social context, Andrews, Bonta, and their associates formulated the Risk/Needs/Responsivity (R/N/R) model of classification-guided rehabilitation using their Level of Service Inventory-Revised (LSI-R) as the preferred classification tool (Andrews & Bonta, 2003, 2010; Andrews et al., 1990; Bonta, 1996).

The *risk principle* focuses on which offenders should be targeted for the most intensive treatment. The Canadian scholars, as they came to be called (Smith, Cullen, & Latessa, 2009), argued that maximum treatment efforts should be directed at the highest-risk offenders who pose the greatest risk to society. Low-risk offenders do best when left to their own devices and should receive only minimal attention. Risk is best assessed by static variables, such as criminal history in actuarial prediction schemes (Andrews & Bonta, 2010).

The *needs principle* focuses on what issues should be targeted in treatment, namely the most criminogenic dynamic factors. The "Big Four" dynamic needs, according to Andrews and Bonta (2003), are antisocial attitudes, associates, behaviors, and personality. These needs, along with problems at home, at school or work, in leisure circumstances, and current substance abuse, constitute the "Central Eight." Other deficits that are not direct causes of criminal behavior, such as anxiety or low self-esteem, should not be the focus of therapeutic interventions aimed at decreasing recidivism (Andrews & Bonta, 2010).

Concentrating on forensic psychiatric patients, Douglas and Skeem (2005) formulated their own list of dynamic risk factors. It included impulsiveness, negative affectivity, psychosis, antisocial attitudes, current substance abuse, problems in interpersonal relationships, therapeutic allegiance, and treatment compliance.

The *responsivity principle,* which has received less attention in the literature, specifies how treatment should be carried out. Andrews and Bonta (2010) stated that interventions should be made in accordance with cognitive social learning practices, individually geared to the offender's strengths, abilities, motivation, personality and demographic characteristics.

The R/N/R model depends heavily on assessment. Each offender's risk, needs, and responsivity should be assessed and monitored if the model is to be implemented properly. Generation 4 instruments, such as the Level of Service/Case Management Inventory (LS/CMI) and Correctional Offender Management Profiling for Alternative Sanctions (COMPAS), are designed to provide this information.

Although Andrews and Bonta (2010) maintain that adherence to the R/N/R model has been shown to reduce recidivism by 35%, the Canadian model is not without its critics, especially when it is applied to female offenders. The "feminist perspective" argues that because men constitute 93% of the correctional population, their characteristics have dominated the research findings on criminal causation, overshadowing the pathways to crime that are more typically found among female offenders (Morash, 2009; Salisbury & Van Voorhis, 2009). Citing a wide array of studies on female offending, Van Voorhis, Wright, Salisbury, and Bauman (2010) stated, "The expanding gender-responsive literature suggests that female offenders are very different from male offenders, as evidenced by their unique paths into criminal behavior, the offenses in which they engage, and their decreased threat of violence across criminal justice settings" (p. 263).

Focusing on life history data, as revealed in interviews and case records, and using path analysis as a tool, feminist researchers have delineated several paths by which women come to be incarcerated. A prototypical pattern might be an early history of physical or sexual abuse or neglect leading to running away from home and culminating with life on the streets or in the juvenile justice system. Low self-esteem, self-medication with drugs and/or alcohol, prostitution, and exploitation are common elements, and issues such as poverty, pregnancy, negative relationships with men, and mental illness are frequent concerns (Chesney-Lind & Shelden, 2004; Daly, 1994; Salisbury & Van Voorhis, 2009; Van Voorhis et al., 2010).

Whereas the Canadian scholars proposed concentrating on the higher risk offenders' most criminogenic needs, gender-responsive approaches advocate treating all female offenders with "wraparound services," which provide a "continuum of care" that addresses all their manifold needs and deficits, whether they relate directly to recidivism (Morash, 2009) or not. According to O'Brien (2001), one female parolee likened this holistic treatment process to "baking a cake" because all the various elements must to come together to have a successful outcome.

While treatment strategies are beyond the scope of this chapter, a number of feminist scholars have questioned the appropriateness of using instruments originally designed for men to classify women offenders (Hannah-Moffett, 2009; Holtfreter & Cupp, 2007; Morash, 2009; Salisbury & Van Voorhis, 2009; Smith et al., 2008; Taylor & Blanchette, 2009). Evidence of the adequacy of the LSI-R for risk assessment among women comes from a meta-analysis of 25 recidivism-prediction studies comprising 14,737 female offenders. After obtaining an average $r = 0.35$, the authors concluded, "Based on the extant data, it seems the LSI-R performs virtually the same for female offenders as it does for male offenders" (Smith et al., 2008, p. 198). Whether it is the best possible classification instrument for women is another issue, especially if it is being used to identify their treatment needs (Hannah-Moffet, 2009; Holtfreter & Cupp, 2007; Taylor & Blanchette, 2009).

Meanwhile, Van Voorhis and her colleagues, working with the National Institute of Corrections in the United States, are developing female-oriented dynamic supplements for risk/needs instruments. They have reported that in six of eight samples, their gender-responsive scales made statistically significant contributions to gender-neutral predictors. They found promising results among female probationers when parental stress, family support, self-efficacy, educational assets, housing safety, anger/hostility, and current mental health were considered; among prisoners, when child abuse, anger/hostility, relationship dysfunction, family support, and current mental health were included; and among released inmates, when adult victimization, anger/hostility, educational assets, and family support were taken into account (Van Voorhis et al., 2010).

## Instruments Used for Risk Assessment

### Personality Tests

Over the years, a number of psychological tests and personality inventories have been applied to the problem of risk assessment, including the MMPI-2 and MCMI-III, which were discussed in Part One. The most effective has been an instrument devised not to predict risk or recidivism but instead to help diagnose psychopathy, the Psychopathy Checklist—Revised (PCL-R; Hare, 2003).

**Psychopathy Checklist—Revised.** The PCL-R was devised to assess the construct of psychopathy as originally delineated by Cleckley (1941/1976). Since 1980, an impressive array of empirical evidence from personality, physiological, and cognitive psychological research, as well as from criminology and corrections, has attested to the construct validity of the PCL-R. Barone (2004) described the PCL-R as the "gold standard" for the measurement of psychopathy.

Although not all psychopaths are criminals and all criminals are certainly not psychopaths (Gendreau, Goggin, & Smith, 2002; Hare, 1996), the PCL-R and its predecessor, the PCL, are often used in risk assessment among criminal offenders. Meloy and Gacono (1995) reported that criminal offenders diagnosed as psychopaths on the basis of their PCL-R scores commit a greater number and variety of criminal offenses, including more predatory violent offenses, and have longer criminal careers than nonpsychopathic offenders. Although violent behavior is not a defining characteristic of psychopathy, psychopathic offenders' impulsivity, poor behavioral control, and lack of empathy for others make them prone to violence (Hart, 1996).

PCL-R assessments require a thorough review of the clinical, medical, and legal records, followed by a semistructured clinical interview in which a complete chronological case history is obtained. The full PCL-R consists of 20 symptoms of psychopathy, each of which is scored on a 3-point scale from 0 (absent) to 2 (clearly present). Interrater reliabilities average .86, and users are advised to base assessments on the average of two or more independent ratings whenever possible (Hare, Harpur, Hakstian, Forth, Hart, & Newman, 1990). A complete PCL-R assessment takes several hours to complete (Hare, 1996). For screening purposes, a 12-item Psychopathy Checklist: Screening Version (PCL-SV; Hart, Hare, & Forth, 1994) can be used, and a youth version (PCL/YV) is available for those age 12 through 18 (Forth, Kosson & Hare, 2003).

The Psychopathy Checklists have two well-defined factors in most analyses. The first reflects an egocentric, selfish interpersonal style with its principal loadings from such items as glibness/superficial charm (.86), grandiose sense of self-worth (.76), pathological lying (.62), conning/manipulative (.59), shallow affect (.57), lack of remorse or guilt (.53), and callous/lack of empathy (.53). The items loading on the second factor suggest the chronic antisocial behavior associated with psychopathy: impulsivity (.66), juvenile delinquency (.59), and need for stimulation, parasitic lifestyle, early behavior problems,

and lack of realistic goals (all loading .56) (Hare et al., 1990).

Reviewing a number of empirical investigations, both retrospective and prospective, Hart (1996) reported that psychopaths, as diagnosed by the PCL-R, had higher rates of violence in the community and in institutions than nonpsychopaths. Psychopathy, as measured by the PCL-R, was predictive of violence after admission to a hospital ward and after conditional release from a hospital or correctional institution. Hart estimated that the average correlation of PCL-R scores with violence in these studies was about .35. In their follow-up of 618 men discharged from a maximum security psychiatric institution, Harris, Rice, and Quinsey (1993) reported that, of all the variables they studied, the PCL-R had the highest correlation (+.35) with violent recidivism, and they included psychopathy, as defined by PCL-R scores > 25, as a predictor in their Violent Risk Appraisal Guide.

In these studies, predictive success is often expressed in terms of "areas under the curve" (AUCs) based on analyses of receiver operating characteristics (ROCs). An AUC of 0.50 indicates predictions at a chance level while an AUC of 1.0 reflects perfect positive predictions. AUCs of .70 or .80 indicate large positive effect sizes (Douglas, Yeomans, & Boer, 2005). Reviewing several studies of the PCL predicting various adverse outcomes, Brennan et al. (2009) reported AUCs ranging from .61 to .75.

Meta-analyses have also shown the PCL-R Factor 1, Factor 2, and total scores of criminal offenders are associated with moderately increased rates of antisocial behavior, recidivism, and violence (Leistico, Salekin, DeCoster, & Rogers, 2000; Salekin, Rogers, & Sewell, 1996). However, Leistico et al. (2000) noted that the association of PCL-R scores with negative behaviors is moderated by gender, race, ethnicity, the country in which the study was carried out, and the setting in which the study was conducted.

As is the case with many risk assessment instruments, PCL-R scores in the clinical range are meaningful, but low scores have no clear relation to behavior. Specifically, they do not guarantee that an offender will never recidivate or be violent. Hart (1996, p. 64) concluded that "predictions of violence using the PCL-R are considerably better than chance, albeit far from perfect."

Although the PCL-R has been mostly used for risk assessment, it also has implications for treatment planning. Psychopaths have a poor prognosis for change (Hare, 1996; Suedfeld & Landon, 1978), and Gendreau et al. (2002) suggested that high PCL-R scores indicate poor responsivity in the R/N/R model. In correctional facilities where treatment resources are scarce and access must be limited to those most likely to profit from interventions, such findings suggest that psychopaths should have lower priority than other offenders.

### Risk/Need Assessment Devices

In addition to personality tests, over 100 objective tools have been specifically devised for assessing risks (Singh & Fazel, 2010). They include instruments used to predict institutional misconduct, violence, recidivism, sexual reoffending, and spouse abuse among adult men and women as well as techniques aimed at forecasting various types of misconduct among adolescents and juveniles (Megargee, 2009, Table 28.1). Among the most widely used are the Dangerous Behavior Rating Scale (Webster & Menzies, 1993); the Historical, Clinical, Risk Management-20 (HCR-20; Douglas & Webster, 1999; Webster, Douglas, Eaves, & Hart, 1997), the Level of Supervision Inventories (LSI and LSI R; Bonta & Motiuk, 1985), the Correctional Offender Management Profiling for Alternative Sanctions (COMPAS; Brennan et al., 2006), the STATIC-99 (Hanson & Thornton, 1999), the Violence Prediction Scheme (VPS; Webster, Harris, Rice, Cormeier, & Quinsey, 1994), the Violence Risk Appraisal Guide (VRAG; Harris et al., 1993; Quinsey, Harris, Rice, & Cormier, 2006), and the Violence Risk Scale (VRS; Wong & Gordon, 2006) (Singh & Fazel, 2010; Viljoen et al., 2010). In this section, I describe the VRAG, the HCR-20, the LSI family of instruments, and the COMPAS.

**Violence Risk Appraisal Guide.**   One of the earliest objective risk assessment instruments, the VRAG (Harris et al., 1993; Quinsey et al, 2006) was actuarially constructed to predict violent recidivism among mentally disordered offenders. It was derived from a population of 618 violent offenders at a maximum-security psychiatric institution, 191 of whom (31%) engaged in further violence after their eventual release. The clinical records of these "violent failures" were combed, coded, and compared with those of the 427 violent offenders who did not subsequently engage in violent recidivism. Multivariate analyses identified 12 static variables from the 50 or so studied that significantly differentiated the two criterion groups. They included three history variables (elementary school maladjustment, separation from parents before age 16, and never marrying), four clinical history variables (history of alcohol abuse, *DSM-III* diagnoses of schizophrenia or personality disorder, and score on the PCL), two overall criminal history variables (record of property offenses and prior failures on conditional release), and three factors regarding the index offense (injuries to the victim,

gender of victim, and age of offender at the time of the offense). Interestingly, the PCL-R was the variable most closely related to violent recidivism. These 12 variables were differentially weighted (with the PCL-R receiving the highest weight) and combined to yield a total VRAG score, which was used to assign the subjects to nine categories ranging from virtually no chance to almost a certain chance of recidivism (Harris et al., 1993).

Actuarially derived tools should be cross-validated on new independent samples before being used, and instruments devised in one setting or locale should be checked for accuracy before they are adopted elsewhere. The VRAG has been successfully cross-validated on new samples of general-population releasees as well as serious mentally disordered offenders by its creators and independent researchers with AUCs ranging from .70 to .77 (Barbaree, Seto, Langton, & Peacock, 2001; Douglas et al., 2005; Grann, Belfrage, & Tengström, 2000; Harris, Rice, & Cormier, 2002; Harris et al., 1993; Kroner & Mills, 2001; Kroner, Statdland, Eidt, & Nedopil, 2007; Loza & Dhaliwal, 1997; Quinsey et al., 2006; Rice & Harris, 1994, 1995).

**Historical, Clinical, Risk Management-20.**   Whereas the VRAG is a purely actuarial predictive instrument, the HCR-20 (Douglas & Webster, 1999; Webster et al., 1997) was rationally constructed to provide data for clinicians to use in structured professional judgment. Items were chosen based on a comprehensive review of the literature and on suggestions made by experienced forensic clinicians (Douglas et al., 2005; Douglas & Webster, 1999).

The HCR-20 is comprised of 20 ratings in three categories, Historical, Clinical, and Risk Management. After reviewing the available records and possibly checking with the offender's friends or family members, HCR-20 raters assess each factor as "Absent," "Possibly Present," or "Definitely Present." The ten Historical (H) items are similar to the items on the VRAG. They include history of (1) previous violence, (2) young age at first violent incident, (3) relationship instability, (4) employment problems, (5) substance abuse, (6) history of major mental illness, (7) psychopathy as measured by the PCL-R, (8) early maladjustment, (9) personality disorder, and (10) prior supervision failure (Douglas & Webster, 1999).

The five Clinical (C) items reflecting current emotional status are (1) lack of insight, (2) negative attitudes, (3) active symptoms of major mental illness, (4) impulsivity, and (5) unresponsiveness to treatment. The five Risk Management (R) items are (1) plans lacking feasibility,

(2) exposure to destabilizers, (3) lack of personal support, (4) lack of compliance with remediation attempts, and (5) stress (Douglas & Webster, 1999). These dynamic C and R items, which can change to reflect a client's current situation, are the clearest difference between the HCR-20 and instruments that are based exclusively on historical or file data. The authors have recommended reviewing these dynamic items at regular intervals to keep the risk appraisal current.

Because it is designed to guide structured clinical judgments, the HCR-20 does not have recommended cutting scores or algorithms that categorize people. Instead, it produces numerical scores on each of its three scales as well as a total score that clinicians are encouraged to consider along with base rate and situational factors when deciding whether people are at low, medium, or high risk of violent offending (Douglas et al., 2005). Nevertheless, a number of researchers have investigated the relationship between HCR-20 scores and various measures of institutional misconduct and recidivism as well as both sexual and nonsexual violent offending and reoffending. These studies indicate that the HCR-20 scales have AUCs, correlations, and effect sizes comparable to the LSI-R, PCL-R, and VRAG (Douglas & Webster, 1999; Douglas et al., 2005; Grann et al., 2000; Kroner & Mills, 2001). In some of these studies, the static Historical items have the highest relations to the criteria, in others the dynamic Clinical and Risk Management factors.

Douglas et al. (2005) also investigated how successfully the HCR-20 guided structured judgments of low, moderate, or high risk for violence. They reported that 19.1% of the low, 58.8% of the moderate, and 85.7% of the high groups were subsequently violent.

**Level of Service Inventories.** The LSI instruments (Andrews & Bonta, 1995; Andrews, Bonta, & Wormith, 2004; Bonta & Motiuk, 1985) have been developed and refined through a systematic program of research over the last quarter century. Whereas the VRAG and HCR-20 both focused on violent reoffending, the original LSI was developed primarily on probationers and short-term prisoners to determine their needs for supervision after transitioning to halfway house or other community placements (Bonta & Motiuk, 1985; Mills, Jones, & Kroner, 2005). Revised and renamed the Level of Service Inventory-Revised (LSI-R) in 1995, it has been widely used in prisons as well as community corrections agencies throughout Canada and has been researched and utilized in Australia (Daffern, Ogloff, Ferguson, & Thomson, 2005), England (Hollin & Palmer, 2006; Palmer & Hollin,

2007), Germany (Dahle, 2006), and the United States (Schlager & Simourd, 2007).

Designed for use with offenders age 16 and older, LSI and LSI-R are based on information from official files plus a 30- to 45-minute structured interview administered by a trained professional. They contain 54 scales covering 10 areas: (1) Criminal History, (2) Education/Employment, (3) Finances, (4) Family/Marital, (5) Accommodations, (6) Leisure/Recreation, (7) Companions, (8) Alcohol/Drug Problems, (9) Emotional/Personal, and (10) Attitudes/Orientation. Each element is scored 0 (absent) or 1 (present). Finances and Leisure/Recreation are omitted from the briefer Level of Service Inventory—Revised: Screening Version (LSI-R:SV), which takes 10 to 15 minutes to complete. The LSIs are thus broader in scope than the VRAG or HCR-20 and utilize both static and dynamic information. In addition to providing an overall risk score, some of the scales provide information that should assist caseworkers in supervising clients in community correctional settings (Bonta & Motiuk, 1985).

Most studies of the LSIs have reported adequate reliability and significant associations of LSI total scores with success or failure in institutional settings, on probation and parole, and with general recidivism among both male and female offenders (Catchpole & Gretton, 2003; Girard & Wormith, 2004; Hollin & Palmer, 2006; Kroner & Mills, 2001; Palmer & Hollin, 2007; Simourd, 2004; Smith et al., 2009). However, Fass et al. (2008) did not find significant associations with recidivism among northeastern, urban, mostly minority males.

The LSI-R's associations with violent recidivism are less robust than those with general recidivism (Daffern et al., 2005; Gendreau et al., 2002). Based on the means obtained in several meta-analyses, Andrews, Bonta, & Wormith (2006) calculated average predictive $rs$ of 0.36 for general recidivism and 0.25 for violent recidivism (Rettinger & Andrews, 2010). Reviewing several studies, Brennan et al. (2009) reported AUCs ranging from .64 to .69 when the LSI-R was used to predict various negative outcomes.

An Ontario revision of the LSI (LSI-OR) designed for use in that province's institutions and community correctional agencies includes a new Specific/Risk section to improve its assessment of aggressive behavior (Girard & Wormith, 2004). In addition, as noted earlier, Van Voorhis et al. (2010) are developing supplements to make the LSI-R and similar instruments more gender responsive.

The most recent additions to the LSI family of instruments are the Level of Service/Case Management

Inventory (LS/CMI; Andrews et al., 2004) and the Youth Level of Service/Case Management Inventory (YLS/CMI; Hoge & Andrews, 2006). Based on official file records, a structured interview, and collateral information, these Generation 4 measures are designed to assess and track adult and youthful offenders' needs and responsivity as well as evaluate their risk factors according to the R/N/R model. The scales permit coding strengths as well as deficits, and they include responsivity measures relevant to each gender as well as to different ethnic groups (Williams, 2010).

The scales in the first section of the LS/CMI assess the Canadian scholars' Central Eight criminogenic risk/needs factors: (1) Criminal History, (2) Employment/Education, (3) Family/Marital, (4) Leisure/Recreation, (5) Companions, (6) Alcohol/Drug Problems, (7) Antisocial Pattern and (8) Procriminal Attitude Orientation. These scales can be combined into an overall General Risk/Need score. Additional case management scales include (a) Barriers to Release, (b) Case Management plan, (c) Progress Record, (d) Discharge Summary, (e) Specific Risk/Needs factors, (f) Prison Experience—Institutional Factors, and (g) Special Responsivity Factors (Andrews et al., 2004).

Thus far, validation studies of the LS/CMI and YLS/CMI have focused on the ability of the General Risk/Need score to predict or postdict general and violent recidivism. Not surprisingly, the findings have been similar to those obtained with the LSI-R (Rettinger & Andrews, 2010; Williams, 2010). Andrews et al. (2006) reported grand mean criterion validity estimates of .41 for general recidivism, .29 for violence, and .37 for reincarceration for a new offense for the adult LS/CMI. The YLS/CMI has been more widely investigated, with positive evidence for its General Need/Risk scale being reported in Australia, Canada, England, and the United States (Bechtel, Lowenkamp, & Latessa, 2007; Catchpole & Gretton, 2003; Holsinger, Lowenkamp, & Latessa, 2006; Jung & Rawana, 1999; Onifade, Davidson, Campbell, Turke, Malinowski, & Turner, 2008; Onifade, Smith-Nyandoro, Davidson, & Campbell, 2010; Rennie & Dolan, 2010; Schmidt, Campbell, & Houlding, 2111; Thompson & Putnins, 2003; Welsh, Schmidt, McKinnon, Chattha, & Meyers, 2008; Williams, 2010). Summarizing a number of these studies, Welsh et al. (2008, p. 105) reported internal consistency correlations ranging from .80 to .91, interrater reliabilities ranging from .71 to .85, test–retest reliabilities for total scores averaging .75, predictive validity correlations for recidivism ranging from .25 to .36, and AUCs ranging from .61 to .67.

There is little research on the correlates of the individual need/risk scale scores on both the LS/CMI and the YLS/CMI. Given their relative brevity, we can anticipate that reliability and validity coefficients will be lower than those for the General Risk/Need measure are. Finding satisfactory independent criterion measures will be challenging. At present, the best evidence for their validity is their manifest content.

**Correctional Offender Management Profiling for Alternative Sanctions.**   COMPAS (Brennan et al., 2006) is a software system that serves as a platform for the Northpointe Institute for Public Management's customized management information systems for jails, prisons, and community corrections agencies. It grew out of a computerized Jail Population Information System (JPIS) developed for jails throughout the State of Michigan in the 1980s with the assistance of the National Institute of Corrections (Wells & Brennan, 2009).

COMPAS features fully computerized assessment and case management systems that can integrate information from different databases and update an offender's current status as new information is entered. The system is designed for use in all stages of criminal justice processing from initial arrest through probation, prison, parole, and community supervision. There is a central Core component as well as risk/needs applications for special populations (COMPAS/Youth, COMPAS/Women, and COMPAS/Reentry.)

COMPAS systems are designed to be adopted agency wide rather than used by individual clinicians or practitioners. Northpointe can adapt its basic systems to each agency's particular population, setting, and needs, taking into account local base rates and existing information systems, reporting requirements, and legal parameters. For example, the scales' decile scores can be computed relative to eight different possible normative comparison groups (Northpointe Institute for Public Management, 2010).

Central to the various COMPAS systems is the Core Risk Assessment, which can be based on official records (i.e., current offense, criminal history) and offender self-report as obtained through questionnaires or structured interviews by trained screeners. Completion of the basic assessment can take from 10 minutes to 1 hour depending on the complexity and extent of the data gathered as well as the mode of collection. The Core Report features color-coded bar graphs with 22 decile scales divided into six categories. In addition, there are three validity scales that "red flag" suspect protocols suggesting possible defensiveness, random responding, or inconsistency (Northpointe Institute for Public Management, 2010).

Because it is computerized, COMPAS can use sophisticated and complex scale scoring procedures. Brennan et al. (2009) described in detail how the score on each Core scale is computed, along with its theoretical and empirical justification. The Core areas assessed include the Central Eight and other familiar variables:

*Category 1, Overall Risk,* has three scales assessing Risk of (1) Violence, (2) Recidivism, and (3) Failure to Appear.

*Category 2, Criminal Involvement,* has four scales assessing (1) Criminal Involvement, (2) History of Non-Compliance, (3) History of Violence, and (4) Current Violence, thus incorporating both static and dynamic variables.

*Category 3, Relationship/Lifestyle,* has five scales assessing (1) Criminal Associates/Peers, (2) Criminal Opportunity, (3) Leisure/Recreation, (4) Social Isolation, and (5) Substance Abuse.

*Category 4, Personality/Attitudes,* has three scales assessing (1) Criminal Personality, (2) Criminal Thinking Self-Report, and (3) Cognitive Behavioral.

*Category 5, Family,* has two scales assessing (1) Family Criminality and (2) Socialization Failure.

*Category 6, Social Exclusion,* has five scales assessing (1) Financial, (2) Vocational/Educational, (3) Social Environment, (4) Residential Instability, and (5) Social Adjustment (Brennan et al., 2009).

In addition to these variables, the COMPAS/Women system includes measures assessing such gender-responsive factors as economic marginalization, mental health, parenting and stress, lack of empowerment, low family support, relationship dysfunction, human capital and abuse/trauma. The Reentry package anticipates the prospective needs of both men and women who are going to transition into the community after relatively lengthy periods of incarceration. The Youth version focuses more on peers, interpersonal relations, school, the behavior and characteristics of the primary socializing family, and the recent family living situation (Northpointe Institute for Public Management, 2010).

I could find only two published peer-reviewed studies testing the validity of the COMPAS. An early study plagued by very small COMPAS samples reported essentially chance results (Fass et al., 2008). A more recent study of 2,238 male offenders reported AUCs for overall predictions of various criteria of general recidivism ranging from .69 to .75 among White men and from .64 to .73 among African American men (Brennan et al., 2009). I could not find any studies investigating the construct validity of the various individual need scales.

### Evaluating Risk Assessment Instruments

Since the first edition of this chapter was written, there have been dramatic developments in the area of risk assessment and a number of new and increasingly sophisticated instruments have been published. Validation has lagged behind. While a number of schemes have been found to be related to various criteria of recidivism and negative behaviors, there has been little published research investigating the validity of the various need scales and responsivity measures. Finding relevant and reliable criterion measures is a challenge, but such studies must be carried out.

Although the emphasis in risk assessment is on diagnosing the most dangerous offenders, the greatest contribution of these classification tools has been to identify low-risk prisoners who could safely be assigned to less secure correctional programs or placed in the community (Austin, 1993; Glaser, 1987; Solomon & Camp, 1993). When making subjective predictions of violence, classifications personnel are often overly conservative, placing many offenders in higher-than-necessary risk categories (Heilbrun & Heilbrun, 1995; Monahan, 1981, 1996; Proctor, 1994; Solomon & Camp, 1993). This is not surprising. The public is rarely incensed if low-risk offenders are retained in more restrictive settings than necessary, but clinicians can expect to be castigated if someone they approved for minimum security or early release goes out to rape, pillage, and plunder the community.

Reducing the extent of overclassification has three important benefits. First, it is the correct thing to do; as noted previously, the courts have consistently ruled that offenders have the right to be maintained in the least restrictive settings consistent with maintaining safety, order, and discipline. Second, less restrictive settings are more economical. Confining an offender in a maximum-security institution costs $3,000 a year more than a minimum-security facility and $7,000 more than a community setting. Third, the residents benefit because more programming is possible in less restrictive settings, and the deleterious effects of crowding are diminished (Proctor, 1994).

Perhaps the greatest limitation on the utilization of objective risk assessment devices is the reluctance of many clinicians and caseworkers to rely on such tools. In his classic paper, "Why I No Longer Attend Case Conferences," Paul Meehl (1977) lamented the tendency for clinicians to place more faith in their subjective impressions than they do in base rates or the results of objective instruments. In a recent risk-assessment study, Kroner and Mills (2001) found that experienced clinicians provided with base rate data apparently ignored them when estimating the likelihood of violent offending. As a result, they did no better than a contrast group of clinicians who had no base rate information.

Hilton and Simmons (2001) reviewed the factors associated with decisions made by the Ontario Review Board on whether mentally disordered offenders charged with serious, usually violent, offenses should be detained in maximum security. VRAG scores, which were provided to the members of the board, were not related to the eventual security-level decisions. The most important single variable was the testimony of the senior clinician, although criminal history, psychotropic medication, institutional behavior, and even the physical attractiveness of the patient also played a role. They concluded that:

> contrary to current optimism in the field, actuarial risk assessment had little influence on clinical judgments and tribunal decisions about mentally disordered offenders in this maximum security setting... It is apparent... that simply creating actuarial instruments and making the results available to decision makers does not alter long-established patterns of forensic decision making. (pp. 402, 406)

With the advent of Generation 3 and 4 instruments, some evidence-based agencies are adopting objective assessments as a matter of policy. However, no matter how much information is provided by these instruments, they have no impact unless the findings influence actual decisions and practices. Staff must be educated, trained, and, most important, convinced of their contribution (Goodloe, 2009). As Andrews and Bonta (2010) recently noted, "Unfortunately, in the 'real world' of routine correctional practice, adhering to the principles is a challenge" (p. 49). Only a relatively small percentage of the studies they reviewed showed caseworkers strictly adhering to their R/N/R policies and principles. Actually implementing agency change is a process that Van Voorhis and Groot (2010) likened to turning a large ship. Vigilant monitoring of actual practices is essential if changes are to be effected.

## REFERENCES

Ægisdóttir, S., White, M. J., Spengler, P. M., Maugherman, A. S., Anderson, L. A., Cook, R. S., ... Rush, J. D. (2006). The meta-analysis of clinical judgment project: Fifty-six years of accumulated research on clinical versus statistical prediction. *Counseling Psychologist, 34,* 341–382.

Aiken, L. R. (2000). *Psychological testing and assessment* (10th ed.). Boston, MA: Allyn & Bacon.

American Correctional Association. (2006). *2006 directory of adult and juvenile correctional departments, institutions, agencies, and probation and paroling authorities.* Alexandria, VA: Author.

American Correctional Association. (2010). *2010* Standards *supplement* (pp. 119–146). Alexandria, VA: Author.

American Correctional Association and Commission on Accreditation. (2002). *Performance-based standards for correctional health care in adult correctional institutions.* Alexandria, VA: Author.

American Psychiatric Association. (1994). *Diagnostic and statistical manual of mental disorders* (4th ed.). Washington, DC: Author.

American Psychiatric Association. (2000). *Guidelines for psychiatric services in jails and prisons: A task force report of the American Psychiatric Association* (2nd ed.). Washington, DC: Author.

American Psychological Association. (2002). Ethical principles of psychologists and code of conduct. *American Psychologist, 57,* 1060–1073.

Anderson, S. T., & Capozzoli, N. (2011). Walking cane use in prison: A medical and cultural analysis. *Journal of Correctional Health Care, 17,* 19–28.

Andrews, D. A., & Bonta, J. (1995). The Level of Service Inventory— Revised. Toronto, Canada: Multi-Health Systems.

Andrews, D. A., & Bonta, J. (2003). *The psychology of criminal conduct* (3rd ed.). Cincinnati, OH: Anderson.

Andrews, D. A., & Bonta, J. (2010). Rehabilitating criminal justice policy and practice. *Psychology, Public Policy, and Law, 16,* 39–55.

Andrews, D. A., Bonta, J., & Hoge, R. D. (1990). Classification for effective rehabilitation: Rediscovering psychology. *Criminal Justice and Behavior, 17,* 19–52.

Andrews, D. A., Bonta, J., & Wormith, S. J. (2004). *The Level of Service/Case Management Inventory.* Toronto, Canada: Multi-Health Systems.

Andrews, D. A., Bonta, J., & Wormith, S. J. (2006). Recent past and near future of risk/need assessment. *Crime and Delinquency, 52,* 7–27.

Anno, B. J. (1991). *Prison health care: Guidelines for the management of an adequate delivery system.* Chicago, IL: National Commission on Correctional Health Care.

Archer, R. P., Buffington-Vollum, J. K., Stredny, R. V., & Handel, R. W. (2006). A survey of psychological test use patterns among forensic psychologists. *Journal of Personality Assessment, 87,* 84–94.

Austin, J. (1993). Objective prison classification systems: A review. In American Correctional Association (Ed.), *Classification: A tool for managing today's offenders* (pp. 108–123). Laurel, MD: Author.

Barbaree, H. E., Seto, M., Langton, C. M., & Peacock, E. J. (2001). Evaluating the predictive accuracy of six risk assessment instruments for adult sex offenders. *Criminal Justice and Behavior, 28,* 490–521.

Bardos, A., & Johnson, K. (2007, August). *Cross-cultural investigation of the General Ability Measure for Adults (GAMA) in Mexico.* Paper presented at the meeting of the American Psychological Association, San Francisco, CA.

Barone, N. (2004). Review of the Psychopathy Checklist-Revised (PCL-R), 2nd ed. *Journal of Psychiatry and Law, 32,* 113–114.

Bechtel, K., Lowenkamp, C. T., & Latessa, E. (2007). Assessing the risk of re-offending for juvenile offenders using the Youth Level of Service/Case Management Inventory. *Journal of Offender Rehabilitation, 45,* 85–108.

Beck, M. D. (1998). Review of Tests of Adult Basic Education, Forms 7, & 8. In J. C. Impara & B. S. Plake (Eds.), *The thirteenth mental measurements yearbook* (pp. 1080–1083). Lincoln, NB: Buros Institute of Mental Measurements of the University of Nebraska, Lincoln.

Ben-Porath, Y. S., & Tellegen, A. (2008). *MMPI-2-RF: Manual for administration, scoring, and interpretation.* Minneapolis: University of Minnesota Press.

Bohn, M. J. Jr. (1979). Inmate classification and the reduction of violence. In *Proceedings of the 109th Annual Congress of Correction* (pp. 63–69). College Park, MD: American Correctional Association.

Bonta, J. (1996). Risk-needs assessment and treatment. In A. T. Harland (Ed.), *Choosing correctional options that work: Defining the demand and evaluating the supply* (pp. 18–32). Thousand Oaks, CA: Sage.

Bonta, J., & Motiuk, L. L. (1985). Utilization of an interview-based classification instrument: A study of correctional halfway houses. *Criminal Justice and Behavior, 12,* 333–352.

Boothby, J., & Clements, C. (2000). A national survey of correctional psychologists. *Criminal Justice and Behavior, 27,* 716–732.

Brennan, T. (1987). Classification: An overview of selected methodological issues. In D. M. Gottfredson & M. Tonry (Eds.), *Prediction and classification in criminal justice decision making* (pp. 201–248). Chicago, IL: University of Chicago Press.

Brennan, T. (1993). Risk assessment: An evaluation of statistical classification methods. In American Correctional Association (Ed.), *Classification: A tool for managing today's offenders* (pp. 46–70). Laurel, MD: Author.

Brennan, T., Dieterich, W., & Ehret, B. (2009). Evaluating the predictive validity of the COMPAS risk and needs assessment system. *Criminal Justice and Behavior, 36,* 21–40.

Brennan, T., Dieterich, W., & Oliver, W. L. (2006). *COMPAS: Technical manual and psychometric report version 5.0.* Traverse City, MI: Northpointe Institute.

Butcher, J. N. (1999). *A beginner's guide to MMPI-2.* Washington, DC: American Psychological Association.

Butcher, J. N. (2006). Pathways to MMPI-2 use: A practitioner's guide to test usage in diverse settings. In J. N. Butcher (Ed.), *MMPI-2: A practitioner's guide* (pp. 3–13) Washington, DC: American Psychological Association.

Butcher, J. N., Dahlstrom, W. G., Graham, J. R., Tellegen, A. M., & Kaemmer, B. (1989). *Minnesota Multiphasic Personality Inventory-2 (MMPI-2): Manual for administration and scoring.* Minneapolis: University of Minnesota Press.

Campbell, M. A., French, S., & Gendreau, P. (2009). The prediction of violence in adult offenders: A meta-analytic comparison of instruments and methods of assessment. *Criminal Justice and Behavior, 36,* 567–590.

Catchpole, R. H., & Gretton, H. M. (2003). The predictive validity of risk assessment with violent young offenders: A 1-year examination of criminal outcome. *Criminal Justice and Behavior, 36,* 688–708.

Chesney-Lind, M., & Shelden, R. G. (2004). *Girls, delinquency, and juvenile justice* (3rd ed.). Belmont, CA: Thompson-Wadsworth.

Clark, D. A. (1994). Behavioural risk assessment: A methodology in practice. In N. K. Clark & G. M. Stephenson (Eds.), *Rights and risks: The application of forensic psychology. Issues in criminological and legal psychology, No. 21.* Leicester, UK: British Psychological Society.

Cleckley, H. (1976). *The mask of sanity.* St. Louis, MO: C. V. Mosby. (Originally published 1941)

Cohen, F. (2008). *The mentally disordered inmate and the law* (2nd ed.). Kingston, NJ: Civic Research Institute.

Cooper, R. P., & Werner, P. D. (1990). Predicting violence in newly admitted inmates. A lens model of staff decision making. *Criminal Justice and Behavior, 17,* 431–447.

CTB/McGraw-Hill. (1987). *Tests of Adult Basic Education (TABE).* Monterey, CA: Author.

Cunningham, M. D., & Reidy, T. J. (1999). Don't confuse me with the facts: Common errors in risk assessment at capital sentencing. *Criminal Justice and Behavior, 26,* 20–43.

Daffern, M., Ogloff, J. R. P., Ferguson, M., & Thomson, L. (2005). Assessing risk for aggression in a forensic psychiatric hospital using the Level of Service Inventory-Revised: Screening Version. *International Journal of Forensic Mental Health, 4,* 201–206.

Dahle, K. P. (2006). Strength and limitations of actuarial prediction of criminal reoffence in a German prison sample: A comparative study of LSI-R, HCR-20, and PCL-R. *International Journal of Law and Psychiatry, 29,* 431–442.

Daly, K. (1994). *Gender, crime, and punishment.* New Haven, CT: Yale University Press.

Davis. A., Bardos, A., & Woodward, K. M. (2006). Convergent validity of the General Ability Measure for Adults (GAMA) with sudden onset neurological impairment. *International Journal of Neuroscience, 116,* 1215–1221.

DeWolfe, A. S., & Ryan, J. J. (1984). Wechsler Performance IQ &gt; Verbal IQ index in a forensic sample: A reconsideration. *Journal of Clinical Psychology, 40,* 291–294.

Doren, D. M., & Megargee, E. I. (1980, February). The nature and prediction of typological changes when employing the MMPI criminal classification system. *The Differential View: A Publication of the International Differential Treatment Association,* 28–41.

Douglas, K. S., & Skeem, J. L. (2005). Violence risk assessment: Getting specific about being dynamic. *Psychology, Public Policy, and Law, 11,* 347–383.

Douglas, K. S., & Webster, C. D. (1999). The HCR-20 violence risk assessment scheme: Concurrent validity in a sample of incarcerated offenders. *Criminal Justice and Behavior, 26,* 3–19.

Douglas, K. S., Yeomans, M., & Boer, D. P. (2005). Comparative validity analysis of multiple measures of violence risk in a sample of criminal offenders. *Criminal Justice and Behavior, 32,* 479–510.

Dyer, F. J., & McCann, J. T. (2000). The Millon Clinical Inventories: Research critical of their forensic application and *Daubert* criteria. *Law and Human Behavior, 24,* 487–498.

Fass, T. L., Heilbrun, K., DeMatteo, D., & Fretz, R. (2008). The LSI-R and COMPAS: Validation data on two risk-needs tools. *Criminal Justice and Behavior, 35,* 1095–1108.

Forth, A. E., Kosson, D. S., & Hare, R. D. (2003). *Psychopathy Checklist: Youth Version (PCL: YV).* Toronto, Canada: Multi-Health Systems.

Fowler, R. (1976). Sweeping reforms ordered in Alabama prisons. *APA Monitor, 7*(4), 1, 15.

Gearing, M. I. II (1981). The new MMPI typology for prisoners: The beginning of a new era in correctional research and (hopefully) practice. [Review of *Classifying criminal offenders: A new system based on the MMPI.*] *Journal of Personality Assessment, 45,* 102–107

Gendreau, P., Goggin, C. E., & Smith, P. (2002). Is the PCL-R really the "unparalleled" measure of offender risk? *Criminal Justice and Behavior, 29,* 397–426.

Girard, L., & Wormith, J. S. (2004). The predictive validity of the Level of Service Inventory—Ontario Revision on general and violent recidivism among various offender groups. *Criminal Justice and Behavior, 31,* 150–181.

Glaser, D. (1987). Classification for risk. In D. M. Gottfredson, & M. Tonry (Eds.), *Prediction and classification in criminal justice decision making* (pp. 249–291). Chicago, IL: University of Chicago Press.

Goeke, R. K., Tosi, D. J., & Eshbaugh, D. M. (1993). Personality patterns of male felons in a correctional halfway house setting: An MMPI typological analysis. *Journal of Clinical Psychology, 49,* 413–422.

Goodloe, N. (2009, Winter). Lessons learned: Evidence-based practices in the real world. *American Probation and Parole Association Perspectives,* 32–42.

Graham, J. R. (2006). *MMPI-2: Assessing personality and psychopathology* (4th ed.). New York, NY: Oxford University Press.

Grann, M., Belfrage, H. & Tengström, A. (2000). Actuarial assessment of risk for violence: The predictive validity of the VRAG and the historical part of the HCR-20. *Criminal Justice and Behavior, 27,* 97–114.

Greene, R. L. (2011). *MMPI-2/MMPI-2-RF: An interpretive manual* (3rd ed.). Boston, MA: Allyn & Bacon.

Groth-Marnat, G. (1997). *Handbook of psychological assessment* (3rd ed.). New York, NY: Wiley.

Grove, W. M., & Meehl, P. E. (1996). Comparative efficiency of informal (subjective, impressionistic) and formal (mechanical, algorithmic) prediction procedures: The clinical-statistical controversy. *Psychology, Public Policy, and Law, 2,* 293–323.

Grove, W. M., Zald, D. R., Lebow, B. S., Snitz, B. E., & Nelson, C. (2000). Clinical vs. actuarial prediction: A meta-analysis. *Psychological Assessment, 12,* 19–30.

Hannah-Moffat, K. (2009). Gridlock or mutability: Reconsidering "gender" and risk assessment. *Criminology and Public Policy, 8,* 209–219.

Hanson, R. K., & Bussicre, M. T. (1998). Predicting relapse: A meta-analysis of sexual offender recidivism studies. *Journal of Consulting and Clinical Psychology, 66,* 348–362.

Hanson, R. K., & Morton-Bourgon, K. E. (2009). Accuracy of recidivism risk for sexual offenders: A meta-analysis of 118 prediction studies. *Psychological Assessment, 21,* 1–21.

Hanson, R. K., & Thornton, D. (1999). *Static-99: Improving actuarial risk assessment for sex offenders* (User Rep. 1999–02). Ottawa, Canada: Department of the Solicitor General of Canada.

Hare, R. D. (1996). Psychopathy: A clinical construct whose time has come. *Criminal Justice and Behavior, 23,* 25–54.

Hare, R. D. (2003). *The Hare Psychopathy Checklist-Revised (PCL R)* (2nd ed.). Toronto, Canada: Multi-Health Systems.

Hare, R. D., Harpur, T. J., Hakstian, A. R., Forth, A. E., & Hart, S. D. (1990). The Revised Psychopathy Checklist: Reliability and factor structure. *Psychological Assessment: A Journal of Consulting and Clinical Psychology, 2,* 338–341.

Harris, G. T., Rice, M. E., & Cormier, C. A. (2002). Prospective replication of the Violence Risk Appraisal Guide in predicting violent recidivism among forensic patients. *Law and Human Behavior, 26,* 377–394.

Harris, G. T., Rice, M. E., & Quinsey, V. L. (1993). Violent recidivism of mentally disordered offenders: The development of a statistical prediction instrument. *Criminal Justice and Behavior, 20,* 315–335.

Hart, S. D. (1996). Psychopathy and risk assessment. In D. J. Cooke, A. E. Forth, J. Newman, & R. D. Hare (Eds.), *International perspectives in psychopathy* (pp. 63–67). *Issues in criminological and legal psychology,* No. 24. Leicester, UK: British Psychological Society, Division of Criminological and Legal Psychology.

Hart, S. D., Hare, R. D., & Forth, A. E. (1994). Psychopathy as a risk marker for violence: Development and validation of a screening version of the revised Psychopathy Checklist. In J. Monahan & H. Steadman (Eds.), *Violence and mental disorder: Developments in risk assessment* (pp. 81–98). Chicago, IL: University of Chicago Press.

Hathaway, S. R., & McKinley, J. C. (1943). Manual for administering and scoring the MMPI. Minneapolis: University of Minnesota Press.

Heilbrun, K., & Heilbrun, A. (1995). Risk assessment with MMPI-2 in forensic evaluations. In Y. S. Ben-Porath, J. R. Graham, G. C. N. Hall, R. D. Hirschman, & M. S. Zaragoza (Eds.), *Forensic applications of MMPI-2* (pp. 160–178). Thousand Oaks, CA: Sage.

Hilton, N. Z., & Simmons, J. L. (2001). The influence of actuarial risk assessment in clinical judgments and tribunal decisions about mentally disordered offenders in maximum security. *Law and Human Behavior, 25,* 393–408.

Hiltonsmith, R. W., Hayman, P. M. & Kleinman, P. (1984). Predicting WAIS-R scores from the Revised Beta for low functioning minority group offenders. *Journal of Clinical Psychology, 40,* 1063–1066.

Hiscock, C. K., Layman, L. B., & Hiscock, M. (1994). Cross-validation of two measures for assessing feigned mental incompetence. *Criminal Justice and Behavior, 21,* 443–453.

Hiscock, C. K., Rustemier, P., & Hiscock, M. (1993). Determination of criminal responsibility: Application of the two-alternative forced-choice strategem. *Criminal Justice and Behavior, 20,* 391–405.

Hoge, R. D., & Andrews, D. A. (2006). *Youth Level of Service/Case Management Inventory user's manual.* North Tonawanda, NY: Multi-Health Systems.

Hollin, C. R., & Palmer, E. J. (2006). The Level of Service Inventory—Revised profile of English prisoners: Risk and reconviction analysis. *Criminal Justice and Behavior, 33,* 347–366.

Holsinger, A. M., Lowenkamp, C. T., & Latessa, E. (2006). Predicting institutional misconduct using the Youth Level of Service/Case Management Inventory. *American Journal of Criminal Justice, 30,* 267–284.

Holtfreter, K., & Cupp, R. (2007). Gender and risk assessment: The empirical status of the LSI-R for women. *Journal of Contemporary Criminal Justice, 23,* 363–382.

House, A. E. (1996). The Wechsler Adult Intelligence Scale—Revised (WAIS-R). In C. S. Newmark (Ed.), *Major psychological instruments* (2nd ed., pp. 329–347). Needham Heights, MA: Allyn & Bacon.

International Association for Correctional and Forensic Psychology, Practice Standards Committee (2010). Standards for psychology services in jails, prisons, correctional facilities, and agencies. *Criminal Justice and Behavior, 37,* 749–808.

Ispas, D., Iliescu, D., Ilie, A., & Johnson, R. E. (2010). Examining the criterion related validity of the General Ability Measure for Adults: A two-sample investigation. *International Journal of Selection and Assessment, 18,* 226–229.

Jung, S., & Rowena, E. (1999). Risk and needs assessment of juvenile offenders. *Criminal Justice and Behavior, 26,* 69–89.

Kay, S. I. (1991). *The constitutional dimensions of an inmate's right to health care.* Chicago, IL: National Commission on Correctional Health Care.

Kellogg, C. E., & Morton, N. W. (1934). Revised Beta examination. *Personnel Journal, 13,* 98–99.

Kellogg, C. E., & Morton, N. W. (1978). *Revised Beta examination—Second Edition.* San Antonio, TX: Psychological Corporation.

Kellogg, C. E., & Morton, N. W. (1999). *Beta III manual.* San Antonio, TX: Pearson.

Kennedy, D. B. (1993). [Review of *Suicide behind bars* by D. Lester & B. L. Danto]. *Criminal Justice and Behavior, 20,* 306–309.

Kroner, D. G., & Mills, J. F. (2001). The accuracy of five risk appraisal instruments in predicting institutional misconduct and new convictions. *Criminal Justice and Behavior, 28,* 471–479.

Kroner, D. G., Statdland, M., Eidt, M., & Nedopil, N. (2007). The validity of the Violence Risk Appraisal Guide (VRAG) in predicting criminal recidivism. *Criminal Behaviour and Mental Health, 17,* 89–100.

Lassiter, K. S., Bell, N. L., Hutchinson, M. B., & Matthews, T. D. (2001). College students' performance on the General Ability Measure for Adults and the Wechsler Intelligence Scale for Adults—Third Edition. *Psychology in the Schools, 38,* 1–10.

Lassiter, K. S., Leverett, J. P., & Safa, T. A., (2000). The validity of the General Ability Measure for Adults: Comparison with WAIS-R IQ scores in a sample of college students with academic difficulties. *Assessment, 7,* 63–72.

Lassiter, K. S., & Matthews, T. D. (1999). Test-retest reliability of the General Ability Measure for Adults. *Perceptual and Motor Skills, 88,* 531–534.

Lassiter, K. S., Matthews, T. D., Bell, N. L., & Maher, C. M. (2002). Comparison of the General Ability Measure for Adults and the Kaufman Adolescent and Adult Intelligence Test with college students. *Psychology in the Schools, 39,* 497–506.

Leistico, A. R., Salekin, R. T., DeCoster, J., & Rogers, R. (2000). A large-scale meta-analysis relating the Hare measures of psychopathy to antisocial conduct. *Law and Human Behavior, 32,* 28–45.

Leverett, J. P., Matthews, T. D., Lassiter, K. S., & Bell, N. L. (2001). Validity comparison of the General Ability Measure for Adults with the Wonderlic Personnel Test. *North American Journal of Psychology, 31,* 173–182.

Levine, R. V. (1969). The MMPI and Revised Beta as predictors of academic and vocational success in a correctional institution. *FCI Research Reports, 1*(3), 1–52.

Levinson, R. (1988). Developments in the classification process: Quay's AIMS approach. *Criminal Justice and Behavior, 15,* 24–38.

Lindner, R. M., & Gurvitz, M. (1946). Restandardization of the Revised Beta Examination to yield Wechsler type of IQ. *Journal of Applied Psychology, 30,* 649–658.

Lissitz, R. W. (1992). Review of Tests of Adult Basic Education, Forms 5 & 6 and Survey Form. In J. J. Kramer & J. C. Conley (Eds.), *The eleventh mental measurements yearbook* (pp. 984–985). Lincoln: Buros Institute of Mental Measurements of the University of Nebraska, Lincoln.

Loring, D. W., & Bauer, R. M. (2010). Testing the limits: Cautions and concerns regarding the new Wechsler IQ and memory scales. *Neurology, 74,* 685–690.

Loza, W., & Dhaliwal, G. (1997). Psychometric evaluation of the Risk Appraisal Guide (RAG): A tool for assessing violent recidivism. *Journal of Interpersonal Violence, 12,* 779–793.

Matthews, T. D., Lassiter, K. S., & Habedenk, H. (2001). Validity of two brief measures: The General Ability Measure for Adults and the Shipley Institute of Living Scale. *Perceptual and Motor Skills, 92,* 881–887.

McNiel, D. E., Binder, R. L., & Robinson, J. C. (2005). Incarceration associated with homelessness, mental disorder, and cooccurring substance abuse. *Psychiatric Services, 56,* 840–846.

Meehl, P. E. (1954). *Clinical versus statistical prediction.* Minneapolis: University of Minnesota Press.

Meehl, P. E. (1957). When shall we use our heads instead of the formula? *Journal of Counseling Psychology, 4,* 268–273.

Meehl, P. E. (1977). Why I do not attend case conferences. In *Psychodiagnosis: Selected papers* (pp. 255–302). New York, NY: Norton.

Megargee, E. I. (1970). The prediction of violence with psychological tests. In C. D. Spielberger (Ed.), *Current topics in clinical and community psychology* (Vol. 2, pp. 97–156). New York, NY: Academic Press.

Megargee, E. I. (1994). Using the Megargee MMPI-based classification system with the MMPI-2s of male prison inmates. *Psychological Assessment, 6,* 337–344.

Megargee, E. I. (1997). Using the Megargee MMPI-based classification system with MMPI-2s of female prison inmates. *Psychological Assessment, 9,* 75–82.

Megargee, E. I. (2003). Psychological assessment in correctional settings. In J. R. Graham & J. A. Naglieri (Eds.), *Handbook of psychology, Vol. 10: Assessment psychology* (pp. 365–388). Hoboken, NJ: Wiley.

Megargee, E. I. (2006). Using the MMPI-2 in criminal justice and correctional settings. Minneapolis: University of Minnesota Press.

Megargee, E. I. (2009). Understanding and assessing aggression and violence. In J. N. Butcher (Ed.), *Oxford handbook of personality assessment* (pp. 542–566). New York, NY: Oxford University Press.

Megargee, E. I., & Bohn, M. J. (1977). A new classification system for criminal offenders, IV: Empirically determined characteristics of the ten types. *Criminal Justice and Behavior, 4,* 149–210.

Megargee, E. I., & Bohn, M. J. Jr., with Meyer, J. Jr., & Sink, F. (1979). *Classifying criminal offenders: A new system based on the MMPI.* Beverly Hills, CA: Sage.

Megargee, E. I., & Carbonell, J. L. (1995). Use of the MMPI-2 in correctional settings. In Y. S. Ben-Porath, J. R. Graham, G. C. N. Hall, R. D. Hirschman, & M. S. Zaragoza (Eds.), *Forensic applications of MMPI-2* (pp. 127–159). Thousand Oaks, CA: Sage.

Megargee, E. I., Carbonell, J. L., Bohn, M. J. Jr., & Sliger, G. L. (2001). *Classifying criminal offenders with MMPI-2: The Megargee system.* Minneapolis: University of Minnesota Press.

Megargee, E. I., Mercer, S. J. & Carbonell, J. L. (1999). MMPI-2 with male and female state and federal prison inmates. *Psychological Assessment, 11,* 177–185.

Meloy, J. R., & Gacono, C. (1995). Assessing the psychopathic personality. In J. N. Butcher (Ed.), *Clinical personality assessment: Practical approaches* (pp. 410–422). New York, NY: Oxford University Press.

Millon, C. (1997). Using the MCMI in correctional settings. In T. Millon (Ed.), *The Millon inventories: Clinical and personality assessment* (pp. 140–153). New York, NY: Guilford Press.

Millon, T. (1977). *Millon Clinical Multiaxial Inventory.* Minneapolis, MN: National Computer Systems.

Millon, T. (1987). *Manual for the MCMI-II* (2nd ed.). Minneapolis, MN: National Computer Systems.

Millon, T., & Davis, R. D. (1996). *Disorders of personality: DSM-IV and beyond.* New York, NY: Wiley.

Millon, T., & Davis, R. D. (1997). The MCMI-III: Present and future directions. *Journal of Personality Assessment, 68,* 69–85.

Millon, T., & Green, C. (1989). Interpretive guide to the Millon Clinical Multiaxial Inventory (MCMI-II). In C. S. Newmark (Ed.), *Major psychological instruments* (Vol. 2, pp. 5–43). Boston, MA: Allyn & Bacon.

Millon, T., & Millon, C. (2006). *MCMI-III (Millon Clinical Multiaxial Inventory-III manual)* (3rd ed.). Minneapolis, MN: NCS Pearson.

Millon, T., & Millon, C. (2009). *MCMI-III (Millon Clinical Multiaxial Inventory-III: Corrections report user's guide)* (rev. ed.). Minneapolis, MN: NCS Pearson.

Mills, J. F., Jones, M. N., & Kroner, D. G. (2005). An examination of the generalizability of the LSI-R and VRAG probability bins. *Criminal Justice and Behavior, 32,* 565–585.

Monahan, J. (1980). *Who is the client? The ethics of psychological intervention in the criminal justice system.* Washington, DC: American Psychological Association.

Monahan, J. (1981). *Predicting violent behavior: An assessment of clinical techniques.* Beverly Hills, CA: Sage.

Monahan, J. (1996). Violence prediction: The past twenty years. *Criminal Justice and Behavior, 23,* 107–120.

Morash, M. (2009). A great debate over using the Level of Service Inventory—Revised (LSI-R) with women. *Criminology and Public Policy, 8,* 173–181.

Mrad, D. F., Kabacoff, R. A., & Duckro, P. (1983). Validation of the Megargee typology in a halfway house setting. *Criminal Justice and Behavior, 10,* 252–262.

Munetz, M. R., & Griffin, P. A. (2006). Use of the Sequential Intercept Model as an approach to decriminalization of people with serious mental illness. *Psychiatric Services, 57,* 544–549.

Naglieri, J. A., & Bardos, A. (1997). *GAMA (General Ability Measure for Adults) manual.* Minneapolis, MN: Pearson.

National Advisory Commission on Criminal Justice Standards and Goals. (1973). *Report on corrections.* Washington, DC: U.S. Department of Justice, Law Enforcement Assistance Administration.

National Center for Education Statistics. (1994). *Literacy behind prison walls: Profiles of the prison population from the National Adult Literacy Survey* (NCES 1994–102). Washington, DC: U.S. Department of Education, Office of Educational Research and Improvement.

National Commission on Correctional Health Care. (2004). *Standards for health services in juvenile detention and confinement facilities.* Chicago, IL: Author.

National Commission on Correctional Health Care. (2008a). *Standards for health services in jails.* Chicago, IL: Author.

National Commission on Correctional Health Care. (2008b). *Standards for health services in prisons.* Chicago, IL: Author.

National Commission on Correctional Health Care. (2008c). *Standards for mental health services in correctional facilities.* Chicago, IL: Author.

Nichols, W. (1980). *The classification of law offenders with the MMPI: A methodological study.* Doctoral Dissertation, University of Alabama, 1979. [*Dissertation Abstracts International, 41*(1), 333-B.]

Northpointe Institute for Public Management. (2010, January 14). *COMPAS Risk and Need Assessment System: Selected Questions Posed by Inquiring Agencies.* Retrieved from www.northpointe.com

O'Brien, P. (2001). "Just like baking a cake": Women describe the necessary ingredients for successful reentry after incarceration. *Families in Society: The Journal of Contemporary Social Services, 82,* 287–295.

Onifade, E., Davidson, W., Campbell, C., Turke, G., Malinowski, J., & Turner, K. (2008). Predicting recidivism in probationers with the Youth Level of Service/Case Management Inventory (YLS/CMI). *Criminal Justice and Behavior, 35,* 474–483.

Onifade, E., Smith Nandoro, A., Davidson, W. S., & Campbell, C. (2010). Truancy and patterns of criminogenic risk in a young offender population. *Youth Violence and Criminal Justice, 8, 3–18.*

Palmer, E. J., & Hollin, C. (2007). The Level of Service Inventory—Revised with English women offenders. *Criminal Justice and Behavior, 34,* 971–984.

Pankratz, L. (1979). Symptom validity testing and symptom retraining: Procedures for assessment and treatment of sensory deficits. *Journal of Consulting and Clinical Psychology, 47,* 409–410.

Patrogiannis, K., Bardos, A. N., & Politko, N. (1999). *A cross-cultural investigation of the General Ability Measure for Adults (GAMA) in Greece.* Paper presented at the International Conference of Test Adaptation, Washington, DC.

Proctor, J. L. (1994). Evaluating a modified version of the federal prison system's inmate classification model: An assessment of objectivity and predictive validity. *Criminal Justice and Behavior, 21,* 256–272.

Puzzanchera, C. (2009), Juvenile arrests, 2007. *Juvenile Justice Bulletin.* Washington, DC: Office of Justice Programs, U.S. Department of Justice.

Quinsey, V. L., Harris, G. T., Rice, M. E., & Cormier, C. A. (2006). *Violent offenders: Appraising and managing risk* (2nd ed.). Washington, DC: American Psychological Association.

Raiford, S. E., & Coalson, D. L. (2008, August). *WAIS-IV revision goals; New, retained, and dropped subtests, and structure.* Paper presented at the meeting of the American Psychological Association, Boston, MA.

Rees, L. M., Tombaugh, T. N., Gansler, D. A., & Moczynski, N. P. (1998). Five validation experiments of the Test of Memory Malingering. *Psychological Assessment, 10,* 10–20.

Rennie, C., & Dolan, M. (2010). Predictive validity of the Youth Level of Service/Case Management Inventory in a custody sample in England. *Journal of Forensic Psychiatry and Psychology, 21,* 407–425.

Rettinger, L. J., & Andrews, D. A. (2010). General risk and need, gender specificity, and the recidivism of female offenders. *Criminal Justice and Behavior, 37,* 29–46.

Retzleff, P. D. (2000). Comment on the validity of the MCMI. *Law and Human Behavior, 24,* 425–444.

Retzleff, P. D. Stoner, J. & Kleinsasser, D. (2002). The use of the MCMI-III in the screening and triage of offenders. *International Journal of Offender Therapy and Comparative Criminology, 46,* 319–332.

Rice, M. E., & Harris, G. T. (1994, May). *The actuarial prediction of violent recidivism among sex offenders.* Paper presented at the conference on the assesment and management of risk in the sex offender, Clarke Institute of Psychiatry, Toronto, Ontario, Canada.

Rice, M. E., & Harris, G. T. (1995). Violent recidivism: Assessing predictive validity. *Journal of Consulting and Clinical Psychology, 63,* 737–748.

Rogers, B. G. (1998). Review of Tests of Adult Basic Education, Forms 7, & 8. In J. C. Impara & B. S. Plake (Eds.), *The thirteenth mental measurements yearbook* (pp. 1083–1085). Lincoln: Buros Institute of Mental Measurements of the University of Nebraska, Lincoln.

Rogers, R., Salekin, R. T., & Sewell, K. W. (1999). Validation of the Millon Clinical Multiaxial Inventory for Axis II disorders: Does it meet the *Daubert* standard? *Law and Human Behavior, 23,* 425–443.

Rogers, R., Salekin, R. T., & Sewell, K. W. (2000). The MCMI-III and the *Daubert* standard: Separating rhetoric from reality. *Law and Human Behavior, 24,* 501–506.

Rowan, J. (1998). *Suicide prevention in custody.* Lanham, MD: American Correctional Association.

Sabol, W. J., West, H. C. & Cooper, M. (2010). *Bulletin of Justice Statistics Bulletin: Prisoners in 2008* (NJC 228417). Issued December 2009; revised June 30, 2010. Washington, DC: U.S. Department of Justice, Office of Justice Programs, Bureau of Justice Statistics.

Salekin, R. T., Rogers, R., & Sewell, K. W. (1996). A review and meta-analysis of the Psychopathy Checklist and the Psychopathy Checklist—Revised. Predictive validity of dangerousness. *Clinical Psychology: Science and Practice, 3,* 203–215.

Salisbury, E., & Van Voorhis, P. (2009). Gendered pathways: A quantitative investigation of women probationers' paths to incarceration. *Criminal Justice and Behavior, 36,* 541–566.

Schlager, M. D., & Simourd, D. J. (2007). Validity of the Level of Service Inventory—Revised (LSI-R) among African American and Hispanic male offenders. *Criminal Justice and Behavior, 34,* 545–554.

Schmidt, F., Campbell, M. A., & Houlding, C. (2111). Comparative analysis of the YLS/CMI, SAVRY, & PCL:YV in adolescent offenders: A 10-year follow-up into adulthood. *Youth Violence and Juvenile Justice, 9,* 23–42.

Schretelen, D. (1988). The use of psychological tests to identify malingered symptoms of mental disorder. *Clinical Psychology Review, 8,* 451–476.

Shaffer, C. E., Pettigrew, C. G., Blouin, D., & Edwards, D. W. (1983). Multivariate classification of female offender MMPI profiles. *Journal of Crime and Justice, 6,* 57–66.

Shutte, J. W. (2001). Using the MCMI-III in forensic evaluations. *American Journal of Forensic Psychology, 19,* 5–20.

Simourd, D. J. (2004). Use of dynamic risk/need assessment instruments among long-term incarcerated offenders. *Criminal Justice and Behavior, 31,* 306–323.

Singh, J. P., & Fazel, S. (2010). Forensic risk assessment: A metareview. *Criminal Justice and Behavior, 37,* 965–988.

Sliger, G. L. (1992). *The MMPI-based classification system for adult criminal offenders: A critical review* (Unpublished manuscript). Florida State University, Department of Psychology, Tallahassee, FL.

Sliger, G. L. (1997). *The applicability of the Megargee MMPI-based offender classification system to the MMPI-2s of women inmates* (Unpublished doctoral dissertation). Florida State University, Tallahassee, FL.

Small, M. A., & Otto, R. K. (1991). Evaluations of competency for execution. Legal contours and implications for assessment. *Criminal Justice and Behavior, 18,* 146–158.

Smith, P., Cullen, F. T., & Latessa, E. J. (2009). Can 14,737 women be wrong? A meta-analysis of the LSI-R and recidivism for female offenders. *Criminology and Public Policy, 8,* 183–208.

Solomon, L., & Camp, A. T. (1993). The revolution in correctional classification. In American Correctional Association (Ed.), *Classification: A tool for managing today's offenders* (pp. 1–16). Laurel, MD: Author.

Spruill, J., & May, J. (1988). The mentally retarded offender: Prevalence rates based on individual intelligence tests. *Criminal Justice and Behavior, 15,* 484–491.

Steadman, H. J., Osher, F. F., Robbins, P. C., Case, B., & Samuels, S. (2009). Prevalence of serious mental illness among jail inmates. *Psychiatric Services, 60,* 761–765.

Steuber, H. (1975). The prediction of academic success with the Minnesota Multiphasic Personality Inventory (MMPI) and the California Psychological Inventory (CPI) in a correctional institution. *FCI Research Reports, 5*(2), 1–28.

Stoner, J. W. (2008). Using the MCMI in corrections. In T. Millon & C. Bloom (Eds.), *The Millon inventories: A practitioner's guide* (2nd ed., pp. 196–243). New York, NY: Guilford Press.

Suedfeld, P., & Landon, P. B. (1978). Approaches to treatment. In R. D. Hare & D. Schalling (Eds.), *Psychopathic behavior: Approaches to treatment.* New York, NY: Wiley.

Taylor, K. N., & Blanchette, K. (2009). The women are not wrong: It is the approach that is debatable. *Criminology and Public Policy, 8,* 221–229.

Teplin, L. (1990). The prevalence of severe mental disorder among urban jail detainees: Comparison with the Epidemiological Catchment Area program. *American Journal of Public Health, 80,* 663–669.

Teplin, L. (1996). Prevalence of psychiatric disorders among incarcerated women. *Archives of General Psychiatry, 53,* 505–512.

Thompson, A. P., & Putnins, A. L. (2003). Risk-need assessment inventories for juvenile offenders in Australia. *Psychiatry, Psychology, and the Law, 10,* 324–333.

Tidmarsh, D. (1997). Risk assessment among prisoners: A view from a Parole Board member. *International Review of Psychiatry, 9,* 273–281.

Tombaugh, T. N. (1997). The Test of Memory Malingering (TOMM): Normative data from cognitively intact and cognitively impaired individuals. *Psychological Assessment, 9,* 260–268.

Torrey, E., Stieber, J., Ezekial, J., Wolfe, S. M., Sharfstein, J., Noble, J. H., & Flynn, L. M. (1992). *Criminalizing the mentally ill: The abuse of jails as hospitals.* Washington, DC: Public Citizen's Health Research Group and the National Alliance for the Mentally Ill.

Towl, G., & Crighton, D. (1995). Risk assessment in prison: A psychological critique. *Forensic Update, 40,* 6–14. (Published by the Division of Criminological and Legal Psychology of the British Psychological Society.)

VandeCreek, L. & Knapp, S. (1989). *Tarasoff and beyond: Legal and clinical considerations in the treatment of life-endangering patients.* Sarasota, FL: Practitioner's Resource Series.

Vanderhoff, H., Jeglic, E. L., & Donovick, P. J. (2011). Neuropsychological assessment in prisons: Ethical and practical challenges. *Journal of Correctional Health Care, 17,* 51–60.

Van Voorhis, P., & Groot, B. (2010, November). *Turning large ships: Effecting agency change through program assessments, action planning, and targeted training.* Paper presented at the annual meeting of the International Community Corrections Association, Louisville, KY.

Van Voorhis, P., Wright, E., Salisbury, E., & Bauman, A. (2010). Women's risk factors and their contribution to existing risk/needs assessment. *Criminal Justice and Assessment, 37,* 261–288.

Viljoen, J. L., McLachlan, K., & Vincent, G. M. (2010). Assessing violence risk and psychopathy in juvenile and adult offenders: A survey of clinical practice. *Assessment, 17,* 377–395.

Webster, C. D., Douglas, K. S., Eaves, D., & Hart, S. D. (1997). *HCR-20: Assessing risk for violence* (Version 2). Burnaby, Canada: Mental Health, Law, & Policy Institute, Simon Fraser University.

Webster, C. D., Harris, G. T., Rice, M. E., Cormier, C., & Quinsey, V. L. (1994). *The Violence Prediction Scheme: Assessing dangerousness in high risk men.* Toronto, Canada: University of Toronto.

Webster, C. D., & Menzies, R. J. (1993). Supervision in the deinstitutionalized community. In S. Hodgins (Ed.), *Mental disorder and crime* (pp. 22–38). Newbury Park, CA: Sage.

Wechsler, D. (1939). *Wechsler Bellevue Intelligence Scale.* New York, NY: Psychological Corporation.

Wechsler, D. (1955). *Wechsler Adult Intelligence Scale.* New York, NY: Psychological Corporation.

Wechsler, D. (1981). *Wechsler Adult Intelligence Scale—Revised.* San Antonio, TX: Psychological Corporation.

Wechsler, D. (1997). *Wechsler Adult Intelligence Scale—Third Edition.* San Antonio, TX: Psychological Corporation.

Wechsler, D., Coalson, D. L., & Raiford, S. E. (2008). *Wechsler Adult Intelligence Test: Fourth Edition. Technical and Interpretive manual.* San Antonio, TX: Pearson.

Wechsler, D., Holdnack, J., & Drozdick, L. W. (2009). *Wechsler Memory Scale: Fourth Edition. Technical and Interpretive manual.* San Antonio, TX: Pearson.

Wells, D., & Brennan, T. (2009). *The Michigan classification project.* Traverse City, MI: Northpointe Institute for Public Management.

Welsh, J. L., Schmidt, F., McKinnon, L., Chattha, H. K., & Meyers, J. R. (2008). A comparative study of adolescent risk assessment instruments: Predictive and incremental validity. *Assessment, 15,* 104–115.

Williams, K. W. (2010, August). *Youth Level of Service/Case Management Inventory 2.0 (YLS/CMI 2.0).* Paper presented at the annual meeting of the American Psychological Association Convention, San Diego, CA.

Wong, S. C. P., & Gordon, A. (2006). The validity and reliability of the Violence Risk Scale: A treatment-friendly violence risk assessment tool. *Psychology, Public Policy, and the Law, 12,* 279–309.

Wright, K. N. (1986). An exploratory study of transactional classification. *Journal of Research in Crime and Delinquency, 23,* 595–618.

Wright, K. N. (1988). The relationship of risk, needs, and personality classification systems and prison adjustment. *Criminal Justice and Behavior, 15,* 454–471.

Zafiris, C., & Bardos, A. (2009, August). *Using the GAMA and the OPIE-3 (MR) formula in estimating pre-morbid functioning.* Paper presented at the meeting of the American Psychological Association, Toronto, Canada.

Zager, L. D. (1988). The MMPI-based criminal classification system: A review, current status, and future directions. *Criminal Justice and Behavior, 15,* 39–57.

CHAPTER 17

# Assessment in Geriatric Settings

BARRY A. EDELSTEIN, RONALD R. MARTIN, AND LINDSAY A. GEROLIMATOS

In 2009 there were 39.6 million adults 65 years of age and older in the United States, representing 12.9% of the population (Administration on Aging, 2009). This percentage is expected to increase dramatically now that baby boomers are reaching the age of 65. There will be approximately 72.1 million older adults by 2030, comprising approximately 19% of the U.S. population (Administration on Aging, 2009). In addition, the older adult population is getting older. From 1920 to 2010, the population of adults age 85 and older is expected to increase 31-fold (Administration on Aging, 2010a). Most adults age successfully (cf. Rowe & Kahn, 1998). In 2008, 39.1% of noninstitutionalized older adults rated their heath as excellent or very good (Administration on Aging, 2010a). When adults age 65 and older were recently asked about their mental health concerns (including stress, depression, and problems with emotion), only 6.5% reported frequent mental distress, where mental distress was defined as 14 or more days of poor mental health (Centers for Disease Control, 2010). Notwithstanding these rather encouraging figures regarding older adult longevity, health, and mental health, older adults do experience mental health problems, and there are age-related increases in chronic health problems. The interaction of these factors with normal human development poses a unique challenge for psychological assessment.

The principal goal of this chapter is to acquaint the reader with assessment issues that are relatively unique to older adults, with a focus on those factors that could influence the process or outcome of clinical assessment. We begin with the discussions of two intra- and interpersonal

variables: bias in the form of ageism and cultural competence. Ignorance of the importance and influence of these variables can lead to the corruption, contamination, and invalidation of the entire assessment enterprise. We then consider biological and medical issues that are more common among older adults that can play a significant role in the interplay between biological and environmental factors. Next we shift to two conceptual issues, beginning with the assessment paradigms within which the clinician performs the assessment. We then address diagnostic issues and question the prudence of utilizing traditional diagnostic taxonomies with older adults. The complexities of carrying out clinical assessments are then addressed through discussions of multiple method and multidimensional assessment. We follow this with a discussion of psychometric considerations for developing or selecting assessment instruments suitable for older adults. We end the chapter with a brief conclusion and discussion of future directions in the assessment of older adults.

## INTRA- AND INTERPERSONAL ISSUES

### Ageism

Ageism involves stereotyping, prejudice, or discrimination based on age (Butler, 1969). Although any age group can experience ageism, it is particularly common among older adults (Kimmel, 1988). In a study of adults age 60 and older, nearly 77% experienced at least one incidence of ageism (Palmore, 2001). Ageism against older adults is a remarkably unique form of discrimination, given that all individuals will grow old (Palmore, 2001). Butler (1980) outlined three components of ageism related to older adults: (1) prejudicial attitudes toward older adults and aging, (2) discriminatory practices against older adults, and (3) institutional policies that limit opportunities available to older adults. Indeed, evidence shows that ageism affects the provision of health services (Gatz & Pearson, 1988; James & Haley, 1995; Robb, Chen, & Haley, 2002), including the assessment process. Many of these prejudicial attitudes are borne of myths about the aging process and older adults.

## Negative Myths of Aging

The assessment process is not without ageism (Robb et al., 2002). Clinicians possess ageist attitudes, which can affect screening processes, diagnoses, and treatment. Older adults may receive different screening procedures from younger adults and are more likely to be treated for ailments with medications (James & Haley, 1995; Robb et al., 2002). Recent evidence suggests that age biases may be confounded with health biases, such that those of poorer health receive different medical treatments from healthier adults (Robb et al., 2002). Given that medical problems increase with age, clinicians must be mindful of ageist and biased practices.

With respect to the myths of aging, Thornton (2002) proposed six common misconceptions describing older adults as: (1) poor in health, (2) lacking vigor or activity, (3) senile or declining in cognitive function, (4) unable to learn, (5) sexless, and (6) sad, depressed, or lonely. Many older adults do experience at least one chronic health problem, with hypertension, arthritis, and heart disease among the most common illnesses (Administration on Aging, 2010b). Although the prevalence of illness and comorbidity increases with age, older adults are less likely than young adults to have acute illness or experience accidents and injuries (Palmore, 1999).

Despite these health issues, older adults continue to maintain active lifestyles. For example, the participation of older adults in the labor force has increased substantially over the past few decades. In 2009, adults age 55 and older comprised 19% of the labor force, the highest percentage since 1948 (Johnson & Kaminski, 2010). Therefore, clinicians must recognize that older adults continue to contribute to society.

That older adults experience significant cognitive decline is exaggerated. Whereas normative, age-related declines in cognitive processes such as processing speed (Salthouse, 1994), working memory, and episodic memory (Luo & Craik, 2008) occur, other cognitive abilities are maintained (e.g., recognition, procedural memory, and semantic memory; Luo & Craik, 2008) or increase (e.g., crystallized intelligence) with age. Older adults are able to compensate for some age-related declines with, for instance, enhanced emotion regulation skills (Charles, 2010; Orgeta, 2009). According to Selective Optimization with Compensation theory (Baltes & Baltes, 1990), older adults cope with limitations by selecting situations to focus their resources, optimizing the likelihood of gains, and compensating for any losses. Further, chronological age does not largely affect one's ability to learn (Poon, 1995), and repeated practice or teaching can help older adults retain new skills (Kramer & Willis, 2002). Overall, it appears that older adults do maintain cognitive abilities and are capable of learning new information and skills.

Last, the notion that older adulthood is a time of depression and isolation is unsupported. Only 1% to 5% of older adults suffer from depression, which is lower than the prevalence of depression in the general population (Beekman, Copeland, & Prince, 1999). Also, older adults continue to maintain positive social support networks. The size of social networks decrease in late life, though the qualities of the social relationships are maintained (e.g., Fung, Carstensen, & Lang, 2001). The trade-off between size and quality of relationships enhances older adults' abilities to meet their emotional needs as they near the end of life (Carstensen, 1991). Loneliness and isolation are not common experiences of adults over the age of 65; however, isolation does appear to disproportionally affect the oldest old (Dykstra, 2009). In general, many older adults report that they are happy (Palmore, 1999).

## Effects of Myths on Assessment

Many of the myths just described affect the assessment process. For example, the notion that older adults have poorer health may result in more referrals to physicians for medications. Similarly, the belief that older adults cannot learn new skills and are less likely to demonstrate progress in treatment (James & Haley, 1995) may result in fewer older adults referred for mental health services (Gatz & Pearson, 1988). Given that older adults tend to take more than one medication, the reliance on medications for treatment of psychological problems, in lieu of therapy, is alarming as it may increase the risk of adverse drug reactions (Qato, Alexander, Conti, Johnson, Schumm, & Lindau, 2008).

There is also a tendency to attribute many presenting problems to age, such as assuming depressive symptoms are a normal part of the aging process. In addition, the older adult is more likely to receive a diagnosis of dementia relative to younger adults (Gatz & Pearson, 1988), which may reflect the misconception that older adults are likely to experience significant cognitive decline. A focus on cognitive decline and dementia may detract from other problems the older adult may be experiencing (e.g., depression in dementia). Therefore, older adults may be denied appropriate services as a result of ageist beliefs.

## Positive Ageism

In addition to negative stereotypes of aging, there are also positive stereotypes of the older adult, though less attention had been afforded this phenomenon. Palmore (1999) identified eight characteristics often attributed to older adults: They are kind, wise, dependable, affluent, have substantial political power, have the freedom to engage in any activities they want, are eternally youthful, and are generally happy. However, positive stereotypes can also have deleterious effects on the assessment process. For instance, there may be a tendency to exaggerate the competencies of the aged or overlook some shortcomings, which can lead to erroneous diagnoses and treatment plans (Gatz & Pearson, 1988). These efforts to avoid negative discrimination may in fact be a disservice to meeting the needs of the older client.

To avoid the effects of ageism, both positive and negative, professionals should learn about the aging process and gain more exposure to older adults. Clinicians should also become aware of and examine their personal feelings about aging. As part of this process, clinicians need to challenge their own beliefs and seek evidence to refute their assumptions. It is also essential that professionals assess how biases may affect their professional performance. Finally, it is important to appreciate that ageism can affect older adults' behavior, as they come to learn about and adopt these attitudes themselves.

## CULTURAL AND ETHNIC ISSUES

The influence of ethnicity and culture on the assessment process is becoming an increasingly important consideration in providing mental health services to older adults. In 2010, 20% of Americans age 65 and older and 15% of adults 85 and older identified as an ethnic minority (Vincent & Velkoff, 2010). Among American adults age 65 and older, 9% identified as African American, 7% as Latino, and 3% as Asian. These numbers are expected to grow considerably in the next 40 years (Vincent & Velkoff, 2010). Furthermore, the number of individuals

identifying as biracial is also expected to increase considerably (Vincent & Velkoff, 2010). The growing number of non-White older adults necessitates culturally competent assessment.

With respect to cultural competence, the American Psychological Association (2003) recommended several guidelines. A culturally competent psychologist must be committed to cultural awareness of the self and others and must recognize that all individuals possess various social identities (e.g., gender, sexual orientation, socioeconomic status). Both the clinician and the client bring their own cultural perspectives to the assessment process, and these facets must be acknowledged. A culturally competent clinician should integrate culturally appropriate skills into practice, such as using suitable, empirically supported assessments with certain groups. As a first step in increasing competence, clinicians must gain knowledge about various cultural and ethnic groups.

One important consideration for assessment is that symptoms may present differently for older adults in various ethnic groups. In particular, somatization is more common in ethnic minority groups, especially among Asians and African Americans (Kirmayer & Young, 1998). It is important to note that somatization occurs in all cultures but is more common among certain groups or subgroups (Kirmayer, 2001). In addition, the ways in which ethnic minority older adults describe the symptoms can differ across various groups (Kirmayer, 2001). For example, the term nerves or nervios may be used to describe the experience of anxiety (Kirmayer, 2001). Similarly, there are disorders that are unique to certain ethnic groups. The Hopi Indians of Arizona have a major depression–like disorder that lacks the dysphoria component (Mouton & Esparza, 2000). In Japan, a disorder known as taijin kyofusho resembles social phobia, though the concern centers on upsetting others rather than embarrassing the self (Kirmayer, 2001). Finally, the means by which individuals cope with their psychological distress can differ across cultures. Within the African American population, it is not uncommon to cope with symptoms of depression via prayer or by engaging in activities to distract oneself (Conner et al., 2010).

Often, greater stigma is attached to mental illness within ethnic minority communities. Older Korean Americans are more likely than younger Korean Americans to believe that mental illness is a sign of personal weakness and that mental health problems can bring shame to a family (Jang, Chiriboga, & Okazaki, 2009). Older African Americans view professional treatment for depression as a "last resort" (Conner et al., 2010). Therefore, the clinician must be mindful of older adults' reluctance to discuss mental health problems for fear of stigmatization. Additionally, older ethnic minority clients may be less knowledgeable about mental illness in general. A study of African American and Mexican American older adults (Choi & Gonzalez, 2005) found that both groups lacked knowledge about the referral process, which hampered their ability to seek and receive mental health services. Both groups also demonstrated a lack of awareness about the nature of mental illness. Interestingly, Conner and colleagues (2010) found that African American older adults understood the symptoms of depression but had difficulty identifying these symptoms in themselves. Participants in this study also identified racism as contributing to their depressive symptoms, which clinicians should consider as a topic of assessment.

Last, the professional working with an ethnic minority older adult must be mindful of the limitations of current measures. Evidence shows that some cognitive assessments may be biased against African Americans, in that members of this group perform poorer compared to White older adults (Jones, 2003; Sloan & Wang, 2005). Further, many measures have not been normed on ethnic minority populations and therefore may not accurately capture the distress experienced by older ethnic minority adults. Use of such measures should be done with caution.

To overcome obstacles related to the evaluation of older adults from different ethnicities, professionals need to increase their knowledge about these groups. However, clinicians must be careful not to stereotype members of an ethnic group, as there is considerable variability within groups. Additionally, to assist ethnic minority older adults in receiving adequate mental health care, clinicians should elicit the support of family members, make appropriate referrals, and request the assistance of bilingual speakers if necessary (Choi & Gonzalez, 2005).

## BIOLOGICAL AND MEDICAL FACTORS

Numerous biological and medical factors can directly or indirectly influence the assessment process and outcome. A comprehensive discussion of these factors is beyond the scope of this chapter. We have chosen to focus on selected factors that are likely to impact assessment and, in some cases, factors that are often overlooked in older adult assessment (e.g., biological rhythms).

### Sensory Changes Associated With Aging

As individuals age, they are at greater risk of developing chronic health problems. Some of these health problems may be associated with the senses, which can significantly contribute to a decrease in overall functioning (Whitbourne, 2002). Awareness of physiological changes associated with aging is essential to facilitate accurate assessments and diagnoses. Due to space limitations, we address age-related changes in visual and auditory systems only.

### *Vision*

Age-related visual deficits are common in late life. Approximately 17.5% of adults over the age of 80 years old have myopia (i.e., nearsightedness) and 23.6% have presbyopia (i.e., farsightedness; National Eye Institute, 2011). More serious diseases of the eye that can substantially impair vision include cataracts, glaucoma, macular degeneration, and diabetic retinopathy (Whiteside, Wallhagen & Pettengill, 2006). Cataracts are the most common visual illness, affecting 20% of 60- to 69-year-olds, increasing to 68.3% of adults over the age of 80 (National Eye Institute, 2011).

Normative age-related changes in the visual system affect visual acuity. In particular, the lens of the eye becomes thicker and less elastic, which hinders the ability to focus on objects (Whitbourne, 2002). This change largely explains the increased incidences of presbyopia (difficulty seeing small, up-close objects) in late life. Older adults also experience poorer depth perception, greater sensitivity to light, and slower dark adaptation. Cataracts, which are increasingly common with age, diminish the ability to see color and can enhance sensitivity to glare. Finally, older adults exhibit difficulty tracking visual objects. The ramifications of these visual changes are considerable: Older adults may be more likely to fall due to poorer depth perception and slow dark adaptation, and the likelihood of motor vehicle accidents increase as a result of glare and changing light intensities (Edelstein, Drozdick, & Kogan, 1998). In addition, changes in social interactions may occur due to failure to recognize close friends and family.

These changes in the visual system can largely impact assessment results. Paper-and-pencil self-report measures may not be easily read by the client with visual impairment. Some clients may not readily admit to visual deficits and may attempt to complete these self-report measures. Visual impairment is also related to cognitive performance. Individuals with greater visual impairment show decreased performance on tests of cognitive abilities (Glass, 2007). Visual impairment also predicts cognitive and functional decline in older women (Lin et al., 2004). Clinicians administering a cognitive assessment battery should consider how visual difficulties may impact the results. For visually impaired patients, measures that do not rely on visual cues may be a better measure of cognitive ability. Additionally, clinicians should recognize that individuals with vision problems are more likely to display depressive symptoms (Tolman, Hill, Kleinschmidt, & Gregg, 2005) and functional impairment (Jang, Mortimer, Haley, Small, Chisolm, & Graves, 2003), which may necessitate additional areas of assessment.

When assessing the older adult, measures with at least 14-point print font should be used (Vanderplas & Vanderplas, 1981). Assessments should be administered in well-lit areas, though lights that are too bright can exacerbate problems with glare. Glossy paper also increases glare, so materials should be printed on matte paper. Finally, older adults are likely to wear corrective lenses to compensate for poor vision, and they may have to switch between pairs of glasses to view close, middle, and far distances. It is important to be patient during assessment and to quell assumptions that slowness during testing is due to cognitive decline.

### Hearing

Approximately one in three adults over the age of 60 suffers from hearing loss, with half of adults age 75 and older reporting hearing difficulties (National Institute on Deafness and Other Communication Disorders, 2009). One of the most common problems in the auditory system is tinnitus. Tinnitus is marked by ringing, clicking, or hissing sounds in the ear. Prevalence rates of tinnitus are 12.3% of men and 14% of women. Also common is presbycusis, loss of hearing for high-pitched sounds, which occurs naturally across the life span. Presbycusis makes it difficult for older adults to hear female voices, which tend to be of higher pitch than men's voices. Women should be careful to make their voices deeper when assessing older clients. Age-related changes in the auditory system include thickening of ear wax, which can stifle the ability to hear sounds. Also, the auditory canal tends to shift inward, which makes audition more difficult (Whitbourne, 2002).

Hearing problems can have substantial impact on the assessment process. Notably, the client may have difficulty hearing questions and either may fail to respond or may respond incorrectly. It is important to remember that hearing loss can be stigmatizing (Wallhagen, 2009), and clients may be reluctant to admit to difficulties hearing a question. Older adults may spend a great deal of effort trying to listen and tend to auditory questions and commands. This effortful processing can impair subsequent performance on tests of memory (Tun, McCoy, & Wingfield, 2009). Consequently, hearing-impaired individuals

may demonstrate poorer cognitive performance on assessments, though their cognitive abilities are intact. Finally, hearing loss impacts social functioning. Given that conversing with others relies heavily on being able to hear, older adults with hearing impairment may be more likely to withdraw from social interactions (Jang et al., 2003). Once again, hearing loss should be factored into the assessment of social, cognitive, and functional impairment in older adults.

To improve the assessment process, the clinician should face the client and conduct the assessment in a well-lit area, so as to allow the client to read lips and rely on other nonverbal cues. Extraneous noise should be minimized to the greatest extent possible, as older adults often have difficulty maintaining a conversation amid background noise (a phenomenon known as masking). Assessments may need to occur in isolated, quiet areas to enhance the client's ability to hear. When speaking, the clinician should speak loudly and enunciate. However, the clinician should be careful not to speak too loudly or overenunciate, as these behaviors can be interpreted as condescending. Finally, the clinician should not assume that slowness in answering or inattention is due to cognitive impairment.

## Biological Rhythms and Assessment

Mounting chronobiological and psychological evidence indicates that clinicians should not ignore the time of day during which adults are assessed. The human biological clock, or circadian system, controls a wide range of biological and psychological processes (e.g., body temperature regulation, hormone secretion, sleep/wake cycles) through circadian rhythms. Each of these processes show peaks and troughs throughout the 24-hour cycle. Evidence suggests that various cognitive processes follow similar rhythms, with peak performance associated with peak periods of physiological arousal (e.g., Bodenhausen, 1990; Schmidt, Fabienne, Cajochen, & Peigneux, 2007; West, Murphy, Armilio, Craik, & Stuss, 2002). For example, May, Hasher, and Stoltzfus (1993) found memory for prose to be most accurate when participants were tested during their period of peak circadian arousal, typically during the early morning or late afternoon. Interestingly, researchers have found that such peak performance periods vary by age (e.g., May et al., 1993). These age-related differences in performance also correspond to subjective ratings of peak and off-peak times of the day (e.g., Horne & Osterberg, 1976). For example, approximately 40% of college students (age 18–25) tend to experience peak performance in the evening, whereas most (approximately

70%) older adults (age 60–75) tend to peak in the morning (Yoon, May, & Hasher, 1997). Yoon et al. (1997), citing the work of Ishihara, Miyake, Miyasita, and Miyata (1991), noted that the shift toward peak morning performance appears to begin around the age of 50. The effects of time of day on cognitive processes appear to vary across processes. More cognitively demanding processes (e.g., problem solving, planning) appear more likely to be influenced (West et al., 2002). Tasks involving more automatic processes (e.g., vocabulary tests, simple trivial questions) appear less influenced (Schmidt et al., 2007; Yang, Hasher, & Wilson, 2007).

There is considerable evidence of age-related declines in the inhibition of task-irrelevant information (e.g., Alain & Woods, 1999). Hasher and colleagues (Hasher, Goldstein, & May, 2005; Hasher & Zacks, 1988) have suggested that older adults whose inhibitory processes are impaired are more likely to experience impairment in working memory due to the presence of distracting, irrelevant information generated by the individual (e.g., related cognitions) or by the external environment (e.g., noise). Hasher and colleagues (e.g., Hasher, Goldstein, & May, 2005; Hasher & Zacks, 1988) have compiled an impressive amount of data suggesting that the changes in cognitive functioning that occur at off-peak times are due to deficits in inhibition related to circadian rhythm.

The research addressing the performance effects of off-peak assessment has very important implications for the assessment of older adult cognitive functioning. Neuropsychological assessment should probably be conducted during an individual's peak time period if one is seeking optimal performance. More specifically, cognitive assessment of older adults ideally should take into consideration the individual's peak and off-peak performance periods. Finally, the assessment of other domains that involve cognitive performance (e.g., decision-making capacity) is also potentially susceptible to circadian rhythms. At the very least, clinicians should record the time of day during which each element of the assessment process occurs.

The aforementioned physiological changes can significantly alter the behavior of the client and unintentionally contribute to erroneous conclusions if one is ignorant of these changes and their potential consequences. Clinicians must be vigilant about assessing for the presence and degree of physiological and sensory changes associated with aging and must consider them when formulating a conceptualization of the client's presenting problems. Similarly, erroneous assumptions made by clinicians with regard to the characteristics of older adults can lead to faulty conclusions. Clinicians must be careful to not misattribute symptoms of disease to normal aging processes or assume that impairments in sensory symptoms are not amenable to intervention.

## Psychological Presentations of Physical Disease

A number of the most common medical conditions may precipitate psychological symptoms. Sometimes these conditions can also present with features that mimic mental health problems. Often medical professionals are insufficiently prepared to recognize or assess for psychological concomitants of physical disease. Similarly, mental health practitioners may be unaware of possible underlying medical problems associated with psychological distress. This section addresses physical disorders that can cause or may share features with psychological problems.

### Parkinson's Disease

Parkinson's disease is marked by stiff and slow motor movements, including hand tremors. Patients with Parkinson's may be unsteady when standing or walking. Initiating motor activity, such as walking, may be particularly difficult. A common cooccurring psychological disorder is depression, which affects 58% of older adults with Parkinson's disease (Quelhas & Costa, 2009). Of those 58%, approximately 84% present with moderate to severe depressive symptoms (Quelhas & Costa, 2009). Anxiety is also common among individuals with Parkinson's disease. Qualhas and Costa (2009) found that 55% of individuals with Parkinson's disease had anxiety, with 33% of those individuals presenting with moderate to severe symptoms. Finally, dementia is more likely to occur in the older client with Parkinson's disease. Studies show that 40% of Parkinson's patients have dementia. Furthermore, postural instability gait difficulty (a subtype of Parkinson's characterized by motor difficulties) is associated with greater cognitive decline compared to other subtypes of Parkinson's disease (Burn, Rowan, Allan, Molloy, O'Brien, & McKeith, 2006).

### Cancer

Depression is also a common concomitant of cancer, with 18% of cancer patients presenting with major depression and 33% meeting criteria for dysthymic disorder (Fann, Fan, & Unützer, 2009). In pancreatic cancer, depression can be an early sign of the disease (Carney, Jones, Woolson, Noyes, & Doebbeling, 2003; Frazer, Leicht, & Baker, 1996). The likelihood of depression in cancer increases with disease severity and symptoms, such as pain and fatigue (Spiegel & Giese-Davis, 2003). The onset of depression in cancer patients has been linked to social changes associated with cancer, such as increased isolation and lack of social support. For example, social support from partners and adult children has been shown to protect against depression in older women with cancer (Maly, Umezawa, Leake, & Silliman, 2005). Similarly, social support has also been shown to reduce depression, anxiety, and pain and may also increase survival time (Spiegel & Giese-Davis, 2003). Therefore, it is important to assess social support networks of individuals suffering from cancer.

It is also possible that common treatments for cancer, such as chemotherapy and radiation therapy, precipitate depressive symptoms (Greenberg, 1989). Additionally, evidence suggests that chemotherapy may have deleterious effects on cognitive functioning, in particular processing speed (Kvale et al., 2010). Finally, psychophysiological changes associated with cancer, such as the dysregulation of the hypothalamic-pituitary-adrenal axis, may result in depressive symptomatology (Spiegel & Giese-Davis, 2003). Another important consideration is that many cancer patients experience worry and anxiety during the course of cancer and after remission (Deimling, Bowman, Sterns, Wagner, & Kahana, 2006).

### Chronic Obstructive Pulmonary Disease

Chronic obstructive pulmonary disease (COPD) consists of a group of degenerative diseases of the respiratory system. Chronic bronchitis and emphysema are the most common forms of COPD. Dyspnea (inability to obtain enough air), chronic cough, and increased sputum production are the prominent symptoms of COPD. Both depression and anxiety are common psychological features associated with the disease. In a study of COPD patients, approximately 11% showed moderate to severe depressive symptoms, whereas 38% showed moderate to severe anxiety symptoms (Cully et al., 2006). Some symptoms of COPD may mimic signs of depression; for example, individuals with COPD often have low energy due to low oxygen levels as a result of dyspnea. Additionally, COPD is associated with greater social isolation (Nazir & Erbland, 2009). These features can be misinterpreted as depressive symptoms. Anxiety related to difficulties getting oxygen is also common (Frazer et al., 1996). Dyspnea is associated with an increased risk of panic attacks (Nazir & Erbland, 2009) and difficulties with physical functioning, such as walking even short distances (Cully et al., 2006).

### Cardiovascular Disease

Cardiovascular disease (CVD), including hypertension, coronary artery disease, valvular heart disease, arrhythmias, heart failure, and peripheral vascular diseases, all involve difficulty sustaining a regular, sufficient blood supply throughout the body (Frazer et al., 1996). Rates of depression are approximately twice as high in individuals with CVD compared to those without (15.8% compared to 7.1%; Fan, Strine, Jiles, & Mokdad, 2008). Additionally, having three or more CVD conditions is associated with an increase in depressive symptoms (Bogner, Ford, & Gallo, 2006). Depressive symptoms in CVD are likely to persist over time. A study of patients hospitalized for congestive heart failure found that rates of depression in these individuals were maintained 6 months following hospitalization for the disease (Fulop, Strain, & Stettin, 2003). Some symptoms of CVD, such as lack of energy due to decreased cardiac output, mimic depressive symptoms (Kim, Braun, & Kunik, 2001). Functional impairment as a result of CVD can also resemble anhedonia, as many individuals limit their involvement in activities (Kim et al., 2001).

Anxiety is also associated with CVD. Just over 16% of older adults with a history of CVD report anxiety symptoms (Fan et al., 2008), and a CVD diagnosis is related to generalized anxiety disorder (GAD), panic, and specific phobia (Goodwin, Davidson, & Keyes, 2009). The symptoms of some CVDs can resemble anxiety. For example, individuals with myocardial infarction are often agitated or restless, and some medications for hypertension can produce side effects similar to anxiety (Kim et al., 2001). Also, panic can become exacerbated by coronary artery disease (Kim et al., 2001). Finally, CVD can impact mental status. Some evidence suggests cognitive decline predicts myocardial infarction (Frazer et al., 1996), whereas others suggest decline may result from CVD. Individuals with CVD often complain of increased distractibility and difficulties sustaining attention, though these symptoms may be better explained by depression associated with CVD (Gunstad, Cohen, Paul, Tate, Hoth, & Poppas, 2006).

### Cerebrovascular Disease

Cerebrovascular conditions are closely related to cardiovascular conditions. When heart disease or atherosclerosis leads to interruption in blood flow to the brain, the patient will experience cognitive effects from the resulting anoxia. The most common cerebrovascular condition in older adults is stroke, which is associated with a 50% increase in depressive symptoms (Beekman et al., 1998). Forty percent of ischemic stroke victims report clinically significant depression 3 to 4 months following stroke (Vataja et al., 2001), and depressive symptoms can persist 2 years after stroke (Whyte, Mulsant, Vanderbilt, Dodge, & Ganguli, 2004). Depressive symptoms following stroke are independent of functional impairment (Whyte et al., 2004), though much research has suggested functional impairment as a mechanism for depression. With respect to cognitive function, the site of the stroke determines the impact on cognitive abilities (e.g., stroke in the left hemisphere will have a significant impact on language; Mansueti, de Frias, Bub, & Dixon, 2008). Often there are difficulties with attention, which may be related to impairment in daily functioning (McDowd, Filion, Pohl, Richards, & Stiers, 2003).

### *Diabetes*

Diabetes mellitus involves hyperglycemia (high blood sugar) due to absent or reduced insulin secretion or ineffective insulin action. Diabetes is divided into Type I (insulin-dependent diabetes mellitus [IDDM]) and Type II (non-insulin-dependent diabetes mellitus [NIDDM]), with more older adults diagnosed with NIDDM. The prevalence rate of depression in older adults with diabetes is estimated at 17.6% (Ali, Stone, Peters, Davies, & Khunti, 2006). Depression is twice as high in individuals with Type II diabetes compared to those without diabetes (R. J. Anderson, Clouse, Freedland, & Lustman, 2001). In a study of adults with comorbid depression and diabetes, 77.8% demonstrated significant functional impairment in 12 routine tasks, including walking, bending, carrying groceries, participating in social activities, and handling small objects (Egede, 2004). Depression is related to poor glucose control (Lustman, Griffith, Clouse, & Cryer, 1986), such that blood glucose levels tend to improve with remission of depressive symptoms (Talbot & Nouwen, 2000). Similarly, poor glycemic control is associated with greater cognitive decline (Awad, Gagnon, & Messier, 2004), though the effects are small for adults under the age of 70. These cognitive declines are attenuated by increased glycemic management (Awad et al., 2004). As part of the assessment process, the clinician should ensure that blood glucose levels are managed appropriately.

Clinicians must be knowledgeable of the frequent comorbidity of medical and mental disorders. With enhanced awareness of the interaction between medical and mental health problems, assessments can be thorough and interventions can be more specifically and appropriately focused.

## Medication Use

With age, the likelihood of developing a chronic disease increases. Most older adults, approximately 80%, suffer from at least one chronic disease (Knight, Santos, Teri, & Lawton, 1995). As described earlier, some of the most common include hypertension (41%), arthritis (49%), heart disease (39%), and cancer (22%; Administration on Aging, 2010b). The number of chronic diseases is accompanied by an increase in the number of medications taken by older adults. Although older adults represent approximately 15% of the U.S. population, they use one third of all prescription drugs and 40% of all over-the-counter medications (Maiese, 2002). Community-dwelling older adults take between two and nine prescription drugs per day (Hajjar, Cafiero, & Hanlon, 2007).

There is a greater chance that older adults will be taking more medications than necessary than younger adults (Hajjar & Hanlon, 2006), which increases the risk of adverse drug effects. In a study on community-dwelling older adults' medication use, 4% of adults were at risk for adverse drug interactions (Qato et al., 2008). Furthermore, 45.8% were prescribed a drug that was inappropriate given their health problems (Shiyanbola & Farris, 2010). In another study, 58.9% of older adults were prescribed at least one or more unnecessary medications (Rossi et al., 2007). Use of several drugs is known as polypharmacy, which increases the risk for mortality and morbidity (Hajjar et al., 2007).

The metabolization of medications changes as a result of age-related changes in the body. Turnheim (2003) identified several physiological changes that can affect metabolism. First, excretion of drugs by the kidneys declines in late life, which increases the amount of time the drug stays in the body. Additionally, the body's water content decreases and fat content increases. Therefore, the same dose of a water-based drug given to a younger adult and an older adult will result in a higher concentration in the older adult's body, whereas a fat-based drug will have a lower concentration in the body. Homeostatic regulation also changes in late life, with longer time required for the body's systems to return to baseline. This pattern places older adults in an increased risk for adverse drug reactions. Finally, some drugs, especially anticonvulsant or psychotropic medications, can impact cognitive function and motor coordination. Some antidepressants and neuroleptic medications can cause delirium, agitation, and confusion. Clinicians must be aware of what medications their clients are taking at the time of assessment to determine the extent to which presenting problems are due to medication side effects.

# METHODOLOGICAL AND PROCEDURAL ISSUES

## Assessment Paradigms

A variety of assessment paradigms guide our approaches to assessment. A brief discussion of the two dominant paradigms is important before proceeding with our discussion of older adult assessment methods and instruments. An assessment paradigm is a set of principles, beliefs, values, hypotheses, and methods advocated in an assessment discipline or by its adherents (Haynes & O'Brien, 2000, p. 10). Consequently, the paradigm determines the nature of the questions addressed, settings in which information is obtained, nature of assessment instruments, the manner in which data obtained from assessment instruments are used, inferences that may be drawn from assessment data, how the clinician proceeds from assessment to intervention when change is desirable, and so on. In summary, a clinician's assessment paradigm determines how he or she approaches the systematic examination of behavior, which is essentially the task of psychological assessment.

The two principal assessment paradigms are traditional and behavioral. It would be simplistic to attempt a clear distinction between these two paradigms, as they share elements. Moreover, neither is monolithic, with each having subparadigms (cf. Haynes & O'Brien, 2000). For example, within the traditional paradigm, one might find trait-oriented psychodynamic personality, intellectual, neuropsychological, diagnostic, and family systems subparadigms. Within the behavioral paradigm, one might find behavior-analytic, social learning, and cognitive-behavioral subparadigms. (See Kazdin & Wilson, 1978.)

Behavioral and traditional paradigms can be distinguished in a variety of ways. (See Haynes & O'Brien, 2000; Nelson & Hayes, 1986.) For the purposes of this chapter, two distinctions will be useful. First, one can distinguish between behavioral and traditional paradigms in terms of their philosophical assumptions regarding descriptions and causes of behavior. Traditional approaches tend to emphasize descriptions of an individual's dispositional characteristics (e.g, personality traits) or what he or she *has* (cf. Mischel, 1968), which is often inferred from observed behavior, self-reports of feelings, attitudes, and behavior. The behavior of the individual tends to be explained by these personal characteristics. In contrast, behavioral approaches focus on the identification of environmental conditions that reliably produce the behaviors of interest. The behavior of the individual is explained by describing the conditions under which the behavior of interest occurs. This might include a description, for example, of the environmental conditions and schedule of reinforcement that is maintaining the aggressive behavior of an individual with dementia or the low level of social engagement of a depressed individual. A lower level of inference is required in behavioral assessment, as the phenomenon of interest is usually behavior (including thoughts or cognitions) rather than inferences drawn from the behavior.

Another way of characterizing the differences between traditional and behavioral paradigms is by distinguishing between idiographic and nomothetic approaches to assessment. In general, the nomothetic approach is used to examine commonalities among individuals, whereas the idiographic approach is used to ascertain the uniqueness of an individual. Nomothetic assessment typically involves the use of assessment instruments that have been standardized with a large number of individuals. The same instrument is used to assess multiple individuals. The results of the assessment (e.g., scores on a measure of depression) are compared against the results obtained with a standardization population (normative sample). An idiographic approach to assessment involves the "measurement of variables and functional relations that have been individually selected, or derived from assessment stimuli or contexts that have been individually tailored, to maximize their relevance for the particular individual" (Haynes, Mumma, & Pinson, 2009, p. 180). Multiple idiographic methods may also be utilized. For example, a socially anxious individual might be assessed via a role-play with familiar individuals and strangers, a direct observation instrument that targets relevant overt behaviors under a wide range of conditions, and a set of self-report questions specifically tailored for the client that focus on cognitions (e.g., self-statements regarding fear of negative evaluation), experiences of anxiety (e.g., heart rate, tightening chest, sweaty palms), and knowledge of effective conversational skills. There is typically no attempt to compare the assessment results with those obtained with other individuals. The criteria or standards used by the clinician are individually determined. Mischel (1968) noted that "behavioral assessment involves an exploration of the unique or idiosyncratic aspects of the single case, perhaps to a greater extent than any other approach" (p. 190).

Though the traditional and behavioral paradigms are quite different in many respects, their characteristic assessment methods and instruments can be combined (cf. Haynes et al., 2009). For example, a clinician might use a standardized depression assessment instrument to obtain information for use in a behavioral analysis. In addition to comparing a total depression score with population norms (traditional nomothetic approach), the individual depression inventory items could be used to characterize the individual (ideographic) (e.g., Mumma, 2004). Thus, one might determine that an individual is probably clinically depressed using a total score and then examine individual test items to gain an understanding of how the individual is experiencing and expressing depression.

As one moves from cognitively intact to cognitively impaired individuals, there is a necessary shift from more traditional to more behavioral, idiographic assessment approaches. Moderate to severe cognitive impairment typically precludes accurate and reliable self-report. Thus, assessment questions are less likely to focus on the person's personality, cognitions, and self-reported behavior and more likely to focus on the person's observed behavior and the environmental conditions that are maintaining it. The question, Why is this person behaving this way? becomes, Under what conditions is this person exhibiting this behavior? Questions asked might include: What time of day, in whose presence, and how often does the behavior occur? Similarly one typically asks: What happens after the behavior occurs? Of equal importance is the question of the conditions under which the behavior does *not* occur. The assessment methods become more circumscribed and direct, relying principally on reports by others and direct observation.

## Diagnostic Issues

### Differential Diagnosis

Older adults are often referred to clinicians when a new diagnosis may be required or when an existing diagnosis may need to be reevaluated. Initially, clinicians may need to use their expertise to determine whether the older adult's presenting signs and symptoms are merely manifestations of normal, age-related changes (e.g., distinguishing between delirium and dementia). If the older adult's problems appear beyond normal age-related changes, a diagnosis may be needed. The process of working toward an accurate diagnosis may be challenging, given that the older adult's presenting signs and symptoms may fall within more than one diagnostic category. When this occurs, clinicians are faced with the task of making a differential diagnosis. This entails determining which disorder or disorders best account for the symptoms that are present. Consider the example of an older adult who presents with these symptoms: memory difficulty, sleep disturbance, a change in psychomotor activity, and poor concentration. Without any additional information, one might speculate that

the older adult is experiencing some form of anxiety or mood disorder, a dementing illness, the sequelae of a medical condition, or the side effects of a medication or other ingested substance. What is needed at this point are data that can be used to differentiate between the possible diagnoses. Ideally, clinicians will set aside enough time to conduct a thorough evaluation, which may include any or all of these components:

1. Structured or unstructured clinical interviews with older adults to gather information regarding the older adult's presenting problems, mental status, capacity, and psychosocial and medical history
2. Measures that are standardized and possibly norm-referenced
3. Self-report or behaviorally based measures
4. Formal neuropsychological evaluations
5. Data gathered from significant others
6. Direct observation
7. Functional evaluations
8. Physiological data
9. Medical examinations and tests
10. Lists of medications and substances that are being used, along with the individual and compounded side effects possible

## Epidemiological Issues

Estimates reveal that only a small percentage of older adults (i.e., approximately 1%) between the ages of 60 and 70 experience some form of mental impairment, but this figure rises considerably (approximately 25%) when the upper age limit is extended into the mid-80s and beyond (Gatz, Kasl-Godley, & Karel, 1996). Similarly, data from the National Comorbidity Survey Replication (Kessler, Berglund, Demler, Jin, Merikangas, & Walters, 2005) indicated that the lifetime prevalence for any psychological disorder (i.e., using the fourth edition of the *Diagnostic and Statistical Manual of Mental Disorders*, text revision [*DSM-IV-TR*], American Psychiatric Association, 2000) was approximately 26% for adults age 60 years and over. Knowledge regarding the prevalence of various psychological disorders among older adults in community and inpatient settings may be useful in dispelling some of the myths about mental health and aging, providing mental health practitioners with a basic appreciation of the pervasiveness or rarity of various disorders among older adults and in formulating long-term projections for the treatment needs of seniors.

## Dementia and Delirium

The results from a nationally representative, population-based study of dementia in the United States revealed that the prevalence of dementia among individuals age 71 and older was 13.9%, comprising about 3.4 million individuals in 2002. The prevalence of Alzheimer's disease and vascular dementia was estimated to be 9.7% (2.4 million individuals) and 2.4% (594,000 individuals), respectively (Plassman et al., 2007). The prevalence of dementia increases with age, from 5.0% of those age 71 to 79 years to 37.4% of those age 90 and older. In contrast, the prevalence of dementia among adults age 60 to 65 years and over appears to be slightly lower in other countries. Estimates range from 1% to 3% in India and sub-Saharan Africa to approximately 5% to 10% in some Asian, Latin American, and western European countries (Ferri et al., 2005; Kalaria et al., 2008; Winblad, Viramo, Remes, Manninen, & Jokelainen, 2010). Although national estimates of the prevalence of dementia may vary considerably, there is strong agreement that the prevalence of dementia increases with age (i.e., roughly 30% of seniors age 85 years and over), and that Alzheimer's disease is the most common form of dementia (Zarit & Zarit, 2007a). The cardinal symptoms of dementia include: (a) memory impairment and impairment in at least one other domain of cognitive functioning, (b) impairment in social or occupational functioning as a result of cognitive dysfunction, and (c) decline from a previously level of functioning (American Psychiatric Association, 2000).

Clinicians who work with older adults should become very familiar with the process of conducting differential diagnoses among delirium, dementia, and other psychiatric disorders (e.g., depression). Although the prevalence of delirium among community-dwelling seniors is low (i.e., 1%), summaries of prevalence estimates provided by Inouye (2006) and Fearing and Inouye (2009) indicate that delirium affects approximately 14% to 56% of hospitalized elderly patients, 15% to 53% of older postoperative patients, 70 to 87% of older adults in intensive care, up to 60% of patients in long-term care or postacute care settings, and approximately 80% of all patients at the end of life. The cardinal symptoms of delirium include inability to sustain attention, disorganized thinking, rapid onset of symptoms with fluctuating course, and at least two of the following: perceptual disturbance, sleep-wake cycle disturbance, psychomotor increase or decrease, disorientation, and memory impairment (American Psychiatric Association, 2000). The accurate and timely diagnosis of delirium is critical, given that it is often a reversible condition and one that is very harmful and potentially life-threatening if left untreated.

## Mood and Anxiety Disorders

The National Comorbidity Survey Replication (Byers, Yaffe, Covinsky, Friedman, & Bruce, 2010) provided nationally representative estimates of age-specific 12-month prevalence rates of mood, anxiety, and comorbid disorders among community-dwelling older adults age 55 years and over, using the *DSM-IV-TR* (American Psychiatric Association, 2000). In reference to the total sample, these prevalence estimates were reported for mood disorders: any mood disorder (4.9%); major depressive disorder (4.0%); dysthymia (0.8%); and bipolar I or II disorder (0.9%). Prevalence estimates for anxiety disorders among the total sample were: any anxiety disorder (11.6%); specific phobia (6.5%); social phobia (3.5%); posttraumatic stress disorder (2.1%); GAD (2.0%); panic disorder (1.3%); and agoraphobia without panic (0.8%). In addition, approximately 2.8% of the sample experienced a comorbid disorder. A recent review of research concerning the prevalence of anxiety disorders among community-dwelling older adults revealed estimates ranging from 1% to 15%, with anywhere from 15% to 52% of seniors experiencing anxiety symptoms (Bryant, Jackson, & Ames, 2008). In general, specific phobia and generalized anxiety disorder are the two most common forms of anxiety disorder among seniors (Bryant et al., 2008). Byers et al. (2010) further reported that the prevalence of mood and anxiety disorders in late life tended to decline with age but remained common, especially among women. A recent comprehensive and rigorous review of prevalence studies that focus on anxiety disorders among older adults also indicated that anxiety disorders are common among older adults, but less common than in younger adults, and that anxiety disorders are highly comorbid with depression and a number of medical illnesses (Wolitzky-Taylor, Castriotta, Lenze, Stanley, & Craske, 2010).

Higher prevalence rates for depression may be observed among seniors residing in long-term care, with 15% to 32% of residents experiencing depressive disorders (Anstey, von Sanden, Sargent-Cox, & Luszcz, 2007; McDougall, Matthews, Kvaal, Dewey, & Brayne, 2007). When subsyndromal depressive symptoms are considered along with depressive disorders, the prevalence rate may rise to 44% (Canadian Institute for Health Research, 2010). A review of research regarding the prevalence of anxiety disorders among older adults in clinical settings revealed estimates ranging from 1% to 28%, with anywhere from 15% to 56% experiencing anxiety symptoms (Bryant et al., 2008).

### Suicide

Older adults are at a higher risk for completed suicide than any other segment of the population (National Institute of Mental Health [NIMH], 2007; Turvey et al., 2002). According to facts reported by the NIMH, although 12% of the U.S. population was comprised of older adults in 2004, they disproportionately accounted for 16% of suicide deaths. Further, non-Hispanic White males age 85 years and over were at greatest risk for suicide. Paradoxically, although older adults are more likely than any other age group to commit suicide, suicidal ideation and suicide attempts may be less common among older adults (Conwell, Duberstein, & Caine, 2002). Although mood disorders are often linked with suicide among older adults (Szanto, Prigerson, & Reynolds, 2001), psychotic disorders (i.e., schizophrenia, schizoaffective disorder, delusional disorder), personality disorders, and anxiety disorders may play a smaller role in completed suicides among this group. Similarly, disorders related to the use of alcohol and other substances may be less common among older than younger victims of suicide (Conwell et al., 2002). Other research has revealed that depressed older adults with lower cognitive functioning and impairments in physical self-care may be vulnerable to impulsive suicidal behavior (Conner et al., 2007).

### Schizophrenia

The prevalence of schizophrenia among adults age 65 years and over has been estimated to be approximately 1% (C. I. Cohen et al., 2000). The median age for admission to a nursing home is 65 years for those persons with schizophrenia, compared to age 80 years for those with no mental illness (Andrews, Bartels, Xie, & Peacock, 2009). Further, middle-age persons with schizophrenia are almost four times more likely to undergo early institutionalization in nursing homes compared with their same-age peers with no mental illness. The prevalence of schizophrenia in nursing homes is estimated to range from 5.9% to 12% (McCarthy, Blow, & Kales, 2004; Mechanic & McAlpine, 2000).

### Personality Disorders

Estimates of the prevalence of personality disorders among older adults (i.e., age 50 years and over) range from 10% to 20% (Abrams & Horowitz, 1996, 1999; Morse & Lynch, 2000; Widiger & Seidlitz, 2002). There is general consensus that the rates of personality disorders are lower among older adults than in younger individuals. Further, there is evidence to suggest that rates of Cluster B disorders (i.e., involving antisocial and impulsive behavior) are less common among seniors than younger individuals and that Cluster C disorders (i.e., involving anxious or fearful behaviors) may become more common with advanced age (Zarit & Zarit, 2007b).

## Unique Presentations of Disorders Among Older Adults

### Age-Related Changes and Differences in Axis I Disorders

The presentations of psychological disorders vary across different age groups. Both physiological changes associated with age and unique life circumstances in late adulthood contribute to differences in presentation. It is not uncommon for older adults to experience subsyndromal presentations of a disorder. Though these features may not meet criteria for a disorder, they can still have a significant impact on functioning. For example, subthreshold late-life anxiety is associated with increased distress, health-care utilization, and risk for developing additional psychiatric disorders (de Beurs, Beekman, van Balkom, Deeg, van Dyck, & van Tilburg, 1999).

Older adults may describe the experiences of disorders differently. With masked depression, older adults present with physical rather than psychological symptoms (Yesavage, 1992). Similarly, older adults are more likely to complain of somatic symptoms than affective or cognitive features (Fountoulakis et al., 2003). Older adults with GAD endorse fewer somatic symptoms (e.g., muscle tension, nausea), and cognitive symptoms (e.g., negative self-evaluation) of anxiety relative to middle and young adults (Brenes, Knudson, McCall, Williamson, Miller, & Stanley, 2008). This finding underscores the notion that older adults often have fewer symptoms of psychological distress than younger adults.

Overall, older adults tend to report less negative affect compared to younger age groups (Brenes et al., 2008). As described in the *DSM-IV-TR*, older adults with depression are more likely to present with melancholic features (American Psychiatric Association, 2000), which includes early-morning awakenings, poor mood in the morning, excessive weight loss or lack of eating, and psychomotor changes. Although guilt may be a sign of depression, Fountoulakis and colleagues (2003) suggested that older adults are not likely to report this symptom. In addition, it is not uncommon for depressed mood to be completely absent from the presentation of depression in the older adult. In bipolar disorder, older adults are more likely to experience rapid cycling (American Psychiatric Association, 2000) and tend to have less intense manic episodes (Depp & Jeste, 2004).

Differences in symptom presentation may result from age-related variations in the description of psychological disorders. Wetherell and colleagues (2009) found that older and younger adults often describe the symptoms of depression and anxiety differently. Older adults were poorer at identifying somatic, affective, and cognitive features of anxiety and depression compared to younger adults. Older adults were slightly better at identifying the symptoms of depression compared to anxiety, and symptoms of anxiety were more likely to be attributed to physical health problems. This study suggests that older adults do not necessarily experience fewer or unique symptoms of anxiety; rather, they may misattribute the cause of their symptoms.

### Age-Related Changes and Differences in Axis II Disorders

Personality disorders are defined in the *DSM-IV-TR* (American Psychiatric Association, 2000) as rigid and inflexible personality traits present since adolescence or early adulthood that cause functional problems. Older adults with personality disorders have likely had a long history of distress. Often there will be an indication or diagnosis of a personality disorder in a client's previous clinical reports (Zweig, 2008). Assessment of the older adult with a personality disorder is complicated due to comorbidity with one or more Axis I diagnoses. Also, interviews with clients can be difficult because of the nature of interpersonal problems associated with personality disorders (Zweig, 2008). Information regarding the changes in personality disorders with advancing age is very limited, as there is a marked paucity of longitudinal data. Some evidence suggests that the emotional and dramatic symptoms associated with antisocial, histrionic, and borderline personality disorders may become less pronounced with age (American Psychiatric Association, 2000; Zweig, 2008), although these findings may reflect issues with diagnostic criteria and measurement rather than true personality change (Tackett, Balsis, Oltmanns, & Krueger, 2009). That is, current diagnostic criteria and assessments for personality disorders are based on presentations in young adults. Therefore, criteria often do not account for age-related changes (e.g., many personality disorder features, such as impulsivity and sexual behaviors, tend to decrease in late life), rendering the current nosology ill-fitting to older adults (Tackett et al.,

2009; Van Alphen, Engelen, Kuin, & Derksen, 2006). For additional information regarding Axis II presentation in late life, the interested reader is referred to Zweig (2008).

### Aging and DSM-IV-TR Criteria

Age-related changes have been documented across numerous symptom dimensions (i.e., cognitive, biological, social). In many instances, normative, age-related changes in these symptoms overlap with the *DSM-IV* diagnostic criteria (American Psychiatric Association, 2000). Consider, for example, changes in sleep patterns in late life. Older adults sleep less, experience more awakenings, but report comparable levels of fatigue to younger adults (Buysse, Monk, Carrier, & Begley, 2005). Other changes include increased difficulty filtering out distractions when working on cognitive tasks (Tun, O'Kane, & Wingfield, 2002), and a reduction in social networks (Fung et al., 2001). All of these changes are normative in later adulthood but may be interpreted as part of the diagnostic criteria for a major depressive episode (i.e., sleep disturbance, poor concentration, and declines in social functioning). As described earlier, many characteristics or behaviors associated with personality disorders (e.g., risky sexual behavior) are less likely to be endorsed by older adults (Tackett et al., 2009; Van Alphen et al., 2006). These examples illustrate how the current diagnostic system may not be especially appropriate for older populations.

Proposed changes for the fifth edition of the *DSM* may result in criteria that are better suited to the needs of older adults. The adoption of a dimensional approach to classification, which considers a broader range of symptoms as well as the severity of these symptoms, may more accurately capture subsyndromal and unique presentations of disorders in older adults (American Psychiatric Association, 2010). Research on the usefulness of dimensional assessment is currently under way.

## MULTIMETHOD ASSESSMENT

Clinicians have long been encouraged to employ multiple methods in the measurement of clinical phenomena (e.g., Campbell & Fiske, 1959; Eid & Diener, 2006). Each method (e.g., interview, direct observation, self-report, report by others, psychophysiological recording) has strengths and weaknesses. Moreover, each can portray a different picture of the phenomenon of interest, which is often characterized as method variance (cf. Campbell & Fisk, 1959). The relative strengths and weaknesses of each method can be minimized by using multiple assessment methods, such as a self-report instrument, a rating scale completed by a proxy, direct observation of relevant behavior, and a brief structured interview completed by a mental health professional. The use of such methods can offer both unique and corroborative information. The strengths and weaknesses of some of these methods, particularly with regard to older adults, are discussed next.

## Self-Report

The self-report method is arguably the most frequently used assessment method for young and older adults. The reliability and validity of assessment information obtained via self-report with older adults are vulnerable for a variety of reasons, some of which are more likely to be age related. For example, the specific wording of questions, question format, and question context can influence the results obtained from the self-report method with older adults (Schwarz, 1999), particularly with age-related impairment in cognitive functioning. Self-reporting can be particularly problematic with older adults who are experiencing communication-related cognitive deficits. Overall, the evidence supporting the accuracy, reliability, and validity of older adult self-reports is mixed. For example, older adult estimates of their functional ability have been questioned, with some overestimating their functional ability (e.g., Rubenstein, Schairer, Weiland, & Kane, 1984) and others both under- and overestimating their abilities (e.g., Sager, Dunham, Schwantes, Mecum, Havorson, & Harlowe, 1992). Self-reports of memory impairment among older adults may be inaccurate (e.g., Sunderland, Watts, Baddeley, & Harris, 1986), and self-reports of health service use may be substantially underreported by older adults (e.g., Wallihan, Stump, & Callahan, 1999). When asked about past experiences, older adults tend to underreport symptoms of psychological distress, report more intense affect than younger adults (Alea, Bluck, & Semegon, 2004), and minimize or deny symptoms (Blazer, 2009).

A variety of factors can contribute to the inaccuracies of self-reported information among older adults. These might include, for example, physical and mental health status, affective responses to acute illness, changes from previous levels of physical functioning occurring during hospitalization, and the presence of acute or chronic cognitive impairment (Sager et al., 1992). Cognitively impaired older adults pose a formidable assessment challenge. Evidence for the validity of many psychological assessment instruments for use with cognitively impaired

older adults is lacking. In addition, older adults may be unable to comprehend questions or the nature of information requested. Numerous studies have questioned the accuracy of self-reports by cognitively impaired older adults (e.g., Farias, Mungas, & Jagust, 2005). For example, Feher, Larrabee, and Crook (1992) found that older adults with dementia who denied memory loss also tended to deny the presence of other symptoms. Kiyak, Teri, and Borsom (1994) found that self-reports of functional health of demented individuals were consistently rated as poorer than reports by family members. Similarly, Kelly-Hayes, Jette, Wolf, D'Adostino, and O'Dell (1992) found low rates of agreement between self-reports of cognitively impaired individuals and performance-based measures. In contrast, Feher et al. (1992) argued that self-report instruments designed to measure recent mood may be utilized with older adults experiencing mild to moderate dementia, noting that accurate self-report of recent mood requires only minimal memory ability.

Evidence regarding the accuracy of unimpaired older adults is more encouraging. For example, self-reported activities of daily living (ADLs) correlate highly with performance measures in outpatient settings (Sager et al., 1992). Older adults are also as accurate as younger adults when replying to survey questions (Rodgers & Herzog, 1987). Similarly, older adult self-reports of insomnia are accurate, when compared against polysomnography (e.g., Reite, Buysse, Reynolds, & Mendelson, 1995), the gold standard for sleep disorder assessment.

In summary, self-report can be a rich source of valuable assessment information with unimpaired older adults. However, this method becomes increasingly unreliable with older adults whose physical, cognitive, and mental health status are compromised. In such cases, multimethod assessment is particularly valuable.

## Interview

The interview is the most commonly used clinical assessment instrument and arguably the most important means of gathering assessment data. Interviews afford one the opportunity to observe directly behavioral indicators of psychopathology in addition to obtaining information through strategic queries. Though the principles of young-adult interviewing apply to older adults, the interviewing of older adults requires knowledge of possible age-related psychological and physiological changes. For example, when contrasted with younger adults, older adults refuse to participate in surveys at a higher rate (e.g., DeMaio, 1980; Herzog & Rodgers, 1988), refuse to answer certain types of questions (e.g., Gergen & Back, 1966), and respond "don't know" (Colsher & Wallace, 1989) more often. Older adults also tend to be more cautious when responding (Okun, 1976) and give more acquiescent responses (N. Kogan, 1961). The older adult's physical stamina, cognitive skills, and sensory deficits can all play a role in determining the accuracy, reliability, and validity of information obtained.

Interviews vary in structure, ranging from structured and semistructured diagnostic interviews (e.g., Structured Diagnostic Interview for *DSM-IV-TR*; First, Spitzer, Gibbon, & Williams, 2002) to unstructured, free-flowing, nonstandardized clinical interviews. Though highly structured interviews offer diagnostic precision, they lack the flexibility and forgiving nature of unstructured interviews. The unstructured interview permits rephrasing of questions that appear unclear to the interviewee and the exploration of topic areas that may be tangential but relevant to the presenting problems (Edelstein, Staats, Kalish, & Northrop, 1996). Moreover, the unstructured interview permits one to prompt and encourage responses and maintain the attention of interviewees who experience difficulty concentrating.

## Self-Report Inventories

Self-report inventories can be very useful in the assessment of older adults, particularly because they permit the older adult to respond to questions at his or her own pace. Sadly, few existing instruments have psychometric support for use with older adults (Edelstein et al., 2008), though self-report instruments are being developed specifically for use with older adults (e.g., J. Kogan & Edelstein, 2004; Pachana, Byrne, Siddle, Koloski, Harley, & Arnold, 2007; Wisocki, Handen, & Morse,1986). The physical and cognitive demands of self-report inventories must be considered when selecting instruments, as most require good vision, adequate reading comprehension, and at least modest perceptual-motor skills. Problems in any of these domains can influence the reliability and validity of information obtained via questionnaires and inventories.

Self-report measures continue to be the mainstay of clinicians and are an important source of information. Their uses will undoubtedly grow as more current self-report instruments are revised for use with older adults and more instruments are developed specifically for use with the older adults. Self-reported information should, however, be considered in combination with information obtained through other assessment methods.

## Report by Others

The report-by-other (e.g., spouse, caregiver, adult child) assessment method can be a rich source of unique and verifying data, particularly regarding contextual factors relating to the problem(s) in question (Edelstein, Martin, & McKee, 2000). Reports by others can be particularly valuable with older adults who are incapable of conveying accurate information (e.g., when demented). Even when the ability to self-report is unimpaired, reports by others can offer an additional method for gathering convergent information. As with any source of information, reports by others are subject to the same potential problems of unreliability, invalidity, and inaccuracy as other assessment methods. For example, caregivers overestimate the level of older adult cancer patient pain (Redinbaugh, Baum, DeMoss, Fello, & Arnold, 2002). Characteristics of caregivers also can influence their accuracy. Accuracy of caregiver reports of patient ADLs among individuals with mild dementia can be influenced by the caregiver's depressive symptoms and burden (e.g., Zanetti, Geroldi, Frisoni, Bianchetti, & Trabucchi, 1999). Moreover, the accuracy of the caregiver varies across activities (e.g., walking, telephone use, money use, shopping; Zanetti et al., 1999).

## Direct Observation

Direct observation of behavior can be a rich, accurate, and often more valid measure than self-report and report by others (Yoder & Symons, 2010). Moreover, overt behavior is often the ultimate focus of assessment. This method can be incorporated into many of the other methods discussed. For example, one can begin one's observation with an ambulatory patient as he or she walks down the hall of a clinical facility to one's office and continue during an interview and formal testing. Unreported symptoms can also be noted during the assessment process.

There are several advantages of using direct observation. Direct observation can be useful when assessing older adults who are uncooperative, unavailable for self-report, or severely cognitively or physically impaired (Goga & Hambacher, 1977). In addition, simple observational procedures can be taught easily to individuals with little or no previous experience (Edelstein et al., 2000). Direct observation data are of particular value in institutional settings, where the often-profound effects of environmental factors can be observed and addressed through institution-wide systems. Moreover, multiple staff members can monitor behavior changes over time, thereby offering convergent evidence for sometimes idiosyncratic variations in behavior as a function of environmental stimuli.

The potential disadvantages of direct observation methodology are both financial and practical. Reliable direct observation can be quite time consuming, depending on the nature and frequency of the behaviors in question. Such observations can become quite complicated when complex behavior coding systems are employed. One must balance the richness of data provided by complex coding systems with the demands of other staff responsibilities.

### Psychophysiological Assessment

Psychophysiological assessment typically is performed in the clinical context as an index of autonomic nervous system arousal. For the most part, such assessment is limited to the assessment of anxiety-related responses. Psychophysiological methods have enabled researchers to understand better the basic processes related to the etiology and maintenance of anxiety disorders, clarify the boundaries and relations between subtypes of anxiety disorders, and assess anxiety states and treatment progress (Turpin, 1991). Unfortunately, apparently no published studies have examined age-related changes in autonomic arousal in young and older adults with anxiety disorders. There are, however, several laboratory studies of autonomic arousal in older adults from which one can draw. (See Lau, Edelstein, & Larkin, 2001, and Uchino, Birmingham, & Berg, 2010, for reviews.) In general, autonomic arousal appears to diminish with age (Appenzeller, 1994). Resting heart rate tends to decrease with age and skin conductance levels in response to behavioral and sensory stressors diminish with age (N. B. Anderson & McNeilly, 1991; Appenzeller, 1994; Juniper & Dykman, 1967). In contrast, older adults exhibit greater stress-induced blood pressure reactivity than younger adults when exposed to pharmacologic, behavioral, and cognitive challenges (McNeilly & Anderson, 1997; Uchino et al., 2010). Finally, increased age is associated with decreased heart rate reactivity in the laboratory (Uchino et al., 2010).

These changes in autonomic arousal are believed to result from multiple age-related physiological and neurochemical changes (J. Kogan, Edelstein, & McKee, 2000). In light of results of laboratory studies of autonomic arousal of older adults, one might expect similar age-related patterns of responding when older adults face anxiety arousing stimuli outside the laboratory. If this is the case, one must be cautious in interpreting arousal patterns using normative data based on younger adults.

## PSYCHOMETRIC CONSIDERATIONS

In recent years, a great deal of progress has been made in addressing and improving the psychometric properties of instruments used to assess older adults (Edelstein et al., 2008). Although academics and health professionals are well aware of the importance of using psychometrically strong measures, instruments that are reliable and valid for use with older adults have been lacking. Many measures have been (and continue to be) developed and normed for use with younger populations, with little or no attention paid to the potentially unique clinical presentation and characteristics of older adults. It is unlikely that such instruments would be judged as psychometrically sound when used with seniors. This fact underscores the importance of investigating the psychometric properties of any instruments that are used in the assessment of older adults.

### Reliability

An assessment instrument is judged to be reliable when it yields consistent and stable results from the same person across multiple administrations, regardless of who administers the test. In order to judge whether a given test is reliable, we examine various estimates of reliability (e.g., internal consistency, test–retest reliability).

Measures of internal consistency estimate reliability based on the average correlation among test items (Nunnally & Bernstein, 1994). Different measures of internal consistency may be reported, including coefficient alpha (J. Cohen, 1960), the Kuder Richardson-20 for dichotomous items (Kuder & Richardson, 1937), split-half, and alternate forms. An instrument with good internal consistency is assumed to measure one construct. Low estimates of internal consistency may indicate that either the test is too short or the items have little in common. Further, if a test originally developed for use with younger populations is administered to older adults, estimates of internal consistency may differ substantially. This fact underscores the idea that reliability is a function of *samples*, not tests (Vacha-Haase, Kogan, & Thompson, 2000). One way to improve the internal consistency of a measure is to increase the number of quality test items that sample the intended content domain. There may be practical limitations to using this strategy, however, given that chronic health problems (e.g., arthritis) or fatigue may interfere with the completion of longer assessments.

In some cases, clinicians and researchers may administer a test to an older adult on multiple occasions (e.g., memory or IQ testing). In these cases, the test–retest reliability of a measure may be examined to gauge its temporal stability. This indicator of reliability is most relevant when measures are used to assess constructs that are expected to remain relatively consistent over time (e.g., one would not expect significant change in the IQ of a healthy adult over a 1-month interval, but one would expect to see more variation if mood were assessed over the same time period). If a clinician or researcher intends to use an instrument on two different occasions, it is important to consider the optimal test–retest interval. Again, estimates of test–retest reliability may differ between younger and older samples (Vacha-Haase et al., 2000).

## Validity

Validity has been defined by Aiken and Groth-Marnat (2006) as the "extent to which a test measures what it was developed to measure" (p. 97). How well a test measures the construct it was designed to measure is usually expressed as a validity coefficient, which is derived by calculating a statistical correlation between the measure in question and other criterion measures (Aiken & Groth-Marnat, 2006; Anastasi & Urbina, 1997). Three forms of validity that are commonly addressed include criterion-related validity, content validity, and construct validity.

Criterion-related validity is relevant when one measure (X) is used to predict another criterion measure (Y). If the criterion measure (Y) is obtained some time after the original measure (X) is given, then predictive validity is being assessed. However, if both measures are administered at essentially the same time, concurrent validity is being studied (Cronbach & Meehl, 1955).

Content validity involves the extent to which an instrument samples the domain of interest (Cronbach, 1971). In order to establish content validity, it is necessary first to define the relevant domain and then to ensure a representative sampling from this domain when selecting items for inclusion in an assessment instrument. In reference to older populations, it is important for clinicians to confirm that the items on an assessment instrument pertain to the construct of interest as it applies to older adults. To illustrate, older adults experiencing depression may be less likely than younger adults to report suicidal ideation (Blazer, Bachar, & Hughes, 1987) and dysphoria (Gallo, Rabins, & Anthony, 1999) but more likely to report hopelessness and helplessness (Christenden et al., 1999), psychomotor retardation, and somatic symptoms (Gallo, Anthony, & Muthén, 1994).

Construct validity is defined as the degree to which scores from an instrument accurately measure the psychological construct of interest (Cronbach & Meehl, 1955). Clinicians and researchers should become familiar with the concepts of *measurement equivalence* and *factorial invariance* as these are crucial when comparing groups (e.g., younger versus older adults) on a construct of interest or when conducting longitudinal studies that examine changes in constructs (e.g., intelligence) over time.

## CONCLUSIONS AND FUTURE DIRECTIONS

As the ranks of the baby boomer generation continue to swell, the proportion of older adults in our society is projected to increase. As a result, there is an increased likelihood that clinicians will encounter older clients in their practices. In order to assess older populations in an ethical and sound manner, it is necessary to gain a better understanding of the aging process and the ways that geriatric assessment differs from the assessment of younger populations. Graduate programs that train professionals to work directly with older adults should include curricula that address the unique aspects of geriatric assessment.

At the societal level, clinicians and researchers must be aware of the influence of ageism and negative myths of aging when developing new assessment instruments, selecting and administering existing tests, and interpreting assessment results. Within the United States, it is also important to acknowledge that the culture of managed care will continue to exert an influence on the assessment of seniors in health-care settings. Managed care organizations place restrictions on the content and length of psychological services, which may mean that clinicians are less able to tailor their services to suit the needs of individual clients (e.g., providing more time for older adults with cognitive, sensory, and health problems to complete assessments). However, recent changes in health-care legislation in the United States under the Patient Protection and Affordable Care Act of 2010 may provide additional opportunities for older adults to gain access to assessment services.

Ideally, geriatric assessments should incorporate multiple methods and take into account the multidimensional nature of the phenomena of interest. When clinicians and researchers engage in diagnostic assessments, they should be familiar with the differences between pathology and normal age-related change, comorbidity issues among seniors, and the importance of conducting thorough and accurate differential diagnoses. Further, diagnostic assessments should go beyond simply arriving at a diagnosis and include sufficient commentary on the older adult's strengths, weaknesses, and functional capabilities.

As the future of geriatric assessment unfolds, it is likely that computers will play a greater role in the assessment process. This likelihood raises concerns about the interaction between older clients and the computerized assessment format. (For a comprehensive review of computer use by older adults, see Wagner, Hassanein, & Head, 2010.) Although older adults may be the fastest-growing users of computers and the Internet, more senior cohorts may be more likely to report higher levels of anxiety regarding the use of computers than younger adults (Karavidas, Llim, & Katsikas, 2002). It is likely that successive cohorts of older adults may be more at ease with the use of computers, as training programs and computer interfaces are redesigned to accommodate the needs of older users. There are certain advantages to the use of computerized assessments with older populations. For example, ageism or stereotypes that may be harbored by clinicians would be negated by the greater standardization of testing conditions. In addition, it is feasible that assessment software packages could be designed to take into account an older adult's cognitive, sensory, or motor deficits. For example, an older adult with limited motor skills could interact verbally with an assessment device that also takes into consideration his or her unique hearing deficits by amplifying selected sound frequencies. Partially sighted individuals also could interact with such a device. Fatigue could be minimized through branching programs that permitted the skipping of various contents areas when warranted. The words, sentence structures, and information complexity and quantity used in the assessment process could be tailored to the individual's probable cognitive deficits as determined by a screening instrument. Information also could be conveyed via digital video systems that would permit rapid replays and enhance information recall through the use of multisensory (e.g., olfactory, auditory, visual) contextual cues. With the aid of telemetry devices and satellite technology, patterns of behavior could also be monitored from great distances.

While the format of the assessment process may change over time (i.e., toward the greater use of electronics), the underlying goals of the assessment process may also change in the future. As mentioned earlier in the chapter, a departure from the traditional approach of syndromal classification may occur. The forthcoming *DSM-5* may include criteria that are better suited to the needs of older adults. A move toward a dimensional approach to classification that considers a broader range of symptoms, and the severity of those symptoms, may better capture subsyndromal and unique presentations of disorders among older adults.

As always, clinicians and researchers are urged to carefully consider the psychometric properties of any assessment instruments that are used. Tests that were developed for use with younger adults may not be reliable or valid for use with older adults. Further, there is widespread consensus that large, representative samples (according to national census data) of older adults are needed when developing and standardizing assessment instruments that may be used in geriatric assessment. Moreover, the data collected regarding standardization samples should include information that goes beyond age and gender (e.g., the inclusion of data on racial/ethnic background, health status, living arrangements), as older adults are not a uniform group.

# REFERENCES

Abrams, R. C., & Horowitz, S. V. (1996). Personality disorders after age 50: A meta-analysis. *Journal of Personality Disorders*, *10*, 271–281.

Abrams, R. C., & Horowitz, S. V. (1999). Personality disorders after age 50: A meta-analytic review of the literature. In E. Rosowsky, R. C. Abrams, & R. A. Zweig (Eds.), *Personality disorders in older adults: Emerging issues in diagnosis and treatment* (pp. 55–68). Mahwah, NJ: Erlbaum.

Administration on Aging. (2009). *A profile of older Americans: 2009*. Retrieved from www.aoa.gov/aoaroot/aging_statistics/Profile/2009/docs/2009profile_508.pdf

Administration on Aging. (2010a). *Older Americans 2010: Key Indicator of Well Being*. Retrieved from www.agingstats.gov/agingstatsdotnet/Main_Site/Data/2010_Documents/Docs/OA_2010.pdf

Administration on Aging. (2010b). *Profile of Older Americans: 2009*. Retrieved from www.aoa.gov/AoARoot/Aging_Statistics/Profile/2009/14.aspx

Aiken, L. R., & Groth-Marnat, G. (2006). *Psychological testing and assessment* (12th ed.). Boston, MA: Pearson Education.

Alain, C., & Woods, D. L. (1999). Age-related changes in processing auditory stimulus during visual attention: Evidence for deficits in inhibitory control and sensory memory. *Psychology and Aging*, *14*, 507–519.

Alea, N., Bluck, S, & Semegon, A. B. (2004). Young and older adults' expression of emotional experience: Do autobiographical narratives tell a different story? *Journal of Adult Development*, *11*, 235–250.

Ali, S., Stone, M. A., Peters, J. L., Davies, M. J., & Khunti, K. (2006). The prevalence of comorbid depression in adults with Type II diabetes: A systematic review and meta-analysis. *Diabetic Medicine*, *23*, 1165–1173.

American Psychiatric Association. (2000). *Diagnostic and statistical manual of mental disorders* (4th ed., text rev.). Washington, DC: Author.

American Psychiatric Association. (2010). *Proposed draft revisions to DSM disorders and criteria*. Retrieved from www.dsm5.org/ProposedRevisions/Pages/Default.aspx

American Psychological Association. (2003). Guidelines on multicultural education, training, research, practice, and organizational change for psychologists. *American Psychologist*, 58, 377–402.

Anastasi, A., & Urbina, S. (1997). *Psychological testing* (7th ed.). Upper Saddle River, NJ: Prentice-Hall.

Anderson, N. B., & McNeilly, M. (1991). Age, gender, and ethnicity as variables in psychophysiological assessment: Sociodemographics in context. *Psychological Assessment*, 3, 376–384.

Anderson, R. J., Clouse, R. E., Freedland, K. E., & Lustman, P. J. (2001). The prevalence of comorbid depression in adults with diabetes. *Diabetes Care*, 24, 1069–1078.

Andrews, A. O., Bartels, S. J., Xie, H., & Peacock, W. J. (2009). Increased risk of nursing home admission among middle aged and older adults with schizophrenia. *American Journal of Geriatric Psychiatry*, 17(8), 697–705. doi:10.1097//JGP.0b013e3181aad59d

Anstey, K. J., von Sanden, C., Sargent-Cox, K., & Luszcz, M. (2007). Prevalence and risk factors for depression in a longitudinal, population-based study including individuals in the community and residential care. *American Journal of Geriatric Psychiatry*, 15, 497–505.

Appenzeller, O. (1994). Aging, stress, and autonomic control. In M. L. Albert & J. E. Knoefel (Eds.), *Clinical neurology of aging* (pp. 651–673). New York, NY: Oxford University Press.

Awad, N., Gagnon, M., & Messier, C. (2004). The relationship between impaired glucose tolerance, type II diabetes, and cognitive function. *Journal of Clinical and Experimental Neuropsychology*, 26, 1044–1080.

Baltes, P. B., & Baltes, M. M. (1990). Psychological perspectives on successful aging: The model of selective optimization with compensation. In P. B. Baltes & M. M. Baltes (Eds.), *Successful aging: Perspectives from the behavioral sciences* (pp. 1–34). New York, NY: Cambridge University Press.

Beekman, A. T., Copeland, J. R., & Prince, M. J. (1999). Review of community prevalence of depression in later life. *British Journal of Psychiatry*, 174, 307–311.

Beekman, A. T. F., Penninx, B. W. J. H., Deeg, D. J. H., Ormel, J., Smit, J. H., Braam, A. W., & van Tilburg, W. (1998). Depression in survivors of stroke: A community-based study of prevalence, risk factors, and consequences. *Social Psychiatry and Psychiatric Epidemiology*, 33, 463–470.

Blazer, D. G., Bachar, J. R., & Hughes, D. C. (1987). Major depression with melancholia: A comparison of middle-aged and elderly adults. *Journal of the American Geriatrics Society*, 35, 927–932.

Blazer, D. G. (2009). The psychiatric interview of older adults. In D. G. Blazer & D. C. Steffens (Eds.), *The American Psychiatric Publishing textbook of geriatric psychiatry* (4th ed., pp. 187–200). Arlington, VA: American Psychiatric Publishing.

Bodenhausen, G. V. (1990). Stereotypes and judgmental heuristics: Evidence of circadian variations in discrimination. *Psychological Science*, 1, 319–322.

Bogner, H. R., Ford, D. E., & Gallo, J. J. (2006). The role of cardiovascular disease in the identification and management of depression by primary care physicians. *American Journal of Geriatric Psychiatry*, 14, 71–78.

Brenes, G. A., Knudson, M., McCall, W. V., Williamson, J. D., Miller, M. E., & Stanley, M. A. (2008). Age and racial differences in the presentation and treatment of generalized anxiety disorder in primary care. *Journal of Anxiety Disorders*, 22, 1128–1136.

Bryant, C., Jackson, H., & Ames, D. (2008). The prevalence of anxiety in older adults: Methodological issues and a review of the literature. *Journal of Affective Disorders*, 109, 233–250.

Burn, D. J., Rowan, E. N., Allan, L. M., Molloy, S., O'Brien, J. T., & McKeith, I. G. (2006). Motor subtype and cognitive decline in Parkinson's disease, Parkinson's disease with dementia, and dementia with Lewy bodies. *Journal of Neurology, Neurosurgery, and Psychiatry*, 77, 585–589.

Butler, R. (1969). Ageism: Another form of bigotry. *Gerontologist*, 9, 243.

Butler, R. (1980). Ageism: A foreword. *Journal of Social Issues*, 36, 8–11.

Buysse, D. J., Monk, T. H., Carrier, J., & Begley, A. (2005). Circadian patterns of sleep, sleepiness, and performance in older and younger adults. *Sleep*, 28, 1365–1376.

Byers, A. L., Yaffe, K., Covinsky, K. E., Friedman, M. B., & Bruce, M. L. (2010). High occurrence of mood and anxiety disorders among older adults. *Archives of General Psychiatry*, 67, 489–496.

Campbell, D. T., & Fiske, D. W. (1959). Convergent and discriminant validation by the multitrait-multidimensional matrix. *Psychological Bulletin*, 56, 81–105.

Canadian Institute for Health Information. (2010). *Depression among seniors in residential care*. Retrieved from http://secure.cihi.ca/cihiweb/products/ccrs_depression_among_seniors_e.pdf

Carney, C. P., Jones, L., Woolson, R. F., Noyes, R., & Doebbeling, B. N. (2003). Relationship between depression and pancreatic cancer in the general population. *Psychosomatic Medicine*, 65, 884–888.

Carstensen, L. L. (1991). Socioemotional selectivity theory: Social activity in life-span context. *Annual Review of Gerontology and Geriatrics*, 17, 195–217.

Centers for Disease Control. (2010). *The state of mental health and aging in the America*. Retrieved from www.cdc.gov/aging/pdf/mental_health.pdf

Charles, S. T. (2010). Strength and vulnerability integration: A model of emotional well-being across adulthood. *Psychological Bulletin*, 136, 1068–1091.

Choi, N. G., & Gonzalez, J. M. (2005). Barriers and contributors to minority older adults' access to mental health treatment. *Journal of Gerontological Social Work*, 44(3), 115–135.

Christenden, H., Jorm, A. F., MacKinnon, A. J., Korten, A. E., Jacomb, P. A., Henderson, A. S., et al. (1999). Age differences in depression and anxiety symptoms: A structural equation modelling analysis of data from a general population sample. *Psychological Medicine*, 29, 325–339.

Cohen, C. I., Cohen, G. D., Blank, K., Gaitz, C., Katz, I. R., Leuchter, A., & Shamoian, C. (2000). *American Journal of Geriatric Psychiatry*, 8, 19–28.

Cohen, J. (1960). A coefficient of agreement for nominal scales. *Educational and Psychological Measurement*, 20, 37–46.

Colsher, P., & Wallace, R. B. (1989). Data quality and age: Health and psychobehavioral correlates of item nonresponse and inconsistent responses. *Journal of Gerontology: Psychological Sciences*, 44, P45–P52.

Conner, K. O., Lee, B., Mayers, V., Robinson, D., Reynolds, C. F., Albert, S., et al. (2010). Attitudes and beliefs about mental health among African American older adults suffering from depression. *Journal of Aging Studies*, 24, 266–277.

Conner, K. R., Duberstein, P. R., Beckman, A., Heisel, M. J., Hirsch, J. K., Gamble, S., & Conwell, Y. (2007). Planning of suicide attempts among depressed inpatients ages 50 and over. *Journal of Affective Disorders*, 97, 123–128.

Conwell, Y., Duberstein, P. R., & Caine, E. D. (2002). Risk factors for suicide in later life. *Society of Biological Psychiatry*, 52, 193–204.

Cronbach, L. J. (1971). Test validation. In R. L. Thorndike (Ed.), *Educational measurement* (2nd ed., pp. 443–507). Washington, DC: American Council on Education.

Cronbach, L. J., & Meehl, P. E. (1955). Construct validity in psychological tests. *Psychological Bulletin*, 52, 281–302.

Cully, J. A., Graham, D. P., Stanley, M., Ferguson, C. J., Sharafkhaneh, A., Souchek, J., et al. (2006). Quality of life in patients with chronic obstructive pulmonary disease and comorbid anxiety or depression. *Psychosomatics*, 47, 312–319.

de Beurs, E., Beekman, A. T. F., van Balkom, A. J. L. M., Deeg, D. J. H., van Dyck, R., & van Tilburg, W. (1999). Consequences of anxiety in older persons: Its effect on disability, well-being and use of health services. *Psychological Medicine*, *29*, 583–593.

Deimling, G. T., Bowman, K. F., Sterns, S., Wagner, L. J., & Kahana, B. (2006). Cancer-related health worries and psychological distress among older adult, long-term cancer survivors. *Psycho-Oncology*, *15*, 306–320.

DeMaio, T. (1980). Refusals: Who, where and why. *Public Opinion Quarterly*, *44*, 223–233.

Depp, C. A., & Jeste, D. V. (2004). Bipolar disorder in older adults: A critical review. *Bipolar Disorders*, *6*, 343–367.

Dykstra, P. A. (2009). Older adult loneliness: Myths and realities. *European Journal of Ageing*, *6*, 91–100.

Edelstein, B. A., Drozdick, L. W., & Kogan, J. N. (1998). Assessment of older adults. In A. S. Bellack & M. Hersen (Eds.), *Behavioral assessment: A practical handbook* (4th ed., pp. 179–209). Needham Heights, MA: Allyn & Bacon.

Edelstein, B. A., Martin, R. R., & McKee, D. R. (2000). Assessment of older adult psychopathology. In S. K. Whitbourne (Ed.), *Psychopathology in later adulthood*. (pp. 61–88). New York, NY: Wiley.

Edelstein, B. A., Staats, N., Kalish, K., & Northrop, L. (1996). Assessment of older adults. In M. Hersen & V. Van Hasselt (Eds.) *Psychological treatment of older adults: An introductory textbook* (pp. 35–68). New York, NY: Plenum Press.

Edelstein, B., Woodhead, E., Segal, D., Heisel, M., Bower, E., Lowery, A., & Stoner, S. (2008). Older adult psychological assessment: Current instrument status and related considerations. *Clinical Gerontologist*, *31*, 1–35.

Egede, L. E. (2004). Diabetes, major depression, and functional disability among US adults. *Diabetes Care*, *27*, 421–428.

Eid, M., & Diener, E. (2006). *Handbook of multimethod measurement in psychology*. Washington, DC: American Psychological Association.

Fan, A. Z., Strine, T. W., Jiles, R., & Mokdad, A. H. (2008). Depression and anxiety associated with cardiovascular disease among persons aged 45 years and older in 38 states of the United States, 2006. *Preventive Medicine*, *46*, 445–450.

Fann, J. F., Fan, M., & Unützer, J. (2009). Improving primary care for older adults with cancer and depression. *Journal of General Internal Medicine*, *24*, 417–424.

Farias, S. T., Mungas, D., & Jagust, W. (2005). Degree of discrepancy between self and other-reported everyday functioning by cognitive status: Dementia, mild cognitive impairment, and healthy elders. *International Journal of Geriatric Psychiatry*, *20*, 827–834.

Fearing, M. A., & Inouye, S. K. (2009). Delirium. In D. G. Blazer & D. C. Steffens (Eds.), *Textbook of geriatric psychiatry* (4th ed., pp. 229–242). Arlington, VA: American Psychiatric Publishing.

Feher, E. P., Larrabee, G. J., & Crook, T. J. (1992). Factors attenuating the validity of the geriatric depression scale in a dementia population. *Journal of the American Geriatrics Society*, *40*, 906–909.

Ferri, C. P., Prince, M., Brayne, C., Brodaty, H., Fratiglioni, L., Ganguli, M. . . . & Scazufca, M. (2005). Global prevalence of dementia: A Delphi consensus study. *Lancet*, *366*, 2112–2117.

First, M. B., Spitzer, R. L., Gibbon, M., & Williams, J. B. W. (2002). *Structured Clinical Interview for DSM-IV-TR Axis I disorders, research version, patient edition*. (SCID-I/P). New York, NY: Biometrics Research, New York State Psychiatric Institute.

Fountoulakis, K. N., O'Hara, R. O., Iacovides, A., Camilleri, C. P., Kaprinis, S., Kaprinis, G., & Yesavage, J. (2003). Unipolar late-onset depression: A comprehensive review. *Annals of General Hospital Psychiatry*, *2*. doi:10.1186/1475–2832–2–11

Frazer, D. W., Leicht, M. L., & Baker, M. D. (1996). Psychological manifestations of physical disease in the elderly. In L. L. Carstensen, B. A. Edelstein, & L. Dornbrand (Eds.) *The practical handbook of clinical gerontology*. Thousand Oaks, CA: Sage.

Fulop, G., Strain, J. J., & Stettin, G. (2003). Congestive heart failure and depression in older adults: Clinical course and health services use six months after hospitalization. *Psychosomatics*, *44*, 367–373.

Fung, H. H., Carstensen, L. L., & Lang, F. R. (2001). Age-related patterns in social networks among European Americans and African Americans: implications for Socioemotional Selectivity Theory across the lifespan. *International Journal of Aging and Human Development*, *52*, 185–206.

Gallo, J. J., Anthony, J. C., & Muthén, B. O. (1994). Age differences in the symptoms of depression: A latent trait analysis. *Journal of Gerontology: Psychological Sciences*, *49*, P251–P264.

Gallo, J. J., Rabins, P. V., & Anthony, J. C. (1999). Sadness in older persons: 13-year follow-up of a community sample in Baltimore, Maryland. *Psychological Medicine*, *29*, 341–350.

Gatz, M., & Pearson, C. G. (1988). Ageism revised and the provision of psychological services. *American Psychologist*, *43*, 184–188.

Gatz, M., Kasl-Godley, J. E., & Karel, M. J. (1996). Aging and mental disorders. In J. Birren & K. W. Schaie (Eds.), *Handbook of the psychology of aging* (4th ed., pp. 365–382). New York, NY: Academic Press.

Gergen, K. J., & Back, K. W. (1966). Communication in the interview and the disengaged respondent. *Public Opinion Quarterly*, *30*, 385–398.

Glass, J. M. (2007). Visual function and cognitive aging: Differential role of contrast sensitivity in verbal versus spatial tasks. *Psychology and Aging*, *22*, 233–238.

Goga, J. A., & Hambacher, W. O. (1977). Psychologic and behavioral assessment of geriatric patients: A review. *Journal of the American Geriatrics Society*, *25*, 232–237.

Goodwin, R. D., Davidson, K. W., & Keyes, K. (2009). Mental disorders and cardiovascular disease among adults in the United States. *Journal of Psychiatric Research*, *43*, 239–246.

Greenberg, D. B. (1989). Depression and cancer. In R. G. Robinson & P. V. Rabins (Eds.), *Depression and coexisting disease* (pp. 103–115). New York, NY: Igaku-Shoin.

Gunstad, J., Cohen, R. A., Paul, R. H., Tate, D. F., Hoth, K. F., & Poppas, A. (2006). Understanding reported cognitive dysfunction in older adults with cardiovascular disease. *Neuropsychiatric Disease and Treatment*, *2*, 213–218.

Hajjar, E. R., & Hanlon, J. T. (2006). Polypharmacy in the elderly. In K. Calhoun & E. E. Eibling (Eds.), *Geriatric otolaryngology* (pp. 667–673). New York, NY: Taylor & Francis.

Hajjar, E. R., Cafiero, A. C., & Hanlon, J. F. (2007). Polypharmacy in elderly patients. *American Journal of Geriatric Pharmacology*, *5*(4), 345–356.

Hasher, L., Goldstein, D., & May, C. (2005). It's about time: Circadian rhythms, memory and aging. In C. Izawa & N. Ohta (Eds.), *Human learning and memory: Advances in theory and application* (pp. 199–217). Mawah, NJ: Erlbaum.

Hasher, L., & Zacks, R. T. (1988). Working memory, comprehension, and aging: A review and a new view. In G. H. Bower (Ed.), *The psychology of learning and motivation* (Vol. 22, pp. 193–225). New York, NY: Academic Press.

Haynes, S. N., & O'Brien, W. H. (2000). *Principles and practice of behavioral assessment*. New York, NY: Kluwer.

Haynes, S. N., Mumma, G. H., & Pinson, C. (2009). Idiographic assessment: Conceptual and psychometric foundations of individualized behavioral assessment. *Clinical Psychology Review*, *29*, 179–191.

Herzog, A. R., & Rodgers, W. L. (1988). Age and response rates to interview sample surveys. *Journals of Gerontology*, *43*, S200–S205.

Horne, J., & Osterberg, O. (1976). A self-assessment questionnaire to determine morningness-eveningness in human circadian rhythms. *International Journal of Chronobiology*, *4*, 97–110.

Inouye, S. K. (2006). Delirium in older persons. *New England Journal of Medicine*, *354*, 1157–1165.

Ishihara, K., Miyake, S., Miyasita, A., & Miyata, Y. (1991). Morningness-eveningness preference and sleep habits in Japanese office workers of different ages. *Chronobiologia*, *19*, 9–16.

James, J. W., & Haley, W. E. (1995). Age and health bias in practicing clinical psychologists. *Psychology and Aging*, *10*, 610–616.

Jang, Y., Chiriboga, D. A., & Okazaki, S. (2009). Attitudes toward mental health services: Age-group differences in Korean American adults. *Aging and Mental Health*, *13*, 127–134.

Jang, Y., Mortimer, J. A., Haley, W. E., Small, B. J., Chisolm, T. E., & Graves, A. B. (2003). The role of vision and hearing in physical, social, and emotional functioning among older adults. *Research on Aging*, *25*, 172–191.

Johnson, R. W., & Kaminski, J. (2010). Older adult's labor force participation since 1993: A decade and a half of growth. *Fact Sheet on Retirement Policy*. Retrieved from www.retirementpolicy.org

Jones, R. N. (2003). Racial bias in the assessment of cognitive functioning of older adults. *Aging and Mental Health*, *7*, 83–102.

Juniper, K., & Dykman, R. A. (1967). Skin resistance, sweat gland counts, salivary flow, and gastric secretion: Age, race, and sex differences and intercorrelations. *Psychophysiology*, *4*, 216–222.

Kalaria, R. N., Maestre, G. E., Arizaga, R., Friedland, R. P., Galasko, D., Hall, K., & Antuono, P. (2008). Alzheimer's disease and vascular dementia in developing countries: Prevalence, management, and risk factors. *Lancet Neurology*, *7*, 812–826. doi:10.1016/S1474-4422(08)70169–8

Karavidas, M., Llim, N. K., & Katsikas, S. L. (2002). The effects of computer on older adult users. *Computers in Human Behavior*, *21*, 697–711.

Kazdin, A., & Wilson, G. T. (1978). *Evaluation of behavior therapy: Issues, evidence, and research*. Cambridge, MA: Ballinger.

Kelly-Hayes, M., Jette, A. M., Wolf, P. A., D'Agostino, R. B., & Odell, P. M. (1992). Functional limitations and disability among elders in the Framingham study. *American Journal of Public Health*, *82*, 841–845.

Kessler, R. C., Berglund, P., Demler, O., Jin, R., Merikangas, K. R., & Walters, E. E. (2005). Lifetime prevalence and age-of-onset distributions of *DSM-IV* disorders in the National Comorbidity Survey Replication. *Archives of General Psychiatry*, *62*, 593–602.

Kim, H. F. S., Braun, U., & Kunik, M. E. (2001). Anxiety and depression in medically ill older adults. *Journal of Clinical Geropsychology*, *7*, 117–130.

Kimmel, D. C. (1988). Ageism, psychology, and public policy. *American Psychologist*, *43*, 175–178.

Kirmayer, L. J. (2001). Cultural variations in the clinical presentation of depression and anxiety: Implications for diagnosis and treatment. *Journal of Clinical Psychiatry*, *62*, 22–28.

Kirmayer, L. J., & Young, A. (1998). Culture and somatization: Clinical, epidemiological, and ethnographic perspectives. *Psychosomatic Medicine*, *60*, 420–430.

Kiyak, H. A., Teri, L., & Borsom, S. (1994). Physical and functional health assessment in normal aging and Alzheimer's disease: Self-reports vs. family reports. *Gerontologist*, *34*, 324–330.

Knight, B. G., Santos, J., Teri, L., & Lawton, M. P. (1995). The development of training in clinical geropsychology. In B. G. Knight, L. Teri, P. Wolford, & J. Santos (Eds.), *Mental health services for older adults: Implications for training and practice in geropsychology* (pp. 1–8). Washington, DC: American Psychological Association.

Kogan, J., & Edelstein, B. (2004). Modification and psychometric examination of a self-report measure of fear in older adults. *Journal of Anxiety Disorders*, *18*, 397–409.

Kogan, J., Edelstein, B., & McKee, D. (2000). Assessment of anxiety in older adults: Current status. *Journal of Anxiety Disorders*, *14*, 109–132.

Kogan, N. (1961). Attitudes towards old people in an older sample. *Journal of Abnormal and Social Psychology*, *62*, 616–622.

Kramer, A. F., & Willis, S. L. (2002). Enhancing the cognitive vitality of older adults. *Current Directions in Psychological Science*, *11*, 173–177.

Kuder, G. F., & Richardson, M. W. (1937). The theory of the estimation of reliability. *Psychometrika*, *2*, 151–160.

Kvale, E. A., Clay, O. J., Ross-Meadows, L. A., McGee, J. S., Edwards, J. D., Unverzagt, F. W., et al. (2010). Cognitive speed of processing and functional declines in older cancer survivors: An analysis of data from the ACTIVE trial. *European Journal of Cancer Care*, *19*, 110–117.

Lau, A., Edelstein, B., & Larkin, K. (2001). Psychophysiological responses of older adults: A critical review with implications for assessment of anxiety disorders. *Clinical Psychology Review*, *21*, 609–630.

Lin, M. Y., Gutierrez, P. R., Stone, K. L., Yaffe, K., Ensrud, K. E., Fink, H. A., . . . Study of Osteoporotic Fractures Research Group. (2004). Vision impairment and combined vision and hearing impairment predict cognitive and functional decline in older women. *Journal of the American Geriatrics Society*, *52*, 1996–2002.

Luo, L., & Craik, F. I. M. (2008). Aging and memory: A cognitive approach. *Canadian Journal of Psychiatry*, *53*, 346–353.

Lustman, P. J., Griffith, L. S., Clouse, R. E., & Cryer, P. E. (1986). Psychiatric illness in diabetes mellitus: Relationship to symptoms and glucose control. *Journal of Nervous and Mental Disease*, *174*, 736–742.

Maiese, D. R. (2002). Healthy people 2010: Leading health indicators for women. *Women's Health Issues*, *12*, 155–164.

Maly, R. C., Umezawa, Y., Leake, B., & Silliman, R. A. (2005). Mental health outcomes in older women with breast cancer: Impact of perceived family support and adjustment. *Psycho-Oncology*, *14*, 535–545.

Mansueti, L., de Frias, C. M., Bub, D., & Dixon, R. A. (2008). Exploring cognitive effects of self reported mild stroke in older adults: Selective but robust effects on story memory. *Aging, Neuropsychology, and Cognition*, *15*, 545–573.

May, C. P., Hasher, L., & Stoltzfus, E. R. (1993). Optimal time of day and the magnitude of age differences in memory. *Psychological Science*, *4*, 326–330.

McCarthy, J. F., Blow, F. C., & Kales, H. C. (2004). Disruptive behaviors in Veterans Affairs nursing home residents: How different are residents with serious mental illness? *Journal of the American Geriatrics Society*, *52*, 2031–2038.

McDougall, F. A., Matthews, F. E., Kvaal, K., Dewey, M. E., & Brayne, C. (2007). Prevalence and symptomatology of depression in older people living in institutions in England and Wales. *Age and Ageing*, *36*, 526–568.

McDowd, J. M., Filion, D. L., Pohl, P. S., Richards, L. G., & Stiers, W. (2003). Attentional abilities and functional outcomes following stroke. *Journal of Gerontology: Psychological Sciences*, *58B*, P45–P53.

McNeilly, M., & Anderson, N. B. (1997). Age differences in physiological responses to stress. In P. E. Ruskin & J. A. Talbott (Eds.), *Aging and posttraumatic stress disorder* (pp. 163–201). Washington, DC: American Psychiatric Press.

Mechanic, D., & McAlpine, D. D. (2000). Use of nursing homes in the care of persons with severe mental illness: 1985–1995. *Psychiatric Services*, *51*, 354–358.

Mischel, W. (1968). *Personality and assessment*. New York, NY: Wiley.

Morse, J. Q., & Lynch, T. R. (2000). Personality disorders in late life. *Current Psychiatry Reports*, *2*, 24–31.

Mouton, C. P., & Esparza, Y. B. (2000). Ethnicity and geriatric assessment. In J. J. Gallo, T. Fulmer, G. J. Paveza, & W. Reichel (Eds.), *Handbook of geriatric assessment* (pp. 13–28). Gaithersburg, MD: Aspen.

Mumma, G. H. (2004). Validation of idiographic cognitive schema in cognitive case formulations: An intraindividual idiographic approach. *Psychological Assessment*, *16*, 211–230.

National Eye Institute. (2011). Prevalence of blindness data. Retrieved from www.nei.nih.gov/eyedata/pbd_tables.asp

National Institute of Mental Health. (2007). *Older adults: Depression and suicide facts (fact sheet)*. Retrieved from www.nimh.nih.gov/health/publications/older-adults-depression-and-suicide-facts-fact-sheet/index.shtml#cdc

National Institute on Deafness and Other Communication Disorders. (2009). *Hearing loss and older adults*. Retrieved from www.nidcd.nih.gov/health/hearing

Nazir, S. A., & Erbland, M. L. (2009). Chronic obstructive pulmonary disease: An update on diagnosis and management issues in older adults. *Drugs and Aging*, *26*, 813–831.

Nelson, R., & Hayes, S. (Eds.). (1986). Conceptual foundations of behavioral assessment. New York, NY: Guilford Press.

Nunnally, J. C., & Bernstein, I. H. (1994). *Psychometric theory* (3rd ed.). New York, NY: McGraw-Hill.

Okun, M. (1976). Adult age and cautiousness in decision: A review of the literature. *Human Development*, *19*, 220–233.

Orgeta, V. (2009). Specificity of age differences in emotion regulation. *Aging and Mental Health*, *13*, 818–826.

Pachana, N. A., Byrne, G. J., Siddle, H., Koloski, N., Harley, E., & Arnold, E. (2007). Development and validation of the Geriatric Anxiety Inventory. *International Psychogeriatrics*, *19*, 103–114.

Palmore, E. (2001). The Ageism survey: First findings. *Gerontologist*, *41*, 572–575.

Palmore, E. B. (1999). *Ageism: Negative and positive* (2nd ed.). New York, NY: Springer.

Plassman, B. L., Langa, K. M., Fisher, G. G., Heeringa, S. G., Weir, D. R., Ofstedal, M. B., & Wallace, R. B. (2007). Prevalence of dementia in the United States: The Aging, Demographics, and Memory Study. *Neuroepidemiology*, *29*, 125–132. doi: 10.1159/000109998

Poon, L. (1995). Learning. In G. Maddox, (Ed.), *The encyclopedia of aging* (pp. 380–381). New York, NY: Springer.

Qato, D. M., Alexander, G. C., Conti, R. M., Johnson, M., Schumm, P., & Lindau, S. T. (2008). Use of prescription and over-the-counter medication and dietary supplements among older adults in the United States. *Journal of the American Medical Association*, *24*, 2867–2878.

Quelhas, R., & Costa, M. (2009). Anxiety, depression, and quality of life in Parkinson's disease. *Journal of Neuropsychiatry and Clinical Neuroscience*, *21*, 413–419.

Redinbaugh, E. M., Baum, A., DeMoss, C., Fello, M., & Arnold, R. (2002). Factors associated with the accuracy of family caregiver estimates of patient pain. *Journal of Pain and Symptom Management*, *23*, 31–38.

Reite, M., Buysse, D., Reynolds, C., & Mendelson, W. (1995). The use of polysomnography in the evaluation of insomnia. *Sleep*, *18*, 58–70.

Robb, C., Chen, H., & Haley, W. E. (2002). Ageism in mental health and health care: A critical review. *Journal of Clinical Geropsychology*, *8*, 1–12.

Rodgers, W. L., & Herzog, A. R. (1987). Interviewing older adults: The accuracy of factual information. *Journal of Gerontology*, *42*(4), 387–394.

Rossi, M. I., Young, A., Maher, R., Rodriguez, K. L., Appelt, C. J., Perera, S., et al. (2007). Polypharmacy and health beliefs in older outpatients. *American Journal of Geriatric Pharmacotherapy*, *5*, 317–323.

Rowe, J. W., & Kahn, R. L. (1998). *Successful aging*. New York, NY: Pantheon Books.

Rubenstein, L. Z., Schairer, C., Wieland, G. D., & Kane, R. (1984). Systematic biases in functional status assessment of elderly adults:

Effects of different data sources. *Journal of Gerontology*, *39*(6), 686–691.

Sager, M. A., Dunham, N. C., Schwantes, A., Mecum, L., Haverson, K., & Harlowe, D. (1992). Measurement of activities of daily living in hospitalized elderly: A comparison of self-report and performance-based methods. *Journal of the American Geriatrics Society*, *40*, 457–462.

Salthouse, T. A. (1994). The nature of the influence of speed on adult age differences in cognition. *Developmental Psychology*, *30*, 763–776.

Schmidt, C., Fabienne, C., Cajochen, C. & Peigneux, P. (2007). A time to think: Circadian rhythms in human cognition. *Cognitive Neuropsychology*, *24*, 755–789.

Schwarz, N. (1999). Self-reports of behavioral and opinions: Cognitive and communicative processes. In N. Schwarz, D. C. Park, B. Knauper, & S. Sudman (Eds.). *Cognition, aging, and self-reports* (pp. 17–44). Philadelphia, PA: Psychology Press.

Shiyanbola, O. O., & Farris, K. B. (2010). Concerns and beliefs about medicines and inappropriate medication: An Internet-based survey on risk factors for self-reported adverse drug events among older adults. *American Journal of Geriatric Pharmacotherapy*, *8*, 243–257.

Sloan, F. A., & Wang, J. (2005). Disparities among older adults in measure of cognitive function by race or ethnicity. *Journal of Gerontology: Psychological Sciences*, *60B*, P242–P250.

Spiegel, D., & Giese-Davis, J. (2003). Depression and cancer: Mechanisms and disease progression. *Biological Psychiatry*, *54*, 269–282.

Sunderland, A., Watts, K., Baddeley, A. D., & Harris, J. E. (1986). Subjective memory assessment and test performance in elderly adults. *Journal of Gerontology*, *41*(3), 376–384.

Szanto, K., Prigerson, H. G., & Reynolds, C. F. III (2001). Suicide in the elderly. *Clinical Neuroscience Research*, *1*, 366–376.

Tackett, J. L., Balsis, S., Oltmanns, T. F., & Krueger, R. F. (2009). A unifying perspective on personality pathology across the lifespan: Developmental considerations for the fifth edition of the *Diagnostic and Statistical Manual of Mental Disorders*. *Developmental Psychopathology*, *21*, 687–713.

Talbot, F., & Nouwen, A. (2000). A review of the relationship between depression and diabetes in adults. *Diabetes Care*, *23*, 1556–1562.

Thornton, J. E. (2002). Myths of aging or ageist stereotypes. *Educational Gerontology*, *28*, 301–312.

Tolman, J., Hill, R. D., Kleinschmidt, J. J., & Gregg, C. H. (2005). Psychosocial adaptation to visual impairment and its relationship to depressive affect in older adults with age-related macular degeneration. *Gerontologist*, *45*, 747–753.

Tun, P. A., McCoy, S., & Wingfield, A. (2009). Aging, hearing acuity, and the attentional costs of effortful listening. *Psychology and Aging*, *24*, 761–766.

Tun, P. A., O'Kane, G., & Wingfield, A. (2002). Distraction by competing speech in young and older adult listeners. *Psychology and Aging*, *17*, 453–467.

Turnheim, K. (2003). When drug therapy gets old: Pharmacokinetics and pharmacodynamics in the elderly. *Experimental Gerontology*, *38*, 843–853.

Turpin, G. (1991). The psychophysiological assessment of anxiety disorders: Three-systems measurement and beyond. *Psychological Assessment*, *3*, 366–375.

Turvey, C. L., Conwell, Y., Jones, M. P., Phillips, C., Simonsick, E., Pearson, J. L., & Wallace, R. (2002). Risk factors for late-life suicide: A prospective, community-based study. *American Journal of Geriatric Psychiatry*, *10*, 398–406.

Uchino, B. N., Birmingham, W., & Berg, C. A. (2010). Are older adults less or more physiologically reactive? A meta-analysis of age-related differences in cardiovascular reactivity to laboratory tasks. *Journals of Gerontology: Series B*, *65B*(2), 154–162.

Vacha-Haase, T., Kogan, L. R., & Thompson, B. (2000). Sample compositions and variabilities in published studies versus those in test manuals: Validity of score reliability inductions. *Educational and Psychological Measurement*, *60*, 509–522.

Van Alphen, S. P. J., Engelen, G. J. J., Kuin, Y., & Derksen, J. J. L. (2006). The relevance of a geriatric sub-classification of personality disorders in the *DSM-V*. *International Journal of Geriatric Psychiatry*, *21*, 205–209.

Vanderplas, J. H., & Vanderplas, J. M. (1981). Effects of legibility on verbal test performance of older adults. *Perceptual and Motor Skills*, *53*, 183–186.

Vataja, R., Pohjasvaara, T., Leppavuori, A., Mantyle, R., Aronen, H. J., Salonen, O., et al. (2001). Magnetic resonance imaging correlates of depression after ischemic stroke. *Archives of General Psychiatry*, *58*, 925–931.

Vincent, G. K., & Velkoff, V. A. (2010). The older population in the United States: 2010 to 2050. *Current Population Reports*, 25–1138. Washington, DC: U.S. Census Bureau.

Wagner, N., Hassanein, K., & Head, M. (2010). Computer use by older adults: A multi-disciplinary review. *Computers in Human Behavior*, *26*, 870–882.

Wallhagen, M. I. (2009). The stigma of hearing loss. *Gerontologist*, *50*, 66–75.

Wallihan, D., Stump, T., & Callahan, C. (1999). Accuracy of self-reported health services use and patterns of care among urban older adults. *Medical Care*, *37*, 662–670.

West, R., Murphy, K. J., Armilio, M. L., Craik, F. I., & Stuss, D. T. (2002). Effects of time of day on age differences in working memory. *Journals of Geronotology Series B: Psychological and Social Sciences*, *57*, 3–10.

Wetherell, J. L., Petkus, A. J., McChesney, K., Stein, M. B., Judd, P. H., Rockwell, E., et al. (2009). Older adults are less accurate than younger adults are identifying symptoms of anxiety and depression. *Journal of Nervous and Mental Disease*, *197*, 623–626.

Whitbourne, S. K. (2002). *The aging individual: Physical and psychological perspectives* (2nd ed.). New York, NY: Springer.

Whiteside, M. M., Wallhagen, M. I., & Pettengill, E. (2006). Sensory impairment in older adults: Part 2: Vision loss. *American Journal of Nursing*, *106*, 52–61.

Whyte, E. M., Mulsant, B. H., Vanderbilt, J., Dodge, H. H., & Ganguli, M. (2004). Depression after stoke: A prospective epidemiological study. *Journal of the American Geriatrics Society*, *52*, 774–778.

Widiger, T. A., & Seidlitz, L. (2002). Personality, psychopathology, and aging. *Journal of Research in Personality*, *36*, 335–362.

Winblad, I., Viramo, P., Remes, A., Manninen, M., & Jokelainen, J. (2010). Prevalence of dementia: A rising challenge among ageing populations. *European Geriatric Medicine*, *1*, 330–333.

Wisocki, P. A., Handen, B., & Morse, C. K. (1986). The worry scale as a measure of anxiety among homebound and community active elderly. *Behavior Therapist*, *5*, 369–379.

Wolitzky-Taylor, K. B., Castriotta, N., Lenze, E. J., Stanley, M. A., & Craske, M. G. (2010). Anxiety disorders in older adults: A comprehensive review. *Depression and Anxiety*, *27*, 190–211.

Yang, L., Hasher, L., & Wilson, D. E. (2007). Syndrony effects in automatic and controlled retrieval. *Psychonomic Science & Review*, *14*, 51–56.

Yesavage, J. A. (1992). Depression in the elderly: How to recognize masked symptoms and choose appropriate therapy. *Postgraduate Medicine*, *91*, 255–261.

Yoder, P., & Symons, F. (Eds.). (2010) *Observational measurement of behavior*. New York, NY: Springer.

Yoon, C., May, C. P., & Hasher, L. (1997). Age differences in consumers' processing strategies: An investigation of moderating influences. *Journal of Consumer Research*, *24*, 329–342.

Zanetti, O., Geroldi, C., Frisoni, G. B., Bianchetti, A., & Trabucchi, M. (1999). Contrasting results between caregiver's report and direct assessment of activities of daily living in patients affected by mild and very mild dementia: The contribution of the caregiver's personal characteristics. *Journal of the American Geriatrics Society*, *47*, 196–202.

Zarit, S. H., & Zarit, J. M. (2007). *Mental disorders in older adults: Fundamentals of assessment and treatment* (2nd ed., pp. 40–77). New York, NY: Guilford Press.

Zweig, R. A. (2008). Personality disorder in older adults: Assessment challenges and strategies. *Professional Psychology: Research and Practice*, *39*, 298–305.

# PART III

# Assessment Methods

# CHAPTER 18

# Assessment of Intellectual Functioning

JOHN D. WASSERMAN

I hate the impudence of a claim that in fifty minutes you can judge and classify a human being's predestined fitness in life. I hate the pretentiousness of that claim. I hate the abuse of scientific method which it involves. I hate the sense of superiority which it creates, and the sense of inferiority which it imposes.

—Walter Lippmann (1923, p. 146)

The study of intelligence and cognitive abilities dates back more than a century and has been characterized by some of the best and worst of aspects of science—the development of new methodologies, research breakthroughs, and vigorous scholarly debates as well as bitter rivalries, allegations of academic fraud, and the birth of a commercial testing industry that generates hundreds of million dollars in annual revenue. The assessment of intelligence can understandably elicit strong individual reactions, such as that expressed by progressive journalist Walter Lippmann as part of an exchange with Stanford-Binet author Lewis M. Terman in a prescient series of *The New Republic* magazine articles in the 1920s (Lippmann, 1922a–f, 1923). Intelligence testing gave rise to divisive public controversies at regular intervals throughout the 20th century, most recently after the 1994 publication of *The Bell Curve* by Richard J. Herrnstein and Charles Murray. Even with its more controversial aspects, however, intelligence remains a robust and important scientific construct. As of this writing, the American Psychological Association (APA) database PSYCInfo reports nearly 50,000 scholarly publications with *intelligence* as a keyword, and the concept of *general intelligence* has been described as "one of the most central phenomena in all of behavioral science, with broad explanatory powers" (Jensen, 1998, p. xii).

This chapter describes contemporary approaches to the assessment of cognitive and intellectual functioning with an emphasis on omnibus intelligence tests. Seven major intelligence tests are presented in terms of their history, theoretical underpinnings, standardization features and psychometric adequacy, and interpretive indices and applications. These tests include the Cognitive Assessment System (CAS; Naglieri & Das, 1997a, 1997b), Differential Ability Scales (DAS-II; C. D. Elliott, 2007a, 2007b, 2007c), Kaufman Assessment Battery for Children (KABC-II; Kaufman & Kaufman, 2004), Reynolds Intellectual Assessment Scales (RIAS; Reynolds & Kamphaus, 2003), Stanford-Binet Intelligence Scales (SB5; Roid, 2003a, 2003b, 2003c), Wechsler Intelligence Scale for Children and Wechsler Adult Intelligence Scale (WISC-IV and WAIS-IV; Wechsler, 2003a, 2003b, 2008a, 2008b), and Woodcock-Johnson Tests of Cognitive Abilities (WJ III NU Cog; Woodcock, McGrew, & Mather, 2001a, 2007a). The most common diagnostic applications for intelligence testing are provided. Finally, the status of intelligence assessment as a maturing clinical science is assessed.

## DESCRIPTIONS OF THE MAJOR INTELLIGENCE TESTS

This section presents seven of the leading individually administered intelligence tests, along with brief reviews and critical evaluations. The descriptions are limited to intelligence tests that purport to be reasonably comprehensive and multidimensional, covering a variety of content areas; more specialized tests (such as nonverbal cognitive batteries) and group-administered tests (usually administered in large-scale educational testing programs) have been excluded. Students of intellectual assessment will notice considerable overlap and redundancy between many of these instruments, in large part because they tend to measure similar psychological constructs with similar procedures, and in many cases they have similar origins.

The tests are presented in alphabetical order. For each test, its history is briefly recounted followed by a description of its theoretical underpinnings. Basic psychometric features, including characteristics of standardization, reliability, and validity are presented. Core interpretive indices are also described in a way that is generally commensurate with descriptions provided in the test manuals. Emphasis is placed on the interpretive indices that are central to the test, but not the plethora of indices that are available for some tests. Applications, strengths, and limitations of each test are discussed.

Some generalizations may be mentioned at the outset. First, it is apparent that contemporary intelligence measures are much more similar than different. While each instrument has some characteristic limitations, all of them are fairly adequate from a psychometric point of view. They all have satisfactory normative samples, and their composite scales tend to meet at least minimal standards of measurement precision. Second, while a few eschew Spearman's general factor of intelligence (psychometric $g$), most of them end up yielding good overall estimates of $g$. Third, while several different structural models are presented, there is considerable overlap in the constructs being tapped, epitomized by Kaufman and Kaufman's (2004) acknowledgment that their scales can be validly interpreted according to multiple theoretical perspectives, based on the user's theoretical inclinations. Finally, it is becoming increasingly clear that the traditional dichotomy between verbal and nonverbal intelligence overlaps with and is somewhat redundant with the Cattell-Horn-Carroll (CHC) crystallized and fluid ability dichotomy. It is no accident that tests of crystallized ability are overwhelmingly verbal while tests of fluid ability are consistently nonverbal and visual-spatial.

## Cognitive Assessment System

The Das-Naglieri Cognitive Assessment System (CAS; Naglieri & Das, 1997a, 1997b) is a cognitive processing battery intended for use with children and adolescents 5 through 17 years of age. The origins of the CAS may be traced to the work of A. R. Luria, the preeminent Russian neuropsychologist whose work has been highly influential in American psychology. Beginning in 1972, J. P. Das initiated a program of research based on the simultaneous and successive modes of information processing suggested by Luria. Ashman and Das (1980) first reported the addition of planning measures to the simultaneous-successive experimental tasks, and separate attention and planning tasks were developed by the end of the decade (Naglieri & Das, 1987, 1988). The work of Luria and Das influenced Alan and Nadeen Kaufman, who published the K-ABC (see section below) in 1983. Jack A. Naglieri, a former student of Kaufman's who had assisted with the K-ABC development, met J. P. Das in 1984 and began a collaboration to assess Luria's three functional systems. Thirteen years and some 100 studies later, the CAS was published.

CAS is available in two batteries: an 8-subtest basic battery and a 12-subtest standard battery. The basic battery can be administered in about 40 minutes while the standard battery requires about 60 minutes. Translations/adaptations of CAS are now available in Dutch, Chinese, Greek, Italian, Japanese, Korean, Norwegian, and Spanish.

### Theoretical Underpinnings

The CAS has its theoretical underpinnings in Luria's (1970, 1973, 1980) three functional units in the brain: (1) the first unit regulates cortical tone and alertness and arousal (interpreted by the test authors as *attention*); (2) the second unit receives, processes, and retains information in two basic forms of integrative activity (*simultaneous* and *successive*); and (3) the third unit involves the formation, execution, and monitoring of behavioral *planning*. Luria (1966) credited Russian physiologist Ivan M. Sechenov with the concept of *simultaneous* and *successive* processing, which he introduced in this way:

> The first of these forms is the integration of the individual stimuli arriving in the brain into *simultaneous, and primarily spatial, groups,* and the second in the integration of individual stimuli arriving consecutively in the brain *into temporally organized, successive series.* We shall refer conventionally to these as simultaneous and successive syntheses. (p. 74; emphasis in the original)

Simultaneous processing tends to be parallel or synchronous, in which stimuli are perceived and processed as a whole. Successive processing tends to involve a serial, chainlike progression of processing, in which information is processed in order and each activity is related to those that preceded it. Simultaneous and successive cognitive processes formed the core elements of the dual processing system (Das, Kirby, & Jarman, 1975, 1979) that was later expanded and articulated as PASS theory, using the acronym for planning, attention, simultaneous, and successive processes (Das, Naglieri, & Kirby, 1994).

In 1986 Das defined *intelligence* as "the sum total of all cognitive processes" (p. 55; see also Das, 2004, p. 5). According to Naglieri (1999), "the single most important goal of the Cognitive Assessment System is to encourage an evolutionary step from the traditional IQ, general ability approach to a theory-based, multidimensional view with constructs built on contemporary research in human cognition" (p. 9).

### Standardization Features and Psychometric Adequacy

The CAS was standardized from 1993 through 1996 on 2,200 children and adolescents from 5 through 17 years of age, stratified on 1990 census figures. Sample stratification variables included race, ethnicity, geographic region, community setting, parent educational attainment, classroom placement, and educational classification. The standardization sample was evenly divided between males and females, in nine age groups, with $n = 300$ per year for ages 5 through 7 years, $n = 200$ per year for ages 8 through 10 years, and $n = 200$ per 2- or 3- year intervals for ages 11 through 17 years. Demographic characteristics of the standardization sample are reported in detail across stratification variables in the CAS interpretive handbook and closely match the targeted census figures (Naglieri & Das, 1997b).

The reliability of the CAS is generally adequate. Internal consistency was computed through the split-half method with Spearman-Brown correction, and test–retest stability was the basis for estimating the reliability of the Planning and Attention subtests as well as a single Successive Processing subtest (Speech Rate). Stability coefficients were measured with a test–retest interval from 9 to 73 days, with a median of 21 days. Across these two methods of determining score reliability, the average reliabilities for the PASS and Full Scale composite scores across age groups ranged from .84 (Attention, Basic Battery) to .96 (Full Scale, Standard Battery). Average subtest reliability coefficients across age groups ranged from .75 to .89, with a median reliability of .82. A total of 9 of 13 subtests yielded reliability estimates at or above .80. Half (50%) of the composite score reliabilities were at .90 or higher.

Corrected for variability of scores from the first testing, the stability coefficients are somewhat less adequate with

median values of .73 for the CAS subtests and .82 for the Basic and Standard Battery PASS scales. Only 16% of the subtests had corrected stability coefficients at or above .80, and no composite standard scores had corrected stability coefficients at or above .90.

CAS floors and ceilings tend to be adequate for school-age children. Test score floors extend 2 or more standard deviations (*SD*s) below the normative mean beginning with 6-year, 4-month-old children, so discrimination at the lowest processing levels is somewhat limited with 5-year-olds, particularly for simultaneous subtests. Test score ceilings extend more than 2 *SD*s above the normative mean at all age levels. Standard scores range from about 45 to 153 for the PASS scales, with a range of 40 to 160 for the Full Scale IQ (FSIQ).

Exploratory and confirmatory factor analyses of the CAS provide support for either a three- or four-factor solution (Naglieri & Das, 1997b). The four-factor solution is based on the four PASS dimensions whereas the three-factor solution combines Planning and Attention to form a single dimension. The decision to utilize the four-factor solution was based on the test's underlying theory, meaningful discrepancies between planning and attention performance in criterion populations (e.g., attention-deficit/hyperactivity disorder [ADHD], traumatic brain injury), and differential response to treatments in intervention studies (e.g., planning-based intervention).

Critics have asserted that CAS interpretive structure (i.e., the PASS framework) does not match its factor structure, and questions have emerged about what constructs that the PASS scales actually measure. On a data set based on the tryout version of the CAS, Carroll (1995) argued that the planning scale, in which all subtests are timed, may be best conceptualized as a measure of perceptual speed. Keith, Kranzler, and Flanagan challenged the CAS factor structure based on reanalyses of the standardization sample and analyses with new samples (Keith & Kranzler, 1999; Keith et al., 2001; Kranzler & Keith, 1999; Kranzler, Keith, & Flanagan, 2000). These investigations have generally reported that the planning and attention subtests lack the specificity and factorial coherence to be interpreted separately, that they are more appropriately collapsed into a single factor strongly related to speed, and that the simultaneous and successive factors may best be reconceptualized as tapping visualization and short-term memory span. In responding to these types of criticisms, Puhan, Das, and Naglieri (2005) offered other sources of validity evidence for the factor structure of the CAS. Haddad (2004) studied the relationship between speed and planning on the CAS Planned Codes subtest and concluded that the subtest is better described as a measure of planning than speed. More recently, Deng, Liu, We, Chan, and Das (2011) found that either a four-factor PASS model or a three-factor (PA)SS model fit the data well in a confirmatory factor analysis of the Chinese-language adaptation of CAS with a Chinese sample. After conducting hierarchical exploratory factor analyses, Canivez (2011b) and the test's complex structure may have distorted the CFA results of Kranzler and Keith (1999), leading them to overestimate planning and attention factor correlations.

The CAS also deemphasizes interpretation of the overall composite g estimate (the Full Scale standard score) in favor of an emphasis on the four PASS scales (e.g., Naglieri, 1999). In a series of analyses, Canivez (2011a, 2011b, 2011c, 2011d) reported mixed support for this approach. Based on hierarchical exploratory factor analyses with the Schmid-Leiman procedure, Canivez (2011a, 2011b) reported that within the age 5 to 7 group, only the Number Detection subtest yields a high g loading, and within the ages 8 to 17 group, only Planned Connections yields a high g loading, seemingly supporting the interpretation of CAS as a low g test. However, Canivez (2011b) concluded that most of the total and common CAS variance was indeed associated with a second-order g factor, and interpretation of CAS at this level is supported, even if few subtests are good g measures. Even so, he notes that CAS yielded greater proportions of subtest variance apportioned to first order factors (i.e., PASS, or [PA]SS) than most other intelligence tests although some factors (planning and successive) appeared to explain much more variance than the simultaneous factor. Canivez (2011b) concludes, "Further research will help determine the extent to which CAS PASS scores possess acceptable incremental validity and diagnostic utility" (p. 314).

Evidence of convergent validity with other composite intelligence test scores indicates that the CAS overall composite has high correlations with other intelligence test composites—that is, with the WISC-III FSIQ ($r = .69$), the WJ III Cog Brief Intellectual Ability ($r = .70$; from McGrew & Woodcock, 2001) and the Wechsler Preschool and Primary Scale of Intelligence (WPPSI-R) FSIQ ($r = .60$) (Naglieri & Das, 1997b). Evidence of convergent validity for the four individual PASS scales is not reported in the CAS *Interpretive Handbook,* and surprisingly neither the CAS nor the K-ABC or KABC-II have convergent validity studies with each other, in spite of their shared theoretical underpinnings. Some investigations suggest limitations in the validity of the PASS

scales; for example, in separate investigations, the CAS Planning scale has been shown to yield low correlations with Tower of London performance (Naglieri & Das, 1997b; Ciotti, 2007), long considered a criterion measure of planning (e.g., Shallice, 1982). The CAS Planning scale also is not significantly correlated with parent and teacher reports of student planning and organizational ability (Ciotti, 2007).

CAS Full Scale standard scores also have high correlations with achievement test results. Based on a large sample ($n = 1600$) used as a basis for generating ability-achievement comparisons, the CAS Full Scale standard scores yield high correlations with broad reading and broad mathematics achievement ($r = .70$ to .72; see Naglieri & Das, 1997b). Correlations of the CAS with achievement test composites have been shown to be higher than those found for most other intelligence tests (Naglieri & Bornstein, 2003; Naglieri, DeLauder, Goldstein, & Schwebech, 2006; Naglieri & Rojahn, 2001). The comparatively high ability-achievement correlations may be interpreted as supporting a strong and possibly causal linkage between cognitive processes and the academic performances to which they may contribute.

CAS is unique among tests of cognitive abilities and processes insofar as it has been studied with several research-based programs of intervention, specifically programs of cognitive instruction that are concerned with the interface between psychology and education, particularly the cognitive processes involved in learning (e.g., Mayer, 1992). The *Process-Based Reading Enhancement Program* (PREP; see e.g., Carlson & Das, 1997; also Das & Kendrick, 1997) is a PASS theory intervention consisting of a series of exercises in global processing (to facilitate strategy development, independent from reading content) and curriculum bridging (to intervene in processing, but with similar content as required for reading) with the ultimate goal of improving word-reading and decoding skills. Another form of cognitive instruction related to PASS theory is the planning facilitation method described by Cormier, Carlson, and Das (1990); Kar, Dash, Das, and Carlson (1992); and Naglieri (1999); in it students have been shown to differentially benefit from a verbalization technique intended to facilitate planning. Participants who initially perform poorly on measures of planning earn significantly higher postintervention scores than those with good scores in planning. Extended accounts of research with CAS linking assessment to educational interventions are available (e.g., Naglieri, 1999; Naglieri & Das, 1997b; Naglieri & Otero, 2011; Naglieri & Pickering, 2010).

## Interpretive Indices and Applications

The CAS yields four standard scores corresponding to the PASS processes as well as a full scale standard score. Although the subtests account for high levels of specific variance, the focus of CAS interpretation is at the PASS Scale level, not at the subtest level or full scale composite level. PASS theory guides the examination of absolute and relative cognitive strengths and weaknesses. Table 18.1 contains interpretations for each of the PASS scales.

The CAS authors suggest that the test is potentially useful in diagnosis, classification, and eligibility decisions for specific learning disabilities, attention deficit, intellectual disabilities, and giftedness as well as for planning treatment, instructional, or remedial interventions (Naglieri & Das, 1997b). Special population studies reported in validity studies include children diagnosed with ADHD, reading disabilities, intellectual disabilities/mental retardation, traumatic brain injury, serious emotional disturbance, and giftedness. Children with selected exceptionalities appear to show characteristic impairment on PASS processes or combinations of processes. Reading-disabled children tend as a group to obtain their lowest scores on measures of successive processing (Naglieri & Das, 1997b), presumably due to the slowed phonological temporal processing thresholds that have been identified as a processing deficit associated with delayed reading acquisition (e.g., Anderson, Brown, & Tallal, 1993). Children diagnosed

**TABLE 18.1  Cognitive Assessment System (CAS) Core Interpretive Indices**

| Composite Indices | Description |
| --- | --- |
| Full Scale | An index of complex mental activity involving the interaction of diverse cognitive processes |
| Planning | An index of the process by which an individual determines, selects, applies, and evaluates solutions to problems; involves generation of strategies, execution of plans, self-control, and self-monitoring |
| Attention | An index of the process of selectively focusing on particular stimuli while inhibiting response to competing stimuli; involves directed concentration and sustained focus on important information |
| Simultaneous Processing | An index of the process of integration of separate stimuli into a single perceptual or conceptual whole; applies to comprehension of relationships and concepts, understanding of inflection, and working with spatial information |
| Successive Processing | An index of the process of integrating stimuli into a specific, temporal order that forms a serial progression; involves sequential perception and organization of visual and auditory events and execution of motor behaviors in order |

with the hyperactive-impulsive subtype of ADHD tend to characteristically have weaknesses in planning and attention scales (Paolitto, 1999), consistent with the newest theories reconceptualizing ADHD as a disorder of executive functions (Barkley, 1997). Characteristic weaknesses in planning and attention have also been reported in samples of traumatically brain-injured children (Gutentag, Naglieri, & Yeates, 1998), consistent with the frontal-temporal cortical impairment usually associated with closed head injury.

Like most of the other intelligence tests for children and adolescents, CAS is also empirically linked to achievement tests (Woodcock-Johnson–Revised and the WJ III Tests of Achievement). Through the use of simple and predicted differences between ability and achievement, children who qualify for special education services under various state guidelines for specific learning disabilities may be identified. Moreover, CAS permits the identification of selected cognitive processes (planning, attention, simultaneous, and successive processes) that if impaired may contribute to the learning problems. CAS has minimal acquired knowledge and academic skill requirements, although there are low-level requirements for fast recall of alphabetic letter sequences (Planned Connections), rapid word reading (Expressive Attention), and comprehension of language syntax (Verbal-Spatial Relations and Sentence Questions).

CAS also provides normative reference for the use of metacognitive problem-solving strategies that may be observed by the examiner or reported by the examinee on planning subtests. These strategies have been analyzed relative to developmental expectations and effectiveness in enhancing task performance (Winsler & Naglieri, 2003; Winsler, Naglieri, & Manfra, 2006). The inclusion of age-referenced norms for strategy usage provides an independent source of information about the efficiency, implementation, and maturity with which an individual approaches and performs complex tasks.

## Strengths and Limitations

The CAS offers several progressive advances in intelligence testing. Its most important contribution is to include executive functions as a core element in the assessment of intelligence, a decision that preceded the inclusion of executive function subtests in the KABC-II (Kaufman & Kaufman, 2004), WISC-III as a Process Instrument (WISC-III PI; Kaplan, Fein, Kramer, Delis, & Morris, 1999) and WISC-IV Integrated (Wechsler, Kaplan, Fein, Kramer, Morris, Delis, & Maerlender, 2004), and the WJ III Cog (Woodcock, McGrew, &

Mather, 2001a). The inclusion of objective, norm-referenced problem-solving strategies also provides a potentially valuable metacognitive process-based assessment. The demonstration in CAS of higher correlations with basic academic skills (with minimal emphasis on acquired knowledge) than other intelligence tests (e.g., Naglieri & Bornstein, 2003; Naglieri et al., 2006; Naglieri & Rojahn, 2001) speaks to the merits of tapping cognitive processes over crystallized knowledge in intelligence assessment. Efforts to systematically link CAS performance with associated intervention approaches also are forward-looking and strongly needed in this field. By virtue of its theoretical underpinnings and linkages to diagnosis and treatment, the CAS builds on the earlier advances offered by the KABC (Kaufman & Kaufman, 1983a, 1983b). In an early review, Meikamp (1999) observed, "The CAS is an innovative instrument and its development meets high standards of technical adequacy. Despite interpretation cautions with exceptional populations, this instrument creatively bridges the gap between theory and applied psychology" (p. 77).

The chief limitations of the CAS stem from its ambitious yet flawed operationalization of Luria's theory of the functional systems of the brain and a mismatch between its theoretical interpretive framework (PASS) and its structure according to factor analyses. Theoretical shortcomings include a misinterpretation of Luria's first functional unit as regulating higher-order attentional processes; his first functional unit is actually associated with limbic system activation (and inhibition) of generalized arousal and alertness:

> The reticular activating formation, the most important part of the first functional unit of the brain,...affects all sensory and all motor [cortical] functions of the body equally, and...its function is merely that of regulating states of sleep and waking—the non-specific background against which different forms of activity take place. (Luria, 1973, p. 52)

The arousal and alertness mediated by the reticular system may be considered a prerequisite for attention (since a minimal level of arousal is necessary to pay attention), but not higher forms of attention per se. Higher-order attentional processes are now thought to be mediated by at least two attentional systems: a posterior cortical system associated with orienting and foveation and an anterior cortical system associated with signal detection and focal processing (e.g., Posner & Petersen, 1990). CAS attentional subtests almost certainly involve the latter system, which is associated with the same prefrontal processes that some of the planning subtests are believed

to involve (e.g., Derrfuss, Brass, Neumann, & von Cramon, 2005). By including attention tasks and planning tasks, the CAS authors in effect set up two scales tapping prefrontal executive functions and Luria's third functional unit.

A second theoretical limitation was first observed in Das's early work by Paivio (1976), who asserted that the successive-simultaneous processing distinction is confounded by verbal-nonverbal sensory modality assessment methodologies. In other words, successive tasks are predominantly verbal and simultaneous tasks are predominantly visual-spatial, making it difficult to demonstrate that the two cognitive processes transcend sensory modality as Luria believed.

Problems with the CAS theoretical and interpretive structure have been documented in confirmatory factor analyses (Keith & Kranzler, 1999; Keith et al., 2001; Kranzler & Keith, 1999; Kranzler et al., 2000), providing evidence that CAS factors may more appropriately be interpreted as measuring processing speed (rather than planning and attention), memory span (rather than successive processing), and a mixture of fluid intelligence and broad visualization (rather than simultaneous processing), with a higher-order general intelligence factor (approximated by the Full Scale standard score). Hierarchical exploratory factor analyses have documented the low amounts of specificity and incremental validity offered by the PASS scales beyond the Full Scale standard score (Canivez, 2011a, 2011b, 2011c, 2011d).

Some of these challenges could be readily addressed in a revised edition, through the inclusion of untimed subtests in planning and attention domains, nonverbal or nonmemory subtests in the successive processing domain, and verbal subtests in the simultaneous domains. In an explicit acknowledgment that the Lurian dimensions may be readily reinterpreted from the CHC framework, Kaufman and Kaufman (2004) offered a dual theoretical perspective in which successive (sequential) and simultaneous processing may be just as easily viewed as memory span and broad visualization. To demonstrate the structural integrity of the CAS and correspondence of the PASS processes to Luria's functional systems, the next edition of the CAS will have to redesign the content of some subtests so as to clarify the constructs they measure and to conduct the basic brain–behavior research needed to establish the subtests' neural correlates. In an examination of CAS and its underpinnings in Luria's conceptualization of the brain, McCrea (2009) recommended that CAS subtests and scales be examined through functional neuroimaging studies and brain lesion studies to more clearly establish their neural sensitivity and specificity.

## Differential Ability Scales—Second Edition

The Differential Ability Scales—Second Edition (DAS-II; C. D. Elliott, 2007a, 2007b, 2007c) offer ability profiling with 20 subtests divided into two overlapping batteries standardized for ages $2\frac{1}{2}$ through 17 years. The DAS-II is a U.S. adaptation, revision, and extension of the British Ability Scales (BAS; C. D. Elliott, Murray, & Pearson, 1979). Development of the BAS originally began in 1965, with plans to develop a test to measure Thurstone's (1938) seven primary mental abilities and key dimensions from Piagetian theory. Colin D. Elliott, a teacher, university faculty, and school psychologist trainer, became the director of the project in 1973. Elliott spearheaded decisions to deemphasize IQ estimation and to provide a profile of meaningful and distinct abilities as well as to support the introduction of item response theory in psychometric analyses. The first edition of the British Ability Scales was published in 1979 with an amended revised edition published in 1983 (BAS-R; C. D. Elliott et al., 1983). The development of the American edition began in 1984, and the first edition of the DAS was published in 1990. Second editions followed—the BAS-II in 1996 and the DAS-II in 2007—so that over four decades have passed since work on the BAS actually began.

The DAS-II consists of four core subtests (lower level) or six core subtests (upper level) for the Early Years Battery (ages 2:6–6:11) and six core subtests for the School-Age Battery (ages 7:0–17:11). Separate diagnostic subtests may be administered in clusters to assess working memory, phonological processing, processing speed, and foundational abilities for early school learning. The core School-Age battery typically requires about 30 to 40 minutes. Additional time is required for administration of optional diagnostic clusters in School Readiness (15–20 minutes), Working Memory (10–15 minutes), Processing Speed (10 minutes), and Phonological Processing (10 minutes). Spanish-language instructions are provided, but only for subtests that do not require a verbal response from the examinee.

## Theoretical Underpinnings

The DAS-II was developed to accommodate diverse theoretical perspectives, but it now aligns most closely with the CHC framework. It is designed to yield an estimate of higher order general intelligence, the General Conceptual Ability (GCA) score, and lower order broad cognitive factors or diagnostic clusters: Verbal Ability (Gc), Nonverbal Reasoning Ability (Gf), Spatial Ability (Gv), Working Memory (Gsm), and Processing Speed (Gs). The DAS avoids use of the terms *intelligence* and *IQ,* focusing instead on profiles of cognitive abilities and processes that are either strongly related to the general factor or thought to have value for diagnostic purposes.

The GCA captures test performance on subtests that have high *g* loadings, in contrast to some intelligence tests in which all subtests (high and low *g* loading) contribute to the overall IQ composite. Through this approach, it also avoids the problems found on the Wechsler scales in which circumscribed processing deficits (such as low processing speed) depress overall ability estimates. Confirmatory factor analyses reported in the *Introductory and Technical Handbook* (C. D. Elliott, 2007b) show the *g* loadings of core subtests (i.e., those that contribute to the GCA) to range from .66 to .76 for ages 6:0 to 12:11 and from .65 to .78 for ages 6:0 to 17:11. By Kaufman's (1994) criteria, half of the DAS-II subtests are good measures of general intelligence and the remaining core subtests are fair measures of general intelligence. As expected, the diagnostic subtests do not fare as well as measures of *g*.

At a level below the GCA in hierarchical structure are cluster scores that uniformly have sufficient specific variance for interpretation (C. D. Elliott, 2007b). For children from ages $2\frac{1}{2}$ years through $3\frac{1}{2}$ years (Early Years Battery Lower Level), only Verbal Ability and Nonverbal Ability cluster scores may be derived. For older preschool children and school-age children, three cluster scores may be computed from core subtests: Verbal Ability, Nonverbal Reasoning Ability, and Spatial Ability, with the option to compute a Special Nonverbal Composite. From diagnostic subtests, Working Memory and Processing Speed cluster composites may be generated above age $3\frac{1}{2}$, and a School Readiness composite may also be computed from diagnostic subtests in the Early Years Battery Upper Level. The increased cognitive differentiation (i.e., from two core cluster scores to three core cluster scores) from the Early Years Battery Lower Level to the Upper Level and the School-Age Battery is consistent with the fundamental developmental tenet that cognitive abilities tend to become differentiated with maturation (H. Werner, 1948).

### *Standardization Features and Psychometric Adequacy*

Through over six years of research and development, the DAS-II underwent a national pilot, tryout, and standardization study. The standardization edition was normed on a representative U.S. sample of 3,480 children and adolescents, between ages 2:6 and 17:11. Using 2002 Current Population Survey census figures, the normative sample was stratified on the basis of race/ethnicity, parent education level, and geographic region. The sample was balanced by age and sex. Age was divided into 18 age levels, including 6-month bands for the Early Years Battery preschool ages and 12-month bands at and above age 5 years for the School-Age Battery. A total of $n = 176$ was sampled per age band for preschoolers, with $n = 200$ per age band for ages 5 through 17 years. The composition of the normative sample is detailed across stratification variables in the *DAS-II Introductory and Technical Handbook* (C. D. Elliott, 2007b) and appears to closely match its 2002 census target figures. The standardization sample inclusion criteria required English as the primary language of the examinee; prospective examinees were excluded (or referred to special population studies) when they had received diagnoses or services for any delay in cognitive, motor, language, social-emotional, or adaptive functioning.

Individual items were statistically evaluated for fit, reliability, bias, and difficulty through Rasch scaling, which was also used to divide subtests into item sets. The DAS-II reports the relative difficulty of individual items for each subtest (C. D. Elliott, 2007b, Appendix A), thereby providing item difficulty gradients. Raw score to ability score conversion tables are also reported (Appendix A), including the standard error of each ability score, from which local reliabilities may be manually calculated if desired.

The score reliabilities of the DAS-II subtests and composites were computed through calculation of coefficient alpha or item response theory (IRT) proxies for reliability (C. D. Elliott, 2007b). DAS-II subtests are administered in predetermined item sets rather than with formal basal and discontinue rules. This means that starting points and stopping decision points (as well as alternative stopping points) are designated on the Record Form according to the child's age or ability level. Within any given item set, at least three items passed and at least three items failed provide support that the appropriate item set was administered. If an examinee passes fewer than three items, a lower item set should be administered; if an examinee fails fewer than three items, a higher item set should be administered. Ideally, an examinee's performance has been optimally assessed when approximately half of the items are passed and half are failed. Through the use of item sets, examinees receive a form of tailored, adaptive testing, in which they are given items closest to their actual ability levels.

C. D. Elliott (2007b) reports that the average reliability coefficients of Early Years Battery subtests ranged from .79 (Recall of Objects-Immediate, Recognition of Pictures, Word Definitions) to .94 (Pattern Construction). A total of 86% of subtests had average reliabilities across ages at or above .80, and no subtests had substantially lower internal consistency. For cluster and composite scores, average reliabilities ranged from .89 (Nonverbal and Nonverbal Reasoning Ability and Processing Speed) to .95 (Spatial Ability, GCA, and SNC). A total of 75% of composites and cluster scores had average reliabilities at or above .90.

Average reliability coefficients of the School-Age Battery subtests ranged from .74 (Recognition of Pictures) to .96 (Pattern Construction), with 90% of subtests yielding $\alpha \geq .80$. The diagnostic subtest Recognition of Pictures is the only subtest with consistently inadequate reliability. For clusters and composites, 88% of School-Age Battery composites and cluster scores had average reliability greater than or equal to .90, with the average GCA at .96. Altogether and with the exception of the Recognition of Pictures subtest, these findings indicate that the internal consistency of DAS-II tasks and composite scores are consistently adequate.

Internal consistencies are also reported for 12 special populations, including samples of individuals diagnosed with intellectual disability, intellectual giftedness, attention deficits, learning disorders, and limited English proficiency, among others. Isolated subtests show low reliabilities, suggesting the possibility that some subtests should be interpreted cautiously in selected groups, although clearly more research on reliability generalization would be beneficial. In general, however, DAS-II subtest internal reliability coefficients appear fully adequate.

Stability coefficients were computed for 369 examinees in three age groups undergoing test and retest intervals of 1 to 9 weeks (mean interval = 23 days), with correction for restriction of range on the initial score. When these groups are combined, subtest test–retest corrected stability coefficients ranged from .63 to .91, while cluster and composite corrected stabilities ranged from .81 to .92. The stability of the GCA ranged from .91 to .94 across the three groups, indicating fully adequate test–retest stability. In general, these findings suggest that isolated subtests may not be particularly stable at specific ages, but composite score stability coefficients tend to be fairly adequate. Examinations of test–retest gain scores (i.e., practice effects) show that improvements over the span of about a month are largest for Nonverbal Reasoning (5.8 standard score points), School Readiness (5.2 points), and the GCA (5.1 points). The largest composite score practice effects are small to medium, in terms of effect sizes.

Interscorer agreement for the normative sample ranged from .98 to .99, based on double-scoring of all standardization cases. Four subtests that require scoring of drawings or verbal responses according to objective criteria were further investigated. In a stratified sample of 60 cases scored independently by four scorers, the interscorer reliability coefficients ranged from .95 (Copying) to .97 (Recall of Designs) to .99 (Word Definitions and Verbal Similarities), all of which fall within an acceptable range.

The DAS-II composites and clusters scores have considerable range, extending 9 standard deviations (SD) from low standard scores of about 32 (−4.5 SD) to ceiling scores of 169 or 170 (+4.6 SD). DAS-II subtest floors are sufficiently low so that its T scores extend 2 SD below the normative mean with 2½-year-old children with developmental delays. Use of Rasch scaling extrapolation also permits GCA and other composite norms to be extended downward, to standard scores as low as 32, enhancing the discriminability of the DAS-II with individuals with moderate to severe impairment including intellectual disability. DAS-II subtest ceilings are sufficiently high that they extend +4 SD above the normative mean for all but a single subtest (Sequential and Quantitative Reasoning, which extends +3.1 SD) at the highest age range served by the DAS-II. Composite and cluster score ceilings consistently extend as high as 169 or 170, to support the identification of highly gifted individuals. Subtests in the Early Years Battery Upper Level and the School-Age Battery have overlapping norms for children between the ages of 5:0 and 8:11, thereby raising the test ceiling for high-functioning younger children and lowering the test floor for low-functioning older children, permitting out-of-level assessments.

The DAS-II tends to show considerable convergence with other intelligence and achievement tests. According to analyses from C. D. Elliott (2007b), the DAS-II GCA correlates highly with composite indices from Bayley-III Cognitive Scale (r = .59), the WPPSI-III FSIQ (r = .87 for the preschool battery), the WISC-IV FSIQ (r = .84 for the school-age battery), the Wechsler Individual Achievement Test (WIAT-III) Total Achievement composite score (r = .82; see Pearson research staff, 2009), the WJ III Total Achievement Score (r = .80), the Kaufman Test of Educational Achievement (KTEA-II), and Comprehensive Achievement Composite (r = .81). Two investigations have supported the value of multiple specific DAS-II core and diagnostic scores (in lieu of the GCA composite) in predicting academic reading performance (C. D. Elliott, Hale, Fiorello, Dorvil, & Moldovan, 2010) and mathematics performance (Hale, Fiorello, Dumont, Willis, Rackley, & Elliott, 2008).

Confirmatory factor analyses reported in the *Introductory and Technical Handbook* (C. D. Elliott, 2007b) provide general support for the interpretive structure of the test. For the upper level of the Early Years Battery, a three-factor model (Verbal, Nonverbal Reasoning, and Spatial) fit the data significantly better than one- or two-factor models. When the six core subtests alone were examined for ages 7:0 to 17:11, a three-factor solution (Verbal, Nonverbal Reasoning, and Spatial) yielded optimal fit. When all core and diagnostic subtests were included in analyses for ages 6:0 to 12:11, a seven-factor model (Gc, Gf, Gv, Gsm, Glr, Gs, and Ga) provided the best fit with the data. For ages 6:0 to 17:11, a six-factor model (Gc, Gf, Gv, Gsm, Glr, and Gs) produced good fit. Independent higher-order confirmatory factor analyses by Keith and his colleagues (2010) supported the DAS-II structure, with minor exceptions, as well as supporting the factorial invariance of the DAS-II CHC model across the 4- to 17-year age span.

### Interpretive Indices and Applications

The DAS-II involves some score transformations based on item response theory. Raw scores are converted first to latent trait ability scores based on tables appearing in the record form; ability scores are in turn translated into T scores (M = 50, SD = 10), percentile ranks, and age equivalent scores. T scores may be summed to produce the GCA and cluster scores (M = 100, SD = 15), percentiles, and confidence intervals. The GCA is derived only from subtests with high g loadings, and cluster scores consist of subtests that tend to factor together. The diagnostic subtests measure relatively independent abilities. The clusters and diagnostic subtests have adequate specific variance to support their interpretation independent from g. Table 18.2 contains the basic composite and cluster indices.

Dumont, Willis, and Elliott (2009) described evidence for use of DAS-II in assessment of individuals with specific learning disabilities, attention-deficit/hyperactivity disorders, intellectual disability, intellectual giftedness, language disabilities, and autism spectrum disorders, noting that the specificity of DAS-II subtests and composites enhances decision making:

When we are asked to evaluate an individual's cognitive development or aspects of the individual's ability in

**TABLE 18.2  Differential Ability Scales—Second Edition Core Interpretive Indices**

| Composite Indices | Description |
| --- | --- |
| *General Conceptual Ability (GCA)* | An index of ability to perform complex mental information processing, including conceptualization and transformation; derived from subtests with high *g* loadings |
| *Special Nonverbal Composite* | An alternative measure of general ability to be used when verbal subtest performances are considered invalid measures of examinee ability (e.g., when an examinee is not proficient in spoken English) |
| *Verbal Ability* | A cluster score measuring acquired verbal concepts and knowledge |
| *Nonverbal Reasoning Ability* | A cluster score measuring nonverbal mental processing, including inductive reasoning for abstract, visual problems |
| *Spatial Ability* | A cluster score measuring complex visual-spatial processing, including ability in spatial imagery and visualization, perception of spatial orientation, attention to visual details, and analytic thinking |
| *School Readiness* | A multidimensional cluster score tapping the growth of skills and abilities fundamental to early school learning, including number concepts, matching of simple graphic figures, and phonological processing (appropriate for examinees ages 5:0 to 8:11 taking the upper Early Years battery) |
| *Working Memory* | A cluster score tapping auditory short-term memory and working memory, including integration of visualization with verbal short-term memory |
| *Processing Speed* | A cluster score measuring general cognitive processing speed for simple mental operations, including visual comparison and lexical access |

information processing, we need to do this in a way that will clearly identify distinctive, interpretable cognitive factors, systems, or processes with as little overlap and ambiguity as possible. That is the reason we need subtests and composites that are not only reliable but which also have high specificity.... [T]he DAS-II has been designed for this purpose. It has between 10% and 20% more reliable specificity in its subtests and clusters than other cognitive test batteries. (p. 248)

C. D. Elliott (2007b) reported DAS-II special population studies for children identified with intellectual disability, intellectual giftedness, reading disorders, reading and written expression disorder, mathematics disorder, ADHD, ADHD and learning disorders, expressive disorders, mixed receptive-expressive language disorder, limited English proficiency, and developmental risk. Special population group mean scores are each compared with demographically matched comparison groups drawn from the standardization sample.

## Strengths and Limitations

The DAS-II is widely considered to be a psychometrically superlative test battery ranking among the best preschool and school-age cognitive test batteries available. In a critical review, Davis and Finch (2008) wrote:

> The evidence around the psychometric properties of the instrument was generally well presented and of high technical quality. The psychometric properties of the DAS-II are well documented and quite stellar... Across all age ranges, this revision continues to be child-friendly, psychometrically sound, and of high utility. There is a wealth of technical data, much of which will be excessive for the typical user, but examiners will find that virtually any imaginable psychometric study has been conducted with at least adequate results. Additionally, the development and standardization of the DAS-II set a high standard from which many other tests could benefit. Clearly, the DAS-II has been well studied and the evidence presented in the technical report supports the contention that the instrument was found to be both reliable and valid across a variety of samples.

The strengths of the DAS-II should not be wholly surprising, as it has benefited from three predecessor British editions (BAS, BAS-R, BAS-II) as well as the DAS, making it the equivalent of a fifth edition with the same lead author. It overlaps substantially in content with the Wechsler scales but is now aligned with the CHC framework and offers supplemental diagnostic subtests and scales, which will not depress the overall GCA if diagnostic impairment is present. In total, it ranks among the best intelligence tests of this era.

Hill (2005) explained the continued preference of British assessment practitioners for the Wechsler scales over the BAS-II:

> Many psychologists feel that more contemporary psychometric assessments, for example, the BAS-II, lack either the history or the extensive research profile of the Wechsler scales. In a litigious context it appears that some psychologists feel the Wechsler scales provide greater professional security. (p. 89)

The same sentiment may explain preference of American assessment practitioners for the Wechsler scales over the DAS-II (e.g., Camara, Nathan, & Puente, 2000), in spite of its technical excellence. With its assets noted, research is sorely needed to systematically link DAS-II cognitive ability profiles with academic and nonacademic interventions for children and adolescents.

## Kaufman Assessment Battery for Children, Second Edition

When Alan S. Kaufman's book, *Intelligent Testing with the WISC-R*, was published in 1979, he became the leading authority after David Wechsler himself on the Wechsler intelligence scales, the most dominant tests of our era. Kaufman and his wife, Nadeen, released the Kaufman Assessment Battery for Children (K-ABC; Kaufman & Kaufman, 1983a, 1983b) just four years later, and it constituted the boldest challenge yet encountered by the Wechsler scales. These landmark works have gone through successive editions, along with many other accomplishments, making Alan Kaufman the leading influence on the practice of applied intelligence testing in the last 30 years. In the words of his students Randy W. Kamphaus and Cecil R. Reynolds (2009), Kaufman's contribution having the greatest long-term impact was his "joining of the two disciplines of measurement science and clinical assessment practice" (p. 148).

Kaufman and Kaufman are the coauthors of the Kaufman Assessment Battery for Children, Second Edition (KABC-II; Kaufman & Kaufman, 2004) and Kaufman Adolescent and Adult Intelligence Test (KAIT; Kaufman & Kaufman, 1993). They have a unique training and academic lineage, and have in turn exerted strong influences on several leading test developers. Their history here is summarized from the Kaufmans' own telling (Cohen & Swerdlik, 1999). Alan Kaufman completed his doctorate from Columbia University under Robert L. Thorndike, who would head the restandardization of the Stanford-Binet L-M (Terman & Merrill, 1973) and serve as senior author of the Stanford-Binet Fourth Edition (Thorndike, Hagen, & Sattler, 1986). Kaufman was employed at the Psychological Corporation from 1968 to 1974, where he worked closely with David Wechsler on the WISC-R. Nadeen L. Kaufman completed her doctorate in special education with an emphasis in neurosciences from Columbia University, where she acquired a humanistic, intraindividual developmental approach to psychological assessment and learning disabilities that would blend uniquely with her husband's psychometric approach. Following his departure from the Psychological Corporation, Alan Kaufman joined the Educational and School Psychology Department at the University of Georgia. According to the Kaufmans, the K-ABC was conceptualized and a blueprint developed on a 2-hour car trip with their children in March of 1978. In a remarkable coincidence, they were contacted the next day by the director of test development at American Guidance Service (AGS), who asked if they were interested in developing an intelligence test to challenge the Wechsler scales. At the University of Georgia, Alan and Nadeen worked with a gifted group of graduate students on the K-ABC. Among their students were Bruce Bracken, Jack Cummings, Patti Harrison, Randy Kamphaus, Jack Naglieri, and Cecil Reynolds, all influential school psychologists and test authors.

The KABC-II measures cognitive abilities and processing in children and adolescents from age 3 years through 18 years. It consists of core and supplementary tests and may be interpreted according to a dual theoretical foundation, either the CHC psychometric model or Luria's functional systems. The KABC-II is also conormed with the Kaufman Test of Educational Achievement, Second Edition (KTEA-II), facilitating score comparisons between cognitive ability/processes and academic skills. Depending on the theoretical framework selected (the CHC model requires more tests), KABC-II batteries consist of 5 to 7 core subtests and 3 supplemental subtests at age 3; 7 to 9 core subtests and 3 supplemental subtests at age 4; 7 to 9 core subtests and 6 supplemental subtests at age 5; and 8 to 10 core subtests and 5 to 7 supplemental subtests for ages 6;0 to 17:11. The KABC-II may be administered in about 25 to 30 minutes (the core battery at youngest age) to 50 to 70 minutes (the core battery in adolescence); or 35 to 55 minutes (the expanded battery at youngest age) to 75 to 100 minutes (the expanded battery in adolescence).

The KABC-II includes Spanish-language instructions for all subtests with sample or teaching items. For items requiring verbal responses, the examiner may accept responses in any language, and the KABC-II materials list correct and incorrect verbal responses in Spanish as well as English. The Nonverbal Scale of the KABC-II is explicitly intended for use with children who are not fluent in English.

### Theoretical Underpinnings

The KABC-II was developed with an unusual dual theoretical foundation, lending itself to interpretation with either the CHC framework or a Lurian neuropsychological processing framework. There was precedent for this dual foundation in the Kaufmans' body of work; after having developed the original K-ABC (Kaufman & Kaufman, 1983a) to tap Lurian processing, the Kaufmans proposed a "theoretical rerouting" based primarily on extended Gf-Gc theory when they published the KAIT (Kaufman & Kaufman, 1993). For the KABC-II, Kaufman and Kaufman (2004) added planning tasks with low speed requirements (tapping fluid reasoning, or Gf), learning tasks (thereby tapping retrieval, or Glr), while retaining measures of acquired knowledge (thereby tapping Gc). Accordingly, the KABC-II established two parallel structural frameworks. The CHC framework measures Gf, Glr, Gsm, Gv, and Gc, while the Lurian framework featured planning, learning, sequential processing, and simultaneous processing (which could be summarized by the acronym P-L-S-S and which endeavors to exclude acquired knowledge from the assessment). The KABC-II composite using the CHC framework is called the Fluid-Crystallized Index (FCI), whereas the composite using the Lurian framework is the Mental Processing Index (MPI). The authors explain that the CHC model is preferred unless the examinee comes from a background (or is diagnosed with a condition) in which verbal functioning and knowledge acquisition may be depressed, distorting the examinee's actual level of ability:

> The CHC model should generally be the model of choice, except in cases where the examiner believes that including measures of acquired knowledge/crystallized ability would compromise the validity of the FCI. In those cases, the Luria-based global score (MPI) is preferred. The CHC model is given priority over the Luria model because the authors believe that Knowledge/Gc is, in principle, an important aspect of cognitive functioning (Kaufman & Kaufman, 2004).

### Standardization Features and Technical Adequacy

The KABC-II underwent national standardization from 2001 through 2003, and norms are based on a sample of 3,025 children and adolescents between the ages of 3 and 18 years. The sample was collected to be representative according to 2001 U.S. census figures, based on the stratification variables of parent education level, race/ethnicity, geographic region, and educational placement. Sample sizes were set at $n = 200$ per 12-month interval from ages 3 through 14 years; and at $n = 125$ to 150 per year for ages 15 through 18 years. Standardization sample participants were randomly selected to meet stratification targets from a large pool of potential examinees. A review of the standardization sample demographic breakdowns indicates that the KABC-II normative sample closely matches census target figures.

The score reliabilities of the K-ABC were computed with a Rasch adaptation of the split-half method, with Spearman-Brown correction (Kaufman & Kaufman, 2004). For ages 3 to 6 years, 82% of subtest score reliabilities were at or above .80; for ages 7 through 18, 73% of subtest score reliabilities were at or above .80. Reliabilities of the global scale indexes are uniformly

high, averaging in the mid- to upper .90s for the FCI and MPI and in the low .90s for the Nonverbal Index (NVI). All average composite indices including global and factor scale index were at or above .90 across ages 3 to 6 years; 63% of all average composites were at or above .90 across ages 7 to 18 years.

Test–retest stability coefficients were examined for a sample of $n = 250$ children and adolescents undergoing reevaluations after an average interval of about four weeks. When correlations were adjusted for initial score, 26% of composite indices yield a correlation at or above .90 across all ages; 36% of subtest scores yield a correlation at or above .80 across all ages. These stability coefficients are somewhat low.

While exploratory factor analyses were used to guide test development, the authors reported only the results of hierarchical confirmatory factor analyses of the normative standardization sample (Kaufman & Kaufman, 2004). The core subtest configuration (a superordinate $g$ and four or five CHC factors, depending on age level) fit the data well, yielding high confirmatory fit indexes (CFIs) and low root mean squared errors of approximation (RMSEAs). Independent follow-up higher-order confirmatory factor analyses by Reynolds, Keith, Fine, Fisher, and Low (2007) concluded that the "the KABC-II factor structure for school-age children is aligned closely with five broad abilities from CHC theory, although some inconsistencies were found" (p. 511). Reynolds and his colleagues (2007) also found core subtests to be age-invariant measures of their assigned constructs. More recently, Morgan, Rothlisberg, McIntosh, and Hunt (2009) found support for the KABC-II hierarchical structure ($g$ plus four CHC factors) in confirmatory factor analyses with a preschool sample.

Subtest $g$-loadings were examined using the Kaufman (1994) guidelines from a single unrotated factor of the normative sample via principal axis factor analysis (Kaufman & Kaufman, 2004). For ages 3 to 4 years, only 3 subtests were good measures of $g$, four were fair measures of $g$, and five were poor measures of $g$. For ages 5 to 6 years, four subtests were good measures of $g$, 10 were fair measures of $g$, and two were poor measures of $g$. For ages 7 to 18 years, three subtests were good measures of $g$, nine subtests were fair measures of $g$, and two subtests were poor measures of $g$. The subtests tapping Knowledge (Gc) were the most consistent good measures of $g$.

KABC-II composites tend to show high levels of convergent validity with other intelligence tests (Kaufman & Kaufman, 2004). The KABC-II FCI, MPI, and

NVI respectively yield corrected correlations of .89, .88, and .79 with the WISC-IV FSIQ; .81, .76, and .81 at ages 3 to 4 and .81, .73, and .43 at ages 5 to 6 with the WPPSI-III FSIQ; .91, .85, and .77 with the KAIT Composite Intelligence Scale; and .78, .77, and .74 with the WJ III Cog GIA.

KABC-II composites also show high correlations with achievement test scores (Kaufman & Kaufman, 2004). The KABC-II FCI, MPI, and NVI respectively yield corrected correlations of .67, .69, and .66 for grades 1 to 4 and .73, .67, and .32 for grades 5 to 9 with Peabody Individual Achievement Test (PIAT-R) Total Test Achievement; .72, .65, and .52 for grades 2–5 and .87, .83, and .78 for grades 7–10 with the WIAT-II Total Achievement score; and .70, .63, and .51 for grades 2 to 5 and .79, .77, and .71 for grades 6 to 10 with WJ III Ach Total Achievement score.

### Interpretive Indices and Applications

The KABC-II consists of core and supplementary subtests that vary according to the age of the examinee and the purpose of the assessment. For examinees at age 3, up to seven core subtests may be given as well as three supplementary subtests. From ages 4 to 6 years, up to 11 subtests are core with eight supplementary subtests. For ages 7 to 18 years, up to 11 subtests are core, and seven subtests are supplementary. All subtests have a normative *mean* scaled score of 10, *SD* of 3.

The KABC-II yields three global composite indices (the FCI, the MPI, and the NVI). It yields either four or five composite scales, depending on the battery given: Sequential/Gsm, Simultaneous/Gv, Learning/Glr, Planning/Gf, and Knowledge/Gc. All composite standard scores have a normative mean of 100, *SD* of 15. Table 18.3 includes basic interpretations for the KABC-II global and composite scales.

Every subtest has an optional list of Qualitative Indicators (QIs) appearing on the record form that may either disrupt or enhance task performance (e.g., "perseveres," "fails to sustain attention," "reluctant to respond when uncertain"). QIs listed with a minus sign may detract from task performance, while QIs with a plus sign may positively affect performance. The KABC-II record form has a summary page that permits QIs to be listed at a glance for all subtests. QIs can be used to facilitate checks of test validity and reliability as well as to inform observation of problem-solving processes. However, the QIs are not normed and should be compared to behaviors noted outside of the testing situation (Kaufman, Lichtenberger, Fletcher-Janzen, & Kaufman, 2005).

**TABLE 18.3   Kaufman Assessment Battery for Children—Second Edition Core Interpretive Indices**

| Composite Indices | Description |
| --- | --- |
| *Mental Processing Composite (MPC)* | An aggregate index of information processing proficiency intended to emphasize problem-solving rather than acquired knowledge and skills |
| *Fluid-Crystallized Index (FCI)* | An index of general cognitive ability according to the CHC perspective and including measures of acquired knowledge |
| *Nonverbal Index (NVI)* | An estimate of cognitive ability based on task performances that may be administered in pantomime and responded to motorically; appropriate for students with limited English proficiency, speech or language impairments, or other language-related disabilities |
| *Sequential Processing scale/Gsm* | An index of cognitive processes that arrange input in sequential or serial order during problem solving, where each stimulus is linearly or temporally related to the previous one/Gsm = taking in and holding information and then using it within a few seconds |
| *Simultaneous Processing scale/Gv* | An index of proficiency at processing stimuli all at once, in an integrated manner interrelating each element into a perceptual whole/Gv = perceiving, storing, manipulating, and thinking with visual patterns |
| *Learning/Glr* | An index of ability to learn and retain new information with efficiency/Glr = storing and efficiently retrieving newly learned, or previously learned information |
| *Planning/Gf* | An index of proficiency at high-level, decision-making, executive processes/Gf = solving novel problems by using reasoning abilities such as induction and deduction |
| *Knowledge/Gc* | An index of breadth and depth of knowledge acquired from one's culture (included in the CHC model but not included in the Luria model). |

Potential applications of the KABC-II include assessment of individuals with intellectual disability/mental retardation, ADHD, and learning disabilities as well as individuals who may be disadvantaged by a verbally loaded assessments (e.g., individuals who are deaf and hard of hearing, individuals with autism spectrum disorders, and individuals with speech and language disorders) (Kaufman et al., 2005). The KABC-II Manual reports clinical validity studies with children and adolescents diagnosed with specific learning disabilities (in reading, mathematics, written expression), intellectual disability, intellectual giftedness, autism spectrum disorder, ADHD, emotional disturbance, and hearing loss (Kaufman & Kaufman, 2004).

### Strengths and Limitations

The K-ABC was introduced in 1983 with genuine innovations, including a theory-driven model of cognitive processing, careful minimization of acquired knowledge requirements, demonstration of reduced racial and ethnic group mean score differences, and conceptual links of assessment to intervention. Its subtests appeared qualitatively different from Wechsler and Binet-style procedures, it permitted examinees to be taught the task to ensure that no children do poorly because they did not understand what to do, and its easel-based test administration format quickly became the industry standard. Through various marketing campaigns the K-ABC was

> hyped by its publishers as a "revolutionary new way to define and measure intelligence!" . . . Doing away with the notion of IQ, the Kaufmans have designed the K-ABC to measure a purer form of "mental processing ability"; and in doing so, they claim, they have gone a long way toward minimizing the racial and cultural biases that plague existing tests. ("The K-ABC–Will It Be the SOMPA of the 80's?" 1984, pp. 9–10)

After the promotional efforts subsided, Kline, Snyder, and Castellanos (1996) drew some sobering lessons from the K-ABC, including (a) the need to analyze the processing demands in all tasks and scoring systems; (b) the need to critically examine test interpretive practices (i.e., subtest profile analysis) that have dubious validity; (c) the problematic position that IQ scores reflect ability (independent from achievement) even while touting unusually high correlations with achievement; and (d) the failure of efforts to match instruction to learning profiles in K-ABC's remedial model. At the very least, the advances in assessment practice made by the K-ABC may have been overshadowed by its failure to deliver on its initial promise.

The KABC-II appears to continue the advances of its predecessor edition and substantively address some limitations. Its administration remains examinee friendly and clinically flexible. It is conormed with a well-developed achievement test, the KTEA-II. Its dual theoretical model represents an unusual compromise between two opposing theoretical perspectives (CHC and Lurian) without doing damage to either. Its capacity to reduce racial/ethnic mean group score differences is reported more objectively than such findings were publicly represented on the K-ABC. (See, e.g., Kaufman et al., 2005, pp. 223–233.) Its system for identifying strengths and weaknesses is based largely on sets of subtests (scales) rather than individual subtests, thereby addressing concerns about K-ABC subtest profile

analysis by Kline and his colleagues (1996) as well as criticisms of the practice by other researchers (e.g., Livingston, Jennings, Reynolds, & Gray, 2003; Macmann & Barnett, 1997; Watkins, 2000; Watkins & Canivez, 2004).

The KABC-II does have some potential weaknesses. Use of the dual theoretical model effectively causes the CHC framework to dominate the Lurian framework, and it is not clear how supportive research can be interpreted as supporting one theory or the other. The contents and processes involved in subtests are not always clear: for example, the KABC-II Manual documents instances in which subtests (e.g., the Rover subtest, see Kaufman & Kaufman, 2004) were assigned to different scales than originally intended based on factor-analytic findings. This type of discrepancy between test content and factor structure supports Kline and colleagues' (1996) call for detailed componential analyses of tasks and scoring systems, given the many cognitive processes that may be involved in cognitive test performance.

## Reynolds Intellectual Assessment Scales

The Reynolds Intellectual Assessment Scales (Reynolds & Kamphaus, 2003) offer a four- or six-subtest measure of general intelligence and two primary factors, verbal and nonverbal intelligence, normed for use with individuals between the ages of 3 years and 94 years. The RIAS is authored by Cecil R. Reynolds and Randy W. Kamphaus, both former students of Alan Kaufman at the University of Georgia and prolific authors and distinguished scholars in their own right. The RIAS is designed to be a practical and economical intelligence measure that requires no reading, motor coordination, or visual-motor speed.

The four intelligence subtests on the RIAS typically can be administered in less than a half hour through verbally administered or pictorial items appearing in a stimulus book. Instructions are brief and succinct. Following administration of one or two sample items, items are typically administered beginning at a start point, with the option to reverse, until a basal of two consecutive correct items is attained. Items are administered until a discontinue/end rule of two or three consecutive incorrect items is reached. For nonverbal subtests, the examinee is given two chances to respond to each item.

Raw subtest scores are converted to age-adjusted $T$ scores ($M = 50$, $SD = 10$), which may be used to generate up to four composite index scores ($M = 100$, $SD = 15$). $T$ scores for the two verbal subtests, Guess What and Verbal Reasoning, may be used to calculate a Verbal Intelligence Index (VIX). $T$ scores for the two nonverbal subtests, Odd-Item Out and What's Missing, may be used to calculate a Nonverbal Intelligence Index (NIX). Results for the four intelligence subtests are used to calculate a Composite Intelligence Index (CIX). Two memory subtests, Verbal Memory and Nonverbal Memory, are available to supplement intelligence testing and generate a Composite Memory Index (CMX).

### Theoretical Underpinnings

The RIAS was developed to provide efficient measurement in terms of time, cost, and yield. It emphasizes the general intelligence factor, *g*, as the most reliable factor in intelligence, measured on the RIAS with the CIX score. Drawing on the CHC framework, it also taps crystallized and fluid intelligence through its VIX and NIX scores, respectively. Reynolds and Kamphaus (2003) explained: "From our research, we have concluded that a strong measure of *g*, coupled with strong measures of verbal and nonverbal intelligence, account for nearly all of the reliable and interpretable variance in the subtests of good intelligence measures. Others have reached similar conclusions" (p. 10). The memory subtests and composite are optional but can be used to tap an additional CHC factor.

The four subtests that contribute to the CIX appear to be fair to good measures of psychometric *g*. Through exploratory principal factor analyses of the standardization sample and examination of the first unrotated factor, the *g* loadings of RIAS subtests ranged from .62 to .78 for ages 3 to 5 years, .49 to .81 for ages 6 to 11 years, .60 to .88 for ages 12 to 18 years, .66 to 87 for ages 19 to 54 years, and .69 to .85 for ages 55 to 94 years (Reynolds & Kamphaus, 2003). By Kaufman's (1994) criteria, the four RIAS subtests that contribute to CIX are good measures of general intelligence in about two-thirds of analyses conducted across five age groups. The two verbal subtests, Guess What and Verbal Reasoning, consistently have good *g* loadings (≥.70), while the two nonverbal subtests do not fare quite as well. Across age groups, Odd-Item Out has fair to good *g* loadings, and What's Missing is consistently just fair (.50 to .69) in its *g* loading. Bracken (2005) concluded that the verbal subtests are the only consistently good measures of general intelligence. In an independent investigation, hierarchical exploratory factor analyses with the Schmid-Leiman procedure yielded fair *g*-loadings for the four core subtests across nearly all age ranges (Dombrowski et al., 2009).

Support for the RIAS verbal/nonverbal two-factor structure shows evidence of weakness. Exploratory factor analyses with principal factors of the four subtest core

battery supports labeling the Guess What and Verbal Reasoning subtests as verbal (with factor pattern coefficients consistently greater than .65 across ages), but the Odd-Item Out subtest yields not-insubstantial loadings on the same factor from .30 to .50. A second factor is defined by factor pattern coefficients ranging from .53 to .67 on Odd-Item Out and What's Missing. However, the verbal subtests also show significant loading on this factor (.32 to .50). Nelson, Canivez, Lindstrom, and Hatt (2007) found from an independent sample that hierarchical exploratory factor analysis supported only the extraction of a general intelligence factor, accounting for the largest amount of subtest, total, and common variance. In another hierarchical exploratory factor analysis, Dombrowski et al. (2009) concluded of the RIAS factor structure: "The verbal subtests produced fair to poor factor loadings with the verbal factor, whereas the nonverbal subtests produced poor factor loadings on the nonverbal factor across all age ranges" (p. 501). Beaujean, McGlaughlin, and Margulies (2009) reanalyzed data from the standardization sample as well as from the J. M. Nelson, Canivez, Lindstrom, and Hatt (2007) sample, along with a new sample of referred cases, reporting that confirmatory factor analyses supported the two-factor structure of the RIAS although "the verbal factor showed much stronger invariance, construct reliability, and overall interpretability than did the nonverbal factor" (p. 932).

### Standardization Features and Psychometric Adequacy

The RIAS was standardized from 1999 to 2002, with stratification targets based on 2001 Current Population Survey census figures. The national normative standardization sample consisted of 2,438 children, adolescents, and adults between the ages of 3 and 94 years. Sixteen age groups were established, beginning at 1-year intervals for ages 3 through 10, 2-year intervals for ages 11 to 16, and larger multiyear intervals for ages 17 through 94 years. A minimum of $n = 100$ participants were included in each interval, which may potentially be inadequate during the preschool and early school years when cognitive capacities are developing rapidly. The standardization sample exclusion criteria included color blindness, hearing or vision loss, alcohol or drug dependence, current treatment with psychotropic medication, any history of posttraumatic loss of consciousness, and any history of electroconvulsive therapy. The presence of a neuropsychiatric or psychoeducational disorder did not, however, lead to exclusion from participation in the normative standardization sample. The sample was stratified on the basis of sex, ethnicity, educational attainment, and geographic region. An examination of standardization sample demographic breakdowns suggests that while minorities as a whole were oversampled, several age groups show 3% to 4% underrepresentation for African Americans and Hispanic Americans. As a correction after stratification, standardization participants were weighted on an individual basis to precisely match census targets, and continuous norming procedures were applied to generate norms.

The internal consistency reliability of the RIAS subtest scores were computed with Cronbach's coefficient alpha. Median score reliabilities for the four RIAS intelligence subtests, and for the two memory subtests as well, range from .90 to .95 across age levels for the standardization sample. The composite scores (VIX, NIX, CIX, and CMX) show median reliabilities of .94 to .96. Reliabilities reported in the Professional Manual across gender and race are comparably high. Subtest internal consistencies are very high, sufficiently so to suggest that concern may be merited over excessively narrow, homogeneous content.

Test–retest stability coefficients for RIAS subtests were studied for $n = 86$ examinees across a broad age range from 3 through 82 years of age ($M = 11$ years, $SD = 15$) over a median time interval of 21 days (ranging from 9 to 39 days). Corrected test–retest subtest correlations ranged from .76 to .89, while corrected correlations for composite scores ranged from .83 to .91. These findings suggest that RIAS subtests appear reasonably stable over 3-week intervals. A comparison of test–retest mean composite scores suggests small practice effects, from about 2 to 4 points, over the 3-week interval.

In summary, examinations of RIAS score reliabilities indicate very high internal consistency and fairly adequate temporal stability. A small interscorer agreement study ($n = 35$) with only two raters indicated exceptionally high agreement ($r = .95$ to $1.00$) between scorers of completed protocols.

In terms of floors and ceilings, the four RIAS intelligence subtests tend to have limited floors, good ceilings, and some gaps in score gradients. For preschool and school-age children, the subtests consistently extend at least two $SD$s below the normative mean of 50 $T$, down to 30 $T$, but there are some concerns with $T$ score difficulty gradients. For example, answering two items on Verbal Reasoning at age 3 is enough to change resulting subtest scores by 12 $T$ points, more than 1 $SD$. Across all school ages, the four intelligence subtest ceilings extend to just above $+2$ $SD$ (e.g., What's Missing ceiling at age 17 is 71 $T$; Odd-Item Out ceiling is 73 $T$). For ages 7 to 8 years, when students are commonly selected for gifted

and talented programs, RIAS subtest ceilings extend about 3 to 4 $SD$s above the normative mean, a ceiling that is certainly high enough to identify cognitively advanced students.

Correlations between RIAS scores and the WISC-III FSIQ are between .60 and .78. Correlations between RIAS scores and the WAIS-III FSIQ are above .70. Edwards and Paulin (2007) reported that, for a sample of young referred children, the correlation between the CIX and WISC-IV FSIQ was .90, while the correlation between the CIX and the WISC-IV GAI was also .90. Krach, Loe, Jones, and Farrally (2009) reported a corrected correlation of .75 between the RIAS CIX and the WJ III GIA.

Reynolds and Kamphaus (2003) report that the VIX correlates .86 and .44 respectively with the WISC-III VIQ and PIQ, while the NIX (in a pattern opposite to expectations) correlates .60 and .33 respectively with the VIQ and PIQ. The VIX correlates .71 and .61 with the WAIS-III VIQ and PIQ, while the NIX correlates .67 with the VIQ and .71 with the PIQ. These findings do not provide clear support for convergent validity of the NIX. Edwards and Paulin (2007) reported that the correlations between the RIAS VIX and WISC-IV VCI and PRI were .90 and .71, while the correlations between the NIX and the WISC-IV VCI and PRI were .53 and .72, somewhat more in line with expectations, although the magnitude of the correlations suggests that general intelligence pervades the VIX and NIX. Krach et al. (2009) reported that the VIX yields high corrected correlations of .88 and .64 with WJ III Gc and Gf, respectively, while NIX yields corrected correlations of .57 and .54 with Gc and Gf.

There are several isolated reports that RIAS yields significantly higher scores than the WISC-IV and WJ III Cog (Edwards & Paulin, 2007; Krach et al., 2009), although a validity study reported in the RIAS Professional Manual show that WISC-III yielded a significantly higher FSIQ than the RIAS CIX.

### Interpretive Indices and Applications

RIAS subtest raw scores are converted to $T$ scores, and age-equivalent scores corresponding to subtest raw scores are available. Subtest $T$ scores may be summed to look up the composite standard scores. As reported, RIAS composites include the VIX, NIX, and CIX. The CMX may also be derived if the memory subtests are given. Composite indices are accompanied by percentile ranks and 90% and 95% confidence intervals. Table 18.4 contains descriptions of the basic composite indices.

The RIAS provides the option in Appendix I to include the memory subtests in the calculation of total composite

**TABLE 18.4    Reynolds Intellectual Assessment Scales Core Interpretive Indices**

| Composite Indices | Description |
| --- | --- |
| Composite Intelligence Index (CIX) | Summary estimate of general cognitive ability |
| Verbal Intelligence Index (VIX) | An estimate of verbal reasoning ability and crystallized intellectual functioning |
| Nonverbal Intelligence Index (NIX) | An estimate of nonverbal reasoning ability and fluid intellectual functioning |
| Composite Memory Index (CMX) | An estimate of verbal and nonverbal memory functions for material that is meaningful, concrete, or abstract |

scores. In this framework, the Total Verbal Battery (TVB) is based on the sum of $T$ scores for the three verbal subtests, the Total Nonverbal Battery (TNB) is based on the sum of $T$ scores for the three nonverbal subtests, and the Total Test Battery (TTB) is derived from the sum of $T$ scores for all six RIAS subtests. These total battery scores are not recommended by the authors, and available research does not tend to support their use.

Subtests scores and composite scores may be compared on a pairwise basis, based on the statistical significance of differences and normative frequencies of discrepancies for a given age group in the standardization sample. For example, the statistical significance and cumulative frequency of a discrepancy between verbal and nonverbal intelligence (VIX and NIX) may be easily estimated. The discrepancy between composite intelligence and memory (CMX and CMX) is a traditional comparison used to help identify memory disorders.

Potential applications of the RIAS include identification of individuals with learning disability, intellectual disability/mental retardation, intellectual giftedness, neuropsychological impairment, memory impairment, and emotional disturbance (Reynolds & Kamphaus, 2003). The RIAS Professional Manual includes clinical samples diagnosed with intellectual disability/mental retardation, traumatic brain injury, stroke/cerebrovascular accident, seizure disorder, dementia, learning disabilities, anxiety disorders, depression, schizophrenia, bipolar disorder, and polysubstance abuse.

### Strengths and Limitations

The RIAS represents a reliable, efficient, and economical measure of general intelligence. Dombrowski and Mrazik (2008) commented on its efficiency: "Although the RIAS may be expediently administered, it provides a global measure of intelligence consistent with tests more than twice its length" (p. 229). R. W. Elliott (2004) concluded

that RIAS is a time and cost effective means of conducting intellectual assessments: "The RIAS will become a very popular measure of intelligence for school districts that are under serious pressure to provide measures of intelligence for determination of special education and program needs, but to do so at a lower cost and in a more rapid fashion" (p. 325).

The RIAS, however, has limitations in at least two major aspects of its validity: the degree to which its subtests all measure general intelligence and the difficulty supporting its two-factor verbal/nonverbal structure. While J. M. Nelson and his colleagues (2007) found that general intelligence accounted for a large amount of test variance, Bracken (2005) noted that the majority of RIAS subtests have loadings on the $g$ factor that are considered fair or poor. The equivocal support for the factorial extraction of two factors (e.g., Dombrowski et al., 2009) is further complicated by Bracken's (2005) observation that the NIX has correlations as high or higher with the Wechsler verbal subtests as with the Wechsler nonverbal/performance subtests. He was concerned that subtests often have a large (i.e., greater than or equal to .35) secondary loading on the opposite factor, undermining the distinctiveness of the verbal and nonverbal factors. Beaujean et al. (2009) concluded that "there appears to be a growing literature questioning the utility of interpreting the NIX score" (p. 948).

### Stanford-Binet Intelligence Scales

The oldest of intelligence tests is the Stanford-Binet Intelligence Scales, now in its fifth edition (SB5; Roid, 2003a, 2003b, 2003c). The Stanford-Binet has a distinguished lineage, having been the only one of several adaptations of Binet's 1911 scales to survive to the present time. According to Théodore Simon (cited by Wolf, 1973, p. 35), Binet gave Lewis M. Terman at Stanford University the rights to publish an American revision of the Binet-Simon scale "for a token of one dollar." Terman (1877–1956) may arguably be considered the single person most responsible for spawning the testing industry that dominates contemporary intelligence and educational testing. The editions of the Stanford-Binet created by Terman (1916; Terman & Merrill, 1937) remain remarkable technical innovations even today. For example, the first executive function measure explicitly intended to measure planning and organization was Terman's Ball-and-field test (Terman, 1916; see also Littman, 2004), eight decades before Naglieri and Das (1997a, 1997b) reintroduced executive functions to intelligence assessment.

A SB5 test session begins with administration of a nonverbal routing subtest (Nonverbal Fluid Reasoning) and a verbal routing subtest (Verbal Knowledge). Scores on these two subtests each provide guidance specifying which level to begin testing in the nonverbal and verbal batteries. In this manner, the SB5 lends itself to adaptive, tailored testing. It is also possible to use the routing tests as a short form, generating an Abbreviated IQ (ABIQ). The five nonverbal battery subtests are typically completed first, followed by the five verbal battery subtests, with a basal and ceiling ultimately completed for each subtest. A unique feature of the SB5 is that at different stages in development, the tasks, manipulatives, and procedures intended to tap the targeted construct (indicated by the name of the subtest) may change. The SB5 features age-appropriate tasks from 2 through 85+ years delivered in the classic spiral omnibus testing format in which a small number of items (clustered in testlets) from each of the core factors are presented at a given developmental level, before the sequence starts anew at the next developmental level.

### Theoretical Underpinnings

The fourth edition of the Stanford-Binet, published in 1986, was the first intelligence test to adopt Cattell and Horn's fluid-crystallized model of cognitive abilities, with a hierarchical organization in which psychometric $g$ was at the apex, and four broad group factors—crystallized ability, fluid-analytic ability, quantitative reasoning, and short-term memory—were at the second, subordinate level. The SB5 represents an ambitious effort to integrate the CHC model with the traditional verbal-nonverbal dichotomy by measuring each of five CHC factors (termed Fluid Reasoning, Knowledge, Quantitative Reasoning, Visual-Spatial Processing, and Working Memory, corresponding respectively to Gf, Gc, Gq, Gv, and Gsm) with separate verbal and nonverbal subtests. The SB5 deviates from the CHC approach through its inclusion of Quantitative Reasoning as a cognitive factor and its attempt to provide separate verbal and nonverbal measures of each CHC broad factor. The inclusion of Quantitative Reasoning provided continuity with the SB Fourth Edition and has a long-standing prominence among human cognitive abilities, although it was not accorded independent stratum 2 status in Carroll's (1993) three-stratum model. Still, it features prominently in other models of human cognitive abilities. A numerical facility factor appeared in Thurstone's (1938) primary mental ability structure; a quantitative reasoning factor (RQ) and broad mathematical factor (Gq) were identified by Carroll (1993, 2003);

a numerical agency was specified by Cattell (1998); and a second-order quantitative knowledge (Gq) factor was identified by Horn (e.g., Horn & Blankson, 2005). There is somewhat less of a theoretical foundation for verbal and nonverbal measurement of each of the five factors, although each of the factors is thought to transcend sensory modality.

The SB5 appears to provide a sound measure of general intelligence. The $g$-loadings of individual SB5 subtests tend to be high (Roid, 2003c). Through principal axis factor analyses, the average $g$ loadings of SB5 subtests across all ages are good (i.e., $>.70$) for nine of the 10 subtests; only Nonverbal Fluid Reasoning has a fair $g$ loading (.66). Normally the Nonverbal Fluid Reasoning subtest (a matrix reasoning task) would be considered to be an optimal measure of psychometric $g$. From ages 2 to 5 years, 60% of SB5 subtests are good measures of $g$ and 40% are fair measures. From ages 6 to 16 years, 60% to 70% of the subtests are good measures of $g$ and the remaining subtest are fair measures of $g$. For adults, 100% of the subtests are good measures of $g$ (Roid, 2003c).

Factor analyses of SB5 subtests provide strong support for interpretation of the general intelligence factor but little support for the five-factor structure and for the division of tasks into verbal and nonverbal modalities (e.g., Canivez, 2008; DiStefano & Dombrowski, 2006; Ward, Rothlisberg, McIntosh, & Bradley, 2011; Williams, McIntosh, Dixon, Newton, & Youman, 2010). An examination of test content provides possible explanations, such as the inclusion of pictorial absurdities tasks (which elicit a verbal response) among the SB5 nonverbal tasks, or the inclusion of an analogies task (dependent on word knowledge) at the highest levels of fluid reasoning. Moreover, the correlations between the VIQ and NVIQ in the entire standardization sample is unusually high ($r = .85$), providing further evidence that the verbal and nonverbal scales are not distinct. As a result, the SB5 theoretical and interpretive structure cannot be said to match its factor structure.

### Standardization Features and Psychometric Adequacy

The SB5 was standardized from 2001 to 2002 on 4,800 children, adolescents, and adults in 30 age levels from 2 through 85+ years. The sampling plan provided for narrower age gradations during periods of rapid development or potential loss of function when greater cognitive change may be expected (i.e., during the preschool period and older adulthood). For the preschool ages 2 through 4 years, the age levels were divided into 6-month intervals; for child and adolescent ages 5 years through

16 years, 1-year intervals were used; for young adulthood, the intervals were 17 to 20, 21 to 25, and 26 to 29; middle adulthood intervals were by decade (30–39, 40–49, and 50–59); older adulthood (60+ years) was divided into 5-year intervals. The sample size at each age level was $n = 100$, with the exception of young adulthood, which was slightly more variable but still adequate.

The normative sample used 2001 U.S. Census figures to set sampling targets for these stratification variables: sex (balanced for most ages, except older examinees where females are more highly represented), race/ethnicity, geographic region, and socioeconomic level (level of education). Participants were excluded from the normative sample if they qualified for significant special education services, if they had any of a variety of severe medical conditions, if they had severe sensory or communication deficits, or if they were diagnosed with severe behavioral/emotional disturbance. Examinees with limited English proficiency were also excluded. Detailed breakdowns of stratification sampling sizes are reported in the SB5 Technical Manual (Roid, 2003c), and an examination of sampling proportions on the margins suggests that sampling representation was fairly accurate, compared to census proportions. There is, however, anecdotal evidence that examinees from a highly gifted special population study were added to the normative sample, with an unknown impact on mean scores (Andrew Carson, personal communication, March 9, 2010). Normative tables were produced with continuous norming methods that should correct for any vagaries at specific age levels.

The internal consistency score reliabilities of the SB5 subtests and composites appear fully adequate. Roid (2003c) reported that the average subtest score reliabilities computed with the split half method, with Spearman-Brown correction, range from .84 to .89. Average composite score reliabilities range from .90 to .98, with the Full Scale IQ yielding the highest internal consistency. Test consistency across racial/ethnic groups was compared using Feldt's (1969) $F$-test procedure, which yielded only a single statistically significant difference in internal consistency between Asian, Hispanic, White, and African American groups—specifically a finding that for ages 6 to 10, Hispanic groups show significantly higher reliability than Whites for the verbal subtests.

Test–retest stability coefficients were computed for four age cohorts over an interval ranging from 1 to 39 days (*Median* $= 7$ days). Corrected subtest test–retest correlations range from .76 to .91 for preschool children; .76 to .91 for school-age children and adolescents; .66 to .93

for adults; and .77 to .91 for older adults. The highest stability may generally be found on the Verbal Knowledge subtest, the lowest on Nonverbal Fluid Reasoning. Composite score stabilities across these cohorts range from .79 to .95, with the factor indices and ABIQ (each derived from a pair of subtests) generally being lowest, the Verbal IQ and Nonverbal IQ being higher, and the Full Scale IQ having the greatest stability. The Nonverbal IQ consistently has lower stability than the Verbal IQ, and the Fluid Reasoning Index consistently ranks near the least stable of the factor index scores.

Interscorer agreement studies were conducted by comparing three sets of ratings of polychotomously scored items (i.e., those scored as 0, 1, or 2) for clusters of items (testlets) appearing in four of the five SB5 factors. Across all polychotomous items, interscorer correlations ranged from .74 to .97, with an overall median of .90 (Roid, 2003c).

Stanford-Binet subtest floors begin to look adequate for the assessment of potentially disordered children by about ages 4 or 5 years. For 2-year-olds, subtest floors extend from $-1.33$ to $-2.67$ $SD$ below the normative mean, based on the lowest scores corresponding to a raw score of 1. It is not until age 4 years, 4 months that norms for every subtest extend at least 2 $SD$s below the general population mean, to the range associated with developmental disabilities. Based on earning the lowest possible nonzero raw score on every subtest, however, composite test score floors extend down to a Full Scale IQ of 64 at age 2, fully adequate for assessing children with various impairments.

Stanford-Binet subtest ceiling scores consistently extend to scaled scores of 19 ($+3$ $SD$) for perfect scores for all subtests at all ages, yielding a Full Scale IQ of 160 if every item is successfully answered on the test. Roid (2003b) also offered an experimental alternative to the Full Scale IQ, called an Extended IQ (EXIQ), that is capable of describing *more* extreme scores extending up through 225. There is, however, no research as yet on this experimental index. Ceiling content may also be reason to be concerned with SB5 ceilings. For example, the Nonverbal Knowledge subtest has two items dependent on a narrow knowledge of geography at its highest level.

Cross-sectional growth curves for Rasch-based change-sensitive scores appear in the SB5 technical manual (Roid, 2003c) providing evidence of the relationship between SB5 factors and normative cognitive development. Although these scores are not directly comparable, they show that different cognitive abilities develop at different rates, that all develop rapidly through adolescence, that fluid reasoning peaks in young adulthood while acquired knowledge peaks in middle to late adulthood. Growth trends may be considered a unique way to demonstrate test construct validity.

Only confirmatory factor analyses are reported in the SB5 technical manual (Roid, 2003c), while a lengthy discussion (pp. 108–109) explains the conspicuous omission of exploratory factor analyses. Ironically, new exploratory factor analyses are actually reported for the much-older Stanford-Binet Form L (Roid, 2003c). Confirmatory factor analyses were conducted with two split-half versions of each subtest, altogether yielding 20 scores. Results were interpreted as supporting the verbal-nonverbal dichotomy as well as the five-factor structure.

Canivez (2008) conducted a hierarchical exploratory factor analysis of the SB5 standardization sample and found that large portions of total and common variance were accounted for by second-order, general intelligence, with no evidence for a five-factor (Fluid Reasoning, Knowledge, Quantitative Reasoning, Visual-Spatial Processing, and Working Memory) or two-factor (verbal/nonverbal) solution at any level:

> On balance, it appears that the SB-5 is a strong measure of general intelligence in children and adolescents, but little empirical evidence for additional factors was found. As such, clinicians would be wise to concentrate their interpretation on the overall global IQ score from the SB-5, even with the youngest age groups. (Canivez, 2008, pp. 539–540)

Similar concerns about SB5 factor structure have been reported by DiStefano and Dombrowski (2006), who conducted exploratory and confirmatory factor analyses with the standardization sample, concluding that the verbal/nonverbal domains were identifiable with subjects younger than 10 years of age whereas a single factor was readily identified with older age groups.

Williams and her colleagues (2010) conducted confirmatory factor analyses on a sample of 201 high-achieving third-grade students and concluded that a hierarchical, four-factor (fluid reasoning and knowledge were combined into a single factor), post hoc model provided the best fit to the data.

The SB5's overall convergence with other measures of intelligence and achievement appears fully adequate. The SB5 Full Scale IQ has an uncorrected correlation of $r = .90$ with the previous edition (SB IV) Composite Standard Age Score and .85 with the 1972 SB Form L-M IQ. The SB5 FSIQ has a corrected correlation of .83 with the WPPSI-R FSIQ, .84 with the WISC-III FSIQ, .82 with the

WAIS-III FSIQ, and .78 with the WJ III Cog GIA. These correlations provide evidence of high convergent validity with other intelligence test composites. In addition, the SB5 FSIQ has corrected correlations ranging from .50 to .84 with WJ III achievement scores and a corrected correlation of $r = .80$ with the WIAT-II Total Achievement composite (Roid, 2003c).

### Interpretive Indices and Applications

The Stanford-Binet yields 10 subtest scaled scores (with a mean of 10, *SD* of 3), five factor indices, a Nonverbal IQ (NVIQ) and a Verbal IQ (VIQ), and an overall composite score, the Full Scale IQ. Core composite interpretive indices, with a mean of 100 and *SD* of 15, appear in Table 18.5. The SB5 interpretive manual (Roid, 2003b) recommends a seven-step interpretive approach that first considers assumptions, purpose, and context, followed by interpretation of nonverbal versus verbal performance, interpretation of Full Scale IQ, interpretation of factor indexes, subtest profile analysis, and qualitative interpretation.

**TABLE 18.5  Stanford-Binet Intelligence Scales—Fifth Edition Core Interpretive Indices**

| Composite/Factor Indices | Description |
| --- | --- |
| *Full Scale IQ* | Overall cognitive functioning across a sample of verbal and nonverbal tasks |
| *Nonverbal IQ* | Estimate of functioning on problem-solving tasks with minimal or reduced language demands |
| *Verbal IQ* | Estimate of functioning on knowledge and problem-solving tasks with high language demands |
| *Fluid Reasoning* | An estimate of novel problem-solving facility, based on performance on a sample of nonverbal tasks (e.g., analysis of figural analogies and sequences) and verbal tasks (e.g., explanation of verbal absurdities, verbal analogies) |
| *Knowledge* | An estimate of previously acquired declarative and procedural learning, based on performance on a sample of nonverbal tasks (e.g., knowledge of how to perform simple tasks, identification of absurd or missing elements in pictures) and verbal tasks (ability to define words) |
| *Quantitative Reasoning* | An estimate of mathematical problem solving in words and pictures, ranging from elementary number concepts to higher order mathematical operations |
| *Visual-Spatial Processing* | An estimate of spatial cognitive ability, based on reproduction of visual-spatial patterns and capacity to verbally process spatial concepts like position and direction |
| *Working Memory* | Immediate and short-term recall/mental holding capacity, mental operating space, and the ability to mentally manipulate verbal and visual-spatial contents |

Several additional SB5 scores may be of value. The change-sensitive scores (CSS) are Rasch-derived scores that measure performance on a developmental yardstick. Ironically, there is no evidence that change-sensitive scores are actually sensitive to the effects of cognitive, educational, or therapeutic interventions. Other scores, such as the EXIQ score that promises to raise composite IQ scores, should be considered experimental at this time.

Special population studies appearing in the SB5 technical manual include individuals diagnosed with ADHD, autism spectrum disorder, developmental disability, English language learners, intellectually gifted, intellectually disabled/mentally retarded, specific learning disabilities, speech and language impairment, deafness and hard of hearing, and serious emotional disturbance (Roid, 2003c).

### Strengths and Limitations

The SB5 is a fast-moving, engaging, sound measure of general intelligence. In praise of its administrative qualities, Bain and Allin (2005) commented:

> The SB5 represents some departures from previous editions in organization and content while retaining some of the item variation and charm that made administration of the earlier SB L-M a pleasure, particularly with young children. We found administration time using the SB5 to be briefer than the SB-IV... Pacing of subtests is easy, as long as manipulative items are well organized. The younger children we have observed during testing have remained interested in the colorful test stimuli throughout. (p. 94)

The limitations of the SB5 stem principally from its structural difficulties and its yet-to-be-demonstrated clinical relevance. Factor analyses do not support its five-factor interpretive structure or the verbal/nonverbal interpretive dichotomy (e.g., Canivez, 2008). Consequently, the SB5 appears to represent a bold (but failed) effort to expand the CHC model by providing both verbal and nonverbal measures for each of five factors. It is not entirely clear whether the conceptualization or execution of the test was the failure, because some "nonverbal" tests actually require verbal responses, an obvious failure in developing nonverbal tests. Alternatively, CHC constructs may simply not permit equivalent verbal and nonverbal measurement, the clearest evidence of which is the prevailing tendency for all crystallized tests to be mainly verbal, all fluid ability tests to be mainly visual-spatial and nonverbal, and all short-term/working memory tests to be auditory-verbal but not spatial. If the interpretive structure

of the SB5 lacks validity, as research seems to suggest, than it is invalid to interpret any indices but the FSIQ in clinical and educational decision making.

## Wechsler Intelligence Scales

No brand name in psychology is better known than Wechsler, now applied to a series of intelligence scales spanning the ages 2½ through 90 years, an adult memory scale covering ages 16 through 90 years, and an achievement test covering ages 4 through 50 years as well as several ancillary tests. The remarkable success of the Wechsler measures is attributable to David Wechsler (1896–1981), a pioneering clinician and psychometrician with a well-developed sense of what was practical and clinically relevant. Decades after Wechsler's death, his tests continue to dominate intellectual assessment among psychologists (Camara et al., 2000).

Wechsler's role in the history of intelligence assessment is beginning to be critically assessed (e.g., Wasserman, 2012), but the origins of his subtests can be readily traced to testing procedures developed from the 1880s through the 1930s (e.g., Boake, 2002). Wechsler was introduced to most of the procedures that would eventually find a home in his intelligence and memory scales as a graduate student at Columbia University (with faculty including J. McKeen Cattell, Edward L. Thorndike, and Robert S. Woodworth) and as an army mental examiner in World War I. He developed his first test battery for his master's thesis completed in 1917, establishing a pattern he would later follow of appropriating practical and clinically useful procedures from other authors, making slight improvements and modifications, and synthesizing them into a streamlined battery of his own. During his military service in 1918, he learned the group-administered Army mental tests (the Army alpha and beta) as well as leading individual intelligence and performance tests, testing many recruits who suffered from limited English proficiency and illiteracy. It was during his time as an army examiner that many of Wechsler's core ideas about assessment were born, especially his idea to construct an intelligence scale combining verbal and nonverbal tests, paralleling the Army alpha and Army beta/performance exams (Wechsler, 1981). Matarazzo (1981) related that Wechsler realized the value of individual intelligence assessment after seeing recruits who functioned quite adequately in civilian life in spite of subnormal results on the group-administered tests. As part of an educational program intended for American soldiers serving overseas, Wechsler attended the University of London in 1919, where he spent some 3 months studying with Charles E. Spearman, an experience that impressed him deeply. Later Wechsler sought training from several of the leading clinicians of his day, including Augusta F. Bronner and William Healy at the Judge Baker Foundation in Boston and Anna Freud at the Vienna Psychoanalytic Institute (for 3 months in 1932). By virtue of his education and training, Wechsler should properly be remembered as one of the first scientist-clinicians in psychology.

Wechsler first introduced the Bellevue Intelligence Tests (later named the Wechsler-Bellevue; Wechsler, 1939), followed by the Wechsler Intelligence Scale for Children (WISC; Wechsler, 1949), the Wechsler Adult Intelligence Scale (WAIS; Wechsler, 1955), and the Wechsler Preschool and Primary Scale of Intelligence (WPPSI; Wechsler, 1967). With some variation, these tests all utilize the same core set of subtests and interpretive scores. The most recent editions of Wechsler's intelligence scales are the WPPSI-III (Wechsler, 2002), the WISC-IV (Wechsler, 2003a, 2003b), the WAIS-IV (Wechsler, 2008a, 2008b), and a two- or four-subtest short form named the Wechsler Abbreviated Scale of Intelligence (WASI-II; Wechsler, 2012). Since Wechsler's death, these updates have generally been developed by research and development psychologists working with expert advisory panels. The WISC-IV and WAIS-IV are emphasized in this section.

### Theoretical Underpinnings

The Wechsler intelligence scales are decidedly atheoretical, beyond their emphasis on psychometric $g$, and in recent years they have appeared to be a test in search of a theory. As originally conceptualized by David Wechsler (1939), they were clearly intended to tap Spearman's general intelligence factor, $g$: "The only thing we can ask of an intelligence scale is that it measures sufficient portions of intelligence to enable us to use it as a fairly reliable index of the individual's global capacity" (p. 11). Wechsler purposefully included a diverse range of tasks so as to avoid placing disproportionate emphasis on any single ability: "My definition of intelligence is that it's not equivalent to any single ability, it's a global capacity . . . The tests themselves are only modes of communication" (Wechsler, 1975, p. 55). Wechsler kept in contact with Spearman long after World War I, even attempting (unsuccessfully) to identify a general emotional factor as a parallel to the general intellectual factor (Wechsler, 1925). In 1939 Wechsler wrote that Spearman's theory and its proofs constitute "one of the great discoveries of psychology" (p. 6).

Wechsler did not believe that division of his intelligence scales into verbal and performance subtests tapped separate dimensions of intelligence; rather he felt that this dichotomy was diagnostically useful (e.g., Wechsler, 1967). In essence, the verbal and performance scales constituted different means by which $g$ could be assessed. Late in his life Wechsler described the verbal and performance tests merely as ways to "converse" with a person—that is, "to appraise a person in as many different modalities as possible" (Wechsler, 1975, p. 55). Wechsler's intelligence scales sought to capitalize on the established preferences of practitioners to administer both verbal and performance tests as part of a comprehensive assessment, and by packaging both sets of measurements in a single test battery, he was able to meet the needs of applied psychologists. It was not his intent to treat verbal and performance IQ as independent dimensions of intelligence:

> It was not until the publication of the Bellevue Scales that any consistent attempt was made to integrate performance and verbal tests into a single measure of intelligence. The Bellevue tests have had increasingly wider use, but I regret to report that their popularity seems to derive, not from the fact that they make possible a single global rating, but because they enable the examiner to obtain separate verbal and performance I.Q.'s with one test. (Wechsler, 1950, p. 80)

Wechsler was cognizant of multifactor models of intelligence, but he placed little emphasis on them in his writings because after the contribution of the general factor of intelligence was removed, the group factors (e.g., verbal, spatial, memory) accounted for little variance in performance (e.g., Wechsler, 1961). Wechsler also rejected the separation of abilities because he saw intelligence as resulting from the collective integration and connectivity of separate neural processes. He believed that the integrative function of intelligence would never be localized in the brain and observed, "While intellectual abilities can be shown to contain several independent factors, intelligence cannot be so broken up" (Wechsler, 1958, p. 23). Even so, Wechsler (1950) acknowledged the validity of Thurstone's (1938) primary mental abilities:

> What are the elements which factor analysis has shown our intelligence tests to measure? . . . By the use of his [Thurstone's] expanded technique, it has now been shown that intelligence tests, such as they are, contain not one but several independent factors. Some five or six have been definitely identified; they are, to repeat, induction, verbal, spatial,

numerical, and one or two other factors. Notice, however, that these factors, like Spearman's eduction, are all cognitive. (p. 80)

Following Wechsler's death in 1981, the tests have slowly gravitated toward a multifactor interpretive model. Coverage expanded to four factors in the 1991 WISC-III (verbal-comprehension, perceptual-organization, freedom from distractibility, and processing speed) and four factors in the 1997 WAIS-III (verbal-comprehension, perceptual-organization, working memory, and processing speed). With the publication of the WISC-IV (Wechsler, 2003a, 2003b) and the WAIS-IV (Wechsler, 2008a, 2008b), both major tests now feature four identical factors (verbal comprehension, perceptual reasoning, working memory, and processing speed), and the verbal and performance IQs are no longer computed.

### Standardization Features and Psychometric Adequacy

The Wechsler scales are renowned for their rigorous standardizations, with new editions being released about every 10 to 15 years. The Wechsler scales tend to utilize a demographically stratified (and quasi-random) sampling approach, collecting a sample at most age levels of about $n = 200$ usually divided equally by sex.

The WISC-IV normative sample consisted of 2,200 children and adolescents in 11 age groups between the ages of 6 years and 16 years. Unexpectedly, the Arithmetic subtest was normed on only 1,100 participants, half of the normative sample (Wechsler, 2003b). The normative sample was stratified according to race/ethnicity, parent education level, and geographic region. Some 5% to 6% of participants from special population studies were added to the normative sample. At each age, an equal number of males and females were tested. The WAIS-IV normative sample included 2,200 participants in 13 age groups, with 200 examinees in all but the four oldest age groups (70–74, 75–79, 80–84, and 85–90), which consisted of 100 examinees in each group (Wechsler, 2008b). The sample was stratified according to race/ethnicity, educational level, and geographic region. The gender composition of the five oldest age groups was based on census proportions.

The technical manuals for the Wechsler scales report the demographic breakdown of the normative samples in tables that permit several stratification variables to be examined at once in cross-tabulations (e.g., Percentages of the Standardization Sample and U.S. Population by Age, Race/Ethnicity, and Parent Education Level). These cross-tabulations make it possible to verify that stratification characteristics were accurately and proportionally distributed across groups rather than concentrated in a single group. A review of these tables for the WISC-IV and WAIS-IV indicates a fairly close correspondence to census proportions.

Internal consistency with coefficient alpha tends to be fully adequate for the Wechsler subtests and composite scales. On the WISC-IV, all subtest scaled scores had an average reliability coefficient across age groups of .80 or greater, and all composite indexes had reliability coefficients of .90 or greater. B. Thompson (2005) commented on enhanced WISC-IV reliability coefficients relative to the previous edition: "Most reliability coefficients for WISC-IV scores on the 10 retained subtests improved substantially (e.g., Arithmetic, from .78 to .88), and scores on the five new WISC-IV subtests tended to have reliability coefficients (.79 to .90) higher than those for WISC-III scores" (p. 263). For the WAIS-IV, every subtest yields an average reliability coefficient of .80 or greater, and every composite yields an average reliability coefficient of .90 or greater. Speeded subtests (Coding, Symbol Search, and Cancellation) do not lend themselves to internal consistency analyses, so test–retest stability coefficients were used to estimate reliability. Stability coefficients were slightly below .80 for Cancellation (WISC-IV and WAIS-IV) and Symbol Search (WISC-IV only), and the Processing Speed Index was slightly below .90 for the WISC-IV but not the WAIS-IV. It is noteworthy that process scores for Cancellation (Random and Structured) have stability coefficients that are significantly lower than .80 on the WISC-IV, so these scores should be interpreted with some caution.

The WAIS-IV takes a major step forward for the Wechsler scales by reporting subtest reliability coefficients for special population studies, the first step in reliability generalization. While the sample sizes used to calculate reliability coefficients in these studies are relatively small, there are several findings of interest. For example, the low coefficient alpha of .70 for WAIS-IV Letter-Number Sequencing in the small reading disordered sample ($n = 34$) may suggest that this subtest behaves less consistently for at least some learning-disabled individuals (perhaps due to reduced phonological awareness); not surprisingly, Letter-Number Sequencing shows the greatest effect size standard difference for any subtest ($ES = 1.03$) when a reading-disordered group and matched control group are compared.

Test–retest stability tends to be fairly adequate for WISC-IV and WAIS-IV subtests and composite indices, although some subtests (and nearly all process indices) have less than optimal stability. A sample of $n = 243$

participants underwent testing and retesting with the WISC-IV, with an average test–retest interval of 32 days. A sample of $n = 298$ participants underwent retesting with the WAIS-IV over a mean test–retest interval of 22 days. Across all ages for the WISC-IV, the corrected stability coefficient was greater than or equal to .80 for 12 of 15 subtests (with only Picture Concepts being substantially lower), below this benchmark for all process scores, and at or above .90 for two of five composite indices (with the PSI being substantially lower at .86). Across all ages for the WAIS-IV, the corrected stability coefficients were greater than or equal to .80 for 10 of 15 subtests (with Matrix Reasoning and Visual Puzzles substantially lower), below this benchmark for all process scores, and at or above .90 for two of five composite indices (with the remaining composite scores approaching this level).

As with previous editions of the Wechsler intelligence scales, practice effects over several weeks are reported. Over an average interval of 3 to 4 weeks, the most pronounced average practice effects on the Wechsler scales may be expected for Picture Completion (+1.8 scaled score points for the WISC-IV and +1.9 for the WAIS-IV), the Processing Speed Index (+10.9 for the WISC-IV and +4.4 for the WAIS-IV), and FSIQ (+8.3 for the WISC-IV and +4.3 for the WAIS-IV). These findings are much improved relative to older editions of the Wechsler scales and do not provide support for the commonplace recommendation that individuals undergo testing only once a year.

A final issue about the temporal stability of intelligence test results merits discussion, specifically the poor reliability of subtest profile analyses. In the last two decades, the dismal reliability of Wechsler subtest profiles (i.e., patterns of intraindividual strengths and weaknesses) has been definitively established, leading researchers to conclude that the stability of subtest profile configurations is too low for use in clinical and educational decision making (e.g., Livingston et al., 2003; Macmann & Barnett, 1997; McDermott, Fantuzzo, Glutting, Watkins, & Baggaley, 1992; Watkins, 2000; Watkins & Canivez, 2004). While intraindividual subtest profile analysis to identify relative strengths and weaknesses is still featured in most test interpretive manuals, the reliability and validity of composite scores is substantially higher and more suitable for decision making (e.g., Watkins, 2003).

In exploratory analyses documented in the WISC-IV *Technical and Interpretive Manual* (Wechsler, 2003b), the factor structure of the WISC-IV yields four clear factors (verbal comprehension, perceptual reasoning, working memory, and processing speed) that correspond to the four interpretive indices (VCI, PRI, WMI, PSI). Watkins (2006) conducted a hierarchical exploratory factor analysis with the WISC-IV standardization sample and reported a prominent general factor, g, that accounted for the greatest amount of common and total variance. Altogether, the general factor and four first-order factors accounted for 53.7% of the total variance. Watkins, Wilson, Kotz, Carbone, and Babula (2006) demonstrated for a clinical sample that the general factor accounts for more than 75% of the common variance, providing compelling evidence that there is considerable value in interpreting the WISC-IV at the general ability level.

Confirmatory factor analyses with multiple fit indices are reported in the technical manual for the WISC-IV and indicate that a four-factor model tends to best fit the data across multiple age groups (Wechsler, 2003b). A model with a fifth factor (arithmetic reasoning) is viable but offers little improvement over the four-factor model. Keith, Fine, Taub, Reynolds, and Kranzler (2006) conducted confirmatory factor analyses on the WISC-IV normative standardization sample and argued that a CHC-derived five-factor theoretical structure better describes the abilities underlying the WISC-IV than the four-factor model. They suggested that perceptual reasoning subtests measure a mixture of visual processing (Gv) and fluid reasoning (Gf) and that the Arithmetic subtest measures fluid reasoning more than working memory. Bodin, Pardini, Burns, and Stevens (2009) conducted confirmatory analyses with a clinical sample and reported that the second-order general intelligence factor accounted for the largest proportion of variance in the first-order latent factors and in the individual subtests. With a sample of clinically referred students, Watkins (2010) conducted confirmatory factor analyses and reported that the general factor accounted for the predominant amount of variation among the subtests, accounting for 48% of the total variance and 75% of the common variance. Watkin (2010) concluded that the general intelligence score should be the primary basis of test score interpretation.

For the WAIS-IV, the technical manual reported no exploratory factor analyses (Wechsler, 2008b). Canivez (2010) noted that fundamental psychometrics that directly affect test interpretation, such as the proportions of variance accounted for by the higher-order g-factor and the four first-order factors, as well as subtest specificity estimates, are also not reported in WAIS-IV technical materials. Accordingly, Canivez and Watkins (2010a, 2010b) conducted hierarchical exploratory factor analyses and reported that the general factor accounted for major portions of total and common variance and that all WAIS-IV subtests were associated with their theoretically proposed first-order factors. They further noted that the four factors accounted for small amounts of the total and common variance after a general factor was extracted. Confirmatory factor analyses reported in the WAIS-IV technical manual show that four-factor models fit the standardization data well, but that better fit is achieved when two split loadings are specified (i.e., Arithmetic is allowed to load on both the verbal comprehension and working memory factors, and Figure Weights is allowed to load on both the perceptual reasoning and working memory factors), and covariance of error is permitted for subtests that share method variance (i.e., Digit Span and Letter-Number Sequencing) (Wechsler, 2008b).

Convergent validity studies indicate that the Wechsler scales are strongly related to scores from intelligence tests and achievement tests. The WISC-IV FSIQ yields corrected correlations of .91 with the WAIS-IV FSIQ (Wechsler, 2008b), .86 with the WASI four-subtest FSIQ (Wechsler 2003b), and .84 with the DAS-II GCA (C. D. Elliott, 2007b). The WISC-IV FSIQ also has a corrected correlation of .82 with WIAT-III Total Achievement composite, and the FSIQ has correlations between .63 and .75 with all but one WIAT-III composite (Pearson research staff, 2009). Likewise, the WAIS-IV FSIQ correlates at .82 with WIAT-III Total Achievement composite, with correlations between .59 and .80 for all WIAT-III composites (Pearson research staff, 2009).

WISC-IV and WAIS-IV subtest floors and ceilings are improved relative to previous editions. Defined as a scaled score corresponding to a raw score of 1, subtest floors on the WISC-IV extend 2 *SD*s below the normative mean for all subtests and 3 *SD*s below the normative mean for one third of the subtests for the youngest age group (for which floor issues are particularly salient), yielding a floor FSIQ in the 40s (Wechsler, 2003a). The 2008 publication of extended WISC-IV norms raised the subtest scaled score ceiling from 19 to 28 and composite standard scores from 160 to 210 (Zhu, Cayton, Weiss, & Gabel, 2008). For the WAIS-IV oldest age group, 100% of subtests extend 2 *SD*s below the normative mean, and half of the subtests extend 3 SDs below the normative mean (Wechsler, 2008a). The WAIS-IV FSIQ ranges from 40 to 160.

### Interpretive Indices and Applications

Wechsler is reported to have administered and interpreted his own tests in a clinically flexible way that would be considered unacceptable today. For example, in practice he was known to administer the Vocabulary in isolation to estimate intelligence and personality (Adam F.

Wechsler, personal communication, December 3, 1993). Weider (1995) reported, "He never gave the Wechsler the same way twice" and considered the standardization of his tests to be imposed on him by the test publisher. Kaufman (1994) has described Wechsler's clinical approach to interpreting the scales, along with his interest in qualitative aspects of examinee responses to emotionally loaded verbal and pictorial stimuli. One needs only to read Wechsler's (1939) *Measurement of Adult Intelligence* to see that he qualitatively interpreted every test behavior, every item response, every response error, and every problem-solving strategy.

Even so, most contemporary interpretive guidelines emphasize an objective psychometric approach to interpretation of the Wechsler scales, beginning with the FSIQ, followed by the four factor scores, then profile analysis of strengths and weaknesses, and finally process analyses (see e.g., Wechsler, 2008b). The composite index scores that constitute the foundation for Wechsler scale interpretation appear in Table 18.6; these scores are the most reliable scores for interpretation.

**TABLE 18.6  Wechsler Intelligence Scales (WISC-IV and WAIS-IV) Core Interpretive Indices**

| Composite Indices | Description |
| --- | --- |
| *Full Scale IQ (FSIQ)* | Estimate of overall cognitive functioning across a sample of verbal and nonverbal tasks; weighted to emphasize reasoning and knowledge (60%) over information processing speed and capacity (40%) |
| *General Ability Index (GAI)* | Estimate of general cognitive functioning based on performance of subtests associated with reasoning and knowledge, i.e., those strongly associated with psychometric *g* |
| *Cognitive Proficiency Index (CPI)* | Estimate of information processing efficiency, based on performance on subtests associated with processing speed and capacity (working memory); available for WISC-IV only |
| *Verbal Comprehension Index (VCI)* | Estimate of verbal reasoning and knowledge abilities, based on responses to language-based tasks requiring abstract problem solving and retrieval of previous learning |
| *Perceptual Reasoning Index (PRI)* | Performance on tasks requiring abstract visual-spatial perception, processing, and reasoning |
| *Working Memory Index (WMI)* | Auditory immediate/working memory capacity, dependent on capacity and complexity of mental operations as well as facility with number processing |
| *Processing Speed Index (PSI)* | Speed of performance on psychomotor tasks with low difficulty; nonspecifically sensitive to any source of disruptions in cognitive processing efficiency |

The limitations of subtest profile analyses have already been described, although this approach remains common and recommended by some authorities in applied practice (e.g., Flanagan & Kaufman, 2009).

Two new composite indices of intelligence are available for the WISC-IV (Raiford, Weiss, Rolfhus, & Coalson, 2005; Saklofske, Weiss, Raiford, & Prifitera, 2006; Weiss, Saklofske, Schwartz, Prifitera, & Courville, 2006). The General Ability Index (GAI) provides an estimate of general intelligence or ability without penalizing for cognitive inefficiencies, such as reduced processing capacity or speed. The GAI includes subtests thought to have high *g* saturation and thereby emphasizes reasoning ability and acquired knowledge over processing capacity and speed. The GAI is also available for the WAIS-IV (Wechsler, 2008b). The Cognitive Proficiency Index (CPI) provides an estimate of mental efficiency (i.e., how much and how quickly an individual can process information). When information processing efficiency is low, the GAI may provide a more accurate estimate of reasoning and problem-solving ability than the WISC-IV FSIQ.

A few aspects of process-based test interpretation are built into the main Wechsler scales (e.g., Block Design No Time Bonus [BDN], Digit Span subtest fractionation [DSF, DSB, and DSS], and Cancellation subtest fractionation [CAS versus CAR]). Still, the process approach is exemplified in a companion battery entitled WISC-IV Integrated (Wechsler et al., 2004), which merges the WISC-IV with standardized measures of test behavior, problem-solving style, and cognitive processes, building on process-based test procedures first introduced in the WAIS-R as a Neuropsychological Instrument (WAIS-R NI; Kaplan, Fein, Morris, & Delis, 1991) and the WISC-III as a Process Instrument (WISC-III PI; Kaplan et al., 1999). The WISC-IV Integrated includes optional process-based subtests in each of the four factor-defined domains on the WISC-IV (i.e., multiple choice versions of verbal subtests; Block Design Multiple Choice, Block Design Process Approach, Elithorn Mazes; Visual Digit Span, Spatial Span, Letter Span, Letter-Number Sequencing Process Approach, Arithmetic Process Approach, Written Arithmetic; and Coding Recall and Coding Copy). The multiple-choice subtest procedures are typically administered after the standard (free-recall) verbal subtests have been administered, in an effort to discern whether difficulties are attributable to memory retrieval problems (poor performance in free recall but better performance in multiple choice recognition) or a failure to have ever encoded the knowledge in long-term memory (poor performance

in both free-recall and multiple-choice recognition). The child's visual search pattern on the Cancellation subtest may be used to assign a process observation score for each item (Cancellation Random Strategy [CARS] and Cancellation Structured Strategy [CASS]), thereby facilitating comparison of planfulness and accuracy in both disorganized and organized situations. Likewise, observation of errors on Block Design permits objective norm-referenced measurement of breaks in the square $2 \times 2$ or $3 \times 3$ design configurations, which are associated with more severe visual-spatial processing deficits. WISC-IV Integrated options for the Coding subtest permit clarification as to whether difficulties were due to impaired associative learning and memory (Coding Recall) or psychomotor speed (Coding Copy). The WISC-IV Integrated also includes base rate information for the normative number of *Don't Know, No Response, Self-Correction, Repetition,* and *Prompt* response occurrences observed during specific procedures in the test session. The normative frequencies for specific test observations may potentially support various diagnostic inferences, such as an increased number of requests for item repetition in individuals diagnosed with attention deficit or language disorders. Several supplemental subtests offer additional information that extends beyond the traditional Wechsler framework for interpretation, For example, the optional Elithorn Mazes subtest is an explicit measure of planning performance and efficiency, and the Spatial Span subtest is intended as a nonverbal analogue to Digit Span. Ultimately, the WISC-IV Integrated is intended to clarify the nature of any spared and impaired cognitive processes, facilitate identification of problem-solving strategies, and enhance the interpretation of both correct and incorrect responses (e.g., Kaplan, 1988). It remains to note that the usefulness of process-based approaches has yet to be fully demonstrated in the research literature.

Supplemental tasks and procedures designed to facilitate WAIS-IV interpretation may be found in *Advanced Clinical Solutions for the WAIS-IV and WMS-IV* (ACS; Pearson, 2009a). The ACS contains tasks, procedures, and scores that yield information about cognitive processes including new subtests tapping social cognition and motivation/effort, as well as procedures for adjusting standard scores according to demographic characteristics, measuring clinically significant change across serial WAIS-IV administrations, and predicting premorbid cognitive abilities in order to quantify how much cognitive functioning may have been lost from disorders such as traumatic brain injury or Alzheimer's disease.

## Strengths and Limitations

The Wechsler intelligence scales offer reliable and valid measurement of general intelligence and functioning in the areas of verbal and nonverbal intellectual ability, information processing capacity (i.e., working memory) and information processing speed. Since David Wechsler's death, his publisher continues to revise his tests according to high psychometric standards. In a review of the WISC-IV, B. Thompson (2005) commented, "Obviously, considerable resources have been invested in developing the present Wechsler revision. The marriage of resources and reflection inexorably yields impressive progeny" (p. 263). Likewise, the WAIS-IV is considered by reviewers as "one of the best measures of general intellectual functioning available . . . [I]t is extremely comprehensive and provides a reliable and valid measure of intellectual functioning relative to the demands of schooling and academic success" (Canivez, 2010, p. 688).

Yet as the industry leader and most researched of intelligence tests, the Wechsler scales have become the face of intelligence testing, and most appraisals of intelligence testing, whether positive or negative, seem to reflect the qualities (and limitations) of these scales. Among the weaknesses of the Wechsler scales are their limited coverage of the CHC broad factors (e.g., Flanagan & Kaufman, 2009), their continued support of intraindividual subtest profile analyses in spite of considerable evidence against this practice, their shrinking relevance to diagnosis (see the "Diagnostic Applications" section later in the chapter, specifically the deemphasis of intelligence tests in the identification of specific learning disabilities), and their irrelevance for intervention planning. Swanson (2010) observed that "the link between IQ and teaching is obscure (to some it may be nonexistent)" (p. 1), and it may be argued that this failure may be laid at the feet of the Wechsler scales. At the same time, efforts to keep the Wechsler scales fresh and innovative, as by extending WISC-IV norms and developing experimental products like the WISC-IV Integrated and Advanced Clinical Solutions, may help the Wechsler brand remain contemporary while advancing the science and practice of intelligence assessment.

## Woodcock-Johnson Tests of Cognitive Abilities

The Woodcock-Johnson III Normative Update Tests of Cognitive Abilities (WJ III NU Cog; Woodcock, McGrew, & Mather, 2001a, 2007a) represent the most recent revision of an assessment battery with prior

editions from 1977 and 1989. Normed for use from ages 2 through 90 plus years, the WJ III NU Cog is conormed with a leading achievement test, the WJ III NU Tests of Achievement (WJ III NU Ach; Woodcock, McGrew, & Mather, 2001b, 2007b). The battery's origins may be traced back to Richard W. Woodcock's early adult employment in a sawmill and a butcher shop after completion of his World War II navy military service. Upon reading Wechsler's *Measurement and Appraisal of Adult Intelligence*, Woodcock was inspired to study psychology; he quit his jobs and joined the Veteran's Testing Bureau for a wage of 55¢ per hour. Woodcock began active development of the WJ Cog in 1963 in a series of controlled learning experiments that led to development of measures of broad retrieval (now termed Glr) ability. In 1972 Woodcock formed the test development company, Measurement Learning Consultants (MLC), which developed most of his tests. During a 1974–1975 fellowship in neuropsychology at Tufts University, he created an adaptation of the Halstead Category Test that continues to be used as a measure of fluid reasoning (now termed Gf) in the WJ III NU Cog. The original Woodcock-Johnson Psycho-Educational Battery (Woodcock & Johnson, 1977) was envisioned by its primary author as being part of a comprehensive assessment system that measured cognitive abilities and aptitudes, academic achievement skills, scholastic and nonscholastic interests (the Tests of Interest Level), and adaptive functioning (separately measured by the Scales of Independent Behavior) (Woodcock, 1977). The interest inventory was dropped for subsequent editions. The 1989 Woodcock-Johnson Psycho-Educational Battery—Revised (Woodcock & Johnson, 1989, 1990) had the distinction of being the second cognitive test based on the Cattell-Horn theory of fluid and crystallized abilities (after the 1986 Stanford-Binet, Fourth Edition), not wholly surprising since consultants to its development included John L. Horn and John B. Carroll. In 2001 the third edition of the Woodcock-Johnson was published, with the WJ III Cog positioned as an intelligence test tapping general intellectual ability and specific cognitive abilities (Woodcock et al., 2001a, 2007a). A normative update (NU) edition was published in 2007.

Originally finding its primary audience with educators and best known for its companion achievement tests, the WJ III NU Cog is increasingly being utilized by psychologists in educational settings due to its CHC structural underpinnings as well as the popularity of the WJ III NU Ach. The WJ III NU Cog consists of two batteries: a 10-test standard battery and a 20-test extended battery. The Woodcock-Johnson III Diagnostic Supplement to the Tests of Cognitive Abilities (Woodcock, McGrew, Mather, & Schrank, 2003, 2007) includes an additional 11 tests. All items are administered from an easel or compact disc/audiotape. The WJ III NU Cog requires computer scoring and cannot be scored by hand. A parallel Spanish-language battery of cognitive and achievement tests is available in the 2011 Batería III Woodcock-Muñoz NU.

### Theoretical Underpinnings

The WJ III NU Tests of Cognitive Abilities is based on the CHC theory of cognitive abilities. The theory is a hierarchical, multiple-stratum model with $g$ or general intelligence at the apex (or highest stratum), between seven to 10 broad factors of intelligence at the second stratum, and at least 69 narrow factors at the first stratum. The model has been termed an integrated or synthesized CHC framework (McGrew, 1997; McGrew & Flanagan, 1998), and it forms the basis for the cross-battery approach to cognitive assessment (e.g., Flanagan, Ortiz, & Alfonso, 2007). The WJ III NU Cog taps seven broad cognitive abilities in the CHC framework: Gc, Glr, Gv, Ga, Gf, Gs, and Gsm. When the achievement battery is also examined, the additional factors of Gq (mathematics) and language emerge (Carroll, 2003).

Individual tests are differentially weighted in the calculation of the General Intellectual Ability (GIA) score, an estimate of psychometric $g$. The WJ III NU technical manual (McGrew et al., 2007) reports the smoothed $g$ weights for individual subtests, and the largest contribution to GIA consistently comes from the Verbal Comprehension test, a measure of crystallized knowledge. The weights assigned to other tests vary by age and battery. Fluid reasoning tests are never the most weighted tests, representing a major point of departure from prior investigations (e.g., Carroll, 1993; Gustafsson, 1984, 1988; Undheim, 1981) establishing Gf as the most substantial contributor to $g$. In practical terms, this finding expresses the idea that on the WJ III NU Cog, the facts you know contribute more to your intelligence than your ability to reason. It is possible that the unexpected performance of Gf in the WJ III NU Cog may be attributed to its inadequate measurement (Carroll, 2003).

A limitation of the CHC framework is that it is more a compilation of factor analytically derived cognitive abilities than an integrated, coherent theory. Its proponents assert that it has abundant empirical support, but closer examination shows that much of the validity evidence is fragmentary, applied to parts of the model rather than the model as a whole. Even Carroll's (1993) landmark study included only a handful of datasets with all of the stratum 2 broad factors. Moreover, the CHC framework was derived through factor analyses and remains somewhat method dependent. Following the lead of Thurstone, who viewed factor analysis as an early stage in theory development, Carroll (1983) himself identified a number of additional forms of validation that transcend factor analysis, including establishing the nature of a factor, its developmental characteristics, its genetic and environmental determinants, the presence of any demographically based group mean differences, its susceptibility to intervention or more transient influences such as drugs or fatigue, its relationship to noncognitive variables, its ecological relevance and validity, and its implications for psychological theory as a whole. Unfortunately, most of these forms of validity remain to be fully explored as they apply to the factors identified in the CHC framework. The WJ III Cog's dependence on factor analysis is reminiscent of Eysenck's (1993) observation that a psychological model based primarily on factor analysis resembles a chimera ("a fabulous beast made up of parts taken from various animals" [p. 1299]).

In terms of the glue holding together the elements of a well-articulated theory, Woodcock's (1993, 1998a) cognitive performance/information processing model is a beginning to possible integration of factors in the CHC framework. It posits four higher order processes that combine to produce cognitive and academic performance: thinking abilities (Gf, Glr, Ga, Gv), stores of acquired knowledge (Gc, Grw, Gq), cognitive efficiency (Gsm, Gs), and facilitators-inhibitors (e.g., motivation, interest, attention). It also offers testable hypotheses (e.g., all performance, automatic or new learning, is constrained by the relevant stores of knowledge) that have yet to be seriously investigated.

Although McGrew and Woodcock (2001) boldly assert that "CHC taxonomy is the most comprehensive and empirically supported framework available for understanding the structure of human cognitive abilities" (p. 9), Horn and Blankson (2005) make the argument more modestly and objectively: "The extended theory of fluid and crystallized (Gf and Gc) cognitive abilities is wrong, of course, even though it may be the best account we currently have of the organization and development of abilities thought to be indicative of human intelligence" (p. 41). Arguably, scientific validation of the CHC framework is best served by objective, measured conclusions rather than dogmatic advocacy.

### Standardization Features and Psychometric Adequacy

The psychometric characteristics of the WJ III NU Cog are complementarily documented in the normative update technical manual (McGrew, Schrank, & Woodcock, 2007) and the original technical manual (McGrew & Woodcock, 2001).

The WJ III NU Cog was standardized from 1996 through 1999 on 8,782 children, adolescents, and adults from ages 2 through 90+. The school-age sample consisted of 4,740 participants. Stratification targets were originally based on 1996 census projections for the year 2000, but the 2007 normative update was based on actual census 2000 findings. Sample stratification variables included sex, race, ethnicity, type of school, geographic region, community size, adult education, and adult occupation. The sample consisted of over 200 participants at each age year from 2 through 19, over 1,000 participants in their 20s, over 200 participants per decade from 30 to 59, and about 150 participants per decade after age 60. The sample was statistically weighted to correct for proportional underrepresentation of selected groups, including Hispanics and parents with education levels below high school completion. It is not possible to assess the degree to which the sample is representative of the general population, because accuracy is only reported "on the margins" without detailed reporting across stratification variables.

The need for a normative update a mere six years after the publication of the WJ III Cog has been attributed to discrepancies in the 1996 projections for the 2000 U.S. Census and actual year 2000 census statistics (McGrew, Dailey, & Schrank, 2007). The normative update resulted in as much as a 10-point standard score change, with standard score changes tending to be largest in the extreme age ranges (preschool and old age). Bootstrap sampling with replacement was used to provide stable estimates of standard error (and confidence bands). While the rationale and the methodology for the normative update is understandable, it is of concern that it was necessary and that it produced some score changes of large magnitude.

Based on examination of the two WJ III technical manuals (McGrew, Schrank, & Woodcock, 2007; McGrew & Woodcock, 2001), there appear to be some serious problems with the standardization and norming of the WJ III Cog—principally that some tests were administered to only a small number of standardization participants. For example, of the 2,216 children from ages 9 to 13 reported in the normative sample (p. 23), only 1,865 completed the Verbal Comprehension test, only 1443 took the Planning test, and only 548 obtained scores on the Pair Cancellation test (McGrew, Schrank, et al., 2007, p. 167). The small size of the Pair Cancellation sample suggests that as much as 75% of the normative sample may have not taken some tests during standardization of the WJ III Cog. It is not possible to determine whether the subsample actually given these tests is representative of the general population, although bootstrap sampling may help stabilize test parameters. It is also unclear why the sample size in this age group dropped by $n = 25$ from 2,241 (McGrew & Woodcock, 2001, p. 18) to 2,216 in the normative update (McGrew, Schrank, et al., 2007, p. 23). From the 2001 edition to the 2007 normative update, the total normative sample decreased by 36 participants.

Test internal consistency was calculated with the split-half procedure with Spearman-Brown correction and with Rasch procedures for tests that were either speeded or contained multiple point scoring. Test score reliability appears to be fully adequate, with median values across age falling below $r = .80$ for Picture Recognition and Planning only. Some 94% of WJ III Cog NU tests yield split-half or Rasch-derived consistency of .80 or higher. The standardized cluster scores also tend to be fairly reliable, with all but three having median values at or above .90 (the exceptions are Long Term Retrieval at .88, Visual Spatial Thinking at .81, and Short-Term Memory at .88), and across all age groups and all batteries, 84% of the clusters meet the .90 criterion. The overall composite GIA has a median reliability of .97 for the standard battery and .98 for the extended battery. Rasch scaling permits local reliabilities to be calculated:

> The Rasch procedures that underlie the W scale provide a unique estimate of the standard error of measurement for the ability score associated with each raw score for every person in the norm sample. When individual error (SEM) scores are available for all subjects who completed a test, it is possible to directly calculate test reliability. (McGrew, Schrank, et al., 2007, p. 42)

It is unfortunate that the test authors passed on the opportunity to generate automated local score reliabilities via the WJ III Cog NU's computer scoring program.

Temporal stability of WJ III Cog NU tests was not measured according to the conventional 1-month retest approach, so it is difficult to make comparisons with other intelligence tests. For the six WJ III NU Cog speeded tests administered in counterbalanced order with a test–retest interval of only a single day, 44% of the subtests yielded 1-day stability of .80 or better. When a median retest interval of over 1 year is employed, the median reliabilities for the selected tests range from .61 to .86. These long-term score stability coefficients are of considerable potential value to both practitioners and researchers, but the results are not adequately reported, missing data on most WJ III Cog NU tests, absent documentation of practice effects, and absent corrections for variability on first assessment. It also appears implausible that a test like Visual Matching should have median long-term stability of .78 to .86 over a retest interval of <1 year to 10 years, when its 1-day stability ranges from .68 to .87 across different age groups.

WJ III Cog floors and ceilings are difficult to formally evaluate because the test may only be computer-scored and no printed norms are available. The examiner's manual reports that test standard scores extend from 0 to over 200 (Mather & Woodcock, 2001), but this range seems inflated given that adequate test floors tend to be difficult to achieve with certain age groups, such as preschool children. For example, when raw scores of 1 (the best value to use to identify meaningful test floors) are entered for every test administered at the lowest level for a 6-year-old child, the resulting cluster standard scores range from 3 (Visual-Spatial Thinking) to 72 (Fluid Reasoning).

In deriving the standard scores and percentile ranks that are most commonly used for test score interpretation, the WJ III NU uses Rasch scaling to derive interval unit W-scores on a sort of yardstick of absolute performance across the life span, centered at a W of 500 for an average fifth-grade student. These scores permit developmental growth curves to be generated from the cross-sectional age samples in the normative data set, a form of evidence for test score validity that is not found in most intelligence tests. The cross-sectional growth curves suggest that fluid reasoning (Gf), processing speed (Gs), and short-term memory (Gsm) reach their highest levels at approximately age 25 to 30 before beginning a gradual decline, while comprehension-knowledge (Gc) does not reach a peak until age 50 to 60. The curves for long-term retrieval (Glr), auditory processing (Ga), and visual processing (Gv) demonstrate relatively little change with age (McGrew, Schrank, & Woodcock, 2007). These findings provide compelling evidence for the differential rates of development for the CHC broad abilities.

The WJ III GIA score tends to be highly correlated with composites from other intelligence tests, although correlations are not corrected for restricted or expanded score ranges. According to McGrew and Woodcock (2001), the standard battery WJ III Cog GIA correlates .67 to .76 with the DAS GCA; .75 with the KAIT Composite Intelligence Scale; .76 with the Stanford-Binet IV Composite SAS; .71 with the WISC-III FSIQ; and .67 with the WAIS-III FSIQ. Across all school-age groups, median

correlations of the standard battery WJ III NU Cog GIA with WJ III Nu Ach scores are .76 for Total Achievement, .70 for Broad Reading, .67 for Broad Math, and .65 for Broad Written Language (McGrew, Schrank, et al., 2007). These correlations are derived from the normative update as a whole and suggest that the GIA is highly predictive of academic achievement. A number of recent investigations have examined the multivariate capacity of the WJ III Cog broad and narrow ability scores to predict academic performance in specific domains (a long-time objective of multifactor theorists; see e.g., McNemar, 1964), with results indicating that the differential prediction of academic skills varies across age and shows evidence of both direct and indirect cognitive effects (Benson, 2008; Evans, Floyd, McGrew, & Leforgee, 2002; Floyd, Evans, & McGrew, 2003; Floyd, Keith, Taub, & McGrew, 2007; Floyd, McGrew, & Evans, 2008). The WJ III NU software scoring programs offer three methods to predict academic performance for computation of ability-achievement discrepancies: predicted achievement derived from WJ III NU Cog ability scores regressed against achievement, predicted achievement based on GIA score, or predicted achievement based on the Oral Language Ability-Extended score. Unfortunately, the beta weights used in predicted achievement regression equations are not reported.

Factor-analytic studies of the WJ III constitute an area of concern for a test battery that has historically based its foundation on the work of Cattell, Horn, and Carroll. Exploratory factor analyses are not reported in the 2001 or 2007 technical manuals, although the addition of eight new subtests to the WJ III Cog certainly justifies these analyses. The new WJ III Cog subtests purport to measure working memory, planning, naming speed, and attention. Moreover, hierarchical exploratory factor analyses conducted by John B. Carroll (using the same approach described in his 1993 book) have been previously reported for the WJ-R (see also McGrew, Werder, et al., 1991, p. 172; reprinted in McGrew, 1997, pp. 176–177); these analyses yield findings of first-order and second-order factors that are not entirely congruent with the structure of the WJ Cog. As a basis for comparison, other tests in their third editions (e.g., WISC-III, WAIS-III) continued to report exploratory factor analyses.

Previous exploratory analyses have revealed inadequately defined factors that appear to have not been addressed in the WJ III NU Cog. For example, after conducting a hierarchical exploratory factor analyses on the WJ-R standardization data set ($n = 2,261$), Carroll (2003) wrote: "There is still a problem with *Gf*, namely, that it appears to be a rather weak, poorly defined factor, at least in the dataset examined here. Note the relatively small factor loadings for the two tests indicated as measuring *Gf* (p. 14)." The two tests comprising fluid reasoning (Gf) are identical from the WJ-R to the WJ III: Concept Formation and Analysis Synthesis. It may be worthwhile to consider improving these measures or substituting new procedures to tap fluid reasoning in the WJ IV, given the critical importance of this broad ability to assessment in the CHC framework.

The confirmatory factor analyses (CFAs) reported in the WJ III technical manual (McGrew & Woodcock, 2001) appear to provide marginal support for a seven-factor structure relative to two alternative models, but the RMSEA, which should ideally be less than .05 with good model fit, does not support good model fit at any age level. The CFAs involve a contrast between the seven-factor CHC structure, a WAIS-based model, and a Stanford-Binet–based model, the latter two with model specifications that Wechsler or Stanford-Binet devotees would likely argue are misrepresentations. None of the models is hierarchical; none includes a superordinate *g*; and none includes the higher-order dimensions suggested by Woodcock in his cognitive performance model. Moreover, only three goodness-of-fit indices are included whereas best practice with CFAs suggests that fit statistics should ideally include indices sensitive to model fit, model comparison, *and* model parsimony. On a model built on multifactor foundations, it may be argued that a more rigorous CFA test of alternative models is appropriate.

### Interpretive Indices and Applications

Including the Diagnostic Supplement, the WJ III NU Cog consists of 31 tests purporting to measure seven broad cognitive factors and nine cluster scores. The tests are organized into a standard battery (tests 1 through 7, with three supplemental tests) and an extended battery (tests 1 through 7 and tests 11 through 17, with six supplemental tests). The Diagnostic Supplement adds more tests. The WJ III NU Cog is normed for ages 2 years through 90+ years and is conormed with 22 tests in an achievement battery, WJ III NU Tests of Achievement (Woodcock, McGrew, & Mather, 2001b, 2007b). Table 18.7 contains the fundamental interpretive indices, the most important of which are GIA and the factor-derived cluster scores: Gc, Glr, Gv, Ga, Gf, Gsm, Gs. Verbal Ability, Thinking Ability, and Cognitive Efficiency are part of Woodcock's cognitive performance model.

Cognitive cluster scores are conceptually derived and may include tests with heterogeneous content. Clusters

**TABLE 18.7  Woodcock-Johnson III Normative Update Tests of Cognitive Abilities Core Interpretive Indices**

| Composite Indices | Description |
| --- | --- |
| *General Intellectual Ability (GIA)* | A weighted estimate of general cognitive ability |
| *Verbal Ability* | Acquired knowledge in semantic and quantitative symbol systems; includes verbal conceptual knowledge (Gc), quantitative knowledge (Gq, from achievement tests), and reading-writing knowledge (Grw, from achievement tests) |
| *Thinking Ability* | Abilities that allow an individual to process information that has been placed in short-term memory but that cannot be processed automatically; consists of long-term storage and retrieval (Glr), visual processing (Gv), auditory processing (Ga), and fluid reasoning (Gf) |
| *Cognitive Efficiency* | Capacity to hold, rapidly, and automatically process information; includes short-term memory (Gsm) and processing speed (Gs) |
| *Comprehension-Knowledge (Gc)* | Breadth and depth of prior learning in culturally valued verbal areas as well as the capacity for further verbal learning |
| *Long-Term Retrieval (Glr)* | Ability to efficiently acquire and store information, measured by long-term and remote retrieval processes |
| *Visual-Spatial Thinking (Gv)* | Analysis and synthesis of spatial-visual stimuli, and the ability to hold and manipulate mental images |
| *Auditory Processing (Ga)* | Ability to discriminate, analyze, and synthesize auditory stimuli; also related to phonological awareness |
| *Fluid Reasoning (Gf)* | Ability to solve novel and abstract problems, usually of a visual and nonverbal nature |
| *Short-Term Memory (Gsm)* | Ability to hold, transform, and act on auditory information in immediate awareness; auditory-verbal mental holding capacity |
| *Processing Speed (Gs)* | Speed and efficiency in performing easy cognitive tasks |

include Phonemic Awareness, Working Memory, Cognitive Fluency, Perceptual Speed, Associative Memory, Visualization, Sound Discrimination, Auditory Memory Span, and Numerical Reasoning.

In terms of research on clinical and educational applications, the WJ III NU Technical Manual (McGrew, Schrank, et al., 2007) reports data for clinical samples totaling as much as $n = 1,281$, although the entire battery was not administered to every clinical sample, demographic characteristics and criteria for specific diagnoses are not fully presented, and the performance of demographically matched normative control groups are not compared with the performance of clinical samples. Among the clinical groups studied are intellectually gifted, intellectually disabled, ADHD, anxiety spectrum disorders, autism spectrum disorders, depressive spectrum disorders, head injury, language disorders, mathematics disorder, reading disorder, and written expression disorder.

### Strengths and Limitations

The WJ III NU Cog represents an important step forward for intelligence assessment through its fit with the CHC model of cognitive abilities and conorming with the WJ III NU Tests of Achievement, but it largely lacks an integrated theoretical framework, established clinical correlates, and empirically demonstrated treatment utility.

The Woodcock-Johnson III Cog NU model is an elegant exemplar of the multifactor approach to cognitive abilities. Its factor-analytic lineage may be most clearly traced from the pioneering efforts in factor analysis of ability tests by Thurstone (1938) and the encyclopedic tome by Carroll (1993), along with seminal contributions by Cattell and Horn. In fact, Horn and Carroll were consultants in the development of the WJ III Cog. It is this association to a large body of factor analytic research that constitutes the WJ III Cog's main strength. It is notable, however, that as of this writing, no hierarchical exploratory factor analysis (of the type previously conducted by Carroll) has been published for the WJ III Cog or its normative update.

Unfortunately, a systematic overreliance on this same body of factor-analytic research as its primary evidence of test validity constitutes the most substantial weakness of the WJ III NU Cog. The WJ III Cog structure is a structural model missing the integrative, explanatory, and predictive glue that constitutes a scientific theory. Woodcock's (1993, 1998a) cognitive performance/information processing model represents a start toward an integrated model but requires further development and validation. To their credit, authors and advocates for the WJ Cog have acknowledged the current shortcomings of their theoretical foundation: "*Gf-Gc* provides little information on how the *Gf-Gc* abilities develop or how the cognitive processes work together. The theory is largely product oriented and provides little guidance on the dynamic interplay of variables (i.e., the processes) that occur in human cognitive processing" (Flanagan, McGrew, & Ortiz, 2000, p. 61).

The validity of the WJ III NU Cog with special populations is an emerging area of investigation (e.g., Schrank & Flanagan, 2003). The 2007 technical manual lists standard scores for a number of clinical samples, but it does not describe these samples in any detail or provide demographically matched normative comparison groups with effect size differences (McGrew, Schrank, & Woodcock, 2007). For example, the sample designated as gifted ($n = 124$) earned a median GIA (Standard) of 116 with median cluster standard scores ranging from 103 to 116. These scores would be unlikely to independently qualify most students for gifted and talented placements. More plausibly, the intellectually disabled/mentally retarded sample ($n = 93$) yielded a median GIA (Std) of 58, with cluster standard scores ranging from 56 to 77. Clearly much more research as to the clinical applications of the WJ III NU Cog is needed.

The WJ III Cog offers little in the way of empirically based assessment intervention linkages. While logical interventions are offered in Mather and Jaffe (2002; see also Wendling & Mather, 2009), there is a conspicuous absence of empirical verification for these assessment-intervention linkages directly connecting the intervention with WJ III NU Cog performance.

Finally, the claims made by WJ III NU Cog authors are frequently overstated, and research findings have a quality of being selectively reported. As an example of overstatement, the technical manual (McGrew, Schrank, et al., 2007) claims to provide "more precise measures and a wider breadth of coverage of human cognitive abilities than are found in any other system of psychological and educational assessment" (p. 3). Selective reporting extends to disproportionate emphasis on specific methodologies (e.g., CFAs, cross-battery analyses, developmental growth curves) while completely neglecting some important psychometrics (comprehensive DIF studies, hierarchical exploratory factor analyses, normative tables that can be independently reviewed, regression equations used to predict achievement, the magnitude of convergent validity correlations corrected for range restriction, or detailed descriptions of the samples used for special population studies). A more complete discussion of WJ III Cog strengths and limitations, including a dozen unanswered questions, may be found in Wasserman and Maccubbin (2004).

## DIAGNOSTIC APPLICATIONS

There are numerous substantive reasons to give intelligence tests. The most common reasons among psychologists working in education and health care are to facilitate diagnosis, determine the nature of difficulty, and estimate capacity/potential (e.g., Camara et al., 2000; Harrison, Kaufman, Hickman, & Kaufman, 1988; Rabin, Barr, & Burton, 2005; Reschly, 2000). These priorities may shift as legal classification guidelines undergo change for various diagnoses. School psychologists typically spent approximately two-thirds of their time in special education eligibility determination, primarily through testing (e.g., Gresham & Witt, 1997) before the 2004 reauthorization of the Individuals with Disabilities Education Act (IDEA), which fundamentally changed procedures to assess eligibility for some exceptionalities.

In this section, a few of the most common applications of intelligence tests are described, especially in diagnostic determination. At the outset, it is noted that there is not necessarily a strong relation between the science of intelligence assessment (empirical demonstrations of value) and its various applications (i.e., those sanctioned by public institutions, based on public policy decisions). Camara (1997) effectively summarized the plethora of legal, ethical, and professional pressures impinging on assessment practices. One illustrative case showing how legislation may throw intelligence assessment practices into turmoil may be found in federal regulations for *specific learning disability*. In the Individuals with Disabilities Education Act (1997, 1999), federal legislation explicitly required a "severe discrepancy between achievement and intellectual ability" as part of the criterion for special education eligibility. Just 5 years later, the Individuals with Disabilities Education Improvement Act (variously referred to as IDEA or IDEIA, 2004) stated that educators "shall not be required to take into consideration whether a child has a severe discrepancy between achievement and intellectual ability" for specific learning disability eligibility, instead leading to the newer approach of response to intervention (RTI)." Predictably, this reversal of legal standards in a 5-year period left psychologists working in schools considerably confused about the potential value of intelligence tests in the identification of students with possible learning disability (Cangelosi, 2009). The anticipated 2013 publication of the fifth edition of *Diagnostic and Statistical Manual of Mental Disorders (DSM-5)*, with its committee-based decision-making processes, will also likely be accompanied by debate for its new diagnostic methodologies. (See Widiger, 2011, for an illustration.) This section describes the role of intelligence tests in diagnostic decision making in the most recent edition, the fourth edition of the *Diagnostic and Statistical Manual of Mental Disorders, Text Revision (DSM-IV-TR*; American Psychiatric Association, 2000) as well as changes that appear likely for the *DSM*-5.

Beyond diagnostic decision making, several theories also posit that intelligence has a potentially far-reaching nonspecific influence on the development of psychopathology in youth (e.g., Rutter, 1987) and neuropathology in adulthood and older ages (e.g., Stern, 2002, 2009). In these models, often derived from longitudinal studies, intelligence is generally treated as a moderator variable—that is, a variable that "affects the direction and/or strength of the relation between an independent or predictor variable and a dependent or criterion variable" (Baron & Kenny, 1986, p. 1174). For Rutter (1987), intelligence is a type of protective mechanism that "is a modification of the person's response to the risk situation . . . that in ordinary circumstances leads to a maladaptive outcome" (p. 317).

In childhood psychopathology, models of risk and resilience frequently list intelligence as a protective factor or protective process facilitating an individual's ability to deal with risk-elevating factors and adverse life experiences (e.g., Rutter, 1987). Given any child's developmental history with factors that normally predict negative outcome, an average- or above-average intelligence is considered to play some role in producing developmentally appropriate and positive outcomes, while lower intelligence is associated with greater vulnerability to risk and less adaptive outcomes (e.g., Masten, 1994). E. E. Werner (2000) explained that enhanced use of coping and problem-solving strategies and better ways of responding to the risk situation are thought to account for the moderating influence of intelligence for the at-risk child across a wide range of populations:

> Youngsters who are better able to appraise stressful life events correctly are also better able to figure out effective strategies for coping with adversity, either through their own efforts or by actively reaching out to other people for help. This finding has been replicated with children from all socioeconomic groups and from diverse ethnical backgrounds, in studies of African American, Asian American, and Caucasian children who grew up under a variety of high-risk conditions, including poverty, parent mental illness, and substance abuse, as well as family discord and child abuse. (pp. 122–123)

A number of longitudinal investigations have demonstrated that childhood intelligence appears protective against later maladjustment, even into adulthood (Burt & Roisman, 2010; Egeland, Carlson, & Sroufe, 1993; Loeber, Pardini, Stouthamer-Loeber, & Raine, 2007; Luthar, D'Avanzo & Hites, 2003; Masten, Burt, Roisman, Obradovic, Long, & Tellegen, 2004; Radke-Yarrow & Sherman, 1990; E. E. Werner, 1993).

In adulthood and old age, the concept of *cognitive reserve* arises from the observation that there does not appear to be a direct relationship between the degree of brain damage and the clinical-behavioral manifestation of that damage:

> The concept of cognitive reserve provides a ready explanation for why many studies have demonstrated that higher levels of intelligence, and of educational and occupational attainment are good predictors of which individuals can sustain greater brain damage before demonstrating functional deficit. Rather than positing that these individuals' brains are grossly anatomically different than those with less reserve (e.g., they have more synapses), the cognitive reserve hypothesis posts that they process tasks in a more efficient manner. (Stern, 2002, pp. 450–451)

Individuals with high cognitive reserve are thought to better tolerate acquired brain damage, normal age-related changes in cognitive ability, and degenerative neuropathology because their cognitive processing capacities seem to compensate for (or successfully mask) the cognitive and behavioral manifestations of underlying changes in the brain. A corollary to the cognitive reserve hypothesis is that once an individual can no longer effectively compensate for underlying brain damage, any latent level of neuropathological impairment and rate of deterioration may appear more severe, no longer adequately concealed by cognitive processing efficiency. The best-known longitudinal study supporting the cognitive reserve hypothesis is known as the Nun Study (e.g., Snowdon, Greiner, Mortimer, Riley, Greiner, & Markesbery, 1997). Launched in 1986 with elderly nuns who agreed to participate in annual testing of physical and mental functions as well as to donate their brains for study upon death, the study provided compelling evidence that it was possible for individuals to present as cognitively intact even when their brains on autopsy showed prominent evidence of the structural changes associated with advanced Alzheimer's disorder. In general, the better the early language, the higher the education, and the more the positive emotional outlook that the nuns showed in early adulthood, the less prone to cognitive disability and dementia they proved to be. Scarmeas and Stern (2003) assert that through the proposed mechanism of cognitive reserve, "innate intelligence or aspects of life experience like educational or occupational attainments may supply reserve, in the form of a set of skills or repertoires that allows some people to cope with progressing Alzheimer's disease (AD) pathology better than others" (p. 625).

## Dementia/Neurocognitive Disorders

Neuropsychological evaluation and cognitive testing remain among the most effective differential diagnostic methods in discriminating pathophysiological dementia from age-related cognitive decline, cognitive difficulties that are depression-related, and other related disorders. Even after reliable biological markers have been discovered, neuropsychological evaluation and cognitive testing will still be necessary to determine the onset of dementia, the functional expression of the disease process, the rate of decline, the functional capacities of the individual, and hopefully, response to therapies. (APA Task Force to Update the Guidelines for the Evaluation of Dementia and Age-Related Cognitive Decline, 2011, p. 2)

The diagnostic term *dementia,* likely to be replaced with the term *major neurocognitive disorder* in the *DSM-5* (Ganguli et al., 2011), refers to a deterioration in (or loss of) cognitive functions, relative to a higher premorbid level of functioning. The *DSM-IV-TR* specifies that dementia is characterized by the development of multiple cognitive deficits including memory impairment and at least one of the following: aphasia, apraxia, agnosia, or a disturbance in executive functioning. Cognitive deficits must be sufficiently severe to cause impairment in occupational or social functioning and must represent a decline from a previously higher level of functioning (American Psychiatric Association, 2000). In recognition that different dementias may present with unique sequential courses and patterns of cognitive deficits (with memory loss not always the initial presenting concern), the *DSM-5* will likely deemphasize the sole criterion of memory, requiring deficits in at least one (typically two or more) of these areas: complex attention, executive functions, memory, language, visuoconstructional ability, or social cognition (American Psychiatric Association, 2011). At the time of this writing, the proposed *DSM-5* criteria require that the severity of any domain-based cognitive performance impairment must be 2 or more *SD*s below the normative mean (i.e., below the third percentile) for a diagnosis of major neurocognitive disorder, and impairment must be sufficiently severe so as to interfere with functional independence (American Psychiatric Association, 2011).

An associated diagnostic term, *mild neurocognitive disorder* (also known as *mild cognitive impairment*; see Petersen, Smith, Waring, Ivnik, Tangalos, & Kokmen, 1999; Petersen et al., 2009) has been proposed in the *DSM-5* for individuals with mild cognitive deficits in one or more of the cognitive domains but with an intact capacity for functional independence in activities of daily living. This diagnosis may serve to identify the earliest features of Alzheimer's disease and other dementias and is characterized by test performance between the 3rd and 16th percentile (i.e., 1 to 2 SDs below the normative mean) (American Psychiatric Association, 2011). As might be expected, individuals with this diagnosis show only slightly lower performances than control participants on intelligence and nonmemory cognitive performances, but their performance on memory tasks shows more prominent difficulties (Petersen et al., 1999). When familial Alzheimer's disease is present, prodromal/presymptomatic cognitive deficits appear prominently in the areas of general intelligence and memory (Godbolt, Cipolotti, Watt, Fox, Janssen, & Rossor, 2004).

As part of a neuropsychological assessment, intelligence testing has value in the identification of dementias, differentiation from normal age-associated cognitive changes, differential diagnosis between dementias, and monitoring of the course of cognitive decline (e.g., Petersen et al., 1999; Petersen, Stevens, Gangulli, Tangalos, Cummings, & DeKosky, 2001; Ritchie & Tuokko, 2010). However, intelligence tests by themselves are clinically considered insufficient for dementia diagnosis. Intelligence tests rank among the most frequently used measures in American neuropsychological assessments (Camara et al., 2000), but there are no surveys on American practitioner test preferences in dementia assessments. In Europe, an estimated 88% of countries use some version of the WAIS in dementia evaluations (Maruta, Guerreiro, de Mendonça, Hort, & Scheltens, 2011).

Quantification of cognitive decline, describing how much function has been lost from dementia or acquired brain injury, is an important part of monitoring the course of a disorder and estimating the magnitude of disability. There are several methods available to estimate how much cognitive function has been lost, with most methods examining the discrepancy between estimated premorbid ability and current cognitive performance. Specific ways to estimate premorbid levels of ability include: (a) review of premorbid academic or occupational test or achievement scores (e.g., Baade & Schoenberg, 2004); (b) prediction of premorbid ability based on demographic characteristics (e.g., age, education, sex, race/ethnicity; see Barona, Reynolds, & Chastain, 1984); and (c) prediction of premorbid ability based on current test performance in areas known to be resilient to brain injury (e.g., reading recognition for words with irregular phoneme-grapheme spelling; see H. E. Nelson, 1982). The WAIS-IV supplemental materials *Advanced Clinical Solutions for the WAIS-IV and WMS-IV* (Pearson, 2009a) provide estimates of premorbid intellectual and memory functioning based on methods

(b) and (c), in conjunction with a new reading measure, the Test of Pre-Morbid Functioning (TOPF; Pearson, 2009b).

## Intellectual Disability/Mental Retardation

Intellectual disability is characterized by significant limitations both in intellectual functioning and in adaptive behavior as expressed in conceptual, social, and practical adaptive skills. This disability originates before age 18. (Schalock and the Ad Hoc Committee on Terminology and Classification, 2010, p. 1)

This 2010 definition from the Ad Hoc Committee on Terminology and Classification of the American Association on Intellectual and Developmental Disabilities (AAIDD; formerly American Association on Mental Retardation [AAMR]) defines *intellectual disability* (ID; formerly known as *mental retardation*; Schalock et al., 2007) in terms of intellectual functioning and functional adaptation in activities of daily living, both equal in importance and interpreted in a multidimensional, ecological context (not appearing in this main part of the definition just given). The context extends to the environmental supports needed for the individual to participate in activities linked with normative human functioning. As such, intellectual disability is considered to reside not within the individual but instead in the (mis)fit between the individual's capacities and the demands of the environmental context (microsystem, mesosystem, and macrosystem) in which the individual is expected to function (Schalock et al., 2010).

For the diagnosis of *mental retardation,* the *DSM-IV-TR* (American Psychiatric Association, 2000) requires significantly subaverage general intellectual functioning accompanied by significant limitations in adaptive functioning in at least two of these skill areas: communication, self-care, home living, social/interpersonal skills, use of community resources, self-direction, functional academic skills, work, leisure, health, and safety. Onset must occur during the developmental period, and deficits are expected to adversely affect an individual's educational performance. Based on proposed changes, the *DSM-5* appears likely to rename the diagnosis *intellectual disability* or *intellectual development disorder*, aligning it with the AAIDD definition. Among the proposed criteria are a current deficit in general mental abilities approximately 2 or more SDs in IQ below the population mean for a person's age and cultural group; significant impairment in adaptive functioning requiring ongoing support at school, work, or independent life; and onset during the developmental period.

In both *DSM* and AAIDD diagnoses, intellectual functioning is listed as "the first, and the most salient, criterion in the definition of ID" (Borkowski, Carothers, Howard, Schatz, & Farris, 2007), although it is clear that functional adaptation, environmental context, and person–environment fit are essential considerations that have risen in relative importance compared to intelligence. Both AAIDD and *DSM-5* appear to have accorded the *general* factor of intelligence (usually represented by an overall composite score, such as the FSIQ) as the most relevant estimate of cognitive and intellectual ability. Both definitions also specify that the intellectual functioning criterion for a diagnosis of intellectual disability is approximately 2 *SD*s or more below the normative mean, but factors such as test score statistical error (standard error of measurement), test fairness, normative expectations for the population of interest, the Flynn effect, and practice effects from previous testing need to be considered before arriving at any diagnosis. In practical terms, this criterion usually corresponds to a composite IQ score below 70 or 75 (the higher number including standard error and other factors).

The severity of intellectual disability remains stratified by four levels of composite IQ scores in the *DSM-IV-TR* (American Psychiatric Association, 2000), but these levels have been omitted from the last two editions of the AAMR/AAIDD manuals and probably for the *DSM-5* to reflect an emphasis on functional adaptation and the intensity of needed environmental support rather than cognitive-intellectual ability. The levels of intellectual disability based on IQ scores, however, still appear commonly in practice and the research literature and may be summarized in this way:

- *Mild* (IQ level 50–55 to approximately 70–75). Approximately 85% of individuals with intellectual disability fall into this range, and individuals so labeled have historically been considered *educable*. These individuals may be able to acquire basic reading and mathematics literacy and are often able to successfully hold jobs and live independently, with vocational training and community and social support.
- *Moderate* (IQ level 35–40 to 50–55). Encompassing about 10% of individuals with intellectual disability, persons within this level are often considered *trainable* and may acquire academic skills at the kindergarten or first-grade level. They are likely to require regular support and supervision to function in everyday activities, and they may be able to perform repetitive employment tasks in a highly structured and sheltered environment.
- *Severe* (IQ level 20–25 to 35–40). Approximately 3% to 4% of individuals with intellectual disability fall into this group, and they will typically have low communication and social skills, with marked developmental delays. A curriculum emphasizing self-help skills (toileting, dressing with assistance) is provided with high levels of supervision and environmental support.
- *Profound* (IQ level below 20 or 25). About 1% to 2% of individuals with intellectual disabilities are in this IQ range, and they typically require lifelong care and supervision. They are typically unable to walk, talk, or carry out most basic activities of daily living, often suffering from significant physical abnormalities and sensory impairments.

The 10th edition of the AAMR definition and classification manual (Luckasson et al., 2002) enumerated four classification levels for mental retardation, based not on intelligence but rather on the level of environmental support needed: *intermittent* (need for support during stressful or transition periods but not constantly), *limited* (less intense, consistent supports needed, but needs are time-limited for changing situations), *extensive* (long-term consistent support at work and/or home), and *pervasive* (very intense, long-term, constant support needed across most or all situations). These levels do not appear in the 11th edition (Schalock & Ad Hoc Committee, 2010), which emphasizes frequency and duration of needed supports in select areas over global ratings of support needs.

## Intellectual Giftedness

Gifted individuals are those who demonstrate outstanding levels of aptitude (defined as an exceptional ability to reason and learn) or competence (documented performance or achievement in the top 10% or rarer) in one or more domains. Domains include any structured area of activity with its own symbol system (e.g., mathematics, music, language) and/or set of sensorimotor skills (e.g., painting, dance, sports). (Siegle & McCoach, 2010, p. 6)

In 2010 the board of directors of the National Association of Gifted Children formally approved this new definition of giftedness, based on the recommendations of a committee of 15 experts. It represented the culmination of nearly four decades of research after the first federal definition of gifted and talented, based on a 1972 report to Congress from former U.S. Commissioner of Education Sidney P. Marland:

> Gifted and talented children are those, identified by professionally qualified persons, who by virtue of outstanding abilities are capable of high performance. These children require differentiated programs and/or services beyond those normally provided by the regular school program in order to realize their contribution to self and society. Children capable of high performance include those with demonstrated high achievement and/or potential ability in any of the following areas, singly or in combination; general intellectual ability, specific academic aptitude, creative or productive thinking, leadership ability, visual and performing arts, and/or psychomotor ability. (p. 2)

These definitions share an emphasis on requiring high levels of ability or performance in either general ability or specific narrower abilities as part of a gifted eligibility determination. Federal laws do not, however, mandate educational services for gifted and talented learners, and states and individual school districts vary widely as to how they define and determine giftedness.

Norm referenced group and/or individual intelligence tests constitute the leading criterion by which giftedness is identified, but it is considered best practice to base assessments on multiple methods providing different types of information (e.g., National Association for Gifted Children, 2008). Robertson, Pfeiffer, and Taylor (2011) reported that the most common assessment tools used by school psychologists in the identification of gifted and talented students were, in descending order, the Wechsler intelligence scales (used frequently or very frequently by 51%), Woodcock-Johnson Tests of Cognitive Abilities (24%), Stanford-Binet Intelligence Scales (17%), Differential Ability Scales (13%), and Kaufman Assessment Battery for Children (10%). Other criterion measures may include ratings of student products or portfolio, observation of in-classroom behavior, formal teacher-completed rating scales, interviews, letters of support, norm-referenced achievement test performances, curriculum-based measurement/performance assessment, and history of academic accomplishments (e.g., grades, awards), among others. Concerns about the proportional underrepresentation of minorities in gifted education programs have led to the increasing use of nonverbal intelligence tests and alternative assessment methods, but early research indicates that students identified through such methods tend to be less successful in gifted curriculums (e.g., Van Tassel-Baska, Feng, & Evans, 2007).

Characteristics associated with giftedness often include early language development, early acquisition of reading skills, high levels of memory, extended attention span, and an intense curiosity and self-motivated interest in learning and problem-solving. During their earliest school years, gifted students are typically described as active learners seeking in-depth understanding about subjects of interest and making connections between seemingly unrelated events and ideas (e.g., Damiani, 1997; Harrison, 2004; Hodge & Kemp, 2000; Jackson, 2003; Kitano, 1995; Rotigel, 2003; Sankar-DeLeeuw, 2004; Walker, Hafenstein, & Crow-Enslow, 1999). In a large sample of regular education primary school teachers for kindergarten through second grade, Moon and Brighton (2008) reported that 95% or more of primary school teacher respondents agreed with each of these characteristics of gifted learners:

- Transfers learning into other subjects or real-life situations
- Tries to understand the how and whys of things
- Has a large store of general knowledge
- Has an active imagination
- Likes to make three-dimensional structures from blocks and other manipulatives
- Completes assignments faster than same-age peers
- Can devise or adapt strategies to solve problems
- Can carry on a meaningful conversation with an adult
- Can successfully carry out multiple verbal instructions
- Demands a reason for things

While these ratings suggest that educators have meaningful insights into characteristics of giftedness, it has been known for nearly a century that teachers commonly fail to identify gifted learners who do not present as model students. Lewis M. Terman (1916) observed (as Alfred Binet had written before him) that teachers are unreliable evaluators of student cognitive ability:

> Psychological tests show that children of superior ability are very likely to be misunderstood in school. The writer has tested more than a hundred children who were as much above average intelligence as moron defectives are below. The large majority of these were found located below the school grade warranted by their intellectual level. One third had failed to reap any advantage whatever, in terms of promotion, from their very superior intelligence. Even genius languishes when kept over-long at tasks that are too easy.

> Our data show that teachers sometimes fail entirely to recognize exceptional superiority in a pupil, and that the degree of superiority is rarely estimated with anything like the accuracy which is possible to the psychologist after a one-hour examination. (p. 13)

In 1921–1922, Terman, the founder of the gifted child movement, launched the longest longitudinal study in the history of psychology on gifted children. With a grant from the Commonwealth Fund, Terman initiated a study entitled Genetic Studies of Genius (later renamed the Terman Study of the Gifted) that was intended to describe the characteristics of gifted children and follow their development over time. Results from this study were interpreted as dispelling misconceptions about the inadequacies of highly intelligent children, demonstrating that children with high IQ are healthier, better adjusted, better leaders, and higher academic achievers than normatively expected. Terman's findings also disproved the prevailing beliefs of the era that gifted individuals were more at risk, neurotic, or prone to mental illness as adults (e.g., "Precocity is not a menace," 1925). Neihart's (1999) review and update largely agreed but noted that the psychological well-being of gifted children is related to the type of giftedness, the quality of educational fit, and the child's personal characteristics, such as self-perceptions, temperament, and life circumstances.

In terms of intelligence tests, giftedness has traditionally been defined in terms of elevated general intelligence (e.g., Hollingworth, 1942; Terman, 1925), emphasizing the $g$ factor as represented by composite intelligence test scores. Kaufman and Sternberg (2008) stated that general intelligence remains of primary importance in gifted eligibility decisions: "In the United States, a global IQ score is still the dominant criterion used for acceptance into gifted programs at the grade-school level" (p. 80).

As previously discussed, the overall composite score in intelligence tests is not always the best measure of $g$. When tests such as the WISC-IV offer an overall composite (the Full Scale IQ) and a narrower score explicitly intended to measure the $g$ factor (the GAI), authorities in gifted assessment have tended to recommend use of the $g$ factor score (e.g., National Association for Gifted Children, 2010). In part, this recommendation has come from findings that subtests with lower $g$ loadings, such as speed measures, are quite commonly the lowest scores among gifted learners (e.g., Newman, Sparrow, & Pfeiffer, 2008), who tend to be more reflective, contemplative, or methodical in their problem-solving styles. In a consecutive series of 219 students referred for assessment for gifted program eligibility who earned a WISC-IV Full Scale IQ of 120 or higher, Wasserman (2010) reported that processing speed was the lowest index score in 59.4% of the sample; additionally, in 47.5% of the sample, processing speed fell in the average range or lower *and* was the lowest index score. Not surprisingly, gifted learners tend to earn lower composite scores on measures of cognitive processes in comparison with higher $g$-loaded tests. (See Kaufman & Kaufman, 2004, in which a gifted and talented sample earned a mean MPI of 118.7, $SD = 11.9$; see also Naglieri & Das, 1997b, in which a gifted sample earned a mean Full Scale standard score of 118.2, $SD = 10.0$).

Even as defining characteristics of psychometric $g$ such as reasoning ability are usually emphasized when identifying gifted learners, there is a long-held contradictory belief that for higher levels of ability, the general factor $g$ may not explain extraordinary performance as much as narrower and more independent factors. This line of research may be traced to Spearman's (1927) observation in *The Abilities of Man* that "the influence of $g$ on any ability [grows] less—in just the classes of person which, on the whole, possess this $g$ more abundantly" (p. 219). Now referred to as Spearman's Law of Diminishing Returns (SLODR; Jensen, 1998, pp. 585–588), this hypothesis predicts that the $g$ saturation of intelligence tests, derived from test intercorrelations, declines as ability level increases. SLODR has received substantial, but somewhat equivocal, support in the research literature (e.g., Jensen, 1998; te Nijenhuis, & Hartmann, 2006). Adapting Spearman's original analogy, adding fuel (i.e., the mental energy that is $g$) to an automobile's engine will only increase its speed (i.e., the gifted learner's performance) up to a point before the benefits start to wane. Extending the analogy, as a test's difficulty increases, the $g$ loadings are thought to decrease.

While some gifted children show fairly global and uniform elevations across all cognitive abilities, it has long been evident that subtypes of giftedness may be defined by relative superiority in narrower and specific cognitive or academic domains. The most researched domain-specific subtypes of giftedness are verbal/linguistic and logical/mathematical (e.g., Lubinski, Webb, Morelock, & Benbow, 2001; Matthews, 1997; Matthews & Keating, 1995). These subtypes not only describe cognitive profiles but also preferences in education and occupation:

> In general and irrespective of gender, students with tilted intellectual profiles tend to gravitate toward their area of strength. Those with exceptional mathematical abilities relative to verbal abilities tend to gravitate toward mathematics, engineering, and the physical sciences, while those with the inverse pattern are more attracted to the humanities, law, and social sciences. (Benbow, Lubinski, Shea, & Eftekhari-Sanjani, 2000, p. 474)

Another proposed subtype is visual-spatial giftedness (e.g., Humphreys, Lubinski, & Yao, 1993; Silverman,

2002b). The presence of superior visual-spatial ability has been shown to predict self-selected educational and occupational tracks, including architecture, cartography, chemistry, engineering, medical-surgery, and physics (e.g., Humphreys et al., 1993), but individuals with spatial gifts tend to be disproportionately undereducated and underemployed when compared with comparably gifted individuals with strengths in verbal and mathematical domains (Gohm, Humphreys, & Yao, 1998).

Another well-known longitudinal investigation of highly gifted children, lasting some four decades, is the Study of Mathematically Precocious Youth (SMPY), started by Julian C. Stanley in 1971 (Benbow & Stanley, 1983; Lubinski & Benbow, 2006). Its participants were originally intended to be mathematically advanced but actually included many students with greater verbal than mathematical abilities, first identified at about ages 12 or 13 through high school achievement test performances followed by out-of-level testing with the SAT in math and verbal areas while still in early middle school. Participants could be subdivided into at least three subtypes, one of which was defined by exceptional mathematical reasoning relative to verbal ability (e.g., Lubinski et al., 2001). Research findings showed that when provided with fast-paced mathematics classes, SMPY participants were twice as likely to be in math-science career tracks in their mid-20s and in their mid-30s. This study also yielded compelling evidence that gifted students benefit from being provided with educational opportunities tailored to their rates of learning:

> Intellectually able adolescents scoring 500 or more on SAT-M or SAT-V before age 13 (top 1 in 2000) can assimilate a full high school course (e.g., chemistry, English, mathematics) in 3 weeks at a summer residential program for intellectually precocious youth; yet exceptionally able adolescents, those scoring 700 or more (top 1 in 10,000), can assimilate at least twice this amount. (p. 318)

Use of the SAT by middle school students (as in the SMPY) is one way to reliably identify students with abilities in the top 0.01% (1 in 10,000) of the general population. Although descriptive classifications in the uppermost ranges of intelligence are less well known and less researched than those in the lowermost ranges, there appears to be a newfound interest in identifying and differentiating highly gifted students, considering the extended normative capacities built into the WISC-IV (Zhu et al., 2008) and the Stanford-Binet (Roid, 2003c, p. 22). While norm-referenced IQ scores have typically topped out at about 150 to 160 for decades, there is

actually a long-standing tradition of identifying the highly gifted, dating back to Galton's (1869/1892) rankings of genius (eminently gifted and illustrious) and Terman's (1916) designation of near genius or genius for IQs above 140. Building on the rich qualitative descriptions generated by Leta Hollingworth (1942; see also Stanley, 1990) to describe exceptionally and profoundly gifted children, Miraca Gross (2000) identified students as highly gifted with IQs from 145 to 159, exceptionally gifted with IQs of 160 to 179, and profoundly gifted with IQs of 180 or higher (with an estimated population frequency of less than 1 per 1 million). A full range descriptive classification appears in Table 18.8 and is designed to be symmetrical around the normative mean of 100, but any descriptive system may be used to denote the highly gifted and draw attention to their unique needs. WISC-IV composite scores now extend up to 210 (Zhu et al., 2008), joining other cognitive ability tests with composite scores that also extend to 200 and beyond (e.g., Roid, 2003c; Woodcock, McGrew, & Mather, 2001a). Ironically, the Wechsler-Bellevue (Wechsler, 1939) originally yielded Full Scale IQ scores ranging up to 195, so the practice of extending norms is not particularly new.

The concept of *asynchrony* (e.g., Columbus Group, 1991) or *dyssynchrony* (Terrassier, 1985), which may be defined in gifted individuals as referring to "a lack of synchronicity in the rates of their cognitive, emotional and physical development" (Morelock, 1992, p. 11), is an apt way to close this section. With variable rates of development for the different qualities and behaviors described long ago in gifted individuals by Hollingworth (1931) and

**TABLE 18.8 Descriptive Ability Levels Across an Extended IQ Range**

| Descriptive Level | Ability/IQ Range | Normal Curve Cut Points |
|---|---|---|
| Profoundly advanced/gifted | above 176 | +5.1 SD and above |
| Exceptionally advanced/gifted | 161 to 175 | +4.1 to +5.0 SD |
| Highly advanced/gifted | 146 to 160 | +3.1 to +4.0 SD |
| Advanced/gifted | 131 to 145 | +2.1 to +3.0 SD |
| Superior | 121 to 130 | +1.4 to +2.0 SD |
| High average | 111 to 120 | +0.7 to +1.3 SD |
| Average | 90 to 110 | +0.67 to −0.67 SD |
| Low average | 80 to 89 | −0.7 to −1.3 SD |
| Borderline | 70 to 79 | −1.4 to −2.0 SD |
| Mildly delayed/impaired | 55 to 69 | −2.1 SD to −3.0 SD |
| Moderately delayed/impaired | 40 to 54 | −3.1 SD to −4.0 SD |
| Severely delayed/impaired | 25 to 39 | −4.1 SD to −5.0 SD |
| Profoundly delayed/impaired | below 25 | −5.1 SD and below |

*Note.* IQ range scores are for a test with a standard score mean of 100 and SD of 15.

Terman (1931), the most basic and universal aspect of asynchronous development in the gifted is that cognitive development nearly always progresses at a considerably faster rate than physical development (N. M. Robinson, 2008). Asynchrony also encompasses uneven development of cognitive abilities and acquired skills, meaning that gifted individuals may commonly show a striking pattern of strengths and weaknesses, with performance discrepancies appearing more pronounced in younger students and those who are highly gifted (Gilman, 2008; Webb, Gore, Amend, & DeVries, 2007). Tolan (1994) described the complex behavioral presentation resulting from asynchrony:

> The young gifted child may appear to be many ages at once. He may be eight (his chronological age) when riding a bicycle, twelve when playing chess, fifteen when studying algebra, ten when collecting fossils and two when asked to share his chocolate chip cookie with his sister. (pp. 2–3)

Roedell (1989) described the discrepancies in intelligence, social knowledge, and actual social behaviors that are not unusual in gifted children: "It is unsettling to hold a high-level conversation with a 5-year-old who then turns around and punches a classmate who stole her pencil" (p. 22). The implications of asynchrony for understanding and counseling the gifted are quite profound (Silverman, 1993, 2002a, 2009, 2012), but for our purposes it is critical to note that uneven development of cognitive, emotional, physical, and social abilities should be normatively expected in gifted children, especially highly gifted children. An inspection of developmental growth trends suggests that cognitive abilities that are more strongly related to general intelligence tend to develop more uniformly, whereas more unique and low-$g$ abilities often have different and distinctive developmental trajectories (Wasserman, 2007).

## Specific Learning Disabilities

> The term "specific learning disability" means a disorder in 1 or more of the basic psychological processes involved in understanding or in using language, spoken or written, which disorder may manifest itself in the imperfect ability to listen, think, speak, read, write, spell, or do mathematical calculations.... Such term includes such conditions as perceptual disabilities, brain injury, minimal brain dysfunction, dyslexia, and developmental aphasia.... Such term does not include a learning problem that is primarily the result of visual, hearing, or motor disabilities, of mental retardation, of emotional disturbance, or of environmental, cultural, or economic disadvantage. (IDEA, 2004, 20 U.S.C. § 1401, 118 Stat. 2657)

While the definition of *specific learning disabilities* (SLDs) appearing in IDEA 2004 federal legislation has remained largely unchanged since 1968, the methods for SLD eligibility determination have changed significantly. In a notable scientific-legislative development, the federal government forbade the requirement for (but not the use of) the ability-achievement discrepancy method in SLD eligibility determination in favor of a Response To Intervention (RTI) methodology. The replacement of the discrepancy method, with its empirically demonstrated limitations, by the RTI method, which had little empirical support at the time of its adoption and which continues to have a weak evidence base at the time of this writing, has led some authorities to wonder if RTI is a "politically rather than scientifically motivated" model (Kavale, Kauffman, Bachmeier, & LeFever, 2008, p. 135). In this section, current federal SLD guidelines are described along with the diminished but still potentially valuable role of intelligence testing in the identification of SLDs.

From 1977 through about 2004 to 2006, the discrepancy between intellectual ability and performance on academic achievement tests was the primary federal criterion for defining specific learning disabilities in clinical and educational practice ("Procedures for evaluating specific learning disabilities," 1977). The origins of SLD discrepancy methods may be traced to Franzen's (1920) accomplishment quotient (the ratio of an educational quotient to the intelligence quotient) and Monroe's (1932) reading index (a discrepancy between actual and expected level of reading achievement). Samuel Kirk first used the term *learning disability* in print in 1962, defining it as "a retardation, disorder, or delayed development in one or more of the processes of speech, language, reading, writing, arithmetic, or other school subject" (p. 263). It was Kirk's former student, Barbara Bateman, who reintroduced the discrepancy model in 1965: "Children who have learning disorders are those who manifest an educationally significant discrepancy between their estimated potential and actual level of performance related to basic disorders in the learning process" (p. 220). Michael L. Rutter's Isle of Wight studies (Rutter, 1978; Rutter & Yule, 1973, 1975) are generally credited with having differentiated two types of reading-impaired groups: a general reading backwardness group (an ability-achievement nondiscrepant group, with less than two standard errors of estimate from the reading achievement predicted from performance IQ) and a specific reading retardation group (an ability-achievement discrepant group, with reading more than two standard errors of the estimate below the grade level predicted from performance IQ). The two groups differed in both their cognitive characteristics and their educational prognoses.

In 1975 the Education for All Handicapped Children Act (Public Law 94–142), was signed into federal law and defined *specific learning disability* as well as promulgating the severe discrepancy approach to SLD eligibility through U.S. Office of Education regulations in 1977.

As described in the introduction to this section, federal law last reaffirmed the ability-achievement discrepancy methodology in 1999, reversing itself in IDEA (2004) by mandating that ability-achievement discrepancies may *not* be required in the determination of eligibility for specific learning disabilities, a directive that many educators and psychologists mistakenly understood as precluding the use of ability-achievement discrepancies.

Over the last two decades, a number of researchers effectively challenged the rationale, validity, reliability, and fairness of discrepancy methodologies in identification of students with SLD. For example, Stanovich (1991a, 1991b) criticized the implicit assumption in discrepancy methodologies that intelligence predicts reading potential. The concept that students must wait years until their reading achievement deficiencies have grown large enough to reach the number required for a "severe discrepancy" with intelligence was criticized as a "wait to fail" index of SLD, which unnecessarily delayed delivery of interventions (e.g., Stage, Abbott, Jenkins, & Berninger, 2003; Stuebing, Fletcher, LeDoux, Lyon, Shaywitz, & Shaywitz, 2002). Several important validity investigations, including meta-analyses, failed to support meaningful distinctions between ability-achievement discrepant and nondiscrepant groups in terms of their academic performance, cognitive/achievement characteristics, educational prognosis, and response to intervention (Fletcher et al., 2002; Francis, Shaywitz, Stuebing, Shaywitz, & Fletcher, 1996; Hoskyn & Swanson, 2000; Shaywitz, Escobar, Shaywitz, Fletcher, & Makuch, 1992; Stage et al., 2003; Stanovich & Siegel, 1994; Stuebing et al., 2002; Vellutino, Scanlon, & Lyon, 2000). The reliability and stability of discrepancy scores were also effectively challenged (e.g., Francis, Fletcher, Stuebing, Lyon, Shaywitz, & Shaywitz, 2005). Finally, the disproportionate identification of minority students in high-incidence special education classifications including SLD was attributed to the use of intelligence tests. The 2002 report of the President's Commission on Excellence in Special Education reported, "The Commission found that several factors were responsible for this over-representation [of minority students in special education], including the reliance on IQ tests that have known cultural bias" (U.S. Department of Education, Office of Special Education and Rehabilitative Services, 2002, p. 26). The commission left little doubt of its low regard for intelligence tests in special education:

> There is little justification for the ubiquitous use of IQ tests for children with high-incidence disabilities, except when mild mental retardation is a consideration, especially given their cost and the lack of evidence indicating that IQ test results are related meaningfully to intervention outcomes. (p. 25)

The solution in federal regulations to the discrepancy methodology was termed *Responsiveness To Intervention* (also *Response To Intervention,* or *RTI*), in which students who fail to achieve adequately are provided with a series of increasingly intensive, individualized instructional interventions across multiple conceptual stage (or tiers), coupled with continuous and systematic monitoring of student progress at each stage. Students who fail to respond positively to intervention are considered to be "at risk" for learning disabilities, potentially being referred for psychoeducational assessment in tier 3 to specify the need for special education services. Now, after several years of implementation, increasing concern about the effectiveness of RTI is being expressed (e.g., Reynolds & Shaywitz, 2009). Swanson's (2010) critical appraisal noted:

> At the present time, RTI as an assessment approach to define LD [learning disability] has a weak experimental base. There have been no controlled studies randomly assigning children seriously at risk for LD to assessment and/or delivery models [(e.g., tiered instruction versus special education (resource room placement)] that have measured outcomes on key variables (e.g., over identification, stability of classification, academic and cognitive growth in response to treatment). The few studies that compare RTI with other assessment models (e.g., discrepancy based or low achievement based models) involve post hoc assessments of children divided at post-test within the same sample. In addition, different states and school districts have variations in their interpretations on how RTI should be implemented, thereby weakening any uniformity linking the science of instruction to assessing children at risk for LD. (p. 2)

The only meta-analysis of RTI published to date (Tran, Sanchez, Arellano, & Swanson, 2011; based on 13 studies) indicated that students identified as low responders to tier 1 and tier 2 RTI reading interventions show improvement but do not reach reading levels achieved by the high responders and that students with the lowest pre-intervention reading scores consistently remain the lowest performers, even with the flexibility and breadth of RTI interventions that are delivered. This study suggested that an initial standardized assessment may be most predictive of outcome as well as a way to identify students unlikely to respond to RTI more quickly than by multiple interventions across the RTI tiers. Moreover, even with intensive intervention, significant performance weaknesses remain for some students at risk for LD when compared to students who are more responsive to instruction. According to Tran and his colleagues (2011): "Unfortunately, the validity of RTI procedures, particularly in comparisons to other assessment approaches, has not been adequately established in the present synthesis of the literature" (p. 293).

A number of researchers, awaiting evidence on the effectiveness of RTI across achievement domains, have proposed alternative multimethod assessment approaches to the identification of SLD (e.g., Kavale & Forness, 2000; Kavale, Holdnack, & Mostert, 2005; Kavale, Kaufman, Naglieri, & Hale, 2005; Mather & Gregg, 2006; C. S. Robinson, Menchetti, & Torgesen, 2002). These approaches to identification of SLD have some or all of these elements in common:

1. Document the failure to achieve adequately or make sufficient progress in one or more areas of academic achievement through examination of educational history; class grades; work samples; standardized or curriculum-based measurement; analysis of performance process and quality; teacher, student, and parent reports; and/or response to interventions.

2. Identify one or more specific cognitive abilities or processes (e.g., phonological processing for reading decoding difficulties) that plausibly explain academic performance difficulties. Any contributory impaired abilities/processes need to have a research-based association with the specific domain of academic performance that is impaired. Multiple methods can be used to identify the contributory abilities or processes including standardized cognitive-intellectual test performance and formal observation, teacher ratings, or qualitative analysis of academic performance errors.

3. Rule out other explanations for the academic difficulties including intellectual disability, sensory disability, neurological trauma or condition, emotional-psychiatric disorder, or the consequences of an impoverished, disadvantaged, or culturally/linguistically different environment.

Intelligence tests quantify important personal resources (see the section on resilience and protective factors in the introduction to "Diagnostic Applications"), measure relevant cognitive abilities and processes, and have value in the identification of exclusionary diagnoses, such as intellectual disability. Intelligence tests can also provide information about verbal cognitive abilities and word knowledge, among other predictors of successful academic performance in reading.

Finally, a meta-analytic investigation has also provided evidence that the ability-achievement discrepancy may be effective in predicting intervention outcome within circumscribed ranges. Swanson (2003) reported that studies with aggregated intelligence and reading achievement scores that are both in the low range (<25th percentile, or a standard score of 90) yield significantly higher effect sizes related to intervention outcomes than studies with reading scores in the low range (<25th percentile) but with high IQ scores (e.g., IQ > 100). Accordingly, it appears there is value in the ability-achievement discrepancy method, albeit within specific parameters, and that complete abandonment of this approach may constitute "throwing the baby out with the bathwater" (Scruggs & Mastropieri, 2002, p. 165).

One of the unintended consequences of IDEA 2004's disparagement of ability-achievement discrepancies has been its unfortunate impact on identification of gifted students with specific learning disabilities (also known as *twice-exceptional*, or *Gifted 2e* students). These students are by nature exceptionally bright and often self-motivated, using their strengths to compensate for striking academic weaknesses for as long as they are able. Even when psychometric assessments identify large ability-achievement discrepancies, federal regulations discourage their interpretation and ambiguously promote use of achievement test performance patterns as a basis for identification:

> Discrepancy models are not essential for identifying children with SLD who are gifted. However, the regulations clearly allow discrepancies in achievement domains, typical of children with SLD who are gifted, to be used to identify children with SLD. (Rules and Regulations, *71 Fed. Reg.* 46647, August 14, 2006)

No states, to our knowledge, have published specific guidelines on identification of gifted SLD students, putting these students in the tragic wait-to-fail position that IDEA 2004 was intended to solve. Nicpon, Allmon, Sieck, and Stinson (2011) reported evidence of a pervasive and harmful misconception among educators that inclusion in gifted programs and selection for special education services are mutually exclusive.

## TOWARD A MATURE CLINICAL SCIENCE

Whither goest intellectual assessment?

The future is difficult to predict, but past events suggest that the measurement of intelligence will continue to be a useful professional activity, with continued gradual improvements in practice but with a shrinking number of applications depending on sociopolitical winds and scientific progress.

Actual practice has changed little since the 1960s, when the Wechsler intelligence scales began their dominance. If intelligence tests continue to be revised every 10 to 15 years, then by about 2050 it is reasonable to expect seventh or eighth edition revisions of the Wechsler and Stanford-Binet intelligence scales. There are few changes in diagnostic applications on the horizon, and recent legislation (IDEA, 2004) discouraged the use of intelligence tests in assessment of learning disabilities. The theory of general intelligence, dating back over 100 years, still tends to guide most intellectual applications.

The tenuous link between assessment and intervention continues to be an Achilles' heel for intellectual assessment. Perhaps the most telling indicator of the limited intervention utility of intelligence tests may be found in the Maruish (2004) and Antony and Barlow (2010) volumes, totaling over 1,300 pages, on the use of psychological testing for treatment planning with *no* mention of intelligence or IQ. Ironically, at the start of intelligence testing Alfred Binet (1909/1975) was unequivocal about his belief in the effectiveness of cognitive intervention, describing programs and exercises to enhance the efficiency of cognitive faculties. Efforts to systematically link intelligence assessment and intervention, such as those of Feuerstein (e.g., Feuerstein, Feuerstein, & Falik, 2010), have failed to gain traction.

Progress in reaching scientific consensus on matters related to intelligence and its assessment has been mixed, with two professional consensus statements having been published in the 1990s. The first appeared in the *Wall Street Journal* in 1994, when Linda S. Gottfredson authored a statement with 25 conclusions and 52 signatories, "Mainstream Science on Intelligence" (Gottfredson, December 13, 1994, p. A18; see also Gottfredson, 1997). In 1996 an APA task force issued an authoritative scientific consensus statement about intelligence and its assessment entitled "Intelligence: Knowns and Unknowns" (Neisser et al., 1996). While Spearman's (1904) psychometric $g$ was affirmed in the 1994 statement, the 1996 APA consensus hedged on $g$, stating that "while the $g$-based factor hierarchy is the most widely accepted current view of the structure of abilities, some theorists regard it as misleading" (Neisser et al., 1996, p. 81).

There are signs of potential change and guarded optimism in intelligence assessment. The CHC model offers a potentially unifying foundational structure for thinking about human cognitive abilities and intelligence. Advances in technology would seem to make it inevitable that the tradition of one examiner testing one student with verbal inquiries, stimulus materials, and manipulables will evolve toward increased online/computerized assessment and automated scoring, reporting, and interpretation. Psychometric techniques such as Rasch scaling have had little discernible impact on the material substance of intellectual tests thus far, but they promise the potential to reduce test development time and costs, thereby offering practitioners more choices in intelligence assessment.

An appraisal of the state of the science can lead only to the conclusion that intelligence assessment has yet to achieve status as a mature clinical science. The essential requirements of a mature clinical science, according to Millon (1999; Millon & Davis, 1996), are (a) a coherent foundational theory, from which testable principles and propositions may be derived; (b) a variety of assessment instruments, operationalizing the theory and serving the needs of special populations; (c) an applied diagnostic taxonomy, derived from and consistent with the theory and its measures; and (d) a compendium of change-oriented intervention techniques, aimed at modifying specific behaviors in a manner consistent with the theory. Three of these four criteria may arguably be said to have been met: Substantial advances in theories of intelligence have been made in recent years, a variety of intelligence tests are available, and diagnostic categories related to intelligence are in widespread use. Unfortunately, the field of psychology has yet to develop a systematic model linking intelligence assessment to intervention, making this long-sought objective a sort of holy grail necessary to move forward the science and practice of intelligence assessment.

## REFERENCES

American Psychiatric Association. (2000). *Diagnostic and statistical manual of mental disorders* (4th ed., Text revision). Washington, DC: Author.

American Psychiatric Association. (2011). *DSM-5 development. Major neurocognitive disorder.* Retrieved from www.dsm5.org/ProposedRevision/Pages/proposedrevision.aspx?rid=419#

Anderson, K., Brown, C., & Tallal, P. (1993). Developmental language disorders: Evidence for a basic processing deficit. *Current Opinion in Neurology and Neurosurgery, 6,* 98–106.

Antony, M. M., & Barlow, D. H. (2010). *Handbook of assessment and treatment planning for psychological disorders* (2nd ed.). New York, NY: Guilford Press.

APA Task Force to Update the Guidelines for the Evaluation of Dementia and Age-Related Cognitive Decline. (2011). *Guidelines for the evaluation of dementia and age-related cognitive change.* Washington, DC: American Psychological Association.

Ashman, A. F., & Das, J. P. (1980). Relation between planning and simultaneous-successive processing. *Perceptual and Motor Skills, 51,* 371–382.

Baade, L. L., & Schoenberg, M. R. (2004). A proposed method to estimate premorbid intelligence utilizing group achievement measures from school records. *Archives of Clinical Neuropsychology, 19,* 227–243.

Bain, S. K., & Allin, J. D. (2005). Review: Stanford-Binet Intelligence Scales, Fifth Edition. *Journal of Psychoeducational Assessment, 23,* 87–95.

Barkley, R. A. (1997). *ADHD and the nature of self-control.* New York, NY: Guilford Press.

Baron, R. M., & Kenny, D. A. (1986). The moderator-mediator variable distinction in social psychological research: Conceptual, strategic, and statistical considerations. *Journal of Personality and Social Psychology, 51,* 1173–1182.

Barona, A., Reynolds, C. R., & Chastain, R. (1984). A demographically based index of premorbid intelligence for the WAIS-R. *Journal of Consulting and Clinical Psychology, 52,* 885–887.

Bateman, B. (1965). An educational view of a diagnostic approach to learning disorders. In J. Hellmuth (Ed.), *Learning disorders* (Vol. 1, pp. 219–239). Seattle, WA: Special Child Publications.

Beaujean, A. A., McGlaughlin, S. M., & Margulies, A. S. (2009). Factorial validity of the Reynolds Intellectual Assessment Scales for referred students. *Psychology in the Schools, 46,* 932–950.

Benbow, C. P., Lubinski, D., Shea, D. L., & Eftekhari-Sanjani, H. (2000). Sex differences in mathematical reasoning ability at age 13: Their status 20 years later. *Psychological Science, 11,* 474–480.

Benbow, C. P., & Stanley, J. C. (Eds.). (1983). *Academic precocity: Aspects of its development.* Baltimore, MD: Johns Hopkins University Press.

Benson, N. (2008). Cattell-Horn-Carroll cognitive abilities and reading achievement. *Journal of Psychoeducational Assessment, 26,* 27–41.

Binet, A. (1975). *Modern ideas about children.* (S. Heisler, Trans.). Menlo Park, CA: Suzanne Heisler. (Original work published 1909)

Boake, C. (2002). From the Binet-Simon to the Wechsler-Bellevue: Tracing the history of intelligence testing. *Journal of Clinical and Experimental Neuropsychology, 24,* 383–405.

Bodin, D., Pardini, D. A., Burns, T. G., & Stevens, A. B. (2009). Higher order factor structure of the WISC-IV in a clinical neuropsychological sample. *Child Neuropsychology, 15,* 417–424.

Borkowski, J. G., Carothers, S. S., Howard, K., Schatz, J., & Farris, J. R. (2007). Intellectual assessment and intellectual disability. In J. W. Jacobson, J. A. Mulick, & J. Rojahn (Eds.), *Handbook of intellectual and developmental disabilities* (pp. 261–278). New York, NY: Springer.

Bracken, B. A. (2005). Reynolds Intellectual Assessment Scales and the Reynolds Intellectual Screening Test. In R. A. Spies & B. S. Plake (Eds.), *The sixteenth mental measurements yearbook* (pp. 892–894). Lincoln, NE: Buros Institute of Mental Measurements.

Burt, K. B., & Roisman, G. I. (2010). Competence and psychopathology: Cascade effects in the NICHD Study of Early Child Care and Youth Development. *Development and Psychopathology, 22,* 557–567.

Camara, W. J. (1997). Use and consequences of assessments in the USA: Professional, ethical, and legal issues. *European Journal of Psychological Assessment, 13,* 140–152.

Camara, W. J., Nathan, J. S., & Puente, A. E. (2000). Psychological test usage: Implications in professional psychology. *Professional Psychology: Research & Practice, 31,* 141–154.

Cangelosi, M. D. (2009). Identification of specific learning disability: A survey of school psychologists' knowledge and current practice. *Dissertation Abstracts International: Section B: The Sciences and Engineering,* AAT 3388260.

Canivez, G. L. (2008). Orthogonal higher order factor structure of the Stanford-Binet Intelligence Scales—Fifth Edition for children and adolescents. *School Psychology Quarterly, 23,* 533–541.

Canivez, G. L. (2010). Review of the Wechsler Adult Intelligence Scale—Fourth Edition. In R. A. Spies, J. F. Carlson, and K. F. Geisinger (Eds.), *The eighteenth mental measurements yearbook* (pp. 684–688). Lincoln, NE: Buros Institute of Mental Measurement.

Canivez, G. L. (2011a). *Cognitive Assessment System: An orthogonal hierarchical factor structure investigation.* Paper presented at the annual convention of the Midwestern Psychological Association, Chicago, IL.

Canivez, G. L. (2011b). Hierarchical factor structure of the Cognitive Assessment System: Variance partitions from the Schmid–Leiman (1957) procedure. *School Psychology Quarterly, 26,* 305–317.

Canivez, G. L. (2011c). *Incremental predictive validity of Cognitive Assessment System PASS scores.* Paper presented at the annual convention of the National Association of School Psychologists, San Francisco, CA.

Canivez, G. L. (2011d). *Interpretation of Cognitive Assessment System scores: Considering incremental validity of PASS Scores in predicting achievement.* Paper presented at the annual convention of the American Psychological Association, Washington, DC.

Canivez, G. L., & Watkins, M. W. (2010a). Exploratory and higher-order factor analyses of the Wechsler Adult Intelligence Scale—Fourth Edition (WAIS-IV) adolescent subsample. *School Psychology Quarterly, 25,* 223–235.

Canivez, G. L., & Watkins, M. W. (2010b). Investigation of the factor structure of the Wechsler Adult Intelligence Scale—Fourth Edition (WAIS-IV): Exploratory and higher order factor analyses. *Psychological Assessment, 22,* 827–836.

Carlson, J., & Das, J. P. (1997). A process approach to remediating word-decoding deficiencies in Chapter 1 children. *Learning Disability Quarterly, 20,* 93–102.

Carroll, J. B. (1983). Studying individual differences in cognitive abilities: Through and beyond factor analysis. In R. F. Dillon & R. R. Schmeck (Eds.), *Individual differences in cognition* (pp. 1–33). New York, NY: Academic Press.

Carroll, J. B. (1993). *Human cognitive abilities: A survey of factor analytic studies.* New York, NY: Cambridge University Press.

Carroll, J. B. (1995). Review of the book *Assessment of cognitive processing: The PASS theory of intelligence. Journal of Psychoeducational Assessment, 13,* 397–409.

Carroll, J. B. (2003). The higher-stratum structure of cognitive abilities: Current evidence supports *g* and about ten broad factors. In H. Nyborg (Ed.), *The scientific study of general intelligence: Tribute to Arthur R. Jensen* (pp. 5–21). Boston, MA: Pergamon Press.

Cattell, R. B. (1998). Where is intelligence? Some answers from the triadic theory. In J. J. McArdle & R. W. Woodcock (Eds.), *Human cognitive abilities in theory and practice* (pp. 29–38). Mahwah, NJ: Erlbaum.

Ciotti, R. M. (2007). The relationships among executive function scores: Examining the Cognitive Assessment System (CAS), Tower of London-Drexel (TOLDX), and the Behavior Rating Inventory Executive Function (BRIEF). *ProQuest Dissertations and Theses,* AAT 3267677.

Cohen, R. J., & Swerdlik, M. E. (1999). *Psychological testing and assessment: An introduction to tests and measurement* (4th ed.). Mountain View, CA: Mayfield.

Columbus Group. (1991, July). Unpublished transcript of meeting. Columbus, OH.

Cormier, P., Carlson, J. S., & Das, J. P. (1990). Planning ability and cognitive performance: The compensatory effects of a dynamic assessment approach. *Learning and Individual Differences, 2,* 437–449.

Damiani, V. B. (1997). Young gifted children in research and practice: The need for early childhood programs. *Gifted Child Today, 20*(3), 18–23.

Das, J. P. (1986). On definition of intelligence. In R. J. Sternberg & D. K. Detterman (Eds.), *What is intelligence? Contemporary viewpoints on its nature and definition* (pp. 55–56). Norwood, NJ: Ablex.

Das, J. P. (2004). Theories of intelligence: Issues and applications. In G. Goldstein & S. R. Beers (Eds.), *Comprehensive handbook of psychological assessment (Vol. 1): Intellectual and neuropsychological assessment* (pp. 5–23). Hoboken, NJ: Wiley.

Das, J. P., & Kendrick, M. (1997). PASS Reading Enhancement Program: A short manual for teachers. *Journal of Cognitive Education, 5,* 193–208.

Das, J. P., Kirby, J. R., & Jarman, R. F. (1975). Simultaneous and successive synthesis: An alternative model for cognitive abilities. *Psychological Bulletin, 82,* 87–103.

Das, J. P., Kirby, J. R., & Jarman, R. F. (1979). *Simultaneous and successive cognitive processes.* New York, NY: Academic Press.

Das, J. P., Naglieri, J. A., & Kirby, J. R. (1994). *Assessment of cognitive processes: The PASS theory of intelligence.* Needham Heights, MA: Allyn & Bacon.

Davis, A. S., & Finch, W. H. (2008). Review of Differential Ability Scales, Second Edition. In K. F. Geisinger, R. A. Spies, J. F. Carlson, & B. S. Plake (Eds.), *Eighteenth Annual Mental Measurements Yearbook.* Lincoln, NE: Buros Mental Measurements Institute.

Deng, C., Liu, M., Wei, W., Chan, R. C. K., & Das, J. P. (2011). Latent factor structure of the Das-Naglieri Cognitive Assessment System: A confirmatory factor analysis in a Chinese setting. *Research in Developmental Disabilities, 32,* 1988–1997.

Derrfuss, J., Brass, M., Neumann, J., & von Cramon, D. Y. (2005). Involvement of the inferior frontal junction in cognitive control: Meta-analyses of switching and Stroop studies. *Human Brain Mapping, 25,* 22–34.

DiStefano, C., & Dombrowski, S. C. (2006). Investigating the theoretical structure of the Stanford-Binet, Fifth Edition. *Journal of Psychoeducational Assessment, 24,* 123–136.

Dombrowski, S. C., & Mrazik, M. (2008). Test review: Reynolds Intellectual Assessment Scales. *Canadian Journal of School Psychology, 23,* 223–230.

Dombrowski, S. C., Watkins, M. W., & Brogan, M. J. (2009). An exploratory investigation of the factor structure of the Reynolds Intellectual Assessment Scales (RIAS). *Journal of Psychoeducational Assessment, 27,* 494–507.

Dumont, R., Willis, J. O., & Elliott, C. D. (2009). *Essentials of DAS-II assessment.* Hoboken, NJ: Wiley.

Education for All Handicapped Children Act. Pub. L. No. 94–142 (1975). 20 U.S.C. § 1401 et seq.

Edwards, O. W., & Paulin, R. V. (2007). Referred students' performance on the Reynolds Intellectual Assessment Scales and the Wechsler Intelligence Scale for Children–Fourth Edition. *Journal of Psychoeducational Assessment, 25,* 334–340.

Egeland, B. R., Carlson, E., & Sroufe, L. A. (1993). Resilience as process. *Development and Psychopathology, 5,* 517–528.

Elliott, C. D. (1983). *The British Ability Scales. Manual 1: Introductory handbook.* Windsor, UK: NFER-Nelson.

Elliott, C. D. (2007a). *Differential Ability Scales—Second Edition: Administration and scoring manual.* San Antonio, TX: Pearson.

Elliott, C. D. (2007b). *Differential Ability Scales—Second Edition: Introductory and technical handbook.* San Antonio, TX: Pearson.

Elliott, C. D. (2007c). *Differential Ability Scales—Second Edition: Normative data tables manual.* San Antonio, TX: Pearson.

Elliott, C. D., Hale, J. B., Fiorello, C. A., Dorvil, C., & Moldovan, J. (2010). Differential Ability Scales—II prediction of reading performance: Global scores are not enough. *Psychology in the Schools, 47,* 698–720.

Elliott, C. D., Murray, D. J., & Pearson, L. S. (1979). *British Ability Scales.* Slough, UK: NFER.

Elliott, R. W. (2004). Reynolds Intellectual Assessment Scales. *Archives of Clinical Neuropsychology, 19,* 325–328.

Evans, J. J., Floyd, R. G., McGrew, K. S., & Leforgee, M. H. (2002). The relations between measures of Cattell-Horn-Carroll (CHC) cognitive abilities and reading achievement during childhood and adolescence. *School Psychology Review, 31,* 246–262.

Eysenck, H. J. (1993). Comment on Goldberg. *American Psychologist, 48,* 1299–1300.

Feldt, L. S. (1969). A test of the hypothesis that Cronbach's alpha or Kuder-Richardson coefficient twenty is the same for two tests. *Psychometrika, 34,* 363–373.

Feuerstein, R., Feuerstein, R. S., & Falik, L. H. (2010). *Beyond smarter: Mediated learning and the brain's capacity for change.* New York, NY: Teachers College Press.

Flanagan, D. P., & Kaufman, A. S. (2009). *Essentials of WISC-IV assessment* (2nd ed.). Hoboken, NJ: John Wiley & Sons.

Flanagan, D. P., McGrew, K. S., & Ortiz, S. O. (2000). *The Wechsler intelligence scales and Gf-Gc theory: A contemporary approach to interpretation.* Needham Heights, MA: Allyn & Bacon.

Flanagan, D. P., Ortiz, S. O., & Alfonso, V. C. (2007). *Essentials of cross battery assessment* (2nd ed.). Hoboken, NJ: Wiley.

Fletcher, J. M., Lyon, G. R., Barnes, M., Stuebing, K. K., Francis, D. J., Olson, R. K., . . . Shaywitz, B. A. (2002). Classification of learning disabilities: An evidenced-based evaluation. In R. Bradley, L. Danielson, & D. P. Hallahan (Eds.). *Identification of learning disabilities: Research to practice* (pp. 185–250). Mahwah, NJ: Erlbaum.

Floyd, R. G., Evans, J. J., & McGrew, K. S. (2003). Relations between measures of Cattell- Horn-Carroll (CHC) cognitive abilities and mathematics achievement across the school-age years. *Psychology in the Schools, 40,* 155–171.

Floyd, R. G., Keith, T., Taub, G. McGrew, K. (2007). Cattell-Horn-Carroll cognitive abilities and their effects on reading decoding skills: g has indirect effects, more specific abilities have direct effects. *School Psychology Quarterly, 22,* 200–223.

Floyd, R. G., McGrew, K. & Evans, J. (2008). The relative contributions of the Cattell-Horn- Carroll cognitive abilities in explaining writing achievement during childhood and adolescence. *Psychology in the Schools, 45,* 132–144.

Francis, D. J., Fletcher, J. M., Stuebing, K. K., Lyon, G. R., Shaywitz, B. A., & Shaywitz, S. E. (2005). Psychometric approaches to the identification of learning disabilities: IQ and achievement scores are not sufficient. *Journal of Learning Disabilities, 38*(2), 98–108.

Francis, D. J., Shaywitz, S. E., Stuebing, K. K., Shaywitz, B. A., & Fletcher, J. M. (1996). Developmental lag versus deficit models of reading disability: A longitudinal individual growth curves analysis. *Journal of Educational Psychology, 88,* 3–17.

Franzen, R. (1920). The accomplishment quotient: A school mark in terms of individual capacity. *Teachers College Record, 21,* 432–440.

Ganguli, M., Blacker, D., Blazer, D. G., Grant, I., Jeste, D. V., Paulsen, J. S., . . . Sachdev, P. S. (2011). Classification of neurocognitive disorders in DSM-5: A work in progress. *American Journal of Geriatric Psychiatry, 19*(3), 205–209.

Gilman, B. J. (2008). *Academic advocacy for gifted children: A parent's complete guide.* Scottsdale, AZ: Great Potential Press.

Godbolt, A. K., Cipolotti, L., Watt, H., Fox, N. C., Janssen, J. C., & Rossor, M. N. (2004). The natural history of Alzheimer disease: A longitudinal presymptomatic and symptomatic study of a familial cohort. *Archives of Neurology, 61,* 1743–1748.

Gohm, C. L., Humphreys, L. G., & Yao, G. (1998). Underachievement among spatially gifted students. *American Educational Research Journal, 35,* 515–531.

Gottfredson, L. J. (1994, December 13). Mainstream science on intelligence. *Wall Street Journal,* p. A18.

Gottfredson, L. J. (1997). Mainstream science on intelligence: An editorial with 52 signatories, history, and bibliography. *Intelligence, 24,* 13–23.

Gresham, F. M., & Witt, J. C. (1997). Utility of intelligence tests for treatment planning, classification, and placement decisions: Recent empirical findings and future directions. *School Psychology Quarterly, 12,* 249–267.

Gross, M. (2000). Exceptionally and profoundly gifted students: An underserved population. *Understanding Our Gifted, 12*(2), 3–9.

Gustafsson, J.-E. (1984). A unifying model of the structure of intellectual abilities. *Intelligence, 8,* 179–203.

Gustafsson, J.-E. (1988). Hierarchical models for individual differences in cognitive abilities. In R. J. Sternberg (Ed.), *Advances in the psychology of human intelligence* (Vol. 4, pp. 35–71). Hillsdale, NJ: Erlbaum.

Gutentag, S. S., Naglieri, J. A., & Yeates, K. O. (1998). Performance of children with traumatic brain injury on the cognitive assessment system. *Assessment, 5,* 263–272.

Haddad, F. A. (2004). Planning versus speed: An experimental examination of what Planned Codes of the Cognitive Assessment System measures. *Archives of Clinical Neuropsychology, 19,* 313–317.

Hale, J. B., Fiorello, C. A., Dumont, R., Willis, J .O., Rackley, C., & Elliott, C. (2008). Differential Ability Scales—Second Edition, (neuro)psychological predictors of math performance for typical children and children with math disabilities. *Psychology in the Schools, 45,* 838–858.

Harrison, C. (2004). Giftedness in early childhood: The search for complexity and connection. *Roeper Review, 26,* 78–84.

Harrison, P. L., Kaufman, A. S., Hickman, J. A., & Kaufman, N. L. (1988). A survey of tests used for adult assessment. *Journal of Psychoeducational Assessment, 6,* 188–198.

Herrnstein, R. J., & Murray, C. (1994). *The bell curve: Intelligence and class structure in American life.* New York, NY: Free Press.

Hill, V. (2005). Through the past darkly: A review of the British Ability Scales Second Edition. *Child and Adolescent Mental Health, 10,* 87–98.

Hodge, K. A., & Kemp, C. R. (2000). Exploring the nature of giftedness in preschool children. *Journal for the Education of the Gifted, 24,* 46–73.

Hollingworth, L. S. (1931). The child of very superior intelligence as a special problem in social adjustment. *Mental Hygiene, 15*(1), 3–16.

Hollingworth, L. S. (1942). *Children above 180 IQ (Stanford-Binet): Origin and development.* Yonkers-on-Hudson, NY: World Book.

Horn, J. L., & Blankson, N. (2005). Foundations for better understanding of cognitive abilities. In D. P. Flanagan & P. L. Harrison (Eds.), *Contemporary intellectual assessment: Theories, tests, and issues* (2nd ed., pp. 41–68). New York, NY: Guilford Press.

Hoskyn, M., & Swanson, H. L. (2000). Cognitive processing of low achievers and children with reading disabilities: A selective meta-analytic review of the published literature. *School Psychology Review, 29,* 102–119.

Humphreys, L. G., Lubinski, D., & Yao, G. (1993). Utility of predicting group membership and the role of spatial visualization in becoming an engineer, physical scientist, or artist. *Journal of Applied Psychology, 78,* 250–261.

Individuals with Disabilities Education Act, Pub. L. No. 105–17 (1997, 1999). 20 U.S.C. § 1400 et seq. (Statute). 34 C.F.R. 300 (Regulations).

Individuals with Disabilities Education Improvement Act of 2004, Pub. L. No. 108–446, 20 U.S.C. § 1401, 118 STAT. 2657 (2004).

Jackson, N. E. (2003). Young gifted children. In N. Colangelo & G. Davis (Eds.), *Handbook of gifted education* (3rd ed., pp. 470–482). Boston, MA: Allyn & Bacon.

Jensen, A. R. (1998). *The g factor: The science of mental ability.* Westport, CT: Praeger.

The K-ABC–Will it be the SOMPA of the 80's? (1984). *Ohio School Psychologist* [Ohio School Psychologists Association], *29*(4), 9–11.

Kamphaus, R. W., & Reynolds, C. R. (2009). Kaufman's work in the penumbra between measurement science and clinical assessment. In J. C. Kaufman (Ed.), *Intelligence testing: Integrating psychological theory and clinical practice* (pp. 148–156). New York, NY: Cambridge University Press.

Kaplan, E. (1988). A process approach to neuropsychological assessment. In T. J. Boll & B. K. Bryant (Eds.), *Clinical neuropsychology and brain function: Research, measurement, and practice* (pp. 129–167). Washington, DC: American Psychological Association.

Kaplan, E., Fein, D., Kramer, J., Delis, D., & Morris, R. (1999). *Wechsler Intelligence Scale for Children—Third Edition as a Process Instrument (WISC-III PI).* San Antonio, TX: Psychological Corporation.

Kaplan, E., Fein, D., Morris, R., & Delis, D. (1991). *Wechsler Adult Intelligence Scale—Revised as a Neuropsychological Instrument (WAIS-R NI).* San Antonio, TX: Psychological Corporation.

Kar, B. C., Dash, U. N., Das, J. P., & Carlson, J. S. (1992). Two experiments on the dynamic assessment of planning. *Learning and Individual Differences, 5,* 13–29.

Kaufman, A. S. (1994). *Intelligent testing with the WISC-III.* New York, NY: Wiley.

Kaufman, A. S., & Kaufman, N. L. (1983a). *Kaufman Assessment Battery for Children administration and scoring manual.* Circle Pines, MN: American Guidance.

Kaufman, A. S., & Kaufman, N. L. (1983b). *Kaufman Assessment Battery for Children interpretive manual.* Circle Pines, MN: American Guidance.

Kaufman A. S., & Kaufman, N. L. (1993). *Kaufman Adolescent and Adult Intelligence Test.* Circle Pines, MN: American Guidance.

Kaufman, A. S., & Kaufman, N. L. (2004). *Kaufman Assessment Battery for Children, Second Edition (KABC-II): Manual.* Bloomington, MN: Pearson.

Kaufman, A. S., Lichtenberger, E. O., Fletcher-Janzen, E., & Kaufman, N. L. (2005). *Essentials of KABC-II assessment.* Hoboken, NJ: Wiley.

Kaufman, S. B., & Sternberg, R. J. (2008). Conceptions of giftedness. In S. I. Pfeiffer (Ed.), *Handbook of giftedness in children* (pp. 71–91). New York, NY: Springer.

Kavale, K. A., & Forness, S. R. (2000). What definitions of learning disabilities say and don't say: A critical analysis. *Journal of Learning Disabilities, 33,* 239–256.

Kavale, K. A., Holdnack, J. A., & Mostert, M. P. (2005). Responsiveness to intervention and the identification of specific learning disability: A critique and alternative proposal. *Learning Disability Quarterly, 28,* 2–16.

Kavale, K. A., Kauffman, J. M., Bachmeier, R. J., & LeFever, G. B. (2008). Response-to-Intervention: Separating the rhetoric of self-congratulation from the reality of specific learning disability identification. *Learning Disability Quarterly, 31,* 135–150.

Kavale, K. A., Kaufman, A. S., Naglieri, J. A., & Hale, J. (2005). Changing procedures for identifying learning disabilities: The danger of poorly supported ideas. *School Psychologist, 59,* 16–25.

Keith, T. Z., Fine, J. G., Taub, G. E., Reynolds, M. R., & Kranzler, J. H. (2006). Higher order, multisample, confirmatory factor analysis of the Wechsler Intelligence Scale for Children—Fourth Edition: What does it measure? *School Psychology Review, 35,* 108–127.

Keith, T. Z., & Kranzler, J. H. (1999). The absence of structural fidelity precludes construct validity: Rejoinder to Naglieri on what the Cognitive Assessment System does and does not measure. *School Psychology Review, 28,* 303–321.

Keith, T. Z., Kranzler, J. H., & Flanagan, D. P. (2001). What does the Cognitive Assessment System (CAS) measure? Joint confirmatory factor analysis of the CAS and the Woodcock-Johnson Tests of Cognitive Ability (3rd ed.). *School Psychology Review, 30,* 89–119.

Keith, T. Z., Low, J. A., Reynolds, M. R., Patel, P. G., & Ridley, K. P. (2010). Higher-order factor structure of the Differential Ability Scales-II: Consistency across ages 4 to 17. *Psychology in the Schools, 47,* 676–697.

Kirk, S. A. (1962). *Educating exceptional children.* Boston, MA: Houghton Mifflin

Kitano, M. K. (1995). Language diversity and giftedness: Working with gifted English language learners. *Journal for the Education of the Gifted, 18,* 234–254.

Kline, R. B., Snyder, J., Castellanos, M. (1996). Lessons from the Kaufman Assessment Battery for Children (K-ABC): Toward a new cognitive assessment model. *Psychological Assessment, 8,* 7–17.

Krach, S. K., Loe, S. A., Jones, W. P., & Farrally, A. (2009). Convergent validity of the Reynolds Intellectual Assessment Scales (RIAS) using the Woodcock-Johnson Tests of Cognitive Ability, Third Edition (WJ-III) with university students. *Journal of Psychoeducational Assessment, 27,* 355–365.

Kranzler, J. H., & Keith, T. Z. (1999). Independent confirmatory factor analysis of the Cognitive Assessment System (CAS): What does the CAS measure? *School Psychology Review, 28,* 117–144.

Kranzler, J. H., Keith, T. Z., & Flanagan, D. P. (2000). Independent examination of the factor structure of the Cognitive Assessment System (CAS): Further evidence challenging the construct validity of the CAS. *Journal of Psychoeducational Assessment, 18,* 143–159.

Lippmann, W. (1922a). The mental age of Americans. *New Republic, 32,* 213–215

Lippmann, W. (1922b). The mystery of the "A" men. *New Republic, 32,* 246–248.

Lippmann, W. (1922c). The reliability of intelligence tests. *New Republic, 32,* 275–277

Lippmann, W. (1922d). The abuse of the tests. *New Republic, 32,* 297–298.

Lippmann, W. (1922e). Tests of hereditary intelligence, *New Republic, 32,* 328–330.

Lippmann, W. (1922f). A future for the tests. *New Republic, 33,* 9–10.

Lippmann, W. (1923). The great confusion: A reply to Mr. Terman. *New Republic, 33,* 145–146.

Littman, R. A. (2004). Mental tests and fossils. *Journal of the History of the Behavioral Sciences, 40,* 423–431.

Livingston, R. B., Jennings, E., Reynolds, C. R., & Gray, R. M. (2003). Multivariate analyses of the profile stability of intelligence tests: High for IQs, low to very low for subtest analyses. *Archives of Clinical Neuropsychology, 18,* 487–507.

Loeber, R., Pardini, D. A., Stouthamer-Loeber, M., & Raine, A. (2007). Do cognitive, physiological, and psychosocial risk and promotive factors predict desistance from delinquency in males? *Development and Psychopathology, 19,* 867–887.

Lubinski, D., & Benbow, C. P. (2006). Study of mathematically precocious youth after 35 years: Uncovering antecedents for the development of math-science expertise. *Perspectives on Psychological Science, 1,* 316–345.

Lubinski, D., Webb, R. M., Morelock, M. J., & Benbow, C. P. (2001). Top 1 in 10,000: A 10-year follow-up of the profoundly gifted. *Journal of Applied Psychology, 86,* 718–720.

Luckasson, R., Borthwick-Duffy, S., Buntinx, W. H. E., Coulter, D. L., Craig, E. M., Reeve, A., . . . Tasse, M. J. (2002). *Mental retardation: Definition, classification, and systems of supports* (10th ed.). Washington, DC: American Association on Mental Retardation.

Luria, A. R. (1966). *Human brain and psychological processes.* New York, NY: Harper & Row.

Luria, A. R. (1970). The functional organization of the brain. *Scientific American, 222*(3), 66–78.

Luria, A. R. (1973). *The working brain: An introduction to neuropsychology.* New York, NY: Basic Books.

Luria, A. R. (1980). *Higher cortical functions in man* (2nd ed.; B. Haigh, Trans.). New York, NY: Basic Books.

Luthar, S. S., D'Avanzo, K., & Hites, S. (2003). Maternal drug abuse versus other psychological disturbances: Risks and resilience among children. In S. S. Luthar (Ed.), *Resilience and vulnerability: Adaptation in the context of childhood adversities* (pp. 104–129). New York, NY: Cambridge University Press

Macmann, G. M., & Barnett, D. W. (1997). Myth of the master detective: Reliability of interpretations for Kaufman's "Intelligent Testing" approach to the WISC-III. *School Psychology Quarterly, 12,* 197–234.

Marland, S. P. (1972). *Education of the gifted and talented: Vol. 1. Report to the Congress of the United States by the U.S. Commissioner of Education.* Washington, DC: U.S. Government Printing Office.

Maruish, M. E. (Ed.). (2004). *The use of psychological testing for treatment planning and outcomes assessment. (Vol. 2) Instruments for children and adolescents* (3rd ed.). Mahwah, NJ: Erlbaum.

Maruta, C., Guerreiro, M., de Mendónça, A., Hort, J., & Scheltono, P. (2011). The use of neuropsychological tests across Europe: The need for a consensus in the use of assessment tools for dementia. *European Journal of Neurology, 18,* 279–285.

Masten, A. S. (1994). Resilience in individual development: Successful adaptation despite risk and adversity. In M. C. Wang & E. W. Gordon (Eds.), *Educational resilience in inner-city America: Challenges and prospects* (pp. 1–25). Hillsdale, NJ: Erlbaum.

Masten, A. S., Burt, K. B., Roisman, G. I., Obradovic, J., Long, J. D., & Tellegen, A. (2004). Resources and resilience in the transition to adulthood: Continuity and change. *Development and Psychopathology, 16,* 1071–1094.

Matarazzo, J. D. (1981). Obituary: David Wechsler (1896–1981). *American Psychologist, 36,* 1542–1543.

Mather, N., & Gregg, N. (2006). Specific learning disabilities: Clarifying, not eliminating, a construct. *Professional Psychology: Research and Practice, 37,* 99–106.

Mather, N., & Jaffe, L. E. (2002). *Woodcock-Johnson III: Reports, recommendations, and strategies.* Hoboken, NJ: Wiley.

Mather, N., & Woodcock, R. W. (2001). *Woodcock-Johnson III Tests of Cognitive Abilities examiner's manual: Standard and extended batteries.* Itasca, IL: Riverside.

Matthews, D. J. (1997). Diversity in domains of development: Research findings and their implications for gifted identification and programming. *Roeper Review, 19*(3), 172–177.

Matthews, D. J., & Keating, D. P. (1995). Domain specificity and habits of mind: An investigation of patterns of high-level development. *Journal of Early Adolescence, 15,* 319–343.

Mayer, R. E. (1992). Cognition and instruction: Their historic meeting within educational psychology. *Journal of Educational Psychology, 84,* 405–412.

McCrea, S. M. (2009). A review and empirical study of the composite scales of the Das-Naglieri Cognitive Assessment System. *Psychology Research and Behavior Management, 2,* 59–79.

McDermott, P. A., Fantuzzo, J. W., Glutting, J. J., Watkins, M. W., & Baggaley, A. R. (1992). Illusions of meaning in the ipsative assessment of children's ability. *Journal of Special Education, 25,* 504–526.

McGrew, K. S. (1997). Analysis of the major intelligence batteries according to a proposed comprehensive Gf-Gc framework. In D. P. Flanagan, J. L. Genshaft, & P. L. Harrison (Eds.), *Contemporary intellectual assessment: Theories, tests, and issues* (pp. 151–180). New York, NY: Guilford Press.

McGrew, K. S., Dailey, D. E. H., & Schrank, F. A. (2007). *Woodcock-Johnson III/Woodcock-Johnson III Normative Update score differences: What the user can expect and why (Woodcock-Johnson III Assessment Service Bulletin No. 9).* Rolling Meadows, IL: Riverside.

McGrew, K. S., & Flanagan, D. P. (1998). *The intelligence test desk reference (ITDR): Gf-Gc cross-battery assessment.* Needham Heights, MA: Allyn & Bacon.

McGrew, K. S., Schrank, F. A., & Woodcock, R. W. (2007). *Woodcock-Johnson III Normative Update technical manual.* Rolling Meadows, IL: Riverside.

McGrew, K. S., Werder, J. K., & Woodcock, R. W. (1991). *Woodcock-Johnson Psycho-Educational Battery—Revised (WJ-R) technical manual.* Allen, TX: DLM.

McGrew, K. S., & Woodcock, R. W. (2001). *Technical manual. Woodcock-Johnson III.* Itasca, IL: Riverside.

McNemar, Q. (1964). Lost: Our intelligence? Why? *American Psychologist, 19,* 871–882.

Meikamp, J. (1999). Review of the Das-Naglieri Cognitive Assessment System. In. B. S. Plake & J. C. Impara (Eds.), *The supplement to the thirteenth mental measurements yearbook* (pp. 75–77). Lincoln, NE: Buros Institute.

Millon, T. (1999). Reflections on psychosynergy: A model for integrating science, theory, classification, assessment, and therapy. *Journal of Personality Assessment, 72,* 437–456.

Millon, T., & Davis, R. D. (1996). *Disorders of personality: DSM-IV and beyond* (2nd. ed). New York, NY: Wiley.

Monroe, M. (1932). *Children who cannot read.* Chicago, IL: University of Chicago Press.

Moon, T. R., & Brighton, C. M. (2008). Primary teachers' conceptions of giftedness. *Journal for the Education of the Gifted, 31,* 447–480.

Morelock, M. J. (1992). Giftedness: The view from within. *Understanding Our Gifted, 4*(3), 1, 11–15.

Morgan, K. E., Rothlisberg, B. A., McIntosh, D. E., & Hunt, M. S. (2009). Confirmatory factor analysis of the KABC-II in preschool children. *Psychology in the Schools, 46,* 515–525.

Naglieri, J. A. (1999). *Essentials of CAS assessment.* New York, NY: Wiley.

Naglieri, J. A., & Bornstein, B. T. (2003). Intelligence and achievement: Just how correlated are they? *Journal of Psychoeducational Assessment, 21,* 244–260.

Naglieri, J. A., & Das, J. P. (1987). Construct and criterion related validity of planning, simultaneous, and successive cognitive processing tasks. *Journal of Psychoeducational Assessment, 5,* 353–363.

Naglieri, J. A., & Das, J. P. (1988). Planning-Arousal-Simultaneous-Successive (PASS): A model for assessment. *Journal of School Psychology, 26,* 35–48.

Naglieri, J. A., & Das, J. P. (1997a). *Cognitive Assessment System: Administration and scoring manual.* Itasca, IL: Riverside.

Naglieri, J. A., & Das, J. P. (1997b). *Cognitive Assessment System: Interpretive handbook.* Itasca, IL: Riverside.

Naglieri, J. A., DeLauder, B. Y., Goldstein, S., & Schwebech, A. (2006). WISC-III and D-N CAS: Which correlates higher with achievement for a clinical sample? *School Psychology Quarterly, 21,* 62–76.

Naglieri, J. A., & Otero, T. (2011). Cognitive Assessment System: Redefining intelligence from a neuropsychological perspective. In A. Davis (Ed.). *Handbook of pediatric neuropsychology* (pp. 320–333). New York, NY: Springer.

Naglieri, J. A., & Pickering, E. B. (2010). *Helping children learn: Intervention handouts for use at school and home* (2nd ed.). Baltimore, MD: Brookes.

Naglieri, J. A., & Rojahn, J. (2001). Intellectual classification of Black and White children in special education programs using the WISC-III and the Cognitive Assessment System. *American Journal on Mental Retardation, 106,* 359–367.

Naglieri, J. A., & Rojahn, J. (2004). Construct validity of the PASS theory and CAS: Correlations with achievement. *Journal of Educational Psychology, 96,* 174–181.

National Association for Gifted Children. (2008). *The role of assessments in the identification of gifted students* (NAGC Position Paper). Washington, DC: Author.

National Association for Gifted Children. (2010). *Use of the WISC-IV for gifted identification* (NAGC Position Paper). Washington, DC: Author.

Neihart, M. (1999). The impact of giftedness on psychological well-being: What does the empirical literature say? *Roeper Review, 22,* 10–17.

Neisser, U., Boodoo, G., Bouchard, T. J., Boykin, A. W., Brody, N., Ceci, S. J.,... Urbina, S. (1996). Intelligence: Knowns and unknowns. *American Psychologist, 51,* 77–101.

Nelson, H. E. (1982). *The National Adult Reading Test (NART). Test manual.* Windsor, UK: NFER-Nelson.

Nelson, J. M., Canivez, G. L, Lindstrom, W., & Hatt, C. (2007). Higher-order exploratory factor analysis of the Reynolds Intellectual Assessment Scales with a referred sample. *Journal of School Psychology, 45,* 439–456.

Newman, T. M., Sparrow, S. S., & Pfeiffer, S. I. (2008). The use of the WISC-IV in assessment and intervention planning for children who are gifted. In A. Prifitera, D. H. Saklofske, & L. G. Weiss (Eds.), *WISC-IV clinical assessment and intervention* (2nd ed., pp. 217–272). San Diego, CA: Academic Press.

Nicpon, M. F., Allmon, A., Sieck, B., & Stinson, R. D. (2011). Empirical investigation of twice-exceptionality: Where have we been and where are we going? *Gifted Child Quarterly, 55,* 3–17.

Paivio, A. (1976). Concerning dual-coding and simultaneous-successive processing. *Canadian Psychological Review, 17,* 69–72.

Paolitto, A. W. (1999). Clinical validation of the Cognitive Assessment System with children with ADHD. *ADHD Report, 7,* 1–5.

Pearson. (2009a). *Advanced Clinical Solutions for the WAIS-IV and WMS-IV.* San Antonio, TX: Author.

Pearson. (2009b). *Test of Pre-Morbid Functioning.* San Antonio, TX: Author.

Pearson research staff. (2009). *Wechsler Individual Achievement Test–Third Edition (WIAT-III) technical manual.* San Antonio, TX: Pearson.

Petersen, R. C., Roberts, R. O., Knopman, D. S., Boeve, B. F., Geda, Y. E., Ivnik, R. J.,... Jack, C. R. (2009). Mild cognitive impairment: Ten years later. *Archives of Neurology, 66,* 1447–1455.

Petersen, R. C., Smith, G. E., Waring, S. C., Ivnik, R. J., Tangalos, E. G., & Kokmen, E. (1999). Mild cognitive impairment: Clinical characterization and outcome. *Archives of Neurology, 56,* 303–308.

Petersen, R. C., Stevens, J. C., Ganguli, M., Tangalos, E. G., Cummings, J. L., & DeKosky, S. T. (2001). Practice parameter: Early detection of dementia: Mild cognitive impairment (an evidence-based review). *Neurology, 56,* 1133–1142.

Posner, M. I., & Petersen, S. E. (1990). The attention system of the human brain. *Annual Review of Neuroscience, 13,* 25–42.

Precocity is not a menace. (1925, May 31). *Los Angeles Times,* p. H9.

Procedures for evaluating specific learning disabilities. 42 *Federal Register* 65082 (Dec. 29, 1977).

Puhan, G., Das, J. P., & Naglieri, J. A. (2005). Separating planning and attention: Evidential and consequential validity. *Canadian Journal of School Psychology, 20,* 75–83.

Rabin, L. A., Barr, W. B., & Burton, L. A. (2005). Assessment practices of clinical neuropsychologists in the United States and Canada: A survey of INS, NAN, and APA Division 40 members. *Archives of Clinical Neuropsychology, 20,* 33–65.

Radke-Yarrow, M., & Sherman, T. (1990). Hard growing: Children who survive. In R. E. Rolf, A. S. Masten, D. Cicchetti, K. H. Nuecherlein, & S. Weintraub (Eds.), *Risk and protective factors in the development of psychopathology* (pp. 97–119). New York, NY: Cambridge University Press.

Raiford, S. E., Weiss, L. G., Rolfhus, E., & Coalson, D. (2005/2008). *WISC-IV technical report no. 4 (2008 Update): General Ability Index.* San Antonio, TX: Pearson.

Reschly, D. J. (2000). The present and future status of school psychology in the United States. *School Psychology Review, 29,* 507–522.

Reynolds, C. R., & Kamphaus, R. W. (2003). *Reynolds Intellectual Assessment Scales (RIAS) and the Reynolds Intellectual Screening Test (RIST): Professional manual.* Lutz, FL: PAR.

Reynolds, C. R., & Shaywitz, S. E. (2009). Response to Intervention: Ready or not? Or, from Wait-to-Fail to Watch-Them-Fail. *School Psychology Quarterly, 24,* 130–145.

Reynolds, M. R., Keith, T. Z., Fine, J. G., Fisher, M. E., & Low, J. A. (2007). Confirmatory factor structure of the Kaufman Assessment Battery for Children–Second Edition: Consistency with Cattell-Horn Carroll theory. *School Psychology Quarterly, 22,* 511–539.

Ritchie, L. J., & Tuokko, H. (2010). Patterns of cognitive decline, conversion rates, and predictive validity for 3 Models of MCI. *American Journal of Alzheimer's Disease & Other Dementias, 25,* 592–603.

Robertson, S. G., Pfeiffer, S. I., & Taylor, N. (2011). Serving the gifted: A national survey of school psychologists. *Psychology in the Schools, 48,* 786–799.

Robinson, C. S., Menchetti, B. M., & Torgesen, J. K. (2002). Toward a two-factor theory of one type of mathematics disabilities. *Learning Disabilities Research & Practice, 17,* 81–90.

Robinson, N. M. (2008). The social world of gifted children and youth. In S. I. Pfeiffer (Ed.), *Handbook of giftedness in children: Psycho-educational theory, research, and best practices* (pp. 33–51). New York, NY: Springer Science.

Roedell, W. C. (1989). Early development of gifted children. In J. VanTassel-Baska & P. Olszewski-Kubilius (Eds.), *Patterns of influence on gifted learners: The home, the self, and the school* (pp. 13–28). New York, NY: Teachers College Press.

Roid, G. H. (2003a). *Stanford-Binet Intelligence Scales, Fifth Edition: Examiner's manual.* Rolling Meadows, IL: Riverside.

Roid, G. H. (2003b). *Stanford-Binet Intelligence Scales, Fifth Edition: Interpretive manual. Expanded guide to the interpretation of SB5 test results.* Rolling Meadows, IL: Riverside.

Roid, G. H. (2003c). *Stanford-Binet Intelligence Scales, Fifth Edition: Technical manual.* Rolling Meadows, IL: Riverside.

Rotigel, J. V. (2003). Understanding the young gifted child: Guidelines for parents, families, and educators. *Early Childhood Education Journal, 30,* 209–214.

Rules and Regulations. (2006, August 14). *Federal Register, 71,* 46647.

Rutter, M. (1978). Prevalence and types of dyslexia. In A. L. Benton & D. Pearl (Eds.), *Dyslexia: An appraisal of current knowledge* (pp. 5–28). New York, NY: Oxford University Press.

Rutter, M. (1987). Psychosocial resilience and protective mechanism. *American Journal of Orthopsychiatry, 57,* 316–331.

Rutter, M., & Yule, W. (1973). Specific reading retardation. In L. Mann & D. Sabatino (Eds.), *The first review of special education* (pp. 49–62). Philadelphia, PA: JSE Press.

Rutter, M., & Yule, W. (1975). The concept of specific reading retardation. *Journal of Child Psychology and Psychiatry, 16,* 181–197.

Saklofske, D. H., Weiss, L. G., Raiford, S. E., & Prifitera, A. (2006). Advanced interpretive issues with the WISC-IV Full Scale IQ and General Ability Index scores. In L. G. Weiss, D. H. Saklofske, A. Prifitera, & J. A. Holdnack (Eds.), *WISC-IV advanced clinical interpretation* (pp. 99–138). Burlington, MA: Academic Press.

Sankar-DeLeeuw, N. (2004). Case studies of gifted kindergarten children: Profiles of promise. *Roeper Review, 26,* 192–207.

Scarmeas, N., & Stern, Y. (2003). Cognitive reserve and lifestyle. *Journal of Clinical and Experimental Neuropsychology, 25,* 625–633.

Schalock, R. L., and the Ad Hoc Committee on Terminology and Classification. (2010). *Intellectual disability: Definition, classification, and systems of supports* (11th ed.). Washington, DC: American Association on Intellectual and Developmental Disabilities.

Schalock, R. L., Luckasson, R. A., Shogren, K. A., Borthwick-Duffy, S., Bradley, V., Buntinx, W. H., . . . Yeager, M. H. (2007). The renaming of mental retardation: Understanding the change to the term intellectual disability. *Intellectual and Developmental Disabilities, 45,* 116–124.

Schrank, F. A., & Flanagan, D. P. (Eds.) (2003). *WJ III clinical use and interpretation: Scientist-practitioner perspectives.* San Diego, CA: Academic Press.

Scruggs, T. E., & Mastropieri, M. A. (2002). On babies and bathwater: Addressing the problems of identification of learning disabilities. *Learning Disability Quarterly, 25,* 155–168.

Shallice, T. (1982). Specific impairments of planning. *Philosophical Transactions of the Royal Society of London Series B: Biological Sciences, 298,* 199–209.

Shaywitz, S. E., Escobar, M. D., Shaywitz, B. A., Fletcher, J. M., & Makuch, R. (1992). Distribution and temporal stability of dyslexia in an epidemiological sample of 414 children followed longitudinally. *New England Journal of Medicine, 326,* 145–150.

Siegle, D., & McCoach, D. B. (2010). Redefining giftedness for a new century: Shifting the paradigm. *Journal of Advanced Academics, 22,* 6–8.

Silverman, L. K. (Ed.) (1993). *Counseling the gifted and talented.* Denver, CO: Love.

Silverman, L. K. (2002a). Asynchronous development. In M. Neihart, S. Reis, N. Robinson, & S. Moon (Eds.), *The social and emotional development of gifted children: What do we know?* National Association for Gifted Children (pp. 31–37). Waco, TX: Prufrock Press.

Silverman, L. K. (2002b). *Upside-down brilliance: The visual-spatial learner.* Denver, CO: DeLeon.

Silverman, L. K. (2009). Asynchrony. In B. Kerr (Ed.), *Encyclopedia of giftedness, creativity, and talent* (Vol. 1, pp. 67–70). Thousand Oaks, CA: Sage.

Silverman, L. K. (2012). Asynchronous development: A key to counseling the gifted. In T. L. Cross & J. R. Cross (Eds.), *Handbook for counselors serving students with gifts and talents* (pp. 261–279). Waco, TX: Prufrock.

Snowdon D. A., Greiner, L. H., Mortimer, J. A., Riley, K. P., Greiner, P. A., & Markesbery, W. R. (1997). Brain infarction and the clinical expression of Alzheimer disease. The Nun Study. *Journal of the American Medical Association, 277,* 813–817.

Spearman, C. (1904). General intelligence: Objectively determined and measured. *American Journal of Psychology, 15,* 201–293.

Spearman, C. (1927). *The abilities of man: Their nature and measurement.* New York, NY: Macmillan.

Stage, S. A., Abbott, R. D., Jenkins, J. R., & Berninger, V. W. (2003). Predicting response to early reading intervention from verbal IQ, reading-related language abilities, attention ratings, and verbal IQ-word reading discrepancy: Failure to validate discrepancy method. *Journal of Learning Disabilities, 36,* 24–33.

Stanley, J. C. (1990). Leta Hollingworth's contributions to above-level testing of the gifted. *Roeper Review, 13,* 166–171.

Stanovich, K. E. (1991a). Conceptual and empirical problems with discrepancy definitions of reading disability. *Learning Disability Quarterly, 14,* 269–280.

Stanovich, K. E. (1991b). Discrepancy definitions of reading disability: Has intelligence led us astray? *Reading Research Quarterly, 26,* 7–29.

Stanovich, K. E., & Siegel, L. S. (1994). Phenotypic performance profiles of children with reading disabilities: A regression-based test of the phonological-core variable difference model. *Journal of Educational Psychology, 86,* 24–53.

Stern, Y. (2002). What is cognitive reserve? Theory and research application of the reserve concept. *Journal of the International Neuropsychological Society, 8,* 448–460.

Stern, Y. (2009). Cognitive reserve. *Neuropsychologia, 47,* 2015–2028.

Stuebing, K. K., Fletcher, J. M., LeDoux, J. M., Lyon, G. R., Shaywitz, S. E., & Shaywitz, B. A. (2002). Validity of IQ-discrepancy classifications of reading disabilities: A meta-analysis. *American Educational Research Journal, 39,* 469–518.

Swanson, H. L. (2003). Does IQ and reading level influence treatment outcomes? Implications for the definition of learning disabilities. *Advances in Learning and Behavioral Disabilities, 16,* 205–222.

Swanson, H. L. (2010). What about IQ again and avoiding Poison Oak. *New Times for DLD* [Newsletter for the Division for Learning Disabilities special interest group of the Council for Exceptional Children], *28*(1), 1–3.

te Nijenhuis, J., & Hartmann, P. (2006). Spearman's "law of diminishing returns" in samples of Dutch and immigrant children and adults, *Intelligence, 34,* 437–447.

Terman, L. M. (1916). *The measurement of intelligence.* Cambridge, MA: Riverside Press.

Terman, L. M. (1925). *Genetic studies of genius: Vol. 1. Mental and physical traits of a thousand gifted children.* Stanford, CA: Stanford University Press.

Terman, L. M. (1931). The gifted child. In C. Murchison (Ed.), *A handbook of child psychology* (pp. 568–584). Worcester, MA: Clark University Press.

Terman, L. M., & Merrill, M. A. (1937). *Measuring intelligence: A guide to the administration of the new revised Stanford-Binet tests of intelligence.* Boston, MA: Houghton Mifflin.

Terman, L. M., & Merrill, M. A. (1973). *Stanford-Binet Intelligence Scale: 1973 norms edition.* Boston, MA: Houghton Mifflin.

Terrassier, J.-C. (1985). Dyssynchrony—uneven development. In J. Freeman (Ed.), *The psychology of gifted children: Perspectives on development and education* (pp. 265–274). New York, NY: Wiley.

Thompson, B. (2005). Review of Wechsler Intelligence Scale for Children—Fourth Edition. In R. Spies & B. Plake (Eds.), *The mental measurements yearbook* (16th ed., pp. 262–263). Lincoln, NE: Buros Institute of Mental Measurements.

Thorndike, R. L., Hagen, E. P., & Sattler, J. M. (1986). *The Stanford-Binet intelligence scale: Fourth edition.* Itasca, IL: Riverside.

Thurstone, L. L. (1938). *Primary mental abilities.* Chicago, IL: University of Chicago Press.

Tolan, S. S. (1994). Giftedness as asynchronous development. *Tip Network News, 4*(1), 1, 7. Retrieved from www.stephanietolan.com/gt_as_asynch.htm

Tran, L., Sanchez, T., Arellano, B., & Swanson, H. L. (2011). A meta-analysis of the RTI literature for children at risk for reading disabilities. *Journal of Learning Disabilities, 44,* 283–295.

Undheim, J. O. (1981). On intelligence: II. A neo-Spearman model to replace Cattell's theory of fluid and crystallized intelligence. *Scandinavian Journal of Psychology, 22,* 181–187.

U.S. Department of Education, Office of Special Education and Rehabilitative Services. (2002). *A new era: Revitalizing special education for children and their families.* Washington, DC: U.S. Department of Education Publications Center.

Van Tassel-Baska, J., Feng, A. X., & Evans, B. L. (2007). Patterns of identification and performance among gifted students identified through performance tasks: A three-year analysis. *Gifted Child Quarterly, 51,* 218–231.

Vellutino, F. R., Scanlon, D M., & Lyon, G. R. (2000). Differentiating between difficult-to-remediate and readily remediated poor readers: More evidence against the IQ-achievement discrepancy definition of reading disability. *Journal of Learning Disabilities, 33,* 223–238.

Walker, B., Hafenstein, N. L., & Crow-Enslow, L. (1999). Meeting the needs of gifted learners in the early childhood classroom. *Young Children, 54*(1), 32–36.

Ward, K. E., Rothlisberg, D. E., McIntosh, D. E., & Bradley, M. H. (2011). Assessing the SB-V factor structure in a sample of preschool children. *Psychology in the Schools, 48,* 454–463.

Wasserman, J. D. (2007). Intellectual assessment of exceptionally and profoundly gifted children. In K. Kay, D. Robson, & J. F. Brenneman (Eds.), *High IQ kids: Collected insights, information and personal stories from the experts* (pp. 48–65). Minneapolis, MN: Free Spirit.

Wasserman, J. D. (2010, March). *Recent developments in psychological testing of intelligence with gifted and talented students.* Workshop presentation to the Association of Practicing Psychologists, Montgomery-Prince George's Counties, MD.

Wasserman, J. D. (2012). A history of intelligence assessment: The unfinished tapestry. In D. P. Flanagan & P. L. Harrison (Eds.), *Contemporary intellectual assessment: Theories, tests, and issues* (3rd ed., pp. 3–55). New York, NY: Guilford Press.

Wasserman, J. D., & Maccubbin, E. M. (2004). *Dark science: A critical review of the Woodcock-Johnson III Tests of Cognitive Abilities.* Unpublished test review.

Watkins, M. W. (2000). Cognitive profile analysis: A shared professional myth. *School Psychology Quarterly, 15,* 465–479.

Watkins, M. W. (2003). IQ subtest analysis: Clinical acumen or clinical illusion? *The Scientific Review of Mental Health Practice: Objective Investigations of Controversial and Unorthodox Claims in Clinical Psychology, Psychiatry, and Social Work, 2*(2), 118–141.

Watkins, M. W. (2006). Orthogonal higher-order structure of the Wechsler Intelligence Scale for Children—Fourth Edition. *Psychological Assessment, 18,* 123–125.

Watkins, M. W. (2010). Structure of the Wechsler Intelligence Scale for Children—Fourth Edition among a national sample of referred students. *Psychological Assessment, 22,* 782–787.

Watkins, M. W., & Canivez, G. L. (2004). Temporal stability of WISC-III subtest composite: Strengths and weaknesses. *Psychological Assessment, 16,* 133–138.

Watkins, M. W., Wilson, S. M., Kotz, K. M., Carbone, M. C., & Babula, T. (2006). Factor structure of the Wechsler Intelligence Scale for Children—Fourth Edition among referred students. *Educational and Psychological Measurement, 66,* 975–983.

Webb, J. T., Gore, J. L., Amend, E. W., & DeVries, A. R. (2007). *A parent's guide to gifted children.* Scottsdale, AZ: Great Potential Press.

Wechsler, D. (1925). On the specificity of emotional reactions. *Journal of Psychology, 36,* 424–426.

Wechsler, D. (1939). *The measurement of adult intelligence.* Baltimore, MD: Williams & Wilkins.

Wechsler, D. (1949). *Wechsler Intelligence Scale for Children manual.* New York, NY: Psychological Corporation.

Wechsler, D. (1950). Cognitive, conative, and non-intellective intelligence. *American Psychologist, 5,* 78–83.

Wechsler, D. (1955). *Wechsler Adult Intelligence Scale manual.* New York, NY: Psychological Corporation.

Wechsler, D. (1958). Intelligence et fonction cérébrale. *Revue de Psychologie Appliquée, 8,* 143–147.

Wechsler, D. (1961). Intelligence, memory, and the aging process. In P. Hoch & J. Zubin (Eds.), *Psychopathology of aging* (pp. 152–159). New York, NY: Grune & Stratton.

Wechsler, D. (1967). *Wechsler Preschool and Primary Scale of Intelligence.* New York, NY: Psychological Corporation.

Wechsler, D. (1975). A conversation with Dr. David Wechsler [Interviewers: Jerome E. Doppelt and Roger T. Lennon]. Unpublished transcript of interview. San Antonio, TX: Psychological Corporation.

Wechsler, D. (1981). The psychometric tradition: Developing the Wechsler Adult Intelligence Scale. *Contemporary Educational Psychology, 6,* 82–85.

Wechsler, D. (2002). *Wechsler Preschool and Primary Scale of Intelligence—Third Edition (WPPSI-III).* San Antonio, TX: Psychological Corporation.

Wechsler, D. (2003a). *Wechsler Intelligence Scale for Children—Fourth Edition (WISC-IV): Administration and scoring manual.* San Antonio, TX: Psychological Corporation.

Wechsler, D. (2003b). *Wechsler Intelligence Scale for Children—Fourth Edition (WISC-IV): Technical and interpretive manual.* San Antonio, TX: Psychological Corporation.

Wechsler, D. (2008a). *Wechsler Adult Intelligence Scale—Fourth Edition (WAIS-IV): Administration and scoring manual.* San Antonio, TX: Pearson.

Wechsler, D. (2008b). *Wechsler Adult Intelligence Scale—Fourth Edition (WAIS-IV): Technical and interpretive manual.* San Antonio, TX: Pearson.

Wechsler, D. (2012). *Wechsler Abbreviated Scale of Intelligence—Second Edition (WASI-II) manual.* San Antonio, TX: Pearson.

Wechsler, D., Kaplan, E., Fein, D., Kramer, J., Morris, R., Delis, D., & Maerlender, A. (2004). *Wechsler Intelligence Scale for Children Fourth Edition—Integrated (WISC-IV Integrated) administration and scoring manual.* San Antonio, TX: Harcourt Assessment.

Weider, A. (1995). An interview with Arthur Weider/Interviewer: John D. Wasserman. *Unpublished transcript of interview.* (Available from interviewer.)

Weiss, L. G., Saklofske, D. H., Schwartz, D. M., Prifitera, A., & Courville, T. (2006). Advanced clinical interpretation of WISC-IV index scores. In L. G. Weiss, D. H. Saklofske, A. Prifitera, & J. A. Holdnack (Eds.), *WISC-IV advanced clinical interpretation* (pp. 139–179). Burlington, MA: Academic Press.

Wendling, B. J., & Mather, N. (2009). *Essentials of evidence-based academic interventions.* Hoboken, NJ: Wiley.

Werner, E. E. (1993). Risk, resilience, and recovery: Perspectives from the Kauai Longitudinal Study. *Development and Psychopathology, 5,* 503–515.

Werner, E. E. (2000). Protective factors and individual resilience. In S. J. Meisels & J. P. Shonkoff (Eds.), *Handbook of early childhood intervention* (2nd ed., pp. 115–132). New York, NY: Cambridge University Press.

Werner, H. (1948). *Comparative psychology of mental development.* New York, NY: International Universities Press.

Widiger, T. A. (2011). A shaky future for personality disorders. *Personality Disorders: Theory, Research, and Treatment, 2,* 54–67.

Williams, T. H., McIntosh, D. E., Dixon, F., Newton, J. H., & Youman, E. (2010). A confirmatory factor analysis of the Stanford-Binet Intelligence Scales, Fifth Edition, with a high-achieving sample. *Psychology in the Schools, 47,* 1071–1083.

Winsler, A., & Naglieri, J. A. (2003). Overt and covert verbal problem-solving strategies: Developmental trends in use, awareness, and relations with task performance in children age 5 to 17. *Child Development, 74,* 659–678.

Winsler, A., Naglieri, J. A., & Manfra, L. (2006). Children's search strategies and accompanying verbal and motor strategic behavior: Developmental trends and relations with task performance among children age 5 to 17. *Cognitive Development, 21,* 232–248.

Wolf, T. H. (1973). *Alfred Binet.* Chicago, IL: University of Chicago Press.

Woodcock, R. W. (1977). *Woodcock-Johnson Psycho-Educational Battery. Technical report.* Boston, MA: Teaching Resources.

Woodcock, R. W. (1993). An information processing view of Gf-Gc theory. *Journal of Psychoeducational Assessment Monograph Series: Woodcock-Johnson Psycho-Educational Assessment Battery–Revised*, pp. 80–102. Cordova, TN: Psychoeducational Corporation.

Woodcock, R. W. (1998a). Extending Gf-Gc theory into practice. In J. J. McArdle & R. W. Woodcock (Eds.), *Human cognitive abilities in theory and practice* (pp. 137–156). Mahwah, NJ: Erlbaum.

Woodcock, R. W., & Johnson, M. B. (1977). *Woodcock-Johnson Psycho-Educational Battery.* Boston, MA: Teaching Resources Corporation.

Woodcock, R. W., & Johnson, M. B. (1989, 1990). *Woodcock-Johnson Psycho-Educational Battery—Revised.* Allen, TX: DLM.

Woodcock, R. W., McGrew, K. S., & Mather, N. (2001a, 2007a). *Woodcock-Johnson III Tests of Cognitive Abilities.* Rolling Meadows, IL: Riverside.

Woodcock, R. W., McGrew, K. S., & Mather, N. (2001b, 2007b). *Woodcock-Johnson III Tests of Achievement.* Rolling Meadows, IL: Riverside.

Woodcock, R. W., McGrew, K. S., Mather, N., & Schrank, F. A. (2003, 2007). *Woodcock-Johnson III Diagnostic Supplement to the Tests of Cognitive Abilities.* Rolling Meadows, IL: Riverside.

Zhu, J., Cayton, T., Weiss, L., & Gabel, A. (2008). *WISC-IV extended norms (WISC-IV technical report no. 7).* San Antonio, TX: Pearson.

CHAPTER 19

# Assessment of Neuropsychological Functioning

TULIO M. OTERO, KENNETH PODELL, PHILIP DeFINA, AND ELKHONON GOLDBERG

## HISTORICAL ROOTS

Although the term *neuropsychology* appears to have been first used formally by Sir William Osler in 1913 (Bruce, 1985), Benton (1988) viewed it as a discipline representing the convergence of several fields of study: neurology and psychology, neuroanatomy and neurophysiology, and neurochemistry and neuropharmacology. Neuropsychology, although it is closely related to behavioral neurology, distinguishes itself from both neuropsychiatry and behavioral neurology by its focus on clarifying the mechanisms underlying both abnormal *and* normal behavior. Neuropsychiatry and behavioral neurology focus on the diagnosis and treatment of abnormal behavior only (Bradshaw & Mattingley, 1995). Neuropsychology is the study of brain–behavior relationships. Clinical neuropsychology "is a specialty area... that focuses on how the brain functions within the normal individual and what happens to an individual with brain illness or brain injury. It is considered applied because it deals with the assessment, diagnosis and treatment of those individuals with brain illness or injury" (Holtz, 2011, p. 4).

Neuropsychology and neuroscience in general have a history that is quite a bit older than one would think. Thus, before examining modern neuropsychology and neuropsychological assessment, a brief historical review is in order. Written records of the nervous system date back as far as 1700 BC, when ancient Egyptians appear to have engaged in treating head and brain injuries. For example,

the Edwin Smith Papyrus (2500–3000 BC) provides the earliest written record of medical treatment. Among the 48 cases described are included references to head and brain injury. These descriptions suggest, for the first time, that brain functions are localized in specific parts of the brain. There are references to weakness on one side of the body (hemiplegia) and the buildup of pressure, probably a blood clot in this case. The Egyptian physician was unclear about the relationship between the side of the hemiplegia and the body location because he did not yet know that hemiplegia occurs on the side opposite to the lesion. The physician may have been confused by the presence of a contra-coup injury, in which a brain lesion occurs on the opposite side of the brain from the initial impact (Gross, 1998). But the bulk of knowledge about the brain and its functions did not become known until the 17th century. This is when men like Andres Vesalius, René Descartes, and Thomas Willis began studying the human nervous system and how it worked.

Vesalius (1514–1564) was the first to conduct careful observations of brain anatomy and introduced the anatomical theater in which students and doctors could watch dissections from above. Descartes (1596–1650) was the first scholar of note to make statements about the brain having an effect on behavior. He proposed that movements and subsequent behaviors were caused by the flow of "animal spirits" through the nerves. Descartes saw the nerves as hollow tubes that transported the fluid causing muscles to be stimulated. This is known as the mechanistic view of behavior. The anatomy of the brain was detailed and published by Willis in 1664. Willis had a different view of the brain than did Descartes. He felt that the structures of the brain itself had influence on behavior rather than the cerebral spinal fluid or the ventricles. Thomas also found that there were two types of tissue in the brain—gray matter and white matter. The gray matter made up the outer cortex of the brain while the white matter was the fibrous connective tissue found elsewhere in the brain.

Franz Joseph Gall (1758–1828) introduced the idea that the brain was comprised of separate organs, each *localized* and responsible for a basic psychological trait. For the times, Gall's concepts on brain localization were revolutionary and met with opposition by religious leaders who considered his theory as contrary to religious beliefs. Many scientists questioned the scientific validity of his assertions. Gall developed "cranioscopy," a method to determine the personality and development of mental and moral faculties on the basis of the external shape of the skull. (Cranioscopy was later renamed *phrenology*.) Gall was an accomplished scientist who conducted experiments and extensive structural analyses of the brain (human and animal). He found that the larger the brain, the more complex, flexible, and intelligent behavior the organism could engage in. He also stated that the brain was the center of higher mental activity (Holtz, 2011). Phrenology was later discredited by others who showed that there is no relationship between the bumps on the skull and the underlying brain tissue, nor is there a relationship between the size of an area of brain and the size of the function that it supports. (Skulls are hard, brains are not.) Although he was almost completely incorrect, Gall's phrenology represents the beginning of the strong modern-day localizationist doctrine.

Localization theory postulates that there are specific areas of the brain that perform specific jobs. This concept was supported by the likes of Paul Broca (1824–1880), who was interested in how damage to the brain affected people. One famous case was dealt with a man named "Tan," so named because that is all he could say. After the man died, Broca performed an autopsy and found that a portion of the man's left frontal cortex was damaged by a lesion. From studying the brains of Tan brain and others, Broca found that that specific area of the brain had control over the expression of language. The people with damage to this area can still read and write but have trouble verbalizing. The third convolution of the inferior posterior frontal lobe has since become known as Broca's area, and patients with damage to Broca's area are referred to as having Broca's aphasia.

Several years after Broca presented his cases of frontal lobe lesions, Wernicke (1848–1904) presented cases in which patients had lesions of the superior posterior part of the left hemisphere and had trouble comprehending language. He suspected a relation between the functioning of hearing and that of speech, and he described cases in which aphasic patients had lesions in the auditory projection area that differed from those described by Broca in several important ways. This resulted in Wernicke's idea that different aspects of language were localized. On the basis of Wernicke's observations, the modern doctrine of component process localization and disconnection syndromes developed. This doctrine states that complex mental functions, such as language, represent the combined processing of a number of subcomponent processes represented in widely different areas of the brain and that, in order for these to work, several brain functions and the respective regions must interact.

Localization ideas were challenged by the study of how animals and people recovered function after some injury. The work of Jean Pierre Flourens (1794–1867) is illustrative. Flourens's experimental method consisted of removing parts of the brains of animals to study any changes in behavior produced by these surgeries. He concluded that function is more a product of the amount of damage than the location of where the damage occurred. Furthermore, Flourens observed that if there was enough intact tissue following brain damage, the remaining tissue would compensate and take over the function of the missing area. After the removal of a piece of cortex, with the passage of time, animals with induced lesions would recover to the point that they seemed normal. This pattern of loss and recovery of function held for all Flourens's cortex experiments, seeming to refute the idea that different cortical areas have specialized functions. Other animal experiments conducted by Friedrich L. Gloatz (1834–1902) confirmed Flourens's findings and concluded that the removal of parts of the cortex did not eliminate any function completely; rather, it appeared to reduce all functions to some extent. These findings were a strong argument against localization of function and even cast doubt on the role of the cortex and behavior.

Sergei Sergeievich Korsakoff (1854–1900) was a Russian neuropsychiatrist who in 1887 observed a correlation between memory disorder and toxic metabolic states. His early work also included patients who were heavy and chronic abusers of alcohol. Wernicke observed similar cases that also included acute confusion and other neurological abnormalities. It became clear that the cases seen by Korsakoff and Wernicke were essentially different examples of the same disorder. It was observed that these patients suffered a nutritional deficiency that resulted in lesions of structures in the middle part of the brain, structures involved in remembering new information. The pattern of lesions and symptoms is now referred to as Wernicke-Korsakoff syndrome. Its existence established the fact that memory is mediated by structures in the temporal lobes of the brain.

John Hughlings-Jackson (1835–1911) put forth the concept of *hierarchical organization* of brain functioning. He proposed that each nervous system was organized as a functional hierarchy. Each successively higher level controlled more complex aspects of behavior and did so by means of the lower levels. Hughlings-Jackson suggested that diseases were tissue damage that affects the highest level the brain. Brain lesions to the higher centers would produce *dissolution*. That is, he observed that animals with brain lesions would still have a repertoire of behaviors, but the behaviors would be simpler and were similar to those of animals that had not yet evolved the missing brain structure. Hughlings-Jackson put forth other novel concepts of brain–behavior relationships. For example, he proposed that all parts of the brain could contribute to behavior. In the case of language functioning, he believed that every part of the brain contributes to language, with each part making some special contribution. The relevant question was not where language is localized but what unique contribution each part of the cortex makes.

Alexander Romanovich Luria (1902–1977) was a famous Soviet neuropsychologist and developmental psychologist. He established the theory of function systems, which is the culmination of the localization and connectionist theories begun by Wernicke. Luria viewed the brain as a functional mosaic, the parts of which interact in different combinations to subserve cognitive processing (Luria, 1973). He conceptualized four interconnected levels of brain–behavior relationships and neurocognitive disorders that clinicians need to know: the structure of the brain, the functional organization based on structure, syndromes and impairments arising in brain disorders, and clinical methods of assessment (Korkman, 1999). Luria's theoretical formulations, methods, and ideas are articulated in such seminal works as *Human Brain and Psychological Processes* (1966), *The Working Brain* (1973), *Higher Cortical Functions in Man* (1980), and *The Working Brain* (1973). There is no area of the brain that functions without input from other areas; thus, integration is a key principle of brain function within the Lurian framework. Cognition and behavior then result from an interaction of complex brain activity across

various areas. (For a thorough presentation, see Naglieri & Otero, 2011.) Luria's conceptualization consists of three interacting functional systems:

1. The attention and arousal system, mediated by the brain stem and other subcortical structures
2. The sensory and memory system, located in the posterior parts of the brain
3. The motor control, planning, and evaluation system, utilizing the basal ganglia, cerebellum, motor parts of the cerebral cortex, and the prefrontal cortex

At approximately the same time that Luria was studying the functions of various areas of the brain, Roger Sperry (1913–1994) began studying split-brain subjects: those in whom the corpus callosum had been severed. Sperry demonstrated important consequences for each hemisphere after separation of the corpus callosum. During independent testing of the hemispheres, the left hemisphere was more verbal, rational, and analytical while the right was more spatial and emotional. In 1981 Sperry received a Nobel Prize for his work.

At about the same time Sperry was conducting his initial work on split-brain patients, Ward Halstead (1908–1968) developed the first neuropsychology laboratory in 1935 at the University of Chicago. While there, Halsted began the task of assessing brain impairment. He not only attempted to develop tests to measure brain impairment, but also he wanted his tests to be reliable and valid measures of the constructs he was studying. He developed, in collaboration with Ralph Reitan, the Halstead-Reitan neuropsychological test battery, which has been the most popular and most widely used fixed neuropsychological battery of its kind in the United States and abroad for approximately 50 years (Holtz, 2011). Halstead worked almost exclusively with neurology patients—individuals who had diseases or damage to the central nervous system—and developed assessment devices that differentiated between patients with brain damage and those without.

While at the University of Nebraska, Charles Golden (1949–) developed the Luria-Nebraska Neuropsychological Battery based on Alexander Luria's original ideas of brain functioning (Charles, Ariel, & McKay, 1982). Whereas the Halsted-Reitan neuropsychological test battery was designed to be administered in a standardized fashion to all subjects and allowed for comparability between subjects, the Luria-Nebraska Neuropsychological Battery was designed to fit the needs of individual patients. Administration of test items could be altered to fit individual needs (the flexible battery approach).

The application of Luria's conceptualization of brain function is further represented in a collection of standardized tests called the Cognitive Assessment System (Naglieri & Das, 1997). The authors refined the psychometric characteristics of tests for the assessment of the neurocognitive processes described by Luria to the assessment of children and adolescents. In doing so they also strove to articulate how the assessment of these neuropsychological concepts can be linked to academic and behavioral problems, thus leading to more accurate diagnosis and treatment.

Neuropsychology as a profession has been influenced by many historical factors that have helped to develop and shape the field, both experimentally and clinically.

## NEUROPSYCHOLOGY TODAY

Various internal and external forces have shaped researchers and clinicians in the field of neuropsychology. Internal forces include cutting-edge neuroimaging technology, such as functional magnetic resonance imaging (fMRI), magnetoencephalography (MEG), diffusion tensor imaging (DTI); the development and application of more sophisticated statistical techniques; the development of new neuropsychological tests; and the expansion into new clinical areas (such as sport-related concussion and several of the developmental disabilities). One of the strongest external forces influencing and molding the future of neuropsychology is economics. The current situation in health care has had a particular impact on the development of neuropsychology, especially as a clinical discipline. Numerous graduate and postgraduate training sites have closed due to lack of funding or budget cuts, and up to 23% of graduate students do not match to an internship site (American Psychological Association, 2011). Paradoxically, there has been a slight increase in the number of students entering graduate psychology programs in general with women representing a majority (American Psychological Association Women's Programs Office, 2006). Consequently many students cannot find adequate training; moreover, even if they do find such training, many cannot find an acceptable position. However, the shrinking health-care dollar is causing neuropsychologists to rethink how they administer neuropsychological services (a much-needed self-check) and to be creative and develop or enter new venues for generating revenue.

Probably the best example of new revenue opportunities is the explosion of forensic neuropsychology (Heilbronner, 2004). More and more neuropsychologists have recognized the lucrative area of forensic practice. Although some truly see forensic neuropsychology as a science, others see it merely as a way of increasing revenue. This situation has caused exponential growth in clinical activity, which has in turn stimulated the critical research required to scientifically support this area of neuropsychological practice. This research, in turn, lends support to clinical application and the reputations of neuropsychologists (and probably psychology as a whole) in the forensic arena. Neuropsychologists are expanding clinical practice and research to other fields as well, such as education, business, and sports (sport-related concussion assessment and return-to-play decisions). A growing number of psychologists have been seeking specific training in the subspecialty of school neuropsychology. The focus of this recent specialty involves the integration of neuropsychological principles into educational practice (D. Miller, 2007). Growth in the field has been fueled by revisions of federal education law, national task force reports, and an increase in the number of children with birth trauma and other medical illnesses with direct correlates to later academic and behavior concerns; the growing acknowledgment within the medical and education communities of the neurobiological bases of childhood learning and behavioral disorders; the increased use of medications with school-age children, often including multiple medications with unknown combined risks or potential interactions; and the fact that neuropsychological reports by psychologists not trained in educational matters are often not useful to the schools in developing educationally relevant interventions for children and adolescents (D. Miller, 2010).

## ISSUES IN NEUROPSYCHOLOGY

The rest of this chapter focuses on important issues in neuropsychology. Our intent is to selectively introduce advances and explain some of their basic components. We focus on how these new developments advance experimental and clinical neuropsychology, how they contribute to our knowledge of brain–behavior relationships and treatment of patients, and how they are shaping the field of neuropsychology as a whole.

### Developments in Clinical Application

#### Sport-Related Concussion Assessment

Two major research and practice areas define sport neuropsychology today: sport-related concussion and neurocognitive/medical well-being. Sport-related concussion defines a phenomenon of mild traumatic brain injury (MTBI) that occurs within a sport context. For example, when a hockey player is smashed into the boards and comes off the ice wobbly, confused, and amnestic for the event, an instance of sport-related concussion has occurred (Webbe, 2010a). Between 2002 and 2006, 144,000 children were seen in emergency and outpatient departments for concussion. Most concussions happen in boys and are sport related, with football and ice hockey being the most common sports associated with concussion (Contemporary Pediatrics Staff, 2010). Female participation in sports has increased dramatically in recent decades representing 42% of high school and college athletes. Female college athletes in soccer and basketball sustained significantly more concussions than males (Agel, Evans, Dick, Putukian, & Marshall, 2007): significant declines on simple and complex reaction times compared to baseline have been noted on the computerized Concussion Resolution Index (CRI) compared to males (Broshek, Kaushik, Freeman, Erlanger, Weebe, & Barth, 2005). Because concussions are no longer considered trivial, neuropsychologists are becoming ever more important in helping sport teams assess and manage sport-related concussions.

Large epidemiological studies by J. W. Powell and others (Barth et al., 1989; Guskiewicz, Weaver, Padua, & Garrett, 2000; J. W. Powell & Barber-Foss, 1999) have shown that 5% to 10% of football players are concussed each year. Approximately 5% of participants in various others sports (e.g., soccer and field hockey) suffer the same trauma. In American high school football alone, that would indicate approximately 25,500 concussions per season (a base rate of 2,460 concussions per 100,000 high school football players). McCrea, Hammeke, Olsenq, Leo, & Guskiewicz (2004) have shown that the rate of concussion in college athletes has decreased from about 10% per season (Barth et al., 1989) to about 4%, probably due to rule changes and new and improved equipment (J. W. Powell, 1999).

The large number of brain injuries makes clear the need for better diagnosis, management, and treatment. This is exactly where clinical neuropsychology has played an integral part and is rapidly developing as the standard for measuring the effects of sport-related concussions and return-to-play issues (Aubry et al., 2002). Beyond creating a new area of services, neuropsychology's role in sport-related concussion assessment and management has become a key service for clinical care professional service providers and parents. For example, because of neuropsychology's role in sport-related concussion assessment, neuropsychologists are now presenting to and working with the sports medicine community, athletic trainers, and other physicians who normally would not have been aware of or utilized this service. Several medical journals, such as the *Journal of the American Medical Association*, *Journal of Sports Medicine*, and *Physician and Sports Medicine*, have featured articles written by neuropsychologists, thus also broadening neuropsychology's exposure.

One neuropsychologist who has led both clinical and experimental neuropsychologists into the area of sport-related concussion is Mark R. Lovell. Due to his involvement with concussion committees for the National Football League (NFL) and the National Hockey League (NHL), neuropsychological testing is mandatory in the NHL, and approximately 80% of NFL teams use neuropsychological testing. Additionally, colleges, high schools, and amateur and professional sports teams worldwide have concussion safety programs and guidelines in which players undergo baseline testing during the preseason. If concussed during the season, a player is retested, and his or her results are compared to the baseline. This comparison allows for assessment of intra-individual changes, and the neuropsychologist can use the differences (or lack of differences) in scores to help the team with return-to-play decision making. Lovell and Collins (1998) have demonstrated little change (outside of practice effect) in preseason versus postseason testing in varsity college football players. However, Collins, Grindel, Lovel, Dede, Moser, and Phalin (1999) demonstrated that sport-related concussion in college football players caused significant decrement in memory and attention concentration (consistent with the initial seminal studies of Barth; see Barth et al., 1989). In addition, Collins et al. (1999) found that after a concussion, those with a prior history of concussion performed more poorly than did those without such a history. Moreover, they found that a history of learning disability was a risk factor for greater cognitive impairment following a concussion. Van Kampen, Lovell, Pardini, Collins, and Fu (2006) found that reliance on patients' self-reported symptoms after concussion is likely to result in underdiagnosis of concussion and may result in premature return to play. Neurocognitive testing increases diagnostic accuracy when used in conjunction with self-reported symptoms.

The standard protocol for performing neuropsychological evaluations in sport-related concussions is to use a serial assessment approach, starting with a baseline (e.g., preseason or prior to any concussions) neuropsychological evaluation. Typically, these computerized neuropsychological batteries are relatively short (approximately 20–25 minutes, focusing on working memory, complex attention concentration, reaction time, and anterograde memory). The typical follow-up neuropsychological evaluation is performed within 24 hours of the concussion and is followed by additional postconcussion evaluations at days 3, 5, and 7. After this point, if the athlete is still concussed, additional testing can be done weekly or every other week. Various programs differ from this pattern, but the general idea is to perform a baseline evaluation, an initial postconcussion assessment, and additional follow-up assessments to document recovery of function and help with return-to-play decision making. The role of neuropsychologists in sport-related concussions has expanded the understanding of concussions and their effects on and recovery of cognition and symptomatology. It has also increased concussion awareness in the general public—particularly parents—and has demystified some of the misconceptions about concussion and placed it alongside other common injuries (e.g., sprains) in sports. Neuropsychology has also improved how athletes' concussions are diagnosed, managed, and treated (Webbe, 2010a). The neuropsychological outcomes of sport-related concussions specific to children and adolescents has been well documented and demonstrates the neurocognitive, psychological, educational, and social sequelae (Webbe, 2010b).

Thanks to the activities of neuropsychologists and other professionals, concussions are no longer minimized or ignored; rather, they are diagnosed and treated as the injuries they are. Because of this enlightened attitude and improved awareness and diagnostic accuracy, athletes—especially younger ones—are more accurately (and frequently) diagnosed and treated. This practice allows for appropriate treatment and decreased risk of greater injury by sustaining a second concussion while still concussed from the first one; it may help to reduce greater long-term brain injury and reduce the chance of second-impact syndrome—a rare but often fatal event (Cantu, 1998). Clearly, neuropsychologists' leadership role in this area has had and will continue to have a beneficial effect on athletes.

### Forensic Neuropsychology

The word *forensic* is taken from *forensis,* the legal forum in Rome where legal proceedings were held. Forensic neuropsychology involves the application neuropsychological theory, research, methodology, and knowledge to address legal issues (Greiffenstein & Cohen, 2011). The types of referrals that forensic neuropsychologists deal with may be related to civil litigation, causality, or criminal litigation. Referral questions in civil litigation often involve determination of the presence or absence of neurological and/or psychiatric disorders. Causality-related assessments pertain to a specific event or injury, prognosis, medical necessity of treatment and/or disability status. In criminal litigation, the neuropsychological examination may be used to assist in determining competency to stand trial and issues of responsibility for the crime, or in sentencing/mitigation. The nature of the examination may range from a relatively brief clinical interview to a comprehensive examination that includes extensive psychological or neuropsychological test administration.

Probably the single area within clinical neuropsychology that has seen the greatest growth explosion is forensic neuropsychology; this is due partly to the greater demand by the legal system for expert testimony that can identify neuropsychological deficits (Nies & Sweet, 1994) and also to the potentially lucrative income associated with forensic-related activity. The one area within forensic neuropsychology that has seen the greatest growth clinically is civil litigation—usually traumatic brain injuries (TBIs) suffered in motor vehicle accidents (Ruff & Richardson, 1999). Each year, an estimated 1.7 million people sustain a TBI annually (Faul, Xu, Wald, & Coronado, 2010). Of these, 275,000 are hospitalized and 1.365 million, nearly 80%, are treated and released from an emergency department. TBI is a contributing factor to a third (30.5%) of all injury-related deaths in the United States. Among all age groups, motor vehicle crashes and traffic-related incidents were the second leading cause of TBI (17.3%) and resulted in the largest percentage of TBI-related deaths (31.8%). For a brief introduction into the area of clinical forensic neuropsychological assessment, we use MTBI as a model.

Standardized instruments are used by neuropsychologists to collect information and derive inferences about brain–behavior relationships. Technology, such as magnetic resonance imaging (MRI), fMRI, positron emission tomography (PET), computed tomography (CT), and diffusion tensor imaging, has reduced the need for neuropsychological tests to localize and access brain damage. Neuropsychological tests, however, play an important role in identifying the neurocognitive processes, or abilities, necessary for effective thinking, learning, and behaving while also allowing for judgments regarding the integrity of the brain and functional outcomes (Naglieri & Otero, 2011). It is through standardized neuropsychological instruments and other methods that the forensic psychologist presents evidence to support or refute the presence of central nervous system dysfunction. In forensic cases in which lasting MTBI sequelae is claimed, neuropsychological deficits may persist even when standard neurological examinations and neuroimaging methods fail to be sensitive to subtle deficits (Bigler & Snyder, 1995). In fact, longitudinal and case-controlled studies along with numerous case reports support the use of neuropsychological tests to assess the severity of injury and the prognosis for patients with closed head trauma, to monitor progression, and to provide measures of outcome for determining degree of recovery (Baum et al., 2008; Greve et al., 2008; Kalmar et al., 2008).

Typically, considerable monetary compensation is sought in these cases, which augments the importance of the neuropsychological evaluation. Well over half of TBI cases are mild in nature (Ruff & Richardson, 1999). Although most people with MTBI fully recover, a minority of individuals (ranging from estimates of 7–8% to 10–20%) experience longer-term effects (Bigler, 2008). In reviewing the recent literature related to the long-term neurocognitive sequelae, McAllister (2011) report that MTBI results in measurable deficits information processing speed, memory, and attention in the immediate postinjury period. Recovery from these deficits is the rule for most people, occurring over a variable period from 4 to 12 weeks. For a minority of persons with MTBI, however, recovery from these deficits may occur very slowly or remain incomplete. Individuals with MTBI often have a set of symptoms that may be experienced for weeks, months, or occasionally up to a year or more after a concussion. This constellation of symptoms has been termed the postconcussion syndrome (PCS). The most commonly reported symptoms include irritability, fatigue, difficulty concentrating, memory deficits, headache, dizziness, blurred vision, photophobia, ringing of the ears, and disinhibition and loss of temper (Goodyear & Umetsu, 2002). There has been a great deal of debate concerning persistent PCS; many suggest that it is psychologically rather than neurologically based or that patients are exaggerating symptoms or malingering in order to receive compensation (Mittenberg & Strauman, 2000; Ryan & Warden, 2003). This debate extends across both adult and pediatric populations (Lee, 2007). In one study, 732 TBI subjects and 120 general trauma comparison (TC) subjects provided new or worse symptom information at 1 month and/or 1 year postinjury. Symptom reporting at 1 year postinjury was compared in subgroups based on basic demographics, preexisting conditions, and severity of brain injury. The TBI group reported significantly more symptoms at 1 month and

1 year after injury than the TC group. Although symptom endorsement declined from 1 month to 1 year, 53% of people with TBI and 24% of TC continued to report 3 or more symptoms at 1 year postinjury. Symptom reporting in the TBI group was significantly related to age, gender, preinjury alcohol abuse, pre-injury psychiatric history, and severity of TBI. Thus, symptom reporting by a substantial number of TBI subjects continues across all severity levels at 1 year postinjury (Dikmen, Machamer, Fann, & Temkin, 2010).

Because there is no litmus test to determine the presence of residual MTBI, it can be very difficult to differentiate those who truly have residual deficits from those without deficits who are exploiting their past (recovered) injury for monetary compensation based on self-reported symptomatology only. In fact, the base rates of self-reported symptomatology cannot distinguish between groups with verified MTBI from healthy controls or from those seeking compensation for non-TBI-related injuries (Lees-Haley & Brown 1993; Lees-Haley, Fox, & Courtney, 2001). Therefore, when this difficulty is combined with the lack of any neuroimaging evidence, the neuropsychologist becomes the key to determining and proving the presence of residual MTBI with the use of symptom validity tests as part of a neuropsychological assessment. The National Academy of Neuropsychology presented a position paper on the use of symptom validity tests (SVTs) (Bush et al., 2005); it specifically recommends administration of at least two SVTs in evaluation of symptom validity (Heilbronner et al., 2009). For example, Meyer, Volbrecht, Axelrod, and Reinsch-Boothby (2011) examined a sample of 314 consecutive clinical and forensic referrals with MTBI using the Meyers Neuropsychological Battery (MNB). A comparison was made of the test performance and performance on the embedded SVTs with a control for multicolinearity utilized. The results of this study indicate that there does appear to be a relationship between internal SVT failures and overall neuropsychological test performance. Poor performance on SVTs correlates with poor performance on neuropsychological tests.

From a forensic perspective, the critical question is whether a neuropsychologist who applies various neuropsychological and psychological tests can differentiate between those who truly have residual cognitive or emotional deficits from those who are malingering, exaggerating, or even presenting with a somatoform or factitious disorder? The task of detecting suboptimal performance carries a great responsibility because the decision can determine whether services will be provided for a patient or whether the patient will receive large monetary compensation (Davies et al., 1997; McKinlay, McGowan, & Russell, 2010; Nies & Sweet, 1994). Although the rate of malingering is unknown, estimates range from 7.5% to 15% (Trueblood & Schmidt, 1993) to 18% to 33% (Binder, 1993). More recent data regarding the rate of malingering among personal injury claimants estimates range from 20% to 59% (Rubenzer, 2005). However, it is generally believed that the incidence of exaggeration of symptoms is higher than that of actual malingering (Resnick, West, & Payne, 2008).

There are several ways in which neuropsychological testing can determine whether the test score actually represents a true cognitive deficit or whether it might indicate symptom exaggeration or even malingering. Some of the procedures or tests are more sophisticated and sensitive than others. First, and foremost, the deficits (one of the most common complaints is anterograde memory impairment) must be consistent with the nature of the injury. For example, one cannot have a dense amnesia if the TBI was mild. Similarly, the deficit patterns must make neuropsychological sense and conform to known brain–behavior relationships. For example, worsening memory over time after a MTBI is not consistent with what is known about TBIs. (They are static events from which one can only recover, not worsen over time.) Another method that neuropsychologists use to detect true versus malingered or exaggerated deficits is through the use of tests specifically designed to check for suboptimal performance. Test development in the area of the assessment of malingering has flourished over the past several years, and significant strides have been made. (See Iverson & Binder, 2000; Morgan & Sweet, 2008; and Sweet, 1999, for comprehensive reviews.) The sophistication of the tests developed and refined has improved greatly over the past few years; this is important because lawyers and their clients are becoming more sophisticated and aware of these tests. In fact, plaintiff attorneys have been known to coach their clients about these tests and prepare them for any independent neuropsychological evaluation they may undergo. Such practices have led some researchers to not publish some of their normative data in journal articles in order to protect the integrity and use of the tests. (See Millis, Putnam, Adams, & Ricker, 1995; Sweet et al., 2000.)

### Forced-Choice Recognition Tests

A number of strategies typically are employed to identify malingered performance. The first involves the use of a two alternative forced-choice (e.g., 5-digit numbers) method (Hiscock & Hiscock, 1989). When these tests were first designed and employed in clinical assessments, simple binomial distribution theory was applied to interpret performance. In two-choice recognition tests, the probability of responding correctly on all items by chance alone (i.e., guessing) is 50%. Scores significantly below those predicted by chance are unlikely by chance alone; therefore, such performance is assumed to be the result of deliberate selection of incorrect answers, which is suggestive of exaggeration or malingering of deficits. Without any knowledge of the stimulus (as would occur in the case of amnesia), the patient should answer approximately 50% of the items correctly; a score significantly below 50% suggests that the patient knew the correct answer but deliberately chose the incorrect response. More recently, research has shown that patients with more severe head injury and genuine memory loss typically perform well above the chance level on two-alternative forced choice tests (Binder & Pankrantz, 1987; Binder & Willis, 1991; Guilmette, Hart, & Giuliano, 1993; Prigatano & Amin, 1993). Prigatano and Amin (1993) demonstrated that the performance of postconcussive patients and those with unequivocal history of cerebral dysfunction averaged over 99% correct compared to a group of suspected malingerers who averaged only 73.8% correct. Guilmette et al. (1993) demonstrated that a group of brain-injured and psychiatric patients obtained almost perfect scores whereas simulators obtained scores that were significantly lower. However, only 34% of the simulators obtained scores below chance level. These findings suggest that the development of cutoff scores is necessary in order to improve the sensitivity of this method. A 90% cutoff score has typically been established based on the large body of evidence, which suggests that those with genuine brain injury typically perform above this level on digit recognition procedures.

A number of forced-choice tests have been developed and are briefly reviewed here; they include the Portland Digit Recognition Test (PDRT; Binder, 1993), the Victoria Symptom Validity Test (VSVT; Slick, Hopp, & Strauss, 1998), the Recognition Memory Test (RMT; Warrington, 1984), the Validity Indicator Profile (VIP; Frederick, 1997), the Computerized Assessment of Response Bias (CARB; Allen, Conder, Green, & Cox, 1998), and the Test of Memory Malingering (TOMM; Tombaugh, 1996).

Hiscock and Hiscock (1989) developed a test requiring individuals to choose which of two 5-digit numbers was the same as a number seen prior to a brief delay. The 5-digit number is presented on a card for 5 seconds followed by a delay period, after which another card is presented with the correct choice and a foil. The foil item differs from the target item by two or more digits, including either the first or last digit. A total of 72 items are administered. These 72 items are divided into three blocks with a 5-, 10-, or 15-second delay. The examiner tells the patient that the test is difficult for those with memory deficits and. after the first and second blocks, that the test will be more difficult because of the increasing delay period.

In an attempt to improve the test's sensitivity in detecting suboptimal performance, Binder (1993) refined the Hiscock and Hiscock procedure by developing the PDRT. It is a digit recognition task with three blocks of items differentiated by the length of delay between target presentation and response. Binder's version differed from that of Hiscock and Hiscock in a number of ways such as auditory presentation of the target item followed by visual presentation of the target and distractor item and increased delay periods between presentation and response (5, 15, and 30 seconds). Research suggests that difficult items (30-second delay) are more sensitive to malingered performance than are easy items (Hiscock & Hiscock, 1989). In addition, it has an intervening activity, which requires that the patient count backward during the delay period. This activity makes the task appear even more difficult to the patient.

Binder (1992) found that non-compensation-seeking (NCS) patients with well-documented brain injury performed better than did both mild head trauma and compensation-seeking (CS) patients with well-documented brain injury on the PDRT but that the CS brain-injured group's performance was superior to that of the mild head injury group on other tests. Binder (1993) administered the PDRT and the Rey Auditory Verbal Learning Test (RAVLT) to two groups of CS patients, including a mild head injury and well-documented brain injury group and a group of NCS brain dysfunction patients. His results showed that patients with financial incentives were significantly more impaired on the PDRT but performed as well as the NCS groups did on the RAVLT. Binder and Willis (1991) demonstrated that those with affective disorders performed at a level similar to that of a group of NCS brain-dysfunction patients, which suggests that the performance of the CS groups in this study was not the result of depression. Binder concluded that poor PDRT performance significant enough to raise concern about malingering is probably not caused by either verbal memory deficits or affective disorders, and the PDRT is therefore a useful tool for the detection of exaggerated memory deficits.

Greve et al. (2008) studied the classification accuracy of the PDRT in detecting cognitive malingering in patients claiming cognitive deficits due to exposure to environmental or industrial toxins. Twenty-nine patients alleging toxic exposure were compared to 14 toxic exposure patients testing negative for evidence of malingering. The published cutoffs were associated with a false positive error rate of 0% and sensitivity of more than 50%. When criterion for a PDRT failure was a positive PDRT finding on more than one section, the False Positive rate remained 0% while sensitivity improved to about 70%. Their results indicate that a failed PDRT is an indication of malingering and not the neurological effect of a toxic substance or some other clinical phenomenon. The PDRT can be used with confidence as an indicator of negative response bias in cases of alleged exposure to neurotoxic substances.

Vickery, Berry, Hanlon-Inman, Harris, and Orey (2001) performed a meta-analysis of a number of malingering procedures. The PDRT had high specificity rates at the level of individual classification (97.3%) but only moderate sensitivity (43.3%) because of a high number of performances that were poor but above chance level (Rose, Hall, & Szalda-Petree, 1995). One suggestion to improve the PDRT has been to measure the response latency (Brandt, 1988). It is expected that purposely responding incorrectly to the test items requires increased information processing time. Brandt used a computerized version of the test and found that when response latency and total number correct were used in combination, 32% fewer classification errors were made and the overall hit rate increased from 72% to 81%. It was also demonstrated that coaching affected the total number correct in that all subjects scored above the cutoff; however, there was no difference in response latency.

Slick (Slick et al., 1998) also modified the Hiscock and Hiscock procedure. First, administration time was decreased by decreasing the number of items from 72 to 48, which are presented in three blocks of 16 items each. The delay period is increased in each block from 5 to 10 to 15 seconds. Item difficulty was manipulated by making items appear more difficult (i.e., similarity between the correct item and foils). Strauss et al. (1999) administered the VSVT to simulators and controls three times over a 3-week period. Simulators performed less consistently over the three administrations. Results demonstrated that on the hard items, a deviation of 3 points differentiated the control and malingering groups with 95% probability. A deviation of 1 point differentiated the groups with 95% probability on the easy items. Eighty-eight percent of the control group and 89% of the malingering group were correctly classified. On the VSVT, both response latency and number correct are recorded. Slick, Hopp,

Strauss, Hunter, and Pinch (1994) found that those who produced invalid profiles had significantly longer response latencies, again suggesting the usefulness of this measure. In addition, a new third category of classification is added. Performance below chance is still labeled invalid, and performance significantly above chance is still labeled valid. The third category, *questionable,* consists of scores that fall within the remaining 90% confidence interval of chance performance. The three-category classification system has shown high specificity and good sensitivity (Slick et al., 1994).

One of the criticisms of the VSVT is that although recommended interpretive guidelines are published in the test manual, the samples used in developing interpretive guidelines are small and heterogeneous and concern has been expressed regarding high false negative rates (Macciocchi, Seel, Alderson, & Godsall, 2006). In the Macciocchi et al. study (2006), a homogeneous sample of acute, severely brain-injured persons was used to assess the sensitivity of the VSVT. Results confirmed that acute, severely brain-injured persons ($N = 71$) perform very well on the VSVT. The severe brain-injury population was 99% likely to have between 44.1 and 46.8 correct VSVT Combined Score responses. While the VSVT was insensitive to memory dysfunction, the presence of severe visual perceptual (Benton Visual Form Discrimination Score <21) and verbal fluency (Controlled Oral Word Association Score <15) deficits predicted poor performance on the VSVT. These results provide further evidence that performance expectations currently incorporated in the VSVT manual interpretative criteria are too conservative. Empirically based alternative criteria for interpreting VSVT Combined Scores in the TBI population that are presented by the authors would decrease the false negative decisions regarding neuropsychological test validity. (See Macciocchi et al., 2006, alternative interpretive criteria.)

The VIP (Frederick, 1997) is a computerized, two-alternative forced-choice procedure that incorporates a fourfold classification system based on two test-taking characteristics: motivation (to excel or fail) and effort (high or low). The combination of the concepts of motivation and effort generate four classification schemes: compliant (high effort and motivation), careless (high motivation to perform well but low effort to correctly respond), irrelevant (low effort when motivated to perform poorly), and malingering (high effort and motivation to perform poorly). Only the compliant profile is considered valid. The test contains both verbal (20-minute) and nonverbal (30-minute) subtests. The nonverbal subtest

is a 100-item progressive matrix test modified from the Test of Nonverbal Intelligence (TONI; Brown, Sherbenou, & Johnson, 1982). The verbal subtest contains 78 two-alternative word knowledge items. The VIP uses a performance curve analysis. The performance curve shows the average performance of the test taker across an increasingly difficult range of test items. Compliant responding results in a curve that starts at about 100% and remains at that level until the test taker reaches his or her ceiling of ability (as items increase in difficulty), at which time the curve goes through a period of transition until it results in about 50% correct performance (or random responding). As a result, performance curves for compliant test takers should be similar in shape regardless of ability levels. The VIP underwent renorming in 2003 and has been studied primarily with adult populations. The VIP has also been used with adolescents' ages 15 to 18. Walter (2005) showed that the VIP was consistent in classifying the adolescent population to the same degree that the adult population is correctly classified.

The use of multiple SVT is supported by the work of Greve, Binder, and Bianchini (2009). They compared three symptom validity tests on a sample of mild, moderate, and severe brain-injury cases. Their results indicate that multiple SVTs were more likely to yield below-chance results than a single test and support the use of multiple SVTs in forensic neuropsychological evaluations. The continued use of SVT to assess malingering has been supported by Fox (2011). He examined symptom validity test results from 220 archival cases that were analyzed to determine if failing a symptom validity test (SVT) affects the relationship between neuropsychological tests and brain damage. The results confirmed that failure on an SVT essentially invalidates the relationship between neuropsychological test results and brain damage.

### Standard Clinical Tests

Although there have been several tests developed specifically to assess for malingering, several researchers have taken standard clinical tests and studied their ability to distinguish motivated from possibly malingering-exaggerating (or those acting as malingerers) and TBI patients. Some of the more commonly used tests today include the Wechsler Memory Scale–III (Scott-Killgore & DellaPietra, 2000), the California Verbal Learning Test (R. Baker, Donders, & Thompson, 2000; Millis et al., 1995; Sweet et al., 2000), and the Wisconsin Card Sorting Test (Suhr & Boyer 1999). J. B. Miller et al. (2011) investigated the ability of the Wechsler Memory Scale, Fourth Edition (WMS-IV) and the Advanced Clinical

Solutions (ACS; Pearson, 2009) package, including the new Word Choice Test (WCT; part of the ACS), and provides effort scores when combined with embedded items in the Wechsler Adult Intelligence Scale-IV and WMS-IV to distinguish poor performance due to intentional response bias among simulators of TBI from poor performance due to actual TBI. Participants were 45 survivors of moderate to severe TBI and 39 healthy adults coached to simulate TBI. Their analysis indicated that a five-variable model containing all the ACS variables and a single-variable model using only the WCT were reliable and that adding the WCT to the ACS increased predictive accuracy. Diagnostic efficiency for the full ACS model was recommended (J. B. Miller et al., 2011).

The development of tests used to assess for suboptimal effort has greatly enhanced neuropsychologists' ability to accurately detect malingering and sincere performance. Over the past few years, the tests have become much more sophisticated. However, a few interesting points should be made regarding the development of normative data for these tests as well as the appropriate application of these tests. First, it is almost impossible to *truly* find a known malingering group. By definition, these individuals are trying to fake brain impairment and thus do not admit to malingering. Therefore, the research used in developing these tasks and their normative data has primarily used groups trained to fake brain impairment or has compared groups of TBI patients matched for severity of injury but differing in CS status (e.g., CS versus NCS). Although these substitutes are adequate and quite frankly the best that can be achieved, they do not allow for the assessment of a group of clearly defined true malingerers. All of the aforementioned tests used to help determine level of motivation depend on a conscious response by the subject. It is this response that is under the individual's control. It is up to the neuropsychologist to determine whether the response actually represents the true ability of the individual or whether it was suboptimal (i.e., possibly malingered or exaggerated).

The development of a test that can determine malingering and is not under the conscious control of the client—something akin to a blood test—would be helpful. Cognitive evoked response potentials (ERPs) may be the closest thing we have to a cognitive blood test. (See Rosenfeld & Ellwanger, 1999, for a review.) It has been proposed that cognitive ERP (P300) may be the involuntary psychophysiological test that cannot be faked by an individual; thus, it might give a window into true cognitive deficit or the lack thereof. (Ellwanger, Rosenfeld, Sweet, & Bhatt, 1996; Rosenfeld, Ellwanger, & Sweet,

1995). An evoked potential test measures electrical activity in the brain that is produced (evoked) in response to an external sensory stimulus. Types of stimuli that are commonly used for the test include visual (a flashing light), auditory (a clicking noise delivered to the ear via headphones), or tactile (a light touch or mild electrical shock). The resulting stimulation of a sensory nerve cell (neuron) results in an electrical discharge (depolarization) of the cell, which generates an electrical impulse called an action potential. Action potentials can also be elicited from a cognitive stimulus (recognition of a specified target or pattern) or by the omission of a stimulus (an increased time gap between stimuli). Brain and/or spinal cord electrical activity is recorded by a computer, which then analyzes the speed, duration, and intensity of the neural response. Decreased P300 amplitude has been demonstrated in TBI (see Ellwanger, Tenhulla, Rosenfeld, & Sweet, 1999) even if recognition memory is intact (Ellwanger, Rosenfeld, & Sweet, 1997). Since P300 is not under the conscious control of the client, appropriate changes in P300 would indicate intact electrophysiological functioning, regardless of the client's response. Overall, the evidence suggests that P300 during recognition memory test or during an oddball auditory paradigm is able to accurately detect groups of simulated feigners of memory deficits—especially when it is used in conjunction with other neuropsychological tests of motivation malingering (Ellwanger et al., 1999; Rosenfeld & Ellwanger, 1999; Tardif, Barry, Fox, & Johnstone, 2000).

Other useful proposals for the detection of exaggeration and malingering combine neuropsychological and psychophysiological measures, such as skin conductance and heart rate. Vilar-Lopez, Perez-Garcia, Sanchez-Barrera, Rodriguez-Fernandez, and Gomez-Rio (2011) studied the peripheral psychophysiological response pattern of subjects instructed to exaggerate cognitive deficits (ECD) during the execution of the VSVT and normal effort (NE) conditions. Differences in skin conductance between correct answers and errors limited to the decision-making phase of each conditions. The most important finding of the study was the determination of differences on the electrodermal conductance during the performance of the VSVT when individuals fake compared with when they do their best. The results showed an increase in the skin conductance when participants ECD in comparison to responses in the NE conditions. Specifically, skin conductance registered during erroneous responses was found to be significantly higher than conductance obtained during correct responses in the ECD condition but not in the NE condition. Furthermore, the differences were restricted to the decision-making phase and disappeared after the execution of the response.

One of the major shortfalls in the assessment of malingering is that almost all of these tests are designed for assessment of MTBI, and using them for other populations (e.g., malingering, depression, somatoform or conversion disorders) is difficult. Even if patient scores in the impaired range on these tests, it is not a guarantee of a diagnosis of malingering; this is why many authors like to think of these tests as measuring suboptimal performance and not malingering, per se. For example, if an individual with MTBI seeking compensation performs near the chance level on a forced-choice recognition test, one can say that the test indicated suboptimal performance. However, one cannot conclude that the patient is malingering because issues of depression, anxiety, and even somatoform and conversion disorders could cause poor performance on these tests. Thus, the use of these tests is highly specific and can only be used with the populations for which they were intended, developed, and normed until experimental evidence is produced that supports their use and interpretation within other clinical populations. Finally, the ability to detect malingering does not end with cognitive deficits. It typically extends into the assessment of affect and personality. Ample research has been performed with self-report personality questionnaires in determining malingering and distortion. The most commonly used self-report questionnaire, the Minnesota Multiphasic Personality Inventory–2 (MMPI-2), has been researched extensively in terms of methodology and patterns in detecting malingering or distortion. (See Ben-Porath, Graham, Hall, Hirschman, & Zaragoza, 1995.) For example, the Fake Bad scale (Lees-Haley, English, & Glen, 1991) was designed to detect the endorsement of items rarely identified in known psychopathology.

The MMPI-2 has an "infrequency" scale developed by Megargee (2004) for use in criminal settings called the Criminal Offender Infrequency (Fc) scale. Gassen, Pietz, Spray, and Denney (2007) compared Fc with seven other MMPI-2 validity scales in detecting malingering by obtaining archival data from evaluations of male inmates that used the MMPI-2 and the Structured Interview of Reported Symptoms (SIRS). A cutoff of Fc > 14 produced the highest hit rate of any cutoff on all of the scales examined. Results from this study suggest that Fc may be a useful addition to the MMPI-2 for detecting malingering in criminal settings. The MMPI-2 Fake Bad Scale (FBS) in the detection of incomplete effort in mild head injury was investigated by Ross, Millis, Krukowski, Putnam,

and Adams (2004). Using receiver operating characteristic (ROC) curve analysis, they found that a cutoff score of 21 had a sensitivity of 90% and specificity of 90%, providing an overall correct classificatory rate of 90%. These authors found that a cutoff score only slightly higher than that originally reported by Lees-Haley et al. (1991) resulted in maximum sensitivity and specificity for this scale. Also, a neuro-correction factor for use in TBI patients (Gass, 1991) was developed to try to tease out items that are common in neurological samples (such as MTBI) but otherwise would inflate psychopathology level on the MMPI-2 scales. An updated version of the MMPI-2, the Minnesota Multiphasic Personality Inventory–2 Restructured Form (MMPI-2-RF) (Ben-Porath, & Tellegen, 2008) is composed of 338 items, with the RC (Restructured Clinical) Scales at its core, builds on the strengths of the MMPI 2. It features 50 new and revised empirically validated scales. The test includes a new Infrequent Somatic Responses Scale ($F_S$) and the recently adapted Response Bias Scale (RBS). A study by Rogers, Gillard, Berry, and Granacher (2011) supports the use of these new scales in ruling out a feigned mental disorder but not feigned cognitive disorder.

The Personality Assessment Inventory (PAI; Morcy, 1991) is becoming a widely used self-report personality questionnaire as an alternative to the MMPI-2. The PAI is a multiscale test of psychological functioning that assesses constructs relevant to personality and psychopathology evaluation (e.g., depression, anxiety, aggression) in various contexts, including psychotherapy, crisis/evaluation, forensic, personnel selection, pain/medical, and child custody assessment. The PAI has 22 nonoverlapping scales, providing a comprehensive overview of psychopathology in adults. The PAI contains four kinds of scales:

1. Validity scales, which measure the respondent's approach to the test, including faking good or bad, exaggeration, or defensiveness
2. Clinical scales, which correspond to psychiatric diagnostic categories
3. Treatment consideration scales, which assess factors that may relate to treatment of clinical disorders or other risk factors but which are not captured in psychiatric diagnoses (e.g., suicidal ideation)
4. Interpersonal scales, which provide indicators of interpersonal dimensions of personality functioning

Additionally, the PAI is shorter (344 versus 567 items in the MMPI-2) and requires only a fourth-grade reading level. (The MMPI-2 requires a sixth-grade reading level.) Most important, however, is that the PAI has appropriate application in the forensic setting. Various authors have developed malingering scales that are useful in detecting malingering, exaggeration, or minimalization of psychopathology. (See Morey, 2007.)

Neuropsychological assessments have other forensic applications in addition to civil litigation. For example, neuropsychologists are often asked to perform assessments to help determine issues of guardianship and conservatorship. From a legal perspective, individuals can be assessed to determine their ability to make independent decisions in medical treatment, finances, and caring for themselves. Daniel Marson has applied the legal standards (that vary by state) to these issues and developed a battery of cognitive-based tasks capable of answering these questions (Dymek, Atchison, Harrell, & Marson, 2001; Earnst, Marson, & Harrell, 2000; Larrabee, 2007; Marson, 2001; Marson, Annis, McInturff, Bartolucci, & Harrell, 1999; Marson, Chatterjee, Ingram, & Harrell, 1996; Marson, Cody, Ingram, & Harrell, 1995; Marson, Martin, & Wadley et al., 2009). This area is important for future research in neuropsychological assessment.

## ISSUES IN NEUROPSYCHOLOGICAL ASSESSMENT

Within general neuropsychological assessment, there are new developments worth mentioning. In general, test development has become more rigorous over the years, and many of the standard tests have been redesigned and renormed. Moreover, some specific developments—particularly in the areas of computerized assessment and the development of novel assessment techniques—have made rather significant impacts on the advancement of clinical neuropsychology. Assessment in clinical neuropsychology historically can trace its roots back to two lines of development that (roughly speaking) can be separated into a North American camp and a European-Russian camp. The European and Russian group based their assessments mainly on qualitative features that were developed over time studying brain-injured patients. This approach is very much in the Lurian tradition of neuropsychological assessment. The North American approach is quantitative in nature and has it foundations in more experimentally and empirically based test design. The Halstead-Reitan Neuropsychological Test Battery (Reitan & Wolfson, 1993) is the quintessential example of a strictly formal psychometric approach in neuropsychological assessment. In this approach, all types of patients receive the same tests administered in the exact same way every time. Their data are based almost exclusively on the numerical tests scores. Interpretation is based on actuarial predictions for diagnosis. (See Lezak, Howieson, Bigler, & Tranel, 2012.)

Although there has been much debate over which assessment technique is better—qualitative or quantitative (see Lezak, Howieson, Bigler, & Tranel, 2012), there clearly has been a merging of these two camps over time. Edith Kaplan and Muriel Lezak have probably been the most influential in merging both qualitative and quantitative aspects into current-day clinical neuropsychological assessments. Therefore, some of the developments in clinical neuropsychological testing have to do with combining both qualitative and quantitative features. In addition to merging qualitative and quantitative aspects of testing, other neuropsychological tests represent a blending of various specialties within psychology (e.g., educational psychology) or combine complex theoretical models of cognition. For example, the Cognitive Assessment System (Naglieri & Das, 1997); and soon-to-be published Cognitive Assessment System-2 (Naglieri, Das, & Goldstein, forthcoming) are designed to measure basic neurocognitive processes, including attention-concentration and executive control. The system integrates the assessment of cognitive processes from a Lurian perspective (Naglieri & Otero, 2011) with the advantages of a psychometric tradition using a well-developed theory (PASS; planning, attention, simultaneous, and successive processes) and applies the results to educational and clinical settings. (See Naglieri & Otero, 2011.)

### Computerized Assessment

Neuropsychological testing, like most assessments in psychology, has traditionally been conducted with paper-and-pencil tests; however, more and more neuropsychological testing is becoming computerized. Although computerization has made scoring much simpler and more accurate, it has also allowed for more complicated computations and thus more sophisticated and powerful clinical applications. However, the actual computerization of test administration has had the greatest impact. There are some clear and basic advantages to computerized assessment. It allows for more efficient and standardized testing. For example, it allows for more accurate reaction time measurement, which is important when testing higher-order attention and concentration; also, it can allow for better randomization of stimuli. Computerized test administration also can be very economical because it decreases costs and allows for group administration at times (i.e., less need for a technician-based administration). In addition, computerized testing may be suited for a screening instrument and/or monitoring change in cognitive function(s) over time. However, as usual, there are some disadvantages as well. Computerized testing can be rather inflexible, which can lead to problems testing brain-injured individuals or individuals who do not understand test instructions (especially in a group administration setting). Computerized testing can also reduce the ability to pick up qualitative features of test performance, which are more easily detected with paper-and-pencil testing. What will most likely evolve (and is actually being done in most clinical settings at present) is a combination of both paper-and-pencil and computerized testing. Finally, although many of the same issues apply to computerized testing (Naglieri et al., 2004), several ethical issues may be unique to computerized assessment, and increased awareness of relevant issues will enhance the chances that ethical dilemmas will be navigated successfully (Schulenberg & Yutrzenka, 2004).

Although it is beyond the scope of this chapter to review the full array of computerized neuropsychological assessment, it is worth mentioning its use in one particular area. Neuropsychologists working within sport-related concussion have developed basic assessment techniques to assess and measure the extent of concussion (as defined as decrements in cognitive abilities). Initially, paper-and-pencil tests were used (see Lovell & Collins, 1998), but because of practice effects, accuracy measuring reaction time, and high costs, computerized assessment has become the new standard. Using generic computerized testing techniques (Automated Neuropsychological Assessment Metrics [ANAM]; Reeves, Kane, & Winter, 1996), Joseph Bleiberg and others have demonstrated the cognitive deficits following a concussion and MTBI (Bleiberg, Halpern, Reeves, & Daniel, 1998; Bleiberg, Kane, Reeves, Garmoe, & Halpern, 2000; Warden et al., 2001). Others have developed specific computerized test batteries specifically designed for use in sport-related concussion work. For example, the Immediate Post-Concussion Assessment and Cognitive Testing (ImPACT; see Maroon et al., 2000) consists of six modules assessing working memory, anterograde memory, simple and complex reaction time, and impulsivity. It also assesses concussion symptomatology. It was designed to be very easy to administer (so it can be given by athletic trainers), it requires minimal English skills (for athletes for whom English is second language), and it is very sensitive to the effects of concussion. It can be group administered and uses computer-randomized stimuli to create up to five equivalent versions to minimize practice effects with repeated administration. ImPACT uses self-report symptomatology along with scores from memory, reaction time, and impulsivity indexes derived from the individual modules.

A plethora of computerized test batteries now exist. A recent Internet search revealed several stand-alone computerized cognitive batteries produced by as many as 13 independent developers. Some of the batteries are: CNS-Vital Signs (Gualtieri & Johnson, 2006), Computer-Administered Neuropsychological Screen for Mild Cognitive Impairments (CANS-MCI; Tornatore, Hill, & Laboff, 2005), Cambridge Neuropsychological Test Automated Battery (CANTAB; Sahakian & Owen, 1992), CogSport (www.cogstate.com/go/sport), Headminder (www.headminder.com/site/home.html), MicroCog (D. Powell et al., 2004), MindStreams (www.neurotrax.com/), Fepsy Comprehensive Neuropsychological Test System (www.fepsy.com/), and Neurobehavioral Evaluation System–3 (NES-3; Letz, Green, & Woodard, 1996).

On a cautionary note, the reader in encouraged to keep in mind that neuropsychological tests rely heavily on timing of stimuli and response and consistent presentation of stimuli across all subjects. While computers offer increased accuracy of timing and consistency of presentation, there are several areas of a computer system where errors can occur due to hardware and software interactions (Cernich, Brennana, Barker, & Bleiberg, 2007). As with standard neuropsychological measures, the major issue is method variance. In the computer environment, the hardware, software, and peripherals offer multiple sources of error that can confound timing accuracy and presentation of test stimuli. Although error in some cases must be dealt with at the programming level, in most cases, it is incumbent on the neuropsychologist to ensure that the program is used correctly. For example, ensuring that the assessment program is running with as few other applications open as possible is good practice since many assessment programs utilize a great deal of memory.

## Paper-and-Pencil Testing

Although computerized assessment is a new and viable approach, neuropsychological assessment still depends on paper-and-pencil testing. Some of the more popular tests continually undergo refinement, redevelopment, and renorming (e.g., the Wechsler Memory Scale-IV; Wechsler, 2009) and Wechsler Adult Intelligence Scale-IV; Wechsler, 2008. In fact, test developers are sensitive to the need for shorter yet still reliable tests (in response to managed care) and are trying to develop such instruments. A few examples are the Wechsler Abbreviated Scale of Intelligence-II (WASI-II; Wechsler, 2011), Kaufman Brief Intelligence Test-2 (K-BIT2; Kaufman & Kaufman, 2004), and the General Ability Measure for Adults (GAMA; Naglieri & Bardos, 1997).

Another area in which paper-and-pencil test development has seen some advancement is in the quantification of qualitative aspects of impaired neuropsychological performance. Several prominent neuropsychologists (e.g., A. R. Luria and Edith Kaplan) for decades expressed the importance of understanding *how* the patient responds, not just *what* the patient responds. In the past, one had to have years of experience in order to develop the skills to perform qualitative analysis. Even then, these skills often differed from practitioner to practitioner. However, some tests have been developed to quantify these qualitative features that are often so important in neuropsychological assessments. Kaplan, for example, authored the Wechsler Adult Intelligence Scale—Revised Neuropsychological Investigation (WAIS-R NI; Kaplan, Fein, Morris, Kramer, & Delis, 1991). Other tests such as the Boston Qualitative Scoring System for the Rey Complex Figure Test (R. A. Stern et al., 1999) is an attempt at quantifying various qualitative features found in the responses of brain-injured patients. Several recent tests of ability based on neuropsychological theory, such as the Cognitive Assessment System (CAS; Naglieri & Das, 1997) and the Kaufman Assessment Battery for Children-II (KABC-II; Kaufman & Kaufman, 2004), include options for qualitative observations within the test record forms.

The Executive Control Battery (ECB; Goldberg, Podell, Bilder, & Jaeger, 2000) was developed to quantify various features of executive control deficits often not assessed in other, more frequently used measures of executive control skills (e.g., Wisconsin Card Sorting Test). Clearly, the development of tests that assess qualitative features has improved neuropsychological testing. However, neuropsychological tests in general are limited to measuring ability only. To take the assessment of qualitative features one step further, it would be important to understand not only *ability* (i.e., whether the subject could get the correct answer) but perhaps the subject's *preference* in choosing. At times—particularly in brain-injured patients—it is as important to understand an individual's preference when given a choice in problem solving as it is to understand the ability level per se. For example, we know that patients with prefrontal lobe damage have extreme difficulty functioning in everyday life and sometimes cannot complete basic daily skills,

but they still maintain intact cognitive abilities. (See Goldberg, 2001, 2009, for a description of these types of deficits.) Thus, it may not be the individual's ability per se that interferes with daily functioning but rather his or her preference or, in the case of brain-injured persons, the inability to make an appropriate choice.

Goldberg and colleagues (Goldberg & Podell, 1999; Goldberg, Podell, Harner, Lovell, & Riggio, 1994) have studied the effects of lateralized prefrontal lesions and developed a task specifically designed to assess a person's response preference rather than ability. The Cognitive Bias Task (Goldberg & Podell, 2001) entails a simple, forced-choice perceptual discrimination task with rather ambiguous instructions. After seeing a target card, participants are presented with two stimulus cards and must choose the one they like the best. Of the two stimulus choice cards, one is perceptually more similar to and one is perceptually more different from the target card. The task is set up so that the individual must decide which way he or she is going to respond—more similar to or more different from the target card. There is no feedback after a response. The ambiguity of the instructions is central to making the task a test of preference rather than ability. In fact, it is this ambiguity that allowed Goldberg and colleagues to demonstrate some of the essential cognitive differences between right and left prefrontal functioning as well as a significant gender difference. When the instructions are disambiguated (e.g., choose the more similar or more different stimulus card), all of the subjects—even patients with prefrontal cortical lesions—performed the tasks well. Thus, it was not an issue of ability (e.g., intact performance with disambiguated instructions) but rather preference (e.g., difference with ambiguous instructions).

## RECENT ADVANCEMENTS IN PSYCHOMETRIC APPLICATIONS

Neuropsychologists are typically asked to look at changes in cognitive abilities over time as they relate to a disease process (e.g., dementia), recovery of function (e.g., TBI), or following surgical intervention (e.g., temporal lobectomy for intractable seizure disorder). However, many clinical neuropsychologists (as well as psychologists in general) do not apply well-established, empirically based statistical procedures for determining whether the differences in tests actually represent a *true* (i.e., statistically reliable) change or rather one that can be explained simply by test–retest variance. We believe that this issue is central and pertinent to the practice of clinical neuropsychology and thus worthy of some detailed discussion. Another important development in this area for neuropsychology is the use of ROC curves in determining the sensitivity of a test. Historically, research using neuropsychological tests has relied on strictly using weaker, discriminant analyses and not relying on more sophisticated methods such as ROC curves. As discussed next, the use of more sophisticated statistical methods are starting to come of age in neuropsychological research.

## Reliability of Change Indexes

Repeated administrations of neuropsychological tests frequently yield varying results, even in people who have not experienced any true change in cognitive functioning (Temkin, Heaton, Grant, & Dikmen, 1999). There are a number of reasons for this variance, including less-than-perfect reliability of test instruments, less-than-optimally standardized test administration, fluctuations in a patient's performance related to motivational issues, mood, health status, and so on. The relative contribution of these factors is almost always different for different tests. Many clinical neuropsychologists use a seat of the-pants approach to determine whether changes are to be considered significant; they examine the change in scores and decide whether the difference is significant based on clinical experience and a basic knowledge of statistics. Others use various rules of thumb, such as the change in test scores must be greater than one-half standard deviation of a test's normative sample to be considered significant. Obviously, these methods are highly susceptible to error. Most often these methods conclude that a change is significant when it is in fact not statistically significant. Any change from one testing occasion to another is considered significant if the magnitude of the change is sufficiently large relative to the associated error variance of the test. Determination of the error variance is based on test–retest reliability and variation about the mean of the test (Jacobson & Truax, 1991).

Statistical approaches to determining the significance of a change in test scores are based on predicting the likely range of scores that would be obtained if there were no real change in cognitive functioning. Statistical approaches to predicting scores on retest with concomitant prediction or confidence intervals are much more likely to be accurate and unbiased. Even so, it is not entirely clear what statistical approach is best suited for predicting subsequent scores on a given measure. There is not even a clear consensus about the factors that should be considered in a prediction model beyond the baseline test score

and test–retest reliability. Test factors beyond test–retest reliability may be important; these include internal consistency, susceptibility to practice effects, and test floors and ceilings. Potentially important participant variables include age, education, overall level of neuropsychological test performance at baseline, health status, mood, test-taking attitude, medication and other drug use, and various cognitive risk factors.

The prediction interval, sometimes known as the confidence interval, is a particular kind of interval estimate of a population parameter and is used to indicate the reliability of an estimate. For purposes of determining whether there has been change in functioning over time, the size of the interval is based partly on the standard error of difference ($S$diff) between the two test scores. This in turn is typically based on the standard deviation of scores in the control group and the test's stability coefficient (test–retest reliability). The size of the prediction interval is also based on the clinician or researcher's judgment as to the level of certainty desired. Intervals typically contain 90% of the differences between actual and predicted test scores in a cognitively intact or stable sample (Temkin et al., 1999). The intervals are usually defined so that in a stable sample, 5% of the individuals will be considered to show significant deterioration and 5% will show significant improvement. Intervals of other sizes and the use of one-tailed tests of significance may be more appropriate, depending on the goals of the researcher or clinician (Hinton-Bayre, Geffin, Geffen, McFarland, & Friss, 1999; Jacobson & Truax, 1991).

Various models for determining the significance of changes in test scores have been presented in the research literature. The models have become more sophisticated and the number of potentially important variables considered has increased as this research area has evolved. Early models consisted of simply dividing the change in test scores by the $S$diff between the two test scores (Christensen & Mendoza, 1986). This value is considered to represent significant change if it exceeds the RC $z$ score cut point corresponding to the desired level of certainty. The next step in the evolution of determining the significance of changes involved taking practice effects into account (Chelune, Naugle, Lüders, Sedlak, & Awad, 1993). Performance on many neuropsychological measures is expected to improve with subsequent testing simply because of increased familiarity with the material and because strategies to improve performance are often learned. Another method of determining the significance of changes in test scores is linear regression, which can correct for regression to the mean as well as practice effects (McSweeny, Naugle, Chelune, & Lüders, 1993, cited in Temkin et al., 1999). As Atkinson (1991) noted, the obtained score is not the best estimate of an individual's true score because of the tendency for a person with a score that deviates from the mean to obtain a score closer to the mean on a randomly parallel form of the test. The discrepancy between obtained and predicted true scores will be greater when the obtained score is more extreme, and the discrepancy will be less with tests that are more reliable. Another reason for using predicted true scores is that the original or classic RC index makes the statistical assumption that the error components are normally distributed with a mean of zero and that standard errors of measurement of the difference score are equal for all participants (Maassen, 2000).

Temkin et al. (1999) presented a model that uses stepwise linear regression to predict retest scores using additional factors that might be important. These factors included the test–retest interval; various demographic variables including age, education, sex, and race; and a measure of overall neuropsychological competence at baseline. They also explored the possibility of a nonlinear relationship between test and retest scores by including the square and the cube of the initial score in the variable selection as well as the square and the cube of the test–retest interval. Temkin et al. (1999) compared the exemplars of the various models for assessing the significance of change on several neuropsychological tests using multiple measures of prediction accuracy. They also examined the distribution of the residuals and presented distribution-free intervals for those that had particularly nonnormal distributions, and they explored whether prediction accuracy was constant across different levels of predictor variables. They found that initial test performance is the most powerful predictor of follow-up test performance. For example, they found that for the representative measures from the Halstead-Reitan Neuropsychological Test Battery that they analyzed, initial scores alone accounted for 67% to 88% of the variance in follow-up test scores. The addition of other predictors in the multiple regression model increased explained follow-up test scores between 0.8% and 8.5%. In general, demographic variables tended to exert additional influences on follow-up scores in the same direction as they did on initial test scores. For example, older and less well-educated participants tended to perform worse on follow-up than did younger and better-educated participants with the same initial test scores. Perhaps surprising to many clinicians is the finding that practice effects do not decrease very much over the 2- to 16-month time frame considered in these

studies (Temkin et al., 1999). Temkin et al. (1999) noted that of the four models they compared, the original RC index performed least well. They considered this model inadequate because of its wide prediction intervals and its poor prediction accuracy.

The RC model with correction for practice effects had much better prediction accuracy, but of course the size of the prediction interval is not affected. In fact, the overall prediction accuracy of the RC model with correction for practice effects was similar to that of the multiple regression models, although there were large differences in predicted retest scores at the extremes of initial test performance and extremes of general neuropsychological competence at baseline. For practical purposes, the differences in the size of the prediction intervals are not always clinically significant. For example, the prediction interval size for the Wechsler Adult Intelligence Scale (WAIS) Verbal IQ using the regression model with all predictors was only 0.2 IQ points smaller in each direction (improved and deteriorated) than was the RC index. A larger difference was noted between the two methods for the Halstead Category Test, with a difference of 3.6 errors in each direction. The difference was yet more pronounced when distribution-free intervals were computed for tests with scores that are not normally distributed, such as Trails B and the Tactual Performance Test.

Various authors have reached different conclusions about the most appropriate methods for determining the reliability of change scores. For example, Temkin et al. (1999) concluded from their study that simple models perform less well than do more complex models with patients who are relatively more impaired and those whose demographic characteristics are associated with lower absolute levels of performance. They suggested that because the patients seen in clinical settings are more likely than healthy individuals to obtain relatively extreme test scores, the complex prediction models are likely to be even more advantageous than demonstrated in their study. Maassen (2000) reached a different conclusion based on theoretical and conceptual considerations. He compared null hypothesis methods, of which the original RC index (originally developed by Jacobson, Follette, & Revenstorf, 1984, and refined by Christensen & Mendoza, 1986) is derived, to estimation interval methods, which include the regressed score approach. Although he acknowledged that both general methods probably lead to the same interpretation of observed change, he noted that the probability that observed changes will be erroneously deemed reliable with the null hypothesis method is limited by a low level of significance. This method rules out with high probability that measurement error is a possible explanation for observed change. In contrast, there is no uniform upper limit for the probability of an incorrect conclusion with the estimation interval methods. Trivial effects could potentially lead to an observed change, or even lack of change, being deemed reliable. In fact, an observed change in one direction could be interpreted as reliable change in the other direction.

There are other considerations for the practicing clinical neuropsychologist. For example, the average clinician is highly unlikely to have the data and the necessary time and skills to develop regression models for the other tests that he or she uses in clinical practice. In contrast, the manuals for most standardized tests contain the stability coefficients required for determination of RC indexes with or without practice effects. These approaches are very likely to be much more reliable than a seat-of-the-pants approach or a rule of thumb. Chelune et al. (1993) pointed out another important consideration for the clinician. The formulas that have been developed to date are concerned only with the reliability of change in single test scores. Clinicians very rarely base conclusions about changes in cognitive or other functioning on a single change score. Rather, they look at patterns of change across a number of tests in a battery. The cooccurrence of two or more changes in the same direction is more reliable and robust than are changes on a single measure (Chelune, 2010). Two or more change scores that are each not statistically significant in themselves may represent reliable change when considered together. It is of course important to consider the statistical independence of the scores. The fact that two or more related scores from the same test have changed in the same direction inspires much less confidence than do consistent changes across different tests.

## Receiver Operating Curves

An increasing number of investigators are assessing the accuracy of neuropsychological tests through the use of signal detection statistics and computation of ROC curves (McFall & Treat, 1999). Signal detection statistics provide indexes of the ability to make a clinical decision when faced with a given criterion or test score. The sensitivity of a measure refers to the proportion of individuals with the condition in question whose scores exceed that criterion. Specificity of a measure refers to the number of individuals without the condition classified accurately as not achieving that criterion. The ROC curves provide graphic representations of the trade-off between true-positive and false-positive rates of classification. Calculation of the area under the ROC curve provides an empirical method for determining the diagnostic accuracy of a given test or helping to determine which of two tests is more accurate for diagnosing a certain condition. In other words, ROC curves help the user decide what constitutes normal and abnormal or pathological performance.

Virtually no test can discriminate between normal and pathological with 100% accuracy because the distributions of normal and pathological performances overlap. A score in the overlap area might belong to either the normal or the pathological distribution. Consequently, test users choose a cutoff score. Scores on one side of the cutoff are presumed to be normal, and scores on the other side are presumed to be pathological. The position of the cutoff determines the number of true positives, true negatives, false positives, and false negatives. The exact cutoff chosen is based on the particular use of a test and the user's assessment of the relative costs of different types of erroneous decisions. The *sensitivity* of a cutoff score refers to the proportion of results considered positive relative to the proportion of the sample that is actually part of the positive distribution. In other words, increasing sensitivity results in an increasing number of true positives, but it does so at the expense of also increasing the number of false positives. Conversely, the *specificity* of a cutoff score refers to the proportion of results considered negative relative to the proportion of the sample that is actually part of the negative distribution. In other words, increasing specificity reduces the number of false positives at the expense of also increasing the number of false negatives. There is always a trade-off between sensitivity and specificity. Increasing sensitivity will always result in reduced specificity, and increasing specificity will always result in reduced sensitivity.

ROC curves are plots of a test's sensitivity or true positive rate along the *y*-axis or false positive rate along the *x*-axis (Tape, 2001). As noted, ROC curves graphically demonstrate the trade-off between sensitivity and specificity. The area under the curve is a measure of test accuracy or the potential discriminability of a test. Tests that are more accurate are characterized by ROC curves that closely follow the left-hand border and then the top border of the ROC space. Less accurate tests are characterized by ROC curves that more closely follow a 45-degree diagonal from the bottom left to the upper right of the ROC space. An area of 1.0 represents a perfect test, whereas an area of 0.5 represents a worthless test. (See Figure 19.1.) The main use of ROC curves for practicing clinical neuropsychologists is in test selection. An ROC

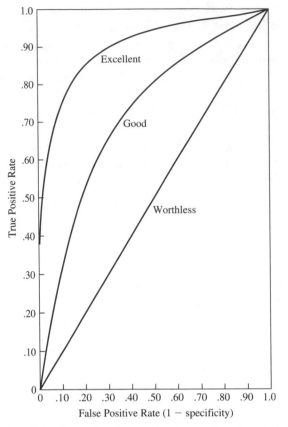

**Figure 19.1** Example of a receiver operating characteristic curve.

curve provides valuable information about the ability of a test to discriminate between normal and pathological or between sufficient and insufficient effort. An ROC curve also provides information about the trade-off between sensitivity and specificity, and it is helpful in guiding decisions about the most appropriate cutoff score to use in a particular situation (e.g., Barr & McCrea, 2001).

## Operating Characteristics: Sensitivity, Selectivity, Positive and Negative Predictive Power

When dealing with a specific individual, the examiner wants to know whether that patient falls within one group or another, such as within a brain-damaged or a control group. The operating characteristics of a neuropsychological measure can provide evidence of scientific validity and accuracy (Gouvier, 1999).

When using operating characteristics, the severity of impairment has no effect on the statistic other than determining which side of a cut point the subject falls. All members of a group on each side of the cut point are treated the same statistically no matter how extreme is

their impairment. Consequently, for clinical purposes in which the question is determining the existence of a condition, statistics based on the operating characteristics of a cut point are more accurate.

A number of different operating characteristics may be used to evaluate a criterion. Several of these characteristics, which are fairly standard (Retzlaff & Gibertini, 2000) include prevalence, sensitivity, specificity, positive predictive power, negative predictive power, and overall predictive power.

These characteristics cover the major measures that can be used to determine the accuracy of a test in terms of correct and incorrect assessments of its criteria. The accuracy of a cut point for a test should be evaluated for each characteristic since each characteristic provides different information concerning the measure. For instance, if we want to know how accurate a test is in predicting a condition, its positive predictive power is the most important characteristic. However, if we want to know how accurate a test is in predicting individuals who do not have the condition (normal subjects), the negative predictive power is required.

*Sensitivity* indicates how responsive a measure is to a condition when the condition is present, such as brain damage. Thus, sensitivity is the ratio of subjects correctly classified as brain damaged compared to all of the brain-damaged subjects. *Prevalence* is the proportion of subjects in the study who have a condition, such as brain damage. It is the number of subjects who demonstrate the condition divided by the total number of subjects. Prevalence is equivalent to base rate. Meehl and Rosen (1955) showed that the probability of valid classifications depends on the base rate or prevalence of the disorder in the clinical sample and that the base rate represents the proportion of valid test positives due to chance alone. They showed that under certain conditions, even tests with very good sensitivity and specificity can result in more classification errors than does chance alone. The sensitivity of a test is most misleading for the clinician when the base rate of a disorder is very low; the specificity is most misleading when the base rate is very high. Rather than using inflexible cutoffs, Meehl and Rosen argued that cutoffs should be adjusted to local base rates to maximize the probability of valid test discriminations.

It should be noted that sensitivity and specificity are not directly affected by base rate. They measure the ratio of correct prediction for each category of a condition independently. The numbers of subjects having a condition (brain damage) varies independently from the numbers of subjects who do not have the condition. Each condition is treated as a separate sample. That is, the number of subjects with brain damage varies independently from the number of those who are normal. If there are 60 subjects with brain damage and the test correctly designates 45 of those subjects as having brain damage, sensitivity is 75%. Since this measure is not concerned with the normal control subjects, there do not need to be any control subjects in the study to obtain this characteristic. Specificity concerns only the subjects who do not have brain damage—in other words, the normals. It specifies the accuracy of the test in correctly determining the number of the normal subjects who do not have brain damage. If the normal group has 100 subjects and the test designates 88 of them as not having brain damage, the test's specificity is 88%.

The two tests of predictive power are less well known, but they are of greatest concern to the examiner who wants to know the accuracy of a measure. They are more directly concerned with the accuracy of a test than sensitivity and specificity. Predictive power measures determine how accurately a test can predict whether a subject is a member of the brain-damaged or normal group. Positive predictive power indicates the probability that a person with a positive score on a test actually has a particular disorder. This statistic takes the base rates of a disorder into account. It is the number of true positives divided by the total number of test positives. Negative predictive power indicates the probability that a person with a negative score on the test will not have the disorder. This is the number of true negatives divided by the total test negatives. This number provides the most direct indication of the accuracy of a test in determining whether a subject is normal (i.e., does not have the condition). Positive predictive power and negative predictive power are reciprocally influenced by prevalence. A lower prevalence rate results in a loss of positive predictive power and a gain in negative predictive power (Elwood, 1993). Although sensitivity and specificity are independent of prevalence, they are still related to positive predictive power and negative predictive power. A loss of specificity (i.e., an increase in false positives) results in reduced positive predictive power, whereas a loss of sensitivity (i.e., an increase in false negatives) results in reduced negative predictive power.

## NEUROIMAGING

Initially, neuroimaging was very static and limited to dry (structural) anatomy. Although these earlier methodologies—head X rays, pneumoencephalography, CT scanning, and static MRI—were progressive and very useful clinically, they were capable of eliciting only correlative data regarding brain structure and brain functioning.

Over the past decade, there has been an explosion of anatomical and functional neuroimaging techniques, allowing exciting investigation of new aspects of the human brain functions with respect to cognition, learning, and memory. These developments have occurred with respect to the machinery (diverse methods of acquisition), the methods for analysis, and the extent of clinical applications. Modern, state-of-the-art neuroimaging techniques such as single-photon emission computed tomography (SPECT), positron emission tomography (PET), functional magnetic resonance imaging (fMRI), magnetic resonance spectroscopy (MRS), and magnetoencephalography (MEG) have drastically advanced our level of understanding of brain–behavior relationships. In essence, we went from a static, correlative model of matching neuropsychological findings to lesions on computed tomography-magnetic resonance imaging (CT-MRI) or electroencephalogram (EEG) to a more dynamic-causative model through understanding cause and effect in healthy subjects. These technological breakthroughs have expanded our understanding of brain–behavior relationships not only from a scientific-research perspective but also in terms of clinical applications. What is unique about functional neuroimaging and neuropsychology is their interdependence. Functional neuroimaging has evolved beyond simple motor-sensory paradigms. To use its full potential, it must rely on sophisticated neuropsychology paradigms to elicit brain activation in heteromodal cortices and limbic regions (required for complex cognition, memory, and behavior). Scientists can now directly test hypotheses of brain–behavior relationships (both experimentally and clinically) and use fundamental experimental psychology principles of manipulating an independent variable (IV; neuropsychological paradigms) and assess change in the dependent variable (DV; brain activation) rather than correlating changes in test scores with lesion location (as has been the tradition with static neuroimaging). Thus, in order to use functional neuroimaging, especially fMRI, one needs the appropriate cognitive paradigms (unique to the knowledge base of neuropsychologists) in order to elicit brain activation.

fMRI is a type of specialized MRI scan. It measures the hemodynamic response (change in blood flow) related to neural activity in the brain. This allows images to be generated that reflect which brain structures are activated (and how) during performance of different tasks fMRI has come to dominate the brain-mapping field due to its relatively low invasiveness, absence of radiation exposure, and relatively wide availability. Functional neuroimaging has already added an incredible amount of scientific information about brain–behavior relationships and has the potential for adding much more.

Consider functional neuroimaging and the evaluation of brain areas in pre-surgery language dominance studies, for example. The research of language dominance using functional neuroimaging provides an important contribution to clinical applications. Evaluation of the language area facilitates an efficient procedure for surgery of brain tumors or untreatable epilepsy to prevent the over-resection of the language area (Szaflarski et al., 2002). Despite the disadvantage that the function of the language is temporarily impaired, the Wada method—the intracarotid amobarbital procedure—has gained wide acceptance as a standard method to decide language dominance despite its somewhat procedural invasiveness that has some risks and limitations. Noninvasive examinations for the evaluation of the language area, consisting of fMRI have been developed as an alternative (Sabbah et al., 2003). fMRI is especially useful for the accurate evaluation of cerebral activity because of its high spatial resolution. Its use increases the posttest probabilities of hemispheric language dominance in multiple subgroups of individuals with and without epilepsy (Medina, Bernal, & Ruiz, 2007).

fMRI has been used in the evaluation of language laterality and activation of modality-specific memory systems (Detre et al., 1998; Killgore et al., 1999). Tantamount to the method's success is the development of the appropriate cognitive assessment paradigms by neuropsychologists. Perhaps one of the most influential findings to come from functional neuroimaging is proof of the concept that complex (and even not-so-complex) behaviors and cognition require the integration of many different brain regions configured into rather large and complex neural networks. This finding clearly dispels the notion of neuropsychological isomorphism between behavior and neuroanatomy (i.e., that discrete areas of the brain are responsible for one and only one function) and the concept of modularity of brain organization. Also, functional neuroimaging—particularly fMRI—is starting to address such issues as cognitive efficiency and how it relates to brain activation (such that more efficient processing requires less activation). Prior to this technological development, such topics were discussed theoretically only.

The next sections provide very brief overviews of particular clinical areas or cognitive processes currently being studied using functional neuroimaging technologies.

## Language

Language is a complex entity involving multiple levels of processing. Expressive language tasks (e.g. verbal fluency) are the most frequently used paradigms to investigate language lateralization (Gallagher et al., 2007). Receptive language tests are more suitable for imaging studies and when working with young children or patients with mental retardation because they do not require a verbal response from the subject (Gallagher et al., 2008).

The brain activation patterns of receptive language processing have been studied mainly with fMRI and PET. However, the invasive and restrictive nature of these techniques often make them inappropriate for young children, epileptic patients, or patients with mental retardation (Gallagher et al., 2007). Near-infrared spectroscopy (NIRS), a noninvasive technique that allows the measurement of blood oxygenation changes related to cerebral activation (Villringer & Chance, 1997), is also known as optical imaging. This technique is based on the light absorption properties of oxyhemoglobin (HbO) and deoxyhemoglobin (HbR). Good agreements have been observed between NIRS and fMRI, MEG, and PET (Kuperberg et al., 2000). However, NIRS has a better temporal resolution than fMRI; its mobile and cheaper nature confers important advantages over the other techniques. Moreover, its configuration does not require subject containment, thus allowing participants to move and speak. This makes it ideal while evaluating cognitive and linguistic functions or for research with young children and special populations (Gallagher et al., 2008).

Paquette et al. (2010) investigated the use of NIRS to assess receptive language patterns using a story listening paradigm. Four native French speakers listened to stories read aloud by a bilingual speaker in both French and Arabic. To determine if the signal recorded was affected by episodic memory processes, a familiar story and an unknown story were presented. Results showed that listening to stories in French elicited a significantly higher left lateralized response than listening to stories in Arabic, independent of the familiarity of the story. These results suggest that NIRS is a useful noninvasive technique to assess receptive language in adults and can be used to investigate language lateralization among children and epileptic patients slated for epilepsy surgery.

Functional neuroimaging in normal populations has been used to explore complex, integrative regions of the brain (secondary unimodal zones and heteromodal or tertiary zones). The studies most related to neuropsychological issues are language, memory, and executive functions.

These functional activation studies are aimed at elucidating specificity of functions in underlying neural networks. Beyond the classical language areas of Broca's and Wernicke's, new areas continue to be identified. Regions contiguous to these known areas of expressive and receptive speech also play important roles in language. New areas identified as playing important roles with receptive language include the middle temporal, inferior temporal, fusiform, supramarginal, and angular gyri. The role of the insular cortex in the rapidity of automatized phonological processing is noteworthy for facilitating fluent reading (Shaywitz et al., 1995). There are data as to gender differences and the functional organization of language (Frost et al., 1997). Similarly, the neural circuitry involved in complex visual object recognition and semantic memory has been mapped using fMRI (Ishai, Ungerleider, Martin, & Haxby, 2000; see Martin & Chao, 2001). Their findings indicate that the cortical areas involved in recalling the names of objects are located near the representation of the physical attributes for the objects and that there is a highly complex distributed network rather than isolated, modular areas of storage.

The network of language pathways has been studied with diffusion tensor MRI (Glasser & Rilling, 2008). Diffusion tensor MRI is an MRI method that produces in vivo images of biological tissues weighted with the local microstructural characteristics of water diffusion. The field of diffusion tensor MRI can be understood in terms of two distinct classes of application: diffusion weighted MRI and diffusion tensor MRI. Diffusion weighted MRI can provide information about damage to parts of the nervous system. Diffusion tensor MRI can provide information about connections among brain regions. DTI has also been used to demonstrate subtle abnormalities in a variety of conditions, including multiple sclerosis and schizophrenia (Chan et al., 2010), TBI (Kraus et al., 2007), and attention-deficit/hyperactivity disorder (Konrad et al., 2010).

### Executive Control and Memory

Another area extremely important in neuropsychology is memory processing. The supervisory attentional system or central executive that modulates the verbal and visual-spatial aspects of short-term memory are a major area of study. fMRI studies can quantitatively assess relationships between brain activation states and higher cognition. The role of the dorsolateral prefrontal cortex (DLPFC) in the shifting, planning, and organizing of mental processes has been demonstrated by various experimental paradigms (Nystrom et al., 2000). The registration of novel information (i.e., anterograde memory processing) and subsequent transfer from short-term storage to long-term storage have been confirmed through fMRI studies showing activation of the bilateral posterior hippocampal formations, parahippocampal gyri, and fusiform gyri (C. E. Stern et al., 1996), whereas the anterior hippocampus may be preferentially involved memory encoding. (See Schacter & Wagner, 1999.) Similarly, others have identified additional brain areas involved in memory processes (primarily prefrontal and mesial temporal structures) and thus have started to show the complex brain circuitry involved in memory. (See Buckner, Logan, Donaldson, & Wheeler, 2000; Cabeza & Nyberg, 2000; Fletcher & Henson, 2001.)

Cognitive control between younger adults and older adults has been investigated by Jimura and Braver (2010), who found that older adults show declines in both sustained and transient cognitive control processes. However, previous neuroimaging studies have primarily focused on age-related change in the magnitude, but not temporal dynamics, of brain activity. Jimura and Braver compared brain activity dynamics in healthy old and young adults during task switching. A mixed blocked/event-related fMRI design enabled separation of transient and sustained neural activity associated with cognitive control. Relative to young adults, older adults exhibited not only decreased sustained activity in the anterior prefrontal cortex during task-switching blocks but also increased transient activity on task-switch trials.

Another pattern of age-related shift in dynamics was present in the lateral prefrontal cortex and posterior parietal cortex, with younger adults showing a cue-related response during task-switch trials in the lateral prefrontal cortex and prefrontal cortex, whereas older adults exhibited switch-related activation during the cue period in the prefrontal cortex only. These qualitatively distinct patterns of brain activity predicted distinct patterns of behavioral performance across the two age groups, suggesting that older adults may shift from a proactive to reactive cognitive control strategy as a means of retaining relatively preserved behavioral performance in the face of age-related neurocognitive changes.

### Schizophrenia

Since the work of Andreasen and colleagues in the early 1990s, we have obtained objective, empirical evidence of structural anomalies associated with schizophrenia (Andreasen et al., 1990; Andreasen et al., 1993; Andreasen et al., 1997). The dilatation of ventricular size in these patients was the earliest potential link between underlying neuropathological changes and psychiatric manifestations. Subsequent MRI studies (Chua & McKenna, 1995) replicated the findings of increased lateral and third ventricle enlargement in persons diagnosed with schizophrenia. Ventricular brain ratio increases were seen most often with persons diagnosed with chronic schizophrenia who consequently had smaller frontal lobes, along with temporal lobe asymmetries and changes related to the size and surface area of the planum temporal and reduction in size and volume of the corpus callosum (Andreasen et al., 1990). Subcortical increases in gray matter in the basal ganglia were also reported (Hokama et al., 1995). Neuropsychological deficit patterns seem to be linked to structural anomalies within the DLPFC, with the left hemisphere demonstrating more significant changes (Lawrie et al., 1997). PET studies over the last two decades have isolated functional metabolic changes through the use of radioactive isotopes such as 2-fluorodeoxyglucose (2-FDG 015). A diminution in glucose metabolism was seen in various regions of the frontal lobes of schizophrenic patients. This hypofrontality became a functional neuroradiological marker associated with this disease entity. Neuropsychological testing of these patients revealed dysexecutive functioning and anterograde memory impairment as associated neurobehavioral sequelae, neuropsychological findings that seem directly related to these metabolic lesions, which may be at the root of the poor reality testing—that is, delusional thinking and disorganized ability to connect cognition to emotions. fMRI research confirms prefrontal dysfunction on tasks of working memory (Perlstein, Carter, Noll, & Cohen, 2001) and verbal fluency tasks (Shergill, 2005; Smee et al., 2006). (See Meyer-Lindenberg & Berman, 2001, for a review prefrontal dysfunction in schizophrenia.)

### Affective Disorders

Structural and functional deviations are also seen on neuroimaging studies of affective disorders (unipolar and bipolar types; Videbech, 1997). The expanded width of the third ventricle and volume reductions of the basal ganglia are notable. Functional imaging with a number of radioisotopes demonstrated pathological changes associated with affective disorders. For depression, left (inferior) prefrontal region and anterior cingulate gyrus hypometabolism is a hallmark finding. (See Bench, Friston, Brown, Frackowiak, & Dolan, 1993; Mayberg, 2001; and Podell, Lovell, & Goldberg, 2001, for reviews.) The neuropsychological and neuroimaging data collectively demonstrate cognitive sequelae linked to metabolic changes within specific brain regions and their interconnecting neural networks. The bilateral inferior frontal gyri and right anterior cingulate gyrus seem to be implicated in the emotional aspects of behavior (George et al., 1993).

Patients with elated and depressed moods demonstrated dysfunctional cognition on verbal fluency tasks. Associated metabolic changes are seen in the thalamus, cingulate gyrus, premotor and prefrontal cortices of the left hemisphere (see Mayberg, 2001). In studies of generalized anxiety disorder (GAD), there were hypermetabolic changes in the frontal, temporal, and parietal cortices, and reductions were seen in the metabolic state of the basal ganglia. Relative to healthy controls, subjects with obsessive compulsive disorder (OCD) demonstrated metabolic increases in the head of the caudate nucleus and orbital gyri. Treatments of OCD patients with selective serotonin reuptake inhibitors showed metabolic decreases in the entire cingulate gyrus (Baxter et al., 1992; Perani et al., 1995). Theoretical models suggest that OCD is related to functional and structural abnormalities in orbitofronto-striatal circuits. Evidence from cognitive and neuroimaging studies (fMRI and MRI and PET) have been supportive of this view despite inconsistencies across the studies.

In summary, there are several notable discrepancies among findings from cognitive studies, neuroimaging studies, and the present theoretical model proposed to underlie OCD. The currently available evidence suggests that the orbitofronto-striatal model may not be sufficient to explain the brain basis of OCD. Menzies et al. (2008) found consistent abnormalities in orbitofronto-striatal and other additional areas in OCD, which have not been considered in current models. These authors advocate an approach where whole brain-based neuroimaging and cognitive studies direct researchers to the study of additional regions outside the orbitofronto-striatal circuit, followed by closer investigation of these regions. Neurochemical changes were noted after behavioral interventions, psychopharmacological interventions, or both were undertaken. Posttreatment data revealed metabolic decreases in the entire cingulate gyrus that were associated with clinical improvement. Also revealed was the role of the amygdale in relation to anxiety producing stimuli. Collectively, neuroimaging studies have linked limbic and paralimbic structures to the processing of emotional behaviors (George et al., 1993).

### Dementia

In dementias, metabolic reductions have been seen in both the anterior and posterior tertiary zones as well as unimodal association areas within all cortices (Frackowiak, 1989; Smith et al., 1992). Dementias have also demonstrated hypometabolic changes in limbic, paralimbic, diencephalic, and periventricular regions (Mielke et al., 1996). Corresponding neuropsychological deficits are most prominent on measures of anterograde memory and executive functioning, with additional material-specific disturbances reported when discrete focal areas were implicated. Distinctive cognitive profiles in Alzheimer's disease and subcortical vascular dementia have been reported by Graham, Emery, and Hodges (2004). Despite a minimal degree of overall dementia, both patient groups had impairments in all cognitive domains. The Alzheimer's patients were more impaired than those with vascular dementia on episodic memory while the patients with vascular dementia were more impaired on semantic memory, executive/attentional functioning, and visuospatial and perceptual skills. Although decline in episodic memory is usually the earliest cognitive change that occurs prior to the development of the Alzheimer dementia syndrome, asymmetry in cognitive abilities may also occur during the preclinical phase of the disease and predict imminent dementia. Discrete patterns of cognitive deficits occur in Alzheimer's disease and several neuropathologically distinct age-associated neurodegenerative disorders. Knowledge of the differences between X and Y helps to distinguish among various causes of dementia and provides useful models for understanding brain–behavior relationships that mediate cognitive abilities affected in various neurodegenerative diseases (Salmon & Bondi, 2009). Modulation within the cholinergic neurotransmitter system is often associated with amnestic changes. The right midfrontal gyrus seems to be linked to both working memory and general executive functioning in support of these activities (Furey et al., 1997). A review of numerous studies has revealed that although serotonergic and cholinergic neurotransmitter systems have been implicated in dementias—especially those of the Alzheimer's type—there are probably many additional neurotransmitter systems involved as well.

### Transcranial Magnetic Stimulation

Transcranial magnetic stimulation (TMS) is a noninvasive method to cause depolarization in the neurons of the brain. TMS uses electromagnetic induction to induce weak electric currents using a rapidly changing magnetic field that causes activity in specific or general parts of the brain and allows brain functioning to be studied. A variant of TMS, repetitive transcranial magnetic stimulation (rTMS), has been tested as a treatment tool for various neurological and psychiatric disorders. TMS can be used clinically to measure activity and function of specific brain circuits in humans. The most robust and widely accepted use is in measuring the connection between the primary motor cortex and a muscle to evaluate damage from strokes, spinal cord injuries, multiple sclerosis, and motor neuron disease (Dimyan & Cohen, 2010; Rossini & Rossi, 2007).

Studies of the use of TMS and rTMS to treat neurological and psychiatric conditions have shown modest effects (Slotema, Blom, Hoek, & Sommer, 2010). However, publications reporting the results of reviews and statistical meta-anaylses of earlier investigations have stated that rTMS appeared to be effective in the treatment of certain types of major depression under certain specific conditions (Schutter, 2008).

## FUTURE DIRECTIONS

Neuropsychology has enjoyed a wide range of growth and development over the past several decades, particularly within the past several years. This growth and development has been fueled by technological advancements, such as more innovative and powerful neurodiagnostic equipment and tests (e.g., fMRI), innovations in computerized and paper-and-pencil assessment techniques, and application of statistical procedures to improve assessment accuracy. Clinical neuropsychology has also grown by creating new clinical niches, such as sport-related concussion assessment, and by improving already existing clinical specialties, such as forensic, clinical, and school neuropsychology. Other issues or factors are on the horizon and should continue to shape neuropsychology in the near future and may have a profound impact on the field. For example, we believe that there is a need for greater consistency within clinical neuropsychological assessments, not only in the tests used but also in the normative data being applied and in the construct validity of tests with diverse populations. Slightly different normative tables may drastically alter test results. Although having various normative tables for the same test is appropriate based on demographic variables, the misuse of normative tables is common. For example, a large normative sample was developed out of the Mayo Clinic called the Mayo Older Adult Normative Study for older subjects (MOANS norms) for various commonly used neuropsychological tests such as Wechsler Memory Scale—Revised and the Mattis Dementia Rating Scale (Ivnik, Malec, Smith, Tangalos, & Petersen, 1996; Ivnik et al., 1992; Lucas et al., 1998). However, this normative sample tends to be highly educated (mean education of 13.1 years) and consists of disproportionately Caucasian suburbanites. Often we have seen clinicians apply these norms to unrepresented samples. When the MOANS norms are compared to those of other recent studies (Banks, Yochim, MacNeill, & Lichtenberg, 2000), one can clearly see the effects the demographic factors have on the test scores and how they can lead to a different interpretation. We would like to see better application of more demographically appropriate normative data.

U.S. demographic and sociopolitical shifts have resulted in a rapidly growing need for culturally competent neuropsychological services. However, clinical neuropsychology as a field has not kept pace with the needs of ethnic minority clients. Three major factors argue for neuropsychology to increase the provision of culturally competent neuropsychological services for ethnic minorities: (1) demographic shifts in the U.S. population, (2) the ethics and ethos of the broader discipline of psychology, and (3) construct validity requirements in neuropsychological evaluation. The U.S. Census Bureau (2007) recently announced that the ethnic minority population reached 100.7 million (34%). In several states, ethnic minority groups already outnumber non-Hispanic whites (U.S. Census Bureau, 2007). By the year 2050, approximately 50% of all U.S. residents will belong to an ethnic minority group. Thus, there is an ethical imperative to provide services in a culturally and linguistically competent manner to these individuals.

American Psychological Association Standard 2.01 (2002; Boundaries of Competence) states that "cultural expertise or competence at the individual level is essential for the clinician who is working with cross-cultural populations." It is clear that neuropsychologists, like all psychologists, have an ethical mandate to provide culturally competent neuropsychological services to ethnic minority clients. Last, fundamental to valid neuropsychological evaluation is the use of valid instruments. APA Ethical Standard 9.02b (2002) states: "Psychologists use assessment instruments whose validity and reliability have been established for use with members of the population tested." Luria (1976) warned that tests developed and validated for use in one culture frequently resulted in experimental failures and were invalid for use with other cultural groups. Similarly, neuropsychological instruments designed to measure constructs in one culture may not be applied to individuals of other cultures with the expectation that they will be equally measuring the same construct.

Recent research has offered promising empirical results in addressing cross-cultural issues in assessment. Tuokko and his colleagues (2009) elegantly addressed the issue of cross-linguistic construct validity in a sample of English- and French-speaking older adults. This study used factor-analytic techniques to examine whether the latent variables underlying the Canadian Study of Health and Aging (CSHA) neuropsychological test battery administered in English or French were the same (i.e., invariant). The results revealed that the best-fitting baseline model, which was established in the English-speaking Exploratory sample ($n = 716$), demonstrated invariance among the English-speaking ($n = 715$) and the French-speaking ($n = 446$) respondents. The study provideed some empirical support for the cross-linguistic construct validity of the CSHA neuropsychological battery utilizing a relatively straightforward multigroup confirmatory factor analysis (CFA) framework.

Another line of research that has shown promise is the assessment and comparison of neurocognitive processes of Hispanic children and adolescents. Naglieri, Rojahn, and Matto (2007) examined Cognitive Assessment System (CAS) scores for 244 Hispanic and 1,956 non-Hispanic children. They found that the two groups differed by 6.1 points when the samples were unmatched samples, 5.1 points with samples matched on basic demographic variables, and 4.8 points when demographics differences were statistically controlled. Naglieri, Otero, Delauder, and Matto (2007) compared the English and Spanish versions of the CAS for bilingual Hispanic children. The children in their study earned very similar CAS Full Scale scores (84.6 and 87.6 for English and Spanish versions, respectively) and deficits in Successive processing were found (78.0 and 83.1 for English and Spanish versions, respectively). The Full Scale scores for the English and Spanish versions of the CAS correlated .96. Importantly, 90% of children who had a PASS weakness on one version of the CAS also had the same PASS weakness on the other version of the CAS. A second study of the English and Spanish version of the CAS yielded very similar findings. Otero, Gonzales, and Naglieri (in press) examined the performance of referred Hispanic English-language learners ($N = 40$) on the English and Spanish versions of the CAS and found no significant differences between the Full Scale scores or in any of the PASS scales. Students earned their lowest scores in Successive processing regardless of the language in which the test was administered. These findings suggest that the CAS may be a useful measure for Hispanic children with underdeveloped English-language proficiency.

Naglieri and Taddei (2006) examined English and Italian versions of the CAS for Italian ($N = 809$) and U.S. ($N = 1,174$) samples matched by age and gender. Small differences between U.S. and Italian samples were found on the PASS and Full Scale standard scores when the U.S. norms were used. The differences between the samples for the PASS scores were trivial except for the Attention Scale ($d = .26$), where Italian sample was slightly higher. The Full Scale standard scores (using the U.S. norms) for the Italian (100.9) and U.S. (100.5) samples were nearly identical. Negligible differences were found for nine of the 13 subtests, 3 showed small $d$-ratios (2 in favor of the Italian sample), and 1 was large (in favor of the U.S. sample). Taken as a whole, these findings for the English/Spanish and English/Italian studies suggest that the PASS theory as measured by CAS yields similar mean scores for samples that differ on cultural and linguistic characteristics. In total, the research demonstrates the utility of using a neuropsychological approach (e.g., PASS theory) as a way to fairly assess diverse populations.

Clinicians often lack in-depth training in assessment of ethnic minorities (Rivera, Mindt, Saez, & Manly, 2010). The Houston Conference guidelines (Hannay et al., 1998) recommend that trainees should gain knowledge about cultural diversity from their core of knowledge of general psychology, and the ability to recognize multicultural issues from their training in assessment. The proceedings contained little detail, however, about the level of multicultural knowledge and skills required to function as a clinical neuropsychologist or how the knowledge and skill was to be achieved. It is clear that neuropsychology training programs will need to formally integrate multicultural issues to foster cultural competence into their curricula, didactics, and training. Equally important in the assessment of diverse groups is the use of tests that are representative of those groups.

Tests used in neuropsychology now have greater degree of fractionation of large normative samples to allow more accurate matching to the individual client. For example, the WMS-IV, NEPSY-Second Edition (NPSY-II), WAIS-IV, KABC-II, CAS, and the NAB, to mention a few are based on large, census-matched normative samples, and normative data are broken down by age, gender and education. Although several tests lack such a data breakdown, it is likely that test publishers will require such information in future iterations of older tests.

Another interesting trend in clinical neuropsychology is the incorporation of other disciplines into assessments. For example, in our clinics we often incorporate functional assessment techniques (such as the Independent Living Scales; Loeb, 1996) into our traditional neuropsychological assessment. (See Baird, Podell, Lovell, & McGinty, 2001.) This practice allows for a more comprehensive assessment that helps to address issues of functioning at home. Such a practice improves the comprehensiveness of the neuropsychological assessment, better helps the patient, and improves the role neuropsychology can have in the care of the patient. Additionally, computer technologies may develop in a way that will provide highly realistic simulations of the cognitive tasks that must be performed in everyday life, tasks on which developmental change or the effects of neurological disease or trauma are first noted. One example is using sophisticated multiple-screen, computerized training simulators that mimic driving a car under a wide variety of circumstances. Technologies such as these have been validated and shown to be sensitive to drug effects (Kay et al., 2004). Future computer-based technologies may allow subjects to enter a new interactive world (a virtual reality) in which they could be called on to perform a wide variety of cognitive tasks while their performance is precisely measured. As neuropsychologists, our ultimate concern is with individuals' ability to function in a cognitively demanding environment, and simulating that environment in cognitive testing may be an important direction for future research and development of the field. Technological breakthroughs in neuroimaging and computer technologies have greatly improved our neuropsychological knowledge base. We believe that we have only seen the tip of the iceberg and that we will continue to see a rapid expansion of knowledge and understanding of brain–behavior relationships for years to come.

Innovations in clinical assessments have led to new clinical niches, such as sport-related concussion assessment and improved forensic assessment techniques. As the economy and health care continue to place pressure on traditional neuropsychological testing, our field will need to be creative in countering the negative impact managed care has on our clinical assessments. One of our fears is how this situation will affect training future neuropsychologists. We have already seen a trend toward shorter test protocols dictated by highly intrusive utilization management by insurance companies. These shorter batteries can compromise clinical training (let alone quality of care) in that limited protocols will not allow trainees to see the full complement of cognitive deficits. Although the field does need some adjustment, there is concern that training will become compromised as large institutions try to keep training programs viable while balancing the need to cut costs (e.g., use shorter protocols) and provide a diverse enough training experience. We also are concerned, as are all those who work in the field of health care, with the potential brain drain that managed care and the shrinking health-care dollar have on attracting talented young individuals to more lucrative professions.

The future of neuropsychology is blossoming with many more exciting developments still to come. However, as in all other health-care fields, neuropsychology is also in the midst of historic changes from external forces (common to all industries). It must be able to weather the storm if it wants to survive as a strong and viable clinical service and area of research growth.

# REFERENCES

Agel, J., Olson, D. E., Dick, R., Arendt, E. A., Marshall, S. W., & Sikka, R. S. (2007). Descriptive epidemiology of collegiate women's basketball injuries: National collegiate athletic association injury surveillance system, 1988–1989 through 2003–2004. *Journal of Athletic Training, 42* (2), 202–210.

Allen, L. M., Conder, R. L. Jr., Green, P., & Cox, D. R. (1998). *Computerized assessment of response bias.* Durham, NC: Cognisyst.

Andreasen, N. C., Flaum, M., Swayze, V., II, O'Leary, D. S., Alliger, R., & Cohen, G. (1993). Intelligence and brain structure in normal individuals. *American Journal of Psychiatry, 150,* 130–134.

Andreasen, N. C., O'Leary, D. S., Flaum, M., Nopoulos, P., Watkins, G. L., Boles Ponto, L. L., & Hichwa, R. D. (1997). Hypofrontality in schizophrenia: Distributed dysfunctional circuits in neuroleptic-naive patients. *Lancet, 349,* 1730–1734.

Andreasen, N. C., Swayze, V. W. II, Flaum, M., Yates, W. R., Arndt, S., & McChesney, C. (1990). Ventricular enlargement in schizophrenia evaluated with computed tomographic scanning. Effects of gender, age, and stage of illness. *Archives of General Psychiatry, 47,* 1008–1015.

American Psychological Association (2002). Ethical principles of psychologists and code of conduct. *American Psychologist, 57,* 12, 1060–1073.

American Psychological Association. (2011). About the internship crisis. Retrieved from www.apa.org/apags/issues/internship.aspx

American Psychological Association Women's Programs Office. (2006). Women in the American Psychological Association: 2006. Retrieved from www.apa.org/pi/women/committee/wapa-2006.pdf

Atkinson, L. (1991). Three standard errors of measurement and the Wechsler Memory Scale—Revised. *Psychological Assessment, 3,* 136–138.

Aubry, M., Cantu, R., Duorak, J., Johnston, K., Kelly, J., Lovell, M. R., . . . Schamosch, P. (2002). Summary agreement statement of the first International Conference on Concussion in Sport. *British Journal of Sports Medicine, 36,* 6–10.

Baker, R., Donders, J., & Thompson, E. (2000). Assessment of incomplete effort with the California Verbal Learning Test. *Applied Neuropsychology, 7,* 111–114.

Baird, A., Podell, K., Lovell, M., & McGinty, S. B. (2001). Complex real-world functioning and neuropsychological test performance in older adults. *Clinical Neuropsychologist, 15,* 369–379.

Banks, A. L., Yochim, B. P., MacNeill, S. E., & Lichtenberg, P. A. (2000). Expanded normative data for the Mattis Dementia Rating Scale for use with urban, elderly medical patients. *Clinical Neuropsychologist, 14,* 149–156.

Barr, W. B., & McCrea, M. (2001). Sensitivity and specificity of standardized neurocognitive testing immediately following sports concussion. *Journal of the International Neuropsychological Society, 7,* 693–702.

Barth, J. T., Alves, W. M., Ryan, T. V., Macciocchi, S. N., Rimel, R. W., Jane, J. A., & Nelson, W. E. (1989). Mild head injury in sports: Neuropsychological sequelae and recovery of function. In H. Levin, H. M. Eisenberg, & A. L. Benton (Eds.), *Mild head injury* (pp. 257–275). New York, NY: Oxford University Press.

Baum, C. M., Connor, L. T, Morrison, T., Hahn, M., Dromerick, D., & Edwards, D. F. (2008). Reliability, validity, and clinical utility of the Executive Function Performance Test: A measure of executive function in a sample of people with stroke. *American Journal of Occupational Therapy, 62* (4), 446–455.

Baxter, L. R. Jr., Schwartz, J. M., Bergman, K. S., Szuba, M. P., Guze, B. H., & Mazziotta, J. C. (1992). Caudate glucose metabolic rate changes with both drug and behavior therapy for obsessive-compulsive disorder. *Archives of General Psychiatry, 49,* 681–689.

Bench, C. J., Friston, K. J., Brown, R. G., Frackowiak, R. S., & Dolan, R. J. (1993). Regional cerebral blood flow in depression measured by positron emission tomography: The relationship with clinical dimensions. *Psychological Medicine, 23,* 579–590.

Ben-Porath, Y. S., Graham, J. R., Hall, G. C. N., Hirschman, R. D., & Zaragoza, M. S. (1995). *Forensic application of the MMPI-2.* Thousand Oaks, CA: Sage.

Ben-Porath, Y. S., & Tellegen, A. (2008). MMPI-2-RF (Minnesota Multiphasic Personality Inventory-2 Restructured Form): Manual for administration, scoring, and interpretation. Minneapolis: University of Minnesota Press.

Benton, A. (1988). Neuropsychology: Past, present and future. In F. Boller & J. Grafman (Eds.), *Handbook of clinical neuropsychology* (Vol. 1, pp. 3–27). Amsterdam: Swets and Zeitlinger B.V.

Bigler, E. D., & Snyder, J. L. (1995). Neuropsychological outcome and quantitative neuroimaging in mild traumatic brain injury. *Archives of Clinical Neuropsychology, 10,* 159–174.

Bigler, E. D. (2008). Neuropsychology and clinical neuroscience of persistent post-concussive syndrome. *Journal of the International Neuropsychological Society, 14* (1), 1–22.

Binder, L. M. (1992). Forced-choice testing provides evidence of malingering. *Archives of Physical Medicine and Rehabilitation, 73,* 377–380.

Binder, L. M. (1993). Assessment of malingering after mild head trauma with the Portland Digit Recognition Test. *Journal of Clinical and Experimental Neuropsychology, 15,* 170–182.

Binder, L. M., & Pankrantz, L. (1987). Neuropsychological evidence of a factitious memory complaint. *Journal of Clinical and Experimental Neuropsychology, 9,* 167–171.

Binder, L. M., & Willis, S. C. (1991). Assessment of motivation after financially compensable minor head trauma. *Psychological Assessment, 3,* 175–181.

Bleiberg, J., Halpern, E. L., Reeves, D. L., & Daniel, J. C. (1998). Future directions for the neuropsychological assessment of sports concussion. *Journal of Head Trauma Rehabilitation, 13,* 36–44.

Bleiberg, J., Kane, R. L., Reeves, D. L., Garmoe, W. S., & Halpern, E. (2000). Factor analysis of computerized and traditional tests used in mild brain injury research. *Clinical Neuropsychologist, 14,* 287–294.

Broshek, D. K., Kaushik, T., Freeman, J. R., Erlanger, D., Webbe, F., & Barth, J. T. (2005). Sex differences in outcome following sports-related concussion. *Journal of Neurosurgery, 102,* 856–863.

Bruce, D. (1985). On the origin of the term "neuropsychology." *Neuropsychologia, 23,* 813–81.

Bradshaw, J. L., & Mattingley, J. B. (1995). *Clinical neuropsychology.* New York, NY: Academic Press.

Brandt, J. (1988). Malingered amnesia. In R. Rogers (Ed.), *Clinical assessment of malingering and deception* (pp. 56–69). New York, NY: Guilford Press.

Brown, L., Sherbenou, R. J., & Johnson, S. K. (1982). *Test of Nonverbal Intelligence.* Austin, TX: ProEd.

Buckner, R. L., Logan, J., Donaldson, D. I., & Wheeler, M. E. (2000). Cognitive neuroscience of episodic memory encoding. *Acta Psychologica, 105,* 127–139

Bush, S. S., Ruff, R. M., Tröster, A. I., Barth, J. T., Koffler, S. P., Pliskin, N. H., . . . Silver, C. H. (2005). Symptom validity assessment: Practice issues and medical necessity NAN policy & planning committee. *Archives of Clinical Neuropsychology, 20,* 419–426.

Cabeza, R., & Nyberg, L. (2000). Neural bases of learning and memory: Functional neuroimaging evidence. *Current Opinions in Neurology, 13,* 415–421.

Cantu, R. C. (1998). Second-impact syndrome. *Clinical Sports Medicine, 17,* 37–44.

Cernich, A. N., Brennana, D. M., Barker, L. M., & Bleiberg, J. (2007). Sources of error in computerized neuropsychological assessment. *Archives of Clinical Neuropsychology, 22,* 1, 39–48.

Chan, W. Y., Yang, G. L., Chia, M. Y., Lau, I. Y., Sitoh, Y. Y., Nowinski, W. L., & Sim, K. (2010). White matter abnormalities in first-episode schizophrenia: A combined structural MRI and DTI study. *Schizophrenia Research, 119,* 52–60.

Charles, C. J., Ariel, R. N., McKay, S. E. (1982). The Luria-Nebraska Neuropsychological Battery: Theoretical orientation and comment. *Journal of Consulting and Clinical Psychology, 50,* 291–300.

Chelune, G. J. (2010). Evidence-based research and practice in clinical neuropsychology. *The Clinical Neuropsychologist, 24*(3): 454–67.

Chelune, G. J., Naugle, R. I., Lüders, H. S. J., Sedlak, J., & Awad, I. A. (1993). Individual change after epilepsy surgery: Practice effects and base-rate information. *Neuropsychology, 7,* 41–52.

Christensen, L., & Mendoza, J. L. (1986). A method of assessing change in a single subject: An alteration of the RC index. *Behavior Therapy, 17,* 305–308.

Chua, S. E., & McKenna, P. J. (1995). Schizophrenia: A brain disease? *British Journal of Psychiatry, 66,* 563–582.

Collins, M., Grindel, S., Lovell, M., Dede, D., Moser, D., & Phalin, B. (1999). Relationship between concussion and neuropsychological performance in college football players. *Journal of the American Medical Association, 282,* 964–970.

Contemporary Pediatrics Staff. (2010, September 1). Sports-related concussions require careful assessment and treatment. Retrieved from www.modernmedicine.com/modernmedicine/Modern+Medicine+Now/Sports-related-concussions-require-carefulassessmt/Article Standard/Article/detail/687328

Davies, H. P., King, J. H., Klebe, K. J., Bajszer, G., Bloodworth, M. R., & Wallick, S. L. (1997). The detection of simulated malingering using a computerized priming test. *Archives of Clinical Neuropsychology, 12,* 145–153.

Detre, J. A., Maccotta, L., King, D., Alsop, D. C., Glosser, G., & D'Esposito, M. (1998). Noninvasive MRI evaluation of cerebral blood flow in cerebrovascular disease. *Neurology, 50,* 926–932.

Dikmen, S., Machamer, J., Fann, J. R., & Temkin, N. R. (2010). Rates of symptom reporting following traumatic brain injury. *Journal of the International Neuropsychological Society, 16,* 401–411.

Dimyan, M. A., & Cohen, L. (2010). Contribution of transcranial magnetic stimulation to the understanding of mechanisms of functional recovery after stroke. *Neurorehabilitation and Neural Repair, 24*(2), 125–135.

Dymek, M. P., Atchison, P., Harrell, L., & Marson, D. C. (2001). Competency to consent to medical treatment in cognitively impaired patients with Parkinson's disease. *Neurology, 9,* 17–24.

Earnst, K. S., Marson, D. C., & Harrell, L. E. (2000). Cognitive models of physicians' legal standard and personal judgments of competency in-patients with Alzheimer's disease. *Journal of American Geriatric Society, 48,* 1014–1016.

Ellwanger, J., Rosenfeld, J. P., Sweet, J. J., & Bhatt, M. (1996). Detecting simulated amnesia for autobiographical and recently learned information using P300 event related potential. *International Journal of Psychophysiology, 23,* 9–23.

Ellwanger, J., Tenhulla, W. N., Rosenfeld, P., & Sweet, J. J. (1999). Identifying simulators of cognitive deficit through combined use of neuropsychological test performance and event-related potentials. *Journal of Clinical and Experimental Neuropsychology, 21,* 866–879.

Elwood, R. W. (1993). Clinical discriminations and neuropsychological tests: An appeal to Bayes' theorem. *Clinical Neuropsychologist, 7,* 224–233.

Faul, M., Xu, L., Wald, M. M., & Coronado, V. G. (2010). Traumatic brain injury in the United States: emergency department visits, hospitalizations, and deaths. Atlanta, GA: Centers for Disease Control and Prevention, National Center for Injury Prevention and Control. Retrieved from www.cdc.gov/traumaticbraininjury/tbi_ed.html

Fox, D. (2011). SVT failure indicates invalidity of neuropsychological tests. *Clinical Neuropsychologist, 25*(3), 488–495.

Fletcher, P. C., & Henson, R. N. (2001). Frontal lobes and human memory: Insights from functional neuroimaging. *Brain, 124,* 849–881.

Frackowiak, R. S. (1989). PET: Studies in dementia. *Psychiatry Research, 32,* 3, 525–549.

Frederick, R. I. (1997). *Validity indicator profile manual.* Minnetonka, MN: NCS Assessments.

Frost, J. A., Springer, J. A., Binder, J. R., Hammeke, T. A., Bellgowan, P. S. F., & Rao. (1997). Sex does not determine functional lateralization of semantic processing: Evidence from fMRI. *Neuroimage, 5,* S564.

Furey, M. L., Pietrini, P., Haxby, J. V., Alexander, G. E., Lee, H. C., & VanMeter, J. (1997). Cholinergic stimulation alters performance and task-specific regional cerebral blood flow during working memory. *Proceedings from National Academy of Science, 94,* 6512–6516.

Gallagher, A., Bastien, D., Pelletier, I., Vannasing, P., Legatt, A. D., Moshé, S. L., . . . Lassonde, M. (2008). A noninvasive, presurgical expressive and receptive language investigation in a 9-year-old epileptic boy using near-infrared spectroscopy. *Epilepsy & Behavior, 12*(2), 340–346.

Gallagher, A., Thériault, M., Maclin, E., Low, K., Gratton, G., Fabiani, M., . . . Lassonde, M. (2007). Near-infrared spectroscopy as an alternative to the Wada test for language mapping in children, adults and special populations. *Epileptic Disorders: International Epilepsy Journal, 9,* 241–255.

Gass, C. S. (1991). MMPI-2 interpretation and closed head injury: A correction factor. *Psychological Assessment, 3,* 27–31.

Gassen, M. D., Pietz, C. A., Spray, B. J., & Denney, R. L. (2007). Accuracy of Megargee's Criminal Offender Infrequency (FC) Scale in detecting malingering among forensic examinees. *Criminal Justice & Behavior, 34*(4), 493–504.

George, M. S., Ketter, T. A., Gill, D. S., Haxby, J. V., Ungerleider, L. G., & Herscovitch, P. (1993). Brain regions involved in recognizing facial emotion or identity: An oxygen-15 PET study. *Journal of Neuropsychiatry and Clinical Neuroscience, 5,* 384–394.

Glasser, M. F., & Rilling, J. K. (2008). DTI tractography of the human brain's language pathways. *Cerebral Cortex, 18*(11), 2471–2482.

Goldberg, E. (2001). *The executive brain: Frontal lobes and the civilized mind.* New York, NY: Oxford University Press.

Goldberg, E. (2009). *The new executive brain: Frontal lobes and the civilized mind.* New York, NY: Oxford University Press.

Goldberg, E., & Podell, K. (1999). Adaptive versus veridical decision making and the frontal lobes. *Journal of Consciousness and Cognition, 8,* 364–377.

Goldberg, E., & Podell, K. (2001). *The Cognitive Bias Test.* Melbourne, Australia: PsychPress.

Goldberg, E., Podell, K., Bilder, R., & Jaeger, J. (2000). *The Executive Control Battery.* Melbourne, Australia: PsychPress.

Goldberg, E., Podell, K., Harner, R., Lovell, M., & Riggio, S. (1994). Cognitive bias, functional cortical geometry, and the frontal lobes: Laterality, sex and handedness. *Journal of Cognitive Neuroscience, 6,* 276–296.

Goodyear, B., & Umetsu, D. (2002). Selected issues in forensic neuropsychology. In B. Van Dorsten (Ed.), *Forensic psychology: From classroom to courtroom* (pp. 289–290). New York, NY: Kluwer Academic/Plenum Press.

Gouvier, W. D. Base rates and clinical decision making in neuropsychology. In J. Sweet (Ed.), *Forensic neuropsychology: Fundamentals and practice.* Royersford, PA: Swets & Zietlinger, 1999.

Graham, N. L., Emery, T., & Hodges, J. R. (2004). Distinctive cognitive profiles in Alzheimer's disease and subcortical vascular dementia. *Journal of Neurology, Neurosurgery and Psychiatry, 75*(1), 61–71.

Greiffenstein, M., & Cohen, L. (2011). Neuropsychology and the law: Principles of productive attorney-neuropsychologist relations. In

G. Larrabee (Ed.), *Forensic neuropsychology: A scientific approach* (pp. 29–91). New York, NY: Oxford University Press.

Greve, K. W., Bianchini, K. J., Heinly, M. T., Love, J. M., Swift, D. A. & Ciota, M. (2008). Classification accuracy of the Portland digit recognition test in persons claiming exposure to environmental and industrial toxins. *Archives of Clinical Neuropsychology, 23*(3), 341–350.

Greve, K. W., Binder, L. M., & Bianchini, K. J. (2009). Rates of below-chance performance in forced-choice symptom validity tests. *Clinical Neuropsychologist, 23*(3), 534–544.

Greve, K. W., Ord, J., Curtis, K. L., Bianchini, K. J., & Brennan, A. (2008). Detecting malingering in traumatic brain injury and chronic pain: a comparison of three forced-choice symptom validity tests. *Clinical Neuropsychologist, 22*(5), 896–918.

Gross, C. G. (1998). *Brain, Vision, Memory: Tales in the History of Neuroscience*. Cambridge: MIT Press.

Gualtieri, C. T., & Johnson, L. G. (2006). Reliability and validity of a computerized neurocognitive test battery, CNS Vital Signs. *Archives of Clinical Neuropsychology, 21*, 623–643.

Guilmette, T. J., Hart, K. J., & Giuliano, A. J. (1993). Malingering detection: The use of a forced-choice method in identifying organic versus simulated memory impairment. *Clinical Neuropsychologist, 7*, 59–69.

Guskiewicz, K. M., Weaver, N. L., Padua, D. A., & Garrett, W. E. (2000). Epidemiology of concussion in collegiate and high school football players. *American Journal of Sports Medicine, 25*, 643–650.

Hannay, H. J., Bieliauskas, L. A., Crosson, B. A., Hammeke, T. A., Hamsher, K. de S., & Koffler, S. (Eds.) (1998). Proceedings of the Houston Conference on Specialty Education and Training in Clinical Neuropsychology: Policy statement. *Archives of Clinical Neuropsychology, 13*, 160–166.

Heilbronner, R. L. (2004, May). A status report on the practice of forensic neuropsychology. *Clinical Neuropsychology, 18*(2), 312–326.

Heilbronner, R. L., Sweet, J. J., Morgan, J. E., Larrabee, G. J., & Millis, S. R., & Conference Participants (2009). American Academy of Clinical Neuropsychology Consensus Conference Statement on the neuropsychological assessment of effort, response bias, and malingering. *Clinical Neuropsychologist, 23*, 1093–1129.

Hinton-Bayre, A. D., Geffin, G. M., Geffen, L. G., McFarland, K. A., & Friss, P. (1999). Concussion in contact sports: Reliable change indices of impairment and recovery. *Journal of Clinical and Experimental Neuropsychology, 21*, 70–86.

Hiscock, M., & Hiscock, C. K. (1989). Refining the forced choice method for the detection of malingering. *Journal of Clinical and Experimental Neuropsychology, 11*, 967–974.

Hokama, H., Shenton, M. E., Nestor, P. G., Kikinis, R., Levitt, J. J., & Metcalf, D. (1995). Caudate, putamen, and globus pallidus volume in schizophrenia: A quantitative MRI study. *Psychiatry Research, 61*, 209–229.

Holtz, J. L. (2011). *Applied clinical neuropsychology: An introduction*. New York, NY: Springer.

Ishai, A., Ungerleider, L. G., Martin, A., & Haxby, J. V. (2000). The representation of objects in the human occipital and temporalcortex. *Journal of Cognitive Neuroscience, 12*, 35–51.

Iverson, G. L., & Binder, L. M. (2000). Detecting exaggeration and malingering in neuropsychological assessment. *Journal of Head Trauma Rehabilitation, 15*, 829–858.

Ivnik, R. J., Malec, J. F., Smith, G. E., Tangalos, E. G., & Petersen, R. C. (1996). Neuropsychological tests' norms above age 55: COWAT, BNT, MAE Token, WRAT-R, AMNART, Stroop, TMT, and JLO. *Clinical Neuropsychologist, 10*, 262–278.

Ivnik, R. J., Malec, J. F., Smith, G. E., Tangalos, E. G., Petersen, R. C., Kokmen, E., & Kurland, L. T. (1992). Mayo's older Americans studies: WMS-R norms for ages 56–94. *Clinical Neuropsychologist, 6*, 49–82.

Jacobson, N. S., Follette, W. C., & Revenstorf, D. (1984). Psychotherapy outcome research: Methods for reporting variability and evaluating clinical significance. *Behavior Therapy, 15*, 336–352.

Jacobson, N. S., & Truax, P. (1991). Clinical significance: A statistical approach to defining meaningful change in psychotherapy research. *Journal of Consulting and Clinical Psychology, 59*, 12–19.

Jimura, K., & Braver, T. S. (2010). Age-related shifts in brain activity dynamics during task switching. *Cerebral Cortex, 20*(6), 1420–1431.

Kalmar, K., Novack, T. A., Nakase-Richardson, R., Sherer, M., Frol, A. B., Gordon, W. A., ... Ricker, J. H. (2008). Feasibility of a brief neuropsychological test battery during acute inpatient rehabilitation after traumatic brain injury. *Archives of Physical Medicine and Rehabilitation, 8*(5), 942–949.

Kaufman, A. S., & Kaufman, N. L. (2004). *Kaufman Brief Intelligence Test* (2nd ed.). San Antonio, TX: Pearson.

Kaufman, A. S., & Kaufman, N. L. (2004). *Kaufman assessment battery for children* (2nd ed). San Antonio, TX: Pearson.

Kaplan, E., Fein, D., Morris, R., Kramer, J. H., & Delis, D. C. (1991). *The WAIS-R NI*. San Antonio, TX: Psychological Corporation.

Kay, G. G., Pakull, B., Clark, T. M., Sea, D., Mays, D. A., & Tulloch, S. J. (2004). *The effect of Adderal XR treatment on driving performance in young adults with ADHD*. Paper presented at the 17th annual U.S. Psychiatric and Mental Health Congress. San Diego, CA.

Killgore, W. D., Glosser, G., Casasanto, D. J., French, J. A., Alsop, D. C., & Detre, J. A. (1999). Functional MRI and the Wada test provide complementary information for predicting postoperative seizure control. *Seizure, 8*, 450–455.

Konrad, A., Dielentheis, T. F., El Masri, D., Bayerl, M., Fehr, C., Gesierich, T., ... Winterer, G. (2010). Disturbed structural connectivity is related to inattention and impulsivity in adult attention deficit hyperactivity disorder. *European Journal of Neuroscience, 31*, 912–919.

Korkman, M. (1999). Applying Luria's diagnostic principles in the neuropsychological assessment of children. *Neuropsychology Review, 9*, 89–105.

Kraus, M. F., Susmaras, T., Caughlin, B., Walke, C. J., Sweeney, J. A., & Little, D. M. (2007). White matter integrity and cognition in chronic traumatic brain injury: A diffusion tensor imaging study. *Brain, 26*(8), 2508–2519.

Kuperberg, G. R., McGuire, P. K., Bullmore, E. T., Brammer, M. J., Rabe-Hesketh, S., Wright, I. C., ... David, A. S. (2000). Common and distinct neural substrates for pragmatic, semantic, and syntactic processing of spoken sentences: An FMRI study. *Journal of Cognitive Neuroscience, 12*(2), 321–341.

Larrabee, G. (2005). *Forensic neuropsychology: A scientific approach*. New York, NY: Oxford University Press.

Larrabee, G. J. (2007). *Assessment of malingered neuropsychological deficits*. New York: Oxford University Press.

Lawrie, S. M., Abukmeil, S. S., Chiswick, A., Egan, V., Santosh, C. G., & Best, J. J. (1997). Qualitative cerebral morphology in schizophrenia: A magnetic resonance imaging study and systematic literature review. *Schizophrenia Research, 25*, 155–166.

Lee, L. K. (2007). Controversies in the sequelae of pediatric mild traumatic brain injury. *Pediatric Emergency Care, 23*(8), 580–583.

Lees-Haley, P., English, L., & Glen, W. (1991). A fake bad scale on the MMPI-2 for personal injury claimants. *Psychological Reports, 68*, 203–210.

Lees-Haley, P. R., & Brown, R. S. (1993). Neuropsychological complain base rates of 170 personal injury claimants. *Archives of Clinical Neuropsychology, 8*, 203–209.

Lees-Haley, P. R., Fox, D. D., & Courtney, J. C. (2001). A comparison of complaints by mild brain injury claimants and other claimants describing subjective experiences immediately following their injury. *Archives of Clinical Neuropsychology, 16*(7), 689–695.

Letz, R. L., Green, R. C., & Woodard, J. L. (1996). Development of a computer-based battery designed to screen adults for neuropsychological impairment. *Neurotoxicology Teratology, 18*, 365–370.

Lezak, M., Howieson, D. B., Bigler, E. D., & Tranel, D. (2012). *Neuropsychological assessment* (5th ed.). New York: Oxford University Press.

Loeb, P. A. (1996). *Independent Living Scales*. San Antonio, TX: Psychological Corporation.

Lovell, M. R., & Collins, M. W. (1998). Neuropsychological assessment of the college football player. *Journal of Head Trauma Rehabilitation, 13*, 9–26.

Lucas, J. A., Ivnik, R. J., Smith, G. E., Bohac, D. L., Tangalos, E. G., & Kokmen, E. (1998). Normative Data for the Mattis Dementia Rating Scale. *Journal of Clinical and Experimental Psychology, 20*, 536–547.

Luria, A. R. (1966). *Human brain and psychological processes*. New York, NY: Harper & Row.

Luria, A. R. (1973). *The working brain: An introduction to neuropsychology*. New York, NY: Basic Books.

Luria, A. R. (1980). *Higher cortical functions in man* (2nd ed.). New York, NY: Basic Books.

Luria, A. R. (1976). *Cognitive development, its cultural and social foundations*. Cambridge, MA: Harvard University Press.

Maassen, G. H. (2000). Principles of defining reliable change indices. *Journal of Clinical and Experimental Neuropsychology, 22*, 622–632.

Macciocchi, S. N., Seel, S. T., Alderson, A., & Godsall, R. (2006) Victoria Symptom Validity Test performance in acute severe traumatic brain injury: Implications for test interpretation. *Archives of Clinical Neuropsychology, 21*(5), 395–404.

Maroon, J. C., Lovell, M. R., Norwig, J., Podell, K., Powell, J. W., & Hartl, R. (2000). Cerebral concussion in athletes: Evaluation and neuropsychological testing. *Neurosurgery, 47*(3), 659–669 (discussion, pp. 669–672).

Marson, D. C. (2001). Loss of competency in Alzheimer's disease: Conceptual and psychometric approaches. *International Journal of Law Psychiatry, 24*(2–3), 267–283.

Marson, D. C., Annis, S. M., McInturff, B., Bartolucci, A., & Harrell, L. E. (1999). Error behaviors associated with loss of competency in Alzheimer's disease. *Neurology, 53*, 1983–1992.

Marson, D. C., Chatterjee, A., Ingram, K. K., & Harrell, L. E. (1996). Toward a neurologic model of competency: Cognitive predictors of capacity to consent in Alzheimer's disease using three different legal standards. *Neurology, 46*, 666–672.

Marson, D. C., Cody, H. A., Ingram, K. K., & Harrell, L. E. (1995). Neuropsychologic predictors of competency in Alzheimer's disease using a rational reasons legal standard. *Archives of Neurology, 52*, 955–959.

Marson, D. C., Martin, R. C., Wadley, V., Griffith, H. R., Snyder, S., Belue, K., Goode, P., Kinney, C., Nicholas, A., Steele, T., Anderson, B., Zamrini, E., Raman, R., Bartolucci, A., Harrell, L. E. (2009). Clinical interview assessment of financial capacity in older adults with mild cognitive impairment and dementia. *Journal of the American Geriatrics Society, 57*, 806–814.

Martin, A., & Chao, L. L. (2001). Semantic memory and the brain: Structure and processes. *Current Opinion in Neurobiology, 11*, 194–201.

Mayberg, H. S. (2001). Frontal lobe dysfunction in secondary depression. In S. P. Salloway, P. F. Malloy, & J. D. Duffy (Eds.), *The frontal lobes and neuropsychiatric illness* (pp. 167–186). Washington, DC: American Psychiatric Press.

McAllister, T. W. (2011). Mild brain injury. In J. M. Silver, T. W. McAllister, & S. C. Yudofsky (Eds.), *Textbook of Traumatic Brain Injury* (2nd ed.). Arlington, VA: American Psychiatric Publishing.

McCrea, M., Hammeke, T., Olsenq, G., Leo, P., & Guskiewicz, K. (2004). Unreported concussion in high school football players: Implications for prevention. *Clinical Journal of Sport Medicine, 14*(1), 13–17.

McFall, R. M., & Treat, T. A. (1999). Quantifying the information value of clinical assessments with signal detection theory. *Annual Review of Psychology, 50*, 215–241.

McKinlay, W. W., McGowan, M., & Russell, J. V. 2010. Forensic issues in neuropsychology. In J. M. Gurd, U. Kischka, & J. Marshall (Eds.). *The handbook of clinical neuropsychology* (2nd ed., pp. 741–761). Oxford, UK: Oxford University Press.

McSweeny, A. J., Chelune, G. J., Naugle, R. I., & Lüders, H. (1993). "T-scores for change:" An illustration of a regression approach to depicting change in clinical neuropsychology. *Clinical Neuropsychologist, 7*, 300–312.

Medina, L. S., Bernal, B., & Ruiz, J. (2007). Role of functional MR in determining language dominance in epilepsy and nonepilepsy populations: A Bayesian analysis. *Radiology, 242*, 94–100.

Meehl, P. E., & Rosen, A. (1955). Antecedent probability and the efficiency of psychometric signs, patterns, or cutting scores. *Psychological Bulletin, 52*, 194–216.

Megargee, E. I. (2004, May). *Development and initial validation of an MMPI-2 Infrequency Scale (Fc) for use with criminal offenders*. Paper presented at the 39th Annual Symposium on Recent Developments on the MMPI-2/MMPI-A, Minneapolis, MN.

Menzies, L., Chamberlain, S. R., Laird, A. R., Thelen, S. M., Sahakian, B. J., & Bullmore, E. T. (2008). Integrating evidence from neuroimaging and neuropsychological studies of obsessive-compulsive disorder: The orbitofronto-striatal model revisited. *Neuroscience & Biobehavioral Reviews, 32*(3), 525–549.

Meyer, J. E., Volbrecht, M., Axelrod, B. N., & Reinsch-Boothby, L. (2011). Embedded symptom validity tests and overall neuropsychological test performance. *Archives of Clinical Neuropsychology, 26*(1), 8–15.

Meyer-Lindenberg, A., & Berman, K. F. (2001). The frontal lobes and schizophrenia. In S. P. Salloway, P. F. Malloy, & J. D. Duffy (Eds.), *The frontal lobes and neuropsychiatric illness* (pp. 187–197). Washington, DC: American Psychiatric Press.

Mielke, R., Kessler, J., Szelies, B., Herholz, K., Wienhard, K., & Heiss, W. D. (1996). Vascular dementia: Perfusional and metabolicdisturbances and effects of therapy. *Journal of Neural Transmission, (Suppl.) 47*, 183–191.

Miller, D. (2007). *Essentials of school neuropsychological assessment*. Hoboken, NJ: Wiley.

Miller, D. (2010). *Best practices in school neuropsychology*. Hoboken, NJ: Wiley.

Miller, J. B., Millis, S. R., Rapport, L. J., Bashem, J. R., Hanks, R. A., & Axelrod, B. N. (2011). Detection of insufficient effort using the Advanced Clinical Solutions for the Wechsler Memory Scale, Fourth Edition. *Clinical Neuropsychologist, 25*(1), 160–172.

Millis, S. R., Putnam, S. H., Adams, K. M., & Ricker, J. H. (1995). The California Verbal Learning Test in the detection of incomplete effort in neuropsychological testing. *Psychological Assessment, 7*, 463–471.

Minnesota Multiphasic Personality Inventory-2-Restructured Form (2008). San Antonio, TX: Pearson.

Morey, L. C. (1991). *Personality Assessment Inventory™*. Odessa, FL: Psychological Assessment Resources.

Mittenberg, W., & Strauman, S. (2000). Diagnosis of mild head injury and the postconcussion syndrome. *Journal of Head Trauma Rehabilitation, 15*, 783–791.

Morey, L. C. (2007). *The Personality Assessment Inventory professional manual*. Lutz, FL: Psychological Assessment Resources.

Morgan, J. E., & Sweet, J. J. (2008) (Eds.). *Neuropsychology of malingering casebook*. New York, NY: Psychology Press.

Naglieri, J. A., & Bardos, A. N. (1997). *General Ability Scale for Adults (GAMA)*. San Antonio, TX: Pearson.

Naglieri, J. A., & Das, J. P. (1997). *Cognitive Assessment System*. Itasca, IL: Riverside.

Naglieri, J. A., Das, J. P., & Goldstein, S. (forthcoming). *Cognitive Assessment System-2*. Dallas, TX: Pro-Ed.

Naglieri, J. A., Drasgow, F., Schmit, M., Handler, L., Prifitera, A., Margolis, A., & Velasquez, R. (2004). Psychological testing on the Internet: New problems, old issues. *American Psychologist, 3,* 150–162.

Naglieri, J. A., & Otero, T. (2011). Cognitive Assessment System: Redefining intelligence from a neuropsychological perspective. In A. Davis (Ed.), *Handbook of pediatric neuropsychology* (pp. 320–333). New York, NY: Springer.

Naglieri, J. A., Otero, T., DeLauder, B., & Matto, H. (2007). Bilingual Hispanic children's performance on the English and Spanish versions of the Cognitive Assessment System. *School Psychology Quarterly, 22,* 432–448.

Naglieri, J. A., Rojahn, J. & Matto, H. (2007). Hispanic and Non-Hispanic children's performance on PASS cognitive processes and achievement. *Intelligence, 35,* 568–579.

Naglieri, J. A., Taddei, S. & Williams, K. (submitted for publication). U.S. and Italian children's performance on the Cognitive Assessment System: A cross cultural equivalence study. Manuscript submitted for publication to Psychological Assessment.

Nies, K. J., & Sweet, J. J. (1994). Neuropsychological assessment and malingering: A critical review of past and present strategies. *Archives of Clinical Neuropsychology, 9,* 501–552.

Nystrom, L. E., Braver, T. S., Sabb, F. W., Delgado, M. R., Noll, D. C., & Cohen, J. D. (2000). Working memory for letters, shapes, and location: fMRI evidence against stimulus-based regional organization in human prefrontal cortex. *Neuroimage, 11,* 424–446.

Otero, T. M., Gonzales, L., & Naglieri, J. A. (in press). The neurocognitive assessment of Hispanic English language learners with reading failure. *Journal of Applied Neuropsychology.*

Paquette, N., Gonzalez-Frankenberger, B., Vannasing, P., Tremblay, J., Florea, O., Beland, R.,...Lassonde, M. (2010). Lateralization of receptive language function using near infrared spectroscopy. *Neuroscience & Medicine, 1,* 64–70.

Pearson Clinical Assessments (2009). *Advanced Clinical Solutions for the WAIS-IV and WMS-IV*. San Antonio, TX: Pearson Education, Inc.

Perani, D., Colombo, C., Bressi, S., Bonfanti, A., Grassi, F., & Scarone, S. (1995). [18F] FDG PET study in obsessive compulsive disorder: A clinical/metabolic correlation study after treatment. *British Journal of Psychiatry, 166,* 244–250

Perlstein, W. M., Carter, C. S., Noll, D. C., & Cohen, J. D. (2001). Relation of prefrontal cortex dysfunction to working memory and symptoms in schizophrenia. *American Journal of Psychiatry, 158,* 1105–1113.

Podell, K., Lovell, M., & Goldberg, E. (2001). Lateralization of frontal lobe functions. In S. P. Salloway, P. F. Malloy, & J. D. Duffy (Eds.), *The frontal lobes and neuropsychiatric illness* (pp. 83–100). Washington, DC: American Psychiatric Press.

Powell, D., Kaplan, E., Whitla, D., Weintraub, S., Catlin, R., & Funkenstein, H. (2004). *MicroCog™: Assessment of Cognitive Functioning Windows® Edition*. New York, NY: Pearson Education.

Powell, J. W. (1999). Epidemiology of sports-related head injury. In J. E. Bailes, M. R. Lovell, & J. C. Maroon (Eds.), *Sports related concussion* (pp. 75–90). St. Louis, MO: Quality Medical.

Powell, J. W., & Barber-Foss, K. D. (1999). Traumatic brain injury in high school athletes. *Journal of the American Medical Association, 282*(10), 958–963.

Prigatano, G. P., & Amin, K. (1993). Digit memory test: Unequivocal cerebral dysfunction and suspected malingering. *Journal of Clinical and Experimental Neuropsychology, 15,* 537–546.

Reitan, R. M., & Wolfson, D. (1993). *The Halstead-Reitan Neuropsychological Test Battery* (2nd ed.). Tucson, AZ: Neuropsychology Press.

Resnick, P. J., West, S., Payne, J. W. (2008). Malingering of post-traumatic disorder. In R. Rogers (Ed.), *Clinical assessment of malingering and deception* (pp. 109–127). New York, NY: Guilford Press.

Reeves, D., Kane, R., & Winter, K. (1996). *ANAM V3.11a/96 User's Manual: Clinical and neurotoxicology subtests*. (Report No. NCRF-TR-96-01). San Diego, CA: National Recovery Foundation.

Retzlaff, P. D., & Gibertini, M. (2000). Neuropsychometric issues and problems. In R. D. Vanderploeg, *Clinician's guide to neuropsychological assessment* (2nd ed., pp. 277–299). Mahwah, NJ: Erlbaum.

Rivera Mindt, M., Saez, P., & Manly, J. (2010). Increasing culturally competent neuropsychological services for ethnic minority populations: A call to action. *Clinical Neuropsychologist, 24*(3), 429–453.

Rogers, R., Gillard, N. D., Berry, D. T. R., & Granacher, R. P. Jr. (2011). Effectiveness of the MMPI-2-RF validity scales for feigned mental disorders and cognitive impairment: A known-groups study. *Journal of Psychopathology and Behavioral Assessment, 33*(3), 355–367.

Rose, F., Hall, S., & Szalda-Petree, A. (1995). Portland Digit Recognition Test—computerized: Measuring response latency improves the detection of malingering. *Clinical Neuropsychologist, 9,* 124–134.

Rosenfeld, J. P., Ellwanger, J. W., & Sweet, J. J. (1995). Detecting simulated amnesia with event-related brain potentials. *International Journal of Psychophysiology, 19,* 1–11.

Rosenfeld, J. P., & Ellwanger, J. W. (1999). Cognitive psychophysiology in detection of malingered cognitive deficits. In J. J. Sweet (Ed.), *Forensic neuropsychology: Fundamentals and practice* (pp. 287–312). Lisse, the Netherlands: Swets & Zeitlinger.

Ross, S. R., Millis, S. R., Krukowski, R. A., Putnam, S. H., & Adams, K. M. (2004). Detecting incomplete effort on the MMPI-2: An examination of the Fake-Bad Scale in mild head injury. *Journal of Clinical & Experimental Neuropsychology, 26*(1), 115–124.

Rossini, P., & Rossi, S. (2007). Transcranial magnetic stimulation: Diagnostic, therapeutic, and research potential. *Neurology, 68*(7), 484–488.

Rubenzer, S. J. (2005). Malingering psychiatric disorders and cognitive impairment in personal injury settings. *For the Defense, 47*(4), 18–25.

Ruff, R. M., & Richardson, A. M. (1999). Mild traumatic brain injury. In J. J. Sweet (Ed.), *Forensic neuropsychology: Fundamentals and practice* (pp. 313–338). Lisse, the Netherlands: Swets & Zeitlinger.

Ryan, L. M., & Warden, D. L. (2003). Post concussion syndrome. *International Review of Psychiatry, 15*(4), 310–316.

Sabbah, P., Chassoux, F., Leveque, C., Landre, E., Baudoin-Chial, S., Devaux, B.,...Cordoliani, Y. S. (2003). Functional MR imaging in assessment of language dominance in epileptic patients. *Neuroimage, 18,* 460–467.

Sahakian, B. J., & Owen, A. M. (1992). Computerized assessment in neuropsychiatry using CANTAB: Discussion paper. *Journal of the Royal Society of Medicine, 85,* 399–402.

Salmon, D. P., & Bondi, M. W. (2009). Neuropsychological Assessment of Dementia. *Annual Review of Psychology, 60,* 257–282.

Schacter, D. L., & Wagner, A. D. (1999). Medical temporal lobe activation in fMRI and PET studies of episodic encoding and retrieval. *Hippocampus, 9,* 7–24.

Schulenberg, S. E., & Yutrzenka, B. A. (2004). Ethical issues in the use of computerized assessment. *Computers in Human Behavior, 20*(4), 477–490.

Schutter, D. (2008). Antidepressant efficacy of high-frequency transcranial magnetic stimulation over the left dorsolateral prefrontal cortex in double-blind sham-controlled designs: A meta-analysis. *Psychological Medicine, 39*(1), 65–75.

Scott-Killgore, W. D., & DellaPietra, L. (2000). Using the WMS-III to detect malingering: Empirical validation of the Rarely Missed Index (RMI). *Journal of Clinical and Experimental Neuropsychology, 22,* 761–771.

Shaywitz, B. A., Shaywitz, S. E., Pugh, K. R., Constable, R. T., Skudlarski, P., & Fulbright, R. K. (1995). Sex differences in the functional organization of the brain for language. *Nature, 373,* 607–609.

Slick, D., Hopp, G., & Strauss, E. (1998). *Victoria Symptom Validity Test*. Odessa, FL: Psychological Assessment Resources.

Slick, D., Hopp, G., Strauss, E., Hunter, M., & Pinch, D. (1994). Detecting dissimulation: Profiles of simulated malingerers, traumatic brain injury patients and normal controls on a revised version of Hiscock and Hiscock's forced choice memory test. *Journal of Clinical and Experimental Neuropsychology, 16,* 472–481.

Slotema, C. W., Blom, J. D., Hoek, H. W., & Sommer, I. E. (2010). Should we expand the toolbox of psychiatric treatment methods to include Repetitive Transcranial Magnetic Stimulation (rTMS)? A meta-analysis of the efficacy of rTMS in psychiatric disorders. *Journal of Clinical Psychiatry, 71*(7), 873–884.

Smee, C., Samson, G., Morley, L., Giampietro, V., Brammer, M., Murray, R., & Shergi. S. (2006). Prefrontal cortical dysfunction in schizophrenia: An fMRI study. *Annals of General Psychiatry, 5*(Suppl. 1): S121.

Smith, G. S., de Leon, M. J., George, A. E., Kluger, A., Volkow, N. D., & McRae, T. (1992). Topography of cross-sectional and longitudinal glucose metabolic deficits in Alzheimer's disease: Pathophysiologic implications. *Archive of Neurology, 49,* 1142–1150.

Stern, R. A., Javorsky, D. J., Singer, E. A., Singer-Harris, N. G., Somerville, J. A., & Duke, L. M. (1999). *The Boston Qualitative Scoring System for the Rey-Osterrieth Complex Figure.* Odessa, FL: Psychological Assessment Resources.

Stern, C. E., Corkin, S., Gonzalez, R. G., Guimaraes, A. R., Baker, J. R., & Jennings, P. (1996). The hippocampal formation participates in novel picture encoding: Evidence from functional magnetic resonance imaging. *Proceedings of National Academy of Science, 93,* 8660–8665.

Strauss, E., Hultsch, D. F., Hunter, M., Slick, D. J., Patry, B., & Levy-Bencheton, J. (1999). Using intraindividual variability to detect malingering in cognitive performance. *Clinical Neuropsychologist, 13,* 420–432.

Suhr, J. A., & Boyer, D. (1999). Use of the Wisconsin Card Sorting Test in the detection of malingering in student simulator and patient samples. *Journal of Clinical and Experimental Neuropsychology, 21,* 701–708.

Sweet, J. J. (1999). Malingering: Differential diagnosis. In J. J. Sweet (Ed.), *Forensic neuropsychology: Fundamentals and practice* (pp. 255–286). Lisse, the Netherlands: Swets & Zeitlinger.

Sweet, J. J., Wolfe, P., Sattlberger, E., Numan, B., Rosenfeld, J. P., & Clingerman, S. (2000). Further investigation of traumatic brain injury versus insufficient effort with the California Verbal Learning Test. *Archives of Clinical Neuropsychology, 15,* 105–113.

Szaflarski, J. P., Binder J. R., Possing, M. S., McKiernan, K. A., Ward, B. D., & Hammeke, T. A. (2002). Language lateralization in left-handed and ambidextrous people: fMRI data. *Neurology, 59*(2), 238–244.

Taddei, S., & Naglieri, J. A. (2006). L'Adattamento Italiano del Das-Naglieri Cognitive Assessment System [Italian adaptation of DAS-Naglieri Cognitive Assessment System]. In J. A. Naglieri, & J. P. Das (Eds.), *Cognitive Assessment System—Manuale.* Firenze, Italy: OS.

Tape, T. G. (2001). ROC curves. In *Interpreting diagnostic tests.* Retrieved from http://gim.unmc.edu/dxtests/Default.htm

Tardif, H. P., Barry, R. J., Fox, A. M., & Johnstone, S. J. (2000). Detection of feigned recognition memory impairment using the old/new effect of the event-related potential. *International Journal of Psychophysiology, 36,* 1–9.

Tellegen, A., & Ben-Porath, Y. S. (2008). *MMPI-2-RF (Minnesota Multiphasic Personality Inventory-2 Restructured Form): Technical manual.* Minneapolis: University of Minnesota Press.

Temkin, N. R., Heaton, R. K., Grant, I., & Dikmen, S. S. (1999). Detecting significant change in neuropsychological test performance: A comparison of four models. *Journal of the International Neuropsychological Society, 5*(4), 357–369.

Tombaugh, T. N. (1996). *Test of memory malingering.* Toronto, Canada: Multi-Health Systems.

Tornatore, J. B., Hill, E., & Laboff, J. A. (2005). Self-administered screening for mild cognitive impairment: Initial Validation of a computerized test battery. *Journal of Neuropsychiatry and Clinical Neurosciences, 17*(1), 98–105.

Trueblood, W., & Schmidt, M. (1993). Malingering and other validity considerations in the neuropsychological evaluation of mild head injury. *Journal of Clinical and Experimental Neuropsychology, 15,* 578–590.

Tuokko, H. A., Chou, P. H. B., Bowden, S. C., Simartd, M., Ska, B., & Crossley, M. (2009). Partial measurement equivalence of French and English versions of the Canadian Study of Health and Aging neuropsychological battery. *Journal of the International Neuropsychological Society, 15,* 416–425.

U.S. Census Bureau. (2007, May 17). *Minority population tops 100 million* [Press release CB07–70].

Van Kampen, D. A., Lovell, M. R., Pardini, J. E., Collins, M. W., & Fu, F. H. (2006). The "value added" of neurocognitive testing after sports-related concussion. *American Journal of Sports Medicine, 34*(10), 1630–1635.

Vickery, C. D., Berry, D. T. R., Hanlon-Inman, T., Harris, M. J., & Orey, S. A. (2001). Detection of inadequate effort on neuropsychological testing: A meta-analytic review of selected procedures. *Archives of Clinical Neuropsychology, 16*(1), 45–73.

Videbech, P. (1997). MRI findings in patients with affective disorder: A meta analysis. *Acta Psychologica Scandinavia, 96,* 157–168

Vilar-Lopez, R., Perez-Garcia, M., Sanchez-Barrera, M. B., Rodriguez-Fernandez, A., & Gomez-Rios, M. (2011). Symptom validity testing and its underlying psychophysiological response pattern: A preliminary study. *Archives of Clinical Neuropsychology, 26*(2), 133–143.

Villringer, A., & Chance, B. (1997). Non-invasive optical spectroscopy and imaging of human brain function. *Trends in Neuroscience, 20*(10), 435–442.

Walter, D. (2005). The use of the Validity Indicator Profile with a 15- to 18-year-old population. ProQuest Dissertations & Theses database, UMI 3164789.

Warden, D. L., Bleiberg, J., Cameron, K. L., Ecklund, J., Walter, J. D., & Sparling, M. B. (2001). Persistent prolongation of reaction time in sports concussion. *Neurology, 57,* 524–526.

Warrington, E. K. (1984). *Recognition memory test: Manual.* Berkshire, UK: NFER-Nelson.

Webbe, F. M. (2010a). Future directions in sport neuropsychology. In F. M. Webbe (Ed.), *Handbook of sport neuropsychology* (pp. 383–392). New York, NY: Springer.

Webbe, F. M. (2010b). Introduction to sport neuropsychology. In F. M. Webbe (Ed.), *Handbook of sport neuropsychology* (pp. 1–16). New York, NY: Springer.

Wechsler, D. (2008). *Wechsler Adult Intelligence Scale—Fourth Edition (WAIS–IV).* San Antonio, TX: Pearson.

Wechsler, D. (2009). *Wechsler Memory Scale—Fourth Edition (WMS-IV).* San Antonio, TX: Pearson.

Wechsler, D. (2011). *Wechsler Abbreviated Scale of Intelligence—Second Edition.* San Antonio, TX: Pearson.

# CHAPTER 20

# Conceptualization and Assessment of Interests

RODNEY L. LOWMAN AND ANDREW D. CARSON

Despite difficulties in reaching a consensus as to exactly what occupational interests are, how they develop, and how best to classify them, psychologists have created a number of assessment tools for measuring them, and the test publishing industry has turned occupational interest inventories—the most common type of interest measure—into a flourishing business. Decades of research (yielding thousands of publications, making this necessarily a highly selective review) have established interests as their own major psychological domain, comparable in scope and importance to abilities and personality traits; assessment of interests has therefore become a mainstay of many psychologists and allied professionals. However, suggestions that group membership (e.g., age, sex, culture) may affect the validity of interpretations of interest measures for some purposes should inspire reasonable caution on the part of researchers and users alike.

In this chapter we address issues related to the psychology and measurement of interests as well as issues relating to future research directions. Specifically, this chapter begins with a discussion of a definition of interests, offering a working definition of the nature of interests. Many of the major interest assessment measures, some of them among the longest-lived and most psychometrically sophisticated measures in psychology, are then presented and briefly discussed. General findings and themes on the reliability and validity of interests are reviewed along with possible issues of group differences in their measurement.

Interests are then placed in a broader context by looking at the relationships among interests and other domains, especially personality and ability. Finally, the chapter outlines some needed research that may help take interests to the next level of understanding and practical applications.

## DEFINITIONS OF INTERESTS

Savickas (1999) and Crites (1969) each provided useful definitions of interests drawn from the major researchers in the field. They noted the impact of definitions of interests proffered by E. K. Strong Jr. Strong (1955) essentially accepted the dictionary definition of *interest*—"a propensity to attend to and be stirred by a certain object"—along with four attributes: *attention* and *feeling* for an object, *intensity* (some activities preferred over others), and *duration*. Savickas suggested that each of these attributes reflects an area of theoretical and research activity related to interests in the first third of the last century. The formal definition of interests offered by Strong was

activities for which we have liking or disliking and which we go toward or away from, or concerning which we at least continue or discontinue the status quo; furthermore, they may or may not be preferred to other interests and they may continue varying over time. Or an interest may be defined as a liking/disliking state of mind accompanying the doing of an activity, or the thought of performing the activity. (p. 138)

For Strong (1943), interests did not require consciousness or even thought; "they remind me of tropisms. We go toward liked activities, go away from disliked activities" (p. 7).

Lowman (2007) similarly defined interests as

relatively stable psychological characteristics of people [that] identify the personal evaluation (subjective attributions of "goodness" or "badness," judged by degree of personal fit or misfit) attached to particular groups of occupational or leisure activity clusters. (p. 477)

Within this definition, *interests* refer both to occupations that a person is likely to find appealing and satisfying and to leisure and avocational activities that are likely to be enjoyable and to bring long-term satisfaction.

## DEVELOPMENT OF INTERESTS

How interests develop has implications for their measurement. Trait theories resting on genetic inheritance models may suggest the possibility of measuring interests reliably from an early age while those based on developmental or situational influence models may imply the need for more state-specific measures.

Several alternative—and not mutually exclusive—conceptualizations of the development of interests have been proposed. Although these approaches have never had the devoted enthusiasts that have attached to, say, approaches to psychotherapy, they still provide a useful categorizing and classifying approach.

Psychoanalytic theories of the development of personality strongly influenced Anne Roe's (1957) early and popular account of the nature of interests. Roe's theory stimulated several studies testing the relationship between quality of the parent–child relationship and subsequent development of the child's vocational interests. However, empirical studies in general found little support for Roe's theory, suggesting that the environment—and especially the early parent–child relationship–may have relatively little lasting effect on the development of interests, seemingly disproving her theory. She (in Roe & Lunneborg, 1990) acknowledged as much. Freud's psychosexual stage model apparently also influenced John Holland's (1959) original statement of his theory of vocational choice (Holland, 1959). Bordin (1994) and S. D. Brown and Watkins (1994) reviewed modern psychodynamic approaches to interests and career issues. In his subsequent broadening of the construct of interests from personal orientations to vocational personality, Holland (1997a) sought to expand it from a focus on only interests to one that spanned personality, skill and ability, and other constructs as well as interests; however, his theory remains at its core one of interests.

The social learning approach to interests assumes that since interests derive from appropriate reinforcements, interests are shaped by the influences of parents and educators or by interactions with the environment (Mitchell & Krumboltz, 1990). Theories with this basis assume, essentially, that people learn to become interested in what they do well and disinterested in what they do poorly, based on feedback from others and on feedback from task performance itself. Holland's (1997a) current version of his widely used vocational personality theory of the development of interests assumes that most interests are acquired through social learning experiences. Whatever biological factors may predispose people to particular interests, environments, Holland contended, are composed of people with more similar than dissimilar interest patterns. Thus, environments both attract others with similar patterns and influence the behavior of others by making those who stay in the environments more like the dominant interest patterns in the group (see L. S. Gottfredson, 1999; Walsh & Chartrand, 1994). Dawis's theory of work adjustment (Dawis, 1991, 2005) also posits the environment as consisting of reinforcers that attract and sustain particular types of people and behavior.

Genetic models of interests (e.g., Lykken, Bouchard, McGue & Tellegen, 1993) assume that interests have considerable heritability, suggesting a more fixed and determinative approach. L. S. Gottfredson (1999) reviewed evidence from the as yet somewhat small behavior–genetic literature on psychological traits, including vocational interests. She concluded that there exists convincing evidence from twin and other studies that a sizable proportion of the variance in measured psychological traits, including interests, has a genetic component and that this proportion tended to increase with age (i.e., environmental effects decreased). In addition, shared family effects on the observed traits (i.e., effects of global factors shared across children in the family) tended to decrease with age, becoming much less of a factor by adolescence. Thus, as represented by their measured characteristics such as abilities and interests, individuals essentially reach a period of maximum independence from the forces of family of origin and genes during their adolescent and early adult years, at the same time that secondary and higher education and the world of work would presumably serve to influence skills and motivations. Increasing research similarly points to the presence of a substantial genetic component to interests and occupational choice (see, e.g., Moloney, Bouchard, & Segal, 1991; Nicolaou & Shane, 2010).

## STRUCTURE AND DIMENSIONALITY OF INTERESTS

The design of assessment instruments to measure interests depends of course on both the definition and the assumed underlying dimensionality of interests. Indeed, the structure of interests is a topic that has concerned both counselors and researchers for some time. For example, approaching the problem from the needs of counselors and educators, Kitson (1937, p. 40) proposed a "vocational hexagon" with six points of view through which an individual's match to occupations might be considered: Physical, Mental, Economic, Moral, Physiological, and Social. However, his inspiration appears to have been his practical experience and not empirical data.

In early studies, essentially theoretical measures such as Strong's (1938b) were often examined factorially to determine their underlying structure. In an early study, Thurstone (1931) extracted four factors in a study of the Strong Vocational Interest Blank (SVIB): science, business, people, and language. Strong's (1943) work in this area identified a similar set of dimensions, plus a things versus people dimension; Strong also bifurcated the business dimension into systems and contact. Roe (1954) proposed an eight-group model, similar to Strong's. Holland's (1959) original theory proposed six interest-based personal orientations, later renamed vocational personality types.

Although a number of empirical efforts to measure and classify interests preceded his work, Holland's remains the dominant structural model of interests (e.g., Campbell & Borgen, 1999). Holland's contribution (Campbell & Borgen, 1999; Holland, 1959, 1997a), among others, was to add theory to empiricism to put factor results into a model that cuts across occupational types, work environments, and cultures.

Holland's (1997a) six-factor interests model (RIASEC; which today might be called the "Big 6" of interest variables) consisted of these factors with their now widely used labels:

1. *Realistic* (preference for "real world" activities involving the manipulation of things and enjoyment of the physical environment)
2. *Investigative* (interest in science and intellectually relevant abstractions; a world of empirically based ideas,

enjoyment of logic, order, and precision rather than subjectivity, elasticity, and fuzziness)
3. *Artistic* (concern with the world of symbolic expression, a preference for subjectively experienced views, esthetic idealism, a need for accurately understanding and communicating, often forcefully, subjectively experienced reality, even, or perhaps especially, when it runs counter to prevailing views of reality or of appropriate behavior, feelings or conduct)
4. *Social* (preference for continual involvements with people, liking to work with and through others and to better others and the human condition more generally)
5. *Enterprising* (more aptly named "managerial," a preference for working with others but from the perspective of managing or leading others, liking of prestige and extrinsic rewards, liking of upward mobility and control over others, liking activities involving persuasion and influence)
6. *Conventional* (preference for orderly and predictable activities involving repetitiveness, numbers or data, and for routine, predictability, and order) (see, among others, Holland, 1997a).

Holland's structural model of interests has been exhaustively studied (Holland, 1997a) in many cultures and populations (see, e.g., Taylor, 2009). Much of the research has been supportive of the idea of six factors and their general relationship with one another regardless of culture (see, e.g., Hedrih, 2008; Nagy, Trautwein, & Lüdtke, 2010). Other reviews (e.g., Armstrong, Smith, Donnay, & Rounds, 2004; Rounds, & Day, 1998; Day, Rounds, & Swaney, 1998; Rounds & Day, 1999; Tracey & Rounds, 1993), however, have challenged the criticality of the six factors and argue that the number of interest factors and their presumed relationship to one another are essentially arbitrary, that they are neither limited to six nor do they necessarily assume the Holland circular/hexagonal structure. Armstrong et al. (2004) labeled their large analyses of the Strong databases the "Strong Ring" intended to describe the structural relationship. Although the sample was quite large, the database was limited to 198 occupational samples. Thus, a number of investigators have begun to search for an underlying, or meta, second-order factor structure of interests or to suggest a few more dimensions to Holland's RIASEC model. However, the idea of a smaller number of underlying dimensions of interests or of an alternative number of dimensions for basic interests has not yet resulted in any practical measures based solely on the presumed underlying dimensional structure.

Most investigators seeking to propose some number of basic interests other than six tend to follow a rule of "six plus or minus four." An exception is a model that has been suggested by authors associated with the StrengthsQuest (Clifton, Anderson, & Schreiner, 2006), a reconfiguration of the Clifton Strengths Finder (Asplund, Lopez, Hodges, & Harter, 2007), which includes 34 scales for strengths that as a group map reasonably well to Holland's six types (Carson, Evans, Gitin, & Eads, 2011). However, though the domains may overlap, the measure, by intention anyway, is more of abilities ("strengths") than of interests.

Before leaving this section, we note that interest assessment measures must almost by definition be multifactorial. The number of expected factors probably needs to be around six, and the factors either need to track with Holland's RIASEC variables or use an alternative conceptual approach to the measurement of interests. However, with the possible exception of Campbell's decision (see Campbell, 2002) to divide the Realistic orientation into two complementary types, we are unaware of research that has sought to apply Holland's (1959) initial proposal that pure subtypes of interests may exist at levels narrower than his six types (or "personal orientations," as he originally termed them).

We turn next examine several of the widely used assessment measures of interests.

## MEASURING INTERESTS

This review of interest theories suggests that theorists have developed somewhat incompatible accounts for the development and measurement of interests. Given this lack of consensus, it may appear surprising how much similarity exists among the widely used measures of interests, which mostly consist of inventories of statements about the strength of an individual's interest in particular activities or occupations. Although a variety of methods of assessing interests developed over the 20th century, most of this diversity flourished only in the first decades of interest measurement and then vanished. Nevertheless, we can discuss different ways to measure interests (most with historical examples) and point to some ongoing efforts—most spurred by the potentially disruptive technology of the Internet—to diversify measurement methods.

The first and most important distinction is between interests as observed behavior versus self-reported feelings or thoughts. By observing people's behavior and pattern of activities, one may infer interests from the behavior, on the assumption that people would not generally engage in behavior if they were not interested in it. Closely related to actually observing behavior is the approach relying on inferring interests from behaviors recorded on behavioral checklists or biographical data forms, both of which often turn out to be strong predictors of job-related performance and presumably therefore of fit to jobs. Crites (1999) noted that although observed behavior could provide indicators of interests, noninterest factors, such as family and social pressures, could affect them more than, say, expressed or inventoried interests. It is much more common to assess interests through self-reports of introspective states such as feelings or thoughts.

The second important distinction is between measures of interests as tests versus inventories. On the assumption that people will learn more about the things in which they are interested, tests can be constructed reflecting knowledge or skills across different occupational or leisure activity areas; individual differences in performance on these tests may reflect differences in practice or attentiveness associated with such activities and therefore serve as indicators of underlying interests. Some vocabulary-based and knowledge based interest inventories saw brief service in the middle of the 20th century, but apparently only briefly, and they were soon displaced by the growing popularity of inventory-based measures, in which answers to items on a questionnaire do not have an objectively correct answer. Super (1949) described and evaluated information tests (such as those on which Super worked during World War II), and the degree to which they might serve as indicators of interests. Crites (1999) concluded that although the idea of an interest test was intriguing, subsequent research has shown them lacking in criterion and predictive validity.

The third important distinction is between expressed versus inferred interests. Inferred interests have been assessed not only by inventories but also by tests and observed behavior. One way to assess a feeling or thought is to ask directly; the direct expression of that feeling or thought may involve different psychological processes than would a more indirect assessment of the same construct. Expressed interests may also be more likely to tap not only an individual's current interests but also the sort of interests he or she wishes to have.

### Specific Measures of Interests

We first discuss several popular or widely used measures of interests, including the Strong Vocational Interest

Blank (SVIB; now marketed as the Strong Interest Inventory, SII), the Campbell Interest and Skill Survey (CISS), the Kuder Occupational Interest Survey (Kuder Career Search, KCS), the Unisex Edition of the ACT Program's Interest Inventory, the Self-Directed Search, the Vocational Preference Inventory, Find Your Interests (FYI), and Johansson's measures. From consultations with colleagues, Savickas (1998) identified the first five as being widely used and included them in a special issue of the *Career Development Quarterly* dedicated to interpreting interest inventories. Our focus is the design and types of scales within each inventory, other similarities and differences between the measures, and how the measures support joint interpretation with other constructs such as abilities and skills. These measures have now, in large measure, been adapted for administration over the Internet via standard Web browsers.

### Strong Interest Inventory

Strong began development of his SVIB in the 1920s (see Donnay, 1997). The current version is the SII (see Donnay, Thompson, Morris, & Schaubhut, 2004), which has several sets of scales, distributed across six sections, formed from 291 items (with most items contributing to several scales). All items use a 5-point Likert format.

The original set of scales in the SVIB and still the most numerous set in the SII are the Occupational Scales, of which the current edition includes 122 pairs, one scale for each sex. These scales offer separate norms for comparisons to women and men in particular occupations. The Occupational Scales include items from the SII that serve to distinguish members of the occupational norm group from members of a general population sample.

The next set of scales developed were the Basic Interest Scales, homogenous scales that measure specialized interests in a presumably pure form. There are 30 Basic Interest Scales in the current edition. Next developed were the General Occupational Themes, based on Holland's six types (Realistic, Investigative, Artistic, Social, Enterprising, and Conventional). (David Campbell and John Holland reportedly selected the original items to comprise the General Occupational Themes [GOTs] based primarily on how much they seemed to relate to Holland's various personal orientations; thus, one could argue that the original themes were based mainly on rational rather than empirical scale construction methods. However, a different and more empirical basis underlies the GOTs in the current edition of the SII.) In addition, both the Occupational and Basic Interest Scales are classified into best-corresponding Holland interest types for purposes

of reporting results. Finally, a set of personality-related scales has been included across various editions of the SVIB; they are now grouped in the Personal Style Scales, for which Lindley and Borgen (2000) have demonstrated predicted relations to the Big Five personality traits. The Personal Style Scales include Work Style, Learning Environment, Leadership Style, Risk Taking, and Team Orientation.

Because the Occupational Scales of the SVIB and SII tend to focus more on occupations requiring a college or professional education, some authors have argued that that the SVIB is relatively less useful for non–college-bound students. Although it is true that the Occupational Scales are more representative of occupations requiring college or professional education, skilled interpretation of the SII may extend its reach to occupations in general. In particular, one may determine a three-letter Holland code from rank ordering of scores on the General Occupational Themes and the other scales organized by Holland's types; one may then, using a crosswalk such as the *Dictionary of Holland Occupational Codes* (G. D. Gottfredson & Holland, 1996) or the U.S. Department of Labor's O*Net system, match an SII profile to almost any occupation.

The SII's publisher reports that the measure requires an eighth-grade reading level. There are also separate profile reports available for secondary and postsecondary populations, along with a more detailed interpretive report not targeted to a specific age group.

The SII's companion measure, the Skills Confidence Inventory (SCI; Betz, Borgen, & Harmon, 1996), assesses self-ratings of skills on dimensions corresponding to many facets of the SII. These dimensions include the Holland personal orientations assessed through the SII's General Occupational Themes.

### Campbell Interest and Skill Survey

The CISS (Campbell, 1995, 2002; Campbell, Hyne, & Nilsen, 1992; Hansen & Neuman, 1999) is one of a family of career assessment measures by Campbell and his colleagues, with companion instruments measuring leadership traits and related constructs of interest to organizations. The CISS consists of 200 interest and 120 skill items. An 11-page report provides scores on seven Orientation Scales (influencing, organizing, helping, creating, analyzing, producing, and adventuring) that generally correspond to Holland's scales except for having two realistic analogues (producing and adventuring). The CISS also includes 29 Basic (interest and skill) Scales (clusters of occupations and skills, such as mathematics and science grouped with "write computer programs . . . perform lab research"), 60 Occupational Scales, and 2 Special Scales (academic focus and extraversion, corresponding to the scales on the previous edition of the SII). This design clearly is similar to that used by the SII, with which it directly competes. Such similarity is hardly surprising, given that Campbell had directed development of the Strong for many years before moving on to develop the CISS.

Perhaps Campbell's most persuasive argument for use of the CISS instead of the SII is that the instrument results in an essentially identical set of scales despite the administration of many fewer (interest) items with the CISS (291 SII items versus 200 interest items for the CISS). Campbell used a 6-response option Likert format for his items. In the current edition of the SII, its authors replaced the multiple item response formats with a single 5-response option Likert format. As with the corresponding scales on the SII, the Orientation and Basic Scales on the CISS are homogeneous, while the Occupational Scales are developed through use of occupational criterion groups.

Another difference between the SII and the CISS is that whereas the SII's occupational norms were developed separately by gender, the CISS relies on combined gender occupational groups. However, a careful review of the number of respondents of each gender who were included in the original samples (see Campbell et al., 1992) suggests that the number of women in the occupational norming group are often significantly lower than the number of men, raising serious questions about the representativeness of the samples no matter how the norms might have been adjusted to reflect such sampling differences. For example, 33 males versus 5 females for the Airline Mechanic interest scales were included; 63 males versus 17 females for the accountant interest scales, 64 male versus 9 female attorneys; 123 males versus 18 female architects, and so on. The Occupational Scale scores are also reported somewhat differently from the corresponding scales on the SII but still make use of comparisons of occupational group responses compared to a general reference group sample (with the general reference sample including both genders).

Another (minor) difference lies in Campbell's use of seven personal orientation categories compared to Holland's six, although two of Campbell's categories combine to map to Holland's Realistic type. The reading level for the CISS (intended to be readable by the average person age 15 or older) appears to be comparable to that of the SII; however, the CISS also offers definitions of occupations, perhaps easing the vocabulary burden, especially for individuals without much exposure to occupational information in their daily lives.

The CISS report provides recommendations for exploration of different occupational options: pursue (high interest, high skill), develop (high interest, low skill), explore (low interest, high skill), and avoid (low interest, low skill). Counselors may similarly compare interest inventory results on the SII (using the SCI for comparison), but such comparisons are not directly built into an automated report.

### Kuder Career Search and Related Measures

Kuder (1939) began to develop his family of interest measures within a decade after the initial publication of the SVIB. Measures in the Kuder line published prior to 1997 that are still available from Kuder.com include the Kuder General Interest Survey Form E and the Kuder Occupational Interest Survey Form DD (KOIS; Diamond & Zytowski, 2000; Kuder, 1991). The KOIS, like the SII, includes criterion-based occupational scales plus college-based major scales. The measure has 100 items, each formed of a triad of options; most and least preferred activities in each triad are chosen. Similarities between an examinee's responses to those typical of an occupation are calculated directly, without reference to differentiation from members of general population samples. The Kuder reportedly has a sixth-grade reading level, but typical use of the measure is grade 11 and above. Those in lower grades may find the reading level challenging.

Today, the primary Kuder assessment is the Kuder Career Search with Person Match (Zytowski, 2001a, 2001b), offered through Kuder.com. Containing 60 triad-based items, the KCS is substantially shorter than the KOIS and reportedly has a reading level that is truly closer to that of sixth graders. It reports results into the same 10 Activity Preference Scales as used by the KOIS, along with six Career Cluster scales (corresponding to Holland's six personal orientations), and Person-Matches corresponding to the 253 occupational classifications reported in the U.S. Department of Labor publications (e.g., U.S. Department of Labor, 1991), extending the KCS's usefulness to include the full range of students, not only those bound for college. However, instead of matching an examinee's results to, say, a norm sample of members of an occupation, what the person-match component of the system does is to match the examinee's responses to the entire sample of profiles in the Kuder match database; after identifying the 25 best-matching cases, that set of similar cases is shared with the examinee, along with the known career history of those cases.

The online resources offered through Kuder.com include both the interest assessment (KCS) and a measure of self-estimated skills, the Kuder Skills Assessment (Zytowski & Luzzo, 2002). This supports direct comparison of assessed interests and self-estimated skills in a manner comparable to that offered through the Strong and its companion skills measure and between the interest and skill subscales of the Campbell measure (Betz & Rottinghaus, 2006).

### Unisex Edition of the ACT Interest Inventory

The ACT Interest Inventory, also known as the Unisex Edition of the ACT (UNIACT) Interest Inventory, is one of the most widely used interest measures in the world, according to one of its authors (Swaney, 1995). The test is not marketed directly to counselors or examinees as a stand-alone measure but rather is available only through bundling with other ACT products, such as through career planning packages sold or licensed to schools or through the ACT college entrance examination.

The UNIACT's manual (ACT, 2009) provides a thorough discussion of two versions of the UNIACT, one for secondary use, the other for postsecondary and adult use. Each version consists of 72 activity-based items (as with the KCS, only activities are used), 12 for each of the six Holland personal orientations, yielding the six Basic Interest Scales (Technical, Science, Arts, Social Service, Business Contact, and Business Operations, corresponding in order to the Holland orientations of Realistic, Investigative, Artistic, Social, Enterprising, and Conventional). Each item offers three response options (like, dislike, indifferent). The UNIACT also organizes its report according to a two-dimensional framework that incorporates the orientations measured by the Basic Interest Scales. The first of these dimensions describes a Data-Ideas dimension (with Business Contact and Operations on the Data extreme and Arts and Sciences on the Ideas extreme). The second delineates a People–Things dimension (with Social Service on the People extreme and Technical on the Things extreme). The UNIACT report makes use of a coordinate system defined by these two bipolar dimensions to locate examinees, academic majors, and occupations within the same two-dimensional space, yielding the World-of-Work map, a practical tool for inventory interpretation and counseling (see Prediger, 2002). Within this map, the UNIACT report clusters 23 job families within 12 regions. Interpretation of UNIACT results relies heavily on the spatial position of the examinee in relation to job families and regions. Perhaps the major difference between the UNIACT and the

previously discussed measures is the decision to seek to eliminate gender-related differences in scale scores by retaining only those items that showed no gender-related differences.

### Self-Directed Search

Holland's Self-Directed Search (SDS; Holland, 1994; Holland, Fritzsche, & Powell, 1994) differs from the previously discussed interest inventories in several important respects. First, examinees can score and interpret it for themselves. (In addition to the self-scoring paper-and-pencil version, there is also a computerized SDS.) Second, self-administration of the SDS encourages reliance on raw scores in lieu of scaled scores and comparisons to normative samples, which provides a simpler, if not always most accurate, understanding for non–technically trained persons.

Spokane and Holland (1995) provided a review of the family of SDS measures, including Form R (Regular) for high school (or younger, for students with a minimum of sixth-grade reading ability) through adult; Form E (for adults and older adolescents with low (grades 4 to 6) reading level; Form CP for higher-level individuals in organizations; a version for use with middle-school students; and versions in other languages. The sections of the SDS include Occupational Daydreams (examinee lists up to eight occupations), Activities (6 scales corresponding to each of the Holland vocational types, 11 items each), Competencies (6 scales, 11 items each), Occupations (6 scales, 14 items each), and Self-Estimates (2 sets of 6 ratings). In all sections except Occupational Daydreams, item response involves simply checking the item to endorse it; scores from each section except Occupational Daydreams contribute to summary scores for each of the six types, from which the examinee may determine his or her three-letter Holland code. Once the code is determined (say, Realistic-Investigative-Enterprising), one may use the code as the basis for exploring classifications of occupations, college majors, and leisure activities for corresponding (reasonable) matches to the code. Prince and Heiser (2000) have offered thorough discussion of additional features of the SDS.

Holland was also the first author to seek to assess and integrate abilities and skills (via self-ratings) with interests within the same assessment system; in this way, the SDS anticipated the CISS, the SCI, the new Kuder self-ratings measure, and even the ability assessment systems into which ACT has embedded the UNIACT. In fact, the market success of the SDS probably spurred these changes in the other major measures.

It is unclear how Holland's death will affect future development of the SDS and his other instruments. Many of his key innovations have already spread throughout all of the assessments previously discussed. The migration of interest assessments to computerized platforms may obviate the benefits of the (traditional) self-scoring version of the SDS, which forces examinees to wait longer and work harder to obtain scores than they would with a computerized assessment. One area for continued use of the SDS may lie in international use; for example, Leung and Hou (2001) reported an adaptation of the SDS for use in China.

### Vocational Preference Inventory

Holland's original measure of personal orientations was the Vocational Preference Inventory (VPI; Holland, 1958, 1985), consisting of 160 occupations representing his six vocational personality types as well as five additional personality traits (Self-Control, Status, Masculinity/Femininity, Infrequency, and Acquiescence). A short form of this measure is also available (see Lowman & Schurman, 1982). Counselors can use (raw) scores from the six personality types to locate matching occupations, majors, or leisure activities in various resources. The measure offers the advantages of brevity and low cost, along with information about some additional personality-related traits, and, unlike the SDS, the examinee does not know how particular items will contribute to various scales. This may recommend it for such purposes as research, where the goal is to obtain efficient markers of Holland's types (e.g., Roberti, Fox, & Tunick, 2003). However, the origin of the test's norms appears not to be clearly defined. At this point they need updating, and the validity evidence for the test could use newer studies, particularly to establish that the occupational titles in the test are still current and differentiating.

### Find Your Interests

Find Your Interests (FYI) is part of the Armed Services Vocational Aptitude Battery (ASVAB) assessment offered for no cost through a majority of American high schools for purposes of military enlisted recruitment and selection (Baker, Styer, Harmon, & Pommerich, 2010). As such, it replaces the ASVAB's Interest-Finder (see Wall & Baker, 1997), swapping the 240-item Interest-Finder with the new 90-item FYI while retaining the Interest-Finder's reporting structure around Holland's six types and supporting mapping results into career clusters associated with these types. The FYI's design in fact appears essentially identical to the UNIACT, down to reliance on three levels of response option per item. As with the UNIACT, development focused on the late-adolescent examinee. The resulting six subscales map to both Holland's hexagonal structure of types and demonstrate predicated correlations with the SII (Baker et al., 2010). Despite its being a relatively new instrument, it apparently receives widespread use, as the ASVAB system of which the FYI is a part is reported to be completed by 25% of all high school students in the United States (Baker, 2002).

### O*Net Interest Profiler

The O*Net Interest Profiler (U.S. Department of Labor, 2000) is one of the assessments offered through the O*Net system produced by the U.S. Department of Labor section on Employment and Training Administration. O*Net provides a range of resources (U.S. Department of Labor, n.d.-c), including assessments, occupational information, and ways of matching the two for purposes of career intervention and job search. Two forms (standard and short) are available across two formats (paper-and-pencil and online). The standard form includes 180 items, with 30 items for each of the six Holland types; each item has three levels of response. The short form (described by Rounds, Su, Lewis, & Rivkin, 2010) includes 60 items, with 10 items for each of the six Holland types.

Examinees and professionals search O*Net's database of over 800 occupations (O*Net online, U.S. Department of Labor, n.d.-b) via reports organized through career clusters, job families, or logical combinations of occupational descriptors (or tags). The career clusters offered by O*Net do not necessarily presume the psychological underpinnings Holland's types. However, they do rely on Holland's system as an organizing framework. The O*Net profile allows for interpretation of the results of the Interest Profiler with reference to O*Net's occupational database. In addition, the reporting system was designed (U.S. Department of Labor, 2000) to further divide the set of career clusters into various "job zones," grouping the occupations by similar training requirements and other features. Results from the Interest Profiler may also be used to search occupations using the other two methods (job families and tags), further moving away from Holland's basic theory.

### Johansson's Measures

Johansson has developed another family of interest inventories, two of which are especially appropriate for use with non–college-bound or nonprofessional populations. The earliest developed—the Interest Determination, Exploration, and Assessment System (IDEAS;

Johansson, 1980)—essentially replicates the SDS. It is a self-directing inventory yielding six Holland orientation scores and associated basic interest scales (all using combined gender norms) organized by orientation, appropriate for use by individuals not bound for college. The Career Assessment Inventory—Vocational Version (CAI-VV; Johansson, 1982) and the Career Assessment Inventory—Enhanced Version (CAI-EV; Johansson, 1986) are modeled closely on the SII, with each including criterion-based occupational scales, basic interest scales, and scales for each of Holland's personal orientations. The CAI-VV's design reflects intention for use with individuals not aiming for careers in the professions. The CAI-EV is intended to be more broadly applicable, through incorporation of more items and reporting more reflective of professional occupations. The manuals report the reading levels for the CAI-VV and CAI-EV to be grade 6 and 8 respectively; however, as with the SII, KOIS, and similar measures, examinee unfamiliarity with some terms (especially occupational titles) suggests the need for caution in administration to younger students (see Vacc & Hinkle, 1994).

### Other Inventories and Methods

Some other inventories of interest include:

- The FOCUS-2 (Career Dimensions, Inc., 2009)
- The very promising CAPA Interest Inventory (Betz & Borgen, 2010)
- The COPSystem (Knapp-Lee, 1995)
- The Harrington-O'Shea Career Decision-Making System (HOCDMS; Harrington & O'Shea, 2000)
- The Jackson Vocational Interest Survey (JVIS; Jackson, 1991)
- An interest measure in the public domain, the Oregon Vocational Interest Scales (Pozzebon, Visser, Ashton, Lee, & Goldberg, 2010)
- The Work Preferences Survey (WPS; Van Iddekinge, Putka, & Campbell (2011)
- The Vocational Interest Inventory (VII; Lunneborg, 1981)
- The Chronicle Career Quest (CCQ, Forms S and L; CGP Research Staff, 1992; see review by Livers, 1994)

We do not know the frequency of use of these measures (some of which are quite new), although we suspect that the FOCUS-2 may have the widest usage, with its publisher reporting use in over 1,500 colleges, universities, and career centers throughout the United States alone (Career Dimensions, Inc., 2009). There are also several

card sorts for measuring interests; Hartung (1999) discussed their rationale, history, and availability, including a review of eight interest card sorts of potential interest to users.

### Conclusions About Alternative Measures of Interests

Which measure of interests is preferable under what circumstances? It is clear that the measures of Holland's interest constructs cannot be used interchangeably (Lowman, Palmer, Santana, & Abbott, 2003). Additionally, no single measure of occupational interests can be declared universally superior for use in all circumstances and with all populations (Eby & Russell, 1998). The relative merits and limitations of each measure are counterbalanced by the merits and limitations of the others. Some measures are preferable for certain age groups or reading levels; others, for particular educational levels. The SVIB includes one of the most impressive normative bases and one that is regularly updated; the SDS lends itself to individual administration, scoring and interpretation; the UNI-ACT attempts to minimize gender differences. All have value and all measures in one way or another incorporate Holland's factors. Nevertheless, more research is needed examining the shared variance across these measures and whether it practically matters, in the measurement of interests, which measure was used. In the meantime, practitioners need carefully to choose measures of interests relevant for the particular assessment population and task at hand. Interpretation of interests should be done in the context of the client's understanding of self and in association with other variables (see Holland, 1996; Lowman & Carson, 2000).

## RELIABILITY AND VALIDITY OF INTEREST MEASURES

In this section we consider the reliability (focusing on short- and long-term stability) and validity of measures of interests. Determination of the validity of interests relates to the question of whether interests are empirically structured in a way consistent with espoused theory, whether they are differentiated from other relevant psychological concepts (such as attitudes, personality, or abilities), and whether they predict behaviorally relevant life and career choices. The first of these issues calls for factorial and internal consistency studies, the second consideration of the extent to which these constructs overlap with other relevant ones (such as personality and values; these matters are discussed in a separate section), and the third to the relationship of interest constructs with relevant criterion measures. Fouad (1999) has provided a good survey of some of the validity issues and research findings. Because of their particular relevance of individual differences (e.g., age, sex, and culture) to validity issues, we also briefly discuss some of these factors here.

## Reliability of Interests

In this section, we discuss some of the issues about the reliability of occupational interest measures.

### Short-Term Stability and Precision of Measurement

Most traditional measures of interests demonstrate high reliability when judged by standard reliability measures such as coefficient alpha's (Blake, 1969; Campbell, 1995; Holland, 1985; Lowman & Schurman, 1982; Prince & Heiser, 2000; Swaney, 1995). These measures typically have reliability coefficients in the .80s to .90s

However, the advent of online assessment of interests, and the consequence of competition for an ever-decreasing pool of time that most examinees appear willing to devote to the task of interest assessment, has created pressures to decrease the length of interest inventories to the point that adequate reliabilities may no longer be assured, even for the latest incarnations of long-established brands of inventories. The trend appears to be the creation of forms that are considerably shorter (e.g., 33% to 50%) than the original forms. However, the reliabilities for subscales of these shorter forms of many apparently popular interest assessments may fall in the .7 or even .6 range, as has been reported for the KCS (Ihle-Helledy, Zytowski, & Fouad, 2004). The short form of the O*Net (Rounds et al., 2010) has reported reliabilities in the .7 to .8 range, somewhat lower than desirable for such scales. It appears that it is not the design of a primarily online test that accounts for these lower reliabilities, as recently published CAPA Interest Inventory (Betz & Borgen, 2010), with 190 items, reports subscale reliabilities above the .8 level. All things being equal, when it comes to reliability, length appears still to matter.

### Long-Term Stability of Interests

For both classical and more recent research, the long-term test reliability of interest test scores has tended to be robust (typically in the .70s or higher over multiyear intervals; see Dawis, 1991). This finding appears to hold independently of specific measurement instrument (see, e.g., Hansen & Johansson, 1972; Johansson & Campbell, 1971;

Lau & Abrahams, 1971; Rottinghaus, Coon, Gaffey, & Zytowski, 2007; Strong, 1952). Perhaps the most systematic longitudinal studies of the stability of interests to date have been those of Strong (1938a, 1938b, 1951, 1952), which persistently found that the interest patterns of men and women were among the most temporally stable of all psychological variables. More recently Swanson (1999) discussed in detail issues concerning the stability of occupational interests and concluded that, although a small proportion of people do change their interests over the course of the life cycle, in general, interests are markedly stable. On the other hand, we did not find any reports, one way or the other, for the long-term (multiple-year) stability of interests assessed through briefer (90-items or under) assessment measures that were administered on line.

## Validity of Interests

Holland's (1997a) six-factor model has been the most widely used and validated model of interest measurements. This may be because the model lends itself to complexity in that people do not have to be classified into one of six categories but rather, if the three most highly endorsed scales are considered, to one of 120 permutations of the three most highly endorsed interest patterns (see Lowman, 1991; Lowman, Williams, & Leeman, 1985). The factors are said to describe and to classify environments as well as individuals, and the question of the "match" between person and occupation or organization is at the heart of most contemporary career assessment and counseling practice. There is considerable evidence for the existence of these factors in a variety of cultural measurements (e.g., Athanasou, O'Gorman, & Meyer, 1981; Day & Rounds, 1998; Fouad & Mohler, 2004).

We and others (e.g., Gottfredson & Johnstun, 2009) suggest that Holland's theory has persisted for over 50 years because: (a) it is based on the empirically verified fact that preferences for a diversity of occupations can meaningfully be grouped into a small number of occupational clusters that have factorial integrity; and (b) the factors or scales or "types" have practical implications that can be readily grasped by end users, such as the general public or career counselors working with clients. Whatever the reasons, Holland's model continues to dominate the interest scene of both research and practice.

Although most (but not all) researchers would likely agree that there is still merit and especially practical utility in Holland's classical and persistent six-factor model of interests, there are exceptions. Campbell's (1995) CISS measure included seven measures of interests and posited the conventional and social (rather than conventional and enterprising) interests as being juxtaposed. Moreover, the structural models of interests also need to incorporate an underlying metastructure that has increasingly been suggested by second-order factor researchers. Most secondary factor structures generally reduce the six-factor solution to two overarching (perhaps, more accurately, undergirding or foundational) dimensions: concern with data versus ideas and concern with people versus things (see Einarsdottir & Rounds, 2000; Gati, 1991; Prediger, 1982; Rounds & Day, 1999; Tracey & Rounds, 1993). Einarsdottir and Rounds also claim to have identified a third structural factor, perhaps best labeled as sex-role congruence.

The practical implications for the underlying two-factor structure of interests remain to be demonstrated. Whether concern for things versus concern with people and concern with ideas versus data is a sufficiently robust or detailed grouping from which individuals can make career decisions and on which career assessors and counselors can provide guidance remains to be demonstrated. The balance between scientific precision or parsimony and practical utility needs to be considered in evaluating the utility of such findings, since occupational choices are generally not experienced by individuals in abstract psychological or conceptual terms. People tend to think about occupational choices concretely: for example, "Should I go to medical school or law school?" Rounds and Day (1999) appropriately argued that the model of interests employed should match the counseling question. In this respect the more detailed models clustering occupations into a larger number of psychologically meaningful dimensions may be more pragmatically useful at this time.

### Criterion-Related Validity: Education-Related Criteria

Some studies have demonstrated the ability of occupational interest test scores to predict well to school major, a common criterion measure. Interest theory suggests that persons with particular interests should prefer particular college majors, generally those consistent with persons in the adult work world corresponding to the college major (e.g., persons with realistic-investigative interests would be predicted to choose both majors and careers in engineering or technology versus, say, art or history). Independent of the instrument used, these occupational interest variables predict well to groupings of like-minded students and to students' choice of college majors (Betz & Taylor, 1982; Borgen & Helms, 1975; Fouad, 1999; Hansen & Neuman, 1999; Hansen & Swanson, 1983; Miller, Newell,

Springer, & Wells, 1992; Naylor & Kidd, 1991; Silver & Barnette, 1970). In addition, use of interest inventories appears to help students to more readily select and be satisfied with college majors (Betz & Borgen, 2010).

### Criterion-Related Validity: Vocational Choices

The research results are generally positive but somewhat more mixed in supporting the validity of interest measures in predicting to real-world occupational and avocational (Super, 1940a) activity choices. In predicting to broadly categorized occupational choices years later, the interest measures on average are quite good in their predictive power (Donnay & Borgen, 1996; G. D. Gottfredson & Holland, 1975; Lowman & Schurman, 1982; Lucy, 1976; Mount & Muchinsky, 1978a, 1978b; Spokane & Decker, 1999; Super, 1940b, 1949; Super & Crites, 1962; Upperman & Church, 1995). The more specific the predictive task, however, the less well the interest measures do (DeFruyt & Mervielde, 1999; Fricko & Beehr, 1992; Upperman & Church, 1995; Zytowski & Hay, 1984).

Various attempts have been made over the years to integrate characteristics of people with presumed-relevant occupational choices. Among the earliest was Strong's (Campbell & Hansen, 1981; Strong, 1955) matching of the expressed interest patterns of happily employed successful individuals in particular occupations. Although this work was significant in that persons in a profession were measured, the number of occupations covered was very small even as the Strong measure evolved over time. G. D. Gottfredson and Holland's (1996) *Dictionary of Holland Occupational Codes* was another such effort. Although it covered a number of different occupations, the methodology was such that characteristics derived from the U.S. Department of Labor's (1991) *Dictionary of Occupational Titles* were matched by a computer program with the supposed interest patterns associated with that occupation. Few of the matches were empirically validated using persons in those occupations and their measured interests.

When it comes to the predictive power of interests, we are also reminded of the old saw of surgeons knowing everything about nothing, psychiatrists knowing nothing about everything, and pathologists knowing everything about everything, but too late. The analogy holds for the former two components as far as mapping from the results of interest assessments to occupational options, with systems that rely on actual interest data from occupational samples being more like surgeons, systems that map to almost all occupations based on indirect or often speculative data being more like psychiatrists, and no system having the perfect (albeit tardy) understanding of the pathologist.

For example, a strength of the O*Net occupational database is that it relies on sampling or expert ratings of a large range of over 800 occupations; however, measurement of ability and skill requirements for the positions was the primary basis for development of that database. To a large degree, mapping from any interest assessment alone to that database requires a degree of faith in the underlying assumption of Holland's later theory statements that interests, abilities, and skills tend to go hand in hand as well as in the accuracy of the expert raters contributing to the mapping of presumed interest patterns to the occupations. However, this criticism might be directed toward any assessment that maps its interest assessment results to occupations without exclusive reliance on empirical data on interests from the system's target occupations, and currently only the Strong and Campbell assessments are immune from this charge; however, they suffer from a shortage of occupations in the database relative to O*Net. Thus, users of any assessment system must choose their poison, and run the risk of incorrectly mapping interest inventory results to a larger range of occupations or correctly matching interest inventory results to a fairly narrow sample of occupations.

### Predicting Work-Related Outcomes

The conventional view is that interest measures usually predict to career satisfaction (liking one's occupational choice) but not to issues related to job satisfaction (liking one's specific job, including the specific work setting) or productivity (e.g., Dawis, 1991; Hogan & Blake, 1996; Schneider, Paul, White, & Holcombe, 1999). The general lack of support for predicting to performance-related outcomes is presumably because many other factors influence the degree to which someone is likely to be productive in a particular application of an occupation, including most notably abilities. Other noninterest factors affecting such outcomes include extrinsic factors, such a salary, satisfaction with coworkers, satisfaction with the quality of supervision, and one's own history with a particular employer and the context in which the employment occurs. For example, the level of unemployment and degree of job availability may affect job satisfaction as much as goodness of interest–career fit.

Research approaches addressing person–environment fit (Spokane, Meir, & Catalano, 2000) provide considerably more sophistication in the definition of the job as it relates to interests theories (e.g., Maurer & Tarullie, 1997), so it is possible that, over time, more complex

predictions of work-related outcomes can be made. In an important recent article, Van Iddekinge et al. (2011) reported on the authors' creation of an interest measure that predicted well to work-related outcomes. Their measure was useful in personnel selection explaining variance above cognitive abilities and Big 5 measures of personality. Tinsley (2006) has argued that degree of fit between general interests and an occupation simply fails to predict relevant outcomes, such as satisfaction or productivity, without consideration of moderating factors, such as the role of personality style in person–environment interaction. Instead, he recommended that we "must abandon our decades-long fixation on Holland's (1997a) hexagonal model as a predictor of vocational outcomes if we are to achieve advances that are presently outside our reach" (p. 287). Tinsley instead recommended complexity and the creation of microtheories operating on "micro work environments," and the replacement of static indicators of person–environment fit or congruence with longitudinal studies involving hit-rate analysis and the consideration of personality style. Concerning congruence, Dik, Strife, and Hansen (2010) also considered whether incongruence between interests and jobs (e.g., a career's calling for use of those interest patterns least endorsed) raised similar "match" concerns as positive fit between most endorsed interests and those called for in a career or job. They concluded that congruence with high-endorsed interests was different in kind from simply avoiding ill-fitting matches.

## GROUP DIFFERENCES IN THE MEASUREMENT OF INTERESTS

Systematic group differences in interest patterns or interest test scores have been a cause of concern for some time, because they may represent bias in a measure, perhaps leading to restriction in the sorts of occupations or other options considered. However, just because groups differ on items or scales does not necessarily indicate bias or invalidity, as observed score differences may reflect true group differences in interests. Groups have most often been compared through absolute levels of interests and by the ways in which interest scores correlate with one another (i.e., the structure of interests). Our focus is on interest inventories and not other methods, such as card sorts. We briefly survey research on differences in interests across groups differing in age, sex and gender, and culture. We do not discuss differences across groups with different disabilities, except to refer interested readers to summaries of the topic (see Lowman, 1997; Klein, Wheaton, &

Wilson, 1997) and to note that most manuals provide scant data about such groups (see Fouad & Spreda, 1995).

## Age

In a thorough review of the literature on stability and change in interests across the life span, Swanson (1999) reported that there are few systematic, normative changes in interests over time, especially after age 30. She also noted that differences observed between groups of individuals at different ages are smaller than between occupational groups. Swanson further reported that one change reported across studies is that interests appear to become better defined over time.

Although focused on leisure rather than occupational interests, Hansen, Dik, and Zhou (2008) reported the results of a cross-section study examining changes in leisure interests across the life span (with samples of college students, working-age adults, and retirees). They found evidence for similarity in the structure of leisure interests across adulthood and at least partial convergence between occupational and leisure interests across the three samples.

## Sex, Gender, and Sexual Orientation

It is useful to distinguish between sex and gender differences, the former related to an examinee's biological sex (male or female) and the latter related to the examinee's sense of gender-role identification (masculine or feminine) and behavior, which is (highly) correlated with biological gender. Gender is more difficult to assess than biological sex and generally requires specialized scales for assessment. Such measures can tap the degree to which a child has been socialized into, say, traditional masculine or feminine roles or the degree to which an adolescent or adult has adopted androgynous characteristics in the course of education, peer socialization, or immersion in the popular culture. Of the extensive research on group differences in interests, almost all has been carried out in relation to biological sex and almost none in relation to gender, although the masculinity–femininity scales included on some—and mostly older—interest inventories (such as the Vocational Preference Inventory; Holland, 1958, 1985) are essentially gender indicators in their own right. (Note that in the literature on sex differences in interests, authors generally use the word *gender* in lieu of *sex,* and often authors' discussions fail to distinguish adequately the two concepts.) Because of the paucity of recent research on gender-related group differences in interests,

our remaining discussion focuses on sex differences; however, until research speaks to the issue, it remains a live possibility that it is primarily gender and not sex per se that accounts for observed sex differences in interests.

Sex-related differences in responses to interest inventory items have been reported since the earliest inventories. In most cases, such differences are more a matter of degree than of kind; in other words, although there may exist sex-related differences in mean level of endorsement of an item, there are usually some members of each sex who will respond on either extreme of endorsement. Typically, however, in broad general population samples, males more highly endorse realistic interests than do women, and women are more likely to endorse social and conventional interests. Such findings should never be used to obscure that the usual purpose of interest measurement is to help people find satisfying careers at the individual, not group, level.

One strategy to eliminate sex differences from a measure is to not include in the final measure any inventory items that evince sex differences. The developers of the UNIACT (Swaney, 1995) followed this approach. Critics of this approach might argue that the resulting measure might not reflect the reality of possible interests on which the sexes may, for whatever reason, really do differ. Fouad and Spreda (1995) reported having found meaningful sex differences in endorsement of 25% of the items of the 1994 edition of the SII. They also reported that even in the UNIACT there were major sex differences in endorsement of some of the scales. Kuder and Zytowski (1991), using KOIS data, reported that men and women in the same occupation have different interests. The conclusion after several decades of research is that the interests of men and women continue to differ at both the item and the scale level (Fouad & Spreda, 1995). Hansen, Collins, Swanson, and Fouad (1993) reported evidence, based on multidimensional scaling, that there are also sex differences in the structure of interests, but some have challenged those findings as being based on samples of inadequate size. However, over the past decade meta-analytic research on a range of data sets associated with a range of major interest assessments seems to have put the question to rest, and decisively so, in defense of the claim that there exist substantial sex differences in vocational interests (Su, Rounds, & Armstrong, 2009). Su et al. further argued that sex differences in vocational interests may contribute to gender differences and sex typing in the various science-technology-engineering-math (STEM) fields; they further suggested that, given the stability in interests across adulthood, if society wishes to spur more women to enter STEM fields, it might focus primarily on shaping young girls' interests in that direction rather than waiting for non-STEM interests to become entrenched by adolescence.

Authors of measures must also decide when to use same-sex or combined sex samples when norming scales. The SII, KOIS, COPSystem, Self-Directed Search, and JVIS are some measures that include scales making use of separate norm groups for men and women. The UNI-ACT and CISS are among the measures using only scales that make use of combined sex norm groups. Again, critics of the practice of using combined sex norm groups point to data suggesting that because men and women in occupations do appear to have different interest patterns, combined norm groups may mask real differences, though they may foster consideration and exploration of occupations that they might not otherwise have considered.

There is little published research on differences in interests based on sexual preference, consistent with Prince's (1997) claim that there has been little research on common assessment measures with gay, lesbian, and bisexual populations. Some authors (see Lowman, 1993; Rothenberg, 1990) have suggested that gay males are disproportionately represented in the arts (although there is no evidence that a majority of gay males are creatively talented; see also Lidderdale, Croteau, Anderson, Tovar-Murray, & Davis, 2007; Pope et al., 2004). Chung and Harmon (1994) compared SDS scores of gay and heterosexual men; gay men scored relatively higher on artistic and social scales and lower on realistic and investigative ones. This research may suggest that, as with sex differences, interests likewise could vary with sexual orientation although much wider and more representative samples would be needed to understand this issue better.

## Culture

Culture is a diverse category; in reporting cultural differences in interests, we focus mainly on ethnicity and race, although a more complete treatment would include language, nationality, religion, and other factors. Most authors of interest inventories have sought to study possible group differences related to race and ethnicity. However, such research generally does a poor job of making clear whether groups were selected on the biological construct race versus the more socially determined construct ethnicity. Also, in most studies examinees are required to choose the single racial or ethnic category that best describes their background (e.g., Black, White). However, a growing proportion of the population has a mixed

background in terms of race (a fuzzy concept to start with), and determining a single ethnic identification is for many a difficult if not impossible task for many individuals enculturated into more than one ethnic tradition. In addition, several authors concerned with career assessment and development also discuss the concept of minority status (see DeVaney & Hughey, 2000) in relation to race or ethnicity, but this likewise has become more problematic as some states no longer have a single racial or ethnic group that can claim a majority and as nearly everyone is a member of a minority group in an increasingly global economy.

For many decades, interest inventories were normed mainly on samples of European descent. Until recently there were relatively few studies of cultural differences in interests. In an important review of the literature on the use of the SVIB and its later versions using Black samples, spanning the period from the 1920s to the 1980s, Carter and Swanson (1990) reported only eight studies (often with small or unrepresentative samples) that suggested that, compared to Whites, Black Americans had relatively higher interests in social and business occupations and relatively lower interests in scientific and technical ones. Over the past two decades, a plethora of articles have appeared on the topic of cultural assessment, including a number directed at issues of interest patterns or structures in specific racial or ethnic groups (e.g., Lattimore & Borgen, 1999; Leong & Leung, 1994; Šverko & Babarović, 2006).

Recently developed or renormed inventories generally seek to sample from diverse and representative ethnic and racial populations and then check to ensure that scale scores are approximately the same across groups. As with sex and gender, a number of studies have investigated whether the structure of interests—generally in reference to Holland's theory—remains the same across ethnic and racial groups (e.g., Gupta, 2009; Gupta, Tracey, & Gore, 2008; Leong & Hartung, 2000; Tak, 2004). For example, using a sample of male and female Native American college students, Hansen and Haviland (2000) reported support for Holland's hexagonal model of interests using the General Occupational Themes from the 1985 edition of the SII, although the results for women slightly better fit the predicted hexagonal shape than did those for men. Fouad and Spreda (1995) summarized such research for the SII, KOIS, UNIACT, and SDS, generally finding great similarity across ethnic and racial groups, and at any rate more similarity than between the sexes. We hasten to add that interests and occupational aspirations are not identical; people can be interested in one type of work but aspire to another that they believe is more realistic or achievable

(L. S. Gottfredson, 1986; Gottfredson & Lapan, 1997). Thus, there may still exist large differences between ethnic and racial groups in occupational aspirations, even when differences in interests are few. Additionally, the validity of interest measures does not speak to the ways in which such measures may best be used in counseling with persons from various ethnic, cultural, or disadvantaged groups (see, e.g., Fouad & Kantamneni, 2008).

## INTERDOMAIN ASSESSMENT: INTERESTS, ABILITIES, *AND* PERSONALITY

The measurement of interests alone as a basis for advising on or understanding career issues is generally insufficient from a research or practice perspective, since interests do not predict in a vacuum and account for only one aspect of what goes into making choices affecting career, job, or life satisfaction. The senior author has been one of the most persistent advocates of the need to measure in multiple domains (see, e.g., Lowman, 1991, 1997). (The general area of this research is labeled interdomain theory.) Real people of course do not consist of interests alone. Rather, they are composites of various combinations of interests that, assuredly, interact with abilities and personality, among other trait variables, to determine occupational histories, best-fitting careers, and appropriateness for particular positions. The issues were well identified in a different context by Martindale (1999): "Creativity is a rare trait. This is presumably because it requires the simultaneous presence of a number of traits (e.g., intelligence, perseverance, unconventionality, the ability to think in a particular manner). None of these traits is especially rare. What is quite uncommon is to find them all present in the same person" (p. 137). Increasingly, researchers are looking for the interaction of interests and other variables, such as personality, ability, motivation, and life experiences (see, e.g., Lapan, Shaughnessy, & Boggs, 1996; Super, Savickas, & Super, 1996). Although there are some (and generally older) studies comparing interest and values (Sarbin & Berdie, 1940; Williams, 1972), we focus on the relations of interests to personality traits and abilities, for which robust literatures are now accruing.

### Interest–Personality Relationships

There is considerable evidence (Hogan & Blake, 1996), some of it (e.g., Ackerman & Beier, 2003; Atkinson & Lunneborg, 1968) not new, that interests overlap substantially with personality characteristics and that these relationships generally follow a predictable path at the aggregated level. Holland (1997b) himself argued that interest inventories actually are, in effect, personality measures. However, considerably more work is needed to determine the relationships other than at the aggregated basis. Thus, understanding relationships among interests, abilities, and personality characteristics of groups of research participants raises different issues than trying to understand interdomain patterns on an individual basis. Grouped overlaps address issues related to factors that tend to move in the same direction, for example, the question of whether there is overlap between conscientiousness as a personality variable and conventional interest patterns. More data are needed not just on the interdomain relationships on the aggregated basis but also in determining the relationships between cross-domain nonmatches (e.g., high conventional interest patterns coupled with low scores on conscientiousness).

By far the most work has been done to date in exploring the relationships between occupational interests and personality using inventoried measures from each domain (Holland, Johnston, & Asama, 1994). The usual research paradigm has been to administer self-report measures of interests and self-report measures of personality and to consider whether (a) there is common variance and (b) whether predicted relationships across domains (e.g., conventional interest pattern and conscientiousness) are correlated in a predictable manner. Generally this research has found overlap between interest areas (typically using Holland's six-factor model) and the corresponding personality variables predicted to co-vary with interests (e.g., artistic vocational interests with the personality variable of openness).

A more complicated question concerns the relationship of interests and what might be called overarching personality variables. Researchers (e.g., Betz & Borgen 2000; Betz & Schifano, 2000; Lapan et al., 1996) have demonstrated that self-efficacy can be a powerful additive, if not overarching, variable in determining whether people make appropriate use of their interest patterns, particularly when confronted with a culturally atypical career preference (e.g., women with realistic interests attracted to male-dominated fields).

### Interest–Ability Relationships

Perhaps the least amount of systematic work to date has been done on measuring the overlap between interests and abilities, despite some early efforts to consider the question (e.g., Hartman & Dashiell, 1919; Lowman, 1991;

Lowman et al., 1985). A literature has begun to emerge in this important area (e.g., Ackerman, 1996; Ackerman, Kyllonen, & Roberts, 1999; Carson, 1996; L. S. Gottfredson, 1996; Lowman & Williams, 1987; Lowman et al., 1985; Proyer, 2006; Randahl, 1991), but it remains limited (see, e.g., Krane & Tirre, 2005; see also Betz, 1993). The measurement of abilities remains complex and hampers progress in this area. Some research, generally measuring abilities through self-ratings (Prediger, 1999a, 1999b; Tracey & Hopkins, 2001) has been reported, including a few detailed studies with comprehensive measures of abilities, but on the basis of this scanty record it is premature to draw many conclusions. So far, the interest and ability domains appear to be separable, interactive, and similarly structured. The several studies (e.g., Prediger, 1999a, 1999b) that have addressed the topic from the perspective of self-ratings of both interests and abilities suffer from the absence of a convincing literature base establishing that self-rating abilities are equivalent to objectively rated ones (see Carson, 1998b; Lowman & Williams, 1987). Not surprisingly, there are generally more powerful results shown in the relationship between self-ratings of abilities and interests, but this may partly be explained by common method variance since identical response formats are generally used. However, Lowman and Williams (1987) demonstrated that against the criteria of objective measures of ability, self-ratings are less than ideal.

Much more research work is needed to better understand how interests relate to abilities and vice versa. An intriguing suggestion is that interests, if in large part essentially inherited and rather fixed characteristics of people, direct activity to specific, interest-related areas. Since ability in contrast to interests requires considerable practice to advance from raw talent to usable skills, it is likely that interests may direct where one's "ability capital" is invested (see Ericsson, 1996, p. 27). According to those in this theoretical group (which would include early psychologist Dewey; see Savickas, 1999, p. 32) the great importance of interests is that they drive practice, and that practice determines skill acquisition.

The nature of abilities themselves is of course not without controversy. By most accounts, abilities are suffused with a general factor, often labeled $g$, or intelligence, and a series of primary abilities, $p$s, which are themselves correlated moderately with $g$ (see Carroll, 1993). The question of whether to evaluate abilities only on the basis of $b$, or also to include $p$s is therefore not without controversy. Separate correlations of $g$ and $g$-free specific abilities may be useful in sorting out interdomain relationships.

## Interest–Ability–Personality Relationships

Very little research has been conducted examining the relationships of interests, abilities, and personality characteristics, measuring all three domains simultaneously (Ackerman, 1996; Ackerman & Beier, 2003; Carless, 1999; Carson, 1998a; Lowman, 1991). The reality of these differences has been demonstrated by various profile studies (e.g., Lowman & Leeman, 1988; Lowman & Ng, 2010; Robertson, Smeets, Lubinski, & Benbow, 2010; Wicherts & Vorst, 2010). Perhaps the most relevant newer work is that of Ackerman and his colleagues. Ackerman's (1996) process, personality, interests, and knowledge (PPIK) model addresses the three major domains so far shown to be important in determining career issues and job placement. However, his models need to be replicated using alternative measures of interests and abilities and with real-world choices as criteria. S. D. Brown, Lent, and Gore (2000) found overlapping but separable information contributed from interests, self-rated abilities, and a personality measure. More recently, Armstrong and Rounds (2010) presented a model attempting to integrate across these domains.

In real life, of course, people are not simply one psychological variable or another. They have specific levels of abilities, specific types of generally quite stable interests, and a personality structure that also has predictability. Theories that relate to all three domains (interests, abilities, and personality) simultaneously are few in number and include Ackerman's (Ackerman, 1996; Ackerman & Heggested, 1997; Ackerman et al., 1999) PPIK, and Lowman's (1991) interdomain theory.

## NEEDED RESEARCH

By any reasonable standard, research in interests is dynamic and flourishing. Nevertheless, more work is needed to address several "next-level" issues. Looking ahead to the next research tasks relevant to interest assessment, we can ask what is there left to do and how should such tasks be prioritized. These tasks can be grouped into several categories:

- Psychobiology of interests
- Specific versus general interest categories
- Commonality and differences of alternative interest measures
- Empirically based occupational and environmental codings
- The structure of interests

- Interdomain relationships
- Additive value of measures related to interests

## Psychobiology of Interests

Although promising, the current research is inadequate for reliably differentiating the amount of variance that is more or less fixed genetically and the amount that can be influenced by environments. Preliminary studies suggest a sizable amount of heritability to interests, but this finding needs replication using alternative measures of interests. Certainly, a finding of high heritability would be expected, given the pronounced stability of interests across the life cycle and the marked efficiency with which people seem to self-select in "right-fitting" occupations. Nonetheless, among those with relatively fixed profiles, it matters which aspects of interests can change or are likely naturally to change, since career choice and satisfaction issues are associated. Conversely, in cases in which interests appear not to be stable, to what extent is the profile, if highly genetic in origin, simply unknown to the person being counseled as opposed to something still in flux? Interest measures need to devote more attention to test–retest reliability over time.

An approach integrating aspects of both the learning and genetic approaches might be to assume that there exist "critical periods" during which interests are modifiable based on environmental reinforcement but after which they are more resistant to modification. Of course, psychoanalytic theories of interests placing special importance on the quality of parent–young child interaction represent a type of critical period theory, but one may hypothesize critical periods for interests extending to much greater ages. One may also classify L. S. Gottfredson's (1996) theory of circumscription and compromise as a critical period model of the development of interests, although her theory focuses mainly on the development of vocational aspirations and only secondarily on interests per se. Critical periods have been proposed for acquiring various cognitive abilities, such as acquisition of accent-free facility in learning a second language or learning musical skills, such as those associated with perfect pitch, although the concept of critical periods in ability acquisition is not without its critics. Carson (1995) proposed such a model of critical periods for the acquisition of interests, noting that several authors had reported that interests in physical sciences appeared to crystallize earlier than those in biological ones (in the early teens and mid-teens, respectively), which crystallized still earlier than interests in the social sciences (by the early 20s). Perhaps there exist a number of potentially strong interests in any child, but without the actual exercise of related skills during a critical period, the opportunity for crystallizing that interest would pass and thereafter becoming exceedingly difficult to revive.

Finally, the degree to which specific psychoactive substances, including medical drugs, recreational drugs, and perhaps even various types of food, may affect levels of interest in different activities and therefore, even if indirectly, types of work, needs further research. There is, for example, growing interest in so-called smart drugs, or nootropics (see Gazzaniga, 2006, p. 184), that appear to enhance specific types of cognitive function that contribute to effective performance in educational and occupational settings. One might similarly wonder whether there may exist "motivator drugs" or "interest nootropics" that boost conative function that support the direction of interest and effort toward specific educational and occupational tasks. A better understanding of such effects might, for example, help us to understand occupational differences in the use of specific substances.

## Specific Versus General Interests Categories

To date, studies have generally taken the easy approach to classifying people on interest patterns, using 1-point codes to establish criterion groups or doing simple correlations between interest and other variables. Such approaches ignore important within-category variance. Taking Holland's six-factor theory as a base, there are 120 possible combinations of three-interest-category codes. Few studies have yet examined the implications of this complexity of interests or the personality or ability differences that may be associated with more complexly measured interest types. Presumably there are significant differences between, say, enterprising-conventional and enterprising-realistic types. Research investigating the underlying structure of a few broad interests should be balanced by another line looking at a more complex and detailed (and narrower) classifications of people (see Tinsley, 2006). With modern computer technology and large sample sizes, we can now study all possible 2- and 3-letter interest combinations.

Commonalities and differences across interest measures need to be better established. There is a paucity of research examining the degree of overlap between measures. Lowman et al. (2003) found an average correlation of only .75 between measures of interests given to the same respondents. This would imply that only half the variance is accounted for when alternative instruments are used to classify people on interests. From a research perspective, this implies that it matters which measure was given to a respondent as to how he or she is classified. For the moment, researchers need to examine the extent to which their results are method bound versus replicating to alternative measures of the same underlying interests.

## Empirically Based Coding of Occupations

Most of the literature on comparing persons' interests with chosen occupations rests on the average coding of job categories using measures such as contained in G. D. Gottfredson and Holland's (1996) *Dictionary of Holland Occupational Codes*. This compendium is based both on empirically validated ratings of occupational interest assignments and those derived from a computer methodology that translated *The Dictionary of Occupational Titles* (U.S. Department of Labor, 1991) data into Holland interest codes. Only measures such as the SVIB (e.g., Hansen & Swanson, 1983) appear to use exclusively empirically derived criterion groups to establish the interest profiles of persons in occupations. However, even those measures inevitably include only a tiny fraction of possible occupations. More recently, the O*Net OnLine has provided a similar service in which interests obtained from any source can (www.onetonline.org/explore/interests) be entered and matched with occupations fitting that code. Of course, the very helpful approach, a free resource, is only as good as the measured interests of the individual using the system and the underlying assessment of the interests said to be associated with particular occupations.

Since the match between individual characteristics and job characteristics is at the base of much of the literature on career assessment and personnel selection, it matters as much whether jobs and occupations are correctly classified as it does that individual interest patterns are (see L. S. Gottfredson & Richards, 1999; Upperman & Church, 1995). Yet the field has been surprisingly cavalier about accepting as valid far less than empirically well established codings of occupations. Additionally, if mean interest profiles are taken as the criterion of what constitutes a particular occupation's code, complex research questions remain. Does not being matched with the average profile established empirically for an occupation result in lower job satisfaction or productivity levels? To what extent can employees be productive in an occupation yet not satisfied in it, as, for example, what might be predicted for those having the requisite abilities for a profession but a lack of interest matching? Finally, there appear to be complex relationships between occupations as classified on job analytic methods and interest themes (Hyland & Muchinsky, 1991). These relationships need further exploration.

## Interdomain Research

Enough research now is available to establish empirically that there are complex empirical relationships among, at the least, interests, abilities, and personality characteristics. The relevance of a multidomain model of career assessment was established some time ago (see Ackerman & Heggestad, 1997; Lowman, 1991), but the specific empirical nature of interdomain relationships has not been fully determined. Having established that interests and personality are highly related, more work is needed to determine ability-interest and ability-interest-personality relationships.

## Adult Development Models of Interests

In the assessment of interests, it matters whether they change over the life cycle in basic interests or their expression in specific jobs. For example, Kanfer and Ackerman (2004) have raised the important and underresearched question about whether interests decrease in intensity over the course of adulthood (see also Ackerman & Rolfhus, 1999).

## SUMMARY AND CONCLUSION

The measurement of interests is a prolific business enterprise and an area that has generated an impressive array of research findings. Interests appear to represent variables with profound significance for predicting individuals' behavior, well-being, and occupational lives.

This chapter has reviewed definitions of interests and suggested an operational definition of the construct. The chapter notes that there is increasing evidence that there is a strong component of heritability to interests that may account for their unusually high test–retest reliability.

Several of the major contemporary measures of interests were discussed, including the Strong Vocational Interest Blank (Strong Interest Inventory), the Campbell Interest and Skill Survey, the Kuder Occupational Interest Survey, the Unisex Edition of the ACT Interest Inventory, the Self-Directed Search, the Vocational Preference Inventory, Johansson's measures, the O*Net Interest Profiler, and the FYI.

The chapter briefly reviewed a large and growing research literature addressing the validity and reliability of interests, concluding that they predict well to school and work choices. There is also both consensus and controversy regarding the existence of six interest factors. (Some say more, some fewer.) It appears that underlying metafactors summarize the six Holland factors typically reported in the literature; however, there may be more practical utility to the six-factor model than to a two-dimensional one. The research literature offers less information on the relationship among interests and other domains, such as abilities and personality variables. There is also little basis from which to determine the specific interest measures that work best for particular assessment tasks.

A number of research issues meriting attention in the next decade were also identified. These include:

- psychobiology of interests,
- specific versus general interest categories,
- commonality and differences of alternative interest measures,
- empirically based occupational and environmental codings,
- the structure of interests,
- interdomain relationships, and
- additive value of measures related to interests.

## REFERENCES

Ackerman, P. L. (1996). A theory of adult intellectual development: Process, personality, interests, and knowledge. *Intelligence, 22,* 227–257. doi:10.1016/S0160–2896(96)90016–1

Ackerman, P. L., & Beier, M. E. (2003). Intelligence, personality, and interests in the career choice process. *Journal of Career Assessment, 11,* 205–218. doi:10.1177/1069072703011002006

Ackerman, P. L., & Heggestad, E. D. (1997). Intelligence, personality, and interests: Evidence for overlapping traits. *Psychological Bulletin, 121,* 219–245.

Ackerman, P. L., Kyllonen, P. C., & Roberts, R. D. (Eds.) (1999). *Learning and individual differences. Process, trait, and content determinants.* Washington, DC: American Psychological Association.

Ackerman, P. L., & Rolfhus, E. L. (1999). The locus of adult intelligence: Knowledge, abilities, and nonability traits. *Psychology and Aging, 14,* 314–330. doi:10.1037/0882–7974.14.2.314

ACT. (2009). *ACT Interest Inventory technical manual.* Retrieved from www.act.org/research/researchers/pdf/ACTInterestInventory TechnicalManual.pdf

Armstrong, P., & Rounds, J. (2010). Integrating individual differences in career assessment: The Atlas Model of Individual Differences and the Strong Ring. *Career Development Quarterly, 59,* 143–153.

Armstrong, P., Smith, T. J., Donnay, D. C., & Rounds, J. (2004). The Strong Ring: A basic interest model of occupational structure. *Journal of Counseling Psychology, 51*(3), 299–313. doi:10.1037/0022–0167.51.3.299

Asplund, J., Lopez, S. J., Hodges, T., & Harter, J. (2007). *The Clifton Strengthsfinder 2.0 technical report: Development and validation.* Omaha, NE: Gallup.

Athanasou, J. A., O'Gorman, J., & Meyer, E. (1981). Factorial validity of the vocational interest scales of the Holland Vocational Preference Inventory for Australian high school students. *Educational and Psychological Measurement, 41,* 523–527.

Atkinson, G., & Lunneborg, C. E. (1968). Comparison of oblique and orthogonal simple structure solutions for personality and interest factors. *Multivariate Behavioral Research, 3,* 21–35.

Baker, H. E. (2002). Reducing adolescent career indecision: The ASVAB Career Exploration Program. *Career Development Quarterly, 50,* 359–370.

Baker, H. E., Styer, J. S., Harmon, L., & Pommerich, M. (2010). *Development and validation of the FYI—A preliminary report.* Paper presented at the meeting of the American Educational Research Association, Denver, CO. Retrieved from www.eric.ed.gov/PDFS/ED509882.pdf.

Betz, N. E. (1993). Issues in the use of ability and interest measures with women. *Journal of Career Assessment, 1,* 217–232. doi:10.1177/106907279300100302

Betz, N. E., & Borgen, F. H. (2000). The future of career assessment: Integrating vocational interests with self-efficacy and personal styles. *Journal of Career Assessment, 8,* 329–338.

Betz, N. E., & Borgen, F. H. (2010). The CAPA Integrative Online System for College Major Exploration. *Journal of Career Assessment, 18,* 317–327.

Betz, N. E., Borgen, F., & Harmon, L. (1996). *Skills Confidence Inventory applications and technical guide.* Palo Alto, CA: Consulting Psychologists Press.

Betz, N. E., & Rottinghaus, P. J. (2006). Current research on parallel measures of interests and confidence for basic dimensions of vocational activity. *Journal of Career Assessment, 14,* 56–76.

Betz, N. E., & Schifano, R. S. (2000). Evaluation of an intervention to increase realistic self-efficacy and interests in college women. *Journal of Vocational Behavior, 56,* 35–52.

Betz, N. E., & Taylor, K. M. (1982). Concurrent validity of the Strong-Campbell Interest Inventory for graduate students in counseling. *Journal of Counseling Psychology, 29,* 626–635.

Blake, R. (1969). Comparative reliability of picture form and verbal form interest inventories. *Journal of Applied Psychology, 53,* 42–44.

Bordin, E. S. (1994). Intrinsic motivation and the active self: Convergence from a psychodynamic perspective. In M. L. Savickas & R. W. Lent (Eds.), *Convergence in career development theories: Implications for science and practice* (pp. 53–61). Palo Alto, CA: Davies-Black.

Borgen, F. H., & Helms, J. E. (1975). Validity generalization of the men's form of the Strong Vocational Interest Blank with academically able women. *Journal of Counseling Psychology, 22,* 210–216.

Brown, S. D., & Brooks, L. (Eds.). (1996). *Career choice and development* (3rd ed.). San Francisco, CA: Jossey-Bass.

Brown, S. D., Lent, R. W., & Gore, P. A. Jr. (2000). Self-rated abilities and self-efficacy beliefs: Are they empirically distinct? *Journal of Career Assessment, 8,* 223–235.

Brown, S. D., & Watkins, C. E. Jr. (1994). Psychodynamic and personological perspectives on vocational behavior. In M. L. Savickas & R. W. Lent (Eds.), *Convergence in career development theories: Implications for science and practice* (pp. 197–205). Palo Alto, CA: Davies-Black.

Campbell, D. P. (1995). The Campbell Interest and Skill Survey (CISS): A product of ninety years of psychometric evolution. *Journal of Career Assessment, 3,* 391–410.

Campbell, D. P. (2002). The history and development of the Campbell Interest and Skill Survey. *Journal of Career Assessment, 10*(2), 150–168.

Campbell, D. P., & Borgen, F. H. (1999). Holland's theory and the development of interest inventories. *Journal of Vocational Behavior, 55,* 86–101.

Campbell, D. P., & Hansen, J. C. (1981). *Manual for the Strong-Campbell Interest Inventory* (3rd ed.). Stanford, CA: Stanford University Press.

Campbell, D. P., Hyne, S. A., & Nilsen, D. L. (1992). *Manual for the Campbell Interest and Skill Survey.* Minneapolis, MN: National Computer Systems.

Career Dimensions, Inc. (2009). *FOCUS-2 Technical Report.* Center Harbor, NH: Author.

Carless, S. A. (1999). Career assessment: Holland's vocational interests, personality characteristics, and abilities. *Journal of Career Assessment, 7,* 125–144.

Carroll, J. B. (1993). *Human cognitive abilities. A survey of factor-analytic studies.* New York, NY: Cambridge University Press.

Carson, A. D. (1995, August). The selection of interests. In A. D. Carson (Chair), *The nature of interests.* Symposium presented at the meeting of the American Psychological Association, New York, NY.

Carson, A. D. (1996). Aptitudes across Holland's types: Implications for school-based counsellors. *McGill Journal of Education, 31*(3), 319–332.

Carson, A. D. (1998a). The integration of interests, aptitudes, and personality traits: A test of Lowman's matrix. *Journal of Career Assessment, 6,* 83–105.

Carson, A. D. (1998b). The relation of self-reported abilities to aptitude test scores: A replication and extension. *Journal of Vocational Behavior, 53,* 353–371.

Carson, A. D., Evans, K., Gitin, E., & Eads, J. (2011). Mapping StrengthsQuest themes to Holland's vocational personality types. *Journal of Career Assessment, 19,* 197–211.

Carter, R. T., & Swanson, J. L. (1990). The validity of the Strong Interest Inventory for Black Americans: A review of the literature. *Journal of Vocational Behavior, 36,* 195–209.

CGP Research Staff. (1992). *CCQ technical manual.* Moravia, NY: Chronicle Guidance.

Chung, Y. B., & Harmon, L. W. (1994). The career interests and aspirations of gay men: How sex-role orientation is related. *Journal of Vocational Behavior, 45,* 223–239.

Clifton, D. O., Anderson, E. C., & Schreiner, L. A. (2006). *StrengthsQuest: Discover and develop your strengths in academics, career, and beyond.* New York, NY: Gallup Press.

Crites, J. O. (1969). *Vocational psychology: The study of vocational behavior and development.* New York, NY: McGraw-Hill.

Crites, J. O. (1999). Operational definitions of vocational interests. In M. L. Savickas & A. R. Spokane (Eds.), *Vocational interests: Meaning, measurement, and counseling use* (pp. 163–170). Palo Alto, CA: Davies-Black.

Dawis, R. V. (1991). Vocational interests, values, and preferences. In M. D. Dunnette & L. M. Hough (Eds.), *Handbook of industrial and organizational psychology* (pp. 833–871). Palo Alto, CA: Consulting Psychologists Press.

Dawis, R. V. (2005). The Minnesota Theory of Work Adjustment. In S. D. Brown, R. W. Lent, S. D. Brown, R. W. Lent (Eds.), *Career development and counseling: Putting theory and research to work* (pp. 3–23). Hoboken, NJ: Wiley.

Day, S. X., & Rounds, J., (1998). Universality of vocational interest structure among racial and ethnic minorities. *American Psychologist, 53,* 728–736.

Day, S. X., Rounds, J., & Swaney, K. (1998). The structure of vocational interests for diverse racial-ethnic groups. *Psychological Science, 9,* 40–44.

DeFruyt, F., & Mervielde, I. (1999). RIASEC types and big five traits as predictors of employment status and nature of employment. *Personnel Psychology, 52,* 701–727.

DeVaney, S. B., & Hughey, A. W. (2000). Career development of ethnic minority students. In D. A. Luzzo (Ed.), *Career counseling of college students: An empirical guide to strategies that work* (pp. 233–252). Washington, DC: American Psychological Association.

Diamond, E. E., & Zytowski, D. G. (2000). The Kuder Occupational Interest Survey. In C. E. Watkins Jr. & V. L. Campbell. (Eds.), *Testing and assessment in counseling practice* (2nd ed.). *Contemporary topics in vocational psychology* (pp. 263–294). Mahwah, NJ: Erlbaum.

Dik, B. J., Strife, S., & Hansen, J. C. (2010). The flip side of Holland type congruence: Incongruence and job satisfaction. *Career Development Quarterly, 58,* 352–358.

Donnay, D. A. C. (1997). E. K. Strong's legacy and beyond: 70 years of the Strong Interest Inventory. *Career Development Quarterly, 46,* 2–22.

Donnay, D. A. C., & Borgen, F. H. (1996). Validity, structure, and content of the 1994 Strong Interest Inventory, *Journal of Counseling Psychology, 43,* 275–291.

Donnay, D. A. C., Thompson, R. C., Morris, M. L., & Schaubhut, N. A. (2004). *Technical brief for the Newly Revised Strong Interest Inventory Assessment: Content, reliability, and validity.* Mountain View, CA: CPP.

Eby, L. T., & Russell, J. E. A. (1998). A psychometric review of career assessment tools for use with diverse individuals. *Journal of Career Assessment, 6,* 269–310.

Einarsdottir, S., & Rounds, J. (2000). Application of three dimensions of vocational interests to the Strong Interest Inventory. *Journal of Vocational Behavior, 56,* 363–379.

Ericsson, K. A. (1996). The acquisition to expert performance: An introduction to some of the issues. In K. A. Ericsson (Ed.), *The road to excellence: The acquisition of expert performance in the arts and sciences, sports and games* (pp. 1–50). Mahwah, NJ: Erlbaum.

Fouad, N. A. (1999). Validity evidence for interest inventories. In M. L. Savickas & A. R. Spokane (Eds.), *Vocational interests: Meaning, measurement, and counseling use* (pp. 193–209). Palo Alto, CA: Davies-Black.

Fouad, N. A., & Kantamneni, N. (2008). Contextual factors in vocational psychology: Intersections of individual, group, and societal dimensions. In S. D. Brown, R. W. Lent, S. D. Brown, & R. W. Lent (Eds.), *Handbook of counseling psychology* (4th ed., pp. 408–425). Hoboken, NJ: Wiley.

Fouad, N. A., & Mohler, C. J. (2004). Cultural validity of Holland's theory and the Strong Interest Inventory for five racial/ethnic groups. *Journal of Career Assessment, 12,* 423–439.

Fouad, N. A., & Spreda, A. L. (1995). Use of interest inventories with special populations: Women and minority groups. *Journal of Career Assessment, 3,* 453–468.

Fricko, M. A., & Beehr, T. A. (1992). A longitudinal investigation of interest congruence and gender concentration as predictors of job satisfaction. *Personnel Psychology, 45,* 99–117.

Gati, I. (1991). The structure of vocational interests. *Psychological Bulletin, 109,* 309–324.

Gazzaniga, M. S. (2006). *The ethical brain: The science of our moral dilemmas.* New York, NY: Harper Perennial.

Gottfredson, G. D. (1999). John L. Holland's contributions to vocational psychology: A review and evaluation. *Journal of Vocational Behavior, 55,* 15–40.

Gottfredson, G. D., & Holland, J. L. (1975). Vocational choices of men and women: A comparison of predictors from the Self-Directed Search. *Journal of Counseling Psychology, 22,* 28–34.

Gottfredson, G. D., & Holland, J. L. (1996). *Dictionary of Holland occupational codes* (3rd ed.). Odessa, FL: Psychological Assessment Resources.

Gottfredson, G. D., & Johnstun, M. L. (2009). John Holland's contributions: A theory-ridden approach to career assistance. *Career Development Quarterly, 58,* 99–107.

Gottfredson, L. S. (1986). Special groups and the beneficial use of vocational interest inventories. In W. B. Walsh & S. H. Osipow (Eds.), *Advances in Vocational Psychology: Vol. I. The assessment of interests* (pp. 127–198). Hillsdale, NJ: Erlbaum.

Gottfredson, L. S. (1996). Gottfredson's theory of circumscription and compromise. In D. Brown & L. Brooks (Eds.), *Career choice and development* (3rd ed., pp. 179–232). San Francisco, CA: Jossey-Bass.

Gottfredson, L. S. (1999). The nature and nurture of vocational interests. In M. L. Savickas & A. R. Spokane (Eds.), *Vocational interests: Meaning, measurement, and counseling use* (pp. 57–85). Palo Alto, CA: Davies-Black.

Gottfredson, L. S., & Lapan, R. T. (1997). Assessing gender-based circumscription of occupational aspirations. *Journal of Career Assessment, 5,* 419–441.

Gottfredson, L. S., & Richards, J. M. Jr. (1999). The meaning and measurement of environments in Holland's theory. *Journal of Vocational Behavior, 55,* 57–73.

Gupta, S. (2009). Structural analysis and cross-racial/cultural validity of Holland's theory of vocational interests as measured by the UNIACT. *Dissertation Abstracts International, 69*(12B), 7795.

Gupta, S., Tracey, T. G., & Gore, P. A Jr. (2008). Structural examination of RIASEC scales in high school students: Variation across ethnicity and method. *Journal of Vocational Behavior, 72*(1), 1–13. doi:10.1016/j.jvb.2007.10.013

Hansen, J. C., Collins, R. C., Swanson, J. L., and Fouad, N. A. (1993). Gender differences in the structure of interests. *Journal of Vocational Behavior, 42,* 200–211.

Hansen, J. C., Dik, B. J., & Zhou, S. (2008). An examination of the structure of leisure interests of college students, working-age adults, and retirees. *Journal of Counseling Psychology, 55,* 133–145.

Hansen, J. C., & Haviland, M. G. (2000). The interest structure of Native American college students. *Journal of Career Assessment, 8,* 159–165.

Hansen, J. C., & Johansson, C. B. (1972). The application of Holland's vocational model to the Strong Vocational Interest Blank for women. *Journal of Vocational Behavior, 2,* 479–493.

Hansen, J. C., & Neuman, J. L. (1999). Evidence of concurrent prediction of the Campbell Interest and Skill Survey (CISS) for college major selection. *Journal of Career Assessment, 7,* 239–247.

Hansen, J. C., & Swanson, J. L. (1983). Stability of interests and the predictive and concurrent validity of the 1981 Strong-Campbell Interest Inventory for college majors. *Journal of Counseling Psychology, 30,* 194–201.

Harrington, T., & O'Shea, A. (2000). *The Harrington-O'Shea Career Decision-Making System revised.* Circle Pines, MN: American Guidance Service.

Hartman, R., & Dashiell, J. F. (1919). An experiment to determine the relation of interests to abilities. *Psychological Bulletin, 16,* 259–262.

Hartung, P. J. (1999). Interest assessment using card sorts. In M. L. Savickas & A. R. Spokane (Eds.), *Vocational interests: Meaning, measurement, and counseling use* (pp. 235–252). Palo Alto, CA: Davies-Black.

Hedrih, V. (2008). Structure of vocational interests in Serbia: Evaluation of the spherical model. *Journal of Vocational Behavior, 73,* 13–23.

Hogan, R., & Blake, R. J. (1996). Vocational interests. Matching self-concept with the work environment. In K. R. Murphy (Ed.), *Individual differences and behavior in organizations* (pp. 89–144). San Francisco, CA: Jossey-Bass.

Holland, J. L. (1958). A personality inventory employing occupational titles. *Journal of Applied Psychology, 42,* 336–342.

Holland, J. L. (1959). A theory of vocational choice. *Journal of Counseling Psychology, 6,* 35–44.

Holland, J. L. (1985). *Vocational Preference Inventory manual.* Odessa, FL: Psychological Assessment Resources.

Holland, J. L. (1994). *The Self-Directed Search.* Odessa, FL: Psychological Assessment Resources.

Holland, J. L. (1996). Integrating career theory and practice: The current situation and some potential remedies. In M. L. Savickas & W. B. Walsh (Eds.), *Handbook of career counseling theory and practice* (pp. 1–12). Palo Alto, CA: Davies-Black.

Holland, J. L. (1997a). *Making vocational choices: A theory of vocational personalities and work environments* (3rd ed.). Odessa, FL: Psychological Assessment Resources.

Holland, J. L. (1997b). Why interest inventories are also personality inventories. In M. L. Savickas & A. R. Spokane (Eds.), *Vocational interests: Meaning, measurement, and counseling use* (pp. 87–101). Palo Alto, CA: Davies-Black.

Holland, J. L., Fritzsche, B. A., & Powell, A. B. (1994). *The Self-Directed Search technical manual.* Odessa, FL: Psychological Assessment Resources.

Holland, J. L., Johnston, J. A., & Asama, N. F. (1994). More evidence for the relationship between Holland's personality types and personality variables. *Journal of Career Assessment, 2,* 331–340.

Hyland, A. M., & Muchinsky, P. M. (1991). Assessment of the structural validity of Holland's model with job analysis (PAQ) information. *Journal of Applied Psychology, 76,* 75–80.

Ihle-Helledy, K., Zytowski, D. G., & Fouad, N. A. (2004). Kuder Career Search: Test-retest reliability and consequential validity. *Journal of Career Assessment, 12,* 285–297.

Jackson, D. N. (1991). *Manual for the Jackson Vocational Interest Survey.* Port Huron, MI: Research Psychologists Press.

Johansson, C. B. (1980). *Manual for IDEAS: Interest Determination, Exploration, and Assessment System.* Minneapolis, MN: National Computer Systems.

Johansson, C. B. (1982). *Manual for the Career Assessment Inventory* (2nd ed.). Minneapolis, MN: National Computer Systems.

Johansson, C. B. (1986). *Career Assessment Inventory: The enhanced version.* Minneapolis, MN: National Computer Systems.

Johansson, C. B., & Campbell, D. P. (1971). Stability of the Strong Vocational Interest Blank for men. *Journal of Applied Psychology, 55,* 34–37.

Kanfer, R., & Ackerman, P. L. (2004). Aging, adult development, and work motivation. *Academy of Management Review, 29,* 440–458

Kitson, H. D. (1937). *I find my vocation.* New York, NY: McGraw-Hill.

Klein, M. A., Wheaton, J. E., & Wilson, K. B. (1997). The career assessment of persons with disabilities: A review. *Journal of Career Assessment, 5,* 203–211.

Knapp-Lee, L. J. (1995). Use of the COPSystem in career assessment. *Journal of Career Assessment, 3,* 411–428.

Krane, N., & Tirre, W. C. (2005). Ability assessment in career counseling. In S. D. Brown & R. W. Lent (Eds.), *Career development and counseling: Putting theory and research to work* (pp. 330–352). Hoboken, NJ: Wiley.

Kuder, G. F. (1939). The stability of preference items, *Journal of Social Psychology, 10,* 41–50.

Kuder, G. F. (1991). *Occupational Interest Survey, Form DD.* Monterey, CA: CTB McGraw-Hill.

Kuder, F., & Zytowski, D. G. (1991). *Kuder DD/PC: User's guide.* Monterey, CA: CTB Macmillan/McGraw-Hill.

Lapan, R. T., Shaughnessy, P., & Boggs, K. (1996). Efficacy expectations and vocational interests as mediators between sex and choice of math/science college majors: A longitudinal study. *Journal of Vocational Behavior, 49,* 277–291.

Lattimore, R. R., & Borgen, F. H. (1999). Validity of the 1994 Strong Interest Inventory with racial and ethnic groups in the United States, *Journal of Counseling Psychology, 46*, 185–195.

Lau, A. W., & Abrahams, N. M. (1971). Stability of vocational interests within nonprofessional occupations. *Journal of Applied Psychology, 55*, 143–150.

Leong, F. T. L., & Hartung, P. J. (2000). Cross-cultural career assessment: Review and prospects for the new millennium. *Journal of Career Assessment, 8*, 391–401.

Leong, F. T. L., & Leung, S. A. (1994). Career assessment with Asian-Americans. *Journal of Career Assessment, 2*, 240–257.

Leung, S. A., & Hou, Z. (2001). Concurrent validity of the 1994 Self-Directed Search for Chinese high school students in Hong Kong. *Journal of Career Assessment, 9*, 283–296.

Lidderdale, M. A., Croteau, J. M., Anderson, M. Z., Tovar-Murray, D., & Davis, J. M. (2007). Building lesbian, gay, and bisexual vocational psychology: A theoretical model of workplace sexual identity management. In K. J. Bieschke, R. M. Perez, K. A. DeBord, K. J. Bieschke, R. M. Perez, & K. A. DeBord (Eds.), *Handbook of counseling and psychotherapy with lesbian, gay, bisexual, and transgender clients* (2nd ed., pp. 245–270). Washington, DC: American Psychological Association. doi:10.1037/11482–010

Lindley, L. D., & Borgen, F. H. (2000). Personal Style Scales of the Strong Interest Inventory: Linking personality and interests. *Journal of Vocational Behavior, 57*, 22–41.

Livers, D. L. (1994). Review of the Chronicle Career Quest. In J. T. Kapes, M. M. Mastie, & E. A. Whitfield (Eds.), *A counselor's guide to career assessment instruments* (3rd ed., pp. 163–166). Alexandria, VA: National Career Development Association.

Lowman, R. L. (1991). *The clinical practice of career assessment: Interests, abilities, and personality.* Washington, DC: American Psychological Association.

Lowman, R. L. (1993). *Counseling and psychotherapy of work dysfunctions.* Washington, DC: American Psychological Association.

Lowman, R. L. (1997). Career assessment and psychological impairment: Integrating inter-domain and work dysfunctions theory. *Journal of Career Assessment, 5*, 213–224.

Lowman, R. L. (2007). Interests. In R. Fernandez-Ballesteros (Ed.), *Corsini's Encyclopedia of Psychology* (4th ed.). Hoboken, NJ: Wiley.

Lowman, R. L., & Carson, A. D. (2000). Integrating assessment data into the delivery of career counseling services. In D. A. Luzzo (Ed.), *Career development of college students: Translating theory into practice* (pp. 121–136). Washington, DC: American Psychological Association.

Lowman, R. L. & Leeman, G. E. (1988). The dimensionality of social intelligence: Social interests, abilities and needs. *Journal of Psychology, 122*, 279–290.

Lowman, R. L., & Ng, Y. (2010). Interest, ability and personality characteristics of two samples of employed realistic males: Implications for management and assessment. *Psychologist-Manager Journal, 13*(3), 147–163. doi:10.1080/10887156.2010.500259

Lowman, R. L., Palmer, L. K., Santana, R., & Abbott, J. (2003). Executive and career assessment. Can alternative occupational interest measures be used interchangeably? *Psychologist-Manager Journal, 6*, 65–78.

Lowman, R. L., & Schurman, S. J. (1982). Psychometric characteristics of a Vocational Preference Inventory short form. *Educational and Psychological Measurement, 42*, 601–613.

Lowman, R. L., & Williams, R. E. (1987). Validity of self-ratings of abilities and competencies. *Journal of Vocational Behavior, 31*, 1–13.

Lowman, R. L., Williams, R. E., & Leeman, G. E. (1985). The structure and relationship of college women's primary abilities and vocational interests. *Journal of Vocational Behavior, 27*, 298–315.

Lucy, W. T. (1976). An adult population reflects the stability of Holland's personality types over time. *Journal of College Student Personnel, 17*, 76–79.

Lunneborg, P. W. (1981). *The Vocational Interest Inventory manual.* Los Angeles, CA: Western Psychological Services.

Lykken, D. T., Bouchard, T. J., McGue, M. M., & Tellegen, A. (1993). Heritability of interests: A twin study. *Journal of Applied Psychology, 78*(4), 649–661. doi:10.1037/0021–9010.78.4.649

Martindale, C. (1999). Biological bases of creativity. In P. L. Ackerman, P. C. Kyllonen, & R. D. Roberts (Eds.), *Learning and individual differences. Process, trait, and content determinants* (pp. 137–152). Washington, DC: American Psychological Association.

Maurer, T. J., & Tarullie, B. A. (1997). Managerial work, job analysis, and Holland's RIASEC vocational environment dimensions. *Journal of Vocational Behavior, 50*, 365–381.

Miller, M. J., Newell, N. P., Springer, T. P., & Wells, D. (1992). Accuracy of the College Majors Finder for three majors. *Career Development Quarterly, 40*, 334–339.

Mitchell, L. K., & Krumboltz, J. D. (1990). Social learning approach to career decision making: Krumboltz's theory. In D. Brown & L. Brooks (Eds.), *Career choice and development: Applying contemporary theories to practice* (2nd ed., pp. 145–196). San Francisco, CA: Jossey-Bass.

Moloney, D. P., Bouchard, T. J. Jr., & Segal, N. L. (1991). A genetic and environmental analysis of the vocational interests of monozygotic and dizygotic twins reared apart. *Journal of Vocational Behavior, 39*, 76–109.

Mount, M. K., & Muchinsky, P. M. (1978a). Concurrent validation of Holland's hexagonal model with occupational workers. *Journal of Vocational Behavior, 13*, 348–354.

Mount, M. K., & Muchinsky, P. M. (1978b). Person-environment congruence and employee job satisfaction: A test of Holland's theory. *Journal of Vocational Behavior, 13*, 84–100.

Nagy, G., Trautwein, U., & Lüdtke, O. (2010). The structure of vocational interests in Germany: Different methodologies, different conclusions. *Journal of Vocational Behavior, 76*, 153–169. doi:10.1016/j.jvb.2007.07.002

Naylor, F. D., & Kidd, G. J. (1991). The predictive validity of the Investigative scale of the Career Assessment Inventory. *Educational and Psychological Measurement, 51*, 217–226.

Nicolaou, N., & Shane, S. (2010). Entrepreneurship and occupational choice: Genetic and environmental influences. *Journal of Economic Behavior & Organization, 76*, 3–14.

Pope, M., Barret, B., Szymanski, D. M., Chung, Y., Singaravelu, H., McLean, R., & Sanabria, S. (2004). Culturally appropriate career counseling with gay and lesbian clients. *Career Development Quarterly, 53*(2), 158–177

Pozzebon, J. A., Visser, B. A., Ashton, M. C., Lee, K., & Goldberg, L. R. (2010). Psychometric characteristics of a public-domain self-report measure of vocational interests: The Oregon Vocational Interest Scales. *Journal of Personality Assessment, 92*(2), 168–174. doi:10.1080/00223890903510431

Prediger, D. J. (1982). Dimensions underlying Holland's hexagon: Missing link between interests and occupations? *Journal of Vocational Behavior, 21*, 259–287.

Prediger, D. J. (1999a). Basic structure of work-relevant abilities. *Journal of Counseling Psychology, 46*, 173–184.

Prediger, D. J. (1999b). Integrating interests and abilities for career exploration: General considerations. In M. L. Savickas & A. R. Spokane (Eds.), *Vocational interests: Meaning, measurement, and counseling use* (pp. 295–325). Palo Alto, CA: Davies-Black.

Prediger, D. J. (2002). Abilities, interests, and values: Their assessment and their integration via the World-of-Work Map. *Journal of Career Assessment, 10*, 209–232.

Prince, J. P. (1997). Career assessment with lesbian, gay, and bisexual individuals. *Journal of Career Assessment, 5*, 225–238.

Prince, J. P., & Heiser, L. J. (2000). *Essentials of career interest assessment.* New York, NY: Wiley.

Proyer, R. T. (2006). The relationship between vocational interests and intelligence: Do findings generalize across different assessment methods? *Psychology Science, 48*(4), 463–476.

Randahl, G. J. (1991). A typological analysis of the relations between measured vocational interests and abilities. *Journal of Vocational Behavior, 38,* 333–350.

Roberti, J. W., Fox, D. J., & Tunick, R. H. (2003). Alternative personality variables and the relationship to Holland's personality types in college students. *Journal of Career Assessment, 11*(3), 308–327.

Robertson, K., Smeets, S., Lubinski, D., & Benbow, C. P. (2010). Beyond the threshold hypothesis: Even among the gifted and top math/science graduate students, cognitive abilities, vocational interests, and lifestyle preferences matter for career choice, performance, and persistence. *Current Directions in Psychological Science, 19,* 346–351. doi:10.1177/0963721410391442

Roe, A. (1954). A new classification of occupations. *Journal of Counseling Psychology, 1,* 215–220.

Roe, A. (1957). Early determinants of vocational choice. *Journal of Counseling Psychology, 4,* 212–217.

Roe, A., & Lunneborg, P. W. (1990). Personality development and career choice. In D. Brown & L. Brooks (Eds.), *Career choice and development: Applying contemporary theories to practice* (2nd ed., pp. 68–101). San Francisco, CA: Jossey-Bass.

Rothenberg, A. (1990). Creativity, mental health, and alcoholism. *Creativity Research Journal, 3,* 179–201.

Rottinghaus, P. J., Coon, K. L., Gaffey, A. R., & Zytowski, D. G. (2007). Thirty-year stability and predictive validity of vocational interests. *Journal of Career Assessment, 15*(1), 5–22. doi:10.1177/1069072706294517

Rounds, J., & Day, S. X., (1998). Universality of vocational interest structure among racial and ethnic minorities. *American Psychologist, 53,* 728–736.

Rounds, J., & Day, S. X., (1999). Describing, evaluating, and creating vocational interest structures. In M. L. Savickas & A. R. Spokane (Eds.) *Vocational interests: Meaning, measurement, and counseling use* (pp. 103–133). Palo Alto, CA: Davies-Black.

Rounds, J., Su, R., Lewis, P., & Rivkin, D. (2010). *O\*NET Interest Profiler Short Form psychometric characteristics: Summary.* Washington, DC: National Center for O\*NET Development. Retrieved from www.onetcenter.org/dl_files/IPSF_Psychometric.pdf

Sarbin, T. R., & Berdie, R. F. (1940). Relation of measured interests to the Allport-Vernon study of values. *Journal of Applied Psychology, 24,* 287–296.

Savickas, M. L. (1998). Interpreting interest inventories: A "case" example. *Career Development Quarterly, 46,* 307–310.

Savickas, M. L. (1999). The psychology of interests. In M. L. Savickas & A. R. Spokane (Eds.), *Vocational interests: Meaning, measurement, and counseling use* (pp. 19–56). Palo Alto, CA: Davies-Black.

Schneider, B., Paul, M. C., White, S. S., & Holcombe, K. M. (1999). Understanding high school student leaders, I: Predicting teacher ratings of leader behavior. *Leadership Quarterly, 10,* 609–636.

Silver, H. A., & Barnette, W. L. (1970). Predictive and concurrent validity of the Minnesota Vocational Interest Inventory for vocational high school boys. *Journal of Applied Psychology, 54,* 436–440.

Spokane, A. R., & Decker, A. R. (1999). Expressed and measured interests. In M. L. Savickas & A. R. Spokane (Eds.), *Vocational interests: Meaning, measurement, and counseling use* (pp. 211–233). Palo Alto, CA: Davies-Black.

Spokane, A. R., & Holland, J. L. (1995). The Self-Directed Search: A family of self-guided career interventions. *Journal of Career Assessment, 3,* 347–468.

Spokane, A. R., Meir, E. I., & Catalano, M. (2000). Person-environment congruence and Holland's theory: A review and reconsideration. *Journal of Vocational Behavior, 57,* 137–187.

Strong, E. K. (1938a). Predictive value of the vocational interest test. *Journal of Educational Psychology, 26,* 331–349.

Strong, E. K. (1938b). Vocational interest blank for men. Palo Alto, CA: Stanford University Press.

Strong, E. K. (1943). *Vocational interests of men and women.* Palo Alto, CA: Stanford University Press.

Strong, E. K. (1951). Interest scores while in college of occupations engaged in 20 years later. *Educational and Psychological Measurement, 11,* 335–348.

Strong, E. K. (1952). Nineteen-year follow-up of engineer interests. *Journal of Applied Psychology, 36,* 65–74.

Strong, E. K. (1955). *Vocational interests 18 years after college.* Minneapolis, MN: University of Minnesota Press.

Super, D. E. (1940a). *Avocational interest patterns; a study in the psychology of avocations.* Palo Alto, CA: Stanford University Press.

Super, D. E. (1940b). The measurement of interest in an occupation vs. patterns of interests similar to those of persons in that occupation. *Psychological Bulletin, 37,* 450–451.

Super, D. E. (1949). *Appraising vocational fitness by means of psychological tests.* New York, NY: Harper & Brothers.

Super, D. E., & Crites, J. O. (1962). *Appraising vocational fitness by means of psychological tests* (rev. ed.). New York, NY: Harper & Brothers.

Super, D. E., Savickas, M. L., & Super, C. M. (1996). The life-span, life-space approach to careers. In D. Brown & L. Brooks (Eds.), *Career choice and development* (3rd ed., pp. 121–178). San Francisco, CA: Jossey-Bass.

Šverko, I., & Babaroviæ, T. (2006). The validity of Holland's theory in Croatia. *Journal of Career Assessment, 14*(4), 490–507. doi: 10.1177/10169072706288940

Swaney, K. B. (1995). *Technical manual: Revised unisex edition of the ACT Interest Inventory (UNIACT).* Iowa City, IA: ACT.

Swanson, J. L. (1999). Stability and change in vocational interests. In M. L. Savickas & A. R. Spokane (Eds.), *Vocational interests: Meaning, measurement, and counseling use* (pp. 135–158). Palo Alto, CA: Consulting Psychologists Press.

Su, R., Rounds, J., & Armstrong, P. I. (2009). Men and things, women and people: A meta-analysis of sex differences in interests. *Psychological Bulletin, 135,* 859–884.

Tak, J. (2004). Structure of vocational interests for Korean college students. *Journal of Career Assessment, 12,* 298–311.

Taylor, K. (2009). Operationalizing the good lives model: An examination of Holland's RIASEC theory and vocational congruence with offenders 2001–2008. *Dissertation Abstracts International, 70*(4-B), 2067.

Thurstone, L. L. (1931). A multiple factor study of vocational interests. *Personnel Journal, 10,* 198–205.

Tinsley, H. E. A. (2006). A pig in a suit is still a pig: A common on "Modifying the C Index for use with Holland codes of unequal length." *Journal of Career Assessment, 14*(2), 283–288.

Tracey, T. J., & Rounds, J. B. (1993). Evaluating Holland's and Gati's vocational-interest models: A structural meta-analysis. *Psychological Bulletin, 113,* 229–246.

Tracey, T. J. G., & Hopkins, N. (2001). Correspondence of interests and abilities with occupational choice. *Journal of Counseling Psychology, 48,* 178–189.

Upperman, P. J., & Church, A. J. (1995). Investigating Holland's typological theory with Army occupational specialties. *Journal of Vocational Behavior, 47,* 61–75.

U.S. Department of Labor (1991). *Dictionary of occupational titles* (Vol. 1). Chicago, IL: NTC Publishing Group.

U.S. Department of Labor. (2000). *Interest Profiler user's guide, Version 3.0.* Washington, DC: Author. Retrieved from www.onetcenter .org/dl_tools/IP_zips/IP-UG-deskp.pdf

U.S. Department of Labor. (n.d.a). *O\*Net Interest Profiler.* Retrieved from www.onetcenter.org/IP.html

U.S. Department of Labor. (n.d.b). O\*Net online. Retrieved from www.onetcenter.org/online.html

U.S. Department of Labor. (n.d.c). *O\*Net resource center.* Retrieved from www.onetcenter.org/overview.html?p=2

Vacc, N. A., & Hinkle, J. S. (1994). Review of the Career Assessment Inventory—Enhanced Version and Career Assessment Inventory—Vocational Version. In J. T. Kapes, M. M. Mastie, & E. A. Whitfield (Eds.), *A counselor's guide to career assessment instruments* (3rd ed., pp. 145–150). Alexandria, VA: National Career Development Association.

Van Iddekinge, C. H., Putka, D. J., & Campbell, J. P. (2011). Reconsidering vocational interests for personnel selection: The validity of an interest-based selection test in relation to job knowledge, job performance, and continuance intentions. *Journal of Applied Psychology, 96,* 13–33. doi:10.1037/a0021193

Wall, J. E., & Baker, H. E. (1997). The Interest-Finder: Evidence of validity. *Journal of Career Assessment, 5,* 255–273.

Walsh, W. B., & Chartrand, J. M. (1994). Emerging directions of person-environment fit. In M. L. Savickas & R. W. Lent (Eds.), *Convergence in career development theories: Implications for science and practice* (pp. 187–195). Palo Alto, CA: Davies-Black.

Wicherts, J. M., & Vorst, H. M. (2010). The relation between specialty choice of psychology students and their interests, personality, and cognitive abilities. *Learning and Individual Differences, 20*(5), 494–500. doi:10.1016/j.lindif.2010.01.004

Williams, C. M. (1972). Occupational choice of male graduate students as related to values and personality: A test of Holland's theory. *Journal of Vocational Behavior, 2,* 29–46.

Zytowski, D. G. (2001a). *Kuder Career Search: User's manual.* Adel, IA: National Career Assessment Services.

Zytowski, D. G. (2001b). Kuder Career Search with person match: Career assessment for the 21st century. *Journal of Career Assessment, 9,* 229–241.

Zytowski, D. G., & Hay, R. (1984). Do birds of a feather flock together? A test of the similarities within and the differences between five occupations. *Journal of Vocational Psychology, 24,* 242–248.

Zytowski, D. G., & Luzzo, D. A. (2002). Developing the Kuder Skills Assessment. *Journal of Career Assessment, 10*(2), 190–199.

CHAPTER 21

# Assessing Personality and Psychopathology With Interviews

ROBERT J. CRAIG

Interviews are the most basic and most frequently used method of psychological assessment and the most important means of data collection during a psychological evaluation. One review of the practice of psychological assessment by clinical psychologists found that 95% reported the use of clinical interviewing. The other 5% were probably clinical psychologists in administrative positions (Watkins, Campbell, Nieberding, & Hallmark, 1995). Interviews are endemic to the task performance of almost all psychologists—especially clinical and counseling psychologists. During my internship (in a state mental hospital), each intern interviewed a psychiatric patient weekly. Another intern sat in the room taking notes, and the clinical supervisor sat there unobtrusively and later critiqued our commentary on the interview. This process continued for the entire year of our internship. Contemporary supervisors at clinical practica and internships continue to place emphasis on clinical interviewing due to its salient importance in the assessment process. Chapters on clinical interviewing continue to appear in major compendia on personality assessment (Craig, 2003a, 2005a, 2009b, 2010; Hersen & Thomas, 2007; Maruish, 2008).

## HISTORY OF DIAGNOSTIC INTERVIEWING

Diagnosing has a long history. In fact, the conditions that we now label as depression and hysteria appear in both Sumerian and Egyptian literature as far back as 2400 BC (Wiens & Matarazzo, 1983). Initial attempts at formal psychiatric classification began in 1840 and grouped all disorders into two categories: idiotic and insane. In 1880 there were only seven psychiatric disorders in existence: dementia, dipsomania (alcoholism), epilepsy, mania, melancholia, monomania (depression), and paresis. There are now hundreds of diagnoses in *Diagnostic and Statistical Manual of Mental Disorders Fourth Edition* (*DSM-IV*; American Psychiatric Association, 1994). Readers interested in a review of the history of psychiatric diagnosis are referred to Menninger, Mayman, and Pruyser (1963, a 70-page history of psychiatric diagnosis from 2600 BC to 1963) and to the several revisions of *DSM* (American Psychiatric Association, 1980, 1987, 1994).

The word *interview* was initially included in standard dictionaries in 1514 and designated a meeting of persons face-to-face for the purpose of formal conference on some point (Matarazzo, 1965). Initially assessment interviews were modeled on question-and-answer formats. The introduction of psychoanalysis allowed for a more open-ended, free-flowing format. During the 1940s and 1950s, researchers began to study interviews in terms of their content and process, problem-solving versus expressive elements, degree of directedness within an interview, the amount of structure, and the activity of both the respondent and interviewer. Carl Rogers (1961) stimulated much interview research in the 1950s and 1960s by emphasizing personal qualities of the clinician (e.g., warmth, accurate empathy, unconditional positive regard, genuineness). The 1970s introduced the idea of using structured diagnostic interviews, and this trend was further stimulated by the revisions of *DSM-III* (American Psychiatric Association, 1980) with the introduction of diagnostic criteria sets and the requirement to assess for personality disorders for Axis II. Advances in behavioral assessment resulted in more specificity and objectivity in interviews. Seminal behavioral models include such approaches as the BASIC-ID (behaviors, affect, sensation, imagery, cognition, interpersonal relations, and possible need for psychotherapeutic drugs). Since the 1990s there has been increasing appreciation of the role of culture, race, and ethnicity in the development of psychopathology. Managed health care also emphasized brief assessment measures and essentially required psychologists to rely on assessment interviews to the near exclusion of other assessment methods (Groth-Marnatt, 2009).

## PURPOSE OF ASSESSMENT INTERVIEWS

Assessment interviews can be thought of as having four major functions: administration, treatment, research, and prevention (Wiens & Matarazzo, 1983). Sometimes psychologists' interviews are for purposes of fulfilling certain agency requirements, such as determining eligibility for services. The treatment function of the interview might involve assigning differential diagnoses. For example, I received a physician referral to determine whether a patient had a delusional disorder or a borderline personality disorder. If the patient was delusional, the physician was going to treat the patient with medication; if the patient had a borderline condition, the treatment would have been psychotherapy without medication. As director of a drug abuse program, I interviewed every new patient to determine which of our therapists might be a good fit for the patient in order to maximize progress. Assessment interviews are also conducted for research purposes. A salient example is the use of interviews for psychiatric epidemiological research or the use of structured psychiatric interviews to assess the reliability and validity of clinical interviews. Another example would be debriefings after completion of a social psychological research study that involved deception. Finally, the prevention function follows the treatment and research function. If we have a way to reliably classify disorders, we can include homogenous groups of patients into research protocols.

Findings from those studies then could serve a prevention function.

## TYPES OF INTERVIEWS

Several types of interviews have been delineated. They differ in purpose, focus, and duration. Various interviews that have been discussed in the literature are discussed in this section. They are not necessarily mutually exclusive, and they are segmented here for didactic purposes. However, several of these formats can be utilized within a single interview. For example, a clinician can begin with an orientation interview, transition to a screening interview, continue with an interview for etiology, and conclude with an ending interview. There are, however, settings in which each type of interview is conducted separately or perhaps to the exclusion of the others. There is no agreed-on list of interview types, and the list presented in this chapter is somewhat arbitrary, but it provides the reader with a reasonable array of the various kinds of interviews available for clinical use.

### Case History Interviews

Sometimes additional or more elaborate and detailed sequencing of case history material is required in order to make clinical decisions. In this situation, a special interview is completed in which the focus is only on ascertaining the nature of the person's problems in historical sequence, with a possible focus on critical periods of development or events, antecedents and precipitants of behavior, and other matters of clinical interest. Case history interviews can be conducted with the respondent directly, or with the respondent's family, friends, or others.

### Diagnostic Interviews

In a diagnostic interview, the clinician attempts to categorize the behavior of the client into some formal diagnostic system. For psychopathology, two official diagnostic classification systems are in widespread use. The first is the official classification system of the World Health Organization—*International Classification of Disease—Tenth Edition* (*ICD-10*; World Health Organization, 1992). The second is the *Diagnostic and Statistical Manual of Mental Disorders* (*DSM*) (American Psychiatric Association, 1980, 1987, 1994). The fifth edition of the *DSM* is pending. For reimbursement purposes, insurance companies recognize both, but the *DSM* is more popular in the United States and is the more commonly used diagnostic system in psychiatric and psychological clinical research, teaching, and clinical practice. The *DSM* has also become more popular internationally than ICD-10, especially in more westernized countries (Maser, Kaelber, & Weise, 1991). Although there have been calls for considering other classification systems (Dyce, 1994), *DSM* is the predominant diagnostic system in use today. Appendix H of *DSM-IV* lists *DSM-IV* classifications with *IDC-10* codes.

For assessing personality and personality disorders, the issue is a bit more complicated. Most clinicians still use the personality disorder diagnostic categories contained in these two official diagnostic systems, but others prefer to assess people according to more theoretically derived personality classifications, such as Millon's (1991, 2000b) bioevolutionary model, Cattell's (1989) factors, interpersonal models (Benjamin, 1996), the five-factor model (Costa & Widiger, 1997; Samuel & Widiger, 2008), or more biologically based systems (Cloninger, 2000). A recent survey found that a majority of experts on personality disorders were dissatisfied with the current diagnostic systems, and the forthcoming *DSM-5* is unlikely to resolve the problems (Bernstein, Iscan, & Maser, 2007).

### Follow-up Interviews

Follow-up interviews are special-focused interviews that usually have a single purpose. Perhaps it is to review highlights of assessment results or to evaluate quality of services and patient satisfaction received from a health maintenance organization (HMO). Researchers may conduct a debriefing interview when the research involves deception. A medical practitioner will schedule a follow-up interview to judge the effects of psychotropic medication induction.

### Forensic Interviews

Psychologists may be called on to contribute their experience in legal matters that may be complicated by factors related to mental health. These factors include evaluations for dangerousness, competency to stand trial, various insanity pleas, behaviors that may be induced by substance abuse, or custody evaluations, to name a few. Forensic interviews differ in fundamental ways from traditional clinical interviews. While one goal of a clinical interview is the expression of emotions in a nurturing environment, the objective of a forensic interview is the discovery of facts and the truth. Forensic interviews are typically far

more investigative than many other types of interviews, often are of longer duration, and may occur over multiple sessions. Often the person being interviewed is not the client at all but rather the court or perhaps private attorneys who retain these services on behalf of their clients. Forensic evaluations do not carry the same protection of privacy and confidentiality of material obtained in the evaluation as do most other mental health interviews (Craig, 2005b).

### Intake Interviews

Intake interviews are designed to obtain preliminary information about a prospective client and most typically occur within agencies; they may include a determination as to a person's eligibility in terms of the agency's mission. Intake interviews may also be used to acquire information to be presented at a case conference, to help clarify the kind of services available at the agency, to communicate agency rules and policies, or to consider whether the case will be referred elsewhere.

### Interviewing for Etiology

The interview for etiology is designed to determine such matters as etiology and motivational attributions. The interviewer seeks to understand from a theoretical perspective why the person is behaving in a certain way. This kind of interview can be conducted from many theoretical frameworks, such as psychodynamic, behavioral, cognitive-behavioral, family systems, and existential-humanistic perspectives. Also, with each of these defined frameworks are subcategories that also differ from each other. For example, an interview from an analytic perspective can proceed along the line of classical Freudian theory, object relations theory, or self-psychology. An interview from a behavioral perspective can be conducted using Pavlovian (classical conditioning), Skinnerian (instrumental conditioning), or more cognitive-behavioral perspectives. The main point is that interviews for etiology are theory derived and theory driven.

### Mental Status Exams

A special type of interview is the mental status exam, which is conducted to determine the kind and degree of mental impairment associated with a given clinical disorder. Mental status exams traditionally explore such content areas as reasoning, concentration, judgment,

**TABLE 21.1    Common Content Areas in a Mental Status Exam**

| | | |
|---|---|---|
| Appearance | Abnormal Physical Traits | Age Appropriate |
| | Attention to Grooming | Eye Contact |
| | Level of Consciousness | Position of Body |
| Attitude | Cooperative | Dysphoric |
| Mood (affect) | Alexithymic | Euthymic |
| | Anxious | Flat |
| | Apathetic | Hostile |
| | Appropriate | Manic |
| | Depressed | |
| Perception | Depersonalization | Hallucinations |
| | Derealization | Illusions |
| | Déjà vu | Superstitions |
| Orientation | Time | Place |
| | Person | Space and location |
| Thought Processes | | |
| Intellectual | Abstract thinking | Attention span |
| | Impairment in IQ | |
| Judgment | Intact | Impaired |
| Insight | Intact | Impaired |
| Associations | Connected | Directed |
| | Loose | |
| Memory | Immediate | Remote |
| | Recent | |
| Thought Content | Blocking | Overinclusive thinking |
| | Clanging | Perseverations |
| | Compulsions | Phobias |
| | Concrete | Preoccupations |
| | Delusions | Ruminations |
| | Neologisms | Suicidal ideation |
| | Phobias | Violent thoughts |
| Speech and | Articulation | Stream of speech |
| Language | | |
| Movements | Automatic, spontaneous | Voluntary |
| | Compulsions | Tics |
| | Involuntary | |

memory, speech, hearing, orientation, and cognition, and sensorium. They are particularly relevant when evaluating for major psychiatric disorders, neurological involvement, and substance-induced disorders. These exams can be formal, wherein each content area is specifically addressed, or informal, wherein information is ascertained about these content areas while talking to the person about other issues. Table 21.1 presents content areas often addressed in a mental status exam.

## Motivational Interviewing

We need to make a distinction between therapeutic versus assessment interviews. The former includes generic activities within a session designed to advance some treatment goal. The latter includes an array of activities in order to gain information that leads to the development of treatment goals and intervention plans or other decisions,

such as personnel decisions. An example of a therapeutic interview is Miller and Rollnick's (2002) motivational interviewing. Although this approach was developed for the purpose of changing addictive behavior, the principles are generic enough so that the technique could be and has been applied to a number of assessment situations requiring behavior change (Martins & Levitt, 2009).

This approach considers motivation to be a dynamic concept rather than an inherent personality trait. The behavior of the clinician is a salient determinant as to whether change will occur. Miller and Rollnick (2002) recommend that clinicians give *feedback,* emphasize that clients take *responsibility* for change, give clients *advice* and a *menu* of treatment choices and strategies, be *empathic,* and promote *self-efficacy*. The acronym FRAMES is used here as a mnemonic device. The technique also requires that the clinician point out discrepancies in behavior, avoid arguments, roll with resistance, use reflective listening, emphasize personal choice, reframe, and continually support client statements pertaining to self-efficacy. Thus, motivational interviewing can be used as an assessment tool and as an intervention tool.

## Orientation Interviews

Orientation interviews are designed to orient a person to some protocol. They may be used by clinical researchers, who are required to tell each prospective participant the basic procedures of the experiment, any risks associated with it, and the right to withdraw from the study at any point in time. The goal here is to obtain informed consent for the study. The clinician might use this type of interview to inform a new client about treatment options, program policies, rules, and expectations. A psychologist in private practice may use this procedure to orient the client to such matters as confidentiality, cancellation procedures, billing practices, insurance claims, and professional credentials. An industrial psychologist may begin executive assessments with this type of interview in order to prepare the interviewee for what lies ahead. Orientation interviews are particularly useful to help answer any questions the recipient may have and to help develop a client–interviewer contract for services, which may be either a formal document or an informal understanding between both parties.

## Pre- and Posttesting Interviews

Modern methods of psychological assessment require interviews that initially explore with the client particular problem areas prior to more formal psychological assessment and then a posttesting interview, wherein the psychologist reviews or highlights major findings or recommendations derived from the assessment, which may include psychological testing. These findings are also valuable in that hypotheses derived from the assessment can later be explored with the client in the posttesting interview.

### Screening Interviews

Screening interviews are usually brief and designed to elicit information on a specific topic. They may include such areas as determining whether a client is eligible for services, whether the patient is acutely suicidal, whether the patient meets the criteria for a particular diagnosis, or whether the patient needs to be hospitalized as a danger to self or others. Screening interviews are very common in psychology and may in fact be the most frequent kind of clinical interview.

### Specialized Interviews

Sometimes a clinician needs to conduct an interview for a special purpose, such as determining the ability to stand trial, determining legal insanity, assessing the need for psychiatric hospitalization, or making a specific diagnosis

of a particular disorder. Many specialized clinical interviews have been published for these purposes.

### Termination Interview

Very often, clinicians ending services to a client conclude with an interview designed to review treatment goals, progress, and future plans. Clinicians working in inpatient settings often have an ending interview to reinforce the need for continued outpatient follow-up services. Addiction specialists usually have a last session to review planned aftercare and to highlight patient risk factors for relapse. Industrial psychologists meet with a person to review highlights of assessment findings.

Table 21.2 presents topics frequently addressed in assessment interviews.

### CLIENT APPROACH TO THE INTERVIEW

Interviews are influenced by a number of factors. First, is the client's visit *voluntary or involuntary*? Presumably, a voluntary client has noticed there is a problem, has made failed attempts to resolve it—perhaps through discussions with friends or clergy or through self-help methods—and then has sought professional assistance. The client may come with the expectation that the distress (often a particular symptom or cluster of symptoms) will be ameliorated through professional help. This fact tends to increase the truthfulness of client self-reports and promotes a therapeutic working alliance and a more goal-oriented approach within counseling.

When a third party has referred the client, the situation is quite different. There are many cases in which the client is receiving services at the insistence of someone else. Clients arrested for driving under the influence may be sent by a judge for an evaluation to a psychologist. A teenager showing oppositional and conduct-disordered behavior may be taken to a psychologist by his or her parents. A person who is addicted to drugs may come for help at the insistence of a spouse who threatened to leave the relationship unless he or she gets help. In each of these scenarios, the client may not feel the need for help and may actually resist it.

Second, the client's *purpose or motive* for the interview also affects its course and direction. Even if the patient seems to be self-referred, hidden agendas may compromise the purity of the interview. For example, a person may seek help for a problem with incestuous behavior, but the real motive may be to present a facade to the judge in

**TABLE 21.2    Content Areas of Assessment Interviews**

| | |
|---|---|
| History of Problem | Description of the problem |
| | Onset (Intensity, Duration) |
| | Antecedents and consequences |
| | Prior treatment episodes |
| Family Background | Nuclear family constellation |
| | Cultural background |
| | Socioeconomic level |
| | Parents' occupations |
| | Medical history |
| | Family relationships |
| | Family atmosphere |
| Personal History | Developmental milestones |
| | Social and work history |
| | Relationship with parents |
| | History of childhood abuse (physical, sexual) |
| | Current relationships |
| | Vocational problems |
| | Marital-partner history |
| | Emotional stability |
| | History of psychological treatment |
| | Legal problems |
| | Use of illicit substances |
| | Medical problems |

order to escape more severe criminal sanctions and punishment. Another person may present asking for assistance with anxiety or depression, whereas the true motivation is to establish a record of psychological treatment pursuant to a worker's compensation claim for disability. A person with drug addiction may seek inpatient treatment for detoxification but actually may be hiding from the police. A psychiatric patient may allege delusions, hallucinations, and threats of suicide so that he or she is determined to be in need of inpatient care, whereas the true motivation may be to receive basic food and shelter during severe cold weather. It is incumbent on the clinician to ascertain the person's real motivation for assessment and treatment if possible.

Third, client *expectations* can affect the quality of the assessment results. All clients come to the interview with expectations about the nature of the process, how the psychologist may approach the task, and what results the process will have. It is a good idea for psychologists, who will be in a subsequent professional relationship with the client, to clarify any misconceptions and misunderstandings about the interviewing process. In order to explore possible misconceptions, ask the person, "What do you think we are going to do here?" or "What do you expect to happen as a result of our meeting?"

Fourth, the client has *perceptions of the psychologist* that can affect the course and outcome of the interviewing process; analysts have referred to this as object relations. Here, the interviewer embodies all that is contained in a particular role, and all of the client's prior experiences and beliefs of people in this role are then projected onto the psychologist. The patient may be viewing the relationship as parent–child, teacher–student, judged–accused, or lover–love object. These projections are transferences and tend to develop quickly in an ongoing relationship. Sometimes they are outside the client's awareness. At other times they are at the surface and can contaminate the relationship with unreasonable expectations. In fact, a large body of research in social psychology has shown that humans tend to evaluate someone on the basis of their first impression, and all subsequent encounters with that person may be evaluated in the light of those first impressions.

## PSYCHOLOGIST'S APPROACH TO THE INTERVIEW

Psychologists approach an interview with certain preexisting values. The first of these is *philosophical or theoretical orientation*. As clinical psychologists, we do not come to an interview with a blank slate; rather, we bring with us attitudes that influence the structure and process of the interview, the areas of inquiry, the methods and techniques used in the inquiry, how we understand the meaning of a patient's complaints, the words we use to subsequently describe the person, and the goals we set for clients.

There are four main theoretical orientations in mainstream clinical psychology; psychodynamic, cognitive-behavioral, client-centered (now merged with humanistic and existential approaches), and family systems. An eclectic approach draws on each of these orientations depending on the needs of the client. To illustrate how these orientations influence the clinical interview, let us consider the next scenario.

An alcoholic man is brought to counseling by his wife who has threatened to leave him on multiple occasions but has never done so. She alleges that psychotherapy is his last chance or "she will leave." How might the different orientations view this matter? A psychodynamic therapist may determine that the patient has an oral dependent personality and his wife has a masochistic need to suffer. A client-centered therapist will consider the role of alcohol in forestalling self-actualization and personal growth. A cognitive-behaviorist may focus of the antecedent of the man's drinking as well as the consequences and conduct a behavioral analysis identifying the rewards that maintain his alcohol-abusing lifestyle. A family systems therapist may determine that this couple is in a dominant–submissive relationship with the wife controlling the power and desiring to maintain her husband in a dependent relationship. Because the patient fears independence and fears changing family roles, he thereby maintains a homeostatic relationship within the dyad.

Just as the client has certain expectations and beliefs about the nature of the interview, the psychologist also comes to the interview with certain preexisting *beliefs and values* that affect the course of the interview. First, some psychologists value a directed approach while others value a nondirected one. Some value humor whereas others refrain from using it. One psychologist may value discussions about a client's manifest behavior; another may value a focus on a person's inner mental life. Second, psychologists value certain kinds of material more than they do others, and they selectively respond to client material that is considered more important (e.g., more highly valued). Third, psychologists may have a set of assumptions about behavior change and may view the person in the light of those assumptions. There are certainly other areas that could be explicated, but the essential point is that we all come to the interview with preconceived notions and then act according to those preexisting beliefs and assumptions.

Psychologists eventually try to *understand the client and problems* in the light of their theoretical orientation. Most arrive at a diagnosis or some formulation of the problem, but the nature of this description differs. Some may think of the client in terms of oedipal or preoedipal functioning. Others may think of the person in a dominant–submissive relationship against a triangulated third person. Others may couch the problem as a lack of assertiveness because of a history of punishments during attempts at assertiveness. Still others may see the person as dependent with borderline features. All of these characterizations are a diagnosis of a sort, but by the end of the interview, the psychologist is likely to have a hypothesis as to etiology, and most will arrive at a diagnosis on which an intervention approach will be based.

## DIAGNOSTIC INTERVIEWING

Good interviewing consists of putting the client at ease, eliciting information, maintaining control and rapport, and bringing closure. Putting the client at ease consists of attending to privacy and confidentiality issues, reducing anxiety, avoiding interruptions, showing respect by using the client's preferred name, and arranging seating configurations that promote observation and interaction. Eliciting information is accomplished by asking open-ended questions, avoiding unnecessary interruptions, intervening at critical junctions of client elaborations, and clarifying inconsistencies. Controlling the interview does not mean assuming a completely directive interviewing stance; rather, it means that the psychologist has a purpose in mind for the interview itself and engages in behaviors that accomplish this purpose. The psychologist does not dominate the interview but rather guides it along a desired path. Skillfully disrupting client ramblings that are counterproductive, discouraging unnecessary material, and making smooth transitions from one stage of the interview to another can accomplish this goal. Rapport is maintained throughout by being nonjudgmental, displaying empathy, using language appropriate to the client, addressing salient client issues, and communicating a sense that the client's problems are understood and can be helped. Finally, the psychologist brings closure to the interview by informing the person about the next step in the process.

## Structure of the Clinical Interview

The interpersonal psychiatrist, Harry Stack Sullivan (1954) suggested a format for the clinical interview, conceiving it as a phase-sequenced process consisting of (a) the formal inception, (b) reconnaissance, (c) detailed inquiry, and (d) termination. This model remains viable even today (Craig, 2005a).

In the *formal inception*, (e.g., introduction) phase, the clinician learns what brought the client to the interview and explains to the client what will transpire within the interview. Sometimes all that is necessary in the introductory phase is to tell the client: *We're going to put our heads together and see if we can find ways to help you*. Next, tell the client what information you already know. If little or no information is available, it is acceptable to communicate that as well.

The *reconnaissance* (e.g., exploration) is the phase in which the clinician learns some basic information about the interviewee. The client will present what has come to be called the *presenting complaint*. Aside from demographics, the clinician also assesses for clinical syndromes and personality disorders during this part of the process. Sullivan (1954) believed this phase should not take longer than 20 minutes.

By assessing the syndrome, clinicians convey that they understand the problem. Consider a patient who is new in town, is looking for a primary care provider to manage type 2 diabetes, and has narrowed the search down to two physicians. Dr. A takes a history, records the patient's current symptoms, reviews the most recent glucose levels, and gives the patient a prescription for metformin 500 mg once a day. Dr. B does the same thing but also inquires about the patient's kidney function; examines the heart, eyes, and feet; asks whether there is any numbness in the feet; and prescribes 500 mg metformin daily. The patient also is advised to see an ophthalmologist to screen for diabetic retinopathy. In other words, by these actions, Dr. B is telling the patient that she or he knows about diabetes and its consequences and assesses for them. Other things being equal, the patient would probably select Dr. B as the provider, feeling a sense of competence in the inquiry. Dr. A may be just as competent in managing diabetes but failed to communicate that to the patient through a systematic review of the disease. This same process is recommended in mental health interviews. Show the client you understand the problem or syndrome by assessing major symptoms associates with the disorders, and comorbidities.

The third phase is called the *detailed inquiry* (e.g., hypothesis testing). Here the initial impression gained during the first two phases is further assessed, and the clinician interviews for an understanding of why the client is in the present situation and exhibits particular behaviors and coping styles. I call this phase interviewing for etiology. Again, the clinician can frame the etiology within a preferred theoretical framework, citing such concepts as negative reinforcements, unbalanced family systems, or oral fixation. The crucial point is to develop a working hypothesis that will account for the behavior. At the end of this phase, the clinician should have a working hypothesis as to the source of the problem.

I prefer to call the final phase, which Sullivan called *termination, planning, and intervention*. Here the clinician makes a summary statement (e.g., feedback) as to what has been learned in the session; this is not a mere repetition of what the interviewee has said but rather a clinical assessment from the interviewer's perspective. It can be framed in psychodynamic, behavioral, existential-humanistic, or family systems perspectives, but in any case, it tells the client that you understand the problem. It lays the groundwork for how the problem will be addressed. An important point in this phase is to communicate that you can help the client. You understand the problem and can address it so that you can give the client hope and an expectation of improvement. At this phase, basic procedural issues are also discussed. These issues include things such as frequency of visits, issues of confidentiality, fees, or emergency calls. I believe that if the clinician follows this format and satisfactorily addresses the items to be assessed in it, the probability that the client will return for therapeutic work is maximized.

## INTERVIEWING TECHNIQUES

Regardless of one's theoretical position (for the most part), clinicians rely on a finite set of interviewing techniques that cut across interviewing systems.

### Questioning

The questioning interviewing technique is certainly the one that is most often utilized. Clients rarely spontaneously reveal the kind of information necessary, and the interviewer must, perforce, ask questions to get more precise information. Questions may be either closed-ended or open-ended. In *closed-ended questions*, the interviewee is asked a specific question that often is answered in a yes–no format. There is little opportunity for elaboration. As example of a closed-ended question is "Have

you lost any weight within the past 30 days?" In contrast, an *open-ended question* allows for a full range of responses and for client elaboration. An example would be "How does your spouse feel when you keep losing your job?" Both open-ended and closed-ended questions are necessary, but clinicians should try to avoid too many close-ended questions because they inhibit free-flowing communication.

### Clarification

The clarification technique is often necessary because the nature of a person's response may remain obscure; it is usually done by using one of the other interviewing techniques (e.g., questioning, paraphrasing, restating) and is often appreciated by clients because it gives them a continued opportunity to tell their story.

### Confrontation

Confrontation is a technique whereby the clinician points out the discrepancy between what is stated and what is observed. It has frequently been used with substance abusers who continue to deny or minimize their drinking and drug abuse. It is also used with persons with character disorder diagnoses to break down their defenses. When done in a nonhostile and factual manner, it can be helpful, but too often it is done in a destructive manner that increases client resistance. Neophyte interviewers often have a problem with this technique because they may not be prepared to deal with the client's response if the technique is mishandled. This technique probably should be rarely used because more recent evidence has called into question its utility (Miller & Rollnick, 2002).

### Exploration

Some areas may require a review that is more in depth than what is initially presented by the client. In the exploration technique, the clinician structures a more thorough inquiry into a given area. Most clients expect to be questioned about certain issues and may wonder why this was not done. Clinicians should not be reluctant to explore areas that may be considered sensitive.

### Humor

There is increasing recognition that humor does play a role in clinical interviews. It should not be overdone and should always be done to benefit the client. It can reduce anxiety, facilitate therapeutic movement, and enhance the flow of the session. On the flip side, the client may perceive that you are not taking him or her seriously.

## Interpretation

The interpretation technique has a long history in clinical psychology and emanates from the Freudian tradition, which considers much of human motivation outside of conscious awareness. It is probably the most difficult technique to use successfully because it requires good knowledge of the client's personality, motivation, and dynamics. Interviewers in training should not employ this technique without first processing it with their supervisor. It is important to recognize that many clients will acquiesce to the authority of the clinician and agree with the interpretation when in fact it may be erroneous.

## Reflection

In reflection, the clinician skillfully and accurately restates what the client has just said to show that feelings and statements have been understood. The technique has enjoyed a fruitful history with client-centered therapists, who have used this technique almost to the exclusion of others (C. R. Rogers, 1961).

## Reframing

The reframing technique is sometimes called cognitive restructuring. In it, attitudes, opinions, beliefs, or feelings are rephrased so that they correspond more to reality. Reframing can provide a client with a new perspective and may undercut negative self-statements that are often irrational and maladaptive. Reframing also suggests new ways of thinking and behaving.

## Restatement

The restatement technique is sometimes called paraphrasing. It differs from reflection primarily in purpose. Restatement is most often used to promote understanding and clarification whereas reflection is used primarily as a therapeutic tool.

## Self-Disclosure

A long tradition in psychoanalytic psychotherapy argued that the analyst maintain a blank slate within therapy to allow transference to develop. From this tradition grew a belief that the therapist should not reveal personal information. This idea has evolved into a position that argues that therapist self-disclosure can be used for therapeutic gain, as long as it is not overdone and is used for therapeutic purposes (Henretty & Levitt, 2010; Knox & Hill, 2003).

## Silence

Sometimes the best response is no response. Silence can provide the client with an opportunity to process and understand what just has been said. It should be done to promote introspection or to allow clients to compose themselves after an emotional catharsis. It needs to be done in such as way that the client understands that the clinician is using silence for a reason and is still attending to client needs (Hill, Thompson, & Ladany, 2003).

The basic techniques of interviewing and examples illustrating these techniques are presented in Table 21.3.

**TABLE 21.3   Basic Interviewing Techniques**

| Technique | Patient Statement | Interviewer Response |
| --- | --- | --- |
| Clarification | Sometimes my husband doesn't come home for days. | What do you think he's doing when this happens? |
| Confrontation | I no longer abuse my wife. | You hit her yesterday! |
| Exploration | In the service I saw a lot of guys get killed. | Did you have any bad dreams afterward? |
| Humor | Sometimes, Doc, I act so crazy I think I got a split personality. | In that case, that will be $50 each. |
| Interpretation | I took my father's Xanax and flushed them down the toilet. | If he was able to stand up to your mother, then you would not have to behave so aggressively toward her. |
| Reflection | I'm not getting anywhere. | Your lack of progress frustrates you |
| Reframing | My boyfriend left me for someone else. | While it is upsetting now, it gives you a chance to meet someone else. |
| Restatement | I hear voices and get confused. | These strange things are disturbing to you. |
| Self-disclosure | I just can't learn like the other kids. | I'm dyslexic too. It need not hold you back. You just have special needs.(no response) |
| Silence | Someday I'm going to tell her exactly how I feel. | |
| Questioning | As a youth, I was in a detention home. | What did you do to get in there? |

# INTERVIEWING MODELS

In this section, we review the basic theoretical models that influence the clinical interview.

## Medical Model

Many psychologists have argued that interviewing from the medical model is inappropriate. The medical model assumes that the symptoms are developed due to external pathogens; heritable vulnerabilities that are biologically determined; or structural, anatomical, or physiological dysfunctions and abnormalities. These problems can only be corrected or ameliorated through surgery, medicine, or rehabilitation techniques. One can think of the medical model as having two broad functions. The first is to guide classification, diagnosis, and, ultimately, treatment and prevention. The second major function is to control, both socially and legally, the health practices of society. Some psychologists would prefer we adopt a *biopsychosocial* model, which admits the role of biological processes in the development of disorders but which also includes the role of psychological and social factors in their etiology, course, and treatment.

## Behavioral Model

Many psychologists prefer a behavioral model to a medical model of interviewing. Behavioral psychologists do not espouse the idea that health-related problems are rooted in biology. Rather, they believe that contingencies of reinforcement occurring in the context of certain environments are primarily responsible for problematic behaviors. Thus, they deny medical terminology and nosology in favor of such concepts as response patterns, positive and negative reinforcements, and antecedents and consequences. A behaviorally based interview might analyze the problem by taking a reinforcement history, looking for patterns of rewards and punishments following critical behaviors, and carefully defining and quantifying each targeted behavior for intervention. This is referred to as a *functional analysis of behavior*. The chapter by O'Brien and Young in this volume discusses behavioral interviewing at greater length.

## Interview Biases

Interviews are not without problems, and many sources of interviewer biases have been researched. These biases include such factors as positive and negative halo; reliance on first impressions; client attractiveness; theoretical biases (e.g., insisting that one theory can explain all forms of behavior); emphasizing trait, state, or situational determinants of behavior to the exclusion of the others; and conceptualizing behavior as a static rather than a dynamic process.

One problem with the assessment interview is the extent to which bias exists throughout the entire process (Farmer, 2000). One bias that has been particularly addressed is gender bias. There are other sources of bias, including biased constructs, biased criteria for making diagnosis, biased sampling populations to study the issue, biased application of the diagnostic criteria, biased assessment instruments and gender biases to assess diagnostic entities (Widiger & Spitzer, 1987), and cultural biases. (See Lindsay, Sankis, & Widiger, 2000.) Hartung and Widiger (1998) have provided the most recent summary of prevalence rates of various diagnoses by gender, but these rates are not immune to systematic distortions, as mentioned previously, and some studies find no gender differences (Grilo, 2002).

Brown (1990) proposed a model for integrating gender issues into the clinical interview. It includes preassessment activities, such as familiarizing oneself in the scholarship and research on gender and its relationship to clinical judgments; it also includes suggestions to attend to one's activities within the assessment process. These activities include inquires that will help the clinician determine the meaning of gender membership for the client and the client's social and cultural environment, determine gender-role compliance or variation, notice how the client attends to the evaluator's gender, and guard against inappropriate gender stereotyping.

# ASSESSING PSYCHOPATHOLOGY WITH CLINICAL INTERVIEWS

Clinical interviews may be structured, semistructured, or unstructured, though, as we have seen, even the so-called unstructured interview has a structure to it. In this section, we review these differences.

## Structured Versus Unstructured Interviews

Interviews to assess for psychopathology vary considerably in how they are conducted. A basic dimension of interviews is their degree of structure. *Structured interviews* follow rigid rules. The clinician asks specific questions that follow an exact sequence and that include well-defined rules for recording and judging responses. This practice minimizes interview biases and unreliable judgments, hence providing more objective information. Although structured interviews generally have better psychometric properties than unstructured ones, structured interviews may overlook idiosyncrasies that add to the richness of personality, artificially restraining topics covered within the interview. They also may not create much rapport between client and clinician. An example of structured interviewed style can be found in Craig (2009a).

*Semistructured interviews* are more flexible and provide guidelines rather than rules. There are neither prepared questions nor introductory probes. These types of interviews may elicit more information than would emerge from structured interviews because the clinician is allowed more judgment in probative questioning. In completely *unstructured interviews,* the clinician assesses and explores conditions believed to be present within the interviewee. These hypotheses are generated from the person's elaborations during the interview. In clinical practice, diagnoses are more often established using unstructured interviews, whereas in a research context, diagnoses are more often established by using a structured or semistructured interview.

The introduction of *DSM-III* (American Psychiatric Association, 1980) ushered in renewed interest in the reliability of psychiatric diagnosis. Clinicians devoted a substantial amount of effort to improving diagnostic categories and to establishing psychiatric diagnoses. These trends continued through subsequent revisions of the *DSM*. To respond to this challenge, clinical psychologists relied on their history of measuring individual differences in personality via structured inventories. Psychiatrists relied on their history of observation and interviews to establish a diagnosis, and they developed a variety of structured psychiatric interviews for an array of problems and disorders. This move was an attempt to reduce subjective clinical judgments. Table 21.4 presents a selected review of available psychiatric interviews for a variety of conditions along with a brief summary of the most frequently used structured diagnostic interviews. Although each of the structured instruments was designed for somewhat different purposes and was to be used with its companion diagnostic system, all have been revised and can be used with *DSM-IV*.

The structured psychiatric interviews that have received the most attention are the Schedule of Affective Disorders and Schizophrenia (SADS; Endicott & Spitzer, 1978), the Diagnostic Interview Schedule (DIS; Robins,

**TABLE 21.4   Selected Structured Psychiatric Interviews**

| | |
|---|---|
| *General Interview Schedules* | |
| Diagnostic Interview Schedule | Robins, Cottler, Bucholz, Compton, North, & Rourke, 2000 |
| **For DSM-IV** | |
| Schedule for Affective Disorders and Schizophrenia | Endicott & Spitzer, 1978 |
| Structured Clinical Interview for DSM-IV-TR | First, Spitzer, Gibbon, & Williams, 1997 |
| Structured Interview for *DSM* disorders | Pfhol, Stangl, & Zimmerman, 1995 |
| (i) Axis I Disorders | |
|   Acute stress disorder | Bryant, Harvey, Dang, & Sackville, 1988. |
|   Anxiety | Spitzer & Williams, 1988 |
|   Affective disorders and schizophrenia | Endicott & Spitzer, 1978 |
|   Depression | Jamison & Scogin, 1992; Zimmerman, Thomas, & Young, 2003 |
|   Dissociative disorders | Steinberg, Cicchetti, Buchanan, & Hall, 1993 |
|   Eating disorders | Cooper & Fairbairn, 1987 |
|   Hypocondriasis | Barsky, Cleary, Wyshak, Spitzer, Williams, & Klerman, 1992 |
|   Kleptomania | Grant, Suck, & McCabe, 2006 |
|   Panic disorder | Williams, Spitzer, & Gibbon, 1992 |
|   Posttraumatic stress disorder | Watson et al., 1991 |
| (ii) Axis II Disorders | |
|   Personality disorders | Stangl, Pfohl, Zimmerman, Bowers, & Corenthal, 1985 |
| | Selzer, Kernberg, Fibel, Cherbuliez, & Mortati, 1987 |
| | Zanarini, Frankenberg, Chauncy, & Gunderson, 1989 |
| | Zanarini, Frankenberg, Chauncy, & Yong, 1995 |
| | Loranger, Susman, Oldham, & Russakoff, 1987; Loranger et al., 1994 |
| | Widiger, Mangine, Corbitt, Ellis, & Thomas, 1995 |
|   Borderline personality disorder | Zanarini, Gunderson, Frankenburg, & Chauncy, 1989 |
|   Depressive personality disorder | Gunderson, Phillips, Triebwasser, & Hirshfield, 1994 |
| Narcissism | Gunderson, Ronningstam, & Bodkin, 1990 |
| Psychopathy | Hare, 2003; Gacono, 2005 |
| *Miscellaneous* | |
| Suicide | Reynolds, 1990 |
| | Sommers-Flanagan & Sommers-Flanagan, 1995 |
| Symptoms | Andreasen, Flaum, & Arndt, 1992 |

Helzer, Croughan, & Ratcliff, 1981), and the Structured Clinical Interview for DSM Disorders (SCID; Spitzer, Williams, Gibbon, & First, 1992).

The SADS is a standardized, semistructured diagnostic interview that was initially developed to make a differential diagnosis among 25 diagnostic categories in the Research Diagnostic Criteria, a precursor to *DSM-III*. The clinician uses a set of introductory probes and further questions to determine whether the responses meet the diagnostic criteria. The SADS has two main sections. In the first section, the interviewer ascertains a general overview of the client's condition by using detailed questions about current symptoms and their severity. Level of impairment is determined through the use of standard descriptions and is not left to clinical judgment. The second section covers the patient's history of mental disorders; questions are clustered within each diagnosis. It assesses psychopathology and functioning in the current episode and also mood, symptoms, and impairment. Current functioning is defined as level of function 1 week prior to the interview. The final results yield both current and lifetime diagnoses, and the interview requires 1 to 2 hours to administer. There are three versions of the SADS: a lifetime version (SADS-L), a change version (SADS-C) that can be used to evaluate treatment effectiveness, and a children's version (K-SADS-P). The SADS screens for over 30 *DSM-IV* diagnoses.

The DIS is a completely structured diagnostic interview, designed to be used by lay interviewers. It was developed by the National Institute of Mental Health to assess current and lifetime diagnosis in large-scale epidemiological surveys of psychopathology and psychiatric disorders, although it is also has been used in clinical research studies. To administer the DIS, the interviewer reads the questions exactly as they are provided in the interview booklet. In general, there is no probing, although a separate problem flowchart can be used for organic diagnosis with psychiatric syndromes. Separate sections are provided for 32 specific diagnoses containing 263 items. Current symptoms are assessed for four time periods: the past 2 weeks, the past month, the past 6 months, and the past year. Administration time is about 45 to 90 minutes. Much of the research with the DIS has compared it to psychiatric-clinician diagnosis established by traditional means. There are child and adolescent versions of the DIS, and both are available in a computerized DIS (C-DIS) program.

The SCID is a semistructured diagnostic interview designed to be used by clinical interviewers and was intended to have an administration time shorter than that of the SADS. It takes 60 to 90 minutes to administer and assess problems within the past month (current) and lifetime. The interview begins with a patient's description of his or her problems. After the clinician has an overview of the client's difficulties, the more structured section begins, organized in modular format depending on suspected diagnosis. The questions are open ended. After each section, the interviewer scores the disorder for severity (*mild, moderate, severe*) within the past month, according to symptoms and functional impairment. The interview follows a hierarchical structure that appears in *DSM*. There are several versions of the SCID. One is designed for use with inpatients (SCID-P), one with outpatients (SCID-OP), and one with nonpatients (SCID-N). Subsequently, the SCID-II was developed to diagnose personality disorders. The SCID has been translated into several foreign languages and is the most researched psychiatric interview.

Should you use a structured psychiatric interview? They can be useful to teach diagnostic interviewing for clinicians in training. They may be more valuable than unstructured interviews are in certain forensic applications. They can provide an automatic second opinion, and some may save valuable time for the professional because they are administered by mental health paraprofessionals. However, for routine clinical practice, structured clinical interviews are cumbersome and time consuming and seem more appropriate when methodological rigor is required for research diagnoses.

Psychometric properties, so often discussed in the context of assessing psychological tests, may also be applied to clinical interviews that assess psychopathology (Blashfield & Livesley, 1991). These interview schedules were developed to improve the reliability of psychiatric diagnosis. Nevertheless, serious problems in assessment reliability continue to exist even when using structured interviews; response sets, both in the interviewer and patient, can affect the outcome of the evaluation (Alterman, Snider, Cacciola, Brown, Zaballero, & Siddique, 1996).

One outcome of the development of structured clinical interviewing has been the inquiry about comorbidities of Axis I disorders with Axis II disorders (and vice versa). For example, disorders that have been studied include eating disorders (Kaye, Bulik, Thornton, Barbarich, Masters, & Price Foundation, 2004), psychotic disorders (Cassano, Saettoni, Rucci, & Del'Osso, 1998), and substance abuse (Hasin, Samet, Nunes, Meydan, Mateseoane, & Waxman, 2006). These findings are presented in Table 21.5 later in this chapter. It is incumbent on the interviewer to assess those disorders that may be associated with an Axis I or Axis II disorder.

Many factors interact and complicate the process of using interviews to assess psychopathology. These factors include but are not limited to definitional ambiguities (e.g., when does spontaneity become impulsiveness?), criterion unreliability, overlapping symptoms, contextual moderators, multidimensional attributes, population heterogeneity, and deficits in the instruments and processes (e.g., interviews) that we as clinicians use to assess psychopathology (Millon, 1991). Additionally, the diagnostic system we use (*DSM-IV*) is imperfect. Complaints about this system include conceptual obscurity (Russ, Shedler, Bradley, & Westen, 2008), confusion, a questionable broadening of the range and scope of categories classified as mental disorder, use of a categorical rather than a dimensional model, poor applicability to disorders in children, and issues of the medicalization of mental health disorders.

## ASSESSING PERSONALITY WITH CLINICAL INTERVIEWS

In this section, we address assessing personality versus personality disorders and review some problems in assessing these constructs with clinical interviews.

### Personality Assessment Versus Assessing Personality Disorders

It is one thing to assess personality and quite another to assess personality disorders. The latter is substantially easier because there are diagnostic criteria codified in official diagnostic classification systems (e.g., *DSM,* ICD-10). To make the diagnosis, one merely has to determine whether the client meets the criteria. Furthermore. both structured clinical interviews (R. Rogers, 2001) and psychometric tests are available to supplement the clinical interview (Widiger & Francis, 1987) with more continuing to be developed (Craig, 2009b). Because there is no agreed-on classification system for personality, the clinician typically looks for certain traits that are related to the referral or treatment issue.

### Problems in Assessing Personality and Personality Disorders With Clinical Interviews

Many assessment difficulties complicate the diagnosis of personality disorders. Many issues have occupied the field of personality assessment (Zimmerman, 1994) and need to be considered by an individual clinician when interviewing for personality characteristics and personality disorders. Here we focus on seven of these issues.

1. The lines of demarcation between normal and pathological traits are porous and not well differentiated (Strack & Lorr, 1997; Widiger & Clark, 2000). The normal–pathology continuum can be viewed from different theoretical positions, making it difficult for the clinician to determine whether the behavior observed in the interview is normative or aberrant.

2. Official diagnostic classification systems have adopted a categorical system for personality disorders (Widiger, 1992). One criticism of this approach is that it artificially dichotomizes diagnostic decisions into present or absent categories when they are inherently continuous variables. From this perspective, personality disorders have no discrete demarcations that would provide qualitative distinction between normal and abnormal levels (Widiger, 2000). In contrast, a dimensional approach assumes that traits and behaviors are continuously distributed in the population and that a particular individual may have various degrees of each trait or behavior being assessed. Dimensional systems are seen as more flexible, specific, and reliable whereas categorical systems lose too much information and can result in classification dilemmas when a client meets the criteria for multiple disorders. However, dimensional systems are too complex for practical purposes. For example, categorical systems of color (red, yellow, green) work quite well in describing a dress, but if we need more specificity, we need to discuss the properties of light, such as wavelengths. What we gain in specificity we lose in our ability to describe the dress. Determining the optimal point of demarcation between normal and abnormal would be difficult from a dimensional perspective.

3. Many have lamented that the *DSM* personality disorder section lacks a theoretical approach to the understanding and classification of personality disorders. While models exists (Cattell, 1989; Digman, 1990; Millon, 2000a) and while efforts have been made to apply these theories to the assessment of personality disorders (Costa & McCrae, 2005; Costa & Widiger, 1997; Millon, 1994), some efforts have been strained and not without controversy (Rottman, Woo-Kyoung, Sainslow, & Kim, 2009; Saulsman & Page, 2004).

4. Fixed decision rules—as contained in official diagnostic systems—decrease diagnostic efficiency when the cutoff points for diagnosis are not adjusted for local base rates.

5. Affective disorders can influence the expression of traits and confound diagnostic impressions. For example, many patients with clinical depression appear to also have a dependent personality. However, when their depression

abates, they may no longer appear to be dependent. Patients with bipolar manic disorder may appear histrionic during the acute phase of the manic-depression but not when the affective disorder has stabilized. Affective disorders complicate the diagnosis of personality disorders.

6. Is the behavioral manifestation or expression seen in diagnostic interviews due to endemic personality traits, or is the manifestation situationally induced? Specific life circumstances can change behavior and confuse the diagnosis of personality disorders. However, while personality traits fail to predict behavior in a single situation, they predict quite well for behaviors aggregated over several situations (Matthews, Deary, & Whiteman, 2009).

7. Patients often meet diagnostic criteria for more than one personality disorder, and the optimal number of diagnostic criteria needed for an individual diagnosis remains unclear.

One trend in the assessment literature has been to study the role of personality disorders in Axis I syndromes (Zimmerman, Rothchild, & Chelminski, 2005). There is now recognition that personality disorders can influence the expression, course, and duration of Axis I disorders as well as be the focus of treatment in their own right (Markowitz et al., 2007). Table 21.5 presents the personality disorders most often diagnosed in selected Axis I disorders. Clinicians who assess for specific Axis I disorders should evaluate for the presence of personality disorders commonly associated with those syndromes (Livesley, 2001; Millon & Davis, 1996).

One continuing concern is that although the reliability of personality disorder diagnosis has improved, discriminant validity continues to be a problem. This means that there will continue to be high levels of comorbid personality disorder diagnoses within an individual patient, due

to overlap in official diagnostic criteria in classification systems, (e.g., "impulsivity" is a criterion for borderline, histrionic, and antisocial personality disorders) and to item redundancies in psychometric tests used to diagnose personality disorders.

## Role of Culture

We are only beginning to appreciate the role of culture and how it affects behavior. *DSM-IV* recognizes many cultural manifestations that are viewed as common within a designated culture. However, while *DSM-IV* includes Axis I cultural considerations in the appendix, it has been slow to consider the role of cultural considerations and to apply them to the diagnostic criteria for Axis II disorders.

## Reliability of Clinical Interviews and Psychiatric Diagnoses

Most clinicians make a personality disorder diagnosis by listening to the person describe interpersonal interactions and by observing behavior in the interview itself (Westen, 1997). However, even with the introduction of criteria sets, personality disorder diagnoses generally obtain lower levels of reliability compared to Axis I disorders (Widiger & Francis, 1985). This is because the clinician has to address the issues of boundary overlap; the possible influences of state, role, and situational factors on behavioral expression; the client's inability or unwillingness to report symptoms; and the difficulty of determining whether a trait is pervasive and maladaptive within the confines of a brief psychiatric interview.

Prior to *DSM-III,* the mean interrater reliability (kappa, a statistic that corrects for chance agreement) for the diagnosis of personality disorders was .32. *DSM-III* introduced criteria sets for the establishment of a diagnosis. It also included field trials of reliability of the proposed diagnoses using over 450 clinicians involving over 800 patients, including adults, adolescents, and children. For personality disorders in adults, results indicated that overall kappa coefficient of agreement on diagnosis was .66 after separate interviews. High kappas (.70 and above) reflect generally good agreement. With the introduction of criteria sets, the mean kappa for *DSM-III* personality disorders was .61 for joint assessments and .54 using a test–retest format when the decisions was *any personality disorder* but only a median of .23 for individual disorders (Perry, 1992; Spitzer & Williams, 1988).

**TABLE 21.5  Personality Disorders With Higher Prevalence Rates for Selected Axis I Syndromes**

| Clinical Syndrome | Personality Disorder |
| --- | --- |
| Anxiety Disorders, General | Borderline |
| Panic Disorders | Avoidant, dependent, obsessive-compulsive |
| Social Phobia | Avoidant |
| Agoraphobia | Avoidant |
| Somatoform | Avoidant, paranoid |
| Depression: Dysthymia | Avoidant, borderline, histrionic |
| Major Depression | Borderline |
| Bipolar | Histrionic, obsessive-compulsive |
| Borderline | Paranoid |
| Bulimia | Dependent, histrionic, borderline |
| Substance Abuse (Alcohol/drug) | Antisocial, narcissistic |

*DSM-IV* conducted 12 separate field trials at 70 multisite locations involving over 6,000 patients. This prodigious amount of research is available elsewhere and too cumbersome to report here. The interested reader should consult Widiger, Francis, Pincus, Russ, First, Davis, and Kline (1998) for details.

For the personality disorders section, field trial information was provided only for the disorder of antisocial personality disorder (APD). A total of 401 patients were tested at four different sites. Patients were given these measures: Millon Clinical Multiaxial Inventory-II, Self-Report Psychopathy Scale, the Psychopathy Check List, and a semistructured diagnostic interview for *DSM-III-R* APD—either the Diagnostic Interview for Personality Disorders or the Personality Disorder Examination. The correlation between the diagnosis of APD and test scores (collapsed for ease of reporting) ranged from .44 to .89 with a median of .71 (Widiger, Cadoret, et al., 1998). Providing information on APD and omitting similar data of the other personality disorder diagnoses stacks the deck a bit in favor of the *DSM* since APD historically had the highest levels of reliability of any personality disorder diagnosis.

However, method variance contributes significantly to the observed results. Reliability estimates change depending on whether the reliability is based on unstructured interviews, semistructured interviews or joint-interviewee raters compared to single-interview raters (Zimmerman, 1994) as well as long versus short test–retest intervals. Perry (1992) reported that the diagnostic agreement between a clinical interview and a self-report measure of personality disorders was not significantly comparable across methods. Even when using a structured psychiatric interview, a clinician must use a considerable amount of judgment and inferences, resulting in variability of results across research findings (Widiger, Cadoret, et al., 1998). In fact, certain domains that are part of the clinical diagnostic picture of a personality disorder may not be reliably assessed by either structured clinical interviews or self-report measures because these domains pertain to implicit processes that may be outside the awareness of the client.

It is no longer scientifically accurate to discuss the reliability of clinical interviews because reliability will change based on (a) diagnosis, (b) instrument used to assess reliability, and (c) the method used to determine reliability. Psychiatric research now addresses reliability and validity (usually concurrent diagnosis) among the various structured and semi-structured techniques.

There are three strategies to evaluate the reliability of structured psychiatric interviews. In the first strategy (test–retest methodology), two or more clinicians interview the same patient on two separate occasions and independently establish a diagnosis. In the second method, two raters interview the patient simultaneously, and the raters make independent judgments as to diagnosis. Often researchers using this method provide the raters with an audio- or videotape of the interview. In the third method, two or more structured psychiatric interviews, self-report tests, or both are given to the same patient (e.g., Smith, Klein, & Benjamin, 2003). In all methods, the extent of agreement between interviewers as to the presence or absence of a particular disorder is determined by using the kappa statistic. By consensus, kappa values greater than .70 are considered to reflect good agreement, values .50 to .70 reflect fair to good agreement, and values less than .50 reflect poor agreement. Values less than .00 reflect less than chance agreement between raters.

The SCID for *DSM* diagnosis (First, Spitzer, Gibbon, & Williams, 1995a, 1995b; First, Spitzer, Williams, & Gibbon, 1997; Spitzer, Williams, Gibbon, & First, 1992) has been the diagnostic instrument used most often in psychiatric research, and researchers have considerable reliability data on this instrument. Our discussion on reliability of psychiatric diagnoses concentrates on research using this instrument.

The SCID and SCID-II were designed for use by experienced diagnosticians. It has different modules, including all Axis I and Axis II groups of disorders. SCID-I assesses 33 of the more commonly diagnosed *DSM-IV* disorders. The structured format requires the interviewer to read the questions exactly as they are printed (in the first three columns) and to determine the presence or absence of criteria, which appear in the second column. The third column contains three levels of certainty—*yes, no,* or *indeterminate*—as to whether the patient met the criteria. The structured clinical interview allows the clinician to probe and restate questions, challenge the response, and ask for clarification in order to determine whether a particular symptom is present. The use of operational criteria has improved the selection of research participants, thereby improving participant homogeneity and reducing interviewer bias. But potential sources of bias, such as cultural bias, are present, which can influence the expression of psychiatric symptoms and psychopathology as well as the interpersonal nature of the diagnostic process between patient and interviewer (Lesser, 1997). However, these issues exist in all structured clinical interviews. Prevalence rates of disorders also affect diagnostic agreement statistics.

Two major literature reviews have been published concerning the reliability of the SCID-I for Axis I and SCID-II for Axis II disorders (R. Rogers, 2001; Segal, Hersen, & Van Hasselt, 1994). Segal's review found kappa values for the SCID-II ranging from −.03 to 1.00. (It is interesting to note that both of these values were for the somatoform diagnosis in separate studies.) The median kappa values for 33 different diagnoses reported in the literature was .78. Median kappa values for SCID-II reliability studies for Axis I disorders ranged from .43 (histrionic personality disorder) to 1.00 (dependent, self-defeating, and narcissistic personality disorders), with a median of .74.

R. Rogers (2001) found "good-to-superb reliability" of the SCID-I when the criteria were for current episode. Test retest correlations were in the moderate range for clinical samples. He reported on convergent validity samples including posttraumatic stress disorder (PTSD), panic disorders, depression, substance abuse, and psychotic disorders and reported that studies found only modest evidence for diagnostic agreement.

One problem in studying the validity of the SCID and similar instruments is that there is no biological marker or any gold standard against which to compare a given instrument. Using a clinician-derived interview as the standard is inherently problematic because the SCID was designed to improve on clinician-derived interviews. One approach has been to use the "LEAD" standard, which entails conducting a longitudinal assessment (L) (e.g., using data accumulated over time), that were collected by experts (E), using all data (AD), such as a review of medical records, family informants, and so on. While this sounds satisfactory, it is rarely used because of its difficulty in implementation.

Most of the studies against which the SCID-I was compared contrasted this instrument with specialized scales of individual disorders. This methodology would require that those scales have also been well validated. If Measure A (e.g., SCID) is compared to Measure B and if Measure B is flawed, then Measure A will also appear as a poor measure of the construct under investigation. However, R. Rogers (2001) concluded that the SCID-I is a well-validated Axis I interview.

Validity studies have compared the SCID-II with either another structured psychiatric clinical interview or with a self-report inventory assessing personality disorders. Concerning the SCID-II (First, Gibbon, Spitzer, Williams, & Benjamin, 1997), R. Rogers (2001) cited eight studies of convergent validity with similar measures and the correlations ranged from .49 to .91 with a median value of .73 when the criterion was any personality disorder.

However, this does not address the issue of relationships between measuring instruments of a specific personality disorder, which is a far better criterion of convergent validity. Rogers reported on four studies addressing this matter with a modest level of agreement (.30).

A more recent study by Rettew, Lynch, Achenbach, Dumenci, and Ivanova (2009) reported on a meta-analysis of the diagnostic agreement between diagnoses made from clinical interviews and structured psychiatric interviews. Based on 38 studies published between 1955 and 2006 (representing 16,967 patients), the mean kappas between diagnoses from clinical interview compared to a structured psychiatric interview was .27 overall. It was .29 for externalizing disorders and .28 for internalizing disorders. Kappas for specific disorders ranged from .19 (generalized anxiety disorders) to .86 (anorexia nervosa). The median was .48.

Research has found little agreement between the SCID-II and the Minnesota Multiphasic Inventory (MMPI) (Butler, Gaulier, & Haller, 1991) and the Millon Clinical Multiaxial Inventory(MCMI; Marlowe, Husband, Bonieske, & Kirby, 1997; Messina, Wish, Hoffman, & Nemes, 2001; Renneberg, Chambless, Dowdall, Fauerbach, & Gracely, 1992). A similar pattern emerges when two structured clinical interviews are compared; that is, there is often low agreement between instruments on specific disorders and many false positives (Murphy, Monson, Laird, Sobol, & Leighton, 2000; Tenney, Schitte, Denys, van Megan, & Westenberg, 2003). Evidence for this conclusion is derived from studies comparing the SCID-II with the Personality Disorder Questionnaire— Revised (PDQ-R) (Fossati et al., 1998), the Personality Disorder Examination (Lenzenweger, Loranger, Korfine, & Neff, 1997; Modestin, Enri, & Oberson, 1998; O'Boyle & Self, 1990), and miscellaneous structured clinical interviews (Eaton, Neufeld, Chen, & Cai, 2000). Also, using two separate structured psychiatric interviews reveals a different pattern of comorbidity of personality disorders (Oldham et al., 1992), although prevalence rates of antisocial disorders appear to be quite consistent independent of measuring instrument (Craig, 2003b). Because the false negatives rates between these instruments tends to be low, one way to improve convergent validity is to have a clinician question only those diagnostic elements endorsed in the self-report instrument (Jacobsberg, Perry, & Francis, 1995), but this has not been done to date.

In summary, the available data suggests that although structured psychiatric interviews are reliable, they show low to modest agreement at the level of specific diagnoses. This is true not only for the SCID but for other major structured clinical interviews as well. Also, diagnostic agreement is higher between instruments of a similar methodology (e.g., comparing a structured psychiatric interview with another structured psychiatric interview; comparing a self-report personality disorder questionnaire with another self-report personality disorder questionnaire) than when comparing two instruments with different methodology (e.g., comparing a structured clinical interview with a self-report questionnaire). Validity coefficients for externalizing disorders are higher than for internalizing disorders.

## Incremental Validity

A computer search for the terms *incremental validity* and *clinical interviews* found no references pertaining to the question of whether adding an interview adds any information that was attainable through other means (e.g., psychological tests, collateral information). This may be because the clinical interview is the primary way to collect information prior to a diagnostic decision or a clinical intervention. Incremental validity studies are readily available for such entities as the addition of a particular test to a test battery (Weiner, 1999); the prediction of a specific behavior, such as violence (Douglas, Ogcuff, Nicholls, & Grant, 1999); various constructs, such as anxiety sensitivity (McWilliams & Asmund, 1999) or depression (Davis & Hays, 1997); and adding a given test to another measuring tool (Simonds, Handel, & Archer, 2008; Wygant, Sellbom, Graham, & Schenk, 2006), to name a few. However, the criteria in these studies were all established using other self-report inventories rather than a clinical interview.

Studies have appeared that documented the fact that structured clinical interviews yield higher rates of various disorders than do unstructured interviews. For example, comparing comorbidities among 500 adult psychiatric patients assessed at intake with routine clinical interview and 500 patients assessed with the SCID, results showed that 33% of the patients assessed with structured diagnostic interview had three or more Axis I diagnoses compared to only 10% of patients assessed with an unstructured clinical interview. In fact, 15 disorders were more frequently diagnosed with the SCID than with routine clinical assessment; they occurred across mood, anxiety, eating, somatoform, and impulse-control disorders (Zimmerman & Mattia, 1999a). Similarly, PTSD has been overlooked in clinical practice when PTSD symptoms are not the presenting complaint. However, PTSD was more frequently diagnosed using a structured clinical interview

such as the SCID (Zimmerman & Mattia, 1999b). Also, Zimmerman and Mattia (1999c) found that without the benefit of detailed information provided by structured interviews, clinicians rarely diagnose borderline personality disorder during routine intake evaluations.

These studies attest to the fact that *structured clinical interviews diagnose more clinical disorders than do routine clinical interviews*. The need for incremental validity studies with clinical interviews is apparent. We especially need studies that compare clinical interviews to other assessment methods. Several studies have reported rates of diagnostic agreement between clinician-derived or structural clinical interviews compared to self-report measures, such as the MCMI, but they are reliability studies and not studies of incremental validity.

## RECENT TRENDS

In this section, we report on two recent trends in clinical interviewing: the use of computers to establish diagnoses and telepsychiatry.

## Computer-Assisted Diagnosis and Computer Interviews

The use of computers to interview patients has been attempted, mostly in research contexts (Bloom, 1992). The potential advantages of computer use include increased reliability of the information, an increased ability to obtain specific data about a patient, greater comprehensive evaluations compared to traditional interviews, and more consistent coverage of the range of mental disorders. Critics complain that computer interviews are too impersonal and miss subtle aspects of a patient's problem (e.g., body language). Furthermore, computer interviews generate many false positives (Garb, 2007). Perhaps the most promising use of computer interviewing is in highly focused evaluations of a particular problem, such as depression, substance abuse, or sexual disorders.

Computers and technological advances will eventually permeate future diagnostic studies. Indeed, researchers have already established the fact that it is feasible to do diagnostic work via the computer (Keenan, 1994; Kobak et al., 1997; Neal, Fox, Carroll, Holden, & Barnes, 1997). Automated screening can record basic client information—particularly as it pertains to demographics—even before clients see a clinician for their initial assessment, and clients view this as helpful to their treatment (Sloan, Eldridge, & Evenson, 1992).

Computerization of standardized clinician-administered structured diagnostic interviews has also been shown to have validity comparable to that obtained in face-to-face contexts (Levitan, Blouin, Navarro, & Hill, 1991; Lewis, 1994). Outpatients in an acute psychiatric setting, who had been diagnosed by computer, actually liked answering questions on the computer (94%), understood the questions without difficulty (83%), and even felt more comfortable with the computerized interview than with a physician (60%). However, psychiatrists agreed with only 50% of the computer-generated diagnoses, and only 27% of psychiatrists believed that the computer generated any useful new diagnoses (Roseman, Levings, & Korten, 1997).

A more recent study by Chinman, Young, Schell, Hassell, and Mintz (2004) reported similar findings. Patients with schizophrenia, bipolar, or schizoaffective disorders were assessed with either an audio computer-assisted self-assessment or via an in-person interview. A large proportion of patients rated the computer-assisted interview as more enjoyable, more private, and more preferable if interviews were to be conducted as part of regular follow-up. And computer versus in-person interviews were highly correlated (e.g., .78).

One study by Wolford, Rosenberg, Rosenberg, Swartz, Butterfield, Swanson, and Jankowski (2008) compared clinician interviews with computer-assisted interviews for 245 patients with severe mental illness. They examined such disorders as substance abuse, risk of blood-borne diseases, trauma history, and PTSD. Results indicated that the patients enjoyed the computer-assisted interviews, the results were comparable to face-to-face diagnostic conclusions, and they were cost effective. This study confirms a previous report that computer-assisted interviews can be utilized successfully even with severely mentally ill patients (Chinman et al., 2004). Furthermore, use of this technology has been shown to reduce clinician evaluation time by up to 50% (Hughes, Enslie, Wohlfahrt, Winslow, Kashsen, & Rush, 2005).

Evidence continues to appear suggesting that telephone administration of psychiatric interviews for specific disorders (Baer, Brown-Beasley, & Henriques, 1993), and for more mainstream psychiatric interviews (e.g., SCID) can be done reliably with few differences between methods of administration and psychometrically acceptable kappa levels in the .70s (Shore, Savin, Orton, Beals, & Manson, 2007).

Computer-based systems usually provide a list of probable diagnoses and do not include personality descriptions, in contrast to computer-derived psychological test interpretations (Butcher, Perry, & Atlis, 2000). Logic-tree systems are designed to establish the presence of traits or symptoms that are specified in the diagnostic criteria and thereby lead to a particular diagnosis. While several examples of this process have been published (CIDI-Auto; First, 1994; Peters & Andrews, 1995), research in this area has more commonly evaluated the computerized version of the Diagnostic Interview Schedule. This research has found that kappa coefficients for a variety of disorders ranged from .49 to .68, suggesting fairly comparable agreement between clinician-determined and computer-based psychiatric diagnosis (Butcher et al., 2000).

Research has consistently shown that computer-assisted diagnostic interviews yield more disorder diagnoses than do routine clinical assessment procedures. In fact, respondents seem more willing to reveal personal information to a computer than to a human being and tend to prefer a computer-assisted interview to a clinician-conducted interview (Sweeny, McGrath, Leigh, & Costa, 2001). This is probably because respondents felt more judged when interviewed in person than when identical questions were administered from a computer. However, some evidence exists suggesting that computer diagnostic assessment, although reliable, shows poor concordance with SCID diagnoses, except for the diagnoses of antisocial and substance abuse (Ross, Swinson, Doumani, & Larkin, 1995; Ross, Swinson, Larkin, & Doumani, 1994).

Advances in technology are likely to find applications in the diagnostic process as more refinements are added to this methodology. Technology, however, will not obviate the essential difficulties in the diagnostic process as described throughout this chapter—computer-assisted diagnostic formats contain the same problems inherent in a face-to-face diagnostic interview.

One computer-assisted interview that has received acceptable clinical application and utilization is the Addiction Severity Index (McLellan, Cacciola, Iterman, Rikoon, & Carise, 2006). This instrument assesses the severity of alcohol- and drug-abusing behavior in the areas of drug and alcohol, legal, vocational, psychiatry/psychological, medical, and social/familial domains. It allows for targeted interventions since addiction does not affect all domains equally. The Department of Veterans Affairs has used this instrument as an index of treatment improvement, requiring addiction treatment programs to administer this instrument every 6 months and to note changes in severity levels. Also, many addiction researchers use this instrument as a measure of addiction severity in research protocols.

## Telepsychiatry

Telepsychiatry involves using audio or visual media to provide psychiatric services. This kind of technology would be particularly useful for rural areas where there is a paucity of access to mental health services (Shore & Manson, 2005) and also to provide psychiatric consultation through network hookups where an expert could interview the patient and then consult with the attending psychiatrist. Studies have shown that the assessment of psychiatric disorders can be reliably done via the telephone (Cacciola, Alterman, Rutherford, McKay, & May, 1999; Monnier, Knapp, & Freuh, 2003; Rushkin et al., 1998) and such assessment compares favorably with face-to-face interviews (Crippa et al., 2008). Hyler and Gangure (2003) looked at the cost effectiveness of telepsychiatry. They determined that in 12 studies, 7 reported it was worth the cost, 1 reported it was not financially viable, 3 reported on the break-even point compared to in-person psychiatry, and 1 was unable to determine the cost.

While this chapter focuses on interviewing, it must be reported that telepsychiatry has also been used for the management of outpatient antidepressant medication (Simon, Lordmar, & Operskalski, 2006), for psychotherapy for HIV-positive patients in rural areas (Ransom, Herkman, Anderson, Garske, Halrotyd, & Basta, 2008), and for telephone-administered psychotherapy for depression (Mohr, Hart, Julian, Cuttledge, Homos-Webb, Vella, & Tasch, 2005). Recent evidence also suggests that psychologists are using telepsychology increasingly by psychologists for such clinical services as psychotherapy, consulting, and supervision with about 10% of psychologists using the method at least weekly (*Monitor on Psychology,* 2010).

## MISUSE OF THE INTERVIEW

Many clinicians have such faith in the clinical interview (and their own skills) that they can misuse interviews. One such current venue is that occasioned by managed care constraints that often preclude other methods (e.g., psychological tests, collateral interviews) that would either add incremental validity in clinical practice or possibly confirm hypotheses gleaned from the interview itself. Psychologists need to guard against such practices and to advocate for the best possible psychological practice for a given problem.

## WHAT NEEDS TO BE DONE?

In any classification system of personality disorders, most problems are endemically and systematically related to the issue of construct validity. One continuing problem in assessment is that it has been extremely difficult to find independent operationalizations of personality traits and personality disorder constructs that are consistent across assessment devices. Convergent validity between self-report measures and interview-based assessments range from poor to modest. Median correlations between structured psychiatric interviews range from .30 to .50; median correlations between self-report measures range from .39 to .68; and median correlations between questionnaires and structured interviews range from .08 to .42. Consistently moderate correlations between questionnaires have been reported for the diagnoses of borderline, dependent, passive-aggressive, and schizotypal personality disorders. Better convergent validity between questionnaires and clinical interviews has been found for the diagnoses of borderline and avoidant personality disorders. Good convergent validity between instruments of both kinds has been found for disorders with clear behavioral manifestations (e.g., substance abuse, antisocial behavior) but less so for disorders with less behavioral anchors.

Although method variance and general measurement error may account for some of the findings, *the real problem is a lack of clear and explicit definitions of the diagnostic constructs and behavioral anchors* that explicate specific items that define the disorder and aid the diagnostician (and researcher) to diagnose it. For example, with a criteria set of eight items, of which five are needed to make a diagnosis of borderline personality disorder, there are 95 different possible sets of symptoms that would qualify for this diagnosis. Are there really 95 different types of borderline personality disorders? The criteria merely reflect our confusion on the diagnosis itself. This situation is clearly absurd and serves to illustrate the problems that ensue when the construct and the defining criteria are obfuscating. Similarly, the problem of a patient meeting two or more of the personality disorder diagnoses will continue to exist, due largely to definitional problems. A clinician can reduce this bias somewhat by carefully assessing all criterion symptoms and traits, but the problem in the criteria themselves remains.

Associated with the need for more conceptual clarity is *the need to reduce terminological confusion inherent in the criteria set*. For example, as mentioned earlier, when does spontaneity become impulsivity? There is also a need for improved accuracy in clinician diagnosis. Evidence exists that trained interviewers are able to maintain high levels of interrater reliability, diagnostic accuracy, and interviewing skills, such that quality assurance procedures should be systematically presented in both research and clinical settings (Ventura, Liberman, Green, Shaner, & Mintz, 1998). For example, 18 clinical vignettes were sent to 15 therapists, along with *DSM* personality disorder criteria sets. Fourteen of the vignettes were based on *DSM* criteria, and 14 were made up and suggested a diagnosis of no personality disorder. Results showed an 82% rate of agreement in diagnosis. This type of procedure can be cost effective to establish and to assess continuing competency in diagnosing personality disorders (Gude, Dammen, & Friis, 1997).

There have been many calls for an explicit recognition of dimensional structures in official classification systems because such structures would recognize the continuous nature of personality functioning. Millon (2000b) called for a coherent classification-guiding theory. However, it is unlikely that theorists would ever agree as to *the* parsimonious system to be adopted. Another possibility is the use of prototype criteria sets to define pure cases, but such prototypes might be observed only rarely in clinical practice; hence such a system might have little practical utility, although Millon (2000b) has persuasively argued otherwise. He has also called for the inclusion of personality disorder *subtypes* hierarchically subsumed under the major prototypes. Others have called for the inclusion of level of functioning (e.g., mild, moderate, severe) within the personality diagnostic systems. Cloninger (2000) suggested that personality disorders be diagnosed in terms of four core features: (1) low affective stability, (2) low self-directedness, (3) low cooperativeness, and (4) low self-transcendence. Perhaps a blend of both categorical and dimensional systems is preferable. The clinician could diagnose a personality disorder using a categorical system, reference personality (disorder) traits that are salient to the individual, and include a specifier that depicts level of functioning.

Karg and Wiens (1998) have recommended these activities to improve clinical interviewing in general:

- *Prepare for the initial interview.* Get as much information beforehand as possible; be well informed about the patient's problem area. This preparation will allow you to ask more meaningful questions. There may be important information learned from records or from other sources that warrant more detailed inquiry within the assessment interview. If this information is not available to you at the time of the interview, the opportunity for further inquiry may be lost.

- *Determine the purpose of the interview.* Have a clear understanding of what you want to accomplish. Have an interview structure in mind and follow it.

- *Clarify the purpose and parameters of the interview to the client.* If the client has a good understanding of what is trying to be accomplished, his or her willingness to provide you with meaningful information should increase.

- *Conceptualize the interview as a collaborative process.* Explain how the information will be used to help the client with his or her situation.

- *Truly hear what the interviewee has to say.* This can be accomplished with *active listening* and by clarifying the major points of understanding with the interviewee during the interview.

- *Use structured interviews.* These interviews promote a systematic review of content areas and are more reliable.

- *Encourage the client to describe complaints in concrete behavioral terms.* This will help you to understand the client better and will provide examples of potential problematic behavior in relevant context.

- *Complement the interview with other assessment methods, particularly psychological testing.* This may provide both convergent and incremental validity.

- *Identify the antecedent and consequences of problem behaviors.* This will provide more targeted interventions.

- *Differentiate between skill and motivation.* Some patients may have a desire to accomplish goals that are beyond their capacities, and vice versa.

- *Obtain base rates of behaviors.* This will provide a benchmark for later assessment of progress.

- *Avoid expectations and biases.* Self-monitor your own feelings, attitudes, beliefs, and countertransference to determine whether you are remaining objective.

- *Use a disconfirmation strategy.* Look for information that may disprove your hypothesis.

- *Counter the fundamental attribution error.* This attribution error occurs when a clinician attributes the cause of a problem to one set of factors when it actually may be due to another set of factors.

- *Combine testing with interviewing mechanistically.* Combining interview material with data from other sources will provide more accurate and valid than data from one source alone.

- *Delay reaching decisions while the interview is being conducted.* Do not rush to judgments or conclusions.

- *Consider the alternatives.* Offering a menu of choices and possibilities should engender greater client acceptance of goals and interventions.
- *Provide a proper termination.* Suggest a course of action, a plan of intervention, recommended behavioral changes, and so on, that the person can take with him or her from the interview. It is pointless to conduct thorough assessments and evaluations without providing some feedback to the client.

The future will no doubt actively address, research, refine, and even eliminate some of the problems discussed in this chapter. We can look forward to improvements in diagnostic criteria, improved clarity in criteria sets, increased training so clinicians can self-monitor and reduce any potential biases in diagnostic decision making, and take the role of culture more into account in the evaluation of clients. It is hoped that these advances will lead to improvements in therapeutic interventions designed to ameliorate pathological conditions.

## REFERENCES

Alterman, A. I., Snider, E. C., Cacciola, J. S., Brown, L. S., Zaballero, A., & Siddique, N. (1996). Evidence for response set effects in structured research interviews. *Journal of Nervous and Mental Disorders, 184,* 403–410.

American Psychiatric Association. (1980). *Diagnostic and statistical manual of mental disorders* (3rd ed.). Washington, DC: Author.

American Psychiatric Association. (1987). *Diagnostic and statistical manual of mental disorders* (3rd ed., rev.). Washington, DC: Author.

American Psychiatric Association. (1994). *Diagnostic and statistical manual of mental disorders* (4th ed.). Washington, DC: Author.

Andreasen, N., Flaum, M., & Arndt, S. (1992). The comprehensive assessment of symptoms and hi story (CASH). *Archives of General Psychiatry, 49,* 615–623.

Baer, J. H., Brown-Beasley, J. S., & Henriques, A. (1993). Computer-assisted telephone administration of a structured interview for obsessive-compulsive disorder. *American Journal of Psychiatry, 150,* 1737–1738.

Barsky, A. J., Cleary, P. D., Wyshak, G., Spitzer, R. L., Williams, J. B., & Klerman, G. L. (1992). A structured diagnostic interview for hypocondriasis. *Journal of Nervous and Mental Disease, 180,* 20–27.

Benjamin, L. S. (1996). A clinician-friendly version of the Interpersonal Circumplex Structured Analysis of Social Behavior. *Journal of Personality Assessment, 66,* 248–266.

Bernstein, D. P., Iscan, C., & Maser, J. (2007). Opinions of personality disorder experts regarding the *DSM-IV* personality disorder classification system. *Journal of Personality Disorders, 21,* 536–551.

Blashfield, R. K., & Livesley, W. J. (1991). Metaphorical analysis of psychiatric classification as a psychological test. *Journal of Abnormal Psychology, 100,* 262–270.

Bloom, B. L. (1992). Computer-assisted psychological intervention: A review and commentary. *Clinical Psychology Review, 12,* 169–198.

Brown, L. S. (1990). Taking account of gender in the clinical assessment interview. *Professional Psychology: Research and Practice, 21,* 12–17.

Bryant, R. A., Harvey, A. G., Dang, S. T., & Sackville, T. (1988). Assessing acute stress disorder: Psychometric properties of a structured clinical interview. *Psychological Assessment, 10,* 215–220.

Butcher, J. N., Perry, J. N., & Atlis, M. M. (2000). Validity and utility of computer- based test interpretation. *Psychological Assessment, 12,* 6–18.

Butler, S. F., Gaulier, B., & Haller, D. (1991). Assessment of Axis II personality disorders among female substance abusers. *Psychological Reports, 68,* 1344–1346.

Cacciola, J. S., Alterman, A. I., Rutherford, M. J., McKay, J. R., & May, D. J. (1999). Comparability of telephone and in-person Structured Clinical Interview for *DSM-III-R* (SCID) diagnoses. *Assessment, 6,* 235–242.

Cassano, G. B., Saettoni, M., Rucci, P., & Del'Osso, L. (1998). Occurrence and clinical correlates of psychiatric comorbidity in patients with psychotic disorders. *Journal of Clinical Psychiatry, 59,* 60–68.

Cattell, R. B. (1989). *The 16PF: Personality in depth.* Champaign, IL: Institute for Personality and Ability Testing.

Chiman, M., Young, A. S., Schell, T., Hassell, M. A., & Mintz, J. (2004). Computer-assisted self-assessment in persons with severe mental illness. *Journal of Clinical Psychiatry, 65,* 1343–2012.

Cloninger, C. R. (2000). A practical way to diagnose personality disorders: A proposal. *Journal of Personality Disorders, 14,* 99–108.

Cooper, Z., & Fairbairn, C. G. (1987). The eating disorder examination: A semi-structured interview for the assessment of the specific psychopathology of eating disorders. *International Journal of Eating Disorders, 6,* 1–8.

Costa, P. T., & McCrae, R. R. (2005). A five-factor model perspective on personality disorders. In S. Strack (Ed.), *Handbook of personology and psychopathology* (pp. 257–270). Hoboken, NJ: Wiley.

Costa, P. T., & Widiger, T. A. (Eds.). (1997). *Personality disorders and the five-factor model of personality.* Washington, DC: American Psychological Association.

Craig, R. J. (2003a). Assessing personality and psychopathology with interviews. In J. R. Graham and J. A. Neglieri (Eds.), *Assessment psychology,* Vol. 10 in I. B. Weiner (Editor-in-Chief), *Handbook of psychology* (pp. 487–508). Hoboken, NJ: Wiley.

Craig, R. J. (2003b) Prevalence of personality disorders among cocaine and heroin addicts. *New directions in addiction treatment and prevention* (pp. 33–42). Long Island City, NY: Hatherleigh.

Craig, R. J. (Ed.). (2005a). *Clinical and diagnostic interviewing* (2nd ed.). Lanham, MD: Rowman & Littlefield.

Craig, R. J. (2005b). *Personality-guided forensic psychology.* Washington, DC: American Psychological Association.

Craig, R. J. (2009a). The clinical interview. In J. N. Butcher (Ed.), *Handbook of personality assessment* (pp. 201–225). New York, NY: Oxford University Press.

Craig, R. J. (2009b). *The Personality Disorder Adjective Checklist (PDACL).* Palo Alto, CA: Mind Garden.

Craig, R. J. (2010). Interview assessment. In. I. B. Weiner & W. E. Craighead (Eds.), *The Corsini's encyclopedia of psychology* (pp. 865–868). Hoboken, NJ: Wiley.

Crippa, J. A., De Lima, O., Flavia, D., Cristina, M., Filho, A. S., da Silva, F., . . . Loureiro, S. R. (2008). Comparability between telephone and face-to-face Structured Clinical Interview for *DSM-IV* in assessing social anxiety disorder. *Perspectives in Psychiatric Care, 44,* 241–247.

Davis, S. E., & Hays, L. W. (1997). An examination of the clinical validity of the MCMI-III Depression Personality scale. *Journal of Clinical Psychology, 53,* 15–23.

Digman, J. M. (1990). Personality structure: Emergence of the five-factor model. *Annual Review of Psychology, 41,* 417–440.

Douglas, K. S., Ogcuff, J. R., Nicholls, T. L., & Grant, I. (1999). Assessing risk for violence among psychiatric patients: The HCR-20 Violence Risk Assessment scheme: Screening version. *Journal of Consulting and Clinical Psychology, 67,* 917–930.

Dyce, J. A. (1994). Personality disorders: Alternatives to the official diagnostic system. *Journal of Personality Disorders, 8,* 78–88.

Eaton, W. W., Neufeld, K., Chen, L. S., & Cai, G. (2000). A comparison of self-report and clinical diagnostic interviews for depression: Diagnostic Interview Schedule and Schedule for Clinical Assessment in Neuropsychiatry in the Baltimore Epidemiologic Catchment Area follow-up. *Archives of General Psychiatry, 57,* 217–222.

Endicott, J., & Spitzer, R. L. (1978). A diagnostic interview: The Schedule of Affective Disorders and Schizophrenia. *Archives of General Psychiatry, 35,* 837–844.

Farmer, R. F. (2000). Issues in the assessment and conceptualization of personality disorders. *Clinical Psychology Review, 7,* 823–851.

First, M. B. (1994). Computer-assisted assessment of *DSM-III-R* diagnosis *Psychiatric Annals, 24,* 25–29.

First, M. B., Gibbon, M., Spitzer, R. L., Williams, J. B., & Benjamin, L. (1997). *Structured Clinical Interview for DSM-IV Axis II personality disorders.* Washington, DC: American Psychiatric Press.

First, M. B., Spitzer, R. L., Gibbon, M., & Williams, J. B. (1995a). The Structured Clinical Interview for *DSM-III-R* personality disorders (SCID-II): I. Description. *Journal of Personality Disorders, 9,* 82–91.

First, M. B., Spitzer, R. L., Gibbon, M., & Williams, J. B. (1995b). The Structured Clinical Interview for *DSM-III-R* personality disorders (SCID-II): II. Multi-site test-retest reliability study. *Journal of Personality Disorders, 9, 92 101.*

First, M. B., Spitzer, R. L., Williams, J. B., & Gibbon, M. (1997). *The Structured Clinical Interview for DSM-IV disorders (SCID).* Washington, DC: American Psychiatric Press.

Fossati, A., Maffei, C., Bagnato, M., Donati, D., Donini, M., Fiorelli, M., et al. (1998). Criterion validity of the Personality Diagnostic Questionnaire-R (PDQ-R) in a mixed psychiatric sample. *Journal of Personality Disorders, 12,* 172–142.

Gacono, C. B. (2005). *The clinical and forensic interview schedule for the Hare Psychopathy Checklist: Revised and screening version.* Mahwah, NJ: Erlbaum.

Garb, H. N. (2007). Computer-administered interviews and rating scales. *Psychological Assessment, 19,* 4–13.

Grilo, L. M. (2002). Are there gender differences in *DSM-IV* personality disorders? *Comprehensive Psychiatry, 43,* 427–430.

Groth-Marnatt, G. (2009). *Handbook of psychological assessment* (5th ed.). Hoboken, NJ: Wiley.

Grant, J. E., Suck, W. K., & McCabe, J. S. (2006). A structured clinical interview for kleptomania (SCI-K): preliminary and validity testing. *International Journal of Methods in Psychiatric Research, 15,* 83–94.

Gude, T., Gammen, T., & Frilis, S. (1997). Clinical vignettes in quality assurance: An instrument for evaluating therapist's diagnostic competence in personality disorders. *Nordic Journal of Psychiatry, 51,* 207–212.

Gunderson, J. G., Phillips, K. A., Triebwasser, J., & Hirshfield, R. M. (1994). The diagnostic interview for depressive personality. *American Journal of Psychiatry, 151,* 1300–1304.

Gunderson, J. G., Ronningstam, E., & Bodkin, A. (1990). The diagnostic interview for narcissistic patients. *Archives of General Psychiatry, 47,* 676–680.

Hare, R. D. (2003). Manual for the *HARE* Psychopathy Checklist—Revised (2nd ed.). Toronto, Canada: Multi-Health Systems.

Hartung, C. M., & Widiger, T. A. (1998). Gender differences in the diagnosis of mental disorders: Conclusions and controversies of the *DSM-IV. Psychological Bulletin, 123,* 260–278.

Hasin, D., Samet, S., Nunes, E., Meydan, J., Mateseoane, K., & Waxman, R. (2006). Diagnosis of comorbid psychiatric disorders in substance abusers assessed with the Psychiatric Research Interview for Substance and Mental Health Disorders for *DSM-IV. American Journal of Psychiatry, 163,* 689–696.

Henretty, J. R., & Levitt, H. M. (2010). The role of therapist self-disclosure in psychotherapy: A qualitative review. *Clinical Psychology Review, 30,* 63–77.

Hersen, M., & Thomas, J. C. (2007). *Handbook of clinical interviewing with adults.* Thousand Oaks, CA: Sage.

Hill, C. E., Thompson, B. J., & Ladany, N. (2003). Therapist use of silence in therapy: A survey. *Journal of Clinical Psychology, 59,* 513–524.

Hughes, C. W., Enslie, G. J., Wohlfahart, H., Winslow, R., Kashsen, T. M., & Rush, J. (2005). Efforts of structured interviews in evaluation time in pediatric community mental health settings. *Psychiatric Services, 56,* 1098–1103.

Hyler, S. E., & Gangure, D. P. (2003). A review of the costs of telepsychiatry. *Psychiatric Services, 54,* 976–980.

Jacobsberg, L., Perry, S., & Francis, A. (1995). Diagnostic agreement between the SCID-II screening questionnaire and the Personality Disorder Examination. *Journal of Personality Disorders, 65,* 428–433.

Jamison, C., & Scogin, F. (1992). Development of an interview-based geriatric depression rating scale. *International Journal of Aging and Human Development, 35,* 193–204.

Karg, R. S., Wiens, A. N. (1998). Improving diagnostic and clinical interviewing. In G. Koocher, J. Norcross, & S. Hill III (Eds.), *Psychologist's desk reference* (pp. 11–14). New York, NY: Oxford University Press.

Kaye, W. H., Bulik, C. M., Thornton, L., Barbarich, N., Masters, K., & the Price Foundation Collaboration Group. (2004). Comorbidity of anxiety disorders with anorexia and bulimia nervosa. *American Journal of Psychiatry, 161,* 2215–2221.

Keenan, K. (1994). Psychological/Psychiatric Status Interview (PPSI). *Computers in Human Services, 10,* 107–115.

Knox, S., & Hill, C. E. (2003). Therapist self-disclosure: Research-based suggestions for practitioners. *Journal of Clinical Psychology, 59,* 529–539.

Kobak, K. A., Taylor, L. H., Dottl, S. L., Greist, J. H., Jefferson, J. W., Burrows, D. et al. (1997). Computerized screening for psychiatric disorders in an outpatient community mental health clinic. *Psychiatric Services, 48,* 1048–1057.

Lenzenweger, M. F., Loranger, A. W., Korfine, L., & Neff, C. (1997). Detecting personality disorders in a non-clinical population: Application of a 2-stage process for case identification. *Archives of General Psychiatry, 54,* 345–351.

Lesser, I. M. (1997). Cultural considerations using the Structured Clinical Interview for *DSM-III* for mood and anxiety disorders assessment. *Journal of Psychopathology and behavioral Assessment, 19,* 149–160.

Levitan, R. D., Blouin, A. G., Navarro, J. R., & Hill, J. (1991). Validity of the Computerized DIS for diagnosing psychiatric patients. *Canadian Journal of Psychiatry, 36,* 728–731.

Lewis, G. (1994). Assessing psychiatric disorder with a human interviewer or a computer. *Journal of Epidemiology and Community Health, 48,* 207–210.

Lindsay, K. A., Sankis, L. M., & Widiger, T. A. (2000). Gender bias in self-report personality disorder inventories. *Journal of Personality Disorders, 14,* 218–232.

Livesley, W. J. (2001). *Handbook of personality disorders: Theory, research, and treatment.* New York, NY: Guilford Press.

Loranger, A. W., Sartorius, N., Andreoli, A., Berger, P., Buchheim, P., Channabasavanna, S. M., . . . Regier, D. A. (1994). The International Personality Disorder Examination: The World Health Organization/Alcohol, Drug Abuse, and Mental Health Administration international pilot study of personality disorders. *Archives of General Psychiatry, 51,* 215–224.

Loranger, A. W., Susman, V. L., Oldham, J. M., & Russakoff, L. M. (1987). The Personality Disorder examination: A preliminary report. *Journal of Personality Disorders, 1,* 1–13.

Markowitz, J. C., Skodol, A. E., Skodol, M. D., Petkova, E., Cheng, J., Sanislow, C. A., . . . McGlashan, T. H. (2007). Longitudinal effects of personality disorders on psychosocial functioning of patients with major depressive disorder. *Journal of Clinical Psychiatry, 68,* 186–193.

Marlowe, D. B., Husband, S. D., Bonieske, L. K., & Kirby, K. C. (1997). Structured interview versus self-report tests vantages for the assessment of personality pathology in cocaine dependence. *Journal of Personality Disorders, 11,* 177–190.

Martins, P. K., & Levitt, H. M. (2009). The role of motivational interviewing in promoting health behaviors. *Clinical Psychology Review, 29,* 283–293.

Maruish, M. (2008). The clinical interview. In R. P. Archer & S. R. Smith (Eds.), *Personality assessment* (pp. 37–80). New York, NY: Routledge.

Maser, J. D., Kaelber, C., & Weise, R. E. (1991). International use and attitudes towards *DSM-III* and *DSM-III-R*: Growing consensus on psychiatric classification. *Journal of Abnormal Psychology, 100,* 271–279.

Matarazzo, J. D. (1965). The interview. In B. Wolman (Ed.), *Handbook of clinical psychology* (pp. 403–452). New York, NY: McGraw-Hill.

Matthews, G., Deary, I. J., & Whiteman, M. C. (2009). *Personality traits* (3rd ed.). New York, NY: Cambridge University Press.

McLellan, A. T., Cacciola, J. C., lterman, A. I., Rikoon, S. H., & Carise, D. (2006). The Addiction Severity Index: Origins, contributions and translations. *American journal on Addictions, 15,* 113–124.

McWilliams, L. A., & Asmund, G. J. (1999). Alcohol consumption in university women: A second look at the role of anxiety sensitivity. *Depression and Anxiety, 10,* 125–128.

Menninger, K., Mayman, M., & Pruyser, P. (1963). *The vital balance: The life process in mental health and illness*. New York, NY: Viking.

Messina, N., Wish, E., Hoffman, J., & Nemes, S. (2001). Diagnosing antisocial personality disorder among substance abusers: The SCID versus the MCMI-II. *American Journal o Drug and Alcohol Abuse, 27,* 699–717.

Miller, W. R., & Rollnick, S. (2002). *Motivational interviewing: Preparing people for change*. New York, NY: Guilford Press.

Millon, T. (1991). Classification in psychopathology: Rationale, alternatives, and standards. *Journal of Abnormal Psychology, 100,* 245–261.

Millon, T. (1994). *Millon Clinical Multiaxial Inventory—III: Manual*. Minneapolis, MN: National Computer Systems.

Millon, T. (2000a). Reflections on the future of *DSM* Axis II. *Journal of Personality Disorders, 14,* 30–41.

Milllon, T. (2000b). *Towards a new personology*. New York, NY: Wiley.

Millon, T., & Davis, R. (1996). *Disorders of personality: DSM-IV and beyond*. New York, NY: Wiley.

Modestin, J., Enri, T., & Oberson, B. (1998). A comparison of self-report and interview diagnosis of *DSM-III-R* personality disorders. *European Journal of Personality, 12,* 445–455.

Mohr, D. C., Hart, S. L., Julian, L., Cuttledge, C., Homos-Webb, L., Vella, L., & Tasch, E. T. (2005). Telephone-administered psychotherapy for depression. *Archives of General Psychiatry, 62,* 1007–1014.

*Monitor on Psychology*. (2010). Telepsychology is on the rise. Washington, DC: American Psychological Association, p. 11.

Monnier, J., Knapp, R. G., & Freuh, C. (2003). Recent advances in telepsychiatry: An updated review. *Psychiatric Services, 54,* 1604–1609.

Murphy, J. R., Monson, R. R., Laird, N. B., Sobol, A. M., & Leighton, A. H. (2000). A comparison of diagnostic interviews for depression in the Striling County study. *Archives of General Psychiatry, 57,* 30–236.

Neal, L. A., Fox, C., Carroll, N., Holden, M., & Barnes, P. (1997). Development and validation of a computerized screening test for personality disorders in *DSM-III-R*. *Acta Psychiatrica Scandinavia, 95,* 351–356.

O'Boyle, M., & Self, D. (1990). A comparison of two interviews for *DSM-III-R* personality disorders. *Psychiatric Research, 32,* 85–92.

Oldham, J. M., Skodol, A. E., Kellman, H. D., Hyde, E., Dodge, N., Rosnick, L., et al. (1992). Comorbidity of Axis I and Axis II disorders. *American Journal of Psychiatry, 152,* 571–578.

Perry, J. C. (1992). Problems in the considerations in the valid assessment of personality disorders. *American Journal of Psychiatry, 149,* 1645–1653.

Peters, L., & Andrews, G. (1995). Procedural validity of the computerized version of the Composite International Diagnostic Interview (CIDI-Auto) in anxiety disorders. *Psychological Medicine, 25,* 1269–1280.

Ransom, D., Herkman, T. G., Anderson, T., Garske, J., Halrotyd, K., & Basta, T. (2008). Telephone-derived interpersonal psychotherapy for HIV-infected rural persons with depression: A pilot study. *Psychiatric Services, 59,* 871–877.

Renneberg, B., Chambless, D. L., Dowdall, D. J., Fauerbach, J. A., & Gracely, E. J. (1992). The Structured Clinical Interview for *DSM-III-R*, Axis II and the Millon Clinical Multiaxial Inventory: A concurrent validity study of personality disorders among anxious outpatients. *Journal of Personality Disorders, 6,* 117–124.

Rettew, D. C., Lynch, A. D., Achenbach, T. M., Dumenci, L., & Ivanova, M. Y. (2009). Meta-analysis of agreement between diagnoses made from clinical evaluations and standardized diagnostic interviews. *Journal of Methods in Psychiatric Research, 18,* 169–184.

Reynolds, W. M. (1990). Development of a semi-structured clinical interview for suicide behaviors in adolescents. *Psychological Assessment, 2,* 382–390.

Robins, L. N., Cottler, L. B., Bucholz, K. K., Compton, W. M., North, C. S., & Rourke, K. (2000). *The Diagnostic Interview Schedule for DSM-IV* (DSI-IV). St. Louis, MO: Washington University School of Medicine.

Robins, L. N., Cottler, L. B., Bucholz, K. K., Compton, W. M., North, C. S., & Rourke, K. (2000). *The Diagnostic Interview Schedule for DSM-IV* (DSI-IV). St. Louis, MO: Washington University School of Medicine.

Robins, L. N., Helzer, J. E., Coughhan, J., & Ratcliff, K. S. (1981). National Institute on Mental Health Diagnostic Interview Schedule. *Archives of General Psychiatry, 38,* 381–389.

Rogers, C. R. (1961). *On becoming a person*. Boston, MA: Houghton Mifflin.

Rogers, R. (2001). *Handbook of diagnostic and structured interviewing*. New York, NY: Guilford Press.

Roseman, S. J., Levings, C. T., & Korten, A. E. (1997). Clinical utility and patient acceptance of the computerized Composite International Diagnostic Interview. *Psychiatric Services, 48,* 815–820.

Ross, H. E., Swinson, R., Doumani, S., & Larkin, E. J. (1995). Diagnosing comorbidity in substance abusers: A comparison of the test-retest reliability of two interviews. *American Journal of Drug and Alcohol Abuse, 21,* 167–185.

Ross, H. E., Swinson, R., Larkin, E. J., & Doumani, S. (1994). Diagnosing comorbidity in substance abusers: Computer assessment and clinical validation. *Journal of Nervous and Mental Disease, 192,* 556–563.

Rottman, B. M., Woo-Kyoung, A., Sainslow, C. A., & Kim, N. S. (2009). Can clinicians recognize *DSM-IV* personality disorders from Five-Factor model descriptions of patient cases? *American Journal of Psychiatry, 166,* 427–433.

Rushkin, P. E., Reed, S., Kumar, R., Kling, M. A., Siegel-Eliot, R., Rosen, M. R., & Hauser, P. (1998). Reliability and acceptability of psychiatric diagnosis via telecommunication and audiovisual technology. *Psychiatric Services, 35,* 316–327.

Russ, E., Shedler, J., Bradley, R., & Westen, D. (2008). Refining the construct of narcissistic personality disorder: Diagnostic criteria and subtypes. *American Journal of Psychiatry, 165,* 1473–1481.

Samuel, D. B., & Widiger, T. A. (2008). A meta-analytic review of the relationship between the five-factor model and the *DSM-IV-TR* personality disorders: A facet level analysis. *Clinical Psychology Review, 28,* 1326–1342.

Saulsman, L. M., & Page, A. C. (2004). The five-factor model and personality disorder empirical literature: A meta-analytic review. *Clinical Psychology Review, 23,* 1001–1169.

Segal, D. L., Hersen, M., & Van Hasselt, V. B. (1994). Reliability of the Structured Clinical Interview for *DSM-III-R*: An evaluative review. *Comprehensive Psychiatry, 35,* 316–327.

Selzer, M. A., Kernberg, P., Fibel, B., Cherbuliez, T., & Mortati, S. (1987). The personality assessment interview. *Psychiatry, 50,* 142–153.

Shore, J. H., & Manson, S. M. (2005). A developmental model for rural telepsychiatry. *Psychiatric Services, 56,* 976–980.

Shore, J. H., Savin, D., Orton, H., Beals, J., & Manson, S. M. (2007). Diagnostic reliability of telepsychiatry in American Indian veterans. *American Journal of Psychiatry, 164,* 115–118.

Simon, G. E., Lordmar, E. J., & Operskalski, B. H. (2006). Randomized trial of a telephone care management program for outpatients starting antidepressant treatment. *Psychiatric Services, 57,* 1441–1445.

Simonds, E. C., Handel, R. W., & Archer, R. P. (2008). Incremental validity of the Minnesota Multiphasic Personality Inventory–2 and Symptom Checklist Revised with mental health inpatients. *Assessment, 15,* 78–86

Sloan, K. A., Eldridge, K., & Evenson, R. (1992). An automated screening schedule for mental health centers. *Computers in Human Services, 8,* 55–61.

Smith, T. L., Klein, M. H., & Benjamin, L. S. (2003). Validation of the Wisconsin Personality Disorders Inventory–IV with the SCID-II. *Journal of Personality Disorders, 17,* 173–187.

Sommers-Flanagan, J., & Sommers-Flanagan, R. (1995). Intake interviewing with suicidal patients: A systematic approach. *Professional Psychology: Research and Practice, 26,* 41–47.

Spitzer, R., & Williams, J. B. (1988). Revised diagnostic criteria and a new sructured interview for diagnosing anxiety disorders. *Journal of Psychiatric Research, 22* (Supp. 1), 55–85.

Spitzer, R., Williams, J. B., Gibbon, M., & First, M. B. (1992). *Structured Clinical Interview for DSM-III-R (SCID II).* Washington, DC: American Psychiatric Association.

Stangl, D., Pfohl, B., Zimmerman, M., Bowers, W., & Corenthal, M. (1985). A structured interview for the *DSM-III* personality disorders: A preliminary report. *Archives of General Psychiatry, 42,* 591–596.

Steinberg, M., Cicchetti, D., Buchanan, J., & Hall, P. (1993). Clinical assessment of dissociative symptoms and disorders: The Structured Clinical Interview for *DSM-IV* Dissociative Disorders. *Progress in the Dissociative Disorders, 6,* 3–15.

Strack, S., & Lorr, M. (1997). Invited essay: The challenge of differentiating normal and disordered personality. *Journal of Personality Disorders, 11,* 105–122.

Sullivan, H. S. (1954). *The psychiatric interview.* New York, NY: Norton.

Sweeny, M., McGrath, R. E., Leigh, E., & Costa, G. (2001, March). *Computer-assisted interviews: a meta-analysis of patient acceptance.* Paper presented at the annual meeting of the Society for Personality Assessment, Philadelphia, PA.

Tenney, N. H., Schitte, C. K., Denys, D. A., van Megan, H. J., & Westenberg, H. G. (2003). Association of *DSM-IV* personality disorders on obsessive-compulsive disorders: Comparison of clinical diagnosis, self-report questionnaire, and semi-structured interview. *Journal of Personality Disorders, 17,* 550–561.

Ventura, J., Liberman, R. P., Green, M. F., Shaner, A., & Mintz, J. (1998). Training and Quality assurance with Structured Clinical Interview for *DSM-IV* (SCID-IV). *Psychiatry Research, 79,* 163–173.

Watkins, C. E., Campbell, V. L., Nieberding, R., & Hallmark, R. (1995). Contemporary practice of psychological assessment by clinical psychologists. *Professional Psychology: Research and Practice, 26,* 54–60.

Watson, C. G., Juba, M. P., Manifold, V., Kucala, T., & Anderson, P. E. (1991). The PTSD interview: Rationale, description, reliability and concurrent validity of a *DSM-III*-based technique. *Journal of Clinical Psychology, 47,* 179–188.

Weiner, I. (1999). What the Rorschach can do for you: Incremental validity in clinical application. *Assessment, 6,* 327–340.

Westen, D. (1997). Differences between clinical and research methods for assessing personality disorders: Implications for research and the evaluation of Axis II disorders. *American Journal of Psychiatry, 154,* 895–903.

Widiger, T. A. (1992). Categorical versus dimensional classification: Implications from and for research. *Journal of Personality Disorders, 6,* 287–300.

Widiger, T. A. (2000). Personality disorders in the 21st century. *Journal of Personality Disorders, 14,* 2–16.

Widiger, T. A., Cadoret, R., Hare, R. D., Robins, N., Rutherford, M., et al. (1998). *DSM-IV sourcebook: Vol. IV.* Washington, DC: American Psychiatric Association.

Widiger, T. A., & Clark, L. A. (2000). Toward *DSM-V* and the classification of psychopathology. *Psychological Bulletin, 126,* 946–963.

Widiger, T. A., & Francis, A. (1985). Axis II personality disorders: Diagnostic and treatment issues. *Hospital and Community Psychiatry, 36,* 619–627.

Widiger, T. A., & Francis, A. (1987). Interviews and inventories for the measurement of personality disorders. *Clinical Psychology Review, 7,* 49–75.

Widiger, T. A, Francis, A. J., Pincus, H. A., Russ, D., First, M. B., Davis, W. W. & Kline, M. (1998). *DSM-IV sourcebook: Vol. IV.* Washington, DC: American Psychiatric Association.

Widiger, T. A Mangine, S., Corbitt, E. M., Ellis, C. G., & Thomas, G. V. (1995) *Personality Disorder Interview–IV: A semi-structured interview for the Assessment of personality disorders.* Odessa, FL: Psychological Assessment Resources.

Widiger, T. A., & Spitzer, R. L. (1987). Sex bias in the diagnosis of personality disorders Conceptual and methodological issues. *Clinical Psychology Review, 7,* 49–75.

Wiens, A. N., & Matarazzo, J. D. (1983). Diagnostic interviewing. In M. Hersen, Kazdin, & A. Bellak (Eds.), *The clinical psychology handbook* (pp. 309–328). New York, NY: Pergamon Press.

Williams, J. B., Spitzer, R. L., & Gibbon, M. (1992). International reliability of a diagnostic intake procedure for panic disorder. *Journal of Psychiatry, 149,* 560–562.

Wolford, G., Rosenberg, S. D., Rosenberg, H., Swartz, M. S., Butterfield, M. T., Swanson, J. W., & Jankowski, M. K. (2008). A clinical-based comparing interviews and computer-assisted assessment among clients with severe mental illness. *Psychiatric Services, 9,* 769–775.

World Health Organization. (1992). *The ICD-10 classification of mental and Behavioral disorders.* Geneva, Switzerland: Author.

Wygant, D. B., Sellbom, M., Graham, J. R., & Schenk, P. W. (2006). Incremental validity of the Minnesota Multiphasic Personality Inventory-2 PSY-5 scales in assessing self-reported personality disorder interview. *Assessment, 13,* 178–186.

Zanarini, M., Frankenburg, F. R., Chauncy, D. L., & Yong, L. (1995). *Diagnostic Interview for DSM-IV Personality Disorders,* Cambridge, MA: Harvard University Press.

Zanarini, M., Gunderson, J., Frankenburg, F. R., & Chauncy, D. L. (1989). The revised Diagnostic Interview for Borderlines: Discriminating borderline personality disorders from other Axis II disorders. *Journal of Personality Disorders, 3,* 10–18.

Zimmerman, M. D. (1994). Diagnosing personality disorders: A review of issues and research methods. *Archives of General Psychiatry, 51,* 225–245.

Zimmerman, M. D., Rothchild, L., & Chelminski, I. (2005). The prevalence of *DSM-IV* personality disorders in psychiatric outpatients. *American Journal of Psychiatry, 162,* 1911–1918.

Zimmerman, M. D., & Mattia, J. I. (1999a). Psychiatric diagnosis in clinical psychiatry: Is comorbidity being missed? *Comprehensive Psychiatry, 40,* 182–191.

Zimmerman, M. D., & Mattia, J. I. (1999b). Is posttraumatic stress disorder under-diagnosed in routine clinical practice? *Journal of Nervous and Mental Disorders, 187,* 420–428.

Zimmerman, M. D., & Mattia, J. I. (1999c). Differences between clinical and research practices in diagnosing borderline personality disorder. *American Journal of Psychiatry, 156,* 1570–1574.

Zimmerman, M. D., Thomas, S., & Young, D. (2003). The Diagnostic Inventory for Depression: A self-report scale to diagnose *DSM-IV* major depressive disorder. *Journal of Clinical Psychology, 60,* 87–110.

CHAPTER 22

# Assessment of Psychopathology

## Behavioral Approaches

WILLIAM H. O'BRIEN AND KATHLEEN M. YOUNG

## INTRODUCTION

Clinicians face many assessment questions that emphasize prediction. Prototypical questions may be related to risk for harm (e.g., Will a client harm self or others?), likelihood of skill acquisition or treatment outcome (e.g., Is a client able to inhibit anger in order to avoid future conflict with a partner? or What is the likelihood that the client will comply with a treatment program?), and types of environmental changes that are needed to enhance functioning (e.g., What learning classroom environment would be most helpful for a child with poor attention and concentration skills?).

Clinicians must also address assessment questions related to intervention design. Here the focus is on determining what techniques will be most effective for changing a given client's behavior problems. In this domain, questions are focused more on description (e.g., What are the specific behavior problems and goals for treatment?) and causal analysis (e.g., What variables affect behavior problems?).

What theories and perspectives guide the focus of behavioral assessment, and how do these theories and perspectives differ from those generated by nonbehavioral therapists? What methods are used to assess client

difficulties? What sort of information is yielded by these methods, how is it evaluated, and how valid are the conclusions derived from the evaluation? How is the information used?

These and other important questions related to behavioral assessment are discussed in this chapter. Rather than emphasize applications of behavioral assessment in research, we concentrate on how behavioral assessment methods are conducted in clinical settings. We initially examine the conceptual foundations of behavioral assessment and how these foundations differ from other approaches to assessment. Then we review the more commonly used behavioral assessment techniques. Finally, we discuss how assessment information can be organized and integrated into a case conceptualization.

## BASIC ASSUMPTIONS OF
## BEHAVIORAL ASSESSMENT

The core characteristics of behavioral assessment are clarified when they are compared to a psychodynamic approach. The prototypical psychodynamic approach hypothesizes that target behaviors (target behavior refers to any overt-motor, cognitive, emotional, or physiological response that is the focus of assessment) are principally *caused* by stable, internal, and dysfunctional psychological processes that often lie outside of the client's awareness. Some examples of such dysfunctional internal psychological processes are ego defenses, impaired object relations, and disordered personality.

Because dysfunctional internal psychological processes are presumed to be the primary cause of problematic behavior, psychodynamic approaches emphasize the measurement of these unobservable and inferred constructs. Additionally, situational factors that can exert an important influence on target behaviors are deemphasized. The Rorschach is an example of this inferential and nonsituational measurement approach. In a typical Rorschach assessment, clients are presented with ambiguous inkblots and asked to provide a verbal account of what they "see." The examiner prompts for clarification of vague responses but is also cautioned to be as neutral as possible. The clients' verbal responses are recorded verbatim, and these verbatim accounts are coded along a number of dimensions (e.g., verbalizing the use of form, color, shading, white space), often using a manual developed by Exner (1986, 1991). The coded responses then are aggregated in multiple ways to derive various indices of clients' internal dynamics.

A key assumption underlying the Rorschach is that a client's perceptions of the inkblots reveal critical information about his or her personality dynamics and unconscious conflicts. For example, the color-affect hypothesis, which is derived from psychodynamic theory about emotional regulation, posits that inkblots with color (e.g., red, blue, green) elicit emotional activation (Exner, 1991). If a client explicitly reports that color was used in forming his or her perception (e.g., "It looks like an undersea landscape with different colors of coral"), it is thought that he or she has diminished self-regulation (or ego strength) because the emotional reaction elicited by the inkblot colors were not adequately suppressed. This poor self-regulation would be taken as an index of risk for impulsivity, an affective disorder, or psychosis. Alternatively, if the client does *not* report the use of color in many responses, he or she is thought to have excessive self-regulation consistent with repression and anxiety disorders.

As is evident in the Rorschach example, the test is used to infer unobservable internal psychological processes based on verbal responses to test stimuli. The scoring and interpretation system does not allow for interpretation of client responses in relation to ongoing and/or recent situational events that may exert significant impact on verbal responding such as recent life stressors. These two characteristics (validity of inferences about internal states and lack of situational measurement) of the Rorschach have been extensively researched in the past decade. Although there is continuing debate, it appears that the test can be scored reliably but that the validity of many summary scores is poor or undetermined (Acklin, McDowell, Verschell, & Chan, 2000; Lilienfeld, Wood, & Garb, 2000). Further, key psychodynamic assumptions (e.g., the color-affect hypothesis) have not been supported (Frank, 1993). Finally, there is ample evidence indicating that life stressors and ongoing contextual factors exert a significant influence on Rorschach responding (Exner & Sendin, 1997). Taken together, these flaws in the Rorschach system have resulted in a number of researchers recommending that there be a moratorium on its use (e.g., Garb, 1999). Despite continued critiques of the Rorschach system (e.g., Garb, Wood, Lilienfeld, & Nezworski, 2005) and evidence challenging the validity of the Rorschach (e.g., Wood et al., 2010), the measure continues to be utilized frequently by psychologists as an assessment tool (Musewicz, Marczyk, Knauss, & York, 2009).

Personality assessment is similar to psychodymanic approaches because it is thought that responses to paper-and-pencil questions yield information about unobservable internal psychological processes. Additionally, like psychodynamic approaches, the measurement of contextual factors is deemphasized. The Minnesota Multiphasic Personality Inventory (MMPI), a commonly used personality measure, illustrates these two characteristics. Items on the MMPI are carefully worded to avoid linking the item to a specific situation or time frame. For example, a client can respond only "yes" or "no" to broadly worded items, such as "I feel uncomfortable in public." Thus, there is no possibility for measuring how discomfort in public situations varies across situations (e.g., giving a public presentation, sitting in a classroom, using public transportation) and time. Additionally, a "yes" response will be interpreted as an indicator of a stable internal psychological process, such as introversion.

A behavioral assessment approach finds fault with psychodynamic and personality-oriented approaches in two important ways. First, because unobservable internal constructs are presumed to be the primary cause of target behavior, circular reasoning is not uncommonly encountered. An example of such circular reasoning occurs in inpatient medical settings. Specifically, a common referral concern is that a patient may be using his or her call-light excessively and/or yelling out for help from nursing staff. Upon arrival to the patient's room, the nursing staff may find that the patient is experiencing what the nurse determines to be a minor concern. The nursing staff may then apply a dispositional approach and suggest that the patient is "a whiner" or "attention seeking." Note here that the locus of cause is an internal unobserved dispositional characteristic of the patient ("attention-seeker") rather than some event occurring in the environment. This is an example of circular reasoning. The call-light use is presumed to be caused by an internal state (e.g., attention seeking). However, the presence of the internal state is exclusively based on the call-light behavior itself.

Interestingly, the patient will also typically generate a disposition-based and circular reasoning account of the nursing staff behavior. So, when the patient is asked why he or she is using the call-light frequently, often the patient will respond that the nursing staff are "uncaring" and need multiple reminders. Again, the locus of cause in this account resides within the dispositions of the nursing staff rather than the environment.

A behavioral approach to this problem is quite different. Rather than restrict the causal search to internal dispositional factors, the behavior therapist (we use the term *behavior therapist* to refer to any behavioral scientist or mental health worker who conducts assessments and/or interventions based on learning theory and behavioral principles) would examine observable events, such as the relationship between the nursing staff behavior and patient behavior. When this approach is taken, an alternative account of excessive call-light use is evident: Call-light use is being shaped and maintained by negative reinforcement.

The process unfolds in this way. The patient experiences distress and/or discomfort. He or she then presses the call light to obtain assistance. The nursing staff members initially provide relatively quick and consistent responding to the call light. When nursing staff arrive to provide assistance, the patient's distress and discomfort are lessened. This provides negative reinforcement for call-light use. However, after members of the nursing staff conclude that the patient has no "real problem" and is "attention seeking," they begin to delay or withhold responding to the call light. From an operant perspective, this is an example of withdrawing negative reinforcement for call-light use. The patient then experiences increased distress and discomfort. Given intensified distress and withdrawal of reinforcement for call-light use, the client will escalate the use of the call light and engage in additional help-seeking behaviors, such as calling out. This is an example of the well-documented extinction burst

that occurs for a period of time after reinforcement for a behavior is removed. The nursing staff eventually respond after multiple call-light presses and/or when the client begins calling out verbally. Here, from an operant perspective, staff members selectively reinforce higher rates of call-light use and higher intensity help-seeking behavior (calling out). This process is known as shaping.

It is important to note that this behavioral formulation of call-light use is not based on an assumption that an unobservable internal psychological characteristic is causing call-light use. Instead, the formulation is based on observable and measureable interactions between the patient and the nursing staff. Further, this formulation is noncircular because the causal variable (nursing staff reinforcement schedule) is different from the target behavior (call-light use). Finally, this behavioral formulation is closely tied to a potential intervention—having nursing staff provide consistent reinforcement for *not* using the call light (e.g., nursing staff members visit the patient consistently when he or she is quiet). This is known as differential reinforcement for incompatible behavior and has been shown to be an effective intervention for a wide variety of problem behaviors.

The second major criticism leveled at psychodynamic approaches to assessment has been the lack of research support for the main assumptions that: (a) internal psychological characteristics account for meaningful amounts of variance in target behavior occurrence and (b) assessment of these factors leads to effective interventions. This lack of research support is, at least partially, a function of the use of poorly defined internal psychological constructs in many investigations. Additionally, interventions targeting modification of myriad internal psychological characteristics, such as cognitive structures and personality traits, have yielded inconsistent outcomes relative to behavioral interventions (Hayes, 2004).

In contrast to psychodynamic and personality approaches just described, behavioral assessment and the accompanying functional analysis (the functional analysis is a case conceptualization or model of client problems that is derived from the behavioral assessment) emphasizes the evaluation of *behavior in context*. Thus, the onset, maintenance, and termination of any target behavior (a target behavior is any behavior that is the focus of assessment. It can be a problem behavior, an adaptive behavior, or a goal) is thought to arise out of an interaction between individual characteristics (i.e., learning history and biological characteristics) and the events occurring in the environment. Focusing on a single component of this complex interaction (i.e., internal personality characteristics) is thought to be excessively narrow and likely to yield an inadequate account of how and why behavior occurs. Next, we review the core assumptions and theories underlying behavioral assessment.

## Learning Theory

As the field of behavioral therapy has evolved, the characteristic assumptions, theories and accompanying assessment techniques, goals of assessment, and functional analytic accounts of target behavior have also changed. Hayes (2004) argued that this evolutionary process can be organized into three waves. During the first wave, behavioral assessment and functional analyses were primarily based on principles of respondent and operant conditioning. During the second wave, cognitive variables were incorporated into behavioral assessment and functional analyses as important causal variables and target behaviors. During the third wave, principles of functional contextualism were added. We briefly review each of these epochs of behavior therapy evolution and how they are relevant to behavioral assessment and the functional analysis.

### Wave 1: Classical and Operant Conditioning Applied to Observable Target Behaviors and Contextual Factors

Drawing from experimental works in respondent conditioning, first-wave researchers demonstrated how classical conditioning principles could account for the onset, maintenance, and change in many target behaviors. Joseph Wolpe is an excellent example of a wave 1 behavioral researcher. Through thoughtful and meticulous experimentation, Wolpe (cf. 1952a, 1952b) demonstrated that anxiety states, or "neuroses," could be produced using classical conditioning procedures. He also demonstrated that these same anxiety responses could be reduced using graded exposure combined with relaxation (Wolpe, 1958, 1963, 1997; Wolpe & Lazarus, 1966; Wolpe, Salter, & Reyna, 1964).

Other researchers were also exploring how classical conditioning could explain the onset and maintenance of many other target behaviors. Additionally, researchers began to use classical conditioning principles, such as exposure, to create effective treatments for many target behaviors, such as eating disorders, sexual disorders, and psychophysiological disorders.

Operant conditioning was the other major learning theory that was being explored during this first wave. Drawing on the theoretical and empirical work of Watson (1919), Skinner (1938, 1974), and Hull (1952),

researchers were evaluating how principles of reinforcement and punishment as well as stimulus control could account for the acquisition, maintenance, and change in target behaviors. Many behavioral interventions were developed using operant conditioning principles. Further, randomized control outcome trials and single-subject investigations demonstrated that these interventions were consistently effective.

The success of the first wave of behavior therapy laid the foundation for the entire behavior therapy movement. As noted, through the use of sound theory, experimentation, and empiricism, these early behavior therapy pioneers made strong arguments that the focus of assessment ought to be on observable target behaviors and environmental events that were exerting significant causal effects on them.

### Wave 2: Incorporation of Cognitive and Emotional Experiences

Hayes (2004) argued that the second wave of behavior therapy partially emerged because there was a disquieting sense that important areas of unobservable human experiences, such as thoughts and feelings, were inadequately represented in wave 1 theories, assessments, and interventions. Researchers thus began exploring how cognitive variables and emotional variables could be integrated with behavioral theories, behavioral assessments, and functional analyses. The essential position embraced by these researchers was that cognitive variables acted either as causal variables (i.e., thoughts were the principal cause of a target behavior occurrence) or mediators between observable situational events and observable target behaviors.

A classic example of a cognitive perspective is Beck's model of depression (cf. Beck, Rush, Shaw, & Emery, 1979). According to Beck and colleagues, a person with depression may encounter an environmental event that is threatening or challenging (e.g., an invitation to attend a party). Exposure to this event "triggers" a number of dysfunctional and automatic thoughts about the self (e.g., "I am unpopular," "I am boring"), life in general (e.g., "The world is unfair," "It is unfair that I was saddled with this burden"), and the future (e.g., "I will never have friends," "My future is lonely"). In turn, these thoughts cause the person to have negative emotional experiences and engage in maladaptive behaviors (e.g., social avoidance).

Because cognitive variables were thought to be critical causal variables, behavioral assessment techniques developed during this period were often designed to measure their occurrence and effects. Additionally, therapy techniques were developed in which clients were encouraged to identify, stop, confront, and/or nullify the problematic thoughts and feelings. These cognitive therapy techniques were typically combined with wave 1 techniques in order to promote behavior change.

The effectiveness of a great many cognitive-behavioral interventions has been well documented (e.g., Butler, Chapman, Forman, & Beck, 2006). Despite this success, however, some authors began questioning the core assumptions of wave 2 cognitive models. For example, cognitive models presume that learning to *control or correct* dysfunctional cognitive experiences is a critical element of treatment. However, a large-scale component analysis of a cognitive-behavioral treatment for depression demonstrated that the cognitive therapy techniques did not appear to produce improvements over and above those obtained by the wave 1 techniques (behavioral activation, exposure) alone (Jacobson, Martell & Dimidijan, 2001). Others have argued that it is really not possible to effectively control the onset, duration, or intensity of cognitive experiences (Hayes, 2004).

In summary, wave 2 behavior therapies added cognitive variables into behavioral conceptualizations of disordered behavior. Accordingly, behavioral assessment techniques were expanded so that cognitive variables could be measured and quantified. The second wave also broadened therapy techniques and added techniques designed to help patients reduce the frequency, intensity, and/or duration of target cognitions using principles of classical and operant conditioning.

## Wave 3: Functional Contextualism

The behavioral theories and models from the first and second waves of behavior therapy created immense improvements in how psychological disorders and problems were assessed and treated. In recent years, however, a growing number of new behavioral assessment procedures and interventions have been developed that are substantially different from their predecessors. Examples of these third-wave approaches include: acceptance and commitment therapy (Hayes, Strosahl, & Wilson, 1999), dialectical behavior therapy (Linehan, 1993), functional analytic psychotherapy (Kohlenberg, Kanter, Bolling, Wexner, Parker, & Tsai, 2004; Tsai, Kohlenberg, Kanter, Kohlenberg, Follette, & Callighan, 2008), and mindfulness-based cognitive therapy (Segal, Williams, & Teasdale, 2002). These new therapies diverge from wave 1 and wave 2 approaches in terms of philosophical stance, theoretical formulations, and treatment aims. These differences have important implications for behavioral assessment and the functional analysis.

As noted by Hayes (2004), the third wave of behavior therapy represents a movement away from the positivism and "cognitivism" that was embedded in the second-wave approaches. Hayes also argued that the third-wave therapies embrace a recommitment to radical behaviorism and *functional contextualism*. The differences between wave 1 and 2 philosophical stances relative to wave 3 are substantial. From the point of view of waves 1 and 2, overt behavior, cognitive events, and other "private experiences" (e.g., emotional experiences) can be decomposed, or broken down into parts. Then the relationships among these parts can be studied, analyzed, and understood. From this perspective, it is logical to take the position that a thought such as "I am boring" can *cause* a problematic behavioral response such as social avoidance. Further, the thought itself can be labeled as "dysfunctional" because it *causes* maladaptive behavior. Finally, it is therefore important to stop, alter, or control the occurrence of this dysfunctional thought in order to stop social avoidance.

In contrast to the positivistic stance just described, functional contextualism takes the position that cognitive, emotional, and motor responses occur in *relation to, and derive meaning from,* ongoing internal and external events. Consider again the thought "I am boring." From a functional contextual perspective, the thought is neither functional nor dysfunctional. It is simply a cognitive experience not unlike any one of thousands of thoughts that pass through the mind of a client on any given day. Of importance from the functional contextual position is the *relationship* between the thought and other behaviors. Thus, for example, if the thought is *believed to be literally true* and this belief in its "trueness" leads to social avoidance, then treatment would target modification of the patient's tendency to treat the thought as if it were true. That is, the client would be encouraged simply to view the thought as a series of words that he or she has rehearsed. Following this, the client would be encouraged *not* to attempt to control the thought but instead accept it as one of many cognitive experiences that occur thousands of times per day. Additionally, the client would be encouraged to use techniques that reduce the extent to which the thought is believed to be literally true (e.g., defusion techniques) and reduce the strength of its relationship with other target behaviors (e.g., mindfulness techniques that involve noting the thought and allowing it to occur without taking action). Acceptance and commitment therapy uses metaphors to convey this powerful idea to clients. One particularly helpful metaphor involves treating the thoughts as "passengers in the bus or car." The client is encouraged to imagine the thought "You're boring" along with other unhelpful thoughts (e.g., "You're dumb," "No one likes you," etc.) as "passengers" in the seats behind the driver. The goal is to learn to simply "drive" (i.e., go to a social event) without reacting to the thoughts, attempting to control them, or letting them take over the "driving."

A patient who presented with major depression symptoms provides an illustration of the functional contextual approach. The patient, whom we will name Dave, reported that he was experiencing persistent negative thoughts about himself, the future, and the world in general. Dave reported that whenever he observed a family interacting happily, he would experience both hopeful and hopeless thoughts about the possibility for happiness in his own life. These thoughts, in turn, led to feelings of sadness and anger. Shortly after experiencing the sadness and anger, he would report that he would find himself reflecting on how the world was "going to hell" and that having children was actually quite selfish and immoral. Interestingly, this second set of thoughts created feelings of relief. The structure of the relationship among environmental events (observing family), cognitive experiences, and emotional reactions are diagramed in Figure 22.1.

The functional analytic causal model in Figure 22.1 provides insight into the function of cognitive experiences for Dave. The initial event, observing a family, provokes alternating predictions (hopeful/hopeless) about his future. This cognitive struggle ultimately activates sadness and anger. The sadness and anger then prompts a second set of thoughts about the world ("The world is a terrible place"). This second set of thoughts allows Dave to momentarily escape from the sadness and anger (negative reinforcement). These thoughts also justify not taking action

(which would require effort and discomfort). Importantly, although the thoughts about the world appear to be "dysfunctional" from a wave 2 perspective, they are actually escape responses that provide momentary relief from sadness and anger. Further, they will continue until the client learns other ways of reducing the sadness and anger (e.g., mindfulness skills, cognitive deconstruction skills).

The implications of third-wave innovations for functional analysis are becoming clearer and a great deal of research is needed. First, there is a pressing need to develop reliable and valid measures of key constructs, such as the function of thoughts and emotional experiences, acceptance, experiential avoidance, and mindfulness. Second, there is a need to develop and validate case conceptualizations and/or functional analytic causal models that depict client difficulties from a functional-contextual perspective. Finally, there is a need for a better understanding of how important principles derived from first- and second-wave approaches can be integrated with third-wave assessments and interventions.

### Empiricism

A second key foundation of behavioral assessment is that problem behavior can be understood most effectively when an empirical approach is used with clients. Thus, the behavior therapist strives to obtain information that will allow him or her to develop unambiguous and measurable operational definitions of problem behaviors, contextual factors, and the relationships among them.

The importance of an empirical approach in behavioral assessment cannot be overstated. As noted earlier, there is a tendency for clients, staff, therapists, and significant others to misattribute the causes of problem behavior to internal dispositional factors and thereby generate tautological explanations for client behavior. One can pose two types of questions to determine whether an explanation for a particular behavior is tautological. The first question elicits the causal explanation. The second question is designed to obtain evidence that is used to support the causal assertion. An example follows.

*Interviewer:* What are some possible reasons for the patient's excessive pain complaints and refusals to go to physical therapy?

*Nurse:* He's manipulative. (The presumed cause is described as an internal, dispositional, and unobservable characteristic.)

*Interviewer:* How is it that you know he is manipulative? (This question is designed to elicit evidence supporting the causal inference.)

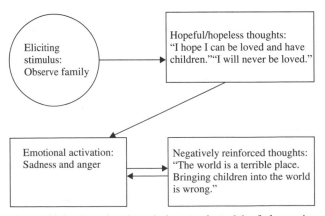

**Figure 22.1** Functional analytic causal model of depressive cognitions and emotional experiences for "Dave."

*Nurse:* Because he starts complaining of pain when we tell him it is time to go to physical therapy. Then when we let him skip a session, he stops complaining.

In this example, the nurse has offered a tautological explanation for the patient's behavior. Specifically, the occurrence of pain complaints and therapy refusal are used to support the presence of manipulativeness. In turn, manipulativeness is used to explain why pain complaints and therapy refusals occur. Note that there is no direct evidence of manipulativeness. It is inferred from the refusal behavior itself.

From an empirical perspective, however, the only observable causal sequence provided in this scenario is the relationship between nursing behavior and pain complaints and therapy refusal. Manipulativeness has not been demonstrated, but nurse reinforcement of pain complaints and therapy refusal has been demonstrated.

By adopting an empirical approach, a functional analysis will emphasize articulating relationships between the *observable* environmental events and *observable* behavioral responses. (It is important to note that many internal events, such as thoughts and emotional experiences, can be made observable using well-validated self-report inventories and psychophysiological recording.) This focus on empirical strategies, in turn, permits the behavior therapist to generate potentially testable hypotheses about behavior and then collect data that can plausibly confirm or disconfirm their verity.

## Additional Core Assumptions

A number of additional assumptions about behavior are embedded in behavioral assessment. These additional assumptions characterize the evolution of thought in behavioral assessment and emerging trends in learning theory and behavioral research. The first of these corollary assumptions is an endorsement of a scholarly, hypothetico-deductive approach to assessment (Haynes & O'Brien, 2000; Haynes, O'Brien, & Kaholokula, 2011). Using this approach, a behavior therapist will strive to design an assessment strategy where client behavior is measured under different conditions so that one or more hypotheses about its function can be empirically tested. Excellent examples of this methodology are the functional analytic experimental procedures developed by Iwata and colleagues for the assessment and treatment of self-injurious behavior (Iwata & Dozier, 2008; Iwata, Smith, & Michael, 2000) and the functional analytic psychotherapy approach developed by Kohlenberg (Tsai

et al., 2008), which provides a learning-based account of client–therapist interactions.

A second corollary assumption is that cause–effect relationships between and among environmental events and behavior are conditional. That is, they arise out of complex interactions occurring among environmental causal events and individual differences (e.g., a client's learning history and biological characteristics). This assumption supports the expectation that behaviors often vary greatly from place to place, moment to moment, and person to person. As such, behavioral assessment will often emphasize measurement in multiple settings.

A third corollary assumption is behavioral plasticity (Haynes et al., 2011; O'Brien & Haynes, 1995). Given that target behaviors are thought to arise from complex learning-based causal interactions between environmental events and individual difference variables, it is reasonable to posit that *any* behavior can be modified so long as one can: (a) discover what variables and combination of variables are exerting causal effects on the target behavior and (b) modify these causal variables in order to produce change. This is a powerful and important assumption in the behavioral assessment paradigm. It is also quite evident in the history of behavioral assessment and behavior therapy wherein many target behaviors that were at one time viewed as untreatable (e.g., psychotic behavior, aggressive behavior among the developmentally disabled) were found to be modifiable when interventions using the correct configuration of learning principles were developed and applied.

A fourth corollary assumption, multivariate multidimensionalism, posits that target behaviors and environmental events are often molar constructs that are comprised of many lower-level and qualitatively distinct modes and dimensions of responding. Consider, for example, "depression." Depression can be comprised of many distinct modes of responding, such as: cognitive experiences (e.g., thoughts of worthlessness, guilt, pessimism), physiological symptoms (e.g., fatigue, sleep difficulties, appetite disturbance, muscle aches and pains), affective states (e.g., subjective feelings of sadness, crying, agitation), and overt behavioral responses (e.g., social withdrawal, low activity level, slowed speech, slowed motor movements,). Additionally, each of these responses can be measured along several different dimensions, such as rate (how a response occurs across a specific time interval), duration (how long each response occurs), intensity (how vivid or believable a given thought may be or how disruptive a given affective response may be), and variability (e.g., how much day-to-day variation there is in the experiencing of a particular physical symptom).

In a similar way, environmental events can be partitioned into distinct modes and dimensions. Consider, for example, the concept of work stress. "Work" is a complex set of environmental events that could include coworker interactions, supervisor/supervisee interactions, workload, work setting, noise levels, lighting, and myriad other variables. Because target behaviors and/or environmental events can be operationalized in many ways, the multidimensional assumption supports the use of multimethod and multifaceted assessment strategies.

A fifth corollary assumption, temporal variability, is that relationships among causal events and problem behaviors are dynamic—they change over time. Consequently, it can be the case that variables causing the onset of a target behavior differ from variables that maintain it. Chronic smoking behavior is an excellent example of this. Specifically, factors that promote the initiation of smoking (e.g., perceived social reinforcement) are different from factors that maintain smoking behavior such as nicotine addiction.

### Implications of Basic Assumptions

The aforementioned conceptual assumptions have a number of implications. First, it is critical that persons who endorse a behavioral approach to assessment be familiar with learning principles and how they apply to behavior problems. Familiarity with learning principles, in turn, permits the behavioral therapist to better understand processes governing the onset, maintenance, and cessation of target behaviors. In addition to being well-versed in learning theory, behavior therapists must also be able to carefully operationalize target behaviors and environmental events so that unambiguous measures of each can be either created or selected from the many measures developed by other researchers. This requires a deliberate and scholarly approach to assessment as well as familiarity research methods related to construct development, measurement, and psychometrics. Finally, behavior therapists must know how to conduct assessments that permit identification and measurement of complex causal relationships among target behaviors and contextual variables.

In the next sections, we review procedures used by behavioral assessors to operationalize, measure, and evaluate problem behavior and situational events. As part of the review, we highlight decisional processes that guide the implementation of these procedures. Prior to presenting this information, however, we provide an overview of the primary goals of behavioral assessment.

## TOPOGRAPHICAL ANALYSIS OF BEHAVIOR

A primary goal of the functional analysis is to generate unambiguous operational definitions of target behaviors. This, in turn, permits accurate measurement. To generate operational definitions, the behavior therapist must initially inquire about the many possible behaviors that are creating difficulty for the client and then select a subset of target behaviors that will be the focus of the intervention.

Once a set of target behaviors has been identified, the behavior therapist must then determine the essential characteristics of each. In other words, operational definitions must be generated. Complex target behaviors can be partitioned into at least three interrelated modes of responding: cognitive-verbal behaviors, physiological-affective behaviors, and overt-motor behaviors. (See Table 22.1.) The cognitive-verbal mode subsumes cognitive experiences such as self-statements, images, irrational beliefs, and attitudes. The physiological-affective mode subsumes physiological responses and felt emotional states. Finally, the overt-motor mode subsumes observable actions.

The process of operationally defining a target behavior requires careful behavioral interviewing. For example, a client who is described as having chronic pain may be presenting with many cognitive, emotional, and overt-motor behaviors, including catastrophic beliefs about outcomes, negative expectancies for the future, social withdrawal, verbal complaints, overt-motor expressions of pain, medication use, and expressed distress. However, another patient with chronic pain may present with a very different configuration of verbal-cognitive, physiological-affective, and overt-motor behaviors. Thus, if the behavior therapist investigates only a restricted number of response modes

**TABLE 22.1   Target Behavior Modes and Contextual Variable Classes**

| Contextual Variable Class | Target Behavior Modes | | |
| --- | --- | --- | --- |
| | Cognitive-Verbal | Affective-Physiological | Overt-Motor |
| Social/Environmental | | | |
| Nonsocial/ Environmental | | | |
| Intrapersonal/ Cognitive-Verbal | | | |
| Intrapersonal/Affective-Physiological | | | |
| Intrapersonal/ Overt-Motor | | | |

(e.g., focusing only on what the patient is feeling), the functional analysis may be adversely affected.

Once a target behavior has been operationalized in terms of mode, its parameters must be articulated. The most commonly used parameters are frequency, duration, and intensity. *Frequency* refers to how often the behavior occurs across a relevant time interval (e.g., number per day, per hour, per minute). *Duration* refers to the time that elapses between the onset and termination of a response. *Intensity* refers to the "force," or salience, of the behavior. Often intensity can be gauged by using a rating scale (e.g., a 0–10 scale, grades) or a visual analog scale (e.g., fear thermometer).

In summary, one of the initial goals of the behavioral assessment is to learn about the three modes of target behavior responding and the parameters of responding. This preliminary operationalization of the problem behavior allows the client, significant others, and the behavior therapist to gain a precise and consensual understanding of target behaviors. In essence, during this initial phase of the behavioral assessment, the behavior therapist will have translated what are often informal and dispositionally biased descriptions of problem behaviors into terms that are (a) consistent with learning theory, (b) observable, and (c) quantifiable.

## TOPOGRAPHICAL ANALYSIS OF CONTEXT

Subsequent to the topographical analysis of target behaviors, the behavior therapist will need to develop operational definitions of key contextual variables. Contextual variables are internal and external events that precede, cooccur with, and/or follow the target behavior and *exert important causal influences on it* (Haynes et al., 2011). Contextual factors can be sorted into two broad classes: environmental/contextual factors and intrapersonal/contextual factors. Environmental/contextual factors can be further divided into social context (e.g., interactions with others) and physical context (e.g., interactions with built environment, temperature, noise levels, lighting levels). Intrapersonal contextual factors include verbal-cognitive, affective-physiological, and overt-motor behaviors that may exert significant causal effects on the target behaviors.

The contextual factor measurement parameters are similar to those used with target behaviors. That is, frequency, duration, and intensity of occurrence are most often assessed. For example, the intensity and duration of exposure to adult attention can be reliably measured and has been shown to have a significant impact on the frequency and magnitude of medication use, pain complaints, immunological functioning, and infection rates.

In summary, the topographical analysis of target behaviors and contextual variables are two of the primary goals of the behavioral assessment. Target behaviors can be partitioned into three modes, and within each mode, several dimensions of measurement may be used. Similarly, contextual variables can be partitioned into classes and measured along specific dimensions. (See Table 22.1.) The operationalization and quantification of target behaviors and contextual factors can serve important functions in behavioral assessment. First, operational definitions can help the client and the behavior therapist think carefully and objectively about the nature of the target behaviors and the contexts within which they occur. This type of consideration can guard against oversimplified, biased, and nonscientific descriptions of target behaviors and contexts. Second, operational definitions and quantification allow the clinician to evaluate the social significance of the target behavior or the stimulus characteristics of a particular context relative to relevant comparison groups or comparison contexts. Finally, operationalizing target behaviors and contexts is a critical step in determining whether behavioral criteria are met for establishing a psychiatric diagnosis. This latter process of rendering a diagnosis is not without controversy in the behavioral assessment literature. However, with the increasing development of effective diagnosis-specific treatment protocols, the generation of a diagnosis can be a critical element of pretreatment assessment and intervention design.

## SAMPLING AND SETTINGS

Given that target behaviors and contextual factors have been operationalized, the behavior therapist must collect data on these variables. Two types of decisions are required to address this aspect of assessment. The first set of decisions is related to sampling: How, where, and when should the target behaviors and contextual factors be measured? The second set of decisions is related to technique: What behavioral assessment methods should be used to gather information? Sampling strategies and assessment techniques are discussed next.

### Time Sampling

Behavior is continuously occurring and changing across time and contexts. Because we cannot observe all behaviors at all times, and in all contexts, sampling strategies must be used. A major factor in deciding on a sampling strategy is degree of generalizability. Specifically, often we are interested in gathering data that will allow us to validly infer how a client behaves in the natural, or "criterion," contexts.

Target behaviors and contextual variables can be sampled in many ways. However, five sampling strategies are most often used in the behavioral assessment literature. Each strategy has advantages and disadvantages. *Event sampling* refers to a procedure in which the occurrence of a target behavior or contextual variables is recorded whenever it occurs. For example, when conducting a classroom observation, we might record each occurrence of yelling by a child (target behavior) and the teacher's responses to it (contextual factor). A frequency estimate is most often calculated using event sampling. Frequency estimates are simply the number of times the behavior occurs within a particular time interval (e.g., minutes, hours, days, or weeks). Event sampling is most appropriate for target behaviors and contextual variables that have distinct beginning and end points. It is also more workable for behaviors that do not occur at a high level of frequency.

*Duration sampling* refers to the amount of time that elapses between the beginning and end of target behaviors and contextual variables. Returning to the classroom observation example, we might be interested not only in how often yelling occurs but also how long it lasts. Like event sampling, duration sampling is applicable to target behaviors and contextual variables that have distinct beginning and end points.

*Interval sampling* involves dividing time into discrete intervals that can range from seconds to hours or days. For example, the behavior therapist may choose to divide the aforementioned child's day into 5-minute observation intervals. In partial interval sampling, the behavior therapist would simply indicate that the target behavior has occurred if yelling was observed at *any point* during a specific 5-minute interval (i.e., there is no counting of individual responses as in event sampling). In whole-interval sampling, the behavior therapist would indicate that the target behavior has occurred only if yelling is observed *during the entire* 5-minute interval. Partial- and whole-interval sampling are recommended for target behaviors and contextual variables that have ambiguous beginning and endpoints. They are also well suited for target behaviors and contextual variables that occur at a high rate of frequency.

*Real-time sampling* involves measuring chronological time at the beginning and end of each target behavior and contextual variable occurrence. A key advantage of real-time sampling is that it can simultaneously yield data about the frequency and duration of target behaviors and contextual variables. Like event and duration sampling, real-time sampling requires distinct beginning and end points.

*Momentary-time sampling* is a sophisticated strategy that can be used to gather data on several clients in a particular context or a single client across multiple contexts. In the former case, the procedure involves conducting a brief observation (e.g., 20 seconds) of a client, recording whether the target behavior or contextual factor occurred during that brief moment of observation, and then repeating this procedure for all clients being evaluated. In our classroom example, we might choose to observe a few students in order to gain a better understanding of the extent to which our client differs from others in terms of yelling. Thus, we would observe our client for a brief moment (and record if yelling is occurring), then observe a comparison student for a brief interval, return to our client, and so on. In the latter case, the momentary time sampling typically involves having a single client target behaviors and contextual variables across time and settings using some form of written or electronic diary. In most cases, the client is prompted by a timer, pager, or some other signaling device to take note of what is happening at that exact moment in time. The client then records target behavior and contextual variable occurrence in his or her diary.

## Setting Sampling

The setting where the measurement occurs is a critical element of behavioral assessment. The setting can be evaluated on a number of dimensions. One important dimension is the degree to which the setting represents the client's natural environment. At one end of the continuum are naturalistic settings. Naturalistic settings are those in which variation in target behaviors and contextual variables arises as a function of nonmanipulated or naturally occurring events. Assessment data collected in naturalistic settings have high ecological validity. One of the principal limitations of naturalistic sampling, however, is that the inability to control target behavior or causal factor occurrences makes it difficult to assess infrequent behaviors. For example, physical aggression may be a low-frequency behavior that occurs in only a very specific context (e.g., with a particular student, in a particular location, coinciding with a particular activity). Consequently, a naturalistic assessment approach may not adequately capture the key characteristics of physical aggression for a particular child.

Analog settings are at the other end of the continuum. In analog settings, the behavior therapist varies some aspect of one or more hypothesized contextual factors while measures of target behaviors are collected. A number of single-subject design strategies can be used to evaluate the direction and strength of the relationships between the target behaviors and contextual variables. There are many different types of analog sampling, including: role playing, marital interaction assessments, behavioral approach tests, and functional analytic experiments. Unlike naturalistic sampling, analog procedures are well suited for low-frequency behaviors. Returning to the physical aggression example, the behavior therapist could arrange to have the client be observed under conditions that systematically vary the presence of other persons and activities to determine what contextual factors trigger the response.

In summary, sampling from natural settings allows for measurement of target behaviors and contextual variables in ecologically valid environments. However, infrequent behaviors and an inability to control the occurrence of critical causal variables can introduce significant limitations with this sampling strategy. Assessment in analog settings allows for measurement of infrequent target behaviors because the assessor can introduce specific causal variables that may bring about their occurrence. Because the analog setting is highly controlled, however, one cannot know how well the assessed behavior represents behavior in naturalistic contexts.

## ASSESSMENT TECHNIQUES

Prior surveys of behavior therapists indicate that the most commonly reported behavioral assessment methods are behavioral interviewing, questionnaire administration, behavioral observation, and self-monitoring (Spiegler & Guevremont, 1998). These assessment methods are briefly described next.

### Behavioral Interviewing

Behavioral interviewing differs from other forms of interviewing primarily in terms of structure and focus. Structurally, behavioral interviewing tends to conform with the goals of behavioral assessment identified earlier in the chapter. Specifically, the assessor structures questions that prompt the client to provide information about the topography and function of target behaviors. Topographical questions direct the client to describe the mode and parameters of target behaviors and/or causal factor occurrences. Functional questions direct the client to provide information about how target behaviors may be affected by possible causal factors.

Despite the fact that the interview is a very commonly used method, very little is known about its psychometric properties. For example, Hay, Hay, Angle, and Nelson (1979) and Felton and Nelson (1984) presented behavior therapists with videotaped interviews of a confederate who was acting as a client. Subsequently, they measured the extent to which the therapists agreed on target behavior identification, causal factor identification, and treatment recommendations. Low to moderate levels of agreement were observed. These authors suggested that these results indicated that behavioral interviews do not appear to yield similar judgments about target behavior topography and function. However, these studies were limited because the therapists could evaluate only information that was provided in response to another interviewer's questions. Thus, they could not follow up with clarifying questions or direct the client to provide greater details about various aspects of the target behavior. Further research is clearly needed to improve our understanding of the psychometric properties of behavioral interviews.

### Behavioral Observation

Systematic observations can be conducted by nonparticipant observers and participant observers. Nonparticipant observers are persons who are specifically trained to record target behaviors and contextual variable occurrence using any of the aforementioned sampling methods. Professional observers, research assistants, and volunteers have been used to collect observational data in treatment outcome studies. Nonparticipant observers are often able to collect data on complex behaviors and contextual variables because their essential role is to record behavior.

Participant observers are persons who have alternative responsibilities and typically also share a relationship with the client. In most cases, participant observers are family members, coworkers, friends, or caregivers. Because participant observers are already involved in the client's life, they are able to conduct observations in many settings. The major drawback associated with participant observation, however, is limited focus and inaccuracy. That is, because participant observers have multiple responsibilities, a smaller number of target behaviors and contextual variables can be reliably and accurately observed.

### Self-Monitoring

Self-monitoring is an assessment method that involves having clients systematically sample and record their own behavior. Because clients can access all three modes of responding (cognitive, affective, overt-motor) in multiple naturalistic contexts, self-monitoring has become a popular and sophisticated assessment method, particularly through the use of mobile technology (e.g., Wenze & Miller, 2010). To maximize accuracy, target behaviors must be clearly defined so that clients can consistently record target behavior and contextual variable occurrence.

Self-monitoring has many advantages as an assessment method. As noted, clients can observe all modes of behaviors with self-monitoring. Additionally, hidden behaviors (e.g., alcohol use, drug use, sexual behavior) are more readily measured with self-monitoring. Finally, self-monitoring has a reactive effect that often promotes reductions in undesirable target behavior occurrence and increases in desired target behavior occurrence.

A principal limitation of self-monitoring is reactivity. Specifically, a client may not accurately record target behavior occurrence due to a number of factors, including: expectations for positive or negative consequences, lack of awareness of target behavior occurrence, the cueing function of self-monitoring behavior, and application of a criteria for target behavior occurrence that is different from those of the therapist. Additionally, noncompliance, and the resultant missing data, can be problematic with self-monitoring procedures. This risk for noncompliance can be reduced, however, by involving the client in the development of the self-monitoring system and providing consistent reinforcement for compliance through regular review and discussion of collected data.

### Behavioral Questionnaires

Most questionnaires used in psychological assessment and research are not particularly useful in behavioral assessments. There are two primary reasons for this. First, many of these more typical questionnaires yield summary scores of global constructs, such as "depression," by aggregating responses or ratings of multiple behaviors. Second, most questionnaires do not assess the conditional nature of target behaviors. That is, they do not provide information about how target behaviors may vary as a function of time and context.

In behavioral assessment, questionnaires that have specific qualities are preferred. (See Haynes et al., 2011, for a review of self-report questionnaires often used in behavioral assessment.) As noted earlier, a target behavior will often have multiple response modes and dimensions. Thus, in behavioral assessment, there is preference for questionnaires that measure the specific behaviors using key parameters of measurement. For example, a clinically useful questionnaire of "depression" would provide measures of its different response modes (e.g., affective-cognitive and psychophysiological) along multiple dimensions (e.g., frequency, severity, duration).

A second questionnaire quality that is important in behavioral assessment is the capacity for measuring functional relations. For example, the Questions about Behavioral Function (Paclawskyj, Matson, Rush, Smalls, & Vollmer, 2000) and the Motivation Assessment Scale (Durand & Crimmins, 1992) provide estimates of the extent to which a behavior problem will be observed under specific reinforcement conditions. Similarly, the Inventory of Gambling Situations (Weiss & Petry, 2008) provides a measure of the extent to which problematic gambling will occur under specific antecedent conditions.

A third questionnaire quality important in behavioral assessment is sensitivity to change. Thus, questionnaires that measure the state of a behavior (i.e., current behavior in a specific context) versus those that measure the trait of a behavior (i.e., noncontextual, past behavior) are preferred. Thus, behavioral questionnaires are more likely to have time frames that are shorter and context-specific.

## SUMMARY OF SAMPLING, SETTINGS, AND ASSESSMENT METHODS

Different combinations of sampling and measurement strategies can be used to gather information about the topography target behaviors and contextual variables. Event, duration, and real-time sampling are most applicable to target behaviors that have distinct beginning and endpoints. Conversely, interval sampling and momentary times sampling are more suitable for high-frequency behavior and behaviors with ambiguous beginning and end points. Assessment locations can range from naturalistic settings to controlled analog settings. Analog settings allow for enhanced precision in target behavior measurement and the measurement of infrequently occurring behaviors. Alternatively, naturalistic settings allow for enhanced generalizability and evaluation of behavior in settings that present multiple and complex stimuli.

Behavioral interviewing, self-monitoring, and questionnaire administration can be used to assess all modes of target behaviors and contextual variables. In contrast, systematic observation is restricted to the measurement of observable target behaviors. In addition to differences in capacity for measuring target behavior mode, each assessment method has advantages and disadvantages in terms of convenience, cost, and validity. (For more complete reviews of the psychometric issues related to the various assessment methods, see Haynes & O'Brien, 2000; Haynes et al., 2011.)

The strengths and limitations of behavior sampling strategies, setting sampling strategies, and assessment methods must be considered in the design and implementation of a behavioral assessment. Because unique errors are associated with each method, it is prudent to use a multimethod assessment strategy. Further, it is beneficial to collect target behavior data in multiple contexts.

## METHODS USED TO IDENTIFY CAUSAL FUNCTIONAL RELATIONSHIPS

The aforementioned assessment methods allow the behavior therapist to collect basic information about the topography of target behaviors and contextual factors. After collecting basic information, however, the behavior therapist must attempt to identify and estimate the magnitude of causal relationships among target behaviors and contextual factors. That is, the behavior therapist must identify which contextual variables are exerting important causal effects on target behaviors. Identifying these causal relationships is vitally important for intervention design because most interventions work by modifying causal relationships. Consider, for example, depressed mood. If variation in depressed mood is primarily caused by marital distress, an effective intervention for depressed mood would focus on reducing marital distress. Alternatively, if variation in depressed mood is primarily caused by a reduction in access to reinforcing activities (as is often the case for patients placed in nursing homes), an effective intervention would focus on increasing access to, and involvement in, reinforcing activities.

Reliable covariation between a target behavior and a contextual variable is the most essential requirement for identifying a causal functional relationship. However, covariation alone does not imply causality. To differentiate causal functional relationships from noncausal functional relationships, the behavior therapist must demonstrate (a) temporal order (the changes in the hypothesized causal variable precede effects on the target behavior), (b) a logical basis or research-supported explanation for the relationship, and (c) the exclusion of plausible

**TABLE 22.2  2 × 2 Table Illustrating Essential Conditions for Causal Assertion**

| | Causal Variable Present | Causal Variable Absent |
|---|---|---|
| **Target Behavior Present** | Evidence supporting causation (necessary condition) | Evidence against causation |
| **Target Behavior Absent** | Evidence against causation | Evidence supporting causation (sufficient condition) |

alternative explanations. Table 22.2 illustrates four important conditional relationships that are required to evaluate the plausibility of causation. The primary assessment method used by behavior therapists to initially identify causal relationships is behavioral interviewing. Specifically, the client or significant others typically are asked to provide an explanation as to "why" the target behavior is occurring. For example, the behavior therapist might ask a client, "What do you think causes you be experience more headache pain on weekdays compared to weekends?" The client's response to this question is then treated as an index of the presence of a *possible* causal functional relationship.

Although interviewing is the primary method used to identify causal relationships, it is important to note that interview-based causal assertions have very limited or unknown validity. The essential difficulty is that the interviewer cannot know how well the client's reports of causation mirror causal relationships in criterion (i.e., real-world) settings. Factors that influence the validity of client causal reports include cognitive capacity to recognize and understand casual relationships, social desirability, capacity to adequately express the nature of causal relationships to the interviewer, and a host of commonly occurring judgment errors (e.g., illusory correlation, availability heuristic, anchoring effects, recency effects, and confirmatory biases [De Los Reyes & Kazdin, 2005; Johnston & Murray, 2003]). In addition, the interviewer's own cognitive biases will influence how questions are posed (which leads to variability in client reporting) and what information is encoded and recalled.

To enhance the validity of client reports of causal relationships, the interviewer should carefully and systematically inquire about covariation, temporal order, and the logical basis for the causal assertion. To accomplish this, the interviewer can envision a 2 × 2 table (see Table 22.3) and ask a series of questions that will provide information relevant to each cell. In the table, the interviewer is evaluating whether work attendance is causally related to reports of headaches.

**TABLE 22.3  Prototypical Questions That Pertain to Each Causal Assertion Condition**

|  | Causal Variable Present | Causal Variable Absent |
|---|---|---|
| **Target Behavior Present** | Conditional probability of occurrence questions: General format: "When the causal event occurs, what is the likelihood that the target behavior will occur?" Example: "On a workday, how likely is it that you will have a headache?" | Base rate of occurrence questions: General format: "When the causal event does not occur, what is the likelihood that the target behavior will occur?" Example: "On a weekend, how likely is it that you will have a headache?" |
| **Target Behavior Absent** | Conditional probability of nonoccurrence: General format: "When the causal event occurs, what is the likelihood that the target behavior will not occur?" Example: "On a workday, how likely is it that you will feel fine and not have a headache?" | Base rate of nonoccurrence: General format: "When the causal event does not occur, what is the likelihood that the target behavior will not occur?" Example: "On a weekend, how likely is it that you will feel fine and have no headache?" |

Behavioral data collected with functional analytic experiments can, and should, be used to evaluate the validity of causal relationships identified during behavioral interviews. Functional analytic experiments involve systematically modifying some aspect of the context or interview process and observing consequent changes in the target behavior. This hypothesis-testing approach has been extensively developed and validated by Kohlenberg (e.g., Kohlenberg et al., 2004; Tsai et al., 2008) and Iwata and colleagues (e.g., Iwata & Dozier, 2008; Iwata et al., 2000). For example, we recently interviewed a young girl with significant fears of "bad weather" and tornadoes. The girl was interviewed with the window shades drawn and then opened using an ABAB design (A = shades drawn, B = shades open). It was observed that the frequency and intensity of checking (glancing out the window) and fear ratings covaried with the two conditions. Specifically, higher rates of checking and higher reports of fear were observed when the window shades were open. Upon further investigation, it was observed that the girl principally evaluated the extent to which the tree limbs swayed as an index of likelihood that bad weather or a tornado was imminent. It thus became apparent that school refusal and severe anxiety were more closely associated with tree limb movement than weather reports or the presence of dark clouds. Further, an intervention targeting graded exposure to wind was designed and implemented.

Functional analytic experiments such as this have gained renewed interest in recent years because they are particularly well suited for establishing causal relationships between target behaviors and causal variables. They have also been extensively evaluated as a tool for generating interventions. Finally, they can be readily incorporated into commonly used assessment procedures (e.g., interviews) and contexts (inpatient, outpatient clinics).

When a functional analytic experiment is not feasible, the behavior therapist can evaluate the plausibility of causal inferences gathered during a behavioral interview using self-monitoring data or observational data. In both circumstances, the behavior therapist would evaluate the extent to which variation in the target behaviors is systematically related to variation in one or more potential causal variables. Conditional probability analysis is an easily applied statistical technique that can evaluate this type of covariation. The conditional probability analysis assumes that causal relationships are evident in elevated conditional probabilities. An *elevated conditional probability* simply means that the likelihood of observing a change in a target behavior, given that some hypothesized contextual event has occurred (i.e., its conditional probability), is greater than the probability of observing a change in a target behavior without considering the occurrence of the hypothesized contextual factor (i.e., its base rate or unconditional probability).

To illustrate, let A = pain complaints from a patient (yes/no), B = presence of absence of spouse (coded as present/absent), and P = probability. A relationship between pain complaints and spouse presence would be inferred if the probability of pain complaints given spouse presence ($P[A|B]$), is greater than the base rate probability pain complaints ($P[A]$). Conditional probability analyses have three important strengths.

1. A small number of data points can yield reliable estimates of association (Schlundt, 1985).
2. The statistical concepts underlying the methodology are easily understood and can be shared with the client in a therapy session using simple tables.
3. Many statistical programs can be used to conduct conditional probability analyses; if none is available, the computations can be easily done by hand using Bayes theorem or chi-square analyses.

Time series analyses, time-lagged correlation, and hierarchical linear modeling can also be used to evaluate relationships between target behaviors and contextual variables. Typically, these approaches require that the client collect data on both sets of variables across fairly lengthy time intervals. The magnitude of causal relationships then can be estimated by calculating a measure of association between controlling variables and target behaviors after partitioning out the variance accounted for by autocorrelation (Wei, 2006).

## INTEGRATING ASSESSMENT USING CAUSAL CASE MODELING

Often the information yielded by interviewing, observation, self-monitoring, and experimentation is complex and difficult to disentangle and communicate with client and significant others. Causal modeling is one strategy that can be used to aid in the explanation of a case conceptualization. Functional analytic case models summarize the functional analysis using vector diagrams. Variables included in the clinical case model include target behaviors, contextual variables, and the relationships among them (Haynes & O'Brien, 2000; Haynes et al., 2011). The construction of a functional analytic case model involves seven key steps.

1. Identify the target behaviors.
2. Specify the response modes (cognitive-verbal, affective-physiological, overt-motor) and dimensions (frequency, intensity, duration, etc.) of the target behaviors.
3. Estimate the relative importance (based on client report, degree of severity, or other indicator) of each target behavior. (Typical importance ratings are low, medium, and high.)
4. Estimate or calculate the strength of relationships (low, medium, high) among target behaviors.
5. Identify the contextual causal variables associated with each target behavior.
6. Estimate or calculate the direction and strength of relationships between causal variables and target behaviors.
7. Construct causal model.

There are several potential advantages for using clinical case modeling. One is that it can aid in the clinical decision-making process by encouraging the clinician to attend to the complexity of the case and whether sufficient information has been collected and/or analyzed to support the inferences about causality. It also promotes greater integration of assessment data and treatment design. Finally, it can provide a parsimonious and more accessible explanation of the many factors influencing target behaviors.

## CASE ILLUSTRATION: USE OF FUNCTIONAL ANALYTIC CASE MODELING WITH SOMATOFORM DISORDER

This case involved a 24-year-old man who was referred for treatment of a "chronic dizziness," extremely limited activity (he had essentially been living on a couch for over 6 months in his parents' home), fatigue, and a host of other vague and difficult-to-measure symptoms. The young man had been evaluated by dozens of physicians, all of whom were unable to generate a "medical diagnosis," according to the young man and his mother.

During the first interviews, the young man presented as an anxious, soft-spoken, and friendly individual. He provided very detailed and colorful descriptions of his various symptoms and had been making daily recordings of his difficulties on a tape recorder and video camera. Despite having excellent capacity for providing descriptions of his symptoms and being quite capable of ambulating without difficulty during the interview, the young man reported he was continuously "foggy" (unable to concentrate) and highly unsteady. Subsequent interviews with the young man and his parents indicated that there was significant family discord related to his condition. Additionally, the young man was receiving high levels of supportive "nursing-like" behavior from his mother. Finally, attempts at encouraging the young man to obtain employment or more independent living typically produced an exacerbation of symptoms. Importantly, the young man was not malingering or engaging in a conscious attempt to manufacture symptoms.

After identifying key target behaviors and contextual factors during the interviews, a self-monitoring form was developed for the client. On the self-monitoring form, he rated dizziness, "fogginess," stomach upset, and anxiety levels 4 times per day. He also rated activity levels (initially time off the couch and later mileage with a pedometer). In addition to self-monitoring, the client was evaluated in our psychophysiology laboratory, where we measured cardiovascular functions and self-ratings of symptoms during various types of activities (sitting, standing, walking, etc.).

A functional analytic causal model of this client's difficulties is presented in Figure 22.2. In this figure, it is hypothesized that upon exposure to standing, movement, or activity, the client generated catastrophic thoughts

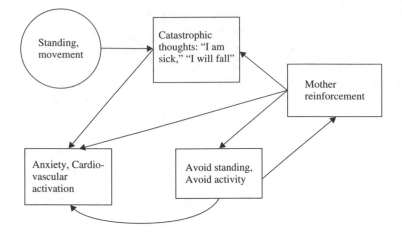

**Figure 22.2** Functional analytic case model of somatoform disorder

about being ill and possible falling and becoming injured. In turn, these thoughts provoked fear and an accompanying *and normal* state of cardiovascular activation. The client interpreted the cardiovascular activation as an indicator of a harmful physiological process. Thus, he would discontinue the activity and return to lying on the couch. Upon lying down, the client would experience relief from fear and cardiovascular activation (negative reinforcement). Additionally, his mother would express her concern about his health and provide him with various special meals, conversation, and support so that he would not feel "upset" and become fearful again.

A behavioral intervention was readily designed from this model. First, the client was provided with education that his cardiovascular activation was normal. Second, and in line with acceptance and commitment therapy, the client was encouraged to note that he had many unhelpful thoughts that were essentially "hijacking" his life—taking control of his daily activities and preventing him from engaging in age-appropriate developmental tasks (e.g., developing romantic relationships, separating from parents, etc.). He was then provided with mindfulness training in an effort to help him learn to observe these thoughts in a more objective and dispassionate manner. It is important to note that the goal here was not to try to suppress the thoughts but simply to learn to note them while he simultaneously began engaging in the pursuit of important life tasks and goals. Third, the client was encouraged to begin increasing activity levels without engaging in avoidance. This was essentially exposure therapy. Finally, the client's mother was encouraged to stop providing social reinforcement for "sick role behaviors" and instead provide reinforcement for adaptive age-appropriate independent living behaviors.

## SUMMARY

Behavioral assessment and the accompanying functional analysis are based on several conceptual foundations. Specifically, a behavior therapist who aims to conduct behavioral assessments must be familiar with the basic learning theory and also become conversant with evolving theories, such as functional contextualism. Second, the behavior therapist must have solid knowledge of empiricism, the hypothetico-deductive method, the conditional nature of behavior disorders, reciprocal causation, and multideterminism. Third, a behavior therapist must be skilled in sampling and assessment techniques that will yield information about the topography of target behaviors, contextual variables, and the relationships among them. Finally, it is important to be able to integrate assessment information using causal modeling and statistical procedures that can test the validity of key causal assumptions about client behavior.

## REFERENCES

Acklin, M. W., McDowell, C. J., Verschell, M. S., & Chan, D. (2000). Interobserver agreement, interobserver reliability, and the Rorschach comprehensive system. *Journal of Personality Assessment, 74,* 15–47.

Beck, A. T., Rush, A. J., Shaw, B. F., & Emery, G. (1979). *Cognitive therapy of depression.* New York, NY: Guilford Press.

Butler, A. C., Chapman, J. E., Forman, E. M., & Beck, A. T. (2006). The empirical status of cognitive-behavioral therapy: A review of meta-analyses. *Clinical Psychology Review, 26,* 17–31.

De Los Reyes, A., & Kazdin, A. E. (2005). Informant discrepancies in the assessment of childhood psychopathology: A critical review, theoretical framework, and recommendations for further study. *Psychological Bulletin, 131,* 483–509.

Durand, V. M., & Crimmins, D. B. (1992). *The Motivation Assessment Scale (MAS) administration guide*. Topeka, KS: Monaco and Associates.

Exner, J. E. (1986). *The Rorschach: A comprehensive system, Volume 1*. New York, NY: Wiley.

Exner, J. E. (1991). *The Rorschach: A comprehensive system, Volume 2*. New York, NY: Wiley.

Exner, J. E., & Sendin, C. (1997). Some issues in Rorschach research. *European Journal of Psychological Assessment, 13*, 155–163.

Felton, J. L., & Nelson, R. O. (1984). Inter-assessor agreement on hypothesized controlling variables and treatment proposals. *Behavioral Assessment, 6*, 199–208.

Frank, G. (1993). On the validity of hypotheses derived from the Rorschach: The relationship between color and affect. *Psychological Reports, 73*, 12–14.

Garb, H. (1999). Call for a moratorium on the use of the Rorschach inkblot test in clinical and forensic settings. *Assessment, 6*, 313–317.

Garb, H. N., Wood, J. M., Lilienfeld, S. O., & Nezworski, M. T. (2005). Roots of the Rorschach controversy. *Clinical Psychology Review, 225*, 97–118.

Hay, W. M., Hay, L. R., Angle, H. V., & Nelson, R. O. (1979). The reliability of problem identification in the behavioral interview. *Behavioral Assessment, 1*, 107–118.

Hayes, S. C. (2004). Acceptance and commitment therapy, relational frame theory, and the third wave of behavioral and cognitive therapies. *Behavior Therapy, 35*, 639–665.

Hayes, S. C., Strosahl, K., & Wilson, K. G. (1999). *Acceptance and commitment therapy: An experiential approach to behavior change*. New York, NY: Guilford Press

Haynes, S. N., & O'Brien, W. H. (2000). *Principles and practice of behavioral assessment*. New York, NY: Plenum Press.

Haynes, S. N., O'Brien, W. H., & Kaholokula, K. (2011). *Behavioral assessment and case formulation*. Hoboken, NJ: Wiley.

Hull, C. L. (1952). *A behavior system: An introduction to behavior theory concerning the individual organism*. New Haven, CT: Yale University Press.

Iwata, B. & Dozier, C. (2008). Clinical application of functional analysis methodology. *Behavior Analysis in Practice, 1*, 3–9.

Iwata, B. A., Smith, R. G., & Michael, J. (2000). Current research on the influence of establishing operations on behavior in applied settings. *Journal of Applied Behavior Analysis, 33*, 411–418.

Jacobson, N., Martell, C. R., Dimidjian, S. (2001). Behavioral activation for depression: Returning to contextual roots. *Clinical Psychology: Science and Practice, 8*, 255–270.

Johnston, C., & Murray, C. (2003). Incremental validity in the psychological assessment of children and adolescents. *Psychological Assessment, 15*, 496–507.

Kohlenberg, R. J., Kanter, J. W., Bolling, M., Wexner, R., Parker, C., & Tsai, M. (2004). Functional analytic psychotherapy, cognitive therapy, and acceptance. In S. C. Hayes, V. M. Follette, & M. M. Linehan (Eds.), *Mindfulness and acceptance: Expanding the cognitive-behavioral tradition* (pp. 96–119). New York, NY: Guilford Press.

Lillienfeld, S. O., Wood, J. M., & Garb, H. N. (2000). The scientific status of projective techniques. *Psychological Science in the Public Interest, 1*, 27–66.

Linehan, M. M. (1993). *Skills training manual for treating borderline personality disorder*. New York, NY: Guilford Press.

Musewicz, J., Marczyk, G., Knauss, L., & York, D. (2009). Current assessment practice, personality measurement, and Rorschach usage by psychologists. *Journal of Personality Assessment, 91*, 453–461.

O'Brien, W. H., & Haynes, S. N. (1995). A functional analytic approach to the assessment and treatment of a child with frequent migraine headaches. *In Session: Psychotherapy in Practice, 1*, 65–80.

Paclawskyj, T. R., Matson, J. L., Rush, K. S., Smalls, Y., & Vollmer, T. R. (2000). Questions about behavioral function (QABF): A behavioral checklist for functional assessment of aberrant behavior. *Research in Developmental Disabilities, 21*, 223–229.

Schlundt, D. G. (1985). An observational methodology for functional analysis. *Bulletin for the Society of Psychologists in Addictive Behaviors, 4*, 234–249.

Segal, Z. V., Williams, J. M., & Teasdale, J. D. (2002). *Mindfulness-based cognitive therapy for depression: A new approach to preventing relapse*. New York, NY: Guilford Press.

Skinner, B. F. (1938). *The behavior of organisms: An experimental analysis*. Oxford, UK: Appleton-Century.

Skinner, B. F. (1974). *About behaviorism*. Oxford, UK: Knopf.

Spiegler, M. D., & Guevremont, D. C. (1998). *Contemporary behavior therapy*. Boston, MA: Brookes/Cole.

Tsai, M., Kohlenberg, R., Kanter, J. W., Kohlenberg, B., Follette, W. C., & Callighan, G. M. (2008). *A guide to functional analytic psychotherapy: Awareness, courage, love, and behaviorism*. New York, NY: Springer.

Watson, J. B. (1919). *Psychology from the standpoint of a behaviorist*. Philadelphia, PA: Lippincott.

Wei, W. S. (2006). *Time series analysis: Univariate and multivariate methods* (2nd ed.). Boston, MA: Pearson.

Weiss, L. M., & Petry, N. M. (2008). Psychometric properties of the inventory of gambling situations with a focus on gender and age differences. *Journal of Nervous and Mental Disorders, 196*, 321–8.

Wenze, S. J., & Miller I. W. (2010). Use of ecological momentary assessment in mood disorders research. *Clinical Psychology Review, 30*, 794–804.

Wolpe, J. (1952a). Experimental neurosis as learned behavior. *British Journal of Psychology, 43*, 243–268.

Wolpe, J. (1952b). The formation of negative habits: A neurophysiological view. *Psychological Review, 59*, 290–299.

Wolpe, J. (1958). *Psychotherapy by reciprocal inhibition*. Oxford, UK: Stanford University Press.

Wolpe, J. (1963). Psychotherapy: The nonscientific heritage and the new science. *Behavior Research and Therapy, 1*, 23–28.

Wolpe, J. (1997). From psychoanalytic to behavioral methods in anxiety disorders: A continuing evolution. In J. K. Zeig (Ed.), *The evolution of psychotherapy: The third conference* (pp. 107–116). Philadelphia, PA: Brunner/Mazel.

Wolpe, J., & Lazarus, A. A. (1966). *Behavior therapy techniques: A guide to the treatment of neuroses*. Elmsford, NY: Pergamon Press.

Wolpe, J., Salter, A., & Reyna, L. J. (1964). *The conditioning therapies*. Oxford, UK: Holt, Rinehart and Winston.

Wood, J. M., Lilienfeld, S. O., Nezworski, M. T., Garb, H. N., Allen, K. H., & Wildermuch, J. L. (2010). Validity of Rorschach inkblot scores for discriminating psychopaths from nonpsychopaths in forensic populations: A meta-analysis. *Psychological Assessment, 22*, 336–349.

CHAPTER 23

# Performance Assessment of Personality and Psychopathology

DONALD J. VIGLIONE AND BRIDGET RIVERA

Performance-based personality measures require an individual to perform a task that is designed to elicit information about the personality in action. Ideally, this performance demonstrates one's personality characteristics, problems in living, or processing and coping style, just as cognitive performance tests reveal one's intelligence or neuropsychological deficits. The methodologies are highly diverse. They might, for example, involve completing a sentence, narrating a vignette while listening to music, characterizing an emotion associated with a distant memory, describing an important person or event, or finishing a phrase to construct a sentence. The task stimulus itself is typically incomplete, contradictory, ambiguous, evocative, or suggestive. With little external structure, direction, or guidance provided, the respondent must rely on him- or herself in formulating a solution so as to maximize the effects of his or her interpretation, processing, and personality. These tests bring the individual aspects of relevant behavior, associations, perceptions, organizations, emotions, and interpersonal components into the consulting room to be observed, documented, and measured. Rather than attributing one trait, behavior, or characteristic to one's self, as with a self-report test, the respondent actually demonstrates the target behavior by doing something while the administrator observes and distills the behavior's relevant dimensions. Thus, the interpretive dimension is implicit in the respondent's behavior, whether it is a story, sentence completion, early memory, description, or other type of production. By

examining complex behaviors, inferring covert mental processes, aggregating these occurrences to attain reliable inferences, performance assessment techniques yield rich information about an individual. Given this freedom, it is understandable that these tests are thought to access what makes an individual unique.

This chapter answers some basic questions about these highly diverse tests: What are performance tests of personality? What are their distinctive characteristics? How should we understand and interpret them? What do they add to assessment? The chapter addresses these questions by providing the reader with a meaningful, comprehensive, and historically informative conceptual framework for understanding the tests. This framework emphasizes a response process that includes both self-expressive and organizational components—that is, what the respondent says and how he or she structures the response. The chapter addresses implication of the framework for performance tests of personality and contributions of this type of testing to assessment at large. In the course of this discussion, we hope to correct some common misperceptions about performance tests and to establish a more informed approach to using them.

It is clear that performance tests of personality have value in the assessment process. This chapter provides a broad overview of their value, incorporating performance tests and methods within a single domain. The need to encompass all these diverse instruments necessitates our inclusive, global approach and precludes detailed, test-specific characterizations. In general, we have reserved our comments about specific tests to the Rorschach, Thematic Apperception Test (TAT), figure drawings, sentence completion tests, and the early memory tests, but we also discuss the Music Apperception Test, a recently developed instrument (van den Daele, 2007). An evaluation of the specific strengths and weaknesses of these or any other individual performance measure awaits others' initiatives.

Traditionally, these tests have been referred to as projective tests and are probably best known by that name. Accordingly, we begin our review with an examination of the problems associated with the term *projective* and why it has been recently replaced with the term *performance* or *performance based*. This recent change in terminology complicates our task.

## "PROJECTIVE" MODEL PROBLEMS

Anastasi and Urbina (1996) characterized what was previously known as a projective test as a "relatively unstructured task, that is, a task that permits almost an unlimited variety of possible responses. To allow free play to the individual's fantasy, only brief, general instructions are provided" (p. 411). This global, descriptive definition identifies some important elements of projective or performance tests. Ironically, however, this definition and others like it impede our understanding of these instruments, when such tests are casually juxtaposed against so-called objective tests. Many American psychologists automatically categorize tests according to a projective–objective dichotomy. In thinking and communicating about assessment instruments, characteristics of each class of instrument are treated as mutually exclusive or as polar opposites. For example, because "objective" tests are thought of as unbiased measures, "performance tests" in the guise of "projective" tests, by default, are assumed to be subjective. As another example, because "objective" tests are seen as having standardized administration and scoring, so-called "projective" tests are assumed to lack empirical rigor. There are a number of reasons why this projective–objective dichotomy leads to an oversimplified and biased understanding of performance tests of personality.

### Why the Projective–Objective Dichotomy Is Misleading

The projective–objective dichotomy is misleading for a number of reasons. First, it often results in misleading reductionism. Instruments under the rubric of "projective" are assumed to be uniform in content, purpose, and methodology. For example, all these instruments are often reduced and treated as equivalent to a classic exemplar, such as the Rorschach. Reducing performance instruments and tasks to the Rorschach ignores their incredible diversity. Not only do these tests target many different domains of functioning, but they also employ a great variety of methodologies for the purposes of inducing very different response processes. For example, early instruments included an indistinct speech interpretation, word association, cloud perception, hand positioning perception, comic strip completion, and musical reverie tests (Anastasi & Urbina, 1996; Campbell, 1957; Frank, 1939/1962; Murray, 1938). Moreover, this great variety of task suggests that processes accessible to performance tests are ubiquitous and are involved in many real-life behaviors.

Second, this projective–objective dichotomy implies that there are characteristics unique to each class of test, but these supposed hallmarks are misleading. For example, test elements identified as "projective," such as the flexible response format and ambiguous or incomplete stimuli, are employed by tests generally considered to be models of objectivity and quantification. Murstein (1963) noted from the flexible response format of some cognitive ability tests that "we learn a great deal about the person who, on the vocabulary subtests of the Wechsler Adult Scale of Intelligence, when asked to give the meaning of the word 'sentence,' proceeds to rattle off three or four definitions and is beginning to divulge the differences between the connotations and denotations of the word when he is stopped" (p. 3). Kaplan's (1991) approach to neuropsychological testing focused on process, similar to the response process approach in performance assessment of personality testing. Similarly, Meehl pointed out the projective element of stimulus ambiguity in self-report personality tests. In his Dynamics of Structured Personality Testing (1945/1956), Meehl noted that many Minnesota Multiphasic Personality Inventory (MMPI) items, such as "Once in a while I laugh at a dirty joke," contain ambiguities. At the most basic level, it is not clear whether "once in a while" refers to once a day, once a week, or once in a month.

Third, the stereotypic juxtaposition of "objective" and "projective" testing lends a pejorative connotation to these tests that suggests they lack objectivity. This is misleading, and it fortifies historical bias against performance tests. As an example of such bias, Masling (1997) questioned whether the data supporting of the Rorschach would change the mind of the critics, given the persistent history of bias. Subsequent evidence about the reliability of the Rorschach, for example (e.g., Gacono & Evans, 2008; Hiller, Rosenthal, Bornstein, Berry, & Brunell-Neuleib, 1999; Meyer & Archer, 2001; Viglione & Hilsenroth, 2001) has been largely ignored. One wonders whether emerging neuropsychological support for Rorschach interpretations will also be ignored (Asari, Konishi, Jimura, Chikazoe, Nakamura, & Miyashita, 2008, 2010; Giromini, Porcelli, Viglione, Parolin, & Pineda, 2010; Minassian, Granholm, Verney, & Perry, 2004; Pineda, Giromini, Porcelli, Parolin & Viglione, 2011).

As Masling (1997) concluded his paper on "projective" testing: "Psychology is fortunate to have available two such different means of assessing human behavior, each placing different emphasis on the importance of motive, rational thinking, fantasy, self-reflection, and defense. A wise discipline would value and embrace such differences rather than find fault and lack of respectability in either one" (p. 266).

Many of these performance tests are quantified and standardized in terms of administration, and more should be. If we take the example of cognitive performance tests, the style or process of the response can be systematically observed, quantified, and standardized. This qualitative-to-quantitative test development strategy is exactly the same procedure used in sophisticated quantification of performance tests. The Rorschach Comprehensive System (Exner, 2003), the Rorschach Performance Assessment System (Meyer, Viglione, Mihura, Erard, & Erdberg, 2011), the Washington Sentence Completion Test (Loevinger & Wessler, 1970), approaches to the TAT, and other apperception tests (Jenkins, 2008) use a systematic and standardized system. Similarly, a recently introduced test with promise, the Music Apperception Test, also uses a qualitative to quantitative test development strategy (van den Daele, 2007). Such approaches can result in psychometrically sound quantification and standardization. For example, Joy, Fein, Kaplan, and Freedman (2001) utilized this procedure to standardize observation of the Block Design subtest from the Wechsler scales. Other research summaries and observations (e.g., Rivera & Viglione, 2010; Stricker & Gold, 1999; Weiner, 2001, 2003) indicate that behavioral observation during performance tasks can be used to elaborate previously developed hypotheses and to synthesize inferences about the respondent. These same authors also demonstrated such tactics in case examples.

Of course, quantification and reducing examiner bias—that is, variability introduced by examiners—are important goals in improving psychological assessment. Indeed, one of the major goals of the new Rorschach

Performance Assessment System is to reduce examiner variability (Meyer et al., 2011). Nonetheless, reducing examiner variability is not the only goal of assessment and is not equivalent to validity and utility. Indeed, further research should address the extent to which the examiner's input is induced by the subject, as would be the case with reciprocal determinism, which thereby increases the ecological validity of performance tests (Bandura, 1978; Fischer, 1994; Viglione & Perry, 1991). Furthermore, one may speculate that overemphasis on eliminating examiner variability so as to achieve objectivity can increase test reliability at the expense of validity when it limits salient observations by the examiner.

Finally, performance-based tests and objective tests resemble each other in that they share the same goal: the description of personality, psychopathology, and problems in living. However, the dichotomy highlights the differences in method and overlooks fundamental differences in their approach to understanding personality. Furthermore, when data obtained from both types of tests are integrated, we gain a deeper understanding of the individual. Rather than competing with each other, these tests can complement one other, both striving to meet the goal of describing and understanding our client. Later sections of this chapter highlight some of these fundamental differences. As we show, the differences may be more in the philosophy of the psychologist using the tests rather than in the tests themselves.

In an effort to advance the science of assessment, Meyer and Kurtz (2006) suggested that we retire the terms *objective* and *projective*. They suggested that researchers, clinicians, and teachers find a substitute term; if one is not suitable, people should refer to the test by its specific name, such as "Early Memories." Experts and users have disagreed on a suitable substitute term, with possibilities including *performance tasks, behavioral tasks, constructive methods,* and *free response methods*. As stated, we prefer the term *performance* or *performance-based tests of personality.*

## Conclusion

We have provided just a few examples of the distortions involved in the unexamined use of both the projective–objective dichotomy and the term *projective.* This familiar dichotomy damages the reputation of so-called projective tests and misleads students. Many graduate programs use the terms *projective* and *objective* in course titles, further complicating this issue (Meyer & Kurtz, 2006). A more informed approach to this type of testing is needed. We juxtapose performance tests of personality against self-report tests in the remainder of this chapter.

## PROBLEMS WITH COMMON METAPHORS AND MODELS

The common metaphors and models used to describe the performance response process can also be grossly misleading. The two well-known metaphors of the response process are the blank screen and the X-ray machine. Each metaphor contains an implicit theoretical model of assessment that shapes our understanding of the performance test response process. In this section we critically examine both metaphors.

### Blank Screen Metaphor

The most common and stereotypic metaphor is that of the "blank screen," an image that is particularly associated with the projective processes. (Figure 23.1 presents a schematic for this and other models.) In this metaphor, the test stimulus is portrayed as a blank screen or canvas upon which the respondent projects his or her inner world

(Anastasi & Urbina, 1996). In the reductionistic application of this metaphor, response content is treated as a direct representation of the respondent's inner life. For example, when a respondent projects his or her aggression onto the stimuli, the response content contains aggressive themes as a result. The examiner then equates these aggressive themes with the personality trait of aggression. When taken to the extreme, the blank screen metaphor has had two consequences on our approach to performance assessment of personality: An overemphasis on response content and an underappreciation for the role of the test stimulus and the examination context. By "examination context" we mean the various situational factors as experienced by the respondent. These include the demands on the respondent given the circumstances of the evaluation, the implicit and explicit consequences of the examination, and the interaction between the examiner and respondent.

The blank screen metaphor suggests that the only necessary components to performance test stimuli are ambiguity and a lack of structure. These components are thought to facilitate response content, that is, the free expression of the respondent's internal world. The more ambiguous and unstructured the stimulus, the more it was presumed that personality would be directly expressed in the response. Historically, this simplistic view has led to

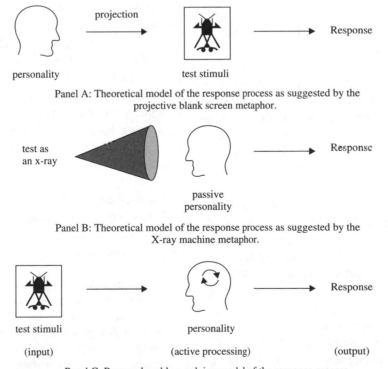

Panel A: Theoretical model of the response process as suggested by the projective blank screen metaphor.

Panel B: Theoretical model of the response process as suggested by the X-ray machine metaphor.

Panel C: Proposed problem-solving model of the response process.

**Figure 23.1**   Metaphors and models of the response process

an emphasis on response content and to the interpretive viewpoint that the test was equivalent to or symbolized an internal response or reality (Murstein, 1963). Aspects of test responses are often seen as symbolic of and equivalent to personality and constituted the basis for grand interpretations.

However, increasing the "blankness" of the screen by increasing the ambiguity of the stimuli does not necessarily produce more useful or valid information. Research into the relationship between amount of ambiguity and structure of pictorial stimuli and test validity has not led to consistent findings (Murstein, 1961, 1963, 1965). For example, the blank TAT card, Card 16, produces relatively conventional responses that are less revealing of the individual than are the rest of the cards, all of which include either a picture of a person, group of people, or some other scene. Moreover, eliminating the more recognizable and salient visual aspects of the Rorschach stimuli—what Exner (1996) called the critical bits—does not lead to more productivity. In fact, the available research supports the view that it is the suggestive aspects of the stimulus rather than the lack thereof that are important. Empirical data clearly demonstrate that the physical stimulus is crucial (Exner, 1974, 1980; Murstein, 1961; Peterson & Schilling, 1983).

What we know about Herman Rorschach's work in developing his test attests to the fact that it is not ambiguity or lack of structure that contributes to the test's usefulness. It appears that each stimulus plate was designed to contain visually recognizable forms, or critical bits, along with some arbitrary and contradictory components (Exner, 1996). Rorschach may have included the arbitrary contours to interfere with the processing of these suggestive, recognizable forms. The plates were carefully chosen, painted, and repainted (i.e., is refined and shaped) so that many versions existed before Rorschach finalized the designs. If you have ever made inkblots, you know that most products look just like inkblots and are not suggestive of other forms or objects. Thus, it seems that the stimulus plates were intended to be evocative to respondents but unclear enough to engage their problem-solving skills. This inconsistency between the recognizable or suggestive components of the inkblot designs and the more arbitrary forms is critical because it constitutes a problem to be solved. In this sense, performance test stimuli have a clear purpose: to present the respondent with a problem-solving task. For example, a major part of the Rorschach task is to reconcile visual and logical inconsistencies among blot details and between the blot and the objects seen. It is the idiosyncratic ways in which respondents solve the problem, rather than merely the content they project onto a blank screen, that reveals useful and valid information. Thus, understanding performance test stimuli as blank screens rather than as problems to be solved is a fundamental misconception that can lead to inaccurate interpretations of test behaviors.

## X-Ray Metaphor

Another common metaphor is that of an X-ray machine. In this metaphor, the test acts as "an X-ray of the mind," which allows the interpreter to observe directly the contents of the respondent's mind. (See Figure 23.1.) Both Frank (1939/1962) and Murray (1938) mentioned this image in their seminal work; thus, it has historical precedents. However, like the blank screen metaphor, this metaphor leads to a focus on response content and the way in which the content directly represents personality. More important, the X-ray metaphor diminishes the role of the respondent in the response process.

Examining Frank's (1939/1962) original work on projective tests and the projective hypothesis allows one to achieve a more adequate understanding of his purpose for using the X-ray metaphor. When Frank first discussed it, he compared learning about personality to the then-current technologies in medical and physical science that allowed one to study internal anatomical structures through noninvasive techniques. However, Frank included a critical distinction between performance tests and medical tools, a distinction that is typically excluded from today's common understanding of the X-ray metaphor. Frank noted that, unlike the target of an X-ray machine, personality is not a passive recipient of attention. In responding to test stimuli, personality does not simply cast a shadow of its nature onto a plate. Rather, Frank contended that *personality is an active organizing process.*

Despite being written over 70 years ago, Frank's ideas reveal a complex and informed perspective on personality, one that is especially relevant to understanding the nature of performance testing:

> Personality is approachable as a process or operation of an individual who organizes experience and reacts affectively to situations. This process is dynamic in the sense that the individual personality imposes upon the common public world of events (what we call nature), his meanings and significances, his organization and patterns, and he invests the situations thus structured with an affective meaning to which he responds idiomatically. (1939/1962, p. 34)

Frank went on to describe personality as a "dynamic organizing process." He contrasted this subjective, synthetic, dynamic process of personality to the objective, external, concrete reality of the world, including the respondent's culture's shared conventional experiences. In Frank's view, the world of culture also influences the personality and its understanding of the external world but cannot account for personality processes and behavior.

Later in this paper, Frank described what we are calling performance techniques as essentially inducing the activity and processing of the personality:

> In similar fashion we may approach the personality and induce the individual to reveal his way of organizing experience by giving him a field (objects, materials, experiences) with relatively little structure and cultural patterning so that the personality can project upon that plastic field his way of seeing life, his meanings, significances, patterns, and especially his feelings. Thus, we elicit a projection of the individual personality's private world because he has to organize the field, interpret the material and react affectively to it. More specifically, a projection method for study of personality involves the presentation of a stimulus-situation designed or chosen because it will mean to the subject, not what the experimenter has arbitrarily decided it should mean (as in most psychological experiments using standardized stimuli in order to be "objective"), but rather whatever it must mean to the personality who gives it, or imposes it, his private, idiosyncratic meaning and organization. (1939/1962, p. 43)

These quotations make it clear that the respondent's organizational style and affect are critical to the performance testing process and that the process involves more than simply adding content to a stimulus field. And unlike self-report tests, performance test stimuli and tasks give respondents an opportunity to express their organizational style and affect. Thus, these tests allow the examiner to observe personality in action with cognitive, affective, interpersonal, and meaning-making activities.

### Need for an Informed Conceptual Framework

This critical review of traditional metaphors and models for performance testing points to their serious shortcomings and oversimplifications. In contrast to a projective testing blank screen metaphor, the stimuli of these tests are more like problem-solving tasks. In contrast to a passive personality that unknowingly projects itself onto a blank screen or that is examined with X-ray vision, personality in performance testing is seen as much more of an active, organizing, and selective process. Perhaps the

most accurate portrayal of projection is that *the personality does not project light onto the blank screen of the test but, rather, the test projects itself through the active organizing process of the personality to the response. In other words, the individual's personal characteristics are observable in the refracted light—that is, the manner in which the person responds to the test.* In sum, there is a need for a broader and more informed conceptual framework for understanding these tests. As noted, earlier the more appropriate name for these tests is *performance* or *performance-based personality assessment.*

From comparisons between the overt stimuli and response, the interpreter infers the covert personality process. This input-processing-output sequence is the essence of our model for performance testing and is presented in the next section. Such a framework goes beyond projection and response content by embracing a problem-solving perspective.

## PROBLEM-SOLVING MODEL

The behavioral response process utilizes the input-processing-output sequence as a problem-solving model when the "problem" of the performance test is being solved.

### Introduction

A problem-solving model leads us to approach personality as a processor of information. Rather than interpreting a response as a symbolic representation of personality, a response is interpreted in the context of the stimulus situation and is used to build a model of the respondent's processing and problem-solving style. Rather than using a static conceptualization of "personality," this problem-solving approach incorporates a model of personality as a problem-solving processor of life's ongoing challenges.

The performance test response can be seen as the development and formulation of a solution to a problem, the structure and content of which reveals something about the individual. All performance tests involve a task, which we can understand as a problem to be solved. For example, the TAT demands the creation of a story that reconciles the suggestive elements of the pictures with ambiguous and missing cues. As another example, the Early Memory Test involves constructing, typically without a complete sense of certainty, a memory dating back to the beginning of one's life. The self-expressive and adequacy of these solutions can be the object of the interpretive system (e.g., for the TAT, see Ronan, Colavito, & Hammontree, 1993).

The history of performance assessment and misuses in current practice reveal that we have drifted from the focus on input-processing-output as first described by Frank. This drift has led to two gross oversimplifications in the name of projective testing: (1) Test responses are inappropriately equated with personality, and (2) verbal and motor behaviors within test responses are thought to symbolize large patterns of life behavior. In contrast, an informed response process approach entails inferring a model of an individual's personality and behavior from how the individual performs during the test as demonstrated in the task solutions based on a thorough understanding of the stimuli, task demands, and processing involved. The future of performance assessment depends on advancing this response process and problem-solving approach, in addition to specifying the evidence base of the individual instruments.

The Standards for Educational and Psychological Testing (American Educational Research Association, American Psychological Association, & National Council on Measurement in Education, 1999) incorporate this interest in the response process. According to the Standards, evidence based on examination of the response process, including eye movements and self-descriptions of the respondent's experience, should be used to validate tests inferences. Response process research is extremely valuable as a basis for clinical inference (e.g., Exner, Armbruster, & Mittman, 1978). The response characteristics of each commonly used performance test should be researched and delineated. Because each test differs in its response process, each test must be addressed and mastered separately, even if these tests share some common processes and principles.

## Self-Expressive and Organizational Components

Within the response process in performance testing, two components have traditionally been identified: (1) a content or self-expressive component and (2) a formal or organizational component. Often these components are referred to respectively as projective and problem-solving components, but these terms are subject to misinterpretation. This chapter refers to them as the *self-expressive and organizational components of performance testing*.

To oversimplify, the self-expressive component largely involves content features of the response (i.e., what the subject says, writes, or draws and what associations the individual brings to the task). Self-expression occurs because performance test stimuli provoke the imagination, acting as a "stimulus to fantasy" (Exner & Weiner, 1995; Goldfried, Sticker, & Weiner, 1971). Thus, respondents react to content suggestions in a task (a sentence stem, picture, a recognizable or evocative form of an inkblot design, or musical composition) and rely on themselves to go beyond that content to access and express information from their own store of images, experiences, feelings, and thoughts or, alternatively fears, worries or concerns.

In contrast, the organizational component involves the formal or structural features of the response: how the individual answers the questions, solves the task, structures the response, and makes decisions. For example, the organizational component includes how the stimulus details are incorporated into TAT or Rorschach responses and whether the stimulus features are accurately perceived or not. Use of detail and the accuracy of the response are organizational features, which can be applied to almost all performance tests. These measures all pose problems to solve; the adequacy, style, and structure of the solutions to the problems are encompassed by the organizational component.

As noted earlier, the common oversimplification in conceptualizing performance testing is to limit its scope to the self-expressive or projective component. Doing so leads one to interpret only response content themes. Even if the organizational component is recognized, often it is conceptualized as independent from the content component.

We believe that separating the self-expressive and organizational components is another misconception that should be corrected. If one examines the respondent's real-time processing while solving the task and developing a response, one observes that self-expressive and organizational aspects are simultaneous and interconnected. One solves the problem by not only organizing the input and the output but also by selecting one's own self-expression to add to the response. For example, if someone were to offer some depressive or self-doubting sentence completions and then finish the sentence stem "I like . . ." with "for sure, NOT this test" the individual has suggested that such distress or doubt (self-expressive) leads to a abandonment of the task at hand (organizational) and a behavioral hypothesis to be tested with other data and observations. From another perspective, including self-expression is not just a "projection" of a trait, need, or perception. Thus, we are making an important distinction here: *Problem-solving within performance tests encompasses both content and formal, both self-expressive and organizational facets.* What are conventionally considered content/self-expressive components are actually best understood as part of a single problem-solving process. Thus, the respondent's way of problem solving may involve, for example, invoking dependent themes. A respondent's adding of certain thematic interpretations, motives, interests, or fantasies to test responses, thus, is part of the problem-solving component of these tests.

Moreover, there may be individual differences, both within an assessment and in one's everyday life, in terms of how much content is projected. Some people may project more personalized content than others. Others who express less personalized content might be characterized as stereotyped, overtly conventional (Schafer, 1954) or, alternatively, as efficient and economical (Exner, 2003). We elaborate on this problem-solving process as the centerpiece of this chapter. We rely on information processing and behavioral approaches in specifying its subcomponents.

## Performance Test Stimulus Situation

In our view, the performance test stimulus encompasses a set of complex factors. It is more than the concrete stimulus itself (i.e., more than merely a picture, a sentence stem, a Rorschach plate, or an invitation to remember). Masling's (1997) work with the Rorschach and a variety of studies with the TAT (Murstein, 1961, 1963) reveal that situational, contextual, and interpersonal stimuli influence the response process. Extrapolating from these findings, we propose that the actual stimulus for a performance test is the entire situation, or what we are calling the *stimulus situation.* Rather than merely being concrete stimuli, the stimulus situation encompasses the interpersonal interaction with the examiner, what the respondent is asked to do with the stimulus, and contextual issues such as the reason for referral. For example, the TAT stimulus situation involves the fact that the respondent is being called on to tell a story to reveal something about the self in front of another person, typically a stranger with some authority and power, about whom the respondent knows very little. Accordingly, when the test is administered individually, there is also a strong interpersonal component to the stimulus situation. Furthermore, this interpersonal component is implicit, yet probably less prominent, in paper-and-pencil performance tests. It is also present in self-report tests of personality, although often it is ignored.

A critical component of the stimulus situation is the respondent's awareness of the obvious potential for the response to reveal something of himself or herself. Reactions to the pressure to self-disclose are invoked by the stimulus situation. Accordingly, response sets, defensiveness, expression of social desirability, and response manipulation are fundamental to the response process. As will be addressed later, these are more than impediments or moderators of test validity.

## Processing the Stimulus Situation

Taking all of these issues into consideration suggests that the respondent reacts to an overall situation, including both concrete and experiential components, as a pattern or field. Such patterning is a well-known fact in the study of human perception. The respondent organizes that field into figure and ground, responding more distinctly to the figural components of the stimulus situation. This figure-ground patterning exists not only within the processing of the concrete test stimulus but also with the entire stimulus situation. Accurate interpretation depends on considering the concrete stimuli element in terms of, for example, Rorschach card pull, sentence stem characteristics, and salient stimuli components for individual cards from storytelling tasks (Exner, 1996; Murstein, 1961, 1963; Watson, 1978). These prominent, recognizable aspects of the concrete stimulus elicit common or popular responses. Peterson and Schilling (1983) have written an informative conceptual article that frames these issues for the Rorschach. Knowledge of the test and its input, processing, and output characteristics provides a context within which to understand the implication of responses for personality. Standardization data and empirical descriptions, the examiner's experience with the stimuli situation, recognition of the response pull for individual test stimuli, and knowledge of conventional and common responses all contribute to optimally valid interpretation.

## Free Response Format

When the examinee is not bound by any external controls or environmental demands, there is freedom in the stimulus situation, which is known as the free response format.

### Freedom in the Stimulus Situation

Freedom and lack of direction are crucial characteristics of the performance test stimulus situation. The individualistic idiographic feature of the response process starts with the individual differences in the perception of the stimulus situation (Colligan & Exner, 1985; Exner, 1980; Perry,

Felger, & Braff, 1998). The individual can choose to attend to different components of the stimuli situation, focusing on, for example, a particular element of the physical stimuli, a demand within the task, or some interpersonal aspect related to the task. The individual may offer an overall Gestalt or focus on a single element or on inconsistencies between stimulus subcomponents. Accordingly, when one identifies what the individual responds to in the stimulus situation, one can assess the individual's self-regulation through stimulus control during performance testing, in terms of what a person attributes to a stimulus.

Another important, related feature of the processing of the stimulus situation is decision making. For example, respondents must decide what to reveal or focus on within the story, image, early memory, or sentence completion item. Decision making also requires reconciling contradicting elements and completing unfinished information. The test stimulus situation does not provide much information to assist the respondent in evaluating the appropriateness and adequacy of a response. In contrast to ability tests, there are no obvious right answers. The lack of information in the stimulus situation interacts with the free response format to impede attempts at self-evaluation of the appropriateness of the response. Thus, decision making and processing in the face of minimal external guidance with concomitant insecurity is also a major component of the response process and the performance test task. In other words, coping with insecurity and uncertainty without sufficient information about the adequacy of one's response is part of the response process.

### Response Characteristics

With self-report tests, the interpretive dimensions (e.g., depression for scale 2 of the MMPI) are predetermined and then attributed to the self during the test administration. In contrast, in performance tests, interpretive dimensions arise during the test process itself and implicit or demonstrated in the test behavior. The interpreter observes the respondent's behavioral patterns in order to construct the dimensions to be described. For example, implicit motives organize stories to pictures (McClelland, Koestner, & Weinberger, 1989), and the interpreter describes these dimensions within the interpretation. As noted earlier, a crucial aspect of the performance test stimulus situation is the lack of information regarding the adequacy of the response. As suggested by Campbell, these tests are "typically open-ended, free, unstructured, and have the virtue of allowing the respondent to project

his own organization on the material" (1957, p. 208). In other words, it is the respondent who accounts for a great majority of the variation in the test responses in terms of their self-expressive and organizational components (Viglione & Perry, 1991). The fact that the response is wholly formed and created by the respondent has been referred to by Beck as the "gold" of the Rorschach (Beck, 1960), and thus the response becomes applicable to performance assessment at large.

The fixed test stimuli and limited response options in self-report tests account for more variation among test responses or behaviors compared to those that do not include fixed response options. Test developers predetermine structured test behaviors and, as a result, limit the freedom of response. In other words, there is much less variation in "true" versus "false" responses as compared to TAT responses or earlier memories. Historically, this fixed item and response format was typical of the personality and attitude measurement devices that dominated during the mental testing period from 1920 to 1935, and against which the early projective testers rebelled. Free responses are not essential for a performance test because multiple-choice or rating scale response formats have been used (Campbell, 1957). Nevertheless, the dominant performance tests in clinical practice use a free response format. Multiple-choice and rating scale formats have been used primarily for research on test validity and the response process (e.g., Exner et al., 1978).

Within the free response format, the respondent creates or organizes a response and expresses him- or herself through its content. The response content is neither preselected nor prestructured by the test developer; it is an expression of the given individual in the context of the exam. In an article introducing a conceptual model for psychopathology and the Rorschach, Viglione and Perry (1991) couched this free response format in terms of the limited environmental influence on Rorschach responses. This argument can be extended to some degree to all performance testing. As described by Viglione and Perry, performance test behaviors are largely influenced by the internal world rather than the test environment and stimuli. The content, structure, adequacy, and evaluation of the adequacy of the response come from the individual. The interpretive system accompanying the test is an aid to learn directly about the individual through analyzing the self-expressive and organizational aspects of these behavioral productions.

The free response format maximizes the expression of individual variance. The population of possible answers is unbounded in free response tasks; for this reason, the response itself can capture much more individual variation than can an item in a self-report personality test. In this way performance tests maximize salience and relevance of the response to the individual, a characteristic that has been referred to as the idiographic focus of this type of assessment. Indeed, the complexity and variety of the responses on such tests have made it difficult to create comprehensive scoring systems. The complexity and variability of stories for the apperception tests have been chief impediments to developing widely used and comprehensive coding systems for the TAT (Jenkins, 2008). From a psychometric perspective, this complexity and variety may translate to less reliability and more interpreter bias but, nevertheless, more validity.

### Interpretive Implications

What has been called expressive style is an example of the organizational component of a performance test response (Bellak, 1944). The free response component allows expressive style to emerge. It can be characterized by these questions: "Does he talk very fast or stammer badly? Is he verbose or terse? Does he respond quickly or slowly?" (Murstein, 1963, p. 3). Expressive style is also captured in nonverbal ways, which are important to understanding an individual's functioning and interpersonal relationships. In drawing and sentence completion blanks, does the respondent use space neatly? Is the respondent overly concerned with wasting space and time or sure to involve elaborate and elegant use of symbolic flair in his or her presentations? Indeed, the nonverbal mode of functioning and being in the world is accessed or represented behaviorally in task solutions (i.e., test responses). In support of this importance of nonverbal functioning, neuropsychological research would suggest that aspects of interpersonal and emotional functioning are differentially related to visual-spatial, kinesthetic, and tactile modes in comparison to verbal modes. Future research might attempt to investigate the relative contributions of expressive style and nonverbal modes to validity and utility.

The multimodal characteristic of the performance test response greatly multiplies its informational value. For example, a behavioral observation of (a) tearfulness at a particular point in an early memory procedure, (b) a man's self-critical humor during a TAT response that describes stereotypic male behavior, (c) fits and starts in telling a story with sexual content, (d) a seemingly sadistic chuckle with "a pelt, it's road kill" Rorschach response, (e) rubbing a Rorschach plate to produce a response, or (f) a lack of positive, playful affect throughout an early memory testing are all critical empirical data subject to

interpretation. Such test behaviors can lead to important hypotheses and allow one to synthesize various components of the test results by placing them in the context of the individual's life. These insights are not readily available or subject to systematic observation through other means in an assessment session. These are examples of the fundamental purpose of performance tests: to gather an otherwise unavailable sample of behavior to illuminate referral issues and questions emerging during the exam.

In addition, performance assessment tasks provide a rare opportunity to observe idiographic issues interacting with the instrumental dimension of behavior. Levy (1963) defined the instrumental dimension of behavior as the adequacy or effectiveness of the response in reaching some goal. In cognitive ability testing, this dimension could be simplified to whether a response is right or wrong. As noted earlier, as in ability, cognitive, or neuropsychological tests, in performance assessments, respondents perform a task. To varying degrees, all performance assessment task solutions can be evaluated along a number of instrumental dimensions, including accuracy, synthesis, meaningfulness, relevance, consistency, conciseness, and communicability. For example, the instrumental dimension relates to the quality, organization, and understandability of a TAT story or early memory as explained to the examiner (Ronan, Gibbs, Dreer, & Lombardo, 2008; Ronan et al., 1993). In ability tests, we concern ourselves mostly with the adequacy of the respondent's outcome, answer, or product. In contrast, with performance tests of personality, we are concerned not only with the adequacy of the outcome but also with the process and behavior involved in producing the outcome. In our nomenclature, the stimulus situation permits one to observe the interaction between the self-expressive and instrumental components of behavior, in other words, how adequate a response is in light of how someone solves a problem. Extending this interaction, performance test behavior also allows the examiner to observe the impact of emotional and interpersonal pressures on the adequacy and approach to solving problems. A crucial contribution of these tests to the assessment enterprise is their providing an interpretive link between findings from self-report tests and ability tests.

## Behavioral Approach to Validity

A behavioral view of the response process is necessary to fully understand the problem-solving model. Such a view provides a sample of behavior that can be viewed as a small representation of the test taker's real-life behavior.

### Behavioral Characteristics

Problem-solving in performance personality testing entails a behavioral view of the response process. This behavioral approach is consistent with Anastasi and Urbina's definition of psychological tests as an "essentially objective and standardized measure of a sample of behavior" (1996, p. 23). Psychological tests are undertaken when we cannot directly access behaviors important to assessment goals (Levy, 1963; Meehl, 1945/1956). In performance tests we induce a sample of behavior to observe that is similar to the behaviors of interest in real life.

Performance tests are attempts to bring aspects of relevant behavior, associations, perceptions, organizations, and affective and interpersonal components into the consulting room to be observed. Such a tactic is eloquently described by Levy (1963):

> We will be better able to predict this person's behavior in a given situation if we can bring a different frame of reference into play. We feel that in order to do this we will have to draw a different sample of behavior from that available to us now. Specifically, we want a sample of behavior that is amenable to description in our frame of reference, one that was designed with our particular language system in mind. (pp. 6–7)

Thus, performance tests induce a behavioral sample, which we can observe and explore so as to synthesize a more valid picture of the life predicament of the respondent. From this behavioral perspective, a test response or behavior is not a chance event but a behavior sample collected under controlled conditions, subject to behavioral laws.

In the section on free response format, we established that *variety* is a hallmark of performance test responses. They also are distinguished by their richness. The overall complexity of the stimulus situation elicits rich responses. Complex stimulus situations produce complex real-life, in vivo behaviors that generalize to complex nontest behaviors in complex situations (Viglione, 1999). By design in projective tests, meaningful behavior is mediated by personality processes and invoked by the stimulus situation.

One might elucidate these ideas by contrasting performance and self-report testing. The test behavior involved in self-report personality tests differs greatly from performance test behavior in terms of richness and variety. Typically, self-report test behavior is merely an endorsement of true and false or a rating of an opinion or sentiment along some dimension. The variety and richness of performance test responses allows the potential for generalizability to meaningful and salient real-life behavior. In contrast, within self-report testing there is no inherent similarity between (a) the act of responding true to aggressive risk items and (b) real life aggressive risk.

### Generalizability and Interpretation

In interpreting performance tests, we observe test behavior and then generalize it to similar behavior in other situations. When considering these tests as behavioral problem-solving tasks, the question of validity, according to Foster and Cone (1995), is one of topographic similarity and functional equivalency. *Topographic similarity* refers to the degree to which the test behavior resembles the nontest behavior in concrete, physical, and descriptive terms. *Functional equivalence* refers to the degree to which the antecedents and consequences of a test behavior correspond to the antecedent and consequences of real-life behavior. Topographically, an aggressive attribution on a TAT response is similar to an aggressive attribution in real life.

To understand topographical similarity within performance tests, one must examine the behavior induced by test demands. These tests incorporate complex stimulus situations and induce rich and complex behaviors that vary greatly from person to person. Test behaviors, such as explaining what one sees and how one sees it (i.e., Rorschach; Viglione, 1999), creating a story to understand a suggestive interaction (TAT), recalling and explaining a personally salient memory (Early Memories), and interpreting or finishing a fragment of a sentence (sentence completion), are all topographically similar to important and familiar life tasks. They are all aspects of what one frequently does in real life—expressions of one's "way of seeing and feeling and reacting to life, i.e. personality" (Frank, 1939/1962, p. 34). For example, it would not take much empirical support to justify the generalization of thought-disordered communication on the Rorschach or TAT to thought-disordered behavior in other contexts. The test behavior and target or in vivo behaviors are topographically and experientially quite similar and thus behaviorally equivalent. It is not surprising then that there is a great amount of empirical support for thought-disorder indices on the Rorschach (Acklin, 1999; Holzman, Proctor, Levy, Yasillo, Meltzer, & Hurt, 1974; Kleiger, 1999; Perry & Braff, 1994; Perry, Geyer, & Braff, 1999; Perry, Viglione, & Braff, 1992; Viglione, 1999; Weiner, 1966).

Performance tests collect standardized samples of real-life behavior; the problem solving of the personality operations in real life. This view of personality incorporates thought organization and disorder as the problem solving of the personality manifest in behavior. Moreover, the behavioral population of interest for performance tests is real-life behavior, just as the population for performance tests is the expression of abilities. More symbolic interpretations, for example, using Rorschach color responses as a symbol of emotionality, lack topographical and experiential similarity. Accordingly, symbolic interpretations, as with self-report test findings, require much more empirical support.

In considering topographical similarity and generalizability, one must also appreciate the examination context and the stimulus situation. In this context performance test activities such as a child's ripping apart stimulus materials or a felon's expressing obvious pleasure in describing malevolent acts are exceptional behaviors. Such behaviors that (a) oppose the social demands of the assessment interpersonal context and (b) possess obvious clinical implications may be understood as corresponding to salient nontest behaviors of interest. They are very-low-probability events that are much more likely to spring from the individual rather than from situational factors. Thus, they are generalizable rare events, even if infrequent.

### Experiential Interpretation

In performance testing, we extend the behavioral notion of topographic similarity to incorporate *experiential* elements. These include subjective and covert problem solving, elements such as self-expressive and internal phenomena associated with the response process. Schachtel (1966) with the Rorschach and Riethmiller and Handler (1997) with the Draw-A-Person demonstrated the value of this approach. For the Rorschach, it would mean asking what processes are involved in avoiding the complexity and contradictions of a blot so as to give simplistic, uninvolved answers. For the Draw-A-Person, the experience-near approach would take into consideration not only the product (i.e., the drawing) but also the process of creating it. Experiential interpretation of a figure drawing might also require such questions as "What experiences or covert processes might accompany drawing this frightening person? What would it be like to meet or have a conversation with this frightening person?" Answers to these questions are more likely to have nontest referents than the nonexperiential detail-oriented questions that have dominated some approaches to drawings (i.e., "How long are the arms? Are the hands represented? Did the respondent mention the head? Was shading involved?"). Answers to the experience-near questions are the real behavioral patterns to be generalized from performance tests to real-life behavior. Given this

stimulus situation, identifying experience-near components involves being in an interpersonal relationship with the respondent and empathizing with his or her process and experience (Riethmiller & Handler, 1997). As research has demonstrated, this interpersonal component is a strength of performance tests given that it is an essential ingredient of the stimulus situation (Stricker & Healy, 1990). For example, figure drawing interpretation is essentially an analysis of the interaction between the examiner and examinee. The examiner asks the respondent to "draw a person," requiring him or her to be open and vulnerable, as he or she recognizes that the drawing will be scrutinized. This interpersonal situation will lead the client to make use of his or her defensive structure, which is designed to shape the reactions of those getting to know him or her (i.e., the drawing he or she has been asked to produce) (Handler & Riethmiller, 1998).

Examining the three-dimensional vista response on the Rorschach might elucidate the experiential and contextual components of interpretation. These three-dimensional, shading responses might mean very different things in different contexts. From an experiential problem-solving perspective, the vista response involves a more precise way of dealing with the blots in which one experiences the self as stepping back and evaluating. Within the context of an inpatient's depression, such an activity might generalize to negative evaluation of the self, others, and the future that compromises adaptation. In the case of a passive but largely successful executive in a nonclinical examination, the vista response might be related to an analytic, evaluative ability to step back and gain perspective and an ability to evaluate the self. Under stress, this capacity may be associated with self-criticism that, although painful, may lead to adjustments and improved functioning. In the context of an assessment of an incarcerated murderer, the vista responses may generalize to situational induced self-criticism, possibly guilt, or alternatively an analytic approach to crime. Accordingly, test behaviors that are identical along overt, topographical parameters may correspond to different covert experience and in vivo behaviors. These distinctions, in turn, are based on the context of the exam and base rate factors. Research on psychological assessment and clinical judgment and decision theory has not addressed these ecologically valid interpretive inferences.

### Functional Equivalence and Generalization

This interaction among interpretation, examination contexts, and topographical and experiential phenomena relates to functional equivalence and generalization. As noted earlier, *functional equivalence* refers to the degree to which the antecedents and consequences of a test behavior correspond to the antecedent and consequences of real-life behavior. The antecedents and consequences of test behaviors are encompassed by the stimulus situation, and the stimuli situations or test environments to some extent vary from test to test and occasion to occasion. However, from the broadest and most inclusive point of view, performance tests involve new and unfamiliar situations in which one organizes incomplete, contradictory, and ambiguous material without any direct feedback from observers or authorities. Also, they involve little implicit feedback from the task about adequacy of performance within an interaction with another individual. Applying the principle of functional equivalence, we are safest when we generalize performance test behaviors to situations with the similar characteristics. Thus, to some degree, interpretations may be context dependent rather than pervasive. Test interpretation may apply to situations with more individual control and less environmental control. More colloquially, these are situations in which the respondent has to make his or her own way and fend for him- or herself.

Functional equivalence helps us to interpret contradictory information so often produced during assessment. Let us say that we observe evidence of depression and distortion of incoming information in a seemingly content and psychologically healthy individual. With such an individual, these data are likely to be related to circumscribed rather than pervasive problems. Functional equivalence and the performance test stimulus situation guide the interpretation and generalization of these test behaviors. With healthy individuals, one could safely generalize the depression and distortion to occasional vulnerability to mistakes in judgment, self-doubt, and distress in new and unfamiliar situations. Alternatively, such negative information might be used to describe worst-case scenarios or self-defeating patterns or potentials. In the context of an exam with a psychiatric inpatient, these same data would suggest much more pervasive difficulties. Thus, the stimulus situation and functional equivalency guides generalization and interpretation of test behaviors along a situation-specific versus pervasive dimension. As interpretation becomes more specific, it should be confined to situations that more closely resemble the performance test stimulus situation.

### Conclusion

The current approach to performance testing needs to adopt this experience-near perspective to identify problem-solving correlates of test behaviors. In addition, interpreters and researchers must recognize that these test behaviors have different implications in different situations. Technically, the problem-solving approach can use differential base rates, conditional probabilities, statistical interactions, or moderator variables to investigate performance testing. Thus, the problem-solving approach to performance assessment challenges the notion that test behaviors are always generalizable to personality at large. This may be true much of the time, but the nature of behavior and contextual factors influence the pervasiveness and situational specificity of generalizations. Many dominant interpretations—for example, those with the Rorschach Comprehensive System—often are based on research and formulations with clinically compromised individuals. Accordingly, many of these interpretations overemphasize the more pathological or problematic correlates of the test behavior. This fact probably contributes to the error of overly negative interpretations of performance tests related to the neglect of base rates (Finn & Kamphuis, 1995; Murstein & Mathes, 1996; Viglione & Hilsenroth, 2001). More positive and accurate interpretations are emerging with new systems with more adequate normative data (e.g., Jenkins, 2008; Meyer et al., 2011; van den Daele, 2007).

## INTERPRETATIVE AND CONCEPTUAL ISSUES

This chapter highlights important characteristics of the performance assessment stimulus situation and the integration of organizational and self-expressive components in the response process. In turn, these factors induce characteristic patterns and methods of interpretation. Interpretation of test responses emphasizes synthetic and individualistic approaches to interpretation (Rabin, 1981), given the prominent role these approaches play in the responses. In practice, those psychologists who are more inclined to emphasize the complexities of the individual are probably more inclined to use performance tests. The "Free Response Format" section outlined the individual or idiographic component of the solutions to performance test tasks, a characteristic that induces a similar focus on individual or idiographic approaches to interpretation.

### Synthetic, Configurational Interpretation

As established in discussing the test stimulus situation and the response process, performance testing accesses multiple dimensions and allows one to elaborate on hypotheses derived earlier in the interpretive process. These factors induce the interpreter to adopt a synthetic or configurational approach in formulating interpretations (Stricker & Gold, 1999). Performance test data present connections and associations between various characteristics from different domains. For example, in the TAT, we can associate a problem-solving failure or cognitive slip to sexual or intimate themes stimulated by a particular card when such themes are mentioned but not meaningfully integrating into a jumbled and unrealistic story. In terms used earlier in this chapter, performance test results bridge self-expressive, organizational, and response set domains. One score or response parameter is analyzed in its relationship to another or in relationship to moderator variables and collateral, nontest variables. Temporal, spatial, and language factors—that is, when and how behaviors occur—allow interpreters to identify how various content and organizational aspects of an individual work together, how they interrelate, and how they may interact with different environmental conditions. Advocates of performance testing are not interested in isolated bits of behavior but study how it comes together in a whole person within a life predicament (Stricker & Gold, 1999; Viglione, 1999; Viglione & Perry, 1991, Weiner, 1999, 2001). Performance test data assist us in putting the person in his or her life context and help us to understand the relationship between internal issues and a person's biography and background. Murstein (1963) called this "configurational dominance" (p. 4). This synthetic or configurational approach can be attributed to Gestalt, field theory, and psychodynamic influences on performance testing (Frank, 1939/1962).

Among the connections made possible by performance tests are those between personality factors and cognitive functions. Conceiving of the tasks in these tests as problems to be solved allows the integration of nonintellectual issues with intellectual ones. From a configurational point of view, the relationships of abilities to affects, interests, motivations, and discriminative stimuli are addressed. A related advantage of performance tests is that they provide a foundation for the examiner to make inferences about motivation. Other performance tests—that is, ability tests—assume and attempt to induce optimal motivation. In real life, however, motivational variation is crucial to understanding personality and behavior.

We can conclude then that part of the utility of performance assessment—in more concrete terms, its added value relative to self-report tests—is that it provides meaningful connections among different characteristics so as to understand a whole person. Because the individual respondent produces the constructs and their

interrelationships with the solutions to the task and associated behaviors in the free response format, we know that the configurational information is relevant and possibly unique to the individual being assessed.

In synthesizing the picture of the individual within this performance assessment perspective, one constructs or builds an integrated picture of the person within a situation. Extrapolating from the original work of Kaufman on *Intelligent Testing with the WISC-R* (1979), each construction, each person's theory, is different in terms of concepts and relationships among concepts. Reflecting this uniqueness of each individual, we strive to construct a different theory for each respondent. Along these lines, an important phenomenon is that performance testing often reveals striking, remarkable aspects or concerns that become important hallmarks or organizing features in understanding an individual. Accordingly, assessment report writers often excerpt quotes from sentence completion responses or responses from other tests to communicate vividly the respondent's experience in his or her own words (Holaday, Smith, & Sherry, 2000).

Invariably, this synthetic and constructive approach leads to discovering contradictions among test data. Resolving these contradictions often provides added insight into the individual. Recognition of contradictions—for example, depressed but overly impressed with the self—is based on nomothetic notions. In other words, we see depression and self-importance as being contradictory when we conceive of them as abstract concepts. Within a single individual, these characteristics need not be contradictory. We find that real people appear to possess both overly negative and overly positive views of the self. Positive views may ward off negative views. Positive views may arise in one situation but not another—for example, among children, positive views may arise in academic situations but not at home. It follows then that the inevitable contradictions among performance test data induce, if not necessitate, a dynamic view of individuals. This dynamic view entails opposing forces operating in the behavior, affect, motivation, and cognition in a way that reflects the opposing excitatory and inhibitory organization of the nervous system.

## Performance Assessment

As suggested by the early leaders in assessment (Frank, 1939/1962; Mayman, Schafer, & Rapaport, 1951; Meehl, 1945/1956), the difference between what were once called "projective" and "objective tests" may lie not so much in the tests but in the interpretive approach—a difference that is induced by the data themselves, by their complexity and richness and their relevance to the individual. These performance tests induce an individualistic, synthetic and configurational, and constructive approach to interpretation that incorporates a view of the individual as embodying contradictions which might be explained dynamically. This approach also involves affects and interpersonal issues. In turn, those holding such a view of interpretation are probably more inclined to use performance tests. The interpreter is involved directly in the assessment administration process, because the individualistic and configurational issues are best known and explored by an active interpreter in a relationship with the respondent. In summary, one's preference for these individualistic tests may largely reflect a philosophical approach to human nature (Mayman et al., 1951).

### Self-Disclosure and Response Sets

"It would be very unsafe, unwise, and incorrect to assume that a patient either can or wants to present all aspects of his or her personality fully to the examiner" (Klopfer, 1981, p. 259). Indeed, this is a central problem that clinicians have struggled with in the practice of assessment over the years. Surveys on assessment practice have not explored the extent to which this unsafe assumption is made implicitly in the interpretation of self-report personality tests. In the early part of the 20th century, the original "projective" testing grew out of the practical need to access what the individual may be unwilling or unable to communicate directly (Frank, 1939/1962; Murray, 1938; Murstein, 1961; Viglione, 1999). This is the fundamental challenge or paradox in assessment: What is most important to know is often what the person is most unwilling or unable to divulge. To uncover this information, performance tests go about the task of accessing behavior and problem solving indirectly. Task instructions (e.g., "Tell a story," "What might this be?," "Complete the sentence . . .") distract the respondent from the interpretive goals of the examination. This is a fundamental projective phenomenon, and when tests function in this way, they are attempts to access the private world of the individual through projection, to get to it more efficiently than through other means (Frank, 1939/1962; Viglione & Hilsenroth, 2001; Viglione & Perry, 1991).

The reactions to pressures to self-disclose in an indirect stimulus situation are not captured neatly within individual scales on any test. Operating in every individual, idiosyncratically, is a conflict between pressures for self-disclosure versus self-protection. This conflict involves (a) a willingness and an ability to be self-revealing versus (b) rational and irrational concerns about negative consequence to self-disclosure accompanied by (c) a motivation to create a favorable impression. Examination of the nuances of self-revealing behaviors and attitudes to testing in the context of the relationship with the examiner allows us to examine this *struggle over self-disclosure.*

Strict adherence to administration principles, examiner training, self-observation, as well as observations of the respondent, are necessary to manage and observe the respondent's struggle over self-disclosure. For example, the Rorschach Comprehensive System (Exner, 1974, 2003; Exner et al., 2001); the Rorschach Performance Assessment System (Meyer et al., 2011); the TAT (Jenkins, 2008); the Early Memory Test; and the Music Apperception Test (van den Daele, 2007) go to great lengths to minimize and to systematize examiner and contextual influences. Moreover, being sensitive to and evaluating these influences help one to assess their impact on the test findings and inferences (Schafer, 1954). However, the influence of conflicts about self-disclosure and response sets cannot be eliminated. Performance tests offer an opportunity to observe, identify, and characterize them as a part of the ongoing interaction between the personality and stimulus situation.

### *Interpretive Implications of the Pressure to Self-Disclose*

The pressure to self-disclose within the stimulus situation leads to a number of interpretive issues. Accordingly, studying and characterizing the response style of the individual is a crucial interpretive goal in all assessment. Response set is an important and complex moderator variable that should be scrutinized in each assessment through observation and analysis of all test data and collateral information. Test findings should be interpreted differently as a function or response set so that the response set acts as a moderator variable for interpretive purposes and validity (Meyer, 1999).

More explicitly, within the interpretive process, results from performance testing can be characterized along the self-protection versus self-disclosure dimension. Stereotypic, brief test protocols, or poorly or quickly executed productions with insufficient effort (e.g., in drawings), can be seen as attempts to suppress or resist pressure from the examiner to reveal one's self. Thus, some test findings may have more to do with how the respondent protects the self or suppresses, defends, or avoids. Looking at these efforts as a moderator variable, such self-protective test protocols may lead to an underestimate of personality tendencies and weaknesses and to false negative findings. From a behavioral perspective, this response set can be seen as an attempt to suppress or defend against self-disclosure. In such cases, the test findings do not survey the full array of personality processes and features, so that the findings may not reveal the personality as a whole. Moreover, these self-protective or suppressive response sets can result in inconsistencies among performance test data, self-report findings, and collateral information (Meyer, 1999).

In contrast, longer, complex test responses may represent an effort to self-disclose or to express or engage fully in the examination. Such records survey the personality more fully. Alternatively, some overly long and involved test records may represent a respondent's effort to present the self in positive light by demonstrating to the examiner talents and problem-solving skills (Viglione, 1996). Nevertheless, too much productivity on any projective test may be associated with overestimation of pathology and false positive results (Murstein & Mathes, 1996; Viglione & Meyer, 2008).

It is well-established that response sets vary along this *self-protection/self-disclosure or suppressive/expressive continuum* and that this continuum acts as an important moderator variable in assessment interpretation. Self-report instruments such as the MMPI and PAI contain response set measures as validity scales and moderator variables. These scales are most useful in measuring the quantitative dimensions of response set. Performance test data are instrumental in individualizing and identifying nuances and complexities in that response set. For example, sentence completion methods illuminate individual styles, worries, motives, and interests in presenting one's self in an overly positive or negative manner. In that sense, performance testing, and sentence completion tasks in particular, add content to what we might learn from the validity scales of an MMPI.

Response sets have implications beyond the interpretation of a given test protocol. Attitudes toward self-disclosure/self-protection are fundamental issues in any change process, whether in a clinical, forensic, or organizational setting. Accordingly, the respondent's engagement in testing has implications for motivation to self-disclose in response to interventions in the real world. Similar issues emerge in assessment of risk of dangerousness. In these contexts, respondents' attitudes toward assessment may also resemble attitudes toward cooperation with management of the test taker's risk. Accordingly, these attitudes as a component of the response set are critical important assessment targets and need to be observed closely.

Response set is important not only as a mediator and discriminative stimulus for test validity but as a target of assessment in and of itself.

Extreme response sets sometimes emerge as malingering and feigned presentations. For respondents to performance tests, adopting such a response set is quite challenging because of the complexity of the stimulus situation, the active role of the examiner, and the freedom allowed within the test responses. In general, malingering or faking successfully may be more difficult to achieve in performance testing than in self-report testing. A study by Shedler, Mayman, and Manis (1993) revealed that in self-report, a substantial portion of respondents may incorporate this false positive bias in their response style so as to obscure test sensitivity to problems. These data suggest that such tests may more accurately describe individuals' functioning. Regarding individual tests, Rorschach research suggests that in some respects, it is more resistant than self-report to response manipulation (Bornstein, Rossner, Hill, & Stepanian, 1994; Viglione, 1999).

### Note of Caution

Nevertheless, the broad claim that the respondent has no control over the content of performance tests is a myth that does not withstand logical and empirical scrutiny. Accumulated research on faking and experimentally induced response sets suggest that a respondent can control content to some extent on many performance tests including the Rorschach. For example, aggression and sexual content themes, but not dependent and many other themes, are routinely subject to considerable control (Exner, 2003; Viglione, 1999). On the TAT, many themes are relatively easily controlled (Holmes, 1974; Murstein, 1961).

### Test or Method and Individualizing Interpretation?

Another long-standing controversy concerns whether performance instruments are actually tests or merely methods or techniques. A *psychological test* can be defined as a standardized administration with an interpretive system that is quantified and subjected to scientific validation. In contrast, a *method* is defined as a systematic way of collecting behavioral observations. Both a test and a method may produce valid interpretations. Within a method, the technique and strategies of interpretation, rather than quantities produced by scales, would be subject to scientific verification. An example of using a performance instrument as a method would be recognizing that completing the sentence stem "I was bothered by" with this written phrase, "the way you looked at me when I was putting the blocks together," may have special interpretative significance for the interpretation of Block Design and interpersonal performances. Asking a respondent what he or she had in mind when endorsing "I have two personalities inside of me" would be an example of using a self-report test as a method. Thus, both self-report and performance instruments could be used as methods. In fact, one might argue that using them as a method enhances interpretation.

### Method Argument

These issues have been addressed in the literature. For example, Weiner (1994) published an article on the Rorschach that stimulated considerable controversy about its status as a test versus a method. He suggested that the Rorschach was foremost a method because the instrument is a means of collecting information about how people structure their experience, express themselves, and interact affectively and interpersonally. Similarly, Klopfer, Ainsworth, Klopfer, and Holt (1954) advocated for calling the test a "technique," so that individualistic processing could be emphasized. From a more extreme but current viewpoint, Aronow, Reznikoff, and Moreland (1994) focused on response content and regards the Rorschach as a structured interview. Most practitioners do not score the TAT, and Little and Schneidman (1955) described it as a "sample of verbal behavior." Earlier, Tomkins (1947) had declared that the TAT was a systematic methodology for personality study, not a test itself. Finally, early memory, sentence, and drawing tasks are routinely used as methods without scoring to collect behavioral observations and personal productions.

Clearly, some advocates of performance testing support the term *method* for these performance procedures. Beyond precision of language, they are concerned that essential qualitative and descriptive information will be excluded from consideration if this information is not captured in formal scoring. Critics of performance tests endorse the term *method*, claiming that the nonquantified components are not worthy of consideration. This extremist view excludes from consideration response nuances and connotations, test behaviors, and emotional expressions as well as the interaction between examiner and the respondent. These characteristics constitute important empirical and objective observations. They are the essence of behavioral assessment and are not captured within the reductionistic view that only test quantities be considered. In cases when they are relevant (i.e., related to other hypotheses firmly grounded in test-based inferences), behavioral and empirical data derived from using performance instruments as methods must be included in the interpretive process.

### Methods, Clinical Utility, and the "N of 1" Problem in Assessment

How does one fit a group or statistical concept—for example, depression or aggressive risk—to individuals and describe its idiosyncratic experience and function within the individual? From a statistical viewpoint, if it is highly likely that a person is depressed based on a score, how do we confirm it with the particular individual we are evaluating? These questions reflect the "N of 1" problem in assessment—that is, the challenge of applying abstracted group-derived constructs and measurements to a single individual. Within individuals, constructs like aggression or depression exist only in idiosyncratic forms. Accordingly, within a performance test protocol, idiosyncratic evidence of depression may serve to confirm and individualize this person's expression of depression. In this way, using these instruments as a method helps address the N of 1 problem in assessment by contextualizing and individualizing abstract concepts and group data.

This N of 1 problem is often framed in terms of the distinction between nomothetic and idiographic science and knowledge (Murstein, 1963). Nomothetic science addresses laws and abstractions applicable across circumstances and individuals. Within psychology, it would be associated with group psychological principles, constructs, and data across individuals and situations. These abstractions may not actually exist in any individual case but are hypothetical constructs created for the purpose of explaining and summarizing relationships among groups of individuals. In contrast, idiographic science is concerned with understanding of a particular event—for example, what led to a particular historical event or decision (in other words, how and why something happened). The aim of assessment, to characterize a unique individual within a life context, is an idiographic goal. Certainly, nomothetic science, methods, and comparisons are critical and necessary to addressing this goal, but they are not sufficient to achieve it fully. Idiographic and configurational information from a method perspective is necessary to address the uniqueness of each case. Thus, performance test data and observations are helpful in translating group, nomothetic, or actuarial data to the individual N of 1 case. Stricker and Gold (1999) stated that the relationship between the idiographic and nomothetic approach to assessment is quite complicated. Obviously, nomothetic findings are always the starting point of the assessment process; however, idiographic data provide us with a deeper and more individual understanding of the client. Ultimately, the nomothetic and idiographic findings complement one another, providing clinicians with a whole and integrated picture of clients.

In terms of clinical utility, using an instrument as a method offers considerable advantage over only using instruments as tests. Observations and inquiries can be adapted to address any purpose. One cannot imagine all of the questions that will come up in an assessment. Thus, one method might replace many tests, offering considerable efficiency and cost savings. The superior status of tests in terms of the validity of a specific interpretation relies on stringent research validation of the test for that particular purpose. Yet it is impossible to develop, research, and master a test for every purpose. Accordingly, performance test methods, interviews, and observations are always necessary for a comprehensive assessment, lest we give up all idiographic assessment goals.

At the broadest level, research supporting the validity of a method addresses whether a performance test of personality can produce valid and useful information when the instrument is used in the standard way. The research clearly supports the conclusion that the chief procedures and tasks employed in personality tests (inkblot perception and representation, storytelling, sentence completion, early recollection, and figure drawing) can yield valid and useful information. However, the limits of these methods and the limits of data they produce are not fully appreciated by some performance test advocates. Further research needs to identify the types of inferences and generalizations that can be made about particular personality processes and from which types of data.

### Conclusion and Recommendations for Tests and Methods

Performance tests of personality, like all psychological tests, can function as both methods and tests. In both roles they should be administered in a standardized fashion. When they are viewed as tests, the administrator relies on quantification, comparison to comparison group data, and preestablished criterion validity. These factors lead to a strong scientific foundation for interpretation for tests. Because of the less sturdy support for inferences based only on using the instruments as methods, inferences derived from methods need additional support from other sources. Within a given assessment, this support can be accomplished by addressing hypotheses that have derived initial support from data encountered earlier in the assessment process. For example, in established

cases of depression, the TAT may yield important information about the idiographic experience of that depression and its interpersonal correlates. Early Memories may provide subjective and experiential patterning associated with this depression. If we establish from a self-report test that the respondent is describing him- or herself in an overly positive and defensive fashion, an examination of sentence completion results and observations about the examiner–respondent interaction may lead to important information about the character and motivation associated with that defensiveness. If new hypotheses emerge from method data, they must be supported by other data from other observations and findings, in a way that we would not require for an interpretation from an instrument used as a test. Thus, when these procedures are used as methods and not tests, they should generally be used as ancillary or elaborative procedures.

Comprehensive System Rorschach interpretation is a good example of an instrument used as a test and a method. One first interprets structural quantitative data, then modifies these foundational interpretations with the Rorschach used as a method (i.e., through response verbalizations and behavioral observations). In this way, method findings are used to refine, elaborate, and qualify previously formulated general hypotheses.

### Contribution to Assessment Relative to Self-Report Tests

One way to address the question of what performance personality testing contributes to assessment is to identify situations in which self-report tests do not yield clear and definitive findings. This approach is consistent with the current concerns about incremental validity. Many have noted that performance tests contribute most in contexts in which the person may be unwilling or unable to provide the sought after information through more direct means (Bagby, Nicholson, Buis, & Radovanovic, 1999; Bathurst, Gottfried, & Gottfried, 1997; Bornstein, 1999; Meyer & Archer, 2001; Viglione, 1999). Some might contend that to some degree, no respondent can fully reveal critical information about the self in an efficient manner.

The traditional view, as first elaborated by Frank (1939/1962), is that performance testing goes beyond socially conventional meanings and roles. From this perspective, self-report items, typically a sentence or phrase, presume a conventional, widely shared understanding of their meaning. In these conventional contexts, individual behavior is best explained by situational phenomena as interpreted with shared cultural norms. Frank contrasted these conventional contexts to situations in which behavior is explained by the individual's unique way of ascribing meaning to the world and organizing the world. In fact, the individual's unique way of ascribing meaning to and organizing the world is the fundamental component of personality, according to Frank. Moreover, performance tests correspond to the self-expressive and organizational components of performance tests addressed earlier in this chapter. By design these tests access these individualistic functions and thus reveal personality activity directly.

This linking of self-report tests to conventional contexts and performance tests to individualistic ones has led some to speculate about the relative contributions of these tests. For example, Hutt (1945) speculated that self-report tests may be valid only when the respondent is willing and capable of self-rating on a known dimension. Meehl (1945/1956) disagreed by objecting that respondents may understand self-report test items differently, but such differences are not relevant to validity. He claimed that validity of self-report tests is not a function of a conventionally, socially prescribed understanding of the test items. Rather, it is a function of empirical relationships with external criteria. This empirical keying approach assumes that the content of the item really does not matter, only its empirical relationship with meaningful criteria.

Despite Meehl's assertions, evidence suggests that what the item means to the respondent does make a difference in the validity of a self-report personality test. On the MMPI, it is well established that obvious items are more valid than subtle items (Graham, 2006; Greene, 2000; Gynther & Burkhart, 1983). In other words, when an item's content is semantically related to the scale on which it resides or the construct it measures, it works better. Also, the largely rationally derived content scales on the MMPI-2 rival the empirically keyed clinical scales in terms of validity (Graham, 2006; Greene, 2000), again suggesting that item content matters. The current test development practice is to pick the item pool for content validity (i.e., what the item means to the respondent; American Educational Research Association, American, Psychological Association, & National Council on Measurement in Education, 1999; Anastasi & Urbina 1996; Morey, 1996). Again, the validity of these scales is partly based on an unequivocal meaning of the item to the respondent. As Frank (1939/1962) asserted theoretically and McClelland et al. (1989) and Bornstein et al. (1994) demonstrated with data, self-report personality tests reveal information about relevant but conventional, culturally prescribed dimensions.

The interpretive implication of all of these data is that self-report personality tests tell us the most about behavior related to social roles, how one acts in the role of a father or in the role of a rebellious adolescent in our society. These tests work best when the examinee translates individual items in conventional ways and when the examinee's response set reflects the host culture's norms. Psychometrically, this occurs when validity scales (e.g., *L, F, K* with the MMPI) are near-average values. Atypical, unconventional response sets, in terms of excessive defensiveness or exaggeration, reflect unconventional approaches to the tests, and atypical translation of test items, in turn, limit the validity of self-report personality tests (Meyer, 1999). Conversely, performance tests have the most to offer in understanding and predicting behavior outside of prescribed social roles and demands across situation and time as well as for issues that are idiographic, idiosyncratic, or implicit. (See Bornstein, 1999; Shedler et al., 1993; Viglione, 1999.) These would include environmental contexts or patterns of behavior that are structured by individual personality rather by than social roles and conventions.

## TEST CONTROVERSY FROM A HISTORICAL PERSPECTIVE

The misgivings and misunderstandings addressed earlier in this chapter about the characterization of performance testing are grounded in a historical perspective. Undeniably, historical developments have influenced our understanding of focal psychological constructs, even when we believe that these constructs are grounded in empirical science. For example, as a result of the Wechsler and Stanford-Binet scales, our implicit and conventional understanding of intelligence emphasizes the quantitative perspective at the expense of the conceptual and developmental aspects as articulated within the Piagetian approach. Self-report personality assessment has led us to simplify adult personality into an aggregate of traits demonstrated by subgroups of individuals. Response set or response manipulation has been reduced to quantitative notions about exaggeration and defensiveness (e.g., as defined through the *L, F,* and *K* scales on the MMPI). Thus, history and our experience have shaped our views, constructs, and what we consider to be science.

It is surprising to learn that controversy about the utility of performance tests has existed since their introduction (Hirt, 1962; Murstein, 1965; Rabin, 1981). The popular academic position dating back to the 1920s is that performance tests of personality are flawed. Periodically, this view has been a rallying cry of academic psychologists. In the 1920s and 1930s, American academic psychology focused on distinguishing psychology by making it a science with mathematical foundations much like physics. It is not surprising that it did not produce many concepts, facts, and methods applicable to clinical work. At that time, applied work in clinical psychology was largely diagnostic and descriptive in support of psychiatrists' work with individuals with mental disorders. The clinical and practical demands of psychologists oppose the academic interests in developing the discipline and science of psychology. It is not surprising that clinical and applied assessment interest and questions advance more quickly than scientific and academic developments. As society changes, this pressure to address advanced and complex questions in everyday practice will certainly persist. Performance-based tests of personality will always be important in answering these vexing questions, revealing the individual and unique traits of the person, and helping us to appreciate how various characteristics come together in complex coping behaviors.

## CONCLUSION

One challenge in writing this chapter has been discussing the great diversity of performance-based tests of personality under one umbrella. The extant research data and the response process model itself would suggest that the next step would be to adapt the problem-solving model to individual tests. This would include developing paradigms to address topographical and experiential similarity, functional equivalence, and personality as problem solving in real life. The challenge in this research is to access the idiographic characteristics of the individual as validity criteria. This is not a simple manner and may require incorporating qualitative research with more traditional quantitative work. Research should also tackle the international and cultural challenges. Performance testing has great potential in these applications, as demonstrated by international normative data sets with the Rorschach (Meyer, Erdberg, & Shaffer, 2007) and traditional and new apperception technique applications (Jenkins, 2008). Every effort should be made to standardize administrations and coding of responses. It is not clear that we can progress much further by lumping these tests together. Rather, the response process and generalization characteristics for each test can be researched and developed separately. Research in performance assessment of

personality testing should address the interpretive process itself. Much more sophisticated clinical judgment studies are needed so as to make them relevant to clinical practice (Karon, 2000; Levine, 1981; Viglione & Hilsenroth, 2001). Such research should include investigations of these instruments as methods.

## REFERENCES

Acklin, M. W. (1999). Behavioral science foundations of the Rorschach test: Research and clinical applications. *Assessment, 6,* 319–324.

American Educational Research Association, American Psychological Association, & National Council on Measurement in Education. (1999). *Standards for educational and psychological testing.* Washington, DC: American Educational Research Association.

Anastasi, A., & Urbina, S. (1996). *Psychological testing* (7th ed.) New York, NY: Macmillan.

Aronow, E., Reznikoff, M., & Moreland, K. (1994). *The Rorschach technique: Perceptual basics, content interpretation, and applications.* Boston, MA: Allyn & Bacon.

Asari, T., Konishi, S., Jimura, K., Chikazoe, J., Nakamura, N., & Miyashita, Y. (2008). Right temporopolar activation associated with unique perception. *NeuroImage, 41,* 145–152.

Asari, T., Konishi, S., Jimura, K., Chikazoe, J., Nakamura, N., & Miyashita, Y. (2010). Amygdalar enlargement associated with unique perception. *Cortex, 46,* 94–99.

Bandura, A. (1978). The self-system in reciprocal determinism. *American Psychologist, 33,* 344–358.

Bagby, R. M., Nicholson, R. A., Buis, T., & Radovanovic, H. (1999). Defensive responding on the MMPI-2 in family custody and access evaluations. *Psychological Assessment, 11,* 24–28.

Bathurst, K., Gottfried, A. W., & Gottfried, A. E. (1997). Normative data for the MMPI-2 in child custody litigation. *Psychological Assessment, 7,* 419–423.

Beck, S. J. (1960). *The Rorschach experiment: Ventures in blind diagnosis.* New York, NY: Grune & Stratton.

Bellak, L. (1944). The concept of projection: An experimental investigation and study of the concept. *Psychiatry, 7,* 353–370.

Bornstein, R. F. (1999). Criterion validity of objective and projective dependency tests: A meta-analytic assessment of behavioral prediction. *Psychological Assessment, 11,* 48–57.

Bornstein, R. F., Rossner, S. C., Hill, E. L., & Stepanian, M. L. (1994). Face validity and fakability of objective and projective measures of dependency. *Journal of Personality Assessment, 63,* 363–386.

Campbell, D. T. (1957). A typology of tests, projective and otherwise. *Journal of Consulting Psychology, 21,* 207–210.

Colligan, S. C., & Exner, J. E. (1985). *Responses of schizophrenics and nonpatients to a tachistoscopic presentation of the Rorschach.* Paper presented at the 11th International Rorschach Congress (1984, Barcelona, Spain). *Journal of Personality Assessment, 49,* 129–136.

Exner, J. E. (1974). *The Rorschach: A comprehensive system* (Vol. 1). New York, NY: Wiley.

Exner, J. E. (1980). But it's only an inkblot. *Journal of Personality Assessment, 44,* 563–576.

Exner, J. E. (1996). Critical bits and the Rorschach response process. *Journal of Personality Assessment, 67,* 464–477.

Exner, J. E. (2003). *The Rorschach: A comprehensive system,* Volume 1. (4th ed.). Hoboken, NJ: Wiley.

Exner, J. E., Armbruster, G., & Mittman, B. (1978). The Rorschach response process. *Journal of Personality Assessment, 42,* 27–38.

Exner, J. E., Colligan, S. C., Hillman, L. B., Metts, A. S., Ritzler, B., Rogers, K. T.,... Viglione, D. J. (2001). *A Rorschach workbook for the Comprehensive System* (5th ed.). Asheville, NC: Rorschach Workshops.

Exner, J. E., & Weiner, I. B. (1995). *The Rorschach: A comprehensive system. Vol. 3, Assessment of children and adolescents* (2nd ed.). New York, NY: Wiley.

Finn, S. E., & Kamphuis, J. H. (1995). What a clinician needs to know about base rates (pp. 224–235). In J. N. Butcher (Ed.), *Clinical Personality Assessment*. New York, NY: Oxford University Press.

Fischer, C. T. (1994). Rorschach scoring questions as access to dynamics. *Journal of Personality Assessment, 62,* 515–525.

Foster, S. L., & Cone, J. D. (1995). Validity issues in clinical assessment. *Psychological Assessment, 7,* 248–260.

Frank, L. K. (1939/1962). Projective methods for the study of personality. In M. Hirt (Ed.), *Rorschach science* (pp. 31–52). New York, NY: Free Press.

Gacono, C. B, & Evans, F. B. with N. Kaser-Boyd (2008) *Handbook of forensic Rorschach psychology*. Mahwah, NJ: Erlbaum.

Giromini, L., Porcelli, P., Viglione, D., Parolin, L., & Pineda, J. (2010). The feeling of movement: EEG evidence for mirroring activity during the observations of static, ambiguous stimuli in the Rorschach cards. *Biological Psychology, 85,* 233–241.

Goldfried, M. R., Stricker, G., & Weiner, I. B. (1971). *Rorschach handbook of clinical and research applications*. Englewood Cliffs, NJ: Prentice-Hall.

Graham, J. R. (2006). *MMPI-2: Assessing personality and psychopathology* (4th ed.). New York, NY: Oxford University Press.

Greene, R. (2000). *The MMPI-2 An interpretive manual* (2nd.ed.). Needham Heights: Allyn & Bacon

Gynther, M. D., & Burkhart, B. R. (1983). Are subtle MMPI items expendable? In J. N. Butcher & C. D. Spielberger (Eds.), *Advances in personality assessment* (Vol. 2, pp. 115–132). Hillsdale, NJ: Erlbaum.

Handler, L. & Riethmiller, R. (1998). Teaching and learning the administration and interpretation of graphic techniques (pp. 270–272). In L. Handler & R. Hilsenroth (Eds.), *Teaching and learning personality assessment*. Mahwah, NJ: Erlbaum.

Hiller, J. B., Rosenthal, R., Bornstein, R. F., Berry, D. T. R., & Brunell-Neuleib, S. (1999). A comparative meta-analysis of Rorschach and MMPI validity. *Psychological Assessment, 11,* 278–296.

Hirt, M. (1962). *Rorschach science: Readings in theory and method*. New York, NY: Free Press.

Holaday, M., Smith, D. A., & Sherry, A. (2000). Sentence Completion Tests: A review of the literature and results of a survey of members of the society for personality assessment. *Journal of Personality Assessment, 74,* 371–383.

Holmes, D. S. (1974). The conscious control of thematic projection. *Journal of Consulting and Clinical Psychology, 42,* 232–329.

Holzman, P. S., Proctor, L. R., Levy, D. L., Yasillo, N. J., Meltzer, H. Y., & Hurt, S. W. (1974). Eye-tracking dysfunctions in schizophrenic patients and their relatives. *Archives of General Psychiatry, 31,* 143–151.

Hutt, M. L. (1945). The use of projective methods of personality measurement in army medical installations. *Journal of Clinical Psychology, 1,* 134–140.

Jenkins, S. R. (Ed.). (2008). *A handbook of clinical scoring systems for thematic apperceptive techniques*. Mahwah, NJ: Erlbaum.

Joy, S., Fein, D., Kaplan, E., & Freedman, M. (2001). Quantifying qualitative features of block design performance among healthy older adults. *Archives of Clinical Neuropsychology, 16,* 157–170.

Kaplan, E. (1991). A process approach to neuropsychological assessment. In T. Boll & B. K. Bryant (Eds.), *Clinical neuropsychology and brain function: Research, measurement, and practice* (pp. 125–168). Washington, DC: American Psychological Association.

Karon, B. P. (2000). The clinical interpretation of the Thematic Apperception Test, Rorschach, and other clinical data: A reexamination of statistical versus clinical prediction. *Professional Psychology: Research and Practice, 31,* 230–233.

Kaufman, A. S. (1979). *Intelligent testing with the WISC-R*. New York, NY: Wiley.

Kleiger, J. H. (1999). *Disordered thinking and the Rorschach: Theory, research, and differential diagnosis*. Hillsdale, NJ: Analytic Press.

Klopfer, B., Ainsworth, M. D., Klopfer, W. G., & Holt, R. R. (1954). *Developments in the Rorschach technique. Vol. I, Technique and theory*. Yonkers-on-Hudson, NY: World Book.

Klopfer, W. G. (1981). Integration of projective techniques in the clinical case study. In A. I. Rabin (Ed.), *Assessment with projective techniques: A concise introduction* (pp. 233–263). New York, NY: Springer.

Levine, D. (1981). Why and when to test: The social context of psychological testing. In A. I. Rabin (Ed.), *Assessment with projective techniques: A concise introduction* (pp. 553–580). New York, NY: Springer.

Levy, L. H. (1963). *Psychological interpretation*. New York, NY: Holt, Rinehart & Winston.

Little, K. B., & Shneidman, E. S. (1955). The validity of thematic projective technique interpretations. *Journal of Projective Techniques, 23,* 285–294.

Loevinger, J., & Wessler, R. (1970). *Measuring ego development: Construction and use of a Sentence Completion Test* (Vol. 1). San Francisco, CA: Jossey-Bass.

Masling, J. (1997). On the nature and utility of objective tests and projective tests. *Journal of Personality Assessment, 69,* 257–270.

Mayman, M., Schafer, R., & Rapaport, D. (1951). Interpretation of the Wechsler-Bellevue Intelligence Scale in Personality appraisal. In H. H. Anderson & G. L. Anderson (Eds.), *An introduction to projective techniques* (pp. 55–98). New York, NY: Prentice-Hall.

McClelland, D. C., Koestner, R., & Weinberger, J. (1989). How do self-attributed and implicit motives differ? *Psychological Review, 96,* 690–702.

Meehl, P. E. (1945/1956). The dynamics of "structured" personality tests. In G. S. Welsh & W. G. Dahlstrom (Eds.), *Basic readings on the MMPI in psychology and medicine* (pp. 5–11). Minneapolis: University of Minnesota Press.

Meyer, G. J. (1999). The convergent validity of MMPI and Rorschach scales: An extension using profile scores to define response-character styles on both methods and a re-examination of simple Rorschach response frequency. *Journal of Personality Assessment, 72,* 1–35.

Meyer, G. J., & Archer, R. P. (2001). The hard science of Rorschach research: What do we know and where do we go? *Psychological Assessment, 13,* 486–502.

Meyer, G. J., & Kurtz, J. E. (2006). Advancing personality assessment terminology: Time to retire "objective" and "projective" as personality test descriptors. *Journal of Personality Assessment, 87,* 223–225.

Meyer, G. J., Erdberg, P., & Shaffer, T. W. (2007). Toward international normative reference data for the Comprehensive System. *Journal of Personality Assessment, 89,* 201–216.

Meyer, G. J., Viglione, D. J., Mihura, J. L., Erard, R. E., & Erdberg, P. (2011). *Manual for the Rorschach Performance Assessment System*. Toledo, OH: R-PAS.

Minassian, A., Granholm, E., Verney, S., & Perry, W. (2004). Pupillary dilation to simple vs. complex tasks and its relationship to thought disturbance in schizophrenia patients. *International Journal of Psychophysiology, 52,* 53–62.

Morey, L. C. (1996). *An Interpretive Guide to the Personality Assessment Inventory (PAI)*. Odessa, FL: Psychological Assessment Resources.

Murray, H. A. (1938). *Explorations in personality*. New York, NY: Oxford University Press.

Murstein, B. I. (1961). Assumptions, adaptation-level, and projective techniques. *Perceptual and Motor Skills, 12,* 107–125.

Murstein, B. I. (1963). *Theory and research in projective techniques (emphasizing the TAT).* New York, NY: Wiley.

Murstein, B. I. (1965). *Handbook of projective techniques.* New York, NY: Basic Books.

Murstein, B. I., & Mathes, S. (1996). Projection on projective techniques = pathology: The problem that is not being addressed. *Journal of Personality Assessment, 66,* 337–349.

Perry, W., & Braff, D. L. (1994). Information-processing deficits and thought disorder in schizophrenia. *American Journal of Psychiatry, 151,* 363–367.

Perry, W., Felger, T., & Braff, D. (1998). The relationship between skin conductance hyporesponsivity and perseverations in schizophrenia patients. *Biological Psychiatry, 44,* 459–465.

Perry, W., Geyer, M. A., & Braff, D. L. (1999). Sensorimotor gating and thought disturbance measured in close temporal proximity in schizophrenic patients. *Archives of General Psychiatry, 56,* 277–281.

Perry, W., Viglione, D., & Braff, D. L. (1992). The Ego Impairment Index and schizophrenia: A validation study. *Journal of Personality Assessment, 59,* 165–175.

Pineda, J., Giromini, L., Porcelli, P., Parolin, L. & Viglione, D. (2011). Mu suppression and human movement responses to the Rorschach test. *NeuroReport, 22*(5): 223–226.

Peterson, C. A., & Schilling, K. M. (1983). Card pull in projective testing. *Journal of Personality Assessment, 47,* 265–275.

Rabin, A. I. (1981). *Assessment with projective techniques: A concise introduction.* New York, NY: Springer.

Riethmiller, R. J., & Handler, L. (1997). The great figure drawing controversy: The integration of research and clinical practice. *Journal of Personality Assessment, 69,* 488–496.

Rivera, B., & Viglione, D. (2010). Conceptualization of children's interpersonal relatedness with the Rorschach: A qualitative multiple case study. *Journal of Personality Assessment, 92,* 377–389.

Ronan, G. F., Colavito, V. A., & Hammontree, S. R. (1993). Personal problem-solving system for scoring TAT responses: preliminary validity and reliability data. *Journal of Personality Assessment, 61,* 28–40.

Ronan, G. F., Gibbs, M. S., Dreer, L. E., Lombardo, J. A. (2008). In S. R. Jenkins (Ed.), *A handbook of clinical scoring systems for Thematic Apperceptive Techniques* (pp. 181–207). Mahwah, NJ: Erlbaum.

Schachtel, E. G. (1966). *Experiential foundations of Rorschach's test.* New York, NY: Basic Books.

Schafer, R. (1954). *Psychoanalytic interpretation in Rorschach testing.* New York, NY: Grune & Stratton.

Shedler, J., Mayman, M., & Manis, M. (1993). The illusion of mental health. *American Psychologist,* 1117–1131.

Stricker, G., & Gold, J. R. (1999). The Rorschach: Toward a nomothetically based, idiographically applicable configurational model. *Psychological Assessment, 11,* 240–250.

Stricker, G., & Healy, B. D. (1990). Projective assessment of object relations: A review of the empirical literature. *Psychological Assessment: A Journal of Consulting and Clinical Psychology, 2,* 219–230.

Tomkins, S. S. (1947). *The Thematic Apperception Test* (rev. ed.). New York, NY: Grune & Stratton.

van dan Daele, L. (2007). *Music Apperception Test manual.* Las Vegas, NV: Psychodiagnostics.

Viglione, D. J. (1999). A review of recent research addressing the utility of the Rorschach. *Psychological Assessment, 11,* 251–265.

Viglione, D. J. (1996). Data and issues to consider in reconciling self-report and the Rorschach. *Journal of Personality Assessment, 67,* 579–587.

Viglione, D. J., & Hilsenroth, M. (2001). The Rorschach: Facts, fictions, and future. *Psychological Assessment, 13,* 452–471.

Viglione, D. J., & Meyer, G. J (2008). An overview of Rorschach psychometrics for forensic practice. In C. B. Gacono & F. B. Evans with N. Kaser-Boyd (Eds.) *Handbook of forensic Rorschach psychology.* (pp. 22–54). Mahwah, NJ: Erlbaum.

Viglione, D. J., & Perry, W. (1991). A general model for psychological assessment and psychopathology applied to depression. *British Journal of Projective Psychology, 36,* 1–16.

Watson, R. I. (1978). The Sentence Completion Method. In B. B. Wolman (Ed.), *Clinical diagnosis of mental disorders: A handbook* (pp. 255–280). New York, NY: Plenum Press.

Weiner, I. B. (1966). *Psychodiagnosis in schizophrenia.* New York, NY: Wiley.

Weiner, I. B. (1994). The Rorschach Inkblot Method (RIM) is not a test: Implications for theory and practice. *Journal of Personality Assessment, 62,* 498–504.

Weiner, I. B. (1999). What the Rorschach can do for you: Incremental validity in clinical applications. *Assessment, 6,* 327–338.

Weiner, I. B. (2001). Advancing the science of psychological assessment: The Rorschach Inkblot Method as exemplar. *Psychological Assessment, 13,* 423–432.

Weiner, I. B. (2003). *Principles of Rorschach interpretation* (2nd ed.). Mahwah, NJ: Erlbaum.

# CHAPTER 24

# Self-Report Inventories

## Assessing Personality and Psychopathology

YOSSEF S. BEN-PORATH

Self-report inventories (SRIs) have been a mainstay of assessment psychology for over eight decades. Researchers and clinicians use them frequently in a broad range of settings and applications. These assessment devices require that a test taker respond to a series of stimuli, the test items, by indicating whether, or to what extent, they describe some aspect of his or her functioning. The response format varies from a dichotomous "true" or "false" to a Likert scale indication of degree of agreement with the statement as a self-description. Some SRIs focus primarily on abnormal functioning or psychopathology whereas others concentrate more on normal personality characteristics. Still others cover both normal and abnormal aspects of personality and psychopathology.

Self-report inventories differ in several notable ways in addition to their relative emphasis on normal versus abnormal personality. One important variable is their conceptual basis. Some SRIs are developed with guidance from a particular personality or psychopathology theory or model whereas others are based more on the results of empirical analyses. In this context, Ben-Porath (2006) noted that personality test developers have typically pursued their efforts from two broad, non–mutually exclusive perspectives. One approach, the clinical perspective, is designed to produce clinically useful instruments that help detect and characterize psychopathology. Self-report inventory developers who follow this approach typically are clinically trained psychologists who focus on conducting applied research. Test developers working from

the normal personality perspective typically have backgrounds in personality or developmental psychology and often seek to construct measures of normal-range personality constructs that can serve as tools in basic personality research. Self-report inventories can also be distinguished in terms of the approaches used to construct and interpret scores on their scales, the methods used to derive standard scores for these scales, and the availability and types of scales and techniques designed to monitor individuals' test-taking attitude and its impact on scale scores.

This chapter first describes the history and development of SRIs and summarizes early criticisms of this technique. Next, current issues in SRI interpretation are described and discussed. Finally, directions for future SRI research are outlined.

## EARLY HISTORY

Ben-Porath and Butcher (1991) identified three primary personality assessment techniques and differentiated between them based on the means and sources used for data collection. Behavioral observations include methods in which personality is assessed by systematically recorded observations of an individual's behavior. Examples include Cattell's (1965, 1979) T (systematic experimentation) and L (behavioral observation) data. Somatic examinations consist of techniques that rely on some form of physical measurement as the basis for assessing psychological functioning. Examples include various psychophysiological measures (e.g., Keller, Hicks, & Miller, 2000). Verbal examinations rely on verbalizations (oral, written, or a combination of the two) produced by the individual being assessed or another person who presumably knows the assessment target. Self-report inventories, as defined earlier, are a subclass of the verbal examination techniques. Projective or performance-based assessment techniques (e.g., the Rorschach and Thematic Apperception Test [TAT]) also fall under this definition.

Ben-Porath and Butcher (1991) traced the early origins of verbal examinations to an elaborate system of competitive examinations (described in detail by DuBois, 1970) used for over 3,000 years to select personnel for the Chinese civil service. Candidates for government positions were tested (and retested every three years) to determine their suitability for these prestigious appointments. Examinees were required to write essays for hours at a time, over a period of several successive days. The essays were used (among other purposes) to gauge the candidates' character and fitness for office (DuBois, 1970).

In the modern era, Sir Francis Galton was the first to suggest and try out systematic procedures for measuring psychological variables based on verbalizations (as well as some novel approaches to behavioral observations). Influenced heavily by the writings of his cousin, Charles Darwin, Galton was interested in devising precise methods for measuring individual differences in mental traits he believed were the product of evolution. Laying the foundations for quantitative approaches to personality assessment, Galton wrote:

> We want lists of facts, every one of which may be separately verified, valued, and revalued, and the whole accurately summed. It is the statistics of each man's conduct in small everyday affairs that will probably be found to give the simplest and most precise measure of his character. (1884, p. 185)

Most of Galton's efforts to elicit such information through verbalizations focused on devising various associative tasks.

The Dutch scholars Heymans and Wiersma (1906) were the first to devise a questionnaire for the task of personality assessment. They constructed a 90-item rating scale and asked some 3,000 physicians to use the scale to describe people with whom they were well acquainted. Based on correlations they found among traits that were rated, Heymans and Wiersma, in essence, developed a crude, hierarchical, factor-analytically generated personality model. They proposed that individuals may be described in terms of their standing on eight lower-order traits: Amorphous, Apathetic, Nervous, Sentimental, Sanguine, Phlegmatic, Choleric, and Impassioned. These traits consisted, in turn, of various combinations of three higher-order traits labeled Activity, Emotionality, and Primary versus Secondary Function. This structure bears substantial similarity to Eysenck's three-factor (Extraversion, Neuroticism, Psychopathy) personality model (Eysenck & Eysenck, 1975) and the three higher-order factors of Tellegen's (forthcoming) Multidimensional Personality Questionnaire.

Hoch and Amsden (1913) and Wells (1914) provided further elaboration on the Heymans and Wiersma (1906) model's utility for personality description and assessment by adding to it various psychopathology symptoms. Their work, in turn, laid the foundations for the first systematic effort to develop a self-report personality questionnaire, Woodworth's (1920) Personal Data Sheet. Woodworth developed the Personal Data Sheet to assist in identifying psychoneurotic individuals who were unfit for duty in the U.S. military during World War I. This need arose because of the large number of combat personnel who had developed shell shock during the conflict. The questionnaire was to be used as a screening instrument so that recruits who exceeded a certain threshold would be referred for follow-up examinations.

DuBois (1970) reported that Woodworth initially compiled hundreds of "neurotic" items from various sources as candidates for inclusion on his questionnaire. Candidate items were selected if their content was judged to be potentially relevant to identifying neurosis. Items were phrased in question form, and test takers were instructed to answer "yes" or "no" to indicate whether each item described them accurately. Woodworth conducted a series of empirical investigations and eliminated items answered "yes" by large numbers of normal individuals. The final questionnaire consisted of 116 items. All were keyed such that a "yes" response was an indication of psychoneurosis. Although the Personal Data Sheet was never used for the purposes for which it was constructed—the war had ended by the time it was completed—both its items and Woodworth's reliance (in part) on empirical analyses for its construction served as the cornerstones for most subsequent self-report personality inventories.

With the conclusion of World War I, Woodworth abandoned his test development efforts and refocused his attention on experimental psychology. However, a number of researchers in the then-novel subdiscipline of personality psychology followed in his footsteps. Downey's (1923) Will-Temperament tests, Travis's (1925) Diagnostic Character Test, Heidbreder's (1926)

Extraversion-Introversion test, Thurstone's (1930) Personality Schedule, and Allport's (1928) Ascendance-Submission measure were among the more prominent early successors to Woodworth's efforts. Over the next three decades, a substantial literature evaluating the SRI technique's merits accumulated. Two comprehensive reviews of this methodology reflected the normal personality and clinical perspectives on assessing personality and psychopathology by self-report. Both Allport (1937), adopting a normal personality perspective, and Ellis (1946), from the clinical perspective, noted the rapid proliferation of SRIs while expressing concern (for somewhat different reasons) about their scientific foundations.

## Allport's Critique

Allport (1937), among the originators of the field of personality psychology, anticipated (correctly) that SRIs would enjoy widespread use in personality research and compared them (somewhat skeptically) with the then more established use of behavioral ratings as a source for quantitative personality data:

> Though less objective than behavioral scales, standardized questionnaires have the merit of sampling a much wider range of behavior, through the medium of the subject's report on his customary conduct or attitudes in a wide variety of situations. These paper and pencil tests are popular for a number of reasons. For one thing, they are fun to construct and fun to take. Students find them diverting, and teachers accordingly use them as agreeable classroom demonstrations. Furthermore, the scores on the tests can be manipulated in diverse ways, and when the quantitative yield of the coefficients and group differences is complete, everyone has a comforting assurance concerning the "scientific" status of personality. (p. 448)

In considering self-report personality questionnaires' merits, Allport (1937) identified several limitations that remain salient in current applications of this methodology. One was that "[i]t is a fallacy to assume that all people have the same psychological reasons for their similar responses [to self-report items]" (p. 449). Allport answered this concern by quoting Binet: "Let the items be crude if only there be enough of them.... One hopes through sheer length of a series that the erroneous diagnoses will to a certain extent cancel one another, and that a trustworthy residual score will remain" (p. 449).

In describing a second major limitation of personality tests, Allport (1937) stated:

Another severe criticism lies in the ability of the subject to fake the test if he chooses to do so...Anyone by trying can (on paper) simulate introversion, conservatism, or even happiness. And if he thinks he has something to gain, he is quite likely to do so.... Even well intentioned subjects may fail insight or slip into systematic error or bias that vitiates the value of their answers. (p. 450)

Thus, Allport listed their transparent nature and susceptibility to intentional and unintentional manipulation among the major limitations of SRIs.

In reviewing the major SRIs of his time, Allport (1937) singled out the Bernreuter Personality Inventory (BPI; Bernreuter, 1933). The BPI consisted of 125 items (originating from several previous SRIs including the Personal Data Sheet) phrased as questions with a "yes" "no" or "?" (i.e., cannot say) response format. The items yielded scores on four common personality traits, labeled Dominance, Self-Sufficiency, Introversion, and Neuroticism. Each of the 125 items was scored on all four scales (although some were scored zero), according to empirically derived criteria. For example, if answered "?," the item "Do you often feel just miserable" was scored $-3$ on introversion, $-1$ on dominance, 0 on neuroticism, and 0 on self-sufficiency. Allport questioned the logic of this approach and recommended instead that items be scored on single scales only.

Finally, Allport (1937) grappled with the question of whether multiscaled SRIs should be designed to measure independent traits or constructs. Commenting on the then-budding practice of factor-analyzing scores on multiscale SRIs to derive "independent factors," Allport noted:

> Unnecessary trouble springs from assuming, as some testers do, that independent factors are to be preferred to interdependent traits. What if certain scales do correlate with each other.... Each scale may still represent a well-conceived, measurable common trait.... No harm is done by overlap; indeed, overlap is a reasonable expectation in view of that roughness of approximation which is the very nature of the entire procedure (also in view of the tendency of certain traits to cluster). Well-considered scales with some overlap are preferable to ill-conceived scales without overlap. To seek intelligible units is a better psychological goal than to seek independent units. (p. 329)

By "overlap," Allport was referring to statistical association, not item overlap, which, as just noted, he counseled against in constructing SRIs.

In summary, viewing SRIs from the normal personality perspective, Allport (1937) raised several important concerns regarding the early successors to Woodworth's

Personal Data Sheet. Recognizing their simplicity of use and consequent appeal, Allport cautioned that SRIs, by necessity, distill human personality to common traits at the expense of a more complete, individually crafted personality description. He emphasized SRIs' tremendous vulnerability to intentional and unintentional distortion, viewing it as an inherent feature of this methodology. He criticized the BPI's method of scoring the same item on multiple scales as well as early efforts by factor analysts to reduce multiscale instruments such as the BPI to a small number of independent factors. Allport offered this rather ambivalent concluding appraisal of the nascent area of personality assessment by self-report: "Historically considered the extension of mental measurements into the field of personality is without doubt one of the outstanding events in American psychology during the twentieth century. The movement is still in its accelerating phase, and the swift output of ingenious tests has quite outstripped progress in criticism and theory" (p. 455).

## Ellis's Review of Personality Questionnaires

Ellis (1946), writing from the clinical perspective, offered a comprehensive appraisal of personality questionnaires near the midpoint of the 20th century. He opened his critique with this generalization:

> While the reliabilities of personality questionnaires have been notoriously high, their validities have remained more questionable. Indeed some of the most widely known and used paper and pencil personality tests have been cavalierly marketed without any serious attempts on the part of their authors to validate them objectively . . . no real endeavors have been made to show that, when used according to their standard directions, these instruments will actually do the clinical jobs they are supposed to do: meaning, that they will adequately differentiate neurotics from non-neurotics, introverts from extroverts, dominant from submissive persons, and so on. (p. 385)

Ellis noted that several authors had preceded him in criticizing SRIs and outlined these emerging points of concern:

- Most empirical SRI studies have focused on their reliability (which has been established) while ignoring matters of validity.
- SRIs do not provide a whole, organismic picture of human behavior. Although they may accurately portray a group of individuals, they are not useful in individual diagnosis.

- Some questionnaires (like the BPI) that purport to measure several distinct traits are, at best, measuring the same one under two or more names.
- Different individuals interpret the same SRI questions in different ways.
- Most subjects can easily falsify their answers to SRIs and frequently choose to do so.
- SRIs' "yes/?/no" response format may compromise the scales' validity.
- Lack of internal consistency may invalidate a questionnaire, but presence of internal consistency does not necessarily validate it.
- SRIs' vocabulary range may cause misunderstandings by respondents and thus adversely affect validity.
- Testing is an artificial procedure, which has little to do with real-life situations.
- Some personality questionnaires are validated against other questionnaires from which their items were largely taken, thus rendering their validation spurious.
- Even when respondents do their best to answer questions truthfully, they may lack insight into their true behavior or may unconsciously be quite a different person from the picture of themselves they draw on the test.
- Armchair (rather than empirical) construction and evaluation of test items is frequently used in personality questionnaires.
- Uncritical use of statistical procedures with many personality tests adds a spurious reality to data that were none too accurate in the first place.
- Many personality tests that claim to measure the same traits (e.g., introversion-extroversion) have very low intercorrelations with each other.
- There are no statistical shortcuts to the understanding of human nature; such as the ones many test users try to arrive at through involved factorial analyses.

Although generated from a notably different perspective, Ellis's (1946) concerns overlap substantially with Allport's (1937) reservations. The two authors also shared consternation that, in spite of these glaring deficiencies, SRIs had become quite popular: "In spite of the many assaults that have been made against it, the paper and pencil personality test has got along splendidly as far as usage is concerned. For there can be little doubt that Americans have, to date, taken more of the Woodworth-Thurstone-Bernreuter type of questionnaires than all other kinds of personality tests combined" (Ellis, 1946, p. 388).

To explain their seemingly unfounded popularity, Ellis (1946) identified several advantages that their proponents claimed for SRIs:

- They are relatively easy to administer and score.
- Even if the respondent's self-description is not taken at face value, it may itself provide some clinically meaningful information.
- Although scale scores may be meaningless, examination of individual responses by experienced clinicians may provide valid clinical material.
- Statistical analyses had shown that the traits posited by questionnaires were not simply the product of chance factors.
- Normal and abnormal test takers tended to give different answers to SRI items.
- It does not matter if respondents answer untruthfully on personality questionnaires, since allowances are made for this in standardization or scoring of the tests.
- Traditional methods of validating questionnaires by outside criteria are themselves faulty and invalid; hence, validation by internal consistency alone is perfectly sound.

Having outlined the prevailing pros and cons for personality questionnaires (from a decidedly con-slanted perspective), Ellis (1946) proceeded to conduct a comprehensive, albeit crude, meta-analysis of the literature on the validity of personality tests, differentiating between two methods for validating personality questionnaires. He dubbed one method subjective and described it rather derogatorily as consisting of "checking the test against itself: that is[,] seeing whether respondents answer its questions in a manner showing it to be internally consistent" (p. 390). He described the second method, labeled objective personality test validation, as:

> checking a schedule, preferably item by item, against an outside clinical criterion. Thus, a questionnaire may be given to a group of normal individuals and to another group of subjects who have been diagnosed by competent outside observers as neurotic, or maladjusted, or psychotic, delinquent, or introverted. Often, the clinically diagnosed group makes significantly higher neurotic scores than does the normal group, [so] the test under consideration is said to have been validated. (p. 390)

Ellis questioned whether the subjective method had any bearing on tests' validity, stating that "[i]nternal consistency of a questionnaire demonstrates, at best, that it is a reliable test of something; but that something may still

have little or no relation to the clinical diagnosis for which the test presumably has been designed" (p. 391). He also found very limited utility in the objective methods of test validation, citing their sole reliance on questionable validity criteria. Nonetheless, he proceeded to review over 250 published objective validation studies classified into six types based on the method used to generate criterion validity data. Ellis sought to quantify his analysis by keeping count of the number of positive, negative, and questionable findings (based on whether these were statistically significant) in each category of studies. Overall, he found positive results in 31% of the studies, questionable ones in 17%, and negative findings in 52% of the publications included in his survey. Ellis concluded, "Obviously, this is not a very good record for the validity of paper and pencil personality questionnaires" (p. 422).

In selecting studies for inclusion in his analysis, Ellis (1946) singled one instrument out for separate treatment and analysis, the then relatively unknown Minnesota Multiphasic Personality Inventory (MMPI; Hathaway & McKinley, 1943). Ellis explained that, unlike the more established instruments included in his review, which were administered anonymously by paper and pencil to groups of subjects, the MMPI was administered individually, simulating more accurately a clinical interview. Of the 15 MMPI studies he reviewed, Ellis reported positive results in 10 studies, questionable ones in 3, and negative findings in 2 investigations.

Ellis's overall conclusions regarding validity of SRIs were quite negative:

> We may conclude, therefore, that judging from the validity studies on group-administered personality questionnaires thus far reported in the literature, there is at best one chance in two that these tests will validly discriminate between groups of adjusted and maladjusted individuals, and there is very little indication that they can be safely used to diagnose individual cases or to give valid estimations of the personality traits of specific respondents. The older, more conventional, and more widely used forms of these tests seem to be, for practical diagnostic purposes, hardly worth the paper on which they are printed. Among the newer questionnaires, the Minnesota Multiphasic schedule appears to be the most promising one—perhaps because it gets away from group administration which has hitherto been synonymous with personality test-giving. More research in this direction is well warranted at the present time. (1946, p. 425)

Judged with the hindsight of 66 years, Ellis's critique appears rather naive and substantially flawed. Ellis himself questioned the utility of the validation methods used in the studies he included in his analyses, noting (correctly) that many, if not most, relied on questionably valid criteria. Given this limitation, these studies could not adequately demonstrate the validity or invalidity of SRIs. Although the tests he reviewed were indeed psychometrically inadequate, Ellis's effort to appraise them empirically was hampered significantly by limitations in the literature he reviewed. Moreover, his summary dismissal of internal consistency as having little or no bearing on validity was overstated.

Nonetheless, Ellis's review, published in the prestigious *Psychological Bulletin*, had a devastating effect on the position of SRIs within the budding field of clinical psychology. Dahlstrom (1992) described the widespread skepticism with which all SRIs were perceived in the 10 years following this and several similar analyses. Indeed, use of tests (such as the BPI) that Ellis had singled out for their lack of validity waned dramatically. Ellis (1946) did, however, anticipate correctly that the MMPI might emerge as a viable alternative to the SRIs of the first half of the 20th century.

Ellis (1953) revisited this issue 7 years later, in an updated review of the validity of personality tests. He concluded that there had been limited progress in developing valid personality SRIs and focused his criticism on the instruments' susceptibility to intentional and unintentional distortion. He was particularly concerned with the effects of unconscious defenses. Ellis again singled out the MMPI as an instrument whose authors had at least made an attempt to correct for these effects on its scale scores, but he expressed skepticism about the success of such corrections. He also observed that the efforts involved in correcting and properly interpreting MMPI scores might better be otherwise invested, stating: "The clinical psychologist who cannot, in the time it now takes a trained worker to administer, score, and interpret a test like the MMPI according to the best recommendations of its authors, get much more pertinent, incisive, and depth-centered 'personality' material from a straightforward interview technique would hardly appear to be worth his salt" (p. 48).

Curiously, Ellis (1953) saw no need to subject the preferred "straightforward interview technique" to the type of scrutiny he applied to SRIs. That task would be left to Meehl (1956) in his seminal monograph comparing the validity of clinical and actuarial assessment techniques.

### Summary of Early History

Self-report inventories emerged as an attractive but scientifically limited approach to personality assessment during the first half of the 20th century. Representing the normal personality perspective, Allport (1937) criticized these instruments for being inherently narrow in scope and unnecessarily divorced from any personality theory. Ellis (1946), writing from the clinical perspective, concluded that there was little or no empirical evidence of their validity as diagnostic instruments. Both authors identified their susceptibility to intentional and unintentional distortion and the implicit assumption that test items have the same meaning to different individuals as major and inherent weakness of SRIs as personality and psychopathology measures.

## CURRENT ISSUES IN PERSONALITY ASSESSMENT BY SELF-REPORT

In spite of their shaky beginnings, SRIs emerged during the second half of the 20th century as the most widely used and studied method for assessing personality and psychopathology. Modern SRI developers sought to address the limitations of their predecessors in a variety of ways. Various approaches to SRI scale construction are described next, followed by a review of current issues in SRI scale score interpretation. These include the roles of empirical data and item content in interpreting SRI scale scores, methods used to derive standard scores for SRI interpretation, and threats to the validity of individual SRI protocols.

Throughout this section, examples from the SRI literature are cited, and most of these involve either the MMPI or its subsequent versions, the second edition of the MMPI (MMPI-2) (Butcher, Graham, Ben-Porath, Tellegen, Dahlstrom, & Kaemmer, 2001) and MMPI-2-RF (Ben-Porath & Tellegen, 2008a; Tellegen & Ben-Porath, 2008). Emphasis on the MMPI reflects this instrument's central role in the modern personality assessment literature.

### Approaches to SRI Scale Construction

Burisch (1984) described three primary, non–mutually exclusive approaches that have been used in SRI scale construction. The external approach involves using collateral (i.e., extratest) data to identify items for an SRI scale. Here individuals are classified into known groups based on criteria that are independent of scale scores (e.g., psychiatric diagnoses) and items are chosen based on their empirical ability to differentiate among members of different groups. The method is sometimes also called empirical keying. Self-report inventory developers who view personality or psychopathology categorically and seek to develop empirical methods for classifying individuals into predetermined categories typically use the external scale construction method. Often these categories correspond to diagnostic classes, such as schizophrenia or major depression. As would be expected, scale developers who rely on this approach typically assume a clinical perspective on personality assessment.

Ellis (1946) highlighted a major limitation of the external approach in his critique of SRIs as measures of personality and psychopathology. That is, their validity is constrained by the criteria used in their development. Absent consensually agreed-on criteria for classification (a situation not uncommon in psychological assessment, and what typically motivates efforts to develop a scale to begin with), test developers must rely on imperfect or controversial external criteria for subject group assignment, item selection, and subsequent cross-validation. Consequently, scales developed with this method have generally not fared well as predictors of the class membership status that they were designed to predict. However, in some instances (e.g., the MMPI clinical scales), empirical research subsequent to their development has guided fruitful application of externally developed scales in ways other than those in which their developers intended originally that they be used, by identifying clinically meaningful correlates of these scales and the patterns of scores among them.

Scale developers who follow the inductive approach, according to Burisch (1984), assume that there exists a basic, probably universal, personality structure, which they attempt both to discover and to measure. The approach is considered inductive because its adherents do not set out to measure a preconceived set of traits but instead leave it up to empirical analyses to reveal important personality dimensions and the relations among them. In the process, an SRI is developed to measure the discovered personality structure. Scale developers who apply the inductive approach often adhere to a normal personality perspective on assessment. They typically rely on various forms of factor analysis, and the constructs they identify characteristically are dimensional. A leading example of an inductively derived SRI is Cattell's 16 Personality Factor Questionnaire (16PF; Cattell, Cattell, & Cattell, 1993). Inductive scale development ideally follows an iterative process of item writing, data collection, factor analysis, and item revision, followed by subsequent rounds of data collection, analysis, and item modification (e.g., Tellegen & Waller, 2009).

Finally, Burisch (1984) described the deductive approach to personality scale construction as one in which developers start with a conceptually grounded personality model and rationally write or select items that are consonant with their conceptualization. Most early personality and psychopathology SRI developers followed this approach in developing the MMPI precursors so devastatingly criticized by Allport (1937) and Ellis (1946). Consequently, deductive scale construction was viewed for many years as an inferior, less sophisticated form of SRI development. Burisch argued and demonstrated that these seemingly less sophisticated scale development techniques often yield measures that compare quite favorably with products of external and inductive scale construction.

The three approaches to scale construction are not mutually exclusive. Any combination of the three may be used in constructing an SRI scale, or different sets of scales within the same instrument. For example, the MMPI-2 (Butcher et al., 2001) contains three sets of scales, each initially based on a different one of the three approaches to scale construction—the Clinical Scales (Hathaway, 1956; Hathaway & McKinley, 1940, 1942; McKinley & Hathaway, 1940, 1942, 1944), originally based on the external method; the Content Scales (Butcher, Graham, Williams, & Ben-Porath, 1990), constructed with a modified deductive approach; and the Personality Psychopathology Five (PSY-5; Harkness, McNulty, & Ben-Porath, 1995), the end product of an inductive research project (Harkness & McNulty, 1994).

Several variations and combinations of these approaches were used in developing the MMPI-2-RF as well (Tellegen & Ben-Porath, 2008). In describing the development of the first set of scales to be added to the MMPI-2-RF, the Restructured Clinical (RC) Scales, Tellegen, Ben-Porath, McNulty, Arbisi, Graham, and Kaemmer (2003) noted that limitations of both the deductive and inductive approaches weighed against applying them exclusively in an effort to address significant limitations of the original Clinical Scales. Specifically, they argued that factorially pure dimensions, which would result from application of the inductive approach reflected in Cattell's work, may miss clinically important phenomena—ones that are rare and/or do not conform to the requirements of simple structure. Conversely, Jackson's (1971) recipe for deductive scale construction required convergence on a consensual set of target constructs, a state that had yet to be accomplished in personality or clinical psychology. Thus, beginning with a set of scales constructed following the external approach, Tellegen at al. (2003) applied a combined scale construction approach that retained the use of inductive, exploratory factor analyses to guide the identification of targets for scale development while adopting a flexible, conceptually and empirically grounded deductive approach to the process of assembling a revised set of scales from the entire MMPI-2 item pool. Similar methods were followed in constructing other MMPI-2-RF scales (Tellegen & Ben-Porath, 2008).

## Approaches to SRI Scale Score Interpretation

Two general approaches to SRI scale score interpretation can be identified based on their sources for interpretive conclusions. Empirically grounded interpretations rely on empirical data to form the basis for ascribing meaning to SRI scale scores. Content-based interpretations are guided by SRI scales' item content. Traditionally, empirically grounded approaches played a more central role in personality and psychopathology SRIs; however, more recently, content-based interpretation has gained increasing recognition and use. As is discussed after the two approaches are described, they are not mutually exclusive.

### Empirically Grounded Interpretation

Meehl (1945) outlined the basic logic of empirically grounded SRI scale interpretation in his classic article, "The Dynamics of 'Structured' Personality Inventories." Responding to early SRI critics' contention that the instruments are inherently flawed because their interpretation is predicated on the assumption that test takers are motivated, and able, to respond accurately to their items, he stated:

> A "self-rating" constitutes an intrinsically interesting and significant bit of verbal behavior, the non-test correlates of which must be discovered by empirical means. Not only is this approach free from the restriction that the subject must be able to describe his own behavior accurately, but a careful study of structured personality tests built on this basis shows that such a restriction would falsify the actual relationships that hold between what a man says and what he is. (p. 297)

Thus, according to Meehl, empirical interpretation is neither predicated nor dependent on what the test taker says (or thinks he or she is saying) in responding to SRI items but rather on the empirical correlates of these statements (as summarized in SRI scale scores).

Two subclasses can be distinguished among the empirical approaches to SRI scale interpretation. Scales constructed with the external approach are expected, based on the method used in their construction, to differentiate empirically between members of the groups used in

their development. This form of empirical interpretation, which may be called empirically keyed interpretation, is predicated on the assumption that if members of different groups (e.g., a target group of depressed patients and a comparison sample of nonpatients) answer a set of items differently, individuals who answer these items similarly to target group members likely belong to that group (i.e., they are depressed). This turns out to be a problematic assumption that requires (and often fails to achieve) empirical verification. Consequently, empirically keyed interpretations, as defined here, are used infrequently in current SRI applications.

The second approach to empirical interpretation is predicated on post hoc statistical identification of variables that are correlated with SRI scale scores (i.e., their empirical correlates). The empirical correlate interpretation approach is independent of the method used to develop a scale and may be applied to measures constructed by any (one or combination) of the three methods just outlined. Unlike the empirically keyed approach, it requires no a priori assumptions regarding the implications of one scale construction technique or another. All that is required are relevant extratest data regarding individuals whose SRI scale scores are available. Statistical analyses are conducted to identify variables that are correlated empirically with SRI scale scores; these are their empirical correlates. For example, if a scale score is empirically correlated with extratest indicators of depressive symptoms, individuals who score higher than others on that scale can be described as more likely than others to display depressive symptomatology.

Empirical correlates can guide SRI scale interpretation at two inference levels. The example just given represents a simple, direct inference level. The empirical fact that a scale score is correlated with an extratest depression indicator is used to gauge the depression of an individual who produces a given score on that scale. The correlation between scale and external indicator represents its criterion validity, which in turn reflects the confidence level we should place in an interpretation based on this correlation.

Although the concept of interpreting scale scores based on their criterion validity represents a simple and direct inference level, the process of establishing and understanding criterion validity of SRIs is complex and challenging. As already noted, the absence of valid criteria often motivates scale development to begin with. In addition, as with any psychological variable, criterion measures themselves are always, to some extent, unreliable. Consequently, validity coefficients—the observed correlations between SRI scale scores and criteria—always underestimate the scales' criterion validity. If a criterion's reliability can be reasonably estimated, through correction for attenuation due to unreliability it is possible to derive a more accurate estimate of criterion validity. However, this is rarely done, and it does not address limitations of criterion validity coefficients imposed by the imperfect validity of the criterion measures. Self-report inventory critics often point to rather low criterion validity coefficients as indications of these instruments' psychometric weakness, without giving adequate consideration to the limitations just noted.

A second, more complex, and less direct inference level in empirical interpretation of SRI scale scores involves reliance on their construct validity. Cronbach and Meehl (1955) indicated:

> Construct validation is involved whenever a test is to be interpreted as a measure of some attribute or quality that is not operationally defined.... When an investigator believes that no criterion available to him is fully valid, he perforce becomes interested in construct validity because this is the only way to avoid the infinite frustration of relating every criterion to some more ultimate standard.... Construct validity must be investigated whenever no criterion or universe of content is accepted as entirely adequate to define the quality to be measured. (p. 282)

Cronbach and Meehl (1955) described construct validation as an ongoing process of learning (through empirical research) about the nature of psychological constructs that underlie scale scores and using this knowledge to guide and refine their interpretation. They defined the seemingly paradoxical bootstraps effect, whereby a test may be constructed based on a fallible criterion and, through the process of construct validation, that same test winds up having greater validity than the criterion used in its construction. As an example, they cited the MMPI Pd scale, which was developed using an external scale construction approach with the intent that it be used to identify individuals with a psychopathic personality. Cronbach and Meehl noted that the scale turned out to have a limited degree of criterion validity for this task. However, as its empirical correlates became elucidated through subsequent research, a construct underlying Pd scores emerged that allowed MMPI interpreters to describe individuals who score high on this scale based on both a broad range of empirical correlates and a conceptual understanding of the Pd construct. The latter allowed for further predictions about likely Pd correlates to be made and tested empirically. These tests, in turn,

broadened or sharpened (depending on the research outcome) the scope of the Pd construct and its empirical correlates.

Knowledge of a scale's construct validity offers a rich, more comprehensive foundation for empirical interpretation than does criterion validity alone. It links the assessment process to theoretical conceptualizations and formulations in a manner described by Cronbach and Meehl (1955) as involving a construct's nomological network, "the interlocking system of laws which constitute a theory" (p. 290). Thus, empirical research can enhance our understanding of (and ability to interpret) psychological test results by placing them in the context of well-developed and appropriately tested theories.

Whether it is based on criterion or construct validity, or both, empirically grounded SRI interpretation can occur at two levels, focusing either on individual scale scores or on configurations among them. Configural interpretation involves simultaneous consideration of scores on more than one SRI scale. Linear interpretation involves separate, independent consideration and interpretation of each SRI scale score.

Much of the literature on this topic involves the MMPI. The move toward configural MMPI interpretation came on the heels of the test's failure to meet its developers' original goal, differential diagnosis of eight primary forms of psychopathology. Clinical experience, bolstered by findings from a series of studies (e.g., Black, 1953; Guthrie, 1952; Halbower, 1955; Hathaway & Meehl, 1951), led MMPI interpreters to conclude that robust empirical correlates for the test were most likely to be found if individuals were classified into types based on the pattern of scores they generated on the test's clinical scales. Based partly on this development, Meehl's (1954) treatise on clinical versus actuarial prediction advocated that researchers pursue a three-pronged task: First, they must identify meaningful classes within which individuals tend to cluster. These would replace the Kraepelinian nosology that served as the target for the original development of the MMPI clinical scales. Next, investigators would need to devise reliable and valid ways of identifying to which class a given individual belongs. Finally, they would identify the empirical correlates of class membership.

In his subsequent call for a so-called cookbook-based interpretation, Meehl (1956) proposed that MMPI profiles could serve all three purposes. Patterns of scores (i.e., configurations) on MMPI clinical scales could be used to identify clinically meaningful and distinct types of individuals; these scores could be used (based on a series of classification rules) to assign individuals to a specific profile type; and empirical research could be conducted to elucidate the correlates of MMPI profile type group membership. Several investigators (most notably Marks & Seeman, 1963, and Gilberstadt & Duker, 1965) followed Meehl's call and produced such MMPI-based classification and interpretation systems.

Underlying configural scale score interpretation is the assumption that there is something about a combination of scores on SRI scales that is not captured by consideration of each scale score individually (i.e., a linear interpretation) and that the whole is somehow greater than (or at least different from) the sum of its parts. For example, there is something to be learned about an individual who generates his or her most deviant scores on MMPI scales 1 (Hypochondriasis) and 3 (Hysteria) that is not reflected in the individual's scores on these scales when they are considered separately. Statistically, this amounts to the expectation of an interaction among scale scores in the prediction of relevant extratest data. Surprisingly (given that it emerged as the dominant approach to MMPI clinical scale score interpretation), the assumption of an interaction among scales that make up the configuration has not been extensively tested.

### Content-Based Interpretation

Content-based SRI interpretation involves reliance on item content to interpret scale scores. For example, if a scale's items contain a list of depressive symptoms, scores on that scale are interpreted to reflect the individual's self-reported depression. It is distinguished from deductive SRI scale construction in that the latter involves using item content for scale development, not necessarily interpretation. Indeed, scales constructed by any of the three primary approaches (external, inductive, or deductive) can be interpreted based on their item content, and SRI measures constructed deductively can be interpreted with an empirically grounded approach.

Content-based SRI interpretation predates empirically grounded approaches and was the focus of many aspects of both Allport's (1937) and Ellis's (1946) early SRI critiques. Meehl's (1945) rationale for empirically grounded SRI scale score interpretation was a reaction to the criticism that content-based interpretation was predicated on the questionable assumptions that test items have the same meaning to test takers that they do to scale developers and that all respondents understand items comparably and approach testing in a motivated and cooperative manner. Meehl (1945) agreed (essentially) that such assumptions were necessary for content-based interpretation and that they were unwarranted. His influential paper on this topic left content-based interpretation in ill repute among sophisticated SRI users for the next 20 years.

Content-based SRI interpretation began to make a comeback when Wiggins (1966) introduced a set of content scales developed with the MMPI item pool. Using a deductive scale development approach complemented by empirical refinement designed to maximize their internal consistency, Wiggins constructed a psychometrically sound set of 13 MMPI content scales and proposed that they be used to augment empirically grounded interpretation of the test's clinical scales. In laying out his rationale for developing a set of content scales for the MMPI, Wiggins commented: "The viewpoint that a personality test protocol represents a communication between the subject and the tester (or the institution he represents) has much to commend it, not the least of which is the likelihood that this is the frame of reference adopted by the subject himself" (p. 2). He went on to acknowledge that

> Obviously, the respondent has some control over what he chooses to communicate, and there are a variety of factors which may enter to distort the message.... Nevertheless, recognition of such sources of "noise" in the system should not lead us to overlook the fact that a message is still involved. (p. 25)

Wiggins was keenly aware of the inherent limits of SRI assessment in general, and content-based interpretation in particular. However, he argued that how an individual chooses to present him- or herself, whatever the reasoning or motivation, provides useful information that might augment what could be learned from empirically grounded interpretation alone. Wiggins (1966) advocated that although we need (and, indeed, should) not take it at face value, how a person chooses to present him- or herself is inherently informative and that it is incumbent upon SRI interpreters to make an effort to find out what it was that an individual sought to communicate in responding to an SRI's items. By developing internally consistent (both statistically and content-wise) SRI scales, psychologists could provide a reliable means for communication between test takers and interpreters.

### Empirically Grounded and Content-Based SRI Interpretation

Empirically grounded and content-based interpretations are not mutually exclusive. Often scale scores intended for interpretation based on one approach can also be (and are) interpreted based on the other. For example, although the MMPI-2 clinical scales are interpreted primarily based on their empirical correlates, the Harris-Lingoes subscales augment clinical scale interpretation by identifying content areas that may primarily be responsible for elevation on a given clinical scale. Conversely, although their interpretation is guided primarily by item content, the MMPI-2 Content Scales (Butcher et al., 1990) also are interpreted based on their empirical correlates. Because they are linked empirically and conceptually to well-known psychological constructs, have a broad range of empirical correlates, and are made up of internally consistent items (both statistically and content-wise), MMPI-2-RF RC Scale interpretation is guided by an approach that combines consideration of construct validity, criterion validity, and item content (Ben-Porath & Tellegen, 2008b).

A primary distinction between empirically grounded and content-based interpretation is that the latter (as SRI critics have long argued) is more susceptible to intentional and unintentional distortion. However, as discussed in detail in the section titled "Threats to SRI Protocol Validity," appropriate application of SRIs requires that test-taking attitude be measured and considered as part of the interpretation process. Because of its inherent susceptibility to distortion, content-based interpretation requires that an SRI be particularly effective in measuring and identifying misleading approaches and that its users apply tools designed to do so appropriately.

### Generating Scores for SRI Interpretation: Standard Score Derivation

Depending on their response format, SRI raw scores consist either of a count of the number of items answered in the keyed (true or false) direction or a sum of the respondent's Likert scale ratings on a scale's items. These scores have no intrinsic meaning. They are a function of arbitrary factors, such as the number of items on a scale and the instrument's response format. Raw scores typically are transformed to some form of standard score that places an individual's SRI scale raw score in an interpretable context. Standard scores are typically generated by a comparison of an individual's raw score on a scale to that of a normative reference group(s) composed of the instrument's standardization or normative sample(s). Because of the critical role of standard scores in SRI interpretation, it is important to understand how they are derived as well as the factors that determine their adequacy.

The most common standard score used with SRIs is the T score, which expresses an individual's standing in reference to the standardization sample on a metric having

a mean of 50 and a standard deviation of 10. This is typically accomplished through the following transformation:

$$T = \frac{RS - MRS}{SDRS} \times 10 + 50$$

where $T$ is the individual's T score, $RS$ is his or her raw score, $MRS$ is the standardization sample's mean score, and $SDRS$ is the sample's standard deviation ($SD$) on a given SRI scale. A T score of 50 corresponds to the mean level for the standardization sample. A T score equal to 60 indicates that the person's score falls 1 $SD$ above the normative mean. The choice of 50 and 10 for the standard scores' mean and $SD$ is arbitrary but has evolved as common practice in many (although not all) SRIs.

Standard scores provide information on where the respondent stands on the construct(s) measured by a SRI scale in comparison with a normative reference. A second important and common application of standard scores is to allow for comparisons across SRI scales. Given the arbitrary nature of SRI scale raw scores, it is not possible to compare an individual's raw scores on, for example, measures of anxiety and depression. Transformation of raw scores to standard scores allows the test interpreter to determine whether an individual shows greater deviation from the normative mean on one measure or another. Such information could be used to assist an assessor in differential diagnostic tasks or, more generally, to allow for configural test interpretation, which, as described earlier in this chapter, involves simultaneous consideration of multiple SRI scale scores.

The accuracy and utility of standard scores rest heavily on the nature and quality of the normative reference sample. To the extent that they aptly represent the target population, standard scores will provide an accurate gauge of the individual's standing on the construct(s) of interest and allow for comparison of an individual's standing across constructs and, more generally, facilitate configural SRI interpretation. Conversely, if the normative reference scores somehow misrepresent the target population, the resulting standard scores will hinder all of the tasks just mentioned. Several factors must be considered in determining whether a normative reference sample represents the target population appropriately. These involve various types and effects of normative sampling problems.

### Types and Effects of Normative Sampling Problems

Identifying potential problems with standard scores can be accomplished by considering the general formula for transforming raw score to standard scores:

$$SS = \frac{RS - MRS}{SDRS} \times NewSD + NewMean,$$

where $SS$ is the individual's standard score, $RS$ is his or her raw score, $MRS$ is the standardization sample's mean score, $SDRS$ is the sample's $SD$ on a given SRI scale, $NewSD$ is the target $SD$ for the standard scores, and $NewMean$ is the target mean for these scores. As discussed earlier, the target mean and $SD$s are arbitrary, but common practice in SRI scale development is to use T scores that have a mean of 50 and an $SD$ of 10. An important consideration in evaluating the adequacy of standard scores is the extent to which the normative reference (or standardization) sample appropriately represents the population's mean and $SD$ on a given SRI scale.

Examination of the general transformation formula shows that if a normative sample's mean ($MRS$) is higher than the actual population mean, the resulting standard score will underestimate the individual's standing in reference to the normative population. Consider a hypothetical example in which T scores are used, the individual's raw score equals 10, the normative sample's mean equals 12, the actual population mean equals 8, and both the sample and population $SD$s equal 5. Applying the T score transformation formula provided earlier,

$$T = \frac{10 - 12}{5} \times 10 + 50 = 46$$

we find that this normative sample yields a T score of 46, suggesting that the individual's raw score falls nearly half an $SD$ below the normative mean on this construct. However, had the sample mean reflected accurately the population mean, applying the T score transformation formula

$$T = \frac{10 - 8}{5} \times 10 + 50 = 54$$

would have yielded a T score of 54, indicating that the individual's raw score falls nearly half an $SD$ above the population mean. Larger discrepancies between sample and population mean would, of course, result in even greater underestimates of the individual's relative standing on the construct(s) of interest. Conversely, to the extent that the sample mean underestimates the population mean, the resulting standard scores will overestimate the individual's relative position on a given scale.

A second factor that could result in systematic inaccuracies in standard scores is sampling error in the $SD$. To the extent that the normative sample's $SD$ underestimates the population $SD$, the resulting standard score will overestimate the individual's relative standing on the scale. As we apply again the T score transformation formula, consider an example in which the individual's raw score equals 10, the sample and population means both equal 8, and the sample $SD$ equals 2, but the population $SD$ actually equals 5. Applying the formula based on the sample data

$$T = \frac{10 - 8}{2} \times 10 + 50 = 60$$

yields a T score of 60, indicating that the individual's score falls 1 $SD$ above the normative mean. However, an accurate estimate of the population $SD$

$$T = \frac{10 - 8}{5} \times 10 + 50 = 54$$

would have produced a T score of 54, reflecting a score that falls just under $\frac{1}{2}$ $SD$ above the normative mean. Here, too, a larger discrepancy between the sample and population $SD$ results in an even greater overestimation of the individual's standing on the construct(s) of interest; conversely, an overestimation of the population's $SD$ would result in an underestimation of the individual's relative score on a given measure.

## Causes of Normative Sample Inadequacies

In light of the importance of standardization samples in determining the adequacy of standard scores, it is essential to identify (and thus try to avoid) reasons why such samples may inaccurately estimate a target population's mean or $SD$ on an SRI scale. Three general types of problems may generate inaccurate normative means and $SD$s: sampling problems, population changes, and application changes. Two types of sampling problems error may occur. The simplest among these is random sampling error, in which, as a result of random factors associated with the sampling process, the normative sample mean or $SD$ fails to represent accurately the relevant population statistics. This can be minimized effectively by collecting sufficiently large normative samples.

Systematic sampling errors occur when, due to specific sampling flaws, the sample mean or $SD$ reflects inaccurately the relevant population statistics. In such cases a normative sample fails to represent accurately one or more segments of the target population as a result of sampling bias. This will negatively affect the normative sample's adequacy if two conditions are met: (1) a sample fails to represent accurately a certain population segment, and (2) the inadequately represented population segment differs systematically (in its mean, its *SD,* or both) from the remaining population on a particular SRI scale. For example, if as a consequence of the sampling method used younger adults are underrepresented in a normative sample that is designed to represent the entire adult population, and younger adults differ systematically from the remaining adult population on the scale being standardized, this could result in biased estimates of both the population mean and its *SD.* This might occur with a scale designed to measure depression, a variable that tends to vary as a function of age.

If younger adults are represented inadequately in a normative sample (this could occur if the sampling process failed to incorporate college students and military personnel) used to develop standard scores on a depression scale, the normative sample would overestimate the population mean on the scale and underestimate its *SD,* resulting in the effects discussed previously.

Note that in order for systematic sampling error to affect scale norms, both conditions just specified must be met. That is, a population segment must be misrepresented and this segment must differ systematically from the remaining population on the scale being standardized. If only the first condition is met, but the misrepresented segment does not differ systematically from the remaining population, this will not result in biased estimates of the population mean and *SD.* Such a scenario occurred with the updated normative sample used to standardize the MMPI-2 (Butcher, Dahlstrom, Graham, Tellegen, & Kaemmer, 1989) and MMPI-2-RF (Tellegen & Ben-Porath, 2008). Data included in the MMPI-2 manual indicated that this sample differed substantially from the general adult population in education. Specifically, the normative sample significantly underrepresented individuals with lower levels of education and overrepresented people with higher levels of education in the general adult population. Some authors (e.g., Duckworth, 1991) expressed concern that this may introduce systematic bias in the updated norms. However, subsequent analyses demonstrated that this sampling bias had no significant impact on resulting test norms because education is not correlated substantially with MMPI scale scores (Schinka & LaLone, 1997).

Population changes are a second reason why normative samples may inadequately represent their target population. These occur when, over the course of time, the target population changes on the construct that a scale measures.

For example, Anastasi (1985), in a review of longitudinal research on intelligence, found a trend for population-wide increases in intelligence over the first half of the 20th century. These were the result primarily of increases in population education levels in general and literacy levels in particular. To account for the effects of these changes on their norms, it has been necessary for intelligence test developers to periodically collect new normative data. To the extent that constructs measured by SRIs are affected similarly by population changes, it becomes necessary to update their normative databases as well. This was one of the considerations that led to the development of new norms for the MMPI (Butcher et al., 1989). However, personality changes do not occur as frequently as do advances in cognitive functioning. For example, Tellegen and Ben-Porath (2008) found that two cohorts tested more than 20 years apart produced essentially interchangeable scores on the 51 scales of the MMPI-2-RF.

Application changes are a third reason why normative samples may misrepresent target populations. Two types of application changes can be distinguished. Changes in administration practices may affect normative data adequacy. For example, the original MMPI normative data were collected using the test's so-called Box Form. Each of the test's items was typed on a separate card, and test takers were instructed to sort the cards (which were presented individually in a random order) into three boxes representing a "true," "false," or "cannot say" response. The instructions given to the original normative sample did not discourage the "cannot say" option. However, after the normative data were collected, an administration change was introduced and test takers were instructed to "be sure to put less than 10 cards behind the 'cannot say'" (Dahlstrom, Welsh, & Dahlstrom, 1972, p. 32). Later still, the Box Form was largely superseded by the MMPI Group Form, a booklet that presented the test's items in a fixed order and required that the test taker record his or her responses (true, false, or cannot say) on an answer sheet. Here, too, test takers were admonished to attempt to answer all of the test items.

To the extent that either of these changes in administration practices affected individuals' responses to the test items, this could have resulted in the original normative sample data's misrepresenting population statistics under the revised administration procedures. In fact, the MMPI-2 norms turned out to be significantly different from the original norms in both their means and *SD*s, and to some extent these shifts are likely a product of the administration changes just described. For example, as a result of the change in instructions regarding the "cannot say" option, the newer normative sample members omitted far fewer items than did their original counterparts, which in turn probably contributed to the new sample's higher mean raw scores on many of the test's original scales. In other words, the original normative sample underestimated the target population's mean raw scores on the MMPI scales given the shift in administration procedure, contributing partly to the artificially elevated T scores generated by individuals and groups tested with the original MMPI when they were transformed to standard scores based on the original test norms.

A more recent change in SRI administration practices followed the introduction of computer technology. Although most SRI norms were collected using booklet forms, software is now available to administer most tests by computer. Such a change in administration practice could also, potentially, affect norm adequacy of these instruments if the different administration format resulted in a systematic change in responses to SRI items. Reassuringly, a meta-analysis by Finger and Ones (1999) demonstrated that computerized test administration does not affect group means or $SD$s (and thus would have no negative impact on the test's norms) on MMPI scales.

A second type of application change that could potentially affect the adequacy of norms involves expansion of the target population. When an SRI developed for use with a rather narrowly defined population is considered for application to a broader population, the possibility that its norms will no longer accurately reflect the expanded population's means and $SD$s on its scales needs to be considered. For example, the MMPI was developed originally for use at the University of Minnesota Hospital, and its normative sample, made up primarily of a group of Caucasian farmers and laborers with an average of 8 years of education, represented fairly well this target population. As the test's use expanded to the broader U.S. population, concerns were raised (e.g., Gynther, 1972) about the adequacy of the MMPI norms for interpreting scores generated by minorities, primarily African Americans, who were not included in the original normative sample.

The effects of expanding an SRI's population on its normative sample's adequacy depend on the new population segment's performance on its scales. To the extent the new segment differs systematically from the original on a scale's mean or $SD$, this would necessitate an expansion of the instrument's normative sample to reflect more accurately the expanded population's scale parameters. This was one of the primary considerations that led to the collection of new normative data for the MMPI and publication of the MMPI-2 (Butcher et al., 1989).

Similarly, as the test's use has expanded beyond the United States to other countries, cultures, and languages, researchers throughout the world have collected new normative data for MMPI and later MMPI-2 application in an ever-increasing number of countries (cf. Butcher, 1996).

The effects of expanding an SRI's target population on normative data adequacy should not be confused with questions about an instrument's validity across population segments, although frequently these very separate concerns are confounded in the literature. Ensuring that various population segments are represented adequately in an SRI's normative sample is not sufficient to guarantee that the test is as valid an indicator of its target psychological constructs in the new segment as it was in the original. To the extent that an instrument's interpretation is predicated on an SRI's empirical correlates, its construct validity, or the combination of the two (as discussed earlier), its application to the expanded population is predicated on the assumption that these test attributes apply comparably to the new population segment.

## General Population Versus Population Subsegment Norms

A final consideration in evaluating normative data adequacy is whether an SRI's standard scores are derived from general or more narrowly defined and specific normative samples. When a general population normative sample is used, the same set of standard scores is applied regardless of the assessment setting or the individual's membership in any specific population subsegments. Thus, for example, the MMPI-2 and MMPI-2-RF have just one set of standard scores generated based on a normative sample designed to represent the general U.S. population. The same set of standard scores is used regardless of where the test is applied.

A more recently developed SRI, the Personality Assessment Inventory (PAI; Morey, 1991, 2007) provides two sets of norms for its scales, based on a sample of community-dwelling adults and a clinical sample. Morey (1991) explained that clinical norms are designed to assist the interpreter in tasks such as diagnosis:

> For example, nearly all patients report depression at their initial evaluation; the question confronting the clinician considering a diagnosis of major depression is one of relative severity of symptomatology. That a patient's score on the PAI DEP [Depression] scale is elevated in comparison to the standardization sample is of value, but a comparison of the elevation relative to a clinical population may be more critical in formulating diagnostic hypotheses. (p. 11)

The ability to know how an individual compares with others known to have significant psychological problems may indeed contribute useful information to test interpretation. However, this particular approach to generating such information has a significant drawback. If, using Morey's example, nearly all members of a clinical reference sample report depression when their normative data are collected, a typical patient experiencing significant problems with depression will produce a nondeviant score on the instrument's clinically referenced depression measure, thus obscuring depression's prominence in the presenting clinical picture.

An alternative approach to providing information on how a test taker's scores compare with a defined group of individuals is reflected in the inclusion of Comparison Group data in the MMPI-2-RF Technical Manual (Tellegen & Ben-Porath) and scoring software (Ben-Porath & Tellegen, 2008c). Means and SDs on the 51 scales of the test are provided for a range of settings (e.g., psychiatric inpatients) and/or populations (e.g., bariatric surgery candidates). These statistics are expressed in standard T score values, demonstrating, as expected, that psychiatric inpatients do indeed show greater evidence of depression than what is found in the general population. For example, a sample of 498 female psychiatric inpatients produced a mean T score of 64 and an SD of 17 on a measure of anhedonic depression. A woman tested on admission to an inpatient facility who produces a T score of 65 (the level at which clinical significance is typically attributed to a deviant test score) would instead have a T score of 50 based on population subsegment norms. With the combined use of a single normative reference sample and comparison groups, it is readily evident that although this test taker is no more depressed than the average psychiatric inpatient, she is, nonetheless, likely experiencing significant emotional dysfunction.

## Threats to SRI Protocol Validity

The impact of test-taking approaches on SRIs has been the focus of heated debate. As reviewed earlier in this chapter, early SRI critics (e.g., Allport, 1937; Ellis, 1946) cited their vulnerability to intentional and unintentional distortion by the test taker as the primary, inherent limitation of SRIs. The basic concern here is that, even if he or she is responding to a psychometrically sound SRI, an individual test taker may, for a variety of reasons, approach the assessment in a manner that compromises the instrument's ability to gauge accurately his or her standing on the construct(s) of interest. In such cases, a psychometrically valid test may yield invalid results.

Use of the term *validity* to refer to both a test's psychometric properties and an individual's test scores can be confusing. A distinction should be drawn between instrument validity and protocol validity. *Instrument validity* refers to a test's psychometric properties and is typically characterized in terms of content, criterion, and construct validity. *Protocol validity* refers to the results of an individual test administration. Use of the term *validity* to refer to these two very different aspects of SRI assessment is unfortunate but sufficiently well grounded in practice that introduction of new terminology at this point is unlikely to succeed.

A need to distinguish between psychometric and protocol validity was highlighted in a debate involving the widely studied NEO Personality Inventory—Revised (NEO-PI-R). Responding to suggestions by Costa and McCrae (1992a; the NEO-PI-R developers) that practitioners use this test in clinical assessment, Ben-Porath and Waller (1992) expressed a concern (among others) that the absence of protocol validity indicators on the NEO-PI-R may limit the instrument's clinical utility. Costa and McCrae (1992b) responded that validity scales were unnecessary, in part because evidence has shown that test scores may be psychometrically valid even in instances in which validity indicators showed evidence of limited protocol validity.

Piedmont, McCrae, Riemann, and Angleitner (2000) sought to demonstrate this point by showing that scores on an SRI's validity scales (designed to assess protocol validity) were unrelated to the NEO-PI-R's psychometric validity. However, their analyses were based on data generated by research volunteers who completed the instruments anonymously. Thus, unlike respondents in most clinical assessment settings, these research volunteers had nothing at stake when responding to the NEO-PI-R. In contrast, as reviewed next, test takers in clinical settings may be motivated by various factors to present themselves in a particular manner. Moreover, psychometric validity in this and similar studies was established based on statistical analyses of group data, whereas protocol validity pertains to individual test results. If, for example, one of the participants in such a study marked his or her answer sheet randomly, without actually reading the SRI items, his or her resulting scale scores are completely invalid and uninterpretable, regardless of how others in the sample responded.

More recently, based on a selective review and analysis of the validity of validity indicators, McGrath, Mitchell,

Kim, and Hough (2010) argued that scales used in a variety of settings have insufficient data to support their use in everyday clinical practice: "a sufficient justification for [their] use ... in applied settings remains elusive" (p. 450). In a rebuttal, Rohling et al. (2011) pointed out that (a) McGrath et al.'s inclusion criteria for relevant studies were too narrow; (b) the authors made errors in interpreting results of the empirical research they did include; and (c) evidence supporting the validity of validity indicators was overlooked.

Consideration of protocol validity is one aspect of SRI-based assessment in which users are able to take an individualized perspective on a generally normative enterprise. Allport (1937) distinguished between idiographic (individualized) and nomothetic (generalized) approaches to personality research and assessment. Drawing an analogy to the diagnostic process in medicine, he noted that the two approaches are not mutually exclusive. Rather, a combined idiographic/nomothetic approach is likely to yield the optimal perspective on diagnosis and assessment. Consideration of protocol validity offers an important window into idiographic aspects of SRI-based assessment.

In sum, instrument validity is necessary but insufficient to guarantee protocol validity. Although it sets the upper limit on protocol validity, information regarding instrument validity does not address a critical question that is at issue in every clinical assessment: Is there anything about an individual's approach to a particular assessment that might compromise its user's ability to interpret an SRI's scores? To answer this question, users must be aware of various threats to protocol validity.

## Types of Threats to Protocol Validity

Threats to SRI protocol validity need to be considered in each SRI application because of their potential to distort the resulting test scores. This information can be used in two important ways. First, knowledge of threats to protocol validity makes it possible for test users to attempt to prevent or minimize their occurrence. Second, this information makes it possible to anticipate invalid responding's potential impact on the resulting test scores and, on the basis of this information, provide appropriate caveats in test interpretation. Such statements may range from a call for caution in assuming that an interpretation will likely reflect accurately the individual's standing on the construct(s) of interest to an unambiguous declaration that protocol validity has been compromised to a degree that makes it impossible to draw any valid inferences about the test taker from the resulting SRI scale scores.

**TABLE 24.1  Threats to Self-Report Inventory Protocol Validity**

Non-content-based invalid responding
    Nonresponding
    Random responding
        Intentional random responding
        Unintentional random responding
    Fixed responding
Content-based invalid responding
    Overreporting
        Intentional overreporting
           Exaggeration versus fabrication
        Unintentional overreporting
    Underreporting
        Intentional underreporting
           Minimization versus denial
        Unintentional underreporting (social desirability)

Threats to protocol validity fall broadly into two categories that reflect the role of test item content in the invalid responding. Important distinctions can be made within each of these categories as well. Table 24.1 lists the various non-content- and content-based threats to protocol validity identified and discussed in this chapter.

### Non-Content-Based Invalid Responding

Non-content-based invalid responding occurs when the test taker's answers to an SRI are not based on an accurate reading, processing, and comprehension of the test items. Its deleterious effects on protocol validity are obvious: To the extent that a test taker's responses do not reflect his or her actual reactions to an SRI's items, then those responses cannot possibly gauge the individual's standing on the construct of interest. This invalidating test-taking approach can be divided further into three modes: nonresponding, random responding, and fixed responding.

*Nonresponding* occurs when the test taker fails to provide a usable response to an SRI item. Typically this takes the form of failing to provide any response to an SRI item, but it may also occur if the test taker provides more than one response. Nonresponding may occur for a variety of reasons. Test takers who are uncooperative or defensive may fail to respond to a large number of an SRI's items. Less insidious reasons why individuals may fail to respond appropriately to a SRI may include an inability to read or understand its items, cognitive functioning deficits that result in confusion or obsessiveness, or limits in the test taker's capacity for introspection and insight.

Nonresponding's effect on protocol validity depends, in part, on the SRI's response format. In tests that use a true/false response format, a nonresponse is treated typically as a response in the nonkeyed direction. In SRIs with a Likert scale response format, a nonresponse typically receives the value zero. These ipso facto scores can by no means be assumed to provide a reasonable approximation of how the respondent would have answered had he or she chosen or been able to do so. Therefore, to the extent that nonresponding occurs in a given SRI protocol, this will distort the resulting test scores. For example, in a true/false response format, a respondent's failure to respond appropriately to a large number of items will result in artificial deflation of his or her scores on the instrument's scales, which, if not identified and considered in scale score interpretation, may result in underestimation of the individual's standing on the constructs measured by the affected scales.

*Random responding* (more accurately characterized as quasi-random) is a test-taking approach characterized by an unsystematic response pattern that is not based on an accurate reading, processing, and understanding of an SRI's items. It is not a dichotomous phenomenon, meaning that random responding may be present to varying degrees in a given test protocol. Two types of random responding can be distinguished. Intentional random responding occurs when the individual has the capacity to respond relevantly to an SRI's items but chooses instead to respond irrelevantly in an unsystematic manner. An uncooperative test taker who is unwilling to participate meaningfully in an assessment may engage in intentional random responding rather than becoming embroiled in a confrontation with the examiner over his or her refusal to participate. In this example, the test taker provides answers to an SRI's items without pausing to read and consider them. He or she may do this throughout the test protocol or at various points along the way in responding to an SRI's items. Unintentional random responding occurs when the individual lacks the capacity to respond relevantly to an SRI's items, but, rather than refraining from doing so, he or she responds without having an accurate understanding of the test items. Often these individuals are not aware that they lack this capacity and have failed to understand and respond relevantly to an SRI's items.

Several factors may lead to unintentional random responding. Reading difficulties may compromise the test taker's ability to respond relevantly to an SRI's items. Most current SRIs require anywhere from a fourth- to a sixth-grade reading level for the test taker to be able to read, comprehend, and respond relevantly to the items. Regrettably, this is not synonymous with having completed four to six years of education. Some high school graduates cannot read at the fourth-grade level. If the examiner has doubts about a test taker's reading ability,

a standardized reading test should be administered to determine his or her reading level. For individuals who do not have the requisite reading skills, it may still be possible to administer the test if the problem is strictly one of literacy rather than language comprehension. In such cases, an SRI's items can be administered orally, using standard stimulus materials, such as an audio-recorded reading of the test items.

Comprehension deficits can also lead to random responding. In this case the individual may actually be able to read the test items but does not have the necessary language comprehension skills to process and understand them. This could be a product of low verbal abilities. In other instances, comprehension deficits may be found in those lacking familiarity with English-language nuances, for example, among individuals for whom English is not their primary language.

Unintentional random responding can also result from confusion and thought disorganization. In some instances, these types of problems may have prompted the assessment and SRI administration. Whereas reading and comprehension difficulties tend to be relatively stable test-taker characteristics that probably will compromise protocol validity regardless of when an SRI is administered, confusion and thought disorganization are often (although not always) transitory conditions. If and when the individual's sensorium clears, she or he may be able to retake an SRI and provide valid responses to its items.

Finally, random responding may result from response recording errors. Many SRIs are administered by having the respondent read a set of items from a booklet and record the responses on a separate answer sheet. If the respondent marks his or her answer to an SRI's items in the wrong location on an answer sheet, he or she is essentially providing random responses. This could result from the test taker's missing just one item on the answer sheet or from an overall careless approach to response recording.

*Fixed responding* is a non-content-based invalidating test-taking approach characterized by a systematic response pattern that is not based on an accurate reading, processing, and understanding of an SRI's items. In contrast to random responding, here the test taker provides the same non-content-based responses to SRI items. If responding to a true/false format SRI, the test taker indiscriminately marks many of the test items either "true" or "false." Note that if the test taker provides both "true" and "false" responses indiscriminately, he or she is engaging in random responding. In fixed responding, the indiscriminant responses are predominantly either "true" or "false." In fixed responding on a Likert scale, the test taker marks items at the same level on the Likert rating scale without properly considering their content. Like nonresponding and random responding, fixed responding is a matter of degree rather than a dichotomous all-or-none phenomenon.

Unlike nonresponding and random responding, fixed responding has received a great deal of attention in the SRI-based assessment literature. Jackson and Messick (1962) sparked this discussion when they proposed that much (if not all) of the variance in MMPI scale scores was attributable to two response styles, termed acquiescence and social desirability. Acquiescence was defined as a tendency to respond "true" to MMPI items without consideration of their content. This type of non-content-based responding is labeled fixed responding in this chapter.

A detailed examination of Jackson and Messick's arguments and the data they analyzed in its support is beyond the scope of this chapter. Essentially, Jackson and Messick factor-analyzed MMPI scale scores in a broad range of samples and found recurrently that two factors accounted for much of the variance in these scores. They attributed variance on these factors to two response styles, acquiescence and social desirability, and cautioned that MMPI scale scores appear primarily to reflect individual differences on these nonsubstantive dimensions. They suggested that MMPI scales were particularly vulnerable to the effects of acquiescence and its counterpart, counteracquiescence (a tendency to respond "false" to self-report items without consideration of their content), because their scoring keys were unbalanced. That is, for some MMPI scales many, if not most, of the items were keyed "true," whereas on other scales most of the items were keyed "false."

In an extensive and sophisticated series of analyses, Block (1965) demonstrated that the two primary MMPI factors reflected substantive personality dimensions rather than stylistic response tendencies. With regard specifically to acquiescence, he showed that completely balanced MMPI scales (i.e., ones with equal numbers of "true" and "false" keyed items) yielded the same factor structure that Jackson and Messick (1962) attributed to the effect of response styles. He showed further that the so-called acquiescence factor was correlated with substantive aspects of personality functioning. Block (1965) labeled this factor ego control and demonstrated that its association with extratest data was unchanged as a function of whether it was measured with balanced or unbalanced scales.

It is important to note that Block's analyses did not indicate that acquiescence is never a problem in SRI-based assessment. In the relatively rare instances when they occur, acquiescence and counteracquiescence can indeed jeopardize protocol validity. In the most extreme case of acquiescence, if a respondent answers "true" to all of a scale's items without reference to their content, his or her score on that scale is obviously invalid. In addition, use of a Likert scale format does not obviate the potential effects of this response style, because with this format, as well, it is possible for test takers to provide a fixed response that is independent of item content. In fact Likert scale response formats offer more options for fixed responding.

Block's compelling demonstration notwithstanding, Jackson and Messick and their followers continued to advocate the response style position and argue that acquiescence represented a serious challenge to MMPI use and interpretation. For example, Helmes and Reddon (1993) revisited this issue and criticized the MMPI and MMPI-2 (among other things) for their continued susceptibility to the effects of acquiescence. These authors again identified the test's unbalanced scoring keys as a primary reason for its susceptibility to acquiescence. In constructing his own SRI, the Basic Personality Inventory (BPI), Jackson (1989) indeed adopted the balanced scoring key solution for its scales, each of which is made up of 20 items, half keyed "true" and the others keyed "false." However, balanced scoring keys actually provide no protection whatsoever against the protocol-invalidating effects of fixed responding. Consider the hypothetical example just mentioned, in which a test taker responds "true" to all 20 BPI scale items without actually referring to their content. The only effect a balanced key might have in this instance might be to instill a false sense of security in the test interpreter that the scale is not susceptible to the protocol invalidating effects of acquiescence, when, in fact, it is.

In summary, although fixed responding does not pose as broad a threat to protocol validity as Jackson and Messick (1962) would argue, in cases in which a test taker uses this response style extensively, the resulting SRI scale scores will be invalid and uninterpretable. Constructing scales with balanced keys or Likert scale response formats does not make an SRI less susceptible to this threat to protocol validity. Self-report inventory users need to determine in each instance that a test is used whether, to what extent, and with what impact fixed responding may have compromised protocol validity. Doing this requires that the SRIs include measures of fixed responding.

### Content-Based Invalid Responding

Content-based invalid responding occurs when the test taker skews his or her answers to SRI items and, as a result, creates a misleading impression. This test-taking approach falls broadly into two classes that have been discussed under various labels in the literature. The first of these has been termed alternatively overreporting, faking bad, and malingering. The second type of content-based invalid responding has been labeled underreporting, faking good, and positive malingering. In this chapter, they are discussed under the more neutral labels of over- and underreporting.

*Overreporting* occurs when, in responding to an SRI, a test taker describes him- or herself as having more serious difficulties, a greater number of them, or both, than he or she actually has. Underlying this definition is the hypothetical notion that if a completely objective measure of psychological functioning were available, the overreporter's subjective self-report would indicate greater dysfunction than does the objective indicator. Two non–mutually exclusive types of overreporting can be distinguished. *Intentional overreporting* occurs when the individual knowingly skews his or her self-report. This test taker may be motivated by some external gain and thus fit the definition of malingering in the text revision of the fourth edition of the *Diagnostic and Statistical Manual* (*DSM-IV-TR;* 2000).

It is important to note that intentional overreporting is not in itself an indication that psychopathology is absent. That is to say, if an individual intentionally overreports in responding to a SRI, that, in itself, does not indicate that he or she is actually free of bona fide psychological dysfunction. It is, in fact, possible for someone who has genuine psychological difficulties to amplify their extent or significance when responding to SRI items. Some people who intentionally overreport in response to an SRI actually do have no problems, however. The distinction here is between exaggeration and fabrication of difficulties. Both forms of intentional overreporting fall under the *DSM-IV-TR* definition of malingering: "the intentional production of false or grossly exaggerated physical or psychological symptoms, motivated by external incentives such as avoiding military duty, avoiding work, obtaining financial compensation, evading criminal prosecution, or obtaining drugs" (American Psychiatric Association, 2000, p. 739). In practice, distinguishing between exaggeration and fabrication in SRI protocol validity determination is challenging.

In *unintentional overreporting,* the test taker is unaware that she or he is deviating from a hypothetically objective self-description and describing her- or himself in an overly negative manner. Here it is the test taker's self-concept that is skewed. Individuals who engage in this test-taking approach believe mistakenly that they are providing an accurate self-description when in fact they are overreporting their difficulties. Individuals with somatoform disorders, for example, report significant somatic symptoms that cannot be explained by medical findings (Lamberty, 2007). Regardless of intentionality, overreporting in response to SRI items results in scale scores that overestimate the extent or significance of psychological problems the respondent experiences.

*Underreporting* occurs when in responding to an SRI a test taker describes him- or herself as having less serious difficulties, a smaller number of difficulties, or both, than he or she actually has. To refer back to the hypothetical objective functioning indicator, in underreporting, the individual's self-report reflects better functioning than would be indicated by an objective assessment. Here, too, a distinction may be drawn between intentional and unintentional underreporting. In *intentional underreporting,* the individual knowingly denies or minimizes the extent of his or her psychological difficulties or negative characteristics. As a result, the individual's SRI scale scores underestimate his or her level of dysfunction. Differentiation between denial and minimization is important but complex. The distinction here is between an individual who blatantly denies problems that he or she knows exist and one who may acknowledge some difficulties or negative characteristics but minimizes their impact or extent.

*Unintentional underreporting* occurs when the individual unknowingly denies or minimizes the extent of his or her psychological difficulties or negative characteristics. Here, too, objective and subjective indicators of psychological functioning would be at odds; however, in unintentional underreporting, this discrepancy results from the individual's self-misperception rather than an intentional effort to produce misleading test results.

Much of the discussion of this topic in the assessment literature has appeared under the label social desirability. Edwards (1957) defined social desirability as "the tendency of subjects to attribute to themselves, in self-description, personality statements with socially desirable scale values and to reject those socially undesirable scale values" (p. vi). Edwards (1970) differentiated between social desirability and what he called "impression management," a deliberate attempt to lie or dissimulate for ulterior motives, that is, intentional underreporting as defined in this chapter. Thus, as conceptualized by Edwards (1957,

1970), social desirability is a form self-deception, that is, an unintentional underreporting in response to SRI items.

Edwards (1957) argued that much of the variance in MMPI scale scores could be attributed to social desirability. He based this conclusion on research he did with an MMPI scale he constructed and labeled social desirability. The scale was made up of 39 items that 10 judges unanimously deemed to reflect highly desirable self-statements. Edwards (1957, 1970) reported that this scale was correlated highly with most MMPI scales in general and the strong, omnipotent first factor that emerged from factor analyses of MMPI scale scores. He concluded that MMPI scale scores were thus hopelessly confounded with the social desirability response style and, therefore, could not be used to identify meaningful (rather than stylistic) individual differences.

As was the case with Jackson and Messick's (1962) argument regarding acquiescence (see the discussion of fixed responding), Block (1965) provided a definitive refutation of Edwards's (1957) social desirability critique. Block demonstrated that Edwards's social desirability scale was in fact a marker of a substantive personality dimension he termed ego resiliency. Following the earlier work of Wiggins (1959), Block developed an ego resiliency–free measure of social desirability and found much lower levels of overlap with substantive MMPI scale scores than Edwards reported for his social desirability scale. Moreover, Block demonstrated that both a social-desirability-independent ego resiliency scale he constructed and Edwards's social desirability scales were correlated with meaningful non-MMPI variables that reflected substantive individual differences.

Commenting on Edwards's (1957) claim that the MMPI scales were hopelessly confounded with social desirability, Block (1965) observed:

> Confounding is a blade that, if held too tightly, will cut its wielder. With the same logic advanced for social desirability as underlying MMPI scales, one can argue that the [first] factor of the MMPI represents a personality dimension that is vital to understanding the SD [Social Desirability] scale. Many of the MMPI scales have empirical origins and demonstrable validity in separating appropriate criterion groups. The high correlations found between these scales and the SD measure therefore plausibly suggest—not an artifact or naiveté in the construction of the earlier scales—but rather that the SD scale, wittingly or not, is an excellent measure of some important variable of personality. (pp. 69–70)

Reflecting on the methods Edwards (1957) used to construct his social desirability scale, the resulting confound

is readily understood. Stated simply, psychopathology is undesirable. Ask a group of persons to identify SRI items that reflect undesirable characteristics, and, if they are included in the pool, participants will undoubtedly generate a list of items describing negative psychological characteristics. Edwards's assumption that individuals' responses to such items reflect a substantively meaningless response style proved to be unwarranted and was refuted by Block's (1965) analyses.

## Implications of Threats to Protocol Validity

The issues discussed and highlighted in this section illustrate the crucial role played by respondents' test-taking approaches in determining the interpretability of SRI scale scores. Allport (1937) and Ellis (1946) foresaw accurately that reliance on an individual's willingness and ability to generate an accurate self-portrayal when responding to test items were among the greatest challenges facing SRI developers and users. Subsequent decades of research and practice have illuminated a host of threats to protocol validity (just described), all manifestations of the kinds of concerns identified early on by Allport and Ellis. Self-report inventory developers have responded to these threats in various ways, ranging from the development of validity scales, SRI measures designed to assess and, in some instances, correct for the effects of protocol invalidating test-taking approaches, to declaration and attempts to demonstrate that these threats do not really amount to much (Costa & McCrae, 1992a; Piedmont et al., 2000) and the consequent decision not to include validity scales on some instruments (e.g., the NEO-PI-R; Costa & McCrae, 1992c). Commenting on the then-prevalent paucity of efforts by SRI developers to address threats to protocol validity, Meehl and Hathaway (1946) observed:

> It is almost as though we inventory-makers were afraid to say too much about the problem because we had no effective solution for it, but it was too obvious a fact to be ignored so it was met by a polite nod. Meanwhile the scores obtained are subjected to varied "precise" statistical manipulations which impel the student of behavior to wonder whether it is not the aim of the personality testers to get as far away from any unsanitary contact with the organism as possible. Part of this trend no doubt reflects the lack of clinical experiences of some psychologists who concern themselves with personality testing. (p. 526)

Acting on this concern, Hathaway and McKinley incorporated two validity scales, L and F, in their original MMPI development efforts. The MMPI was not the first

SRI to make validity scales available to its users. Cady (1923) modified the Woodworth Psychoneurotic Inventory (derived from of the original Personal Data Sheet) to assess juvenile incorrigibility and incorporated negatively worded repeated items in the revised inventory to examine respondents' "reliability." Maller (1932) included items in his Character Sketches measure designed to assess respondents' "readiness to confide." Humm and Wadsworth (1935), developers of the Humm-Wadworth Temperament Scales, incorporated scales designed to identify defensive responding to their SRI. Ruch (1942) developed an "honesty key" for the BPI, the most widely used SRI prior to the MMPI.

Hathaway and McKinley's inclusion of validity scales on the original MMPI was thus consistent with growing recognition among SRI developers of the need to incorporate formal means for assessing and attempting to correct for threats to protocol validity. The most recent version of the test, the MMPI-2-RF (Ben-Porath & Tellegen, 2008b) includes nine validity scales designed to detect the various threats to protocol validity just discussed.

## FUTURE DIRECTIONS AND CONCLUSIONS

Self-report inventories are used commonly and routinely in various applied assessment tasks, and they have been the focus of thousands of empirical investigations. Considerable progress was made in developing this technology over the course of the 20th century, and many of the concerns identified early on by Allport (1937) and Ellis (1946) have been addressed in modern self-report measures. However, as noted, most empirically grounded SRI scale score interpretation has followed the empirical correlate approach. Much of the research in this area has focused on the direct, simple inference level afforded by knowledge of a scale score's criterion validity. Twentieth-century SRI research did not adequately mine the prospects of construct validity. In the case of the MMPI, Meehl's expectation that the code type–based approach to interpreting clinical scale scores would yield a conceptually grounded alternative to the Kreapelinian nosology was not realized. Although a substantial literature on the empirical correlates of the code types became available to guide their interpretation, the next step in establishing their validity as constructs—placing the code types within meaningful nomological networks—did not follow.

Construction of more recently developed MMPI measures (e.g., the Personality Psychopathology Five [PSY-5] Scales [Harkness et al., 1995], Restructured

Clinical [RC] Scales [Tellegen et al., 2003], and other MMPI-2-RF scales) has been guided by conceptually grounded models of personality and psychology, laying the foundation for construct validity-based interpretation of scores and linking the test to current developments in the fields of personality and psychopathology. These necessary first steps will need to be followed by systematic efforts to elucidate the nomological networks associated with the newer measures and incorporate the findings of this research in MMPI-2-RF interpretation.

This chapter provided an overview of the historical foundations and early criticisms of self-report measures, current issues and challenges in SRI interpretation, and needs for future research in this area. A great deal of progress has been made in developing this technology's conceptual and empirical foundations. These efforts have been documented in an elaborate body of scholarly literature that, of course, goes well beyond the scope of this chapter. Other chapters in this volume cover additional aspects of this literature. Overall, these chapters indicate that assessment of personality and psychopathology by self-report rests on solid foundations that leave this technology well positioned for future research and development efforts.

## REFERENCES

Allport, G. W. (1928). A test for ascendance-submission. *Journal of Abnormal and Social Psychology, 23,* 118–136.

Allport, G. W. (1937). *Personality: A psychosocial interpretation.* New York, NY: Henry Holt.

American Psychiatric Association. (2000). *Diagnostic and statistical manual of mental disorders* (4th ed., text revision). Washington, DC: Author.

Anastasi, A. (1985). Some emerging trends in psychological measurement: A fifty year perspective. *Applied Psychological Measurement, 9,* 212–138.

Ben-Porath, Y. S. (2006). Differentiating normal and abnormal personality with the MMPI-2. In S. Strack (Ed.), *Differentiating normal and abnormal personality* (2nd ed., pp. 337–381). New York, NY: Springer.

Ben-Porath, Y. S., & Butcher, J. N. (1991). The historical development of personality assessment. In C. E. Walker (Ed.), *Clinical psychology: Historical and research foundations* (pp. 121–156) New York, NY: Plenum Press.

Ben-Porath, Y., & Tellegen, A. (2008a). Empirical correlates of the MMPI-2 Restructured Clinical (RC) scales in mental health, forensic, and nonclinical settings: An introduction. *Journal of Personality Assessment, 90,* 119–121.

Ben-Porath, Y. S., & Tellegen, A. (2008b). *Minnesota Multiphasic Personality Inventory—Restructured Form: Manual for administration, scoring, and interpretation.* Minneapolis: University of Minnesota Press.

Ben-Porath, Y. S., & Tellegen, A. (2008c). *Minnesota Multiphasic Personality Inventory—Restructured Form: Users guide for reports.* Minneapolis: University of Minnesota Press.

Ben-Porath, Y. S., & Waller, N. G. (1992). "Normal" personality inventories in clinical assessment: General requirements and potential for using the NEO Personality Inventory. *Psychological Assessment, 4,* 14–19.

Bernreuter, R. J. (1933). Theory and construction of the personality inventory. *Journal of Social Psychology, 4,* 387–405.

Black, J. D. (1953). The interpretation of MMPI profiles of college women. *Dissertation Abstracts, 13,* 870–871.

Block, J. (1965). *The challenge of response sets: Unconfounding meaning, acquiescence, and social desirability in the MMPI.* New York, NY: Appleton-Century-Crofts.

Burisch, M. (1984). Approaches to personality inventory construction: A comparison of merits. *American Psychologist, 39,* 214–227.

Butcher, J. N. (1996). *International adaptations of the MMPI-2: Research and clinical applications.* Minneapolis: University of Minnesota Press.

Butcher, J. N., Dahlstrom, W. G., Graham, J. R., Tellegen, A., & Kaemmer, B. (1989). *The Minnesota Multiphasic Personality Inventory-2 (MMPI-2): Manual for administration and scoring.* Minneapolis: University of Minnesota Press.

Butcher, J. N., Graham, J. R., Ben-Porath, Y. S., Tellegen, A., Dahlstrom, W. G., & Kaemmer, B. (2001). *The Minnesota Multiphasic Personality Inventory-2 (MMPI-2): Manual for administration, scoring, and interpretation* (revised ed.). Minneapolis: University of Minnesota Press.

Butcher, J. N., Graham, J. R., Williams, C. L., & Ben-Porath, Y. S. (1990). *Development and use of the MMPI-2 content scales.* Minneapolis: University of Minnesota Press.

Cady, V. M. (1923). The estimation of juvenile incorrigibility. *Elementary School Journal, 33,* 1–140.

Cattell, R. B. (1965). *The scientific analysis of personality.* Baltimore, MD: Penguin Books.

Cattell, R. B. (1979). *Personality and learning theory* (Vol. 1). New York, NY: Springer.

Cattell, R. B., Cattell, A. K., & Cattell, H. E. (1993). *Sixteen Personality Factors Questionnaire* (5th ed.). Champaign, IL: Institute for Personality and Ability Testing.

Costa, P. T., & McCrae, R. R. (1992a). Normal personality assessment in clinical practice: The NEO Personality Inventory. *Psychological Assessment, 4,* 5–13.

Costa, P. T., & McCrae, R. R. (1992b). Normal personality inventories in clinical assessment: General requirements and the potential for using the NEO Personality Inventory. A reply. *Psychological Assessment, 4,* 20–22.

Costa, P. T., & McCrae, R. R. (1992c). *Revised NEO Personality Inventory (NEO-PI-R) and NEO Five Factor Inventory (NEOFFI) professional manual.* Odessa, FL: Psychological Assessment Resources.

Cronbach, L. J., & Meehl, P. E. (1955). Construct validity in psychological tests. *Psychological Bulletin, 52,* 281–302.

Dahlstrom, W. G. (1992). The growth in acceptance of the MMPI. *Professional Psychology: Research and Practice, 23,* 345–348.

Dahlstrom, W. G., Welsh, G. S., & Dahlstrom, L. E. (1972). *An MMPI handbook, Vol. 1: Clinical interpretation* (revised ed.). Minneapolis: University of Minnesota Press.

Downey, J. E. (1923). *The will-temperament and its testing.* New York, NY: World Book.

DuBois, P. L. (1970). *A history of psychological testing.* Boston, MA: Allyn & Bacon.

Duckworth, J. C. (1991). The Minnesota Multiphasic Personality Inventory-2: A review. *Journal of Counseling and Development, 69,* 564–567.

Edwards, A. L. (1957). *The social desirability variable in personality assessment and research.* New York, NY: Dryden.

Edwards, A. L. (1970). *The measurement of personality traits by scales and inventories.* New York, NY: Holt, Reinhart, and Winston.

Ellis, A. (1946). The validity of personality questionnaires. *Psychological Bulletin, 43,* 385–440.

Ellis, A. (1953). Recent research with personality inventories. *Journal of Consulting Psychology, 17,* 45–49.

Eysenck, J. J., & Eysenck, S. B. G. (1975). *Manual for the Eysenck Personality Questionnaire.* San Diego, CA: Educational and Industrial Testing Service.

Finger, M. S., & Ones, D. S. (1999). Psychometric equivalence of the computer and booklet forms of the MMPI: A meta-analysis. *Psychological Assessment, 11,* 58–66.

Galton, F. (1884). Measurement of character. *Fortnightly Review, 42,* 179–185.

Gilberstadt, H., & Duker, J. (1965). *A handbook for clinical and actuarial MMPI interpretation.* Philadelphia, PA: W. B. Saunders.

Guthrie, G. M. (1952). Common characteristics associated with frequent MMPI profile types. *Journal of Clinical Psychology, 8,* 141–145.

Gynther, M. D. (1972). White norms and black MMPIs: A prescription for discrimination? *Psychological Bulletin, 78,* 386–402.

Halbower, C. C. (1955). *A comparison of actuarial versus clinical prediction of classes discriminated by the MMPI.* (Unpublished doctoral dissertation), University of Minnesota, Minneapolis, MN.

Harkness, A. R., & McNulty, J. L. (1994). The Personality-Psychopathology Five: Issues from the pages of a diagnostic manual instead of a dictionary. In S. Strack & M. Lorr (Eds.), *Differentiating normal and abnormal personality* (pp. 291–315). New York, NY: Springer.

Harkness, A. R., McNulty, J. L., & Ben-Porath, Y. S. (1995). The Personality Psychopathology Five (PSY-5) Scales. *Psychological Assessment, 7,* 104–114.

Hathaway, S. R. (1956). Scales 5 (Masculinity-Femininity), 6 (Paranoia), and 8 (Schizophrenia). In G. S. Welsh & W. G. Dahlstrom (Eds.), *Basic readings on the MMPI in psychology and medicine* (pp. 104–111). Minneapolis: University of Minnesota Press.

Hathaway, S. R., & McKinley, J. C. (1940). A Multiphasic Personality Schedule (Minnesota): I. Construction of the schedule. *Journal of Psychology, 10,* 249–254.

Hathaway, S. R., & McKinley, J. C. (1942). A Multiphasic Personality Schedule (Minnesota): II. The measurement of symptomatic depression. *Journal of Psychology, 14,* 73–84.

Hathaway, S. R., & McKinley, J. C. (1943). *The Minnesota Multiphasic Personality Inventory.* Minneapolis: University of Minnesota Press.

Hathaway, S. R., & Meehl, P. E. (1951). The Minnesota Multiphasic Personality Inventory. In *Military clinical psychology* (Department of the Army Technical Manual TM 8:242; Department of the Air Force AFM 160–145). Washington, DC: U.S. Government Printing Office.

Heidbreder, E. (1926). Measuring introversion and extraversion. *Journal of Abnormal and Social Psychology, 21,* 120–134.

Helmes, E., & Reddon, J. R. (1993). A perspective on developments in assessing psychopathology: A critical review of the MMPI and MMPI-2. *Psychological Bulletin, 113,* 453–471.

Heymans, G., & Wiersma, E. (1906). Beitrage zur spezillen psychologie auf grund einer massenunterschung [Contribution of psychological specialists to personality analysis]. *Zeitschrift fur Psychologie, 43,* 81–127.

Hoch, A., & Amsden, G. S. (1913). A guide to the descriptive study of personality. *Review of Neurology and Psychiatry, 11,* 577–587.

Humm, D. G., & Wadsworth, G. W. (1935). The Humm-Wadsworth temperament scale. *American Journal of Psychiatry, 92,* 163–200.

Jackson, D. N. (1989). *Basic Personality Inventory manual.* Port Huron, MI: Sigma Assessment Systems.

Jackson, D. N. (1971). The dynamics of structured personality tests. *Psychological Review, 78,* 229–248.

Jackson, D. N., & Messick, S. (1962). Response styles on the MMPI: Comparison of clinical and normal samples. *Journal of Abnormal and Social Psychology, 65,* 285–299.

Keller, J., Hicks, B. D., & Miller, G. A. (2000). *Psychophysiology in the study of psychopathology.* In J. T. Caciopo & L. G. Tassinary (Eds.), *Handbook of psychophysiology* (pp. 719–750). New York, NY: Cambridge University Press.

Lamberty, G. J. (2007). *Understanding somatization in the practice of clinical neuropsychology.* NY: Oxford University Press.

Maller, J. B. (1932). The measurement of confict between honesty and group loyalty. *Journal of Educational Psychology, 23,* 187–191.

Marks, P. A., & Seeman, W. (1963). *The actuarial description of abnormal personality: An atlas for use with the MMPI.* Baltimore, MD: Williams & Wilkins.

McGrath, R. E., Mitchell, M., Kim, B. H., & Hough, L. (2010). Evidence for response bias as a source of error variance in applied assessment. *Psychological Bulletin, 136,* 450–470.

McKinley, J. C., & Hathaway, S. R. (1940). A Multiphasic Personality Schedule (Minnesota): II. A differential study of hypochondriasis. *Journal of Psychology, 10,* 255–268.

McKinley, J. C., & Hathaway, S. R. (1942). A Multiphasic Personality Schedule (Minnesota): IV. Psychasthenia. *Journal of Applied Psychology, 26,* 614–624.

McKinley, J. C., & Hathaway, S. R. (1944). A Multiphasic Personality Schedule (Minnesota): V. Hysteria, Hypomania, and Psychopathic Deviate. *Journal of Applied Psychology, 28,* 153–174.

Meehl, P. E. (1945). The dynamics of "structured" personality tests. *Journal of Clinical Psychology, 1,* 296–303.

Meehl, P. E. (1954). *Clinical versus statistical prediction: A theoretical analysis and review of the evidence.* Minneapolis, MN: University of Minnesota Press.

Meehl, P. E. (1956). Wanted—A good cookbook. *American Psychologist, 11,* 263–272.

Meehl, P. E., & Hathaway, S. R. (1946). The K factor as a suppressor variable in the MMPI. *Journal of Applied Psychology, 30,* 525–564.

Morey, L. C. (1991). *Personality Assessment Inventory: Professional manual.* Odessa, FL: Psychological Assessment Resources.

Morey, L. C. (2007). *Personality Assessment Inventory Professional Manual* (2nd ed.). Odessa, FL: Psychological Assessment Resources.

Piedmont, R. L., McCrae, R. R., Riemann, R., & Angleitner, A. (2000). On the invalidity of validity scales: Evidence from self-reports and observer ratings in volunteer samples. *Journal of Personality and Social Psychology, 78,* 582–593.

Rohling, M. L., Larrabee, G. J., Greiffenstein, M. F., Ben-Porath, Y. S., Lees-Haley, P., Green, P., & Greve, K. W. (2011). A misleading review of response bias: Comment on McGrath, Mitchell, Kim, and Hough (2010). *Psychological Bulletin, 137*(4), 708–712.

Ruch, F. L. (1942). A technique for detecting attempts to fake performance on a self-inventory type of personality test. In Q. McNemar & M. A. Merrill (Eds.), *Studies on personality* (pp. 61–85). New York, NY: Saunders.

Schinka, J. A., & LaLone, L. (1997). MMPI-2 norms: Comparisons with a census-matched subsample. *Psychological Assessment, 9,* 307–311.

Tellegen, A. (forthcoming). *The Multidimensional Personality Questionnaire.* Minneapolis: University of Minnesota Press.

Tellegen, A., & Ben-Porath, Y. S. (2008). *Minnesota Multiphaisc Personality Inventory-2 Restructured Form (MMPI-2-RF): technical manual.* Minneapolis: University of Minnesota Press.

Tellegen, A., Ben-Porath, Y. S., McNulty, J. L., Arbisi, P. A., Graham, J. R., & Kaemmer, B. (2003). *MMPI-2 Restructured Clinical (RC) Scales: Development, validation, and Interpretation.* Minneapolis: University of Minnesota Press.

Tellegen, A., & Waller, N. G. (2009). Exploring personality through test construction: Development of the Multidimensional Personality Questionnaire. In G. J. Boyle, G. Matthews, & D. H. Saklofske (Eds.), *The SAGE handbook of personality theory and assessment, Vol. 2. Personality measurement and testing* (pp. 261–292). Thousand Oaks, CA: Sage.

Thurstone, L. L. (1930). A neurotic inventory. *Journal of Social Psychology, 1,* 3–30.

Travis, R. C. (1925). The measurement of fundamental character traits by a new diagnostic test. *Journal of Abnormal and Social Psychology, 18,* 400–425.

Wells, F. L. (1914). The systematic observation of the personality—In its relation to the hygiene of the mind. *Psychological Review, 21,* 295–333.

Wiggins, J. S. (1959). Interrelations among MMPI measures of dissimulation under standard and social desirability instruction. *Journal of Consulting Psychology, 23,* 419–427.

Wiggins, J. S. (1966). Substantive dimensions of self-report in the MMPI item pool. *Psychological Monographs, 80*(22, Whole No. 630).

Woodworth, R. S. (1920). *Personal data sheet.* Chicago, IL: Stoeling.

# CHAPTER 25

# Current Status and Future Directions of Assessment Psychology

JACK A. NAGLIERI AND JOHN R. GRAHAM

## BRIEF HISTORY

Assessment psychology can be dated to as early as 2200 BC when the Chinese emperor Wu of Han had individuals examined to determine their fitness for public office (DuBois, 1970). In the late 18th and early 19th centuries, civil service tests, patterned after those of the Chinese, were introduced in Europe. In 1883 the United States endorsed the use of tests for the screening of applicants for civil service jobs (Graham & Lilly, 1984). At about the same time, Sir Francis Galton's work on the genetic transmission of characteristics required the development of measures to quantify the characteristics under study. The simple sensorimotor tasks that Galton developed were later introduced in the United States by James McKeen Cattell. Alfred Binet and Theodore Simon, working in France, adapted some of these sensorimotor tasks and added others when they developed methods for assessing ability in schoolchildren. Their scales were modified for use in the United States by Lewis Terman and further adapted in part by the U.S. Army for evaluation of military personnel. David Wechsler's dissatisfaction with the Binet scales in his work with psychiatric patients led to the development of the first of the Wechsler intelligence scales. The availability of standardized methods for assessing intellectual ability provided American psychologists with unique skills that helped to establish their professional identity in clinical and educational settings. Moreover, these tools to measure ability have had

tremendous impact on our society and the practice of psychology.

## Current Status

The proportion of psychologists' time spent conducting psychological assessments has declined over time. In 1959 psychologists practicing in clinical settings spent 44% of their time conducting psychological assessments (Groth-Marnat, 1999), but by 1998 psychologists in similar clinical settings were spending only 16% of their time conducting psychological assessments (Phelps, Eisman, & Kohout, 1998). However, assessment is still a very important and viable specialty within psychology, especially among professionals working in educational, mental health, medical, forensic, and correctional settings. Earlier chapters in this volume elucidated some of the factors that have affected the use of assessment procedures. A recurring theme has been that economic factors, most currently represented by managed care programs, have had significant impact on assessment practices. Piotrowski, Belter, and Keller (1998) surveyed psychologists listed in the National Register of Health Service Providers in Psychology and found that 70% saw managed care as negatively affecting psychological assessment. Psychologists reported less reliance on procedures requiring much clinician time and more emphasis on briefer instruments. They also reported less emphasis on comprehensive assessments of general psychological functioning and more emphasis on techniques that were directly responsive to specific referral questions. Unfortunately, the validity of many of the specific and abbreviated procedures currently being used has not been adequately demonstrated.

Economic pressures have also forced psychologists to demonstrate that assessment activities contribute significantly to positive outcomes in a variety of settings (e.g., mental health, medical, business, education). Other chapters in this volume offer evidence concerning these contributions. For example, in his chapter in this volume Maruish presents some convincing arguments that assessment procedures can facilitate effective psychological interventions. An especially promising area is the development of standardized assessment procedures for documenting the effectiveness of treatment interventions. Likewise, the chapters in this volume by Sweet, Tovian, Breting and Suchy and by Otero, Podell, DeFina, Barrett, McCullen, and Goldberg document the contributions of psychological assessment in relation to a variety of medical procedures, including surgical interventions, organ transplantation, and physical conditions (e.g., neuropsychological dysfunction). Similarly, in their chapter in this volume Wasserman and Bracken highlight new advances in assessment of cognitive processing that have been shown to be relevant to academic interventions. An important role for assessment psychologists will be to further develop effective ways to assess patients' psychological coping and adjustment to their diseases and also to show relevance to treatment.

The Board of Professional Psychology of the American Psychological Association (APA) established the Psychological Assessment Work Group (PAWG) to examine the current status of psychological assessment and to make recommendations concerning its future. The work group documented the impact of managed care on psychological assessments (Eisman et al., 2000). Although many managed care companies argue that traditional psychological assessments do not add significantly enough to treatment to justify their cost and that less costly interviews are sufficient, the PAWG concluded that these views are not accurate and offered recommendations for rebutting them and preserving the stature of psychological assessment in the health care marketplace. In a subsequent report, PAWG offered evidence from the research literature that some psychological assessment procedures are as valid as (and in some cases more valid than) medical procedures that are readily accepted by many as valid and necessary (Meyer et al., 2001). For example, the relationship between long-term verbal memory tests and differentiation of dementia from depression was of the same

magnitude as the relationship between exercise echocardiography results and identification of coronary artery disease (effect size for both about .60). Neither the use of routine ultrasound examinations for predicting successful pregnancies nor the use of Minnesota Multiphasic Personality Inventory (MMPI) Ego Strength scale scores to predict subsequent psychotherapy outcome can be supported by empirical research findings (effect size for each less than .10). The report emphasized that both psychological and medical procedures have varying degrees of validity and that the validity and utility of each technique has to be demonstrated empirically. The PAWG concluded that "formal psychological assessment is a vital element in psychology's professional heritage and a central part of professional practice today" and that there is "very strong and positive evidence that already exists on the value of psychological testing and assessment" (Meyer et al., 2001, p. 155). It is the responsibility of assessment psychologists, individually and collectively, to use existing evidence to support assessment activities in a variety of settings and to generate additional evidence of the validity and efficiency of psychological assessment procedures in health care and other settings (e.g., business, forensic) where assessment is taking place.

## ASSESSMENT SETTINGS

### Child Mental Health

The chapter in this volume by Wrobel and Lachar on assessment in child mental health settings illustrates the importance that psychological assessment services have in intake evaluation, treatment planning, and subsequent outcome review. The chapter specifically illustrates the interplay of psychology and business and how delivery of services can be related to a variety of factors, including annual institutional budgets from which resources are allocated and the extent to which associated expenses can be reimbursed. These realities of service delivery have considerable impact on children who receive mental health services because of emotional and behavioral adjustment problems.

Wrobel and Lachar describe how psychological assessment in child mental health settings focuses on the identification and quantification of symptoms and problems that should lead to the development of treatment strategies. A detailed discussion of the forms of psychological assessment that can be applied to answer specific diagnostic inquiries includes careful analysis of assessment instruments as well as topics such as qualifications of persons who conduct psychological assessment services, supervision issues, and certification and license considerations. Wrobel and Lachar recognize that well-trained and well-supervised professionals are needed to manage the difficulties of making a diagnosis in an informational environment that can be complicated by problems such as comorbidity and disparate reports from parents. Despite the challenges, psychological assessments ultimately play a pivotal role in the determination of the nature of the problem and the eventual effectiveness of the treatment. Because of the importance assessment plays in meeting the mental health needs of the client, Wrobel and Lachar note that proper assessment should make use of multiple methods (e.g., behavioral rating scales, direct observation, interviews) by multiple informants (e.g., parents, teachers, the children themselves) of behavior in multiple settings (e.g., home, school). The ultimate success of treatment is, of course, related to the value of the methods used to obtain information and select treatments.

Importantly, the discussion by Wrobel and Lachar of methods used by psychologists in this field, and especially the results of surveys of the assessment tools used in the child mental health arena, have shown that traditional tests of intelligence (e.g., Wechsler scales) and personality (e.g., MMPI; Rorschach; Thematic Apperception Test) remain standards in the profession. They also note that recent surveys suggest the growing use of parent and teacher rating scales in a variety of areas (from rating scales of depression and attention deficit hyperactivity disorder to family adjustment scales). Additionally, Wrobel and Lachar note the influence of managed care in reducing the use of some of the most labor-intensive psychological assessment procedures.

They conclude that multidimensional multi-informant objective assessment makes a unique contribution to the assessment of youth adjustment, but more research is needed. They suggest that the validity of objective measures of youth adjustment should be more fully examined and especially the construct and actuarial validity of popular child and adolescent adjustment measures. They stress that validity will be best demonstrated when a measure contributes to the accuracy of routine decision making that occurs in clinical practice (e.g., differential diagnosis or the selection of an optimal treatment plan). Further research is also needed on agreement among informants who have completed rating scales, in particular, the clinical implications of the results obtained from each informant rather than the magnitude of correlations. Additionally, researchers should examine incremental

validity obtained from the use of a variety of objective assessment instruments. These and other issues presented by Wrobel and Lachar illustrate the important topics yet to be examined in this vibrant area of assessment psychology.

## Adult Mental Health

In their chapter in this volume concerning assessment in adult mental health settings, Sellbom, Marion, and Bagby conclude that the main goals of assessment in such settings are providing an accurate description of the client's problems, determining what interpersonal and environmental factors precipitated and are sustaining the problems, and making predictions concerning outcome with or without intervention. Assessments are also useful in planning treatment programs, evaluating the effectiveness of treatment interventions, and guiding discharge and follow-up plans. Sellbom et al. believe that assessments need to be comprehensive and that clients and patients are disadvantaged by trends toward abbreviated assessment instruments and procedures.

In inpatient settings, assessments often address questions of differential diagnosis. Although they discuss the limitations of the categorical approach to diagnosis underlying the fourth edition of the *Diagnostic and Statistical Manual of Mental Disorders* (*DSM-IV*), Sellbom et al. believe that instruments that cover a broad array of symptoms (e.g., MMPI-2) are especially useful in addressing diagnostic questions. Sellbom et al. believe that assessments in adult mental health settings need to be evidence-based and multimodal. Psychologists conducting assessments should choose their tools and make their interpretations of the resulting data using the best available empirical evidence. They echo the opinion expressed by Spengler (this volume) that judgments more closely tied to empirical data will be more accurate than those based on clinical experience and clinical impressions. However, they acknowledge that there is likely to be some clinical judgment involved in most decisions, predictions, or inferences based on assessment data. They also believe that multiple data sources are necessary for reliable and valid inferences to be made about patients and clients. They prefer more structured interviews and more objective instruments, because in their judgment these approaches are more clearly supported by empirical evidence. Sellbom et al. describe and embrace the involvement of clients in the assessment process and identify Finn's Therapeutic Assessment approach as a structured way of increasing client involvement.

## Geriatric

Edelstein, Martin, and Gerolimatos note in their chapter in this volume that the population of the United States is aging rapidly. The number of persons 85 years old or older has expanded 31-fold, and it is estimated that by 2030 there will be 72.1 million adults 65 years or older. Data suggest that approximately 80% of older adults suffer from some chronic health problem and about one fourth meet criteria for a diagnosable mental disorder. Thus, assessment of older adults will become more and more important over time. Edelstein and colleagues discuss the importance of bias in the form of ageism and the cultural competence of those who assess older adults.

Although there are many similarities in the assessment of younger and older adults, there also are some unique considerations when assessing older adults. Older adults may have deficits in vision, hearing, or cognitive processes that make completion of standard assessment procedures difficult or impossible. The presentation of major psychological disorders for older adults is often different from that for younger adults. For example, clinically depressed older adults are more likely than younger adults to present with somatic instead of psychological symptoms. All of these issues present significant challenges in assessing older adults that may best be met through the development of techniques and instruments tailored to the differing abilities and problems of older adults.

Edelstein and colleagues conclude that it is more important to assess the adaptive functioning of older adults than to describe clinical syndromes. Instruments and procedures for assessing the activities of daily living (ADLs; e.g., dressing, bathing) and instrumental activities of daily living (IADLs; e.g., meal preparation, money management) will become more important as the population continues to age. Also, because of an increasing awareness of the importance of social support (real and perceived) to the well-being of older adults, instruments and techniques for effective assessment of social support will become increasingly important.

## Industrial/Organizational

In their chapter in this volume on assessment in industrial/organizational settings, Klimoski and Wilkinson describe the important work psychologists have done to aid companies in their attempts to improve performance by better understanding how people think and behave. As is the case with other settings in which assessment is important, psychologists working in this field initially

used tests developed by the U.S. military (also discussed by Wasserman, this volume) to measure ability as well as for personnel selection, evaluation of social competence, and prediction of behaviors such as absenteeism. Many of the tests used in industrial/organizational settings today were translated or adapted by former military officers who went into the private sector after military service (e.g., Otis and Wechsler). Although versions of these early methods are still in use today (e.g., Army Beta test), Klimoski and Wilkinson's chapter also provides information about the enlargement of the assessment batteries. This is especially important within the context of political considerations, including accommodation for disability and equal opportunities for employment, that must be taken into account in industrial decision-making processes.

Assessment in industrial/organizational settings, like assessment in educational settings (see Braden, this volume), has been influenced by the social context within which the measures and procedures are used. Not only have society's views of assessment issues shaped how assessment is conducted, but federal and state laws and regulations have also had a major impact on the field. In today's industrial/organizational settings, these considerations can be as important as psychometric issues such as reliability and validity, especially as they relate to problems such as job discrimination (fairness based on race, sex, ethnicity, age, or disability), equal opportunity, neutrality of decision makers, and so on. The role of psychologists as assessors within the industrial/organizational setting has also been influenced by the demand for these valuable professionals. Business leaders have seen the advantages to industry provided by psychologists who can assist with selection, promotion, and career planning decisions so that the best people for specific jobs may be found. This has led psychologists to study and utilize a variety of instruments in addition to tests of intelligence and personality, to evaluate things like teamwork and interpersonal skills, specific knowledge and skills pertinent to the job, honesty and integrity, ability to learn, the five-factor structure of personality, and ratings of actual job performance.

Klimoski and Wilkinson discuss challenges facing the field of industrial/organizational psychology. These include research on determining the best prediction and criterion variables. Some researchers have argued that job performance itself is the best criterion, but definition of job performance can be difficult. Similarly, although researchers have found that factors such as ability and personality play an important role in overall job performance, many times the instruments selected were not developed for the purposes for which they are applied. For example, researchers have questioned the application of a test of personality like the MMPI in industrial/organizational settings because it was not developed for this purpose. How can a test like the MMPI be used to determine suitability for a particular job when it was developed to measure psychopathology, not personality factors associated with how well a person can perform a specific task? Another challenge facing industrial/organizational psychologists, and almost every other person in the assessment field, is the movement toward online testing, computer-adaptive tests, and other advances that result from the use of the World Wide Web. Such developments further illustrate the unique demands of those who work in the industrial/organizational field—an environment driven by the intersection of the science of testing, public opinion, and politics and the culture of the business world.

## Forensic Psychology

In their chapter in this volume, Ogloff and Douglas state that forensic psychology involves the application of the principles of psychology to legal questions and issues. Although psychologists have been involved in offering expert testimony in court since the early 1900s, it was not until 1962 that the U.S. District Court of Appeals for the District of Columbia in *Jenkins v. U.S.* clearly recognized psychologists as experts in court. In 2001 the Council of Representatives of the American Psychological Association voted to recognize forensic psychology as a specialty area in psychology.

Because the primary task of forensic psychologists as experts typically is to evaluate the extent to which individuals meet various legal standards and criteria (e.g., competency to stand trial, insanity), assessment is one of the most important tasks that forensic psychologists perform. Several factors have limited the contributions that psychologists have made in this area. Many psychologists, including some who practice forensic psychology on a regular basis, have not been trained in forensic psychological assessment. Although there are similarities between clinical and forensic assessments, there are also important differences. Ogloff and Douglas point out that forensic constructs and questions rarely map directly on to traditional psychological constructs. Thus, persons not adequately trained in forensic assessment will not be able to understand and specify the legal principles and standards relevant to a particular assessment issue. In addition, traditional assessment instruments (e.g., MMPI, Wechsler scales) were not developed within legal contexts

and according to legal principles, so they are far less useful in forensic than in clinical evaluations.

Ogloff and Douglas believe that the role of psychologists in conducting assessments in the legal arena will continue to increase. However, several important changes are indicated if psychologists are to make significant contributions in forensic settings. First, formal forensic training programs need to be developed. Most psychologists currently conducting forensic evaluations have no formal training in forensic psychology. Second, formal procedures for credentialing and certifying forensic psychologists must be expanded. Currently, only nine states in the United States have certification procedures. Although the American Board of Forensic Psychology has procedures for establishing credentials for forensic psychological practice, relatively few psychologists undergo this voluntary evaluation process. The Ethical Guidelines for Forensic Psychologists, which were published in 2001 and revised in 2011, established standards that forensic psychologists are expected to maintain. Third, more research is needed to determine the extent to which traditional psychological assessment instruments and procedures can be used to address specific forensic constructs. Finally, psychologists should use their expertise in test construction and statistical methodologies to develop forensic psychological instruments designed specifically to address forensic questions and issues. Although Ogloff and Douglas believe that we have accomplished a great deal in a relatively short time in forensic psychology, there are significant issues associated with training and instrument development that remain to be addressed.

## Medical Psychology

In their chapter in this volume, Sweet et al. state that assessment activities of psychologists in medical settings have become so commonplace that they are taken for granted. Recently trained physicians expect to have psychological assessment resources available in the settings in which they practice. In general, psychological assessments in medical settings should contribute to a broader understanding of patients. More specifically, assessments should document patients' response to disease and changes (both positive and negative) associated with medical procedures and treatments.

Traditional assessment procedures (e.g., MMPI-2, Rorschach) may contribute significantly to the understanding of patients' psychological status and personality characteristics, but the validity of traditional measures to do so must be demonstrated in medical settings. The issue of using general population norms versus norms for particular medical populations is a complex one that is dependent on the purpose for which the assessments are conducted. For example, if the referral question is whether a patient's emotional distress is severe enough to warrant intervention, general population norms are likely to provide the most useful information. However, if the referral question concerns a patient's adjustment to a specific illness at a particular stage in comparison to that of the typical patient, then illness-specific norms may be more appropriate.

In applied medical settings, the efficiency and cost effectiveness of assessment procedures are being increasingly emphasized. Psychologists must be in a position to demonstrate that psychological assessments contribute significantly to effective treatment programs for patients and that they do so in a cost-effective manner. Economic considerations have resulted in the development of many brief, narrow-band assessment instruments. Although such instruments can be quite valuable, matters of efficiency and cost effectiveness often overshadow more traditional issues, such as reliability and validity in evaluating them. There is likely to be a concomitant emphasis on actuarial judgments over clinical ones. In their chapter, Sweet and colleagues concluded that both clinical and actuarial judgments make significant contributions in medical settings.

## Correctional Psychology

In his chapter in this volume, Megargee points out that more than 7.3 million men and women in the United States are under some form of correctional supervision (i.e., jail, prison, probation, parole). The number of persons in jails and prisons has increased 28% since 2003. With such large numbers of persons to service with limited resources, assessment and classification in correctional settings are extremely important. In 1973 the National Advisory Commission on Criminal Justice Standards and Goals called for immediate implementation of comprehensive classification at all levels of the criminal justice system. In the case of *Palmigiano v. Garrahy* (1977), the courts agreed that accurate classification is essential to the operation of safe prisons.

Megargee discusses in detail the purposes for which assessments are conducted in correctional settings and the instruments and procedures that have been used. Two purposes seem to be most important: the prediction of violence and/or recidivism and classification that can be used to make decisions about matters such as housing and programming.

There clearly has been a move away from using offense data for classification and prediction and toward consideration of individual needs, including psychological ones, of those assessed. Often instruments and procedures developed for use in other (e.g., mental health) settings have been employed in correctional settings. The validity of such applications has not often been studied, but available research indicates little support for the routine use of clinical instruments for correctional assessment. Many instruments and scales have been developed specifically for use in correctional settings, but the methodologies used typically have been inadequate and data concerning validity for the intended purposes are lacking.

One of the most promising approaches to psychological assessment and classification in corrections settings has been the MMPI–MMPI-2 system developed by Megargee and his colleagues (Megargee, Carbonell, Bohn, & Sliger, 2001). In a technique based on cluster analytic procedures, subtypes of inmates were identified using MMPI scores, and classification rules, which can be applied by computers, were developed to assign inmates to types. Megargee has demonstrated that his system is appropriate for local, state, and federal prison systems, with large proportions of inmates being classified in the various settings. External correlates, including institutional adjustment and postrelease behaviors, have been established for many of the Megargee types.

Megargee points out that there has been inadequate attention to the role of situational variables in predicting behaviors in correctional settings. Rather, many psychologists assume that personality variables, as assessed by traditional psychological tests, are the best predictors of such behaviors. While probably of great importance, the interaction of situational and personality variables also has been understudied.

Although the standards of the American Association of Correctional Psychologists and other organizations have recommended minimal qualifications for mental health workers providing services in correctional settings, there are few procedures for establishing that psychologists conducting assessments in correctional settings are adequately trained and competent to do so. Uniform standards and procedures for credentialing and certifying correctional psychologists are badly needed.

## Educational Psychology

In the chapter in this volume on assessment psychology in educational settings, Braden begins by distinguishing psychological assessment in the schools from psychological assessment in other settings. He carefully describes how assessment in schools is conducted for screening and diagnostic purposes, for example, for the identification of children with special education needs. Other purposes of assessment in educational settings include the design of educational interventions as well as evaluation, selection, and certification functions. Braden also reviews more specific methods, such as interviews and reviews of student records, observational systems, and response-to-intervention approaches. More specific checklists and self-report techniques, projective techniques, and standardized tests are also included. Braden also provides a summary of methods used to assess academic achievement particularly because of the importance these tests play in identification of children's academic deficiencies and in psychoeducational diagnosis. The relationships between the use of these tests and educational accountability and standards-based educational reforms are also discussed. Braden's chapter concludes with the suggestion that assessment tools need to be in line with current scientific and technical advances and educational standards of learning. Additionally, assessments must be appropriate for diverse learners and have utility for instructional interventions.

## TYPES OF ASSESSMENT

### Cognitive/Intellectual Assessment

Wasserman's chapter in this volume provides a review of how the assessment of intelligence has had a long history in psychology and can be credited with being one of the most influential constructs in psychology and education. IQ tests have provided a structured method of evaluating ability that has been used in most settings within which psychologists work. Wasserman provides a discussion of how IQ tests have been used, but, more important, he also provides important historical facts on the origins of these tests as well as a discussion of their utility. Like the Reynolds and Suzuki chapter in this volume, which discusses the most controversial topic surrounding IQ tests (the question of bias), Wasserman's coverage of the more politically focused issues gives the reader a greater understanding of the complexities of this topic. Controversies notwithstanding, the contributions intelligence tests have made to our field are reflected in the many settings within which tests are used (schools, hospitals, clinics, industry, etc.) as well as the purposes for which they have been used (diagnosis of learning disorders, giftedness, mental retardation, attention deficits, etc.).

Wasserman emphasizes the importance of understanding the history behind conventional IQ tests, which goes back to the Army Mental Testing Program (Yoakum & Yerkes, 1920) so that instruments can be seen in perspective. He argues that the study of intelligence can be "characterized by the best and worst of science—scholarly debates and bitter rivalries, research breakthroughs and academic fraud, major assessment paradigm shifts, and the birth of a commercial industry that generates hundreds of millions of dollars in annual revenue." He makes the important suggestion that the study of intelligence has yet to claim status as a mature clinical science, despite some signs of progress.

Wasserman's view that the study of intelligence needs an evolutionary step is based on the recognition that this technology (like others in psychology) is dominated by tests created before 1930. He recognizes the tremendous advances in electronic scoring, analysis, and reporting of test results, but these advances are based on instruments that are close to 100 years old (e.g., Wechsler and Binet scales). Wasserman suggests that if the past provides the best prediction of the future, then by about 2050 we may expect seventh-edition revisions of the Stanford-Binet, the Wechsler Intelligence Scale for Children (WISC), and the Wechsler Adult Intelligence Scale (WAIS). His discussion begs the question "Are these tests so valid that they should remain psychologists' primary tools in the 21st century?"

Wasserman argues that changes in fundamental assessment paradigms are needed so that psychological assessment results for a child referred for learning problems, for example, will (a) give information about how learning occurs, (b) describe the relevant impaired cognitive abilities or processes, (c) assess the degree to which the child's ability or process profile resembles that obtained by specific diagnostic groups (e.g., learning disability or attention-deficit hyperactivity disorder), and (d) prescribe interventions that have demonstrated effectiveness for children with similar test score profiles. He believes that well-developed theory, valid and reliable tests, a cognitive diagnostic nomenclature related to abilities and processes, and effective interventions linked to assessment combined may enable the intelligence assessment field to become a mature applied clinical science one day.

### Interests Assessment

The chapter on interests by Lowman and Carson begins with an important recognition of the fact that psychologists have not reached a consensual definition of what interests are, how they develop, and how best to classify them. Nevertheless, as described by Wasserman in the intelligence testing chapter in this volume, the lack of consensus has not blocked the creation of a number of assessment tools for measuring interests, and the test publishing industry has evolved into a flourishing business. This has resulted in a situation in which the measures used to assess interests have defined the field, especially in the eyes of those professionals who use the inventories. Again, as in the situation in intelligence testing, Lowman and Carson see assessment of interests as a field that is comparable in scope and importance to abilities and personality traits. The problems they discuss in the assessment of interests parallel those found in the assessment of intelligence as it relates to issues of gender, age, race, and ethnic factors that may affect the validity of interpretations of interest measures.

The chapter on interests concludes with suggestions for research on a number of important topics, including the heritability of interests. Although Lowman and Carson suggest that high heritability would be expected because of the stability of interests across the life cycle and the efficiency with which people seem to self-select occupations that fit their characteristics, they note that further research is needed in this area. They also recognize the need to study the possibility of critical periods in the development of interests, especially to examine whether children have a number of potentially strong interests that become more stable with the development of related skills during a critical time period.

Other areas of future research include further examination of the commonality and differences of alternative interest measures, empirically based coding of occupations, and the specific empirical nature of interdomain relationships. Finally, having established that interests and personality are highly related, Lowman and Carson indicate that more work is needed to determine ability-interest and ability-interest-personality relationships. This area, like others in assessment psychology, is ripe with ample research opportunities.

## Neuropsychology Assessment

The chapter on neuropsychological assessment in this volume by Otero et al. is unique because neuropsychology has undergone considerably more advancement than many disciplines in psychology, especially in the assessment methods used. As the authors reflect on the history of the field, it becomes clear that most of neuropsychology is based on the large amount of clinical information obtained from studying World War II veterans who experienced brain damage. Psychologists used the understanding of the relationships between brain injury and performance deficits to help determine the likelihood and possible location of brain damage and associated cognitive impairments in a wide variety of clients since that war. Recent advances in cutting-edge neuroimaging technology, such as functional magnetic resonance imaging (fMRI) and magnetoencephalography (MEG), enable today's neuropsychologists to study the brain's functioning more directly. These advances have allowed much greater evaluative ability than ever before and have revolutionized how neuropsychologists perform their job.

Despite the considerable advances these technologies have provided, economic factors have also had a substantial influence on the current and future status of neuropsychology. The current health-care system has had a significant impact on the development of neuropsychology as a clinical discipline, as it has influenced others in the private practice arena. Reduction in funding opportunities has led to fewer graduate and postgraduate training programs, which in turn reflects the reduced availability of well-paying jobs in neuropsychology. The shrinking health-care dollar has also caused neuropsychologists to reexamine how they administer services and to consider alternative employment opportunities, such as forensic and sports neuropsychology. In the latter setting, for example, neuropsychologists have found a new and important role in helping teams assess and manage sport-related concussions. They have been helpful in evaluating the effect of a concussion and using this information to help the team trainer and physicians determine when an athlete is able to return to play. This opportunity is, of course, an expansion of the field that reflects changes in health-care delivery more than advancements in technology. These economic stressors along with new technologies have transformed neuropsychology into a more diverse and scientific subspecialty of psychology.

Otero et al. illustrate how the subspecialty of neuropsychology has evolved and reinvented itself as the technology and demands of the profession have changed. Although this field is still wedded to many traditional instruments and methods (e.g., Wechsler scales), it has experienced a widening through the inclusion of assessment tools that have made some rather significant impacts in advancing neuropsychology (e.g., in the areas of computerized assessment and the development of novel assessment techniques). Computerized testing techniques, such as the Automated Neuropsychological Assessment Metrics and the Immediate Post-Concussion Assessment and

Cognitive Testing approaches, allow for effective evaluation of a variety of factors (e.g., working memory, reaction time, concussion symptomatology). Novel assessment techniques have included those that blend neuropsychology with educational psychology as well as combining complex theoretical models of cognition to measure critical cognitive abilities such as attention and executive control (Cognitive Assessment System; Naglieri & Das, 1997), which is also discussed by Wasserman (this volume). These new methods, combined with traditional tests, new neuroimaging techniques, and the changing economic situations, have facilitated the advancement of the discipline of neuropsychology in important ways. Not only is neuropsychology in an important transition period, as are all other health care related fields, but it is also in the midst of historical changes from external forces, and it must be able to withstand new challenges to survive as a strong and viable clinical service.

## Personality and Psychopathology Assessment

The assessment of personality and psychopathology has long been a part of psychology, and the techniques and methods used in assessment have been quite varied. Performance measures (see Viglione & Rivera, this volume) have involved human figure drawings, responses to inkblots, and stories about ambiguous pictures. Self-report measures (also see Ben-Porath, this volume) have been constructed to assess normal personality (e.g., California Psychological Inventory) and psychopathology (e.g., MMPI-2). As Craig notes in his chapter in this volume, interviews of various kinds have been widely used for years by psychologists and members of other professions.

Much has been said and written about the assumptions underlying the various assessment approaches and their relative advantages and disadvantages in assessing personality and psychopathology. Virtually every technique for assessing personality and psychopathology has been criticized by some and defended by others, and examples abound. Criticisms that the MMPI Clinical scales measure only acquiescence or social desirability response sets (Edwards, 1957, 1964; Messick & Jackson, 1961) were rebutted by Block (1965) and others. The validity of many Rorschach Comprehensive System scores and indexes and the adequacy of its norms have been called into question (Lilienfeld, Wood, & Garb, 2000; Shaffer, Erdberg, & Haroian, 1999) and subsequently defended by Bornstein (2001), Meyer (2000), Meyer and Archer (2001), and Weiner (2000, 2001). Unfortunately, the controversies surrounding assessment of personality and psychopathology

have not led to constructive conclusions about validity or subsequent changes or modifications in the way the assessment techniques are used. Despite the criticisms, however, assessment of personality and psychopathology remains a hallmark of assessment psychology.

## Interviews

Interviewing is the oldest and most widely used assessment method, with almost every psychological evaluation including some kind of interview data. Unstructured clinical interviews are more commonly used than structured interviews in applied clinical settings. Structured diagnostic interviews, such as the Structured Clinical Interview for *DSM-IV* Axis I Disorders (SCID) or Diagnostic Interview Schedule (DIS), are widely used in research studies. In his chapter in this volume, Craig points out that structured interviews generally lead to more reliable inferences and judgments than unstructured interviews. However, he also acknowledges that diagnoses resulting from one structured interview do not necessarily agree with those resulting from other structured interviews. Craig concludes that relatively little information exists about the validity of interviewing as an assessment method, largely because interview-based data typically are used as criterion measures against which other methods are evaluated. This is especially true with structured diagnostic interviews, which often are seen as the gold standard. Craig maintains that a basic problem that limits the reliability and validity of interview-based judgments is the lack of clear and explicit definitions and criteria for determining the presence and extent of specific personality characteristics and symptoms of psychopathology.

Craig points out that there is an increasing use of computer-assisted interviewing, and some of the structured diagnostic interviews were designed specifically for computerized use. Computerized interviews utilize less professional time and therefore are more cost effective. It is interesting to note that most people have a positive reaction to the computerized interview format and are more likely to acknowledge problems and symptoms in a computerized interview than in a clinician-conducted interview. Computerized interviews generally lead to more reliable inferences or judgments about patients than do clinician-conducted interviews. In addition, they are likely to reduce sources of error associated with interviewer biases. Craig also acknowledges the increasing use of telepsychiatry and telepsychology and the use of interviews utilizing these approaches. He calls for increased training in interviewing so that clinicians can self-monitor and reduce potential biases in diagnostic decision-making. It is also important for clinicians to understand clearly the role of culture and take it into account in conducting interviews.

## Behavioral Approaches

The behavioral assessment chapter in this volume by O'Brien and Young describes an approach that is founded on assumptions of empiricism and environmental determinism that arose from new developments in theory and research in the behavioral sciences. The authors recognize that cognitive-behavioral conceptualizations of behavior have become increasingly complex due to advances in research and a broadening of assumptions. A typical assessment, therefore, requires that the behaviorally oriented researchers and clinicians recognize the increasing complexities of human behavior in order to decipher the functional relationships among target behaviors and contextual factors. O'Brien and Young also discuss the need for familiarity with new sampling and assessment methods combined with strategies for identifying functional relationships to empirically identify the root causes of behaviors. The authors note that each method has strengths and limitations that influence the degree of clinical utility.

O'Brien and Young indicate that intuitive and statistical procedures can be used to evaluate hypothesized causal functional relationships, but intuitive evaluation is often inaccurate. (Also see Spengler, this volume.) They urge the use of statistical approaches that can provide better information on the strength of functional relationships, and they suggest that practitioners use conditional probability analyses because they require only a modest amount of data, are easily understood, and are convenient to use. They note, however, that this approach is limited to the evaluation of only a few variables and appears to be incompatible with typical clinical settings.

O'Brien and Young suggest a number of avenues for future research, including the examination of the treatment utility of behavioral assessment. They suggest that it will be especially important to examine the extent to which individualized treatments based on behavioral assessment outperform other treatment protocols. They strongly urge researchers to determine the treatment utility of behavioral assessment in relation to idiographic treatment design and standardized treatment–client matching. Their chapter, like others in this volume, illustrates the evolution of behavioral methods and the increasing recognition of the complexities of human performance.

## Performance Approaches

Projective techniques have long been a part of psychological assessments, although recent surveys suggest that their popularity in most settings has been declining somewhat (e.g., Camara, Nathan, & Puente, 2000). In fact, the Rorschach inkblots are almost synonymous with psychology in the minds of many laypersons. In their chapter in this volume, Viglione and Rivera discuss the misunderstandings and distortions that arise from categorizing tests as projective or objective. They make a cogent argument to instead use the term *performance tests* instead of projective tests. They also discuss various approaches to the interpretation of performance test data.

In most settings, content analysis, in which responses are seen as a reflection of a person's unconscious, has given way to more empirically based approaches (e.g., Exner's Comprehensive System). A newer approach to performance test interpretation, the Rorschach Performance Assessment System (Meyer, Viglione, Mihura, Erard, & Erdberg, 2011), takes into account the self-expressive and organizational components of examinees' responses. Although the more structured approaches have become quite popular, critics have raised questions about the reliability and validity of interpretations based on the scoring systems and about the norms used to generate interpretive statements (e.g., Lilienfeld et al., 2000).

Supporters of the Rorschach and other performance-based techniques have responded to the criticisms of Lilienfeld et al. by pointing out methodological deficiencies in many of the studies reviewed (e.g., use of untrained examiners, unrepresentative samples) and suggesting that the reviews is not objective and scientific (Meyer, 2000; Weiner, 2000, 2001). It is beyond the scope of this chapter to reach conclusions about these issues. However, it seems clear to us that we need less emotional approaches to the issues and methodologically sophisticated research studies designed to address specific issues.

Viglione and Rivera (this volume) suggest that the debate about the relative validity of self-report and performance-based approaches to assessment may reflect differences between psychologists in academic and applied settings. They see academic psychologists as needing to promote their scientific status and doing so by attacking performance-based techniques. They see psychologists in clinical settings as being rather uncritical in their acceptance of the validity and usefulness of a wide variety of assessment and therapeutic techniques. Viglione and Rivera see the continuing debate as philosophical and moral, not scientific. They emphasize that each assessment approach has its strengths and weaknesses and that we all should be trying to determine how they could be combined to achieve a better understanding of those we evaluate.

Viglione and Rivera describe an approach to Rorschach interpretation that views a performance test as involving a new and unfamiliar situation in which one organizes incomplete, contradictory, and ambiguous material without any direct feedback from observers or authorities. How respondents complete this problem-solving task should have implications for how they deal with many important tasks in their real lives. Of course, relationships between problem solving in responding to performance test stimuli and problem solving in real-life situations need to be demonstrated empirically.

## Self-Report Approaches

Self-report approaches in psychological assessment typically involve asking respondents to indicate whether— and sometimes to what extent—particular symptoms, behaviors, and personality descriptors are characteristic of them. Survey data indicate that self-report inventories generally, and the MMP-2 specifically, are the most widely used methods of psychological assessment in the United States (Camara et al., 2000).

In his chapter in this volume, Ben-Porath traces the use of self-report measures over more than seven decades, pointing out the major strengths and weakness of this assessment approach. Self-report inventories have been developed to assess various dimensions of psychopathology as well as normal personality functioning. Early scales were constructed using empirical procedures and gave little attention to the content of items. More contemporary scales (e.g., MMPI-2 Content scales) have emphasized the selection of items based on the relevance of their content to the constructs being assessed. Ben-Porath indicates that it is important to demonstrate the content validity (i.e., the extent to which items adequately cover the relevant content domain for the constructs being assessed) and the empirical validity and eventually the construct validity of these content-based scales.

Ben-Porath discusses criticisms of self report inventories (especially the MMPI/MMPI-2) by those convinced that their scales measure only response sets such as social desirability and acquiescence (e.g., Edwards, 1964; Messick & Jackson, 1961) and the rebuttals by those who demonstrated empirically that the scales account for valid variance even when the effects of these response sets are removed (e.g., Block, 1965). It is extremely difficult to determine to what extent the manner in which respondents approach self-report inventories represents error variance as opposed to valid variance in the constructs being assessed. One advantage of some self-report inventories (e.g., MMPI-2, Personality Assessment Inventory) is that they include scales and indexes for assessing tendencies of respondents to over- or underreport problems and symptoms to create the impression of being more adjusted or maladjusted than they really are. Much evidence has accumulated, for example, suggesting that the validity scales of the MMPI-2 can detect malingering and defensiveness even when respondents have been given information about the disorders to be feigned or denied and the validity scales designed to detect their invalid responding.

Self-report inventories lend themselves readily to computer administration, scoring, and interpretation. In his chapter in this volume Butcher describes ways in which computer technology contributes to psychological assessment. Ben-Porath stresses the need to demonstrate that scores based on standard administration of tests are applicable to computer-administered versions, and Butcher emphasizes the importance of determining empirically the validity of computer-generated inferences and statements.

Ben-Porath argues for more emphasis on construct validity. More recently developed self-report measures (e.g., Personality Psychopathology-Five scales [Harkness, McNulty, & Ben-Porath, 1995]; Restructured Clinical scales [Tellegen et al., 2003]; MMPI-2 Restructured Form scales [Ben-Porath & Tellegen, 2008]) have been based on conceptually grounded models of personality and psychopathology, providing the basis for construct-validity based interpretation of scores.

## CONCLUDING ISSUES IN ASSESSMENT PSYCHOLOGY

Assessment psychology is an important and viable specialty within the discipline of psychology and in many areas is at a defining point in its development. Many of the methods of assessment in use today were developed during the early part of the 20th century, and the field is now in need of redefinition.

The considerable base of knowledge that has defined the field as a subdiscipline in psychology is both an advantage and a limitation. The vast amount of research and knowledge in the field provides considerable advantage. We have been able to better detect and understand various attributes of people and how these attributes relate to a variety of factors, such as job performance, academic achievement, personality, social interactions, and so on. The accumulation of information creates a base of knowledge that has been used by researchers and clinicians alike as the foundation of their efforts. Although this base provides a comfortable footing for practice, it is not without limitations.

The current state of the art in assessment psychology raises a variety of important issues. For example, procedures are being used in settings different from those in which they were developed and normed. The MMPI was developed for diagnosis in inpatient psychiatric settings, but it is used now in personnel selection, medical settings, correctional settings, and others. The adequacy of the original norms and the validity of inferences in these broader settings must be demonstrated empirically. The limitation on generalizability of interpretive inferences in these other settings warrants greater attention. Similarly, conventional IQ tests were originally developed to sort people on the basis of overall general ability; now the tests are used for many types of diagnostic purposes (learning disabilities, attention deficit disorders, etc.) for which they were not intended and for which research has not supported. (See Wasserman, this volume.)

Another of the more thorny issues in assessment psychology involves the debate on clinical versus actuarial (statistical) decision making. The debate continues between those who advocate practices supported by clinical experience and those who stress the need for empirically supported decision making. This issue cuts across many dimensions of assessment psychology and involves most tests and methods. For example, research on clinical judgment (see Spengler, this volume) alerts practitioners that they need to know the empirical support for the methods they use and that they should *not* use an instrument or treatment method merely because it seems to work. Similarly, interpretations of subtest or subscale scores obtained from tests of personality and intelligence, for example, that have not been empirically validated should not be made. This tendency is especially evident in the practice of intelligence test subtest analysis. The limitations of assessment psychology have not gone unnoticed by those who pay for this information, especially the insurance industry.

The influences of managed care companies and the resulting reduction in reimbursements for evaluation and treatment pose a considerable challenge to assessment psychology. Clinicians have seen how managed care has encouraged brief, symptom-focused measures and the need to demonstrate that assessment contributes to successful outcomes in efficient, cost-effective ways. One new effort in assessment psychology that fits some of these needs is the application of computer technology, which can reduce costs by utilizing less expensive methods of administration, scoring, and interpretation of assessment instruments. Another new technology is adaptive testing, which, like others, requires considerable empirical justification but represents an important evolution in the field of assessment psychology.

Perhaps the most serious impediment to the future advancement of assessment psychology is the conservative nature of the industry and of many in the profession, which has led to the overreliance on conventional practices. Apparent in many of the chapters in this volume, with some notable exceptions (e.g., neuropsychology), is a strong reliance on traditional instrumentation. Clinicians tend to use what they learned in their training programs and are resistant to change. For example, despite that fact that the Wechsler scales represent a technology developed in the early 1900s, the instrument continues to be widely used in a variety of settings.

Moreover, training of new graduate students is inadequate, is limited to traditional instruments, and emphasizes tests over a problem-solving approach that views tests and other evaluative methods as part of an overall assessment process. (See Handler & Smith, this volume.) The future development of assessment psychology will determine whether the field can evolve into the mature science described by Wasserman in his chapter in this volume on assessment of intelligence. The field has excellent potential, which is perhaps most apparent in its emergence as a viable specialty within the discipline of psychology. The American Psychological Association (APA) has now recognized personality assessment as a proficiency in professional psychology. Division 12 (Clinical Psychology) of the APA has approved an assessment psychology section, and the American Board of Assessment Psychology continues to evaluate credentials of assessment psychologists and to advocate for assessment as an important part of the science and practice of psychology.

Despite these successes, there are important challenges ahead for assessment psychology. Changes in the way graduate students are educated must occur if assessment psychology is to evolve into a mature science. There has been far too much emphasis on traditional instruments and approaches. For example, the MMPI-2, Wechsler scales, TAT, and Rorschach are still the most widely taught and used assessment instruments, and not enough training has occurred on innovative approaches. Some examples of more innovative approaches include the five-factor model of personality and resulting instruments (PSY-5 scales for MMPI-2; Harkness et al., 1995), neuroimaging techniques in neuropsychology (fMRI), and cognitive processing approaches to intelligence (e.g., Cognitive Assessment System; Naglieri & Das, 1997). These new efforts require attention in training programs, and these programs need to focus more on the purposes for which the assessments are conducted than on the tests themselves. Additionally, there is a dire need to demonstrate more clearly the link between assessment and intervention, especially as it relates to cognitive measures and educational interventions as well as personality measures and treatment planning (e.g., therapeutic assessment work by Finn, 1996, and colleagues). Finally, credentialing and certification of assessment psychologists that includes uniform standards and compulsory evaluation of those conducting assessments should be mandated. The future advancement of assessment psychology will also be related to how well disputes in the field can be resolved. Although there is very strong and positive evidence on the value of psychological testing and assessment and much research has been accumulated, virtually every approach and technique has been criticized by some and defended by others. Some of the controversies (e.g., the dispute over performance-based tests) have led to conclusions that a particular method should not be used. Rather than arguing against use of a method, we believe that the worth of any assessment technique must be determined empirically through systematic research. An important focus of this type of research is to demonstrate that inferences based on the technique are related to *specific* uses that occur in *specific* applications of the *specific* instrument. For example, is the form quality of responses by adults to inkblots related to disturbed thinking? Are scores on the Depression Content scale of the MMPI-2 related to symptoms of clinical depression? Can results for a particular type of performance test (e.g., Draw-A-Person) be used for general identification of emotional problems rather than the specific diagnosis of children? In other words, for what purposes (and in what circumstances) are various scales and measures valid? Some argue that advancement in assessment psychology is limited because the issues involved are so complex. Others suggest that researchers advocating any method or instrument (e.g., behavioral versus performance; MMPI-2 versus Rorschach) are not very objective. Still others contend that we can expect only limited advances in assessment psychology as long as we continue to use and study instruments and approaches that are many decades old. Additionally, some argue that instruments and procedures developed for use in one setting have been employed in

other settings without adequate examination of the validity of such applications. We believe that all of these factors contribute to limited advancements in assessment psychology. It seems that what is needed are comprehensive and innovative studies conducted by reasonably impartial assessment researchers.

Our position is that the validity and usefulness of any psychological instrument or procedure must be established empirically for the specific purposes and in the specific settings in which the instruments are to be used. This is equally true for interviews, tests of cognitive processes, interest and achievement tests, objective approaches, and performance-based techniques. As Weiner emphasizes in the opening chapter to this volume, and as others have echoed in subsequent chapters, the most valid and useful psychological assessments are likely to result when data from various sources and instruments are integrated to address important questions and problems.

## FUTURE OF ASSESSMENT PSYCHOLOGY

Assessment psychology is alive and well and taking place in many different settings. Although considerable work is needed to demonstrate the validity and cost effectiveness of assessment, much evidence already exists that psychologists can use to promote assessment. Although managed care may be seen as a threat to assessment psychology, it also provides opportunities and stimulus to help the profession grow into a more mature science. (See Maruish, this volume.) Only time will tell if the next 100 years of assessment psychology will be more of the same or if innovative approaches will develop and be embraced. However, it is clear that although traditional instruments and methods have allowed assessment psychology to develop into a viable subdiscipline of psychology, they cannot sustain the field for another 100 years because so many of the goals of assessment have changed. The assessment needs of today and tomorrow are not the same as those present when traditional tests and methods were developed in the early 1900s. Assessment psychology must meet these new demands to continue its evolution into a mature science and a strong subdiscipline of psychology.

## REFERENCES

Ben-Porath, Y. S., & Tellegen, A. (2008). *Minnesota Multiphasic Personality Inventory-2-Restructured Form: Manual for administration, scoring, and interpretation*. Minneapolis: University of Minnesota Press.

Block, J. (1965). *The challenge of response sets: Unconfounding meaning, acquiescence, and social desirability in the MMPI*. New York, NY: Appleton-Century-Crofts.

Bornstein, R. F. (2001). Clinical utility of the Rorschach Inkblot Method: Reframing the debate. *Journal of Personality Assessment, 77,* 48–70.

Camara, W. J., Nathan, J. S., & Puente, A. E. (2000). Psychological test usage: Implications in professional psychology. *Professional Psychology: Research and Practice, 31,* 141–154.

DuBois, P. H. (1970). *A history of psychological testing*. Boston, MA: Allyn & Bacon.

Edwards. A. L. (1957). *The social desirability variable in personality assessment and research*. New York, NY: Dryden.

Edwards, A. L. (1964). Social desirability and performance on the MMPI. *Psychometrika, 29,* 295–308.

Eisman, E. J., Dies, R. R., Finn, S. E., Eyde, L. D., Kay, G. G., Kubiszyn, T. W.,...Moreland, K. (2000). Problems and limitations in using psychological assessment in the contemporary health care delivery system. Professional *Psychology: Research and Practice, 31,* 131–140.

Finn, S. E. (1996). *Manual for using the MMPI-2 as a therapeutic intervention*. Minneapolis: University of Minnesota Press.

Graham, J. R., & Lilly, R. S. (1984). *Psychological testing*. Englewood Cliffs, NJ: Prentice-Hall.

Groth-Marnat, G. (1999). Financial efficacy of clinical assessment: Rational guidelines and issues for future research. *Journal of Clinical Psychology, 55,* 813–824.

Harkness, A. R., McNulty, J. L., & Ben-Porath, Y. S. (1995). The personality psychopathology five (PSY-5): Constructs and MMPI-2 scales. *Psychological Assessment, 7,* 104–114.

Lilienfeld, S. O., Wood, J. M., & Garb, H. N. (2000). The scientific status of projective techniques. *Psychological Science in the Public Interest, 1,* 27–66.

Megargee, E. I., Carbonell, J. L., Bohn, M. J., & Sliger, G. L. (2001). *Classifying criminal offenders with the MMPI-2: The Megargee system*. Minneapolis: University of Minnesota Press.

Messick, S., & Jackson, D. N. (1961). Acquiescence and the factorial interpretation of the MMPI. *Psychological Bulletin, 58,* 299–304.

Meyer, G. J. (2000). On the science of Rorschach research. *Journal of Personality Assessment, 75,* 46–81.

Meyer, G. J., & Archer, R. P. (2001). The hard science of Rorschach research: What do we know and where do we go? *Psychological Assessment, 13,* 486–502.

Meyer, G. J., Finn, S. E., Eyde, L. D., Kay, G. G., Moreland, K. L., Dies, R. R.,...Reed, G. M. (2001). Psychological testing and psychological assessment: A review of evidence and issues. *American Psychologist, 56,* 128–165.

Meyer, G. J., Viglione, D. J., Mihura, J. L., Erard, R. E., & Erdberg, P. (2011). *Manual for the Rorschach Performance Assessment System*. San Diego, CA: R-PAS.

Naglieri, J. A., & Das, J. P. (1997). *Cognitive Assessment System*. Itasca, IL: Riverside.

*Palmigiano v. Garrahy*, 443 F. Supp. 956 (D.R.I. 1977).

Phelps, R., Eisman, E. J., & Kohout, J. (1998). Psychological practice and managed care: Results of the CAPP practitioner survey. *Professional Psychology: Research and Practice, 29,* 31–36.

Piotrowski, C., Belter, R. W., & Keller, J. W. (1998). The impact of "managed care" on the practice of psychological testing: Preliminary findings. *Journal of Personality Assessment, 70,* 441–447.

Shaffer, T. W., Erdberg, P., & Haroian, J. (1999). Current nonpatient data for the Rorschach, WAIS, and MMPI-2. *Journal of Personality Assessment, 73,* 305–316.

Tellegen, A., Ben-Porath, Y. S., McNulty, J. L., Arbisi, P. A. Graham, J. R., & Kaemmer, B. (2003). *MMPI-2 Restructured Clinical (RC) scales: Development, validation, and interpretation*. Minneapolis: University of Minnesota Press.

Weiner, I. B. (2000). Making Rorschach interpretation as good as it can be. *Journal of Personality Assessment, 74,* 164–174.

Weiner, I. B. (2001). Considerations in collecting Rorschach reference data. *Journal of Personality Assessment, 77,* 122–127.

Yoakum, C. S., & Yerkes, R. M. (1920). *Army mental tests*. New York, NY: Holt.

# Author Index

Cizek, G. J., 66
Claiborn, C., 226
Clair, D., 148
Clarizio, H. F., 305
Clark, D. A., 411
Clark, D. M., 337
Clark, J. A., 18
Clark, L., 244
Clark, L. A., 67, 167, 244, 245, 570
Clark, T. M., 527
Clarkin, J., 147
Clarkin, J. F., 12, 65, 241, 245, 246, 256
Clay, O. J., 431
Cleary, P. D., 568
Cleary, T. A., 74, 83, 101, 102
Cleckley, H., 414
Clemence, A., 228
Clements, C., 401, 403, 406
Cleveland, J. N., 349, 363
Cleveland, L. A., 265
Clifton, D. O., 537
Cline, T., 27, 36
Clingerman, S., 509, 511
Cloninger, C. R., 337, 560, 577
Clopton, J. R., 147, 246
Clouse, R. E., 432
Coady, M., 118
Coalson, D. L., 403, 406, 407
Cody, H. A., 514
Coffey, P., 338
Coffman, W. E., 306
Cohen, A. S., 131
Cohen, C. I., 436
Cohen, F., 410
Cohen, G., 523
Cohen, G. D., 436
Cohen, J., 26, 51, 440
Cohen, J. D., 523, 524
Cohen, J. W., 159
Cohen, L., 333, 507, 525
Cohen, R. A., 431
Cohen, R. J., 461
Coie, J. D., 292, 298
Colavito, V. A., 606, 609
Cole, M., 119
Coles, M. E., 180
Colligan, S. C., 607, 614
Collins, C. A., 229
Collins, F. L., 316
Collins, F. S., 334
Collins, M., 506
Collins, M. W., 506, 515
Collins, R. C., 546
Colombo, C., 524
Colsher, P., 439
Compton, W. M., 273, 568
Comrey, A. L., 55
Conder, R. L., 509
Condon, C. A., 52

Cone, J. D., 67, 69, 610
Connelly, M. S., 367
Conner, K. O., 427, 428
Conner, K. R., 436
Conners, C. K., 272, 279
Connor, L. T., 508
Conover, N., 263
Conrad, H. S., 28, 31
Constable, R. T., 523
Conte, K. L., 305
Conti, R. M., 426, 432
Contreras-Niño, L. A., 123
Conwell, Y., 436
Cook, D. A., 36
Cook, L. L., 133, 134
Cook, L. M., 180
Cook, L. P., 156
Cook, R. S., 14, 26–40, 42, 412
Cook, T. D., 60
Cooke, D. J., 381
Cooke, J. K., 31
Coolidge, F. L., 264
Coon, K. L., 543
Cooper, A., 33
Cooper, M., 394, 400, 410
Cooper, R. P., 411
Cooper, Z., 568
Copeland, J. R., 426
Coppotelli, H., 298
Corbitt, E. M., 568
Cordell, A., 267
Cordoliani, Y. S., 522
Corenthal, M., 568
Corkin, S., 523
Cormier, C., 415
Cormier, C. A., 32, 381, 415
Cormier, P., 454
Cornell, J., 228
Coronado, V. G., 507
Corrigan, S. K., 19
Cortina, J. M., 67
Costa, G., 575
Costa, M., 430
Costa, P. T., 62, 254, 357, 358, 570, 636, 641
Costanza, D. P., 367
Costello, A. J., 263
Costello, E. J., 263
Cottler, L. B., 273, 568
Coughhan, J., 568
Coulter, D. L., 486
Courtney, J. C., 508
Courville, T., 476
Coury, D. L., 279
Covinsky, K. E., 435
Cox, D., 33
Cox, D. N., 382, 384
Cox, D. R., 509
Coyne, I., 166, 170, 181

Coyne, J. C., 230
Craddick, R. A., 31, 33
Craft, L., 174
Craig, E. M., 486
Craig, R. J., 247, 558, 560, 568, 570, 573
Craik, F. I., 429, 430
Craik, F. I. M., 426
Cramer, A. O. J., 59
Cramer, P., 223
Craske, M. G., 435
Crawford, E. R., 363
Crenshaw, B., 326
Crighton, D., 411
Crimmins, D. B., 594
Crippa, J. A., 576
Cristina, M., 576
Crites, J. O., 534, 537, 544
Crits-Christoph, P., 33
Crocker, L., 60, 61
Cronbach, L. J., 59, 64, 66, 67, 127, 133, 353, 441, 630
Crook, T. J., 438
Crossley, M., 526
Crosson, B. A., 527
Croteau, J. M., 547
Crowder, R. C., 63
Crow-Enslow, L., 487
Crowther, J. H., 147
Cryer, P. E., 432
Crystal, D. S., 272
Csikszentmihalyi, M., 20, 233
Cubic, B. A., 328
Cuéllar, I., 224
Cuellar, I., 118, 120
Cukrowicz, K. C., 242, 253
Cullen, F. T., 412, 416
Cullen, M. J., 130
Cully, J. A., 431
Culpepper, W. J., 143
Cumella, E., 179
Cumella, E. J., 178
Cummings, A. L., 37, 38
Cummings, J. L., 485
Cummins, J., 117
Cunningham, M. D., 394
Cunningham, W. E., 340
Cupp, R., 413
Curiel, A. R., 178
Curry, K. T., 225, 227
Cuttledge, C., 576


Dadds, M. R., 273
D'Adostino, R. B., 438
Daffern, M., 416
Dahle, K. P., 416
Dahlstrom, L. E., 634
Dahlstrom, N. G., 385

# Subject Index